Group Policy

Fundamentals, Security, and the Managed Desktop

Third Edition

Group Policy

Fundamentals, Security, and the Managed Desktop

Third Edition

Jeremy Moskowitz

SYBEX®
A Wiley Brand

Senior Acquisitions Editor: Kenyon Brown
Development Editor: Sara Barry
Technical Editor: Alan Burchill
Production Editor: Elizabeth Campbell
Copy Editor: Judy Flynn
Editorial Manager: Mary Beth Wakefield
Production Manager: Kathleen Wisor
Associate Publisher: Jim Minatel
Book Designers: Judy Fung and Bill Gibson
Compositors: Craig Woods and Kate Kaminski, Happenstance Type-O-Rama
Proofreaders: Jenn Bennett, Jen Larsen Word One New York
Indexer: Johnna VanHoose Dinse
Project Coordinator, Cover: Brent Savage
Cover Designer: Wiley
Cover Image: © Mehmet Hilmi Barcin / iStockPhoto

For L, A, M, J, B, E, J, and E as we journey through life together.
—Jeremy

Acknowledgments

I want to thank Alan Burchill for the second time in taking on the not-so-glamorous job of technical editor. I'm really glad to have you on my team, helping me clean up the little messes I made during the writing process and taking on a heavy responsibility. Note: If there are still any technical problems with the book, blame me, not him. Alan was awesome.

I want to thank Sara Barry for taking my initial chapters and kneading them from a wad of dough into tasty pizza. And to Elizabeth Campbell, who has worked with me through every major project to completion for almost 15 years now. We joke that she's "been making Jeremy sound like Jeremy since 2001." And it's mostly true. Thank you.

Special thanks to my Sybex and Wiley compatriots: Ken Brown, Mariann Barsolo, Jim Minitel, Mary Beth Wakefield, and everyone else on the Sybex/Wiley team. Once again, your dedication to my book's success means so much to me. You take everything I create and deal with it so personally, and I really know that. Thank you, very sincerely.

Thanks to Jeff Hicks, PowerShell MVP, who helped me write Appendix A on Group Policy and PowerShell. Jeff, you did a smashing job as usual. Thank you.

Thank you to Microsoft Group Policy team and the Group Policy MVPs who support me directly and indirectly, and help me out whenever they can.

Thank you, Mark Minasi, for being a trusted friend and a great inspiration to me personally and professionally.

A special thanks to my GPanswers.com and PolicyPak Team: You are awesome and it's great to work with you every day.

Finally, I want to thank you. If you're holding this book, there's a good chance you've owned a previous edition, or multiple previous editions. Thank you for your trust, and for purchasing and repurchasing each edition of this book I work so hard to bring you each time.

When I meet you, the reader of this book, in person, it makes the hours and hours spent on a project like this vaporize away to a distant memory. Thank you for buying the book, for joining me at my live events and at GPAnswers.com, and for using my PolicyPak software. You all make me the best "me" I can be. Thanks.

About the Author

Jeremy Moskowitz   Group Policy MVP, is the founder of GPanswers.com and PolicyPak Software (PolicyPak.com). He is a nationally recognized authority on Windows Server, Active Directory, Group Policy, and Windows management. He is one of fewer than a dozen Microsoft MVPs in Group Policy. His GPanswers.com is ranked by Computerworld as a "Top 20 Resource for Microsoft IT Professionals." Jeremy is a sought-after speaker and trainer at many industry conferences and, in his training workshops, helps thousands of administrators every year do more with Group Policy. Contact Jeremy by visiting www.GPanswers.com or www.PolicyPak.com.

About The Contributors

Jeffery Hicks is an IT veteran with over 25 years of experience, much of it spent as an IT infrastructure consultant specializing in Microsoft server technologies with an emphasis in automation and efficiency. He is a multi-year recipient of the Microsoft MVP Award in Windows PowerShell. He works today as an independent author, trainer, and consultant. He has taught and presented on PowerShell and the benefits of automation to IT pros all over the world. Jeff has written for numerous online sites and print publications, is a contributing editor at Petri.com, a Pluralsight author, and a frequent speaker at technology conferences and user groups. His latest book is *PowerShell In Depth: An Administrator's Guide, Second Edition*, with Don Jones and Richard Siddaway (Manning Publications, 2013). You can keep up with Jeff on Twitter (http://twitter.com/JeffHicks) and on his blog (http://jdhitsolutions.com/blog).

Alan Burchill works as a manager for Avanade Australia based in Brisbane. He has a normal day job as the lead global Active Directory administrator for a large multinational corporation. Alan has been working with Microsoft technologies for over 17 years and is a regular speaker at Microsoft TechEd and Ignite conferences. He has been a Microsoft Valuable Professional in the area of Group Policy for the past six years. He regularly blogs about Group Policy and other related topics at his website called Group Policy Central at www.grouppolicy.biz. Alan also runs the Brisbane Infrastructure Users Group (www.bigau.org), where he organizes monthly meetings about Microsoft Infrastructure-related topics, and he is the organizer of the annual Infrastructure Saturday event (www.infrastructuresaturday.com), which is a full-day community event about Microsoft Infrastructure Technologies. You can reach him via his website or via Twitter @alanburchill.

Contents at a Glance

Contents

Introduction

Windows 10 is here.

Alas, Windows 8 and 8.1, we hardly knew ye.

And Windows 9—we just skipped you entirely and jumped ahead to Windows 10.

For people buying this book for the first time, welcome. For people who have bought previous editions and are returning again (or again and again and again)—thank you for coming back.

Group Policy and Active Directory go hand in hand. If you have Active Directory, you get Group Policy.

If you're very new to Group Policy, here's the inside scoop. Group Policy has one goal: to make your administrative life easier. Instead of running around from machine to machine, tweaking a setting here or installing some software there, you'll have ultimate control from on high.

Like Zeus himself, controlling the many aspects of the mortal world below, you will have the ability, via Group Policy, to dictate specific settings pertaining to how you want your users and computers to operate. You'll be able to shape your network's destiny. You'll have the power. But you need to know how to tap into this power and what can be powered.

In this introduction and throughout the first several chapters, I'll describe just what Group Policy is all about and give you an idea of its tremendous power. Then, as your skills grow, chapter by chapter, we'll build on what you've already learned and help you do more with Group Policy, troubleshoot it, and implement some of its most powerful features.

For those of you who are already somewhat Group Policy savvy, there is some good and some bad news (which is the same news): From a Group Policy perspective, Windows 10 is not radically different from its Windows 7 or Windows 8 siblings.

Ironically, Group Policy's innards did get the most recent update between Windows 8 and Windows 8.1, and those carry forward to Windows 10. I'll explain these when the time comes, so you can understand the behavior changes. Take a look at Table I.1 for how the Windows Group Policy engine evolved when the internal version number changed.

TABLE I.1 How Windows and Group Policy evolved

Product Name	Internal Windows Version Number	Changes to Group Policy Engine
Windows XP	5.0	Big changes from Windows 2000
Vista	6.0	Big changes from XP
Windows 7	6.1	Not so big changes from Windows Vista
Windows 8	6.2	Not so big changes from Windows 7

TABLE I.1   How Windows and Group Policy evolved *(continued)*

Product Name	Internal Windows Version Number	Changes to Group Policy Engine
Windows 8.1 and Windows 8.1 with Update	6.3	Medium changes from Windows 8
Windows 10	6.4 when it was in beta. But now at release Microsoft smartly jumped it up to 10.	No changes from Windows 8.1

Again, Table I.1 shows changes from a "Group Policy guts" perspective and is not necessarily reflective of what you can do (the actions you can perform) with Group Policy.

Knowing what's changed within the Group Policy guts is a dual-edged sword. On the one hand, you could say to yourself, "Awesome! If I'm already an expert at Windows 7 and Group Policy, there's not a huge hill to climb!" And that would be true. On the other hand, it's also true that because Windows 8 through 10 didn't shake things up too much, with regard to Group Policy "guts," there's not a lot of whiz-bang newness to uncover and show off. That being said, the updates in Windows 8.1 (which carry forward to Windows 10) will be covered in Chapter 3.

In a way, I really like the dual-edged sword. I like that there are a variety of new goodies and things you can do with Group Policy for Windows 10, some interesting updates, but not a radical head-spinning change. I like the fact that what is already working in practice doesn't change that much. I like knowing that the time already invested in getting smarter in Group Policy isn't for nothing, and you and I won't have to relearn everything we ever knew all over again.

So, even though the "guts" haven't changed all the much, there's always new "stuff" you can accomplish with Group Policy as each operating system comes out.

As you likely already know, Group Policy is, at its heart, an "on-prem" system for management. Isn't this antithetical to Microsoft's new battle cry of "Mobile first, cloud first?"

If you want to read Microsoft's own perspective on this, see:

http://news.microsoft.com/2014/03/27/satya-nadella-mobile-first-cloud-first-press-briefing/

Shouldn't Group Policy get a huge overhaul in its underlying technology to align with "Mobile first, cloud first?"

Perhaps it doesn't need it. Because Group Policy is, by its very nature, extensible, we can extend Group Policy to the cloud when needed if paired with (at least two) "add-ons." Microsoft DirectAccess (beyond the scope of this book, but briefly touched upon in Chapter 3) enables Windows machines to act as if they are *always* connected on-premise, even though they might be over the Internet at a coffee shop. That being said, DirectAccess only works with the more pricey Enterprise version of the Windows client.

PolicyPak Cloud (demonstrated in Chapter 3 and "name dropped" throughout the book) can take existing Group Policy directives and get them to the cloud for use on traveling and even non-domain-joined machines. PolicyPak Cloud works with any version of Windows and isn't limited to the more pricey Enterprise version.

If you've done some work already with Group Policy, you might notice that it could be described as various components under one roof; it roughly breaks down as follows:

- Group Policy Administrative Templates
- Group Policy Security Settings
- Group Policy Preferences
- Everything else, including third-party extensions

With all that power, and extendibility, Group Policy continues to stay not just relevant but, indeed, *central* to any Active Directory administrator's tool belt of required knowledge.

And because Group Policy is extensible, it can keep working in a "Mobile first, cloud first" world.

Group Policy Defined

If we take a step back and try to analyze the term *Group Policy*, it's easy to become confused. When I first heard the term, I didn't know what to make of it.

I asked myself, "Are we applying 'policy' to 'groups'? Is this some sort of old-school NT 4 System Policy applied to Active Directory groups?"

Turns out, "Group Policy" as a name isn't, well, excellent. At cocktail parties, when I tell the person next to me that I teach, write about, and make software to extend Group Policy, they don't get what "Group Policy" means.

If I said something like "I teach databases," he would cheerfully go back to his scotch and soda and leave me alone. But because I say, "I teach Group Policy to smart people looking to get smarter and build software that hooks into Group Policy," he (unfortunately) wants to know more. He'll say something like "What does that mean? I've never heard of Group Policy before." And while I love talking about Group Policy with you, my friendly IT geeks, at a cocktail party full of stuffed shirts, I just want to get another canapé.

So, the name "Group Policy" can be kind of confusing, but it's also intriguing. Microsoft's perspective is that the name "Group Policy" is derived from the fact that you are "grouping together policy settings." I don't really love the name "Group Policy"—but it's the name we have, so that's what it's called. As Juliet said in *Romeo and Juliet* (II, ii, 43–44), "What's in a name? That which we call a rose by any other name would smell as sweet."

For me, if I was consulted, I might have named it Windows Policy or Microsoft Policy. But, alas. Group Policy is the name it has.

 Group Policy is, in essence, rules that are applied and enforced at multiple levels of Active Directory. Policy settings you dictate must be adhered to by your users and computers. This provides great power and efficiency when manipulating client systems.]

Instead of running around from machine to machine, you're in charge (not your users).

When going through the examples in this book, you will play the various parts of the end user, the OU administrator, the domain administrator, and the enterprise administrator. Your mission is to create and define Group Policy using Active Directory and witness it being automatically enforced. What you say goes! With Group Policy, you can set policies that dictate that users quit messing with their machines. You can dictate what software will be deployed. You can determine how much disk space users can use. You can do pretty much whatever you want—it is up to you. With Group Policy, you hold all the power. That's the good news.

And this magical power only works on Windows 2000 and later machines. For the sake of completeness, this includes all versions of Windows 2000 and later: workstation and server. Of course, this includes all the modern Windows systems you would use, like Windows 10 and Windows Server 2016.

I'll likely say this again in multiple places, but I want to get one "big ol' misconception" out of the way right here, right in the introduction. The Group Policy infrastructure does not care what mode your domain is in. If you have only one type of Domain Controller or a mixture of Domain Controllers, 100 percent of everything we cover in this book is valid.

Said another way, even if your domain level is the oldest-of-the-old Windows 2000 mixed mode, you're still pretty much 100 percent covered here. Group Policy is all about the client (the target) operating system and not the Domain Controllers or domain modes.

> **TIP** It is true that wireless settings and BitLocker key storage require schema updates to play nicely with Group Policy. But even then, Group Policy will still work running with the oldest-of-the-old servers.

If the range of control scares you, don't be afraid! It just means more power to hold over your environment. You'll quickly learn how to wisely use this newfound power to reign over your subjects, er, users.

Group Policy vs. Group Policy Objects vs. Group Policy Preferences

Before we go headlong into Group Policy theory, let's get some terminology and vocabulary out of the way:

- *Group Policy* is the concept that, from on high, you can do all this "stuff" to your client machines.

- A *policy setting* is just one individual setting that you can use to perform some specific action.

- *Group Policy Objects (GPOs)* are the "nuts and bolts" contained within Active Directory Domain Controllers, and each can contain anywhere from one to a zillion individual policy settings.

- The *Group Policy Preferences* is a newer add-on to the existing set of the "original" Group Policy settings and abilities many have come to know and love. Group Policy Preferences (sometimes shortened to GPPrefs) don't act quite the same as their original cousins. We'll cover the Group Policy Preferences in detail in Chapter 5.

- *Preference item* is a way to describe one "Group Policy Preferences directive." It's like a "policy setting," but for the Group Policy Preferences.

It's my goal that after you work through this book, you'll be able to jump up on your desk one day and use all the vocabulary at once. Like this: "Hey! *Group Policy* isn't applying to our client machines! Perhaps a *policy setting* is misconfigured. Or, maybe one of our *Group Policy Objects* has gone belly up! Heck, maybe one of the *preference items* is misconfigured. I'd better read about what's going on in Chapter 7, 'Troubleshooting Group Policy.'"

This terminology can be a little confusing—considering that each term includes the word *policy*. In this text, however, I've tried especially hard to use the correct nomenclature for what I'm describing. If you get confused, just come back here to refresh your brain about the definitions.

> **NOTE** Note that there is never a time to use the phrase "Group Policies." Those two words together shouldn't exist. If you're talking about "multiple GPOs" or "multiple policy settings" or "policy settings vs. preference items," these are the preferred phrases to use, and never "Group Policies."

Where Group Policy Applies

Group Policy can be applied to many machines at once using Active Directory, or it can be applied when you walk up to a specific machine. For the most part, in this book I'll focus on using Group Policy within an Active Directory environment, where it affects the most machines.

A percentage of the settings explored and discussed in this book are available to member or stand-alone Windows machines—which can either participate (that is, be "joined" to Active Directory) or not participate (that is, it's "non-domain-joined") in an Active Directory environment.

However, the Folder Redirection settings (discussed in Chapter 10) and the Software Distribution settings (discussed in Chapter 11) are not available to stand-alone machines (that is, computers that are not participating in an Active Directory domain). In some cases, I will pay particular attention to non–Active Directory environments. However, most of the book deals with the more common case; that is, we'll explore the implications of deploying Group Policy in an Active Directory environment.

The "Too Many Operating Systems" Problem

If we line up all the operating systems that you (a savvy IT person) might have in your corporate world, we would likely find one or more of the following (presented here in date-release order):

- Windows 2000 (Workstation and Server), RTM through SP4
- Windows Server 2003, RTM through SP2
- Windows XP, RTM through SP3
- Windows Vista, RTM through SP2
- Windows Server 2008, RTM (known as SP1, actually) through SP2
- Windows 7 RTM, through SP1
- Windows Server 2008 R2, through SP1
- Windows Server 2012, RTM
- Windows Server 2012 R2
- Windows 8 client, RTM
- Windows 8.1 client, RTM
- Windows 8.1 Update 1
- Windows 10, RTM
- Windows Server 2016, RTM

For the love of Pete (whoever Pete is), that's a *lot* of potential operating systems. Okay, okay—perhaps you don't have *all* of them. You likely don't have any more Windows 2000 (or maybe you *do*, tucked in a back room somewhere, quietly processing something or other).

The point, however, is that Group Policy can apply to *all* of these systems. Under most circumstances, "old stuff" will work correctly on newer machines. That is, generally, something that could affect, say, an XP machine will also (generally) continue to affect a Windows 10 machine.

With that in mind, here's an example of what I'm *not* going to do. I'm *not* going to show you an example of something in the book, then say something like, "and this example is valid for Windows XP, Windows Vista, Windows Server 2008, Windows Server 2008 R2, Windows 7, Windows 8, Windows 8.1, Windows 8.1 Update 1, Windows Server 2012, Windows Server 2012 R2, Windows 10, and Windows Server 2016."

My head (and yours) will just explode if I do that and you need to read it each time. So, here's what I *am* going to do. You'll read my discussion about something, then I'll say something like, "and this example is valid for Windows XP and later." That would mean that the thing I'm about to show you (for example, a policy setting) should work A-OK for XP and later machines (all the way to Windows 10 and also usually for servers, like Windows Server 2016, too). Similarly, if I say, "and this is valid for Windows Vista and later," that means you'll be golden if the target machine is Windows Vista and later (all the way through Windows 10 and Windows Server 2016).

Of course, there are a handful of exceptions: things that only work on one particular operating system in a possibly peculiar way. For instance, there are a handful of Windows Vista–only settings that aren't valid for Windows 7 and Windows 8. There are Windows 10–specific settings that won't work on older machines. Again, I'll strive for clarity regarding the exceptions—but the good news is, those are few and far between.

If you get lost, here's a quick cheat sheet to help you remember "which machines act alike":

- Windows 2000 Workstation and Windows Server
- Windows Server 2003 and Windows XP
- Windows Server 2008 and Windows Vista
- Windows 7 and Windows Server 2008 R2
- Windows 8 and Windows Server 2012
- Windows 8.1 and Windows Server 2012 R2
- Windows 10 and Windows Server 2016

Just to be even more specific, Windows 7, Windows 8, Windows 8.1, Windows Server 2008 R2, Windows Server 2012, Windows Server 2012 R2, Windows 10, and Windows Server 2016 are ludicrously close brothers. They look alike, throw the same temper tantrums, and enjoy the same kinds of movies. But they're not identical. They are, in fact, different, but in most cases, they're super-duper similar and will react the same way when poked.

For this edition of the book, we decided to make a conscious choice about how to present Group Policy. Most of the walk-throughs, examples, and screen shots in the book will be of Windows 10 and Windows Server 2016.

Since I wrote the last edition of this book, two friends have passed away. Those friends, of course, are Windows XP and Windows Server 2003. It's impossible to know how much XP is still out there, but my unscientific guess would be that 30 percent of the PCs in the business world are still using XP as I write these words. That's not a lot, but it's certainly not a little either.

As far as I'm concerned though, XP and Windows Server 2003 are dead ends. I mean, they really are: Microsoft has stopped supporting them except in extreme circumstances and special handling cases.

But I do want to be super-clear about something: I am also specifically going to note and talk about the differences between the various operating systems. For instance, I'll definitely be expressing some concepts as originally found in Windows 2000, and also Windows XP and Windows Vista—things that were originally in these operating systems' behaviors but are absent or changed now.

When explaining Group Policy, I like to explain how Group Policy evolved from Windows 2000 through Windows XP and Vista and now on to Windows 10. I like to talk about the "old-school" stuff sometimes, because I find it helps explain why Windows does some things today that seem, well, odd or confusing. If I explain the older operating systems, for example, Windows 2000 and Windows XP, it's actually *easier* to understand modern Windows. But as far as actual examples go in this book, *sayonara* XP (and Windows Server 2003). When it's necessary to get a deeper perspective on details of Windows XP, I might refer you to previous editions of this book.

And now, a quick word about Windows Vista.

Yes, friends. Vista happened.

We also cannot deny the existence of Windows Vista and that it actually came and went without anyone caring at all.

That being said, even though Microsoft "didn't quite get the taste right" with regard to Windows Vista, the individual ingredients continue to be the base of our Windows soup going forward. So, that means Windows 7, 8, and 10 are honestly very minor upgrades from Vista.

And pretty much everything that was once valid for Vista is *also* valid for Windows 7, Windows 8, and Windows 10. Therefore, you'll see me write a lot about, "and this works for Windows Vista and later," or in some places, like table listings, you'll see "Valid for Vista+"—meaning that whatever I'm referencing will work on Vista (if you have it), but it will also work on Windows 7, almost always Windows 8, and onward to Windows 10.

A Little about Me, This Book, PolicyPak, and Beyond

Group Policy is a big concept with some big power. This book is intended to help you get a handle on this new power to gain control over your environment and to make your day-to-day administration easier. It's filled with practical, hands-on examples of Group Policy usage and troubleshooting. It is my hope that you enjoy this book and learn from my experiences so you can successfully deploy Group Policy and manage your desktops to better control your network. I'm honored to have you aboard for the ride, and I hope you get as much out of Group Policy as I do.

I've had and continue to have a long history with Group Policy.

I've been writing about and speaking about Group Policy in my hands-on workshops for over 10 years.

I've been one of about a dozen Group Policy MVPs, as anointed by Microsoft for 12 years.

And, I've also founded a company called PolicyPak Software, which extends Group Policy to do more amazing things than what is possible with what is in the box alone. For instance, here are some of the things you can do with the products from PolicyPak:

- Manage just about any third-party application using Group Policy (like Java, Flash, Firefox, Lync [now Skype for Business], OpenOffice, and hundreds more).

- Craft exactly when and how Group Policy Admin Template template settings will be applied to users or computers.

- Keep Group Policy Preferences items working—even when the computer goes offline.

- Learn when a machine is in compliance and out of compliance with what you need it to be.

- Deploy almost all Group Policy directives over the Internet and on to machines that might never otherwise be able to get Group Policy.

So, I'm going to try to walk a fine line here. With your permission, I am going to, from time to time, describe when something from PolicyPak could enhance a situation or solve a problem that cannot be solved out of the box. I'll show you real examples of how to solve real problems.

And I'm doing it not to sell you something, but if that happens, that's okay, too. The point, really, is to demonstrate a problem or situation that might not have any other way out of it. So basically, if I didn't explain that the "PolicyPak possibility" to fix a particular problem existed, you wouldn't know about it and you'd still always be stuck in a rut.

Meanwhile, as you read this book, it's natural to have questions about Group Policy or managing your desktops. To form a community around Group Policy, I have a popular community forum that can be found at www.GPanswers.com.

I encourage you to visit the website and post your questions to the community forum or peruse the other resources that will be constantly renewed and available for download. For instance, in addition to the forum at www.GPanswers.com, you'll find these resources:

- Full downloadable PowerShell scripts from the PowerShell chapter
- Tips and tricks
- A third-party *Group Policy Solutions Guide*, and lots, lots more!

If you want to meet me in person, book me for onsite training, or attend my live public Group Policy courses; my website at www.GPanswers.com has a calendar with upcoming events. I'd love to hear how this book met your needs or helped you out.

Thanks again for being a part of the journey.

1

Group Policy Essentials

In this chapter, you'll get your feet wet with the concept that is Group Policy. You'll start to understand conceptually what Group Policy is and how it's created, applied, and modified, and you'll go through some practical examples to get at the basics.

The best news is that the essentials of Group Policy are the same in all versions of Windows 2000 on. So as I stated in the introduction, if you've got Windows XP, Windows 7, Windows 8, Windows 10—whatever—you're golden.

Learn the basics here, and you're set up on a great path.

That's because Group Policy isn't a server-driven technology. As you'll learn in depth a little later, the magic of Group Policy happens (mostly) on the client (target) machine. And when we say "client," we mean anything that can "receive" Group Policy directives: Windows 8, Windows XP, or even the server operating systems such as Windows Server 2016 or Windows Server 2008 R2; they're all "clients" too.

So, if your Active Directory Domain Controllers are a mixture of Windows Server 2008, Windows Server 2012, and/or Windows Server 2016, nothing much changes. And it doesn't matter if your domain is in Mixed, Native, or another mode—the Group Policy engine works exactly the same in all of them.

There are occasional odds and ends you get with upgraded domain types. When the domain mode is Windows 2003 or later schema, you'll get something neat called WMI filters (described in Chapter 4, "Advanced Group Policy Processing"). Also note that in a Windows 2008 Functional mode domain level or later, the replication of the file-based part of a Group Policy Object (GPO) can be enhanced to use distributed file system (DFS) replication instead of system volume (SYSVOL) replication.

Regardless of what your server architecture is, I encourage you to work through the examples in this chapter.

So, let's get started and talk about the essentials.

Getting Ready to Use This Book

This book is full of examples. And to help you work through them, I'm going to suggest a sample test lab for you to create. It's pretty simple really, but in its simplicity we'll be able to work through dozens of real-world examples to see how things work.

Here are the computers you need to set up and what I suggest you name them (if you want to work through the examples with me in the book):

DC01.corp.com   This is your Active Directory Domain Controller. It can be any type of Domain Controller (DC). For this book, I'll assume you've loaded Windows Server 2016 and later on this computer and that you'll create a test domain called Corp.com.

In real life you would have multiple Domain Controllers in the domain. But here in the test lab, it'll be okay if you just have one.

I'll refer to this machine as DC01 in the book. We'll also use DC01 as a file server and software distribution server and for a lot of other roles we really shouldn't. That's so you can work through lots of examples without bringing up lots of servers. Bringing up a modern DC requires the use of Server Manager. Check out the sidebar "Bringing Up a Windows Server as a Domain Controller" if you need a little guidance.

Win10.corp.com   This is some user's Windows 10 machine and it's joined to the domain Corp.com. I'll refer to this machine as WIN10 in the book. Sometimes it'll be a Sales computer, other times a Marketing computer, and other times a Nursing computer. To use this machine as such, just move the computer account around in Active Directory when the time comes. You'll see what I mean.

Win10management.corp.com   This machine belongs to you—the IT pro who runs the show. You could manage Active Directory from anywhere on your network, but you're going to do it from here. This is the machine you'll use to run the tools you need to manage both Active Directory and Group Policy. I'll refer to this machine as WIN10MANAGEMENT. As the name implies, you'll run Windows 10 from this machine. Note that you aren't "forced" or "required" to use a Windows 10 machine as your management machine—but you'll be able to "manage it all" if you do.

You can see a suggested test lab setup in Figure 1.1.

Note that from time to time I might refer to some machine that *isn't* here in the suggested test lab, just to illustrate a point. However, this is the minimum configuration you'll need to get the most out the book.

To save space in the book, we're going to assume you're using a Windows 10 machine as your management machine. You can also use a Windows 8 or 7 management machine as well and be able to work through pretty much everything in the book, barring a few new things that got born in Windows 8.1 and are still present on a Windows 10 management machine. If you're forced by some draconian corporate edict to use a Windows Vista or Windows XP (or earlier) machine as a management machine, you'll have to refer to previous editions of the book to get the skinny about using them.

FIGURE 1.1 Here's the configuration you'll need for the test lab in this book. Note that the Domain Controller can be 2000 or above, but Windows Server 2016 is preferred to allow you to work through all the examples in this book.

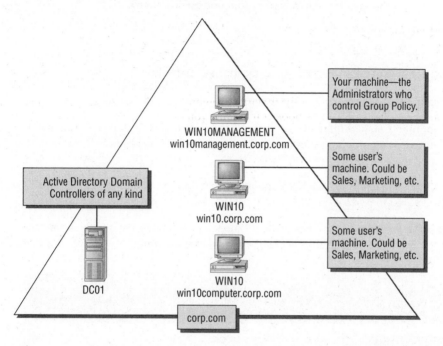

For working through this book, you can build your test lab with real machines or with virtual hardware. Personally, I use VMware Workstation (a pay tool) for my testing. However, Microsoft's Hyper-V is a perfectly decent choice as well. Indeed, Hyper-V is now available built into Windows 8 and later. So, you could bring up a whole test lab to learn Windows 10—on your Windows 10 box! What a mindblower! Here's an (older) overview of Windows 8's Hyper-V if you care to use it: http://tinyurl.com/3r99nr9. Note there are also other alternatives, such as Parallels Desktop and VMware Fusion (both of which run on a Mac) and Oracle VM VirtualBox.

In short, by using virtual machines, if you don't have a bunch of extra physical servers and desktops around, you can follow along with all the examples anyway.

I suggest you build your test lab from scratch. Get the original media or download each operating system and spin up a new test lab.

Here is where to find trial downloads for Windows 7, Windows 8.1, Windows 10, and Windows Server 2016:

www.microsoft.com/en-us/evalcenter/evaluate-windows-8-1-enterprise

Microsoft usually also makes prebuilt virtual hard disk (VHD) images for use with Virtual PC and now, more recently, Hyper-V. It's your choice of course, but I prefer to fresh-build my lab instead of using the preconfigured VHD files.

And that's what I'll be doing for my examples in this book. If the URLs I've specified change, I'm sure a little Googling, er, Bing-ing will Bing it, er, bring it right up.

Because Group Policy can be so all-encompassing, I highly recommend that you try the examples in a test lab environment first before making changes for real in your production environment.

Bringing Up a Windows Server as a Domain Controller

The DCPROMO.EXE you knew and loved is dead as of Windows Server 2012.

Before continuing, ensure that your server is already named DC01. If it isn't, rename it and reboot before continuing. Additionally, ensure that DC01 has a static IP address and is configured to use itself as the DNS server.

Now, you'll need to use the Server Manager's "Add Roles and Features Wizard" to add the roles required to make your server a DC. It's not hard. Here's a sketch of the steps.

First, fire up Server Manager, which is the leftmost icon when you're on the server. Next, click Dashboard and select "Add roles and features," as seen here.

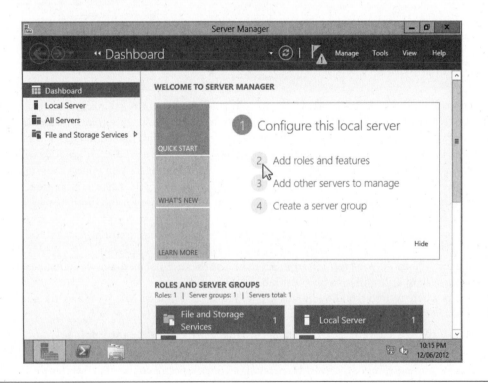

Then you'll be at the "Add Roles and Features Wizard," as seen here.

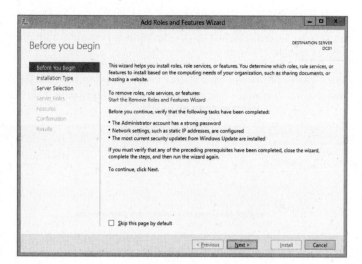

Click Next to visit the Installation Type screen and select "Role-based or feature-based installation." Then click Next.

At Server Selection, click "Select a server from the server pool" and select your only machine: DC01.

At Server Roles, select Active Directory Domain Services, as seen here, and say yes when prompted to load the additional items, which must come along for the ride.

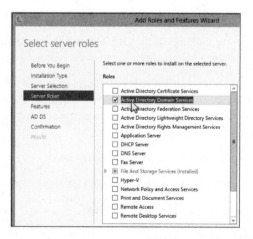

At the Features screen, click Next.

At the AD DS screen, click Next.

At the Confirmation screen, select "Restart the destination server automatically if required" and then click Install.

Next, Active Directory components will be installed on DC01 along with the GPMC. When done, you'll be able to select "Promote this server to a domain controller," as seen here.

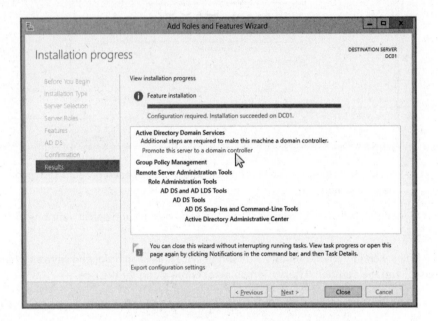

At this point it should be pretty familiar. At the Deployment Configuration page, select "Add a new forest" and type **Corp.com** as the root domain name. Click Next.

At the Domain Controller Options page, leave the defaults as is. Provide a Directory Services Restore Mode (DSRM) password. I recommend **p@ssw0rd**. (My suggested password in all my books is p@ssw0rd. That's a lowercase *p*, the at sign, an *s*, an *s*, a *w*, a zero, then *r*, and *d*.) Click Next to continue.

At the DNS Options page, you might get a warning; click Next.

At the Additional Options page, leave the defaults and click Next.

At the Paths page, leave the defaults as is and click Next.

At the Review Options page, click Next.

At the Prerequisites Check page, make sure there are no showstoppers. Finally, click Install on that same page.

The computer should restart automatically and reboot.

Congrats! You have your first Domain Controller!

Getting Started with Group Policy

Group Policy is a big, big place. And you need a road map. Let's try to get a firm understanding of what we're about to be looking at for the next several hundred pages.

Group Policy Entities and Policy Settings

Every Group Policy Object contains two halves: a User half and a Computer half. These two halves are properly called *nodes*, though sometimes they're just referred to as either the *User half* and the *Computer half* or the *User branch* and the *Computer branch*.

A sample Group Policy Object with both the Computer Configuration and User Configuration nodes can be seen in Figure 1.2 (in the upcoming section, "Local Group Policy Editor"). Don't worry; I'll show you how to get there in just a second.

Just to make things a little more complicated, if you're deploying settings using Active Directory (the most usual case) as opposed to walking up and creating a "local GPO" as we do later in Figure 1.2, the interface is a wee bit different and shows the Group Policy Preferences node. Hang tight for more on that.

The first level under both the User and the Computer nodes contains Software Settings, Windows Settings, and Administrative Templates. If we dive down into the Administrative Templates of the Computer node, underneath we discover additional levels of Windows Components, System, Network, and Printers. Likewise, if we dive down into the Administrative Templates of the User node, we see some of the same folders plus some additional ones, such as Shared Folders, Desktop, Start Menu, and Taskbar.

In both the User and Computer halves, you'll see that policy settings are hierarchical, like a directory structure. Similar policy settings are grouped together for easy location. That's the idea anyway—though, admittedly, sometimes locating the specific policy or configuration you want can prove to be a challenge.

When manipulating policy settings, you can choose to set either computer policy settings or user policy settings (or both!). You'll see examples of this shortly. (See the section "Searching and Commenting Group Policy Objects and Policy Settings" in Chapter 2,

"Managing Group Policy with the GPMC and via Powershell," for tricks on how to mini-mize the effort of finding the policy setting you want.)

Most policy settings are not found in both nodes. However, there are a few that overlap. In that case, if the computer policy setting is different from the user policy setting, the computer policy setting generally overrides the user policy setting. But, to be sure, check the Explain text associated with the policy setting.

Wait... I Don't Get It. What Do the User and Computer Nodes Do?

One of the key issues that new Group Policy administrators ask themselves is, "What the heck is the difference between the Computer and User nodes?"

Imagine that you had a combination store: Dog Treats (for dogs) and Candy Treats (for kids). That's right; it's a strange little store with seemingly two types of incompatible foods under the same roof. You wouldn't feed the kids dog treats (they'd spit them out and ignore the treat), and you wouldn't feed the kids' candy to a dog (because the dogs would spit out the sour candy and ignore the treat).

That's the same thing that happens here. Sure, it looks tempting. There are lots of treats on both sides of the store, but only one type of customer will accept each type of treat.

So, in practical terms, the Computer node (the first part of the policy) contains policy settings that are relevant only for computers. That is, if there's a GPO that contains Computer-side settings and it "hits" a computer, these settings will take effect. These Computer-side settings could be items like startup scripts, shutdown scripts, and how the local firewall should be configured. Think of this as every setting relevant to the *computer itself*—no matter who is logged on at that moment.

The User node (the second part of the policy) contains policy settings that are relevant only for users. Again, if there's a GPO that contains User-side settings and it "hits" a user, these settings will take effect for that user. These User-side items make sense only on a per-user basis, like logon scripts, logoff scripts, availability of the Control Panel, and lots more. Think of this as every setting relevant to the currently logged-on user—and these settings will follow the user to every machine they pop on to.

Feeding users dog treats, er, Computer-side settings doesn't work. Same thing with feed-ing computers User-side settings. When a GPO hits user objects with Computer policy settings or computer objects with User policy settings, it simply will *not* do anything. You'll just sit there and scratch your head and wonder why it doesn't work. But it's not that it's not working; this is how it's designed.

Computer settings are for computer objects, and User settings are for user objects. If this is bad news for you, there are two ways to get out of the problem. One way is an in-the-box advanced technique called *loopback processing* that can help you out. Look for more information on loopback processing in Chapter 4. The other way is via a third-party tool called PolicyPak, which (among other things) can permit computers to embrace User-side settings. More on this in Chapter 6, "Managing Applications and Settings Using Group Policy.

Active Directory and Local Group Policy

Group Policy is a twofold idea. First, without an Active Directory, there's one and only one Group Policy available.

Officially, this policy directly on the workstation is called a *local policy*, but it still resides under the umbrella of the concept of Group Policy. Later, once Active Directory is available, the nonlocal (or, as they're sometimes called, *domain-based* or *Active Directory–based*) Group Policy Objects come into play, as you'll see later. Let's get started and explore both options.

Then, here's the weird thing: after I've fully described Active Directory's Group Policy, we're going to take a second visit back to Local Group Policy. That's because with Windows Vista and later, there's a special superpower I want to show you, but I only want to explain it after we've explored the first two concepts. So, in summary, here's the short-term road map:

- Local Group Policy for Windows XP and later
- Active Directory Group Policy for all operating systems
- Multiple Local Group Policy (MLGPO) for Windows Vista and later

Trust me; it's easier to learn it this way, even though we're taking two passes at one concept.

While you're plunking around inside the Group Policy editor (also known as the Group Policy Management Editor, or Group Policy Object Editor), you'll see lots of policy settings that are geared toward a particular operating system. Some are only for specific operating systems, and others are more general. If you happen to apply a policy setting to a system that isn't listed, the policy setting is simply ignored. For instance, policy settings described as working "Only for Windows 8" machines will not typically work on Windows XP machines. All policy settings have a "Supported on" field that should be consulted to know which operating systems can embrace which policy setting. Many of them will say something like "At least Windows XP" to let you know they're valid for, say, XP and on.

Understanding Local Group Policy

Before we officially dive into what is specifically contained inside this magic of Group Policy or how Group Policy is applied when Active Directory is involved, you might be curious to see exactly what your interaction with Local Group Policy might look like.

Local Group Policy is best used when Active Directory isn't available, say either in a Novell NetWare environment or when you have a gaggle of machines that simply aren't connected to a domain.

Local Group Policy Editor

The most expeditious way to edit the Local Group Policy on a machine is to click Start ➤ Run and type in **GPEDIT.MSC**. This pops up the Local Computer Policy Editor.

You are now exploring the Local Group Policy of this workstation. Local Group Policy is unique to each specific machine. To see how a Local Group Policy applies, drill down through the User Configuration ➤ Administrative Templates ➤ System ➤ Ctrl+Alt+Del options and select **Remove Lock Computer**, as shown in Figure 1.2. As seen in the figure, the default for all policy settings is Not Configured. To make this policy setting perform its magic, choose the Enabled radio button and click OK.

When you do, within a few seconds you should see that if you press Ctrl+Alt+Del, the Lock Computer option is unavailable.

To revert the change, simply reselect **Remove Lock Computer** and select Not Configured. This reverts the change.

 You can think of Local Group Policy as a way to perform decentralized administration. A bit later, when we explore Group Policy with Active Directory, we'll saunter into centralized administration.

This Local Group Policy affects everyone who logs onto this machine—including normal users and administrators. Be careful when making settings here; you can temporarily lock yourself out of some useful functions.

If you're thinking to yourself, "Yep, I've done that," then stay tuned. After the next section is complete, we'll return to Local Group Policy and discuss the idea of Multiple Local Group Policy Objects, which can help ensure that you escape from this very jam.

Before we leave Local Group Policy (for now), remember something that I stated in the introduction. That is, many of the settings we'll explore in this book are available to workstations or servers that aren't joined to an Active Directory domain. Just poke around here in Local Group Policy to get a feel for what you can and cannot do without Active Directory. However, many functions, like Folder Redirection settings (discussed in Chapter 10, "Implementing a Managed Desktop, Part 1: Redirected Folders, Offline Files, and the Synchronization Manager"), the Software Distribution settings (discussed in Chapter 11, "The Managed Desktop, Part 2: Software Deployment via Group Policy"), and others require Active Directory present to embrace these Group Policy directives.

You can point to other computers' local policies by using the syntax gpedit.msc /gpcomputer:"*targetmachine*" or gpedit.msc / gpcomputer:"*targetmachine.domain.com*"; the machine name must be in quotes.

FIGURE 1.2   You can edit the Local Group Policy using the Local Group Policy Editor (GPEDIT.MSC).

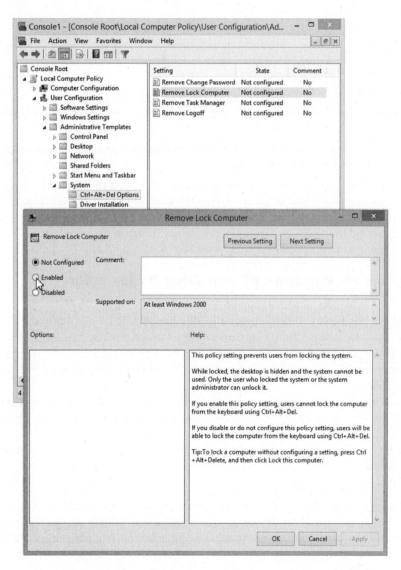

Active Directory–Based Group Policy

To use Group Policy in the most meaningful way, you'll need an Active Directory environment. An Active Directory environment needn't be anything particularly fancy; indeed, it could consist of a single Domain Controller and perhaps just one Windows 10 workstation joined to the domain.

But Active Directory can also grow extensively from that original solitary server. You can think of an Active Directory network as having four constituent and distinct levels that relate to Group Policy:

- The local computer
- The site
- The domain
- The organizational unit (OU)

The rules of Active Directory state the following:

- Every server and workstation must be a member of one (and only one) domain and be located in one (and only one) site.
- Every user must be a member of one (and only one) domain and may also be located within one OU (and only one OU).

One of the most baffling questions people have when they start to dig into Group Policy is, "If a user can only be a member of one OU, how do I apply multiple Group Policy Object directives to one user?" I know it seems almost impossible based on the constraints listed, but I promise I'll explain exactly how to do that in Chapter 2 in the section "Filtering the Scope of Group Policy Objects with Security."

Full Windows vs. Windows RT and What It Means for Group Policy

Windows has two big flavors: full Windows and Windows RT.

Windows RT is the tablet edition that runs on ARM-based devices. Microsoft is not permitting Windows RT machines to join Active Directory. Therefore, there is no way to get Active Directory–based Group Policy on Windows RT. However, Windows RT will support Local Group Policy.

In this book we're not going to be spending much time on Windows RT, because most of what we'll do, we'll do within the domain—and Windows RT machines are left out of the fun.

Windows RT has some non–Group Policy management capability so that administrators can control basic security settings. For more information about this feature, visit

`http://tinyurl.com/6ufn565`

Sadly, Windows RT has been out a few years (with the birth of Windows 8) and there still isn't any way to manage these devices using Group Policy. If there ever comes a time that Windows RT machines can join the domain and get Active Directory Group Policy, I'll write about it at www.GPanswers.com. But don't hold your breath, as all indications suggest Windows RT will likely be depreciated and Microsoft will only be updating Windows RT to keep the lights on.

Group Policy and Active Directory

As you saw, when Group Policy is created at the local level, everyone who uses that machine is affected by those wishes. But once you step up and use Active Directory, you can have nearly limitless Group Policy Objects (GPOs)—with the ability to selectively decide which users and which computers will get which wishes (try saying that five times quickly). The GPO is the vessel that stores these wishes for delivery.

Actually, you can have only 999 GPOs applied and affecting a user or a computer before the system "gives up" and won't apply any more.

You'll create GPOs using the Group Policy Management Console, or GPMC for short. The GPMC can be added to a Windows Server 2016 computer or Domain Controller (see the section "Using a Windows Server 2016 Machine as Your Management Station"). The GPMC can also be added to a Windows 7, Windows 8, Windows 8.1, or Windows 10 machine via an extra download and install called RSAT. RSAT stands for Remote Server Administration Tools, and after installing it, you'll find tools like Active Directory Users and Computers as well as the GPMC, which we'll use right around the bend.

When we create a GPO that can be used in Active Directory, two things happen: we create some brand-new entries within Active Directory, and we automatically create some brand-new files within our Domain Controllers. Collectively, these items make one GPO.

You can think of Active Directory as having three major levels:

- Site
- Domain
- OU

Additionally, since OUs can be nested within each other, Active Directory has a nearly limitless capacity for where we can tuck stuff away.

In fact, it's best to think of this design as a three-tier hierarchy: site, domain, and each nested OU. When wishes, er, policy settings, are set at a higher level in Active Directory, they automatically flow down throughout the remaining levels.

So, to be precise:

- If a GPO is set at the site level, the policy settings contained within affect those accounts within the geography of the site. Sure, their user account could be in one domain and their computer account could be in another domain. And of course, it's likely that those accounts are in an OU. But the account is affected only by the policy settings here because the account is in a specific site. And logically, when a computer starts up in a new site, the User object will also get its site-based Group Policy from the same place. This is based on the IP subnet the user is a part of and is configured using Active Directory Sites and Services.

▪ If a GPO is set at the domain level, it affects those users and computers within the domain and all OUs and all other OUs beneath it.

▪ If a GPO is set at the OU level, it affects those users or computers within the OU and all other OUs beneath it (usually just called child or sub-OUs).

By default, when a policy is set at one level, the levels below *inherit* the settings from the levels above it. You can have "cumulative" wishes that keep piling on.

You might wonder what happens if two policy settings conflict. Perhaps one policy is set at the domain level and another policy is set at the OU level, which reverses the edict in the domain. The result is simple: policy settings further down the food chain take precedence. For instance, if a policy setting conflicts at the domain and OU levels, the OU level "wins." Likewise, domain-level settings override any policy settings that conflict with previously set site-specific policy settings. This might seem counterintuitive at first, so bear with me for a minute.

Take a look at the following illustration to get a view of the order of precedence.

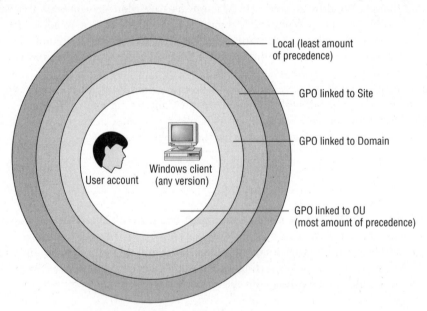

The golden rule with Group Policy is truly, "Last writer wins." Another way to say it is, "If any GPOs conflict, the settings contained in the last-written GPO win."

However, don't forget about any Local Group Policy that might have been set on a specific workstation. Regardless, once that local policy is determined, only *then* do policy settings within Active Directory (the site, domain, and OU) apply. So, sometimes people refer to the *four* levels of Group Policy: local workstation, site, domain, and OU. Nonetheless, GPOs set within Active Directory always trump the Local Group Policy should there be any conflict.

If this behavior is undesirable for lower Active Directory levels, all the settings from higher Active Directory levels can be blocked with the "Block Inheritance" attribute on a given OU. Additionally, if a higher-level administrator wants to guarantee that a setting is inherited down the food chain, they can apply the "Enforced" attribute via the GPMC interface. (Panic not! Chapter 2 explores both "Block Inheritance" and "Enforced" attributes in detail.)

Note that you cannot "Block Inheritance" between Local GPOs and Active Directory GPOs. But it is true that anything you set within Active Directory to inverse a Local GPO setting is always honored. Said another way, Active Directory edicts trump local edicts. You can, however, literally "turn off" Local Group Policy Objects from processing. In Windows Vista and later, there is a policy setting found in Computer Configuration ➢ Policies ➢ Administrative Templates ➢ System ➢ Group Policy entitled **Turn off Local Group Policy Object processing**, which, when set to Enabled, will prevent Local Group Policy Objects from affecting the machine.

Don't sweat it if your head is spinning a little now from the Group Policy application theory. I'll go through specific hands-on examples to illustrate each of these behaviors so that you understand exactly how this works.

Linking Group Policy Objects

Another technical concept that needs a bit of description here is the "linking" of GPOs. When a GPO "appears" to be "created" at the site, domain, or OU level via the GUI (which we'll do in a moment), what's really happening is quite different. It's created in one set "place," then merely "linked" there. (Yes, I know there are a lot of "quotes" in the last sentence, but sometimes that's how I "write.")

Anyway, when you tell the system, "I want to affect an OU with this new GPO," the system automatically creates the GPO in the fixed location and then associates that GPO with the level at which you want to affect. That association is called *linking*.

Linking is an important concept for several reasons. First, it's generally a good idea to understand what's going on under the hood. However, more practically, the Group Policy Management Console (GPMC), as we'll explore in just a bit, displays GPOs from their linked perspective.

Let's extend the metaphor a little more.

You can think of all the GPOs you create in Active Directory as children in a big swimming pool. Each child has a tether attached around their waist, and an adult guardian is holding the other end of the rope. Indeed, there could be multiple tethers around a child's waist, with multiple adults tethered to one child. A sad state indeed would be a child who has no tether but is just swimming around in the pool unsecured. The swimming pool in this analogy is a specific Active Directory container named Policies (which we'll examine closely in Chapter 7, "Troubleshooting Group Policy"). All GPOs are born and "live" in that specific domain. Indeed, they're replicated to all Domain Controllers. The adult guardian in this analogy represents a *level* in Active Directory—any site, domain, or OU.

In our swimming pool example, multiple adults can be tethered to a specific child. With Active Directory, multiple levels can be linked to a specific GPO. Thus, any level in Active Directory can leverage multiple GPOs, which are standing by in the domain ready to be used.

Remember, though, unless a GPO is specifically linked to a site, a domain, or an OU, it does not take effect. It's just floating around in the swimming pool of the domain waiting for someone to make use of it.

I'll keep reiterating and refining the concept of linking throughout the first four chapters. And, as necessary, I'll discuss why you might want to "unlink" a policy.

This concept of linking to GPOs created in Active Directory can be a bit confusing. It will become clearer later as we explore the processes of creating new GPOs and linking to existing ones. Stay tuned. That discussion is right around the corner.

Multiple Local GPOs (Vista and Later)

Okay, as promised, we need to take a second swipe at Local GPOs.

Starting with Vista and continuing on through Windows 10, there's a secret superpower that takes Local Group Policy to the next level.

The last time I discussed Local GPOs, I stated this:

> *This Local Group Policy affects everyone who logs onto this machine—including normal users and administrators. Be careful when making settings here; you can temporarily lock yourself out of some useful functions.*

True—for pre-Vista machines, like Windows XP. On Vista and later, however, the superpower feature is that you can decide who gets which settings at a local level. This feature is called Multiple Local GPOs (MLGPOs).

MLGPOs are most often handy when you want your users to get one gaggle of settings (that is, desktop restrictions) but you want to ensure that your access is unfettered for day-to-day administration.

Now, in these examples we're going to use Windows 10, but this same feature is available on Vista and later (including Windows Server 2008 and later). It's just not all that likely you'll end up using it on a Windows Server.

Understanding Multiple Local GPOs

The best way to understand MLGPOs is by thinking of the end product. That is, when we're done, we want our users to embrace some settings, and we (administrators) want to potentially embrace some settings or *avoid* some settings. We can even get granular and dictate specific settings to just one user.

By typing **GPEDIT.MSC** at a command prompt, you're running the utility to affect all users—mere mortals *and* administrators.

But with Vista and later, there are actually three "layers" that can be leveraged to ensure that some settings affect regular users and other settings affect you (the administrator).

Let's be sure to understand all three layers before we get too gung ho and try it out. When MLGPOs are processed, Windows Vista and later checks to see if the layer is being used and if that layer is supposed to apply to that user:

Layer 1 (Lowest Priority)   The Local Computer Policy. You create this by running GPEDIT.MSC.

- The settings you make on the Computer Configuration side are guaranteed to affect all users on this computer (including administrators).

- The settings you make on the User Configuration side may be trumped by Layer 2 or Layer 3.

Layer 2 (Next Highest Priority)   Is the user a mere mortal *or* a local administrator? (One account cannot be both.) This layer cannot contain Computer Configuration settings.

Layer 3 (Most Specific)   Is this a specific user who is being dictated a specific policy? This layer cannot contain Computer Configuration settings.

You can see this graphically laid out in Figure 1.3.

If no conflicts exist among the levels, the effect is additive. For instance, let's imagine the following:

- Layer 1 (Everyone): The wish is to restrict "Lock this PC" from the Ctrl+Alt+Del area in Windows 10. We'll use the **Remove Lock Computer** policy setting that we already saw in Figure 1.2.

- Then, at Layer 2 (Users, but not Administrators): We say "All local users" will have Task Manager gone from the Ctl+Alt+Del screen in Windows 10.

- Then, at Layer 3 (a specific user): We say Fred, a local user, will be denied access to the Control Panel.

The result for Fred will be the sum total of all edicts at all layers.

But what if there's a conflict between the levels? In that case, the layer that's "closest to the user" wins (also known as "Last writer wins"). So, if at the Local Computer Policy the wish is to **Remove Lock Computer** from the Ctrl+Alt+Del area but that area is expressly granted to Sally, a local user on that machine, Sally will still be able to use the Lock command. That's because we're saying that she is expressly granted the right at Layer 3, which "wins" over Layers 1 and 2.

FIGURE 1.3   A block diagram of how MLGPOs are applied to a system

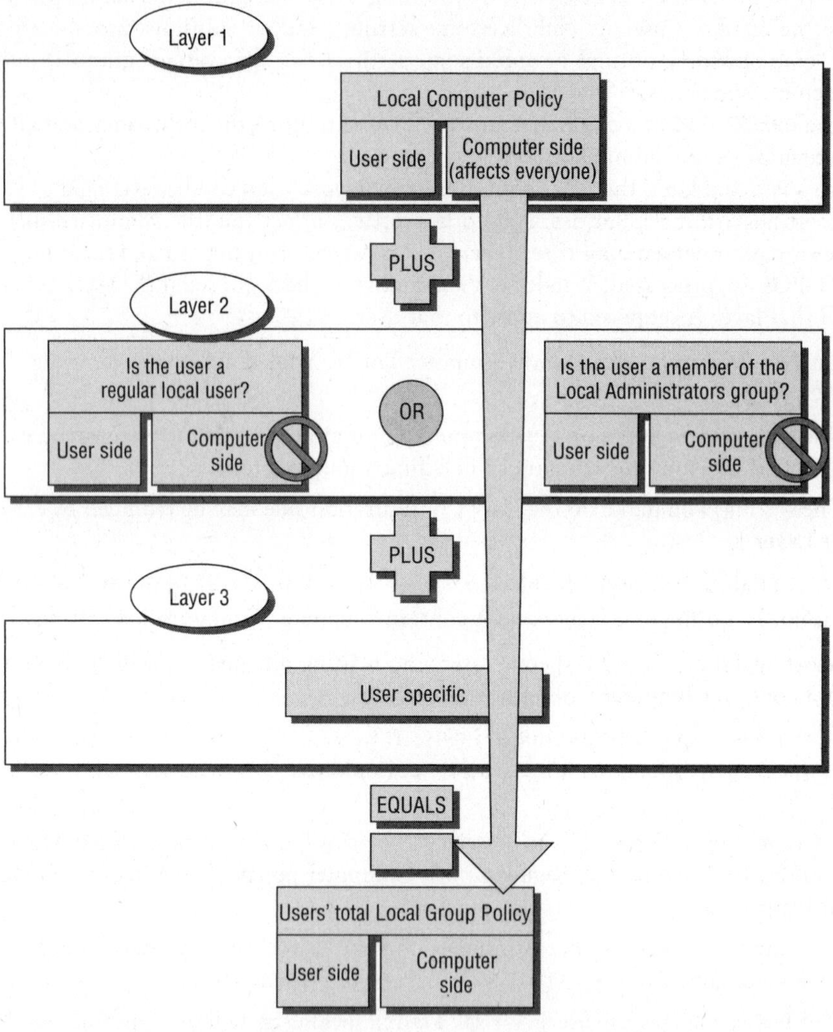

Layer 1

Local Computer Policy

| User side | Computer side (affects everyone) |

PLUS

Layer 2

| Is the user a regular local user? | | Is the user a member of the Local Administrators group? |

| User side | Computer side | | User side | Computer side |

OR

PLUS

Layer 3

User specific

EQUALS

Users' total Local Group Policy

| User side | Computer side |

Trying Out Multiple Local GPOs on Windows 10

Just typing **GPEDIT.MSC** at the Start screen doesn't give you the magical "layering" super-power. Indeed, just typing **GPEDIT.MSC** performs the exact same function as it did in Windows XP. That is, every edit you make while you run the Local Computer Policy affects all users logged onto the machine.

To tell Vista and later you want to edit one of the layers (as just described), you need to load the Group Policy Object Editor by hand. We'll do this on WIN10.

On WIN10, to load the Group Policy Object Editor by hand, follow these steps:

1. From the Start screen, start typing `MMC` (which will bring up the Search box). A "naked" MMC appears. Note that you may have to approve a User Access Control (UAC) dialog message (UAC is discussed in detail in Chapter 8, "Implementing Security with Group Policy").

2. From the File menu, choose Add/Remove Snap-in to open the Add/Remove Snap-in dialog box.

3. Locate and select the Group Policy Object Editor Snap-in and click Add (don't choose the Group Policy Management Snap-in, if present—that's the GPMC that we'll use a bit later).

4. At the Select Group Policy Object screen, note that the default Local Computer Policy is selected. Click Browse.

5. The "Browse for a Group Policy Object" dialog box appears. Select the Users tab and select the layer you want. That is, you can pick Non-Administrators or Administrators, or click a specific user, or choose the Administrator account, as seen in Figure 1.4.

FIGURE 1.4 Edit specific layers of Windows MLGPOs by first adding the Group Policy Object Editor into a "naked" MMC. Then browse for the Windows Local Group Policy by firing up GPEDIT.MSC.

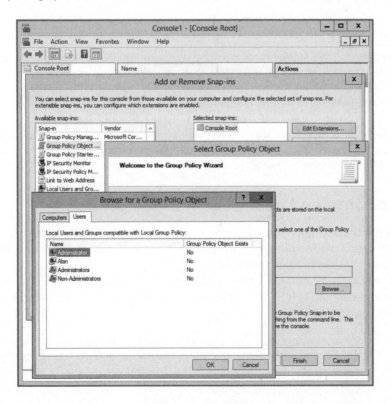

In the Group Policy Object Exists column in the Users tab, you can also tell whether or not a local GPO layer is being used.

6. At the "Select Group Policy Object" dialog box, click Finish.

7. At the "Add or Remove Snap-ins" dialog box, click OK.

You should now be able to edit that layer of the local GPO. For instance, Figure 1.5 shows that I've chosen to edit the Non-Administrators portion of the GPO (which is on level 2).

FIGURE 1.5   Below the words *Console Root*, you can see which layer of the local GPO you're specifically editing.

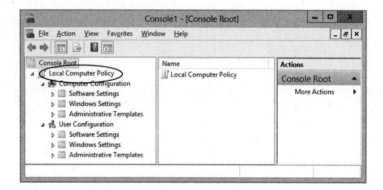

To edit additional or other layers of the local GPO, repeat the previous steps.

Here's an important point that bears repeating: Layers 2 and 3 of the MLGPO *cannot* contain overriding computer settings from Layer 1. That's why in Figure 1.5 you simply don't see them—they're not there. If you want to introduce a Computer-side setting that affects everyone on the machine, just fire up GPEDIT.MSC and you'll be off and running. That's Layer 1, and it affects everyone.

Final Thoughts on Local GPOs

You can think of Local Group Policy as a way to perform desktop management in a decentralized way. That is, you're still running around, more or less, from machine to machine where you want to set the Local Group Policy.

The other strategy is a centralized approach. Centralized Group Policy administration works only in conjunction with Active Directory and is the main focus of this book.

 For more information, check out the article "Step-by-Step Guide to Managing Multiple Local Group Policy" from Microsoft. At last check, the URL was http://tinyurl.com/oqgl8at. The steps should work for all versions of Windows starting with Vista.

In case you're curious, Local Group Policy is stored in the `%windir%\system32\grouppolicy` directory (usually `C:\windows\system32\grouppolicy`). The structure found here mirrors what you'll see later in Chapter 7 when we inspect the ins and outs of how Group Policy applies from Active Directory. Windows Vista and later store Level 2 (Admin/Non-Admin Local Policies) and specific Local User Policies (Level 3) inside `%windir%\system32\grouppolicyusers`.

You will notice one folder per user policy you have created, each named with the Security ID (SID) of the relevant user object.

An Example of Group Policy Application

At this point, it's best not to jump directly into adding, deleting, or modifying our own GPOs. Right now, it's better to understand how Group Policy works "on paper." This is especially true if you're new to the concept of Group Policy, but perhaps also if Group Policy has been deployed by other administrators in your Active Directory.

By walking through a fictitious organization that has deployed GPOs at multiple levels, you'll be able to better understand how and why policy settings are applied by the deployment of GPOs.

Let's start by taking a look at Figure 1.6, the organization for our fictitious example company, Example.com.

This picture could easily tell a thousand words. For the sake of brevity, I've kept it down to around 200. There are two domains: Example.com and Widgets.example.com. Let's talk about Example.com:

- The domain Example.com has two Domain Controllers. One DC, named EXAMPLEDC1, is physically located in the California site. Example.com's other Domain Controller, EXAMPLEDC2, is physically located in the Phoenix site.

- As for PCs, they need to physically reside somewhere. SallysPC is in the California site; BrettsPC and AdamsPC are in the Delaware site. JoesPC is in the Phoenix site. FredsPC is in the California site, and MarksPC is in the New York site.

- User accounts may or may not be in OUs. Dave's and Jane's account are in the **Human Resources** OU.

- Computer accounts may or may not be in OUs. FredsPC is in the **Human Resources** OU. AdamsPC is specifically placed within the **High Security** OU. And that **High Security** OU is actually within the **Human Resources** OU (also known as a sub-OU.). JoesPC, SallysPC, BrettsPC, and MarksPC are hanging out in a container and aren't in any OUs.

Using Active Directory Sites and Services, you can put in place a schedule to regulate communication between EXAMPLEDC1 located in California and EXAMPLEDC2 located in Phoenix. That way, the administrator controls the chatter between the two Example.com Domain Controllers, and it is not at the whim of the operating system.

FIGURE 1.6 This fictitious Example.com is relatively simple. Your environment may be more complex.

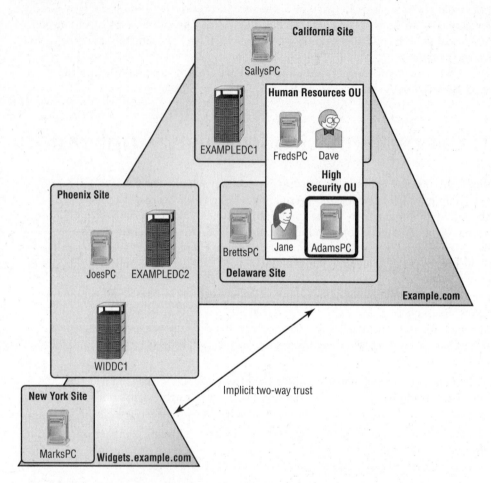

Another domain, called Widgets.example.com, has an implicit transitive two-way trust to Example.com. There is only one Domain Controller in the Widgets.example.com domain, named WIDDC1, and it physically resides at the Phoenix site. Last, there is MarksPC, a member of the Widgets.example.com domain, and it physically resides in the New York site and isn't in any OU.

Understanding where your users and machines are is half the battle. The other half is understanding which policy settings are expected to appear when they start logging onto Active Directory.

Examining the Resultant Set of Policy

As stated earlier, the effect of Group Policy is cumulative as GPOs are successively applied—starting at the local computer, then the site, the domain, and each nested OU. The end result of what affects a specific user or computer—after all Group Policy at all levels has been applied—is called the *Resultant Set of Policy (RSoP)*. This is sometimes referred to as the *RSoP calculation*.

Throughout your lifetime working with Group Policy, you will be asked to troubleshoot the RSoP of client machines.

> Many of our dealings with Group Policy will consist of trying to understand and troubleshoot the RSoP of a particular configuration. Getting a good, early understanding of how to perform manual RSoP calculations on paper is important because it's a useful troubleshooting skill. In Chapters 3 and 7, we'll also explore additional RSoP skills—with tools and additional manual troubleshooting.

Before we jump in to try to discover what the RSoP might be for any specific machine, it's often helpful to break out each of the strata—local computer, site, domain, and OU—and examine, at each level, what happens to the entities contained in them. I'll then bring it all together to see how a specific computer or user reacts to the accumulation of GPOs. For these examples, assume that no local policy is set on any of the computers; the goal is to get a better feeling of how Group Policy flows, not necessarily what the specific end state will be.

At the Site Level

Based on what we know from Figure 1.6, the GPOs in effect at the site level are shown here:

Site	Computers Affected
California	SallysPC, EXAMPLEDC1, and FredsPC
Phoenix	EXAMPLEDC2, JoesPC, and WIDDC1
New York	MarksPC
Delaware	AdamsPC and BrettsPC

If we look at the graphic again, it looks like Dave, for instance, resides in California and Jane, for instance, resides in Delaware. But I don't like to think about it like that. I prefer to say that their accounts reside in OUs.

But users are affected by site GPOs *only* when they log onto computers that are at a specific site.

In Figure 1.6, we have Dave's and Jane's accounts in the **Human Resources** OU. And that's great. But they're only affected by California site-level GPOs if they travel to California. It doesn't matter where they usually reside; again, they're only affected by the site-level GPOs when they're physically present in that site. So if they travel to California, they will get the GPOs related to California first; then other GPOs (described later) will apply.

So, don't think that user accounts *reside* at the site level. Rather, they reside in the OU level but are using computers in the site and, hence, get the properties assigned to all users at that site.

Sites are defined using the Active Directory Sites and Services tool. IP subnets that constitute a site are assigned using this tool. That way, if a new computer turns on in Delaware, Active Directory knows what site the computer is in.

At the Domain Level

Here's what we have working at the domain level:

Domain	Computers/Users Affected
Example.com Computers	SallysPC, FredsPC, AdamsPC, BrettsPC, JoesPC, EXAMPLEDC1, and EXAMPLEDC2
Example.com Users	Dave and Jane
Widgets.example.com Computers	WIDDC1 and MarksPC

At the OU Level

At the organizational unit level, we have the following:

Organizational Unit	Computers/Users Affected
Human Resources OU Computers	FredsPC is in the **Human Resources** OU; therefore, it is affected when the **Human Resources** OU gets GPOs applied. Additionally, the **High Security** OU is contained inside the **Human Resources** OU. Therefore, AdamsPC, which is in the **High Security** OU, is also affected whenever the **Human Resources** OU is affected.
Human Resources OU Users	The accounts of Dave and Jane are affected when the **Human Resources** OU has GPOs applied.

Bringing It All Together

Now that you've broken out all the levels and seen what is being applied to them, you can start to calculate what the devil is happening on any specific user and computer combination. Looking at Figure 1.6 and analyzing what's happening at each level makes adding things together between the local, site, domain, and organizational unit GPOs a lot easier.

Here are some examples of RSoP for specific users and computers in our fictitious environment:

FredsPC	FredsPC inherits the settings of the GPOs from the California site, then the Example.com domain, and last, the **Human Resources** OU.
MarksPC	MarksPC first accepts the GPOs from the New York site and then the Widgets.example.com domain. MarksPC is not in any OU; therefore, no organizational unit GPOs apply to his computer.
AdamsPC	AdamsPC is subject to the GPOs at the Delaware site, the Example.com domain, the **Human Resources** OU, and the **High Security** OU.
Dave using AdamsPC	AdamsPC is subject to the computer policies in the GPOs for the Delaware site, the Example.com domain, the **Human Resources** OU, and finally the **High Security** OU. When Dave travels from California to Delaware to use Adam's workstation, his user GPOs are dictated from the Delaware site, the Example.com domain, and the **Human Resources** OU (where Dave's account is actually contained).

At no time are any domain GPOs from the Example.com parent domain automatically inherited by the Widget.example.com child domain. Inheritance for GPOs only flows downward to OUs within a single domain—not between any two domains—parent to child or otherwise, unless you explicitly link one of those parent GPOs to a child Domain Container.

If you want one GPO to affect the users in more than one domain, you have four choices:

- Precisely re-create the GPOs in each domain with their own GPO.
- Copy the GPO from one domain to another domain (using the GPMC, as explained in Chapter 2 in the section "Basic Interdomain Copy and Import").
- Use a third-party tool that can perform some magic and automatically perform the copying between domains for you.
- Do a generally recognized no-no called *cross-domain policy linking*. (I'll describe this no-no in detail in Chapter 7 in the section "Group Policy Objects from a Domain Perspective.")

Also, don't assume that linking a GPO at a site level necessarily guarantees the results to just one domain. In this example, as in real life, there is not necessarily a 1:1 correlation between sites and domains. Indeed, without getting too geeky here, sites technically belong to the forest and not any particular domain.

At this point, we'll put our example Example.com behind us. That was an on-paper exercise to allow you to get a feel for what's possible in Group Policy–land. From this point forward, you'll be doing most items in your test lab and following along.

Group Policy, Active Directory, and the GPMC

The Group Policy Management Console (GPMC) was created to help administrators work in a "one-stop-shop" place for all Group Policy management functions. Since 2003, it was freely downloadable as an add-on to either Windows XP or Windows Server 2003 systems.

Today, the GPMC is built into the server operating systems (Server 2008 R2, Windows Server 2016, etc.). And it's also available for download as part of the RSAT tools for your own machine (say, Windows 7 or 10).

Even though I've said it before, it bears repeating: it doesn't matter if your Active Directory or domains or Domain Controllers are Windows 2000, Windows 2003, Windows 2008, Windows 2008 R2, Windows 2012, Windows 2012 R2, Windows Server 2016, or whatever. The Group Policy infrastructure doesn't care what domain type or Domain Controllers you have.

The GPMC's name says it all. It's the Group Policy Management Console. Indeed, this will be the MMC snap-in that you use to manage the underlying Group Policy mechanism. The GPMC just helps us tap into those features already built into Active Directory. I'll highlight the mechanism of how Group Policy works throughout the next three chapters.

One major design goal of the GPMC is to get a Group Policy–centric view of the lay of the land. The GPMC also provides a programmatic way to manage your GPOs. In fact, the GPMC scripting interface allows just about any GPO operation. You can do the same "stuff" with the GPMC that you do with the mouse programmatically with VBScript and PowerShell.

We'll explore scripting Group Policy operations normally performed with the GPMC, but instead using PowerShell in Appendix A, a downloadable bonus chapter, "Scripting Group Policy Operations with Windows PowerShell."

 The VBScript GPMC scripts, which were previously part of the downloadable GPMC package, are not included in the newest GPMC. You have to specifically download them from the GPMC scripting center at http://tinyurl.com/23xfz3 or search for "Group Policy Management Console Sample Scripts" in your favorite search engine.

There are lots of ways you *could* manage your Group Policy universe. Some people walk up to their Domain Controllers, log onto the console, and manage their Group Policy infrastructure there. Others use a *management workstation* and manage their Group Policy infrastructure from their own Windows 10 workstation (suggested).

I'll talk more about the use and best practices of a Windows 10 management workstation in Chapter 6.

Implementing the GPMC on Your Management Station

As I mentioned, the GPMC isn't built into Windows 10. But it is built into Windows Server 2016. Remember earlier I stated that you could manage your Active Directory from anywhere. And this is true. You *could* walk up to a Domain Controller, you *could* install the GPMC on a Windows Server 2016 server, or you *could* use Terminal Services to remotely connect to a Domain Controller.

But in this book, you won't be. Your ideal management station is a Windows 10 machine (where we'll manually introduce the GPMC) or a Windows Server 2016 machine (which is ready to go, no pesky downloads needed).

Windows 7 and Windows Server 2008 R2 are perfectly fine choices as well, but there is a small downside with those GPMCs. That is, they aren't the "latest, greatest" and do lack some of the newest features, which we'll explore in the next chapter. One good example of this is that the Windows 7 version of GPMC will not have the Group Policy Preferences item type for Internet Explorer 10. The idea is that Microsoft will only put new or updated functionality in the latest, greatest GPMC, and today, that GPMC is Windows 10's (and Windows Server 2016's). (They share the same guts.) That being said, if you only had a Windows 7 GPMC to use, it wouldn't be the end of the world, and you'll likely be pretty happy.

If you must use something else (Windows XP, Windows Server 2003, or Windows Vista), you'll see me pepper in some advice for those. But you'll really want to use the recommended set to get the most out of this book

Using a Windows 10 or Windows Server 2016 Management Station

For this book, and for real life, I recommend that you use what's known as a Windows 10 management station. And, to make use of it to implement Group Policy in your domain, you'll need to introduce the downloadable GPMC on it.

Note that you could *also* use a Windows Server 2016 machine as your management station. Honestly, the Windows 10 GPMC that you'll download and the built-in GPMC for Windows Server 2016 are equals. There's no difference. But it's simply not likely you're going to install Windows Server 2016 on your laptop or desktop.

So, just to be clear, the following two ways to create and manage GPOs are equal:

▪ Windows 10 and the downloadable GPMC (contained within the RSAT tools)

▪ Windows Server 2016 with its built-in GPMC

I'll usually just refer to a Windows 10 management station, and when I say that, I mean what I have in that first bullet point. Just remember that you can use a Windows Server 2016 machine as your management station, too.

Now, to be super-crazy, ridiculously clear: you could also use any of the other GPMCs out there, and things will basically "work." I delve into this in serious detail in Chapter 6, but here's the CliffNotes, er, JeremyNotes version of "What GPMC should I use?":

▪ Always strive to use Windows 10 (or Windows Server 2016) as your management station and you'll always be able to control all operating systems' settings from all operating systems. If by the time you read this book, something after Windows 11 is out—use that GPMC. Always use the latest GPMC.

▪ The next best choice would be Windows 8.1 (with Update 1) and RSAT or Server 2012 R2.

▪ After that, the next best choice would be Windows 7 or Windows Server 2008 R2, which has "almost" all the same stuff as Windows 8's GPMC (but not quite).

Everything else would be suboptimal to use.

But if you have even one Windows 10 client machine (say in Sales or Marketing), in order to manage all its settings you're going to need to manage the machine using a "modern" GPMC. So I'm suggesting you just bite the bullet and get yourself a copy of Windows 10 and do your management from there.

Again, more details later, but here's the warning. If you create a GPO using a "newer GPMC" (say, using a Windows 10 or Windows Server 2016 GPMC) but then edit it using an older operating system (say, a Windows 7 or XP GPMC), you might not be able to "see" all the configurable options. And what's worse, some settings might be set (but you wouldn't be able to see them!). Only the newest GPMC can see the "stuff" that the newest GPMC puts into the GPO.

What if you're not "allowed" to load Windows 10, 8.1, or 7 on your own management station? Well, you've got another option. Perhaps you can create a Windows 10 or Windows Server 2016 machine to act as your management station, say in the server room. Or, use VMware Workstation or another virtualization tool to make an "almost real" management machine. Or, do create a real machine but set up Terminal Services or Remote Desktop to utilize the GPMC remotely.

Again, in our examples we'll call our machine WIN10MANAGEMENT, but you can use either a Windows 10 or Windows Server 2016 for your best management station experience.

Using a Windows Server 2016 Machine as Your Management Station

The latest GPMC is available in Windows Server 2016. However, it's not magically installed in most cases. The only time it is just "magically there" is when you make your Windows Server 2008, Windows Server 2008 R2, or Windows Server 2016 machine a Domain Controller. In that case, the GPMC is automatically installed for you. You don't need to do the following procedure.

And, if you're following along in the labs, you've likely already made your server a Domain Controller. But for practice, if you want to learn how to install it for when your server is not acting as a Domain Controller, there are two ways to install the GPMC: using Server Manager and also by the command line.

To install the GPMC using Server Manager:

1. From the Start screen, select Server Manager.

2. Click Dashboard, then select "Add roles and features."

3. In the "Add Roles and Features" wizard, you'll eventually get to the Features screen. Be sure Group Policy Management is selected.

4. Click Install.

Close Server Manager once you're done.

You can also install the GPMC using the command line:

1. Open a PowerShell prompt as an Administrator.

2. In PowerShell, type **Add-WindowsFeature GPMC**.

3. Close the command prompt when the installation has been completed.

Using Windows 10 as Your Management Machine

The first step on your Windows 10 management-station-to-be is to install Windows 10.

RSAT comes as a Microsoft Update Standalone Package and installs like a hotfix, and you may or may not need to reboot after installation. At last check, you can download the Windows 10 RSAT from www.microsoft.com/en-us/download/details.aspx?id=45520.

All the tools installed automatically when you install the Update Package. You can see the tools already installed in Figure 1.7.

Once you're done, close the Windows Features window and, if prompted, reboot your Windows 10 machine. The next time you boot, you'll have Active Directory Users and Computers, the GPMC, and other tools available for use in the rest of the book.

If you cannot use a Windows 10 management machine and can only use a Windows 8.1 or 7 management machine, then the steps are the same for Windows 7, except the RSAT download is different. The RSAT for Windows 8.1 RSAT can be found at http://tinyurl.com/win81rsat and the Windows 7 SP1 can be found at http://tinyurl.com/win7rsat-sp1.

FIGURE 1.7 The RSAT tools installed in Windows Features in the Control Panel ➢ Programs ➢ "Turn Windows features on or off"

Creating a One-Stop-Shop MMC

As you'll see, the GPMC is a fairly comprehensive Group Policy management tool. But the problem is that right now the GPMC and the Active Directory Users and Computers snap-ins are, well, separate tools that each do a specific job. They're not integrated to allow you to work on the idea of Users and Computers *and* Group Policy at the same time.

Often, you'll want to change a Group Policy linked to an OU and then move computers to that OU. Unfortunately, you can't do so from the GPMC; you must return to Active Directory Users and Computers to finish the task. This can get frustrating quickly. But that's the deal.

As a result, my preference is to create a custom MMC that shows both the Active Directory Users and Computers and GPMC in a one-stop-shop view. You can see what I mean in Figure 1.8.

You might be wondering at this point, "So, Jeremy, what are the steps I need in order to create this unified MMC console you've so neatly described and shown in Figure 1.8?"

Just click Start and type **MMC** at the Search prompt. Then add in both the Active Directory Users and Computers and Group Policy Management snap-ins, as shown in Figure 1.9.

You won't need the Group Policy Management Editor (which allows you to edit one Group Policy Object at a time), the Group Policy Object Editor (for Local Group Policy), or the Group Policy Starter GPO Editor (which we use in Chapter 2).

FIGURE 1.8   Use the MMC to create a unified console.

FIGURE 1.9   Add Active Directory Users and Computers and Group Policy Management to your custom view.

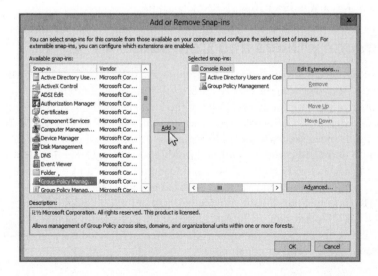

Once you have added both snap-ins to your console, you'll have a near-unified view of most of what you need at your fingertips. Both Active Directory Users and Computers and the GPMC can create and delete OUs. Both tools also allow administrators to delegate permissions to others to manage Group Policy, but that's where the two tools' functionality overlap ends.

The GPMC won't show you the actual users and computer objects inside the OU, so deleting an OU from within the GPMC is dicey at best because you can't be sure of what's inside!

You can choose to add other snaps-ins, too, of course, including Active Directory Sites and Services or anything else you think is useful. The illustrations in the rest of this book will show both snap-ins loaded in this configuration. I suggest you save your "one-stop shop" to the Desktop and give it catchy name so you can quickly find it later when you need to.

Group Policy 101 and Active Directory

Let's start with some basics to ensure that things are running smoothly. For most of the examples in this book, you'll be able to get by with just the one Domain Controller and one or two workstations that participate in the domain, for verifying that your changes took place.

> For the examples in this book, I'll refer to our sample Domain Controller, DC01, which is part of my example Corp.com domain. For these examples, you can choose to rename the Default-First-Site-Name site or not—your choice.

Again, I encourage you to try these examples in your test lab and not to try them directly on your production network. This will help you avoid a CLM (career-limiting move).

For our examples, we'll assume you're using WIN10MANAGEMENT as your management station, which is a Windows 10 with RSAT machine.

Active Directory Users and Computers vs. GPMC

The main job of Active Directory Users and Computers is to give you an Active Directory object–centric view of your domain. Active Directory Users and Computers lets you deal with users, computers, groups, contacts, some of the Flexible Single Master Operations (FSMO) roles, and delegation of control over user accounts as well as change the domain mode and define advanced security and auditing inside Active Directory. You can also create OUs and move users and computers around inside those OUs. Other administrators can then drill down inside Active Directory Users and Computers into an OU and see the computers, groups, contacts, and so on that you've moved to those OUs.

But the GPMC has one main job: to provide you with a Group Policy–centric view of all you control. All the OUs that you see in Active Directory Users and Computers are visible in the GPMC. Think about it—it's the same Active Directory behind the scenes "storing" those details about the OU and its contents.

However, the GPMC just doesn't have a way to "view" the users, computers, contacts, and such. When you drill down into an OU inside the GPMC, you'll see but one thing: the GPOs that affect the objects inside the OU.

In Figure 1.8, you were able to see the Active Directory Users and Computers view as well as the GPMC view—rolled into one MMC that we created earlier. Even though it's not super-obvious from the screen shot, the Active Directory Users and Computers view of an OU and the GPMC view of the same OU are radically different. For instance, in Figure 1.8 I've added (for the sake of this discussion) an OU called **Temporary Office Help** and some other OUs, too, for fun.

When focused at a site, a domain, or an OU within the GPMC, you see only the GPOs that affect that level in Active Directory. You don't see the same "stuff" that Active Directory Users and Computers sees, such as users, computers, groups, or contacts.

The basic overlap in the two tools is the ability to create and delete OUs. If you add or delete an OU in either tool, you need to refresh the other tool by pressing F5 to see the update. For instance, in Figure 1.8 you could see that my Active Directory has several OUs, including the one I added named **Temporary Office Help**.

 Deleting an OU from inside the GPMC is generally a bad idea. Because you cannot see the Active Directory objects inside the OU (such as users and computers), you don't know how many objects you're about to delete. So be careful!

If I delete the **Temporary Office Help** OU in Active Directory Users and Computers, the change is not reflected in the GPMC window until it's refreshed. And vice versa.

So, let's summarize with three key points:

- Understanding that the two tools are "separate" and work on the same underlying database is key.

- Understanding that what you do in one tool (e.g., delete an OU) affects the other tool (because it's affecting the same underlying database) is also key.

- The final key is realizing that you will need to occasionally "refresh" the view of each tool. This is because other administrators might be "doing stuff" to the GPOs and/or Active Directory user accounts. You won't see their changes until you refresh *your* view.

Adjusting the View within the GPMC

The GPMC lets you view as much or as little of your Active Directory as you like. By default, you view only your own forest and domain. You can optionally add in the ability to see the sites in your forest as well as the ability to see other domains in your forest or domains in other forests, although these views might not be the best for seeing what you have control over.

Here's how to view the various other items you may need to within the GPMC:

Viewing Sites in the GPMC   When you create GPOs, you won't often create GPOs that affect sites. The designers of the GPMC seem to agree; it's a bit of a chore to apply GPOs to sites. To do so, you need to link an *existing* GPO to a site. You'll see how to do this a bit later in this chapter.

However, you first need to expose the site objects in Active Directory. To do so, right-click the Sites object in GPMC, choose Show Sites from the context menu (see Figure 1.10), and then click the check box next to each site you want to expose.

FIGURE 1.10   You need to expose the Active Directory sites before you can link GPOs to them.

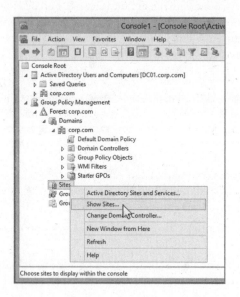

In our first example, we'll use the site level of Active Directory to deploy our first Group Policy Object. At this point, go ahead and enable the Default-First-Site-Name so that you can have it ready for use in our own experiments.

Viewing Other Domains in the GPMC   To see other domains in your forest, drill down to the Forest folder in Group Policy Management, right-click Domains, choose Show Domains, and select the other available domains in your forest. Each domain will now appear at the same hierarchical level in the GPMC.

Viewing Other Forests in the GPMC   To see other forests, right-click the root (Group Policy Management) and choose Add Forest from the context menu. You'll need to type the name of the Active Directory forest you want to add. If you want to add or subtract domains within that new forest, follow the instructions in the preceding paragraph.

Now that we've adjusted our view to see the domains and forests we want, let's examine how to manipulate our GPOs and GPO links.

You can add forests with which you do not have a trust. However, GPMC defaults will not display these domains as a safety mechanism. To turn off the safety mechanism, choose View ➢ Options to open the Options dialog box. In the General tab, clear Enable Trust Detection and click OK.

The GPMC-centric View

As I stated earlier, one of the fundamental concepts of Group Policy is that the GPOs *themselves* live in the "swimming pool" inside the domain. Then, when you want to utilize a GPO from that swimming pool against a level in Active Directory, you simply link a GPO to that level.

Figure 1.11 shows what our swimming pool will eventually look like when we're done with the examples in this chapter.

FIGURE 1.11   Imagine your about-to-be-leveraged GPOs as just hanging out in the swimming pool of the domain.

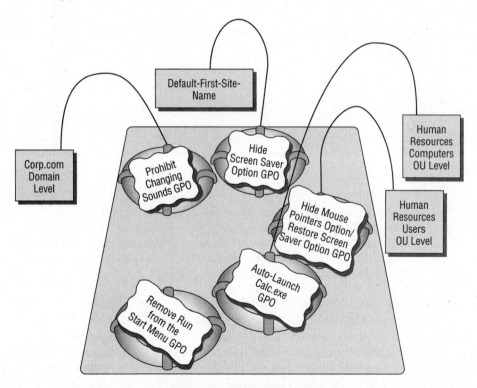

The Corp.com GPO Swimming Pool

Our swimming pool will be full of GPOs, with various levels in Active Directory "linked" to those GPOs. To that end, you can drill down, right now, to see the representation of the swimming pool. It's there, waiting for you. Click Group Policy Management ➢ Forest ➢ Domains ➢ Corp.com ➢ Group Policy Objects to see all the GPOs that will exist in the domain by the time we're done (see Figure 1.12).

FIGURE 1.12 The Group Policy Objects folder highlighted here is the representation of the swimming pool of the domain that contains your actual GPOs.

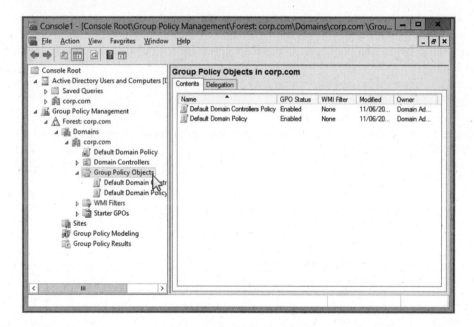

If you're just getting started, it's not likely you'll have more than the "Default Domain Controllers Policy" GPO and "Default Domain Policy" GPO. That's okay. You'll start getting more GPOs soon enough. Oh, and for now, please don't modify the default GPOs. They're a bit special and are covered in great detail in Chapter 8.

All GPOs in the domain are represented in the Group Policy Objects folder. As you can see, when the **Temporary Office Help** OU is shown within the GPMC, a relationship exists between the OU and the "Hide Desktop Settings Option" GPO. That relationship is the tether to the GPO in the swimming pool—the GPO is linked back to "Hide Desktop Settings Option." You can see this linked relationship because the "Hide Desktop Settings Option" icon inside **Temporary Office Help** has a little arrow icon, signifying the link back to the actual GPO in the domain. The same is true for the "Default Domain Policy," which is linked at the domain level, but the actual GPO is placed below the Group Policy Objects folder.

Our Own Group Policy Examples

Now that you've got a grip on honing your view within the GPMC, let's take it for a quick spin around the block with some examples!

For this series of examples, we're going after the users who keep fiddling with their display doo-dads in Windows 10.

If you want to see these examples in action using Windows 10, start out on WIN10 by looking at the "Change the visuals and sounds on your computer" page, which is located by right-clicking the Desktop and choosing Personalize. In the left column, you'll see items including "Change desktop icons" and "Change mouse pointers." In the bottom section, you'll see several entries, including Desktop Background, Window Color, Sounds, and Screen Saver, as shown in Figure 1.13.

FIGURE 1.13   The Windows 10 Personalization page—unconfigured by Group Policy

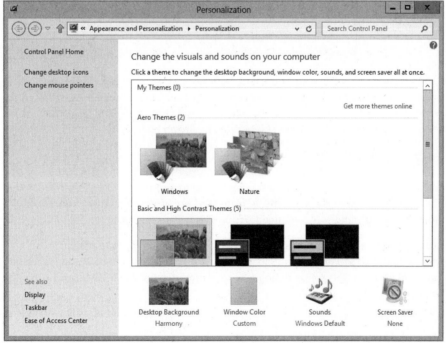

For our first use of Group Policy, we're going to produce four "edicts" (for dramatic effect, you should stand on your desk and loudly proclaim these edicts with a thick British accent):

- At the site level, there will be no ability to change screen savers.
- At the domain level, there will be no ability to change Windows' sounds.

- At the **Human Resources Users** OU level, there will be no way to change the mouse pointers. And, while we're at it, let's bring back the ability to change screen savers!

- At the **Human Resources Computers** OU, we'll make it so whenever anyone uses a Human Resources computer, calc.exe automatically launches after login.

Following along with these concrete examples will reinforce the concepts presented earlier. Additionally, they are used throughout the remainder of this chapter and the book.

Understanding GPMC's Link Warning

As you work through the examples, you'll do a lot of clicking around. When you click a GPO link the first time, you'll get this message:

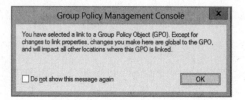

This message is trying to convey an important sentiment—that is, multiple levels in Active Directory may be linked back and use the exact same GPO. The idea is that multiple levels of Active Directory could use the exact same Group Policy Object contained inside the Group Policy Objects container—but just be linked back to it.

What if you modify the policy settings by right-clicking a policy link and choosing Edit from the context menu? All instances in Active Directory that link to that GPO embrace the new settings. If this is a fear, you might want to create another GPO and then link it to the level in Active Directory you want. More properties are affected by this warning, and we'll explore them in Chapter 4, "Advanced Group Policy Processing."

If you've squelched this message by selecting "Do not show this message again," you can get it back. In the GPMC in the menus, choose View ➤ Options and select the General tab, then select "Show confirmation dialog box to distinguish between GPOs and GPO links" and click OK.

More about Linking and the Group Policy Objects Container

The GPMC is a fairly flexible tool. Indeed, it permits the administrator to perform many tasks in different ways. One thing you'll do quite a lot in your travels with the GPMC is create your own Group Policy Objects. Again, GPOs live in a container within Active Directory and are represented within the Group Policy Objects container (the swimming pool) inside the domain (seen in Figure 1.11, earlier in this chapter). Any levels of Active Directory—site, domain, or OU—simply link back to the GPOs hanging out in the Group Policy Objects container.

To apply Group Policy to a level in Active Directory using the GPMC, you have two options:

- Create the GPOs in the Group Policy Objects container first. Then, while focused at the level you want to command in Active Directory (site, domain, or OU), manually add a link to the GPO that is in the Group Policy Objects container.

- While focused at the level you want to command in Active Directory (domain or OU), create the GPOs in the Group Policy Objects container and automatically create the link. This link is created at the level you're currently focused at *back* to the GPO in the Group Policy Objects container.

Which is the correct way to go? Both are perfectly acceptable because both are doing the same thing.

In both cases the GPO itself does not "live" at the level in Active Directory at which you're focused. Rather, the GPO itself "lives" in the Group Policy Objects container. The link back to the GPO inside the Group Policy Objects container is what makes the relationship between the GPO inside the Group Policy Objects container swimming pool and the level in Active Directory you want to command.

To get the hang of this, let's work through some examples. First, let's create our first GPO in the Group Policy Objects folder. Follow these steps:

1. Launch the GPMC. Click Start, and then in the search box, type **GPMC.MSC**.

2. Traverse down by clicking Group Policy Management ➢ Forest ➢ Domains ➢ Corp. com ➢ Group Policy Objects.

3. Right-click the Group Policy Objects folder and choose New from the context menu, as shown in Figure 1.14, to open the New GPO dialog box.

4. Let's name our first edict, er, GPO, something descriptive, such as "Hide Screen Saver Option."

5. Once the name is entered, you'll see the new GPO listed in the swimming pool. Right-click the GPO and choose Edit, as shown in Figure 1.15, to open the Group Policy Management Editor.

6. To hide the Screen Saver option, drill down by clicking User Configuration ➢ Policies ➢ Administrative Templates ➢ Control Panel ➢ Personalization. Double-click the **Prevent changing screen saver** policy setting to open it. Select the Enabled setting, and click OK.

7. Close the Group Policy Management Editor.

FIGURE 1.14   You create your first GPO in the Group Policy Objects container by right-clicking and choosing New.

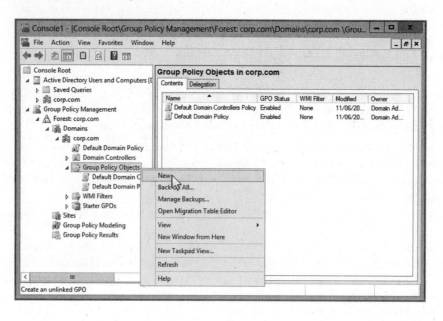

FIGURE 1.15   You can right-click the GPO in the Group Policy Objects container and choose Edit from the context menu to open the Group Policy Management Editor.

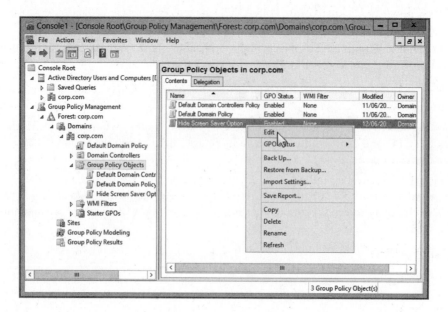

Note that in earlier iterations of the GPMC, this setting was named differently and placed in another node. It used to be called **Hide Screen Saver Tab** and was located in the Display node within Control Panel. As you can see, as the operating system evolves, so do the names of the policy settings, Group Policy Preference items (described in Chapter 5), and the capabilities within the GPMC itself. This is why it's pretty important to always use the "latest, greatest" GPMC, as we are doing in this book.

Understanding Our Actions

Now that we have this "Hide Screen Saver Option" edict, er, GPO floating around in the Group Policy Objects container—in the representation of the swimming pool of the domain—what have we done? Not a whole lot, actually, other than create some bits inside Active Directory and on the Domain Controllers. By creating new GPOs in the Group Policy Objects folder, we haven't inherently forced our desires on *any* level in Active Directory—site, domain, or OU.

To make a level in Active Directory accept our will, we need to *link* this new Group Policy Object to an existing level. Only then will our will be accepted and embraced. Let's do that now.

Applying a Group Policy Object to the Site Level

The least-often-used level of Group Policy application is at the site. This is because it's got the broadest stroke but the bluntest application. And more and more organizations use high-speed links everywhere, so it's not easy to separate computers into individual sites because (in some organizations) Active Directory is set up to see the network as just one big site!

Additionally, since Active Directory states that only members of Enterprise Administrators (EAs) can modify sites and site links, it's equally true that only EAs (by default) can add and manipulate GPOs at the site level.

When a tree or a forest contains more than one domain, only the EAs and the Domain Administrators (DAs) of the root domain can create and modify sites and site links. When multiple domains exist, DAs in domains other than the root domain cannot create sites or site links (or site-level GPOs).

However, site GPOs might come in handy on occasion. For instance, you might want to set up site-level GPO definitions for network-specific settings, such as Internet Explorer proxy settings or an IP security policy for sensitive locations. Setting up site-based settings is useful if you have one building (set up explicitly as an Active Directory site) that has a particular or unique network configuration. You might choose to modify the Internet Explorer proxy settings if this building has a unique proxy server. Or, in the case of IP security, perhaps this facility has particularly sensitive information, such as confidential records or payroll information.

Therefore, if you're not an EA (or a DA of the root domain), it's likely you'll never get to practice this exercise outside the test lab. In upcoming chapters I'll show you how to delegate these rights to other administrators, like OU administrators.

For now, we'll work with a basic example to get the feel of the Group Policy Management Editor.

We already stood on our desks and loudly declared that there will be no Screen Saver options at our one default site. The good news is that we've already done two-thirds of what we need to do to make that site accept our will: we exposed the sites we want to manage, and we created the "Hide Screen Saver Option" GPO in the Group Policy Objects container.

WARNING   Implementing GPOs linked to sites can have a substantial impact on your logon times and WAN (wide area network) traffic if not performed correctly. For more information, see Chapter 7 in the section "Group Policy Objects from a Site Perspective."

Now all we need do is to tether the GPO we created to the site with a GPO link.

To remove the Screen Saver option using the Group Policy Management Editor at the site level, follow these steps:

1. Inside the GPMC snap-in, drill down by clicking the Group Policy Management folder, the Forest folder, and the Sites folder.

2. Find the site to which you want to deliver the policy. If you have only one site, it is likely called Default-First-Site-Name.

3. Right-click the site and choose "Link an Existing GPO," as shown in Figure 1.16.

4. Now you can select the "Hide Screen Saver Option" GPO from the list of GPOs in the Group Policy Objects container within the domain.

Once you have chosen the GPO, it will be linked to the site.

WARNING   Did you notice that there was no "Are You Sure You Really Want To Do This?" warning or anything similar? The GPMC trusts that you set up the GPO correctly. If you create GPOs with incorrect settings and/or link them to the wrong level in Active Directory, you can make boo-boos on a grand scale. Again, this is why you want to try any setting you want to deploy in a test lab environment first.

Again, there is a good reason GPOs for sites must be pre-created. Since Sites does not belong to a specific domain but rather the forest, you cannot assume which "domain swimming pool" a particular GPO should be added to. By creating them this way, you know which domain you created them in first and then to what site you want them linked.

FIGURE 1.16   Once you have your first GPO designed, you can link it to your site.

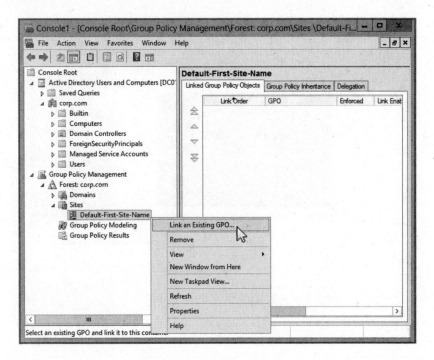

Verifying Your Changes at the Site Level

Now, log onto any workstation or server that falls within the boundaries of the site to which you applied the sitewide GPO. If you didn't change any of the defaults, you should be able to log onto any computer in the domain (say, WIN10) as any user you have defined— even the administrator of the domain.

Right-click the Desktop and select Personalize. Then click Lock Screen on the left, and try the Screen Saver option toward the bottom of the page. When you try it, you'll see what happens, which you can also see in Figure 1.17.

Don't panic if you do not see the changes reflected the first time you log on. See Chapter 3, "Group Policy Processing Behavior Essentials," in the section "Background Refresh Policy Processing" to find out how to encourage changes to appear. To see the Screen Saver tab disappear right now, log off and log back on. The policy should take effect.

FIGURE 1.17 In Windows 10 the Screen Saver entry on the Personalization page is disabled.

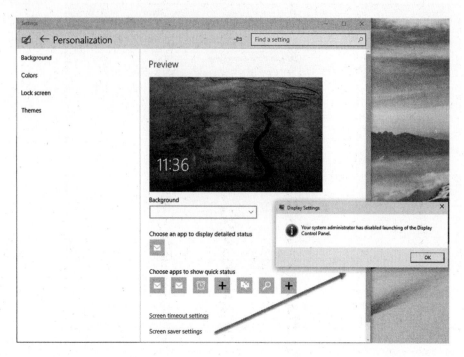

This demonstration should prove how powerful Group Policy is, not only because everyone at the site is affected, but more specifically because administrators are not immune to Group Policy effects. Administrators are not immune because they are automatically members of the Authenticated Users security group. (You can modify this behavior with the techniques explored in Chapter 3.)

Applying Group Policy Objects to the Domain Level

At the domain level, we want to deliver an edict that says that the Sounds option in the Windows Personalization page should be removed.

Active Directory domains allow only members of the Domain Administrators group the ability to create and link Group Policy directly on the domain level. Therefore, if you're not a DA (or a member of the EA group), or you don't get delegated the right, it's likely that you'll never get to practice this exercise outside the test lab. (A bit later we'll talk more about how to give others besides Domain Admins rights to create and link GPOs.)

To apply the edict, follow these steps:

1. In the GPMC, drill down by clicking Group Policy Management ➢ Forest ➢ Corp.com.

2. Right-click the domain name to see the available options, as shown in Figure 1.18.

FIGURE 1.18   At the domain level, you can create the GPO in the Group Policy Objects container and then immediately link to the GPO from here.

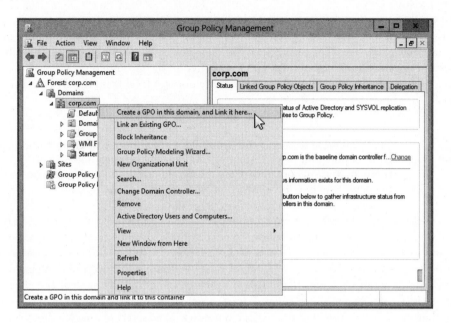

"Create a GPO in this domain, and Link it here" vs. "Link an Existing GPO"

In the previous example, we forced the site level to embrace our "Hide Screen Saver Option" edict. First, we created the GPO in the Group Policy Objects folder, and then in another step we linked the GPO to the site level. However, at the domain level (and, as you're about to see, the OU level), we can take care of both steps at once via the "Create a GPO in this domain, and Link it here" command. (Note, in previous versions of the GPMC, this was confusingly called "Create And Link A GPO Here." Being a grammar snob, this was a personal wish of mine to have clarified, and I'm happy to see Microsoft agreed and corrected it.)

This command tells the GPMC to create a new GPO in the Group Policy Objects folder and then automatically link the new GPO back to this focused level of Active Directory. This is a time-saving step so we don't have to dive down into the Group Policy Objects folder first and then create the link back to the Active Directory level.

So why is the "Create a GPO in this domain, and Link it here" option possible only at the domain and OU level and not the site level? Because Group Policy Objects linked to sites can often cause excessive bandwidth troubles when the old-school way of doing things is used. With that in mind, the GPMC interface makes sure that when you work with GPOs that affect sites, you're consciously choosing from *which* domain the GPO is being linked.

Don't panic when you see all the possible options. We'll hit them all in due time; right now we're interested in the first two: "Create a GPO in this domain, and Link it here" and "Link an Existing GPO."

Since you're focused at the domain level, you are prompted for the name of a new Group Policy Object when you right-click and choose "Create a GPO in this domain, and Link it here." For this one, type a descriptive name, such as "Prohibit Changing Sounds." Your new "Prohibit Changing Sounds" GPO is created in the Group Policy Objects container and, automatically, a link is created at the domain level from the GPO to the domain.

Take a moment to look in the Group Policy "swimming pool" for your new GPO. Simply drill down through Group Policy Management ➢ Forest ➢ Domains ➢ Corp.com and locate the Group Policy Objects node. Look for the new "Prohibit Changing Sounds" GPO.

Right-click the link "Prohibit Changing Sounds" (or the GPO itself) and choose Edit to open the Group Policy Management Editor. To make your wish come true and affect the sounds applet Windows 10 Personalization page, drill down through User Configuration ➢ Policies ➢ Administrative Templates ➢ Control Panel ➢ Personalization, and double-click **Prevent changing sounds**. Change the setting from Not Configured to Enabled, and click OK. Close the Group Policy Management Editor to return to the GPMC.

Note that the policy setting will only affect Windows 7 and later, so any Windows XP machines (if you have any) will ignore the policy setting.

Verifying Your Changes at the Domain Level

Now, log on as any user in the domain. You can log onto any computer in the domain (say, WIN10) as any user you have defined—even the administrator of the domain.

On WIN10, right-click the Desktop and click Personalize ➢ Themes ➢ Go to Advanced sound settings.

You'll see in Figure 1.19 the before and after. On the left, you'll see that before the policy applies, there are four tabs in the Sound applet. After the policy applies, there are three tabs in the Sounds applet.

The actual policy name was called **Prevent changing sounds**. Note that it didn't prevent access to the Sounds applet, but instead removed the most critical tab, the Sounds tab, in the Sound applet.

Once again, administrators are not immune to Group Policy effects. You can change this behavior, as you'll see in Chapter 2.

FIGURE 1.19   The Sounds applet goes from four tabs to three tabs because the user is affected by the domain-level policy

 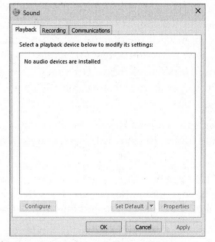

Applying Group Policy Objects to the OU Level

OUs are wonderful tools for delegating away unpleasant administrative duties, such as password resets or modifying group memberships. But that's only half their purpose. The other half is to be able to apply Group Policy.

You'll likely find yourself making most Group Policy additions and changes at the OU level, because that's where you have the most flexibility and the OU is the most refined instrument to affect users. Once OU administrators become comfortable in their surroundings, they want to harness the power of Group Policy.

Preparing to Delegate Control

To create a GPO at the OU level, you must first create the OU and a plan to delegate. For the examples in this book, we'll create three OUs that look like this:

- **Human Resources**
- **Human Resources Users**
- **Human Resources Computers**

Having separate OUs for your users and computers is a good idea—for both delegation of rights and GPO design. Microsoft considers this a best practice. In the **Human Resources Users** OU in our Corp.com domain, we'll create and leverage an Active Directory security group to do our dirty work. We'll name this group HR-OU-Admins and put our first users inside the HR-OU-Admins security group. We'll then delegate the appropriate rights necessary for them to use the power of GPOs.

To create the **Human Resources Users** OU using your WIN10MANAGEMENT machine, follow these steps:

1. Earlier, you created a "unified console" where you housed both Active Directory Users and Computer and the GPMC. Simply use Active Directory Users and Computers, right-click the domain name, and choose New ➢ Organizational Unit, which will allow you to enter a new OU name. Enter **Human Resources** as the name. (Note that newer versions of Active Directory Users and Computers will ask you if you want to "Protect container from accidental deletion." It's your choice. I typically deselect the check box.)

2. Inside the **Human Resources** OU, create two more OUs—**Human Resources Computers** and **Human Resources Users**, as shown in Figure 1.20.

FIGURE 1.20   When you complete all these steps, your Human Resources OU should have a Human Resources Users OU and Human Resources Computers OU. In the users' side, put Frank Rizzo and the HR-OU-Admins.

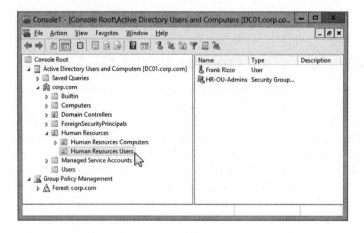

Alternatively, you can create the OU in the GPMC. Just right-click the domain and choose New Organizational Unit from the context menu.

To create the HR-OU-Admins group, follow these steps:

1. In Active Directory Users and Computers, right-click the new **Human Resources Users** OU and choose New ➤ Group.

2. Create the new group HR-OU-Admins as a new global security group.

To create the first user to go inside HR-OU-Admins, follow these steps:

1. In Active Directory Users and Computers, right-click the **Human Resources Users** OU and choose New ➤ User.

2. Name the user **Frank Rizzo,** with an account name of **frizzo,** and click Next.

3. Modern domains require a complex password for a user. Again, my suggested password is p@ssw0rd. That's a lowercase *p*, the at sign, an *s*, an *s*, a *w*, a zero, then *r*, and *d*.

4. Finish and close the wizard.

If you're following along, Frank Rizzo's login will be `frizzo@corp.com`.

Easily Manage New Users and Computers

The Computers folder and Users folder in Active Directory Users and Computers are *not* OUs. They are generic *containers*. You'll notice that they are not present when you're using the GPMC to view Active Directory. Because they are generic containers (and not OUs), you cannot link Group Policy Objects to them. Of course, these objects will receive GPOs if linked to the domain, because the containers are still *in* the domain. They just aren't OUs in the domain.

These folders have two purposes:

- If you ever did an upgrade from NT 4 domains to Active Directory, these User and Computer accounts would wind up in these folders. (Administrators are then supposed to move the accounts into OUs.)

- The two folders are the default location where older tools drop new accounts when creating new users and computers. Additionally, command-line tools, such as net user and net group, will add accounts to these two folders. Similarly, the Computers folder is the default location for any new client workstation or server that joins the domain. The same goes when you create computer accounts using the net computer command.

So, these seem like decent "holding pens" for these kinds of objects. But ultimately, you don't want your users or computers to reside in these folders for very long—you want them to end up in OUs. That's where the action is because you can apply Group Policy to OUs, not to these folders! Yeah, sure, these users and computers are affected by site- and domain-level GPOs. But the action is at the OU level, and you want your computer and user objects to be placed in OUs as fast as possible—not sitting around in these generic Computers and Users folders.

To that end, domains that are at least at the "Windows 2003 functional level" have two tools to redirect the default location of new users and computers to the OUs of your choice. For example, suppose you want all new computers to go to a **NewComputers** OU and all new users to go to a **NewUsers** OU. And you want to link several GPOs to the **NewUsers** and **NewComputers** OUs to ensure that new accounts immediately have some baseline level of security, restriction, or protection. Without a little magic, new user accounts created using older tools won't automatically be placed there.

Starting with Windows 2003 Active Directory, Microsoft provided REDIRUSR and REDIRCMP commands that take a distinguished name, like this:

```
REDIRCMP ou=newcomputers,dc=corp,dc=com and/or
REDIRUSR ou=newusers,dc=corp,dc=com
```

Now if you link GPOs to these OUs, your new accounts will get the Group Policy Objects dictating settings to them at an OU level. This will come in handy when users and computers aren't specifically created in their final destination OUs.

To learn more about these tools, see the Microsoft Knowledge Base article 324949 at http://support.microsoft.com/kb/324949.

To add Frank Rizzo to the HR-OU-Admins group, follow these steps:

1. Double-click the HR-OU-Admins group.

2. Click the Members tab.

3. Add Frank Rizzo.

When it's all complete, your OU structure with your first user and group should look like Figure 1.20, shown previously.

Delegating Control for Group Policy Management

You've created the **Human Resources** OU, which contains the **Human Resources Users** OU and the **Human Resources Computers** OU and the HR-OU-Admins security group. Now, put Frank inside the HR-OU-Admins group, and you're ready to delegate control.

Performing Your First Delegation

You can delegate control to use Group Policy in two ways: using Active Directory Users and Computers and using the GPMC.

> For this first example, we'll kick it old school and do it the Active Directory Users and Computers way. Then, in Chapter 2, I'll demonstrate how to delegate control using the GPMC.

To delegate control for Group Policy management, follow these steps:

1. In Active Directory Users and Computers, right-click the top-level **Human Resources** OU you created and choose Delegate Control from the context menu to start the "Delegation of Control Wizard."

2. Click Next to get past the wizard introduction screen.

3. You'll be asked to select users and/or groups. Click Add, add the HR-OU-Admins group, and click Next to open the "Tasks to Delegate" screen, shown in Figure 1.21.

FIGURE 1.21   Select the "Manage Group Policy links" task.

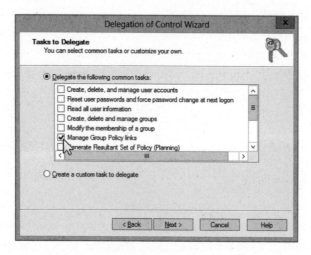

4. Click "Manage Group Policy links," and then click Next.

5. At the wizard review screen, click Finish.

> You might want to click some or all the other check boxes as well, but for this example, only "Manage Group Policy links" is required. Avoid selecting "Generate Resultant Set of Policy (Planning)" and "Generate Resultant Set of Policy (Logging)" at this time. You'll see where these options come into play in Chapter 2.

NOTE The "Manage Group Policy links" delegation assigns the user or group Read and Write access over the gPLink and gPOptions properties for that level. To see or modify these permissions by hand, open Active Directory Users and Computers and choose View ➢ Advanced Features. If later you want to remove a delegated permission, it's a little challenging. To locate the permission that you set, right-click the delegated object (such as OU), click the Properties tab, click the Security tab, choose Advanced, and dig around until you come across the permission you want to remove. Finally, delete the corresponding access control entry (ACE).

Adding a User to the Server Operators Group (Just for This Book)

Under normal conditions, nobody but Domain Administrators, Enterprise Administrators, or Server Operators can walk up to Domain Controllers and log on. For testing purposes only, though, we're going to add our user, Frank, to the Server Operators group so he can easily work on our DC01 Domain Controller when we want him to.

To add a user to the Server Operators group, follow these steps:

1. In Active Directory Users and Computers, double-click Frank Rizzo's account under the **Human Resources Users** OU.

2. Click the Member Of tab and click Add.

3. Select the Server Operators group and click OK.

4. Click OK to close the Properties dialog box for Frank Rizzo.

Normally, you wouldn't give your delegated OU administrators Server Operators access. You're doing it solely for the sake of this example to allow Frank to log on locally to your Domain Controllers.

Testing Your Delegation of Group Policy Management

At this point, on your WIN10MANAGEMENT machine, log off as Administrator and log in as Frank Rizzo (frizzo@corp.com).

Now follow these steps to test your delegation:

1. Choose Start and type **GPMC.MSC** at the Start Search prompt to open the GPMC.

2. Drill down through Group Policy Management, Domains, Corp.com, and Group Policy Objects. If you right-click Group Policy Objects in an attempt to create a new GPO, you'll see the context menu shown in Figure 1.22.

As you can see, Frank is unable to create new GPOs in the swimming pool of the domain. Since Frank has been delegated some control over the **Human Resources** OU (which also contains the other OUs), let's see what he *can* do. If you right-click the **Human Resources** OU in the GPMC, you'll see the context menu shown in Figure 1.23.

FIGURE 1.22   Frank cannot create new GPOs in the Group Policy Objects container.

FIGURE 1.23   Frank's delegated rights allow him to link to existing GPOs but not to create new GPOs.

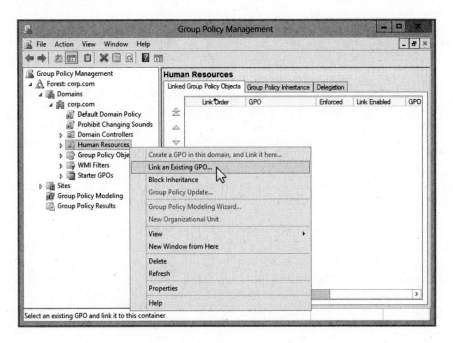

Because Frank is unable to create GPOs in the swimming pool of the domain (the Group Policy Objects container), he is also unable by definition to "Create a GPO in this domain, and Link it here." Although Frank (and more specifically, the HR-OU-Admins) has been delegated the ability to "Manage Group Policy links," he cannot *create* new GPOs. Frank (and the other potential HR-OU-Admins) has only the ability to *link* an existing GPO.

Understanding Group Policy Object Linking Delegation

When we were logged on as the Domain Administrator, we could create GPOs in the Group Policy Objects container, and we could "Create a GPO in this domain, and Link it here" at the domain or OU levels. But Frank cannot.

Here's the idea about delegating the ability to link to GPOs: someone with a lot of brains in the organization does all the work in creating a well-thought-out and well-tested GPO. Maybe this GPO distributes software, maybe it sets up a secure workstation policy, or perhaps it runs a startup script. You get the idea.

Then, others in the organization, like Frank, are delegated just the ability to *link* to that GPO and use it at their level. This solves the problem of delegating perhaps too much control. Certainly some administrators are ready to create their own users and groups, but other administrators may not be quite ready to jump into the cold waters of Group Policy Object creation. Thus, you can design the GPOs for other administrators; they can just link to the ones you (or others) create.

When "Link an Existing GPO" is selected (as seen in Figure 1.23), any GPO which lives in the Group Policy Objects "swimming pool" can be selected.

In this example, the HR-OU-Admins members, such as Frank, can leverage any currently created GPO to affect the users and computers in their OU—even if they didn't create it themselves. In this example, Frank has linked to an existing GPO called "Word 2003 Settings." Turns out that some other administrator in the domain created this GPO, but Frank wants to use it. So, because Frank has "Manage Group Policy links" rights on the **Human Resources** OU (and OUs underneath it), he is allowed to link to it.

But, as you can see in Figure 1.24, he cannot edit the GPOs. Under the hood, Active Directory doesn't permit Frank to edit GPOs he didn't create (and therefore doesn't own).

> In Chapter 2, I'll show you how to grant specific rights to allow more than just the original creator (and now owner) of the object to edit specific GPOs.

Giving the ability to just link to existing GPOs is a good idea in theory, but often OU administrators are simply given full authority to create their own GPOs (as you'll see later). For this example, don't worry about linking to any GPOs. Simply cancel out of the Select GPO screen, close the GPMC, and log off from the server as Frank Rizzo.

FIGURE 1.24   The GPMC will not allow you to edit an existing GPO if you do not own it (or do not have explicit permission to edit it).

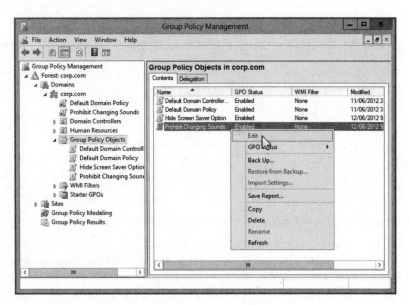

Granting OU Admins Access to Create New Group Policy Objects

By using the "Delegation of Control Wizard" to delegate the "Manage Group Policy links" attribute, you performed half of what is needed to grant the appropriate authority to Frank (and any additional future HR-OU-Admins) to create GPOs in the Group Policy Objects container and link them to the **Human Resources** OU, the **Human Resources Users** OU, or the **Human Resources Computers** OU (though we really don't want to link many GPOs directly to the **Human Resources** OU).

You can grant the HR-OU-Admins the ability to create GPOs in the Group Policy Objects container in two ways. For now, I'll show you the old-school way; in Chapter 2, I'll show you the GPMC way.

One of Active Directory's built-in security groups, Group Policy Creator Owners, holds the key to the other half of our puzzle. You'll need to add those users or groups that you want to have the ability to create GPOs to a built-in group, cleverly named Group Policy Creator Owners. To do so, follow these steps:

1. Log off and log back on as Domain Administrator.

2. Fire up Active Directory Users and Computers.

3. By default, the Group Policy Creator Owners group is located in the Users folder in the domain. Double-click the Group Policy Creator Owners group and add the HR-OU-Admins group and/or Frank Rizzo.

In Chapter 2, you'll see an alternate way to allow users to create GPOs.

Creating and Linking Group Policy Objects at the OU Level

At the site level, we hid the Screen Saver option. At the domain level, we chose to get rid of the Sounds option in the Windows 10 Personalization page.

At the OU level, we have two jobs to do:

- Prevent users from changing the mouse pointers (a Windows 7 and later policy setting)
- Restore the Screen Saver option that was taken away at the site level

To create a GPO at the OU level, follow these steps:

1. Since you're on WIN10MANAGEMENT, log off as Administrator and log back on as Frank Rizzo (frizzo@corp.com).

2. Choose Start and type **GPMC.MSC** in the Start Search prompt.

3. Drill down until you reach the **Human Resources Users** OU, right-click it, and choose "Create a GPO in this domain, and Link it here" from the context menu to open the New GPO dialog box.

4. In the New GPO dialog box, type the name of your new GPO, say "Hide Mouse Pointers Option / Restore Screen Saver Option." This will create a GPO in the Group Policy Objects container and link it to the **Human Resources Users** OU.

5. Right-click the Group Policy link and choose Edit from the context menu to open the Group Policy Management Editor.

6. To hide the mouse pointers option in the Group Policy editor, drill down through User Configuration ➢ Policies ➢ Administrative Templates ➢ Control Panel ➢ Personalization and double-click the **Prevent changing mouse pointers** policy setting. Change the setting from Not Configured to Enabled, and click OK.

7. To restore the Screen Saver setting for Windows 10, double-click the **Prevent Changing Screen Saver** policy setting. Change the setting from Not Configured to Disabled, and click OK.

8. Close the Group Policy Management Editor to return to the GPMC.

By disabling the **Hide Screen Saver Tab** policy setting, you're reversing the Enable setting set at a higher level. See the sidebar "The Three Possible Settings: Not Configured, Enabled, and Disabled" later in this chapter.

Verifying Your Changes at the OU Level

On your test WIN10 machine, log back on as Frank. Because Frank's account is in the OU, Frank is destined to get the site, domain, and now the new OU GPOs with the policy settings.

On WIN10, right-click the Desktop and choose Personalize from the context menu to open the Display Properties dialog box.

You can now (as Frank) click Themes, and when you then try to click on "Go to mouse pointer settings" you will see what's in Figure 1.25.

You should also now (as Frank) be able to click within Personalization upon the Lock Screen menu, and when you try to click on "Screen saver settings" you will be able to open it.

In Figure 1.25, you can see the before (left) and after (right) when the policy is applied. Look closely, and note that the "Pointers" option in the Mouse Properties applet is removed and that the Screen Saver option is no longer grayed out and is now available.

FIGURE 1.25   On the top, we have Frank's Personalization page where Frank can now get to his Screen Saver settings. On the bottom (left) you can see Frank's Mouse Properties before the policy applies. On the bottom (right) you can see Frank's Mouse Properties after the policy applies (and note the missing "Pointers" tabs).

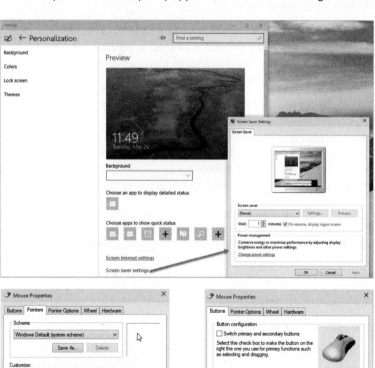

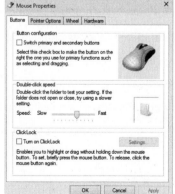

This test proves, once again, that even OU administrators are not automatically immune from policy settings. Chapter 2 explains how to change this behavior.

Group Policy Strategy: Should I Create More or Fewer GPOs?

At times, you'll want to lock down additional functions for a collection of users or computers. For example, you might want to specify that no users in the **Human Resources Users** OU can use the Control Panel.

At the **Human Resources Users** OU level, you've already set up a GPO that contained a policy setting to hide the mouse pointers option in the Windows 10 Personalization page. You can create a new GPO that affects the **Human Resources Users** OU, give it a descriptive name—say, **No One Can Use Control Panel**—and then drill down through User Configuration➢ Policies ➢ Administrative Templates ➢ Control Panel and enable the policy setting **Prohibit Access to Control Panel**.

Or you could simply modify your existing GPO, named Hide Mouse Pointers Option/ Restore Screen Saver Option, so that it contains additional policy settings. You can then rename your GPO to something that makes sense and encompasses the qualities of all the policy changes—say "Our Human Resources Users' Desktop Settings."

Here's the quandary: the former method (one policy setting per GPO) is certainly more descriptive and definitely easier to debug should things go awry. If you have only one policy set inside the GPO, you have a better handle on what each one is affecting. If something goes wrong, you can dive right into the GPO, track down the policy setting, and make the necessary changes, or you can disable the ornery GPO (as discussed in Chapter 2 in the section "Stopping Group Policy Objects from Applying").

The second method (multiple policy settings per GPO) is a teeny-weeny bit faster for your computers and users at boot or logon time because each additional GPO takes some miniscule fraction of additional processing time. But if you stuff too many settings in an individual GPO, the time to debug should things go wrong goes up exponentially. Group Policy has so many nooks and crannies that it can be difficult to debug.

So, in a nutshell, if you have multiple GPOs at a particular level, you can do the following:

- Name each of them more descriptively.
- Debug them easily if things go wrong.
- Disable individually misbehaving GPOs.
- Associate a specific GPO more easily to a WMI filter (explored in Chapter 6).
- More easily delegate permissions to any specific GPO (explored in Chapter 2).

If you have fewer GPOs at a particular level, the following is the case:

- Logging on is slightly faster for the user (but only slightly).

- Debugging is somewhat more difficult if things go wrong.

- You can disable individually misbehaving GPOs or links to misbehaving GPOs. (But if they contain many settings, you might be disabling more than you desire.)

So, how do you form a GPO strategy? There is no right or wrong answer; you need to decide what's best for you. Several options, however, can help you decide.

One middle-of-the-road strategy is to start with multiple GPOs and one lone policy setting in each. Once you are comfortable that they are individually working as expected, you can create another new GPO that contains the sum of the settings from, in this example, **Prevent Changing Mouse Pointers** and **Prohibit Access to Control Panel**, and then delete (or disable) the old individual GPO.

Another middle-of-the-road strategy is to have a single GPO that contains only the policy settings required to perform a complete "wish." This way, if the wish goes sour, you can easily address it or disable it (or whack it) as needed.

Here's yet another strategy. Some Microsoft documentation recommends that you create GPOs so that they affect only the User half or the Computer half. You can then disable the unused portion of the GPO (either the Computer half or the User half). This allows you to group together policy settings affecting one node for ease of naming and debugging and allows for flexible troubleshooting. However, be careful here because after you disable half the GPO, there's no iconic notification (though there is a column labeled GPO Status that does show this). Troubleshooting can become harder if not performed perfectly and consistently. In all, I'm not a huge fan of disabling half the GPO.

Creating a New Group Policy Object Affecting Computers in an OU

For the sake of learning and working through the rest of the examples in this section, you'll create another GPO and link it to the **Human Resources Computers** OU. This GPO will autolaunch a very important application for anyone who uses these machines: calc.exe.

 The setting we're about to play with also exists under the User node, but we'll experiment with the Computer node policy.

First, you'll need to create the new GPO and modify the settings. You'll then need to move some client machines into the **Human Resources Computers** OU in order to see your changes take effect.

To autolaunch `calc.exe` for anyone logging into a computer in the **Human Resources Computers** OU, follow these steps:

1. If you're not already logged in as Frank Rizzo, the **Human Resources** OU administrator, do so now on WIN10MANAGEMENT.

2. Choose Start and type **GPMC.MSC** in the Start Search prompt.

3. Drill down until you reach the **Human Resources Computers** OU, right-click it, and choose "Create a GPO in this domain, and Link it here" from the context menu.

4. Name the GPO something descriptive, such as "Auto-Launch calc.exe."

5. Right-click the GPO, and choose Edit to open the Group Policy Management Editor.

6. We want to affect our client computers (not users), so we need to use the Computers node. To autolaunch `calc.exe`, drill down through Computer Configuration ➢ Policies ➢ Administrative Templates ➢ System ➢ Logon, and double-click **Run these programs at user logon**. Change the setting from Not Configured to Enabled.

7. Click the Show button, and the Show Contents dialog box appears. You'll see that this policy setting has a little "table editor" associated with it. In the first "row," simply enter the full path to `calc.exe` as **c:\windows\system32\calc.exe** and click OK, as shown in Figure 1.26. Click OK to close the Show Contents dialog box, and click OK again to close the **Run these programs at user logon** policy setting.

FIGURE 1.26 When this policy setting is enabled and `calc.exe` is specified, all computers in this OU will launch `calc.exe` when a user logs in.

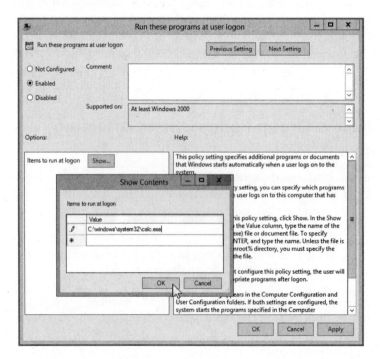

8. Close the Group Policy Management Editor to return the GPMC.

> Be aware of occasional strange Microsoft verbiage when you need to enable a policy to *disable* a setting. Since Windows 2003, most policy settings have been renamed to "Prohibit *<whatever>*" to reflect the change from confusion to clarity.

Moving Computers into the Human Resources Computers OU

Since you just created a policy that will affect computers, you'll need to place a workstation or two inside the **Human Resources Computers** OU to see the results of your labor. You'll need to be logged on as Administrator on DC01 or WIN10MANAGEMENT to do this.

> Quite often computers and users are relegated to separate OUs. That way, certain GPOs can be applied to certain computers but not others. For instance, isolating laptops, desktops, and servers is a common practice.

In this example, we're going to use the Find command in Active Directory Users and Computers to find your workstation named WIN10 and move it into the **Human Resources Computers** OU.

To find and move computers into a specific OU, follow these steps:

1. In Active Directory Users and Computers, right-click the domain, and choose Find from the context menu to open the "Find Users, Contacts, and Groups" dialog box.

2. From the Find drop-down menu, select Computers. In the Name field, type **WIN10** to find the computer account of the same name. Once you've found it, right-click the account and choose Move from the context menu, as shown in Figure 1.27. Move the account to the **Human Resources Computers** OU.

3. Now that you've moved WIN10 (or other example machines) into the new OU, be sure to reboot those client computers.

> After you move the computer accounts into the **Human Resources Computers** OU, it's very important to reboot your client machines. As you'll see in Chapter 3, the computer does not recognize the change right away when computer accounts are moved between OUs.

As you can see in this example (and in the real world), a best practice is to separate users and computers into their own OUs and then link GPOs to those OUs. Indeed, underneath a parent OU structure, such as the **Human Resources** OU, you might have more OUs (that is, **Human Resources Laptops** OU, **Human Resources Servers** OU, and so on). This will give you the most flexibility in design between delegating control where it's needed and the balance of GPO design within OUs. Just remember that for GPOs to affect either a user or computer, that user or computer must be within the scope of the GPO—site, domain, or OU.

FIGURE 1.27 Use the Find command to find computers in the domain, then right-click the entry and select Move to move them.

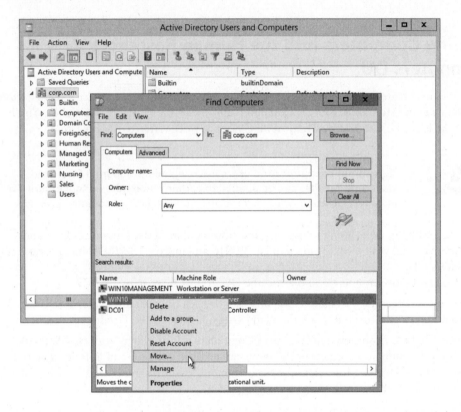

Verifying Your Cumulative Changes

At this point, you've set up three levels of Group Policy that accomplish multiple actions:

- At the site level, the "Hide Screen Saver Option" GPO is in force for users.
- At the domain level, the "Prohibit Changing Sounds" GPO is in force for users.
- In the **Human Resources Users** OU, the "Hide Mouse Pointers Option/Restore Screen Saver Option" GPO is in force for users.
- In the **Human Resources Computers** OU, the "Auto-Launch calc.exe" GPO is in force for computers.

At this point, take a minute to flip back to Figure 1.11 (the swimming pool illustration) to see where we're going here. To see the accumulation of your policy settings inside your GPOs, you'll need to log on as a user who is affected by the **Human Resources Users** OU and at a computer that is affected by the **Human Resources Computers** OU. Therefore, log on as Frank Rizzo at WIN10.

If you're using Windows 10, right-click the Desktop and choose Personalize. Note that the removal of "Change mouse pointers" is still in force (and the Screen Saver entry is restored). And, when you logged in as Frank Rizzo, did the computer GPO autolaunch Windows Calculator?

These tests prove that even OU administrators are not automatically immune from GPOs and the policy settings within. Under the hood, they are in the Authenticated Users security group. See Chapter 2 for information on how to modify this behavior.

The Three Possible Settings: Not Configured, Enabled, and Disabled

As you saw in Figure 1.2 earlier in this chapter, nearly all administrative template policy settings can be set as Not Configured, Enabled, or Disabled. These three settings have very different consequences, so it's important to understand how each works.

Not Configured   The best way to think about Not Configured is to imagine that it really says, "Don't do anything" or even "Pass through." Why is this? Because if a policy setting is set to Not Configured, then it honors any previously set setting (or the operating system default).

Enabled   When a specific policy setting is enabled, the policy will take effect. In the case of the **Prohibit Changing Sounds** policy setting, the effect is obvious. However, lots of policy settings, once enabled, have myriad possibilities *inside* the specific policy setting! (For a gander at one such policy setting, use the Group Policy Management Editor and drill down to User Configuration ▸ Policies ▸ Administrative Templates ▸ Windows Components ▸ Internet Explorer ▸ Toolbars and select the policy setting named **Configure Toolbar Buttons**.) So, as you can see, Enabled really means "Turn this policy setting on." Either it will then do what it says or there will be more options inside the policy setting that can be configured.

Disabled   This setting leads a dual life:

- Disabled usually means that if the same policy setting is enabled at a higher level, reverse its operation. For example, we chose to enable the **Prevent Changing Screen Saver** policy setting at the site level. If at a lower level (say, the domain or OU level), we chose to *disable* this policy setting, the Screen Saver option will pop back at the level at which we *disabled* this policy. You can think of Disabled (usually) as "reverse a policy setting coming from a higher level."

- Disabled sometimes has a special and, typically, rare use. That is, something might already be hard-coded into the Registry to be "turned on" or work one way, and the only way to turn it off is to select Disabled. One such policy setting is the **Shutdown Event Tracker**. You disable the policy setting, which turns it off, because in servers, it's already hard-coded on. In workstations, it's already hard-coded off. Likewise, if you want to kill the firewall for Windows XP (and later), you need to set **Windows Firewall: Protect All Network Connections** to Disabled. (You can find that policy setting at Computer Configuration ➢ Policies ➢ Administrative Templates ➢ Network ➢ Network Connections ➢ Windows Firewall ➢ Domain Profile (and also Standard Profile). Again, you set it to Disabled because the firewall's defaults are hard-coded to on, and by disabling the policy setting, you're "reverting" the behavior back.

So, think of Not Configured as having neither Allow nor Deny set. Enabled will turn it on, and it will possibly have more functions. Disabled has multiple uses, and be sure to first read the help text for each policy setting. Most times it's simply directly spelled out what Enabled and Disabled does for that particular setting. Last, test, test, test to make sure that once you've manipulated a policy setting, it's doing precisely what you had in mind.

Final Thoughts

The concepts here are valid regardless of what your domain is running. It doesn't matter if you have a pure or mixed Active Directory domain with various and sundry Domain Controller types. The point is that to make the best use of Group Policy, you'll need an Active Directory.

You'll also need a Windows 10 or Windows Server 2016 management station to do your Group Policy work. Again, we talk more about why you need a Windows 10 management station in Chapters 3 and 6 and elsewhere.

Remember, the GPMC is built into Windows Server 2016, but it's not installed unless the machine is also a Domain Controller. The GPMC isn't built into Windows 10 and is only available through the downloadable RSAT tools.

Even though most of the examples of a target computer are Windows 10 in this book, you can usually substitute a Windows 7 or 8 machine as your target and see similar (if not often identical) results.

The more you use and implement GPOs in your environment, the better you'll become at their basic use while at the same time avoiding pitfalls when it comes to using them. The following tips are scattered throughout the chapter but are repeated and emphasized here for quick reference, to help you along your Group Policy journey:

GPOs don't "live" at the site, domain, or OU level.   GPOs "live" in Active Directory and are represented in the swimming pool of the domain called the Group Policy Objects container. To use a GPO, you need to link a GPO to a level in Active Directory that you want to affect: a site, a domain, or an OU.

GPOs apply locally and also to Active Directory sites, domains, and OUs.   There is a local GPO that can be used with or without Active Directory. Everyone on that computer must embrace that local GPO. Then, Active Directory Group Policy Objects apply: site, domain, and then OU. Active Directory GPOs "trump" any local policy settings if set within the Local Group Policy. Active Directory is a hierarchy, and Group Policy takes advantage of that hierarchy.

Avoid using the site level to implement GPOs.   Users can roam from site to site by jumping on different computers (or plugging their laptop into another site). When they do, they can be confused by the settings changing around them. Use GPOs linked to the site only to set up special sitewide security settings, such as IPsec or the Internet Explorer Proxy. Use the domain or OU levels when creating GPOs whenever possible.

Implement common settings high in the hierarchy when possible.   The higher up in the hierarchy GPOs are implemented, the more users they affect. You want common settings to be created and set one time. It's not optimal to create many GPOs performing the same functions at other lower levels, which will just clutter your view of Active Directory with the multiple copies of the same policy setting.

Implement unique settings low in the hierarchy.   If a specific collection of users is unique, try to round them up into an OU and then apply Group Policy to them. This is much better than applying the settings high in the hierarchy and using Group Policy filtering later.

Use more GPOs at any level to make things easier.   When creating a new wish, isolate it by creating a new GPO. This will enable easy revocation by unlinking it should something go awry.

Strike a balance between having too many and too few GPOs.   There is a middle ground between having one policy setting within a single GPO and having a bajillion policy settings contained within a single GPO. At the end of your design, the goal is to have meaningfully named GPOs that reflect the "wishes" you want to accomplish. If you should choose to end those wishes, you can easily disable or delete a specific GPO.

As you go on your Group Policy journey...   Don't go at it alone. There are some nice third-party independent resources to help you on your way. I run www.GPanswers.com, which has oodles of resources, downloads, a community forum, downloadable eChapters, video tutorials, links to third-party software, and my in-person and online versions of my hands-on training seminars. Think of it as your secret Group Policy resource.

My pal (and technical editor for this edition of the book) Alan Burchill runs www.group-policy.biz and has a wonderful set of step-by-step articles and tips and tricks and such.

My pal (and technical editor for a previous edition) Darren Mar-Elia runs "GPO Guy," which is part of his software company, SDM Software. Check it out at http://sdmsoftware.com/gpoguy/.

My pal (and technical editor for a previous edition) Jakob Heidelberg has a lot of great articles (mostly on Group Policy topics) at www.heidelbergit.dk/.

2

Managing Group Policy with the GPMC and via PowerShell

In Chapter 1, "Group Policy Essentials," you got to know how and when Group Policy works. We used Active Directory Users and Computers to create and manage users and computers, but we used the Group Policy Management Console (GPMC) to manage Group Policy. We got a little workout with the GPMC when creating new GPOs and linking them to various levels in Active Directory.

And, for just a moment, we went back to the old-school way to delegate control to Frank and the HR-OU-Admins group to link existing GPOs to their **Human Resources** OU structure.

In this chapter, I'll cover the remainder of the daily tasks you can perform using the GPMC. As a reminder, the GPMC is for all implementations of Active Directory. That is, you can use the GPMC to manage your Active Directory—whatever the Domain Controllers are that constitute it.

You just need the GPMC loaded up on some machine. Now, in the previous chapter, I put a pretty fine point on it: you want this machine to be one of the latest machines possible, either a Windows 10 or a Windows Server 2016 machine. There are some older editions, but I don't recommend you use them.

For this edition of the book, I've decided to also show the PowerShell equivalent of the GPMC process. In other words, for almost all the things you can do in the GPMC, you could, if you wanted, use PowerShell.

But first, let's answer the question, Why would you want to do the items within the GPMC using PowerShell? Said another way, if the clickety-clicks are straightforward and easy, why would you want to make it harder on yourself and typety-type your way through the same process?

The answer to that would be if you need to do anything that's repeatable process. For instance, in this chapter, you're going to learn how to do things like this:

- Create a Group Policy Object and give it a name.
- Link a Group Policy Object to an OU.
- Order Group Policy Objects at a level, say, the OU level.

Yep, I'm definitely going to show you how to clickety-click your way to success here. But I'm also going to show you the typety-type way using PowerShell. So if you needed to do the same thing over and over again, you could recycle the typety-types and make it a repeatable script.

If you wanted to fully ignore all the PowerShell text, and focus just on the GPMC clickety-clicks, you could do that.

Also, that being said, I'm not going to be going deep into PowerShell, syntax rules, or actually making scripts. There are zillions of PowerShell tutorials and books that talk about how to do that. And, one of the appendices, entitled "Scripting Group Policy Operations with Windows PowerShell," has a mini-section right at the top entitled "Preparing for Your PowerShell Experience." There you'll learn what I think are the three most important pieces of getting started with PowerShell:

- Getting PowerShell up and running

- Downloading the latest help from Microsoft

- Setting up to run actual scripts (which shouldn't be needed for the one-liners in this chapter)

So, here's my recommendation for using this chapter:

1. Read this chapter, and do the clickety-clicks.

2. If you're already reasonably PowerShell savvy, then just go for the PowerShell examples in this chapter if you want to try them out.

3. If you're warming up to PowerShell, jump to the appendix entitled "Scripting Group Policy Operations with Windows PowerShell" and read the section "Preparing for Your PowerShell Experience," get set up, then come back to this chapter as a reference for most of what can be done with Group Policy and PowerShell.

Again, you should have already created your management station with the GPMC in the previous chapter. Remember, if you don't use a Windows 10 machine (or Windows Server 2016) as your management station, you won't have access to all the latest awesome powers in the Group Policy arsenal. In this chapter, you're going to be working again with your WIN10MANAGEMENT machine where you've already loaded the updated GPMC.

With that in mind, let's get to know the GPMC a bit better.

I'm going to assume you've already installed the GPMC on either your Windows 10 management station (WIN10MANAGEMENT) or your Windows Server 2016 Domain Controller (DC01). If you haven't tackled those installation steps, go back to Chapter 1 and find the section "Implementing the GPMC on Your Management Station."

Once you're ready to get started, from the Start screen, type **GPMC.MSC**.

Common Procedures with the GPMC and PowerShell

In Chapter 1, we created and linked some GPOs, which we can see in the Group Policy Objects container, to determine how, at each level, we were affecting our users. In the following sections, we'll continue by working with some advanced options for applying, manipulating, and using Group Policy.

Since we didn't use PowerShell at all in the last chapter to create and link GPOs, let's take 30 seconds to do the equivalent of what we did in the last chapter and do it right here, right now, using PowerShell. In short, let's create a new, blank Group Policy Object, call it GPO123, then link it to the **Human Resource Users** OU (which is tucked within the **Human Resources** OU, which itself is within the domain Corp.com).

Before we get started though, if you're using an older version of Windows (and/or and older version of PowerShell) you might need to specify the command to import the Group Policy cmdlets before you get anything useful to happen. So if nothing appears to be working in PowerShell, start out with the command import-module grouppolicy (which can be seen in Figure 2.1).

 If you are not running as the Built-In Administrator account, you will need to launch a PowerShell command prompt with Administrator permissions because you are doing something that requires elevated access and a PowerShell. You can do this by right-clicking the shortcut and then clicking the "Run as Administrator" option.

Now, here are the two PowerShell commands you could type to do the job.

Once you are running with Administrator permissions, you're ready to continue on as follows. For instance, to create a new Group Policy Object, it's as simple as:

```
New-GPO -name GPO123
```

or

```
New-GPlink -name GPO123 -target "ou=Human Resources Users, ou=Human Resources,
dc=corp, dc=com"
```

Note how the domain name is proceeded by dc= and the OUs (parent and child) are proceeded by ou= in the PowerShell command.

The result can be seen in Figure 2.1.

Note that this didn't do any real "work" inside the Group Policy Object; it just created it and linked it to our existing OU. If we go back to using the GPMC, you should be able to refresh the GPMC and then verify that the Group Policy Object is now linked to the right OU.

While still in the GPMC, clicking a GPO (or a link) lets you get more information about what it does. For now, feel free to click around, but I suggest that you don't change anything until we get to the specific examples.

FIGURE 2.1 You can create and link GPOs using PowerShell. Be sure to put items with spaces in double quotes.

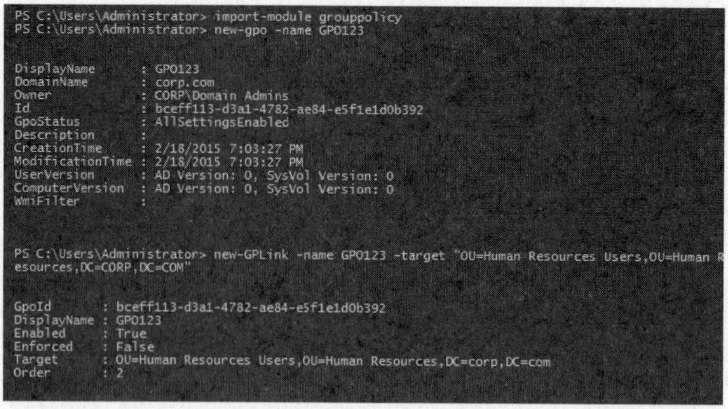

```
PS C:\Users\Administrator> import-module grouppolicy
PS C:\Users\Administrator> new-gpo -name GPO123

DisplayName       : GPO123
DomainName        : corp.com
Owner             : CORP\Domain Admins
Id                : bceff113-d3a1-4782-ae84-e5f1e1d0b392
GpoStatus         : AllSettingsEnabled
Description       :
CreationTime      : 2/18/2015 7:03:27 PM
ModificationTime  : 2/18/2015 7:03:27 PM
UserVersion       : AD Version: 0, SysVol Version: 0
ComputerVersion   : AD Version: 0, SysVol Version: 0
WmiFilter         :


PS C:\Users\Administrator> new-GPLink -name GPO123 -target "OU=Human Resources Users,OU=Human R
esources,DC=CORP,DC=COM"

GpoId             : bceff113-d3a1-4782-ae84-e5f1e1d0b392
DisplayName       : GPO123
Enabled           : True
Enforced          : False
Target            : OU=Human Resources Users,OU=Human Resources,DC=corp,DC=com
Order             : 2
```

Various tabs are available to you once you click the GPO or a link. For instance, let's locate the GPO that's linked to the **Human Resources Users** OU. We'll do this by drilling down to Group Policy Management ≻ Forest ≻ Domains ≻ Corp.com ≻ **Human Resources** ≻ **Human Resources Users** and clicking the one GPO that's linked there: "Hide Mouse Pointers Option/Restore Screen Saver Option." With that in mind, let's examine the various sections of a policy setting; you can flip through each of the tabs to get more information about the GPO you just found.

The Scope Tab Clicking a GPO or a GPO link opens the Scope tab. The Scope tab gives you an at-a-glance view of where and when the GPO will apply. We'll examine the Scope tab in the sections "Deleting and Unlinking Group Policy Objects" and "Filtering the Scope of Group Policy Objects with Security" later in this chapter and in the WMI section of Chapter 4. For now, you can see that the "Hide Mouse Pointers Option/Restore Screen Saver Option" GPO is linked to the **Human Resources Users** OU. But you already knew that.

Using Microsoft's own Group Policy PowerShell cmdlets to detail *what* Group Policy Objects are linked *where* is possible, but actually a little tricky. So, we cover how to do that in the PowerShell appendix, in the section "Documenting GPO Links."

That being said, there is another quick way to do this, if you're willing to download a third-party (but free) PowerShell cmdlet set from my pal Darren Mar-Elia from SDM Software at:

http://sdmsoftware.com/group-policy-management-products/freeware-group-policy-tools-utilities/.

You're looking for the SDM GPMC PowerShell cmdlets.

Once the set is downloaded and installed, just re-open PowerShell, then import his cmdlets and run Darren's command Get-SDMgplink, which lists all GPOs at a level. You simply specify the level. The two commands would be:

```
Import-Module SDM-GPMC
Get-SDMgplink -Scope "OU=Human Resources Users, OU=Human Resources, DC=corp, DC=com"
```

The result using the free SDM GPMC PowerShell cmdlet can be seen here. You can see that the line starting with Name details the one Group Policy Object (in my case) that is linked to that particular scope.

```
PS C:\Users\Administrator> Import-Module SDM-GPMC
PS C:\Users\Administrator> Get-SDMgplink -Scope "OU=Human Resources Users, OU=Human Resources, DC=corp, DC=com"


Enabled      : True
Enforced     : False
GPODomain    : corp.com
GPOID        : {A69968E7-A3C8-4EB5-8641-2A9EE88E7259}
Name         : Hide Mouse Pointers Option/Restore Screen Saver Option
Scope        : OU=Human Resources Users, OU=Human Resources, DC=corp, DC=com
SOMLinkOrder : 1
```

The Details Tab   The Details tab contains information describing who created the GPO (the owner) and the status (Enabled, Disabled, or Partially Disabled) as well as some nuts-and-bolts information about its underlying representation in Active Directory (the GUID). We'll examine the Details tab in the sections "Disabling 'Half' (or Both Halves) of the Group Policy Object" and "Understanding GPMC's Link Warning" later in this chapter.

Should you change the GPO status here by, say, disabling the User Configuration of the policy, you'll be affecting all other levels in Active Directory that might be using this GPO by linking to it. See the section "Understanding GPMC's Link Warning" as well as the sidebar "On GPO Links and GPOs Themselves" a bit later in the chapter.

You can see these details in the GPMC (top), and using PowerShell, you can use the Get-GPO cmdlet as seen in the screenshot on the (bottom).

Hide Mouse Pointers Option/Restore Screen Saver Option

Scope | Details | Settings | Delegation

Domain:	corp.com
Owner:	Domain Admins (CORP\Domain Admins)
Created:	11/16/2014 11:33:18 AM
Modified:	11/16/2014 11:33:18 AM
User version:	0 (AD), 0 (SYSVOL)
Computer version:	0 (AD), 0 (SYSVOL)
Unique ID:	{A69968E7-A3C8-4EB5-8641-2A9EE88E7259}
GPO Status:	Enabled
Comment:	

```
PS C:\Users\Administrator> Get-GPO "Hide Mouse Pointers Option/Restore Screen Saver Option"


DisplayName      : Hide Mouse Pointers Option/Restore Screen Saver Option
DomainName       : corp.com
Owner            : CORP\Domain Admins
Id               : a69968e7-a3c8-4eb5-8641-2a9ee88e7259
GpoStatus        : AllSettingsEnabled
Description      :
CreationTime     : 11/16/2014 11:33:18 AM
ModificationTime : 11/16/2014 11:33:18 AM
UserVersion      : AD Version: 0, SysVol Version: 0
ComputerVersion  : AD Version: 0, SysVol Version: 0
WmiFilter        :
```

The Settings Tab   The Settings tab gives you an at-a-glance view of what's been set inside the GPO. In our example, you can see the Enabled and Disabled status of the two policy settings we manipulated. You can click Hide (or Show) to contract and expand all the configured policy settings.

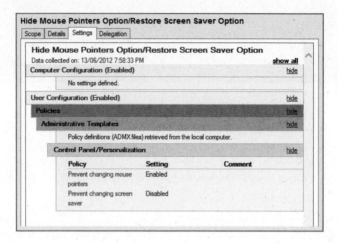

- Clicking Hide at any level tightens that level. You can expose more information by clicking Show.

- Clicking the policy setting name—for example, **Prevent Changing Mouse Pointers**—displays the help text for the policy setting (but note that this is only applicable to Administrative Template settings). This trick can be useful if someone set up a GPO with a kooky name and you want to know what's going on inside that GPO.

- If you want to change a setting, right-click the settings area and select Edit. The familiar Group Policy Management Editor will appear. Note, however, that the Group Policy Management Editor will not "snap to" the policy setting you want to edit. The editor always starts off at the root.

- Additionally, at any time you can right-click over this report and select Save Report, which does just that. It creates an HTML or XML report that you can then e-mail to fellow administrators or the boss, and so on. This is a super way of documenting your Group Policy environment instead of writing down everything by hand.

You can use PowerShell to save a report of a specific Group Policy Object or all GPOs using the cmdlet Get-GPOReport. For instance, you could type:

```
Get-GPOReport –Name GPO123 –ReportType HTML –Path C:\temp\out1.html
```

You could also do something like:

```
Get-GPOReport -ALL -ReportType HTML -Path C:\temp\ALL.html
```

```
PS C:\Users\administrator> import-module grouppolicy
PS C:\Users\administrator> Get-GPOReport -Name GPO123 -ReportType HTML -Path c:\temp\out1.html
PS C:\Users\administrator> Get-GPOReport -ALL -ReportType HTML -Path c:\temp\ALL.html
PS C:\Users\administrator> _
```

Both examples assume C:\temp\ is present. Note the second command is a little weird and dumps *all* the reports of *all* the GPOs into one *big* HTML file.

If you'd like to see the "trick" for having a single report for each Group Policy Object, check out the section "Creating GPO Reports" in the PowerShell appendix.

Now, I've said it before, but it bears repeating: You can also edit the settings by clicking the GPO or any GPO link for that object and choosing Edit. However, you *always* affect all containers (sites, domains, or OUs) to which the GPO is linked. It's one and the same object, regardless of the way you edit it. See the sidebar "On GPO Links and GPOs Themselves" a bit later in the chapter to get the gist of this.

Out, Out Annoying Internet Explorer Pop-ups!

If you chose to run the GPMC on a Windows Server, you may run into security pop-ups when clicking the Settings tab. Certain aspects of the GPMC, such as the Settings tab, utilize Internet Explorer to display their contents.

Since Internet Explorer is "hardened" on Windows Server machines, you will have limited access to the whole picture. When showing the Settings within the GPMC, you'll be presented with a warning box:

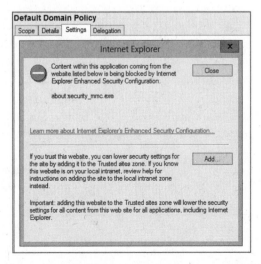

You can bypass this by simply adding `security_mmc.exe` as a trusted website. This should make your problems go away.

Optionally, you can also turn off Internet Explorer Enhanced Security Configuration. In Windows Server 2012 and later, you use Server Manager. Then select Local Server on the left side and select IE Enhanced Security Configuration on the right side. Finally, choose Off in the pop-up window that appears:

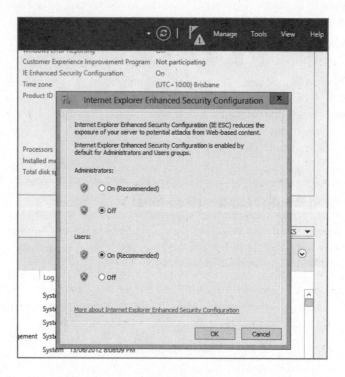

This is where you'll be able to enable or disable the annoying, I mean, informative pop-ups. This approach is recommended in test labs but not recommended on production servers.

The Delegation Tab   The Delegation tab lets you specify who can do what with GPOs, their links, and their properties. You'll find the Delegation tab in a lot of places, such as when you do the following:

- Click a GPO link or click a GPO in the Group Policy Objects container
- Click a site
- Click a domain
- Click an OU

- Click the WMI Filters node
- Click a WMI (Windows Management Instrumentation) filter itself (covered in Chapter 4)
- Click on the Starter GPOs section

The PowerShell cmdlet to get the state of delegation (which could also be thought of as permissions) is `Get-GPPermission`, and the cmdlet to set or change the state of delegation would be `Set-GPPermission`.

We'll not jump into these PowerShell cmdlets here. We'll use these cmdlets a little later in the section "Filtering the Scope of Group Policy Objects with Security."

At each of these locations, the tab allows you to do something different. I'll discuss what each instance of this tab does a bit later in the section "Security Filtering and Delegation with the GPMC."

Raising or Lowering the Precedence of Multiple Group Policy Objects

You already know that the "flow" of Group Policy is inherited from the site level, the domain level, and then from each nested OU level. But, additionally, *within* each level, say at the **Temporary Office Help** OU, multiple GPOs are processed in a ranking precedence order. Lower-ranking GPOs are processed first, and then the higher GPOs are processed.

In Figure 2.2, you can see that an administrator has linked two GPOs to the **Temporary Office Help** OU. One GPO is named "Enforce 50 MB Disk Quota" and another is named "Enforce 40 MB Disk Quota."

If the policy settings inside these GPOs both adjust the disk quota settings, which one will "win"? Client computers will process these two GPOs from *lowest-link order* to *highest-link order*. Therefore, the "Enforce 40 MB Disk Quota" GPO (with link order 2) is processed before "Enforce 50 MB Disk Quota" (link order 1). Hence, the GPO with the policy settings to dictate 50 MB disk quotas will win.

So, if two (or more) GPOs within the same level contain values for the same policy setting (or policy settings), the GPOs will be processed from lowest-link order to highest-link order. Each consecutively processed GPO is then written. If there are any conflicts, the highest link order "wins." This could happen where one GPO has a specific policy setting enabled and another GPO at the same level has the same policy setting disabled.

Just to clear up a confusing little point: it turns out the highest-link order is not the highest numbered GPO listed at a level. Oh no—that would be too easy. Indeed, the highest-link order is shown as the lowest displayed number. Great. Just another fun fact to keep you on your toes.

Changing the order of the processing of multiple GPOs at a specific level is an easy task with the GPMC. For instance, suppose you want to change the order of the processing so that the "Enforce 40 MB Disk Quota" GPO is processed after the "Enforce 50 MB Disk Quota" GPO. Simply click the policy setting you want to process last and click the down arrow icon. Similarly, if you have additional GPOs that you want to process first, click the GPO and click the up arrow icon. The multiple arrow icons will put the highlighted GPO either first or last in the link order—depending on the icon you click.

FIGURE 2.2 You can link multiple GPOs at the same level.

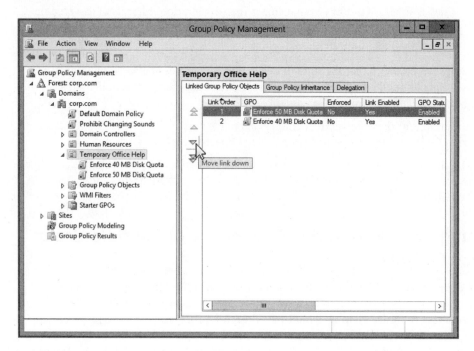

Using PowerShell, the cmdlet would be as follows to set a specific Group Policy Object ("Enforce 40 MB Disk Quota") to link order 2:

```
Set-GPlink –Name "Enforce 40MB Disk Quotas" –Target "ou=Temporary Office Help,
dc=corp, dc=com" –Order 2
```

Again—the "most last" applied GPO wins. So the GPO with a link order of 1 is always applied last and, hence, has the final say at that level. This is always true unless the Enforced function is used (as discussed later).

Understanding GPMC's Link Warning

In the previous chapter, I pointed out that anytime you click a GPO link, you get the informational (or perhaps it's more of a warning) message shown in Figure 2.3.

FIGURE 2.3 You get this message anytime you click the icon for a link.

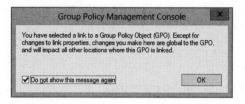

This message is trying to convey an important sentiment: No man is an island, and neither is a Group Policy Object. Just because you created a GPO and it is seen swimming in the Group Policy Objects container doesn't mean you're the only one who is possibly using it.

As we work through examples in this chapter, we'll manipulate various characteristics of GPOs and links to GPOs. If we manipulate any characteristics of a GPO we're about to play with, such as the following, then all other levels in Active Directory that also link to this GPO will be affected by our changes:

* The underlying policy settings themselves
* The security filtering (on the Scope tab)
* The WMI filtering (on the Scope tab)
* The GPO status (on the Details tab)
* The delegation (on the Delegation tab)

For instance, imagine you had a GPO linked to an OU called **Doctors** and the same GPO linked to an OU called **Nurses**. If you edit the GPO in the swimming pool, or click the link to the GPO in *either* **Doctors** *or* **Nurses** and click Edit, you're doing the same thing. Any changes made within the GPO affect *both* the **Doctors** OU and the **Nurses** OU.

This is sometimes a tough concept to remember, so it's good to see it here again. You can choose to squelch the tip if you like. Just don't forget its advice.

> The difference between the GPO itself and the links you can create can be confusing. Be sure to check out the sidebar "On GPO Links and GPOs Themselves" a bit later in the chapter.

Another way to see this principle in action is by locating the "Auto-Launch calc.exe" GPO in either the link in the **Human Resources Computers** OU or the object itself within the Group Policy Objects container. Next, go to the Details tab and change the GPO status to some other setting. Then, go to the link or the actual GPO and see that your changes are reflected. You can even create a new OU, link the GPO, and *still* see that the change is there. This is because you're manipulating the *actual* GPO, not the link. If you choose to squelch the message, you can get it back by choosing View ➢ Options ➢ General and selecting "Show confirmation dialog to distinguish between GPOs and GPO links."

Stopping Group Policy Objects from Applying

After you create your hierarchy of Group Policy that applies to your users and computers, you might occasionally want to temporarily halt the processing of a GPO—usually because a user is complaining that something is wrong. You can prevent a specific GPO from processing at a level in Active Directory via several methods, as explained in the following sections.

Preventing Local GPOs from Applying

Before we get too far down the path with Active Directory–based GPOs, let's not forget that you might also want to stop a local GPO from applying. I mentioned this tidbit in the previous chapter, but I'll mention it here again for emphasis.

Here's the scenario: you might have walked up to 50 Sales computers and created a local GPO that prevents access to the Control Panel. However, now you want to reverse that edict. Instead of walking around to those 50 computers, you can just zap a Group Policy Object to those computers containing a setting to inhibit the processing of local GPOs. Here's the trick, though: this technique only works for Windows Vista or later machines—not for earlier versions of the operating system.

To do this trick, you'll use the policy setting found at Computer Configuration ➢ Administrative Templates ➢ System ➢ Group Policy, and it's called **Turn off Local Group Policy objects processing**. Just remember to ensure that your computers are in the OU where this GPO is targeted to take effect.

Disabling the Link Enabled Status

Remember that all GPOs are contained in the Group Policy Objects container. To use them at a level in Active Directory (site, domain, or OU), you link back to the GPO. So, the quickest way to prevent a GPO's contents from applying is to remove its Link Enabled status. If you right-click a GPO link at a level, you can immediately see its Link Enabled status, as shown in Figure 2.4.

To prevent this GPO from applying to the **Human Resources Users** OU, click Link Enabled to remove the check mark. This will leave the link but disable it, rendering it innocuous.

To use PowerShell to disable the status of a link, you would use the cmdlet Set-GPLink. You would specify the OUs, preceded by OU=, and the name of the domain (pieces, anyway) with DC=, as seen in this snippet:

```
Set-GPLink -Name "Hide Mouse Pointers Option/Restore Screen Saver Option"
-Target "ou=Human Resources Users, ou=Human Resources, dc=corp, dc=com"
-LinkEnabled No
```

```
PS C:\Windows\system32> Set-GPLink -Name "Hide Mouse Pointers Option/Restore Screen Saver Optio
n" -Target "ou=Human Resources Users, ou=Human Resources, dc=corp, dc=com" -LinkEnabled No


GpoId       : f890fc91-33d2-447d-9929-aa990ec50f8c
DisplayName : Hide Mouse Pointers Option/Restore Screen Saver Option
Enabled     : False
Enforced    : False
Target      : OU=Human Resources Users,OU=Human Resources,DC=corp,DC=com
Order       : 2
```

FIGURE 2.4   You can choose to enable or disable a GPO link.

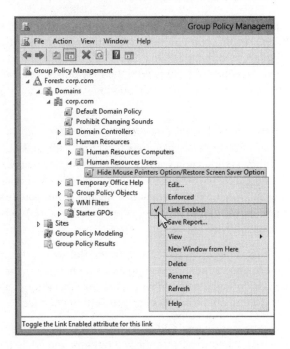

You can flip it back to enabled by substituting Yes for No next to the `-LinkEnabled` parameter.

Back in the GPMC (after a refresh), the icon to the left of the name of the GPO will change to a scroll with the link arrow dimmed. You'll see a zoomed-in picture of this later in the section "GPMC At-a-Glance Icon View."

Disabling "Half" (or Both Halves) of the Group Policy Object

The second way to disable a specific GPO is by disabling just *one-half* of a Group Policy Object. You can disable either the User half or the Computer half. Or you can disable the entire GPO.

You might be wondering why you would want to disable only half of a GPO. On the one hand, disabling a GPO (or half of a GPO) makes startup and logon times a teeny-weeny bit faster for the computer or user, because each GPO you add to the system adds a smidgen of extra processing—either for the user or the computer. Once you disable the unused portion of the GPO, you've shaved that processing time off the startup or logon time. Microsoft calls this "modifying Group Policy for performance."

Don't go bananas disabling your unused half of a GPO just to save a few cycles of processing time. Trust me, it's just not worth the headaches figuring out later where you did and did not disable a half of a policy.

Why Totally Disable a Group Policy Object?

One good reason to disable a specific GPO is if you want to manually "join" several GPOs together into one larger GPO. Then, once you're comfortable with the reaction, you can re-create the policy settings from multiple GPOs into another new GPO and disable the old individual GPOs. If there are signs of trouble with the new policy, you can always just disable (or delete) the large GPO and re-enable the individual GPOs to get right back to where you started.

You might also want to immediately disable a new GPO even before you start to edit it. Imagine that you've chosen "Create and link a new GPO here" for, say, an OU. Then, imagine you have lots of policy settings you want to place inside this new GPO. Remember that each setting is immediately written inside the Group Policy Management Editor. GPOs are replicated across all DCs (on their own schedule; not when you desire them to), and computers are continually requesting changes when their Background Refresh interval triggers.

The affected users or computers might hit their Background Refresh cycle and start accepting the changes before you've finished writing all your changes to the GPO! Therefore, if you disable the GPO before you edit and re-enable the GPO after you edit, you can ensure that your users are getting all the newly changed settings at once.

This tip works best only when creating new GPOs; if you disable the GPO *after* creation, there's an equally likely chance that critical settings will be removed while the GPO is disabled when clients request a Background Refresh. We'll discuss the ins and outs of Background Refresh in Chapter 3.

Disabling half of the GPO makes troubleshooting and usage quite a bit harder, as you might just plumb forget you've disabled half the GPO. Then, down the road, when you modify the disabled half of the policy for some future setting, it won't take effect on your clients! You'll end up pulling your hair out wondering why once things *should* change, they just don't!

To disable an unused half of a GPO, follow these steps:

1. Select the GPO you want to modify. In this case, select "Auto-Launch calc.exe" and select the Details tab in the right pane of the GPMC.

2. Since the policy settings within the "Auto-Launch calc.exe" GPO modify only the Computer node, it is safe to disable the User node. Again, I'm not a big fan, but if you want to practice it anyway, select the GPO Status: dropdown, then select "User configuration settings disabled," as shown in Figure 2.5.

FIGURE 2.5 You can change the default from Enabled (shown here) to "User configuration settings disabled" to disable half the GPO to make Group Policy process a wee bit faster.

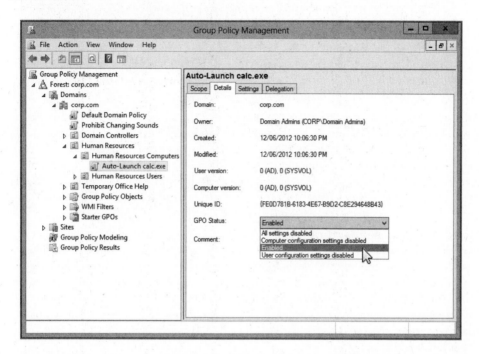

3. You will be prompted to confirm the status change. Choose to do so.

In PowerShell, you can also dictate the status of the Group Policy Object. But it takes more than one line in PowerShell. In short, you hold the contents of the Group Policy Object in a variable of your choosing. Then, you set the GpoStatus bit as you see fit. You can then verify that the change took as expected by showing that bit. So that's three lines as follows:

```
$gpo = Get-GPO "Auto-Launch calc.exe"
$gpo.GpoStatus = "UserSettingsDisabled"
$gpo.GpoStatus
```

Valid values for `GpoStatus` are `AllSettingsEnabled`, `AllSettingsDisabled`, `UserSettingsDisabled`, and `ComputerSettingsDisabled`. These correspond to the four items seen within the dropdown in Figure 2.5.

Here are some additional items to remember regarding disabling portions of a GPO:

- It is possible to disable the entire GPO (both halves) by selecting the GPO, clicking the Options button, and selecting the All Settings Disabled option. If you select All Settings Disabled, the scroll icon next to the name of the GPO "dims" to show that there is no way it can affect any targets. You'll see a zoomed-in picture of this later in the section "GPMC At-a-Glance Icon View."

- As I stated earlier in the section "Understanding GPMC's Link Warning," changing the GPO Status entry (found on the Details tab) will affect the GPO—everywhere it is linked—at any level, anywhere in the domain. You cannot just change the GPO status for the instance of this link—this setting affects all links to this GPO! The good news here is that only the person who created the GPO itself (or anyone who has permissions to it) can manipulate this setting. To get the full thrust of this, be sure to read the sidebar "On GPO Links and GPOs Themselves" later in this chapter.

- In day-to-day use of this feature, the GPMC doesn't do a great job indicating (other than this "GPO status" area) that the link has been fully or half disabled. It's true that if you click the Group Policy Objects Container node (the swimming pool) and look at the GPOs in a list, you will see a column for GPO status. But I don't do that particular action much. Interestingly, in the old-school "Active Directory Users and Computers" interface in Windows 2003's old-and-crusty UI, you would at least see a yellow triangle warning icon next to the name of the GPO. But not in the GPMC. Weird (and potentially unsafe).

Deleting and Unlinking Group Policy Objects

As you just saw, you can prevent a GPO from processing at a level by merely removing its Link Enabled status. However, you can also choose to remove the link entirely. For instance, you might want to return the normal behavior of any affected computers so that `calc.exe` isn't launched whenever someone uses an affected machine. You have two options:

- Delete the link to the GPO
- Delete the GPO itself

Deleting the Link to the Group Policy Object

When you right-click the GPO link of "Auto-Launch calc.exe" in the **Human Resources Computers** OU, you can choose Delete. When you do, the GPMC will confirm your request and remind you of an important fact, as shown in Figure 2.6.

FIGURE 2.6   You can delete a link (as opposed to deleting the GPO itself).

Using PowerShell, you would use the `Remove-GPlink` cmdlet:

```
Remove-GPLink -Name "Auto-Launch calc.exe" -Target "ou=Human Resources
Computers, ou=Human Resources, dc=corp,dc=com"
```

```
PS C:\Users\Administrator> Remove-GPLink -Name "Auto-Launch calc.exe" -Target "ou=Human Resourc
es Computers, ou=Human Resources, dc=corp,dc=com"


DisplayName      : Auto-Launch calc.exe
DomainName       : corp.com
Owner            : CORP\Domain Admins
Id               : 8d2c9ff4-9070-48c5-a83c-0b38539400d2
GpoStatus        : UserSettingsDisabled
Description      :
CreationTime     : 2/9/2015 8:24:37 PM
ModificationTime : 2/9/2015 9:22:00 PM
UserVersion      : AD Version: 0, SysVol Version: 0
ComputerVersion  : AD Version: 0, SysVol Version: 0
WmiFilter        :
```

Recall that the GPO itself doesn't "live" at a level in Active Directory; it lives in a special container in Active Directory (and can be seen via the Group Policy Objects container in the GPMC). We're just working with a link to the real GPO. And, in Chapter 4, "Advanced Group Policy Processing," you'll see where this folder relates directly within Active Directory itself.

When you choose to delete a GPO link, you are choosing to stop using it at the level at which it was created but keeping the GPO alive in the representation of the swimming pool—the Group Policy Objects container. This lets other administrators at other levels continue to link to that GPO if they want.

Truly Deleting the Group Policy Object Itself

You can choose to delete the GPO altogether—lock, stock, and barrel. The only way to delete the GPO itself is to drill down through Group Policy Management ≻ Domains ≻ Corp.com, locate the Group Policy Objects container, and delete the GPO. It's like plucking a child directly from the swimming pool. Before you do, you'll get a warning message, as shown in Figure 2.7.

To have the PowerShell cmdlet do the same thing would be `Remove-GPO -name` "Auto-Launch `calc.exe`." The "not exactly incredibly interesting" result returned from PowerShell can be seen in Figure 2.8.

FIGURE 2.7   Here, you're deleting the GPO itself.

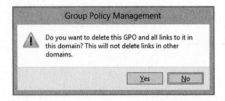

FIGURE 2.8   You can remove a link to a Group Policy Object using PowerShell

This action will remove the bits on the Domain Controller and obliterate it from the system. No other administrators can then link to this GPO.

Once it's gone, it's gone (unless you have a backup).

If you delete the GPO altogether, there's only one problem. There is no indication sent to the folks who are linking to this GPO that you've just deleted it. You might be done with the "Auto-Launch calc.exe" GPO and might not need it anymore to link to *your* locations in Active Directory, but what about other administrators? In this case, while I was out to lunch, Freddie, the administrator for the **Temporary Office Help** OU, has already chosen to link the "Auto-Launch calc.exe" GPO to his OU, as shown in Figure 2.9.

FIGURE 2.9   The "Auto-Launch calc.exe" GPO (lowest circle) is linked at both the Temporary Office Help OU (middle circle) and this Human Resources Computers OU (topmost circle).

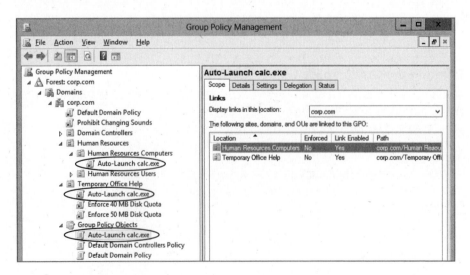

What if I had deleted the "Auto-Launch calc.exe" GPO? I'm pretty sure I would have received an angry phone call from Freddie. Or, maybe not—if Freddie didn't know who created (and owned) the GPO.

Since we only have a handful of OUs, this link back to the GPO was easy to find. However, once you start getting lots of OUs, locating additional links back to a GPO will become much harder. Thankfully, the GPMC shows you if anyone else is linked to a GPO you're about to delete. I call this ability "look before you leap." You can just look on the Scope tab under the Links heading, as indicated in Figure 2.9. There you can see that both the **Temporary Office Help** OU and the **Human Resources Computers** OU are utilizing the GPO "Auto-Launch calc.exe."

If you're confident that you can still continue, you can delete the GPO contained within the Group Policy Objects container. However, for now, let's leave this GPO in place for use in future examples in the book.

The Scope tab shows you the links to the GPOs from your own domain. It is possible for *other* domains to leverage your GPOs and link to them. This is generally considered a "no-no" and is called cross-domain linking. When you delete a GPO forever (and wipe it out of your swimming pool), you're deleting the ability for other domains to utilize that GPO as well. Note that there is a dropdown in the Scope tab labeled "Display links in this location." If you want, you can show Entire Forest. That way, if a GPO is being leveraged by doing a cross-domain link, you can at least see if this GPO is linked to other areas you might not have intended it to be.

For now, don't delete the GPO. We'll use it again in later chapters. If you want to play with deleting a GPO, create a new one and delete it.

Block Inheritance

As you've already seen, the normal course of Group Policy inheritance applies all policy settings within GPOs in a cumulative fashion from the site to the domain and then to each nested OU. A setting at any level automatically affects all levels beneath it. But perhaps this is not always the behavior you want. For instance, we know that an edict from the Domain Administrator states there will be no Sounds option in the Windows 10 Personalization page.

This edict is fine for most of the OU administrators and their subjects who are affected. But Frank Rizzo, the administrator for the **Human Resources** OU structure, believes that the folks contained within his little fiefdom can handle the responsibility and gravitas of being able to change their own sounds. Remember, a policy at the domain level has performed this action. He also feels that they are grown-up enough to manage their own Screen Saver options (a policy at the site level that has performed this action). Now, he wants to bring them back to his users. (But he's not ready to give back the ability to play around with the mouse pointer settings—a policy that is set at his level, the **Human Resources** OU level.)

In this case, Frank can prevent GPOs (and the policy settings within them) defined at higher levels (domain and site) from affecting his users, as shown in Figure 2.10. If Frank chooses to select Block Inheritance, Frank is choosing to block the flow of *all* GPOs (with all their policy settings) from *all* higher levels.

FIGURE 2.10   Use the Block Inheritance feature to prevent all GPOs (and the policy settings within them) from all higher levels from affecting your users and computers.

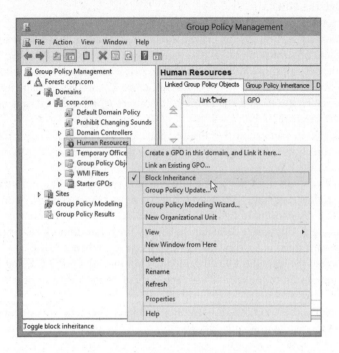

Block Inheritance upon a level (site, domain, or OU) can also be performed using PowerShell. The cmdlet to perform the same Block Inheritance of **Human Resources** OU would be:

```
Set-GPinheritance -Target "ou=Human Resources,dc=corp,dc=com" -IsBlocked Yes
```

You can see the result in Figure 2.11. Note that the field `GpoInheritenceBlocked` is now set to Yes.

FIGURE 2.11   PowerShell can be used to Block Inheritance of GPOs at a specific scope level.

When Frank performs the Block Inheritance, the **Human Resources** OU icon (when refreshed within the GPMC) changes to include a blue exclamation point (!), as seen in Figure 2.10. Once the Block Inheritance upon the OU is performed and the GPOs are reprocessed on the client, only those settings that Frank dictates within his **Human Resources** OU structure will be applied.

If you want to see the effect of Block Inheritance, ensure that the check is seen, as shown in Figure 2.10. Then, log on as any user affected by the **Human Resources** OU—say, Frank Rizzo. You'll notice that the Screen Saver options have returned (if you go to Personalize ➤ Lock Screen ➤ Screen saver settings), as did the ability to manipulate sounds (Personalize ➤ Themes ➤ Go to advanced sound settings.) But you'll also notice that the Mouse Pointers option in the Windows 10 Personalization page (Themes ➤ Go to mouse pointer settings) is prohibited because that edict is contained within a GPO that's explicitly defined at the **Human Resources Users** OU level, which contains Frank's user account.

The Enforced Function

Frank Rizzo and his Human Resources folks are happy that the Screen Saver and Sounds options have made a triumphant return.

There's only one problem: the Domain Administrator has found out about this transgression and wants to ensure that the Sounds option in Windows 10 is permanently revoked.

The normal flow of inheritance is site, domain, and then OU. Super. If you've set a Block Inheritance on an OU (say, the **Human Resources** OU), then *all* settings to that OU are null and void.

But shouldn't there be some power to allow "bigger" administrators to get their wills enforced? Enforced! Heck, what a great term. I should trademark that. To trump a lower level's Block Inheritance, a higher-level administrator will use the *Enforced* function.

 NOTE   Enforced was previously known as No Override in old-school parlance.

The idea behind the Enforced function is simple: It guarantees that policy settings within a specific GPO from a higher level are always inherited by lower levels. It doesn't matter if the lower administrator has blocked inheritance or has a GPO that tries to disable or modify the same policy setting or settings.

In this example, you'll log on as the Domain Administrator and set an edict to force the removal of the Sounds option in the Windows 10 Personalization page (Themes ➤ Go to advanced sound settings).

To use Enforced to force the settings within a specific Group Policy Object setting, right-click the "Prohibit Changing Sounds" GPO link and select Enforced, as shown in Figure 2.12.

FIGURE 2.12 Use the Enforced option to guarantee that settings contained within a specific GPO affect all users downward via inheritance.

The same procedure to perform an Enforce of the Group Policy's link can be done using the Set-GPlink command:

```
Set-GPlink –Name "Prohibit Changing Sounds" –Target "dc=corp, dc=com" –Enforced
Yes
```

When you refresh the GPMC, notice that the GPO link now has a little "lock" icon, demonstrating that it cannot be trumped. You can see this in the "Prohibit Changing Sounds" GPO link icon in Figure 2.10. You'll see a zoomed-in picture of this later in the section "GPMC At-a-Glance Icon View."

To test your Enforced edict, log on as a user affected by the **Human Resources** OU—Frank Rizzo. In the Display Properties dialog box, the Sounds option in the Windows 10 Personalization page (Themes ➢ Go to advanced sound settings) should be prevented because it is being Enforced at the domain level even though Block Inheritance is used at the OU level.

On GPO Links and GPOs Themselves

The GPMC is a cool tool, but it shows you a bit *too* much. Sometimes, it can be confusing as to what can be performed on the GPO's link and what can be performed on the GPO itself. Remember that GPOs themselves are displayed in the GPMC via the Group Policy Objects container. The links back to them are shown at the site, domain, and OU levels. So here's a list of what you can "do" to a GPO link and what you can "do" to a GPO *itself*.

You can only do three things on a GPO link that applies to a site, a domain, or an OU:

- Link Enable (that is, enable or disable the settings to apply at this level).
- Enforce the link (and force the policy settings).
- Delete the link.

Everything else is always done on the *actual* GPO itself:

- Change the policy settings inside the GPO (found on the Settings tab).
- Apply security filters, rights (such as the "Apply Group Policy" privilege), and delegation (such as the "Edit this GPO" privilege), discussed in the section "Security Filtering and Delegation with the GPMC" later in this chapter.
- Enable/disable the Computer and/or User half of the GPO via the GPO status (found on the Details tab).
- Place a WMI filter on the GPO (discussed in Chapter 4).

If this seems clear as mud, consider this scenario:

- Fred and Ginger are the two Domain Administrators. By definition, they can create GPOs.
- Imagine that Fred designs the "Our Important Stuff" GPO (a poorly named GPO), which contains policy settings that affect both users and computers. Perhaps one user policy setting is **Remove Run off Start Menu**. Perhaps one computer policy setting is **Enforce disk quota limit**. And Fred sets the quota limit to 50MB.
- Fred links the Sounds GPO to the **Dancers** OU as well as the **Audition Halls** OU.
- Ginger gets a phone call from the folks in the **Audition Halls** OU. The users in the **Audition Halls** OU report that the 50MB disk quotas are too restrictive. "Can they just turn off the Computer-side settings for us Audition Halls folks?" one of them cries.

- Ginger goes to the "Sounds" GPO link (which is linked to the **Audition Halls** OU), clicks the Details tab, and disables the computer settings using the GPO Status drop-down box.

- Fred then gets a phone call that the **Dancers** OU no longer has disk quotas being applied.

Why did this happen?

Because the Group Policy engine has certain controls on the GPO *itself* and has other controls on the Group Policy *link*. Because Fred and Ginger are both Domain Administrators, they jointly have ownership of the ability to change the GPO and the GPO link.

Whenever Ginger modifies any characteristic in the previous bulleted list, she's changing it "globally" for any place in Active Directory that might be using it. That's what the warning in Figure 2.3, earlier in this chapter, is all about.

If you'll allow me to get on my soap box for the next 10 seconds, the level of finite control over what Ginger can and cannot do to the GPO itself is fairly limited.

In any event, delegating what we can control over the GPO itself is precisely what the next sections are about, specifically the section "User Permissions on Group Policy Objects."

Security Filtering and Delegation with the GPMC

You wouldn't want everyone in your domain to get every GPO applied to them. That would be crazy.

Likewise, you wouldn't want everyone in your domain to be able to modify every GPO. That would be "mega-crazy."

So the following sections will deal with both aspects of making sure users only get access (and application) to what they're supposed to. We'll talk about filtering a user (or computer) from getting specific GPOs. Then we'll move on to talking about ensuring that only the right users and admins have access to the underlying Group Policy system—by properly delegating who should have the ability to do what.

Turns out, to craft the solution to both of these problems, you leverage security pieces upon certain Active Directory aspects and also on specific GPOs.

It's not hard, but let's tackle these questions one at a time to locate all the places users and admins touch our Group Policy infrastructure, look at their access, and see where that access can be managed.

Filtering the Scope of Group Policy Objects with Security

The normal day-to-day Human Resources workers in the **Human Resources** OU structure are fine with the facts of life:

- The Enterprise Administrator says "Good bye to screensavers" (that is, that no one at the site will have the option to use the Screen Saver option).

- The Domain Administrator says that no one will have the ability to use the Sounds option within the Windows 10 Personalization page. He is forcing this edict with the Enforced option.

- Frank Rizzo, the **Human Resources** OU manager, says that for the **Human Resources Users** OU, he wants to prevent the use of the Mouse Pointers applet but restore the Screen Saver option. For the **Human Resources Computers** OU, he'll want to make sure that calc.exe launches whenever someone uses a Human Resources computer.

- Additionally, at the top-level **Human Resources** OU, he will set Block Inheritance. This will return the normal function of the Screen Saver option (originally removed by the Enterprise Administrator at the site level). But Frank is forced to live with the fact that he won't be able to return the Sounds option in the Windows 10 Personalization page to his people. The Domain Administrator has Enforced this idea—taken it away and that's that.

But Frank and other members of the HR-OU-Admins security group are getting frustrated that they cannot access the Display Settings tab. And they're also getting a little annoyed that every time they use a Human Resources machine, calc.exe pops up to greet them.

Sure, it was Frank's own idea to make these two policy settings—one that affects the users he's in charge of and one that affects the computers he's in charge of. The problem is, however, it also affects Frank (and the other members of the HR-OU-Admins team) when they're working, and you can see where that can be annoying.

Frank needs a way to filter the *Scope of Management (SOM)* of the "Hide Mouse Pointers Option/Restore Screen Saver Option" GPO as well as the "Auto-Launch calc.exe" GPO. By scope, or SOM, I mean how far and wide the GPOs we set up will be embraced.

 Occasionally you will see references to SOM in your travels with Group Policy. An SOM is simply a quick-and-dirty way to express the idea of where and when a GPO might apply. An SOM can be nearly any combination of things: linking a GPO to the domain, linking a GPO to an OU, and linking a GPO to a site. However, if you start to filter GPOs within the domain, that's also an SOM. In essence, an SOM indicates *when* and *where* a GPO applies to a level in Active Directory.

In our case, the idea is twofold:

- Frank and his team are excluded from the "Hide Mouse Pointers Option/Restore Screen Saver Option GPO" edict.

- The specific computers that Frank and his team use are excluded from the "Auto-Launch calc.exe" GPO edict.

Recall from Chapter 1 that, despite the wording of the term *Group Policy*, Group Policy does not directly affect security groups. You cannot just wrap up a bunch of similar users or computers in an Active Directory security group and thrust a GPO upon them. There's nowhere to "link" to. You need to round up the individual user or computer accounts into an OU first and then link the desired GPO on that OU.

Here's the truly strange part: even though you can't round up users in security groups and apply GPOs to them, it's the security group that we'll leverage (in most cases) to enable us to filter Group Policy applications!

In order for users to get GPOs to apply to them, they need two under-the-hood access rights to the GPO itself:

- Read

- Apply Group Policy (known in shorthand as the AGP rights)

These permissions must be set on the GPO in question. By default, all Authenticated Users are granted the Read and AGP rights to all new GPOs. Therefore, anyone who has a GPO geared for them will process it.

The following two things might not be immediately obvious:

- Administrators are not magically exempt from embracing Group Policy; they, too, are members of Authenticated Users. You can change this behavior with the techniques described in the next section.

- Computers need love, too. And for computers to apply their side of the GPO, they need the same rights: "Read" and "Apply Group Policy." Since computers are technically Authenticated Users, the computer has all it needs to process GPOs meant for it.

With these fundamental concepts in mind, let's look at several ways to filter who gets specific GPOs.

If you want to filter GPOs for either specific users or specific computers, you have three distinct approaches. For our three examples (which will all do the exact same thing), we want the "Hide Mouse Pointers Option/Restore Screen Saver Option" GPO to "pass over" our heroes in the HR-OU-Admins security group but to apply to everyone else who should get them. We also want the "Auto-Launch calc.exe" GPO to pass over the specific computers our heroes use at their desks.

Group Policy Object Filtering Approach #1: Leverage the Security Filtering Section of the Scope Tab in GPMC

In the first approach, you'll round up only the users, computers, or security groups who should get the GPO applied to them. To make things easier, let's first create two Active Directory security groups—one for our users who will get the GPO and one for computers who will get the GPO. Good names (for learning purposes) might be:

People-Who-Get-the-HideDisplayMousePointersOption-and-RestoreSS

and:

Computers-That-Get-the-Auto-Launch calc.exe

Remember, back when we created GPO, its goal was twofold: so we've named it "Hide Changing Mouse Pointers / Restore Screen Saver Option." Making a group with something easy to remember but still only 64 characters can be tough. So, again, I'm recommending a group named People-Who-Get-the-HideDisplayMousePointersOption-and-RestoreSS.

The second group, for computers, is a little easier to make. The GPO we'll want to leverage with this group only does one thing: it automatically launches calc.exe. So, my suggested name is Computers-That-Get-the-Auto-Launch calc.exe.

Go ahead and do this in Active Directory Users and Computers, as seen in Figure 2.13.

FIGURE 2.13 Create a new Active Directory security group to which you want the GPO to apply. Create security groups for both users and computers based on the GPO you want to filter.

Next, add all user accounts that you want to embrace the GPO into the first security group.

You would then add all computer accounts that you want to get the GPO into the security group named Computers-That-Get-the-Auto-Launch calc.exe.

Because we don't want these GPOs to apply to Frank or Frank's computer (WIN10), don't add Frank to the first group (which contains users) and don't add WIN10 to the second group (which contains computers).

Next, click the link to the "Hide Mouse Pointers Option/Restore Screen Saver Option" GPO found in Group Policy Management ➢ Forest ➢ Domains ➢ Corp.com ➢ **Human Resources** OU ➢ **Human Resources Users** OU. In the Security Filtering section, you can see that Authenticated Users is listed. This means that any users inside the **Human Resources Users** OU will certainly get this GPO applied.

However, now we're about to turn the tables. We're going to click the Remove button to remove the Authenticated Users in the Security Filtering section; then we're going to add the People-Who-Get-the-HideDisplayMousePointersOption-and-RestoreSS security group, as shown in Figure 2.14.

The PowerShell way to perform this same function would be the following two commands:

```
Set-GPPermissions -Name "Hide Mouse Pointers Option/Restore Screen Saver Option"
-Replace -PermissionLevel None -TargetName 'Authenticated Users' -TargetType
group

Set-GPPermissions -Name "Hide Mouse Pointers Option/Restore Screen Saver
Option" -PermissionLevel gpoapply -TargetName "People-Who-Get-the-
HideDisplayMousePointersOption-and-RestoreSS" -TargetType group
```

```
PS C:\Users\Administrator> Set-GPPermissions -Name "Hide Mouse Pointers Option/Restore Screen S
aver Option" -Replace -PermissionLevel None -TargetName 'Authenticated Users' -TargetType group

DisplayName       : Hide Mouse Pointers Option/Restore Screen Saver Option
DomainName        : corp.com
Owner             : CORP\Domain Admins
Id                : f890fc91-33d2-447d-9929-aa990ec50f8c
GpoStatus         : AllSettingsEnabled
Description       :
CreationTime      : 2/9/2015 8:24:01 PM
ModificationTime  : 2/18/2015 7:15:42 PM
UserVersion       : AD Version: 2, SysVol Version: 2
ComputerVersion   : AD Version: 0, SysVol Version: 0
WmiFilter         :

PS C:\Users\Administrator> Set-GPPermissions -Name "Hide Mouse Pointers Option/Restore Screen S
aver Option" -PermissionLevel gpoapply -TargetName "People-Who-Get-the-HideDisplayMousePointers
Option-and-RestoreSS" -TargetType group

DisplayName       : Hide Mouse Pointers Option/Restore Screen Saver Option
DomainName        : corp.com
Owner             : CORP\Domain Admins
Id                : f890fc91-33d2-447d-9929-aa990ec50f8c
GpoStatus         : AllSettingsEnabled
Description       :
CreationTime      : 2/9/2015 8:24:01 PM
ModificationTime  : 2/18/2015 7:15:42 PM
UserVersion       : AD Version: 2, SysVol Version: 2
ComputerVersion   : AD Version: 0, SysVol Version: 0
WmiFilter         :
```

Next, in the GPMC, click the "Auto-Launch calc.exe" GPO link (which is under the **Human Resources Computers** OU). In the Security Filtering section of the Scope tab, you'll remove Authenticated Users and add the Computers-That-Get-the-Auto-Launch calc.exe security group.

 In both cases, what we're doing under the hood is giving these new security groups the ability to Read and Apply Group Policy. You'll see this under-the-hood stuff in a minute.

If you're following along with PowerShell, those two commands would be:

```
Set-GPPermissions -Name "Auto-Launch calc.exe" -Replace -PermissionLevel None
-TargetName "Authenticated Users" -TargetType group

Set-GPPermissions -Name "Auto-Launch calc.exe"  -PermissionLevel gpoapply
-TargetName "Computers-That-Get-the-Auto-Launch calc.exe" -TargetType group
```

FIGURE 2.14   When you remove Authenticated Users, no one will get the effects of the GPO. Add only the users or groups you want the GPO to affect.

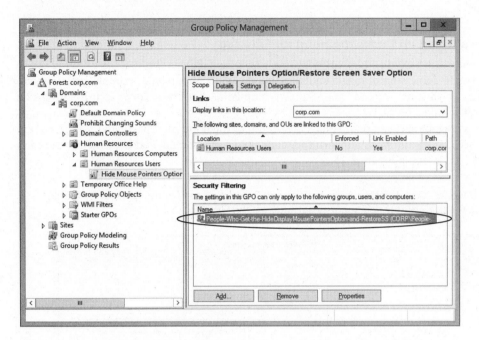

Testing Your First Filters

To see if this is working, log on to WIN10 as Frank (frizzo). Even though the GPO applies to the **Human Resources Users** OU, the GPO will pass over him and anyone else not explicitly put into that security group since Frank is not a member of the People-Who-Get-the-HideDisplayMousePointersOption-and-RestoreSS security group.

For another test, add a new user account or two to the **Human Resources Users** OU (via Active Directory Users and Computers). Then, log on as one of these new users (in the OU) and verify that they, indeed, do not get the GPO. This is because the GPO is only set to apply to members of the security group. Then, add the user to the security group and log on again. The GPO will then apply to your test users (inside the security group) as well. In fact, you can add users to the security group by simply clicking the Properties button in the Security Filtering section. Doing so opens the Security Group Membership dialog box, in which you can add or delete users or computers.

Repeat your tests by adding WIN10 into the security group named Computers-That-Get-the-Auto-Launch calc.exe. When the computer is in the group, it will apply the GPO. Now, try removing WIN10 and see what happens. When the computer is out of the group, the GPO will pass over the computer.

You will have to reboot the machine to immediately see Computer-side results.

What's Going on Under the Hood for Filtering

As I implied, when you add security groups to get the GPOs in the Security Filtering section, you're doing a bit of magic under the hood. Again, that magic is simply granting two security permissions, "Read" and "Apply Group Policy," to the users or security groups on the GPOs linked to the OU.

To see which security permissions are set under the hood for a particular GPO (or GPO link, because it's the same information), click the Delegation tab and click the Advanced button, as shown in Figure 2.15.

FIGURE 2.15 Clicking Advanced on the Delegation tab for the GPO (or GPO link) shows the under-the-hood security settings for the GPO.

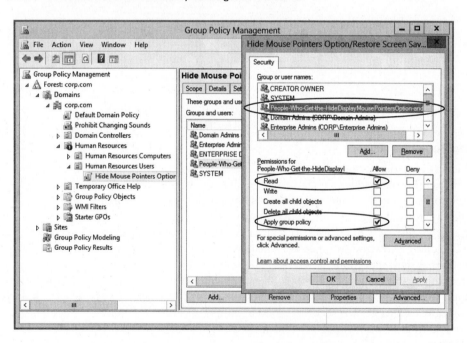

When you do, you can see the actual permission on the GPO itself. You can easily locate the security group named People-Who-Get-the-HideDisplayMousePointersOption-and-RestoreSS and see that they have both the "Read" and "Apply Group Policy" access rights set to Allow. This is why they will process this GPO.

Using PowerShell, the command to see the permissions underneath the hood would be:

```
get-gppermission -Name "Hide Mouse Pointers Option/Restore Screen Saver Option"
-all
```

```
PS C:\Users\Administrator> get-gppermission -Name "Hide Mouse Pointers Option/Restore Screen Sa
ver Option" -all

Trustee      : HR-OU-Admins
TrusteeType  : Group
Permission   : GpoCustom
Inherited    : False

Trustee      : Authenticated Users
TrusteeType  : WellKnownGroup
Permission   : GpoApply
Inherited    : False

Trustee      : Domain Admins
TrusteeType  : Group
Permission   : GpoEditDeleteModifySecurity
Inherited    : False

Trustee      : Enterprise Admins
TrusteeType  : Group
Permission   : GpoEditDeleteModifySecurity
Inherited    : False

Trustee      : ENTERPRISE DOMAIN CONTROLLERS
TrusteeType  : WellKnownGroup
Permission   : GpoRead
Inherited    : False

Trustee      : SYSTEM
TrusteeType  : WellKnownGroup
Permission   : GpoEditDeleteModifySecurity
Inherited    : False
```

Note that PowerShell only shows the Group Policy–specific "Apply" attribute and not the more general (not Group Policy–specific) "Read" attribute.

Filtering Approach #2: Identify Those You Do Not Want to Get the Policy

The other approach is to leave the default definition in for the GPO such that the Authenticated Users group is granted the "Read" and "Apply Group Policy" attributes. Then, figure out who you *do not* want to have the policy applied to, and use the "Deny" attribute over the "Apply Group Policy" right.

When Windows security is evaluated, the designated users or computers will not be able to process the GPO due to the "Deny" attribute; hence, the GPO passes over them.

See the sidebar "Positive or Negative?" later in this chapter before doing this in your real (production) environment.

For our examples, we want the "Hide Mouse Pointers Option/Restore Screen Saver Option" GPO to pass over our heroes in the HR-OU-Admins security group but to apply to everyone else by default. We also want the "Auto-Launch calc.exe" GPO to pass over the specific computers our heroes use at their desks.

To use this second technique, we'll use the "Deny" permission to ensure that the HR-OU-Admins security group cannot apply (and hence process) the "Hide Mouse Pointers Option/Restore Screen Saver Option" GPO. We'll also prevent Frank's computer, WIN10, from processing the "Auto-Launch calc.exe" GPO.

Again, you'll do this using the GPMC upon the GPO (or the GPO link, because it's the same information); click the Delegation tab, and then click the Advanced button. Follow these steps:

1. Locate the People-Who-Get-the-HideDisplayMousePointersOption-and-RestoreSS security group and remove it.

2. Add the Authenticated Users group, and select the "Read" permission.

3. If you used Frank's account originally to create this GPO, he is specifically listed in the security list. You want to remove Frank and add the HR-OU-Admins group. Click Frank, and then click Remove. Click Add, and add the HR-OU-Admins group.

4. Then click Advanced and select the Allow option for the "Apply Group Policy" permission for the Authenticated Users group.

5. Now make sure the Apply Group Policy check box is set to Deny for the HR-OU-Admins group, as shown in Figure 2.16.

   Do not set the Deny check box for the "Read" and "Write" attributes from the HR-OU-Admins (the group you're currently a member of when logged in as Frank). If you do, you'll essentially lock yourself out, and you'll have to ask the Domain Administrator to grant you access again.

FIGURE 2.16   Use the "Deny" attribute on the "Apply Group Policy" right to prevent Group Policy from applying.

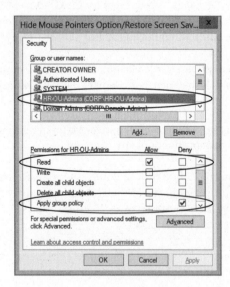

6. Click OK to close the Group Policy Settings dialog box. In the warning box that tells you to be careful about "Deny" permissions, click Yes.

7. Click OK to close the OU Properties dialog box.

In both cases (using the GUI or via PowerShell), what you're doing is specifically adding the "Deny" right.

Below is the PowerShell equivalent, which, unfortunately, takes a little work and appears a lot more complicated. That's because PowerShell does not have any native way to easily apply the "Deny" permission to a Group Policy Object. The commands to type would be as follows:

```
$gpo = Get-GPO -Name "Hide Mouse Pointers Option/Restore Screen Saver Option"
$adgpo = [ADSI]"LDAP://CN=`{$($gpo.Id.guid)`},CN=Policies,CN=System,DC=corp,DC=com"

$rule = New-Object System.DirectoryServices.ActiveDirectoryAccessRule(
          [System.Security.Principal.NTAccount]"CORP\HR-OU-Admins",
          "ExtendedRight",
          "Deny",
          [Guid]"edacfd8f-ffb3-11d1-b41d-00a0c968f939"
        )

$acl = $adgpo.ObjectSecurity
$acl.AddAccessRule($rule)
$adgpo.CommitChanges()
```

The result from the PowerShell commands can be seen here:

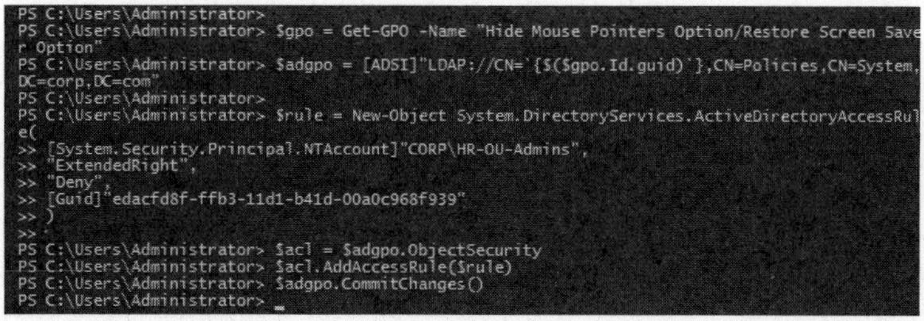

To test your first filter again, log onto WIN10 as Frank Rizzo. Note that the Settings tab has returned to him because he is part of the HR-OU-Admins group. The "Hide Mouse Pointers Option/Restore Screen Saver Option" GPO has passed over him because he is unable to process the GPO.

To bypass the "Auto-Launch calc.exe" GPO on WIN10, you'll perform a similar operation. That is, you'll modify the security on the GPO to pass over the computers our heroes use by denying those specific computer accounts the ability to Apply Group Policy. You can then test your second filter by logging on as anyone to WIN10. You should then see that calc.exe will not launch when a user uses that machine.

Turns out, however, there's something of note when using the aforementioned method. That is, if you performed the previous exercise and used the "Deny" attribute to pass over the HR-OU-Admins group using the security on the GPO, you've got a small problem. Sure, it worked! That's the good news. The bad news is that GPMC isn't smart enough to demonstrate what you did back on the Scope tab in the Security Filtering section shown in Figure 2.17.

FIGURE 2.17   The Security Filtering section on the Scope tab will not show you any use of "Deny" attributes under the hood.

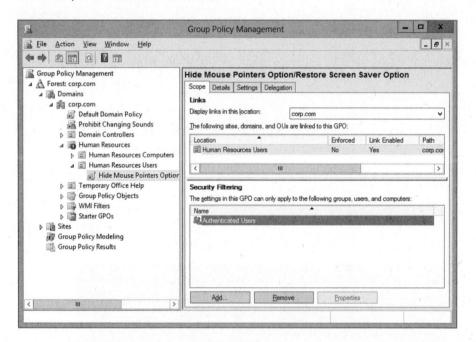

Yes, it's technically true what the Security Filtering section says: Authenticated Users will apply this GPO. However, it doesn't tell us the other important fact: the HR-OU-Admins group *will not* process this GPO because they were denied the ability to Apply Group Policy.

The only way to get the full, true story of who will get the GPO applied to them is to look back within the GPO (or GPO link, because it's the same information), select the Delegation tab, and click the Advanced button to see who has "Read" and "Apply Group Policy;" then also see who is denied access to process the GPO via the "Deny" attributes.

With the GPMC (see the upcoming section "Searching and Comment-ing Group Policy Objects and Policy Settings"), you can leave a comment inside the GPO for others to read regarding who has been specifically denied AGP access. The only problem is someone might not read it.

The moral of the story? Always consult the Advanced tab to get the whole truth as to the security on the GPO.

Positive or Negative?

Now that you can see the two ways to filter users from processing GPOs, which should you use: Approach 1 (adding only those you want to get the GPO) or Approach 2 (denying only those you don't want to get the GPO)? The data reflected within the GPMC's Scope tab clearly wants you to take the first approach. However, many Active Directory imple-mentations I know take the second approach (and, in fact, it was my advice to do so in the first several editions of this book).

Now, you and your team need to make a choice for your approach. As you saw, when you create new GPOs, you can choose to filter via the Scope tab or the Delegation tab's Advanced button. So which do you choose? If you're going to be religious about using the first approach, you can then be reasonably confident that only the users, groups, and computers listed in the Security Filtering section of the Scope tab will, in fact, be the only users, groups, and computers that will get the GPO. You can then reduce your need to dive into the Security Editor, as seen in Figure 2.15 and Figure 2.16, earlier in this chapter.

However, if you (or other administrators) occasionally choose to use the "Deny" attribute on users, computers, and groups to keep them from getting the GPO, you'll need to addi-tionally inspect the Security Editor dialog box, which, again, you'll find by clicking the Advanced button within the Delegation tab, as seen in Figure 2.15 and Figure 2.16.

The GPMC encourages you to use Approach 1 for filtering. If you have older GPOs in your Active Directory that already use Approach 2 for filtering, consider changing it so that GPMC's Scope tab will reflect who will get the GPO.

There's no right or wrong answer here. The challenge is simply that the GPMC will not show who is expressly denied the ability to process the GPO. If you have an in-house system to compensate for that shortcoming (or you use the GPMC Comment feature, which I'll explain later in this chapter), you might be able to make better use of Approach 2.

User Permissions on Group Policy Objects

You already know the three criteria for someone to be able to edit or modify an existing GPO:

- They are a member of the Domain Admins group.
- They are a member of the Enterprise Admins group.
- They created the GPO themselves and hence are the owner. (We saw this in Figure 1.24 in Chapter 1 when Frank could edit his own GPOs but couldn't edit the GPOs he didn't create.)

But sometimes, you also want to add rights on a GPO so other admins can modify it. As I previously suggested, the Delegation tab for a GPO (or GPO link, which reflects the same information) has a second purpose: to help you grant permissions to groups or users over the security properties of that GPO.

If you click Add on the Delegation tab, you can grant any mere mortal user, an admin, or group (even in other domains) the ability to manipulate a particular GPO, as seen in Figure 2.18.

FIGURE 2.18   You can set permissions of "who can do what" on a GPO.

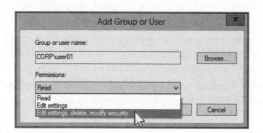

You can also use PowerShell instead of the clickety-clicks by using the Set-GPPermission cmdlet.

Take a peek at Table 2.1, in the first and second column, to know what you want to accomplish. Then replace the permission with the appropriate keyword. So, for instance, if you wanted to specify that Frank Rizzo should be expressly granted "Edit settings, delete, modify security" permissions upon GPO123, you would type:

```
Set-GPPermission -Name GPO123 -PermissionLevel GpoEditDeleteModifySecurity
-TargetName "Frizzo" -TargetType User
```

```
PS C:\Users\Administrator> Set-GPPermission -Name GPO123 -PermissionLevel GpoEditDeleteModifySe
curity -TargetName "Frizzo" -TargetType User

DisplayName      : GPO123
DomainName       : corp.com
Owner            : CORP\Domain Admins
Id               : dedb7af5-8b44-4594-9a8a-1013d1d00452
GpoStatus        : AllSettingsEnabled
Description      :
CreationTime     : 2/9/2015 8:49:51 PM
ModificationTime : 2/18/2015 4:47:00 PM
UserVersion      : AD Version: 0, SysVol Version: 0
ComputerVersion  : AD Version: 0, SysVol Version: 0
WmiFilter        :
```

Once the permissions settings have been applied, the user has that level of rights over the GPO, as you can see in the last column in Table 2.1.

TABLE 2.1 GPMC vs. genuine Active Directory permissions

Permissions option	PowerShell GPPermissionType	Actual under-the-hood permissions
Read	GpoRead	Sets the Allow permission for Read on the GPO.
"Edit settings"	GpoEdit	Sets the Allow permission for Read, Write, Create Child Objects, and Delete Child Objects. See the note regarding under-the-hood attributes.
"Edit settings, delete, modify security"	GpoEditDeleteModifySecurity	Sets the Allow permission for Read, Write, Create Child Objects, Delete Child Objects, Delete, Modify Permissions, and Modify Owner. This is nearly equivalent to full control on the GPO, but note that Apply Group Policy access permission is not set. (This can be useful to set for administrators so they can manipulate the GPO but not have it apply to themselves.)
"Read (from Security Filtering)"	Not applicable for PowerShell	This isn't a permission located in the ACL Editor (see Figure 2.16); rather, this is only visible if the user has Read and AGP permissions on the GPO. This is a reflection of what is on the Scope tab.
Custom	GpoCustom	Any other combinations of rights, including the use of the "Deny" permission. Custom rights are only added via the ACL Editor but can be removed here. They can be removed using the Remove button on the Delegation tab.

If you look really, really closely at the under-the-hood attributes specifically granted to the user when they are given "Edit settings" or "Edit setting, delete, modify security" rights, you'll note that Write isn't expressly listed. However, the ability to perform writes is granted because other subattributes that do permit writing are granted on the entry. To see those attributes for yourself, click the Advanced button while looking at the properties of the security on a GPO (like what we see in Figure 2.16).

Granting Group Policy Object Creation Rights in the Domain

As you learned in Chapter 1, a user cannot create new GPOs unless that user is a member of the Group Policy Creator Owners group. Dropping a user into this group is one of two ways you can grant this right.

However, the GPMC introduces another way to grant users the ability to have Group Policy Creator Owner–style access. Traverse to the Group Policy Objects container as seen in Figure 2.19, and click the Delegation tab. You can now click Add and select any user, including any user in your domain, say a user named Joe User, or users across forests, such as Sol Rosenberg, who is in a domain called bigu.edu. As you can see in Figure 2.19, Sol has been added.

FIGURE 2.19 You can choose to delegate to users in your domain, in other domains, or in domains in other forests.

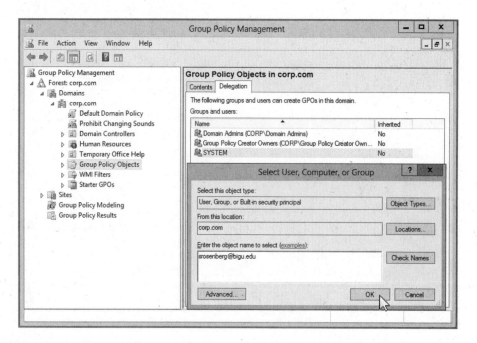

This can be handy if you have trusted administrators in other domains and you want to allow them to create GPOs in your domain. You might want to round them up into a group (instead of just listing them individually as Sol is listed here), but that's your option.

Enabling people to create GPOs is difficult using Microsoft's built-in Group Policy cmdlets. But Darren's free PowerShell cmdlets (which we used earlier) makes quick work of this task you wanted. To enable Sol Rosenberg from the bigu.edu domain to create GPOs in the Corp.com domain using PowerShell, you would use the following command:

```
Add-SDMSOMSecurity -Scope "dc=corp,dc=com" -Trustee "BIGU\srosenberg"
-PermSOMGPOCreate
```

However, in this quick example, I'm using a guy called Testman1 in my Corp domain and giving him those rights.

```
PS C:\Users\Administrator> Add-SDMSOMSecurity -Scope "dc=corp,dc=com" -Trustee "CORP\Testman1"
-PermSOMGPOCreate

Confirm
Are you sure you want to perform this action?
Performing the operation "SOM Permission Change" on target "dc=corp,dc=com".
[Y] Yes  [A] Yes to All  [N] No  [L] No to All  [S] Suspend  [?] Help (default is "Y"): a


Inherited    : False
Inheritable  : False
Denied       : False
Permission   : 1049344
Trustee      : System.__ComObject
```

Special Group Policy Operation Delegations

You can delegate three special permissions at the domain and OU levels, and you can set one of those three special permissions at the site level. Clicking the level, such as an OU, and then clicking the Delegation tab for that level shows the available permissions, as seen in Figure 2.20.

The interface is a bit confusing here. Specifically, you must first select the permission from the drop-down box. This lists the current users who currently have permissions. You can then click the Add, Remove, or Advanced button to make your changes.

You can select three permissions from the drop-down box, as seen in Figure 2.20:

Link GPOs Of the three permissions here, this is the only permission that can be configured at all levels: site, domain, and OU. Recall in Chapter 1 that you ran Active Directory Users and Computers' "Delegation of Control Wizard" (see Figure 1.21). Instead of using Active Directory Users and Computers to perform that task, the GPMC can do the same job—right here.

Perform Group Policy Modeling Analyses This right performs the same function as if we had used Active Directory Users and Computers' "Delegation of Control Wizard" to grant the "Generate Resultant Set of Policy (Planning)" permissions, as you saw in Chapter 1, Figure 1.21. The next section describes how to get more data about what's happening at the client. You'll see how to use this power in the section "What-If Calculations with Group Policy Modeling" later in this chapter. Group Policy Modeling lets you simulate what-if scenarios regarding users and computers.

FIGURE 2.20   These operations enable you to delegate special Group Policy operations.

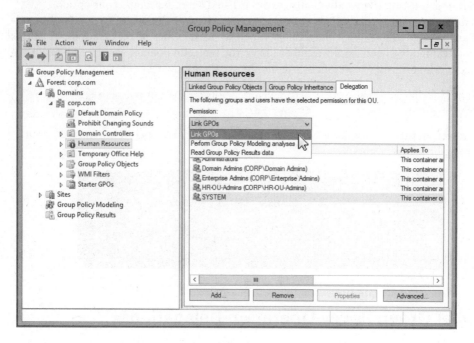

By default, only Domain Admins have the right to perform this task. Domain Admins can grant other users or groups the ability to perform this function, such as the Help Desk, HR-OU-Admins, or your own desktop-administrator teams. You can choose to grant people the ability to perform Group Policy Modeling analyses on this specific container or this specific container and child containers. When you assign this right, the user performing the Group Policy Modeling analysis must have the delegated right on the container containing the what-if user and also the container containing the what-if computer. If you don't grant rights in both containers, only half the analysis is displayed.

Read Group Policy Results Data   This right performs the same function as if we used Active Directory Users and Computers' "Delegation of Control Wizard" to grant the "Generate Resultant Set of Policy (Logging)" permission (which isn't shown in Figure 2.20 but it would be there if you scrolled down a little). You'll see how to use this power in the section "What's-Going-On Calculations with Group Policy Results" later in this chapter. However, if you want to grant this power to others, you can. Again, a typical use is to grant this right to the Help Desk or other administrative authority.

When you assign this right, the user performing the Group Policy Results analysis must have the delegated right on the container containing the target computer. Or this right can be applied at a parent container and the rights will flow down via inheritance. The user or group must also have this right delegated on any container containing any users who have logged onto the machine you want to analyze. If you don't grant rights in both containers, no analysis is displayed.

To add the equivalent permissions via in PowerShell, you need Darren's `Add-SDMSOMSecurity` cmdlet again from his free PowerShell cmdlets download.

You simply specify the name of the person (in this example, I'm using a fake guy called Testman1) and you specify the permissions. The possible entries for permissions are as follows:

* `PermSOMLink Link`—Group Policy Objects
* `PermSOMPlanning`—Perform Group Policy Modeling Analysis
* `PermSOMLogging`—Read Group Policy Results Data

```
Add-SDMSOMSecurity -Scope "ou=human resources, dc=corp,dc=com" -Trustee "corp\
Testman1" -PermSOMLink
```

```
PS C:\Users\Administrator> Add-SDMSOMSecurity -Scope "ou=human resources, dc=corp,dc=com" -Trus
tee "corp\Testman1" -PermSOMLink

Confirm
Are you sure you want to perform this action?
Performing the operation "SOM Permission Change" on target "ou=human resources,
dc=corp,dc=com".
[Y] Yes  [A] Yes to All  [N] No  [L] No to All  [S] Suspend  [?] Help (default is "Y"): a


Inherited   : False
Inheritable : True
Denied      : False
Permission  : 1835008
Trustee     : System.__ComObject
```

Who Can Create and Use WMI Filters?

Okay, okay, okay. I know the subject of WMI filters has come up about 3,000 times already, and every time I refer you, the poor reader, to Chapter 4. Once you've read what they are and how to create them in Chapter 4, please come back here and read how to manage them. In other words, since I'm already talking about the delegation of things inside the GPMC, I'm going to just cover that now. Go learn about what the heck WMI filters *are* in Chapter 4.

That said, two types of people are involved in the management of WMI filters:

* Those who can create them
* Those who can use them

Delegating Who Can Create WMI Filters

By default, only the Domain Administrator can create WMI filters. However, you might have some WMI whiz-kid in your company (and it's a good chance this isn't the same person as the Domain Administrator). With that in mind, the Domain Administrator can grant that special someone the ability to create WMI filters. To do this, drill down to the domain ➢ WMI Filters node, and then select Delegation in the pane on the right. You can now grant one of two rights, as shown in Figure 2.21.

FIGURE 2.21   These are controls over the creation of WMI filters.

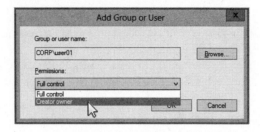

In Figure 2.21, we can see the two rights that appear in the drop-down box:

* Once a user has "Creator owner" rights here, they can create and modify their own WMI filters but they cannot modify others' WMI filters. Note that members of the Group Policy Creator Owners security group have this right by default.

* A user with "Full control" rights here can create and modify their own WMI filters or anyone else's.

Delegating Who Can Use WMI Filters

Once WMI filters are created (again, see Chapter 4), you'll likely want to assign who can apply them to specific GPOs. To do this, drill down to the specific WMI filter, as shown in Figure 2.22. Then click Add, and you'll see that two rights are available for the user you want.

FIGURE 2.22   These are controls over the WMI filters themselves.

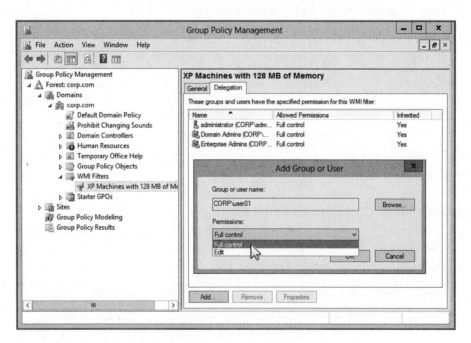

In Figure 2.22, we can see the two rights that appear in the drop-down box:

- Once users have "Edit" rights here, they can edit and tailor the filter, as we do in Chapter 4.
- A user with "Full control" rights here can edit the filter as well as delete it and modify the security (that is, specify who else can get "Edit" or "Full control" rights here).

Performing RSoP Calculations with the GPMC

In Chapter 1, we charted out a fictitious organization's GPO structure on paper. We looked and saw when various GPOs were going to apply to various users and computers. Charting out the RSoP (Resultant Set of Policy) for users and computers on paper is a handy skill for a basic understanding of GPO organization and flow, but in the real world, you need a tool that can help you figure out what's going on at your client desktops.

The GPMC has a handy feature to show us all the GPOs that are going to apply for the users and computers at a specific level in Active Directory. In Figure 2.23, when you click the **Human Resources Users** OU and then click the Group Policy Inheritance tab, you can see a list of all the GPOs that should apply to the **Human Resources Users** OU.

The site level is not shown in this Group Policy Inheritance tab. Because computers, particularly laptops, can travel from site to site, it is impossible to know for sure what site to represent here.

FIGURE 2.23   The Group Policy Inheritance tab shows you which GPOs should apply.

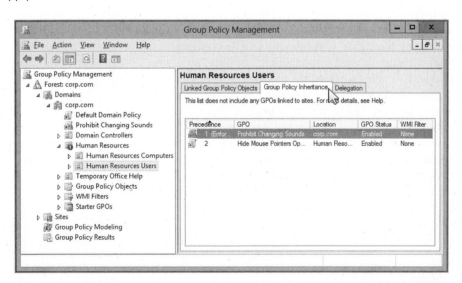

As I said, this tab in Figure 2.23 should tell you what's going to happen. The operative word here is *should*. That's because a lot can go wrong between your wishes and what happens on the client systems. For instance, you already saw how to filter GPOs using security groups, which would certainly change the experience of one user versus another on the very same machine. And in Chapter 4, you'll learn about WMI filters, which limit when GPOs are applied even more.

The point of all this RSoP stuff is to help us know the score about what's going on at machines that could be many hundreds of miles away. When users freak out about getting settings they don't expect or when they freak out about lacking settings they do expect, the point is to know which setting is causing the stir and which GPO is to blame for the errant setting.

We know one thing for sure: users do freak out if anything changes, and it's our job to track down Group Policy issues that could be affecting them. So the point of performing an RSoP calculation is to help you know what is going on and why it's going on that way. The GPMC can help with that.

What's-Going-On Calculations with Group Policy Results

If someone calls you to report that an unexpected GPO is applying, you can find out what's going on by using the GPMC. Once the user with the problem has logged onto the machine in question, you can tap into the WMI provider built into all editions of Windows since Windows XP. Without going too propeller-head here, the upshot of this magic is that the GPMC (and the GPResult command, and Get-GPresultantSetOfPolicy PowerShell cmdlet, as we'll explore more in Chapter 7) can query any particular user who has ever logged on locally. It's then a simple matter to display the sexy results within the GPMC.

Once the results are displayed, you can right-click over the report and save them as an HTML or XML report.

The magic happens when the computer asking "What's going on?" (in this case, the computer running the GPMC) asks the target client computer. The target client computer responds with a result of what has happened—which GPOs were applied to the Computer side and to the User side (provided the user has ever, at least once, logged on).

Let me expand on this important point: This Group Policy Results magic only works if the target user has ever logged onto the target machine. They only need to have ever logged on once, and here's the amazing part: they don't even need to be logged on while you run the test. But if the target user has *never* logged onto the target machine, the Group Policy Results will not allow you to select that user.

You can run your what's-going-on calculations inside the GPMC by right-clicking the Group Policy Results node at the bottom of the GPMC's hierarchy, as shown in Figure 2.24. When you do, you can select the user and the computer and see their interaction.

FIGURE 2.24 The Group Policy Results Wizard performs what's-going-on calculations.

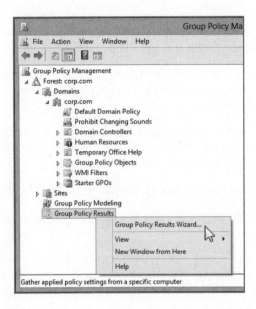

Keep in mind the following before trying to run the Group Policy Results Wizard to figure out what's going on:

- The target computer must be turned on and on the network. If this is not the case, you'll get an error to this effect. It will state that it cannot contact the WMI service via RPC.

- If the target machine has a firewall turned on, it must be disabled. Alternatively (in advance), you can open up ports 135 and 445 on the target machine. See the sidebar "Understanding Windows Firewall Settings (and Dealing with Group Policy Results)" for some ideas on how to mitigate this. If the machine is unreachable because the firewall is blocking access to port 135 or port 445, you'll get the same RPC Error as if the computer was off.

- The Windows Management Instrumentation service must be started.

- The user's local profile cannot be deleted. If the user has logged on but the administrator later whacks the local profile (or a Windows Vista or later–specific policy setting is enabled to auto-whack the local profile), WMI data will not be available.

Remember, the user you want to find out about must have logged onto the target computer *at least once* to be eligible to perform a Group Policy Results calculation.

Understanding Windows Firewall Settings (and Dealing with Group Policy Results)

Since Windows XP SP2 and Windows Server 2008, the Windows Firewall is automatically engaged—protecting your poor machines from the baddies out there.

Now, regular, everyday Group Policy stuff works just fine when the firewall is on. That's because the Group Policy *client* requests what it wants from the server, then the results are returned through the requested ports.

But, as you just learned, the ability to get Group Policy Results is effectively disabled when the Windows Firewall is engaged. That's because firewalls reject unrequested stuff when engaged. So, it feels like the target computer is turned off.

There are some policy settings that will affect Windows XP or later found in two locations:

Administrative Templates ➢ Network ➢ Network Connections ➢ Windows Firewall ➢ Domain Profile

Administrative Templates ➢ Network ➢ Network Connections ➢ Windows Firewall ➢ Standard Profile

You can see that the exact same policy settings are listed for both the Standard Profile and Domain Profile nodes. The Domain Profile settings are what will take effect when users are inside your corporate network; that is, when they're actively logged in by a Domain Controller. The Standard Profile, on the other hand, is used for when users are out of the office (perhaps in a hotel or other public network where they cannot reach your company's Domain Controllers for authentication).

Once a machine receives the policy settings for both the Domain Profile and Standard Profile, that computer is ready to travel both in and out of the office. You can be sure that machine is embracing your company's firewall security policy both in the office and on the road.

If you're interested in learning more about how a computer makes a determination of whether it is supposed to use Domain Profile or Standard Profile policy settings, be sure to read Microsoft's "Network Determination Behavior for Network-Related Group Policy Settings" at https://technet.microsoft.com/library/bb878049 (shortened to http://tinyurl.com/cao73).

Note that the details are different for Vista and later, but the net result is the same: You can use these Standard Profile settings or Domain Profile settings as you need to. You have two options if you want to restore the Group Policy Results functionality when you have Windows XP or later clients with the firewall on:

Approach 1: Kill the Windows XP/SP2 (and later) firewall. Now that you understand how to control Windows XP's (or later versions') firewall settings, one approach is to kill the firewall completely. If you do this, you understand that you're giving up any of the protection that Windows Firewall affords. However, by doing so, you will restore communication to the target computer. To kill the firewall, drill down to Administrative Templates ➢ Network ➢ Network Connections ➢ Windows Firewall ➢ Domain Profile and select **Windows Firewall: Protect all network Connections**. But here's the thing. You don't enable this policy to kill the firewall. You disable it. Yes, you read that right: you disable it. Read the help text in the policy for more information on specific usage examples.

Approach 2: Poke just the required holes in the firewall. Instead of killing the firewall dead, you can simply open up the one port you need. Again, the idea is that if the target computer responds on port 135, you're golden. Windows has a policy setting you can enable named **Windows Firewall: Allow Inbound Remote Administration Exception**, which is located in Computer Configuration ➢ Administrative Templates ➢ Network ➢ Network Connections ➢ Windows Firewall ➢ Domain Profile. Again, when you do this, you're opening up the necessary port 135 (RPC). Note, however, that enabling this policy setting also opens up port 445 (SMB), which some security shops might object to.

The output generated from the GPMC when performing Group Policy Results RSoP calculations is quite powerful. When your GPMC is Windows 8 or later, the level of detail is increased. You now get what is shown in Figure 2.25.

FIGURE 2.25 The Group Policy Results report shows three tabs, starting with Summary.

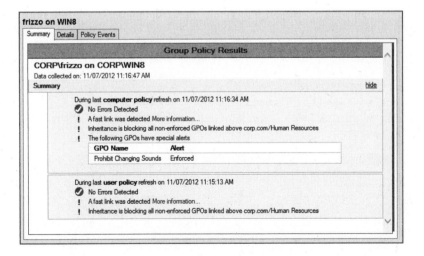

When your GPMC is Windows 8 or later, the Summary tab in the Group Policy Results report shows a true summary of what has occurred. Any "special events" are immediately obvious here on the Summary page. For instance, as Figure 2.25 shows, you can see that specific links to GPOs are called out when they are enforced. Also shown is a specific alert for where Block Inheritance starts.

Additionally, if any errors occurred, those would be present here as well. And you can see hyperlinks to web pages with interesting information for both errors and informational items.

Similar to using the Settings tab, you can expand and contract the report by clicking Show and Hide. Inside, you can clearly see which GPOs have been applied and any major errors along the way. At a glance, you can see which GPOs have Applied and which were Denied (passed over) for whatever reason, such as filtering or that one-half of the GPO was empty.

The Details tab shows the meat of the report, as shown in Figure 2.26. Note that the report is pretty long, so I'm showing you only the bottom half, which is the user portion in Figure 2.26.

FIGURE 2.26   The GPMC Details report shows the settings within the GPOs.

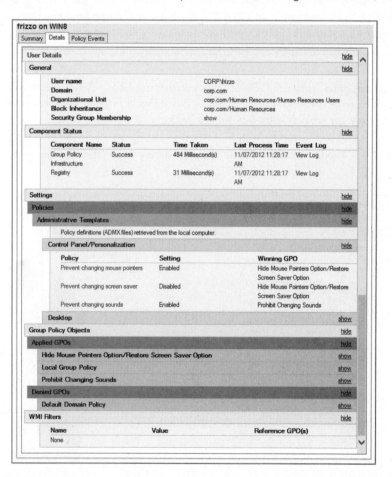

Here you can see which GPOs were Applied and which were Denied. Applied means that on the User or Computer side, the directives inside the Group Policy Object were performed. Denied means that the Group Policy Object's directives were not performed. Denied doesn't necessarily mean there's a problem. Indeed, in Figure 2.26, the Default Domain Policy is listed underneath "Denied GPOs" underneath User Details. But there is no problem here. It simply means that the Default Domain Policy contains no user settings at all, and therefore the User side of Group Policy didn't process anything.

With the Windows 8 and later GPMC, there's also expanded information for "Component Status," which specifies the particular Client Side Extensions (CSEs) that were processed and how long each CSE took to process.

I love this report, because it's clear how long Group Policy took to process something. Oftentimes, Group Policy is blamed for overall computer slowdowns when usually it's not to blame at all. A report like this is a major win for Group Policy "defenders" like me (and probably you, too).

If you click the Settings portion of this report, you get an extra bonus: If conflicts exist along the scope of the GPO, you can see which other GPOs won in the contest for the ultimate Group Policy smackdown! Indeed, you can see this in Figure 2.26. Note, however, that the GPMC doesn't show you which GPOs lost when there was a conflict. This can sometimes mean more troubleshooting to determine other GPOs with conflicting settings.

There are one or two caveats about Group Policy Results data. Specifically, when you produce a Group Policy Results report, some data simply isn't reported! Depending on the circumstances, you might not see some of the following data in a report:

* IPsec policies
* Wireless policies
* Disk quotas policies
* Third-party Client-Side Extension add-ins

Stay away from the tempting right-click Advanced View after the report appears. The Advanced View tool hasn't been updated since XP, so you might get some strange, incorrect, or hard-to-interpret results when using it.

Additionally useful here is the Policy Events tab, which will dive into the target machine's Event Viewer and pull out the events related to GPOs, as shown in Figure 2.27. Just double-click the event to open it. Talk about handy!

The GPMC will also save the query so you can reuse it later if you want to retest your assumptions. For example, you might want to retry this after you've corrected your software installation failure, added a new GPO to the mix, or moved a machine from one OU to another.

If you move a computer from one OU to another, you might not get the correct results right away because the computer may not immediately recognize that it has been moved. If you move a computer from one OU to another, you might want to synchronize your Domain Controllers and then reboot the target machine to get accurate results right away. This is discussed in more detail in Chapter 3.

FIGURE 2.27   The Policy Events tab shows you events specific to this target computer.

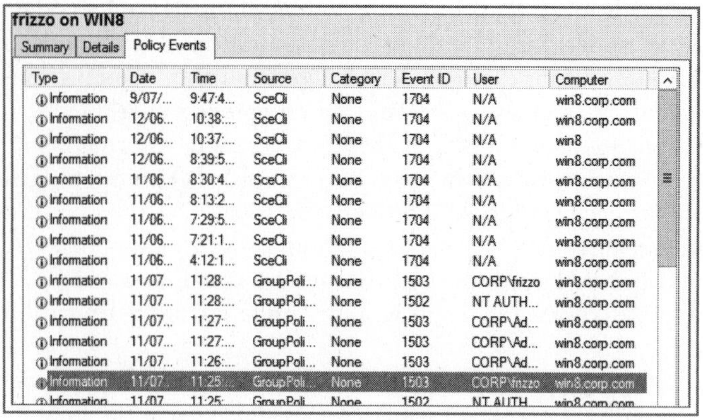

What-If Calculations with Group Policy Modeling

Finding out what's going on is useful if someone calls you in a panic. However, you might also want to plan for the future. For instance, would you be able to easily determine what would happen to the users in the **Human Resources Users** OU if a somewhat indiscriminately named GPO called "Desktop and User Stuff" was linked to it? Maybe or maybe not. (With a horribly named GPO like that, likely not.)

Or, what might happen if Frank Rizzo took a trip to another site? Which GPOs would apply to him then? Or which GPOs would apply if the HR-OU-Admins were granted different security rights (or had them revoked)? The Oracle, er, the Group Policy Modeling Wizard found in the GPMC can answer a million of these questions. Its job is to answer "What happens if?"

This function is available only if the domain schema has been updated for (at least) Windows 2003 and you have at least one Windows 2003 Domain Controller available. This is because a Windows 2003 or later Domain Controller runs a service that must be running for the calculation to occur.

Again, the only catch to this magic is that when you want to run what-if modeling calculations, the processing of the calculations must occur on a Windows 2003 or later Domain Controller. Even if you have the GPMC loaded on a Windows 10 management station, you'll still have to make contact with a Windows 2003 or later Domain Controller to assist in the calculations.

You can kick off a modeling session by right-clicking the domain or any OU (as well as the Group Policy Modeling node) and selecting Group Policy Modeling Wizard. When you do, you'll be presented with the Group Policy Modeling Wizard Welcome screen.

You then choose which Domain Controller (2003 or later) will have the honor of performing the calculation for you. It doesn't matter which Domain Controller you choose—just pick one.

You'll then get to play Zeus and determine what would happen if you plucked a user and/or computer out of a current situation and modified the circumstances. In the wizard screens, you get to choose the following:

- Which user and/or computer (or container) you want to start to play with
- Whether to pretend to apply slow-link processing (if not already present on the target)
- Whether to pretend to apply loopback processing (if not already present on the target)
- The site in which you want to pretend the object is starting
- Where to move the user (if the user account moves at all)
- Where to move the computer (if it moves at all)
- Whether to pretend to change the user's security group membership
- Whether to pretend to change the computer's security group membership
- Whether to pretend to apply WMI filters for users or computers (if not already present on the target)

Now, to be clear: you don't have to tweak *all* these settings—maybe just one or two. Just whatever applies to your situation.

Also note that you will likely get inaccurate results if you try to do something that isn't possible. For instance, you can force the wizard into seeing what happens if Frank Rizzo's account is moved to another domain. But since there isn't a way to actually move Frank's account, the displayed results will be cockeyed. You'll learn more about some of the additional concepts, such as slow-link processing and loopback processing, in Chapter 4. You'll also learn more about WMI filters in Chapter 4.

The output in Figure 2.28 shows what would happen if Frank Rizzo were removed from the **Human Resources Users** OU (and plopped into the root of the domain).

FIGURE 2.28   Here, the Group Policy Modeling summary screen shows you what you're about to simulate. For instance, you can simulate moving a computer and/or a user to other locations.

When the calculations are complete, you'll get a results dialog box that looks quite similar to Figure 2.26. There, you can see how results will be displayed on both the Summary and Details tabs. As a reminder, the Summary tab shows you which GPOs were applied; the Details tab shows you which policies in the GPOs will win if there's a conflict. Present only in Group Policy Modeling output (not shown) is another item, called the Query tab, which can remind you of the choices you made when generating the query.

What to Expect from the Group Policy Modeling Wizard

When you first use the Group Policy Modeling Wizard, you may be surprised to see that it has Loopback, WMI Filters, and Slow Links options. At first, I was curious as to why these were options in the wizard—if the wizard's whole job is to figure out what will be at the end of the simulation.

In a nutshell, the Group Policy Modeling Wizard allows you to simulate these additional items as if they all were *actually* going to be true. This way, you don't have to create an OU and/or a GPO with the specific policy settings (Loopback and so on) *just* to turn it on. This makes sense: if you enable these options on the real OU, you change the live environment.

The point of the Group Policy Modeling Wizard is to let you just simulate *what if* you did this on the target. When using the wizard and selecting Loopback, Slow Links, or WMI Filters, don't expect it to tell you that any of these things *are* true in the target. The simulation demonstrates what would happen *if* these properties came into the mix.

Note that the Group Policy Modeling Wizard is unable to take into account any Local Group Policy Object settings on the potential target workstation. That's because this wizard never queries a target computer. The calculations all happen on a Windows 2003 or later Domain Controller and are then output in the GPMC.

Searching and Commenting Group Policy Objects and Policy Settings

As your Active Directory grows, so will your use of GPOs. However, sometimes remembering the one GPO that you used to do some magic a while ago can be difficult.

And, moreover, with (what seems like) a bajillion policy settings available to choose from, finding the particular policy setting you want in the "policy setting haystack" is harder than ever.

To that end, the GPMC has some basic searching functionality for GPOs (the actual objects) and the Group Policy Management Editor has some filtering functionality for policy settings (the settings themselves, within the GPOs). Additionally, on each (the

GPO itself or a policy setting), you can make "comments" to help you remember why you decided to do something—which can be helpful if you go back six months later and wonder why you did something.

Searching for GPO Characteristics

With the search feature, you can search for GPOs with any (and all) of the following characteristics:

- Display name (that is, friendly name)
- GUID
- Permissions on the GPO itself
- A link, if it exists (used in conjunction with the name, and so on)
- WMI filters used
- Specific Client-Side Extensions if they were used for either the User or Computer side

To be clear, I'm talking about finding a specific GPO itself, not finding the settings *within* a GPO. To learn how to find specific settings contained within GPOs, well, that's coming right up.

To search for a GPO that matches the characteristics you're after, right-click the domain and choose Search, as seen in Figure 2.29. I show it here, specifically, because it can be a little hard to find.

FIGURE 2.29   Right-click the domain name and select Search to start searching for GPO characteristics.

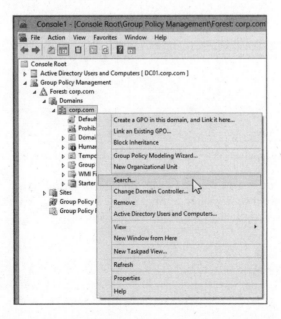

Here's how it works:

- In the Search Item dialog box, pick the pre-canned search type, like GPO Name, or GUID.

- In the Condition dropdown, select your condition, like "Contains" or "Does not contain."

- In the Value field, specifically enter criteria. Note that the Value field can change to a dropdown depending on what's used for the Search criteria, or it can be a free-form text box.

So, in Figure 2.30, I've selected "GPO Name" in the Search Item dropdown, selected "Contains" in the Condition dropdown, and finally entered "hide" for Value. Last, I selected "Add" to add the whole criteria to the search engine, and clicked Search. The results in Figure 2.30 show all GPOs with *Hide* in the name.

FIGURE 2.30   You can locate GPOs with lots of characteristics.

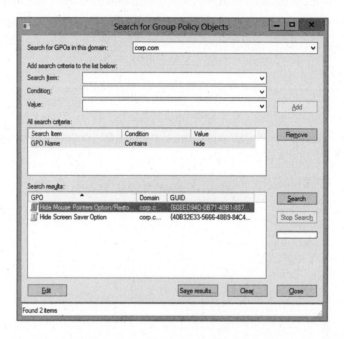

Note that one thing *this* search engine *cannot* do is poke through each and every GPO to see where you configured some policy setting. That's done on a per-GPO basis while editing, which we'll cover, well, right here in the next section.

Filtering Inside a GPO for Policy Settings

How many individual Group Policy settings are there? Lots. There are now almost 4,000 settings that can affect your Windows machines.

So, it's perfectly natural to feel like you're trying to find a needle in a haystack just locating a setting.

Where Did Filtering Come From?

The good news is that Filtering is available within the Group Policy Management Editor (GPME). The bad news is that not every area within the GPME is searchable (boo!). Before we go into what is and is not available for the new search function, let's take a look at the historical archives for the Group Policy Filtering feature.

If you'll recall, the original Group Policy Editor (contained in the downloadable-for-XP version of the GPMC) *always* had a Filtering option. Really? You didn't know this? That's because it wasn't very well documented and kind of tucked away. If you still have an old XP machine with the GPMC kicking around, click View ➢ Filtering, and you'll see the window shown in Figure 2.31.

FIGURE 2.31   The Windows XP and Windows Filtering option

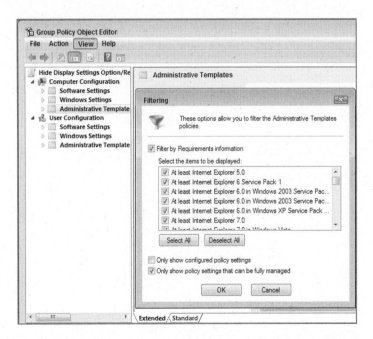

This Filtering option had simple abilities. You can check "Filter by Requirements information" and filter for policy settings that would, for example, work only on Windows XP or newer computers.

When you use the modern GPMC, you get a new ability to filter.

What's Available to Filter

The good news is that filtering is available. The bad news is that only the Administrative Templates Group Policy settings are available to search. So, if you're looking to find that security policy setting that will set **Accounts: Rename guest account** or **Devices: Restrict CD-ROM access to locally logged in user only**, well, you're out of luck. These lie within Computer Configuration ➢ Windows Settings ➢ Security Settings ➢ Local Policies ➢ Security Options.

Anything that's not within the Administrative Template section is off limits to the Filtering feature.

To get to the filter options, click anywhere within the User Configuration ➢ Policies ➢ Administrative Templates or Computer Configuration ➢ Policies ➢ Administrative Templates windows, then click View ➢ Filter Options, or right-click over the words "Administrative Templates" and select Filter Options, as seen in Figure 2.32. Once you do this, you'll get the Filter Options dialog box, shown in Figure 2.33. You could also right-click within Administrative Templates and select Filter Options.

FIGURE 2.32 The GPMC Filter Options selection

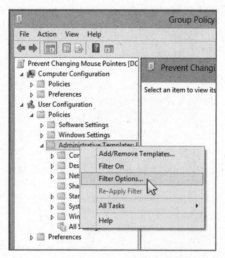

We'll discuss the dialog box in three parts: top (type of settings to display), middle (keyword filters), and bottom (requirements filters). We'll start in the middle with keyword filters, move to the top, and then finally move to the bottom.

FIGURE 2.33   The GPMC Filter Options dialog

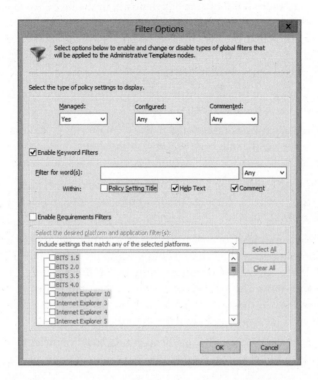

There are numerous reasons you might want to use the Filter Options dialog box. For instance, you might want to show only the policy settings that have been changed from their defaults. You can absolutely do that. But the most common reason for using the Filter Options dialog box is to hunt down settings you think (or hope) might be there. For instance, you already know there are some settings that do something to the Control Panel, but you may not know the exact setting names. You can use this dialog box to find the policy setting you seek.

We'll go through all the options in the Filter Options dialog box, but keep in mind that the most common use is to hunt down settings you want to muck with, er, *experiment* with inside your test lab.

Keyword Filters

Arguably the most useful part of the dialog box, the Keyword Filters option lets you type in something you know you want to do, then see which policy settings match that keyword. You can choose to search in the following three places:

Policy Setting Title   Searches text in the name of a policy setting, like **Prevent access to Control Panel and PC settings**

Help Text (Also Known as Explain Text)   Searches the help text within the Help section of each policy setting. Note that all policy settings that ship in the box have help text (though some policy settings from ADM or ADMX templates that you get on the Internet might not). It should also be noted that the help text keeps getting better and better with each new edition of Windows. Even the Security entries are mostly commented (but again, remember that you cannot filter based on Security entries).

Comment   We'll talk about comments a little later. But, in short, you can search for any text in comments within a particular GPO.

Let's say you wanted to find settings related to the Control Panel. Next to the "Filter for word(s)" line, you can see the default modifier Any, with All and Exact hiding underneath. Here's how the search for "Control Panel" would work with each modifier:

Any   Returns results where either the word *Control* or *Panel* or both are found. So, results like "Turn Off Password Security in Input Panel" would also appear along with "Show Only Specified Control Panel Items."

All   Returns results where both *Control* and *Panel* are found, but would not display settings that contain only one or the other. Results would include "Hide The Programs Control Panel" and "Hide Specified Control Panel Items." If there were a setting called "Control a Panel of Experts to Use Group Policy More," it would return that, too, because both *Control* and *Panel* are in the name, even though they don't appear right next to each other. (Oh, if only there were a setting like that—but I digress.)

Exact   Returns results where the word *Control* is immediately followed by the word *Panel*. If those two words weren't in that exact order, that setting would not show up.

Note that all of these modifiers, including Exact, ignore case. So *Control Panel* is the same as *CoNTrol PANel.*

Type of Settings to Display

This section of the dialog box can be seen in the following image.

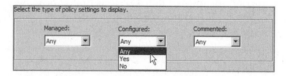

Here you'll be able to select three possible options:

Managed   You'll learn more about Managed (blue dot/list icon) versus Unmanaged (red dot/down arrow icon) policy settings in Chapter 6, "Managing Applications and Settings Using Group Policy." The quick summary in 100 words or fewer is that *managed* policies act like true Group Policy settings and *unmanaged* policies will "tattoo" the Registry. For more information about tattooing, read Chapter 6.

I'm not quite sure why, but the default here is set to Yes. That would mean the results will be *only* Managed policy settings. Just to be on the safe side, selecting Any is likely a better bet because that way, you'll get back both managed and unmanaged policy settings. Again, I'll talk about this more in Chapter 6.

Configured   As you learned in Chapter 1, Administrative Templates policy settings can be set to Enabled, Disabled, or Not Configured. The default for Configured is No, which means the results will show only policy settings that haven't been configured. If you select Yes, the results will show only Enabled or Disabled policy settings. If you choose Any, the results will show Enabled, Disabled, or Not Configured. Selecting Any here seems to be your best bet for finding a policy setting you might want to experiment with.

Commented   You'll learn about comments later in this chapter, so stay tuned. The default here is Any, which means it will look for commented or uncommented policy settings within this GPO. Selecting Yes will show only commented policy settings within this GPO. Choosing No will show only those policy settings without comments (which would typically be most of them).

Requirements Filters

If you click Enable Requirements Filters (seen in Figure 2.33 earlier), you can determine if you want to show policy settings that are meant for particular client types. Again, a Group Policy "client" can be anything that "receives" Group Policy. So, a Group Policy client can be Windows 2000 or later. The available platforms are listed for you to select, and the list includes various operating system parts that policy settings affect, such as Windows Media Player 10, Windows Installer 3.0, or NetMeeting 3.0. Just select the appropriate check boxes.

Note that there's a drop-down that changes the Filter results when you've checked multiple items. You can show All or Any of the selected platforms. To get your head around what these settings do, it's best to run through a "working example" on each:

Include settings that match any of the selected platforms.   For argument's sake, let's say you select two categories using the Any drop-down. Let's say you select Windows XP SP2 and Windows 10. When you do this, you'll see policy settings results that are valid to be applied for lots of machine types: Windows 2000, Windows Vista, Windows 7, Windows 8, Windows 10, Windows Server 2008, Windows Server 2016, and more. That makes sense. But, for example, what you *won't* see are policy settings that apply *only* to Windows 2000 machines. Again, some results (lots of them, actually) will be valid for, say, Windows 2000. And that's because lots of settings that *also* work for Windows XP SP2 and Windows 7 are perfectly happy and embraceable by Windows 2000 machines. But Windows 2000–only settings (that is, settings that Windows 2000 machines can use but other machine types cannot use) are not listed in the results.

Include settings that match all of the selected platforms.   For argument's sake, let's say you select the *same* two categories using the All dropdown. Let's say you select Windows XP SP2 and Windows 10. When you do this, you'll see lots of results. But surprisingly, none of the results show anything for, say, Windows XP SP2, nor do they show anything for Windows 10. You will see a lot of settings that say "At least Windows 2000" and "At least Windows XP Professional." Clear your mind for a second; here's why: The results you get back are correct. You're telling the system, "Show me the settings that are valid only for both Windows XP SP2 and also Windows 10." Well, older settings (Windows 2000–specific and original Windows XP settings) fit that bill. Newer Windows XP settings, specifically Windows XP SP2 settings, might be perfectly valid on Windows 10. But those newest Windows 10 settings are *not* also valid on Windows XP. So the results you get are accurate. You're only seeing settings that will, indeed, *only* work on all the selected platforms—guaranteed. See Figure 2.34 (which shows Vista and Windows XP, but you get the idea).

FIGURE 2.34   You can select to filter by which platforms are supported.

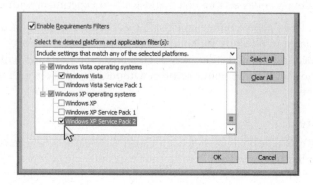

PolicySettings.XLS: Beyond the Filters Node

The Filters node is great. But it's missing one key, well, filtering ability.

It's missing the ability to show specifically what policy settings are available *only* for each operating system. That's right; there's no way of using the Filters to say, "Show me only the new policy settings that apply only for Windows 10."

So, how do you do that?

You can download a spreadsheet from Microsoft at http://tinyurl.com/policysettings-xls. Note, however, that Microsoft's spreadsheet doesn't go into much detail beyond the Explain Text setting for each policy setting. But they're all there and searchable, and you can sort by which operating systems will embrace which policy settings. It's quite good. Also, if you've got an older version of this spreadsheet kicking around, you should note that these settings are always updated whenever a service pack comes out. The older version of the spreadsheet also expresses when a specific policy setting requires a logoff or a reboot.

Nice touch!

Results of Your Filter

Once you've made your selections in the Filter Options dialog box, you're ready to click OK and watch the magic. Let's do a simple filter and look to find any unique Control Panel policy settings that we might want to check out. The filter selections can be seen in Figure 2.35. Here I've made sure to specify "Managed: Any" (which implies managed or unmanaged), policy settings that are configured or not configured, and policy settings that are commented or uncommented (more on comments a little later). And for now, I'm just looking for the words *Control Panel* (in that exact order) to appear in any part of the setting title.

FIGURE 2.35   I changed the Keyword Filter modifier to Exact to ensure that my results contained the exact phrase *control panel*.

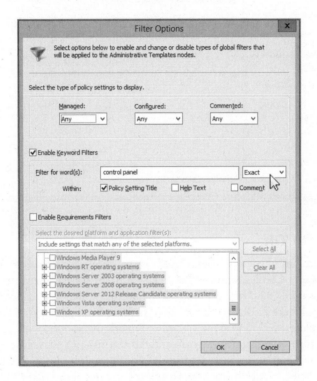

Browsing the Results

The results of applying your filter can be seen in multiple places. You can see the policy settings that affect the Control Panel in the User side by clicking User Configuration ➢ Policies ➢ Administrative Templates ➢ Control Panel (and also the folders within Control Panel named Display and Programs). An example is seen in Figure 2.36.

Note that the filter does not affect the Computer side. The filters are independently set. If you want to turn this on for the Computer side as well, you would need to manually find the Computer Configuration ➢ Policies ➢ Administrative Templates node and create a filter that filtered for the words *Control* and *Panel*.

FIGURE 2.36   Browsing results of running the filter

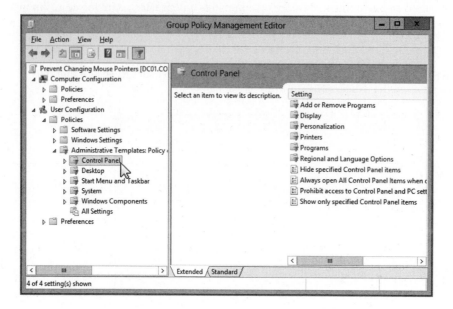

Filter Options On/Off

Once the filter is set to On, the icons around User Configuration ➢ Policies ➢ Administrative Templates and Computer Configuration ➢ Policies ➢ Administrative Templates change. Specifically, the icons take on a "funnel" image to demonstrate that you're looking through the filtered option. In Figure 2.37, I've "blown up" the User Configuration ➢ Policies ➢ Administrative Templates section to show you what I'm talking about.

If you ever want to stop looking at only the filtered settings, it's easy. Just right-click anywhere within User Configuration ➢ Policies ➢ Administrative Templates or Computer Configuration ➢ Policies ➢ Administrative Templates and uncheck Filter On, as seen in Figure 2.38.

FIGURE 2.37   The funnel icon shows you've got filtering enabled.

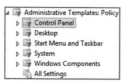

FIGURE 2.38   You can uncheck Filter On to disable the filter.

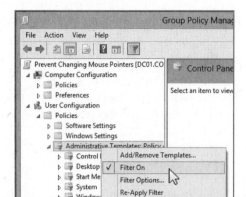

When you do, the filter immediately pops off, and you'll be looking at every possible policy setting again.

 The GPMC filter settings "stick around," meaning that the last filter you use is remembered the next time you apply a filter. This is an advantage if you are searching for a specific setting through different GPOs. Sure, you still need to open each GPO one by one, but at least the last filter you created will be utilized.

Why "Reapply" a Filter?

In Figure 2.38, you can see the Re-Apply Filter option. Here's how that works.

Let's say you apply a filter to show only settings that contain the word *test* in the comment field. Your results show you the policy settings that currently match. However, what if you later add more comments to other policy settings that contain the word *test*? Your results won't show that new change immediately. That is, the change won't show until you reapply the filter!

You can see the same result if you choose to show only Not Configured policy settings but then later change one or a few of those to Enabled. Those changes will not be seen until you reapply the filter.

Reapplying the filter just sets filtering to Off and then turns it back on. Same result (but reapplying the filter is quicker).

The All Settings Node

Along with filters, the All Settings node is a feature in the GPMC. The idea is a little weird, so hang in here with me. There are two ways to leverage the All Settings node: when you're using filtering and when you're not.

Using the All Settings Node in Conjunction with Filtering

The idea is that you can see, at a glance, all the settings that tested "true" for the filter.

Since the results of filtering for *Control Panel* might exist in various nodes (User Configuration ➢ Policies ➢ Administrative Templates ➢ Control Panel, User Configuration ➢ Policies ➢ Administrative Templates ➢ Control Panel ➢ Display, and User Configuration ➢ Policies ➢ Administrative Templates ➢ Control Panel ➢ Programs), there are a lot of places you'd have to click to see all your results.

Instead, you can just click the All Settings node (and there's one for each side: User Configuration and Computer Configuration). There you'll see all the matches at a glance. Check it out in Figure 2.39.

FIGURE 2.39 The All Settings node shows 100 percent of the returned filter results in one view.

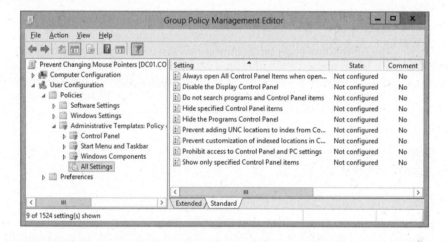

In Figure 2.39, you'll also see some other interesting tidbits of information, like whether the policy is Not Configured or if it has been configured (Enabled or Disabled) or if there's a comment within that policy setting (I promise you, we're getting to comments). Finally, there is also a column (not shown) named Path which shows the path to the policy setting, in case you wanted to show others where to find this policy setting.

The path is always relative to User Configuration ➢ Policies ➢ Administrative Templates or Computer Configuration ➢ Policies ➢ Administrative Templates, because that's the only place filtering is valid.

Using the All Settings Node without the Use of Filtering

There's another interesting way to use the All Settings node—when the filter is off. There are zillions of policy settings inside User Configuration and Computer Configuration.

What if you just wanted to quickly locate the policy settings with comments?

Or the policy settings that are configured?

Or quickly find a policy setting based on its name?

You could set up a filter (as previously discussed), but that takes *several whole seconds*! You don't have time for that! You're a busy IT professional!

If you had no filter configured, you could be a speed demon and just click the All Settings node, then click on the column you wish to sort. In Figure 2.40, I've turned off the filter, then clicked User Configuration ➢ Policies ➢ Administrative Templates ➢ All Settings, and finally clicked the State column heading.

FIGURE 2.40   Using the All Settings node with filtering turned off

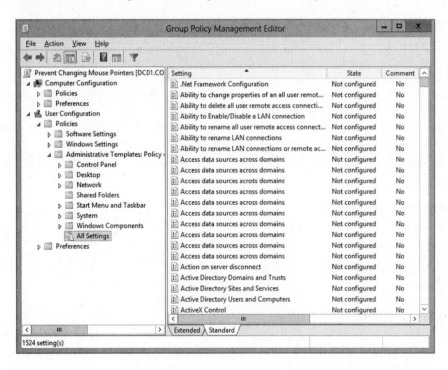

I can immediately see which policy settings have been configured in this particular GPO. No need to click, click, click my way through filters. This is life in the fast lane.

Comments for GPOs and Policy Settings

Imagine for a moment that you're in a large company—maybe you already are and it doesn't require much imagination. Perhaps there are 2, 5, or 50 other administrators. Wouldn't it be nice to be able to leave little messages inside the GPOs and particular GPO settings for other administrators who might happen to find a GPO you create?

That's what the following sections are all about: the Comment feature.

> Again, you'll be able to leave comments and read others' comments only if you use the updated GPMC. Admins using Windows XP (hence, the older GPMC) won't be able to read your comments. It only works with the updated GPMC.

You can leave and read comments in exactly two places: in the GPO itself and inside a GPO's settings. We'll explore these two next.

Comments about a Specific GPO

In the real world, life moves fast. As a result, sometimes administrators don't always spend the time they would like when crafting the name of a GPO. For instance, you might see a poorly named GPO like Our Desktop Settings. It's poorly named because it doesn't explain what those settings are. Is that the Desktop background settings? Or the Control Panel settings? Both? Neither? You get the idea.

Fortunately, now you can choose to leave a comment inside a GPO. Here are some ideas as to what to include when you choose to leave a comment:

- Who's in charge of the GPO
- Who to call if there's a problem with this GPO
- Backup contact information
- Who is supposed to be affected by this GPO
- Detailed information about what the GPO is supposed to do
- Your favorite chocolate chip cookie recipe

Just kidding about that last one. But you get the idea.

Leaving a Comment inside a GPO

Leaving a comment is pretty easy to do, but the problem is that it's not super-duper obvious where to go to leave a comment (and, as you'll see in the next section, not super-duper obvious where to pick them up, either).

To leave a comment, you must first have rights to edit the GPO. Then, while you're editing the GPO, right-click the topmost node with the name of the GPO, then click Properties, as seen in Figure 2.41. Then you can type in your comment and click OK, as shown in Figure 2.42.

FIGURE 2.41   Leave comments while editing a GPO by going to its Properties dialog box.

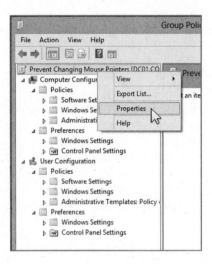

FIGURE 2.42   Entering a comment inside a GPO

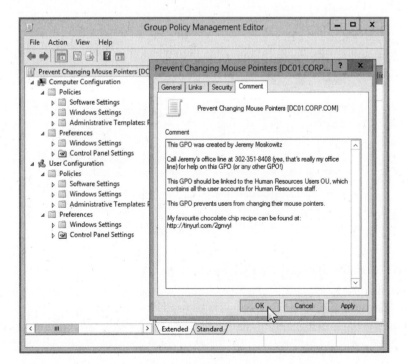

The Comments feature includes some assistance for right-to-left languages like Arabic and Hebrew. You can find these while right-clicking inside the text field. Things like "Right to Left Reading Order," "Show Unicode Characters," and more are there for that kind of input.

Reading a Comment about a GPO

Reading comments sounds as if it should be easy, but for the uninitiated, they're not easy to find. If you're editing the GPO, you can right-click over the top node, select Properties, and click the Comment tab, as you saw in Figure 2.42. Then, instead of leaving a comment, you can just read the existing comment.

But a better option is found within the GPMC itself. Simply click on the GPO (or the link to the GPO), then click the Details tab, seen in Figure 2.43. You'll see the results in the Comment field below. The formatting is mostly kept the same as when the comment was typed into the Comment editor. And what's more, Unicode characters (like Japanese, Hebrew, etc.) are supported in the editor and the resulting display.

FIGURE 2.43   The Details tab within the GPO shows the comments.

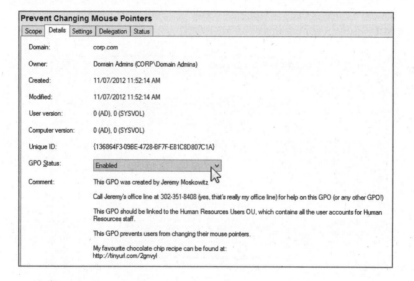

Comments about Specific GPO Settings

Previously you learned how to leave a comment about a particular GPO. Now let's explore the ability to leave comments about a particular Group Policy setting.

Like filters, comments about a specific GPO setting are available only to the Administrative Templates section. You cannot leave comments in other areas, like Security settings (which would be very useful) and the like. Note that Group Policy Preferences, which we talk about in Chapter 5, "Group Policy Preferences," also have a Description field, which is nice.

Leaving a Comment Inside a Specific GPO Setting

For instance, let's say you wanted to explain why a particular policy setting was Enabled (or Disabled). Simply traverse to the policy setting, get to its properties, then select the Comment tab. Leave a comment like the one you see in Figure 2.44.

FIGURE 2.44 Comments are available on a particular Group Policy setting.

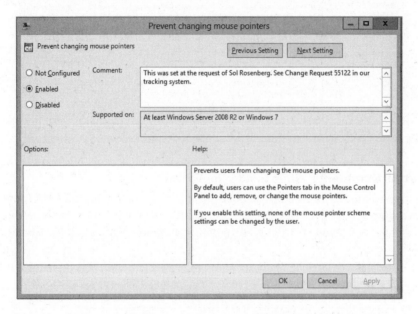

Reading a Comment Inside a Specific GPO Setting

To quickly read any comments inside particular GPO settings, you have two techniques available. First, while you're editing the GPO, you can quickly check to see which policy settings (if any) contain comments. Second, you can see them while tooling around inside the GPMC.

Looking at Comments While Editing the GPO

Remember from my discussion of the All Settings node that if the filter is off, you can then just click either User Configuration ➢ Policies ➢ Administrative Templates ➢ All Settings or Computer Configuration ➢ Policies ➢ Administrative Templates ➢ All Settings and then click the Comment column to sort the ones with comments, which bubble to the top. You can see this in Figure 2.45. Then it's a simple matter of double-clicking the policy setting in question and clicking the Comment tab to read it.

FIGURE 2.45   The All Settings node displays a Comment column that can be sorted.

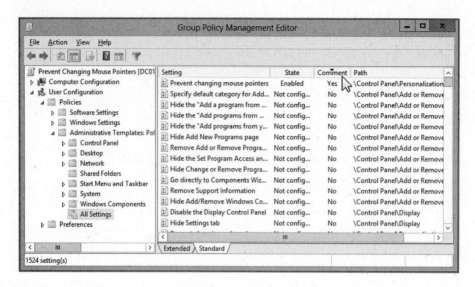

Looking at All Comments While Inside the GPMC

The alternative way to see all comments about the policy settings inside the GPO is to view the settings report. Simply click on the GPO (or the link to a GPO) and click the Settings tab. When you do, any comments about any policy settings are displayed inline, as shown in Figure 2.46.

FIGURE 2.46   The comments can be seen inside your GPMC settings reports.

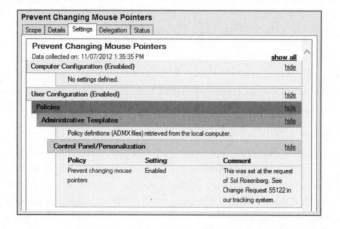

Where and What Are the Comments Anyway?

Behind the scenes, comments are really plaintext or XML files placed in SYSVOL.

General GPO comments are placed in a plaintext file located here:

```
\\<domain>\SYSVOL\<domain>\Policies\<GPO GUID>\GPO.cmt
```

Individual comments for GPO settings are placed in two XML files for each GPO, one for Computer Configuration comments and another for User Configuration comments. The files are placed here:

```
\\<domain>\SYSVOL\<domain>\Policies\<GPO GUID>\Machine\Comment.cmtx
\\<domain>\SYSVOL\<domain>\Policies\<GPO GUID>\User\Comment.cmtx
```

I wrote a blog entry on how to recycle a GPO's comments. You can read that here: www.gpanswers.com/group-policy-talk-is-cheap/.

Microsoft liked that blog entry so much, it made its own showing how you can use PowerShell to automate the idea. You can read that here: `http://tinyurl.com/GP-comment-powershell`.

Starter GPOs

The GPMC has another feature called Starter GPOs.

In big companies, there are often just a handful of people at the top who really "get" Group Policy. But there are a whole lot of people in the company who have to implement it. Not everyone can take a master class on Group Policy (hint, hint: `www.GPanswers.com/training`) or spend the time reading this book and working through all the examples.

With that in mind, Microsoft created Starter GPOs. The idea is that someone can create a GPO with some baseline settings, including comments, and make them available for others as a jumping-off point.

For instance, if you were the Domain Administrator and wanted to make sure that all your OU administrators got a recommended group of settings for desktop configuration, that would be easy. You would create a Starter GPO, then let them know they had a baseline of settings to leverage or to edit as they so desired.

You could think of Starter GPOs as templates for making new policies. That way, you're not back to nothing whenever you need to create a new GPO. The problem is, the word *template* has a special meaning with Microsoft's pay Group Policy management tool—AGPM, the Advanced Group Policy Management. That tool is discussed in Appendix C.

Anyway, AGPM has a similar feature called templates, and that's likely why this feature is called Starter GPOs and *not* Templates.

The GPMC has a new node called Starter GPOs. To get, er, started with Starter GPOs, you need to have the Starter GPOs folder created in the domain. Click on the Starter GPOs node and you'll see what's in Figure 2.47.

FIGURE 2.47   To create the Starter GPOs folder, just click on the big ol' button.

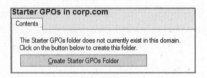

You might be asking yourself, "Where is this Starter GPOs folder being created?" Well, we go into the "internals" of GPOs in the next chapter, but for the curious, its new directory is created in the domain, inside the Domain Controller's SYSVOL container—specifically, the `<Domain>\SYSVOL\<Domain>\StarterGPOs` folder.

During creation, something "extra special" happens.

If you're using the Windows 7 or later GPMC and you click the Create Starter GPOs Folder button, Microsoft will auto-populate the Starter GPOs folder with some preconfigured items for your use. You can see these in Figure 2.48.

FIGURE 2.48   The two types of Starter GPOs are Custom and System.

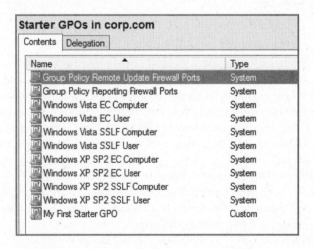

Note that you will not see these preconfigured Starter GPOs unless you're using the Windows 7 and later GPMC. And, you won't see the two Starter GPOs named "Group Policy Remote Update Firewall Ports" and "Group Policy Reporting Firewall Ports" without using the GPMC from Windows 8 or later.

Also note that any new Starter GPOs you create will just appear alongside these existing Starter GPOs (also seen in Figure 2.48). The Type fields for Starter GPOs that Microsoft provides are listed as System. The ones you create will be listed as Custom.

There are some differences in what Microsoft is able to put into its pre-created Starter GPOs vs. what you'll be able to do. We'll explore those differences here and in the section "Should You Use Microsoft's Pre-created Starter GPOs?"

Creating a Starter GPO

Simply right-click the Starter GPOs node and select New. When you do, you'll be prompted to give it a name and make some comments, as you can see in Figure 2.49.

FIGURE 2.49   Add a useful comment when creating a new Starter GPO.

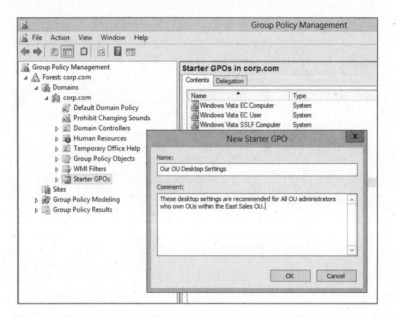

You can also use PowerShell to create a new Starter Group Policy Object. You could use the following to create one:

```
New-GPStarterGPO –Name "My First Starter GPO"
```

Note that running this PowerShell cmdlet really won't work correctly until the built-in Starter GPOs are already showing in the GPMC.

Editing a Starter GPO

Editing a Starter GPO is almost like editing a regular GPO. Just right-click the Starter GPO and select Edit. However, when you do, you'll notice it doesn't look exactly like what you're used to. In fact, only Computer Configuration ➢ Administrative Templates and User Configuration ➢ Administrative Templates are available as editable starter policy settings.

> A keen eye will spot that the Group Policy Object Editor title bar name changes to "Group Policy Starter GPO Editor" when you edit a Starter GPO.

You can see this in Figure 2.50.

FIGURE 2.50   Starter GPOs allow for Administrative Templates settings along with comments inside any Administrative Templates settings.

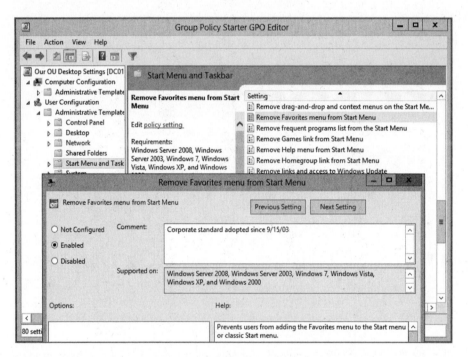

This is a real bummer; most people think (and rightly so) that Starter GPOs should encompass all the areas, not just Administrative Templates. The ability to use all areas, however, is possible, if you step up to Microsoft's pay Group Policy management tool—Advanced Group Policy Management (which we'll talk about in Appendix C). That feature is called Templates. It's like Starter GPOs, but all areas are available. Of course, AGPM costs money, and Starter GPOs are free. So, the free tool has at least something.

At this point, you can edit any settings you wish and even add comments about any particular policy settings.

Once you're finished, close the GPME.

Leveraging a Starter GPO

Now that you've created a Starter GPO, it's time for others to leverage your creation. To do that, an OU administrator (or Domain Admin, etc.) has two options: using the Starter GPOs node or just creating a new GPO as they normally would.

Using the Starter GPOs Node

Right-click the Starter GPO in the Starter GPOs node, and select New GPO From Starter GPO (as seen in Figure 2.51).

FIGURE 2.51   You can spawn a new GPO from the Starter GPOs node.

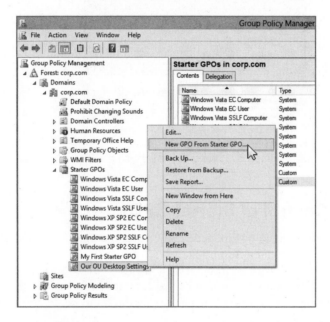

Next, the New GPO dialog box appears, and it auto-fills the Source Starter GPO field, as you can see in Figure 2.52.

FIGURE 2.52   The source Starter GPO is preset when you are modifying a Starter GPO.

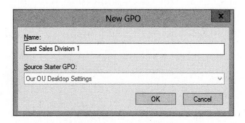

Creating a New GPO and Selecting a Starter GPO

The other way to use a Starter GPO is to create a new GPO. This can be done either by right-clicking the Group Policy Objects node and selecting New or by clicking over the Domain or OU levels and selecting "Create a GPO in this domain, and Link it here." Regardless of which you do, you'll see the New GPO dialog box, shown in Figure 2.53. At this point, you can select Source Starter GPO and choose the Starter GPO you wish to use.

FIGURE 2.53   If you're creating a GPO normally, you can select a Source Starter GPO.

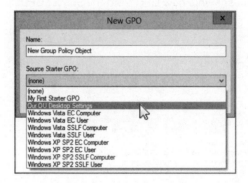

Delegating Control of Starter GPOs

The Starter GPOs section has a bug in its delegation section. That is, Starter GPOs cannot be delegated (beyond the Domain Administrators who already have access).

To access the Starter GPOs Delegation section, just click on the Starter GPOs node, and then click the Delegation tab that is seen in Figure 2.54. In the Delegation tab you could see that, curiously, Authenticated Users is listed as having the ability to "…create Starter GPOs in this domain."

That's not true. And adding in a user you want to sanction, say, Frank Rizzo to the list in the Delegation tab, also yields incorrect results. Also in Figure 2.54, we can see Frank trying to create a new Starter GPO even after he has been specifically delegated access. But creating Starter GPOs fails. Again, only (seemingly) Domain Admins have the ability to create Starter GPOs and not any kind of delegated users.

This bug has been around since Starter GPOs shipped in Windows Vista, and it seems to affect all domain types under all circumstances.

If the status should change, you'll find out about it first with an update at www.GPanswers.com.

FIGURE 2.54 Regular Authenticated users, thankfully, cannot manipulate Starter GPOs.

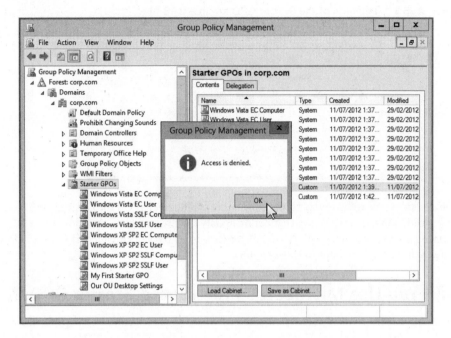

Wrapping Up and Sending Starter GPOs

One of the neat things about Starter GPOs is that you can give them to your friends—even if they belong to other domains. It's sort of like backing up a GPO, except all the guts are wrapped up into one file.

It's simple to do. Just click on the Starter GPOs node in the GPMC. Then find the Starter GPO you want to send to a friend. Then click "Save as Cabinet." This will save the file as a CAB file.

When your friend gets it, they click the Load Cabinet button to reverse the process. You can see the Load Cabinet and "Save as Cabinet" buttons in Figure 2.55.

FIGURE 2.55 You can save and load Starter GPOs from CAB files.

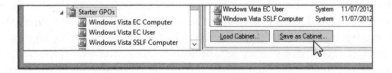

Inside the CAB files are the guts, as seen in Figure 2.56.

FIGURE 2.56   The guts of the Starter GPO are in a CAB file.

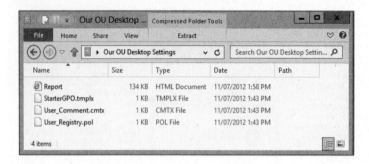

There doesn't seem to be a way to wrap up multiple Starter GPOs into a single CAB file. That would make transporting them enormously easier, but, alas, that doesn't exist. Additionally, note that Starter GPOs are not backed up as part of the normal Group Policy backup (which we explore later in this chapter).

Should You Use Microsoft's Pre-created Starter GPOs?

The pre-created Starter GPOs that Microsoft provides are supposed to be based on the recommendations in the Windows Vista Security Guide and the Windows XP Security Guide. Of course, you don't care about Windows Vista or Windows XP anymore—you want what's "latest." As you might imagine, this introduces several problems for you.

Problem #1: Outdated Settings

You probably won't be using Vista. You've probably rolled out Windows 7 or 8 and are headed toward a Windows 10 rollout. And you have definitely moved past Windows XP SP2. So the pre-created Starter GPOs that are supposed to mirror the Windows Vista and XP SP2 Security Guide could be of limited value to you.

Problem #2: Incomplete Settings

The Starter GPOs that Microsoft has created and supplied are incomplete. Remember, Starter GPOs have a big limitation. When we create our own Starter GPOs, we are only able to manipulate the Administrative Template settings. Turns out, underneath the hood, however, Starter GPOs can also allow for *some* security settings. (Note that we, as non-Microsoft insiders, cannot use Starter GPOs in this way—only the Microsoft templates are capable of leveraging this extra superpower.) But even then, they're still incomplete. If you do an apples-to-apples comparison between the Starter GPOs that are pre-created when you create the Starter GPOs folder against the GPOs that Microsoft originally recommended from its security guidance, you'll find that the Starter GPOs are missing a lot of important stuff.

So, should you use the built-in Starter GPOs that are auto-created?

My advice would be to not use most of them because of the problems noted. However, there are two new, useful Starter GPOs that you'll find when you create the Starter GPOs folder using a Windows 8 or later GPMC:

- Group Policy Remote Update Firewall Ports
- Group Policy Reporting Firewall Ports

These Starter GPOs are there to help you open up the required ports for some GPMC features, which we'll explore in the next chapter. You might want to use these, or you can manually open up the required ports. There's not a big difference.

With regard to the rest of the Starter GPOs, Microsoft's advice (and mine, too) would be to start investigating and using the Microsoft Security Compliance Manager, which is available for download at www.microsoft.com/scm. This utility will download predefined settings from Microsoft and enable you to export them as GPOs for you to test and then deploy.

We'll discuss the SCM tool in Appendix D.

Back Up and Restore for Group Policy

Inadvertently deleting a single GPO can wreak havoc on your domain. Imagine what happens when a bunch of GPOs are inadvertently deleted. Let's just say that the users are suddenly happy because they can do stuff they couldn't normally do, and you're not happy because now *they're* happy. Ironic, isn't it?

It's not just the errant Group Policy deletion that could cause an issue. Another administrator could inadvertently delete a portion of the SYSVOL container on one Domain Controller, which would replicate to all Domain Controllers and quickly damage your GPOs.

In both of these example cases, you'll need a way to restore.

The Backup and Restore functions for GPOs are only meant to work within the same domain. However, you'll see in the section entitled "Migrating Group Policy Objects between Domains" how the GPMC can be used to back up and import a GPO to get the same effect *between* domains.

In our case, if the policy settings inside the "Auto-Launch calc.exe" GPO were wiped out, the name of the GPO can surely help us put it back together. But the name alone might not be an accurate representation of what's going on inside the GPO.

Then, there are still other questions: Where was this GPO linked? What was the security on the GPO? Who owned it?

All said and done, you don't want to get stuck with a deleted or damaged GPO without a backup. Thankfully, the GPMC makes easy work of the once laborious task of backing up and restoring GPOs.

These techniques are valid for both all types and all configurations of Active Directory. So, back up those GPOs today with the GPMC regardless of your domain structure!

Backing Up Group Policy Objects

When you back up a GPO within the GPMC, you also back up a lot of important data:

- The settings inside the GPO.

- The permissions on that GPO (that is, the stuff inside the Delegation tab).

- The link to the WMI filter—however, the actual filter itself is not preserved. (Again, I'll talk about WMI filters in Chapter 4.)

However, it's also important to know what won't be backed up:

- Any WMI filters contained within Active Directory. You must back them up separately. You can see one way to do this in the section "Backing Up and Restoring WMI Filters" later in this chapter.

- IPsec settings themselves aren't backed up via the GPMC Backup and Restore function. They are backed up during a Domain Controller's System State backup. But discussing backing up and restoring them is a bit beyond the scope of this book. My best suggestion: manually document any GPOs with IPsec settings.

- GPO links aren't specifically backed up. Yes, you read that right. But before you panic, let me first explain how this is for your own protection. We'll examine this phenomenon in a bit and try to make you a believer in why this is a good thing.

As you'll learn in Chapter 7, there are two parts of GPOs: the GPT (Group Policy Template) from Active Directory and the GPC (Group Policy Container) from within the SYSVOL. When a backup is performed, the GPT and GPC are wrapped up and placed as a set of files that can be stored or transported.

What's additionally neat is that contained within the backup is a report of the settings inside that GPO you just backed up. So, if someone backs up a GPO named Sounds (again, a horrible name), you can at least see the report of just what is inside the GPO before you restore it to your domain.

To back up a GPO, you need Read access to that GPO, as shown earlier in Figure 2.18. You can start by locating the GPO node in the GPMC and right-clicking it. Select either Back Up All or Manage Backups. For this first time, select Back Up All.

You then select the location for the backup (hopefully someplace secure) and click Backup. You'll then see each GPO being backed up to the target location, as shown in Figure 2.57. When you're finished, you can rest easy (or at least easier) that your GPOs are safe.

You can inspect the directories that the backup produced if you like. You'll see a directory for each GPO, the XML file representing the GPT, and an XML report showing the settings. In the next section, you'll learn how to view the report (easily) by utilizing the View Settings button (shown in Figure 2.58).

FIGURE 2.57   You can back up all your GPOs at once, if desired.

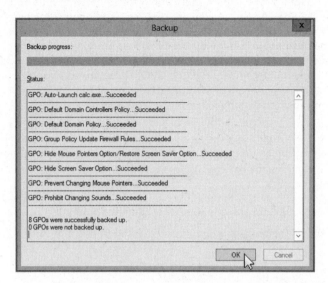

FIGURE 2.58   You can see all backups or just the latest versions.

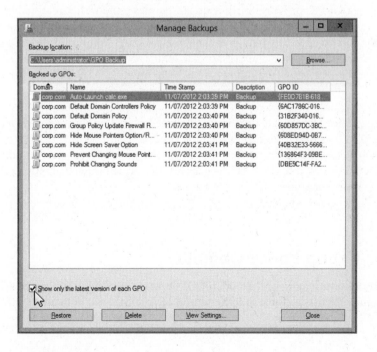

In Chapter 7, you'll learn more about the underlying nuts and bolts of GPOs. Specifically, you'll learn that the underlying name of a GPO relies on a unique GUID name being assigned to the GPO. What isn't immediately obvious here is that the directory names produced by the backup (which take the form of GUIDs) are *not* the same GUIDs that are used for the underlying identification of the GPO. These are additional, unique, random GUID directory names generated just for backup. This seemingly bizarre contradiction becomes useful—just read on.

You can also use PowerShell to perform a backup of all GPOs all in one shot. This assumes you have a backup folder ready and waiting—for instance, a folder named C:\GpoBackups. You can give the backup an optional comment as well. The PowerShell command would be:

```
Backup-Gpo -All -Path C:\GpoBackups -Comment "My First Backup"
```

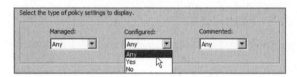

PowerShell shows each Group Policy Object as its being backed up.

The backup (via GPMC or PowerShell) is quick, painless, and rather reasonably sized. The best part about the backup facility is that it's flexible. When you choose to run your next backup, you can keep your backups in the same directory you just chose, and you'll keep a history of the GPOs, should anything change. It's the underlying random and unique GUID names for the directories that allow you to keep plowing more GPO backups right into the same backup directory—there's no fear of overlap. Or you can keep the backups in their own directory; it's your choice.

If you dare, go ahead and delete the "Hide Mouse Pointers Option/Restore Screen Saver Option" GPO. You'll restore it in the next section (I hope).

Now that you've backed up the whole caboodle, it should also be noted that you can back up just a solitary GPO. Right-click the *actual* GPO (which is located only in the Group Policy Objects container) and choose Backup.

Be sure the place where you back up your GPOs is safe and that you can get to it in a pinch.

Restoring Group Policy Objects

The restore process is just as easy. It works for GPOs that were backed up in the same domain. Note that it's also possible to back up and restore between domains, but this is called a GPO Migration (see later in the chapter, "Migrating Group Policy Objects between Domains").

When you restore a GPO, the file object you created in the backup process is "unrolled" and placed within Active Directory. As you would expect, the following key elements are preserved:

- The settings inside the GPO
- The friendly name (which comes back from the dead)
- The GUID (which comes back from the dead)
- The security and permissions on that object (which come back from the dead)
- The link to WMI filters (which comes back from the dead)

 Whomping a GPO doesn't delete any WMI filters associated with a GPO itself. Any WMI filters are stored in a separate place in Active Directory. It's sort of like the Jacuzzi next to the swimming pool.

The GPO does not have to be deleted to do a restore. For instance, if someone changed the settings and you want to simply restore the GPO to get an older version of the policy settings, you can certainly restore over an existing GPO to put a previously known "good" version back in play.

Restoring GPOs requires the following security rights:

- If you want to restore on top of a GPO that already exists, you need Edit, Delete, and Modify rights, as seen back in Figure 2.18.
- If you want to restore a deleted GPO, you need to be a member of the Group Policy Creator Owners (or Domain Admins or Enterprise Admins) security group.

Warning: A Deleted GPO's Links Are Not Restored!

Assuming you went ahead in the last example and deleted the "Hide Mouse Pointers Option/Restore Screen Saver Option" GPO and are now ready to restore it, there is something you need to know before proceeding. One critical item is missing: the Group Policy links to the GPO are *not* restored in this operation. The location of links is backed up, but during a restore, the links are *not* restored. You might be scratching your head wondering why this is.

Let's examine a theoretical timeline:

- On Day 0, a GPO named Sounds is linked to two OUs named **Doctors** and **Nurses**.

- On Day 1, the GPO is backed up.

- On Day 2, a fellow administrator unlinks the GPO from **Doctors**. Now, the GPO is linked only to **Nurses**.

- On Day 3, someone deletes the whole GPO (and hence its links).

- On Day 4, someone recognizes this deletion and restores the GPO.

Here's the $50,000 question: upon restore, where should the links be restored to?

Should the links be restored back to the last way it was *just before* the catastrophe on Day 3? Sure, that would be ideal, but how would the system know what happened between Day 2 and Day 4? As it is, on Day 4, the GPO is now linked *only* to **Nurses**, but how could the system know that now?

Should it link the GPO back to the *original* locations, as it was on Day 1? On Day 1, it was linked to **Doctors** and **Nurses**. But restoring those links to the same location could be a catastrophic mistake. Clearly, on Day 2 an administrator unlinked it from **Doctors** for some good reason! Restoring the link back on the **Doctors** could be detrimental to their health!

Instead of restoring the links, the GPMC does the smartest thing it can do during a restore: it doesn't restore the links. That's right—by not restoring the links, it ensures that you're not inadvertently relinking the GPO back to some location in Active Directory that shouldn't have it anymore.

However, as stated, the backup process does record where the links were at the time of backup. To that end, you can easily see where the links were at the time of backup, and if desired, you can manually relink the GPO back to the locations you want. To see where a GPO had links at backup time, here's what to do:

1. Right-click over the Group Policy Objects node and select Manage Backups.

2. In the Manage Backups dialog box, ensure that you're looking at the directory with the contents of the backup.

3. Locate and then select the GPO that was deleted.

4. Click the View Settings button (seen earlier in Figure 2.58).

A report will be generated that, among other things, shows you where the GPO was linked. Then, once the GPO is restored, you can manually relink it where you need it to be linked.

You can start a restore by right-clicking the Group Policy Objects container and choosing Manage Backups. You'll be able to select a location that will house your GPO backups; you might have multiple locations.

If you've chosen to keep backing up the GPOs into the same backup directory, you can select the "Show only the latest version of each GPO" option, which shows you only the last backed-up version. If you've forgotten what is contained in a backup, click the backup name and choose View Settings. You can see these options in Figure 2.58.

When you're ready, click the GPO to restore, and then click Restore. It's really that easy.

You can also right-click the GPO itself (found only in the Group Policy Objects container) and choose "Restore from Backup," which in fact performs the same function.

You can also use PowerShell to restore a Group Policy Object. But there's a little (well, big) catch. Just now, we used the GUI to restore a Group Policy Object: if it was fully deleted, or if it just needed its guts returned from an errant mistake.

If you want to use PowerShell to restore a Group Policy Object, the Group Policy Object cannot be deleted. Said another way, a "restore" of a Group Policy Object requires that you have in place a Group Policy Object of the *same name*.

Only then can you overwrite its contents and restore it.

It's easiest if you know the GPO's name (though, technically you could restore by GUID):

```
Restore-GPO -Name "GPO123" -Path C:\GPOBackups
```

The Group Policy Object's contents are restored to that existing Group Policy Object (GPO123), which is already in place (that is, not already deleted), as seen here:

```
PS C:\Users\Administrator> Restore-GPO -Name "GPO123" -Path C:\GPObackups

DisplayName       : GPO123
DomainName        : corp.com
Owner             : CORP\Domain Admins
Id                : 4b01bfdf-27b9-413d-bbc8-bc061f401139
GpoStatus         : AllSettingsEnabled
Description       :
CreationTime      : 1/24/2015 7:57:30 AM
ModificationTime  : 1/24/2015 7:57:30 AM
UserVersion       : AD Version: 1, SysVol Version: 1
ComputerVersion   : AD Version: 1, SysVol Version: 1
WmiFilter         :
```

If you have a situation where you've deleted the Group Policy Object, then want to use the `Restore-GPO` cmdlet, it's not going to immediately work. Here's what you get in return when trying to restore a Group Policy Object that has been deleted:

```
PS C:\Users\Administrator> Restore-GPO -Name "GPO123" -Path c:\GPOBackups
Restore-GPO : The "GPO123" GPO was not found in the corp.com domain.
Parameter name: gpoDisplayName
At line:1 char:1
+ Restore-GPO -Name "GPO123" -Path c:\GPOBackups
+ ~~~~~~~~~~~~~~~~~~~~~~~~~~~~~~~~~~~~~~~~~~~~~~~~
    + CategoryInfo          : ObjectNotFound: (Microsoft.GroupPolicy.GPDomain:GPDomain) [Rest
   ore-GPO], ArgumentException
    + FullyQualifiedErrorId : GpoWithNameNotFound,Microsoft.GroupPolicy.Commands.RestoreGpoCo
   mmand
```

Instead, create a totally blank, new Group Policy Object with the same name. Use the GPMC or PowerShell. Then restore the Group Policy Object's contents using PowerShell. You can see me creating the Group Policy Object with the same name and then restoring it here:

```
PS C:\Users\Administrator> Restore-GPO -Name "GPO123" -Path c:\GPOBackups
Restore-GPO : The "GPO123" GPO was not found in the corp.com domain.
Parameter name: gpoDisplayName
At line:1 char:1
+ Restore-GPO -Name "GPO123" -Path c:\GPOBackups
+ ~~~~~~~~~~~~~~~~~~~~~~~~~~~~~~~~~~~~~~~~~~~~~~~~
    + CategoryInfo          : ObjectNotFound: (Microsoft.GroupPolicy.GPDomain:GPDomain) [Rest
   ore-GPO], ArgumentException
    + FullyQualifiedErrorId : GpoWithNameNotFound,Microsoft.GroupPolicy.Commands.RestoreGpoCo
   mmand
```

Here's the very, very weird part: If you go back to the GPMC, you'll see there are now *two* GPOs with the *same name*. One will be empty. It's the totally new one you created right before the restore (see the example on the left). The second one will have the restored contents (see the example on the right).

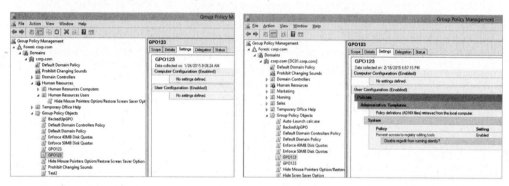

I think this is just a bug in the PowerShell `Restore-GPO` routine. To compensate, merely delete the empty Group Policy Object that needed to be there in order to perform the name match before the restore.

Note, though, that you can do this in one step; well, one step after you create the blank, new Group Policy Object. It's using the `Import-GPO` cmdlet, which is explained a little later. It's a lot like the `Restore-GPO` cmdlet, as you'll see in that section.

Backing Up and Restoring Starter GPOs

We just covered backing up and restoring GPOs. However, it should be noted that the backup you normally do to protect yourself from GPO deletion, corruption, and plain ol' stupidity doesn't protect you here regarding Starter GPOs.

You'll have to occasionally right-click on the Starter GPOs node and select Backup. When you do, you'll be able to back up the Starter GPOs quite like backing up normal GPOs. You can see an example in Figure 2.59.

FIGURE 2.59 Backing up Starter GPOs is similar to backing up regular GPOs.

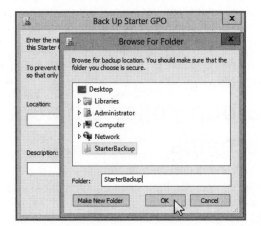

Other functions like Restore are completely analogous to what you just learned.

 Right now, there's no published scriptable interface for backing up and restoring Starter GPOs.

Backing Up and Restoring WMI Filters

As you read about WMI filters in Chapter 4 and learn what a pain in the tush they are to create, you'll be thankful that there's a mechanism that can back up and restore them. They are not backed up or restored in the process we just used. Rather, you must individually back up each WMI filter. Simply right-click the filter and choose Export. To restore, right-click the WMI Filters node and choose Import. Sometimes restoring a WMI filter adds excess and invalid characters to the query. Simply re-edit the query and clean up the characters and you're back in business.

In the previous section, you saw that GPO links are not restored when the GPO is restored. The same is true for WMI filters: the WMI filter links are not restored when the WMI filter is restored. Again, for information on how to automatically document this information, see Chapter 4.

Backing Up and Restoring IPsec Filters

As stated earlier, IPsec filters are not maintained as part of the normal Group Policy backup. I know—it's weird. We don't go much into IPsec policies in this book. But, in short, you create and configure IPsec policies using the Group Policy interface, but they're not stored inside the GPO itself.

With that in mind, to ensure your IPsec policies are backed up, use the IP Security Policy Management console, an MMC snap-in. Then use the All tasks ➤ Export Policies and All tasks ➤ Import Policies commands to, well, export and/or import.

It's still important to back up the GPOs that contain IPsec filters so you can "reconnect" a restored GPO to an IPsec filter—and also so you can "reconnect" a restored IPsec policy to a GPO.

Migrating Group Policy Objects between Domains

What you learned in the last section was Backup and Restore for Group Policy Objects. You might also have the need, however, to take a Group Policy Object (or multiple GPOs) that is born in one domain and get it over to another domain.

This can occur if you have multiple domains in the same forest and you want to take an existing Group Policy Object and utilize it in another domain. Or, this can be a test lab where you have an existing Group Policy Object and want to get your work from that test lab into production. That test lab could be connected to the live network (perhaps another domain in the same forest) or completely disconnected and "air gapped" from the live network.

The GPMC supports all these functions, and that's what we'll explore now. Note that in the following sections, I'll demonstrate fictitious domains that you won't have in your test lab.

Basic Interdomain Copy and Import

Using the GPMC, you can take existing GPOs from any domain and copy them to another domain. The target domain can be a parent domain, a child domain, a cross-forest domain, or a completely foreign domain that has no trusts. Both the Copy and the Import operations transfer only the policy settings; these operations do not modify either the source or the destination links of the GPOs.

The Copy Operation

The interdomain Copy operation is meant to be used when you want to copy live GPOs from one domain to another. That is, you have two domains, connectivity between them, and appropriate rights to the GPOs. To copy the GPO, you need Read rights on the source GPO you want to copy and Write rights in the target domain.

An example of this can be seen in Figure 2.60. Corp.com and Widgets.corp.com are two domains in the same forest.

FIGURE 2.60 If two domains are in the same forest and have connectivity, you can copy GPOs between them.

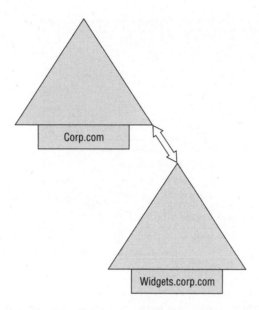

To get started, you'll want to tweak your GPMC console so that you can see the two domains you want. Using the GPMC, you right-click Domains and choose Show Domains from the context menu, as seen in Figure 2.61, to open the Show Domains dialog box. Then, select the domains you want to see. To add other forests, right-click Group Policy Management and choose Add Forest from the context menu (as seen in Figure 2.62) to open the Add Forest dialog box. You can then enter the name of the domain in the forest.

In this first example, we'll copy a GPO from Corp.com to Widgets.corp.com. An Enterprise Administrator will have rights in all domains. For instance, an Enterprise Administrator would have rights in Corp.com (to read) and Widgets.corp.com (to write). Follow these steps:

1. In the Group Policy Objects container, right-click the GPO you want to copy, as shown in Figure 2.63. For this example, I've chosen the "Hide Mouse Pointers Option/Restore Screen Saver Tab" GPO.

2. Adjust your view of the GPMC so that you can see the target domain and its Group Policy Object container.

3. Right-click the target domain's Group Policy Objects container, and choose Paste to start the Cross-Domain Copying Wizard.

4. Click Next to bypass the initial splash screen and open the "Copy GPO" screen, shown in Figure 2.64.

FIGURE 2.61   The GPMC will only show your own domain by default. Use the Show Domains command to see other domains.

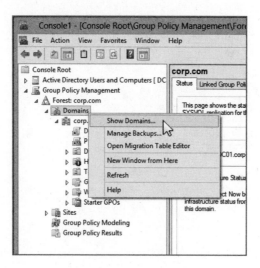

FIGURE 2.62   The GPMC can be told to look for other domains within other forests, as seen here.

FIGURE 2.63 You can copy a GPO from the Group Policy Objects container.

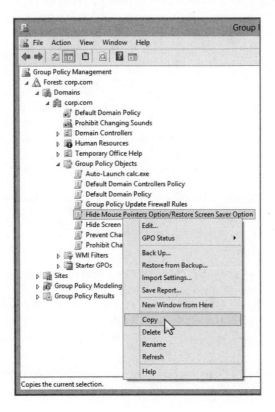

FIGURE 2.64 When you paste a GPO, you can choose how to handle permissions.

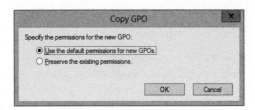

You can now choose to create a GPO with the default permissions or to copy the original permissions to the new GPO. The latter might be useful if you've delegated some special permissions to that GPO and don't want to redo your efforts. Most of the time, however, the first option is fine. You can now zip through the rest of the wizard.

You might see a message about migration tables. Don't fret; they're right around the corner. For this specific GPO, you won't need migration tables, so it won't be an issue.

If you copy a GPO between domains, the WMI filtering is lost because the WMI filter won't necessarily exist in the target domain.

PowerShell can also copy a Group Policy Object from one domain to another. The cmdlet is Copy-GPO. Here's an example copying a Group Policy Object named GPO123 from Corp.com and giving it a new name, MyGPO123, in Widgets.corp.com.

```
Copy-GPO -SourceName GPO123 -SourceDomain corp.com TargetName MyGPO123
-TargetDomain widgets.corp.com
```

The Import Operation

In the previous scenario, we copied a GPO from Corp.com to Widgets.corp.com. We did this when both domains were online and accessible.

But take a look at a different example, say, in Figure 2.65. In this example, the two domains, Corp.com and Testlab.internal.com, have no connectivity. Testlab.internal.com could be in a closet somewhere, completely isolated from the real live production network.

FIGURE 2.65 GPOs can still be migrated between unrelated domains.

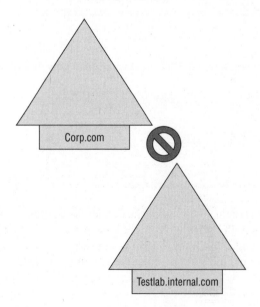

So, how, then, do you take a GPO you created in the isolated test lab and bring it into production? First, create a backup, as described in the earlier section "Back Up and Restore for Group Policy." You'll then have a collection of files that you can put on a USB stick and take out into the real world. You can then create a brand-new GPO (or overwrite an existing GPO) and perform the import! Follow these steps:

1. Right-click the Group Policy Objects container, choose New from the context menu to open the New GPO dialog box, and in the Name Field, enter the name of a new GPO.

2. Right-click that GPO and choose Import Settings from the context menu, as shown in Figure 2.66. This starts the Import Settings Wizard.

FIGURE 2.66   You can import the settings and overwrite an existing GPO.

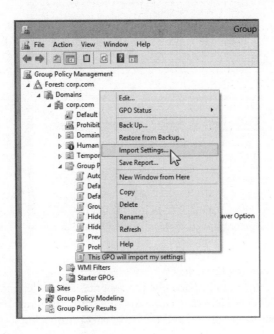

Anyone with Edit rights on the GPO can perform an Import.

You can choose to overwrite an existing GPO, but that's just it. It's an overwrite, not a merge. So, be careful!

3. The wizard then presents the Backup GPO screen, which allows you to back up the newly created GPO; however, this is unnecessary. Backing up is a safety measure should you decide to overwrite an existing GPO. You can then click Next to see the Backup Location screen.

4. In the Backup Location screen, use the "Backup folder" field to input the path to where your backup set is and click Next. The Source GPO screen will appear.

5. At the Source GPO screen, select the GPO from which you want to import settings, as shown in Figure 2.67, and click Next.

FIGURE 2.67   Select a GPO from which you want to import settings.

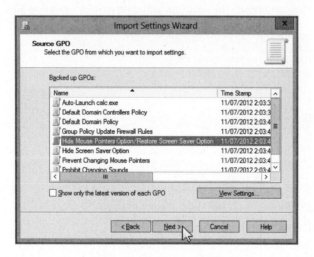

You should now be able to zip through the rest of the wizard. Ignore any references to migration tables; they're coming up next.

PowerShell can also perform an import. Use the `Import-GPO` cmdlet and point toward the name of the Group Policy Object that's already backed up, the name of the Group Policy Object you're about to import to, and the path where the backup is stored:

```
Import-GPO –BackupGpoName BackedUpGPO –TargetName GPO123 –path C:\GPObackups
```

A Word about Drag and Drop

Dragging and dropping a GPO from one domain into another domain can be hazardous. For example, your intention is to copy a GPO named "Restrict Solitaire" from the GPO container in Widgets.corp.com to the **Human Resources Users** OU in Corp.com. It looks like it's going to make sense: You set up your view in the GPMC to show both domains, you can see the Group Policy Objects container in Widgets.corp.com, and you can see the **Human Resources Users** OU in Corp.com. Then, you drag and drop, and you're asked the following question:

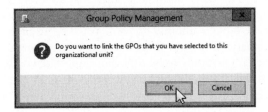

If you click OK, you're not actually copying! Indeed, you're performing a no-no! You are creating a cross-domain link to the GPO, as you can see when you click the Scope tab of the GPO:

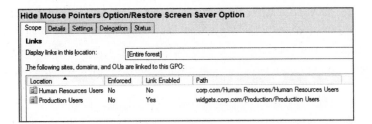

In this example, the Domain field shows that it lives in Widgets.corp.com, even though the GPO is linked to an OU in Corp.com.

Whenever a GPO is linked from across a domain, the GPO must be pulled from a Domain Controller that actually houses it. If it's across the WAN, so be it. And that could mean major slowdowns.

The moral of the story is to be sure you're copying (as described earlier) and not just linking.

Copy and Import with Migration Tables

Basic Backup and Import will work for many scenarios, but, unfortunately, not all of them.

When you create GPOs, occasionally those GPOs will have references to security groups or UNC paths. For instance, in your test lab, you might create a Group Policy Object that has references only to stuff that could be valid inside your test lab and not your real world.

Policy setting types that could have Security Group or UNC references are Folder Redirection, Restricted Groups, Group Policy Software Installation policy settings, and pointers to scripts. If any of these items is in the Testlab.internal.com domain, how will you be able to use it in your live Corp.com domain?

With that in mind, both the Copy and Import functions can leverage *migration tables*. Migration tables let you rectify both security group and UNC references that exist in a GPO when you transfer the GPO to another domain. You'll be given the opportunity to use the migration tables automatically if your Copy or Import operation detects that a policy setting needs it. After the GPO is ready to be copied or imported, you'll be notified that some adjustments are needed. It's that easy.

In the Migrating References screen of the wizard (shown in Figure 2.68), you can choose two paths.

- Selecting "Copying them identically from the source" can be risky. Again, you won't know what the source is using for security groups or UNC paths. The existing security groups and UNC paths may be valid, but they may not be.

- Selecting "Using this migration table to map them in the destination GPO" gives you the opportunity to choose an existing migration table (if you have one), or you can click the New button to open the Migration Table Editor and create one on the fly.

FIGURE 2.68   A migration table can smooth the bumps between domains.

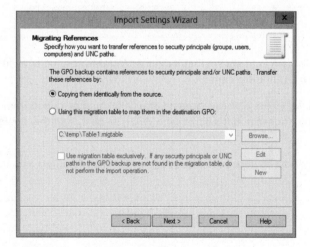

To start, use a new blank migration table (after clicking the New button) and follow these steps:

1. If you're performing a Copy, choose Tools ➢ Populate from GPO to open the Select GPO screen; then select the live GPO. If you're performing an Import, choose Tools ➢ "Populate from Backup" to open the Select Backup dialog box, which allows you to select a GPO from backup.

2. Choose the GPO you're copying or importing to display a list of all the references that need to be corrected.

3. In Figure 2.69, you can see both the Source Name and the Destination Name fields. The Source Name field will automatically be filled in. All that's left is to enter the Destination Name UNC path for the new environment and you're done.

FIGURE 2.69   Enter the UNC paths or other items from the source domain in the Source Name column and the names for the destination in the Destination Name column.

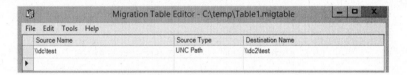

4. Save the file (with a `.migtable` filename extension), and close the Migration Table Editor—New screen.

5. Back at the Migrating References page, click Browse and choose the migration table you just made.

Before clicking the Next button, you can optionally choose the check box that begins with "Use migration table exclusively." In this example, we have but one UNC reference that needs to be rectified. You might have a meaty GPO with 30 UNC paths and another 50 security principals that need to be cleared up. Perhaps you can't locate all the destination names. If you select this check box, the wizard will not proceed unless all the paths in the destination name are valid. Use this setting if you need to be sure all settings will be verified successfully.

When ready, click Next. Click Next again at the summary screen, and you're finished.

PowerShell can also perform an import using a migration table. The migration table file needs to exist already (use the GUI for that since it's easiest). You can do that fast by right-clicking upon the Group Policy Objects folder, as seen here.

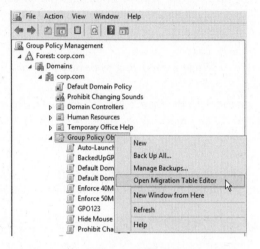

Then after that, simply tack on the -MigrationTable parameter to the Import-GPO cmdlet, as seen here:

```
Import-GPO -BackupGpoName GPO123 -TargetName GPO123 -path C:\GPOBackups
-MigrationTable C:\Temp\Table1.Migtable
```

The result you'll get is similar to what was seen earlier when you imported a Group Policy Object without the migration table, so we'll save space and not show the screen shot here.

The only downside is that migration tables do not honor or care about anything in the Group Policy Preferences. So, if you have references in the original (source) domain, they are usually just copied through, without any possibility of translating them via a migration table. Note that Microsoft's pay product, AGPM 4.0, does have the ability to migrate between domains and includes support for Group Policy Preferences.

Wholesale Backup and Restore of Your Test Lab (or an Easy Way to Migrate to Production)

One more tip before we leave this section: when you're working in your test lab, you might find it necessary to completely demolish and rebuild it for a variety of reasons. However, as noted in this chapter, when a GPO is restored, the links are not restored along with it. Again, this is a protection mechanism for your benefit. However, as they say in the hallowed IT halls, "What you do in the test lab stays in the test lab." So, the test lab is a different animal. And, to that end, you might want to back up a whole gaggle of stuff for safekeeping:

- GPOs
- Group Policy links
- Security groups
- OUs
- Users
- Permissions on GPOs

Then, if you need to demolish your test lab and put it back in order, you'll need a way to perform a wholesale restore of all these objects. The GPMC has a built-in script that will back up all these things into one little package. Then, when you're ready, you run another script that takes the package and expands it back into these objects.

The script that does all the backup stuff is called `CreateXMLFromEnvironment.vbs`. The one that does all the restoring is `CreateEnvironmentFromXML.vbs`. Both scripts are available for download at `http://tinyurl.com/2quhw5`.

The other reason to use these scripts is to do a wholesale migration from the test lab into the real production environment. Personally, I'm not all that keen on a wholesale backup and restore of my test lab into the real world, but I guess if you had nothing at all in the real world, this could be a useful way to get things over lock, stock, and barrel.

Microsoft has various documents about this script, so check out `www.microsoft.com` for some tips about using it. For instance, there's a Microsoft Knowledge Base article on this script at `http://support.microsoft.com/kb/929397`.

GPMC At-a-Glance Icon View

Because the GPMC contains so many icon types, it can be difficult to know specifically what an icon represents. That's what Table 2.2 is all about.

TABLE 2.2 GPMC icon list

Icon	Description	What the icon means
	Scroll.	A GPO itself. You'll only see this in the Group Policy Objects container.
	Scroll with arrow.	A link to an actual GPO.
	Scroll with arrow. Just the arrow is dimmed.	A GPO link that has Link Status disabled.
	Scroll with arrow. The whole icon is dimmed.	A link has been disabled and also the GPO status (on the Details tab) has been set to "All settings disabled."
	Scroll. The whole icon is dimmed.	A GPO whose status (on the Details tab) has been set to "All settings disabled."
	Scroll with arrow; additional lock icon.	Enforced link.
	Blue exclamation point.	Block inheritance at this level.
	Folder with scroll.	Group Policy Objects container that actually holds the GPOs themselves.
	Folder with filter.	WMI Filters node.
	Filter.	A WMI filter.

Final Thoughts

We explored all the major features of the GPMC in this chapter. And we did it using the GPMC's clickety-clicks and using PowerShell with some typety-type. You'll mostly use the GPMC for one-time operations, but it's also good to know the PowerShell equivalents for items you'll use again and again.

Switching gears a little bit, while using the GPMC throughout this chapter, you ran queries and created several reports. What you possibly didn't know is that all that time you were creating HTML reports you can use to document your environment.

So any time you see a Group Policy settings report, you can right-click anywhere in the report and choose Save Report. Since these reports are standard HTML, you have an incredibly easy way to document just about every aspect of your Group Policy universe.

Backing up and restoring with the GPMC is simply awesome. But as you'll recall, when you restore a deleted GPO, you don't restore the links. You'll have to bring them back manually. Having good backups and good documentation about where each GPO is linked will always be your ace in the hole.

Remember that the best GPMC version you can use is always the "latest, greatest"—whatever that is. Today, it's Windows Server 2016 or Windows 10 client with RSAT installed.

Here are some parting tips for daily Group Policy Object management with the GPMC:

Use Block Inheritance and Enforced sparingly.   The less you use these features, the easier it will be to debug the application of settings. Figuring out at which level in the hierarchy one administrator has Blocked Inheritance and another has declared Enforced can eat up days of fun at the office. The GPMC makes it easier to see what's going on, but still, minimize your use of these two attributes.

Remember what can only be applied at the link.   Three and only three attributes are set on a GPO link: "Link Enable" (enable or disable the settings to apply at this level), "Enforce" the link (and force the policy settings), and "Delete" the link.

Remember what can be applied only on the actual GPO itself.   The following attributes must be set on the GPO itself: the policies and settings inside the GPO (found on the Settings tab), Security filters, permissions (as in the "Apply Group Policy" permission), delegation (as in the "Edit this GPO" permission), Enabling/Disabling half (or both halves) of the GPO via the GPO status (found on the Details tab), and WMI filtering (discussed in Chapter 4).

Remember that Group Policy is notoriously tough to debug.   Once you start linking GPOs at multiple levels, throwing in a Block Inheritance, an Enforced, and a filter or two, you're up to your eyeballs in troubleshooting. The best thing you can do is document the heck out of your GPOs. The GPMC helps you determine what a GPO does in the Settings tab, but your documentation will be your sanity check when trying to figure things out.

3

Group Policy Processing Behavior Essentials

After you create or modify a GPO in the domain, the policy's "wishes" are not immediately dropped on the target machines. In fact, they're not dropped on the target machines at all; they're requested by the client computer at various times throughout the day. GPOs are processed at specific times, based on various conditions. You could basically say that GPOs are created from your management machine and plopped on the Domain Controllers for storage. Then those GPOs are simply "pulled" by the client.

It's likely that you have all sorts of client systems, including Windows 7, Windows 8.1, Windows 10, maybe some Windows XP left behind, and various Windows Servers. So, again, when I say "client system" I mean "the client that receives Group Policy"—even if it's a server operating system. Each operating system that receives Group Policy instructions processes Group Policy at different times in different ways. With different operating systems requesting different things at different times, the expected behaviors can get confusing quickly.

Additionally, other factors determine when and how a GPO applies. When users dial in over slow links, things can be—and usually are—different. And you can instruct the Group Policy engine (on a specific computer or all computers) to forgo its out-of-the-box processing behaviors for a customized (and often more secure) way to process.

Often, people throw up their hands when the Group Policy engine doesn't seem to process the dictated GPOs in an expected manner. Group Policy doesn't just process when it wants to; rather, it adheres to a strict set of processing rules. The goal of this chapter and the next is to answer this question: When does Group Policy apply?

Understanding the processing rules will help you better understand when Group Policy processes GPOs the way it does. Then, in Chapter 7, "Troubleshooting Group Policy," you'll get a grip on why and how Group Policy applies. Between these chapters, your goal is to discover how Group Policy can apply under different circumstances and how you can become a better Group Policy troubleshooter.

Group Policy Processing Principles

For you to best understand how modern Windows processes GPOs, I'll first describe how Windows 2000 does its thing.

"What? That's lunacy!" I hear you cry. "Here it is, the year 2015," or later, I suppose, depending on when you're reading this. "And you, Moskowitz, have the audacity to explain to me how a 15-year-old operating system works? Get modern, Mr. Caveman." Seriously. I can hear you—right now. It's like I'm right there.

Anyway, I know it's weird. But since Windows 2000 came out first, its behavior is critically important—especially because (and here's the punch line) I think you'll want to make at least some of your XP (or later) machines act like Windows 2000 by the time you're done reading this section.

You've read that right: I'm guessing you'll want to make your XP and later machines, like Windows 10 desktops, act like the 15-year-old Windows 2000 operating system.

Trust me. You'll want to learn how Windows 2000 does its thing first before trying to understand the rest of the family.

Sure, Windows Servers, like Windows Server 2008, Windows Server 2012, and Windows Server 2016, also process GPOs as a Group Policy client. I'll pepper in that information when necessary. But, as you're reading along, try to focus on the typical client computer.

To get a feel for how GPO processing works, we're going to walk through what happens to four users:

- Wally, who uses only a Windows 2000 Professional machine.

- Xavier, who uses only a Windows XP machine.

- Sven, who uses only a Windows 7 machine. Get it? Sven on Seven? I slay myself. But anyway: Sven could also be using a Windows 8 machine—there is no difference in Group Policy processing between a Windows 7 and a Windows 8 machine.

- Ben, who uses a Windows 10 machine. Note that Ben could be using a Windows 8.1 machine, too. Said another way, the Group Policy "engine" got updated with Windows 8.1, but we'll be using Ben on Windows 10. ("Ben on Ten," get it?)

By using Wally, Xavier, and Sven, and Ben as our four sample users (on our four sample computers), we can see precisely when Group Policy applies to them based on their machines.

Before we go even one step further, let me debunk a popular myth about Group Policy processing: Group Policy is never *pushed* from the server and forced on the clients. Rather, the process is quite the opposite. Group Policy occurs when the Group Policy engine on a Windows client requests Group Policy. This happens at various times, but at no time can you magically declare from on high, "All clients! Go forth and accept my latest GPOs!" It doesn't work like that. Clients request GPOs according to the rules listed in this chapter.

As always, however, there is an exception to the rule, and we will cover that later in this chapter in the section "Manually Forcing Background Policy Processing (Remote *GPUpdate*)," where we talk about Group Policy Update. Even though this seems like a feature that allows administrators to push out a policy update, it's still technically just triggering a pull from the server.

In a nutshell, Group Policy is potentially triggered to apply at four times (and one special case we need to cover). Here's a rundown of those times; I'll discuss them in grueling detail in the next sections.

Initial Policy Processing   Initial policy processing is a fancy way of saying "the first cycle" of Group Policy. That first cycle happens for computers at startup time and for users at logon time.

Background Refresh Policy Processing (Member Computers)   Member machines (that is, non–Domain Controllers) check in with the Domain Controller to see if there are any new or changed Group Policy Objects. This occurs some time after the computer starts up and also for the user after the user logs on (usually at 90-minute intervals or so). A bit later, you'll see how Windows XP and later (like Windows 10) leverage the background policy processing mechanism to a distinct advantage.

Background Refresh Policy Processing (Domain Controllers)   Domain Controllers need love, too, and to that end, all Domain Controllers perform a background refresh every five minutes (after replication has occurred).

Security Policy Processing   For all operating systems, only the security settings within all GPOs are reprocessed and applied every 16 hours regardless of whether they have changed. This safety mechanism prevents unscrupulous local workstation administrators from doing too much harm.

> You can change the default behavior of certain nonsecurity policy settings so they are enforced in a manner similar to the way security settings are automatically enforced. But you have to explicitly turn this feature on, and you have to do so correctly. In the section "Mandatory Reapplication for Nonsecurity Policy," later in this chapter, I describe how to do this and give you several examples of why you would want to do so.

Special Case: Moving a User or Computer Object   Although all the previous items demonstrate a trigger of when Group Policy applies, one case isn't trigger specific; however, it's important to understand a special case of Group Policy processing behavior. You might think that if you move a user or computer around in Active Directory (specifically, from one OU to another), then Group Policy is set to reapply—the system would "know" it's been moved around in Active Directory. But that doesn't happen. When you move a user or a computer from one OU to another, background processing may not immediately understand that something was moved. Some time later, the system should detect the change, and background processing should start normally again.

Don't Get Lost

There are definitely nuances in the processing mechanism among the various operating systems. The good news, if your head starts to swim a bit, is that you can dog-ear this page and highlight this little area for quick reference. If you remember one takeaway from this chapter, it should be that target computers fall into these four behavior types:

Behavior Type 1   Windows 2000 Professional workstations, Windows 2000 member servers through Windows Server 2016 member servers

Behavior Type 2   Domain Controllers of all sorts: Windows 2000 through Windows Server 2016

Behavior Type 3   Windows XP and later, like Windows 7 and 8—though, Windows 8 does have a little trick up its sleeve, as discussed here

Behavior Type 4   Windows 8.1 and later, like Windows 8.1 and Windows 10

It's important to understand the difference between these four behavior types. And once you understand the difference between them, you can decide if you want to take the machines that are in Behavior Types 3 and 4 and make them act like machines that are in Behavior Type 1.

By now, you have likely expunged Windows 2000 systems from your domain. However, I strongly encourage you to read about how all systems are processed.

I recommend this for three reasons:

- The behaviors described in the following sections are all based on the original "baseline" Windows 2000 behavior.

- It's easier to understand the modern Windows behavior if you understand the original Windows 2000 behavior.

- Later in the chapter I'm going to encourage you to make some of your Windows XP and later machines act like Windows 2000. So, if you don't understand the Windows 2000 behavior, you won't know what I'm talking about.

Initial Policy Processing

Recall that each GPO has two halves: a Computer half and a User half. This is important to remember when trying to understand when GPOs are processed. All machines perform what is called *initial policy processing*. Again, that's just a way of saying "the first time policy is checked for after a computer is rebooted" and "the first time policy is checked for after a user logs on."

But Windows XP and later machines don't exactly perform the same steps as their Windows 2000 counterparts. Let's check it all out.

Windows 2000 (and All Server Types) Initial Policy Processing

Our sample computer user Wally walks into his office and turns on his Windows 2000 Professional machine. The Computer half of the policy is always processed at the target machines upon startup as his machine reboots. When a Windows 2000 or any Windows Server operating system machine starts up, it states that it is "Processing security policy" or "Applying Computer Settings." What this should say is "Processing Group Policy" (but it doesn't).

At that time, the workstation logs onto the network by contacting a Domain Controller. It finds the Domain Controller by looking up DNS records that say, "Hey, here's the name of a Domain Controller." The Domain Controller then tells the workstation which site it belongs to, which domain it belongs to, and which OU it is in. The system then downloads and processes the Computer half of Group Policy in that order. When the processing is finished, the "Press Ctrl+Alt+Delete to begin" prompt is revealed, and Wally can log on by pressing Ctrl+Alt+Delete and giving his username and password.

After Wally is validated to Active Directory, the User half of the GPO is downloaded and then processed in the same precise order: site, domain, and then each nested OU.

Wally's Windows 2000 Desktop is manipulated by the policy settings inside any GPOs targeting Wally's user or computer account. Wally's Desktop is displayed only when all the User-side GPOs are processed.

If you look at how all this goes, you'll see it's a lock-step mechanism. The computer starts up and then processes GPOs in the natural order: local, site, domain, and each nested OU. The user then logs on, and Group Policy is processed, again in the natural order: local, site, domain, and each nested OU. This style of GPO processing is called *synchronous processing*. That is, to proceed to the next step in either the startup or logon process, the previous step must be completed. For example, the GPOs at the OU level of the user are never downloaded and applied before the GPOs at the site level. Likewise, the GPOs at the domain level for Windows 2000 (and Windows Server 2003 and Windows Server 2008) are never downloaded before the site GPOs that affect a computer.

Therefore, the default for Windows 2000 (and all server types—up to and including Windows Server 2012 servers), for both the computer startup and the user logon, is that each GPO is processed synchronously. This same process occurs every time.

Again, this synchronous processing style occurs only for Windows 2000 workstations and all server types (by default).

Windows XP and Later Initial Policy Processing

Xavier walks into his office and turns on his Windows XP machine. For a moment, let's assume this is the *first time* that this Windows XP machine has started up since joining the domain. Perhaps it just landed on Xavier's desk after a new desktop rollout of Windows XP. If this is the case, the Windows XP machine will act just like Windows 2000 (as described earlier). It will look to see which site, domain, and OUs the computer account is in and then apply GPOs synchronously. Likewise, let's assume this is the first time Xavier is logging into this Windows XP machine with his user account, which lives in Active Directory. Again, imagine that this machine just arrived after a desktop rollout. In this case, again,

Windows XP will act like Windows 2000 (and synchronously process GPOs based on the site, domain, and OU Xavier is logging on from).

So far, so good. However, Windows XP performs this initial synchronous processing only in this special case described here. That is, either the computer has never started in the domain before or the user has never logged onto this particular Windows XP machine before.

Sven's experience on Windows 7 will be the same as Xavier's. That is, if Sven walks into his office and turns on his Windows 7 machine for the first time and logs into the machine for the first time, it will act like Windows 2000 and process GPOs synchronously for both the computer (during startup) and the user (during login).

The same thing occurs on Windows 8 and with Ben on Windows 10: The first time the computer is ever turned on after joining the domain, or first logged in, it acts like Windows 2000.

To understand Windows XP and later's normal default processing mode, take a deep breath and read on.

Background Refresh Policy Processing

Wally is logged onto Windows 2000 (or any server operating system, like Windows Server 2008 or Windows Server 2012), and Xavier is logged onto Windows XP, and Sven is plugging along on Windows 7, and Ben on Windows 10 is happy as a clam. Things are great—for everyone. As the administrators, we're happy because Wally, Xavier, Sven, and Ben are all receiving our wishes. They're happy because, well, they're just happy, that's all.

But now we decide to add a new GPO or to modify a policy setting inside an existing GPO. What if something is modified in the Group Policy Management Editor that should affect a user or a computer? Aren't Wally, Xavier, Sven, and Ben already logged on—happy as clams? Well, a new setting is destined for an already-logged-in user or computer, and the new changes (and only the new changes) are indeed reflected on the user or computer that should receive them. But this delivery doesn't happen immediately; rather, the changes are delivered according to the *background refresh interval* (sometimes known as the *background processing interval*).

The background refresh interval dictates how often changed GPOs in Active Directory are pulled by the client computer. As I implied earlier, there are different background intervals for the different operating systems' roles (that is, member versus Domain Controller).

When the background refresh interval comes to pass, GPOs are processed *asynchronously*. That is, if a GPO that affects a user's OU (or other Active Directory level) is changed, the changes are pulled to the local computer when the clock strikes the processing time. It doesn't matter if the change happens at any level in Active Directory: OU, domain, or site. When changes are available to users or computers after the user or computer is already logged on, the changes are processed asynchronously. Whichever GPOs at any level have changed, those changes are reflected on the client.

Standard precedence order is still applied: site, domain, OU. In other words, even though a new GPO linked to a site is ready, it isn't necessarily going to trump a GPO linked to the OU.

When does this happen? According to the background refresh interval for the operating system (discussed next).

Background Refresh Intervals for Windows Member Servers (Any Operating System)

It stands to reason that when we change an existing GPO (or create a new GPO), we want our users and computers to get the latest and greatest set of instructions and wishes. With that in mind, let's continue with our example. Remember that Wally is on his Windows 2000 machine, Xavier is on his Windows XP machine, and Sven is on his Windows 7 machine. And Ben is on his Windows 10 machine.

By default, the background refresh interval for Windows 2000 workstations and for all Windows member servers is 90 minutes, with a 0–30-minute positive random differential added to the mix to ensure that no gaggle of PCs will refresh at any one time and clog your network asking for mass GPO downloads from Domain Controllers. Therefore, once a change has been made to a GPO, it could take as little as 90 minutes or as long as 120 minutes for each user or workstation that is already logged onto the network to see that change.

Microsoft's older documentation isn't consistent in this description. Some older Microsoft documentation will say the offset is 30 minutes (which could be interpreted as positive or negative 30 minutes). Indeed, in the first edition of this book, I incorrectly reported that "fact." However, since then, I have verified with Microsoft that the refresh interval is (and has always been) 90 minutes plus (not minus) 0–30 minutes.

Again, this is known as the background refresh interval. Additionally, the background refresh interval for the Computer half of Group Policy and the User half of Group Policy are on their own independent schedules. That is, the Computer half or the User half might be refreshed before the other half; they're not necessarily refreshed at the exact same moment because they're on their own individual timetables. This makes sense: the computer and user didn't each get Group Policy at the precise moment in time in the first place, did they?

You can change the background refresh interval for the Computer half and/or the User half using Group Policy, as described later in the section cleverly titled "Using Group Policy to Affect Group Policy."

How Does the Group Policy Engine Know What's New or Changed?

The Group Policy engine keeps track of what's new or changed via a control mechanism called *version numbers*. Each GPO has a version number for each half of the GPO, and this is stored in Active Directory. If the version number in Active Directory doesn't change, nothing is downloaded. Since nothing has changed, the Group Policy engine thinks it has all the latest and greatest stuff—so why bother to redownload it (which takes time) and reprocess it (which takes more time)?

By default, when a background refresh interval arrives, a timesaving mechanism, "checking the GPO version numbers," is employed to minimize the time needed to get the latest and greatest GPOs. You'll learn more about GPO version numbers in Chapter 7.

To reiterate, when the background refresh interval arrives, only the new or changed GPOs are downloaded and processed.

You can set individual policy settings to prevent specific areas of Group Policy from being refreshed in the background, such as Internet Explorer Maintenance and Administrative Templates. See the section "Using Group Policy to Affect Group Policy" later in this chapter.

Background Refresh Intervals for Windows Domain Controllers

Even though Wally, Xavier, Sven, and Ben are not logging onto Domain Controllers, other people might. And because Domain Controllers are a bit special, the processing for Domain Controllers is handled in a special way.

Because Group Policy contains sensitive security settings (for example, Password and Account Policy, Kerberos Policy, Audit Policy), any policy geared for a Domain Controller is refreshed within 5 minutes. This adds a tighter level of security to Domain Controllers. For more information on precisely how the default GPOs work, see Chapter 8, "Implementing Security with Group Policy.

You can change the background interval for Domain Controllers using Group Policy (as described later in the section "Using Group Policy to Affect Group Policy"). However, you shouldn't mess with the default values here—they work pretty well.

You'll learn more about affecting Domain Controllers' security in Chapter 8.

Background Refresh Exemptions and Special Cases

Wally has been logged onto his Windows 2000 machine for four hours. Xavier has been logged onto his Windows XP machine, and both Sven (on Windows 7) and Ben (on Windows 10) have been logged on for the same amount of time. Clearly, the background refresh interval has come and gone—somewhere between two and three times.

If any GPOs had been created or any existing GPOs had changed while Wally, Xavier, Sven, and Ben were logged on, both their user accounts and their computer accounts would have embraced the newest policy settings. However, four policy categories are exceptions and are never processed in the background while users are logged on:

Folder Redirection (Explored in Detail in Chapter 10)   Folder Redirection's goal is to anchor specific directories, such as the My Documents folder, to certain network shared folders. This policy is never refreshed during a background refresh. The logic behind this is that if an administrator changes this location while the user is using it (and the system responds), the user's data could be at risk for corruption. If the administrator changes Folder Redirection via Group Policy, this change affects only the user at the next logon.

Software Installation (Explored in Detail in Chapter 11)   Software Installation is also exempt from background refresh. You can use Group Policy to deploy software packages, large and small, to your users or to your computers. You can also use Group Policy to revoke already-distributed software packages. Software is neither installed nor revoked to users or computers when the background interval comes to pass. You wouldn't want users to lose applications right in the middle of use and, hence, lose or corrupt data. These functions occur only at startup for the computer or at logon for the user.

Disk Quotas (Explored in Previous Editions of the Book)   Disk quotas run on Windows 8.1 and later when the background processing interval comes around. For previous operating systems, such as Windows 7, they are run (changed, really) only at computer startup.

Logon, Logoff, Startup, and Shutdown Scripts (Explored in Detail in Chapter 12)   Technically, this entry shouldn't be here. Here's why: Yes, it's true that these scripts are run only at the appointed time (at logon, logoff, startup, or shutdown). And, as expected, these scripts are not run again and again when the background processing interval comes around. But, technically, the Client-Side Extension (CSE) that implements scripts does run in the background. If it runs in the background, what is it doing? The Group Policy CSE will update the "values" like location and path changes. This can happen even after the user has already logged on. It's just that, of course, they won't run again until the appointed time. So, the important (and often misunderstood) point is that Group Policy itself doesn't run the scripts. That's handled by the logon process. The Group Policy part of the magic is always happening—just updating values (like location of the script) if they're changed within the GPO.

Group Policy Preferences' Drive Maps (Explored in Chapter 5)   One of the Group Policy Preferences' superpowers is the ability to map drives using Group Policy instead of via login scripts.

On Windows 8 and earlier, when Group Policy refreshes, if the user is *already* logged on, Group Policy Preferences will not touch the existing mapped drives. The user must log out and back on. Sometimes logging off and on twice is required to see that changed drive mapping occur!

On Windows 8.1 and later, when Group Policy refreshes, if the user is *already* logged on, Group Policy Preferences perform an update.

Windows Background Processing

As I stated in the introduction to this section, Windows XP and later do not process new Group Policy updates in the same way that Windows 2000 and all versions of Windows Server do. Let's get a grip on how Windows XP and later work.

Now that Xavier has logged onto his Windows XP machine for the first time, Sven has logged onto his Windows 7 machine for the first time, and Ben has logged onto Windows 10 for the first time, their sessions will continue to process GPOs in the background as I just described: every 90 minutes or so if any new GPOs appear or any existing GPOs have changed. Xavier now goes home for the night. He logs off the domain and shuts down his machine. When he comes in the next morning, he will not process GPOs the same way that Wally will on his Windows 2000 machine.

When Xavier (or Sven or Ben) logs on the second time (and all subsequent times) on a Windows XP or later machine, initial policy processing will no longer be performed as described in the section "Initial Policy Processing" earlier in this chapter. From this point forward, at startup or logon, Windows XP and later will not process GPOs synchronously like Windows 2000; rather, GPOs will be processed only in the background.

If you're scratching your head at this point as to why Windows 2000 is different from Windows XP and later, here's the short answer: When Windows XP was in development, all the stops were pulled to make the "XPerience" as fast as possible. Both boot times and logon times were indeed faster than ever, but the trade-off came at a price.

By default, Windows XP and later won't wait for the network to be there in order to check for any updated GPOs. If the network is unavailable or slow, Windows XP and later will simply utilize the last-known downloaded GPOs as the baseline, even if GPOs have changed in Active Directory while the Windows XP or Windows 10 machine was turned off. Said another way, if Windows XP and later machines can't download anything new (quickly), they just maintain what they have, without any holdups.

While the network card is still warming up and finding the network and the first Domain Controller, the last-used computer GPOs are already just "there." Then, the "Press Ctrl+Alt+Delete to begin" prompt is presented to the user. While this prompt is presented, and once the network is ready, only then does Windows XP and later download and apply any new computer GPOs.

Assuming the user is now logged on, the Desktop and Start menu appear. Again, the system will not synchronously download the latest site, domain, and OU Group Policy Objects and apply them before displaying the Desktop. Instead, other activity is happening while the latest and greatest Group Policy is being downloaded, so the user might not see the effects right away.

Once the computer has started and the user is logged on, the Group Policy settings from "last time" are already there on the machine. Newly downloaded GPOs (and the policy settings inside) are then processed asynchronously in the background. This net result is a bit of a compromise. The user feels that there is a faster boot time (when the GPO contains computer policy settings) as well as faster logon time (when the GPO contains user policy settings). The most important policy settings, such as updated Security settings and Administrative Templates (Registry updates), are applied soon after logon—and no one is the wiser. Microsoft calls this Group Policy processing behavior *Fast Boot* (sometimes called *Logon Optimization*). Yes, it does speed things up a bit, but at a cost.

To keep things simple, we just walked through what would happen for Xavier on his Windows XP machine. However, the exact same behavior would occur for Sven on his Windows 7 machine. There is no difference between Windows 10, Windows 8, Windows 8.1, Windows 7, Windows XP, and Windows Vista in this respect.

Windows XP and Later Fast-Boot Results

Fast Boot affects two major components: Group Policy processing and user-account attribute processing. The (sometimes strange) results occur for users when they have previously logged on. The only one spared the strange behavior is Wally on his Windows 2000 machine, because Windows 2000 doesn't do this modern "Fast Boot" behavior.

WINDOWS XP AND LATER FAST BOOT GROUP POLICY PROCESSING DETAILS

The immediate downside to the Windows XP and later (including Windows 10) Fast Boot approach is that, potentially, a user could be totally logged on but not quite have all the GPOs processed. Then, once they are working for a little while—pop! A setting takes effect out of the blue. This is because not all GPOs were processed before the user was presented with the Desktop and Start menu. Your network would have to be pretty slow for this scenario to occur, but it's certainly possible. This is most commonly seen if you do not have Spanning Tree PortFast set to enabled on your network switches. Without it, a 30- to 50-second delay could be seen with the activation of the network port. And considering Windows 8 and Windows 10 boot a lot faster than Windows 7, you may see this behavior more often in your environment. If you're using Cisco gear, a reference document on this can be found at:

```
http://tinyurl.com/cisco-spanning
```

The next major downside takes a bit more to wrap your head around. Some Group Policy (and Profile) features can potentially take Windows XP and later several additional logons or reboots to actually get the changes you want on them. This strange behavior becomes understandable when we take a step back and think about how certain policy categories are processed on Windows 2000. Specifically, we need to direct our attention to Software Distribution and Folder Redirection policy. I mentioned that on Windows 2000 these two types of policy categories (and some others) *must* be processed in the foreground (or synchronously) to prevent data corruption. That is, if there are Software Distribution or Folder Redirection edicts to embrace, they can happen *only* during startup or login.

But we have a paradox: if Windows XP and later only process GPOs asynchronously, how are the Software Distribution and Folder Redirection polices handled if they must be handled *synchronously*?

Windows XP, and later, fake it and tag the machine when a software package is targeted for the user or system. The *next time* the user logs on (or the computer is rebooted for Computer-side policy), the Group Policy engine sees that the machine is tagged for Software Distribution and switches, just for this one time, back into synchronous mode. The net result: Windows XP and later machines typically require two logons (or reboots) for a user or computer to get a software distribution package.

Again, note that Windows 2000 Professional machines only require one logon (for user settings) or one reboot (for computer settings).

Folder Redirection is a wonderful tool. It has two modes: Basic Folder Redirection (which applies to everyone in the OU) and Advanced Folder Redirection (which checks which security groups the user is in). Windows XP and later machines won't get the effects of Basic Folder Redirection for two logons! And Windows XP and later machines won't get the effects of Advanced Folder Redirection for a whopping three logons. The first logon tags the system for a Folder Redirection change, the second logon figures out the user's security group membership, and the third logon actually performs the new Folder Redirection—synchronously for just that one logon.

We cover Folder Redirection in Chapter 10, "The Managed Desktop, Part 1: Redirected Folders, Offline Files, and the Synchronization Manager."

AUTOMATICALLY KILLING FAST BOOT WITH SPECIAL USER ACCOUNT ATTRIBUTES

Group Policy is only one of two areas affected by the Windows XP and later Fast Boot mechanism. If you change certain key user attributes, you could find that they are not updated until (you guessed it!) two logons. Those key attributes are as follows:

- Roaming profile path (discussed in Chapter 9)
- The home directory
- Old-style logon scripts

But once they are set (and detected), Fast Boot is officially, automatically killed by the system. From that point forward, since Fast Boot is turned off, if you change those values again, it should take only one logon for you to see.

Read more about this topic here: http://support.microsoft.com/kb/305293.

MANUALLY TURNING OFF WINDOWS XP AND LATER FAST BOOT

In previous editions of the book, I recommended that you simply turn off Fast Boot for all operating systems and be done with it. The thrust of my idea was that if you kept Fast Boot on, your machines would be a wee bit faster, but all machines would have decreased consistency.

That also means if you turned off Fast Boot (and went back to the Windows 2000 behavior), you'd be going a wee bit slower but gaining increased consistency.

My updated recommendation is as follows:

* Keep Fast Boot on (the default) for machines that are roaming, traveling, laptop-y, or tablet-y. (Yes, I just made up those two words.)

* Turn Fast Boot off (explained later) for any machines that are desktops, hardwired, or VDI machines.

Fast Boot: First Logins and Side Effects

Again, remember that Fast Boot is automatically disabled the first time any Windows XP, and later, machine is started as a member of the domain. It is also disabled the first time any new user logs onto a Windows XP, and later, client. In these situations, Windows XP and later assume (correctly) that no GPO information is known and therefore must go out to Active Directory to get the latest GPOs. The net effect is that if settings for either (or both) Folder Redirection policy and Software Distribution policy already exist, the user will not require additional logons or reboots *the first time* they log onto a Windows XP, and later, machine or when the computer is started for the first time after joining the domain.

This "Fast Boot" behavior can have another unintended side effect: Group Policy–based logon scripts could possibly run *after* the user has already logged on. If that logon script was there to configure something important, the user's environment might not be ready for work until after this piece was complete!

Why is this my new recommendation?

If you want the long story of why this is my recommendation, I'd like to point you toward a speech I gave at TechEd 2014 entitled "Group Policy: Tips, Tricks and Notes from the Field." At last check the replay of the talk can be found at:

`https://channel9.msdn.com/Events/TechEd/NorthAmerica/2014/WIN-B328#fbid=`

The summary of the recommendation, however, can be broken down into two easy thoughts:

For Laptop-y and Tablet-y Machines   Group Policy can be slowed down over slow links. Therefore, if you have laptop-y or tablet-y machines, they might use a slow link, and you'll want to ensure that their experience is as fast as possible, even if that means that they don't get the latest Group Policy settings right away during a reconnect.

For Hardwired Machines (Typically Desktops and VDI)   They won't be using slow links. So for these machines, go for consistency in how Group Policy applies, even if it takes an extra moment or two during the logon process. It might be a smidgen slower to log on, but honestly, under most conditions you and your users likely wouldn't notice the difference, and you'll be thankful for the consistency.

To take my suggestions, you'll likely need to split machines into different OUs: one OU for traveling machines and one for hardwired machines.

On the OU containing traveling machines, do nothing. Fast Boot is the default, and already on.

On the OU containing the hardwired machines, you will need to create a Group Policy Object that contains a policy setting to revert the behavior of Windows XP and later machines back to the older, more consistent behavior. Enable the policy setting named **Always wait for the network at computer startup and logon**. This policy can be found in Computer Configuration ➢ Policies ➢ Administrative Templates ➢ System ➢ Logon. The name of this policy setting is a bit confusing. It would have been better, in my opinion, to name it **Make Client Machines Process GPOs Like Windows 2000**. But they didn't.

Remember, to force Windows XP and later machines to receive this computer policy (or any computer policy), the computer account must be within the site, domain, or OU where you set the policy.

Last, don't give the name of the policy setting **Always wait for the network at computer startup and logon** too much contemplation, even though it's confusing. It does not mean that the machine will just "hang" there until it sees the network during startup and logon. Its job is only to make Windows XP and later machines process policy in the older, more consistent style.

Manually Starting Background Policy Processing (One at a Time)

You get a phone call from the person who handles the firewalls and proxy servers at your company. He tells you that he's added an additional proxy server for your users to use when going out to the Internet. Excitedly, you add a new GPO that affects Xavier's, Sven's, and Ben's user objects so they can use the new proxy server. But you're impatient.

You know that when you make this setting, it's going to take between 90 and 120 minutes to kick in. And you don't want to tell Sven (and your other users) to log off and log back on to get the policy—they wouldn't like that much.

In cases like these, you might want to bypass the normal wait time before background policy processing kicks in. The good news is that you can run a simple command that tells the client to skip the normal background processing interval and request an update of new or changed GPOs from the server right now. Again, only new GPOs or GPOs that have changed on the server in some way will actually come down and be reflected on your client machines.

But, because you're impatient, you want to see Sven on his Windows 7 machine start using that new proxy server setting that you plunked into that GPO right away. So you physically trot out to his machine and enter the gpupdate command to manually refresh the GPOs.

Note that the gpupdate command can refresh either the User or the Computer half of a GPO, or both. The syntax is gpupdate /Target:Computer, /Target:User, or (again) just gpupdate by itself to trigger both.

Running gpupdate while Sven and Ben are logged on gives those users the new settings in the GPO you just set. This is, of course, provided the Domain Controller that Sven and Ben are using has the replicated GPO information.

Additionally, gpupdate can figure out if newly changed items require a logoff or reboot to be active. For instance, we know that Software Distribution and Folder Redirection settings are processed only at future logon times (and not in the background). Therefore, specifying gpupdate with a /Logoff switch will figure out if a policy has changed such that a logoff is required and then automatically log you off. If the updated GPO does not require a logoff, the GPO settings are applied and the currently logged-on user remains logged on.

Similarly, Software Distribution settings will also require a reboot before the software will be available. Therefore, specifying gpupdate with a /boot switch will figure out if a policy has something that requires a reboot and automatically reboot the computer. If the updated GPO does not require a reboot, the GPO settings are applied, and the user remains logged on.

The /logoff and /boot switches are optional.

One switch has a lot of mystery around it: the /force switch. The /force switch basically says, "Redownload all Group Policy settings from all GPOs, even if nothing has changed." Remember, the Group Policy engine on the client already knows which GPOs it's already downloaded. For more information on this, see the earlier sidebar "How Does the Group Policy Engine Know What's New or Changed?" and also the details in Chapter 7.

So, the /force switch is often not needed in gpupdate, because gpupdate could be run without switches and be equally effective.

So, why run the /force switch with gpupdate at all?

A key case when you *would* need the /force switch would be, say, if someone with local admin rights did a no-no, like change a value that only the protected SYSTEM should get to. For example, say a local administrator deleted a Registry key, which restricted access to the Control Panel or changed how big a log file should be. Now, remember: regular, standard users cannot do this. But local administrators can.

In those cases, running a gpupdate by itself wouldn't fix the problem. Only a gpupdate /force will "re-bring down" the settings—even if the version numbers have not changed.

So, to be clear, in 99 percent of the cases, you shouldn't need to add /force to gpupdate.

That being said, I have seen plenty of times where gpupdate /force is like a "brain reboot" for Group Policy. There is some magical quality about /force that does sometimes jump-start you out of a problem, and—hey now—things seem to work the way you expect.

Manually Forcing Background Policy Processing (Remote *GPUpdate*)

Sometimes, you make a change and you want that change to go out NOW! NOW! NOW! This can happen if you, oops, forgot to perform some critical change or just want to see a gaggle of computers embrace your changes.

When you use the GPMC from Windows 8 or later (preferably Windows 10), you will, indeed, be able to do this very quickly.

Before I show you exactly how to do it, though, let's go over the theory of what is about to happen. First, you cannot stand on your desk and shout at a bunch of users to download their settings NOW! NOW! NOW! It doesn't work like that. Instead, you point at a bunch of computers and tell them to download *their* settings now, and the users who are on those computers also download their settings automatically at the same time. It's a fine distinction, but an important one. So, to recap, you can only select a place (OUs, really), which contains computers, and the settings for the computer as well as the user's settings (for the users on those computers) will also be refreshed.

But there's another small theory point here. The refresh is the equivalent of a gpupdate /force. This means a full "re-application" of all the policy settings will come down. Again, see the previous section for a little more detail on this topic.

So, without further ado, let's see exactly how to get our computers to embrace our changes NOW! NOW! NOW! Okay, that's that last time I'm saying that. I'm not really a shouter.

As I stated, the trick is to find the location with the computers that users are already using. The GPMC limits this trick only to OUs and won't let you perform a remote Group Policy Update upon the whole domain or at a site.

Additionally, this magic only works for Windows 7 and later as target machines. Group Policy on Windows XP machines cannot be remotely updated using the GPMC.

To test this out, I suggest you log on to your Win10 machine as Frank Rizzo. At this point in our story, Frank should be getting a GPO called "Hide Mouse Pointers Option/ Restore Screen Saver Option." You should see that the option to manipulate mouse pointers is prevented. (On the Desktop, right click Personalization ➢ Themes ➢ Mouse pointer settings.) You should see the Pointers tab within the Mouse Properties applet is removed (though other tabs, like Pointer Options and Buttons remain).

So let's set ourselves up for a quick test to force update a GPO to our target computers. For a quick test within the GPMC right-click on the "Hide Mouse Pointers Option/Restore Screen Saver Option" Group Policy Object and uncheck Link Enabled. This will stop the Group Policy Object from affecting the OU that contains Frank.

Don't do this—but at this point, if Frank were to log off and log back on, this change would take effect. But instead, we want to run the Remote Group Policy Update. Do this by finding the **Human Resources Computers** OU, then right-clicking over it and selecting Group Policy Update, as seen in Figure 3.1.

When you do this, you'll get a dialog box like the one in Figure 3.2.

If you make a mistake and select an OU containing only User objects, the Remote Group Policy Update will politely explain the problem, as seen in Figure 3.3.

Note that the Remote Group Policy Update will show you the number of computers that are about to be refreshed. This is great so you don't inadvertently refresh 200,000 computers when you meant to refresh 20.

The next thing that happens is very disappointing. In short, as seen in Figure 3.4, by default this will always fail.

"Why does this fail?" I hear you cry. Because, by default, on these machines, the Windows Firewall is preventing remote access by you—that is, unless, you followed along in Chapter 2, "Managing Group Policy with the GPMC and via PowerShell" specifically in the sidebar "Understanding Windows Firewall Settings (and Dealing with Group Policy Results)." In that sidebar, I showed you how to poke just the right holes in the Windows Firewall to allow remote administration, like what we're trying to do here.

FIGURE 3.1 You can right-click over any OU that contains computers and select Group Policy Update.

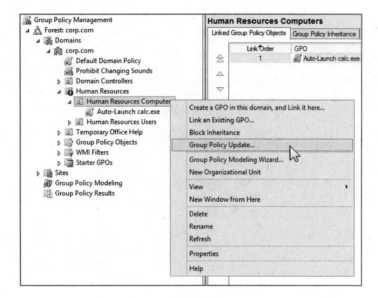

FIGURE 3.2 Remote Group Policy Update shows you how many computers are going to be affected.

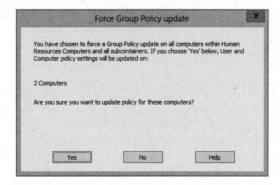

FIGURE 3.3 Remote Group Policy Update won't let you update users—only computers.

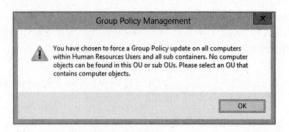

FIGURE 3.4 By default, Remote Group Policy Update won't work because each machine's firewall is preventing the update.

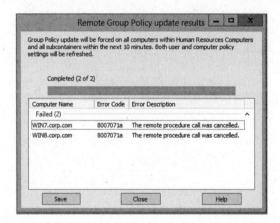

Alternatively, you could also use the Starter GPO we talked about in the previous chapter, specifically the section "Should You Use Microsoft's Pre-created Starter GPOs?" Both methods do ostensibly the same thing but take somewhat different routes to perform the work.

Regardless, once you've poked the hole through the firewall, you're ready to go. At this point, rerunning remote Group Policy Update should succeed, as shown in Figure 3.5.

But wait! Just because it succeeded doesn't mean it will refresh instantly. Indeed, there is a maximum 10-minute wait time between the time you say "Go" and the time the computers say "Done."

Within 10 minutes, in Figure 3.6, you can see what the user sees while Group Policy applies. As far as I know, there is no way to make this "silent." Users on Windows 7 and later see the same dialog box pop up. And, Windows XP users see—nothing, as, again, remote Group Policy Update will not apply to Windows XP machines.

FIGURE 3.5   Remote Group Policy Update succeeds when the firewall holes are poked through.

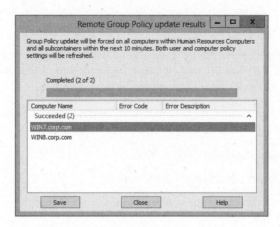

FIGURE 3.6   When Remote Group Policy Update performs its work, it shows this brief pop-up to users.

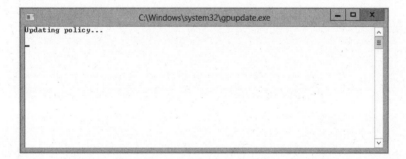

The reason for both the 10-minute delay and the dialog box is that the Remote Group Policy Update actually doesn't perform the update itself. The Remote Group Policy Update does something pretty sneaky: it tells the target computer to add a Scheduled Task to run its own gpupdate /force. For more information on what's going on under the hood, check out the sidebar "Under the Hood with Remote Group Policy Processing."

Security Background Refresh Processing

As I've stated, all Group Policy clients process GPOs when the background refresh interval comes to pass—but only those GPOs that were new or changed since the last time the client requested them.

Under the Hood with Remote Group Policy Processing

As you learned in the section "Manually Forcing Background Policy Processing (Remote *GPUpdate*)," the GPMC with Windows 8 and later has a new superpower.

And, as I stated, the Remote Group Policy Update itself isn't exactly doing what it says it's doing. Instead, it's really putting a scheduled task on your modern Windows machines. Sorry, Windows XP machines are left out of the fun here.

On your Windows 7 and later machine, you must have the following services enabled and ready to go:

- Remote Scheduled Tasks Management (RPC)

- Remote Scheduled Tasks Management (RPD-EPMAP)

- Windows Management Instrumentation (WMI-In)

By default, these services are running on Windows 7 and later. So when you target an OU with computers and pull the trigger, the Remote Group Policy Update Service connects with these services, does a little magic, and then places scheduled tasks into the target machines' task scheduler. You can even see what happens when multiple users are logged on to a particular target machine.

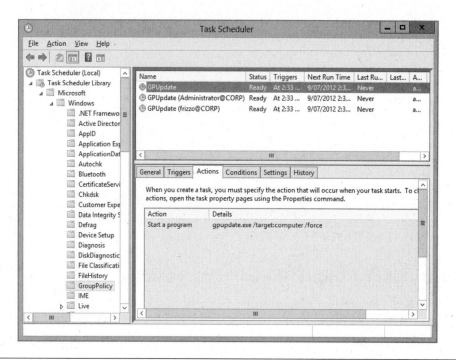

Here, you can see that three scheduled tasks are configured to execute at 2:33 p.m. There's one task for each of the two users currently logged on and one for the computer. For a user, the action is set to "Start a program" and the details are set to run "gpupdate. exe /target:user /force." On the Computer side, the scheduled task is set to run gpupdate `/target:computer /force`.

Remember, in order for Remote Group Policy Refresh to work, you need to be able to remotely make contact with each and every target machine. The computer cannot get the task scheduled and will not respond to the request if the machine has one of the following conditions:

- Is offline

- Has the firewall on or doesn't have the remote management ports open (135 and 445)

- Is Windows XP or older

Wally is on a Windows 2000 machine, and he's been logged on for four hours. Likewise, Xavier has been logged onto his Windows XP machine for four hours, and Sven has been logged onto his Windows 7 machine for four hours. Ben on Windows 10, also four hours.

Imagine for a second that there was a GPO in Active Directory named "Prevent Access to the Control Panel" and it contained a policy setting inside it to do just that. The client would certainly do so according to the initial policy processing rules and/or the background refresh processing rules.

Assuming that the underlying GPO doesn't get any policy settings modified or any new policy settings or that the GPO itself doesn't get removed, the client already knows to accept this edict. The client just accepts that things haven't changed and, hence, keeps on truckin'. Only a change inside the GPO will trigger the client to realize that new instructions are available, and the client will execute that new edict during its background policy processing.

Now, let's assume that we anoint Wally, Xavier, Sven, and Ben as local administrators of their Windows 2000, Windows XP, Windows 7, and Windows 10 machines, respectively. Since Wally, Xavier, Sven, and Ben are now local administrators, they have total control to go around the Group Policy engine processes and make their own changes. These changes could nullify a policy you've previously set with a GPO and allow them to access and change features on the system that shouldn't be changed. In this case, there are certainly going to be situations in which the GPOs on the Domain Controllers don't change, but certain parts of the workstation should remain locked down anyway.

Of course, the right answer is to only give people you absolutely trust access to local Administrator accounts. You should never give regular users Administrator accounts if you can possibly help it.

But, with that being said, let's examine two potential exploits of the Group Policy engine if a local administrator does choose to do so:

Group Policy Exploit Example #1: Going Around an Administrative Template   Consider the `calc.exe` program we are forced to run every time someone uses a computer in Human Resources. We created a GPO named "Auto-Launch calc.exe" and enabled the policy setting named **Run these programs at user logon** within it. We linked the GPO to the **Human Resources Computers** OU. Our edict affected all users on our computers (including our administrators) so that `calc.exe` ran for everyone (because the GPO was linked to an OU containing the computer). Imagine, then, that someone with local administrative privileges (such as Wally) on the workstation changes the portion of the Registry that is affected, as shown in Figure 3.7.

FIGURE 3.7   A simple deletion of the Registry entry will nullify our policy setting.

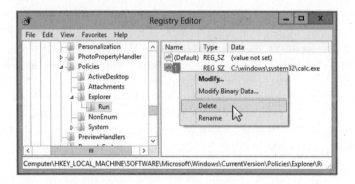

After the local administrator changes the setting, `calc.exe` simply won't run. (Again, only local administrators can make this change. Mere mortals do not have access to this portion of the Registry.) We're now at risk; a local administrator did the dirty work, and now all users on this workstation are officially going around our policy. Ninety minutes or so later, the background refresh interval strikes, and the client computer requests the background refresh from the GPOs in Active Directory. You might think that this should once again lock down the "Auto-Launch calc.exe" ability. But it doesn't. This ability won't get relocked down on reboot, either. Why? Because the Windows client thinks everything is status quo. Because nothing has changed in the underlying GPO in Active Directory that is telling the client its instruction set changed.

In this example, the Group Policy processing engine on the client thinks it has already asked for (and received) the latest version of the policy; the Group Policy processing engine doesn't know about the nefarious Registry change the local workstation administrator performed behind its back. Windows clients are not protected from this sort of attack by default. However, the protection can be made stronger. (See the section "Mandatory Reapplication for Nonsecurity Policy" later in this chapter.) Okay, this example exploit is fairly harmless, but it could be more or less damaging depending on precisely which policy settings we are forcing on our clients (as seen in this next example).

Group Policy Exploit Example #2: Going Around a Security Policy Setting   Imagine we created a GPO with settings that locked down the \MYSECUREDIR directory with specific file ACLs. For this example, imagine we set the \MYSECUREDIR directory so that only the Domain Administrators have access. Then, behind our backs, Sven, now a local administrator, changes these file ACLs to allow everyone full control of these sensitive files. Uh-oh, now we could have a real problem on our hands.

Windows offers protection to handle cleanup for exploits of these two types. Remember, though, in both cases, we're assuming these users are running with Administrative rights—a real no-no. If users are simply standard users, then this "problem" would never really be a problem at all.

Let's see how Windows tries to compensate for these circumstances.

In the first example, we went around the **Run these programs at user logon** policy setting by forcefully modifying the Registry. Running calc.exe for every user on a particular computer isn't considered a security setting. So, *by default* there is no protection for Exploit #1 (note the emphasis on "by default"). But before you start panicking, let's examine Exploit #2, which attempts to go around a security policy we set.

Background Security Refresh Processing

The Group Policy engine tries to clean up after examples such as Exploit #2 by asking for a special background refresh—just for the security policy settings. This is called the *background security refresh* and is valid for every version of Windows.

Every 16 hours, a Group Policy client asks Active Directory for all the GPOs that contain "security stuff" (not just the ones that have changed). And, all that security stuff inside those GPOs is reapplied. This ensures that if a security setting has changed on the client (behind the Group Policy engine's back), it's automatically patched up within 16 hours.

To reiterate, background security refresh helps secure stuff on the client only every 16 hours and only if the setting is security related. So, within a maximum of 16 hours, the \windows\repair directory would have the intended permissions rethrust upon it. Okay, great. But in Exploit #1, our evil administrator went around the **Run these programs at user logon** policy setting. And the background security refresh would *not* have enforced our intended will upon the system. Running calc.exe is not considered a security policy setting. "How do we secure *those* exploits?" I hear you cry. "Read on," I reply. (Hey, that rhymed.)

Changing the Security Refresh Interval

You can manually change this security refresh interval in two ways. First, you can edit the local workstation's Registry at:

```
HKEY_LOCAL_MACHINE\SOFTWARE\Microsoft\
Windows NT\CurrentVersion\Winlogon\GPExtensions\
{827D319E-6EAC-11D2-A4EA-00C04F79F83A}\
MaxNoGPOListChangesInterval
```

and leverage a REG_DWORD signifying the number of minutes to pull down the entire security policy (by default, every 16 hours, so 960 minutes). You can also use the Security Policy Processing policy, which is described in the section "Using Group Policy to Affect Group Policy" later in this chapter. For more information, see Microsoft Knowledge Base article 277543 at http://support.microsoft.com/kb/277543.

Mandatory Reapplication for Nonsecurity Policy

Your network is humming along. You've established the GPOs in your organization, and you've let them sit unchanged for several months. Wally logs on. Wally logs off. So does Xavier. And Sven. And Ben. They each reboot their machines a bunch. But imagine for a moment that the GPOs in Active Directory haven't changed in months.

When your users or computers perform initial Group Policy processing or background policy processing, a whole lot of nothing happens. If GPOs haven't changed in months, there's nothing for the clients to do. Since the engine has already processed the latest version of what's in Active Directory, what more could it possibly need?

True, every 16 hours the security-related policy settings are guaranteed to be refreshed by the background security refresh. But what about Exploit #1 in which Wally (who was anointed as a local workstation administrator) went around the **Run these programs at user logon** policy setting by hacking his local Registry?

Well, running calc.exe isn't a security policy. But it still could be thought of as a security hole you need to fill (if you were running something really important every time a user logged in). With a little magic, you can force the nonsecurity sections of Group Policy to automatically close their own security holes. You can make the nonsecurity sections of Group Policy enforce their settings, even if the GPOs on the servers haven't changed. This will fix exploits that aren't specifically security related. You'll learn how to do this a bit later in the section "Affecting the Computer Settings of Group Policy."

The general idea is that once the nonsecurity sections of Group Policy are told to mandatorily reapply, they will do so whenever an initial policy processing or background refresh processing happens.

You can choose to (optionally) mandatorily reapply the following areas of Group Policy, along with the initial processing and background refresh:

- Registry (Administrative Templates)
- Internet Explorer Maintenance
- IP Security
- EFS Recovery Policy
- Wireless Policy
- Disk Quota
- Scripts (by scripts I mean the notification of changes to scripts, not the actual rerunning of scripts after the appointed time)
- Security
- Folder Redirection
- Software Installation
- Wired Policy

As you'll see in the section "Affecting the Computer Settings of Group Policy," you can use the GUI to select other areas of Group Policy to enforce along with the background refresh.

To recap, if the GPO in Active Directory has *actually* changed, you don't have to worry about whether it will be automatically applied. Rather, mandatory reapplication is an extra safety measure that you can choose to place on your client systems so your will is always downloaded and re-embraced, not only if an existing GPO has changed or a new GPO has appeared. And you can specify Group Policy sections that you wish to do this for.

As you'll see in Chapter 7, a bit more is going on between the client and the server. Underneath the hood, the client keeps track of the GPO *version number*. If the version number changes in Active Directory, the GPO is flagged as being required for download; it is then redownloaded and applied. If the version number stays the same in Active Directory, the Group Policy isn't redownloaded or applied. Stay tuned for more on GPO version numbers in Chapter 7.

Special Case: Moving a User or a Computer Object

When you move a user or a computer within Active Directory, Group Policy may not immediately apply as you think it should. For instance, if you move a computer from the **Human Resources Computers** OU to another OU, that computer may still pull GPOs from the **Human Resources Computers** OU for a while longer. This is because the computer may get confused about where the accounts it's supposed to work with are currently residing.

The userenv process syncs with Active Directory every so often to determine if a user or a computer has been moved.

This happens, at most, about every 30 minutes or so.

Once resynced, background processing continues as it normally would—only this time the user and computer GPOs are pulled from the new destination. If you move a user or a computer, remember that Group Policy processing continues to pull from the old location until it realizes the switch.

And don't forget that replication takes a while within your site and, also, potentially *between* Active Directory sites.

Altogether, the maximum wait time after a move to get GPOs pulled from a new location is as follows:

- 30 minutes (the maximum Active Directory synchronization time) *and*
- 90 minutes (the maximum Group Policy default background refresh rate) *and*
- 30 minutes (the maximum Group Policy default background refresh rate offset)

So that's a grand total maximum of 150 minutes. It could and usually does happen faster than that, but it can't take any longer. This behavior is important to understand if you move an entire OU (perhaps with many computers) underneath another OU!

Windows 7 and later has a special trick up its sleeves. If you know the computer or user account has been moved (and, hence, would get different Group Policy settings), you can just run gpupdate /force, which double-checks where both the user and computer account live in Active Directory. Once the location is found, it applies GPOs specifically for that new location.

In my testing with Windows 7 and later, this does seem to work "pretty well." But, my suggestion is that if you move a user around, to be 100 percent sure, you should then log off and log back on. If you move a computer around, you should then reboot the machine. Only then are you really sure to get the latest settings.

Windows 8, 8.1, and 10 Group Policy: Subtle Differences

Okay, I've waited until now to discuss (and actually re-discuss) a handful of very, very small and possibly inconsequential secrets about how the Group Policy processing engine for Windows 8 and later is ever-so-slightly different from that of Windows past. The changes happened at Windows 8 and again at Windows 8.1 and continue onward to Windows 10. Said another way, Windows 8 had some changes. Then Windows 8.1 had some more changes, and those changes continued through to Windows 10. But Windows 10 itself really didn't have any additional changes.

Secret 1: The Windows Group Policy Service Turns On and Off (Windows 8 and Later)

To save battery life, most Windows 8 and later services will automatically turn off when not needed. When it comes to Group Policy, here's specifically how this works.

When the computer turns on and requests Group Policy, the Group Policy Service starts up, gets Group Policy and then…waits. It waits 10 minutes for any additional requests for

Group Policy. Now, usually during those 10 minutes the user logs on. So the service stays on, processes the User side of Group Policy, then waits another 10 minutes. If nothing happens in 10 minutes, the service goes to sleep. Should you manually run gpupdate or perform a remote Group Policy Refresh, the service takes a second (or three) to start up, performs the request, and then waits for 10 minutes. And the cycle continues. Therefore, if you keep running gpupdate over and over again within 10 minutes, the "countdown" to put the service to sleep restarts every time the Group Policy engine has to do something. Eventually, however, the Group Policy service sleeps until it's next needed.

Microsoft calls this behavior Always On, Always Connected (AOAC). I have no idea why— it's not a very descriptive name for this "Sleep when not needed" process.

This behavior is set by default on all Windows 8 and later clients, including Windows RT. This does mean that the service will take some time to start up before it performs the Group Policy update request if it's asleep. You can revert the behavior back to the "non-sleepy" way by using the Group Policy setting **Turn off Group Policy Client Service AOAC optimization**, which is explored in the section "Using Group Policy to Affect Group Policy" a little later.

This behavior is off by default on Windows Servers. This means that the service never sleeps on Windows Server 2012 and later and is always on.

Secret 2: Windows RT Cannot Get Active Directory–Based Group Policy (Windows 8 and Later)

We talked about this in Chapter 1, so I guess it isn't a secret. But it's still unclear and bears repeating.

In short, Windows RT computers cannot be domain joined and therefore cannot get Active Directory–based Group Policy.

You can, however, run GPEDIT.MSC on Windows RT machines and manually flip the switches of various items.

There doesn't appear to be any way to update a Windows RT machine's Group Policy using some kind of central management. If it ever happens, stay tuned on GPanswers.com for more information as the subject emerges.

Secret 3: If You Use Windows Hiberboot, You (Basically) Lose Computer Processing at Startup (Windows 8 and Later)

Windows 8 and later has a feature called Hiberboot. Hiberboot enables a low-power and quick restart of a system. The user sees the command as "Shut down" in the GUI—except it's not really shut down at all. It's more like "super suspend."

Then, when the system is powered back on and "rebooted," it looks and feels super fast. But it's not a real full power off and full restart reboot. You can read more about Hiberboot and see a video here:

```
http://blogs.msdn.com/b/b8/archive/2011/09/08/delivering-fast-boot-times-
in-windows-8.aspx
```

So, with regard to Group Policy, here's the deal. When you start the computer up from Hiberboot, Group Policy doesn't process the Computer side. That's because the computer was, technically, on already, just in a low-power state. At some point in the computer's distant past, it was completely powered off. And only at that initial completely powered-down point did it get the Computer-side GPOs at startup.

Then, when the user logs in, User-side policy processes as normal after logon. All normal User-side processing works as previously described. And if you've changed Group Policy processing to synchronous mode, then the Group Policy engine will cheerfully perform in synchronous mode, too.

Then, up to 90 minutes after the computer is started, the background refresh interval will kick in for Windows Computer side and process any changed items on the Computer side.

However, there is a big catch here: Remember that some directives cannot process when the computer is already started up—notably, computer-based Group Policy Software Deployment. So, if you're expecting to see your software on the next "reboot," you won't see it, because you're not fully rebooting at all. Instead, the computer would need to be powered off and back on with a "Restart" and not a "Shutdown" (which really, again, isn't a shutdown at all).

If you want to always have full shutdowns, which will enable computer processing every time the computer starts, you will need to disable hibernation, which in turn prevents Hiberboots from occurring.

Secret 4: Group Policy Preferences Drive Maps and Disk Quotas Run in the Background (Windows 8.1 and Later)

Windows 8.1 and later have eliminated the need to log off (for Group Policy Preferences Drive Maps) or to reboot (for Disk Quotas).

If you make a Group Policy Preferences Drive Maps change or a Disk Quota change, you'll see those changes take effect in the background, or when you run gpupdate.

There's a side benefit here, too. Before Windows 8.1, if you used Group Policy Preferences Drive Maps, every other login would be triggered for a foreground update, and every other login would be triggered for a background update.

I call this the "Tick / Tock" problem with Group Policy Preferences Drive Maps. I demonstrated this in my TechEd 2014 talk, again found at:

```
https://channel9.msdn.com/Events/TechEd/NorthAmerica/2014/WIN-B328#fbid=
```

You can jump to the 35- and 46-minute minute marks to see the demo.

So instead of one login being fast-ish and another being slower-ish, when Group Policy Preferences Drive Maps is used, it just becomes more consistent.

That's a big win.

Secret 5: Better Logging from Windows 8.1 and Later

Windows 8.1 and later has added better logging. I'll talk more about Group Policy event logging in Chapter 7. But, starting in Windows 8.1, Group Policy got a handful of new Event IDs that can help you understand and troubleshoot when things go wrong.

In Chapter 7, I provide a list of Event IDs for the Group Policy engine should you want them.

Secret 6: Group Policy Caching (Windows 8.1 and Later)

Windows 8.1 introduced a very unusual feature called Group Policy Caching. The goal of Group Policy Caching is a noble one, but it appears to have missed its mark.

The goal is to minimize over-the-network chatter when two things are true:

- When the link is slow.
- When Group Policy is told to perform a foreground policy process.

Those conditions are rarely ever occurring with Windows 8.1 and later, because Microsoft reduced the Group Policy items that require a foreground process to only Folder Redirection and Group Policy Software Installation. And even then, those items need to be new or changed in the Group Policy Object to trigger a foreground process.

Therefore, the Group Policy cache is rarely, if ever, actually used.

In fact, there's a side effect of the Group Policy cache. If you are on someone's client machine and just run gpupdate, because the Group Policy cache is trying to store these GPOs for later possible use, it takes a lot longer to actually finish a manual gpupdate because of the extra network traffic and disk writes to perform the work. But, again, you would only see this delay if you manually ran gpupdate, and it doesn't affect login time.

My pal Darren Mar-Elia has two blog entries on Group Policy Caching, which are worth a read, if only to see how he breaks down the feature and, like me, decides that this feature misses its mark. Here are the two URLs for extra reading:

```
http://sdmsoftware.com/group-policy-blog/group-policy/understanding-group-
policy-caching-in-windows-8-1/
```

```
http://sdmsoftware.com/group-policy-blog/windows-8-1/clarifying-group-
policy-caching-in-windows-8-1/
```

So, in the end analysis, I think unless the Group Policy cache is updated to support some other use cases, it's not super valuable. And if your machines are always connected and hardwired, there's zero reason to keep the cache working at all. In these cases you can turn off the Group Policy cache with the **Configure Group Policy Caching** policy setting and set it to Disabled as seen in Figure 3.8. It is located in the Computer Configuration ➢ Administrative Templates ➢ System ➢ Group Policy section.

Note there is also a policy setting named **Enable Group Policy Caching for Servers,** which I wouldn't recommend enabling.

Secret 7: When Many GPOs Are Involved, Using Windows 8.1 and Later Could Just "Be Faster"

Starting with Windows 8.1 and later, Microsoft optimized the client when multiple GPOs are requested. If there are a lot of GPOs, the amount of "chatter" has been reduced.

Additionally, if there are slow links involved (see the next section) the downloading of the GPOs can just be a lot faster and more optimized than when Windows 7 was doing it.

Therefore, if you have a lot of GPOs and put a Windows 7 and a Windows 10 machine side by side, it's likely the Windows 10 machine will beat the Windows 7 machine.

There's nothing to configure here; it's all internal starting with Windows 8.1 and continuing onward.

FIGURE 3.8   Configure this setting to Disabled, as shown, if you want to turn off the Group Policy cache.

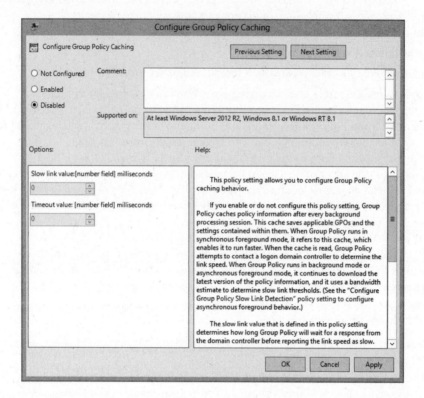

Secret 8: Processing of Logon Scripts Is Delayed 5 Minutes (Windows 8.1 and Later)

Starting with Windows 8.1 and continuing onward, Microsoft decided to delay the processing of login scripts when deployed using Group Policy.

If you think about it, this is a good idea.

When the user is logging on, all this stuff is trying to happen at once:

- Talking over the network.
- Setting up or downloading a profile.
- Explorer is trying to run.
- The Run and Runonce items are trying to fire off.
- Possibly other login actions are trying to fire off as well.

With all this activity that is definitely going to happen anyway, do you really want the additional network chatter and hard drive utilization all at the same exact time as this other stuff?

Said another way, the slowest thing in your computer is your hard drive. If all these items are firing off at the same time (including the login script, if there is one), then it's just going to be a contentious battle for the disk.

So, instead, Microsoft has decided to keep the logon script out of the melee between all the stuff that has to happen and the login script.

The login script is now, by default, delayed 5 minutes, but this delay is configurable to any number you like. This is configurable in the **Configure Login Script Delay** policy setting. You could set it to disabled, or enabled, 0 (zero), which would make the behavior revert back to the old style.

For me, I think you should be able to get out of the dirty business of login scripts altogether. And if you can't, I think it's reasonable to have some kind of delay on it.

That being said, if you've rolled out Solid State Disks (SSDs) to your computers or otherwise find that a login script doesn't add delays, then feel free to turn this feature off by setting the Computer Configuration ➢ Administrative Templates ➢ System ➢ Group Policy ➢ **Configure Login Script Delay** policy setting to zero as seen in Figure 3.9.

FIGURE 3.9   The new default delay for login scripts is 5 minutes after the user logs on. Set this policy setting to zero, as seen here, to revert back to the old behavior.

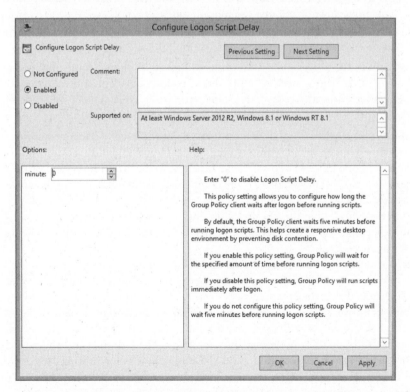

Policy Application via Remote Access, Slow Links, and after Hibernation

You will certainly have situations in which users take their Windows machines on the road and access your Active Directory and servers remotely via dial-up or VPN.

We're going to be talking about Windows Vista and later here. If you want to learn how Windows XP handles slow network connections, you'll have to go to a previous edition of the book.

When and How Does Windows Check for Slow Links?

Windows Vista and later can detect link speed using a Windows component called *Network Location Awareness (NLA)*.

NLA is pretty simple, and there's nothing you need to configure. NLA for Windows Vista and later (like Windows 10) has two jobs:

1. NLA checks to see if the link is slow. This test doesn't use ICMP, so if router administrators have turned off ICMP, the calculation will still work. (See the next section, "What Is Processed over a Slow Network Connection?" for why you should care about what is processed over a slow network connection.)

2. NLA calls out to the universe every so often and asks, "Is there a Domain Controller available NOW?" If the answer is "No!" then Group Policy cannot be updated. Pretty simple. However, if the answer is "Yes!" updated Group Policy could, theoretically, be processed, right?

This might be useful when a user has been working at the beach, disconnected for several days, then finally dials up or comes into the office. However, before doing anything, the Group Policy engine kicks in and asks one more question: "Did I miss the last background refresh interval?" (For instance, if the computer was hibernated, and therefore turned off, for three days).

If the answer is "Yes," then the Group Policy engine immediately performs (what amounts to) a gpupdate (no /force) to refresh Group Policy since the last time the user and computer made contact.

Why is the Group Policy engine so specific about finding out whether it missed the last background refresh interval? The Group Policy engine asks this question because NLA could have determined that the computer was ever-so-briefly off the network—and then back on again. And if that's the case, there was nothing to miss, so nothing is updated. You wouldn't want it to trigger every time it went off and back on the network. That would be a veritable flurry of Group Policy updating! In other words, the Group Policy engine ensures that Windows was off the network for a good amount of time before asking for a refresh.

Again, Windows Vista and later all act the same way, including Windows Server 2008 R2 and later. But it's unlikely you're going to have Windows Server 2016 on a laptop and VPN in from the beach.

What Is Processed over a Slow Network Connection?

So, if the connection is deemed fast enough, *portions* of Group Policy are applied.

Surprisingly, even if the connection is deemed "not fast enough," several sections of Group Policy are *still* applied. Security settings and Administrative Templates are *guaranteed* to be downloaded during logon over a slow connection regardless of the speed. And there's nothing you can do to change that (not that you should want to). Additionally, included in security settings are Software Restriction Policy, EFS (Encrypting File System) Recovery Policy, and IPsec (IP Security) policy. They are also always downloaded over slow links.

 WARNING The Group Policy interface suggests that downloading of EFS Recovery Policy and IPsec policy can be switched on or off over slow links. This is not true. (See the note in the section "Using Group Policy to Affect Group Policy" later in this chapter.)

Other sections of Group Policy are handled as follows during a slow connection:

Folder Redirection Settings   By default, these are not downloaded over slow links. (Again, you can change this condition using the information in "Using Group Policy to Affect Group Policy.")

Scripts (Logon, Logoff, Startup, and Shutdown)   By default, script updates are not downloaded over slow links. (You can change this condition using the information in "Using Group Policy to Affect Group Policy.") Scripts themselves should still run, if the client can reach over the network and perform the run.

Disk Quota Settings   By default, these are not downloaded over slow links. (You can change this condition using the information in "Using Group Policy to Affect Group Policy.") The currently cached disk quota settings are still enforced.

Software Installation and Maintenance   By default, these are not downloaded over slow links. More specifically, the offers of newly available software are not shown to users. Users do have the ability to choose whether to pull down the latest versions of applications at their whim. You can torture your dial-in users by changing the behavior of how offers are handled and by permitting the icons of new software to be displayed. They will hate you after you do this, but that is for you and them to work out. See the corresponding setting described later in this chapter in "Using Group Policy to Affect Group Policy." More information about Group Policy Software Installation can be found in Chapter 11, "The Managed Desktop, Part 2: Software Deployment via Group Policy."

Software Restriction Policy   These are guaranteed to download over slow links. You cannot turn off this ability. More information about Software Restriction Policy can be found in Chapter 8.

802.11 Wireless Policy   By default, these are not downloaded over slow links. (You can change this condition using the information in "Using Group Policy to Affect Group Policy.") The currently cached 802.11 policy settings are still enforced.

802.3 Wired Policy (Windows Vista and Later)   By default, these are not downloaded over slow links. (You can change this condition using the information in "Using Group Policy to Affect Group Policy.")

Administrative Templates   These are guaranteed to download over slow links. You cannot turn off this ability.

EFS Recovery Policy   These are guaranteed to download over slow links. You cannot turn off this ability. The interface has an option that makes it appear as if you can turn off this ability, but you can't.

IPsec Policy   These are guaranteed to download over slow links. You cannot turn off this ability. Again, the interface has an option that makes it appear as if you can turn off this ability, but you can't.

Group Policy Preference Extensions   The Group Policy Preference Extensions, which we'll explore in Chapter 5, "Group Policy Preferences," will by default all download and process over slow links. Usually, people are concerned about getting Group Policy Preferences Drive Maps over a slow link. And starting with Windows 8.1 and continuing onward, Group Policy Preferences Drive Maps (new ones and changes) should download and process over a slow link. Before Windows 8.1, Group Policy Preferences Drive Maps would not process over a slow link (because Group Policy Preferences Drive Maps would not process in the background).

You can change what is considered fast enough for all these policy categories from 500Kbps to whatever speed you desire (independently for the Computer half and the User half). This is detailed in the section "Using Group Policy to Affect Group Policy."

Always Get Group Policy (Even on the Road, through the Internet)

So you want Group Policy to apply to your machines, even if they're not currently physically at your offices or if they rely upon users using a VPN. How can you do that?

There are two ways: One is from Microsoft. The other is (again, I mentioned I would be doing this) from PolicyPak, using PolicyPak Cloud.

Let's explore the two ways.

Group Policy over the Internet Using Unified Remote Access (Formally Known as DirectAccess)

Microsoft has had two technologies for "seamless network access"—DirectAccess (with Windows Server 2008 R2 and Windows Server 2012) has now been morphed into Unified Remote Access for Windows Server 2012 R2 and Windows Server 2016 and Unified Access Gateway (UAG). UAG is being discontinued for mainstream support in 2015, but Unified Remote Access (aka DirectAccess) lives on.

Here's the idea of both (they're built on the same technologies).

In short, both technologies promise a way for laptops to simply "always be on the network"—if they're really at headquarters or in the coffee shop. Now if that sounds a little scary, there's supposed to be lots and lots of security involved IN getting these solutions up and going.

But the *promise* of Unified Remote Access is quite interesting. The promise is that, once your laptops are set up to use Unified Remote Access, your laptops are, well, "always on the network." And if they're always on the network, they just always get Group Policy, naturally. I haven't personally set this up and tested it end to end. I hear generally "good things" from folks who say this works as advertised. It is quite an uphill battle getting all the hardware and software and licenses and such working. But when Unified Remote Access does work, I hear it works great, and Group Policy will magically apply, say, when your users are sipping coffee at Starbucks.

Unified Remote Access has three main problems:

- First, it doesn't work with all flavors of Windows 7, 8, and 10. It only works with the Enterprise versions of Windows, meaning if you have the Professional (or Pro) versions of Windows, you literally cannot use those systems and magically connect using Unified Remote Access.

- Second, all machines must be domain joined before working with Unified Remote Access.

- Last, based upon what people have told me, my understanding is that it's quite a bear to set up and keep working reliably.

That said, here are some links to help you if you decide to try out the Unified Remote Access (aka DirectAccess) route:

For DirectAccess on 2012 R2, I would start with:

`http://technet.microsoft.com/en-us/library/dn636118.aspx`

and:

`http://technet.microsoft.com/en-us/library/dn614138.aspx`

There's a multipart article on DirectAccess 2012 with precise how-to for a test lab here: `http://tinyurl.com/directaccess-2012`. Start with part 1 and continue on. If you're looking for all the articles in the series, try:

`http://blogs.technet.com/b/meamcs/archive/tags/direct+access/`

There's also a more modern book specifically about it found here:

`www.packtpub.com/networking-and-servers/windows-server-2012-unified-remote-access-planning-and-deployment`

Group Policy over the Internet (using PolicyPak Cloud)

If you want your machines to get Group Policy while your users are on the road or at remote offices, without having to buy or build servers or change any architecture at all, then check out PolicyPak Cloud.

PolicyPak Cloud is a service where you can do the following:

- Create XML "directives" based upon contents of real GPOs.
- Upload those XML directives.
- Have computers join your PolicyPak Cloud.
- Have computers download and process your PolicyPak directives.

In Figure 3.10, you can see four XML directives linked to the "All" group in PolicyPak Cloud.

You can literally take just about any piece of a GPO, and upload it to PolicyPak cloud. Client computers simply download and process these directives just like real GPOs and process them. Here's the best part about PolicyPak Cloud:

- There are no servers to buy, build, or install.

- XML directives are created from the contents of real GPOs. Almost all settings within a Group Policy Object can be delivered via PolicyPak Cloud.

- Client machines can be any flavor of Windows (Pro, Professional, or Enterprise).

- Client machines can be domain joined and even non–domain joined. (That's a big, big deal.)

- Clients can use PolicyPak Cloud over encrypted HTTP or HTTPS—behind proxy servers and other weird network setups.

FIGURE 3.10   PolicyPak Cloud starts you off with some preconfigured XML directives

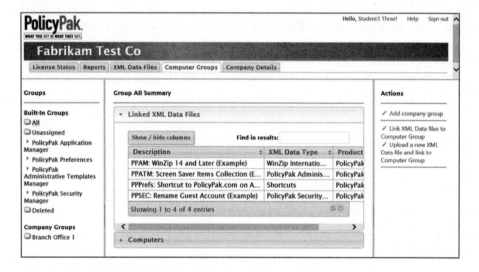

In this way, PolicyPak Cloud is great for IT pros who need to manage non–domain joined machines and machines that don't come back to the office very often or use a VPN. It's also great for Managed Service Providers (MSPs) who want a "one-stop shop" to upload directives and make sure they affect multiple customers at once (based upon customer groupings).

You can see the Quickstart and demos for PolicyPak Cloud on the PolicyPak web page at the following location and then check it out if it seems interesting to you:

`www.policypak.com/support-sharing/policypak-cloud-getting-started.html`

Also, see Appendix D for a PolicyPak Cloud walk-through.

Using Group Policy to Affect Group Policy

At times, you might want to change the behavior of Group Policy. Amazingly, you actually use Group Policy settings to change the behavior of Group Policy! Several Group Policy settings appear under both the User and Computer nodes; however, you must set the policy settings in each section independently.

Affecting the User Settings of Group Policy

The Group Policy settings that affect the User node appear under User Configuration ➢ Policies ➢ Administrative Templates ➢ System ➢ Group Policy. Remember that user accounts must be subject to the site, domain, or OU where these GPOs are linked in order to be affected. Most of these policy settings are valid for any Windows machine, although some are explicitly designed and will operate only on Windows XP, Windows Vista, Windows 7, and so on.

The following sections list the policy settings that affect the User side of Group Policy.

Set Group Policy Refresh Interval for Users

This setting changes the default User node background refresh rate of 90 minutes with a 0–30-minute positive randomizer to almost any number of refresh and randomizer minutes you choose. Choose a smaller number for the background refresh to speed up Group Policy on your machines, or choose a larger number to quell the traffic that a Group Policy refresh takes across your network. There is a similar refresh interval for computers, which is on an alternate clock with its own settings. A setting of 0 is equal to seven seconds. Set to 0 only in the test lab.

Configure Group Policy Slow Link Detection

You can change the default definition of *fast connectivity for users* from 500Kbps to any speed you like. Recall that certain aspects of Group Policy are not applied to machines that are determined to be coming in over slow links. This setting specifies what constitutes a slow link for the User node. There is an identically named policy setting located under the Computer node (explored later in this chapter) that also needs to be set to define what is slow for the Computer node. Preferably set these to the same number. Note that you can set the **Group Policy Slow Link Detection** policy setting to zero to disable it.

Configure Group Policy Domain Controller Selection

GPOs are written to the PDC emulator by default. When users (generally Domain Administrators or OU administrators) are affected by this setting, they are allowed to create new GPOs on Domain Controllers other than the PDC emulator. See Chapter 7 for more information on this setting and how and why to use it.

Create New Group Policy Object Links Disabled by Default

When users (generally Domain Administrators or OU administrators) are affected by this setting, the GPOs they create will be disabled by default. This ensures that users and computers are not hitting their refresh intervals and downloading half-finished GPOs that you are in the process of creating. Enable the GPOs when finished, and they will download during their next background refresh cycle.

Set Default Name for Group Policy Objects

If a user has been assigned the rights to create GPOs via membership in the Group Policy Creator Owners group and has also been assigned the rights to link GPOs to OUs within Active Directory, the default name created for GPOs is "New Group Policy Object." You might want all GPOs created at the domain level to have one name, perhaps "AppliesToDomain-GPO," and all GPOs created at the **Human Resources** OU level (and all child levels) to have another name, maybe "AppliestoHR-GPO." Again, in order for this policy to work, the user's account with the rights to create GPOs must be affected by the policy.

Enforce Show Policies Only

When users (generally Domain Administrators or OU administrators) are affected by this setting, the "Only show policy settings that can be fully managed" setting (explored in Chapter 6, "Managing Applications and Settings Using Group Policy") is forced to be enabled. This prevents the importation of "bad" Administrative Templates (ADM files), which have the unfortunate side effect of tattooing the Registry until they are explicitly removed. (See Chapter 6 for more information on using all types of ADM templates.) Note, however, that the updated GPMC will always show "bad" ADM templates and, hence, this isn't needed when using the updated GPMC (the one with RSAT) on your management station.

Turn Off Automatic Update of ADM Files

You'll learn all about ADM files (and this particular policy setting) in Chapter 6. But, in essence, ADM template files are the underlying "definitions" of what's possible in Group Policy–land (when you use pre-Vista management machines). When you use Vista (and later) management machines (like Windows 10), a new mechanism called ADMX files is used to define policy settings. Here's the 10-second "before Chapter 6" crash course. ADM templates start out in life on your local machine running the older GPMC. Then, they're "pushed up" into the GPO for future reference.

When it comes to ADM template behavior, the default behavior is to check the local machine's default location—that is, the \windows\inf folder—to see if the ADM template (locally) is newer than the one stored inside the GPO. If it's newer—bingo, the one in the GPO is overwritten.

By default, this check for an update occurs every time you double-click the Administrative Templates section of any GPO as if you were going to modify it. However, if you enable this setting, you're saying to ignore the normal update process and simply keep on using the ADM template you initially used. In other words, you're telling the system you'd prefer to keep the initial ADM template regardless of whether a newer one is available. (See Chapter 6 for more info on this topic.)

Determine If Interactive Users Can Generate Resultant Set of Policy Data

Users affected by this setting cannot use gpresult.exe, the Group Policy Modeling, Group Policy Results tasks in the GPMC, or the old-and-crusty RSOP.MSC (which shouldn't be used anyway).

Enabling this setting locks down a possible entry point into the system. That is, it prevents unauthorized users from determining the current security settings on the box and developing attack strategies.

This policy setting is valid only when applied to Windows XP workstations and Windows 2003 Servers (even though the policy specifies "At least XP and Server 2003").

In my testing, this setting did not affect Windows Vista and later machines.

Affecting the Computer Settings of Group Policy

The Group Policy settings that affect the Computer node appear under Computer Configuration ➢ Policies ➢ Administrative Templates ➢ System ➢ Group Policy. Once computers are affected by these policy settings, they change the processing behavior of Group Policy. Remember that the computer accounts must be subject to the site, domain, or OU where these GPOs are linked in order to be affected.

Note that also underneath "Group Policy" is another subcategory called "Logging and Tracing." We'll talk about those policy settings in Chapter 5 when we discuss the Group Policy Preferences. Next, we'll be exploring a lot of settings. If you don't see all the settings on your machine, it's likely because you're using a Windows 10, 8, or 7 management machine and not a Windows Server 2012 or Windows Server 2016 management machine.

If you're missing some settings, be sure to read the section "The Missing Group Policy Preferences' Policy Settings" a little later to understand why.

Preference Extension Policy Processing

Actually, this isn't the name of any specific policy setting. Indeed, you'll find 21 policy settings that manage each of the Group Policy Preferences items. You're looking for names like "Drive Maps preference extension policy processing" or "Printers preference extension policy processing" and the like. All of them have the same look and feel should you click on them, similar to what's seen in Figure 3.11.

Note that when the policy setting is Not Configured, the defaults are set.

Once enabled, each policy setting has four potential options:

Allow Processing Across a Slow Network Connection   Select this check box to allow this particular Group Policy Preferences category to download when logging on over slow links. This is set on by default. You might want to deselect this check box if you want logins to be faster over VPN so the Group Policy Preferences category isn't trying to reinstall over a VPN. Group Policy Preferences Printers is a good one to deselect because installing printers over VPN can be really slow.

Do Not Apply during Periodic Background Processing   If this option is selected, the particular Group Policy Preferences category will not be downloaded or applied during the background refresh. This is not selected by default, meaning that most Group Policy Preferences items will reapply when the user is logged on.

Process Even If the Group Policy Objects Have Not Changed   If this option is selected, it updates and reapplies the policy settings in this category even if the underlying GPO has not changed. Recall that this type of processing is meant to clean up should a user or an administrator have nefariously gone behind our backs and modified a local setting.

Background Priority   I'm not exactly sure why this option is available to us as administrators to tweak, because I've never seen a reason to use it. In short, this sets up how much processing juice this particular CSE will use. To be on the safe side, I would just leave it as Idle.

FIGURE 3.11   You can manage any of the 21 Group Policy Preferences CSEs using individual policy settings.

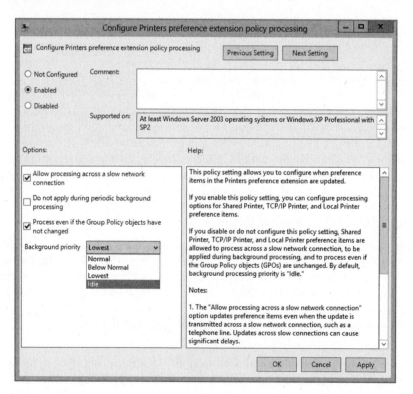

Turn Off Background Refresh of Group Policy

When this setting is enabled, the affected computer downloads the latest GPOs for both the user and the computer, according to the background refresh interval—but it doesn't apply them. The GPOs are applied when the user logs off but before the next user logs on. This is helpful in situations in which you want to guarantee that a user's experience stays the same throughout the session.

Set Group Policy Refresh Interval for Computers

This setting changes the default Computer node background refresh rate of 90 minutes with a 30-minute randomizer to almost any number of refresh and randomizer minutes you choose. Specify a smaller number for the background refresh to speed up Group Policy on your machines, or choose a larger number to quell the traffic a Group Policy refresh causes across your network. A similar refresh interval for the User node is on a completely separate and unrelated timing rate and randomizer. A setting of 0 equals seven seconds. Set to 0 only in the test lab.

Set Group Policy Refresh Interval for Domain Controllers

Recall that Domain Controllers are updated regarding Group Policy changes within five minutes. You can close or widen that gap as you see fit. The closer the gap, the more network chatter. Widen the gap and the security settings will be inconsistent until the interval is hit. A setting of 0 equals seven seconds. Set to 0 only in the test lab.

Configure User Group Policy Loopback Processing Mode

We'll explore this setting in detail in the next chapter.

Allow Cross-Forest User Policy and Roaming User Profiles

This policy is valid only in cross-forest trust scenarios. I'll describe how these work and how this policy works in Chapter 4, "Advanced Group Policy Processing," in the section "Group Policy with Cross-Forest Trusts."

This policy setting is valid only when applied to Windows XP/SP2 systems and later.

Configure Group Policy Slow Link Detection

You can change the default definition of *fast connectivity* from 500Kbps to any speed you like. Recall that certain aspects of Group Policy are not applied to those machines that are deemed to be coming in over slow links. Independently, an identically named policy setting that exists under the User node (explored earlier) also needs to be set to define what is slow for the User node. Preferably, set these to the same number.

Turn Off Resultant Set of Policy Logging

As you'll see in Chapter 7, users on Windows XP can launch the Resultant Set of Policy (RSoP) snap-in by typing **RSOP.MSC** at the command prompt. Enabling this policy setting doesn't prevent its launch but, for all intents and purposes, disables its use. This policy setting disables the use for the currently logged-on user (known as the interactive user) as well as anyone trying to get the results using the remote features of the RSoP snap-in.

This policy setting is valid only when applied to Windows XP workstations and Windows 2003 Servers (even though the policy specifies "At least XP and Server 2003").

In my testing, this setting did not affect Windows Vista and later machines. Your mileage may vary.

> On Windows Vista and later, regular users can only see the User half of the RSoP by default. They must be delegated the "Read Group Policy Results data" right over the computer they want to gather the information for. We talked about this in Chapter 2 in the section "Special Group Policy Operation Delegations."

Remove Users' Ability to Invoke Machine Policy Refresh

By default, mere-mortal users can perform their own manual background refreshes using gpupdate. However, you might not want users to perform their own gpupdate. I can think of only one reason to disable this setting: to prevent users from sucking up bandwidth to Domain Controllers by continually running gpupdate. Other than that, I can't imagine why you would want to prevent them from being able to get the latest GPO settings if they were so inclined. Perhaps one user is performing a denial of service (DoS) attack on your Domain Controllers by continually requesting Group Policy—but even that's a stretch.

Even if this policy is enabled, local administrators can still force a gpupdate. But, again, gpupdate only works when run locally on the machine needing the update.

This policy setting is valid only when applied to Windows XP and newer and requires a reboot to kick in.

Determine If Interactive Users Can Generate Resultant Set of Policy Data

This policy is similar to the **Turn off Resultant Set of Policy logging** setting but affects only the user on the console. Enabling this setting might be useful if you don't want the interactive user to have the ability to generate RSoP data but you still want to allow administrators to get the RSoP remotely.

This policy setting only affects Windows XP (and Windows Server 2003).

Configure Registry Policy Processing

This setting affects how your policy settings in the Administrative Templates subtrees react (and, generally, any other policy that affects the Registry). Once this policy setting is enabled, you have two other options:

Do Not Apply during Periodic Background Processing   Typically, Administrative Templates settings are refreshed every 90 minutes or so. However, if you enable this setting, you're telling the client not to ever refresh the Administrative Templates in the GPOs that are meant for it after the logon. You might choose to prevent background refresh for Administrative Templates for two reasons:

- On Windows XP when the background refresh occurs, the screen may flicker for a second as the system reapplies the changed GPOs (with their policy settings) and instructs Explorer.exe to refresh the Desktop. This could be a slight distraction for the user every 90 minutes or so.

- You might choose to disable background processing so that users' experiences with the Desktop and applications stay consistent for the entire length of their logon. Having settings suddenly change while the user is logged on could be confusing.

This issue was resolved since the release of Windows Vista. My advice is to leave this setting alone unless you're seriously impacted by the background processing affecting your users' experience.

Process Even If the Group Policy Objects Have Not Changed   If this setting is selected, the system will update and reapply the policy settings in this category even if the underlying GPO has not changed when the background refresh interval occurs. Recall that this type of processing is meant to clean up should an administrator have nefariously gone behind our backs and modified a local setting.

 You cannot turn off Registry policy processing over slow links. They are always downloaded and applied.

Configure Internet Explorer Maintenance Policy Processing

Once enabled, this policy setting has three potential options:

Allow Processing across a Slow Network Connection   Select this check box to allow Internet Explorer Maintenance settings to download when logging on over slow links. Enabling this could cause your users to experience a longer logon time, but they will adhere to your latest Internet Explorer wishes.

Do Not Apply during Periodic Background Processing   If this option is selected, the latest Internet Explorer settings in Active Directory GPOs will not be downloaded or applied during the background refresh.

Process Even If the Group Policy Objects Have Not Changed   If this option is selected, it updates and reapplies the policy settings in this category even if the underlying GPO has not changed. Recall that this type of processing is meant to clean up should a user or an administrator have nefariously gone behind our backs and modified a local setting.

Configure Software Installation Policy Processing

Once enabled, this policy setting has two potential options:

Allow Processing across a Slow Network Connection   As I stated, by default, software deployment offers are not displayed to users connecting over slow links. This is a good thing; allowing users to click the newly available icons to begin the download and installation of new software over a 56K dial-up line can be tortuous. Use this setting to change this behavior.

> If you have already distributed software via Group Policy and an offer has been accepted by a client computer (but perhaps not all pieces of the application have been loaded), setting this selection will likely not help, and your users may experience a long delay in running their application over a slow link. For more information on how to best distribute software to clients who use slow links, see Chapter 11.

Process Even If the Group Policy Objects Have Not Changed   For Software Installation, I cannot find any difference whether this option is selected or not, though Microsoft has implied it might correct some actions should the software become damaged. Since software deployment offers are only displayed upon logon or reboot (otherwise known as foreground policy processing), in my testing this setting seems not to have any effect.

> Users can still get caught in a trap regarding Group Policy Software Installation and slow links. That is, if they accept a "partial offer" while connected over a fast link, then try to request more of the same application, the computer will attempt to download that part over a slow link. This happens regardless of how the "Allow Processing across a Slow Network Connection" policy setting is set. See the Software Installation settings described in Chapter 11 for more information.

Configure Folder Redirection Policy Processing

Once enabled, this policy setting has two potential options:

Allow Processing across a Slow Network Connection   Recall that the Folder Redirection policy is changed only at logon time. Chances are you won't want dialed-in users to experience that new change. Rather, you'll want to wait until they are on your LAN. If you want to torture your users and allow them to accept the changed policy anyway, use this setting to change this behavior.

Process Even If the Group Policy Objects Have Not Changed   I cannot find any difference whether this setting is selected or not, though Microsoft has implied it might correct some folder-redirection woes should the username get renamed.

Folder Redirection settings are discussed in detail in Chapter 10.

Configure Scripts Policy Processing

This one is a weird one, so stay with me. If you change this setting, you're *not* saying, "I want to run scripts over a slow link."

What you're saying is, "When I'm over a slow link, I want to accept changes to where I know the scripts are running from."

That's a biiiiiig distinction. Here's the scenario:

- Fred has a GPO that tells him he's got a logon script that runs from \\server15\share10\runme.bat.
- Fred cheerfully runs this script, day in and day out—even over a slow link.
- Then, you change the GPO and point Fred's script to \\server81\share101\runme2.bat.
- Fred's computer will not be updated about the knowledge of the change. Fred will continue to try to run the script from the original location. Oops!

So, the idea is that you'll use this policy setting to change the behavior of the script's CSE if you want to ensure that Fred will receive the updated location—even over a slow link.

So, once enabled, this policy setting has three potential options:

Allow Processing across a Slow Network Connection Recall that, by default, updates to where scripts run are not downloaded over slow networks. Change this option to allow the updates to download over slow links. The actual running of the scripts is a different process; this setting only cares if there is a new or updated reference to a script.

Do Not Apply during Periodic Background Processing This option will not allow the newest script instructions to be downloaded.

Process Even If the GPOs Have Not Changed This option will allow the newest script instructions to be downloaded even if the GPOs have not changed.

Configure Security Policy Processing

Once enabled, this policy setting has two potential options:

Do Not Apply during Periodic Background Processing Recall that the security settings are refreshed on the machines every 16 hours, whether or not they need it. Checking this option will turn off that refresh. I recommend that you leave this as is. However, you might want to consider enabling this setting for servers with high numbers of transactions that require all the processing power they can muster.

Process Even If the GPOs Have Not Changed Recall that after 16 hours, this policy category is always refreshed. With this option enabled, the security policies will be reprocessed during *every* refresh cycle.

Configure IP Security Policy Processing

Once enabled, this policy setting has three potential options:

Allow Processing across a Slow Network Connection   When selected, this setting (shown in Figure 3.12) does nothing. IP Security settings are always downloaded, regardless of whether the computer is connected over a slow network. So, you might be asking yourself, what happens when you select this check box? Answer: nothing—it's a bug in the interface. To repeat: IP Security is always processed, regardless of the link speed.

> IPsec policies act slightly different from other policy setting categories. IPsec policy settings are not additive. For IP Security, the last applied policy wins.

FIGURE 3.12   The "Allow processing across a slow network connection" setting is not used for IP Security or EFS settings (all versions of Windows).

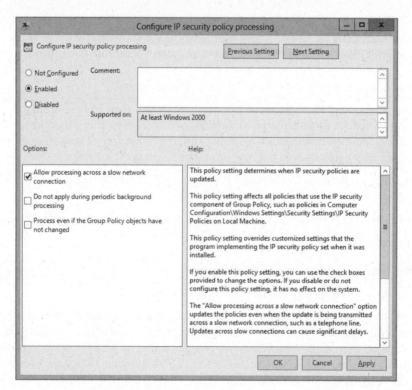

Do Not Apply during Periodic Background Processing   If this option is selected, the latest IP Security settings in Active Directory GPOs will not be downloaded or applied during the background refresh.

Process Even If the Group Policy Objects Have Not Changed   If this option is selected, it updates and reapplies the policy settings in this category even if the underlying GPO has not changed. Recall that this type of processing is meant to clean up should a user or an administrator have nefariously gone behind our backs and modified a local setting.

Configure EFS Recovery Policy Processing

Once enabled, this policy setting has three potential options:

Allow Processing across a Slow Network Connection   When this option is selected, it does nothing.

Like IP Security, the EFS recovery settings are always downloaded—even over slow networks. This is the same bug shown earlier in Figure 3.12. To repeat, EFS recovery policy is always processed, regardless of link speed.

   EFS recovery policies act slightly different from other policy setting categories. EFS recovery policies are not additive; the last applied policy wins.

Do Not Apply during Periodic Background Processing   If this option is selected, the latest EFS recovery settings in Active Directory GPOs are not downloaded or applied during the background refresh.

Process Even If the Group Policy Objects Have Not Changed   If this option is selected, it updates and reapplies the policy settings in this category even if the underlying GPO has not changed. Recall that this type of processing is meant to clean up should a user or an administrator have nefariously gone behind our backs and modified a local setting.

Configure Wireless Policy Processing

If this policy setting is enabled, it has three potential options:

Allow Processing across a Slow Network Connection   Check this option to allow the latest wireless policy settings to download when the user is logging on over slow links. Enabling this could cause your users to experience a longer logon time.

Do Not Apply during Periodic Background Processing   If this option is selected, the latest wireless policy settings will not be downloaded or applied during the background refresh.

Process Even If the Group Policy Objects Have Not Changed   If this option is selected, it updates and reapplies the policy settings in this category even if the underlying GPO has not changed. Recall that this type of processing is meant to clean up should a user or an administrator have nefariously gone behind our backs and modified a local setting.

Configure Wired Policy Processing

This policy setting is valid only when applied to Windows Vista and later. If this policy setting is enabled, it has three potential options:

Allow Processing across a Slow Network Connection   Check this option to allow the latest wired policy settings to download when the user is logging on over slow links. Enabling this could cause your users to experience a longer logon time.

Do Not Apply during Periodic Background Processing   If this option is selected, the latest wired policy settings will not be downloaded or applied during the background refresh.

Process Even If the Group Policy Objects Have Not Changed   If this option is selected, it updates and reapplies the policy settings in this category even if the underlying GPO has not changed. Recall that this type of processing is meant to clean up should a user or an administrator have nefariously gone behind our backs and modified a local setting.

Configure Disk Quota Policy Processing

If this policy setting is enabled, it has three potential options:

Allow Processing across a Slow Network Connection   Check this option to allow the latest disk quota policy settings to download and apply when the user logs on over slow links. Enabling this could cause your users to experience a longer logon time.

Do Not Apply during Periodic Background Processing   If this option is selected, the latest disk quota policy settings will not be downloaded or applied during the background refresh.

Process Even If the Group Policy Objects Have Not Changed   If selected, this option updates and reapplies the policy settings in this category even if the underlying GPO has not changed. Recall that this type of processing is meant to clean up should a user or an administrator have nefariously gone behind our backs and modified a local setting.

Always Use Local ADM Files for Group Policy Object Editor

ADM files are the underlying language that creates policy settings in pre–Windows Vista versions. I'll talk more about ADM files and how to best use them in Chapter 6. However, for reference, if a computer is affected by this policy setting, the Group Policy Object Editor attempts to show the text within the ADM files from your local %windir%\inf directory (usually C:\windows\inf). If the ADM file is different inside the GPO than on your local C:\windows\inf directory, you could end up seeing different settings and Explain text than what's inside the GPO.

WARNING   This policy is valid only when applied to Windows Server 2003 but not (strangely) Windows XP management stations.

Indeed, if this policy is enabled, you might now see totally different policy settings than were originally placed in the GPO. However, you might want to enable this policy setting if you know that you will always be using one specific management station. Stay tuned for Chapter 6 to see how to use this function.

Turn Off Local Group Policy Objects Processing

If a Windows Vista or later computer is affected by this policy setting, then whatever is set within the local GPOs is ignored.

This can be useful if a machine is originally used in a workgroup (non–domain joined environment) and then it's joined to the domain. In that case, you might want to ensure that no user has any lingering policy settings that will specifically affect them. Hence, your desire would be to control everything from Active Directory and not anything from the local level.

Of course, this policy setting only works when being delivered from Active Directory (not when it's set locally).

This policy setting affects only Windows Vista and later machines (including Windows Server 2008 machines and later).

Specify Startup Policy Processing Wait Time

This policy setting helps with timeouts when processing Group Policy. The policy setting only exists for Windows Vista and later; however, the facility to control these timeouts exists in other operating systems (like Windows XP/SP2 with a Registry hack).

Check out KB article 840669 (found here: http://tinyurl.com/88tbo) if you want to implement this setting for Windows XP/SP2 and earlier machines.

Specify Workplace Connectivity Wait Time for Policy Processing

This value is used if you're using workplace connectivity (aka DirectAccess).

If so, your computer can be running in the default of Asynchronous processing mode or be switched back to the Windows 2000 behavior of Synchronous processing mode (my suggestion).

If running Asynchronously, then the computer will continue on whether or not it can see your company across the Internet. The downside here is that you might miss the signal for something that could only process in the foreground (like Group Policy Preferences Drive Maps).

If running in Synchronous processing mode, the computer will wait (by default) 60 seconds to see your company across the Internet. After that, it "gives up" and lets the user log on.

If you want to force the waiting to be longer (in the case of Synchronous processing, or even in the case of Asynchronous processing), then set this value. The computer will wait this many seconds before continuing.

Configure Direct Access Connections as a Fast Network Connection

If you are using DirectAccess—see the section "Always Get Group Policy (Even on the Road, through the Internet)." You might want to treat all DirectAccess connections as fast —even if they aren't.

This seems like a good idea to me, because that way, your users will get the exact same Group Policy experience in the office and out of the office (even if it takes a little bit longer).

This setting only affects Windows 8 and later and Windows Server 2012 and later. If you want to affect a Windows RT machine, you need to specify this setting locally, manually, since Windows RT machines cannot receive Active Directory–based Group Policy.

Allow Asynchronous User Group Policy Processing When Logging On through Remote Desktop Services

Remember: Group Policy will process synchronously for servers of all types and asynchronously for clients (Windows XP and later). By running Group Policy asynchronously, you ensure that logins may run a little bit faster, but at the sacrifice of not always having the latest Group Policy settings at login time.

If you set this policy, you're making your Windows 2008 (and later) Remote Desktop Services (Terminal Servers) work like client systems do by default.

I wouldn't set this setting, personally, because I'm a fan of running synchronously, not asynchronously (even if it means things are a teensy-weensy bit slower at login). But that's just my opinion.

Change Group Policy Processing to Run Asynchronously When a Slow Network Connection Is Detected

This setting tells slow machines to avoid processing any CSE that requires synchronous processing.

I don't recommend having this setting on. Here's why:

- If your user isn't yet logged in and uses the VPN connection, then you'll be specifically avoiding items that process synchronously like Group Policy Preferences Drive Maps (if you use Windows 7 clients).

- If you are already logged in, then the user makes their VPN connection, then—well, it won't matter. That's because if you're already logged in, you would have missed the opportunity to process items like Group Policy Preferences Drive Maps (on Windows 7), because it can only process them at login time.

In short, don't bother with this setting. It makes my head hurt just thinking about what will and won't process. Ow.

Turn Off Group Policy Client Service AOAC Optimization

In the earlier section "Windows 8, 8.1, and 10 Group Policy: Subtle Differences," I described how the Group Policy service on Windows 8 and later will turn itself off after 10 minutes of idle time.

If you wanted to revert back to the Windows 7 style (which leaves the service always on), you would configure this setting to Enabled.

You might want to do this for Windows 8 and later desktops, since there is very little downside. And you might want to leave this behavior as is (that is, leave this setting Not Configured) for Windows 8 and later laptops to squeeze the extra battery life out of them.

Enable AD/DFS Domain Controller Synchronization during policy refresh

The help text description says it all.

"Enabling this setting will cause the Group Policy Client to connect to the same domain controller for DFS shares as is being used for Active Directory."

Therefore, when it's enabled, you are ensuring that the Group Policy client isn't making another connection to some other DC just to get Group Policy if it's also using DFS.

Configure Group Policy Caching and Enable Group Policy Caching for Servers

In the earlier section "Windows 8, 8.1 and 10 Group Policy: Subtle Differences" in Secret 6, I explained Group Policy Caching and talked about these two settings.

Configure Logon Script Delay

In the earlier section "Windows 8, 8.1 and 10 Group Policy: Subtle Differences" in Secret 8, I talked about how Windows will delay login script processing and also showed you this policy setting to tweak and configure if you decided.

The Missing Group Policy Preferences Policy Settings

As I stated, you could use a Windows 10 or Windows Server 2016 machine as your management machine and get the same Group Policy features. This is mostly true, except in one big case.

Seriously, this is weird, so stick with me. In Figure 3.13 you can see two screen shots. The left shows the Windows 10 management machine view of the Computer Configuration ➢ Policies ➢ Administrative Templates ➢ System ➢ Group Policy node. The right shows the same thing, except seen from a Windows Server 2016 management machine.

In fact, the list goes on for so long on the right that I've saved space and cut it off.

So, what are these "missing" definitions? These are the settings used to control, manage, and monitor the Group Policy Preferences (basically, what all of Chapter 5 is about.)

You'll see specific policy definitions to manage and Group Policy Preferences items like **Printers Policy Processing, Shortcuts Policy Processing, Start Menu Policy Processing**, and all sorts of other Group Policy Preferences–specific settings.

Look closely, and you'll also see another whole node *within* the Group Policy node called "Logging and tracing" that's only available in the definitions on Windows Server 2016.

Okay, so what gives?

We'll use and understand these settings in Chapter 5 in the "Troubleshooting: Reporting, Logging, and Tracing" section and learn more about where the definitions come from in Chapter 6.

FIGURE 3.13 For Windows 10 (left) you'll see fewer policy settings in the Group Policy node as compared to Windows Server 2016 (right).

Setting	State
Allow cross-forest user policy and roaming user profiles	Not configured
Always use local ADM files for Group Policy Object Editor	Not configured
Change Group Policy processing to run asynchronously whe...	Not configured
Configure Direct Access connections as a fast network conn...	Not configured
Configure disk quota policy processing	Not configured
Configure EFS recovery policy processing	Not configured
Configure folder redirection policy processing	Not configured
Configure Group Policy slow link detection	Not configured
Configure Internet Explorer Maintenance policy processing	Not configured
Configure IP security policy processing	Not configured
Configure registry policy processing	Not configured
Configure scripts policy processing	Not configured
Configure security policy processing	Not configured
Configure software Installation policy processing	Not configured
Configure user Group Policy loopback processing mode	Not configured
Configure wired policy processing	Not configured
Configure wireless policy processing	Not configured
Determine if interactive users can generate Resultant Set of ...	Not configured
Enable AD/DFS domain controller synchronization during p...	Not configured
Remove users' ability to invoke machine policy refresh	Not configured
Set Group Policy refresh interval for computers	Not configured
Set Group Policy refresh interval for domain controllers	Not configured
Specify startup policy processing wait time	Not configured
Specify workplace connectivity wait time for policy processi...	Not configured
Turn off background refresh of Group Policy	Not configured
Turn off Group Policy Client Service AOAC optimization	Not configured
Turn off Local Group Policy Objects processing	Not configured
Turn off Resultant Set of Policy logging	Not configured

Setting	State
Logging and tracing	
Allow asynchronous user Group Policy processing when log...	Not configured
Allow cross-forest user policy and roaming user profiles	Not configured
Always use local ADM files for Group Policy Object Editor	Not configured
Change Group Policy processing to run asynchronously wh...	Not configured
Configure Applications preference extension policy processi...	Not configured
Configure Data Sources preference extension policy processi...	Not configured
Configure Devices preference extension policy processing	Not configured
Configure Direct Access connections as a fast network conn...	Not configured
Configure disk quota policy processing	Not configured
Configure Drive Maps preference extension policy processing	Not configured
Configure EFS recovery policy processing	Not configured
Configure Environment preference extension policy processi...	Not configured
Configure Files preference extension policy processing	Not configured
Configure Folder Options preference extension policy proce...	Not configured
Configure folder redirection policy processing	Not configured
Configure Folders preference extension policy processing	Not configured
Configure Group Policy slow link detection	Not configured
Configure Ini Files preference extension policy processing	Not configured
Configure Internet Explorer Maintenance policy processing	Not configured
Configure Internet Settings preference extension policy proc...	Not configured
Configure IP security policy processing	Not configured
Configure Local Users and Groups preference extension poli...	Not configured
Configure Network Options preference extension policy pro...	Not configured
Configure Network Shares preference extension policy proc...	Not configured
Configure Power Options preference extension policy proce...	Not configured
Configure Printers preference extension policy processing	Not configured
Configure Regional Options preference extension policy pro...	Not configured
Configure registry policy processing	Not configured
Configure Registry preference extension policy processing	Not configured
Configure Scheduled Tasks preference extension policy proc...	Not configured
Configure scripts policy processing	Not configured
Configure security policy processing	Not configured
Configure Services preference extension policy processing	Not configured
Configure Shortcuts preference extension policy processing	Not configured
Configure software Installation policy processing	Not configured
Configure Start Menu preference extension policy processing	Not configured
Configure user Group Policy loopback processing mode	Not configured
Configure wired policy processing	Not configured
Configure wireless policy processing	Not configured
Determine if interactive users can generate Resultant Set of ...	Not configured
Enable AD/DFS domain controller synchronization during p...	Not configured
Remove users' ability to invoke machine policy refresh	Not configured
Set Group Policy refresh interval for computers	Not configured
Set Group Policy refresh interval for domain controllers	Not configured
Specify startup policy processing wait time	Not configured
Specify workplace connectivity wait time for policy processi...	Not configured
Turn off background refresh of Group Policy	Not configured
Turn off Group Policy Client Service AOAC optimization	Not configured
Turn off Local Group Policy Objects processing	Not configured
Turn off Resultant Set of Policy logging	Not configured

But since you can't wait that long, here's the abbreviated version. In short, the "definitions" of what's possible in Group Policy–land are stored in ADMX files (again, more detail—a lot more detail—in Chapter 6). Turns out, though, that Windows clients and Windows Server don't ship with the exact same definitions.

Kooky. The "missing" Group Policy settings are only available within the set that exists on Windows Server.

In Chapter 6 we'll revisit the topic of where policy definitions come from. I'll show you how to make sure you always have the "latest set" of policy settings, so they're no mystery—you'll always have the latest set.

This blog entry spells it all out (in the section "Logging and tracing missing from RSAT"): http://tinyurl.com/kowj66.

Final Thoughts

Group Policy doesn't just pick and choose when it wants to apply. Rather, a specific set of rules is followed when it comes time to process. Understanding these rules is paramount in helping you prevent potential Group Policy problems.

Here are a few takeaway tips to keep in mind:

Remember background refresh policy processing (member computers).   For all machine types, regular member computers refresh some time after the user is logged on (usually 90 minutes or so).

Remember when GPOs apply and don't apply.   By default, workstations (like Windows 10) will process GPOs *only* in the background (asynchronously). Some features, such as Software Distribution and Folder Redirection, can take two reboots or logons to take effect. Advanced Folder Redirection can take three logons before you see an effect. This is because these special functions can be processed only in the foreground.

Decide when to leave Fast Boot on or turn it off.   You can turn off Fast Boot to make Group Policy process more practicably.

You can leave Fast Boot on to make Group Policy process faster as the user is logging on.

Again, my revised advice is to turn off Fast Boot for well-connected (hardwired) machines and to leave it on for any kind of computer that could roam.

Remember background refresh policy processing (Domain Controllers).   All Domain Controllers receive a background refresh every five minutes (after replication has occurred).

Security policy processing occurs every 16 hours.   For all operating systems, just the security settings within all GPOs are reprocessed and applied every 16 hours, regardless of whether security settings have changed. This ensures that all security functions in all GPOs are reprocessed if someone has manually gone around the security on the system.

4

Advanced Group Policy Processing

In the previous chapter, we talked about basic Group Policy processing principles along with some special cases, including what happens over a slow link and how to manage the Group Policy engine itself—using Group Policy.

In this chapter, we'll explore some advanced scenarios. Here's the quick breakdown of what they are and why I think you'll be interested:

- If you've ever wanted to decide *when* and *where* a particular Group Policy should be applied, you're going to love WMI filters.

- If you've thought to yourself, "How do I get User-side settings to affect my computers?" you're going to love Loopback policy processing.

- And, if you've got multiple Active Directories tied together with cross-forest trusts, you'll want to understand how and when Group Policy applies.

We're also going to explore one of the components of the PolicyPak On-Premise suite, PolicyPak Admin Templates Manager, which helps with the first two bullets in the previous list.

So, let's get started with our advanced Group Policy processing.

Fine-Tuning When and Where Group Policy Applies

Pretend for a second there was exactly one level of Group Policy.

That would make it very difficult to segment out your users and computers into compartments and then link GPOs over to them.

But even then, with the three levels—site, domain, and OU—sometimes it can be a real challenge to get specific GPOs, or specific stuff within GPOs, to hit users and computers within a level.

In the following sections, we'll explore two ways to fine-tune when and where a Group Policy Object (itself) and a Group Policy Object's contents apply.

Using WMI Filters to Filter the Scope of a Group Policy Object (Itself)

In Chapter 2, "Managing Group Policy with the GPMC and via PowerShell," I alluded to a power called WMI filters. I like to think of WMI filters as adding laser-sighting to the gun of Group Policy. With WMI filters, you can dive into and inspect the soul of your client machines, and if certain criteria are met, you can then apply the GPO to them.

While WMI filters can be used with any GPO, I find that people usually use them for targeting software via Group Policy Software Installation (GPSI) or for circumstances where you want machines within an OU to get different settings based upon their operating system.

I explore Group Policy Software Installation in Chapter 11, "The Managed Desktop, Part 2: Software Deployment via Group Policy."

WMI is a huge animal, and you can choose to filter on thousands of items. Hot items to filter on typically include the following:

- The amount of memory
- The available hard-drive space
- CPU speed
- A hotfix
- OS version or service pack level

But you don't have to stop there. You can get creative and filter GPOs on obscure items (if they exist and are supported by the hardware) such as the following:

- BIOS revision
- Manufacturer of the CD drive
- Whether a UPS is connected
- The rotational speed of the fan

The potential esoteric criteria you can query for, and then filter, goes on and on.

A silly example might be "Prevent Access to the Control Panel when the machine has at least 2GB of memory."

Okay, perhaps that's a little too silly. You likely wouldn't care about showing or hiding desktop settings depending on the amount of RAM a computer has. But you can take the ideas here and use them in real examples. You can do things like this:

- "Only deploy DogFoodMaker Professional when I have these hotfixes installed."
- "On Tuesdays at logon time, start up Excel."
- "Only install an operating system service pack when I have at least 3GB of RAM and 10GB of free hard-drive space."

The idea is that either Group Policy will apply the whole contents of the GPO if the WMI filter evaluates to True or it will not apply the contents of the GPO if the WMI filter evaluates to False. Likewise, if "today" the GPO evaluates to True, but "tomorrow" it evaluates to False, the GPO will "fall out of scope" and then un-apply.

To give this a try, we'll first need some tools to help us figure out which pieces of WMI to query. We'll then take what we've learned and use the GPMC to create a WMI filter to specifically target the systems we want.

Unfortunately, I don't have room to dive into how or why WMI works on a molecular level. If you're unfamiliar with WMI, take a peek at:

`http://msdn.microsoft.com/en-us/library/aa394582%28VS.85%29.aspx`

shortened to `http://tinyurl.com/yjpojph`.

So, let's start off by creating a WMI filter and associating it with a GPO. Let's make an example that says, "Turn off the ability to change Windows sounds when the RAM on the machine is over 500MB." Yes, yes, it's a positively silly example. The point is that you'll be able to create your first WMI filter and associate it with a GPO and see that it works (provided your machines have over 500MB of RAM).

Tools (and References) of the WMI Trade

To master WMI, you have to do a lot of work. You'll have to read up on and master four crucial pieces of WMI documentation, three of which are found at the following websites:

`http://msdn2.microsoft.com/en-us/library/ms974579.aspx`

(shortened to `http://tinyurl.com/yt4jlu`)

`http://msdn2.microsoft.com/en-us/library/ms974592.aspx`

(shortened to `http://tinyurl.com/2bjfkb`)

`http://msdn2.microsoft.com/en-us/library/ms974547.aspx`

(shortened to `http://tinyurl.com/2f464f`)

Or work through the zillions of hits when you Google, I mean Bing, "WMI and PowerShell."

What? You don't have time for that? No problem! You can do the next best thing and "wing it." We'll use two tools to create WMI queries, and then we'll manually bend them into WMI filters.

- WMI CIM Studio is available on Microsoft's website. At last check, it was at

  `http://www.microsoft.com/en-us/download/details.aspx?id=24045`

- The Scriptomatic version 2 tool, which we'll be using for these examples, is available at

  `http://www.microsoft.com/en-us/download/details.aspx?id=12028`

The Scriptomatic tool was made by my pals the "Microsoft Scripting Guys." The tool "enumerates" all the available WMI classes and then makes them available for an easy-breezy query. Note that you'll have to run the tool as an Administrator or you'll get errors.

In Figure 4.1, the WMI class `Win32_ComputerSystem` is selected. Then, scriptomagically, all the WMI attributes in that class are exposed in a ready-to-run VBScript application. You can see them in Figure 4.1, including `Systemtype`, `Status`, `WakeUpType`, and the one we're after, `TotalPhysicalMemory`, which expresses the amount of RAM in this machine. Just click the Run button and you can see the output with the values on *this* machine.

FIGURE 4.1   The Scriptomatic version 2 tool from the "Microsoft Scripting Guys"

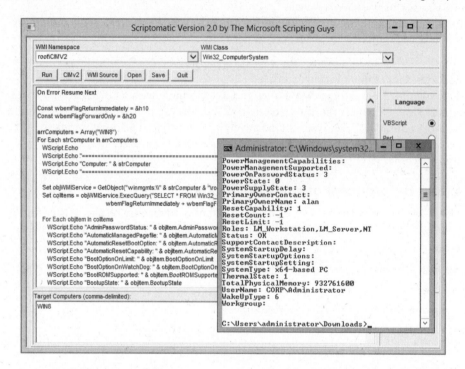

When you click Run, the script runs in a little prompt window. You can see that the `TotalPhysicalMemory` of this box is 932761600, which is about 1GB. The point here, however, is that the unit measurement and expected output of this field is expressed in number of bytes. We'll leverage this information when we bend this WMI query into a WMI filter.

WMI Filter Syntax

You can start nearly all the WMI filters you'll create using Scriptomatic. All that's left is to wrap a little logic around the output. All the WMI filters we'll create have the following syntax:

```
SELECT * from Win32_{something}
WHERE {variable} [=,>,<,is, etc] {desired result}
```

Now, all we have to do is plug in the stuff we already know and we're off and running. In this example, we're using Win32_ComputerSystem. We know the variable we want is *TotalPhysicalMemory,* and we know that we want it to be greater than 1.5GB, which we can represent as > 1500000000. Yes, I know 1500000000 isn't exactly 1.5GB of memory (it's actually less), but it's close enough. Anyway, when you put it all together, you get:

```
SELECT * from Win32_ComputerSystem WHERE TotalPhysicalMemory > 1500000000
```

Easy as pie. However, not all WMI filters are this easy. Some WMI variable entries have text, and you must use quotes to specifically match what's inside the string to what's inside the WMI variable.

Creating and Using a WMI Filter

Once your WMI filter is in the correct syntax, you're ready to inject it into an existing GPO. Again, this can be any GPO you want.

Creating and using a WMI filter is a two-step process: creating and then using. (I guess that makes sense.)

WMI Filter Creation

Before you can filter a specific GPO, you need to define the filter in Active Directory. Follow these steps:

1. Fire up the GPMC, then drill down to the Forest ➤ Domains ➤ WMI Filters node.

2. Right-click the WMI Filters node and select New, as seen in Figure 4.2.

FIGURE 4.2   Right-click the WMI Filters node to create a WMI filter.

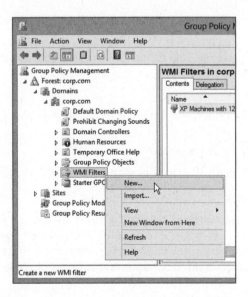

3. When you do, you'll be presented with the New WMI Filter dialog box, seen in Figure 4.3. You'll be able to type in a name and description of your new filter. Then, click the Add button, and in the Queries field, just enter the full SELECT statement from before.

FIGURE 4.3 This WMI query will evaluate to True when the machine has 1.5GB of memory or more.

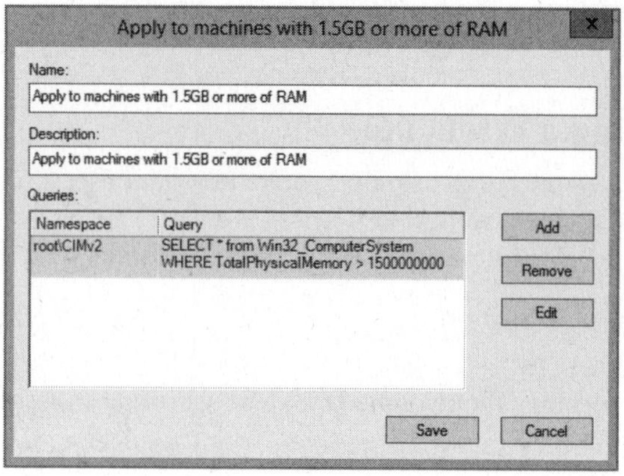

4. When you're done, click Save. Your query is now saved into Active Directory and can be leveraged for any GPO you want. We'll explore how to do that next.

WMI Filter Usage

Using the GPMC, it's easy to find the GPO you want and then leverage the WMI filter you just made. Follow these steps:

1. Locate the "Prohibit Changing Sounds" GPO you created (which should be linked to the domain level).

2. Click the Scope tab of the GPO.

3. In the WMI Filtering section, select the WMI filter you just created, as shown in Figure 4.4.

4. At the prompt, confirm your selection.

Now this GPO will only apply to machines with 1.5GB of RAM or more.

WMI Performance Impact

WMI filters can be a bit tough to create, but they're worth it. You can filter target machines that meet specific criteria for GPOs that leverage GPSI or any other Group Policy function.

Remember, the whole contents of the Group Policy Object will process when the WMI filter evaluates to True, and when the WMI filter evaluates to False, the whole contents will evaluate to False.

FIGURE 4.4   Choose the GPO (or GPO link) and select a WMI filter.

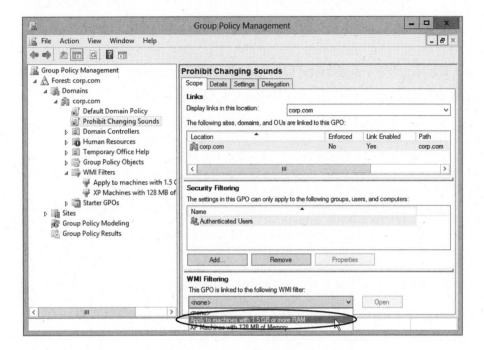

Keep in mind that WMI filters take some percentage of performance away each and every time Group Policy processing is evaluated. Typically the delay is on the order of a few milliseconds to a second or two (with one big exception, noted in a moment).

So, that is, at every logon, at startup, and every 90 minutes thereafter, you'll take a little performance hit because WMI filters are reevaluated. So, be careful and don't link a GPO to the domain level or every single machine will work hard to evaluate that WMI query.

So, my example where I used the WMI filter on a GPO for the whole domain *isn't such a hot idea.* I did it only for the sake of the example, and you should try to avoid that kind of use in the real world.

The upshot: Be careful where you link GPOs with WMI queries. You could affect GPO processing performance. You'll definitely want to test your WMI filters first in the lab for performance metrics before you roll them out company wide.

Here's a big tip: Avoid the Win32_Product class, which handily enables you to verify if a particular piece of software is installed on the machine. If it's so handy, why avoid it? Tests show that it's just awful when it comes to performance. A query to Win32_Product takes an average of about 11 seconds! So you don't want to add 11 seconds of processing time if you don't absolutely have to.

Note that Windows 7 and later improve on WMI performance over XP by some percentage. I've read statistics that it's 20 percent to 50 percent faster, but your experiences may vary.

Return to Chapter 2 to review how to back up and restore WMI filters as well as how to delegate their creation and use.

Using PolicyPak Admin Templates Manager to Filter the Scope of a Group Policy Object's Contents

As a 12-year Group Policy MVP (as of this writing), one question people ask me, over and over again, is, "Is there any way to target *some* of the items within a Group Policy Object to *some* of the people based upon criteria?"

In other words, using just one Group Policy Object, can you get some stuff within that GPO to hit some users (based upon who they are and what they're doing) and other stuff in the same GPO to hit other users (based upon who they are and what they're doing)?

The short answer is yes, if you're using Group Policy Preferences. In the next chapter, I'll dive deep into the idea of Group Policy Preferences' item-level targeting (ILT).

But for the majority of settings within a Group Policy Object, the 3000+ Group Policy Admin Template settings from Microsoft, there is no way to do that. So, I asked the developers at my company PolicyPak to build it, and it's called PolicyPak Admin Templates Manager.

Here's the general idea of PolicyPak Admin Templates Manager:

- Create different "Collections" (like folders).

- Collections can have filters (really, item-level targeting) upon them so they'll only apply when the conditions are True.

- Inside the Collections, you put your policies.

- Policies themselves within Collections can also have filters (really, item-level targeting.)

So in Figure 4.5, you can see a specific Group Policy Object using PolicyPak Admin Templates Manager that contains two Collections (one for "When machines are Windows 7" and another for "When machines are Windows 10"). I just thought this was a good example; your criteria could be just about anything you want, including computer name match, IP range, and lots of other possibilities.

Then inside each folder, put the Admin Templates policy settings you want to fire off (when the Collection's conditions evaluate to True). So in Figure 4.6, within the "When machines are Windows 10" Collection, you can see I've added the policy settings **Prevent access to registry editing tools, Prevent access to the command prompt**, and **Custom User Interface**.

If you look closely at Figure 4.6, you'll see that the **Custom User Interface** policy setting in the column labeled "Item Level Targeting," is set to Yes. This means this particular policy setting will fire off with its own set of conditions. For instance, maybe I only want naughty user Fred to get a **Custom User Interface**, but all others who get this Group Policy Object will merely get the other two policy settings in the Collection (when they use Windows 10).

FIGURE 4.5 Use PolicyPak Admin Templates Manager to create Collections and put filters (item-level targeting) upon them. Policies go inside.

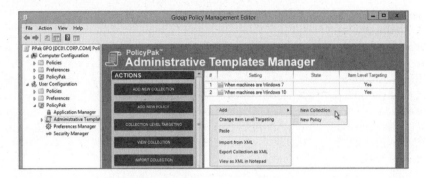

FIGURE 4.6 Specify which Group Policy Admin Template policy settings should take affect within a Collection.

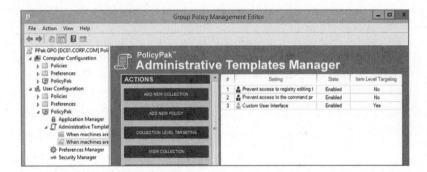

So to be clear, using the in-the-box WMI filters is sufficient if you want to specify when the whole contents of the Group Policy Object will take effect (or not take effect), but if you utilize PolicyPak Admin Templates Manager, you'll get flexibility *inside* a Group Policy Object to target when Group Policy Admin Template Settings will take effect (or not).

To see PolicyPak Admin Templates Manager with Collections and item-level targeting in action, see the video on the following page:

```
http://www.policypak.com/products/admin-template-manager.html
```

Group Policy Loopback Processing

As you know, the normal course of Group Policy scope is local computer, site, domain, and then each nested OU. But sometimes it's necessary to deviate from the normal routine. For instance, you might want all users, whoever they are, to be able to walk up and log onto a specific machine and get the same User node settings. This can be handy in public computing environments such as libraries, nursing stations, and kiosks as well as manufacturing and production assembly environments. This is also critically necessary for Remote Desktops/Terminal Server environments, as discussed in the section "Group Policy Loopback—Replace Mode" later in this chapter.

Wouldn't it be keen if you could round up all the special computers on which users need the same settings for an OU and force them to use these settings? In this way, whoever logs onto those computers would get the same Internet Explorer settings (such as a special proxy) and logon scripts or certain Control Panel restrictions—just for those workstations.

There are two ways to do this: Use Group Policy Loopback processing (in the box from Microsoft) or use PolicyPak (PolicyPak Application Manager and/or PolicyPak Admin Templates Manager).

We'll explore both.

Reviewing Normal Group Policy Processing

Recall that sometimes computers and users can each be relegated into different OUs. Indeed, any user from any other portion of the domain, say the Domain Administrator, could log onto WIN10 located under the **Human Resources Computers** OU.

When a user account contained in one OU logs onto a computer contained in another OU, the normal behavior is to process the computer GPOs based on the site, domain, and OU hierarchy and then process the user GPOs based on the site, domain, and OU hierarchy. This is true just by the rules of time: computers start up, their GPOs are processed, users log on, and their GPOs are processed.

 Even when the default of Fast Boot in Windows XP (and later) is turned off, that's generally the way things happen.

So, if the Domain Administrator were to sit down at the WIN10 machine in the **Human Resources Computers** OU, the normal course of events would apply the policy settings in the Computers node from the Default-First-Site-Name, then the Corp.com domain, and then finally the **Human Resources Computers** OU. Next, the policy settings in GPOs linked to the user account would apply; first from the Default-First-Site-Name and then only from the Corp.com domain (as the Administrator account is not sitting under any OU in our examples).

With Group Policy Loopback processing enabled, the rules change for a client computer.

There are two Group Policy Loopback modes: Merge and Replace. In both, the computer is tricked into forgetting that it's really a computer.

It temporarily puts on a hat that says, "I'm a user," and processes the site, domain, and organizational unit GPOs as if it were a user. Kooky, huh? Let's take a look at the Merge and Replace modes for Loopback processing.

For our examples, we'll pretend to have another machine called WIN10B. This is a new machine, just for this set of examples. It is not listed in Chapter 1 in the section "Getting Ready to Use This Book."

Group Policy Loopback—Merge Mode

When computers are subject to Group Policy Loopback—Merge mode, GPOs process in the normal way at startup (and at background refresh time): Computer node for site, for domain, and then for each nested OU. The user then logs on, and policy settings meant for that user are applied in the normal way: all GPOs are processed from the site, the domain, and then each nested OU.

But when computers are affected by Group Policy Loopback—Merge mode, the system determines where the computer account is and applies another round of User node settings—those contained in all GPOs that lead to that computer (yes, User node settings). This means that the logged-on user gets whacked with two different sets of User node policy settings. Here's the timeline:

- The computer starts up and gets the appropriate Computer node policy settings.

- The user logs on and gets the appropriate User node policy settings.

- The computer then puts on a hat that says, "I'm a user." Then all *User* node policy settings apply to the *computer*. Again, this happens because the computer is wearing the "I'm a user" hat.

The net result is that the user settings from the user's account and the user settings from the computer (which temporarily thinks it's a user) are equal to each other; neither is more important than the other, except when they overlap. In that case, the computer settings win, as usual.

The Group Policy Loopback—Merge mode can be handy when you need to modify a property in the user profile, but do it per computer.

Group Policy Loopback—Replace Mode

When computers are subject to Group Policy Loopback—Replace mode, Group Policy processes in the normal way at startup (and at background refresh time): Computer node for site, domain, and then each nested OU. The user then logs on, and GPOs meant for the user are totally ignored down the food chain for the logged-on user. Instead, the computer puts on an "I'm a user" hat, and the system determines where the computer account is but applies the User node settings contained in all GPOs that lead to that computer. Therefore, you change the balance of power so all users are forced to heed the User settings based on what is geared for the computer.

Group Policy Loopback—Replace mode has one other major use: Remote Desktop Services (which used to be known as Terminal Services). If you have lots of servers and lots of users logging onto them, chances are you want everyone who logs onto your Terminal Services machines to have precisely the same settings, regardless of who they are.

The process of establishing these settings is straightforward:

1. Create an OU for your Terminal Services, I mean, Remote Desktop Services (RDS) computers and give it an appropriate name, such as **Remote Desktop Services** OU.

2. Set Loopback Replace mode to apply to that OU.

3. Stuff your Remote Desktop Services server computer objects into the OU and reboot the RDS machines.

Now any user policy settings within GPOs set on the **Remote Desktop Services** OU and everyone logging onto these Remote Desktop Servers will get the exact same settings.

All Remote Desktop servers respond just fine to Loopback—Replace mode. Just be sure to stuff your RDS (i.e., Terminal Services) computer objects into your designated OU, too, and then manually configure the policy settings on those computers as desired.

As an administrator, you might want to log onto the Remote Desktop Services machines, but you don't want the same settings as everyone else. To configure this, simply use the techniques found in Chapter 2 and filter the GPO containing the policy that performs the lockout for, say, Domain Administrators.

By and large, Group Policy Loopback—Replace mode is more useful than Merge mode and works well in public computing environments such as labs, kiosks, classrooms, training machines, libraries, and so on.

Confused? Let's generate an example to "unconfuse" you.

So let's work through an example to solidify your understanding of Replace mode. In this example, we'll perform a variety of steps:

1. Create a new OU called **Public Kiosk**.

2. Move a Windows 10 machine into the **Public Kiosk** OU. Again, use the WIN10B computer (a new computer for these examples).

3. Create a new GPO for the **Public Kiosk** OU that performs two functions:

   ▪ Disables the Control Panel so users cannot get to it.

   ▪ Performs Group Policy Loopback—Replace mode processing so that *all* users are forced to embrace the setting. That is, everyone logging onto the computers in the **Public Kiosk** OU will get the edict that kills the Control Panel. (So, no one will be able to access the Control Panel.)

Loopback—Merge Mode with Remote Desktop Services

In the section "Group Policy Loopback—Replace Mode," I suggested that using Loopback—Replace mode can be great for RDS, or Remote Desktop Services (previously known as Terminal Services). The issue with that is that you really kind of "separate" your desktop and laptop world from your RDS world. It doesn't have to be that way.

With a little savvy, you could actually use Group Policy Loopback—Merge mode and specify only certain differences between your desktop and laptop world and your RDS world—specifically, things you want different in your RDS world.

Here's a prime example and way to wrap your head around this.

Let's say you have a very handsome corporate background image applied to all your normal workstations. These graphics are typically very detailed and large graphic files.

This is super-duper on your desktops and laptops: you're likely storing the image locally, and it's no problem at all for those detailed images to be displayed. Piece of cake.

On RDS sessions, that's another story.

Via a slow WAN or 3G connection, that background would have to get drawn, over and over again, and that slows the user down every time they log on and during the use of the system. Sure, you could prevent showing the background image at all, but then they see just a lousy black background that, well, simply looks terrible.

So, here's the big idea: Have a separate image just for your RDS sessions that is similar to your normal corporate background image but smaller in size and reduced in detail.

Then, when your users utilize RDS, you want two things to happen: You also want the users' "everyday" policies to be there (that is, all their normal stuff) but the twist is that you want to ensure that they ditch the "complex" background for the "simpler" (but similar) background. The look and feel between the two systems will be (almost) exactly the same and they get to maintain their other normal Group Policy settings!

So, if you're careful, you could use Loopback—Merge such that you don't need to maintain a completely separate set of User-side policy settings: one for your desktops and laptops and one for your RDS world.

Instead, you have all your user settings applied to your user objects (as normal), and you then need only apply the delta of special, optimized User-side settings to your Remote Desktop Services servers.

To do this, you'll need to follow these steps:

1. Create an OU, say, **Remote Desktop Services**, and move your Remote Desktop Services computer accounts into this OU.

2. Create a new GPO on that OU and name it, say, "All Remote Desktop Services Servers."

3. Drill down to the new GPO to Computer Configuration ➢ Policies ➢ Administrative Templates ➢ System ➢ Group Policy ➢ User Group Policy Loopback Processing mode, and specify that it be in Merge mode.

4. Drill down into User Configuration ➢ Windows ➢ Desktop ➢ Desktop. Double-click the **Desktop Wallpaper** policy setting, then enable it and specify the path to the new Desktop wallpaper for the Remote Desktop Services servers.

Now, whenever you log on as any user to Remote Desktop Services, you get a different background image but retain all your other user settings.

Creating a New OU

To create a new OU called **Public Kiosk**, follow these steps:

1. Log onto the Domain Controller DC01 or WIN10MANAGEMENT as Domain Administrator.

2. Choose Start ➢ All Programs ➢ Administrative Tools and select Active Directory Users and Computers.

3. Right-click the domain name, and choose New ➢ Organizational Unit. Enter **Public Kiosk** as the name in the New Object—New Organizational Unit dialog box.

> **WARNING**   You are creating this new OU on the same level as **Human Resources**. Do not create this new OU underneath **Human Resources**.

Moving a Client into the Public Kiosk OU

In this case, we'll move a different computer, say WIN10B, into the **Public Kiosk** OU. Follow these steps:

1. In Active Directory Users and Computers, right-click the domain and choose Find to open the "Find Users, Contacts and Groups" dialog box.

2. In the Find dropdown, select Computers. In the Name field, type **WIN10B** (or the name of some other computer) to find the computer account of the same name. Once

you've found it, right-click the account and choose Move. Move the account to the **Public Kiosk** OU.

Repeat these steps for all other computers you want to move to the **Public Kiosk** OU.

Creating a Group Policy Object with Group Policy Loopback— Replace Mode

We want the Display Properties dialog box disabled for all users who log onto WIN10B. To do this, we need to set two policy settings within a single GPO: **Prohibit Access to the Control Panel** and **User Group Policy Loopback Processing Mode**. Follow these steps using the GPMC:

1. Right-click the **Public Kiosk** OU, and choose "Create a GPO in this domain, and Link it here."

2. In the New GPO dialog box, name the GPO something descriptive, such as "No Control Panel—Loopback Replace."

3. Highlight the GPO and click Edit to open the Group Policy Management Editor.

4. To hide the Settings tab, drill down to User Configuration ➤ Policies ➤ Administrative Templates ➤ Control Panel ➤ and double-click the **Prohibit Access to the Control Panel** policy setting. Change the policy setting from Not Configured to Enabled, and click OK.

5. To enable Loopback processing, drill down to Computer Configuration ➤ Policies ➤ Administrative Templates ➤ System ➤ Group Policy and double-click the **Configure user Group Policy loopback processing mode** policy setting. Change the setting from Not Configured to Enabled; select Replace from the dropdown box, as shown in Figure 4.7, and click OK.

6. Close the Group Policy Management Editor.

Verifying That Group Policy Loopback—Replace Mode Is Working

You'll want to log onto WIN10B, but you'll need to restart it because Loopback processing doesn't seem to ever take effect until a reboot occurs. Since we're using Loopback Policy processing in Replace mode, you can choose any user you have defined—a mere mortal or even the administrator of the domain.

Switch to the Desktop view, right-click on the Desktop, and select Personalize. Note that no one can access the Personalize settings (which is part of Control Panel), as shown in Figure 4.8.

Group Policy Loopback—Replace mode policy processing is powerful but is only useful for specialty machines. Additionally, you'll need to use it sparingly, because Loopback processing is a bit more CPU intensive for the client and servers and quite difficult to troubleshoot should things go wrong.

FIGURE 4.7   Choose the Loopback Processing mode desired; in this case, Replace.

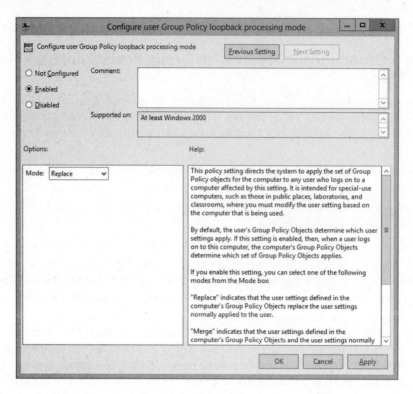

FIGURE 4.8   With Group Policy Loopback—Replace mode processing enabled, all users are affected by a computer's setting.

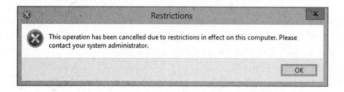

Additional Remote Desktop (Terminal Services) Tips

As a side note, there is a gaggle of policy settings that affect Remote Desktop Services servers.

- To manipulate computer settings for Remote Desktop Services, drill down to Computer Configuration ➢ Policies ➢ Administrative Templates ➢ Windows Components ➢ Remote Desktop Services.

- To manipulate Terminal Services clients, drill down to User Configuration ➢ Policies ➢ Administrative Templates ➢ Windows Components ➢ Remote Desktop Services.

Including information on how best to use these policy settings is beyond the scope of this book. To that end, here's a bunch of recommended reading:

- Windows Server 2008 Terminal Services Resource Kit: `http://tinyurl.com/773x7ws`

- Windows Server 2008 R2 Remote Desktop Services Resource Kit: `http://tinyurl.com/blqm8pt`

Here are three articles that all help with XenApp tuning using Group Policy:

`www.xenappblog.com/2010/xenapp-6-tuning-group-policy-for-windows-2008-r2/`

`www.xenappblog.com/2009/terminal-server-xenapp-tuning-tips-group-policy/`

`http://www.citrixtools.net/articles/article/terminal-server-xenapp-tuning-tips`

My pals Carl Webster and Alex Verboon often blog about Group Policy and Remote Desktops at `www.CarlWebster.com` and `www.verboon.info`, respectively.

One final parting tip regarding Terminal Services, I mean Remote Desktop Services. Microsoft has a nice, older piece of documentation that has a lot of tips and tricks for Terminal Services administrators vis-à-vis Group Policy. The document is named "Step-by-Step Guide for Configuring Group Policy for Terminal Services," and it can be found here: `http://tinyurl.com/7snwgjn`.

Loopback without Loopback (Switched Mode with PolicyPak Application Manager and PolicyPak Admin Templates Manager)

Again: This isn't a commercial, but rather something you should just know about in case you need it.

Before we go onward, let's face it: Loopback processing does work as advertised, but it comes with some strings attached.

Issue 1: Hard to implement.   When you use loopback, you have to go through mental gymnastics to calculate what policy settings are going to affect which people on what machines and what times. Typically, people "give up" on Loopback because it can be unpredictable.

Issue 2: Can slow things down.   When you use Loopback, you're slowing things down at login. This is because you're essentially processing Group Policy twice: once for the user and once again for the computer pretending to be the user. (Remember, the computer puts on an "I'm a user" hat.)

Issue 3: You (often) get more than you bargained for.   The number one problem I see when I review people's use of Loopback processing is that an administrator *wanted* to deliver just one or two User-side settings to all computers but instead implemented a huge gaggle of settings from lots of GPOs (oops) by accident. And it's really, really easy to do. That's because the computer, when in Loopback mode, doesn't concern itself with "just one setting." It's applying *all* settings to the computer as a user.

So is there a way to somehow clean up all three of these issues and deliver exactly the User-side settings I want to all computers within an OU ... without actually using Loopback?

Yes there is. The PolicyPak On-Premise suite enables you to do this in two ways. First, you can deploy application settings to all users on a computer (without using Loopback). Second, you can deploy any Admin Template setting to all users on a computer (again, without using Loopback).

In Figure 4.9, you can see a definition to deliver Firefox, Java, and Lync settings, where the directives are stored on the *Computer side*. In this way, all users on the computers pick up these applications' settings: no Loopback required. All users on these computers just get what you lay down.

In Figure 4.10, you can see two (normally User side) Admin Template policy settings being deployed on the Computer side using PolicyPak Admin Templates Manager. You can see **Prohibit access to Control Panel and PC Settings** and **Password protect the screensaver** User side policy settings... but being delivered on the *Computer* side. In this way, all users on the computers pick up these policy settings: no Loopback required.

In PolicyPak terminology, we call this idea *switched mode*. This is because we're using our own special processing magic while a computer starts up, when gpupdate is run, or after a user logs on. We're switching it up and delivering User-side items to the computer during those times.

Once these are set, there's nothing else to do. Said another way, you don't need to set Loopback at all to do this special switching. It's just automatically going to deliver those User-side settings to all users on those computers at logon time (and in the background).

In short, you get to use the best part of what Loopback tries to do without all the headaches of actually using Loopback.

You can see an example video of PolicyPak Application Manager delivering settings via switched mode here (this video shows Java settings deployed via switched mode): `http://www.policypak.com/video/policypak-manage-and-lock-down-java-site-list-exceptions.html`.

FIGURE 4.9 Use PolicyPak Application Manager to deliver settings to computers (which affects all users) without Loopback.

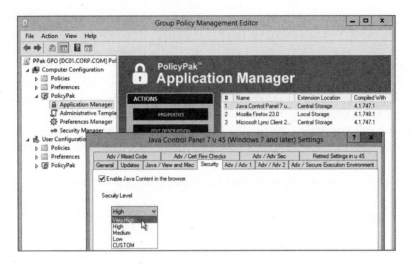

FIGURE 4.10 Use PolicyPak Admin Templates Manager to deliver any User-side Group Policy Admin Template policy setting to computers (which affects all users) without Loopback.

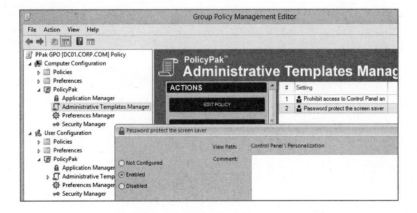

And, you can see a video of PolicyPak Admin Templates Manager and switched mode here: http://www.policypak.com/video/policypak-admin-templates-manager-switched-policies-without-loopback.html.

Group Policy with Cross-Forest Trusts

Windows 2003 domains brought a new trust type to the table: a forest trust (also known as a cross-forest trust). The idea is that if you have multiple, unrelated forests, you can join their root domains with one single trust; then, anytime new domains pop up in either forest, there is an automatically implied trust relationship.

Doing this requires a large commitment from all parties involved (though in most organizations, this requirement is satisfied). That is, all domains must be in at least Windows 2003 Functional mode, and all forests must be in Windows 2003 Functional mode. Only then is it possible to create cross-forest trusts via the Active Directory Domains and Trusts utility. For an example of an organization that might use this, see Figure 4.11.

FIGURE 4.11   Here's one example of how a cross-forest trust can be used.

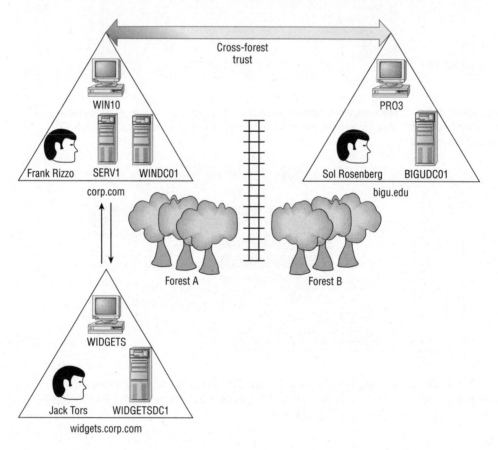

In this example, all domains trust all other domains via the cross-forest trust. Indeed, a user with an account housed in bigu.edu, say, Sol Rosenberg, could sit down at a computer in either Corp.com or Widgets.corp.com and log onto his user account, which is maintained in bigu.edu.

 When Sol (srosenberg) from bigu.edu logs onto any computer in domains below Corp.com (that is, Widgets.corp.com), the logon screen will not present BIGU as an option. To log on, Sol will need to type **srosenberg@ bigu.edu** as his logon ID along with his password. This is one of the limitations of cross-forest trusts.

What Happens When Logging onto Different Clients across a Cross-Forest Trust?

So what happens when Sol from bigu.edu has access to various computer types in the Corp.com forest?

Here's where things get weird, so try to stay with me. Imagine that Sol Rosenberg in bigu.edu is also the SQL database administrator for a server named SERV1 over in Corp.com in the **Human Resources SQL-Servers** OU. From time to time, Sol gets in his car and travels from the BigU campus over to the SERV1 computer sitting at the Corp.com headquarters. He sits down, logs on locally to the console (where he's been granted access), and he *doesn't* get the GPOs meant for him (and therefore doesn't get his own policy settings).

Instead, the server processes GPOs as if it were using Group Policy Loopback Processing in Replace mode. What does this mean?

- The GPOs that would normally apply to Sol's user account in bigu.edu are ignored by the SERV1 computer.

- The computer puts on an "I'm a user" hat and says, "Give me the GPOs that would apply to me if I were a user."

So, in our example, we can see that when Sol from bigu.edu logs onto SERV1 (which could really be any Windows Server 2003 and later machine or Windows XP and later machine), his policy settings are ignored. The computer then looks at the GPOs that would apply to users in the **Human Resources SQL-Servers** OU (where the SERV1 account resides).

Since no GPOs linked to the **Human Resources SQL-Servers** OU contain policy settings geared for users, Sol gets no policy settings applied.

After logging on, you can check out the Application Event Log and see Event ID 1109, which states that Sol is "from a different forest logged onto this machine. Cross forest Group Policy processing is disabled and Loopback processing has been enforced in this forest for this user account."

At this point, you're likely scratching your head in disbelief. Why wouldn't Sol just get the "normal GPOs" that *should* affect him?

The answer is simple: If Sol were assigned software (Chapter 11), logon scripts, Group Policy Preferences (Chapter 5), or other potentially dangerous settings, *our* machine's stability could be affected.

By going into Loopback mode, our systems are protected from stuff that we might not want to happen to it. Since we're not administrating Sol, we don't know what potential harm Sol's settings might do.

Strange? Yes, but it works, and this becomes strangely more logical the more you think about it.

If you put your head around it for a while, you can design your Active Directory to account for this "phenomenon." That is, if you set up User-side policy settings for users and link them to OUs that contain computers, users from "foreign" domains across the cross-forest trust will get the user policy settings *you* intend for them to—not what *their* administrator wanted.

It's a mind-bender.

So, yes, this can be complicated, and thankfully, only a few administrators have to stay up nights thinking about it. But if you have cross-forest trusts—congrats—you're now one of us.

Turns out, something "extra" also occurs here that is out of the ordinary. That is, when users log onto your computers across a cross-forest trust, their user profiles are not allowed to be downloaded onto your machines either. That's right—user profiles from that foreign domain are apparently "potentially dangerous," too, like GPOs from that foreign domain.

So a user logging in from a foreign domain across a cross-forest trust might see something like what's in Figure 4.12.

FIGURE 4.12 When users log on across a cross-forest trust, their access to their own user profiles is restricted.

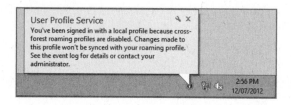

Event ID 1109 will be generated on the client machine in the Application Event Log stating that a user is "...from a different forest."

Disabling Loopback Processing When Using Cross-Forest Trusts

Let's recall the two things that happen across a cross-forest trust:

- Loopback Replace processing is turned on for users who use your computers across a cross-forest trust.

- Roaming user profiles are disabled for users who use your computers across a cross-forest trust.

Perhaps you want to restore the "normal" behavior. You can do that. Once you apply this setting, target users on these machines will get their "usual" set of policy settings (which, again, would come from their domain—not yours).

To do this, you need to locate the **Allow Cross-Forest User Policy and Roaming User Profiles** policy setting. Drill down through Computer Configuration ➢ Policies ➢ Administrative Templates ➢ System ➢ Group Policy. Note that the policy setting says "At least Windows Server 2003," but it will affect Windows XP/SP2 machines and later as well.

Just create a GPO and link it to the computers you want to "make normal" again. But, again, the point is that this decreases the security on the system, because you won't know what "the other administrator" has dictated for the user. And then the user could be running evil, nasty programs or scripts on your client machines.

Understanding Cross-Forest Trust Permissions

If you're going to set up cross-forest trusts, here's a little extra takeaway to get you started.

Windows cross-forest trusts have two modes: Forest-wide authentication and Selective authentication, as shown in Figure 4.13. To view the screen shown here, open Active Directory Domains and Trusts, locate the properties of the trust, and click the Authentication tab.

FIGURE 4.13   You can set Forest-wide authentication or Selective authentication.

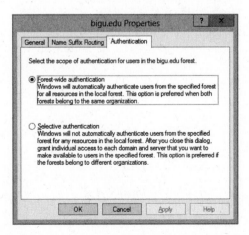

In a Windows 2003 (or later) Active Directory domain, Full Authentication mode enables all users to log onto "the other guys' computers" across the cross-forest trust.

We already know that Sol is the SQL database administrator over at Corp.com, and we saw what happened when he logged onto the Windows member server SERV1. Twice a week, however, Sol works at Widgets.corp.com on the WIDGETS machine for some CAD work. Then, the unthinkable happens.

An attack originating at bigu.edu upon Corp.com's computers gets the two Domain Administrators in a heated battle. The Corp.com Domain Administrator decides he wants to prevent attacks from bigu.edu, so he enables Selective authentication. Now no one from bigu.edu can log onto any of the machines in Corp.com or Widgets.corp.com. Ergo, Sol will not be able to log onto either his SERV1 member server in Corp.com or his WIDGETS machine in Widgets.corp.com. Sol needs the "Allowed to authenticate" right on the computer objects he will use. In this example, you can see what is done for WIDGETS in Figure 4.14.

Additional computers in Corp.com and Widgets.corp.com need these explicit rights if anyone else from bigu.edu is going to use them.

FIGURE 4.14   You need to specifically grant the "Allowed to authenticate" right in order for Sol to use this particular machine.

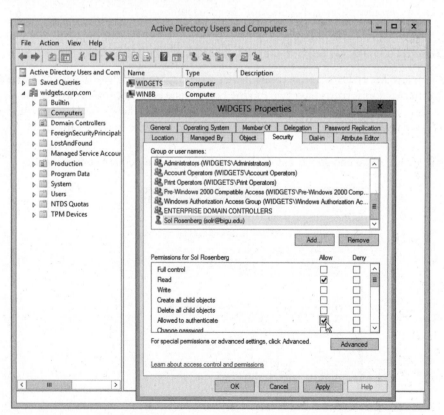

Final Thoughts

In this chapter, you learned ways to utilize Group Policy in some interesting cases.

WMI filters are great; just be careful when you use them. They do take a little while to process on each machine (from milliseconds to several seconds), so be careful in the number of WMI filters you're asking your machines to process. WMI filters, when they evaluate to True, will apply the whole contents of the Group Policy Object.

If instead, however, you want to manage which specific Admin Template settings inside a GPO will get delivered under what conditions, PolicyPak Admin Templates Manager will help you do that.

Loopback processing is great, too; its job is to help you ensure that the same set of user settings affects a machine. It can be confusing to understand and use both at first, and hard to troubleshoot in the long run. It also can slow down login because of the extra work involved by the Group Policy engine. So be sure to try it out in a test lab before running it in your production environment, and document exactly why you decided to use it.

Alternatively, PolicyPak Application Manager and PolicyPak Admin Templates Manager both give you a way to deliver settings to computers (which then affect all users)—without needing Loopback at all. Just set up what you want to do on the Computer side, and all users on those computers will get what you want them to at login time. No Loopback involved.

If you have cross-forest trusts, consider what happens over the trust. You can decide if you want to revert back to "standard" behavior (that is, you can retrain the system to allow Group Policy Objects to affect your user accounts) or stay with the Loopback Replace mode behavior I described earlier. As with all the advice in this book, test, test, test before you deploy.

5

Group Policy Preferences

Take a look at Figure 5.1. You'll see the Preferences node in the Group Policy editor.

FIGURE 5.1   Welcome to the Preferences node in the Group Policy editor.

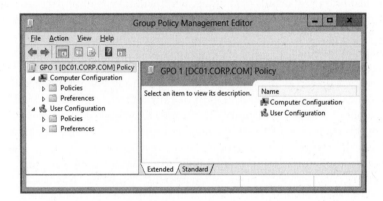

You might be thinking to yourself, "Preferences? What's a preference? I thought this whole book was on Group Policy, so why is there a node called Preferences?"

And others might be thinking, "I've been using Group Policy for a long time and heard about the Preferences, but I never really dove into them. What do I download to start using them?"

The good news is, you likely have everything you need to get started with them.

Recall that a Client-Side Extension (CSE) is a way to "do more stuff" with Group Policy. Windows Vista does more stuff than Windows XP. Windows 7 does more stuff than Vista, and Windows 8 does more stuff than Windows 7. Windows 10 does more stuff than Windows 8 and 8.1.

That's because each operating system has more CSEs, which you learned about in Chapter 3, "Group Policy Processing Behavior Essentials." If you'll remember, they're just bits of code (DLLs actually) that process the directives contained in GPOs.

The Group Policy Preference extensions are simply that: extension DLLs—really, one DLL that does a *lot* of stuff. Because *Group Policy Preferences* is kind of long to say, I'll abbreviate the Group Policy Preferences (the concept) as GPPrefs and a specific Group Policy Preference extension as a GPPref, or just an extension or node—for instance, the Registry preference extension or the Registry node.

You might wonder where the word *Preferences* derived from, since they live in a world of "Group Policy." I'll explain that in detail, too, I promise, but in short, they act like, well, preferences. That is, they don't "clean up" after themselves, like normal Group Policy settings do, and they don't "lock out" or restrict the user interface (under most circumstances). So, in short, GPPrefs aren't policies—they're preferences. They're preferences that live in the "ecosystem" of Group Policy.

Said another way, Group Policy Preferences is a technology that uses the Group Policy mechanism to deliver preferences. (Pretty Zen, right?)

They're settings administrators can deliver but users can work around. Indeed, it should be noted that Group Policy has always been able to deliver preferences; we'll see how to do it using ADM and ADMX files in the very next chapter.

Again, we'll go into these details coming up, but it will take a lot of pages to answer both of these questions thoroughly. So I'll ask you to please hold your horses before running out and trying all these superpowers. You'll be really, really glad you waited and read this whole chapter to truly understand the powers you have rather than doing something you wish you hadn't done.

The technology is powerful and awesome; it extends Group Policy's reach and capabilities an astronomical amount. However, it must be fully understood and used with caution to get the most out of it, and so you don't shoot yourself in the foot as you're using it.

That's what this chapter is all about: the nuts, bolts, general use, and troubleshooting of the Group Policy Preferences. We won't be going over each and every setting. That could be a whole book in and of itself. However, I will have more information about how to do some neat things using GPPrefs magic in Chapter 12, "Finishing Touches with Group Policy: Scripts, Internet Explorer, Hardware Control, Printer Deployment, Local Admin Password Control."

G'bye Logon Scripts, Hello Group Policy Preferences

Here's one takeaway that you should start thinking about as you're reading this chapter: "Is there anything in my logon or startup process that I script today but could now start using Group Policy for?"

Indeed, almost everyone sets Environment variables and maps drive letters using scripts. So, start thinking of pulling those things out of the logon scripts and making them more Group Policy-ish using the Group Policy Preferences.

And, as you'll learn, since the GPPrefs can leverage variables, you'll have a lot more flexibility with GPOs and GPPrefs than you usually do with logon scripts.

So, for this chapter, I'm going use the following road map to help you get a grip on what the GPPrefs are all about. Think about this chapter in four parts:

Powers of the Group Policy Preferences   You want to know what toys are in the toy box. I totally get it. Let's quickly review of all the toys first, and then later you can come back and use them (after you've learned how to do so safely).

Group Policy Preferences Concepts   In this meaty section, you'll learn more about policy versus preference, how the original Group Policy set and Group Policy Preferences can overlap but also work together. You'll also learn about the (sometimes confusing) red and green circles in the user interface. You'll learn about a concept called "CRUD modes" and about the Common tab.

Group Policy Preferences Tips, Tricks, and Troubleshooting   I think you can figure out what we'll learn in this section.

Giving Group Policy Preferences a "Boost"   In this section, I'll show you how you can give Group Policy a little boost to do more. We'll shore up some shortcomings and even get Group Policy Preferences items over the Internet, as well as see how to apply them to non-domain-joined machines.

Note that the Group Policy Preferences are not available as Local Group Policy Objects. The Group Policy Preferences appear only when you use the GPMC and manage Active Directory GPOs. Said another way, Group Policy Preferences isn't available when computers are not domain joined; that is, unless you use PolicyPak Cloud, which has the ability to deploy Group Policy Preferences items to both domain joined and non-domain joined machines. See the section "Giving Group Policy Preferences a 'Boost'" near the end of this chapter for details.

Making the Group Policy Preferences Work on Windows XP, Windows Vista, or Windows Server 2003

Windows 7 and Windows Server 2008 and later already have the moving parts prebaked in and ready to go for the Group Policy Preferences. But Windows XP, Windows Vista, and Windows Server 2003—just don't.

If you still have these older systems in place, here's how to make the magic happen so you can create GPOs with Group Policy Preferences directives and have them apply to and affect your Windows XP, Windows Vista, or Server 2003 machines.

For Windows Server 2003, Windows XP, and Windows Vista, you need to download pieces to make the magic happen. Let's examine each operating system, where to get the downloads, and how to install the pieces by hand.

The "main search" you'll want to look for is KB943729. Here, I've listed, at last check, where you would find the Group Policy Preferences Client Side Extensions for various operating systems. These might change in the future:

> Windows XP/32-bit: `http://tinyurl.com/mac4g7`
>
> Windows XP/64-bit: `http://tinyurl.com/nzafod`
>
> Windows Vista/32-bit: `http://tinyurl.com/ln8aw9`
>
> Windows Vista/64-bit: `http://tinyurl.com/n3va22`
>
> Windows Server 2003/32-bit: `http://tinyurl.com/cr3bwo`
>
> Windows Server 2003/64-bit: `http://tinyurl.com/kkavwm`

Note that Windows XP and Windows Server 2003 machines also need a prerequisite called XmlLite, and it can be found at `http://support.microsoft.com/default.aspx/kb/914783`.

Here's some key points about XmlLite:

- You may already "have all you need." That is, XmlLite is already built in to Windows XP/SP3 and part of IE7. If you have already deployed either of those; skip ahead— you've got XmlLite already.

- Neither the XmlLite prerequisite nor the GPPrefs themselves are MSIs. Nope, they're *patches*. So, for Windows XP and Windows Server 2003, they're .EXE patches.

As we'll explore in Chapter 11, "The Managed Desktop, Part 2: Software Deployment via Group Policy," the Group Policy Software Installation engine cannot install MSP patches and it can't install newer MSU patches.

You can, however, use WSUS and find the Group Policy Preferences bits listed under "Optional Software" to deliver to your clients.

Alternatively, you can use a script here to install all the pre-reqs and the CSEs in one fell swoop:

> `www.heidelbergit.dk/2008/03/how-to-install-gpp-cses-using-startup.html`

Powers of the Group Policy Preferences

Before we dive into the power they hold, we need to first be super clear about how you can utilize them. First things first:

- You don't need to have Windows Server 2016 or really any specific version of Windows Server to use them.

- Neither Group Policy (the system) nor Group Policy Preferences (the function) cares what domain modes, functional levels, or Domain Controller types you have.

Because Group Policy is "client based" and uses CSEs, all that matters is if your clients have the "moving part" on them (the CSE) to receive the GPPrefs' directives from within a GPO.

If you've never seen the Preferences node, that means you likely have been using the older GPMC when editing GPOs. To make the most use of the Group Policy Preferences, you should be using the latest GPMC possible, which today is a Windows 10 machine with RSAT or a Windows Server 2016 machine. Technically, you could go as far back as Windows Vista and get some Group Policy Preferences functionality, but to ensure that you have all the *latest* Group Policy Preferences features and updates, always use the latest, greatest GPMC (which as of this writing is Windows 10).

If you've been accustomed to the older GPMC (without the Preferences node), it doesn't have to be scary. The original "stuff" is now just tucked within the Policies node. Indeed, other than that, not much has changed there.

The new GPPrefs stuff is contained within its own node called Preferences. Again, you won't see it until you use a modern GPMC.

The new Preferences node has lots of categories on both the User and the Computer side—and some even overlap! Indeed, not just overlap with itself (i.e., the same preference extension on both the Computer and User side), but also overlap with original Group Policy settings (which now live in the Policies nodes). Yikes! See the section "The Overlap of Group Policy vs. Group Policy Preferences and Associated Issues" a little later for more information on this particular issue.

In all, the Preferences node has 21 new categories of toys to play with. (Remember, I said I'd describe the powerful new abilities first, and we'll work on the understanding of that power second.)

You'll also see that these new Group Policy options are split between Windows Settings and Control Panel Settings:

GPPrefs, cPassword, and Security

In May 2014, Microsoft closed a well-known security hole in GPPrefs. Specifically, a password can be stored within several GPPrefs items. On the surface this makes sense; here would be several examples of where you would utilize that ability:

- Map a drive to \\server\share, but use Fred's credentials instead of the logged-in user.

- Change the password of XYZ Service to p@ssw0rd.

- Set the Local Admin password to p@ssw0rd on all your systems.

- Create a scheduled task, and run it as Fred instead of system.

This idea is all great, but in practice it leads to a real security hole. Here's the problem, fully spelled out:

- After you (the admin) create the GPPrefs item, it's stored as XML in SYSVOL. The XML contains a hash of the password, not the actual password in cleartext. For instance, if you set an item's password to hello1, the actual text in the XML will show up as gwAaYaZl3kuzY5i3gc8+Wg. You can see this example here:

- Remember that all Group Policy files in SYSVOL are readable to Everyone. So literally anyone in your organization can go to a DC's SYSVOL, find the Policies folder, and find a Group Policy Object that contains the XML that shows this cPassword.

- That cPassword isn't really encrypted; as I stated, it's merely hashed.

- That hash is "well known," which is another term for *published*.

- Therefore, if you find any of these GPOs with cPassword fields, you (or someone that isn't you but wants to be you) can reverse the hash and get the actual password.

What I'm not going to do here is point you toward tools that could do that. Suffice it to say, it can be done, pretty darned easily. So the upshot is that if I'm a bad guy, and I get even one of your users' passwords, then I can use that as a way to read the SYSVOL and find all GPOs that contain these cPassword values. If I'm a bad guy maybe I'll get lucky:

- You encrypted the Local Admin password. (Now I have local admin passwords on some or all of your machines.)

- You encrypted service account passwords. (Now I can be naughty and act as this service.)

- You encrypted the Domain Admin password. (Now I have "God Rights" everywhere.)

There are other scenarios; but those are the major ones Microsoft wanted to protect against.

So, what exactly did Microsoft do in May 2014 to help protect against this issue? At Microsoft TechEd 2014, the folks at Microsoft "anointed me" to speak on their behalf and explain what they were announcing to fix the problem.

That speech can be found at:

```
https://channel9.msdn.com/Events/TechEd/NorthAmerica/2014/WIN-B328
```

You can jump to the announcement at the 1 hour and 7 minute mark.

To get to the heart of the issue, let's look at a Group Policy Preferences Drive Maps item as editable from a GPMC upon Windows Server 2008 R2 or Windows 7.

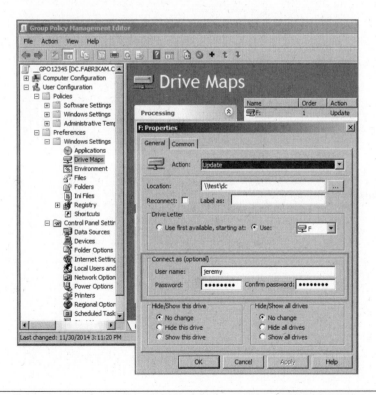

See that the "User name" and Password fields are available to me to put in what I want?

In May 2014, Microsoft released a hotfix for the GPMCs of Windows 7, Windows 2008 R2, Windows 8, and Windows 8.1. When this hotfix is applied, and you go to edit a GPPrefs item that could store cPassword fields (Drive Maps, Local Users and Groups, Scheduled Tasks, Services, and Data Sources), the editor will not permit you to store cPassword data.

And, that hotfix is pre-rolled into the GPMC on Windows 10, so if you try to do the same thing on Windows 10, you'll see what you see here.

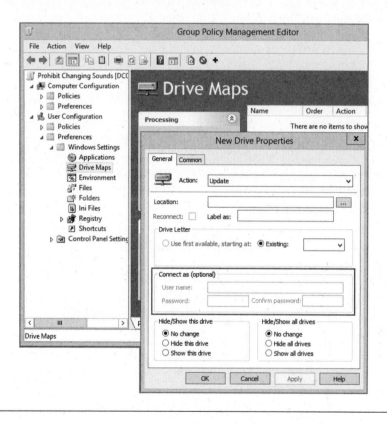

That is, you cannot write to the "User name" or Password field, or any other GPPrefs item that stores cPassword field items. Though some items will make it look like it's allowing you to write cPassword data, when you press OK, you'll get what you see here.

So, the latest GPMC (Windows 10) and the GPMCs with the patches act exactly the same way, preventing admins from writing sensitive cPassword data.

An overview of the hotfix can be found here:

```
https://support.microsoft.com/kb/2962486?wa=wsignin1.0
```

And that page shows lots of screen shots before and after the patch is applied. You'll also see two PowerShell scripts:

* One script helps you set local admin passwords using PowerShell (something that a lot of people were doing with GPPrefs and its Local Users and Groups item type).

* Another script helps you hunt down and find existing GPOs with GPPrefs items that contain cPassword fields. They call it the "Detecting cPassword preferences" scripts.

All that being said, I have referred to this hotfix as the "GPMC Baby Gate" hotfix. Here's why: The hotfix (and also the GPMC within Windows 10) doesn't actually prevent you, if you really know what you are doing, from creating an item (by hand) with cPassword fields and chucking the XML files into the Group Policy Object for processing. And, there's also nothing preventing another administrator on your network, without the hotfix, say, upon his Windows 7 machine, from firing up his GPMC, editing a Group Policy Object, and writing perfectly valid XML data with cPassword fields.

Said another way, the processing of the GPPrefs CSE isn't changed. The only change is in the GPMC, which prevents you from writing the cPassword field data. It's likely a "good enough" solution for now.

But do be careful that all other Admins who edit GPOs are using either the latest GPMC on Windows 10 or have applied the hotfix to their GPMC if their machine is earlier than Windows 10.

One more side note here. This idea is generally called "credential stealing" and also, depending on who you ask, "Pass the Hash." Closing up this cPassword problem is one step toward getting tighter on the Pass the Hash problem. For some interesting additional information, you might want to investigate Microsoft's Pass the Hash portal at:

```
http://technet.microsoft.com/en-us/security/dn785092
```

Computer Configuration ➢ Preferences

Again, this node is split in two: Windows Settings and Control Panel Settings. Let's check out each extension (in brief).

Computer Configuration ➢ Preferences ➢ Windows Settings

The Windows settings are settings you can make that, well, directly affect Windows. I know that's a little vague, but the other big category is Control Panel, which is also a little vague. In short, it doesn't matter why they're broken up this way; they just are.

Environment Extension

You can do two big things with the Environment preference extension:

- You can set user and system Environment variables.
- You can change or update the special Windows system Path variable.

You can best utilize this extension by using it to set specific Environment variables based on certain conditions. Then, in other GPPrefs, you can call these variables. For instance, you can define a variable like the one seen in the following image, where we're defining NURSEFILES as C:\Nursefiles. Then, later, you can recycle this variable when you want to use other GPPrefs to copy or use files based on it.

Files Extension

The Files preference extension lets you copy files from Point A to Point B. Point A can be a UNC path or the local machine, and so can Point B, though Point B usually is the local machine. The most common scenario is to copy a file (or three) from a share on a server to a user's My Documents folder, the Desktop, or C:\ drive.

You can see a screen shot of the Files preference extension in the section "Environment Variables" a little later.

Folders Extension

This extension lets you create new folders and delete existing folders or wipe out their contents. In this example, I'm deleting the contents of the %NURSESFILES% folder, but only if the folder is empty.

.INI Files Extension

This extension allows you to perform a search and replace within existing `.INI` files. I have an example in the section "Environment Variables" a little later.

Registry Extension

This is a very powerful extension that can also be a little hard to handle. We'll use this extension later in some examples, but the idea is simple: punch in a particular Registry setting to your client machines.

You can see in the example here that I'm dictating a particular Registry setting to good ol' Notepad.

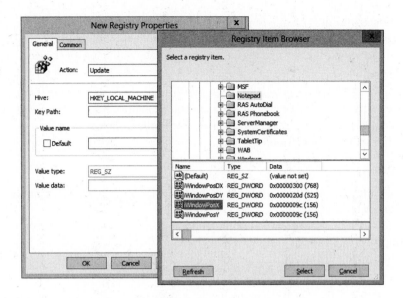

On the Computer side, there's no way to get the HKCU hive except for the `.Default` profile. This is the account you see when no one is logged on, at the "Press Ctl+Alt+Del to Log On" prompt. I'm not sure why this is the only way you can get to the `.Default` profile and not normal users' settings by a computer using GPPrefs. Note, however, that PolicyPak On-Premise suite can overcome this limitation and deliver user-based Registry settings to anyone based on computers (without Loopback).

The Registry extension also allows you to set any type of Registry key, like REG_BINARY values, which has traditionally been impossible using ADM and ADMX files.

However, this extension needs to be handled with caution (as do others), especially when the "Remove this item when it is no longer applied" setting is chosen (which we'll discuss when we explore the Common tab a little later).

There are there several ways to utilize the Registry extension:

Registry Item   This lets you specifically set an individual Registry setting. Again, all the major Registry types are supported (REG_SZ, REG_DWORD, REG_BINARY, REG_MULTI_SZ, and REG_EXPAND_SZ), and you can dictate to HKEY_LOCAL_MACHINE, HKEY_CURRENT_USER, HKEY_CLASSES_ROOT, HKEY_USERS, or HKEY_CURRENT_CONFIG.

Collection Item   This is a fancy way of saying "a folder of stuff I want to lump together as a group." In short, by using this item, you can guarantee that groups of Registry settings will affect the machine at the same time. You'll use item-level targeting (ILT), which we'll discuss later, to ensure that your criteria are met *before* making the group of changes. For instance, you can check that the machine is a laptop before delivering all the Registry items in this group.

Registry Wizard   This is a great way to take a sample machine's Registry, find a particular setting you want to manage, and then manipulate and ultimately deliver the setting. You can select individual Registry settings or a whole Registry branch, change values if you want, and then deliver all the changed values.

Network Shares Extension

This extension allows you to create new shares on workstations, or more commonly, servers. Or you can delete those shares.

You can also turn on Access-based Enumeration (ABE), which will prevent someone who doesn't have proper rights from even seeing the shared directory.

Note that this extension won't create the directory for the share; the directory must already exist. But you can easily create the folders you need using the Folders extension, which we just explored.

Shortcuts Extension

This extension allows you to plunk both program and URL shortcuts on Desktops, in the Startup folder, in the Programs folders, and in a lot of other locations. In this example, I'm plunking a link to www.GPanswers.com on the user's Desktop and selecting the little World icon.

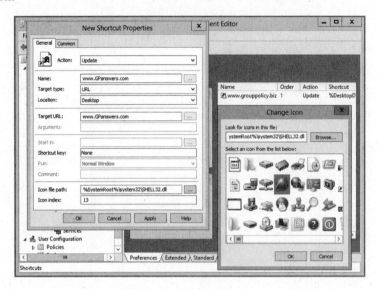

Note that you can also create shortcuts to shell objects. For instance, you can put a link to the Recycle Bin in the folders that users utilize most and even in the "Send to" flyout menu.

Also note that the icon you select is "embedded" inside a DLL of your choosing. Indeed, you're really saying, "I want icon #6 inside Whatever.DLL." So, two things need to be true to get the same icon: that DLL needs to be on the target machine, and the icon needs to be in the same index within the DLL. I've seen people select one icon in the Group Policy editor only to have another icon appear on the target machine. That's because either the DLL was not present on the target machine or the icon wasn't in the same place (the index) of the DLL.

Computer Configuration ➢ Preferences ➢ Control Panel Settings

Again, it's kind of unnecessary to have a division here and call out the specific "Control Panel" settings. But here are the ones listed within the Control Panel node.

Data Sources Extension

The Data Sources extension lets you set Open Database Connectivity (ODBC) data sources via Group Policy. Typically, this can be a 12-step process that you would normally have to run around and perform on every machine. Now it can be done via Group Policy in a snap.

Devices Extension

This extension can disable a specific device or device class. There are similar original Group Policy settings that seemingly conflict with these.

Check out the section "Group Policy Device Installation Restrictions vs. GPPrefs Devices Preference Extension" for more information about which one does what and which ones are best to use.

Folder Options Extension

This extension exists in both the User and Computer sides. However, in the Computer side, it has only one possible function (whereas in the User side it has three functions). That is, you can associate a file extension with a particular class.

This part of this extension corresponds to Explorer's Tools ➢ Options ➢ File Types ➢ Advanced dialog box. Personally, in all my years working with Windows, I've never needed to modify anything in there, but clearly someone needed to or they wouldn't have put it in here.

Local Users and Groups Extension

In Chapter 8, "Profiles: Local, Roaming, and Mandatory," we will explore a Group Policy concept called "Restricted Groups." I don't want to blow my whole story here, but that original tool is a toy compared with the Group Policy Preferences' Local Users and Groups. Here, you can jam users into groups, remove specific users from specific groups, lock out accounts, and set password expirations.

Note that there are two previously available abilities within the Local Users and Groups extension that are not available anymore. One of the more popular uses for the Local Users and Groups extension was the ability to dictate passwords for the local Admin groups. The other, now removed ability was the ability to create new users locally.

This is due to a security problem with the Password field within both of those functions. See the sidebar "GPPrefs, cPassword, and Security" to understand why this is no longer possible with the GPMC for Windows 10 (or an older GPMC with the hotfix applied as described in that sidebar).

Network Options Extension

The Network Options extension allows you to configure the following connection types:

VPN Connections   Previously, setting virtual private network (VPN) connections was tedious, arduous work. Now it's a snap.

DUN Connections   Ditto for dial-up networking (DUN) connections.

Instead of running around to all your laptops and specifying these settings, you can be finished configuring an army of machines before breakfast. This is the "Cadillac" way to get the job done.

Power Options Extension

This preference item allows you to create new Power Schemes and Power Options for Windows XP (and control existing ones) as well as manage Power Plans in Windows 7 and later.

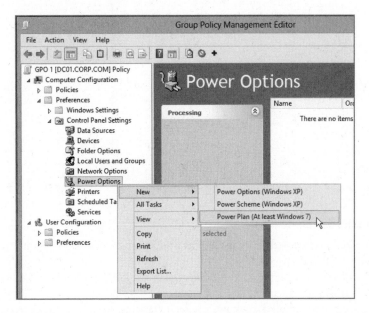

You can set things like the hard disk–spin downtime, how long until the monitor goes into stand-by mode, and what happens to laptops when you hit the power button.

Again, because these settings are merely preferences, users can still change the settings if they want to. So, be careful banking on the users maintaining the settings you wanted.

Printers Extension

The Printers extension option might be one of those things you just fall in love with. But you have to contend with the fact that there's already a way to zap printers down via Group Policy, and we'll talk about it in the section "Group Policy Deployed Printers vs. GPPrefs Printers Extension."

In short, the Printers extension allows you to set shared, TCP/IP, and local printers (though shared printers items are available only on the User side).

Scheduled Tasks Extension

You can set Version 1 scheduled tasks using this preference extension. Version 1 tasks are valid for Windows XP and later.

However, Windows 7 and later have more features available via Version 2 scheduled tasks, like interfacing with the event log and such.

So, you can use the Scheduled Task preference extension to deliver tasks to all operating systems (Windows XP and later), but you cannot use this to take advantage of the Version 2–specific tasks that are available only on Windows 7 and later.

You can set scheduled tasks and immediate tasks. *Immediate* is kind of a misnomer because in Group Policy nothing is really "immediate." In reality, you'll have to wait until Group Policy refreshes on the client. When it does, the task is scheduled to run, and then poof, that's it.

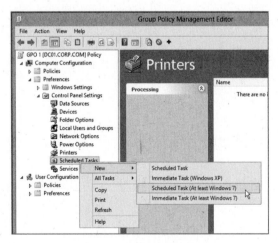

Services Extension

You can manage just about every aspect of a client computer's services. This is especially useful if the target is a server machine and you have a pesky service that's running on multiple machines and you need to configure its behavior a specific way.

You can change the following items:

Startup   If you like, you can change the startup type to Automatic, Manual, or Disabled.

Service action   When the Group Policy runs, you can have it start, stop, or restart a service.

Log on as   You can configure the account that the service uses as well as change the password, as noted earlier.

Recovery   You can specify what will happen if the service fails on first, second, and subsequent failures. This equates to the Recovery options in the normal services dialog box.

Note that the original Group Policy has some ability to work with System Services. Be sure to check out the section "Group Policy System Services vs. GPPrefs Services Preference Extension" a little later for a breakdown on how each compares, head to head.

User Configuration ➤ Preferences

On the User Configuration ➤ Preferences side of things, there are lots of preference extensions that overlap. In the following sections, we'll detail only ones that *don't* specifically overlap (or specific major features that don't overlap).

See Table 5.1 a little later for the bird's-eye view of where the overlaps are and to see what can specifically be accomplished on either the Computer or the User side.

User Configuration ➤ Preferences ➤ Windows Settings

Let's explore the GPPrefs on the User ➤ Windows Settings side.

Applications Extension

This node is special because there are no configurable items available by default and no signs from Microsoft that it will be utilized. This was a special node when it was the pre-Microsoft product, but it doesn't appear Microsoft will be utilizing it. If something changes, I'll let you know on GPanswers.com. I like to say that PolicyPak Application Manager is the "spiritual successor" to the Applications Extension node, because it enables you to deliver, manage, and lock down settings to almost every desktop application.

Drive Maps Extension

When people first check out the Group Policy Preferences, one of their favorites is this one—Drive Maps.

The reason the Drive Maps extension is so great is because it gets you out of the logon script business with tons of "If/Then/Else" scripts.

The Drive Maps preference extension is like the Swiss Army knife of drive mappings, and you can create and delete drive mappings and assign letters with ease.

When this extension is combined with item-level targeting (which we talk about later), you'll be able to dictate drive maps to users based on the circumstances they're in.

Remember that Group Policy Preferences' Drive Maps will only apply in the background when the client machine is Windows 8.1 or later. And Group Policy Preferences Drive Map will only apply in the foreground when the client machine is Windows 8 and earlier.

User Configuration ➢ Preferences ➢ Control Panel

This is the final group of GPPrefs. Here we'll discuss the items that are available only on the User side of the house.

Folder Options Extension

While this exists on both the User and Computer sides, they have different options. On the User side, you can right-click New ➢ Folder Options and see three options:

Folder Options (Windows XP)   This option is shown in the following screen shot. Although you could do many of these little tweaks by editing the Registry directly, there's a lot of "quick power" available in the Folder Options configuration item. These items mostly equate to Explorer's Tools ➢ Folder Options items that you would normally find inside every Explorer window. You can quickly turn on the ability to have Windows Explorer show hidden files, display the full path in the address bar, and show NTFS-compressed files with a different color.

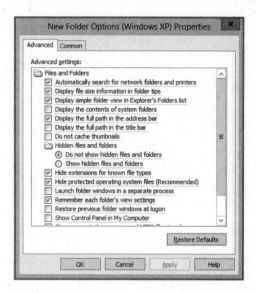

Folder Options (At Least Windows 7)   Very similar items to what's available for Windows XP, but specific to Windows 7 and later, including Windows 8 through Windows 10.

Open With   This enables you to associate (or unassociate) applications from their extensions, so you can quickly configure a specific application on a machine to handle a particular document file.

The only option on the Computer side for Folder Options is File Type.

Internet Settings Extension

You can set one of the following:

- Internet Explorer 5 and 6 settings (that's *one* kind of setting)
- Internet Explorer 7 settings
- Internet Explorer 8 and 9 settings
- Internet Explorer 10 (and later) settings

Note that you won't see "Internet Explorer 8 and 9" or "Internet Explorer 10" unless your GPMC is running on Windows 8 or later.

You can see Internet Explorer 10 and later settings here.

One of the downsides to using Group Policy Preferences IE settings is that if you want to make the same settings across different versions of IE, you would need to make multiple items and ensure that the settings are correctly contained within each item—so, one line item for "Internet Explorer 7" and another one for "Internet Explorer 8 and 9" and another for "Internet Explorer 10 (and later)."

Something weird you might notice here is that I'm using the phrasing "Internet Explorer 10 (and later)" but the user interface only shows "Internet Explorer 10." But underneath the hood, it really is Internet Explorer 10 and later. If you were to peek at the underlying XML of the GPPrefs item that is created, it will apply to "Internet Explorer 10 through 99." So that includes IE 11.

About Windows Edge

Microsoft has a browser that will ship with Windows 10.
Actually, two of them.

Yep, that's right: Windows 10 will have two browsers. One will be the Internet Explorer 11 you know and love; the other will be a new thing called the Windows Edge browser.

As I write this, Microsoft has announced some Group Policy Admin Template settings for Edge, but no Group Policy Preferences support.

The basic party line so far has been: Internet Explorer 11 is still supported and the browser of choice for businesses. Edge, even though it ships in Windows 10, is more geared for consumers, though there is certainly nothing stopping business users from using it, as well.

Lastly, it should be mentioned that there might also be some overlap where the Edge browser picks up at least some of the settings meant for Internet Explorer 11. As of this writing, it's a little too soon to tell, but stay tuned to GPanswers.com for a full analysis when all the dust settles.

In the XML it's displayed as:

```
<FilterFile hidden="1" not="0" bool="AND" path="%ProgramFilesDir%\Internet
Explorer\iexplore.exe" type="VERSION" gte="1" min="10.0.0.0" max="99.0.0.0"
lte="0"/>
```

My pal, and the technical editor for this book, Alan Burchill has a good article on his website here:

www.grouppolicy.biz/2013/11/internet-explorer-11-group-policy-preferences/

Another pal, Darren-Mar Elia, has his own article on this idea here:

http://sdmsoftware.com/group-policy-blog/group-policy-preferences/
gp-preferences-for-internet-explorer-11/

What's also true about the GPPrefs IE item is that there are a lot of user interface elements that seemingly do, well, nothing. Several buttons and other items are entirely grayed out. And, since the item has no superpowers for IE 11, there's nothing special it does for IE 11 either.

And there are other ways to manage IE: the Group Policy ADMX files, the old (and now deprecated) Internet Explorer Maintenance (IEM), and also the script-based Internet Explorer Admin Kit (IEAK). With all these ways of trying to configure IE, people ask me all the time, "Is there just *one* way you would recommend doing it?" Unfortunately, with all the myriad toolkits for managing IE, none of them work very well. I created a whitepaper to explain which tools can do what that you're welcome to download and read. The paper is entitled "What most Internet Explorer Admins don't know about application management" (http://tinyurl.com/o49aobk).

So, one of things I tried to do to help adjust for this problem is to have my team at PolicyPak create a "universal Pak" for all versions of Internet Explorer (which works with PolicyPak Application Manager). First, since it's a universal Pak, you only need to make the setting change once and all versions of IE will pick up what you lay down. This Pak can go beyond what Microsoft was able to do with GPPrefs, Group Policy ADMX, IEM, and IEAK. For instance, PolicyPak Application Manager and its included universal Pak for IE can do the following:

- Site to Zone mapping (for any version of Internet Explorer)
- Import certificates
- Enable/Disable Add-ons
- Create Favorites and Links
- Create Internet Explorer Enterprise Mode site lists (for IE 11) on the fly

And lots more.

Basically, if you can do it in IE, and you need to manage it, we made sure that it was possible using PolicyPak and the IE Pak. If you want to see it in action, you can see the videos with each use case here:

www.policypak.com/products/manage-internet-explorer-using-group-policy-policypak.html

Printers Extension

Although this category exists on both the Computer and User sides, when settings are dictated to users, an additional option is available that allows for managing shared printers. Again, be sure to read the section "Group Policy Deployed Printers vs. GPPrefs Printers Extension" a little later for more information.

Regional Options Extension

This has always been something I wanted to set via Group Policy. It just seems obvious: depending on who the user is, you can immediately change their local settings. Now you can just do that, quickly and easily, using Group Policy.

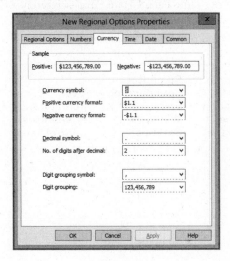

Start Menu Extension

While there are existing settings for controlling the Start Menu, this extension provides an easy way to make your changes. There are Start Menu configurations for Windows XP and "At Least Windows Vista." Note that the user interface could have been clearer here. The "XP" settings will mostly work fine on Windows Server 2003, and the "At Least Windows Vista" settings will mostly work just fine on Windows 7 and Windows Server 2008 R2, but they won't work for Windows 8 and later or Windows Server 2012 R2 and later.

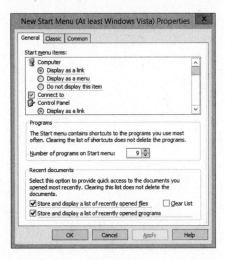

Note that these settings do not change the Windows 8 or Windows 10 tiles on the Start Menu.

Meanwhile, you might not want to try to change any of these settings until you read the section "Group Policy Start Menu Policy Settings vs. GPPrefs Start Menu."

Table 5.1 shows you where to find each Group Policy Preference Extension.

TABLE 5.1   Where to find Group Policy Preferences

	Computer Configuration ➤ Preferences ➤ Control Panel	Computer Configuration ➤ Preferences ➤ Windows Settings	User Configuration ➤ Preferences ➤ Control Panel	User Configuration ➤ Preferences ➤ Windows Settings
Applications				X
Data Sources	X		X	
Devices	X		X	
Drive Maps				X
Environment		X		X
Files		X		X
Folder Options— Folder Options			X	
Folder Options— Open With			X	
Folder Options— File Type	X			
Folders		X		X
INI Files		X		X
Internet Settings			X	
Local Users and Groups—Local Group	X		X	

TABLE 5.1 Where to find Group Policy Preferences *(continued)*

	Computer Configuration ➤ Preferences ➤ Control Panel	Computer Configuration ➤ Preferences ➤ Windows Settings	User Configuration ➤ Preferences ➤ Control Panel	User Configuration ➤ Preferences ➤ Windows Settings
Local Users and Groups—Local User	X		X	
Network Options—VPN Connection	X		X	
Network Options—DUN Connection (Dial-up)	X		X	
Power Options— Power Options	X		X	
Power Options— Power Scheme	X		X	
Power Options—Power Plan (Win7+)	X		X	
Printers— Shared Printer			X	
Printers— TCP/IP Printer	X		X	
Printers— Local Printer	X		X	
Regional Options			X	
Registry		X		X
Scheduled Tasks	X		X	

TABLE 5.1 Where to find Group Policy Preferences *(continued)*

	Computer Configuration ➤ Preferences ➤ Control Panel	Computer Configuration ➤ Preferences ➤ Windows Settings	User Configuration ➤ Preferences ➤ Control Panel	User Configuration ➤ Preferences ➤ Windows Settings
Services	X			
Shortcuts		X		X
Start Menu			X	

Group Policy Preferences Concepts

The Group Policy Preferences look "different" than the rest of the Group Policy universe. That's because they *are* different. They were born at a company called DesktopStandard and then integrated into existing Microsoft technology after Microsoft purchased them. It's kind of like the International Space Station. One minute, you're in the USA section and things are in English. Then you step into the Soyuz escape capsule and all the markings are in Russian. It's not totally like that, but you can certainly see where things are significantly different.

And since there are a lot of holdovers from the originating technology, working with one, then the other, can be a little confusing.

Those confusing (but powerful) elements we'll cover here are as follows:

- The idea that they *aren't really policies* but rather are *preferences*. (Don't worry; we'll clear up this bit of confusion right away.)

- The multicolored and dashed lines that are in some portions of the interface.

- The strange concept called the *CRUD method*.

- The Common tab, which allows you to do some high-power tricks.

- Using Group Policy Preferences "targeting" to further hone your wishes.

In all, it's a cool, cool brave new (or rather *additional*) world. But it does have tricks and pitfalls, and that's what we're going to explore here in this chapter. However, because we can't explore all 21 goodies in this book, <insert shameless plug here> take my live or online Group Policy training class at www.GPanswers.com/training with hands-on labs for more information.

Preference vs. Policy

This is a quote from the Group Policy Preferences help file within the GPMC that pretty much sums it up:

> *Unlike policy settings, by default preference items are not removed*
> *when the hosting GPO becomes out of scope for the user or computer.*

Let's spend a little time breaking this apart, understanding the implications of getting our new superpowers before we proceed to do something we'll later regret.

Let me be really, really clear: please don't mass-deploy Group Policy Preferences settings to your clients until you understand the preference versus policy issues.

Why Group Policy Works—a Review

Let's recall a little more about what Group Policy does for you. Group Policy delivers settings. And the "target application"—say Windows Explorer, or Internet Explorer, or the WSUS client, or Windows Media Player, or whatever—will pick up the settings and change their behavior based on what you want the application to do. For instance, if you use Group Policy and enable a setting like User Configuration ➢ Policies ➢ Administrative Templates ➢ Control Panel ➢ **Prohibit Access to the Control Panel**, your expectation is that Windows Explorer will do the dirty work for you and, well, prohibit access to the Control Panel.

Because that directive is written to a protected part of the Registry—in fact, to the "proper" Policies keys—the user cannot edit the Registry and "scoot" out of getting the setting. Again, we covered this in Chapter 3 and will cover it more in Chapter 6, "Managing Applications and Settings Using Group Policy."

For now, I'll give you the crash course you need, but I won't go overboard.

Why ADM/ADMX Files Are and Aren't So Awesome

The whole idea that Group Policy is a massive "settings delivery machine" is great. And in the next chapter, you'll learn how the "underlying language" of Administrative Template policy settings is either ADM or ADMX. All ADM(X) files are is a simple language to describe what change you want made to the target computers' Registry and where those changes should go.

You'll see that not all settings are exactly alike.

Some settings (indeed, all the ones that Microsoft ships) are "proper Policies." Their directives get put into special "Policies keys" in the Registry. When the GPO no longer applies, the setting is reverted.

We've already seen this in our travels. We create the policy, the action takes place. We remove the policy, the action is reverted. Neat, right?

But this "magic" is contingent on the application knowing to look in these proper "Policies keys" (again, more on this in the next chapter).

Many applications don't know to look in these specialized Policies Keys locations. So, you can implement your own ADM or ADMX file only to push a setting like "Zoom

Level" in Acrobat Reader. But then users can simply "walk around" your suggestion and make their own changes to the zoom level.

That's because Explorer doesn't know to protect that part of the world; it's not contained within the Policies keys.

And that's the same issue with the GPPrefs. The GPPrefs don't write their magical setting to these special Policies keys, like "proper" policy settings do.

And you might be asking yourself why. Again, the answer is simple: the applications they control (Explorer, drive settings, ODBC settings, etc.) don't know to look in the Policies keys to pick up and revert settings. You're changing the values directly.

Group Policy Preferences Are Like ADM/ADMX Files (Mostly)

So, the GPPrefs specify where these applications should look for their settings. But the downsides in this scheme are the same downsides you would get when you create ADM and ADMX files:

- Settings you dictate with ADM/ADMX and GPPrefs can usually be changed, unset, or deleted by the end user (though there are some exceptions).

- If a user moves from one OU to another (or performs in some other way so that they fall out of scope of management), the setting will just stick there, tattooing the machine.

Hence, these new goodies are called Group Policy *Preferences*. And that's because they act more or less like the preferences we created when we created our own ADM and ADMX files.

Group Policy Preferences Advantages over ADM/ADMX Files

However, there is one additional distinction: ADM and ADMX files aren't usually "rewritten" after a user changes settings that are directed for them (though this can be changed via settings located within Computer Configuration ➤ Policies ➤ Administrative Templates ➤ System ➤ Group Policy, as we explored in Chapter 3 in the section "Affecting the Computer Settings of Group Policy").

GPPrefs are different. They hook into the "timing" of the Group Policy engine. So, even if a user changes the underlying settings (say, they delete a shortcut that is supposed to affect them using GPPrefs), the next time Group Policy refreshes, that shortcut will pop right back as if nothing had happened! That said, Group Policy Preferences can only re-apply settings when the machine is on the network and can make contact to a Domain Controller.

 If you want Group Policy Preferences to be maintained even when offline, see the final section in this chapter ("Giving Group Policy Preferences a "boost"), which shows how to keep Group Policy Preferences working offline.

Now, as you'll see a little later, the GPPrefs have some extra superpowers available. These superpowers can all be found on the Common tab, and we'll cover these superpowers in detail a little later on.

Some options go above and beyond the original ADM/ADMX capabilities:

- "Remove this item when it is no longer applied" can help "peel off" settings when the user or computer falls out of scope of management. But this doesn't always work as you might expect, and we'll explore this a little later.

- "Apply once and do not reapply" changes the GPPref's default behavior. So instead of hooking into the timing of the Group Policy engine, settings are simply deployed once and never again—even if the user changes the settings the administrator wanted.

- "Item-level targeting" is sort of like WMI filters on steroids, and it's only available for GPPrefs settings, not original policy settings.

There are some more options where GPPrefs go above and beyond the original ADM/ADMX preferences, but these are the big ones.

The Overlap of Group Policy vs. Group Policy Preferences and Associated Issues

One of the strangest parts of the GPPrefs is that they bring totally new superpowers to the table yet overlap some existing areas. To some, this can be confusing to say the least, because how will you know which one to use?

Classic vs. Group Policy Preferences Overlap Areas

Some items cursorily overlap with other areas of Group Policy. For instance, drive mappings and Environment variables can also be set with login scripts, as can shortcuts and some other areas if you really put your mind to it. But in some instances, there is GPPrefs functionality that seems to "compete" with existing classic Group Policy functionality.

Microsoft doesn't like to think of the features as "competing." The idea is that you'll use some features for some reasons and other features for other reasons.

In practice, though, this is rarely 100 percent true.

In some cases, for some features, I'll make a judgment call. That is, there are "clear winners" in some GPPrefs features that you should simply use and stop using some of the original Group Policy features.

Yet, there are other times where one GPPrefs feature dovetails into an existing Group Policy feature. In those instances, I'll show you how to leverage the two features for a "better together" story.

Let's take a look and see the sights.

Group Policy Deployed Printers vs. GPPrefs Printers Extension

The Group Policy Deployed Printers feature debuted with Windows Server 2003 R2 and then made its way as a mainstream Windows Vista feature. You may be wondering why you've never heard of it and why I'm not covering it in other chapters. Well, in short, the

feature is not wonderful. Check out www.GPanswers.com's Newsletter #17 for more information about deployed printers with Windows Server 2003 R2 and Windows Vista (and
later, actually) if you like. But in short, the "policy-based" feature is difficult to implement,
requires a schema update, and didn't work consistently.

For reference, this feature is found by traversing to Computer Configuration ➢
Policies ➢ Windows Settings ➢ Deployed Printers and User Configuration ➢ Windows
Settings ➢ Deployed Printers. Note that you might not see the Deployed Printers node in
the Group Policy editor if you don't have the print management utilities installed on your
machine.

In contrast, the GPPrefs Printers extension feature is found in two places: in
Computer Configuration ➢ Preferences ➢ Control Panel Settings ➢ Printers and User
Configuration ➢ Preferences ➢ Control Panel Settings ➢ Printers.

The GPPrefs Printers extension allows for TCP/IP, local printers, or shared printers
(User side only); requires no schema changes; and as long as the Group Policy Preferences
are installed on the target machine, makes deploying printers a dream.

This one is a no-brainer: the Printers extension just clobbers the original Group Policy
Printers capability. Start using it right away.

Group Policy Internet Explorer and Group Policy IE Maintenance Configuration vs. the GPPrefs Internet Settings Extension

There was already an overlapping message in Group Policy-land when configuring Internet
Explorer (IE). The original policy settings can be found here:

- Computer Configuration ➢ Policies ➢ Administrative Templates ➢ Windows
  Components ➢ Internet Explorer.

- User Configuration ➢ Policies ➢ Administrative Templates ➢ Windows Components ➢
  Internet Explorer. Inside, you'll see original policy settings for IE 5 and 6, IE 7, IE 8
  and 9, and IE 10 and later.

But then there are also the old and non-working IE Maintenance settings. (They stopped
working with IE 10.) Those were found at User Configuration ➢ Policies ➢ Windows
Settings ➢ Internet Explorer Maintenance. (And you won't see this node if your own
machine has IE 10 or later installed on it.)

So, before we even add the GPPrefs, we have triple overlap.

Now, by adding the GPPrefs, there's a quadruple overlap. The GPPrefs for the IE settings
can be found at User Configuration ➢ Preferences ➢ Control Panel Settings ➢ Internet
Settings, as shown in Figure 5.2.

With the overlap in IE, things get really confusing, really fast. What if you have IE settings contained within three or four areas? See the section "How Does the Group Policy
Engine Deal with Overlaps?" where we discuss that problem.

My basic advice is to try to find settings within the Group Policy Admin Templates first,
because those settings will prevent users from modifying IE's configuration.

Then, if you cannot find the setting you want in the Administrative Templates section,
use Group Policy Preferences where necessary. But note again, users will be able to wiggle
around any preferences you set. And, you'll also need to set up Group Policy Preferences
items for each version of IE you want to support. For instance, if you have both, say, IE 9

and 10 (or later), you would need two Group Policy Preferences items: one for IE9 and one for IE10 such that both IE versions got your intentions.

Between you and me, Microsoft's toolset to manage IE (both Admin Templates and Group Policy Preferences) is really lacking. There's a wide variety of things you simply cannot manage in Internet Explorer, or, if you can, you have to stand on your head to do it. In contrast, PolicyPak Application Manager has a "Universal Pak for Internet Explorer," which enables you to manage, well, pretty much everything about Internet Explorer. Manage add-ons, pop-up blockers, site-to-zone assignment, LAN settings, privacy settings, importing certificates, and on and on. I put together a series of videos and a whitepaper on the subject in case it's your job to really manage IE using Group Policy. Here's the link:

`http://www.policypak.com/products/manage-internet-explorer-using-group-policy-policypak.html`

FIGURE 5.2   This is the IE preference extension.

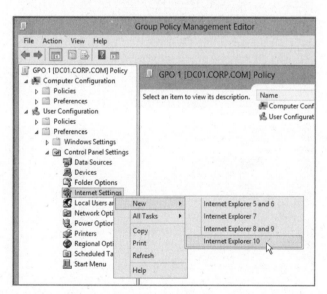

Group Policy Power Management vs. GPPrefs Power Options Preference Extension

Original Power Management options were found in Computer Configuration ➢ Policies ➢ Administrative Templates ➢ System ➢ Power Management (and the various subnodes within). These settings deal with sleep options, what happens when you push various power buttons, spinning down the hard drive, and more.

There is also one lone User-side setting at User Configuration ≻ Policies ≻ System ≻ Power Management that deals with passwords when the laptop comes back from hibernation.

The new Power Options extension settings are found within Computer Configuration ≻ Preferences ≻ Control Panel Settings ≻ Power Options and User Configuration ≻ Preferences ≻ Control Panel Settings ≻ Power Options. In Figure 5.3, you can see the Power Plan settings available.

There is a degree of overlap here. In Figure 5.4, you can see what happens when I set the **Specify the system sleep timeout (plugged in)** policy setting to "300 seconds" (not shown). You can see the result if the "Put the computer to sleep" option is set to five minutes and users are locked out of that setting, plus they get a handy notification bar showing "Some settings are managed by your system administrator." Again, you'll only get the UI lockout and notification bar if you use true policy settings.

FIGURE 5.3   Power Plan settings for Windows 7 and later

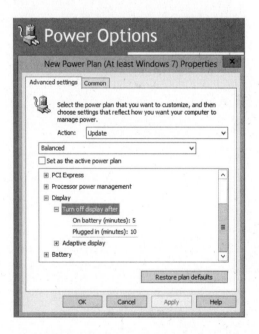

However, you are not able to create new Power Schemes (for XP) or Power Plans (Windows 7 and later) using policy settings. For that, you'll use GPPrefs.

And what's also neat is that you can, say, create a new Power Plan using Group Policy Preferences, set it as the default, then start out to configure all the settings you want using preferences. Then, if there's a particular setting you want to lock down, you can do so, using policy (if it's available).

So, in short, more settings are available using preferences, but only policy performs a true UI lockout.

FIGURE 5.4 You can lock out various power settings using policy.

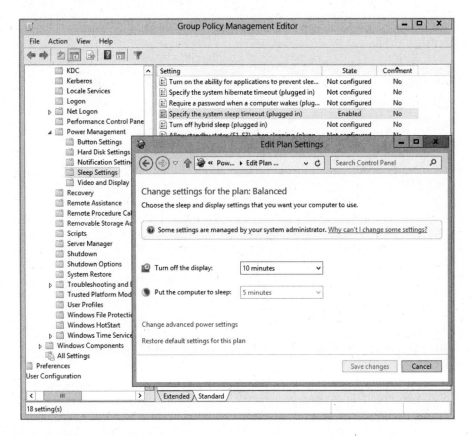

Group Policy File Security vs. GPPrefs Files Preference Extension

Group Policy has a way to set security on files. But until the Files extension came along, there was no way to use Group Policy to get files on the Desktop or into folders (short of using a logon script to do it).

So, this situation is a little weird. It's like two halves that have always wanted to be together. So now with the Files extension (Computer Configuration ➢ Preferences ➢ Windows Settings ➢ Files), you can push a file to a client. And with Group Policy File Security (located within Computer Configuration ➢ Policies ➢ Windows Settings ➢ Security Settings ➢ File System), you can set the ACLs on those files.

What a magic combination!

Group Policy System Services vs. GPPrefs Services Preference Extension

The original way to control services is located in Computer Configuration ➤ Policies ➤ Security Settings ➤ System Services.

The GPPrefs way to control services is located in Computer Configuration ➤ Preferences ➤ Control Panel Settings ➤ Services.

Both have the ability to change the startup mode of a service to Automatic, Manual, or Disabled. However, there are differences between the two tools:

- The original way can also set the security on the account (who can start, stop, and pause the service).

- The GPPrefs way can do the following things that cannot be done the original way:

  - Start or stop the service once the Group Policy applies

  - Change the recovery options if a service fails

  - Change the program to run if a service fails and/or restart the computer if the service fails

So, although there is overlap here, you should ideally use the original way to change the security on the service if necessary but then use the Services extension to manage the rest of the properties, like recovery options.

 Note that the management station needs to be running on a machine with the services you want to manage. This is the same behavior as the original Group Policy services node.

Group Policy Device Installation Restrictions vs. GPPrefs Devices Preference Extension

The original Device Installation Restrictions are found at Computer Configuration ➤ Policies ➤ System ➤ Device Installation ➤ Device Installation Restrictions, and we discuss them in detail in Chapter 8.

The GPPrefs Devices extension node is found in Computer Configuration ➤ Preferences ➤ Control Panel Settings ➤ Devices and User Configuration ➤ Preferences ➤ Control Panel Settings ➤ Devices.

The original way works for only Windows 7 and later. The GPPrefs way works for all operating systems.

However, the two technologies work fundamentally differently. The original technology's job is to prevent users from installing drivers for new hardware. So when you restrict a specific device from your Windows 7 machines, the driver is actually blocked from being installed. And this strategy works great if the device is unplugged and plugged back in a lot because during the next check, it will block the device. So, it works well for things like USB memory sticks and other things that are unplugged and plugged back in. However, the original technology didn't do such a hot job on devices that were already installed on the machine, such as CD-ROMs, SCSI cards, and scanners. Those device drivers are already installed, and you don't usually unplug them and put them back in. So the driver isn't ever rechecked.

The Devices extension technology works differently. Its job is to disable the actual device or port, not prevent the driver from loading. So at first blush it would seem like the Devices extension is the way to go. Except there are two flaws with GPPrefs Devices:

- With the GPPrefs Devices extension, you cannot dictate a specific piece of hardware that you don't already have on your management station. So if you're looking to just ban 32GB iPod Touch devices, you have to track one down and get it hooked into your management station so you can restrict that specific device type. If you can't find one, you can restrict an entire class that links to that, such as USB ports, but then some mice and keyboards won't work.

- Because it only disables the device (and doesn't prevent the device driver from installing), any user with appropriate rights can simply re-enable the device, as seen in Figure 5.5. However, regular users don't have access to this ability, so be sure to test this in your environment to see if it is a good fit.

FIGURE 5.5   If the Devices extension has disabled a device, users with Admin rights can re-enable it.

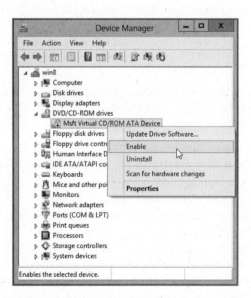

The original technology lets you specify GUIDs of specific hardware IDs. So all you need to do is locate the hardware ID of the device you're after and plunk it into the policy setting and you're golden. Moreover, the original Group Policy settings genuinely prevent the drivers from loading, so there's no way they can just re-enable a device if the drivers aren't even installed.

So, which one do you use where? Here's my advice:

▪ Use the Group Policy Device Installation settings when you have all Windows Vista or later machines. Preventing the driver is a better way to go overall. And, because you always use the Hardware ID when implementing the setting, you can be as specific or generic as you want.

▪ Use the Devices extension settings when you have lots of Windows XP machines. Sure, it's not as industrial strength as preventing the driver from loading, but most users won't know to go around it anyway (and if they don't have rights to, this isn't a problem anyway).

▪ You might want to use Devices extension with Windows 7 and later machines *anyway*, because, don't forget, the Group Policy Device Installation only works when devices are removed and reintroduced. Devices extension works great with devices when they're already used with the machine, such as CD-ROMs and SCSI cards, and so on. But again, it doesn't prevent users with rights from simply enabling these devices if they want to.

▪ Finally, in my testing, Devices extension worked perfectly when I used Computer Configuration ➢ Preferences ➢ Control Panel Settings ➢ Devices. I restricted the hardware and did a gpupdate command, and my hardware was disabled. However, when I did the same thing using User Configuration ➢ Preferences ➢ Control Panel Settings ➢ Devices and restricted the same hardware, it didn't always take effect right away.

 For more on the Devices preference extension versus Group Policy Device Installation settings, be sure to check out Chapter 12, where you'll find additional information on both solutions.

Group Policy Start Menu Policy Settings vs. GPPrefs Start Menu

The original Group Policy Start Menu policy settings are in User Configuration ➢ Administrative Templates ➢ Start Menu and Taskbar.

The GPPrefs Start Menu extension is located within User Configuration ➢ Preferences ➢ Control Panel Settings ➢ Start Menu.

Although there is a lot of overlap, we need to revisit the idea of policy versus preference. Since a policy is going to restrict the operating system (and force the user to accept the change), the policy settings can be heavy-handed. Heck, that may be just what you want.

On the other hand, the Start Menu extension settings are preferences, which means that they're more like suggestions for the user. So, if the user doesn't like your Start Menu preference settings, they can just reverse them if they so choose.

So, there's not one unified answer about which one you would always use.

Choose the Group Policy Start Menu policy settings when you want to guarantee your settings, and use the Start Menu extension settings when you want to set a baseline but permit the user to change them.

That being said, it doesn't appear that the Group Policy Preferences items for the Start Menu have any effect at all on Windows 10. If you want to manage the Start Menu settings for Windows 10, we have a PolicyPak Pak for it.

WARNING   It should be noted that this GPPref (heck, all GPPrefs) will refresh every 90 minutes or so by default and wipe out its changed settings. But you can change this behavior later using information found in the sections about the Common tab, specifically in the section "Apply Once and Do Not Reapply."

Group Policy Restricted Groups vs. Local Users and Groups Preference Extension

The original Group Policy Restricted Groups is located within Computer Configuration ➢ Policies ➢ Security Settings ➢ Restricted Groups. We'll cover it in more detail in Chapter 8 if you're unfamiliar with it.

The GPPrefs Local Users and Groups is located within Computer Configuration ➢ Preferences ➢ Control Panel Settings ➢ Local Users and Groups and User Configuration ➢ Preferences ➢ Control Panel Settings ➢ Local Users and Groups.

Here's the "ever so brief" rundown. The original Group Policy Restricted Groups allows you to affect who is and who is not a member of either domain-based groups or local groups.

However, the Local Users and Groups GPPrefs extension is meant for, well, just local users and groups.

Group Policy Restricted Groups does have some downsides. Its main goal is to strictly control the group membership, which might not be what you're looking to do. Although it's possible to use Group Policy Restricted Groups to simply add a user to a group, it's not intuitive and it's a lot of work.

Moreover, the GPPrefs Local Users and Groups extension is available for both the User and Computer sides (which means it's more flexible), and you can also use it to add a new user account (complete with all account settings) to the computers of your choice. The Local Users and Groups extension can also delete local groups and cherry-pick specific users to delete from groups (super useful if you just want to pluck just one user out of, say, the local Administrators group).

So, the advice is simple:

- If you want to affect domain-based groups (like Backup Operators, Domain Admins, etc.), stick with Group Policy Restricted Groups.

- Use the Local Users and Groups extension for everything else. It's much easier to understand and implement and you'll likely be happier overall.

How Does the Group Policy Engine Deal with Overlaps?

Well, there's the short answer and the long answer. Let's go over both. (We're old friends now—you knew I would anyway, right?)

The Short Answer: Policy Wins over Preferences

The short answer is that if there's a conflict between a policy setting and a preference setting, the policy setting will win. (So, for instance, items in Computer and User Configuration ➢ Policies should always win over Computer or User Configuration ➢ Preferences.)

Why?

Because only policies lock out the user interface of the application they manage (Explorer, Power Settings, etc.).

Preferences don't.

Remember, preferences are suggestions that you can give to the user's application, but the user can usually just wipe them out if they want (although GPPrefs will reapply again at policy refresh time by default).

Here's a quick example to prove the point. In the example in Figure 5.6, I'm clicking Help to ensure that the Help menu is on the Start Menu for all Windows 7 machines. And I'm using GPPrefs to do it. True, this is the default anyway, but by selecting it here, I'm laying down a preference that is always put on the machine.

FIGURE 5.6   By using GPPrefs, you're putting a preference on the client.

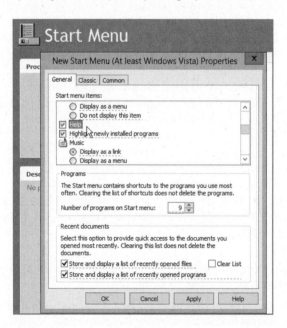

However, if I use the policy setting User Configuration ➢ Policies ➢ Administrative Templates ➢ Start Menu and Taskbar ➢ **Remove Help menu from Start Menu**, as seen in Figure 5.7, the Help option disappears in the Windows 7 Start Menu. (Not Windows 8, of course, because Windows 8 has no Start Menu. And, same for Windows 10, since Windows 10's Start Menu is really a "shortened" Windows 8 Start Menu.)

FIGURE 5.7   This policy will positively remove Help from the Start Menu.

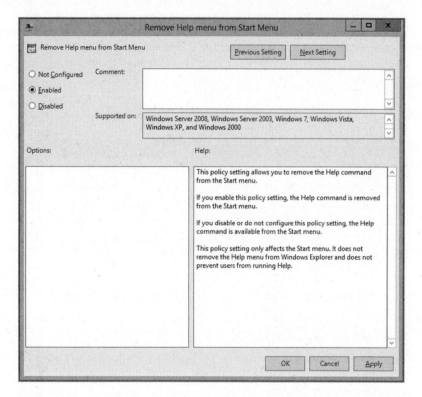

But the general case here is that policies always beat preferences. Rock always beats scissors. Or does it? Can the rock crumble when it's hit by the scissors? Let's continue to see at least one interesting case where it doesn't work that way.

The Long Answer: Understanding CSE Timing and Overlap

Recall that the Group Policy system is a last-written-wins technology. So, if you have an overlap between, say, the domain level and the OU level, the default is that the OU level will win because it was written last.

But now things become markedly more confusing. Not only is there overlap between Active Directory levels (site, domain, OU) for some of the features, there's overlap at the *feature* level, where two or three CSEs compete to write their data last.

Basically, it is possible that you could, in a single Group Policy Object, do something where Preferences "wins" over Policy.

Ow.

There is some order in this chaos. But to understand it you'll need to clear your mind a bit. On any Windows 10 machine, open REGEDIT and head to the following Registry location:

```
HKEY_LOCAL_MACHINE\SOFTWARE\Microsoft\
Windows NT\CurrentVersion\Winlogon\GPExtensions
```

There, you'll see the registrations for all CSEs. The GUID of each CSE dictates the order in which things will process. They'll process alphabetically, by GUID.

So, Wireless Group Policy fires off first (that's a classic Group Policy setting and what's seen in Figure 5.8). Next up is Group Policy Environment (that's a GPPrefs CSE), then Central Access Policy Configuration (that's a CSE that debuted in Windows 8), then Group Policy Local Users and Groups (another GPPrefs CSE), then Group Policy Device Settings (another GPPrefs CSE), and so on.

FIGURE 5.8 All CSEs process in alphabetical order based upon GUID.

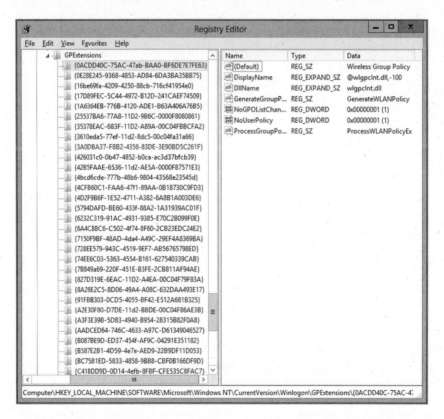

So on the surface, it appears that if you had a conflict with both classic Group Policy settings and newer GPPrefs settings, you could just see which one ran last and bank on that setting always "winning."

But that's only true if the two CSEs end up writing to the *exact same places*.

And this is actually something you could do.

For instance, you could make a Group Policy Admin Templates policy setting that would **Prevent Access to the Control Panel and PC Settings.**

Then, in the same Group Policy Object, you could use a Group Policy Preferences Registry item and set the same value (the exact same value) to zero.

The tie will be broken when an application is coded to look in the proper Policies keys. And, if there's a policy setting in those keys, the target application will honor the policy, not the preference.

If you poke through the list of CSE registrations, you'll see that Group Policy Admin Templates runs first (it's called "Registry"), and then Group Policy Preferences Registry CSE runs second.

Higher up in the list is the CSE for "Registry," which is the old (internal) name for Group Policy's Admin Templates.

Lower down in the registration list is the CSE for Group Policy Preferences Registry items. Which one gets to write last (in the same Group Policy Object)? Group Policy Preferences Registry settings: again, only if you're trying to write to the same exact location using the same single Group Policy Object.

Whew. All this stuff can give you a headache. This "who will win" stuff is really confusing, and I haven't tested every case. Be sure to test all interactions in a test lab before you roll out settings to production (especially if you plan on doing multiple, possibly conflicting things, within one Group Policy Object).

Other Items That Can Affect Group Policy and GPPrefs Processing

Recall that in Chapter 4 you learned about various policy settings found at Computer Configuration ➤ Policies ➤ Administrative Templates ➤ System ➤ Group Policy.

All Group Policy Preferences items will try to reapply, even if nothing has changed within the GPO.

You can disable this behavior and make the Group Policy Preferences item run only one time by locating the corresponding policy setting and unchecking "Process even if the Group Policy objects have not changed" and this behavior will stop.

The Lines and Circles and the CRUD Action Modes

By this time, you might have spent a little time plunking around the new Group Policy Preferences (but you haven't deployed them yet, because you haven't finished reading the whole chapter, right?). And, indeed, you can see that they're really, really different than the original Group Policy settings. Many of them (gasp!) kind of look like the thing they actually manage in the Windows user interface! Mon dieu!

If you haven't yet tried out GPPrefs and want to follow along with these examples, this would be a good time. That's because you'll learn about both the "lines and circles" and Action modes at the same time. I strongly suggest that you try these settings in a test lab and not in production until you've got a real grip on how everything works.

You'll note that many GPPrefs have an action item, and you can set it to Create, Replace, Update, or Delete. This is called the *CRUD method* for short. You'll also notice many GPPrefs have these thin solid green lines or thin dashed red lines underneath certain settings. These colorful lines express which settings could possibly affect your client.

We can use the Power Options preference extension in our examples because it has CRUD ability *and* contains solid green lines for many options. To create a Windows 7 and later power option for your users, dive down to User Configuration ➢ Preferences ➢ Control Panel Settings ➢ Power Options and select New Power Plan (At Least Windows 7). Alternatively, the same node exists on the Computer side if you wanted to play with that. When you do, you'll create a Power Plan Preference item. Drill down into "Hard disk" and "Turn off hard disk after" and see something similar to what is shown in Figure 5.9.

Indeed, to save a little space, I'm showing several items in Figure 5.9. First, you can see I'm pulling down the CRUD action-item modes just to show them off (and selecting Create). You can also see I've typed in the name for a new Power Plan called "Our New Companywide Plan." It's a little hard to see because the Action dropdown is over the text, but it's there. I'm also drilling down to "Hard disk" and the subsection "Turn off hard disk after."

So both the lines and circles and CRUD action-item features can bite you in the butt— if you don't know what they mean and how they work. Let's explore those now. We'll tackle the colored lines first, then the CRUD. (That's it, I'm trademarking that phrase— GPanswers.com: *We Tackle the CRUD*.) Microsoft refers to these abilities as both "CRUD" and "Action Modes."

The Lines and the Circles

Original Group Policy doesn't have any solid and dashed lines, but some of the new GPPrefs items do.

So, what's the deal with those solid and dashed lines? In Figure 5.9, you'll see two thin green lines underneath "On battery (minutes): 0" and "Plugged in (minutes): 0".

The circles and lines are a way to craft which bits and pieces within a GPPrefs item you want to affect a client machine.

Here's an example:

Let's say a user has gone in on their own machine and made some settings they like to use. In our example, we'll assume users on laptops have changed the "Turn off hard disk after" setting, specifically the "Plugged in (minutes)" setting to 15 minutes.

However, we (in the IT department) want to make sure they save power when they're using battery only. No problem! We can use the Power Plan settings to define when the hard disk should turn off when the laptop is plugged in. Again, in Figure 5.9, I'm ready to make changes, but haven't done so yet.

Even though we want to change the "On battery" setting, we already said we don't want to disrupt any settings that might have already been made to the "Plugged In" subsection within "Turn off hard disk after."

So, what are we going to do? If you click around, by default *every* setting on this page has a thin green line beneath it. This means that if you update this power plan and modify even just the "On battery" setting within the "Turn off hard disk after" subsection, *all* green underlined settings will be delivered to the client machine. Ouch! That's exactly what you *don't* want.

FIGURE 5.9   Let's get to know the Action modes and the underlines using Power Plan settings as an example.

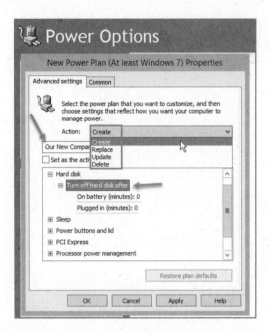

You want a way to update *some* of the settings, and not *all* of the settings. You need a way to prevent the processing of some of the settings on the page. To do this, highlight the setting (actually, drill into the setting first to select it) and then press the F7 key. This will change the thin green line to a thin dashed red line.

You can see in Figure 5.10 that I've updated "On battery (minutes)" to have a thin red dashed line (using the F7 key) and modified "Plugged in (minutes)" to 20 and kept the thin green line.

Now the setting (any ones with the dashed red lines) will be exempt from being applied within the edict.

So here's the thing that's misleading and potentially leads to misunderstanding: It doesn't matter what values you set to those entries with the red dashed underlines—because your client systems will never, ever pick those values up. This is super, duper weird, so stick with me. Look at Figure 5.11. You'll see I changed "On battery (minutes)" to 808. But the setting is still red-dashed, even though I changed the value.

So even though I've changed the value from 0 to 808, because I've set the value to red-dash, it doesn't matter what I've done in that value. Said another way, the Group Policy Preferences engine will ignore all settings with red dashes, because red dashes mean "don't apply."

This same behavior will hold true for check boxes, fill-in-the-blanks, and radio buttons. If there's a red dashed line beneath the setting, your clients simply ignore the setting upon refresh.

FIGURE 5.10   Settings you have modified with red dashed lines will not apply on the client machine.

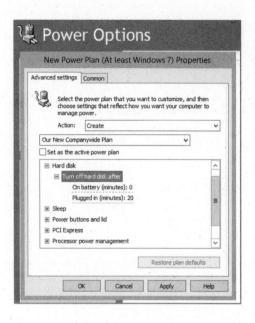

FIGURE 5.11   Even if you change a setting that has red dashes, the engine will not apply these settings.

Microsoft calls this "disabling the policy," but I don't love that term because I don't want to get mixed up in thinking somehow that I'm "disabling the functionality" the setting provides. By *disabling*, Microsoft means "disabling the processing of that particular setting regardless of what the value is set to."

So, wait a minute.

If you just clicked OK and then continued onward, what would be set on the machine?

This is where it gets really bad, really fast. Because we only red-underlined (disabled) *one* of the settings, and on this page *all* the other values are preset to green underlined, this means *all* the values with green underlines will be set to be delivered to the client ... even if you didn't intend for that to be the case.

What you have to do, if you really want to only deliver the "Turn off hard disk after" for "Plugged in" (and nothing else), would be to set all settings on the page to red dashed and just the one item you want to green underlined.

The good news is that there are some "fast keys" you can use to do this quickly within the interface. Here are all the function keys and what they do:

F5   Enables the processing of *all* settings on the page that need to be honored. Useful if you disabled some settings from being honored and want to reset the form.

F6   Enables the processing of one setting on the page that needs to be honored. Useful if you disabled one setting using F7 and want to change it back. Again, merely changing the value will not reset it to a green underline.

F7   Disables the processing of one setting on the page. Useful if you want to keep one setting from being updated or changed on the client.

F8   Disables the processing of all settings on the page. Useful if you want to prevent all the settings on one tab from being honored on the client. Most useful when using the Internet Explorer settings because there are multiple tabs that hold a massive amount of settings. Perhaps you want to disable all settings (which means none will apply) but enable just one tab with two settings.

You'll also see that some settings in the extension have green circles (equivalent to the solid green underline) or red circles à la the "no" sign (which are the equivalent of the thin red dashed line). You can see an example in Figure 5.12, where I've explicitly disabled the processing of two settings within IE 10's Advanced tab. To disable the processing of those items, I simply selected each item and pressed F7. Again, it doesn't matter if the check box is actively checked or not; the value in the check box doesn't get processed if there's a little "no" sign next to it (or it has a red dashed underline).

Warning: Visiting Multiple Tabs Can Be Hazardous to Your Network's Health

There are colored circles and lines for various Group Policy Preferences. Let's again take a look at a GPPrefs item for Internet Explorer 10 (though it's basically exactly the same for the other Internet Explorer Group Policy Preferences items).

So, the Group Policy Preferences item for Internet Explorer 10 (and later), for example, has lots of tabs. So the extension does a little helpful trick for you.

FIGURE 5.12   The red and green circles in some areas of a preference extension are analogous to the red and green underlines.

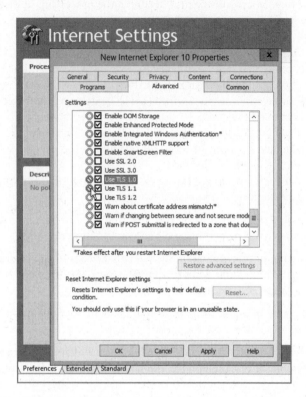

If you visit any tab, you'll see that many settings already have a green underline. You now know that any setting that has a green underline will have its value placed on the client (check box checked, radio button pushed, etc.).

But, again, most tabs have lots of stuff that *already* have green lines on most of the settings within the tabs. Does that mean that all those settings (even ones you likely don't care about) will be delivered to the client?

Well, *possibly*. There are the three cases to consider. We'll use Internet Explorer 8 and 9 properties as our example.

Case 1: Nothing Actually Created   Let's say you just want to poke around and see what's underneath the hood in the tabs. Of course you'll want to; you're naturally curious.

So you open up a Group Policy Object and create a new IE 10 Extension item and start poking around.

You can see it has a gaggle of tabs like General, Security, Privacy, Connections, Programs, and so on. Some tabs have green underlines, and others have red underlines. Others have *both*. You know that green-underlined properties are going to be set on the target machine.

Except you haven't changed anything yet, have you? You're just exploring and poking around.

When you click Cancel, nothing's changed, because the preference item isn't actually created.

Case 2: Quick Visit to Existing Item, but No Changes   Let's say you stumble across someone else's IE 10 item and you want to know what was set within it.

So, you edit the item, and start exploring and poking around *but not changing anything.* You can click the Connections tab and see what's there or click the Advanced tab and see what's there. And you can see what changes were made.

But, again, this is just a quick visit, and you've changed nothing.

When you click Cancel, nothing's changed. That's because you didn't change anything.

Case 3: A Visit with a Change on Any Tab   Let's say you stumbled across someone else's IE 10 item and you want to know what's set in some tabs (like Connections) *and* you want to change an item yourself in another tab (like Privacy).

So you edit the IE 10 item and inspect the Connections tab, shown in the following image. As you can see, no check boxes or other values have been changed by the previous admin. You do see green lines underneath some values, however.

Now you visit the tab you really need to make changes on—the Privacy tab—and you click in one place, and, say, uncheck "Turn on Pop-up Blocker," seen in this screen shot.

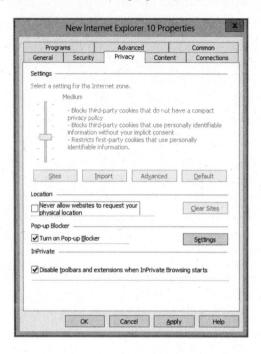

Here's the big warning: Because you initially clicked on a tab (Connections) and that tab has green underlined settings, then you visited a different tab (Privacy) to make a change, the green underlined settings as now specified on the Connections tab *will be set* (as well as all the green underlined settings in Privacy, because they're all green, too!).

This is very counterintuitive because, well, you didn't make any settings changes to Connections! You just visited one tab but made your changes in another tab.

But it doesn't matter. In this case, just looking at the tab (then making changes anywhere) does the damage.

The rule is simple: If you visit a tab (and the tab has green underlines) and you make any changes anywhere within the preference item, any tabs you visited (that have green underlined values) will be part of the delivery—and that's likely not what you want. I suggest instead that you traverse, tab to tab, and change all green underline settings to red-dash settings, just as a safety precaution. Then when you want to make an actual setting change, first set the value to green underline, then finally set the value as you want it delivered.

The CRUD Method: Create, Replace, Update, or Delete

Let's continue with our Power Plan example as we work through the next area: the CRUD method.

CRUD stands for Create, Replace, Update, or Delete. You'll notice these settings in the Action dropdown of many extensions, like the Power Plan extension seen earlier in Figure 5.9.

Here's what happens when an Action mode is chosen:

Create   Create the setting, but only if it does not already exist. Check out Figure 5.9, where I'm creating a new power plan for my whole company. Selecting Replace or Update (the options that follow) wouldn't make sense because I'm not trying to modify an existing scheme. Only Create makes sense, because the whole scheme doesn't yet exist.

Replace   Delete the setting if it already exists. Then push down new settings. For this, the Power Plan preference item, the whole scheme "Our New Companywide Scheme" would be deleted. Then it would be re-created from scratch. A useful scenario might be after some company-wide power plan was defined but perhaps defined incorrectly. In this case, choosing Replace would delete *all* settings if they exist. Then it would lay down all the settings again, ensuring that they were put in place as you wanted them.

Update (Default)   The default action, Update will create any new settings if they don't exist on the client. And if any settings do exist on the client, those with thin green underlines will also be updated with the values in the settings. This is the default because it will overwrite any settings (if present) or create them, as necessary, if they're not present.

Delete   Delete the settings. In our example, Delete would delete the whole power plan, when specifically named. Poof.

Use this CRUD action item with caution. You can delete all sorts of things you wish you hadn't: power schemes, drive mappings, the local Administrators group, and more.

So really watch out, and especially test this action before you implement.

For many GPPrefs, you won't see the Action dropdown. In this case, that means there is only one way for these settings to work. It's usually Update.

Common Tab

If you notice back in some of the figures in this chapter, there's a tab that keeps showing up over and over again. It's called the Common tab, and it's full of many of the superpowers the GPPrefs provide.

If you click on any Common tab, you'll see that they all have exactly the same options, as follows:

- Stop processing items in this extension if an error occurs
- Run in logged-on user's security context (user policy option)
- Remove this item when it is no longer applied
- Apply once and do not reapply
- Item-level targeting

You can see the Common tab in Figure 5.13, with a little extra note when one of the items is selected. (We'll get to that note in this section as well.)

FIGURE 5.13 Be super, extra careful when you select the "Remove this item when it is no longer applied" option in the Common tab.

The idea is that each and every Group Policy Preferences item you create can also optionally choose to leverage one or more of these extra options. Let's examine each of these items now in the following sections.

"Stop Processing Items in This Extension If an Error Occurs"

We'll start out with the least-used item of the bunch. The idea here is that if there's a problem when you're plunking down multiple preference items (within the same extension), then stop when the system encounters that problem. One situation where this might be helpful is when you use the Files extension. Perhaps you didn't want any files to be copied if, for some reason, the source file suddenly didn't exist. So, as soon as the GPPrefs engine realized one source file wasn't available, the whole Files preference extension CSE would stop. Other GPPrefs CSEs, like Drive Maps, Power Options, and Printers, would keep on chuggin'.

Again, this is the least-used option in the bunch.

"Run In Logged-On User's Security Context (User Policy Option)"

By default, the Group Policy engine runs all commands as SYSTEM, even though it's the user who's really logged in. This is awesome because it means you have some crazy super-powers, like the ability to zap any Registry key to anywhere in the Registry, restrict hardware regardless of who is logged on, and schedule tasks to run *right now*, even if no one is logged in.

There might be a time when you want to use this setting, but in my experience the times are few and far between. One example would be if you want to copy files in the user context and not the SYSTEM context.

There might be other times where GPPrefs just don't seem to take effect. One quick GPPrefs troubleshooting tip is to flip this setting on within the Common tab. There might be some occasion when trying to perform the action as the SYSTEM doesn't make the magic happen but performing the same action as the logged-in user does.

The other main use for this setting comes with the use of Environment variables, which we'll talk about later, so hang tight.

Here are some quick notes about some behaviors of this policy:

- Note that this setting is grayed out when dealing with GPPrefs on the Computer side, and the behavior is then to *always* use the SYSTEM account.

- Drive mappings and printers (network printers and TCP/IP printers only) ignore this setting. They *always* use the user context, so checking this check box here shouldn't produce any discernable effect. Note that new drive mappings don't take effect until the next logon and aren't related to this discussion.

"Remove This Item When It Is No Longer Applied"

This is my favorite option because it's full of interesting opportunities, behaviors, and pitfalls. You can see in Figure 5.13, when you click "Remove this item when it is no longer applied," you'll immediately get a pop-up saying, "This will cause a change to 'Replace' mode." If you click back over to, say, the Power Plan tab (or whatever tab your GPPrefs uses that has a CRUD action item), you'll see that the action has automatically been set to Replace and is grayed out to stay that way.

Even though it sets it to Replace mode, you can think of this setting as Delete and not Replace. Heck, Delete isn't strong enough, really. Think of it as Nuke.

That's because it will nuke the settings if the preference goes out of the scope of management. If you'll recall from Chapter 2, a scope change can happen when any of the following are true:

- Group Policy security filters are used and the user/computer is filtered out
- The Group Policy is deleted.
- The Group Policy is unlinked.
- The Group Policy's link is disabled.
- The preference is deleted.
- The WMI filter evaluates to false.
- And now, as you'll learn a little later, if "Item-level targeting" evaluates to false.

If any of these things happens, the target item is nuked.

Nuking an item might be good for a wide variety of reasons. Here are three good real-world examples:

- Someone changes job roles, so they get the S: drive nuked because they're no longer in the Sales OU.
- You deploy a new printer, so the reference to the old printer gets removed.
- An "Emergency Shortcut" is placed on people's Desktops during a crisis, and when the crisis is over, the shortcut should be deleted.

All of these are perfectly excellent examples on how to use Nuke mode. In all these cases the original item was, well, nuked when it was no longer applied.

But, before we can close the case on Nuke mode, let's work through an example with one of my favorites, the Registry extension.

Finding a Value to Change with the Registry Extension

In this example, we're going to change the DoubleClickSpeed entry for all users in the **Human Resources** OU. That includes Frank Rizzo and everyone else who's logged on. (Again, this is a working example to illustrate a point.)

In Figure 5.14, you can see the Mouse properties on the right and the underlying Registry entry HKEY_CURRENT_USER\Control Panel\Mouse\DoubleClickSpeed and its value of 500. If you move the Mouse properties slider to the right by two notches, the result is 340. Knowing this tidbit, if we use the Registry extension to dictate the DoubleClickSpeed value of 340, we'll be forcing our users to double-click slightly faster.

FIGURE 5.14 We can figure out how the DoubleClickSpeed value works by playing with the Mouse Properties applet.

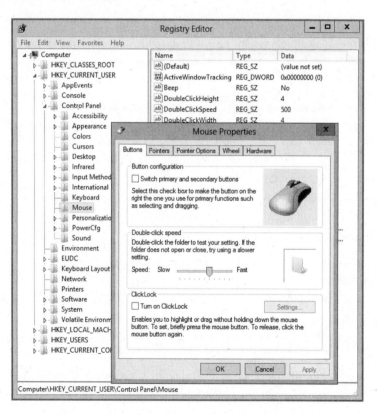

Using the Registry Preference Extension to Dictate the Setting to the Human Resources Users OU

Create and link a GPO over the **Human Resources Users** OU. Then edit the GPO and dive into User Configuration ➢ Preferences ➢ Windows Settings ➢ Registry. Click New ➢ Registry Item.

- For Action, make sure Update is selected.

- For Hive, make sure you've chosen HKEY_CURRENT_USER.

- For Key Path, make sure you've selected (or typed in) Control Panel\Mouse.

- For Value name, make sure DoubleClickSpeed is entered (you can leave the Default check box unchecked).

- For Value type, make sure REG_SZ is selected.

- For Value data, enter **340** (the value we know we want to set).

You can see all of this in Figure 5.15.

FIGURE 5.15 We can dictate specific settings using the GPPrefs' Registry extension. The red triangle next to the preference item shows we're in Replace mode (and also possibly in "Remove this item when it is no longer applied" mode).

Testing the Delivery of Our Settings

At this point, log on as Sol Rosenberg to any machine, then check the double-click speed. You can check the slider in the Control Panel Mouse applet, but an even better check is running REGEDIT. Then dive down into HKEY_CURRENT_USER\Control Panel\Mouse and see if DoubleClickSpeed is set to 340.

Testing the Default Group Policy Preferences Behavior

At this point, move Frank Rizzo's account from the **Human Resources Users** OU to a new OU. For instance, create an OU called **Nurses** and then move him to the **Nurses** OU. (Don't worry; when we're done we'll move him back.)

Log off, and log back on.

Then run the Registry editor (REGEDIT) and dive down into HKEY_CURRENT_USER\Control Panel\Mouse. What happened to the DoubleClickSpeed settings? Answer: Nothing; they stay put because the Group Policy Preferences' default behavior is to maintain, or tattoo, the Registry, even if the user falls out of the scope of management.

Log off as Frank.

Resetting for Our Next Test

At this point, move Frank Rizzo's account from the **Nurses** OU back to the **Human Resources Users** OU.

Make sure you're logged off as Frank Rizzo from the target computer.

Now, we're going to see what happens if we change the default behavior.

Turning on "Remove This Item When It Is No Longer Applied"

Now select the Common tab and select "Remove this item when it is no longer applied." You should get a pop-up box saying the mode has been changed to Nuke, er, Replace.

Back on the General tab, you should see that Replace is on and grayed out so it cannot be changed. Click OK to close the properties page. Now, before we continue, note that there is a signal of the (potential) devastation to come. If you look at the line item that's produced, you'll see a little red triangle next to the name showing you that the system is in Replace mode, also shown in Figure 5.15.

Nothing "bad" will happen until something happens with the scope. Let's examine the normal course of action that could happen up to (and including) that point.

Testing the Redelivery of Our Settings

Just for laughs, while logged on as Sol, reopen the Mouse applet in Control Panel and jam the double-click slider all the way to the left. Now run gpupdate. Close and reopen the Mouse applet.

Did the slider jump back to the faster position we dictated?

Indeed, check the Registry on the machine just to be sure if you're not.

That's good: The default behavior of GPPrefs is working for you. That is, the default is that GPPrefs will always reapply the settings, even if someone changes a setting by hand on the target computer. But, again, redelivery only occurs when the client machine can see a DC. (Again, to keep Group Policy Preferences items "alive" even when the computer goes offline, check out PolicyPak's Group Policy Preferences Manager part of the PolicyPak On-Premise suite, which is described in the PolicyPak Preferences Manager section later.)

Seeing the Result of "Remove This Item When It Is No Longer Applied"

At this point, move Sol Rosenberg's account from the **Human Resources** Users OU to the **Nurses** OU a second time.

Log off, and log back on. Then open re-run the Registry editor tool (REGEDIT) and dive down into HKEY_CURRENT_USER\Control Panel\Mouse.

And make a discovery.

That is, the *whole* DoubleClickSpeed value has been deleted!

You can see this in Figure 5.16. Or, rather, you *can't* see this in Figure 5.16, because it's *gone*.

FIGURE 5.16 Once the "Remove this item when it is no longer applied" setting is checked, the DoubleClickSpeed Registry key is deleted. But, thankfully, the Mouse application doesn't seem to mind very much.

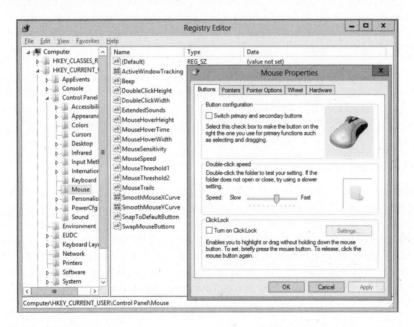

This isn't likely what you expected. You expected it to revert back to 500 or go to 0 or do something else predictable.

Right? Well, it doesn't.

By selecting "Remove this item when it is no longer applied," you nuke the entry. It literally deletes the whole thing you're working on—in this case, a Registry setting, and in other cases, power schemes, local users and groups, data sources, and other things you likely don't want to *delete*.

Putting the World Right Again for Sol

Put Sol's account back into the **Human Resources Users** OU.

Then log out and log back in. You should see the DoubleClickSpeed pop back in place with the value of 340.

Final Thoughts about "Remove This Item When It Is No Longer Applied"

Before we move on to the next topic, I do have some final thoughts about "Remove this item when it is no longer applied."

First, in our DoubleClickSpeed example, we didn't really do any "harm" to the system by deleting the DoubleClickSpeed key. In our examples, double-clicking will continue to work because the people who coded Explorer's mouse double-click feature must have said, "Well, if the DoubleClickSpeed key suddenly goes missing, we'll assume it's, oh, I dunno, how's 500?" And it keeps on working.

But that's because we're lucky!

If this was some Registry key to a custom application, you could have damaged the application, that's for sure.

Next, it isn't the Replace CRUD action that does this deed. It's positively the "Remove this item when it is no longer applied" check box. Again, think of this as Nuke. But the action item shows Replace, which is kind of misleading.

> If you're freaking out right now thinking, "Nuke mode isn't what I want... I want a real way to revert settings back," then don't panic. PolicyPak Admin Templates Manager (back in Chapter 4) will do that as well as PolicyPak Application Manager (in depth in the next chapter) will also do that.

"Apply Once and Do Not Reapply"

This is the other setting in the Common tab that I like a lot. This setting does just what it says: it will plunk down the setting, then never reapply. This is good, and it's bad.

On the one hand, you're able to set a true preference for the user. That is, you're suggesting this setting for them, so it's laid down exactly one time. If they want to change it, they can, and your suggestion never "plows down" back on top of their selected setting.

On the other hand, you might have the occasion to want to perform a baseline push of certain values to the system again. And in that case, not even running gpupdate /force will reset the values.

Targeting Your Preference Items with ILT

The final superpower within the Common tab is item-level targeting (ILT). ILT provides a new way to indicate exactly when a specific preference item should apply. ILT is almost like WMI filters (which we explored in Chapter 4). But ILTs have some advantages over WMI filters:

- They're easier to set up and use immediately. You'll fall in love with the GUI interface of ILTs.

- You can do nested ANDs, ORs, and NOTs within ILTs, making them immediately more flexible than WMI filters.

- ILTs, in general, evaluate faster when run on the client. WMI filters really cut into the machine's heart to see what's going on to evaluate the query. ILTs use code within the GPPrefs CSE to perform the query, so they're usually much faster (in most cases). In most cases, overall there's hardly any processing penalty to using them.

The categories can be seen in Figure 5.17. There are all sorts of queryable items, such as amount of RAM, CPU speed, available disk space, and more.

Note that one category within ILTs *is* WMI queries. So, you can leverage WMI queries within ILTs if you wanted to do something that wasn't part of the native ILT queries. The downside is that item-level targeting is only for GPPrefs and is simply not available for the other areas of original Group Policy.

FIGURE 5.17 Item-level targeting lets you specify when preferences apply.

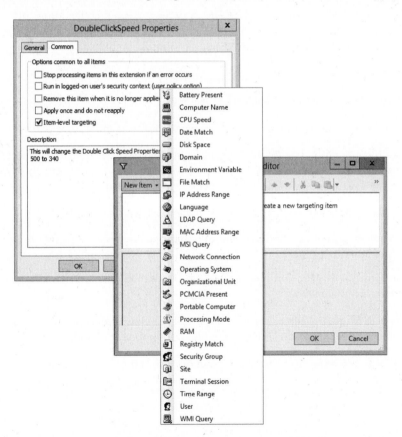

The Targeting Editor

You'll craft your query in the Targeting Editor.

By default, all items are ANDed together. In this way, ILTs can be "banded together" to produce queries where multiple items need to be true for the action to take place.

In Figure 5.18, I've strung together a query to really and truly verify that DogFoodMaker 6.0 is installed on the machine—I'm checking that the MSI product code has been installed on the machine and also that the HKLM\Software\DogFoodMaker hive has a key called Ruff with a value of 6.

Adding Additional Collections

Alternatively, if you want to do something fancier, you can select the Add Collection button and created nested groups of ILTs. For instance, you can have an ILT apply only when it hits User1 or the Administrator account.

To do that, you'd create two collections (be sure they're at the same level; you don't want to nest one within the other). Then, you'd highlight the second collection and click Item Options (next to Add Collection) and select OR. Now your second collection is OR.

Now, add your conditions in the first block and in the second block, and they'll be ORed together, as seen in Figure 5.19.

How Are Item-Level Targeting Items Evaluated?

One question you might be asking yourself is, "In what context is the ILT evaluated?"

In some cases, the logged-in user might not have rights to determine if an item-level targeting item is true or not. Likewise, the computer (SYSTEM) might have too much power and inadvertently say that something is true when really it's not true for the user at all.

Thankfully, these scenarios have been thought out. In short, here's what happens:

- Most ILTs are checked in the SYSTEM context. Because the SYSTEM has more rights than the user, this is desirable.

- However, some items should only be determined from the viewpoint of the logged-on user. Here's the breakdown:

Security Group Targeting Item   Runs from the point of view of the logged-in user (except if you're checking to see if the computer is a member of a group)

Language Targeting Item   Runs from the point of view of the logged-in user

File Match Targeting Item   Runs from the point of view of the logged-in user; then, if that fails, runs in the SYSTEM context as a second try

Other Targeting Editor Tricks

You can usually drag and drop things around without thinking about it too much. The Targeting Editor was rewritten heavily (and heck, renamed!) since the acquisition of the product from DesktopStandard, and they really did a smashing job of cleaning it up and making it easier to use overall.

Be sure to experiment with the cut, paste, and copy items. You'll be able to rapid-fire-create ILTs once you play with these abilities a little more. Additionally, you can add a label to a collection. That way, if you have a complex collection that you're querying for, others can figure out precisely what you were doing. You can see an example of a collection query label in Figure 5.20.

FIGURE 5.18 You can string together items in the Targeting Editor with AND.

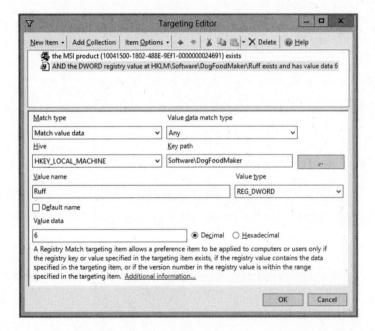

There is one important thing missing from the ILT editor: There is no way to export the potentially rich targeting I created in one item and import it into another GPPrefs item. There simply is no Export/Import feature.

However, a little later, in the section "Drag (or Paste) a Group Policy Preferences Extension to a File," you'll learn how to see the underlying XML code for a GPPrefs item. Inside that XML code is also the ILT information for that item.

With that in mind, you could rip out the well-defined Filter section from one preference item and smash it into the preference item (of another type) you needed. Then, drag and drop the XML file back onto the GPPrefs Editor.

FIGURE 5.19   Using OR, you can ensure that your wishes take place when certain conditions are true.

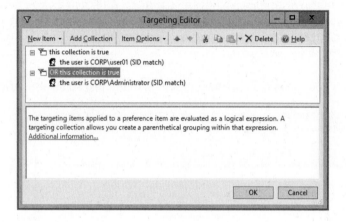

FIGURE 5.20   You can label a targeting item.

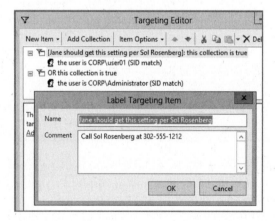

Description Field

This is the final Common entry regarding preference items. Here you're able to put in a simple description of what you're trying to do and notes about ILTs (if any).

It's on the Common tab, as you can see in Figure 5.21.

FIGURE 5.21   Descriptions are GPPrefs item specific and appear in the Description field on the left only when you finally click OK (not Apply).

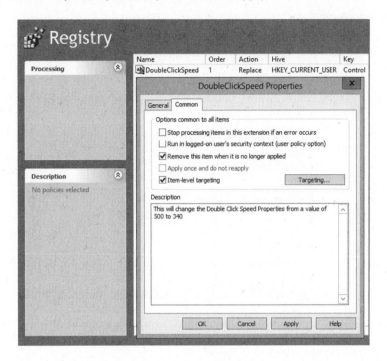

Group Policy Preferences Tips, Tricks, and Troubleshooting

Now that we're past the essentials, we're ready to move on to some useful tips and tricks to make us more productive with GPPrefs. And, of course, if something goes wrong, we'll need to troubleshoot our GPPrefs universe as well.

Quick Copy, Drag and Drop, Cut and Paste, and Sharing of Settings

I know this heading sounds like a lot of stuff, but it's really only one big thought. That is, the interface that allows you to create GPPrefs items lets you treat every setting like an object. I like to call this place the "GPPrefs editor" because it's the place within the Group Policy Management Editor that you create GPPrefs items. So, you can do some neat tricks.

Quick Copy/Paste

In Figure 5.22, I'm about to make a copy of the DoubleClickSpeed Registry punch we dictated in a previous exercise.

FIGURE 5.22   You can right-click a preference item and select Copy (to paste it later).

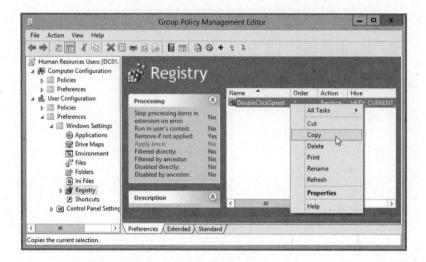

I can now do several things with this copy.

Right below the current entry, right-click and select Paste from the context menu. You'll see that a copy of the DoubleClickSpeed Registry punch is placed right next to it. We'll explore this idea in a little bit so hang tight.

Drag (or Paste) a Group Policy Preferences Extension to a File

Go to your Windows Desktop and click Paste. (Yes, leave the Group Policy Management Editor, find the Windows Desktop, right-click, and select Paste.) A new document is automatically created with an XML extension. Alternatively, you can drag the line item from the GPPrefs editor right to the Desktop or a folder to create a file out of the contents.

You can see my document's icon and the contents of the document in Figure 5.23.

You can see that the file contains the Registry settings as well as the filters built in one neat little package.

Sharing Your Wisdom with Others

At this point, you can e-mail this little gift of a file to a friend and they can drag and drop it into their own Registry Preference item list. In Figure 5.24, you can see what your other Administrator friend would do when she drags the corresponding file into the Registry Preference item list.

FIGURE 5.23   Each preference item is exportable as an XML file.

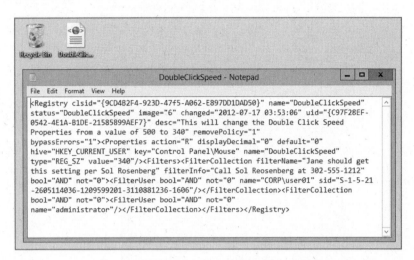

If you're going to share a GPPrefs XML file with other people outside your company, be careful to send only XML files that don't have any sensitive information contained within them, like SIDs, OUs, or encrypted password fields (if you haven't cleaned them out yet). Anything sensitive should be avoided.

Multiple Preference Items at a Level

So an exercise or two ago, we copied our `DoubleClickSpeed` Registry entry. You can see this in Figure 5.14. But why would you want to do such a thing?

To be crafty, that's why!

Let's examine how to take advantage of this neat ability.

Filtering Each Preference Item at a Level

If you copy a preference item (which essentially makes two identical items at the same level), you can put a filter on one preference item and another filter on the other preference item. Of course, you'd change each item to act slightly differently, so that one item hits one set of users and the other item hits another set of users.

For instance, you could say Administrators get a `DoubleClickSpeed` of 300, but Users get a `DoubleClickSpeed` of 480. Just create two preference items (each changed slightly, and each with a different filter).

Again, a silly example, but you get the idea.

But, here's the kicker. GPPrefs process multiple preference items at a level by "counting up sequentially." So, if you had three preference items with the same extension, number 1 would be written first, number 2 would be written next, and number 3 would be written last.

If there was a conflict between any levels, the highest number would win.

FIGURE 5.24   You can share preference items with friends. Have your friend just drag and drop the XML right into the category as a preference item.

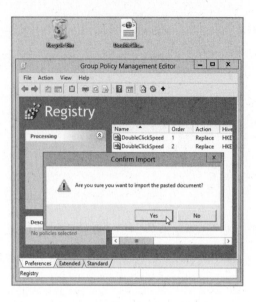

Changing the Order of Preference Items at a Level

You change the order of the levels by clicking on the preference item you want and then using the menu bar's Up and Down arrows to change the order. So, for instance, in Figure 5.25 you can see that there are two preference items in the Start Menu extension. If you wanted to change the order, click on one of them, and then select the menu bar's Up or Down arrow (seen in Figure 5.26). You can also see the full menu bar in Figure 5.26, which we'll refer to throughout the rest of this section.

FIGURE 5.25   You can have multiple, conflicting preference items inside a GPO.

FIGURE 5.26   The menu bar for Group Policy Preferences

This business of counting up sequentially within a GPPrefs extension is a little maddening to a Group Policy guy like me—especially because I usually have to explain how GPOs *themselves* are processed counting *down* sequentially. See the section "Raising or Lowering the Precedence of Multiple Group Policy Objects" in Chapter 2 for more information.

Renaming Preference Items at a Level

Since you copied DoubleClickSpeed, you now have what looks like two identical entries. But you don't. You have one filtered one way and another filtered another way. Why not right-click over each entry and rename it, being specific about what each entry now does, as shown in Figure 5.27?

This will come in handy a little later when you learn about preference items and reporting.

Temporarily Disabling a Single Preference Item or Extension Root

Recall that Group Policy has the ability to remove the Link Enabled status from a GPO. When this happens, the GPO configuration stays in place, but it removes the GPO from processing (and usually reverts the setting back to an original setting).

FIGURE 5.27   If preference items within a GPO might potentially conflict, it's easiest to just rename them.

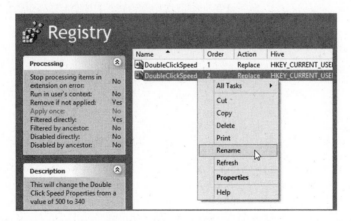

GPPrefs have a similar ability, and it can be done at the preference item level or the GPPrefs extension root level *within* a GPO.

To do this, you can click on a preference item (like DoubleClickSpeed) and click the red No icon on the menu bar.

Or, if you want to do this on a GPPrefs extension root level, click on the Extension root, say the Registry extension, and click the No icon on the menu bar.

In Figure 5.28, I've disabled one preference item within the Registry extension, but I've also disabled the whole Registry extension—right at the root as well, just for show.

When you select the No icon, that icon will automatically change from red to green.

When either happens, the configuration is maintained within the extension, but it's taken out of processing. And, if the "Remove this item when it is no longer applied" setting is checked, the preference item falls out of the scope of management, so that value is usually deleted. So, again, be careful in using that setting.

To restore the preference extension or extension root itself for processing again, click the green No icon, which will put it back in play.

Environment Variables

One of the other superpowers the GPPrefs have is this idea of built-in, addressable variables in addition to the standard Environment variables that Windows automatically sets, or ones that you set with logon scripts, or ones that you set using the Environment extension.

The idea is that GPPrefs bring these *additional* variables that allow you to specify the relative locations of many, many key items.

FIGURE 5.28 In this example, the Group Policy preference item and also the root node are disabled. It might be hard to see in black in white on the page.

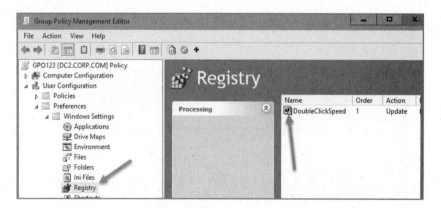

Here's a quick example (and there are about a zillion uses, so it was hard to just pick one). Imagine you had a file on a file share, named Everyone.txt, and you wanted to get it on everyone's machine. But you didn't just want to copy that file directly, no, no! You wanted to rename it in the process to the name of the computer and *also* put it on everyone's Desktop folder. How could you possibly do that? Would you have to create a new GPO for everyone in the company!

Heck no!

With Environment variables, you can do this in one step. In Figure 5.29, I've used the Files Preference extension to specify the source file as \\dc01\share\everyone.txt. But for Destination File, before typing anything in, I hit the F3 key. When you do, the internal Environment variables pop up as a reference and you can select them to be automatically entered for you. For this example, I'll use one internal Environment variable (%CommonDesktopDir%) and one regular Windows Environment variable (%ComputerName%).

So, in Figure 5.29, I've specified %CommonDesktopDir%\%ComputerName%.txt as the destination filename.

Note the curious Resolve Variable check box when you hit the F3 key, as seen in Figure 5.30. The check box is on, which means variables like %ComputerName% resolve to WIN10. That's great; this makes sense and meets our goal.

FIGURE 5.29   Hitting F3 when editing a preference item brings up the "Select a Variable" dialog box.

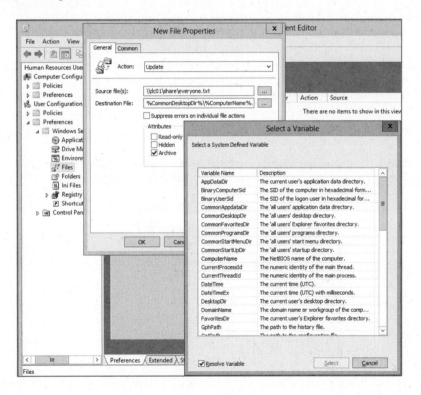

However, strangely, there's also the ability to jam in the words that make up the variables—as variables! So, imagine you had an .INI file you wanted to change, but inside the .INI file, you wanted to jam in an actual variable. For instance, in DogFoodMaker 7.0, you needed to set the ruffcomputer property (located within the [ruffconfig] section) to have the word %ComputerName% (with percent marks included). You would uncheck the

Resolve Variable check box, and what's put into the Property Value field is what's seen in Figure 5.30. That is, the variable name itself is contained within angle brackets (< and >) to signify that the variable %ComputerName% is jammed into the .INI file.

Managing Group Policy Preferences: Hiding Extensions from within the Editor

There might be some times when you'll want to give someone rights to create GPOs but prevent them from utilizing some of the GPPrefs. For instance, maybe you didn't want them to be able to manipulate .INI settings or Registry settings. Well, you can take away that power if you want.

WARNING   I wouldn't exactly call this a "security feature" because someone with enough know-how would be able to use another machine and jam in the underlying XML file into a GPO that they created and/or owned.

If you are logged onto a server, you can see the regular Group Policy settings located at User Configuration ➢ Policies ➢ Administrative Templates ➢ Windows Components ➢ Microsoft Management Console ➢ Restricted/Permitted snap-ins ➢ Group Policy ➢ Preferences can help you perform the restrictions. You can see these policy settings in Figure 5.31.

FIGURE 5.30   It's rare, but you may need to jam in the actual name of a variable, as seen here. Do this by putting angle brackets (< and >) around the variable name.

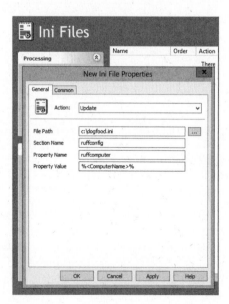

FIGURE 5.31   Use the settings seen here (and select Disabled) to prevent the snap-ins from appearing within the MMC.

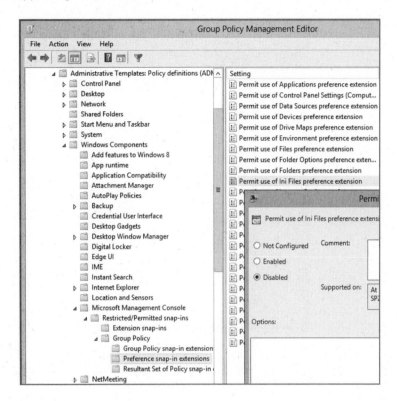

The trick is, the Explain text is awful in these settings. For the ones I've tested, you need to disable the policy setting (yes, disable) to prevent the extension from showing.

In Figure 5.31, you can see I've disabled the .INI Files preference extension via its policy setting. In Figure 5.32, you can see the result; the extension to manipulate the .INI files is just—gone (in both the Computer and User sides)!

> Now, this doesn't mean that GPOs that have any hidden extensions will stop working. It just means that some people (the people affected by these policy settings) cannot use the UI to manage that part of the world.

Troubleshooting: Reporting, Logging, and Tracing

Sometimes, things don't exactly act as they should. This is normal, because we're not perfect and the Group Policy Preferences make it easier than ever to do things we might not even really *want* to do.

FIGURE 5.32   When admins affected by these policy settings try to create GPOs, the snap-ins are simply hidden.

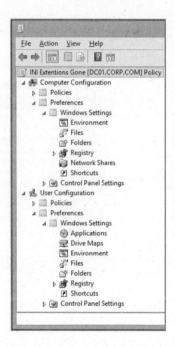

To that end, we may need to spend some time on troubleshooting the Group Policy Preferences. Here are some quick things to check before you start going crazy and working with detailed logs:

- Before you pull your hair out when you're trying to troubleshoot your clients, the very first question you should ask yourself is, "Do my clients have the Group Policy Preferences installed?" Remember, Windows XP, Windows Vista, and Windows Server 2008 machines need the Group Policy Preferences bits installed by you.

- Do you have the GPO linked to the correct place (site, domain, OU), and is the computer or user account in the right place?

- Do you have multiple preference items conflicting at the same level?

There are two places to get some dirt about what's going on: the good ol' Windows event log and also Group Policy Preferences' own Tracing Logs.

Reporting: Settings Tab, GPMC Reporting, and GPResult

We have two usual ways of getting Group Policy results data: the Group Policy Results reports and the GPResult command. Let's see how each one responds to the Group Policy Preferences.

Importing Group Policy Preferences

In Chapter 2, you learned how to use migration tables to migrate GPOs from one domain to another domain. However, it should be noted that migration tables do not support Group Policy Preferences. That is, as GPOs that contain preference items are imported, all settings are simply copied straight through, whether or not the value is valid in the target domain. AGPM (the pay tool from Microsoft we talk about in Appendix C) supports migrating between domains, but again, you have to pay extra for this tool. However, you might also check out a free tool from my pal and fellow Group Policy MVP Mark Heitbrink, at:

www.gruppenrichtlinien.de/artikel/reg2xml-registry-export-file-converter/

It can aid in this area. Don't be afraid of all the German on the page. The website may be in German, but the video demo and the tool itself is in English.

The Group Policy Results Reports from the GPMC

All GPMC HTML reports will work with GPPrefs. The same Group Policy Results and Group Policy Modeling reports you know and love should work just the same with all Group Policy Preferences clients.

There is a little difference here and there, with regard to how original Group Policy "class" reports are delivered. For instance, if more than one preference item is at a level, you can see that within the Settings report of the GPO.

In Figure 5.33, you can see two Start Menu settings that conflicted. Of course, one has to eventually win.

However, when a Group Policy Results report is run, it has to figure not only which GPO wins, but also which preference item within a level wins. In Figure 5.34, we can see a Group Policy Results report, and the results are a little hard to read.

In Figure 5.34, we can see that Test preference item had some "Start Menu (Windows Vista and later)" settings win on the target machine. That's great. But there's like a billion settings within the Start Menu category. Which ones won? Well, even though the preference items are numbered inside the GPPrefs interface (remember Figure 5.25 when we talked about the GPPrefs order?), they're not labeled in the same order within the Group Policy Results reports.

That's a bummer, because that's the kind of thing administrators want to know: which preference item (within the preference item order) won. But here's a tip. If we had used the rename function to rename a GPPrefs item, we can easily see which one won because the winning preference item bubbles up to the top by name.

Additionally, there seems to be no reporting of the ILTs. That's not exactly super helpful; I think I'd like to know why a specific preference item won over another one. So, again, if a specific ILT was found to be true, there doesn't seem to be any way to discover that from the Group Policy Results reports.

FIGURE 5.33 Group Policy Preferences settings are reflected within the report.

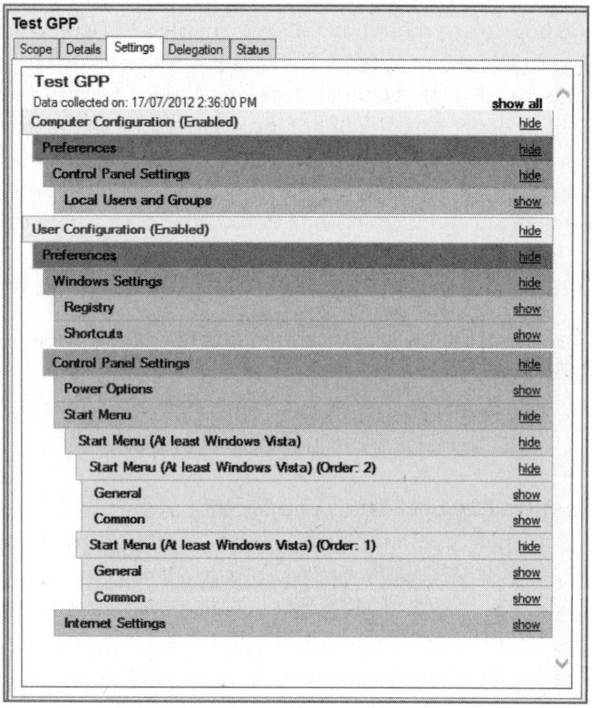

GPResult.exe

I love the GPResult.exe tool. In XP and Vista there was no way to see the Group Policy Preferences "results" inside GPResult. However, with Windows 7 and later, you can run GPResult /H report.html (or any name) and out will pop an HTML file that shows the full RSoP that's occurred—including the Group Policy Preferences items. Again, that's only the HTML report.

If you try to run GPResult /R to get standard (text) output, you'll see the GPOs themselves that affect the user or machine but not the Group Policy Preferences inside those GPOs. Again, to see that data, use GPResult /H report.html.

Event Logs

The Windows Application log contains the really bad news about events that the Group Policy Preferences create. In Figure 5.35, we can see that something went wrong on the target machine (WIN10) when we attempted to apply a Group Policy Preferences Local Users and Group item.

FIGURE 5.34   The winning preference item is the one that bubbles to the top.

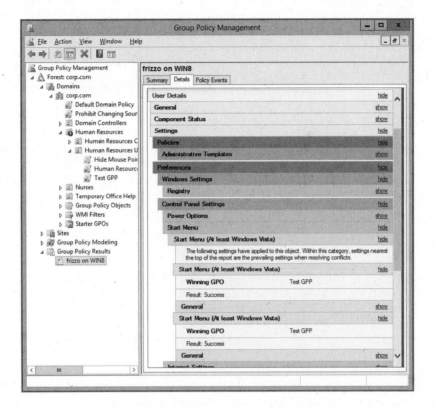

What's interesting is that each and every Group Policy Preference extension category has its own source, so you can create custom views of the Application log, only showing the source you want (this applies to only Windows 7 and later clients). In Figure 5.36, you can see that I'm creating a custom filter where you can select multiple sources (or just one) and show only the errors you want to expose in a single view.

Tracing

Group Policy Preferences have their own mega-detailed logs if you choose to turn them on. The logs are called *Tracing Logs*, and you turn them on them by enabling specific policy settings within Computer Configuration ➢ Policies ➢ Administrative Templates ➢ System ➢ Group Policy ➢ Logging and tracing. What? You've just gone to the Group Policy node on your WIN10MANAGEMENT machine, and you don't see the Logging and Tracing node? Don't panic!

As you learned in Chapter 3, the "missing" Group Policy settings are only built into the server side's "set" of policy definitions. But those missing pieces are downloadable if you don't want to rip them out of an existing Windows Server (or even Windows Server 2008 R2) machine. This blog entry spells it all out: http://tinyurl.com/kowj66. And the downloadable files are here: http://tinyurl.com/mb6x5v.

FIGURE 5.35   Group Policy Preferences' bad news can be found in the Application log.

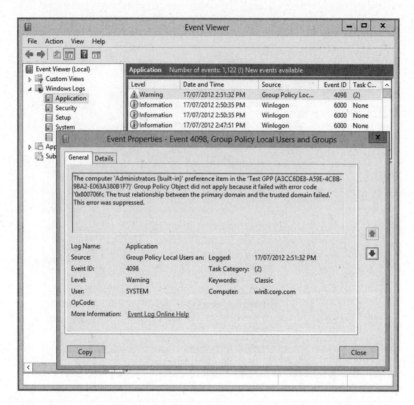

Once you've put the "missing" policy settings in place (see Chapter 6 for a how-to if needed to get all the ADMX and ADML files), you can see the list of policy settings that control Group Policy Preferences in Figure 5.37.

Each Group Policy Preferences log, er, trace, can be set individually. By default they all push information to a shared log for each category.

The Shared User Log   The idea is that if the Group Policy Preferences extension is on the User side, it will write step-by-step data as to what it's doing within this log.

The Shared Computer Log   The idea is that if the Group Policy Preference extension is on the Computer side, it will write step-by-step data as to what it's doing within this log.

The Shared Planning Log   In ye olden days, when the product was younger (and owned by DesktopStandard), there was no GPMC reports integration. If you wanted to troubleshoot and learn what the RSoP was on the client, you needed to run the outmoded RSOP.MSC snap-in on the client system experiencing the problem. Well, those vestiges are still there. You can turn on the Planning log and run RSOP.MSC and see a log generated. There's little reason to do this because you can get reports, as we saw earlier, from GPMC's Group Policy Results reports.

FIGURE 5.36   You can create your own event log filter to just show the Group Policy Preference extension that might be having a problem.

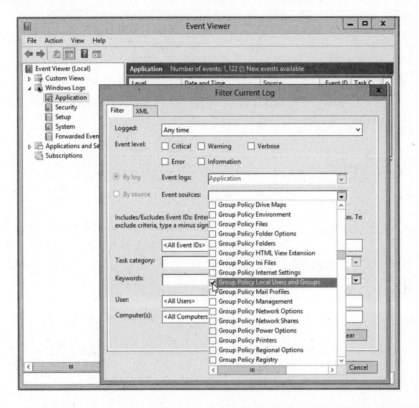

The extra trick is that, after you enable the policy setting and ensure that the log files are in a place you can find, you still need to set the logging level, and then finally (and here's the kicker) click the dropdown next to Tracing and select On. Yep, that's right. You enabled the policy setting, but that's not good enough. You also need to "double-enable" tracing.

FIGURE 5.37 Tracing produces a lot of output. That's why there are two switches to enable it. First, enable the policy setting, and then select On from the Tracing drop-down or Tracing Logs will not be produced.

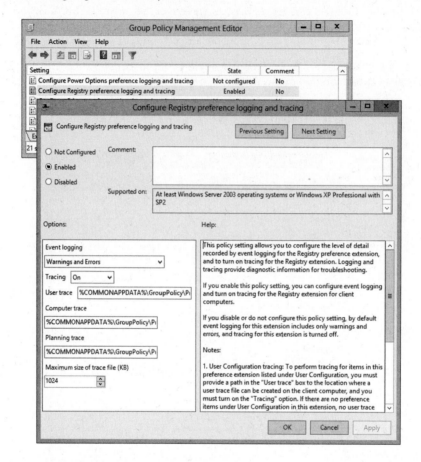

When you do, your log file will appear in:

```
C:\ProgramData\GroupPolicy\Preference\Trace
```

as seen in Figure 5.38.

Finally, you might be asking why some settings, like Internet Settings, have both a Computer and a User log when the extension is applicable only on the User side. In short, it shouldn't be there, and it won't do anything.

FIGURE 5.38   Tracing Logs can be a bit hairy, but useful.

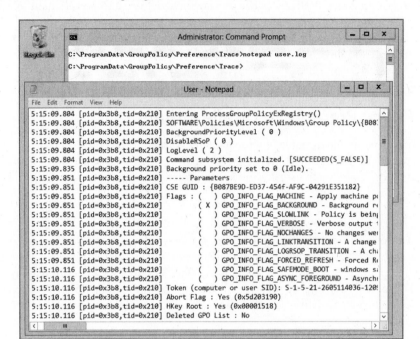

Giving Group Policy Preferences a "Boost" (Using PolicyPak Preferences Manager and PolicyPak Cloud)

As a Group Policy MVP, when Microsoft purchased the Group Policy Preferences and integrated it and released it, I did a dance for joy. I loved all the superpowers I was able to get, like drive maps, printers, shortcuts, and all the other stuff I talked about in this chapter.

That being said, when I started to dive into it, I realized there were four big problems that Group Policy Preferences had that Microsoft would never seemingly resolve.

Problem 1: Group Policy Preferences cannot be maintained when the user goes offline.

Problem 2: Group Policy Preferences has no way to be delivered, say, using SCCM or some other management tool.

Problem 3: Group Policy Preferences has no way to be delivered over the Internet.

Problem 4: Group Policy Preferences has no way to be delivered to non-domain-joined computers.

So being that I love the Group Policy Preferences, I decided to simply give them a "boost" where they needed, and solve all of these problems with my company using PolicyPak.

Using PolicyPak Preferences Manager to Maintain Group Policy Preferences while Offline

Let's re-examine the simple example of what happens when you use Group Policy Preferences to deliver, say, a shortcut or a Registry item to your users using Group Policy.

You create the Group Policy Object. You specify what you want your users to get. They get them.

Yay.

Now the user takes their laptop and goes home.

And then throws the shortcut in the trash (remember, Group Policy Preferences are *preferences* and not policy) or works around a Registry setting you put down.

Now that the computer is offline, what happens when Group Policy goes to reapply and there is no DC to field the request? Answer: Absolutely nothing. Group Policy Preferences has no way to cache and re-deliver Group Policy Preferences that your population has worked around.

PolicyPak Preferences Manager solves this problem. Instead of depending on a DC to be available to refresh Group Policy Preferences settings, PolicyPak caches Group Policy Preferences settings and simply reapplies the settings automatically, even when the computer is offline.

You can see a demo of PolicyPak Preferences Manager redelivering settings automatically when computers go offline here (see the video on left side of the page, and watch the first three minutes):

www.policypak.com/products/policypak-preferences.html

Using PolicyPak Preferences Manager to Deliver Group Policy Preferences Using "Not Group Policy"

Sometimes people want to take the power of the Group Policy Preferences and deploy them using "Not Group Policy." And by "Not Group Policy," I mean, say, using SCCM, KACE, Landesk, or some other existing management system.

Using our tool called the PolicyPak Exporter (included with PolicyPak Preferences Manager), you can take existing Group Policy Preferences items and wrap them up into an MSI file and deploy them using whatever system you like.

You can see a demo of taking existing Group Policy Preferences items, wrapping them into an MSI file, and getting them deployed using SCCM at:

www.policypak.com/products/policypak-preferences.html

See the video on left side of the page, and start at the four-minute mark.

Delivering Group Policy Preferences over the Internet Using PolicyPak Cloud (to Domain-Joined and Non–Domain-Joined Machines)

In Chapter 3 we learned two ways to get Group Policy settings over the Internet:

- Microsoft Unified Remote Access (aka DirectAccess)
- PolicyPak Cloud

Let's recap that section, plus put a fine point on it.

Both technologies will enable you to deliver all categories of Group Policy settings over the Internet.

Remember, though, Microsoft Unified Remote Access requires servers, infrastructure, setup, and care-and-feeding, plus it requires Enterprise versions of the Windows client, which must be domain joined.

PolicyPak Cloud, however, requires no servers, it can use any version of Windows client (Windows 7 and later), and your Windows clients may be domain joined or even non–domain joined.

Remember back in the section entitled "Drag (or Paste) a Group Policy Preferences Extension to a File" and in Figure 5.23, you could literally "snap off" an existing Group Policy Preferences items into a file? Well, that XML file is what you upload to PolicyPak Cloud.

Then your client machines download those over the Internet and perform the work!

You can see how to deploy Group Policy Preferences items over the Internet to both domain joined and non–domain joined machines using the video on the right at:

www.policypak.com/products/policypak-preferences.html

An example of PolicyPak Cloud deploying Group Policy Preferences items (and other settings) to an MSP customer, branch office, or roaming sales team can be seen in Figure 5.39.

FIGURE 5.39   Use PolicyPak Cloud to deploy Group Policy Preferences items (and more) over the Internet (to branch offices or roaming computers).

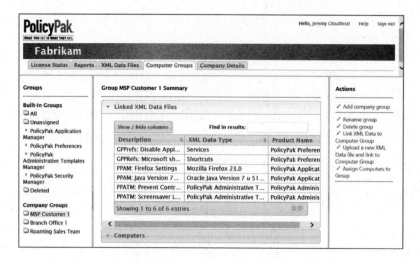

Final Thoughts

Let's do an ever-so-brief review of the top things we've learned about Group Policy Preferences:

- Management station installation: When you use the latest, greatest GPMC management station, you're all set. The GPMC on Windows 10 and Windows Server 2016 would be the most updated right now.

- Group Policy Preferences doesn't care what domain type or domain controllers you have.

- Client piece installation is only required for Windows XP, Vista, and Server 2003. The Group Policy Preferences CSE is built into Windows 7 and later.

- Group Policy Preferences deliver preferences, whereas Group Policy (original) delivers policy settings. This usually means that users can undo settings that you deliver via Group Policy Preferences (but not always).

- There is some overlap between Group Policy (original) and Group Policy Preferences. But really, as we analyzed, there is more harmony between the two than overlap.

- Be sure you understand how the red and green lines and circles work in the interface.

- Know your CRUD Action modes and what each does. When in doubt, use Update. (When *really* in doubt, try it in a test lab first.)

- The Common tab is available for each preference item you create. Inside this tab are some superpowers, like ILT.

- Be super careful using the Common tab element "Remove this item when it is no longer applied." Remember, it's the equivalent of Nuke.

- Use the Windows event logs and Group Policy Preferences tracing logs to help you determine whether or not your Group Policy Preferences wishes are being applied.

- If you want to keep Group Policy Preferences items working even when offline, Policy-Pak Preferences Manager will do that.

- If you want to deploy Group Policy Preferences items using SCCM or some other utility, you can also use PolicyPak Preferences Manager to do that.

- If you want to deploy Group Policy Preferences items over the Internet (or, really any/all Group Policy items), check out PolicyPak Cloud (www.PolicyPak.com).

Again, on www.GPanswers.com in the forums you'll find lots of questions and answers about the Group Policy Preferences.

6

Managing Applications and Settings Using Group Policy

Let's take a step back, go to the 20-yard line, and remember why we're getting jazzed up about Group Policy in the first place.

You're jazzed up because you're starting to realize the potential that Group Policy can bring: dictating settings for your operating system and making your world more "standardized."

As you poke around the Group Policy editor, you'll see there are lots of areas that we've already explored and some we haven't. You've had a chance to handle the Administrative Templates section within policies. You've examined the Group Policy Preferences. In the next chapter you'll learn about the items in the Security section. But let's take some time to focus on an important aspect of Group Policy: extending its use to wider areas of our desktop environment. Sure, Group Policy is neat because it can manage operating system settings—like how you prevented users from getting into the Control Panel, or how you launched calc.exe every time a user logged on.

But let's take it to the next level.

Let's start controlling our applications. True "control freaks" know that it's us, not the users, who should be in charge. And using the power of Group Policy, we can manage our desktop applications like our operating system: let users change only what we want, and also ensure that our corporate controls are in place and that users don't totally run the show.

To accomplish this, we need to understand the Administrative Templates section of the Group Policy editor. We need to know that those bazillions of Administrative Template settings come from somewhere—and we need to understand what they're made of and how they're built.

Even then, those built-in files might not be enough to perform true management under all circumstances. So in this chapter, I also plan on showing you how to use PolicyPak Application Manager to help you specifically manage your applications beyond what's capable "in the box" and take your control-freak tendencies to the next level. Again, it's not a commercial. It's information to help you understand your options, if you're ready to do more than what's already in the box.

Note also that in this chapter there's a lot of "old" Windows XP stuff I talk about. And as I stated in the introduction of this book, I know that Windows 10 is the "latest, greatest."

But I personally find that if I understand where things came from, I can grasp why things work the way they do. So, in many discussions here, you'll see me talk about the "old-school" way that Windows XP did something, then switch gears and show you why we don't do that anymore and that we have a newer way to approach a problem.

Understanding Administrative Templates

To understand how to better manage our world, we need to first understand a little history—where Administrative Templates came from and where they are now.

Additionally, we'll need to clear up some vocabulary around *policy* versus *preference*. Yes, you've just learned about the Group Policy Preferences in the last chapter. But the idea of "what is a preference" can be further refined, as you're about to learn.

Administrative Templates: Then and Now

Take a look at Figure 6.1. First, you'll see the older XP version of the Group Policy editor. Then, you'll see the updated Group Policy editor, found within RSAT. If we ignore the fact that there's a Preferences node, we'll see that the Administrative Templates structure is pretty similar.

FIGURE 6.1   On the left is the updated Group Policy editor. On the right is the older Group Policy editor. They both have Administrative Templates, which contain policy settings.

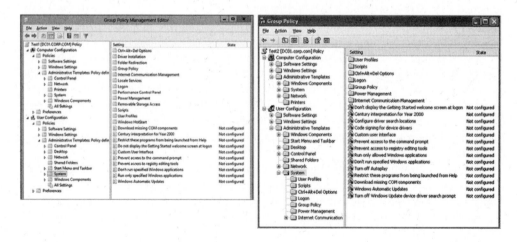

Sure, you'll see a few little differences. Some of the policy settings have different names or have been moved around a bit. But the point is simple: both consoles contain Administrative Templates and both consoles contain policy settings. What's different is where each of these policy settings' definitions come from.

In Windows XP and earlier, the Administrative Templates section is born from what's known as ADM files. In the updated GPMC, that same section comes from a combo of two file types called ADMX and ADML files.

These are the files from which policy settings are born.

The idea behind both older ADM and newer ADMX files is pretty simple:

- Define a setting (i.e., give it a name)
- Describe what Registry setting to control
- Describe how administrators interface with the setting inside the Group Policy editor

Then, once that's wrapped up, we, as administrators, interact with these ADM and/or ADMX files inside the Group Policy editor interfaces (as seen in Figure 6.1). We just click a button, and "flick!" we set the setting, and our Group Policy client machine pulls the setting. "Flick!" again, and that same Registry setting can be toggled off. Our Group Policy client machine pulls the setting again, and magic occurs in the reverse. At least—that's what you likely want to have happen.

In this next section, "Policy vs. Preference," we'll explore the first "flick": what happens when you dictate a Registry setting within a GPO. And, later on, we'll also answer the question about what takes place with the next "flick": what happens when that policy setting is to be removed.

Policy vs. Preference

Microsoft documentation states that four Registry areas are considered the approved places to create policies out of Registry punches:

- Computer settings, the preferred location:

  HKLM\Software\Policies

- Computer settings, an alternative location:

  HKLM\Software\Microsoft\Windows\CurrentVersion\Policies

- User settings, the preferred location:

  HKCU\Software\Policies

- User settings, an alternative location:

  HKCU\Software\Microsoft\Windows\CurrentVersion\Policies

These locations are approved because they have security permissions that do not allow a regular user to modify these keys. Again, the preferred locations are noted here, if any software developers are reading this book (and you know who you are).

When a policy setting is set to Enabled and the client embraces the Group Policy directives, a Registry entry is set in one of these keys. When the GPO that applied the keys is removed, the Registry values associated with it are also removed. However, it should be noted that the application (or operating system component) needs to look for changes to these keys in order for it to take effect. That is, the Group Policy engine doesn't "notify" the application—the application has to do its own checking. So, with this in mind, if an older operating system receives a policy setting for a newer operating system, nothing "bad" happens. It just gets ignored.

WARNING   It should be noted that local administrators have security permissions to these keys and could maliciously modify delivered GPO settings because of rights within this portion of the Registry.

So "normal" Group Policy won't tattoo because it's being directed to go in a nonsticking place in the Registry. Turns out, every single "in the box" policy setting that Microsoft ships within its Administrative Templates section are all "normal" policy settings.

Flick! Hide the Control Panel.

Flick again! Bring it back.

Couldn't be simpler; and, again, it's because the operating system (Explorer.exe in this example) knows to look for proper Policies keys. And when they're not set any longer, poof! The directive is thrown away, and the setting reverts.

Let's take a different example, though.

Let's say you wanted to control a pet application, DogFoodMaker 6.1, that you have deployed in-house. Great—you've decided you want more control. Now, you need to determine which Registry values and data DogFoodMaker 6.1 understands. That could take some time; you might be able to ask the manufacturer for the valid Registry values, or you might have some manual labor in front of you to determine what can be controlled via the Registry. Consider using a tool like Process Monitor:

http://technet.microsoft.com/en-us/sysinternals/bb896645.aspx

or RegShot:

http://sourceforge.net/projects/regshot

You'll then be able to begin to create your own templates (though, by the time you're done with this chapter, I suspect you won't want to anymore).

Anyway, after you've determined how DogFoodMaker 6.1 can be controlled via the Registry, you'll find you have two categories of Registry tweaks:

- Values that fit neatly into the new Policies keys listed earlier

- Values that are anywhere else

You'll have some good news and some bad news.

Good news would be that the application can accept control via the Registry. If this happens, you can still create template files and control the application.

Bad news could take two forms. Bad news could be that the application doesn't store its items in the Registry. If your application is managed using files (like Firefox, Flash, Java, OpenOffice, etc.), then stop right here: ADMX files are not going to help you (but PolicyPak Application Manager can, as we'll see later).

Or, another shot of bad news could be that your application doesn't store its settings in the Policies keys of the Registry. In that case, you will not have proper policies. Rather, they become preferences.

Wait, wait, wait a second. Preferences? "Didn't I just read all about preferences in the last chapter?" Kind of. You read about Group Policy Preferences, or GPPrefs. GPPrefs is a collection of additional stuff you can do—21 functions you couldn't do in the original Group Policy set.

But the word *preference* has a second meaning (oh great). Let's examine the word *preference* itself here for a second. Again, we're talking just about the word *preference*, and not Group Policy Preferences or GPPrefs.

A preference (conceptually) is as follows:

- A Registry setting that is not within the proper Policies keys (listed earlier).

- A setting that, once set, a user can work around. This is because there is no user interface "lockout" from Preferences (as explored in the previous chapter). This is why Group Policy Preferences are called Group Policy Preferences and not Group Policy MorePolicy or something. Remember, as you learned in the last chapter, by and large, Group Policy Preferences can be worked around, even by regular users under most circumstances.

- A setting that, once set, stays set (or tattoos)—even when the setting should no longer apply. This is a weird one, because we're used to the "nice" behavior of Administrative Templates' policy settings. The fact that some settings from the templates that we create or download will stick around makes this idea of preferences kind of messy.

To reiterate, to be truly "policy-enabled," a target application must be programmed to look for values in the Policies keys. Some applications, such as Microsoft Word, are coded to look at Policies keys. Here's an older version of Word that uses this key specifically:

```
HKEY_CURRENT_USER\Software\Policies\Microsoft\Office\9.0\Word\
```

Other applications, such as WordPad, do not "understand" the Policies keys. WordPad stores its settings here:

```
HKEY_CURRENT_USER\Software\Microsoft\Windows\CurrentVersion\Applets\Wordpad
```

Hence, WordPad wouldn't be a candidate to hand-create a template file for the purpose of coding for true policy settings. You could, however, still create your own preferences for WordPad that modify and tattoo the Registry. Therefore, you will have to do the legwork to figure out if your applications are compatible with Policies keys.

Most aren't. Most applications are not still on board the "True Policy" train. Most applications do not ship with any way to control them properly using Group Policy. And, again, even if you hand-created your own ADM or ADMX files, you still do not have the full control that you would likely desire. Again, remember, since most applications don't know to look in the Policies keys, they just store their information "wherever." There's no way to magically create an ADM or ADMX file and somehow make the application behave as if it's under control of true policy. In other words, there's no "in the box" way to policy-enable your apps with true lockdown—because they're not being controlled by true policy.

Because preferences and policies act so differently, you will need to quickly identify them within the Group Policy Object Editor interface. You will want to note whether you're pushing an actual new-style policy to them or a persistent old-style policy.

Take a peek back at Figure 6.1. Look at the "rows" of policy settings. When viewed with the updated GPMC, true policies are designated by little "paper" icons (the screenshot on the left). When viewed on Windows XP (the screenshot on the right), true policies were designated by little blue dots. (I know it's hard to tell they're blue because the book is printed in black and white. But trust me, they're blue.) Again, what you're looking at is "proper" or "true" policy settings because they modify the actual Policies Registry keys listed earlier.

Policies that represent Registry punches in places other than the preferred Microsoft policies are designated another way. Take a look at Figure 6.2. In the updated GPMC editor (top screen shot), they're represented by paper icons with a down arrow. In the older XP GPMC, they're designated by red dots. Again, trust me—it's red.

Don't panic; I'll show you a little later how I added these "extra" templates to my Group Policy editor. Well, honestly, I'm only going to show you how I did it for the updated GPMC. If you really need to still do it for Windows XP, refer to previous editions of this book.

Since the distinction of policies and preferences is an important one for the rest of this chapter, let's recap:

- Policies are temporary Registry changes that are downloaded at log on and startup (and periodically in the background). They don't tattoo the Registry (though they are maintained and stay persistent should the user log on while offline). These are set to modify the Registry in specific Microsoft-blessed Policies keys. Applications need to be coded to recognize the presence of the keys in order to take advantage of the magic of policies. In the updated GPMC's editor, true policies look like little paper icons.

- Preferences are persistent Registry changes delivered using the Group Policy infrastructure. Preferences typically tattoo the Registry until they're specifically changed or removed. In the updated GPMC editor interface, they look like paper icons with a little down arrow. Unlike with policies, if you remove the GPO you "tattoo" or "orphan" the settings on the target computer (no fun at all).

- A preference is just a fancy way of saying "a Registry punch that can live anywhere."

FIGURE 6.2   The updated GPMC shows preferences as seen in the top screen shot. The older GPMC (XP) shows preferences as seen in the bottom screen shot (with red dots).

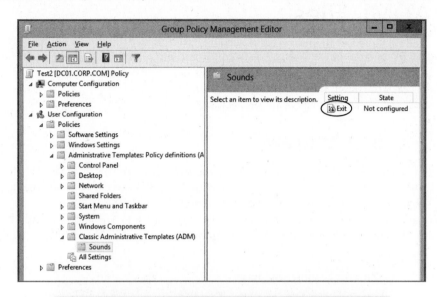

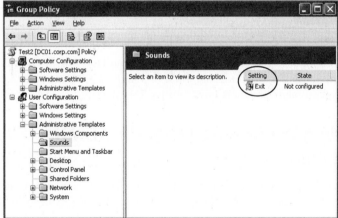

Exploring ADM vs. ADMX and ADML Files

So, the older (XP version) of the Group Policy editor and the newer (RSAT) version of the Group Policy editor present Administrative Templates in a similar fashion. Great.

But underneath the hood, honestly, it's radically different.

That's what we're going to explore in this section.

Looking Back at ADM Files

If you used an older (XP) GPMC to create GPOs, you were using the older ADM (Administrative Templates) files stored on that machine. Those ADM files provide the definitions of "what's possible" in the Administrative Templates section.

Those default templates are stored in the %systemroot%\inf folder, which is usually C:\ windows\inf. The following templates are installed by default on Windows XP machines:

- Conf.adm—NetMeeting settings
- Inetres.adm—Internet Explorer options
- System.adm—Most items in Administrative Templates
- Wmplayer.adm—Windows Media Player settings
- Wuau.adm—WSUS settings

These five ADM templates create both the Computer and User portion within Administrative Templates of a default Group Policy. Windows XP had about 2,400 total settings you could manipulate within Administrative Templates.

Understanding the Updated GPMC's ADMX and ADML Files

As we saw with the older XP GPMC, a mere handful of ADM files made up the bulk of our Administrative Template settings. When you use the updated GPMC, you no longer use built-in ADM files.

Instead, you use built-in ADMX and ADML files. And what was once a handful of files is now an entire growler full.

 NOTE   What's a growler? See http://en.wikipedia.org/wiki/ Beer_bottle#Growler.

The updated GPMC's ADMX files are stored in the %systemroot%\PolicyDefinitions folder, which is usually C:\windows\PolicyDefinitions.

There are now about 176 ADMX files, which roughly cover the same settings found in Windows XP and all the new stuff in Windows Vista and later, including Windows 10. They're generally component specific. For instance, you'll find things like `WindowsMediaPlayer.admx` and `EventLog.admx`, among others.

Here's something neat about ADMX files—they're language neutral. That is, the definitions for the Registry values that are controlled live inside the ADMX file. However, the text strings describing the policy and the Explain text are contained in a separate file called an ADML file—each ADMX file has a corresponding ADML file. These ADML files are located in specific subdirectories for each language within the `C:\windows\PolicyDefinitions` folder. For instance, U.S. English is contained within the en-US directory, which can be seen in Figure 6.3.

FIGURE 6.3   A quick list of some ADMX files. Note the language-specific directory here for English (en-US).

```
Administrator: Command Prompt

C:\Windows\PolicyDefinitions>dir /og
 Volume in drive C has no label.
 Volume Serial Number is F08D-9A74

 Directory of C:\Windows\PolicyDefinitions

05/26/2015  06:10 PM    <DIR>          .
05/26/2015  06:10 PM    <DIR>          ..
05/26/2015  06:10 PM    <DIR>          en-US
05/06/2015  11:36 AM             4,714 AddRemovePrograms.admx
05/06/2015  11:36 AM             1,157 AllowBuildPreview.admx
05/06/2015  11:36 AM             5,203 AppCompat.admx
05/06/2015  11:36 AM             4,152 AppxPackageManager.admx
05/06/2015  11:36 AM             3,975 AppXRuntime.admx
05/06/2015  11:36 AM             5,965 AttachmentManager.admx
05/06/2015  11:36 AM             1,337 AuditSettings.admx
05/06/2015  11:36 AM             3,391 AutoPlay.admx
05/06/2015  11:36 AM             2,968 Biometrics.admx
05/06/2015  11:36 AM            56,679 Bits.admx
05/06/2015  11:36 AM             1,749 CEIPEnable.admx
05/06/2015  11:36 AM             1,837 CipherSuiteOrder.admx
05/06/2015  11:36 AM             1,329 COM.admx
05/06/2015  11:36 AM            13,967 Conf.admx
05/06/2015  11:36 AM             2,600 ControlPanel.admx
05/06/2015  11:36 AM            14,442 ControlPanelDisplay.admx
05/06/2015  11:36 AM             1,293 Cpls.admx
05/06/2015  11:36 AM             4,717 ActiveXInstallService.admx
05/06/2015  11:36 AM            11,354 CredSsp.admx
05/06/2015  11:36 AM             2,254 CredUI.admx
```

The term en-US stands for U.S. English. For other locales, visit `http://tinyurl.com/223ebg`. For instance, HE is for Hebrew, RU is for Russian, DE is for German, and AR is for Arabic.

So, let me spell it out a different way:

- ADMX files store the same stuff as ADM files—except now (whoopee...) they're XML based.

- ADML files are corresponding language files for ADMX files.

You may be wondering, "What special superpowers do I get now that we use ADMX and ADML files?" Well, I dare say that you get "no new superpowers." Just because you're using ADMX/ADML files, you don't somehow magically get to "Group Policy enable" applications and their settings or have more Registry control.

But there has to be some benefit, right? Or else Microsoft wouldn't have done it, right? Yep. They're not superpowers, though. They're fixes to some thorny problems.

Let's compare ADM and ADMX files and then explore the four problems that the construct of ADM files caused and see how the newer construct of ADM and ADMX files fixes each of those problems.

Comparing ADM vs. ADMX Files

Our goal for the rest of this chapter is to give you an in-depth look at both ADM and ADMX files and for you to understand the differences between them. However, before we get going, here's a reference table so you can see where we're going; you can also utilize this table as an ongoing reference.

ADM Files	ADMX Files
Lots and lots of definitions are packed into several large-ish files. The biggest one is SYSTEM.adm.	Definitions are split logically into much smaller ADMX files, generally by Windows feature area.
Each ADM file contains settings in one specific language.	ADMX files are language neutral. Language-specific information is contained within a corresponding ADML file. Language-specific files live in hard-coded directories. For example, U.S. English language files live in %systemroot%\PolicyDefinitions\en-US.
Live on each Windows XP machine in %systemroot%\inf.	Live on each Windows Vista and later machine (including Windows Server 2008 and later) in %systemroot%\PolicyDefinitions.

ADM Files	ADMX Files
Every time a GPO is "born," it costs about 3MB on each Domain Controller because the ADM files are placed inside the GPO.	GPOs created from ADMX files never have big space requirements. That's because the ADMX files are never pushed into the GPO themselves (whether or not the Central Store is used). We'll discuss the Central Store a bit later.
Use their own proprietary ADM syntax for describing Registry policy.	Use standard XML as the syntax for describing Registry policy.

ADMX and ADML Files: What They Do and the Problems They Solve

If ADM files were so wonderful, why did Microsoft have to (basically) dump this "tried and true" way for a newer construct of ADMX and ADML?

At first glance, it seems that ADMX and ADML files are more complex than ADMs. That's true, at least because now inside each file is gobbledygook XML code, and arguably, ADM files are easier to read (when being read by humans). Then, there's the complexity of having two (or more!) files, whereas before, one ADM file seemed to be perfectly sufficient.

Problem is—it just wasn't. Let's examine the four problems that ADMs had and how ADMX and ADML files solve those problems.

Problem and Solution 1: Tackling SYSVOL Bloat

The older Group Policy editor pulls the ADM template files from the computer it is running on. And it copies these ADM template files from %systemroot% \inf—usually C:\windows \inf—directly into each GPO you edit. Each time you do this, you're burning about 3MB of disk space—on every Domain Controller. This is because all material inside the GPO is replicated to every Domain Controller.

Imagine you've created 100 GPOs using the older GPMC. In that case, you're using about 300MB to 500MB of disk space on every Domain Controller to store these ADM files! Ow! This problem is called SYSVOL bloat.

In Figure 6.4, you can see a sample SYSVOL with several GPOs. Recall that GPOs live on every Domain Controller in the sysvol\corp.com\Policies directory underneath their GUID. If you're using the older GPMC, each GPO will have an ADM directory containing the same ADM templates, at about 3MB for each directory.

FIGURE 6.4 Every GPO created with an XP management station pushes about 3MB into SYSVOL.

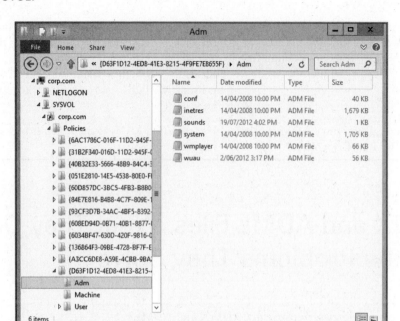

So, what does the updated GPMC do differently? Well, instead of copying stuff up from the local machine into the GPO, it just does "nothing." That's right—nothing. Figure 6.5 shows the difference between the older GPMC and the newer GPMC.

Don't believe it? Let's look at what's generated inside SYSVOL. In Figure 6.6, you can see that the top window was created using a modern GPMC, like what's available for Windows 10 (or really Windows Vista and later). You know this because there's no ADM directory.

So, did we solve problem 1, SYSVOL bloat? You bet. Because there's no ADM directory (and no ADM files inside it) there's no wasted space (SYSVOL bloat) from ADM files.

Problem 2: How Do We Deal with Multiple Languages?

Let's imagine that you're a part of a big company (heck, maybe you are). And in this company you have multiple administrators speaking multiple languages. And these administrators need to modify GPOs. Worse, they sometimes have to modify each other's GPOs.

If you're using the older GPMC (which uses ADM files), this is a real problem. When Vlad in the Russian corporate office edits the GPOs, he wants to see those policy settings and help texts in Russian. When Björn in the Sweden corporate office edits GPOs, he wants to see those policy settings and help texts in Swedish.

FIGURE 6.5 What's copied into the GPO when using the older and the newer GPMC

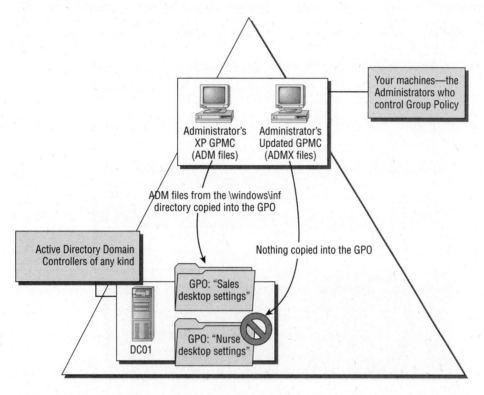

The problem is, if Vlad creates and edits the GPO first using the older GPMC, Vlad's Russian ADM templates (which start out on Vlad's XP machine) go into the GPO. This is no big deal, until Björn wants to edit that same GPO. If Björn's ADM templates on his machine are older or have the same release date, then when Björn goes to edit the GPO that Vlad created, Björn will see the GPO's policy settings and help text in Russian, not Swedish.

So is problem 2, multiple languages solved? Yes, because when admins use the updated GPMC, each admin simply uses his own machine to grab the definitions and it uses his own language.

But, let's read on to problem 3, which is interrelated.

Problem 3: How Do We Deal with "Write Overlaps"?

Let's extend problem 2 a little bit. Let's assume that in the previous example, Vlad's machine was an XP/SP2 machine. Let's also assume that in the previous example, Björn's machine was also an XP/SP2 machine.

FIGURE 6.6 The top window shows a GPO's contents when it's created using an updated GPMC management station. The middle window shows a GPO's contents when it's created using an older GPMC management station. The bottom window shows the contents of the ADM directory for the GPO created using the older GPMC management station.

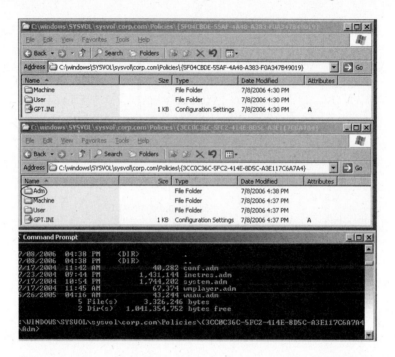

Now, Björn is able to update his machine to XP/SP3, while Vlad still uses XP/SP2 (which is unsupported, I might add). Now when Björn goes to edit the GPO, Björn's ADM templates are newer. And because they're newer, they overwrite the ADM files already inside the GPO.

This is great news for Björn. Now when he edits the GPO, everything inside is Swedish! But this is bad news for Vlad, because now the GPOs he originally created, which had Russian policy settings and help text, will display in Swedish if Björn ever edits them.

Turns out the solution to solving problems 2 and 3 is exactly the same as solving problem 1. To solve the multiple languages problem (that's problem 2) and the "write overlaps" problem (problem 3), the updated GPMC once again simply "does nothing."

Since the modern GPMC doesn't use ADM files, it won't copy any definitions into the GPO at all. Not ADM, not ADMX/ADML. Nothing.

So why does this "do nothing" approach solve the problem? Because now when Vlad edits the GPO, Vlad uses his own local machine (say, a Windows 10 machine) for the Russian definitions. When Björn edits the same GPO, Björn uses his own local Windows 7 Swedish definitions. (Yep, Björn has maintained using his Windows 7 machine, but Vlad has moved on to Windows 10 to get the latest, greatest features.)

Since both Björn and Vlad are using modern GPMCs, magic just happens automatically, and they don't have to do anything special.

This "do-nothing" approach works, because there's never anything written into the GPO regarding definitions. Only the data, the "directives," are inside the GPO. And therefore each administrator simply uses his local %systemroot%\PolicyDefinitions folder to utilize his own ADMX and ADML definitions.

This "do nothing" approach with the updated GPMC seems like a great solution. It's now officially solved three of our four problems. Can we go four for four?

Problem 4: How Do We Distribute Updated Definitions to All Our Administrators?

Let's assume we have some software and the manufacturer created, and then occasionally updates, some policy definition files.

That's great. We get updates from the vendor; now assume we have 20 administrators at our company. Or even two—just Vlad and Björn.

How are we going to get those updated ADM files delivered to those administrators and make sure they're installed correctly? Are we going to e-mail these updates to each of them? Are we going to script these updates and hope the script correctly identifies our administrators and the machines they work upon?

In short, how the heck are we going to get our updated definitions to every administrator in a hurry?

Well, turns out that the updated GPMC has a trick up its sleeve, and it's called the "Central Store." We'll explore the Central Store in an upcoming section, but the idea is simple: rather than trying to get every administrator's machine up to date with ADMs, we'll use ADMX and ADML files, and just plunk them in a centralized place—a "Central Store" if you will.

Stay tuned—I'll show you exactly how that works in the next section.

The Central Store

As we discussed, in the ideal world you'd use only the updated GPMC for your management stations. Sure, that means you'd have to spin up one Windows 10 machine (and download and install the updated GPMC within RSAT or use a Windows Server 2016 machine).

That's easily done in the real world, so we'll assume from here on that you'll be using only updated GPMC as your management station, eschewing older XP/2003 GPMC management stations.

As you're reading this right now, Microsoft has just shipped Windows 10 "out of the box" (also known as RTM, or Released to Manufacturing). But let's fast-forward a bit and assume, oh, that we're up to Windows 10/SP3. Yep, Windows 10 Service Pack 3 has just been released (in my fantasy land) and you need to control the new whiz-bang features that only come with Windows 10/SP3 client computers. (Again, I'm dreaming a little into the future here; new whiz-bang features might or might not come in service packs, but stay with me through this example anyway.)

"No problem!" you say, "I'll just create a Windows 10/SP3 machine and put on the updated GPMC as my management station. That will always have the latest, greatest definitions in the local `PolicyDefinitions` folder." And you'd be right! Except that you already have an updated GPMC machine as your management station. So, you wouldn't want to spin up a whole new machine just for this. You'd want to leverage the updated GPMC management station you already have, right?

Sure!

This is easy! You're a diligent administrator (you bought this book, subscribe to the `www.GPanswers.com` mailing list, and practice good Group Policy hygiene, after all), and you know you have three ways to update your current updated GPMC management station:

- If your updated GPMC management station is Windows 10, you would just apply Windows 10's SP3. That would update the ADMX files that live in `C:\windows\PolicyDefinitions`.

- Or, you could forgo applying SP3 to your Windows 10 management station and simply copy the ADMX (and associated ADML) files from another Windows 10/SP3 machine to your management station. Again, you'll plunk them in the `C:\windows\PolicyDefinitions` directory.

- Or, if your updated GPMC management station is Windows Server 2016, you could also just simply copy the ADMX (and associated ADML) files from another Windows 10 / SP3 machine to your Windows Server 2016's management station. Again, you'll plunk them in the `C:\windows\PolicyDefinitions` directory.

So, the message again sounds simple: whenever Microsoft has new ADMX/ADML files, get them into your updated GPMC management station.

Simple, yes—until you remember that you have 20 administrators in your company, each with their own Windows 10 management station. Or you remember those administrators who love to bounce from machine to machine because they have three sites to manage. Yikes! How are you going to guarantee that all of these administrators will use the updated ADMX files?

Let's assume you've successfully upgraded your Windows 10 management station to SP3, but only some of your 20 administrators successfully upgrade to Windows 10/SP3 (or have created custom ADMX files, or jam the ADMX files into their own local `C:\windows\PolicyDefinitions`).

This becomes a big problem—fast. Here's why: if you create a new GPO, that GPO will have the definitions for all the whiz-bang stuff Windows 10/SP3 has to offer. However, when another administrator (who doesn't have the latest ADMX files) tries to edit or report on that GPO, they simply won't see the policy settings for Windows 10/SP3 available.

GPMC reports about this newly created GPO would show the new whiz-bang features as "Extra Registry Settings," but actually trying to edit the GPO itself will not show them.

What you need is a way to ensure that all administrators who are using updated GPMC management stations have a one-stop-shop way to ensure that they're getting the latest ADMX files. That way, everyone will be on the same page, and there will be no challenges when one administrator creates a GPO and another tries to edit it.

The Windows ADMX/ADML Central Store

As described earlier, the updated GPMC has a trick up its sleeve.

That is, administrators using the updated GPMC can use a Central Store for ADMX and ADML files. Recall that the ADMX files are the definitions themselves and the ADML files are the language-specific files for each ADMX file.

The idea is that the Central Store lives on every Domain Controller. So, after the Central Store is created, your updated GPMC management station simply looks for it—every time it tries to create or edit a GPO—and it will automatically use the definitions contained within the ADMX files inside the Central Store.

This means you don't have to worry about running around to each of your 20 management stations to update them whenever new ADMX files come out. You simply plop them in the Central Store and you're done. You don't even have to tell the updated GPMC management stations you did anything; they'll just automatically look and use the latest definitions!

Here's the best part: It doesn't matter what kind of Domain Controllers you have. Doesn't matter if you have Windows Server 2008, 2012, 2016, or a mix of all of them. It's the updated GPMC that is doing the work to look for the Central Store in the prescribed location (which lives on Domain Controllers).

Wait, I'm going to stop here and take a big deep breath and say it one more time. Because I know you're reading fast and want to get to the good stuff. So, say it out loud if you have to.

It doesn't matter what kind of Domain Controllers you have. You can still make and use the Central Store.

It doesn't matter what domain mode you're in. It's the updated GPMC that is doing the work to look for the Central Store in the prescribed place on the Domain Controller.

Got it? You don't have to "sell" your boss on upgrading the whole Domain Controller back end just to get this cool Central Store stuff. With one updated GPMC management station, you've basically got the magic you need.

So, let's read on and make it happen.

Creating the Central Store

A Domain Administrator must create the Central Store because only a Domain Administrator has the ability to write to the location we need in SYSVOL. You can do this operation on any

Domain Controller, because all Domain Controllers will automatically replicate the changes we do here to all other Domain Controllers via normal Active Directory/SYSVOL replication. However, it's likely best to perform this on the PDC emulator because that's the location the GPMC and Group Policy Object Editor use by default.

To create the Central Store:

1. On the PDC emulator, use Explorer or the command line to create a directory in:

```
%systemroot%\windows\sysvol\sysvol\<domain name>\policies
```

(That's the usual location; yours could be different.) You want to create a directory called PolicyDefinitions, as seen in Figure 6.7.

FIGURE 6.7 Create a new directory called PolicyDefinitions in the Policies folder of SYSVOL.

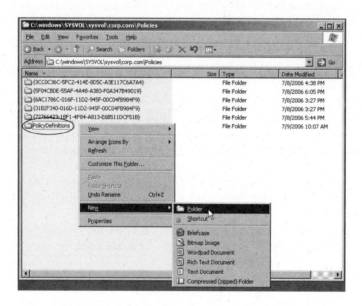

2. We need a location to store our language-specific ADML files. Within PolicyDefinitions you'll create a directory for each locale. Again, U.S. English is en-US. For other locales, visit:

http://msdn.microsoft.com/en-us/goglobal/bb896001.aspx

WARNING Note that the directory name must be the same as specified in the locale reference page. If it's not, the ADMX file will not find its corresponding ADML file for that language.

Populating the Central Store

Now, you simply have to get the latest, greatest ADMX and ADML files from your updated GPMC machine into the Central Store.

There are a zillion possible ways to copy the files there. But the steps are most easily done with two xcopy commands. This will work if your Windows 10 management station has access to the Domain Controller and if you have write rights.

To copy the ADMX files into the Central Store from your Windows 10 management station:

```
xcopy %systemroot%\PolicyDefinitions\*
   %logonserver%\sysvol\%userdnsdomain%\
                policies\PolicyDefinitions\
```

To copy in the ADML files into, say, the U.S. English directory we created earlier:

```
xcopy %systemroot%\PolicyDefinitions\EN-US\*
   %logonserver%\sysvol\%userdnsdomain%\
                policies\PolicyDefinitions\EN-US\
```

You can also use good ol' drag and drop. Here's a YouTube video I created to help you out: http://youtu.be/Q4DBdQo4XZs. I also have another video showing how to upgrade your central store after you download the latest files: http://youtu.be/acYb2wQeL94.

Verifying That You're Using the Central Store

Once you've created the Central Store directories in SYSVOL and copied the ADMX and ADML files to their proper location, you're ready to try it out. Start by closing the updated GPMC if it's already open, then reopen it. You can fire up the GPMC by clicking Start and in the Run box typing **gpmc.msc**.

And then just create and edit a GPO.

However, can you be sure you're really using the Central Store?

The updated GPMC's Group Policy Management Editor will tell you if you're using local policy definitions or using the Central Store. In Figure 6.8, you can see a GPO where the Administrative Templates are retrieved from the local machine. However, as soon as the Central Store is available, that same notice changes to what's seen in Figure 6.9.

There is a secondary test as well to help you verify that you're using the Central Store. That is, when you create and edit a GPO, then click the Settings tab in the GPMC, you'll see a line under either Computer Configuration or User Configuration that says "Policy definitions (ADMX files) retrieved from the central store." You can see this in Figure 6.10.

Updating the Central Store

ADMX and ADML files will be updated at some point.

Likewise, when Windows 10's SP2, SP3, and so on come out, those will be newer still, and so on.

FIGURE 6.8   Policy definitions are originally pulled from the local machine.

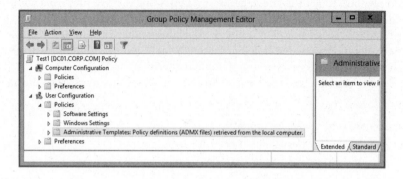

FIGURE 6.9   Policy definitions can be pulled from the Central Store.

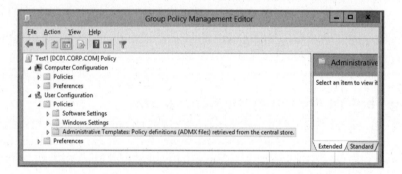

FIGURE 6.10   Anytime you click the Settings tab, the impromptu report will demonstrate if you are using the Central Store for your ADMX files.

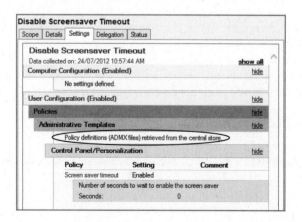

When this happens, you'll need to update the Central Store, which couldn't be easier. Simply copy the latest and greatest ADMX files to the `PolicyDefinitions` directory you created in SYSVOL, and copy the latest and greatest ADML files to the language-specific directory within `PolicyDefinitions`.

Then you're done.

Additionally, other products, like Microsoft Office, have ADMX and ADML files. If you wish to make those available to all administrators, just do the same thing. Drop them into the Central Store and you're done. (More about Office ADMX files a bit later.)

Note that at no time can you put ADM files inside the Central Store. Only ADMX and ADML files (in the Central Store) are valid.

Creating and Editing GPOs in a Mixed Environment

I know I've suggested about 8 million times now that you use the "updated" GPMC. That's the right thing to do when using the power of Group Policy.

The problem is, for many of you, you're ready to upgrade your own management machine to, say, Windows 10 but your friend Billy in the branch office is still using a Windows XP/SP2 machine from 2004.

Ow.

So, here's where things get complicated. That is, you could have the four following situations:

Scenario 1   Start out by creating and editing a GPO on an older GPMC management station (like Windows XP). Continue to edit using another older GPMC management station. In this scenario, no modern Windows is involved.

Scenario 2   Start out by creating and editing a GPO on an older GPMC management station. Edit using a modern management machine station.

Scenario 3   Start out by creating and editing a GPO on a newer management station. Edit using another newer management machine station.

Scenario 4   Start out by creating and editing a GPO on a newer management machine. Edit using an older GPMC (i.e., Windows XP) management station.

Scenario 1: Start by Creating and Editing a GPO Using the Older GPMC; Edit Using Another Older GPMC Management Station

Again, here, the new updated GPMC isn't involved. In this scenario, it's all about using the older GPMC with old-school ADM templates and ADM template behavior. And, of course, note that by creating a GPO using an older GPMC machine, you won't be able to get to any of the modern goodies—that's because all the updated Group Policy Preferences and updated GPMC goodies are available only when you use an updated GPMC management station.

So, let's imagine that you've created 86 GPOs using an old and crusty Windows XP machine with the older GPMC loaded. Of course, all 86 GPOs have the original Windows XP versions of those ADM templates (yes, old and crusty).

The big downside of sticking with the older GPMC is something we already went over: every time you create a new Group Policy Object using XP, you're burning 3MB in the SYSVOL on each Domain Controller.

If you were using the updated GPMC, this waste of space would be totally avoidable. Moreover, there's no universal master update location where you can just "drop in" your latest ADM templates and be done.

Scenario 2: Start by Creating and Editing a GPO with the Older GPMC; Edit Using the Updated GPMC

This will be the common "upgrade" scenario. That is, you've already got a gaggle of GPOs created. You created them "back in the day" using Windows XP's GPMC. Now you've got the updated GPMC installed on, say, a Windows 10 machine, and you're ready to use it. What happens?

Not much! If you start to use a modern GPMC and edit an existing GPO created by XP, nothing happens in SYSVOL. No updated GPMC ADMX files are copied anywhere, and very little happens overall.

However, while you're editing the GPO, you'll have access to all the latest and greatest policy settings, one of which is shown in Figure 6.11.

For argument's sake, let's say you decided to enable **Do not allow taskbars on more than one display**—a feature only on Windows 8 and later.

FIGURE 6.11 Editing an existing GPO with an updated GPMC gives you the ability to see updated settings.

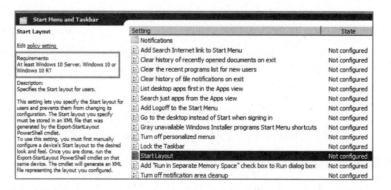

Now, what happens if you try to edit and/or report on those settings using the older GPMC using Windows XP? Short answer: It's not good. That's because the older GPMC doesn't know how to interpret the newer GPMC's specific settings you've set within the GPO. If you try to edit the GPO on an older GPMC machine, you simply won't see the newly available policy setting.

And if you try to look at it using the older GPMC's Settings Report feature, the newer GPMC will give up and simply show it as "Extra Registry Settings," as seen in Figure 6.12.

In Figure 6.12 you can see the Settings tab from GPMC running on an older GPMC machine running Windows XP; it's a report of what's going on inside the GPO.

Again, if you were to continue to use your older GPMC management station to edit the GPO, you simply wouldn't be able to find the **Do not allow taskbars on more than one display** policy setting—or any other more modern specific policy setting for that matter.

> Although it's clearly not a good idea, there is nothing that technically prevents you from using Windows XP to make a change to a GPO that was created using an older GPMC management station. In short, you simply can't see the updated settings.

FIGURE 6.12   Windows XP doesn't know how to interpret newer GPMC settings within a GPO. These settings show up as "Extra Registry Settings."

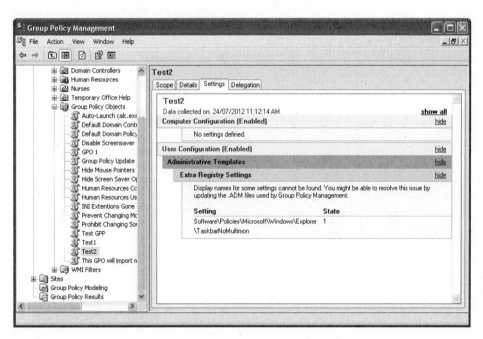

If a custom ADM file has been added to the GPO (yes, ADM), then your updated GPMC will display it.

Scenario 3: Start by Creating and Editing a GPO Using the Updated GPMC; Edit Using Another Updated GPMC Management Station

This is the scenario you want to strive for. That is, always use the updated GPMC to create and edit your GPOs.

Without the Central Store in place, everyone will use their local ADMX and ADML policy definitions. At least the new "do nothing" behavior of the GPMC will cheerfully keep the GPOs "bloat free" and you don't have to worry about multilanguage issues or overwriting each other's definitions inside the GPO.

If you've got the Central Store in place, even better. That way, all your administrators are utilizing the same definitions. Even if various administrators update their own management machines with service packs, everyone is still using the same centralized policy definitions. Then, once those are updated by a domain administrator, again, everyone is immediately updated.

Scenario 4: Start by Creating and Editing a GPO Using an Updated GPMC Management Station; Edit Using an Older GPMC Management Station

Avoid this scenario whenever possible. This is the worst of all worlds because when you originally created the GPO on your updated GPMC management station, you did so without copying the 3MB of ADM files (remember, the updated GPMC doesn't natively use ADM files to define Group Policy settings).

So, you did good here!

However, by editing the GPO using the older GPMC, you end up pushing up the 3MB of ADM files into the GPO (even if you make no changes in the editor). So, every time you do this, you'll see an ADM directory inside the GPO because they were pushed up from your older GPMC machine.

And it's done "invisibly."

So, don't do this. Create a corporate-wide edict to ditch the older GPMC and try to engage all administrators to use the updated GPMC whenever possible to avoid this problem.

Using ADM and ADMX Templates from Other Sources

The templates Microsoft provides with Windows are just the beginning of possibilities when it comes to Administrative Templates. The idea behind additional templates is that you or third-party software vendors can create them to restrict or enhance features of either the operating system or applications.

If you know what to control, you're in business. Just code it up in an ADM or ADMX file and utilize it. Again, however, be mindful that your application itself needs to be coded to be "policy aware" or else you're just zapping Registry edicts around as "preferences."

If you're starting from scratch and have a choice, you'll want to use ADMX files instead of ADM files. That's because you can leverage the Central Store for ADMX files instead of remembering to copy ADM files to every management station.

However, it should be noted that you might already be using an ADM file or three. If you are, how do you get them to the ADMX "promised land"? A free tool, of course. Before we get into that, I will say that's the best option: get those custom and additional ADM files into ADMX format and leverage the Central Store. However, for completeness, I do want to explain what happens if you try to introduce an ADM file directly into a newer GPMC management station.

Recall that ADM templates are the older way to make definitions of what we can control. And recall that there are both true policies and preferences that can be defined within an ADM (or ADMX) file.

Policies write to the "correct" place in the target computer's Registry. And when the user or computer falls out of the "scope of management" of the GPO (that is, it doesn't apply to them anymore), the setting should revert back to the default.

Preferences write anywhere in the Registry. And applications need to be looking for these Registry entries. Preferences tattoo the Registry. So, when the user or computer falls out of the scope of management of the GPO, the setting just sticks around.

You have the ability to get some ADM files from various sources. These ADM files sometimes have definitions for true policies. Other ADM files have definitions for preferences. How do you know which are which? The good news is, the Group Policy Management Editor interface shows you that the two are different. The editor for the older GPMC shows blue for policies and red for preferences. In the updated GPMC, it shows a little paper icon for policies and a paper icon with a down arrow for preferences. That way, you can make an informed decision on whether or not you want to implement a preference.

Using ADM Templates with the Updated GPMC

If you want to leverage and load one of these ADM templates into an existing GPO, simply edit it by using the GPMC and bringing up the Group Policy Object Editor, as shown in Figure 6.13. Then, choose either User Configuration ➢ Policies ➢ Administrative Templates or Computer Configuration ➢ Policies ➢ Administrative Templates, right-click over either instance of Administrative Templates, and choose Add/Remove Templates to open the Add/Remove Templates dialog box.

Click the Add button to open the file requester, and select to load the ADM template you want. I'll show you in the next section or two where to track down more ADM files, but I wanted to show you this first so you'd know how to use them.

The proper name for what we're doing here is *consuming an ADM file*. Remember that every time you consume an ADM template inside a GPO, you're copying that file directly into the GPO within SYSVOL.

 When you're adding an Administrative Template, the interface suggests that you can choose to add it from either the Computer Configuration or the User Configuration node. In actuality, you can add the ADM template from either section and the appropriate policy settings appear under whichever node the ADM template was designed for.

Once ADM templates are added using an updated GPMC management station, they show up within the Group Policy Object Editor under a special node called Classic Administrative Templates (ADM), as seen in Figure 6.14. In Figure 6.14, I've loaded an ADM template from an older version of Word.

FIGURE 6.13   You can still use Add/Remove Templates from a GPO you create with a modern GPMC.

Again, ADM files can have definitions for true policies or for old-style preferences. If you load additional ADM templates into the Group Policy Management Editor that contain old-style preferences, you will also see them. If you go back to Figure 6.2, you'll see it right there.

Once you're editing a preference, you'll notice that old-style preferences have a paper icon with a down arrow on them. This is to indicate that this is a preference and not a true policy, and these values will stick around even after the policy no longer applies to the user or computer. You can see the little down arrow icon for any tattooing preference.

Indeed, the Group Policy Editor is nice enough to even tell you this fact, as you can see in Figure 6.2.

FIGURE 6.14 ADM templates are permitted in GPOs created from newer management stations.

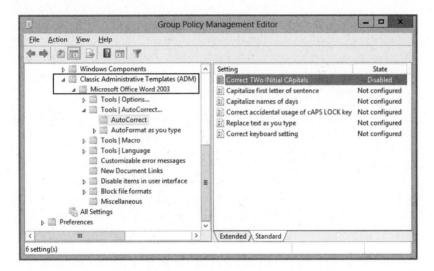

Using ADMX Templates from Other Sources

You'll get ADMX files the same way you got ADM files: companies like Microsoft will make them available to control the products they support, and enterprising geeks will produce ADMX files that control other parts of the operating system and third-party applications.

The same basic note and warning applies, though: ADMX files can contain both (or either) true policies and old-school preferences.

ADMX Templates for Microsoft Office

The most current version of Office, right now, is Office 2013. You can download ADM and ADMX (and a lot of language-specific ADML files) here:

www.microsoft.com/en-us/download/details.aspx?id=35554

I honestly don't know why they have both ADM and ADMX files. Use the ADMX files whenever possible. Note that when you go to download the files, you can choose either 32-bit and/or 64-bit versions, or both. That's because Office itself comes in two versions, 32-bit and 64-bit. And the Registry punches for each product is different, so they needed two ADMX versions. Most organizations deploy the 32-bit version of Office so you'll likely want to use the matching ADMX download too.

The best part is that after you download them, you already know what to do. Just chuck 'em in the Central Store (both ADMX and ADML files in the appropriate places) and you'll be golden. Then all the new GPOs that you create will be able to control Office when you use an updated GPMC management station.

ADMX Templates from Other Sources

Will other Microsoft products have ADMX files? Some already do. Here's a list of items, some of which are ADMs and others that are ADMX files. Other entries are simply additional references, but the web page is definitely worth a look:

http://social.technet.microsoft.com/wiki/contents/articles/4976.aspx

Deciding How to Use ADMX Templates

Once you have the ADMX templates, you need to decide how to use them. If you've already created the Central Store, terrific. Just plop them into the Central Store and you're done. However, note that this means that all administrators who have access to create GPOs using management stations will be able to leverage all ADMX files.

You might not want to enable all administrators to leverage all ADMX templates.

If that's the case, you have only one option: put the specific ADMX files you want only some administrators to get only on the management station you want them to use. The downside, however, is that if another Group Policy administrator (on his management station) tries to edit the GPO or report on it, he won't get the same view of all the settings that you do. That's because his management station doesn't contain the ADMX file you're using.

So, best practice is to use the ADMX file Central Store whenever possible.

ADMX Migrator and ADMX Editor Tools

Yes, it's true. We've just seen that it's possible to import older-school ADM files into GPOs on our updated management machine. Again, the technical term for that is *consuming an ADM file*.

But that procedure gets complex.

Wouldn't it be a better idea to just utilize ADMX files everywhere? That way, you can just plop 'em all in the Central Store and be done. If you already have custom ADM files and need to get them to ADMX land, there's a utility that was written by FullArmor Corporation and licensed by Microsoft to give to you for free.

It's got a silly name: the ADMX Migrator tool. Doesn't it sound like it migrates ADMX files? Well, it doesn't. Maybe it should have been called ADM2ADMX or something, but regardless of the name, that's its job. You can download the tool from Microsoft here: http://tinyurl.com/ydb6ub. Note that it requires the .NET Framework 2.0 to be currently installed.

Additionally, inside the ADMX Migrator tool package is a basic (very, very basic) ADMX editor to help you handcraft your own ADMX files from scratch. The idea is that you don't have to "learn" a new language and hand-code it using, say, Notepad. Just use the tool to create your own ADMX files and you're in business.

> Problem is, though, that the ADMX Migrator tool is not super intuitive. You might also want to check out an alternative ADM and ADMX creation and migration tool from SysPro at www.sysprosoft.com/adm_summary.shtml.

For these examples, I'm running the tools on my WIN10 management station, but they'll work just fine on any machine that has .NET Framework 3.5 loaded from the Windows Feature option in the Control Panel.

ADMX Migrator

There are lots of places you can get premade ADM files. You might try leveraging some right now—some are at www.GPanswers.com; others are found online at various other websites. Here's an example of a simple ADM file if you want to follow along. Just take this text and copy it into Notepad and save it as Sounds.adm:

```
CLASS USER

CATEGORY "Sounds"
    POLICY "Sound to hear when starting Windows XP"
        KEYNAME "Appevents\Schemes\Apps\.Default\SystemStart\.Current"
        PART "What sound do you want? " EDITTEXT REQUIRED
        VALUENAME ".default"
        END PART
    END POLICY

END CATEGORY
```

Then run the FullArmor tool faAdmxConv.exe against the ADM file you have. It can be as simple as just pointing to the file, but there are more switches if you have specific requirements.

Once run, it will create an ADMX and ADML file for the ADM. The documentation swears that it will put them in a temporary directory on the running user's profile, but in my tests, the resulting files seem to go to the root of the C:\ drive. Be sure to look for your new ADMX file in C:\ and the ADML file in C:\en-US.

To prevent this behavior, you can also just specify an output directory like this:

```
faAdmxConv.exe admname.adm C:\outputdirectory
```

Once you're in the directory of your choice, the resulting files are ready to be put in the Central Store (or, if you're not using the Central Store, then with individual updated GPMC management stations). You can see the program run and its output in Figure 6.15.

The ADMX Migrator tool sometimes can't handle the SUPPORTED keyword. In this example, I've removed the SUPPORTED keyword to ensure that conversion occurs properly. However, in the conversion you'll see the warning, as seen in Figure 6.15.

FIGURE 6.15   The `faAdmxConv.exe` tool will take your ADM and convert it into an ADMX and ADML file.

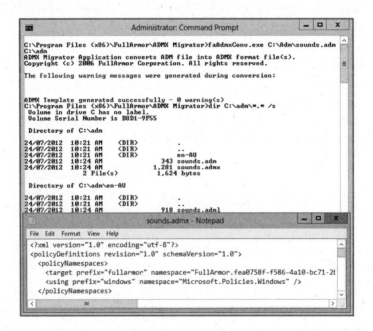

Then, if you want to leverage ADMX and ADML files in the Central Store, put the ADMX file in the \PolicyDefinitions directory within the SYSVOL and the ADML file in the language directory (en-US for English).

The ADMX Migrator tool sometimes appears to be hit or miss during conversion. The latest version (1.3 as of this writing) seems to clear up many of the bugs that I recorded and sent in. Some remain, though, and it's unclear whether FullArmor has intentions of updating the tool in the future.

ADMX Creation and Editor Tools

In the same package as ADMXMigrator, you'll also find an ADMX creation utility. I want to be really honest here and just tell you that I wouldn't recommend it. It's very difficult to use, has no "preview" mode (making edits and re-edits quite hard), and isn't very flexible. However, you're welcome to try it. You would start the ADMX Editor by clicking Start ➤ All Programs ➤ FullArmor ➤ FullArmor ADMX Migrator ➤ ADMX Editor after installing the ADMX Migrator tool installation.

Beyond that, if you're gung-ho to manually create your own ADMX files, you might want to consider the strange route of pre-creating your file as an ADM first, then using the ADMX Migrator utility to convert it. I've seen lots of people do that, and it does work. Editing that ADMX after it's converted can be quite challenging though, because now your "simple" ADM file is converted into a rather "complex" ADMX XML file.

I can suggest two other paths to creating ADMX files:

* There's a script on Microsoft's website called "Convert Registry files (.reg) into ADMX/ADML files for GPO." At last check it was found here: http://tinyurl.com/convert-reg-admx.

* My pals at SysProSoft have an ADM and ADMX editor that has the ability to also convert. So, in short, it has a pleasant editor and a converter built in. You can find that here: www.sysprosoft.com/adm_summary.shtml.

Do remember this key point when creating ADMX files (or ADM files for that matter): You won't get any "magic" ability because you've got an ADM or ADMX file. The target application won't magically perform UI lockout, and settings will stay tattooed on the client when the Group Policy Object is deleted or the user moves to another OU.

If you're looking for that magic, well, it's right around the corner. Read on.

PolicyPak Application Manager

So, I've been working with and teaching Group Policy a long time. As of this writing, I'm a 12-year Group Policy MVP.

But some years back, on one perfectly normal day, it hit me. Like Sir Isaac Newton sitting under the apple tree. Bonk. "There's something missing from the 'in-the-box' stuff: stuff we need. I should invent something. And build a company around solving this problem."

What was my epiphany? What's wrong with Group Policy and Group Policy Preferences "in the box" stuff?

Before we talk about what's wrong—well, if not wrong, then just *missing*—with Group Policy and Group Policy Preferences in the box, let me lead with what works and what's great.

First, using ADM or ADMX templates, you can craft a basic user interface and use it in the GPMC. You can describe and deliver basic Registry punches.

Second, some rare applications support true lockout. That's because those applications are specifically coded to look in the proper Policies keys and coded to perform UI lockout when Registry settings are placed in the proper Policies keys. Again, this is only true for applications using "true policy" (i.e., apps that write to the proper Policies keys) and not preferences (which can write anywhere they feel like).

Third, the Group Policy Preferences Registry extension is neat; it lets you quickly deploy a basic Registry setting just about anywhere.

Now, let's review what's not so hot with Group Policy and Group Policy Preferences:

- Neither Group Policy nor Group Policy Preferences can perform true lockout of an application's UI, unless the application itself is specifically coded for it.

- Those "preference" Registry punches just "stay there" and tattoo after the GPO delivering the setting is removed. There's no way to revert to a known setting.

- Group Policy Preferences has "Nuke mode" (as seen in Chapter 5), which will obliterate settings and not revert them. It's not usually what you're after when you want to revert settings.

- ADMs and ADMXs can only deliver Registry settings. Many applications use more than just the Registry to store application data.

- Creating modern ADMX files is ludicrously painful and sometimes almost impossible.

- Neither Group Policy nor Group Policy Preferences will reapply settings when the computer is offline. If a user manages to change the settings you want them to have, they are maintained (incorrectly) forever until they are back online.

Policy can get you so far. Preferences can get you so far.

I created a series of three videos to demonstrate these problems with the "in-the-box" stuff:

"Group Policy: ADM/X Files – why they cannot prevent user shenanigans"
www.policypak.com/video/admx1

"Group Policy: Understanding ADM-ADMX files tattooing (and what to do about it)"
www.policypak.com/video/admx2

"GPPrefs Registry: Nuke mode, and why users can avoid your GPPrefs settings"
www.policypak.com/video/gpnuke

If you watch these videos, you will see why the "in-the-box" stuff needed a little boost. To me, what was missing was clear.

So I founded a software company, called it PolicyPak, and the first product we created (which has been around the longest) is PolicyPak Application Manager. PolicyPak Application Manager is part of the PolicyPak On-Premise Suite and also the PolicyPak Cloud Suite. It's a commercial product that fills the gap and does all those things I wished Group Policy could do out of the box. So here were the design goals for PolicyPak Application Manager:

- Perform UI lockout for most applications. I don't want to have to wait for a vendor to "catch up" and Group Policy–enable its application.

- Ensure that when a Group Policy Object is removed, all the right settings revert back to the right places. No mystery, no tattooing, and no "nuking."

- Deliver settings to all applications—Registry-based ones and those with exotic file types (INI, XML, JS, JSON, etc.).

- Provide a gaggle of pre-created packs for common applications (Internet Explorer, Acrobat, Lync, Firefox, Java, and more).

- Provide a utility to enable administrators to quickly create their own Paks, instead of hand-creating and editing files. (This idea became the PolicyPak DesignStudio.)

- Ensure that settings will be maintained on computers—even if the computer is offline or if the user tries to work around your desired settings.

 If you're in a hurry and want to see a quick overview of PolicyPak Application Manager, check out www.policypak.com/video/qc6cutrqwk.html.

So, to get you started quickly, PolicyPak comes with over 250 preconfigured Paks for all sorts of applications: AutoCAD, WinZip, Internet Explorer, Firefox, Java, Flash, Acrobat Reader and Pro, and, like I've said, hundreds more. The list is very, very extensive. See the current list here:

www.policypak.com/products/policypak-preconfigured-paks.html

My goal in the following sections is to give you a broad overview of PolicyPak Application Manager, and you can decide if you want to check it out further by coming to a PolicyPak webinar and then trying it all out yourself.

PolicyPak Application Manager is just one component in the PolicyPak suites: you've already seen PolicyPak Admin Templates Manager (Chapter 4) and PolicyPak Preferences Manager (Chapter 5).

But, we didn't really set it up or explain how the moving parts work. I'm going to do that in the following sections.

PolicyPak Concepts and Installation

The PolicyPak suite's job is to help you manage your desktop, system, and application settings using Group Policy.

 You can watch a quick installation of PolicyPak pieces at the following link:

http://www.policypak.com/support-sharing/getting-started.html

What to Install on Your Machine and on Client Machines

Here are the pieces in the download, what they do, and where to install them:

PolicyPak Client-Side Extension.msi (**Client-Side Extension**)   The PolicyPak CSE adds more support where the Group Policy engine leaves off. The PolicyPak CSE is a simple MSI. You can hand-install or use Group Policy Software Installation (Chapter 11) and get it on your client machines. Client machines can be Windows 7 or later 32-bit or 64-bit machines, and RDS/Terminal Services/Citrix. Without the PolicyPak CSE on the client machine, there is no PolicyPak magic.

`PolicyPak Admin Console.msi` (**Adds PolicyPak Node in GPMC**) Hand-install or use Group Policy Software Installation (Chapter 11) and get this file on your machine—where you have the GPMC installed. When you do, you'll see a new PolicyPak node like what's seen in Figure 6.16. So, in your test lab this would be installed on WIN10MANAGEMENT.

FIGURE 6.16 When you add the PolicyPak Admin Console MSI to your GPMC, you get the PolicyPak nodes, as seen here.

Preconfigured Paks PolicyPak comes "ready to rock" with hundreds of popular applications you can manage immediately. You'll put the Paks you want in the PolicyPak Central Store (kind of, almost exactly like Microsoft's Central Store you just learned about).

`PolicyPak Design Studio.msi` This is the PolicyPak Application Manager "Toolkit," which will enable you to create your own Paks. You can install them on the same machine as your management machine or on another machine. We don't have enough space here to cover the PolicyPak Design Studio—but trust me, it's pretty awesome. You can see an example demonstration of the PolicyPak Design Studio at:

www.policypak.com/support-sharing/policypak-designstudio-how-to.html

Getting Started Immediately with PolicyPak's Preconfigured Paks

PolicyPak Application Manager has hundreds of preconfigured Paks. Paks are kinda-sorta like ADMX files, inasmuch as they contain definitions of how to manage the application, and that they be stored in one of two ways:

- Use the Pak "locally" on this machine.
- Use the PolicyPak Central Store!

> PolicyPak Pak files can also be stored in a standard share (like a pseudo-Central Store). Microsoft ADMX files cannot be stored in this way.

PolicyPak honors a central store in almost the precise manner that ADMX files honor a Central Store.

In fact, they live like "neighbors" side by side, as seen in Figure 6.17. You simply manually create the PolicyPak folder, one time, on one Domain Controller. Again, this is super similar to what you did earlier with Microsoft's ADMX Central Store in Figure 6.7. See Figure 6.17 for where to create the PolicyPak folder, as a "peer" next to the `PolicyDefinitions` folder you created earlier.

FIGURE 6.17   You can use the Central Store for Paks, as seen here. Simply copy the Pak DLLs into the PolicyPak central store folder you just created on the Domain Controller.

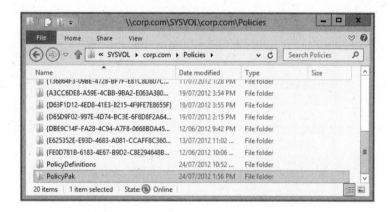

Simply copy any of the PolicyPak preconfigured Paks (DLL files) into the PolicyPak Central Store, and that's it!

All your administrators can utilize the same Paks with the PolicyPak Central Store, in the same way that all your administrators can utilize the same ADMXs with the Microsoft ADMX Central Store!

Top PolicyPak Application Manager Pak Examples

IT admins and MSPs like you use PolicyPak Application Manager for a wide variety of items. Remember, PolicyPak Application Manager ships with over 200 preconfigured Paks (and the DesignStudio to enable you to create your own Paks). That being said, almost everyone who is a PolicyPak customer tends to use at least one of these three example Paks in their world.

Java

If you had a magic wand and wanted to configure Java using Group Policy, I bet these would be your top three items:

- Preventing Java from requesting updates
- Dictating Java's security levels
- Managing Java's exception site lists

Well, now you can do that and just about everything else you would need to configure Java. See Figure 6.18 for how PolicyPak Application Manager's preconfigured Paks for different Java versions can enable you to do these things.

FIGURE 6.18 PolicyPak's preconfigured Pak for Java can stop Java from updating, set security levels, and manage the exception site lists.

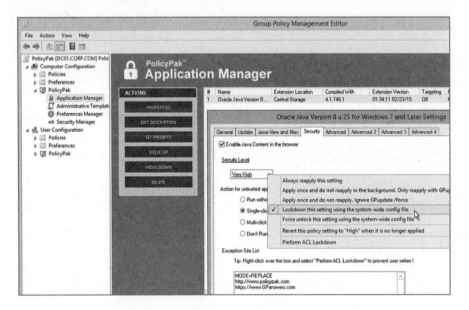

Since Java's configuration is based upon files, and not the Registry, there's no way to manage it using ADMX files or Group Policy Preferences.

To see some videos on using PolicyPak to manage Java, including managing security levels and exception site lists, check out:

www.policypak.com/products/manage-java-jre-with-group-policy.html

Firefox

Firefox has hundreds of configurable items, including the home page, security settings, and "About:Config" settings. PolicyPak can set all of those plus handle complex items like managing certificates for Firefox, blocking extensions, adding sites to the allowed pop-up list, adding bookmarks, and on and on.

In short, if you want to manage Firefox using Group Policy, the preconfigured Pak for Firefox lets you do this, as seen in Figure 6.19.

Since Firefox's configuration is based upon files and not the Registry, there's no way to manage it using ADMX files or Group Policy Preferences.

For a gaggle of how-to manage Firefox using Group Policy and PolicyPak videos, check out:

www.policypak.com/products/manage-firefox-with-group-policy.html

FIGURE 6.19   PolicyPak's preconfigured Pak for Firefox can manage just about everything, from the home page and security settings to certificates, add-ons, and more.

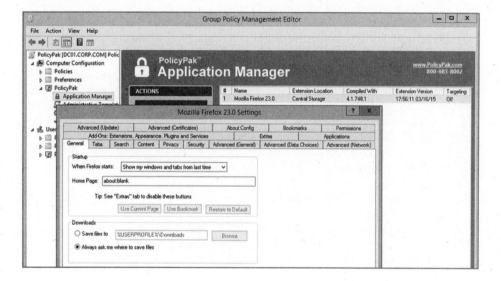

Internet Explorer

On the surface, you might think, "Why would we need another way to manage Internet Explorer?" There's already Group Policy Preferences settings that do this, and there's Group Policy Admin Template policy settings that do this. Turns out there's a huge gap in what's possible with Microsoft's "in the box" abilities.

For starters, PolicyPak unifies the configuration experience of Internet Explorer (bringing the best of the power of policy settings' with the flexibility and look and feel of Group Policy Preferences). As seen in Figure 6.20, the Pak for Internet Explorer looks, well, almost exactly like Internet Explorer.

Beyond that, the Internet Explorer preconfigured Pak takes over the stuff that the now-unavailable Internet Explorer maintenance used to be able to do. For instance, setting Favorites is now possible (again) using the PolicyPak preconfigured Pak for Internet Explorer.

So we ensured that with PolicyPak you could pretty much set anything you needed to. Now you can also manage the following items for all versions of IE 8 and later (including 11, which is the latest as of this writing):

▪ Set primary and secondary start pages

▪ Dictate custom security levels (for Internet, local intranet, trusted sites, and restricted sites)

▪ Set site-to-zone assignment (for Internet, local intranet, trusted sites, and restricted sites)

FIGURE 6.20 PolicyPak's preconfigured Pak for Internet Explorer can manage, well, just about everything with regards to Internet Explorer.

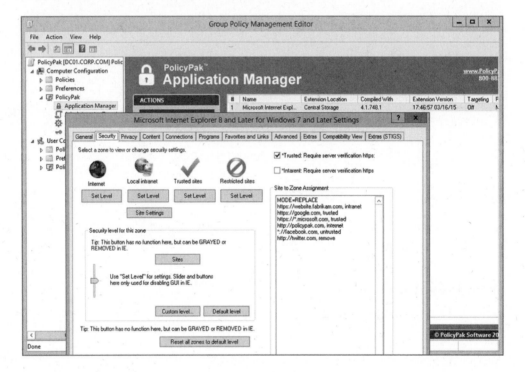

▪ Set privacy and cookies

▪ Manage which sites allow pop-ups

▪ Dictate Content Advisor and block and allow sites

▪ Set LAN settings

- Block add-ons
- Create and remove favorites and links
- Manage advanced settings
- Add/remove certificates
- Add sites to or remove them from Compatibility view
- Add sites to or remove them from Enterprise mode (IE 11 only)

That last one is particularly interesting, and we'll explore both the Microsoft way and the PolicyPak way in Chapter 12. In Figure 6.20, you can see the preconfigured Pak for Internet Explorer managing Site to Zone assignment.

For a gaggle of videos managing every aspect of Internet Explorer using the PolicyPak preconfigured Pak for Internet Explorer, check out

www.policypak.com/products/manage-internet-explorer-using-group-policy-policypak.html

Understanding PolicyPak Superpowers and What Happens When Computers Are Off the Network

As you learned earlier in this chapter, a Group Policy setting is only true policy when it's written to one of the four proper Policies keys. When a value is written to the proper Policies keys, three magical things happen:

- The Registry item is unchangeable by a standard user.
- The item stays compliant even when the computer goes offline.
- The item reverts back to a default when it no longer applies.

This is why, say, when you apply a policy setting that will **Prevent Access to the Control Panel and PC Settings**, the result is that it will:

- Not be changeable or be able to be worked around by a standard user.
- Keep working (enforcing), even if your users go offline.
- Revert when the user doesn't get the Group Policy Object anymore.

The Group Policy engine knows how to do these things—provided the value goes to the proper Policies keys.

And what about Group Policy Preferences? In Chapter 5 you learned that the Group Policy Preferences can reapply only when the computer is online. So when a user goes offline, that's a big, big problem—Group Policy Preferences cannot reapply.

Here's an example of what happens when you try to run gpupdate when the computer has no network connectivity:

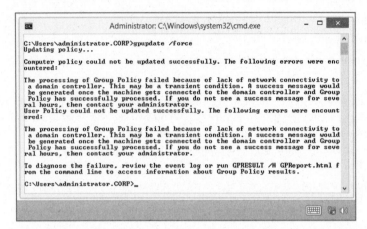

As you can see, Windows just kind of "gives up" because there's no way to make contact.

So, PolicyPak was designed with extra superpowers that neither Group Policy ADM(X) files nor the Group Policy Preferences have.

First, PolicyPak will reapply any settings and make them automatically reapply when one of the following is true:

- The client logs out and back in (online or offline).

- The client manually runs ppupdate.exe, a PolicyPak-specific command, instead of Microsoft's gpupdate.

- Or, the application is simply rerun. Yep—PolicyPak will re-deploy settings to your application, even when offline. All your users have to do is rerun the application.

Here, you can see PolicyPak's ppupdate.exe being run manually and reinforcing any changed settings—even when the computer is off the network. Though, again, running ppupdate.exe isn't normally needed because PolicyPak will simply reapply settings again when the application is relaunched.

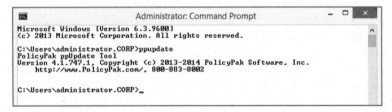

PolicyPak also has an ability to prevent users from working around your dictated settings at all. It's called ACL Lockdown, as seen in Figure 6.21 in the Group Policy editor.

ACL Lockdown ensures that the Registry (in the case of some applications like Internet Explorer) or the configuration file (in the case of other applications like Firefox) will be "owned" by PolicyPak and therefore cannot be worked around *at all* by the standard user, even though they would usually own those files.

In Figure 6.22, you can see what happens when a standard user tries to work around a setting "owned" by PolicyPak ACL Lockdown.

Even the peskiest of users won't be able to work around your settings. Remember, normally items that are in the user's airspace (either HKCU or files in the user's profile) can be managed by *users*. Now with PolicyPak and ACL Lockdown, they're managed and locked down by *you*.

Last, you can export your PolicyPak settings as an XML file and then upload them to the PolicyPak Cloud service, as seen in Figure 6.23.

In this way, you can guarantee settings on-premise (via Group Policy) or to computers off your network using the Internet and the PolicyPak Cloud service.

And, what's more, PolicyPak Cloud delivers settings (application settings and all Group Policy settings) to even non-domain-joined machines. And that's not possible with anything from Microsoft. We'll explore PolicyPak Cloud in Appendix E a bit later.

FIGURE 6.21 Right-click and select ACL Lockdown to secure the Registry settings or files for an application.

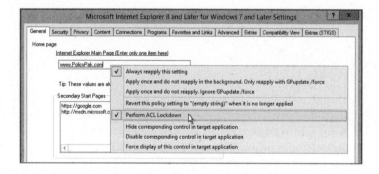

FIGURE 6.22 PolicyPak ACL Lockdown ensures that users cannot work around what you dictate.

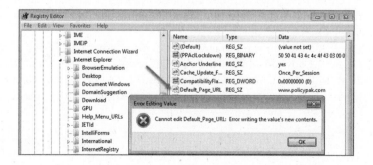

FIGURE 6.23   Upload PolicyPak Application Manager directives to PolicyPak Cloud for use with both domain joined and non-domain-joined machines.

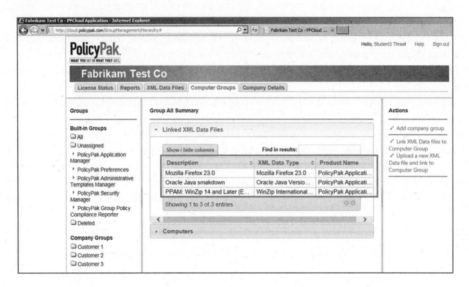

Final Thoughts

Managing your applications requires that you extend Group Policy a bit. You can do so with ADM files, ADMX files, or by using PolicyPak Application Manager. Remember—if you use ADM or ADMX files, only applications smart enough to read Registry settings from the Policies keys will be true policies. They will be applied and removed when different users log on or off. They will not tattoo. They will appear with a paper icon (in the updated GPMC) or a blue dot (in the older GPMC) in the Group Policy Object Editor.

Most applications are not Policies key–aware, which means if the application uses the Registry, then you'll likely need to make those changes into preferences. Preferences do not modify the Policies keys. And they do tattoo the Registry. That means that they're left behind when the policy no longer applies. They will appear with a down arrow (in modern GPMC) or, historically, as a red dot (in XP's GPMC).

If you have an ADM file you want to use in the Central Store, you'll have to convert it to ADMX first. Use the downloadable ADMX Migrator tool to perform that magic. On GPanswers.com, we will also maintain a previous edition's "ADM Template Syntax" chapter as a downloadable PDF should you need that as well. Arguably, it's easier to first create an ADM file by hand and then convert it using the ADMX Migrator tool. Last, check out Microsoft's document Step-by-Step Guide to Managing Group Policy ADMX Files at:

http://go.microsoft.com/fwlink/?LinkId=55414

And for the truly geeky, you can check out the ADMX schema, located at

http://tinyurl.com/28k56v,

if you have wild dreams of hand-coding your own ADMX files—though I'm not sure why you'd ever want to.

Instead of using ADM or ADMX files, consider using PolicyPak Application Manager. PolicyPak Application Manager's goal is to truly policy-enable your applications—even if the underlying Registry punches are really just preferences—or if the application stores its items in places other than the Registry (like Java, Flash, Firefox, or OpenOffice). Or if you need a boost with Internet Explorer, since many of the important items you'll need to configure are simply missing in both Policy and Preferences.

Remember, too, that PolicyPak can also lock down both the user interface and literally take ownership of the underlying settings so users cannot change things, so everything just stays maintained and secure—even when the computer is offline. You can also extend your reach to non-domain-joined machines using the PolicyPak Cloud service.

To get started with PolicyPak, all I ask it that you join me for a webinar first at

www.PolicyPak.com/webinar

and you'll be able to grab the bits and try it all out after the webinar is over.

7

Troubleshooting Group Policy

Working with Group Policy isn't always a bed of roses. Sure, it's delightful when you can set up GPOs with their policy settings from up on high and have them reflected on your users' desktops. However, when you make a Group Policy wish, a specific process occurs before that wish comes true. Indeed, the previous chapter discussed when Group Policy applies. Now you understand the general rules of the game and when they occur.

But what if the unexpected happens? More specifically, it's difficult to determine where a policy setting comes from and how it's applied. Or if Group Policy isn't working, why not, and what's going on? Additionally, you're usually after someone to blame, but that's a task that auditing (discussed in Chapter 8, "Implementing Security with Group Policy") can help with.

A user might call the help desk and loudly declare, "Things have just changed on my Desktop! I want them back the way they were!" Okay, sure, you want things better, too. But a lot of variables are involved. First, there are the four levels: Local Group Policy (and potentially multiple local GPOs in Windows Vista and later), site, domain, and each nested OU (so perhaps even more levels). Then, to make matters worse, what if multiple administrators are making multiple and simultaneous Group Policy changes across your environment? Who knows who has enabled what Group Policy settings and how some user is getting Group Policy applied?

Additional factors are involved as well. For instance, you could have an Active Directory with cross-forest trusts to another forest, and users are logging in all over the place—not to mention a whole litany of things that could possibly go wrong between the time you make your wish and the time the client is expected to honor that wish.

Here's a taste of what to expect while troubleshooting GPOs:

Disabled GPOs   If the GPO is disabled or half the GPO is disabled, you need to hunt it down. Maybe someone decided to disable a GPO link and didn't tell you?

Inheritance Troubles and Trouble with WMI Filtering   Between local, site, domain, and multiple nested OUs, it can be a challenge to locate the GPO you need to fix. Also, introducing WMI filters can make troubleshooting even harder.

GPO Precedence at a Given Level   With multiple GPOs linked to a specific level in Active Directory, you might have some extra hunting to do.

Permissions Problems   Ensuring that users and computers are in the correct site, domain, and OU is one battle; ensuring that they have the correct permissions to access GPOs is quite another.

Replication Problems   The health of the GPO itself on Domain Controllers is important when hunting down policy settings that aren't applying.

Infrastructure Problems   Group Policy processing requires that all pieces of your infrastructure are healthy, including such seemingly unrelated pieces as DNS, the services running on the client, and the ability to pass network protocols between clients and Domain Controllers. Good Active Directory design equals good (consistent) Group Policy processing. The first place to look when Active Directory (or replication) behaves strangely is DNS. As my good friend Mark Minasi likes to say, "The second place to look for replication problems is DNS, too." That's because problems with Active Directory almost always result from the DNS misconfiguration.

Loopback Policy Processing   Sometimes, by mistake, an administrator has enabled loopback policy processing for a computer (or multiple computers). When this happens, the user sees unexpected behavior because the GPOs that would normally apply to him are suddenly out of the ordinary. Just understanding how loopback policy processing works can be a tricky matter. Not only do we have two different modes (Replace or Merge), on top of that you can have complex permission settings on the GPOs themselves, making it hard to calculate which settings a given user will take on.

Slow Links   You've got a VPN for your Windows users or you've rolled out DirectAccess for a seamless VPN experience. Now how and when are your clients going to process GPOs?

These are just a few places where you might encounter trouble. Between various client types with different processing behavior, these problems and the occasional solar flare make things crazy. Troubleshooting can get complicated. Fast.

In this chapter, we'll first dive into where Group Policy "lives" to give you a better sense of what's going on. We'll then explore some techniques and tools that will enable you to get an even better view of why specific policies are being applied.

Now you might be running any number of operating systems at this point: anything from Windows XP to Windows 10, not to mention servers (acting as Group Policy clients), including Windows Server 2003 to Windows Server 2016. Ow.

We'll be focusing on troubleshooting Windows 10 in this chapter. That material should work by and large for Windows 7 and 8, though, as their "guts" are super-duper similar. However, to make a little room for Windows 10 in the book, I did kill some Windows XP information here. You'll be able to find the in-depth Windows XP troubleshooting in previous editions of this book.

That said, here's the "chart" in case you need to understand and troubleshoot other operating systems:

- Windows XP and Windows Server 2003 share the same guts, so they're generally troubleshot the same. Look for references to Windows XP.

- Windows 8, Windows Server 2012, Windows 7, Windows Vista, Windows Server 2008, and Windows Server 2008 R2 are all troubleshot the same. Look for references to Windows 8, Windows 7, or "Windows Vista and later."

- Windows 8.1 and Windows Server 2012 are troubleshot the same.
- Windows 10 and Windows Server 2016 are troubleshot the same, but it should be exactly the same as Windows 8.1 and Server 2012, as there were no earth-shattering updates since Windows 8.1.

There may be a case where one operating system doesn't "fit the mold." In that case, I'll expressly call it out for you.

Under the Hood of Group Policy

As stated in Chapter 1, Group Policy scope has four levels: Local Group Policy (including Multiple Local Group Policy Objects) and then the three levels of Active Directory–based Group Policy—site, domain, and OU. When you're troubleshooting Group Policy, one approach is to first get a firm understanding of what's going on under the hood. As a kid, I took things apart all the time. My parents went mental when they came home and the dishwasher was in pieces all over the kitchen floor. It wasn't broken; I just wanted to know how it worked. If you're like me, the following sections are for you.

Inside Local Group Policy

Remember that a GPO is manipulated when someone walks up to the machine, runs the Local Group Policy Object Editor (GPEDIT.MSC), and makes a wish or three. Remember that in Windows XP, there is only one local GPO on a machine and local GPOs affected everyone who logged on to that machine. In Windows Vista and later, there are Multiple Local GPOs (MLGPOs).

 Enterprise Admins, by default, do not have local administrator rights on individual client machines. Domain Admins, but not Enterprise Admins, have rights to Local Group Policy Objects (LGPOs).

Where Local Group Policy Lives

Once wishes are made with GPEDIT.MSC and a Local Group Policy is modified, the Local Group Policy lives in two places. The first part is file based, and the second part is Registry based:

The File-Based Part of Local Group Policy (All Versions of Windows)   The file-based part of the default local GPO can be found in %windir%\system32\grouppolicy.

The File-Based Part of Local Group Policy for MLGPOs   Remember that in Windows Vista and later there are Multiple Local GPOs (MLGPOs). Because of this, the storage of those user-specific and group-specific GPOs is in a different location than the default local GPOs. Namely, they are stored in a new subfolder of \Windows\SYSTEM32 called GroupPolicyUsers, as shown in Figure 7.1.

FIGURE 7.1   Viewing the directories of Windows 7 local GPOs

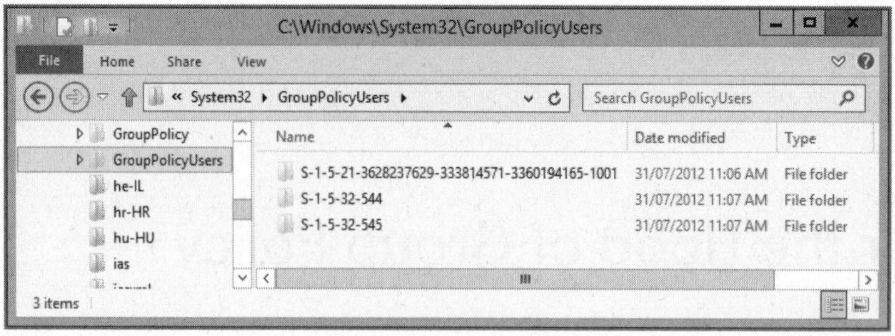

As you can see in Figure 7.1, there are three SID-named folders that contain the user-specific portion of the local GPO. (Remember that the computer portion applies to everyone, and, hence, there is no computer portion represented here.) You might have more than three folders here. In my example, the first SID you see in the list (with a SID of S-1-5-21-3628237629-333814571-3360194165-1001) is the SID of a user account for whom I created a user-specific local GPO.

And, again, as you know from Chapter 1, I could have any number of user-specific local GPOs defined. And each of those user-specific GPOs would have its own SID-based folder.

Folders that you see in Figure 7.1 are like the ones you will find on your Windows Vista and later systems if you decide to define local GPOs. The folder called S-1-5-32-544 defines the Administrators GPO (and not coincidentally, that is the SID of the built-in Administrators group). Likewise, the folder named S-1-5-32-545 is the SID of the built-in Users group, which represents the nonadministrators local GPO.

> Again, you should notice one major difference between the default local GPO and these user-specific local GPOs: the default local GPO includes a computer-specific Machine folder in addition to the default User folder. However, any user-specific local GPO contains only a User folder (since it contains only user-specific policy settings).

The files and folders found in the local GPO mirrors, for the most part, the way the file-based portion of an Active Directory–based GPO stores its stuff. This is good news, as it makes understanding the two types of GPOs (local versus domain-based GPOs) nearly equal.

> Feel free to inspect the %windir%\system32\grouppolicy folder, and then jump to the section "Group Policy Templates" later in this chapter to get the gist of the file structure. Note, however, that not all the structure may be present until the local GPO is edited.

Inside Active Directory Group Policy Objects

Here's the strange part about Group Policy (as if it weren't already strange enough). Chapter 1 discussed how creating a GPO involves two steps. First, the GPO is written in the Group Policy Objects container, and then it is *linked* to a level—site, domain, or OU. So, we know that GPOs don't really "live" at the level where they're linked. Specifically, all GPOs live inside the Group Policy Objects container in the domain. That is, they're always kept nestled inside this container yet are logically linked to (but not stored in) the other levels to which they point. I referred to the GPOs we created as swimming around in a virtual pool within the domain.

So far in our journey, we created four new GPOs that affect our storyline:

- "Hide Screen Saver Option," which we applied to the Default-First-Site-Name site
- "Prohibit Changing Sounds," which we applied to the Corp.com domain
- "Hide Mouse Pointers Option / Restore Screen Saver Option," which we applied to the **Human Resources Users** OU
- "Auto-Launch Calc.exe," which we applied to the **Human Resources Computers** OU

There could also be other GPOs, unlinked and just hanging out in the swimming pool, like "Remove Run from the Start Menu" or others you created.

We can check in with our concept of these GPOs as floating in a swimming pool within the Group Policy Objects container, as shown here.

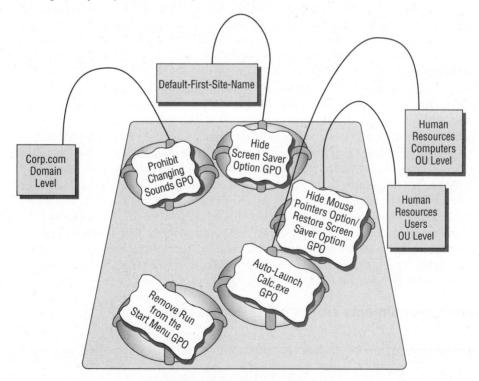

The Corp.com GPO Swimming Pool

As you can see, the GPOs never "live" at any level in Active Directory. They aren't stored at any particular level, although it might appear (using the old-school interface) that they are.

To reiterate, if you leverage a GPO that is supposed to affect a site, an OU, or even a domain, the GPO itself is not stored directly at that level. Rather, the GPO is linked to the level in Active Directory. When a GPO is called to be used, it has to request a Domain Controller to fetch it from the Group Policy Objects container (and from its parts in SYSVOL) and pull the information out.

Each time you create a new GPO, it's born and placed into the swimming pool within the domain—ready for action if linked to a level in Active Directory. You can reuse a GPO at multiple levels in Active Directory by linking it to another level of Active Directory.

So, when GPOs are created for use at the site, domain, or OU level, they're always created within the domain swimming pool, the Group Policy Objects container, where we just link to the GPOs we need when we need them.

We're going to continue this discussion a little out of order here. We'll be talking about domain-linked GPOs, OU-linked GPOs, and then round out with site-linked GPOs. Yes, yes, we all know the "right" order is site, domain, OU—so bear with me here (I think you'll understand why we're going out of order by the time this discussion is complete).

Group Policy Objects from a Domain Perspective

Since we know that all GPOs are just hanging out in the Group Policy Objects container waiting to be used, we can take this one step further. That is, even those GPOs linked to the domain level aren't exempt from having to be "fetched." When clients use domain-linked GPOs, they have to make the same requests and "ask" the Domain Controller for the GPOs that apply to them.

This is usually not a problem; the Domain Controller doesn't have far to go to get the GPO in the swimming pool to apply it to the domain. But this is precisely why doing *cross-domain* GPO linking is so slow and painful.

For instance, in an environment with multiple domains, it might appear to be easier to recycle an existing GPO that lives in another domain. But when it comes time to grab the information inside the GPO, it needs to be brought back all the way from Domain Controllers in the originating domain. Again, this cross-domain GPO linking is very, very painful and should be avoided at all costs. In Chapter 2, "Managing Group Policy with the GPMC and via Powershell," in the section "Basic Interdomain Copy and Import," I discussed the idea of copying GPOs from one domain to another. This avoids the problem altogether because there's no "penalty" for creating a copy from a source domain and then having the copy live in your domain. Sure, it takes up a wee bit of storage in the new domain's swimming pool. But it's better than cross-domain linking.

Group Policy Objects from an OU Perspective

Since GPOs live in the Group Policy Objects container at the domain level, a distinct advantage is associated with the way Group Policy does its thing: it's tremendously easy to move, link, and unlink GPOs to the domain and/or its OUs. You could, if you desired, unlink a GPO in the domain or OU and link it back to some other OU. Or you could link one GPO to the domain and/or multiple OUs.

It's typical and usual that you'll use OUs to apply most of your GPOs. If GPOs live in the Group Policy Objects container swimming pool, it's easy for multiple, unrelated OUs to reuse the same GPOs and just create new links to existing GPOs.

Group Policy Objects from a Site Perspective

Site-level GPOs are a bit unique. If you used (or continue to use) the old-school interface via Active Directory Sites and Services to dictate a site-based GPO, you might be in for a world of pain. By default, all site-level GPOs created using the old-school interface will live in the Group Policy Objects container of the Domain Controllers of the *root* domain—and only the root domain, that is, the first Active Directory domain brought online. Then, every time a GPO meant for a site is called for use by a client system, a Domain Controller from the root domain must fetch that information. If the closest Domain Controller from the root domain is in Singapore, so be it. You can see where the pain could get severe.

The GPMC basically forces us to create site-based GPOs in a thoughtful way. Specifically, you need to create the GPO in the domain swimming pool of your choice. Then, you need to link the GPO from the domain to the site you want. As you saw in Chapter 1, we first create the GPO in the Group Policy Objects container.

The idea is to create the GPO in the domain that makes sense and is closest to where the site-linked GPO will be used. Then, once we expose the site, we just add a link to our existing GPO, which is already in the domain swimming pool. In short, we get the site GPO to leverage the closest domain's swimming pool. Sure, it takes a little extra planning to think about which swimming pool is closest to the users and computers in the site—but it's worth it. That way, we're not asking some Domain Controller in Singapore to serve our New York users.

 Remember, by default, only members of the Enterprise Administrators group (or members of the Domain Admins group in the root domain) can create new site-level GPOs or link to existing GPOs from the site level. Optionally, this right can be delegated.

The Birth, Life, and Death of a GPO

Now that you understand where GPOs live, we can take the next step: understanding the "journey" of a GPO. Specifically, a GPO is born and must stay healthy if it's going to stay alive. If its usefulness becomes depleted, you can call in the Soprano boys to whack it—never to be seen again.

How Group Policy Objects Are "Born"

Before you can give birth to GPOs, you need rights to do so, and you can get these rights in two ways. First, you can be a member of the Group Policy Creator Owners or Domain Admins security group.

> **NOTE**   If you're a member of the Group Policy Creator Owners group, you have rights to create but not link GPOs. Domain Administrators can create GPOs and link them to where they want.

You can also be granted explicit rights via the Delegation tab in the Group Policy Objects container via the GPMC (as you saw in Chapter 2).

A new Group Policy Object is born when you right-click the Group Policy Objects container and choose New. Now you're setting into motion a specific chain of events.

First, by default, the PDC emulator is contacted to see if it's available for writing. If not, the user gets an RPC (Remote Procedure Call) error message, as shown in Figure 7.2.

FIGURE 7.2   If the PDC emulator is not available for writing, and the GPO is started, the user gets an error.

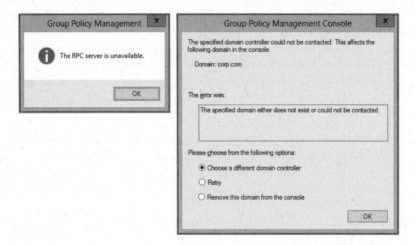

GPOs are initially born when you use the GPMC to create a new GPO. They are created on the PDC emulator, and then, a bit later, they are replicated to the other Domain Controllers within the site and then between sites. Assuming the PDC emulator is available, you can give your GPO a friendly name, say "Hide Mouse Pointers Option / Restore Screen Saver Option," as we did in Chapter 1.

Once that happens, your GPO is officially "born." The PDC emulator has already performed certain functions on your behalf:

- The GPO was given a unique ID that takes its form as a globally unique identifier (GUID).

- It created a *Group Policy Container (GPC)* object in the Policies folder of the system container in the Active Directory domain partition. Think of this as a reference in Active Directory for your new GPO.

- It created a *Group Policy Template (GPT)* folder in the SYSVOL Policies directory of the PDC emulator. This is where the real files that make up your GPO live. They're replicated to every Domain Controller for quicker retrieval.

- Additionally, if "Create a GPO in this domain, and Link it here" is used when focused on the domain or OU level (or the old-school interface is used), the new GPO you just created is automatically *linked* to the current level you were focused at—domain or OU.

When you inspect the properties of any new GPO, you'll see the unique ID it is automatically given, as shown in Figure 7.3.

FIGURE 7.3   Every GPO gets a unique name.

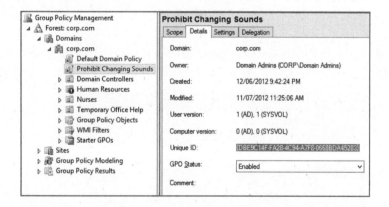

So, every GPO is made up of two components (the GPC and GPT), and those components are split between two places on that Domain Controller. The good news, though, is that it all ties back to the GPO's GUID. We'll explore each of these components in the next two sections.

How a GPO "Lives"

A GPO in Active Directory is made up of two constituent parts. One part isn't enough, and the GPO cannot live without both parts. Both parts are required in order to communicate the GPO message.

As you'll see in a bit, the GPO derives its life from these two parts.

Group Policy Containers (GPCs)

The Active Directory database contains the first half of a GPO. Not to get too geeky, but these are just objects (of class groupPolicyContainer), which we refer to as the Group Policy Containers (GPCs). Each GPO defined in a domain has exactly one GPC object defined for it. Then, it's this GPC object that can hold multiple properties related to the Group Policy Object—for instance, version and display information and some policy settings. A GPC has a unique name that takes the format of a GUID—see the sidebar "GPC Attributes." The GUID is *not* the friendly name we use when administering the GPO. The friendly name is stored as an attribute—called displayName—on that GPC object in Active Directory.

You can see the GPCs for every Group Policy you create by diving into the Active Directory Users and Computers console.

To view the GPCs and their GUIDs, follow these steps:

1. Log onto the server DC01 as Administrator of the domain.

2. Choose Start ➢ All Programs ➢ Administrative Tools ➢ Active Directory Users and Computers.

3. Choose View ➢ Advanced Features, as shown in Figure 7.4, to display the Policies folder.

FIGURE 7.4   Turn on the Advanced Features setting to see the Policies folder (and a whole lot more).

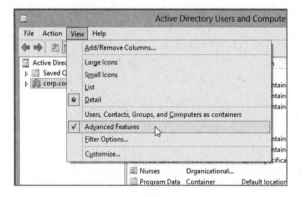

4. Expand the System folder to display the Policies folder along with the GPCs, as shown in Figure 7.5.

Up to this point, we've been using the GPMC interface to create GPOs. When we use the GPMC to create GPOs, we've made reference to the Group Policy Objects container within the GPMC as a representation of the swimming pool. But the GPMC isn't showing you the real swimming pool—it's showing you a *representation* of the swimming pool. What it's showing you is the GPC part of the swimming pool. The other "half" of the swimming pool is the GPT (which we'll talk about next), the files that live in the replicated SYSVOL folder that exists on every domain controller in an Active Directory domain. The path to the GPT is *<domain name>*\sysvol*<domain name>*\policies.

FIGURE 7.5   Expand the Policies folder to expose the underlying GPC objects.

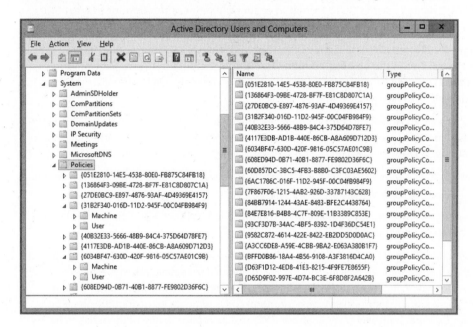

When you drill into a GPC container in Active Directory, you should see one GUID-named folder for every GPO you have created, plus two more for the two default GPOs—the Default Domain Policy and the Default Domain Controllers Policy (which we'll explore in Chapter 8).

Those two default GPOs, in fact, have what are referred to as "well-known GUIDs." That is, the GUID for each of those two GPOs will be the same no matter what AD domain you look at. They are the same in your AD domain as they are mine. That makes it easy to find them. When you're used to seeing those two GUIDs time and again, you will know right away which GPOs they represent.

In Figure 7.5, I have lots of GPOs already created; therefore, I have lots of containers. You might have fewer.

GPC Attributes

When a GPC object is created, it is given several attributes:

Common Name (CN)   In Active Directory, you'll see that this attribute is called cn. An LDAP (Lightweight Directory Access Protocol) designation for the name is assigned to an object. GPC names use the GUID format to ensure uniqueness throughout a forest—for example, CN={2C53BFD6-A2DB-44AF-9476-130492934271}.

Distinguished Name (DN)   In Active Directory, you'll see an attribute called distin-guishedName. This is the object's common name plus the path to the object from the root of the LDAP tree—for example, CN={2C53BFD6-A2DB-44AF-9476-130492934271}, CN=Policies, CN=System, DC=corp, DC=com.

Display Name   In Active Directory, you'll see an attribute called displayName. This is the friendly name assigned to the Group Policy Object in the user interface—for example, the "Hide Screen Saver Option" GPO.

Version   In Active Directory, you'll see an attribute called versionNumber. This is a counter that keeps track of updates to a GPC object (more on this topic a little later).

GUID   In Active Directory, you'll see an attribute called objectGUID. This is the GUID assigned to the object itself.

You might find it a little confusing for the GPC object to have a GUID that refers to the object itself and a name that uses a GUID format. For an important reason, Microsoft needed a way to make the underlying, real name of GPOs unique, independent of their friendly names. Suppose two administrators create two (or more) GPOs with the same friendly name on their own Domain Controllers. When these GPC objects replicate, one of them has to be discarded, overwritten, or renamed, depending on the exact circumstances of the replication collision. That could be a bad thing. Therefore, Microsoft solves this problem by using underlying unique names formatted with the GUID format. There is a negligible chance of identical GUIDs being created, not only within one Active Directory but also across the entire world, should the need arise to coexist with GPOs in other forests (such as with cross-forest trusts).

When you try to drill down into the subcontainers, some will and some will not expand past the {*GUID*}*Machine* and {*GUID*}*User* levels. Those that do expand do so because you have set up policy settings in that specific GPO that Active Directory needs to maintain information on, such as when you Publish or Assign applications. We'll look at where each policy area stores its settings after the section on the GPT.

We explore how to Publish and Assign applications in Chapter 11.

Don't be surprised if, at this stage in working through the book, you do not have any fully expandable subfolders, as shown in Figure 7.5. The subfolders that don't expand simply don't have any Group Policy settings stored within them. Almost everything else the GPO needs in order to be useful is stored in the GPT, which is explored in the section "Group Policy Templates."

Who Really Has Permissions to Do What?

In Chapter 2, we applied various permissions on the GPO, including who had "Read" and "Apply Group Policy" permissions as well as who could see the settings or edit the stuff inside the GPO. The locking mechanism for "Who really has what permissions" on a specific GPO is found right here, at the Policies folder:

- On the one hand, the locking mechanism on the Policies folder itself dictates who can and cannot create GPOs. However, it should be noted that these permissions are not inherited to the GUID-named GPT folder itself.

- See the note following Figure 7.8 for specific information on how to change the default permissions.

- On the other hand, the locking mechanism on the GUID-named GPT folders underneath the Policies folder dictates which users have access to "Read" and "Apply Group Policy" or can change the GPO itself.

In reality, the permissions that you see in GPMC for a given GPO reflect the permissions of *both* the GPC and GPT. Although the permissions that you can grant to an Active Directory object do not map one-to-one to the permissions that you can grant to a file system folder like those found in SYSVOL, they roughly translate into the same permissions. For this reason, it's very important that you *not* try to directly modify the permissions on a GPO by modifying the permissions on either the GPC or the GPT independently. The best tool for this task is the GPMC's security filtering and delegation features.

However, in my GPanswers.com newsletter #13 (found at www.GPanswers .com/newsletter), you will find a tip that does walk through how to expressly change the underlying permissions in an emergency. Note that in that article, it's a special case and, again, should only be performed as described in that particular emergency.

Who Can Create New Group Policy Objects?

Right-click the Policies container, select Properties, and then click the Security tab to display several names, some of which should be familiar, including the Group Policy Creator Owners and Domain Administrators groups. Additionally present will be anyone you explicitly added via the Delegation tab upon the Group Policy Objects container in GPMC. You saw how to do this in Chapter 2. At that time, we added a user named Joe User from our domain.

If you examine the properties of the Policies container (as shown in Figure 7.6), you'll see the Group Policy Creator Owners group. Joe is also listed (because he was expressly granted permission via the GPMC). Note also that the groups named Domain Admins and Enterprise Admins are also present.

FIGURE 7.6   Expand the Policies folder to expose the underlying GPC objects.

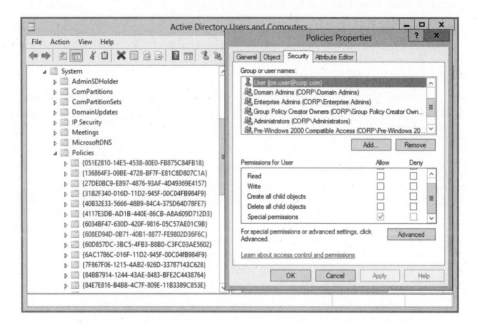

You can click the Advanced button to display Joe's precise "Special Permissions." Indeed, Joe has only one permission, and it's called "Create groupPolicyContainer Objects." Once he has this right, the system permits him to create GPC folders and populate them with Group Policy information when he creates a new GPO.

The Group Policy Creator Owners group has many, many more unnecessary permissions on the Policies folder, including "Create all child objects," "Create User Objects," and a whole lot of stuff that, really, doesn't have anything to do with Group Policy. Indeed, if you log on as someone in the Group Policy Creator Owners group and right-click the Policies folder, you can do some things you really shouldn't do, as you can see in Figure 7.7.

The system (thankfully) won't let you do *all* the functions listed here, but it does let you do *some* of them. And, again, you really shouldn't be poking around like this. Of course, the "right" thing to do is to set permissions only via the GPMC. However, I show you these things for demonstration purposes so you can get a better feeling for what is different between someone in the Group Policy Creator Owners Group versus someone who has been explicitly delegated rights via the Delegation tab upon the Group Policy Objects container in GPMC.

FIGURE 7.7   For the love of Pete, please don't do this.

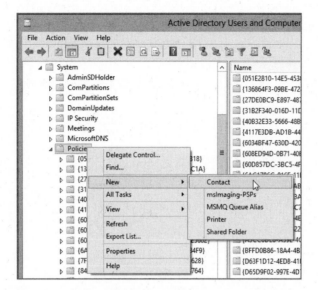

The Domain Administrators group and the Enterprise Administrators group also have explicit permissions here. When they create new GPOs, they do so because of their explicit permissions, not because they are members of the Group Policy Creator Owners group.

Who Can Manipulate and Edit Existing Group Policy Objects?

Right-click a GPO folder (with the name of a GUID) under the Policies folder and choose Properties to display the Security tab (see Figure 7.8), which will show the same information as when, in Chapter 2, you used the Deny attribute to pass over certain security groups. That is, the same information is shown here as when we clicked the Advanced button in the Delegation tab when focused on the GPO (or GPO link, because it's using the same information taken from the actual GPO).

The permissions that a new GPO gets when it's created are controlled by the `DefaultSecurityDescriptor` attribute on the `groupPolicyContainer` class within the Active Directory schema. If you want your GPOs to get different default permissions when they're created, you can modify the schema instance of this attribute. The Microsoft Knowledge Base article at `http://support.microsoft.com/kb/321476/en-us` describes how to do that.

Unless otherwise delegated, the person or group who created the GPO is the only one other than Domain Admins and Enterprise Admins who can modify or delete the GPO. However, this may be a particularly sensitive issue if you have many Domain Administrators—as they all have "joint ownership" of the GPOs they create. There is a serious potential risk in one administrator taking the reins and modifying another administrator's GPOs.

FIGURE 7.8   Each GPC can display the underlying permissions of the GPO.

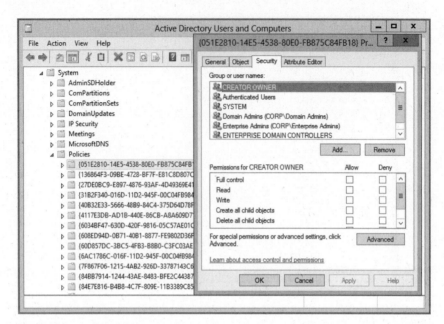

However, as you saw in Chapter 2, you can also grant someone explicit rights via the Delegation tab upon the GPOs container via the GPMC. In this example, I have done this for Joe. Figure 7.9 shows the properties of a GPO that Joe has created.

FIGURE 7.9   If Joe creates a GPO, he owns the GPO. No one else (other than Domain Admins or Enterprise Admins) can edit it.

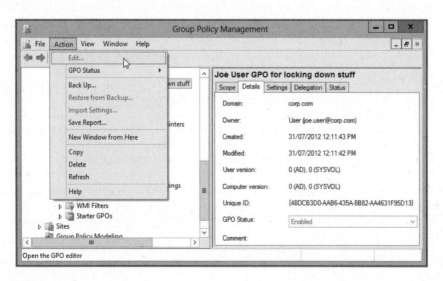

Since Joe has explicit permissions to create GPOs, he becomes the owner of the GPOs he creates. You can clearly see that Joe created it, and now he owns it. Hence, Joe doesn't have to worry about other explicitly anointed users or groups changing the GPOs he creates and owns. Note, however, that the Domain Administrators and Enterprise Administrators groups will, in fact, be able to change any GPOs that Joe creates. Additionally, note that other users within Group Policy Creator Owners cannot dive in and edit Joe's GPOs. Again—Joe owns it; it's his.

Using LDP to See the Guts of a GPC

The GPC object itself holds even more critical attributes for GPOs:

gPCFileSysPath   This is the physical path to the associated Policies folder, or GPT, stored in SYSVOL. The Policies folder has the same name as the GPC, which is another reason that uniqueness is so important. The GPT is discussed in the next section.

gPCMachineExtensionNames   This is a list of GUIDs of the computer-related CSEs (Client-Side Extensions)—and the MMC snap-in that manages them—that will be called for this particular GPO. For instance, if a GPO has policy set on the Administrative Templates node under the Computer Configuration node in the Group Policy Object Editor, the gPC-MachineExtensionNames list includes the GUID of the Registry CSE and the GUID of the MMC snap-in for the Administrative Templates node. CSEs are discussed later in this chapter in the section "How Client Systems Get Group Policy Objects."

gPCUserExtensionNames   This is a list of the GUIDs of the CSEs and their MMC snap-ins, called by a user-related Group Policy. Again, I'll discuss CSEs a bit later in this chapter.

There are several ways you can see this entry. You could use the updated RSAT's Active Directory Users and Computers to see them (on the Attribute Editor tab). Or you could use the ADSI Edit MMC snap-in. I'm suggesting LDP for these examples. LDP lets you perform LDAP queries right into the actual guts of Active Directory. Using LDP, you can see these attributes. Normally, you wouldn't want or need to go poking around in here, but taking the time to learn just where attributes are can help you understand what constitutes a GPO.

To query a specific GPO to see its underlying attributes, follow these steps:

1. After loading the Support tools on the Domain Controller, choose Start ➢ Run to open the Run dialog box, and in the Open field, type **LDP** and press Enter to select the domain of your choice.

2. Choose Connection ➢ Bind, accept the defaults, and click OK.

3. Choose View ➤ Tree to open a dialog box that lets you specify the distinguished name of the domain. If your domain is Corp.com, enter **dc=corp, dc=com**. If you do that correctly, your left pane will show the domain name with a plus (+) sign. You should be able to double-click the plus sign and expand the contents within the domain.

4. Find the System container and double-click it to expand it.

5. Find the Policies container and double-click it to expand it.

6. Find the unique name of the GPO you want to inspect and double-click it to expand it. (For information about how to find a specific unique name of a GPO, see the earlier section "How Group Policy Objects Are 'Born.'") In the following illustration, the attributes are highlighted.

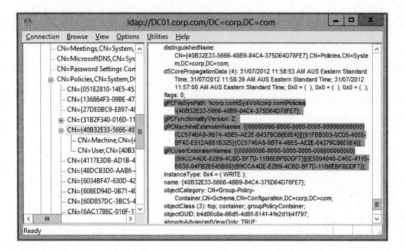

Once you find the unique name, the resultant LDP query will show you the properties on that GPO.

There is one more important attribute to inspect by using LDP: gPLink. Recall that a GPO can be linked by one level, multiple levels, or no levels. If a GPO is to be linked to a site, a domain, or an OU, that level needs to have a *pointer* or *link* to the GPO. When clients log on (computer and user), they use LDAP to query to each level they are a part of (site, domain, OUs) to find out if the level has the gPLink attribute set. If so, the client makes an LDAP query to find out what GPOs are meant for it. With the information in hand, it determines what files to download from the SYSVOL share on its logon server.

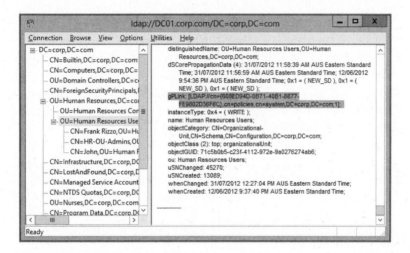

To see the gPLink attribute, you can click the level you want to inspect. In this case, click the **Human Resources Users** OU you created in Chapter 1.

In the right pane, find LDP's query results. The gPLink attribute has LDAP pointers to the unique names of the GPOs. In this case, the **Human Resources Users** OU has links to the "Hide Mouse Pointers Option / Restore Screen Saver Option" GPO, in my case, 608ED94D-0B71-40B1-8877-FE98002D36F6C.

Group Policy Templates

As you just learned, GPCs are stored in the Active Directory database and replicated via normal Active Directory replication. A Group Policy Template (GPT), on the other hand, is stored as a set of files in the SYSVOL share of each Domain Controller. Each GPT is replicated to each Domain Controller through FRS (File Replication Service).

When we used the Properties tab of the GPO, we were able to find its unique name (as we did earlier in Figure 7.3). We can use the unique name to locate the GPC in Active Directory, and it's the same unique name we can use to locate the GPT in the SYSVOL.

To see the GPTs in SYSVOL, follow these steps:

1. On a Domain Controller in the domain, open Windows Explorer.

2. Change the directory to the SYSVOL container. Its usual location is C:\Windows\ SYSVOL\SYSVOL\<domain name> (in this case, C:\Windows\SYSVOL\SYSVOL\corp.com).

3. Change into the Policies folder. You'll see a list of folders. The folder names match the GPC GUID names stored in Active Directory (seen in the previous exercise). Figure 7.10 shows a Policies folder containing many GPOs.

FIGURE 7.10   The unique names of the GPOs are found as folder names in SYSVOL. This is the unique name for the "Hide Mouse Pointers Option / Restore Screen Saver Option" you saw in the last image in the sidebar "Using LDP to See the Guts of a GPC."

Double-clicking a Policies folder inside SYSVOL displays the contents of the GPT. Inside, you'll see several subfolders and a file. The first entry on this list is the file (gpt.ini); the rest are subfolders.

gpt.ini   The one file you will always find under the GUID folder. It holds the version number of the GPT as well as the information that's equivalent to the gpcMachineExtensionName and gpcUserExtensionName attributes found on the GPC object in Active Directory. Namely, these two keys within the gpt.ini list the GUIDs of the CSEs and their associated MMC snap-in extensions that have been implemented within the GPO. This lets the client know which CSEs need to be called when GPOs are processed. (You'll read about version numbers in the section "Understanding Group Policy Version Numbers.") For very old GPOs, you might also see a little text snippet in the gpt.ini that says "displayName=New Group Policy Object." This snippet of text is the same when you're using very old Group Policy creation tools. This entry is vestigial and has never been used.

\Adm If you create your GPOs using a Windows 10 management station (as we discussed in Chapter 1 and explored in depth in Chapter 6, you won't see an ADM directory in any of your newly created GPOs. However, if you ever created GPOs from XP machines, this directory is created to house policy settings called Administrative Template files. In short, when you create or edit a GPO from an XP machine, the Administrative Templates (ADM files) are copied from the \Windows\INF folder. Again, this happens from the machine where you're editing that GPO, into the GPT's \Adm folder.

By default, those ADM files are Conf.adm, Inetres.adm, System.adm, wmplayer.adm, and wuau.adm.

Double-clicking the \Adm folder displays the templates. Note that the \Adm folder will not exist until the GPO is opened for the first time from an XP machine and you click either the Computer or the User Administrative Template node. Again, feel free to review the material in Chapter 6 for more on this topic.

Note that the presence of the \Adm folder in the GPT is an artifact of pre–Windows Vista operating systems. When you create and edit a new GPO using Windows Vista and later, no \Adm folder is created because, for example, your Windows 10 machine no longer copies the ADM files up to the GPT—they are held locally in C:\windows\policydefinitions or in the "Central Store." However, if you edit a GPO that was first created on a modern GPMC, then later edit it using an older GPMC (for example, XP or 2003), the \Adm folder will get created and populated in the GPT. Note that this behavior—editing a GPO from a down-level version of Windows—is generally not a good idea. Once you've started to utilize Windows 10 as your Group Policy creation station, it's best to continue to edit those GPOs using a modern client from then on. You can check out Chapter 6, which describes the Central Store and ADMX files in great detail and explores this particular problem more.

\Machine This folder contains the settings for the Computer side of the GPO, including startup and shutdown scripts (though there's nothing requiring them to live here; they could be located in other places as well), pointers to applications that are assigned, and Registry settings (among other settings). The actual contents of the \Machine folder depend on the computer options specified in the GPO. The potential contents include the following:

The **Registry.pol** File Holds the Registry settings specified in Computer Configuration ➢ Policies ➢ Administrative Templates as well as settings for Software Restriction Policy under Computer Configuration ➢ Policies ➢ Windows Settings ➢ Security Settings ➢ Software Restriction Policies.

The **\Applications** Folder   Stores pointer files called Application Advertisement Scripts, or .AAS files. These files are used in conjunction with Group Policy Software Deployment. These are the instructions that the client computers use to process Software Installation. Software Installation is further discussed in its own chapter, Chapter 11, but .AAS files are described further in the sidebar entitled "Inside .AAS Files."

Inside .AAS Files

The .AAS file serves a specific role in the context of Software Installation policy. This file is created when you first deploy an MSI package. It contains information related to the advertisement of the package.

Advertisement is an MSI feature that allows you to deploy part of an application (you can think of it like a shortcut or file extension association) to a computer or user. The whole application is not installed right away; instead, when the user first clicks the shortcut or activates a file extension associated with the advertised package, the installation proceeds at that time. This feature is known as *Install-On-First-Use*.

The .AAS file holds that advertisement information specific to the package you've deployed. It also contains the hard-coded path to the package you've specified. This is why you cannot easily change the path to a package once you've deployed it via Software Installation policy. This .AAS file must be regenerated and the path to the package that is referenced in the GPC portion of the GPO must also be updated.

The **\Microsoft\Windows NT\Secedit** Folder   Stores a file called GptTmpl.inf. This file holds various computer security settings, defined under the Computer Configuration ➢ Policies ➢ Windows Settings ➢ Security Settings portion of the GPO. You can also set up these settings in advance and deploy them *en masse* using the techniques described in Chapter 8.

The **\Scripts\Shutdown** Folder   Contains the instructions for which shutdown scripts to run and, optionally, the actual files used for computer shutdown scripts. The instructions as to which scripts will run and where the scripts are stored are held in a file called scripts. ini, within this folder. It can be of any scripting file type (that the ShellExecute process can run), including .BAT, .CMD, .VBS, .JS, and others. You'll see how to use this in Chapter 8.

The **\Scripts\Startup** Folder   Contains the instructions for which startup scripts to run and, optionally, the actual files used for computer startup scripts. The instructions as to which scripts will run and where the scripts are stored are held in a file called scripts.ini, within this folder. It can be of any scripting file types (that the ShellExecute process can run), including .BAT, .CMD, .VBS, .JS, and others. You'll see how to use this in Chapter 8.

The \User Folder   This folder contains the settings for the User side of the Group Policy coin, including logon and logoff scripts, pointers to applications that are published or assigned, and Registry settings. Depending on the options used on each GPO, it represents what is in the \User folder under the computer side of the GPT.

The Registry.pol File   Holds the Registry settings set in User Configuration ➢ Policies ➢ Administrative Templates, as well as settings for Software Restriction Policy under User Configuration ➢ Policies ➢ Windows Settings ➢ Security Settings ➢ Software Restriction Policies.

The \Applications Folder   Stores pointer files called .AAS files for applications deployed with Group Policy Software Installation.

The \Documents and Settings Folder   Contains a file called Fdeploy.ini, which stores applicable Folder Redirection settings. You can learn more about Folder Redirection in Chapter 10, "The Managed Desktop, Part 1: Redirected Folders, Offline Files, and the Synchronization Manager."

The \Microsoft\IEAK Folder   Stores files to represent the changes made in User Configuration ➢ Policies ➢ Windows Settings ➢ Internet Explorer Maintenance.

The \Microsoft\RemoteInstall Folder   Stores Oscfilter.ini, which specifies Group Policy Remote Installation Services settings. Remote Installation Services isn't used anymore. Its successor, Windows Deployment Services, doesn't use this entry.

The \Scripts\Logon Folder   Contains the instructions for which logon scripts to run and, optionally, the actual files used for user logon scripts. The instructions as to which scripts will run and where the scripts are stored are held in a file called scripts.ini, within this folder. Can be of any acceptable file type, including .BAT, .VBS, .JS, and others—and, with Windows 7 and later, PowerShell scripts. You'll see how to use this folder in Chapter 12, "Finishing Touches with Group Policy: Scripts, Internet Explorer, Hardware Control, Printer Deployment, Local Admin Password Control."

The \Scripts\Logoff Folder   Contains the instructions for which logoff scripts to run and, optionally, the actual files used for user logoff scripts. The instructions as to which scripts will run and where the scripts are stored are held in a file called scripts.ini, within this folder. Can be of any acceptable file type, including .BAT, .VBS, .JS, and others. You'll see how to use this folder in Chapter 12.

Group Policy Settings Storage

As I've indicated, Group Policy settings, the things that you set when you're editing a GPO, are stored within one-half of the GPO—either the GPC or the GPT. The decision as to which is used to store a given setting varies with the size of the data being stored. Typically, because Active Directory is not designed for storing large blocks of data, those settings that require big chunks of stuff are stored in the GPT instead of the GPC.

But it really does vary by each CSE. Table 7.1 indicates where each CSE stores its settings.

TABLE 7.1 Client-side extensions and their storage locations

Client-side extension	Storage location	Comments
Wireless	Stored in AD, under the GPC container for a given GPO, within the path CN=wireless,CN=Windows, CN=Microsoft,CN=Machine.	Wireless policies are stored in AD as objects of the class msieee80211-Policy. This class is supported only in AD domains of Windows Server 2003 and newer AD domains. So, even though this CSE is on Windows XP, the policy must still be defined in domains that have that minimum schema level. Note that there is also a required schema update to support the enhanced Wireless policy that's only supported on Windows Vista and later clients. This is further explained in Chapter 8.
Folder Redirection	Stored in SYSVOL, under the GPT container for a given GPO. Folder Redirection policy is stored in a file called fdeploy.ini in the subfolder User \Documents and Settings within the GPT.	
Administrative Templates Policy	Stored in SYSVOL, under the GPT container for a given GPO. Administrative Templates policy is stored in a file called registry. pol, which can be defined per user and per computer. Within a given GPT, if you've defined both user and computer Administrative Templates policy, you will see a registry.pol file under both the user and machine subfolders.	If the GPO was created with an older GPMC, then you'll see ADM files for any given GPO that are stored with the GPO in the GPT. Note that ADMs can also be added with the updated GPMC, but not usually. In both cases, you'll find ADMs in a folder called ADM, off the root of the GPT for a given GPO. Thus, each GPO that sets Administrative Templates policy will store its own copy of the ADM files used to edit it, even if they are the same as another GPO. Note that GPOs do not store ADMX files within the GPO, as they are with ADMX files. See the previous chapter for all the gory details.

TABLE 7.1   Client-side extensions and their storage locations *(continued)*

Client-side extension	Storage location	Comments
Disk Quota	Stored in SYSVOL, under the GPT container for a given GPO. Disk quota policy is also stored in registry.pol; however, you'll only find it in the copy of registry.pol stored under the machine folder, as this is a per-machine policy only.	
QoS Packet Scheduler	Stored in SYSVOL, under the GPT container for a given GPO. QoS policy is also stored in registry.pol; however, you'll only find it in the copy of registry.pol stored under the machine folder, as this is a per-machine policy only.	
Startup/Shutdown and Logon/Logoff Scripts	Stored in SYSVOL under the GPT container for a given GPO. Machine-specific scripts are stored in the machine\scripts\startup and machine\scripts\shutdown folders. User-specific scripts are stored in the user\logon and user\logoff folders.	Note that script files themselves do not have to be stored in SYSVOL. You can reference scripts located anywhere on your network, as long as they are accessible to the computer or user. The scripts.ini file found in the computer\scripts folder and user\scripts folder in SYSVOL contains the actual references to any scripts that you've defined.
Internet Explorer Maintenance and Zone Mapping	Stored in SYSVOL under the GPT container for a given GPO. Specifically, IE Maintenance settings are stored in the GPT under the \User\Microsoft\IEAK folder.	Basic "branding" settings are stored in a file under this folder called install.ins. Security zone settings are stored in a subfolder called Branding and are stored as .INF files.
Security Settings	Stored in SYSVOL under the GPT container for a given GPO. Security settings are stored in the Machine\Microsoft\Windows NT\SecEdit folder in a file called GptTmpl.inf.	The format of this file is identical to those created when you use the MMC Security Templates editor to create a Security Template. The exception to this is Software Restriction Policy, which is stored in the registry.pol file.

TABLE 7.1   Client-side extensions and their storage locations *(continued)*

Client-side extension	Storage location	Comments
Software Installation	Stored in both the GPC and the GPT. Within the GPT, deployed package information is stored under the container machine (or user) \Applications, within an Application Advertisement file, or AAS file. Within the GPC, a special object of class packageRegistration is created for each application deployed. This object can be found in the GPC for a GPO under machine (or user)\Class Store\ Packages.	packageRegistration objects found in the GPC contain information such as the path to the .MSI file, any transforms (modifications) that have been selected, and whether the application is published or assigned. (See Chapter 11 for more details.)
IP Security	IPsec policy is a special case. Settings are stored as special objects strictly in Active Directory but *not* within the GPC. Namely, IPsec policy settings are stored under the CN=IP Security, CN=System container within a domain. Therefore, IP Security settings are stored domain wide and can be referenced by any GPO in the domain. When you *assign* a particular IPsec policy to a GPO, an additional object is created within the GPC of the GPO— specifically, an ipsecPolicy object is created under the Machine\Microsoft\Windows container under the GPO. This object stores the association between the available IPsec policies in the domain and that GPO.	

TABLE 7.1 Client-side extensions and their storage locations *(continued)*

Client-side extension	Storage location	Comments
Windows Search (Vista+ only)	Stored in SYSVOL, under the GPT container for a given GPO. Windows Search policy is also stored in `registry.pol`; however, you'll find it only in the copy of `registry.pol` stored under the machine folder, as this is a per-machine policy only.	
Offline Files (Vista+ only)	Stored in SYSVOL, under the GPT container for a given GPO. Offline Files policy is also stored in `registry.pol`, within both the machine and user folders, depending on which side is being set.	
Deployed Printer Connections (Vista+ only)	Stored in AD, under the GPC container for a given GPO, within the path `CN=PushedPrinterConnections`, `CN=Machine` (or `CN=User`).	Deployed Printer Connection policies are stored in Active Directory as objects of class `msPrint-ConnectionPolicy`. This class is only supported in Windows Server 2003 R2 (and later) domains. Therefore, this feature, Deployed Printer Connection policy, can be defined only in domains that have that minimum schema level.
Enterprise QoS Policy (Vista+ only)	Stored in SYSVOL, under the GPT container for a given GPO. Enterprise QoS policy is also stored in `registry.pol`, within both the machine and user folders, depending on which side is being set.	
802.3 and Wireless Policy (Vista+ only)	Both of these policy areas are stored in AD in the GPC but require a schema update.	See Chapter 8 for the required schema update to support both Wired and Wireless schema policy.

Understanding Group Policy Version Numbers

If you take a peek at any GPO's `gpt.ini`, you'll see its version number. You can see the same number if you dive into the GPC using the directions found in the sidebar "Using LDP to See the Guts of a GPC" earlier in this chapter.

So, how is that version number constructed? The idea is that it's a 32-bit value where the most significant 16 bits are the user value and the least 16 significant bits are the computer value.

In decimal, here's the formula:

Version = (Number of user section changes × 65536) + (Number of computer section changes)

So, when you create a new GPO, the version number is 0. Click Edit over a GPO and begin editing, and then the numbers start going up. Enable a policy on the Computer side and click OK. Then set it back to Not Configured. That'll add 2 to the version number. Edit a policy on the User side and click OK. That'll add 65536. Change it back to Not Configured and it'll add another 65536. The version number's largess isn't super important here. That is, it doesn't matter how huge the number gets.

So, how do we, in our daily lives, see the version number? In the Details tab of any Group Policy, as shown here.

In this example, we can see that the User side has been modified twice (2 × 65536) and the computer version has been modified three times (add 3 to that). So, if we peek in the `gpt.ini` of this GPO, the version number should be 131075.

Again, both the GPC and the GPT store the version number for the GPO. But, as we've described, there could be situations where replication hasn't finished and the GPC and GPT version numbers don't agree. In that case, the GPMC (which shows the version numbers via the Details tab of a GPO) will *always* use the GPC version number as the final reference but will give you a message if these are not in sync.

The Group Policy team at Microsoft has an interesting blog entry on the subject. Check it out at `http://tinyurl.com/2gfmmg`.

Verifying That GPCs and GPTs Are in Sync

The two pieces of information that make up a GPO are GPCs and GPTs:

- GPCs are stored in the Active Directory database and are replicated via normal Active Directory replication.
- GPTs are stored in the SYSVOL folders of every Domain Controller and are replicated using FRS replication.

Here's the trick: Back when Group Policy was born (back in Windows 2000 days), Group Policy wouldn't apply on a machine unless both the GPC and the corresponding GPT were synchronized.

Synchronization means that the versionNumber attribute on the GPC object for a given GPO needs to be the same as the versionNumber key found in the GPT's gpt.ini file for that same GPO.

For all versions of Windows after Windows 2000, the GPC and GPT no longer need to have the same version for Group Policy processing of that GPO to occur on a client machine.

Recall that both the GPC and GPT are originally written to the PDC emulator by default. Once they're written, the goal is to replicate the GPC and GPT to other Domain Controllers. With just one Domain Controller in a domain, there are no replication issues because there are no other Domain Controllers to replicate to; it's all happening on one system. But when multiple Domain Controllers in a domain enter the picture, things get a little hairier. This is because normal Active Directory replication and FRS replication are on completely independent schedules (though under normal circumstances, they take the same path).

An administrator can create or modify a GPO, and the GPC might not replicate in lockstep with the files in the GPT. This isn't normally a problem because, over time, all Domain Controllers end up with exactly the same information in their replicas of the Active Directory database and in their SYSVOL folders. But during a given replication cycle, there may be intervals when the GPC and GPT *don't* match on a particular Domain Controller.

Additionally, the GPC and GPT share a *version number* for each half of the GPO—Computer and User. The version numbers are incremented each time the GPO is modified and are included in the list of attributes that are replicated to other Domain Controllers. Remember in Chapter 1 I stated that if a specific GPO doesn't change, the default for the client is to not process the GPO. After all, if nothing's changed, why should the client bother? The client uses these version numbers to figure out if something has changed. The client keeps a cache of the GPOs it last applied along with the version number within the Registry. Then, if the GPO has been touched, say, by the modification of a particular policy setting or the addition of a policy setting, the version number of the GPO in Active Directory changes. The next time the client tries to process GPOs, it will see the change, and the client will download the entire GPO again and embrace the revised instruction set! So, version numbers are important for clients to recognize that new instructions are waiting for them.

So far, so good. Now, there's a bit more to fully understanding version numbers. According to Microsoft, here's the secret to figuring out whether a GPO is going to process on a workstation:

- Both the GPC and GPT parts of the GPO must be present on the Domain Controller the workstation uses to log on.

- If the client processing Group Policy is Windows 2000, then the GPC and GPT must have the same version number.

- If it's XP or later, the GPC and GPT can have different version numbers and Group Policy processing will still occur.

- In all cases, if the version number held in the GPC or GPT is different than the version number held in the Registry from the last time that GPO was processed, Windows considers that a change has occurred and goes ahead and processes policy.

The main point here is that for early versions of Windows (Windows 2000), Group Policy processing would fail if the version numbers didn't match up. Now, it doesn't matter if the version numbers are the same or not. If they are different, Group Policy will try to reapply on the client machine.

It's still important for the two pieces to synchronize at some point. If they aren't synchronized at some point, this implies that one piece doesn't have the latest information for settings. At some point, the replication should complete and all Domain Controllers will have the same Group Policy data; then, machines and users will get the latest version of Group Policy settings. If this *never* happens, you have a problem with your domain and should follow up with the tools and techniques in the following sections.

Version numbers aren't the only thing that would constitute a "change." A change could also be a removed GPO (or added GPO), a change in security group membership, and a new or removed WMI filter. Also, it's important to point out that if one GPO changes, the CSEs that process that GPO must reprocess *all* GPOs in the list, not just the one that changes.

Changing the Default Domain Controller for the Initial Write of Group Policy Objects

GPOs are, by default, created and edited using the Domain Controller that houses the PDC emulator. Of course, over time, those new and modified GPOs make it to all other Domain Controllers using replication. However, sometimes in large Active Directories, you may not want to leverage the PDC emulator as the "go to" place when creating and editing Group Policy.

Imagine this scenario: there is one domain but two sites—the United States and China. The U.S. site holds the Domain Controller designated as the PDC emulator. Therefore, whenever an administrator in China writes a GPO, they must connect across the WAN to write the GPO and then wait for the entire GPO (both the GPC half and the GPT half) to replicate to their local Domain Controllers.

You can, however, specify which Domain Controller to write the GPO to, which is a two-step process:

1. Select a Domain Controller to be *active*. Open the GPMC, right-click the domain name, select Change Domain Controller, and select the Domain Controller to which you want the Group Policy to apply.

2. Create your GPO and edit it. At the root node of the Group Policy snap-in, choose View ➢ DC Options. Now you have the following three choices:

   "The one with the Operations Master token for the PDC Emulator."   The default behavior, this option finds the PDC emulator in the domain and writes the GPO there. Replication then occurs, starting from the PDC emulator.

   "The one used by the Active Directory snap-ins."   Since you just selected the *active* Domain Controller, this is your best bet because you know exactly which Domain Controller you selected in the first step.

   "Any available Domain Controller."   The odds are good that you will get a local Domain Controller to write to (based on Active Directory site information), but not always.

Therefore, the best course of action is to select the Domain Controller you want to initially write to and then select "The one used by the Active Directory snap-ins" to guarantee it.

Sound like too much work for each GPO? Alternatively, you can create a GPO that affects those accounts that can create GPOs. Use the policy setting located at User Configuration ➢ Policies ➢ Administrative Templates ➢ System ➢ Group Policy named **Group Policy Domain Controller Selection**. You'll get the same three choices listed earlier. Set it, and forget it.

Here's a parting tip for this sidebar. Often, GPOs are created with the additional intent to use security groups to filter them. After creating a GPO with the GPMC, an administrator will also create some security groups using Active Directory Users and Computers to filter them. However, after creating the GPO and the security groups, many admins are surprised that the security groups they want to add "now" are not immediately available. This is because the GPMC is using one Domain Controller and the Active Directory Users and Computers tool is using another Domain Controller. Therefore, replication of the group has not yet reached the Domain Controller the GPMC is using! So the tip is to manually focus both the Active Directory Users and Computers and/or GPMCs explicitly on the same Domain Controller (or just the PDC emulator) before creating GPOs where you'll also want to filter using groups.

Using *Gpotool.exe*

If you suspect you're having problems with keeping your GPTs and GPCs in sync, you can use Gpotool.exe, a tool included with the Windows 2003 Resource Kit. At last check, it can be found here:

www.microsoft.com/download/en/details.aspx?id=17657

You can run Gpotool.exe on any Domain Controller to verify that both the GPCs and GPTs are in sync and have consistent data among all Domain Controllers in the domain.

Running the Gpotool command without any parameters verifies that all GPCs and GPTs are synchronized across all Domain Controllers in the domain. If you are having trouble with only one GPO, however, you might not want to go through the intense process required to check every GPO's GPC and GPT on every Domain Controller. Instead, you can use the /gpo: switch, which allows you to specify a friendly name or GUID of a GPO you are having problems with. For instance, if you suspect that you are having problems with the "Hide Mouse Pointers Option / Restore Screen Saver Option" GPO we created in Chapter 1, you can run Gpotool /gpo:Hide to search for all GPOs starting with the word *Hide*. In Figure 7.11, I'm running Gpotool without any switches, which will buzz through all GPOs.

FIGURE 7.11   Use Gpotool to see if your GPCs and GPTs are synchronized across your Domain Controllers.

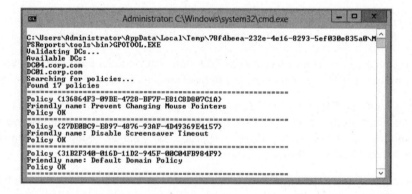

 To specifically verify any specific Group Policy Object, just name it, putting any GPOs with names that have spaces in quotes. Like Gpotool /gpo:"GPO ABC" Note that the /gpo: switch is case sensitive. For instance, running Gpotool x/gpo:"GPO ABC" is different from running GPOTOOL /gpo:"GPO abc".

This example shows when things are going right. This next example (see Figure 7.12) shows when things might be wrong.

FIGURE 7.12   Gpotool has found trouble in paradise.

In this example, we are verifying the synchronization of the GPO named "Broken2." In this case, the versions between the GPC and GPT do not match. You can see this when comparing what the tool calls the DS version with the SYSVOL version. The DS version represents the GPC, and the SYSVOL version represents the GPT.

Before panicking, recall that this "problem" might not actually be a problem. Remember, the GPC and the GPT replicate independently. The DC our clients are currently using might have received the SYSVOL (GPT) changes before the Active Directory changes (GPC), or vice versa. Wait a little while and the two versions might converge. If they do not converge, this problem could indicate either Active Directory or File Replication Service (FRS) replication issues.

Here are some additional tips about using Gpotool:

- Running Gpotool on a large domain with lots of GPOs can take a long time and bog down your Domain Controller performance. If possible, run Gpotool only after hours, when the fewest number of people will be affected.

- If you must run it during working hours, you might want to specify the /dc: option and specify to check only the GPOs on the PDC emulator (the place where GPOs are initially born and initially modified). If you're going to have a problem, it's quite likely to be initially pinpointed on this key Domain Controller.

- Gpotool has one extra superpower: it can also verify the underlying ACLs of the GPT part of a GPO. Recall that the GPT is the part of the GPO that lives in SYSVOL. To perform this extra check, you need to specify it on Gpotool's command line as Gpotool /checkacl. By default, this test is not run because it is additionally time and resource intensive. There is one key point about the /checkacl switch: it checks only the ACL inheritance flag on the SYSVOL Policies folder itself, not the ACLs on the individual folders that contain the guts of the GPO. So, if you have a specific permissions problem on the folder containing a GPO, the /checkacl switch won't help you ferret that out.

- One caveat about Gpotool—it only checks to see if the version numbers are the same between the GPC and GPT. It does not check to see, say, if all the files that are supposed to be in the GPT are there. If you're having FRS replication problems, for example, only some of the GPT files may have replicated to a given DC, and Gpotool won't tell you that if it finds that the gpt.ini file has the information it needs.

Using Windows 10's GPMC's Status Tab

Windows 10 GPMC has a feature that is more or less a graphical version of Gpotool. You find it within the GPMC by clicking on the domain name; in our case, Corp.com. A tab called Status can be seen in Figure 7.13.

FIGURE 7.13   The Status tab in the GPMC, when clicking upon the domain level

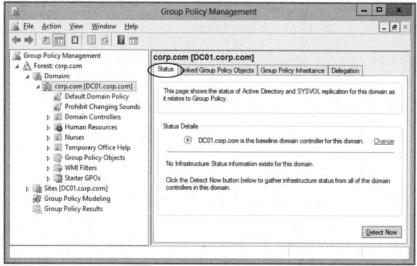

Like gpotool, this Status tab's activities don't run all the time. It's manually kicked off by you by clicking the Detect Now button.

If you're working through the book, then you'll only have exactly one Domain Controller and that means zero replication problems. However, in real life if you have multiple Domain Controllers, you can click the Detect Now button every once in a while to gauge what the overall replication status is.

Again, the Status tab will only show problems, so no news is good news. Additionally, one extra superpower that Status tab has over its older GPOtool cousin is that it is looking for exact matches inside the GPT part of the Group Policy Object. It does this by calculating a file hash for the whole GPT directory. If anything is different on any Domain Controllers, then the Infra Status will send up a red flag that there's a problem with the Group Policy Object.

Additionally, the Status tab can be found when you click on a specific GPO, as seen in Figure 7.14. Instead of checking all of your GPOs, you can click the Detect Now button and that one GPO's status is checked against your Domain Controllers. Handy, if you have a suspect GPO and want to verify that its guts are at least the same on all DCs.

FIGURE 7.14   Status—You can quickly check the status of just one GPO by first clicking on the GPO and then checking the Status tab.

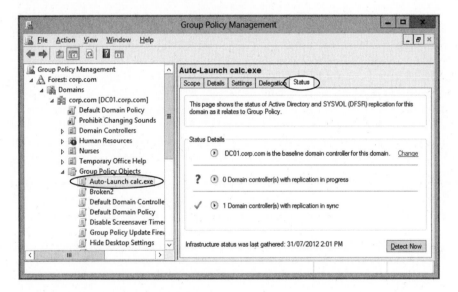

Isolating Replication Problems

If you use GPOtool or the GPMC's Status tab and an error comes back, you'll likely want to drill down and figure out exactly what's wrong.

Remember, Group Policy is two parts: GPC (the Active Directory record) and GPT (the file-based part). You can try to see if Active Directory replication is working (and, hence, if GPC replication is working) by performing several "litmus tests." Here are some examples:

- Create a new GPO in the Group Policy Objects container. Just create it with no policy settings, and don't link it anywhere.

- Create a new OU in Active Directory Users and Computers or the GPMC.

- Add a new user in Active Directory.

In each case, you want to see if these objects are replicated to other DCs. After creating your objects on one Domain Controller, use the Active Directory Users and Computers and/or GPMC to check other Domain Controllers. Right-click the domain and choose another Domain Controller.

If these litmus tests fail, you can try to force replication using Active Directory Sites and Services. If you need extra-strength replication, Repadmin can help force replication in multiple ways.

For some great Repadmin tips, see this Microsoft blog:

http://blogs.technet.com/b/askds/archive/2009/07/01/
getting-over-replmon.aspx

You can try to see if SYSVOL replication is working via FRS (and, hence, if GPT replication is working) by throwing any file—say, a Readme.txt file—into the SYSVOL share of any Domain Controller and seeing if it is replicated to the other Domain Controllers' SYSVOL shares. If it is not automatically copied to the other Domain Controllers, test each machine's connectivity using the ping command.

Microsoft has two tools, Ultrasound and Sonar, that are available on the Microsoft website. At last check, Sonar can be found at http://tinyurl.com/5ouk9 and Ultrasound, which came after Sonar, can be found at http://tinyurl.com/odgu. General FRS troubleshooting and information can be found at http://tinyurl.com/cofstj as of this writing.

The Microsoft Knowledge Base articles Q221112, Q221111, Q272279, and Q229928 are good starting points to learn more about FRS and how to troubleshoot SYSVOL replication problems by debugging FRS. See Q229896 and Q249256 for details on how to debug Active Directory replication.

Twenty-First-Century Replication Using DFSR Instead of FRS

Most Active Directory implementations don't have any issues with the in-the-box replication that has been there since Windows 2000 days: File Replication Service (FRS). FRS is what makes the stuff in SYSVOL "magically" go from Domain Controller to Domain Controller.

However, there is some percentage of customers who have major issues with FRS. FRS kind of "freaks out" when tasked with replicating large files or lots and lots of files. And GPOs (GPTs, really) are just files that FRS moves around. And if FRS freaks out, you could find yourself knee-deep in the ghastly world of morphed files, journal wraps, and a whole lot of other scary errors and conditions.

To that end, it's possible to migrate the SYSVOL replication from FRS to DFSR, the more modern "DFS Replication." You can only opt to do this if all your DCs in a domain are Windows Server 2008 or higher, and once it's performed, there's no going back.

On this page:

http://blogs.technet.com/askds/archive/2009/05/01/sysvol-migration-from-frs-to-dfsr-whitepaper-released.aspx

(http://tinyurl.com/yc634nr), you can find a variety of useful documents to help make that transition:

- SYSVOL Replication Migration Guide: FRS to DFS Replication (TechNet Version)
- SYSVOL Replication Migration Guide: FRS to DFS Replication (Word Doc Version)

You can also find the following "possibly useful" (their words, not mine) documents:

- Verifying File Replication during the Windows Server 2008 DFSR SYSVOL Migration— Down and Dirty Style
- DFSR SYSVOL Migration FAQ: Useful Trivia That May Save Your Follicles
- KB968733 (Hotfix for Migration under Certain RODC Scenarios)
- KB967326 (Hotfix for Migration under Disjoint Name Space Scenarios)

In short, that web page is your "go to" home for FRS-to-DFSR conversion.

Death of a GPO

As you saw in Chapter 2, there are three ways to stop using a GPO at a level in Active Directory. One way is to "Delete the link" to the GPO at the level being used in Active Directory. In the swimming pool analogy, we're removing the tether to our child in the pool, but we're leaving the object swimming in the pool should other levels want to use it.

The other is "Disabling the link." This leaves the tether in place but basically prevents the level from receiving the power within the OU.

The final way to stop using a GPO is to delete it. With the GMPC, you can delete a GPO only by traversing to the Group Policy Objects node, right-clicking it, and choosing Delete, as you saw back in Figure 2.6. But, again, be careful; other levels of Active Directory (including those in other domains and forests) might be using this GPO you're about to whack.

WARNING As we've discussed in previous chapters, cross-domain linking of GPOs is a no-no. And, if you whack the GPO in the source domain, it won't clean up links to *other* (target) domains.

How Client Systems Get Group Policy Objects

The items stored on the server make up only half the story. The real magic happens when the GPO is applied at the client, usually a workstation, although certainly servers behave in the same way. Half of Group Policy's usefulness is that it can apply equally to servers and desktops and laptops. As each new operating system comes out, you can control and configure more stuff than ever. So the details in the following sections are for all "target" machines—regardless of what operating system they run.

When Group Policy is deployed from on high to client systems, the clients always do the requesting. Group Policy's guts are called Client-Side Extensions (CSEs). It's the client who is in charge—not the Domain Controllers. This is why, when the chips are down and things aren't going right, you'll need to check out the target machines' event log (among other troubleshooting areas) to help uncover why the client isn't picking up your desires.

The Steps to Group Policy Processing

Group Policy processing on the client is broken down into roughly two parts. The first part is called "core" or "infrastructure" processing. We'll break it down for Windows XP and modern Windows (like Windows 7, 8.1, and 10, which are all the computer types you're likely to have).

Core Processing for XP Machines

During the core processing stage of Group Policy processing, Windows tries to accomplish a number of tasks. Chief among them:

- To determine if the connection to the Domain Controller is over a slow link
- To discover all of the GPOs that apply to the computer or user

- To discover which Client-Side Extensions have to be called
- To discover whether anything has changed (GPOs, security group memberships, WMI filters) since the last processing cycle
- To create the final list of GPOs that need to be applied

In order to perform these tasks, Windows requires that a number of network protocols be successfully passed between the client and the DC that it's paired with. These protocols, and their usages, are listed here:

- ICMP for slow link detection
- RPC (TCP port 135 and some random port that's greater than port 1024) for authentication to AD
- LDAP (TCP port 389) for querying AD to determine the list of GPOs, group membership, WMI filters, and so on
- SMB (TCP port 445) for querying the GPT in SYSVOL

If the client tries to get to the server and any of the protocols listed here are blocked (usually by a firewall), then all Group Policy processing will fail. Thus it's important that Windows clients have unimpeded access to all potential domain controllers that will respond to authentication and Group Policy requests for these protocols. It's not uncommon for a firewall to be turned on by default on a Windows server, but all the right rules are in place (by default) to allow Group Policy requests to successfully pass.

Another point to note is that Group Policy processing in Windows XP runs within the privileged Winlogon process. Winlogon is a system service and thus has the highest level of privilege within Windows. For that reason, poorly behaved CSEs could potentially crash Windows. This didn't happen often (or ever, to my knowledge, but it was certainly possible). As we'll see in the next section, the inner workings of Group Policy have changed in Windows Vista and later, as we'll see with the *Group Policy Client Service.*

Once the core steps are complete, each CSE DLL is called by the Winlogon process, in the order in which they are registered in the Registry under:

```
HKLM\Software\Microsoft\Windows NT\CurrentVersion\Winlogon\GPExtensions
```

(with the exception of Administrative Templates policy, which always runs first), and each CSE processes the GPOs that have been discovered during the core processing cycle.

Core Processing for Modern Windows

So, Microsoft made a significant change to the Group Policy processing engine in Windows Vista. And that work was maintained in Windows 7 and later (like Windows Server 2008 and Windows Server 2008 R2, Windows 8, etc.). That being said, Windows 8 and later has an "ever so miniscule" tweak, which I'll note in a moment, that Windows 10 maintains.

Starting with Windows Vista, Microsoft moved the engine from Winlogon into a separate service called the *Group Policy Client Service,* or just the Group Policy service for short. This service is "hardened" so that even an administrator cannot easily stop it dead.

This is probably a good thing because there are not too many situations where you'd want to disable Group Policy processing completely. As I mentioned, a normal administrator cannot easily stop the Group Policy Client Service. If you go into the Services MMC snap-in and highlight the service, you'll notice that the options to stop and start the service are grayed out. It takes a bit of work to stop the service, and when you do, it will automatically restart itself after a short period of time. However, if you want to see this in motion, here is the general process.

If you want to try this out (just for fun), you'll need to start the Windows Task Manager and select the Services tab. Locate the service called gpsvc, and note the process ID listed next to it, as shown in Figure 7.15. Next, move to the Processes tab in Task Manager and locate the svchost process with the same process ID as the gpsvc entry. Highlight that svchost process and click the End Process button to end the service.

FIGURE 7.15   Viewing the Group Policy Client Service process

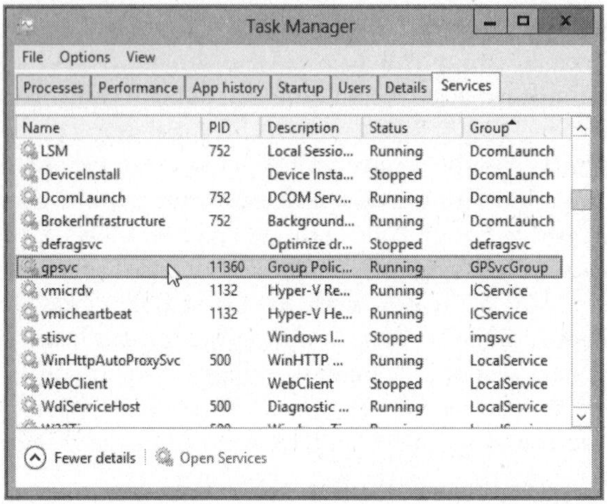

That's all there is to it!

Except in a few minutes, you'll see the gpsvc spring back to life. Which is good.

In Windows 8 and later, the Group Policy service comes alive when the computer is starting up and when the user logs on. Then, after 10 minutes of Group Policy "inactivity," the Group Policy service shuts it down. This is to save battery life on mobile devices like tablets and laptops (though, honestly, I can't see that it would improve battery life all that much). Note that on Windows Server 2012 and later, the Group Policy service does not have this twist because it is active all the time.

In Chapter 3, "Group Policy Processing Behavior Essentials," in the section "Windows 8, 8.1, and Windows 10 Group Policy: Subtle Differences" I talked about a subtle change in the Group Policy engine between Windows 7, 8, 8.1, and 10.

Windows 8 and Later Slow Link Detection

Earlier, I described how Windows XP used ICMP to detect if it was on a slow link.

Windows Vista and later use a completely different mechanism to detect a slow link. Instead of using ICMP pings, Windows Vista and later rely on the Network Location Awareness (NLA) service that is part of the operating system. The NLA service uses a series of higher-level communications with Domain Controllers to determine when a Domain Controller is available and at what link speed the computer has. The NLA process is more dynamic and thus is able to inform the Group Policy engine when a Domain Controller becomes available (where the previous mechanism was not). Because of this, it's important to understand under what scenarios GP processing occurs when NLA detects that a DC is available. We'll discuss this later in the chapter, in the section "Troubleshooting NLA."

If you were to use Windows Server 2012 or later as your Group Policy client over a slow link, it would detect slow links the same way. But how often are you using Windows Server 2012 or later to dial up from a hotel room or over a slow 3G connection?

Client-Side Extensions

When a Group Policy "clock" strikes, the client's Group Policy engine springs into action to start processing your wishes. The GPOs that are meant for the client are downloaded from Active Directory, and then the client pretty much does the rest.

When GPOs are set from on high, usually not all policy setting categories are used. For instance, you might set up an Administrative Templates policy but not an Internet Explorer Maintenance policy. The client is smart enough to know which policy setting groups affect it.

This happens during the "core" processing part of Group Policy. During this core processing cycle, the client queries Active Directory to get its list of GPOs, figures out which ones actually apply to it, and makes a list of the CSEs that will need to run for the GPOs found. Once all that core work is done, each CSE is called in turn to do its thing.

CSEs are really DLLs (Dynamic Link Libraries) that perform the Group Policy processing. These DLLs are called by the system Winlogon process (or the Group Policy Client Service in Windows Vista and later). These CSEs are automatically registered in the operating system and are identified in the Registry by their GUIDs.

Additional CSEs can be created by third-party programmers who want to control their own aspects of the operating system or their own software. See the sidebar "Group Policy Software Vendors with Their Own CSEs" for a sampling.

In Windows 2000, the OS shipped with nine CSEs. In Windows XP and 2003, Microsoft added two more, for a total of 11 CSEs. With Windows XP SP2, another CSE was added. Vista added an additional five for a total of 17.

Once the Group Policy Preferences Extensions are added to Windows XP or Windows Vista, another 21 are added. Or, since they're in the box for Windows Server 2008, the in-the-box number jumps to a total of 38.

Windows 7 contains the 38 CSEs just mentioned plus another five, specific to Windows 7.

Windows 8 adds another three specific to Windows 8 and Windows Server 2012. Windows 8.1 added one more.

Group Policy Software Vendors with Their Own CSEs

The whole idea of CSEs is that if you have a great idea, and if you want to make it happen via Group Policy, you can do it. Several vendors have stepped up and created their own CSEs that implement their ideas. Come to www.GPanswers.com for the latest look at products that have their own CSEs. As of this writing, the following companies have products with their own CSEs:

Specops Software   Specops Software has products that feature CSEs:

Specops Deploy   This CSE enables you to perform several Group Policy Software Installation tasks (discussed in Chapter 11) that you can't natively perform. For instance, you can distribute software to users and computers that are already logged on as well as get a detailed log of which computers received software.

Specops Inventory   This product performs hardware and software inventory via the Group Policy engine and provides detailed reports of what software and hardware your enterprise is using. You can find it here: www.specopssoft.com/products/specops-inventory.

PolicyPak Software   The PolicyPak suite of tools can be found at www.PolicyPak.com. You learned all about PolicyPak Admin Templates Manager in Chapter 4, PolicyPak Preferences Manager in Chapter 5, and PolicyPak Application Manager in Chapter 6. All PolicyPak components are true CSEs and honor all the constructs of Group Policy.

Windows 10 didn't add any more, but they did remove one for some old Internet Explorer functionality that isn't supported anymore.

To take a look at the CSEs on a workstation or server, follow these steps:

1. On Windows WIN10, log on as Administrator.

2. Type **regedit** to open the Registry Editor, shown in Figure 7.16.

3. Drill down into HKLM ➢ Software ➢ Microsoft ➢ Windows NT ➢ Current Version ➢ Winlogon ➢ GPExtensions. Here you will find a list of GUIDs, each representing a CSE.

Let's take a look at the next sections to understand precisely what we're seeing.

CSEs for XP Machines

Figure 7.16 shows a sample CSE and the settings for disk quotas. See Table 7.2 for the CSEs listed by GUID, the functions they perform, and the associated DLLs. Note that a particular DLL can be responsible for more than one function.

FIGURE 7.16 The Client-Side Extension DLLs actually perform the GPO processing.

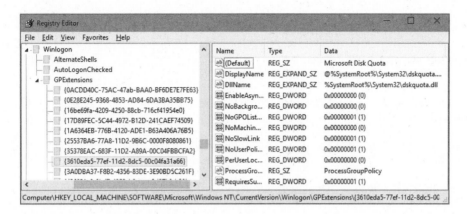

TABLE 7.2 GUIDs, their functions, and their corresponding DLLs for pre–Windows Vista machines

CSE GUIDs	Function	DLL
{C6DC5466-785A-11D2-84D0-00C04FB169F7}	Software deployment	`appmgmts.dll`
{3610EDA5-77EF-11D2-8DC5-00C04FA31A66}	Disk quotas	`dskquota.dll`
{B1BE8D72-6EAC-11D2-A4EA-00C04F79F83A}	EFS recovery	`scecli.dll`
{25537BA6-77A8-11D2-9B6C-0000F8080861}	Folder redirection	`fdeploy.dll`
{A2E30F80-D7DE-11d2-BBDE-00C04F86AE3B}	Internet Explorer settings	`iedkcs32.dll`
{e437bc1c-aa7d-11d2-a382-00c04f991e27}	IP security	`gptext.dll`
{35378EAC-683F-11D2-A89A-00C04FBBCFA2}	Registry settings (Administrative Templates)	`userenv.dll`
{42B5FAAE-6536-11D2-AE5A-0000F87571E3}	Scripts	`gptext.dll`

TABLE 7.2 GUIDs, their functions, and their corresponding DLLs for pre–Windows Vista machines *(continued)*

CSE GUIDs	Function	DLL
{827D319E-6EAC-11D2-A4EA-00C04F79F83A}	Security	scecli.dll
{0ACDD40C-75AC-47ab-BAA0-BF6DE7E7FE63}	Wireless (802.11x) (Windows XP+ only)	gptext.dll
{4CFB60C1-FAA6-47f1-89AA-0B18730C9FD3}	Internet Zone Mapping (Windows XP+)	iedkcs32.dll
{426031c0-0b47-4852-b0ca-ac3d37bfcb39}	Quality of Service Packet Scheduler (Windows XP+ only)	gptext.dll
None	Software Restriction (Windows XP+ only)	None
None	Remote Installation Services (RIS) (Windows Server 2003 and earlier)	None

Why don't all CSEs have DLLs? Neither Remote Installation Services (RIS) nor Software Restriction polices require CSEs to be associated with DLLs. RIS is active *before* the operating system is. Software Restriction policies don't require CSEs because they "tag along" on the functionality of another CSE.

CSEs for Windows Vista and Windows Server 2008 Machines

See Table 7.3 for the Windows Vista–specific CSEs listed by GUID, the functions they perform, and the associated DLLs. Again, all the pre-Vista CSEs are also on Windows Vista, so they're not repeated in this table since they're already listed in Table 7.2. Note that a particular DLL can be responsible for more than one function.

Offline Files existed before Windows Vista (in Windows 2000 and Windows XP), but in Vista it became its own CSE.

TABLE 7.3 CSE GUIDs, their functions, and their corresponding DLLs that exist only on Windows Vista and Server 2008 machines

Class ID	Function	DLL
{7933F41E-56F8-41d6-A31C-4148A711EE93}	Windows Search	srchadmin.dll
{7B983727-8072-47ea-83A4-39C6CE-25BAE6}	Offline Files (see note)	cscobj.dll
{8A28E2C5-8D06-49A4-A08C-632DAA493E17}	Deployed Printer Connections	gpprnext.dll
{B587E2B1-4D59-4e7e-AED9-22B9DF11D053}	802.3 Policy	dot3gpclnt.dll
{FB2CA36D-0B40-4307-821B-A13B252DE56C}	Enterprise QoS	gptext.dll

CSEs for Windows 7 and Windows Server 2008 R2 Machines

It's true that Windows 7 and Windows Server 2008 R2 (and Windows Server 2008 for that matter) all have the Group Policy Preferences CSEs. Table 7.4 lists the specific CSEs that only they have.

TABLE 7.4 Windows 7 and Windows Server 2008 R2 CSE GUIDs, their functions, and their corresponding DLLs that exist only on Windows 7 and Windows Server 2008 R2 machines

GUID	Function	DLL
{7B849a69-220F-451E-B3FE-2CB811AF94AE}	Internet Explorer 8 User Accelerators	iedkcs32.dll
Cc76f039F3-ABA2-41DB-97F2-81E2C5DBFC5D}	Internet Explorer 8 Machine Accelerators	iedkcs32.dll
{CDEAFC3D-948D-49DD-AB12-E578BA4AF7AA}	TCP/IP v6 handlers	gptext.dll
{e437bc1c-aa7d-11d2-a382-00c04f991e27}	IPsec Security Policies	polstore.dll
{fbf687e6-f063-4d9f-9f4f-fd9a26acdd5f}	Connectivity Platform/DirectAccess	gptext.dll

CSEs for Windows 8 and Windows Server 2012 (and Later)

Windows 8 added three specific CSEs that Windows 7 didn't have. You can see these CSEs in Table 7.5. Two are for some new Remote Desktops (Terminal Services) functionality. The other one is for a Windows Server 2012 (and later) feature called Dynamic Access Control that enables admins to specify who can see what kinds of files that live on the server.

TABLE 7.5 Windows 8 (and later) and Windows Server 2012 (and later) CSE GUIDs, their functions, and their corresponding DLLs

GUID	Function	DLL
{16be69fa-4209-4250-88cb-716cf41954e0}	Central Access Policy Con-figuration	auditcse.dll
{4bcd6cde-777b-48b6-9804-43568e23545d}	Remote Desktop USB Redi-rection	TSUsbREdirectionGroupPoli-cyExtension.dll
{4D2F9B6F-1E52-4711-A382-6A8B1A003DE6}	Remote Desktops "Work-space" (TS Workspace)	tsworkspace.dll
{BA649533-0AAC-4E04-B9BC-4DBAc03e025B12}	Windows To Go Startup Options	pwlauncher.dll
{C34B2751-1CF4-44F5-9262-C3FC39666591}	Windows To Go Hibernate Options	pwlauncher.dll

CSEs for Windows 8.1 and Windows Server 2012 R2 (and Later)

Windows 8.1 and Windows Server 2012 R2 got one new CSE for Work Folders. Its GUID is {4d968b55-cac2-4ff5-983f-0a54603781a3} and its DLL is WorkFolderGPExt.dll.

Windows 10 and Windows Server 2016 got zero additional CSEs and carried forward the work done in Windows 8 and Windows 8.1.

Additional CSEs for the Group Policy Preferences

These are the Group Policy preference extensions, which we explored in Chapter 5, "Group Policy Preferences."

Again, to be super clear: they're already in the box for Windows 7 and later (including Windows Server 2008 and later). That being said, they're downloadable for Windows XP, Windows 2003, and Windows Vista. They won't install on Windows 2000.

In Table 7.6, you can see the list of Group Policy Preferences CSEs, their GUIDs, and the corresponding functions.

There's no mistake in Table 7.6. All the new Group Policy preference extensions use the *same* DLL, but if you look at the actual Registry entry, you'll see that each one's Displayname key notes the DLL name (gppprefcl.dll) with an entry point ID.

TABLE 7.6 CSE GUIDs, their functions, and their corresponding DLLs that exist only when you add the Group Policy preference extensions

CSE GUIDs	Function	DLL
{0E28E245-9368-4853-AD84-6DA3BA35BB75}	Group Policy Environment	gpprefcl.dll
{17D89FEC-5C44-4972-B12D-241CAEF74509}	Group Policy Local Users and Groups	gpprefcl.dll
{1A6364EB-776B-4120-ADE1-B63A406A76B5}	Group Policy Device Settings	gpprefcl.dll
{3A0DBA37-F8B2-4356-83DE-3E90BD5C261F}	Group Policy Network Options	gpprefcl.dll
{5794DAFD-BE60-433f-88A2-1A31939AC01F}	Group Policy Drive Maps	gpprefcl.dll
{6232C319-91AC-4931-9385-E70C2B099F0E}	Group Policy Folders	gpprefcl.dll
{6A4C88C6-C502-4f74-8F60-2CB23EDC24E2}	Group Policy Network Shares	gpprefcl.dll
{7150F9BF-48AD-4da4-A49C-29EF4A8369BA}	Group Policy Files	gpprefcl.dll
{728EE579-943C-4519-9EF7-AB56765798ED}	Group Policy Data Sources	gpprefcl.dll
{74EE6C03-5363-4554-B161-627540339CAB}	Group Policy INI Files	gpprefcl.dll
{91FBB303-0CD5-4055-BF42-E512A681B325}	Group Policy Services	gpprefcl.dll

TABLE 7.6 CSE GUIDs, their functions, and their corresponding DLLs that exist only when you add the Group Policy preference extensions *(continued)*

CSE GUIDs	Function	DLL
{A3F3E39B-5D83-4940-B954-28315B82F0A8}	Group Policy Folder Options	gpprefcl.dll
{AADCED64-746C-4633-A97C-D61349046527}	Group Policy Scheduled Tasks	gpprefcl.dll
{B087BE9D-ED37-454f-AF9C-04291E351182}	Group Policy Registry	gpprefcl.dll
{BC75B1ED-5833-4858-9BB8-CBF0B166DF9D}	Group Policy Printers	gpprefcl.dll
{C418DD9D-0D14-4efb-8FBF-CFE535C8FAC7}	Group Policy Shortcuts	gpprefcl.dll
{E47248BA-94CC-49c4-BBB5-9EB7F05183D0}	Group Policy Internet Settings	gpprefcl.dll
{E4F48E54-F38D-4884-BFB9-D4D2c57e029C18}	Group Policy Start Menu Settings	gpprefcl.dll
{E5094040-C46C-4115-B030-04FB2E545B00}	Group Policy Regional Options	gpprefcl.dll
{E62688F0-25FD-4c90-BFF5-F508B9D2E31F}	Group Policy Power Options	gpprefcl.dll
{F9C77450-3A41-477E-9310-9ACD-617BD9E3}	Group Policy Applications	gpprefcl.dll

Inside CSE Values

For each CSE, several values can be set (or not). Not all CSEs use these values. Indeed, Microsoft does not support modifying them in any way.

You can see a list of the values here:

http://msdn.microsoft.com/en-us/library/aa373494%28VS.85%29.aspx

(shortened to http://tinyurl.com/y9ydmcx).

They are presented at that URL for your own edification, but in most circumstances, you should not be modifying them unless explicitly directed to do so by Microsoft Product Support Services (PSS).

Note that many of the options listed at that URL (for example, NoSlowLink, NoBackgroundPolicy, and NoGPOListChanges) can be set within the Computer Configuration ➢ Policies ➢ Administrative Templates ➢ System ➢ Group Policy section of a GPO. When they are set through policy, the values shown in the Registry value column listed in the table are ignored.

I hope you won't have to spend too much time in here. But I present this information so that if you need to debug a certain CSE, you can go right to the source and see how a setting might not be what you want.

Remember that most of these settings are either established by the system default or can be changed. You can modify the settings yourself—such as the ability to process over slow links, the ability to be disabled, or the ability to be processed in the background—using the techniques described near the end of Chapter 3.

Where Are Administrative Templates Registry Settings Stored?

This section is the mini-review of everything you already learned in Chapter 6. But because Administrative Templates is one of the most commonly applied policy settings, let's take a minute to learn how the client processes Administrative Templates.

Here, we're just talking about proper "policies" and not "preferences" (which are discussed in Chapter 5).

Remember, Group Policy's strength is that the "in-the-box" policy settings do not tattoo the Registry. That is, once a setting is applied, it applies only for that computer or user. When the user or computer leaves the scope of the GPO (for example, when you move the user from the **Human Resources Users** OU to the **Accounting Users** OU), the Registry settings that applied to the user are removed and the new Registry settings then apply. Similarly, if a computer was in, say, the **Human Resources Computers** OU and moved to the **Accounting Computers** OU, the settings linked to within the **Human Resources Computers** OU would peel off.

Administrative Templates Group Policy settings are usually stored in the following locations:

User Settings   HKEY_CURRENT_USER\Software\Policies

Computer Settings   HKEY_LOCAL_MACHINE\Software\Policies

Alternatively, some applications may choose the following locations:

User Settings `HKEY_CURRENT_USER\Software\Microsoft\Windows\CurrentVersion\`
`Policies`

Computer Settings `HKEY_LOCAL_MACHINE\Software\Microsoft\Windows\`
`Currentversion\Policies`

> **NOTE** Microsoft is encouraging third-party developers to write their applications so that they utilize `HKEY_CURRENT_USER\Software\Policies` or `HKEY_LOCAL_MACHINE\Software\Policies` to become Group Policy enabled.

Knowing how this works helps us understand why each version of Windows increases the number of Administrative Templates policy settings that can apply to it. It's quite simple: the specific program that's targeted for the policy setting looks for settings at these two Registry locations. Sometimes that application is one we overlook a lot— `Explorer.exe`! It's `Explorer.exe` that can "understand" these policy settings and then do something with that directive. The same is true for Internet Explorer or the Windows Firewall; as they grow up and get "newer" with each operating system, so do the number of items that can be managed.

This also answers the question of why, for instance, Windows XP machines seem to "overlook" policy settings that are designed only for, say, Windows 10 computers.

In short, "older" operating systems (which are really just applications themselves) don't know to "look" for new policy settings (even though those settings are written into the target machine's Registry). So, all operating systems (which, again, are really applications) that can download the policy settings *do*. But who cares? If an older system applies a policy setting, the Registry is modified and then it's generally ignored by the applications running on it. "Old" Windows just doesn't know to look for the new Registry changes. Occasionally, with the release of a service pack, the application in question might get a new lease on life and understand some new policy settings—because the application has now been updated to look for them in the Registry. This has already happened for Explorer, Software Update Services, Windows Media Player, and Office, to name a few.

Because the settings inside Administrative Templates are written to only these four locations, we are free from the bonds of having our Registries tattooed. The Administrative Templates CSE (`Userenv.dll`) applies the settings placed in any of these four locations to the current mix of user and system.

As you move users in and out of OUs, or change group membership, the settings that apply to them change as well. Under the covers, this process is a bit more subtle. The way the nontattooing behavior works is that when Registry settings are first applied, they are merged into files that are stored on the computer in per-computer and per-user areas— each file is called `ntuser.pol`. The next time the Administrative Templates CSE runs, it looks into these stored files and makes a list of all the policy settings that exist in the four "special" keys I mentioned previously (at the beginning of this section). It then deletes all those settings, as specified by that file. Then, the CSE re-creates that file with all the new

Administrative Templates settings that currently apply to the computer or user. Finally, it applies those values to the computer or user portions of the Registry.

Any settings that are outside the four "special" locations are *not* covered by this removal process, and thus you have the tattooing behavior.

 Again, if you use PolicyPak Application Manager (explored in Chapter 6) to deliver settings to your applications, it can properly revert the setting when the policy no longer applies. Therefore, no ugly tattooing.

Why Isn't Group Policy Applying?

At times, you set up Group Policy from on high and your users or workstations do not receive the changes. Why might that be the case?

First, remember how Group Policy is processed:

- The GPO "lives" in the swimming pool in the domain.

- The client requests Group Policy at various times throughout the day.

- The client connects to a Domain Controller to get the latest batch of GPOs. (Group Policy isn't somehow "pushed" from on high.)

- If it's status quo, meaning that:

    - Nothing has changed inside the GPO (based on changed version number).

    - The location of the user or computer hasn't changed in Active Directory.

    - The user or computer hasn't changed group memberships.

    - Any WMI filters set on the GPO haven't changed.

    Then, the default behavior is to not reprocess the GPOs (though this can be changed, as explored in Chapter 3).

- If there is a change (with respect to any of these previous bullet points), then all applicable CSEs reprocess all applicable GPOs.

That's the long and the short of it.

Now, if you think all this is happening properly, try to answer the questions in the following sections to find out what could be damming the proper flow of your Group Policy process.

Reviewing the Basics

Sometimes, it's the small, day-to-day things that prevent a GPO from applying. By testing a simple application that has normal features, you can often find problems and eliminate them, which allows Group Policy to behave the way you expect.

Is the Group Policy Object or Link Disabled?

Recall from Chapter 1 that there are two halves of the Group Policy coin: a Computer half and a User half. Also recall that either portion or both can be disabled. Indeed, a GPO itself can be fully disabled (see Figure 7.17).

FIGURE 7.17   You can disable the entire GPO if desired.

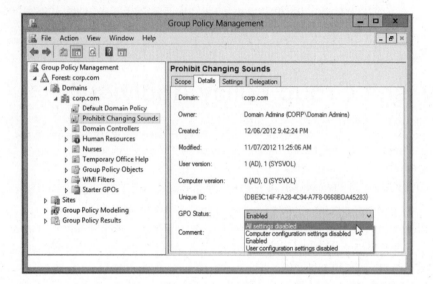

Check the GPO itself or any related GPO links. Click the Details tab and check the GPO Status setting. If it is anything other than Enabled, you might be in trouble.

If you change the status of the GPO, that status changes on all links that use this GPO.

Are You Sure about the Inheritance?

Recall that Group Policy flows downward from each level—site, domain, and each nested OU—and is cumulative. Also recall that in XP, there is only one Local Group Policy for a computer, which is applied first.

And, in Windows Vista and later there are three levels of MLGPOs. See Chapter 1 for the full rundown. Remember, in MLGPOs it's a "last written wins" policy.

Are You Trying to Apply Policy to a Group Inside an OU?

This bears repeating: you can't just plunk an NT-style/Active Directory group that contains users into an OU and expect them to get Group Policy. Group Policy doesn't work that way; you can only apply Group Policy directly to users or computers in an OU—not a group.

Multiple Group Policy Objects at a Level

Also recall that there can be many GPOs at any level, which are applied in the reverse order—that is, from bottom to top, as described in Chapter 2. Since any two (or more) GPOs can contain the same or even conflicting settings, the last-applied GPO wins. If you mean for one GPO to have higher precedence, use the Up and Down buttons to manipulate the order. Remember, the GPO with the *lowest* number gets the *highest* priority. Confusing, I know, but that's the deal.

Examining Your Block Inheritance Usage

The GPMC gives you a quick view of all instances of Block Inheritance with the Blue Exclamation Point (!). Remember, once you select to block inheritance, *all GPOs* from higher levels are considered null and void—not just the one policy setting or GPO you had in mind to block. It's as if you were starting from a totally blank slate. Therefore, whenever you block inheritance, you must start from scratch—either creating and linking new GPOs or linking to existing GPOs already swimming in the GPOs container.

Examining Your "Enforced" Usage

Conversely, be aware of all your "Enforce" directives. The Enforce icon is a little lock next to the GPO link. Enforce specifies that the policy settings selected and contained within a *specific* GPO cannot be avoided at any inherited level from this point forward. Note that Block Inheritance applies to a container in Active Directory (for example, a domain or an OU), whereas Enforced applies to a GPO link. So if you have a GPO linked to four containers in Active Directory, you could have only one of those links "Enforced," two of them, or all of them (or none!). When Block Policy Inheritance and Enforce are seemingly in conflict, Enforce always wins. Recall that Enforce was previously known as No Override in old-school parlance.

Are Your Permissions Set Correctly?

Recall from Chapter 2 that two permissions—"Read" and "Apply Group Policy"—must be set so that the affected user processes a specific GPO. By default, Authenticated Users have these two rights, but you can remove this group and set your own filtering via the Security Filtering section on the Scope tab of a GPO link.

In Chapter 2, I showed you two ways to filter:

* Round up only the users, computers, or security groups who *should* get the GPO applied to them.

* Figure out who you *do not* want to get the GPO applied to them, and use the "Deny" attribute over the "Apply Group Policy" right.

When all is said and done, users will need both "Read" and "Apply Group Policy" permissions on the GPO itself to apply GPOs. And, you can prevent a GPO from applying by setting "Deny" access on one or the other of these two rights. However, if you're going to use this technique, best practices dictate to always try to deny access on "Apply Group Policy" and not "Read."

Try to always deny "Apply Group Policy" (and not "Read") because later that user might need to be able to modify the GPO. And without read access, they cannot modify it.

Having only one of those permissions means that Group Policy will not apply when processing is supposed to occur. Additionally, make sure to remember that the "Deny" attribute always trumps all other permissions. If an explicit "Deny" attribute is encountered, it is as if it were the only bit in the world that matters. Therefore, if a specific GPO is not being applied to a user or a group, make sure that "Deny" isn't somehow getting into the picture along the way.

Any use of the "Deny" attribute is not displayed in the Security Filtering section of the Scope tab, so you have no notification if it's being used. This is a common reason for Group Policy not applying; the old-school way to perform Group Policy filtering involved heavy use of the "Deny" attribute, and now the GPMC will not easily display this fact unless you use the Group Policy Results Wizard (or GPResult.exe).

Advanced Inspection

If you've gone through the basics and nothing is overtly wrong, perhaps a more subtle interaction is occurring. See if any of the following questions and solutions fit the bill.

Is Windows XP (and Later) Fast Boot On?

The default behavior of Windows XP (and later) is different from its original brother—Windows 2000. The default behavior of Windows 2000 is to process GPOs in the foreground (at computer startup or user logon) synchronously. That is, for the policy settings that affect a Windows 2000 computer (which will take effect at startup), every GPO is applied—local, site, domain, and each nested OU—even before the user has the ability to press Ctrl+Alt+Del to log on. Once the user logs on, the policy settings that affect the User side are applied—local, site, domain, and each nested OU—before the user's Desktop is finally displayed and they can start working.

This usually isn't too much of a problem for the policy settings within GPOs that affect computers, but it can seriously affect your user's experience if enabled for user policy processing. Even *after* a user is logged on, GPOs can suddenly be downloaded and policy settings start popping up and changing the user's environment.

Moreover, as I stated in Chapter 3, by default several key items in Windows XP and later take between two and three reboots to become effective. To that end, I suggest you modify the default behavior. The strongest advice I can give you is to create and link a new GPO at the domain level. Name your new GPO something like "Force XP and later machines to act like Windows 2000," and enable the **Always wait for the network at computer startup and logon** policy setting. Then, select Enforced so it cannot be blocked.

To find this policy setting, drill down through the Computer Configuration ➤ Policies ➤ Administrative Templates ➤ System ➤ Logon branch of Group Policy. (For more information, see Chapter 3.)

Therefore, if you have erratic Group Policy application (especially for Software Installation, Folder Redirection, or Profile settings), see if the Windows XP and later default of Fast Boot is still active.

Are Both the GPC and GPT Replicated Correctly?

As stated in the first part of this chapter, Group Policy is made up of two halves:

- The GPC, which is found in Active Directory and replicated via normal Active Directory replication

- The GPT, which is found in the SYSVOL share of one Domain Controller and replicated via FRS to other Domain Controllers

Both the GPC and GPT are replicated independently and can be on different schedules before converging.

Use the techniques described earlier in conjunction with the GPMC's Status tab, Gpotool and Repadmin, to diagnose issues with replicating the GPC and GPT.

Did You Check the DNS Configuration of the Server and Client?

In order for the GPC and GPT to replicate correctly, the DNS structure must be 100 percent kosher at all times—both on the server and at the client. If you suspect that the GPC and GPT are not being replicated correctly, you might try to see if the DNS structure is the way you intend. If it is, I don't recommend you rip it all up and reconfigure it if everything else is working. The Microsoft Knowledge Base article at:

http://support.microsoft.com/kb/291382/en-us

provides a good foundation for understanding how to create a healthy DNS infrastructure.

In some cases, one Domain Controller might not be providing Group Policy to your clients. In the next section, I'll show you how to find out if your clients are really logged on and, if so, what Domain Controller the computer and user are using for logon.

Are You Really Logged In?

Sometimes you can "feel" logged in without actually being logged in. It's a big difference. For instance, if you log on with cached credentials and the Domain Controller didn't return the Kerberos ticket to you, you aren't logged in at all. You just "feel" logged in.

So, to ensure that your user and computer are really logged on the network, you can count on just one tool—Kerbtray (or the command-line equivalent, klist.exe). Kerbtray and klist are found in the Windows 2003 Resource Kit and are small enough to be put on a USB stick and run on a suspect machine. When you run Kerbtray, it puts a little icon in the notification area. If the computer and user have Kerberos tickets, the icon turns green and you know you're really logged on. However, if the Kerbtray returns a graphic of a bunch of loose keys (that, in my opinion, look like question marks), as shown in Figure 7.18, you know you're not logged on and, hence, not downloading the most recent GPOs. Again, if you were really logged on, the graphic would be a green ticket.

FIGURE 7.18 The *LOGONSERVER* variable cannot be trusted. Here, the network is offline, but the *LOGONSERVER* still reports the (wrong) Domain Controller. Use Kerbtray instead, which is shown running in the notification area.

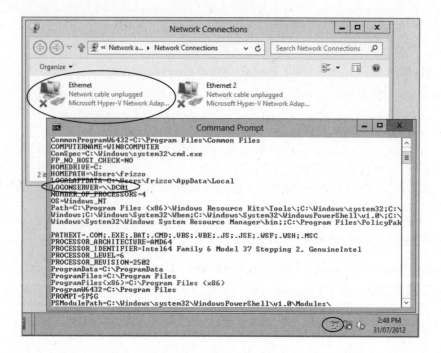

In Figure 7.18, you can see several things:

- The computer's network cards are disconnected (as shown in the Network Connections window).

- The *LOGONSERVER* variable is set to a Domain Controller (as shown in the CMD prompt window). Feel free to say out loud, "If the network card is off, this is bloody impossible."

- Kerbtray, thankfully, returns that icon of a bunch of loose keys verifying that we're not logged on.

So, to find out if you're logged on when using a Windows XP or later computer, it's "Kerbtray or the highway." Once you've validated with Kerbtray that the computer has really logged on, you can *then* use the *LOGONSERVER* variable to determine which Domain Controller the Windows XP or later machine has used—that way, you'll know the truth: whether or not you're really logged on.

Did Something Recently Move?

If a computer account or a user account is moved from one OU to another, Windows (all versions) can wait as long as 30 minutes to realize this fact. Once it does, it might or might not apply background Group Policy processing for another 90 minutes or more! Running gpupdate will not help.

However, if you're expecting a specific setting to take effect on a user or computer that has moved more than 150 minutes ago, you'll then need to figure out if the move has been embraced by the Domain Controller the workstation used to authenticate. (See the previous section for information about how to determine the Domain Controller via the *LOGONSERVER* variable, but make sure you're really logged on!)

You can then fire up Active Directory Users and Computers and connect to the Domain Controller in question, as shown in Figure 7.19.

FIGURE 7.19 You can always manually connect to a Domain Controller to see if Active Directory has performed replication.

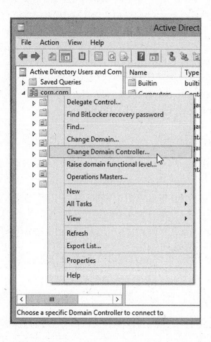

If the target computer's local Domain Controller does not know about the move, you might want to manually kick off replication using Active Directory Sites and Services. If the target computer's local Domain Controller *does* know about the move, you might want to try logging the user off and back on or restarting the computer. Although using gpupdate (for Windows XP and later) to refresh the GPO is a good option, it's best to log off and/or reboot the machine to guarantee that the computer will perform the initial policy processing, as described in Chapter 3.

Running gpupdate /force on a Windows 7 and later machine is supposed to "jump-start" the machine and/or user account into recognizing that it has moved around in Active Directory. I've done extensive testing. It works pretty well with Windows 7 and Windows 8—but even then, I've seen it work and also fail to work. For 100 percent certainty, just reboot the machine.

Is the Machine Properly Joined to the Domain?

This is weird, so stay with me. In short, sometimes you can find yourself in a situation where the computer has de-joined from the domain. This can happen in virtual environments, especially in testing, when a client computer (say, Windows 10) was joined at one time but the virtual machines (VMs) were "rolled back" to an earlier date and time.

There are other circumstances, too, that could cause computer de-joining, but that one happens to me all the time. And here's the weird part: if you try to log on, sometimes it just inexplicably *works*—even though it shouldn't.

But then, as in Stephen King's *Pet Sematary*, suddenly things feel "not quite right." You get User-side policy, and maybe even Computer-side policy—for a while. Then you might lose Computer-side policy. GPresult /R starts to fail with strange error messages.

In short, you're not joined anymore, *and you don't even know it*.

What's happened is that the *computer trust*, also known as a *secure channel*, is broken. To see if the computer trust (secure channel) to the domain is damaged, you can use NLTEST, which is available here: http://tinyurl.com/4uhnu. The verification syntax is nltest /sc_query:domain_name. If the test passes, then you're kosher. If not, the fix is simple: just de-join and rejoin the device to the domain.

Is Loopback Policy Enabled?

Enabling Loopback policy will turn Group Policy on its ear: Loopback forces the same user policy settings for everyone who logs on to a specific computer. If you're seeing user policy settings apply but not computer policies, or if things are applying without rhyme or reason, chances are Loopback policy is enabled. Review Chapter 4, "Advanced Group Policy Processing," to see in depth how it works, when you should use it, and how to turn it off.

In Windows XP, determining you are in Loopback mode is difficult. In Windows Vista and later, it's a little easier. Look for Event ID 5311 in the Windows Group Policy event logs. In the guts of the event, you'll see if Loopback policy processing mode is set to Replace, Merge, or not enabled.

How Are Slow Links Being Defined, and How Are Slow Links Handled?

If you notice that Group Policy is not applied to users coming in over a slow link, remember the rules for slow links:

- Registry and security settings are always applied over slow (and fast) links.

- EFS (Encrypting File System), IPsec (IP Security) policies, Work Folder settings, Windows Search, and Offline Files settings are *always* applied over slow links. You cannot turn off this behavior, even though settings found under the Computer Configuration ➤ Policies ➤ Administrative Templates ➤ System ➤ Group Policy branch imply that you can. This is a bug in the interface, as described in Chapter 3.

- By default, Disk Quotas, Folder Redirection, Internet Explorer settings, old Deployed Printer Connections, and Software Deployment are not applied over slow links. Updated and new logon scripts are also not downloaded over slow links. You can change this default behavior under Computer Configuration ➤ Policies ➤ Administrative

Templates ➢ System ➢ Group Policy, as described in Chapter 3. Note that there is a difference between processing scripts policy and running scripts. The scripts themselves run only during logon and boot (computer startup or user logon), but the *updating* of the list of scripts that needs to run can be done in the background. That updating is what I'm referring to here.

Additionally, you can change the definition of what equals a slow link. By default, a slow link is 500Kb or less. You can change the definition for the user settings in User Configuration ➢ Policies ➢ Administrative Templates ➢ System ➢ Group Policy ➢ **Group Policy Slow Link Detection** and for the computer settings in Computer Configuration ➢ Policies ➢ Administrative Templates ➢ System ➢ Group Policy ➢ **Group Policy Slow Link Detection**. Figure 7.20 shows the user settings. If Group Policy is not being applied to your slow-linked clients, be sure to inspect the slow link definition to make sure they fit.

Last, don't forget about your broadband users on DSL or cable modem. Those speeds are sometimes faster than 500Kb and sometimes slower than 500Kb. This could mean that your broadband users might get GPOs on weekends but not when logged on during peak usage times. Therefore, if this happens, set the definition of slow link up or down as necessary.

Finally, it should be noted that if you set the slow link threshold to 0, the client will always assume it's on a fast link.

FIGURE 7.20   Make sure you haven't raised the bar too high for your slower-connected users to receive Group Policy.

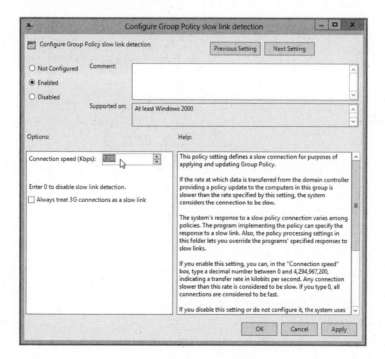

Troubleshooting NLA

If you're working on a Windows Vista or later client, you may need to determine if a Network Location Awareness (NLA) refresh has occurred. As I mentioned earlier, NLA is the service that replaces ICMP slow link detection when determining link speed and Domain Controller availability when your client is Windows Vista and later.

If the Domain Controller is not available to the client, either because the client is remote and not connected to the company network or because the Domain Controller is simply not available, Group Policy processing will fail.

When the Domain Controller becomes available again, NLA will detect its presence and trigger an immediate request to perform a background refresh of Group Policy. But here's the trick: NLA will perform this refresh *only* if the previous refresh of Group Policy has failed. If the previous Group Policy refresh succeeded, and *then* the Domain Controller becomes unavailable and *then* available again (before the next Group Policy processing cycle), NLA will not trigger a background refresh. You will be able to see NLA-based Group Policy refresh by looking at the Group Policy Operational Log, described later in the section "Troubleshooting Using the Group Policy Operational Log." The event will look identical to that shown in Figure 7.21.

FIGURE 7.21   Viewing an event indicating an NLA-based Group Policy refresh

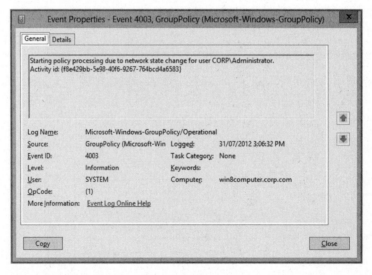

Note that it took as long as 10 minutes for NLA to complete its detection of the Domain Controller and trigger a background Group Policy processing cycle in my testing. So, don't expect an NLA-based Group Policy refresh to happen immediately after your DC becomes available. Depending on your system and network, your mileage may vary.

Are the Date and Time Correct on the Client System?

Time differences greater than five minutes between the client system and the validating Domain Controller will cause Kerberos to not permit the logon. If you don't have Kerberos, you've got a logon problem, and that's going to yield a Group Policy problem.

Are Your Active Directory Sites Configured Correctly?

Sometimes Group Policy won't apply if your client isn't in a properly defined Active Directory site (that has IP information associated with it). With that in mind, check the subnet the client is on, and verify that it is correctly associated to an Active Directory site and that the site has Domain Controller coverage.

Did You Check the DNS Configuration of the Client?

One of the most frequently encountered problems with Active Directory networks is that things just "stop working" when DNS gets out of whack. Specifically, if you're not seeing Group Policy apply to your client machines, make sure their DNS client is pointing to a Domain Controller or other authoritative source for the domain. If it's pointing to the wrong place or not pointing anywhere, Group Policy will simply not be downloaded. As a colleague of mine likes to say, "Healthy DNS equals a healthy Active Directory."

Moreover, since Windows 2003 and its multiple forests with cross-forest trusts, Group Policy could be applying from just about anywhere and everywhere. It's more important than ever to verify that all DNS server pointers are designed properly and working as they should. For instance, if clients cannot access their "home" Domain Controllers while leveraging a cross-forest trust, they won't get Group Policy.

Finally, to put a fine point on it, Group Policy leverages *only* the fully qualified name. It's not enough to verify that you can resolve a computer named WIN10 as opposed to WIN10.corp.com. The first is the NetBIOS name and *not* the fully qualified domain name. The second is the fully qualified domain name. If you find yourself in a DNS resolution situation where resolving the NetBIOS name will work but the fully qualified name will not work, you have a DNS problem that needs to be addressed.

Are You Trying to Set Password or Account Policy on an OU?

As you'll see in Chapter 8, certain Group Policy items, namely password and account policy, cannot be set at the OU level. Rather, these policy settings are only domain wide. The GUI lets you set these policy settings at the OU level, but they don't affect users or machines. Well, that's not true, as you'll see in Chapter 8, but for the purpose of troubleshooting, just remember that you can't have, say, six-character passwords in the **Sales** OU and 12-character passwords in the **Engineering** OU. It won't work. (You will see in Chapter 8 where password policy affects local accounts in an OU.)

Did Someone Muck with Security behind the Group Policy Engine's Back?

As you saw in Chapter 3, there are a number of ways to "go around" the back of the Group Policy engine. Remember, though, that these exploits require local administrative access. However, this implies that users with local administrative access can manually hack the Registry and return their systems to just about however they want. Then, as I've described, Group Policy will not reapply upon background refresh, logon, or reboot. It reapplies changes only when something related to Group Policy has changed, as previously mentioned.

The gpupdate command will refresh changed Group Policy as well, but its /force switch is quite powerful and will reapply all settings—even those that have not changed.

Is the Target Computer in the Correct OU? Is the Target User in the Correct OU?

This is my personal sore point. This is the one I usually check last, and it's usually what's at fault. That is, I've forgotten to place the user object or the computer object into the OU to which I want the GPO to apply. Therefore, the object isn't in the "scope" of where Group Policy will apply.

You can configure all the user or computer policy settings on an OU that you like, but, quite obviously, unless that user or computer object is actually *in* the OU, the target computer will not receive the message you're sending. And, no, you cannot just move a security group that contains the user or computer objects and plunk it in the desired OU. Group Policy doesn't work that way. That actual user or computer object needs to be in the site, domain, or OU that the GPO applies! And since no two objects can be in any two OUs at the same time, this can be a challenge.

Security groups are irrelevant—except for filtering.

Is There a Firewall on (or between) Your Domain Controllers?

All modern Windows operating systems ship with the firewall turned on.

This shouldn't normally be a problem; your Domain Controllers should automatically open up the correct ports when they're upgraded from a mere server to a Domain Controller. However, I have seen times when they haven't. In such a case, you might need to remove the Active Directory "role" and reinstall it to get the ports to open properly.

Likewise, if someone has put up a hardware firewall or some other software firewall barrier between your client and your Domain Controllers and it's blocking some of the core protocols required by the client to communicate with a Domain Controller, you won't be able to get the Domain Controller's attention, and hence you can't download Group Policy.

Did Someone Muck with the ACLs of the GPT Part of the GPO in SYSVOL?

There is very, very little reason to manually dig into the guts of the GPO within SYSVOL (that's the GPT part) and manually manipulate the file ACLs. However, uninitiated administrators will sometimes play—with nasty consequences. And, as stated earlier, Gpotool /checkacl won't validate the file ACLs on the GPO's GPT parts. In other words, if the ACLs on the GPT are damaged, your best bet is to whack the GPO and restore from backup. The restore process should create the GPO with the correct ACLs upon its re-creation. You can also try using the GPMC to simply make a modification to a damaged GPO's ACLs. Any change will do. By doing so, this can sometimes "re-synchronize" the ACLs on the GPC and GPT, though it depends on how badly the GPT's ACLs have been modified as to whether this method will work.

Client-Side Troubleshooting

One of the most important skills to master is the ability to determine what's going on at the client. By and large, the Group Policy Results tool, which you run from the GPMC, should give you what you need. However, occasionally, only trotting out to the client can truly determine what is happening on your client systems.

You could be roaming the halls, just trying to get the last glazed doughnut from the break room, when someone snags you and plops you in their seat for a little impromptu troubleshooting session. They want you to figure out why Group Policy isn't the same today as it was yesterday or why they're suddenly getting new or different settings.

The following sections will describe the various means for determining the RSoP (Resultant Set of Policy) while sitting at a client or using some remote control mechanism such as VNC (Virtual Networking Client), or even using Windows's own Remote Assistance.

As you saw in Chapter 2, the GPMC has two tools to help you tap into this data: Group Policy Results and Group Policy Modeling. However, you have other client-side tools at your disposal. Additionally, I'll describe how to leverage a function to determine a target user's and computer's RSoP remotely.

Let me add a word about general Group Policy troubleshooting techniques before you run off and try to troubleshoot things. There is a good progression to things that is worth following:

1. The first step you should take is to use the RSoP capabilities I describe in the next sections to make sure you know what's happening—which GPOs are applying, which aren't, and why.

2. Once you've got that under your belt and still can't find the problem, the next step is to dive into the logs—starting with the Application Event Log on the problem client.

3. Then proceed to the Group Policy event logs for Windows Vista and later (described later in the section "Troubleshooting Deep Dive").

4. If step 3 doesn't yield results, and you still can't find the problem, progress to CSE-specific logs (if available).

This approach will minimize the time you spend solving a problem and leaves the most complex troubleshooting tasks as a last resort.

RSoP for Windows Clients

In this section, we'll explore several ways to grab an RSoP from a client.

In Chapter 2 (and to a lesser extent in this chapter), we talked about the idea of opening up the Windows Firewall to let us (the admins) see what's happening on users' machines.

The idea is that if you can't remotely grab an RSoP using any of the techniques described here, then you'll need to be able (from your machine) to talk to *their* machine.

To do this, at a minimum you need to open up ports 135 and 445, which is precisely what **Windows Firewall: Allow Inbound Remote Administration Exception** does. Again, this policy setting is located in Computer Configuration ➤ Policies ➤ Windows Firewall ➤ Domain Profile.

GPResult Command-Line Utility

You can run GPResult when you're sitting at a user's desktop or at your own desktop, or you can run it remotely and pretend to be that user.

If you're running it while sitting at someone's desktop, you'll likely use the following options:

- /r is for regular output. (Note: Not required on Windows XP machines.)

- /H:File.html will output the results as HTML to a file named File.html. This output will show the Group Policy Preferences items in the report (Windows 7 and later).

- /X:File.xml will output the results as XML to a filename.

- /v is for verbose mode. It presents the most meaningful information.

- /z is for zuper, er, super-verbose mode. Based on the types of policy settings that affect the user or computer, it displays way more information than you'll likely ever want to see.

- /scope user limits the output to the User-side policy settings, and /scope computer limits the output to the Computer-side policy settings.

WARNING   There was a change in GPResult.exe for Windows Vista and later: As a regular, nonelevated user running GPResult.exe in Vista and later, you will get only User-side results from the tool. If you attempt to report on Computer-side settings, you will get an Access Denied error until you run the command in an elevated context. Note that you could delegate specific users or groups the right to read this data using the GPMC.

You can mix and match the options. For instance, to display verbose output for the user section, you can run GPResult /v /scope user.

Here's the result of running GPResult /r while logged on to the WIN10 workstation (which is in the **Human Resources Computers** OU) as Frank Rizzo (who is in the **Human Resources Users** OU). Note that some of the display might be somewhat different from yours.

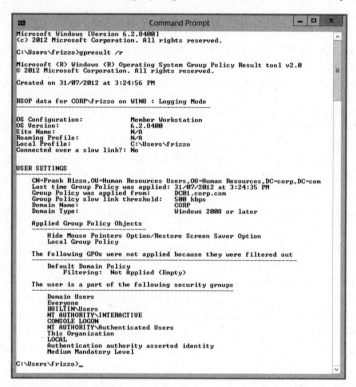

```
Microsoft Windows [Version 6.2.8400]
(c) 2012 Microsoft Corporation. All rights reserved.

C:\Users\frizzo>gpresult /r

Microsoft (R) Windows (R) Operating System Group Policy Result tool v2.0
© 2012 Microsoft Corporation. All rights reserved.

Created on 31/07/2012 at 3:24:56 PM

RSOP data for CORP\frizzo on WIN8 : Logging Mode
-------------------------------------------------

OS Configuration:           Member Workstation
OS Version:                 6.2.8400
Site Name:                  N/A
Roaming Profile:            N/A
Local Profile:              C:\Users\frizzo
Connected over a slow link?: No

USER SETTINGS
-------------
    CN=Frank Rizzo,OU=Human Resources Users,OU=Human Resources,DC=corp,DC=com
    Last time Group Policy was applied: 31/07/2012 at 3:24:35 PM
    Group Policy was applied from:      DC01.corp.com
    Group Policy slow link threshold:   500 kbps
    Domain Name:                        CORP
    Domain Type:                        Windows 2008 or later

    Applied Group Policy Objects
    -----------------------------
        Hide Mouse Pointers Option/Restore Screen Saver Option
        Local Group Policy

    The following GPOs were not applied because they were filtered out
    -------------------------------------------------------------------
        Default Domain Policy
             Filtering:  Not Applied (Empty)

    The user is a part of the following security groups
    ----------------------------------------------------
        Domain Users
        Everyone
        BUILTIN\Users
        NT AUTHORITY\INTERACTIVE
        CONSOLE LOGON
        NT AUTHORITY\Authenticated Users
        This Organization
        LOCAL
        Authentication authority asserted identity
        Medium Mandatory Level

C:\Users\frizzo>_
```

The first thing to note is that the GPResult /r output only shows the User side of Frank's story—and not the Computer side. We'll get to that weird part in a second.

Next, you can glean all sorts of juicy tidbits from GPResult. Here are the key areas to inspect when troubleshooting client RSoP:

- Find the "Applied Group Policy Objects" entries for the user and the computer. Remember that Group Policy is applied from the local computer first, then the site level, then the domain level, and then each nested OU. If a setting is unexpected on the client, use the provided information along with the Group Policy Object Editor to start tracking the errant GPO.

- Use the "Last time Group Policy was applied" entry to see the last time the GPO was applied—via either initial or background refresh processing. Use gpupdate to refresh this, and then ensure that the value is updated when you rerun GPResult.

- Use the spelled-out distinguished name of the computer and user objects (for example, CN=Frank Rizzo, OU=Human Resources Users, DC=corp, and DC=com) to verify that the user and computer objects are located where you think they should be in Active Directory. If they are not, verify the location of the user and computer accounts using Active Directory Users and Computers. You might need to reboot this client machine if the location in Active Directory doesn't check out. Note that this line is absent if you are logging in offline with cached credentials.

- Use "The user is a part of the following security groups" and "The computer is a part of the following security groups" sections to verify that the user or computer is in the groups you expect. Perhaps your user or computer object is inside a group that is denied access to either the "Read" or "Apply Group Policy" permission on the GPO you were expecting. Note that if you make a change to a computer's security group membership, Group Policy will not pick up that change unless you reboot the computer. There is no way around this, unfortunately. The same holds true for user group changes—the user will need to re–log on before the security group changes take.

- Find the "Connected over a slow link?" entry for the log and the "Group Policy slow link threshold" entries for both the user and computer. Remember that the various areas of Group Policy are processed differently when coming over slow links. (See Chapter 3.)

- Find the section "The following GPOs were not applied because they were filtered out" for both the User and the Computer halves. If you have GPOs listed here, the user or computer was, in fact, in the site, domain, or OU that the GPO was supposed to apply to. However, the GPOs listed here have not applied to this user or computer for a variety of reasons. GPResult can tell you why this has happened. Here are some of the common reasons:

Denied (Security)   The user or computer has been explicitly denied "Read" and "Apply Group Policy" rights to process the GPO. For instance, in the previous example, the "Auto-Launch Calc.exe" doesn't apply to WIN10 because in Chapter 2, we explicitly denied the WIN10 computer object the ability to process the "Apply Group Policy" attribute.

Not Applied (Empty)   This GPO doesn't have any policy settings set in the User or Computer half. For instance, in the previous example, the "Prohibit Changing Sounds" GPO doesn't have any Computer-side policy settings. Hence, this GPO doesn't apply to Frank's computer object. Specifically, here the Group Policy engine is seeing that the number of revisions for either the User or Computer half is 0. This is tied to the version number of the GPO, so if the version number is not updated correctly when a GPO change is made, the GPO could be mistakenly viewed as empty.

Not Applied (Unknown Reason)   Usually Block Inheritance has been used, or the user doesn't have rights to read the GPO (though other, truly "unknown reasons" could also be valid). In the previous example, the "Hide Screen Saver Option" GPO, which is set at the site level, won't apply to Frank because we've blocked inheritance at the **Human Resources** OU.

As you just saw in the preceding screen shot, when you run `GPResult /r` as a regular user to get your RSoP data, you'll only be able to see the User-side settings. Why? Because that's all you have access to in this more secure Windows world. To address this, you have two choices:

Choice 1 Run `GPResult` twice: once as the user in question and again as an admin. (You run `GPResult` as an admin by running a command prompt as an administrative user.) This way, you take the User-side RSoP (that you just ran as the user) and the Computer-side RSoP (that you just ran as an administrative user). Then, both of those halves make up the genuine RSoP. Frustrating, but necessary with the way the security within Windows Vista and later prevents regular users from seeing this. What makes this more frustrating is that if you (the Administrator) have never logged in to a particular client machine, you get an error from `GPResult` that expresses that there is no RSoP data for that admin account. So, in the following screen shot, we're logged in as Frank Rizzo trying to get his RSoP data (top window). As stated, the Computer side is inaccessible to him by default. So, we perform the runas command to get our own command-line window as a new Administrator (bottom window). To counter, we then run `GPResult /scope:computer`. We still get an error about the *User* side not having data (bottom window), even though we simply want the *Computer* side of the equation. Frustrating to the max.

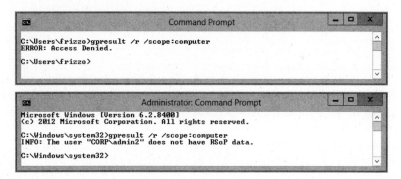

```
                        Command Prompt                     _  □  X
C:\Users\frizzo>gpresult /r /scope:computer
ERROR: Access Denied.

C:\Users\frizzo>
```

```
              Administrator: Command Prompt               _  □  X
Microsoft Windows [Version 6.2.8400]
(c) 2012 Microsoft Corporation. All rights reserved.

C:\Windows\system32>gpresult /r /scope:computer
INFO: The user "CORP\admin2" does not have RSoP data.

C:\Windows\system32>
```

Choice 2 Use the GPMC to delegate users the ability to see their own Computer-side RSoP data. Again, this isn't permitted by default in a Windows Vista and later world. This works just fine for XP machines. So, in my opinion, there's very little reason not to just permit the user to see it.

Assuming you wanted to permit everyone in the domain to see their own RSoP data, we need to review how to perform delegation (discussed in Chapter 2). If we wanted to perform this delegation, we would use the GPMC, click the domain level, and click the Delegation tab. In the Permission dropdown, we would select "Read Group Policy Results data," then add in Authenticated Users (or modify the rights over the Domain Users group, which is always already listed) and select to apply to "This container and all child containers."

You can see a screen shot of this process here:

Again, this is what it takes to get the RSoP of a machine if we're physically sitting down at it. It's a totally different story if you're looking to get this data remotely, from another machine. And the equation gets even more intense if you're looking to delegate rights to a nonadministrative user (like someone on the help desk).

A little later in this chapter, we review how to successfully retrieve Group Policy Results data as a nonadmin user. That section is "Remotely Calculating a Client's RSoP (When You've Delegated Permissions to Someone Who's Not a Local Administrator of the Target Machine)." Be sure to read that section to get the full picture or you'll be left out in the cold wondering why you're getting Access Denied messages.

Remotely Calculating a Client's RSoP (Using *GPresult*)

GPResult relies on the WMI provider built into the operating system. Therefore, you can remotely grab results using GPMC's Group Policy Results Wizard or the GPresult command-line tool by tapping into that data.

You run GPResult, point it to a system, and provide the name of the user whose RSoP data you wish to collect.

There are two more important cautions here. That is, this magic works only if the target user has ever logged on to the target machine. They only need to have logged on just once, and they don't even need to be logged on while you run the test. But if the target user has *never* logged on to the target machine, remotely calculating GPResult for that user will fail. Additionally, remotely trying to get a GPResult will fail if the target machine's Windows Firewall is enabled.

As described in Chapter 2, either turn off the Windows Firewall or enable the policy setting **Windows Firewall: Allow Inbound Remote Administration Exception**, which you can find in Computer Configuration ➢ Policies ➢ Administrative Templates ➢ Network ➢ Network Connections ➢ Windows Firewall ➢ Domain (or Standard) Profile.

Or, for your Windows Vista and later clients, you can really be gung ho and use the new Windows Firewall with Advanced Security (which you'll learn about in Chapter 8), which of course has an alternate method only valid for Windows Vista and later. This would be found under Computer Configuration ➢ Policies ➢ Windows Settings ➢ Security Settings ➢ Windows Firewall with Advanced Security ➢ Inbound Rules.

With that in mind, here are your additional later GPResult options:

- `/s <target system name or IP address>` points to the target system.
- `/user <optional domain\username>` collects RSoP data for the target user.

You can combine any of the aforementioned GPResult switches as well. If you log onto DC01 and want to see only the User-side policy settings when Frank Rizzo logs onto WIN10, type the following:

```
gpresult /user frizzo /s win10 /scope:user /r
```

Again, this command succeeds only if Frank has ever logged on to WIN10 (which he has).

GPResult is much better at telling you *why* a GPO is applying rather than *what* specific policy settings are contained within a GPO. For instance, notice that at no time did GPResult tell us what policy settings were contained in the local GPO. For these tasks, we'll need to use the GPMC (as seen in Chapter 2).

Remotely Calculating a Client's RSoP Using the *Get-GPResultantSetOfPolicy* Cmdlet

You can alternatively use the Get-GPResultantSetOfPolicy cmdlet to remotely grab an RSOP and dump it to either an XML or HTML file. An example command might be something like this:

```
Get-GPResultantSetOfPolicy -ReportType HTML -Computer Win10 -User Frizzo -path
C:\Temp\Report1.html
```

The result of the command can be seen in Figure 7.22.

FIGURE 7.22   Use PowerShell to remotely grab an RSOP report.

Remotely Calculating a Client's RSoP (When You've Delegated Permissions to Someone Who's Not a Local Administrator of the Target Machine)

In the preceding examples, I've made an assumption.

I've assumed you want to view someone's RSoP data and you're also a local administrator on the machine.

But maybe that's not the case in the real world.

Maybe in your real world, you want to delegate rights to, say, the help desk (or another nonadministrative group).

If you do, then you'll need an extra boost to ensure that they can read the RSoP data. (If you need a refresher on how to delegate the permission in the first place, be sure to read the section "Special Group Policy Operation Delegations" in Chapter 2.) Again, this area is located in the Delegation tab on the OU (or domain or site) you want to delegate rights to.

Once you've performed the delegation of the "Read Group Policy Results data" right on the user and/or computer you want, you also need to perform these very important additional delegation steps. (Again, these steps are required only if you've delegated this ability to a nonadministrator of the target machine.)

For instance, let's assume that Tom User (from the help desk) needs access to read Group Policy Results data from a computer that Brett Wier is using (Win10.corp.com). First, you delegate rights on the OU that contains Win10.corp.com and ensure that Tom can "Read Group Policy Results data." But even if you do that, as soon as Tom tries to run the Group Policy Results Wizard, he gets an "Access is denied" message, as seen in Figure 7.23.

To open it up a little (and decrease your security a little as well), you'll need to create and link a GPO that affects the target computer's OU. Then, make sure the following policy settings are enabled within that GPO:

1. We already covered this one, but just to be sure you have it in place: Computer Configuration ➢ Policies ➢ Administrative Templates ➢ Network ➢ Network Connections ➢ Windows Firewall ➢ Domain Profile ➢ **Windows Firewall: Allow Inbound Remote Administration Exception.** Choose which subnets to allow inbound requests from (or specify * to allow all subnets).

2. The other policy setting is located within Computer Configuration ➢ Policies ➢ Windows Settings ➢ Security Settings ➢ Local Policies ➢ Security Options ➢ **DCOM: Machine Access Restrictions in Security Descriptor Definition Language (SDDL) syntax.** When you edit the policy setting, you'll first select "Define this policy setting," then click Edit Security, add in Tom User, and specify to allow Remote Access. When you do this, a security descriptor is (thankfully) automatically built, like O:BAG:BAD:(A;;CDCLC;;;) and is usually quite long. You can see a screen shot of this in Figure 7.24 (though the security descriptor isn't in the screen shot, because I haven't hit OK yet).

FIGURE 7.23　Tom doesn't have access to run Group Policy Results against machines for which he isn't also a local administrator.

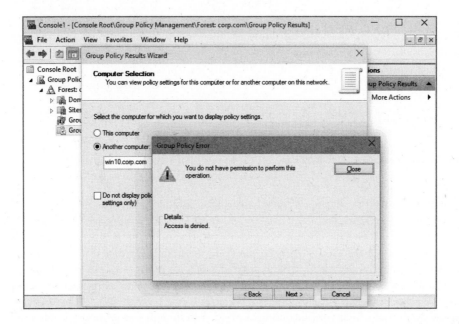

3. The last policy setting is located within Computer Configuration ➢ Policies ➢ Windows Settings ➢ Security Settings ➢ Local Policies ➢ Security Options ➢ **DCOM: Machine Launch Restrictions in Security Descriptor Definition Language (SDDL) syntax.** Again, be sure to click "Define this policy setting." Then, add in the same person (Tom User) and grant the "Remote Launch: Allow" and "Remote Activation: Allow" rights.

FIGURE 7.24 For each DCOM permission, add in the delegated user and specify they have "Remote Access: Allow" permissions.

Since you've changed the Computer-side settings, be sure to run gpupdate /force on the target machine (or just reboot it).

When you do, you'll give the specified nonadministrative users the ability to read another computer's RSoP data using the GPMC's Group Policy Results Wizard.

After these steps are performed, you've delegated a user (or group, like the Help Desk) and have now enabled the ability to "reach out" and see what's going on at other machines—even if they're not a local admin. Don't forget about the golden rule here, though: if the target machine's firewall is blocking your incoming request, even though you've now delegated the permission, it still ain't gonna work.

Advanced Group Policy Troubleshooting with the Event Viewer Logs

We've already explored some of the techniques used to troubleshoot Group Policy applications. You can enable some underlying operating system troubleshooting tools to help diagnose just what the heck is going on when the unexpected occurs.

Quite possibly, the most overlooked and underutilized tool in Windows is the Event Viewer. The client's Event Viewer logs both the successful and unsuccessful application of Group Policy. One such event can be seen in Figure 7.25.

FIGURE 7.25   The Event Viewer is a terrific place to start your troubleshooting journey for both good news (or bad news).

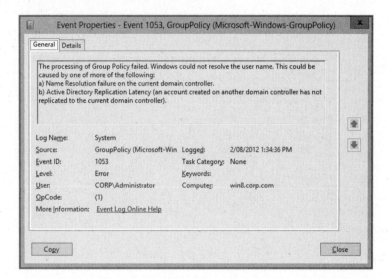

Before beating your head against the wall, check the client's event log for relevant Group Policy records.

In Figure 7.25, the specific Event ID returned was an error code of 1053. Doing a quick search in Microsoft TechNet, you can find a related article, 261007 (http://support .microsoft.com/kb/261007), which shows that the client is pointing to an incorrect DNS server. Again, search the Microsoft Knowledge Base when you find an event that might be at fault. You might find a hidden gem there—perfectly ready to solve your problem.

Troubleshooting Using the Windows System Logs

All major Group Policy–related events are found in the System Log.

A Windows 8 and later system generates Group Policy events with an event source of GroupPolicy (Microsoft-Windows-Group Policy), as shown in the System log in Figure 7.26.

However, note that Windows 7 generates Group Policy events simply as GroupPolicy— without the additional text in parentheses. This does make troubleshooting a little harder if you have both Windows 7 and Windows 8 or later systems, as seen in Figure 7.27. You have to know which event source to look for.

The System Log is designed to give you high-level information about the state of the Group Policy engine. So it will tell you things such as whether computer Group Policy processing succeeded or failed, but it won't necessarily tell you what happened or why.

You can gather details of many events, like what's seen in Figure 7.28.

FIGURE 7.26 Viewing the Windows 7 System Log with Group Policy events

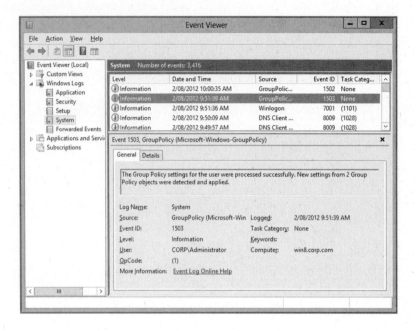

FIGURE 7.27 Viewing the Windows 8 and later System Log with Group Policy events

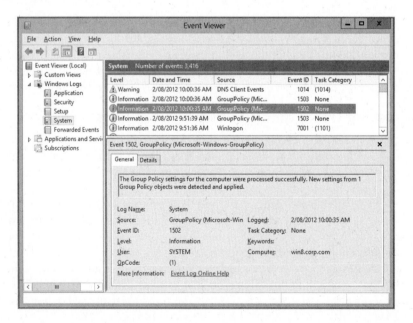

FIGURE 7.28   Viewing the Group Policy processing time

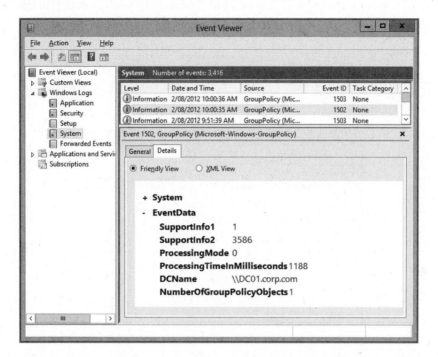

Note that in Figure 7.28, the ProcessingTimeInMilliseconds field shows 1188 milliseconds, or .11 seconds. That is how long it took for computer processing to occur. Also note that the ProcessingMode is listed as 0. That indicates that the computer is working in normal processing mode, as opposed to Loopback processing. If the value were 1 or 2, that would indicate that Loopback in Merge mode or Replace mode, respectively, was enabled. And, of course, the DCName field indicates which Domain Controller serviced the Group Policy engine's request for Group Policy processing during the last cycle.

In addition to telling you when things are good with Group Policy, the System Log will tell you when things aren't so good. The failure logs will also try to give you some hints as to why things aren't working. For example, check out the event in Figure 7.29.

In Figure 7.29, you can see the nature of the failure. Additionally, if you were to click the "Event Log Online Help" link at the bottom of the page, you would be taken to a Microsoft website that contains more detailed information about this event ID. Well, hopefully, anyway. Not every event ID has its own link to a web page, but you can try and check.

The logging of Group Policy events in Windows is on by default, so you don't need to enable anything specifically.

You can simply filter events in this log with a source of GroupPolicy (for Windows 7) or GroupPolicy (Microsoft-Windows-Group Policy) (for Windows 8 and later) and get a snapshot of GP Processing. The events recorded in this log related to Group Policy are a summary of each processing event—they tell you things like whether Group Policy processing proceeded successfully, which Domain Controller was used to process policy, and how many GPOs were processed. They do not provide deep levels of detail. In the next section, we'll talk about how you can get that detail out of the event log in Windows.

FIGURE 7.29   Viewing a Group Policy failure event

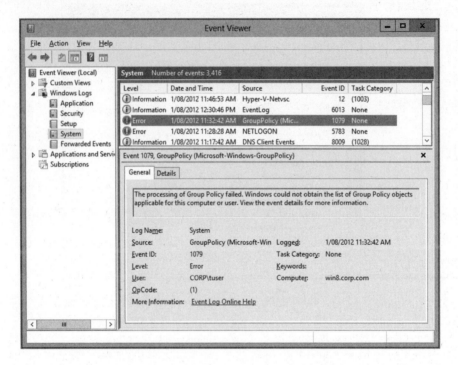

At the time of this writing, the Group Policy event log documentation is found at https://technet.microsoft.com/en-us/library/cc749336.

But it wasn't yet updated for a bunch of event log entries which have been around since Windows 8.1. So to that end, here are the missing un-documented Windows 8.1 (and later) system events you might find.

Event	ID
Get Applicable GPOs Start	4126
Get Applicable GPOs End Success	5126
Get Applicable GPOs End Fail	7126
GPO process sync mode slowlink detected	6344
GPO process sync mode NO DC	6345

Event	ID
GPO process switch sync mode to async	6346
GPsvc start	4115
GPsvc stop	5115
GP session start	4117
GP session return winlogon call	5351
GP session end	5117
GP session end with error	7117
GP save to cache start	4216
GP save to cache end	5216
GP save to cache end with error	7216
GP load from cache start	4217
GP load from cache end	5217
GP load from cache end with error	7217
GP cache first WMI query start	4218
GP cache first WMI query end	5218
GP service init start	4116
GP service init end	5116
GP policy download start	4257
GP policy download end	5257
GP policy download end with error	7257

Troubleshooting Using the Group Policy Operational Log

In the last section we talked about the System Log. I explained that it tells you *what* happened, but isn't really great at the *why*.

The Group Policy Operational log gives you a way to see step by step what occurred in any Group Policy "cycle" and figure out *why* something didn't work.

To find the Group Policy Operational log, open the Event Viewer and drill into Applications and Services Logs ➤ Microsoft ➤ Windows ➤ Group Policy ➤ Operational. What you'll get is a set of events similar to those found in Figure 7.30.

FIGURE 7.30   Viewing the Group Policy Operational log in Windows

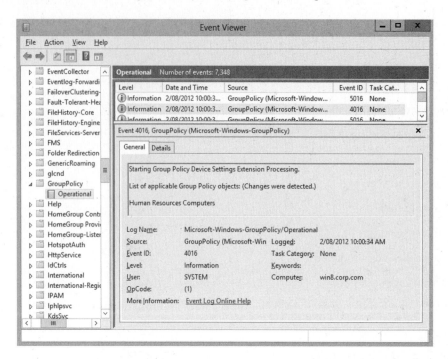

The Group Policy Operational log is going to provide almost all the information you need to track down Group Policy problems. I say "almost" because there are some extra logs that occasionally need to be enabled to get even more data out. (See the sidebar "Other Types of Verbose Logging" a little later.)

Troubleshooting Deep Dive

Again, start with the Windows System Logs when you suspect a problem. It could be very well explained and get you on your way.

Assuming that the System Logs don't help you track down the problem, the next step would be to paw through the Group Policy Operational logs as we just discussed.

But how can you use the Group Policy Operational logs to troubleshoot a problem when there are so many events generated in a given processing cycle? For example, a given Group Policy processing cycle could generate 20 to 30 Operational log events, and the Operational log itself could contain hundreds of these events. The goal is to narrow in on *one* Group Policy processing cycle and walk through the steps that it took to either succeed or fail. You can accomplish this task using a custom view, a feature of the Crimson Event Log system.

Each instance of a Group Policy processing cycle is uniquely identified by a field in the event called *Correlation Activity ID*. By creating a custom view that filters events by this activity ID, you can get a listing of only those Group Policy Operational events related to a given processing cycle. Let's walk through how to do that.

To filter the Operational event logs by a specific Group Policy Activity ID:

1. Start the Event Viewer utility.

2. The first thing you need to do is find the activity ID for the Group Policy processing cycle you're interested in. You can do that by going into the Operational log, finding an event that is part of the cycle in question, and clicking the Details tab in the lower preview pane, as shown in Figure 7.31. Copy this activity ID someplace safe—we'll need it in a second.

FIGURE 7.31   Locating the correlation activity ID in a Group Policy event

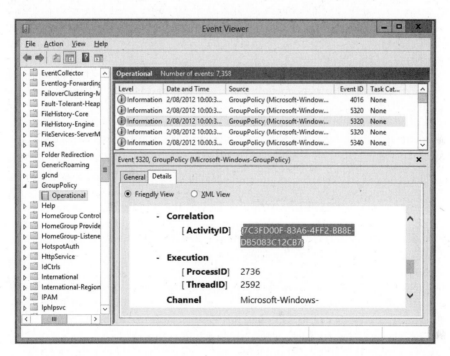

3. On the left-hand pane of the Event Viewer, right-click the Custom Views node and choose Create Custom View.

4. The Create Custom View dialog box appears on the Filter pane, but for this exercise, we're going to enter the XML filter directly rather than using the check boxes. So, click the XML tab and check the box that says "Edit query manually."

5. Copy the text I've written here all as one line. For nice formatting in the book, I've broken it down into what looks like several lines. But imagine it's all one really long line. Type this XML query string into the filter query box:

```
<QueryList><Query Id="0" Path="Application">
<Select Path="Microsoft-Windows-GroupPolicy/Operational"> *[System/
Correlation/@ActivityID='{INSERT ACTIVITY ID
HERE}']</Select></Query></QueryList>
```

6. Place the activity ID you found in step 2 in the spot that says, "INSERT ACTIVITY ID HERE." Once you do that, click OK twice and the upper-right results pane of the Event Viewer will show only a filtered view of your Group Policy events.

GPLogView

Now that we've filtered the events down to a single Group Policy cycle, you might be saying to yourself, "Gee, it's pretty hard to see what's going on given that I have to scroll through each event without getting to see them all in a single view." Well, for that reason, Microsoft has created a tool called GPLogView.

This command-line utility lets you output the events of a Group Policy Operational log to a variety of easy-to-read formats, including straight text and HTML. You can download the tool at http://go.microsoft.com/fwlink/?LinkId=75004.

Here is a taste of what GPLogView can do. You can use it to do the exact same thing we did in the previous custom view description—output the events associated with a single activity ID. To do that, you would run the gplogview command using the following syntax:

```
Gplogview -a 9A867233-04FF-4625-B7D1-6DEB763E2DCA -o ouput.txt
```

This generates a step-by-step listing of all events with the activity ID we've supplied to an output file called output.txt. Figure 7.32 shows a small sample of the output.

Note that it provides useful information such as the bandwidth detected during slow link detection, the time until the next processing cycle, which GPOs were applied and denied, and why.

Additionally, if you look at the actual events in the Event Viewer that correspond to each of the events listed in the output from GPLogView, you can get some more useful information. For example, at the start of every policy processing cycle, useful summary flags are included in each event under the Details tab, as shown in Figure 7.33.

The flags you see in this figure can provide a glimpse into the kind of processing that is occurring. For example, the isBackgroundProcessing = true flag indicates that this is a background processing cycle rather than a foreground one. This is important because certain CSEs, such as Software Installation and Folder Redirection, don't run during background processing. This summary view also provides useful information such as whether processing occurred asynchronously (IsAsyncProcessing) and whether machine or user processing is being logged (IsMachine).

FIGURE 7.32   Viewing the output from GPLogView

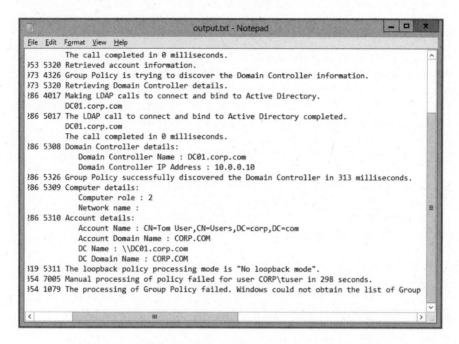

FIGURE 7.33   Viewing summary flags for a Group Policy Operational event

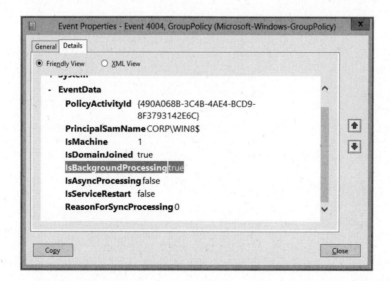

Overall, the Group Policy Operational log is the place to be when it comes to troubleshooting Group Policy problems in Windows Vista and later.

Enabling Tracing for the Group Policy Preference Extensions

The Group Policy Preferences don't produce any direct log files by default. The assumption is that "they're working fine" unless you want to get more information out of them.

To do that, there are a slew of policy settings that enable tracking logs. We explored tracing for the Group Policy Preferences in Chapter 5, but for completeness, I'm putting a reference to their existence here in this troubleshooting chapter as well.

You can find the Group Policy Preference extensions tracing policy settings at Computer Configuration ➢ Policies ➢ Administrative Templates ➢ System ➢ Group Policy ➢ Logging and Tracing.

You can see one of the Group Policy Preference extensions tracing options in Figure 7.34—specifically, for the Group Policy Preferences Drive Maps.

For more information on Group Policy Preferences troubleshooting, check out "Troubleshooting: Reporting, Logging, and Tracing" in Chapter 5.

FIGURE 7.34 You use policy settings like this one to troubleshoot the Group Policy Preference extensions.

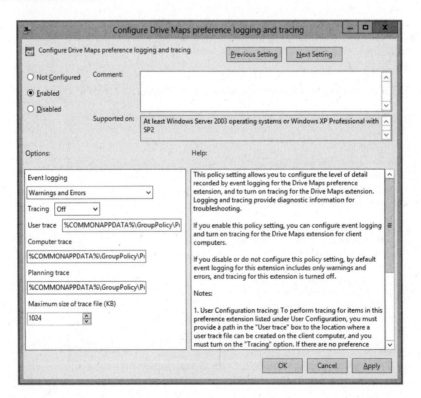

Other Types of Verbose Logging

In addition to using the event logs, some of the individual CSEs provide their own verbose log files that you can enable with Registry tweaks.

When you can't get the information you need from the event logs, your next step is to try to track down the problem with one of these CSE-specific logs. While not every CSE creates its own log file, most of the important ones do, and you can use these logs to get more detailed information about a particular Group Policy area that has gone awry. The following table lists all available CSE-specific logs and Registry values needed to enable them.

Component	Location of log	Location in Registry	Value

Security CSE	`%windir%\`
	`Security\Logs\`
	`WinLogon.log`
		`HKLM\Software\`
		`Microsoft\Windows`
		`NT\CurrentVer-`
		`sion\ Winlogon\`
		`GPExtensions\`
		`{827d319e-6eac-`
		`11d2-a4ea-`
		`00c04f79f83a}`
			`ExtensionDebugLevel`
			`DWORD 2`

Folder Redirection CSE	`%windir%\Debug\`
	`UserMode\FDeploy`
	`.log` (Windows XP and 2003 only) Windows Vista and later log errors to the Application log.
		`HKLM\Software\`
		`Microsoft\Windows`
		`NT\CurrentVersion\`
		`Diagnostics`
			`FDeployDebugLevel`
			`DWORD 0x0B`

Software Installation CSE	`%windir%\ Debug\`
	`UserMode\AppMgmt`
	`.log`
		`HKLM\Software\`
		`Microsoft\Windows`
		`NT\CurrentVersion\`
		`Diagnostics`
			`AppMgmtDebugLevel`
			`DWORD 0x9b`

 See Darren Mar-Elia's website, www.GPOguy.com, for a great ADM template that helps automate these Registry punches, if needed, on your client machines.

Group Policy Processing Performance

I often hear the question, "Is it better to have fewer, bigger GPOs or more GPOs with fewer settings?" The answer to that question is the basis for this section.

The bottom line to Group Policy processing performance is that the time it takes to process Group Policy is highly dependent on what you're doing within a given set of GPOs and the state of your environment. If you think about all the things we've discussed in this chapter about how Group Policy is stored and processed, then you have probably discovered that there is a lot of variability in the process. For example, setting Administrative Templates policy is a lot less time-consuming than re-permissioning a large file tree using File Security policy. Likewise, installing Microsoft Office using Software Installation policy is going to take more time than delivering 10 shortcuts using Group Policy Preferences.

Additionally, the time that Group Policy processing spends during the core processing phase, where the client communicates with AD to determine which GPOs to apply, is typically a small percentage of the overall processing time as compared to the CSE processing part of the cycle. Thus, having to enumerate more GPOs or fewer GPOs will have a negligible effect on the overall processing time as compared to having to perform the more time-intensive CSE processing. And it's also important to remember that Group Policy processing only occurs if something changes in the Group Policy infrastructure for a given computer or user. So, in most environments, days may go by before changes to GPOs are made or a new GPO is created. Given that, the question of performance comes down to what is acceptable in your environment.

The best thing you can do to optimize processing performance is measure and understand where time is being spent during a given processing cycle. You can do this using any number of the tools we've mentioned in this chapter. In addition, you can download a free command-line utility called gptime.exe at https://sdmsoftware.com/gpoguy/free-tools/library/ that outputs the time spent processing Group Policy for either a local or remote computer. Additionally, if you use Windows 8's (and later) GPMC, the Component Status section of a Group Policy Results report can also show you each component's individual processing time.

A number of factors can affect Group Policy processing performance more than just the number of GPOs you have applied to a given user or computer. Some of these are highlighted here:

- Keep the number of security groups applied to a GPO to a minimum. The more security groups a client has to read and process to determine if a GPO applies or does not apply, the more time is spent during the core processing phase.

- Make sure that you are not forcing policy application for a given CSE (by enabling the relevant policy under Computer Configuration\Policies\Administrative Templates\System\Group Policy) during every refresh cycle unless you absolutely have to.

- Make sure that you minimize the amount of "expensive" operations that your GPOs do. Expensive operations include Folder Redirection of large amounts of user data, Software Installation of large applications over the network, and re-permissioning of large file or Registry trees. Additionally, Scripts policy can be problematic if the scripts are performing complex tasks that can hang. The default script time-out in Group Policy is 10 minutes. That means a script could hang there for up to 10 minutes, with your users waiting, until it finally times out.

- WMI filters (discussed in Chapter 5) also take a big chunk of processing time to figure out if the condition is "true" or not. You should use WMI filters if you need them, but not to excess, though WMI filters do process faster on Windows 7 and later than they did on Windows XP.

So, in the end, the question of whether fewer, bigger GPOs perform better than more, smaller GPOs is probably not the right question to ask. The better question is which configuration is easier to manage. Once you answer that question, you can optimize for performance using the tips I've described in this section.

Final Thoughts

You want to be a better troubleshooter for Group Policy issues? You're well on the way.

In the previous chapter, you learned when Group Policy is supposed to apply. It doesn't just happen when it wants to; it happens according to a set of precise timings. In this chapter, you learned two more key items to help on your troubleshooting journey. First, you learned the real story about what's going on under the hood. Then, you learned how to take that knowledge and troubleshoot Group Policy. Hopefully, every page in this chapter will help you further troubleshoot Group Policy should something go awry. However, here are some parting tips for troubleshooting Group Policy:

Check the basics.　When troubleshooting, first check the basics. Make sure you're not using Block Inheritance or Enforced where you shouldn't.

Check permissions.　Users need both "Read" and "Apply Group Policy" permissions to the GPOs. Computers do, too. If a user (or group the user is in) is "Denied" access to either of these permissions, then the GPO will not apply.

Leverage the built-in tools.　Use the built-in debugging tools, such as the Event Viewer, GPResult, and GPMC Results reports to help troubleshoot problems.

Remember which operating systems act alike.　When it comes to troubleshooting, remember that Windows Vista and later are all basically alike. To get very, very specific, Windows 10 and Windows Server 2016 are most alike, Windows 8.1 and Windows Server 2012 R2 are alike, Windows 8 and Windows Server 2012 are alike, followed by Windows 7 and Server 2008 R2. Then Windows Vista and Windows Server 2008. Finally, Windows Server 2003 is just like XP.

Verify that replication is working.　If a client isn't getting the GPOs you think they should, it just may be that normal replication hasn't finished yet. GPCs replicate via Active Directory replication. GPTs replicate via FRS replication. They are supposed to take the same path, but sometimes they don't. Use Gpotool and Repadmin and the GPMC's Status tab to troubleshoot.

Check out Microsoft's troubleshooting documentation.   There are two official white papers on Group Policy troubleshooting from Microsoft. One can be found at http://go.microsoft.com/fwlink/?LinkId=14949.

There's also another version at http://tinyurl.com/gp-trouble2. I was one of the reviewers who provided input into this later document.

8

Implementing Security with Group Policy

There is a little aphorism that's grown on me over time. It's a simple mantra, which hopefully you can agree with:

If you don't know Group Policy, you don't know security.

That's because Group Policy and security are so intrinsically linked. The weird part is that the Group Policy engine *itself* isn't a security mechanism. The Group Policy engine is a settings delivery mechanism. What you're *delivering*, the payload of "instructions," could be security oriented.

But if you don't understand the range of what you can do with Group Policy—either the engine itself or the security payloads it can deliver—then, as my aphorism goes, "You don't know security."

Not only are you setting configuration items (which will make you more secure), and not only are you setting security items (which will also make you more secure), but you also need to know the ins and outs of where Group Policy applies, who it applies to, and when that magic is going to happen.

But Group Policy is a big, big place, and we simply don't have room to go over *all* the stuff you can do with Group Policy or even all the *security* stuff you can do with Group Policy. So I'm picking the most important things to show you in this chapter with the amount of room I have.

In this security chapter we've got an enormous amount to cover. Here's the list:

Default GPOs We'll first look at the two default GPOs—the "Default Domain Policy" GPO and the "Default Domain Controllers Policy" GPO—and how they help tighten security.

Password Policy Ah, passwords. They're so easy to manage, right? I'll show you how to increase your "fun" when it comes to Password Policy in this chapter.

Auditing Servers and Group Policy Usage Who is using our clients and servers? You'll find out how to find out. You'll also discover some new goodies for modern Windows machines.

Restricted Groups You'll learn how to force group membership and nested group membership.

Software Restriction Policies and AppLocker Put the smack down and allow/disallow specific applications to run.

Controlling User Account Control (UAC)   "Are you sure you want to do that?" That question pops up time and time again in Windows Vista and later. Want to control it? This is your section.

Wireless and Wired Network Policies   Windows Vista and later have controls related to wireless and wired network policies. Set up both wired and wireless security using these techniques.

Windows Firewall with Advanced Security   Learn how to configure the Windows firewall in this section.

Obviously, there's a lot more to an overall security strategy. And, in other chapters, and Appendix D, we'll cover some other items you may want to check out if you're crafting a security policy for your environment. Here are the topics I think you should check out:

- Internet Explorer settings (Chapter 12, "Finishing Touches with Group Policy: Scripts, Internet Explorer, Hardware Control, Printer Deployment, Local Admin Password Control")

- Security Compliance Manager (Appendix D)

- ADM/ADMX/PolicyPak Application Manager for controlling your applications (Chapter 6, "Managing Applications and Settings Using Group Policy")

The Two Default Group Policy Objects

Whenever you create a new domain, three things automatically happen:

- The initial (and only) OU, named **Domain Controllers**, is created automatically by the DCPROMO process.

- A default GPO is created and linked to the domain level, and it's called "Default Domain Policy."

- A default GPO is created for the **Domain Controllers** OU, and it's called "Default Domain Controllers Policy."

Let's begin by answering the question, "Why are these GPOs different from all other GPOs?"

These two GPOs are special. First, you cannot easily delete them (though you can rename them). Next, it's a best practice to modify these GPOs only for the security settings that we'll describe right around the corner.. Too often, people will modify the "Default Domain Controller Policy" GPO or "Default Domain Policy" GPO only to mess it up beyond recognition. So, these special default GPOs shouldn't be modified with the "normal stuff" you do day to day. In general, stay clear of them, and modify them only when a setting prescribed for them is required.

Instead of modifying the "Default Domain Controller Policy" GPO or "Default Domain Policy" GPO for normal stuff, you should create a new GPO and link it at the level you want, and then implement your policy settings inside that new GPO. And it's a best practice to always be sure that the defaults are highest in the link order (that means they're the most powerful if anything should conflict in another GPO at the same level).

It's not that the GPOs themselves are all that different, but rather that their location is special, as you'll see later in this chapter. The locations in question are the domain level and the **Domain Controllers** OU.

> The "Default Domain Policy" GPO and "Default Domain Controllers Policy" GPO can be deleted, but I strongly recommend that you *don't ever delete these*. If you truly want to delete either of the default policies, you'll need to add back in the "Delete" access control entry to a group you belong to—Domain Administrators, for instance. Even then, I can't see why you would want to delete them. If you want to disable their link for some reason (again, I can't imagine why), do that, but leave the actual GPOs in place. If you do run into a situation where these are deleted, use the command dcgpofix.exe (described in detail in the section "Oops, the 'Default Domain Policy' GPO and/or 'Default Domain Controllers Policy' GPO Got Screwed Up!") to get them back.

GPOs Linked at the Domain Level

If you take a look inside the domain level, you'll see one GPO that was created by default: "Default Domain Policy." The purpose of this GPO is to set the default configurations for the Account Policies branch in the Group Policy Object Editor. These Account Policies encompass three important domain-wide security settings:

- Password policy
- Account Lockout policy
- Kerberos policy

You can see these settings in Figure 8.1.

Again, the default policy settings are set inside the "Default Domain Policy" GPO and linked to the domain level. However, you can change the defaults of the Account Policies in one of two ways:

- By modifying the "Default Domain Policy" GPO directly
- By creating your own GPO linked to the domain level and changing the precedence order within the domain level

You'll see how shortly.

Again, the special part about the domain level of Group Policy is that this is the only place these three Group Policy settings can be set for the domain, and the default settings for the domain are prespecified in the "Default Domain Policy" GPO.

FIGURE 8.1 The "Default Domain Policy" GPO (linked to the domain level) sets the domain's default Account Policies (Password Policy, Account Lockout policy, and Kerberos policy). If you link GPOs containing these policy settings anywhere else, they are ignored when Active Directory is being used.

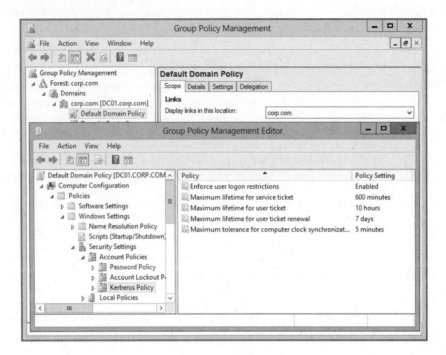

If you try to set Password Policy, Account Lockout policy, or Kerberos policy anywhere else in the domain (say, at any OU or on any site), the settings are ignored when users log onto the domain; they don't matter, and only those linked to the domain level take effect.

Microsoft has taken a lot of heat for the fact that Account Policies must agree for all the accounts in the domain. That meant if two administrators of two OUs couldn't agree on equal Account Policies (usually things like password length), they would have needed to split those users between two domains—a major administrative overhead nightmare.

So Microsoft changed it starting with Windows Server 2008. It's not a light-year improvement, but it does do the job. We'll explore that here as well.

Special Policy Settings for the Domain Level

Along with Password Policy, Account Lockout policy, and Kerberos policy, five additional policy settings take effect only when a GPO is linked to the domain level. They are located under Computer Configuration ➤ Policies ➤ Windows Settings ➤ Security Settings ➤ Local Policies ➤ Security Options.

Network security: Force logoff when logon hours expire You can set up accounts so that users logged onto Active Directory must log off when they exceed the hours available to them.

Accounts: Rename administrator account   You can use this policy setting to forcibly rename the Administrator account. This works only for the Domain Administrator account when set at the domain level. This is useful as a level of "extra protection" so that no matter what the Administrator account is renamed to in Active Directory Users and Computers, it will "snap back" to this name after Group Policy refreshes. The "display name" in Active Directory Users and Computers won't change, but the underlying "real" name of the account will be changed.

Accounts: Rename guest account   You can rename the domain Guest account using this policy setting. This works only for the Guest account when set at the domain level.

Accounts: Administrator account status   You can forcibly disable the Administrator account using this setting. See this tech note for more information: http://bit.ly/wct6W7.

Accounts: Guest account status   You can forcibly disable the Guest account using this setting. See this tech note for more information: http://bit.ly/waRro7.

Setting these five special security settings at any other level has no effect on domain accounts contained within Active Directory. However, if you linked a GPO containing these settings to an OU, the local computer would certainly respond accordingly.

> Again, these policies cannot affect domain accounts when a GPO containing these settings is linked to, say, the **Sales** OU or **Marketing** OU. This is because these policies must specifically affect the Domain Controllers computer objects.

Modifying the "Default Domain Policy" GPO Directly

You can dive into the "Default Domain Policy" GPO in two ways. Use the Group Policy Management Console (GPMC) and click the domain name. You'll see the "Default Domain Policy" GPO linked to the domain level. If you try to edit the GPO at this level, you'll see the standard set of policy settings you've come to know and love while inside the Group Policy Object Editor (though again, as I've stated, you won't want to add "normal stuff" to this GPO).

Here, for instance, you can specify (among other settings) that the password length is 10 characters, the user is locked out after the third password attempt, and Kerberos ticket expiration time is 600 minutes. But these values are only valid for the entire domain.

> Again, if you want to add more policy settings at the domain level (which would affect all users or computers in the domain)—great! But try to leave the "Default Domain Policy" GPO alone, except when you need to change the "special" policy settings, as described earlier.

Creating Your Own Group Policy Object Linked to the Domain Level and Changing the Precedence

Recall that at any level (site, domain, or OU), all the policy settings within all the GPOs linked to a level are merged unless there is a conflict. Then, the GPO with the highest precedence "wins" at a level. I talked about this in Chapter 2, "Managing Group Policy with the GPMC and via PowerShell." The same is true regarding the settings special to the domain level: Password Policy, Account Lockout policy, and Kerberos policy.

The defaults for these three policies are set within the "Default Domain Policy" GPO, but you could certainly create and link more GPOs to the domain level that would override the defaults. That doesn't necessarily mean that you should. Take a look at the example in Figure 8.2.

FIGURE 8.2 If you have a GPO with a higher precedence than the "Default Domain Policy" GPO, it will "win" if there's a conflict.

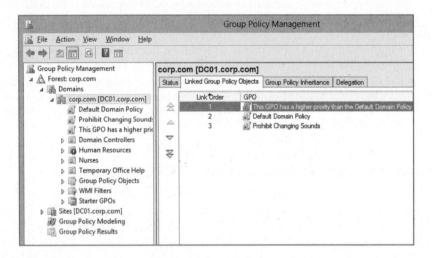

Here, a GPO is higher in priority than the "Default Domain Policy." If you do this, you better know precisely what you are doing. Again, this is because any policy setting within any GPO with a higher priority than the "Default Domain Policy" GPO will "win."

Which Approach Do You Take?

As you've seen, you can either modify the "Default Domain Policy" GPO or create your own GPO and ensure that the precedence is higher than the "Default Domain Policy" GPO. If you need to modify a special domain-wide account policy setting, which approach do you take? Here are the two schools of thought:

School of Thought 1 Modify only the Account Policies settings in the "Default Domain Policy" GPO. Then, ensure that it has the highest precedence at the domain level. This guarantees that if anyone does link other GPOs to the domain level, this one always wins.

School of Thought 2 Leave the defaults in the "Default Domain Policy" GPO. Never modify the "Default Domain Policy" GPO—ever. Create a new GPO for any special settings you want to override in the "Default Domain Policy" GPO. Then, link the GPO to the domain level, and ensure that it has higher precedence than the "Default Domain Policy" GPO (as seen in Figure 8.2).

Various Microsoft insiders have given me different (sometimes conflicting) advice about which to use. So what do I think?

If you want to modify any special domain-wide security settings, use School of Thought 1. This is the simplest and cleanest way. If you do it this way, you'll always treat the "Default Domain Policy" GPO with kid gloves and know it has a special use. And you can check in on it from time to time to make sure no one has lowered the precedence on it. Additionally, some applications will specifically modify the "Default Domain Policy" GPO. Check with your application vendor to be sure. In those cases, if you want that application to run smoothly, it's best to let it do what it wants to do.

School of Thought 2 has its merits. Leave the "Default Domain Policy" GPO clean as a whistle, and then create your own GPOs with higher precedence settings. However, I don't think this is a great idea, because you might forget that you set something important inside this new GPO.

Either way works, but my preference is for School of Thought 1.

Group Policy Objects Linked to the Domain Controllers OU

How is the **Domain Controllers** OU different? You can see there is also a default GPO linked, named the "Default Domain Controllers Policy" GPO. But before we dive into it, let's take a step back. First, it's important to think of all the Domain Controllers as essentially equal. If one Domain Controller gets a policy setting (Security setting or otherwise), they should all be getting the same policy settings. On logon, users choose a Domain Controller for validation at random; however, you want the experience they receive to be consistent, not random. Moreover, when you, as the Domain Administrator, log onto a Domain Controller at the console, you also want your experience to be consistent.

Oh, and did I mention that when servers are finished being promoted into Domain Controllers via DCPROMO, they automatically end up in the **Domain Controllers** OU? So, that's where the "Default Domain Controllers Policy" GPO comes into play. Again, it's easy to find the "Default Domain Controllers Policy" GPO. It's linked to the **Domain Controllers** OU.

Again, since all Domain Controllers are, by default, nestled within the **Domain Controllers** OU, all Domain Controllers are affected by all the aspects inside the "Default Domain Controllers Policy" GPO. Of specific note are the Security Settings, as shown in Figure 8.3.

FIGURE 8.3 The "Default Domain Controllers Policy" GPO affects every Domain Controller in the Domain Controllers OU.

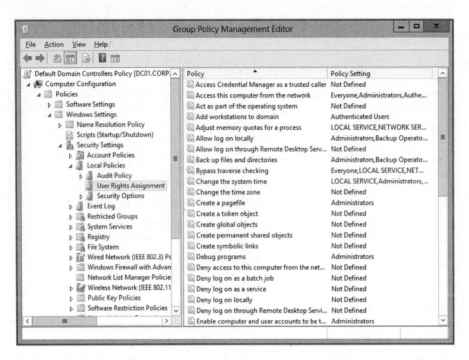

For instance, you'll want the same Event Log settings for all Domain Controllers. You'll want to set it once, inside a GPO linked to the **Domain Controllers** OU, and have it affect all Domain Controllers. By default, the "Default Domain Controllers Policy" GPO has the following set to specific defaults, which should remain consistent among all Domain Controllers.

 Right-click any node and choose Export List from the context menu to export to a text file for an easy way to document complex settings, such as User Rights Assignments.

Audit Policies Located in Computer Configuration ➢ Policies ➢ Windows Settings ➢ Security Settings ➢ Local Policies ➢ Audit Policy. Here you can change the default auditing policies of your domain. We talk about auditing later in this chapter in the section "Inside Basic and Advanced Auditing."

User Rights Assignment Located in Computer Configuration ➢ Policies ➢ Windows Settings ➢ Security Settings ➢ Local Policies ➢ User Rights Assignment. Here you can configure which accounts you will "Allow log on locally" or "Log on as a service" among other specific rights.

Domain Controller Event Log Settings   Located in Computer Configuration ≻ Policies ≻ Windows Settings ≻ Security Settings ≻ Event Log. Set them here, and all Domain Controllers in the **Domain Controllers** OU will obey. Settings such as the maximum size of logs are contained here. Note, however, that decreasing the size of an event log will not take effect on the DCs; you can enforce a log size increase, but not a decrease.

Various Security Options   Located in Computer Configuration ≻ Policies ≻ Windows Settings ≻ Security Settings ≻ Local Policies ≻ Security Options. Here you'll find settings such as "Domain controller: LDAP server signing requirements" and other items that might be specifically relevant to Domain Controllers. Note that GPOs created on the "latest, greatest" GPMC (today, Windows 10) will have more security options available. The Group Policy spreadsheet (found at www.microsoft.com/en-us/download/details.aspx?id=25250) has a list of all the security options and what target machines can be affected.

The same rules apply to the **Domain Controllers** OU as they do for the domain level. That is, you can put a GPO in at a higher precedence than the "Default Domain Controllers Policy" GPO. However, my recommendation is to use the "Default Domain Controllers Policy" GPO for the "special" things that you set at this level and ensure that it's got the highest precedence when being processed within the OU.

Oops, the "Default Domain Policy" GPO and/or "Default Domain Controllers Policy" GPO Got Screwed Up!

If you modify the "Default Domain Policy" GPO or "Default Domain Controllers Policy" GPO such that you want to return it back to the out-of-the-box settings, that is possible. These steps should be performed only as an absolute last resort because it will restore it as if the installation were done out of the box. So, be careful. If you have a backup of your defaults, you should try to perform a restore first—before using this "emergency-only" tool.

If you have the need to restore, say, only the domain's User Rights Assignments, that's possible too, as seen in the sidebar "Resetting User Rights Assignments."

If your Active Directory is functional level 2003, I would perform this on a Windows 2003 server. Likewise, if your domain is functional level 2008, perform on a 2008 machine. 2008 R2? 2008 R2 machine. And, same idea for Windows Server 2012 or Windows Server 2016. Use the tool from whatever server matches your domain's functional level. The basic command to restore the defaults is a command-line tool called DCGPOFIX.

That being said, the tool works "as advertised" with Server 2012 R2 and later but appears to have a bug when run on Server 2008 R2.

Before we get to the weird stuff, let's assume your domain is functional level 2012 or later and you're using a Windows 2012 R2 or later server to make the repairs. To restore the defaults, you can tell DCGPOFIX to restore the "Default Domain Policy" GPO (with the /Target:Domain switch) or the "Default Domain Controllers Policy" GPO (with the /Target:DC switch). Or you can restore both with the /Target:BOTH switch, as shown in Figure 8.4.

FIGURE 8.4 Use DCGPOFIX to restore the defaults if necessary. Say Y(es) when prompted to proceed.

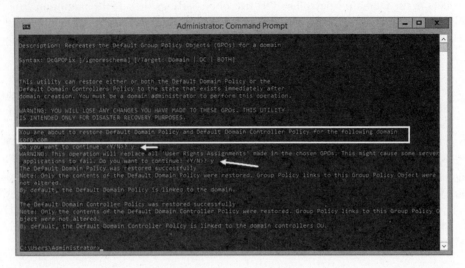

However, you might also encounter a strange situation if you're trying to bring back one of the default GPOs but you've updated the schema to some later version. If that happens, DCGPOFIX won't proceed unless you add the /ignoreschema switch in front.

The idea is that it will bring back the default GPO you choose based on the schema it knows (originally), not the one you might have upgraded to. There's a Microsoft Knowledge Base article (which refers to Server 2003 R2, but is valid for all operating systems and domain functional levels) here: http://support.microsoft.com/kb/932445. In short, you might have to run DCGPOFIX with the /ignoreschema switch, even though it appears there's no reason you might need it.

So, again, when using Server 2012 R2 or Windows Server 2016, everything seems to work just fine. It's if you still must use Windows Server 2008 R2 with this command that I've seen this command just inexplicably fail. The specific bug with Windows Server 2008 R2 is when you need to specifically restore just *one* of the defaults. In these cases here's my little work-around:

1. Make a backup of all your GPOs.

2. Run DCGPOFIX without any arguments or with /ignoreschema if required. This will restore both the "Default Domain Policy" and "Default Domain Controllers Policy."

3. Use the GPMC to restore the one you didn't actually need to repair.

Now, you'll have the one recovered from DCGPOFIX all nice and clean, and the one you restored the settings from using your backup will be perfectly fine from the last backup. Messy, messy. But it works.

If you have to restore the default GPOs for some reason, you might be in a heap of trouble anyway and might want to call Microsoft Product Support Services for extra guidance.

The Strange Life of Password Policy

If you create a new GPO, link it to any OU, and then edit your new GPO, it certainly appears as if you *could* set the Password Policy and Account Lockout policy using a GPO.

But does it do anything? Let's find out.

Additionally, we'll talk about a function in Windows Server 2008 and later domains called Fine-Grained Password Policy.

Resetting User Rights Assignments

Sometimes, people ask me if it's possible to simply reset the User Rights Assignment instead of plowing back the entire "Default Domain Controllers" GPO. You might want to do this if you take over someone else's domain and notice they've left some kind of mess.

To do so, see the Microsoft Knowledge Base article "How to Reset User Rights in the Default Domain Group Policy in Windows Server 2003" (KB 324800) at:

https://support.microsoft.com/en-us/kb/324800?wa=wsignin1.0.

Since the text provided in the article is for Windows Server 2003 domains, if you have a later domain type my advice is to bring up the same domain functional level in a test lab, then copy the GPTTMPL.INF file sections from that test domain into your real world.

So, in short—the advice is good, but the information is old, so use the step-by-step instructions but utilize your own domain type to get the information.

What Happens When You Set Password Settings at an OU Level

For example, I have a **Sales** OU in which I recently placed WIN10. As you can see in Figure 8.5, I created and linked a GPO, called "Sales Password Policy," to the **Sales** OU. I am setting the Password Policy so that the minimum password length is 10 characters.

At first glance this would seem to be counterproductive, because, as already stated, these policy settings only take hold of the accounts in the domain via the "Default Domain Policy" GPO. But administrators might actually want to perform this seemingly contradictory action. That is, when the user logs on locally to the Windows workstation, the account policy settings contained in the GPO linked to the OU will have been magically planted on their machine to take effect for *local* accounts. In Figure 8.6, I have logged in as the local administrator account on the workstation.

FIGURE 8.5   It might seem counterproductive to set the Password Policy at any level but the domain.

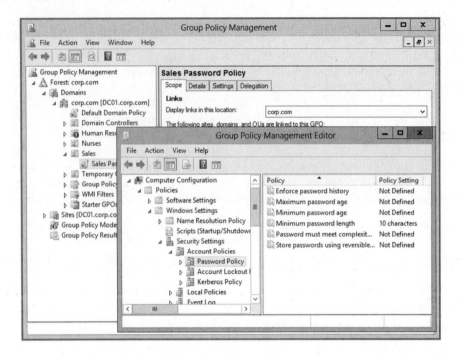

FIGURE 8.6   Setting a Password Policy in the domain (other than at the domain level) will affect passwords used for local accounts on member machines.

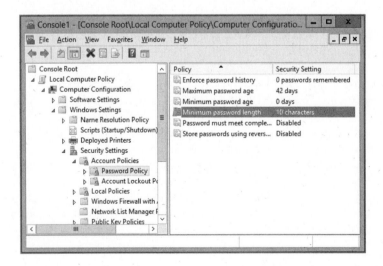

Again, this won't affect users' accounts when users are logging onto the domain; rather, it affects only the local accounts on the targeted computers. This could be helpful if you grant local administrator rights to users on their workstations or laptops and want to set a baseline.

Fine-Grained Password Policy

So if setting Password Policy at an OU level doesn't affect your domain users, is there a way to set password policies on specific users in the domain such that they have different password requirements?

Short answer: yes. It's called Fine-Grained Password Policy (FGPP) and it's built into Windows Server 2008 and later domains.

Longer answer (here goes). You can do this when:

- you have all Domain Controllers that are Windows Server 2008 and later, and
- the domain functional level has been raised to at least Windows Server 2008, and
- you can accept that you can't set Fine-Grained Password Policy on OUs, and
- you accept that you can't use Group Policy to do it.

So, I know I mentioned it, but I think it bears repeating: you can't use Group Policy and affect an entire OU using FGPP. That would be nice, but it's simply not part of the deal here.

Now, this is a Group Policy book, but I'm going to give you the ever-so-brief run-through anyway, because you might want to get a feel for how this works. I'll have some links a little later for you to get super-deep with FGPP if you'd like to.

So, with all those caveats behind us, what does FGPP bring to the table? It brings us the ability to dictate a specific Password Policy for a user account or an Active Directory global security group the user is a member of. The key takeaway here is the word *group* and not *OU*.

Let's check it out to see how it works. You'll want to perform these steps directly using your Windows 10 management machine or your Windows Server 2016 machine acting as your management machine. (These steps work fine with Windows 8 and later, actually, or Windows Server 2012 as your management machine.)

> If you don't have a modern Windows management machine, you can still effectively perform FGPP using Windows Server 2008. I go into detail in the previous edition of the book on how to use ADSI edit to perform the work. If you don't have a copy of the previous edition, check out this article: `http://tinyurl.com/2xld67`.

Getting Ready for Fine-Grained Password Policy

If you're going to make use of this feature, the domain functional level must be Windows Server 2008 or later. You can check and/or raise the functional level by using Active Directory Users and Computers, right-clicking over the domain name, and selecting "Raise domain functional level," as seen in Figure 8.7.

FIGURE 8.7 Use Active Directory Users and Computers to raise the domain functional level (if needed).

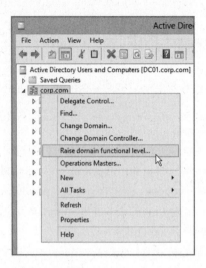

When you do, you can see the current domain functional level and/or change to the Windows Server 2008 or later functional level if necessary, as shown in Figure 8.8. You'll need to do this if you want to proceed.

FIGURE 8.8 If you want to use Fine-Grained Password Policy, the domain functional level must be Windows Server 2008 or later; you can raise it here if necessary.

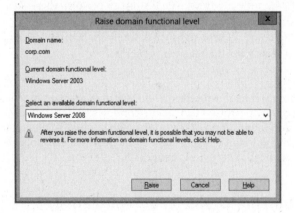

Creating a Password Setting Object

Using Active Directory Administrative Center (ADAC) will help us create the unit we need, called a Password Setting Object (PSO). Here's the breakdown of what we need to do to make the magic happen:

1. Create a PSO in the Password Settings Container (PSC) using ADAC.

2. Configure the PSO options by completing the form.

3. Specify which PSO will affect what user accounts or global security groups.

   So let's get started.

Creating a Password Settings Object

The tool we use is the Active Directory Administrative Console (ADAC). This is the first time we use this tool in the book, so here we go.

Begin by clicking Start, and then locate Active Directory Administrative Center. As shown in Figure 8.9, click on the Tree view; then under System, locate Password Settings Container. Select New ➤ Password Settings, as shown in Figure 8.9.

FIGURE 8.9   Create your PSO using Active Directory Administrative Center.

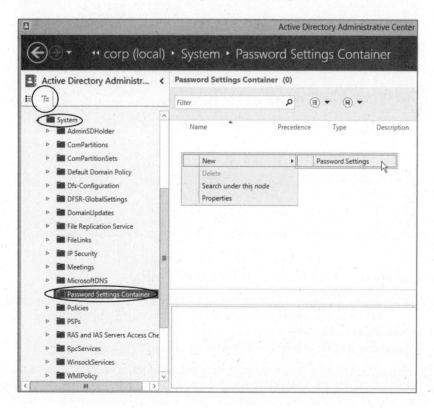

Then it's simply "fill in the blank" time, as seen in Figure 8.10.

Most of the values are self-explanatory. One is a little confusing: Precedence. This number is used as a "cost" for priority between different policies in case a user is hit by multiple PSOs. Be sure to leave space below and above for future use. The stronger the PSO password settings are, the lower the cost should be. In other words, use low numbers for PSOs you want to "win" if there's a precedence collision. (See more on this subject in the next section, "PSO Precedence and the Default Domain Policy.")

When you've finished entering the values in the form, you can select Add next to "Directly Applies To," as also seen in Figure 8.10.

Simply enter specific users or groups to apply your PSO to and click OK.

FIGURE 8.10   Windows Server 2012 and later has a GUI for FGPP.

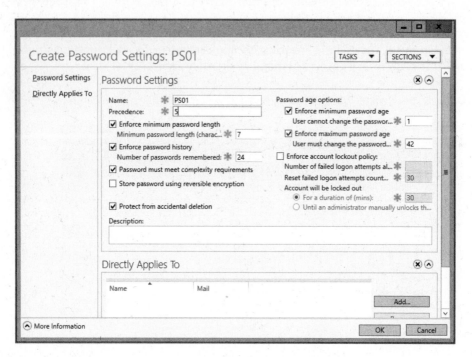

PSO Precedence and the Default Domain Policy

Now in all this hubbub of creating a PSO for your users and groups, you might have forgotten all about the Default Domain Policy. Turns out, it's still working for you, behind the scenes in case you never touch PSOs.

Here's the breakdown of what happens now that you have PSOs set up:

1. If a user has a PSO linked directly to him, that PSO automatically wins. If there are multiple PSOs linked to the user, you'll see a warning in the event log on the Domain Controller, and the one with the *lowest* precedence value is the resultant PSO. If the user doesn't have a PSO linked directly to him, see step 2.

2. If the user is a member of a global security group, he gets a PSO linked to that security group. If the user is a member of multiple groups with PSOs linked to them, see step 3.

3. All the global groups of which the user is a member (and has PSOs linked) are compared. The one with the lowest precedence dictates his resultant PSO.

4. If none of these applies (no PSOs on his account or any group he's a member of), the Default Domain Policy is applied.

So one good strategy is to ensure that your Default Domain Policy password settings are really tough by default. That way, if you make some mistake with FGPP, and someone "defaults" to the Default Domain Policy, you've still got nice, tough security on those passwords. Basically, you'll be "secure by default."

More Information on Fine-Grained Password Policy

Before we leave this topic, it should be noted that there are three attributes that, on a per-user basis, can always override the PSO:

- Reversible password encryption required
- Password not required
- Password does not expire

If any of these attributes are set directly on a user using Active Directory Users and Computers, they will be honored and the PSO policy for those attributes will be ignored.

If you'd like to spend more quality time with FGPP, here are some great sites for you to explore:

- Getting started guide from Microsoft:

  http://technet.microsoft.com/en-us/library/cc770394(v=ws.10).aspx

- Jakob Heidelberg's take on FGPP:

  http://tinyurl.com/2xld67

- And his Part 2:

  http://tinyurl.com/224lyj

- And Ulf B. Simon-Weidner's blog at:

  http://tinyurl.com/22h4sf

Additionally, if you're a command-line freak and don't want to deal with the hassle of the ADSI Edit GUI we saw, Joe from www.Joeware.net has a great tool called PSOMgr that will do just the trick. Just head over to www.joeware.net/freetools/tools/psomgr/index.htm.

I also found a set of tools by Christoffer Andersson that you might find useful. The "Fine Grain Password Policy Tool 1.0" can be found here: http://tinyurl.com/ygwux9w.

Additionally, Microsoft has built-in PowerShell support for Fine-Grained Password Policy. You can start here on your journey:

http://technet.microsoft.com/en-us/library/dd391898(WS.10).aspx

Inside Basic and Advanced Auditing

Auditing is a powerful tool. It can help you determine when people are doing things they shouldn't as well as help you determine when people are doing things they should.

We'll use Group Policy to manage auditing for our Windows Server 2008 R2 and Windows 7 and later machines.

> If you have Windows Vista and Windows Server 2008 machines, they won't know to process the Group Policy settings we're about to explore. Instead they must manually be kicked in the pants using the command-line tool Auditpol.exe. If you need to check that out, please check out previous editions of the book.

Basic Auditable Events Using Group Policy

So, Group Policy can be used to turn on many auditable events.

Certain aspects of auditing you'll turn on at the **Domain Controllers** OU level, inside the "Default Domain Controllers Policy" GPO. Other aspects of auditing you'll typically turn on at other OU levels (via a GPO linked to the OU containing the systems you want to audit).

In Figure 8.11, you can see the default auditing settings contained within the "Default Domain Controllers Policy" GPO. In fact, that screen shot is a little deceiving; specifically, some of those items are hard-coded on by default, even though the Group Policy doesn't have anything enabled. Weird.

The list of possibilities for auditing are numerous and confusing. Table 8.1 shows what can be audited, which items are turned on by default, plus a guideline for where you should perform the audit.

> No matter how much you audit, it does you no good unless you're actually reviewing the logs. There is no way out of the box to centralize the collection of logs from your Domain Controllers, servers, or workstations. Consider a third-party tool. There are many. Just Bingle (that's Google and/or Bing) for "Event Log Monitor tool."

FIGURE 8.11   Windows Server 2008 and later "Default Domain Controller Policy" GPO. Remember, some items are hard-coded on by default (even though you don't see them enabled here).

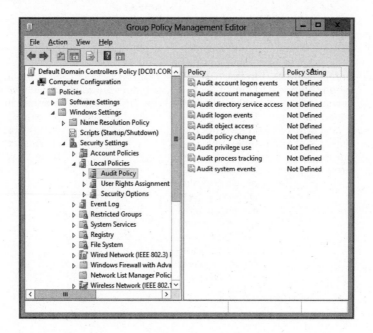

TABLE 8.1   Auditable events

Auditing right	What it does	Where you should set it	Is it on by default in Windows 2008+ Active Directory?	Notes
Audit account logon events	Enters events when someone attempts to log onto Active Directory.	In the "Default Domain Controllers Policy" GPO to monitor when anyone tries to log onto Active Directory.	Yes. Hard-coded on, even though the GPO doesn't show it enabled.	By default, only successes generate events. Settings can be changed to record logon failures as well.

TABLE 8.1   Auditable events *(continued)*

Auditing right	What it does	Where you should set it	Is it on by default in Windows 2008+ Active Directory?	Notes
Audit account management	Enters events when someone creates, deletes, renames, enables, or disables users, computers, groups, and so on.	In the "Default Domain Controllers Policy" GPO to generate events for when users, computers, and so on are created in Active Directory. Set at the OU level to generate events on file servers or workstations for when users and groups are created on member machines.	Yes. Hard-coded on, even though the GPO doesn't show it enabled.	By default, only successful object manipulations generate events. Settings can be changed to record failures as well.
Audit directory service access	Enters events when Active Directory objects are specified to be audited.	In the "Default Domain Controllers Policy" GPO.	Yes. Hard-coded on, even though the GPO doesn't show it enabled.	Works in conjunction with the actual attribute in Active Directory that has auditing for users or computers enabled. Can be used to audit other aspects of Active Directory. See the section "Auditing Group Policy Object Changes."
Audit logon events	Enters events for interactive logon (Local logon) and network logon (Kerberos).	Set at OU level to generate logon events on servers you want to track access for.	Yes. Hard-coded on, even though the GPO doesn't show it enabled.	Set this setting to determine if UserA touches a shared folder on ServerA. This will constitute an auditable event for "Audit logon events."

TABLE 8.1   Auditable events *(continued)*

Auditing right	What it does	Where you should set it	Is it on by default in Windows 2008+ Active Directory?	Notes
Audit object access	Enters events when file objects are specified to be audited.	If you store files on your Domain Controllers, you can set this at the "Default Domain Controllers Policy" GPO. Otherwise, set it at the OU level to monitor specific files within member machines.	No.	Works in conjunction with the actual file on the file server that has auditing enabled. See the section "Auditing File Access."
Audit policy change	Enters events when changes are made to user rights, auditing policies, or trust relationships.	In the "Default Domain Controllers" GPO to monitor when changes are made within Active Directory. Set at OU level to monitor when changes are made on member machines.	Yes. Hard-coded on, even though the GPO doesn't show it enabled.	See discussion in the section "Auditing File Access".

TABLE 8.1   Auditable events *(continued)*

Auditing right	What it does	Where you should set it	Is it on by default in Windows 2008+ Active Directory?	Notes
Audit privilege use	Enters events when any user right is used, such as backup and restore.	In the "Default Domain Controllers Policy" GPO to generate events for when accounts in Active Directory are used. Set at the OU level to generate events on file servers when accounts on member machines are used.	No.	
Audit process tracking.	Enters events when specific programs or processes are running.	In the "Default Domain Controllers Policy" GPO to affect Domain Controllers. Set at the OU level to monitor processes on specific servers within the OU.	No.	This is an advanced auditing feature that can generate a lot of events once turned on. Only turn this on at the behest of Microsoft PSS or another troubleshooting authority.

TABLE 8.1   Auditable events *(continued)*

Auditing right	What it does	Where you should set it	Is it on by default in Windows 2008+ Active Directory?	Notes
Audit system events.	Enters events when the system starts up or shuts down, or any time the security or system logs have been modified.	In the "Default Domain Controllers Policy" GPO to determine when Domain Controllers are rebooted or logs have been modified. Set at an OU level to monitor when member machines are rebooted or logs have been modified.	Yes. Hard-coded on, even though the GPO doesn't show it enabled.	

Auditing File Access

Let's start with something simple.

Let's assume you want to enable auditing when users attempt to access files on file servers. You could run around to each server and turn on file auditing. Or (insert fanfare music here), you could use Group Policy to do it in one fell swoop.

So, to leverage file auditing on a wide scale, you need to do the following within Active Directory:

- Create an OU.
- Move the accounts of those file servers in the OU.
- Create a GPO linked to the OU.
- Enable the **Audit object access** policy setting inside the GPO linked to the OU.

Once you do this, you then specify which files or folders on the target file server you wish to audit. To do so, follow these steps:

1. At the target file server itself, use Explorer to drill down into the drive letter and directory that you want to audit. Right-click the folder (or just one specific file), and choose Properties from the context menu to open the Properties dialog box.

2. Click the Security tab, and then click the Advanced button to open the Advanced Security Settings for the share.

3. Click the Auditing tab.

4. Click Add to open the Auditing Entry dialog box.

5. Click "Select a principal" and type the name of the group for which you want to enable auditing.

6. Click OK, and then click Show Advanced Permissions. As seen in Figure 8.12, this dialog box will allow you to add users to the auditing entries.

FIGURE 8.12   Set auditing for files on the file or folder on the target system.

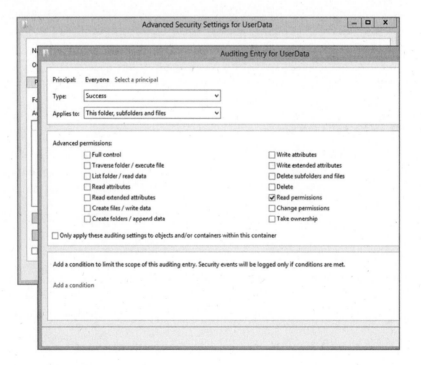

The simplest and most effective entry you can add is the Everyone group, as shown in Figure 8.12.

When anyone tries to touch the file, you can audit for certain triggers, such as the "Read" permission.

Auditing Group Policy Object Changes

You might be asked to determine who created a specific Group Policy and when it was created. To that end, you can leverage Active Directory's auditing capability and use Group Policy to audit Group Policy. Whenever a new Group Policy is born, deleted, or modified, 4662 events (seen in Figure 8.13) are generated.

FIGURE 8.13   There are 4662 events generated when GPOs are created or modified.

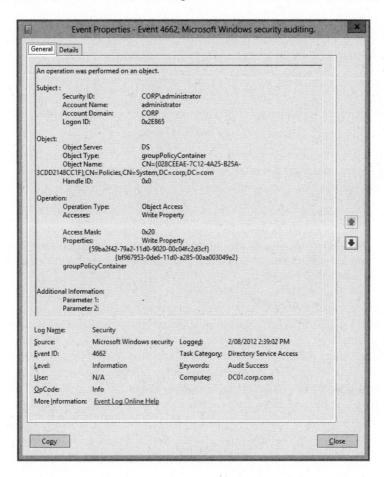

These events are generated on the Domain Controllers because two things are automatically set up by default in Active Directory:

- **Audit directory service access** is simply hard-coded "on" by default regardless of the value in the GUI (as seen in Figure 8.11). This setting likely comes from the security database that is applied during the Domain Controller promotion process.

- Auditing is turned on for the "Policies" object container within Active Directory. The Policies folder is where the GPC (Group Policy Container) for a given GPO is stored in Active Directory. Auditing is turned on so that events are generated when anyone creates, destroys, or modifies any objects inside the folder.

To view the Policies container, follow these steps:

1. Launch Active Directory Users and Computers.

2. Choose View ➤ Advanced Features. This enables you to see some normally hidden folders and security rights within Active Directory Users and Computers.

3. Drill down into Domain ➤ System ➤ Policies.

4. Right-click the Policies folder, and choose Properties from the context menu to open the Properties dialog box.

5. Click the Security tab.

6. Click the Advanced button to open the Advanced Security Settings for Policies window.

7. Click the Auditing tab, which is shown in Figure 8.14.

If you drill down even deeper, you'll discover that the Everyone group will trigger events when new GPOs are modified or created. It is this interaction that generates events, such as those shown in Figure 8.13.

 NOTE   If you wanted to hone in on who triggered events (as opposed to the Everyone group), you could remove the Everyone group from being audited (shown in Figure 8.14) and plunk in just the users or groups you wanted to monitor.

The Event ID to look for is 4662 in Windows Server 2008 and later (it used to be 566 in Windows Server 2003). You saw an example in Figure 8.13, which shows that a specific GPO is being changed.

Reading the event log details of a changed GPO is harder than trying to figure out what's going on in the movie *Pulp Fiction* the first time you watch it.

But it is possible to see that in Figure 8.13 a Group Policy Object was edited. You can't see its Friendly Name, but you can see its GUID (it starts with 028C and goes onward).

You do know who made the change though (in this case, it's CORP\Administrator), but there's nothing to tell you what changed.

For this reason there are various Group Policy change auditor utilities to increase the description of what occurred. To find them, Bingle (again, that's Bing/Google) for "Group Policy Change Auditor" and find a variety of options.

FIGURE 8.14   Auditing for GPO changes is set on the Policies folder within Active Directory Users and Computers.

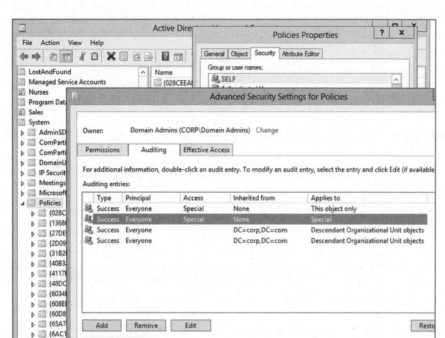

Advanced Audit Policy Configuration

Windows Server 2008 and Windows Vista introduced some potentially useful new auditing capabilities. You have the same general updated abilities when using Windows Server 2012 (or later) and client (or Windows 7 and later), but the way you turn them on is a little different.

I'm not going to be able to go into all the various new capabilities. There's just too many of them. We'll focus on one of them—an important one—in just a bit.

First I'll show you where to find these settings if you want to examine and, optionally, set them. From your Windows 10 management machine, open a new GPO and traverse to Computer Configuration ➢ Policies ➢ Windows Settings ➢ Security Settings ➢ Advanced Audit Policy Configuration, as shown in Figure 8.15.

Now, you might look at this list of 10 categories and 50+ subcategories and think, "Whoa. What does each one do?" Well, the good news is, I'm not going to bore you to death with all that. I am, however, going to point you toward all that boring material for when the time comes: `https://technet.microsoft.com/en-us/library/dn319056.aspx`. In case the article moves, just Bingle for "Advanced Security Audit Policy Settings."

As you can see in Figure 8.16, I'm using that link and drilling down to learn more about the DS Access category and the Audit Detailed Directory Service Replication subcategory. You can see the events it generates and other helpful information. Note that some of that same information is in an Explain tab right inside the policy itself—but I suggest reading both to get super clarity.

So, again, there are lots of Advanced Audit Policy Configuration settings that are perfectly valid on all versions of Windows since Windows Vista.

FIGURE 8.15   We'll explore the "Audit Directory Service Changes" policy.

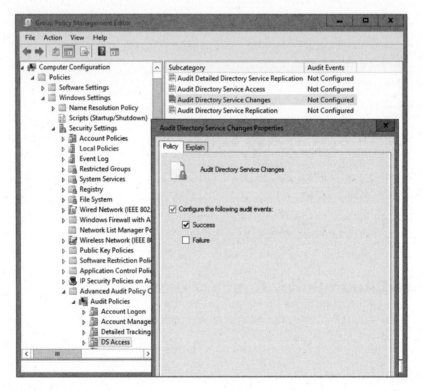

But, let's be super-duper "couldn't be clearer" clear:

- If you turn on these advanced auditing settings using Group Policy, your Windows XP and Windows Server 2003 machines will ignore them.

- If you turn on these advanced auditing settings using Group Policy, your Windows Server 2008 and Windows Vista machines will ignore them.

- If you turn on these advanced auditing settings using Group Policy, your Windows 7 and later (including Windows 10) machines will embrace them.

However, the caveat to bullet 2 is that you can force your Windows Server 2008 and Windows Vista machines to do the advanced auditing if you need them to. The trick is that they use an annoying tool called `Auditpol.exe`, whereas Windows 7 and later are happy as clams to use Group Policy.

FIGURE 8.16   The Microsoft TechNet articles on advanced auditing

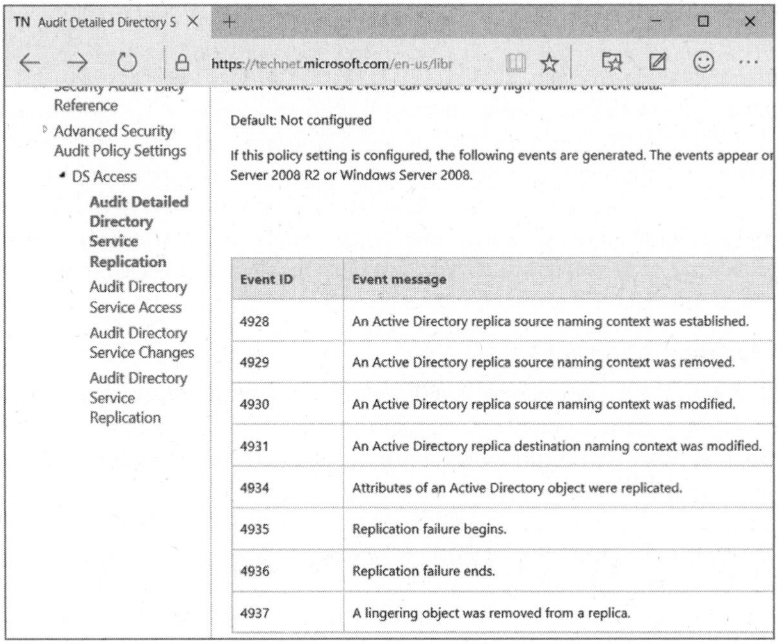

Let's work through one example that might be useful—but I'll do it only on Windows Server 2016 (which is happy to use the built-in Group Policy way to do things).

Advanced Auditing Example: Auditing Directory Service Changes

Let's check out Advanced Auditing using one example category: Audit Directory Service Changes.

Looking up in the Microsoft documentation I pointed to earlier, I learned that I can turn on the ability to show four new Event ID types for when stuff happens in Active Directory. Here are the Event IDs for this category and what they show:

- Event 5136: Show modified attributes
- Event 5137: Show created attributes
- Event 5138: Show undeleted attributes
- Event 5139: Show moved attributes

I was initially excited about these events, thinking that when a Group Policy Object was created or changed it would show me Events 5137 and 5136 and show me the changes *within the GPO*. It doesn't. It tells you a new GPO was created (but I knew that from Event ID 4662).

Oh well.

However, these events *do* show you what has changed in Active Directory after the magic happens. So if EastSalesUser9 was renamed to Sally, you'll get multiple 5136 events because there are a gaggle of things that go on under the hood when a simple user rename occurs.

Make sense?

So how do you enable these new gifts?

Now, before I give you the secret sauce here, you need to ask yourself, "How useful is this going to be for me?" Already you could audit if something changed. The question is, "Do you want to see before and after results of the auditing?" The second question you need to ask yourself is, "Am I prepared to perform multiple steps along anywhere in Active Directory I want to actually audit for these special events?" If the answer is "Yes," then go for it.

Again, I'm picking an example category that makes sense mostly for Domain Controllers. So, that's what I'll show you here.

Enabling Advanced Auditing

Again, enabling Advanced Auditing for Windows Server 2016 (in my example) is easy as pie. Just drill down to the Computer Configuration ➢ Policies ➢ Windows Settings ➢ Security Settings ➢ Advanced Audit Policy ➢ DS Access and enable **Auditing Directory Service Changes**, as seen in Figure 8.15 earlier.

The trick, again, however, is to ensure that your (Windows 7 and later) machine receives the GPO. If a Windows Server 2008 machine (or Windows Server 2003 machine) embraces the GPO, it will do nothing.

Auditing the Specific OU

So you've enabled the configuration using Group Policy.

But wait! There's more you have to do. Specifically, you have to turn on auditing at the OU level. At least, it's an OU in my example; you can audit other areas of Active Directory as well. Here's what to do next:

1. Using Active Directory Users and Computers, right-click the OU (or any object) for which you want to enable auditing, and then click Properties.

2. Click the Security tab, then click Advanced, and finally click the Auditing tab.

3. Click Add, then click "Select a principal" and type **Everyone** (or anyone you want to specifically audit for). Then click OK.

4. In "Apply to," select "Descendant User objects" (which is really far down the list). Note that you could also audit other objects if the container you're auditing contains other objects.

5. Under Access, select the Successful check box for "Write all properties."

6. Click OK in all open windows.

The Results

To see your results, rename a user within that OU you just adjusted for auditing. In Figure 8.17, you can see that I've renamed EastSalesUser9 to Sally.

FIGURE 8.17   Here you can see that the AttributeValue of Sally is placed on the ObjectDN of EastSalesUser9.

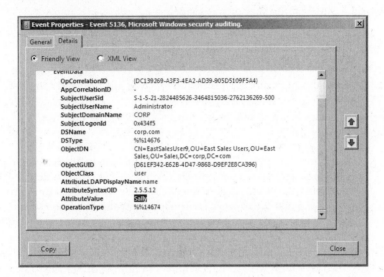

Is this useful? Possibly.

Well, here's the thing: you'd still get 4662 events that express that something's happened to the account anyway. If you want more information from the source, here's a little advanced step-by-step guide: http://tinyurl.com/ykju5q3.

Reading and testing is a must before rolling out into production.

Restricted Groups

We just conquered auditing.

Now, we'll move on to a new topic.

The idea is simple—ensure that the right people are always in the right groups. Sounds easy, right? Well, with a special security-related Group Policy function, you can use Restricted Groups to strictly control the following tasks:

- The membership of security groups that you create in Active Directory

- The security group membership on groups created on member machines (workstations or servers)

- The security groups that are nested within each other

You might want to strictly control these security groups or nestings to make sure that users in other areas of Active Directory, say, other Domain Administrators, don't inadvertently add someone to a group that shouldn't be there. Here are some practical uses of this technology:

▪ Ensure that the domain's Backup Operators group contains only Sally and Joe.

▪ Ensure that the local Administrators group on all desktops contains the user accounts of the help desk and desktop support personnel.

▪ Ensure that the domain's Sales global group contains the domain's East Sales, West Sales, North Sales, and South Sales local groups.

You set up these Restricted Groups' wishes via a GPO. You might be thinking to yourself that if the domain administrator creates the GPO, can't any domain administrator just delete the GPO and work around the point of the Restricted Groups settings? Yes, but the point of Restricted Groups is additional protection, not ultimate protection.

 An analogy might be "museum putty." The idea behind museum putty is that you attach it to your precious objects as extra protection in case an object gets bumped from the shelf. You can see museum putty here: http://tinyurl.com/ycxc78. The idea is that if someone tries to "bump" users in or out of the group, this will keep just the users you want in place.

Here's the trick about the Restricted Groups function: its younger, more capable brother just came back from college with the football trophy. I'm talking about the "Local Users and Groups" Group Policy Preferences function. Here's my honest opinion: I'd rather see you use Local Users and Groups Group Policy Preferences than the Group Policy Restricted Groups function—when it comes to manipulating local computers' groups, like the local Administrators group.

Here's why: It just works.

The interface is obvious about what you want to do, and what's going to happen.

You can easily "laser beam" add or remove a particular user from a group.

With that in mind, if you have a need to manipulate local users and groups—great. Use the Group Policy Preferences and be done. You'll be happier all around.

However, there is one use for Group Policy Restricted Groups that should not be overlooked—and we'll cover it right now. That's when you want to ensure that certain users are members of an Active Directory group.

Ah-ha! So the younger, more capable brother has a little Achilles heel. But this is his only one. So, if you'd like to learn how to utilize Group Policy Restricted Groups to control Active Directory groups, then read on.

To save space, I won't go into detail on how to use Group Policy Restricted Groups for any use on local groups. Again, in those cases, I couldn't recommend the Group Policy Preferences Local Users and Groups (Chapter 5) highly enough.

Strictly Controlling Active Directory Groups

The ideal way to strictly control Active Directory groups with specific Active Directory users is to create a new GPO and link it to the **Domain Controllers** OU.

You *could* modify the "Default Domain Controllers Policy" GPO directly, but as stated earlier, it's better to create a new GPO when dealing with "normal" settings such as this one. This keeps the "Default Domain Controllers Policy" GPO as clean as possible. Likewise, you *could* modify the "Default Domain Policy" GPO. But, again, keeping away from the defaults for other than their special uses (as previously discussed) is preferred.

> If you set up Restricted Groups policies at multiple levels in Active Directory, there is no "merging" between Restricted Groups policy settings. The "last applied" policy wins. For example, if you set up a Restricted Groups policy, link it to the domain level, create another Restricted Groups policy, and link it to the **Domain Controllers** OU, the one linked to the **Domain Controllers** OU "wins."

To get started with Restricted Groups:

1. Open the GPO and traverse to Computer Configuration ➢ Policies ➢ Windows Settings ➢ Security Settings ➢ Restricted Groups.

2. Right-click Restricted Groups, and choose Add Group from the context menu, which opens the Add Group dialog box.

3. Click Browse to open the Browse dialog box, and browse for a group, say, the domain's Backup Operators; then click OK.

4. When you do, the Backup Operator Properties dialog box, shown in Figure 8.18, appears.

You can now choose domain members to place in the "Members of this group" list. In Figure 8.18, I have already added Sally User's account, which is in the domain, and I'm about to add Joe User's domain account.

> Be careful about just typing in the user account names without either browsing the domain or manually entering the domain with the DOMAIN\user syntax. Restricted Groups in Active Directory will not apply correctly unless you do this.

When Restricted Groups Settings Take Effect

After you enter the users in the "Members of this group" list and click OK, you can sit back and wait for all Domain Controllers to get the change and process Group Policy. However, if you have only one Domain Controller in your test lab, this change should occur quickly. You can run gpupdate to make it occur even faster in this case. This happens because any new GPO you create and link to the **Domain Controllers** OU should get picked up and applied right away—about 5 minutes after replication occurs.

Now, take a look inside the Backup Operators group using Active Directory Users and Computers. Sally's and Joe's accounts should be forced inside Backup Operators.

FIGURE 8.18   You can specify which users you want to ensure are in specific groups.

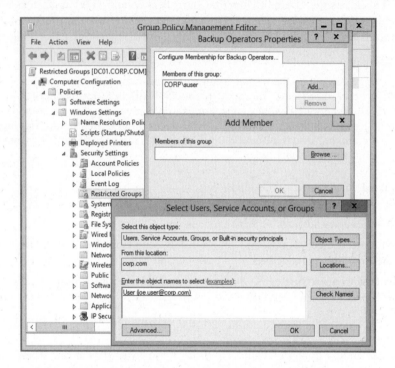

When Restricted Groups Settings Get Refreshed

If someone were to *remove* Sally and Joe from Backup Operators in Active Directory Users and Computers, their accounts would be repopulated during the background security refresh, which is every 16 hours.

As described in Chapter 3, you have two choices if you don't want to wait 16 hours for the background security refresh:

- Link a GPO to the **Domain Controllers** OU level, with the **Security policy processing** policy setting with the "Process even if the Group Policy objects have not changed" flag set. Then, the Background Security Refresh will process with the normal background refresh (every 5 minutes for DCs).

- Force a manual refresh by running gpupdate /force on your Domain Controller. Recall that gpupdate /force may be used when the underlying GPO hasn't changed and you want your changes reflected immediately.

The users removed from Backup Operators will pop right back in!

There is one caveat with the "Members of this group" section of Restricted Groups: this is an explicit list. If you later add more users using Active Directory Users and Computers, they will also be removed when the Restricted Groups policy is refreshed. Only the users listed in the "Members of this group" section will return.

Strictly Applying Group Nesting

Another trick Restricted Groups can perform is that it can ensure that one domain group is nested inside another. Like the "Strictly Controlling Active Directory Groups" trick, you need a GPO linked to the **Domain Controllers** OU.

The interface is a bit counterintuitive; the idea is that you name a group (say, HR-OU-Admins) and then specify the group of which it will be a member.

To nest one group within another:

1. Open the GPO and traverse to Computer Configuration ➢ Policies ➢ Windows Settings ➢ Security Settings ➢ Restricted Groups.

2. Right-click Restricted Groups, and choose Add Group from the context menu, which opens the Add Group dialog box.

3. Click Browse to open the Browse dialog box, and locate the first group. Click OK in the Add Group dialog box to select your group.

4. When you do, the Properties dialog box appears, as shown in Figure 8.18 earlier.

5. Then, you'll click the Add button in the "This group is a member of" section of the Properties dialog box (not shown in Figure 8.18). You'll then be able to specify the second group name.

When you're finished, and the Group Policy applies, the result will be that the first group will be forcefully nested within the second group. In order for this to work well, remember that you can nest global groups into domain local groups. Additionally, global groups can be nested into global groups.

WARNING While you are creating a Restricted Groups policy, take care. Results can be unpredictable when you mix the "This group is a member of" and "Members of this group" sections. If you have ensured a group's membership using the "Members of this group" setting, don't attempt to further modify that group's membership by feeding the "This group is a member of" users (by lying to the Restricted Groups function) to extend the original group's membership! On occasion, "This group is a member of" and "Members of this group" will conflict if you try to add users to both headings.

Which Groups Can Go into Which Other Groups via Restricted Groups?

The processing of Restricted Groups can sometimes be picky depending on the scenario. (This is officially documented in the Microsoft Knowledge Base article 810076 at http://support.microsoft.com/kb/810076.)

Microsoft Knowledge Base article 810076 now has several tables to help you during your testing of this feature. No operating systems past Windows XP are represented in this table yet. While I haven't tested every combination, I'm told iterations of the operating system later than Windows XP/SP2 are supposed to also act like Windows XP/SP2.

Restrict Software Using AppLocker

Windows, as a product, is successful. And the reason for that is pretty simple: it runs a lot of software. Running a lot of software sounds good, until you're on the other end of the equation and, as an IT professional, you want to start *preventing* some of that software from running.

Many viruses show up in your users' inboxes as either executables or .VBS scripting files. Just one launch within your confines and you're cleaning up for a week. Additionally, users will bring in unknown software from home or download junk off the Internet, and then, when the computer blows up, they turn around and blame you. What an injustice!

To that end, there are three separate mechanisms to squelch which software will run—Software Restriction Policies (SRP), AppLocker, and DeviceGuard:

- Software Restriction Policies is available when the target machine is Windows XP or later.

- AppLocker is available when the target is Windows 7 and later or Windows Server 2008 and later.

- DeviceGuard is available when the target is Windows 10.

It's true that Software Restriction Policies originated with Windows XP, but it still works perfectly well on Windows 10.

But it turns out your only choice might be to use Software Restriction Policies instead of AppLocker or DeviceGuard. That's because neither AppLocker nor DeviceGuard is available on every version of Windows 7, Windows 8, and Windows 10.

In this document (http://tinyurl.com/yjvh34d), Microsoft is very clear: AppLocker is only available for the Enterprise (and Ultimate) versions of Windows 7 and later. It is not available in the Professional (or Home) versions of Windows 7 and later.

And as of this writing, which is just before Windows 10 is to be finally released, DeviceGuard (a) isn't finished yet, and (b) is scheduled to work only on Windows 10 Enterprise.

Ouch. That potentially puts these two neat security features out of reach for a lot of people. So, again, if you are using Windows 7 Professional (and later), you do still have access to the Software Restriction Policies, which is up first.

Said another way: all versions of Windows XP, Windows Vista, Windows 7, Windows 8, and Windows 10 will honor Software Restriction Policies. But only Windows 7 Enterprise or Ultimate and Windows 8 Enterprise and Windows 10 Enterprise will honor AppLocker policies.

So, I would say to read the section on Software Restriction Policies to get an overview of some concepts. Then if you have a version of Windows that will honor AppLocker, use AppLocker.

If you're wondering what DeviceGuard is and how it relates to AppLocker, you can jump ahead to the sidebar entitled "AppLocker vs. DeviceGuard."

So if you have a use case for DeviceGuard (and an edition of Windows 10 that supports DeviceGuard), check that out.

If you have no choice *but* to use Software Restriction Policies, then use Software Restriction Policies.

Inside Software Restriction Policies

Software Restriction Policies enables you, the administrator, to precisely dictate what software will and will not run on your Windows XP desktops (or, your Windows 7, Windows 8, or Windows 10 desktops).

You can restrict software for specific users or for all users on a specific machine. You'll find Software Restriction Policies in Computer Configuration ➢ Policies ➢ Windows Settings ➢ Security Settings ➢ Software Restriction Policies. Just right-click over the Software Restriction Policies node, and select New Software Restriction Policies, as shown in Figure 8.19, to get started.

Software Restriction Policies is also available as a node under User Configuration ➢ Policies ➢ Windows Settings ➢ Security Settings ➢ Software Restriction Policies, which can also be seen in Figure 8.19.

Like other policies that affect users or computers, you'll need an OU containing the user or computer accounts you want to restrict, and you'll need a GPO linked to that OU. Or you can set a GPO linked to the domain level, which affects all machines (or, alternatively, users). Typically, you'll use the Computer-side branch of Software Restriction Policies. That way, all users on a specific machine are restricted from using specific "known bad" applications.

 Software Restriction Policies is also valid when set on a local computer within a local policy (via gpedit.msc). This can be particularly useful for a Windows Server acting as a Remote Desktop/Terminal Server.

GPOs containing Software Restriction Policies might be common in environments that include any variety of Windows machines.

FIGURE 8.19 Software Restriction Policies is available in both the Computer and User nodes.

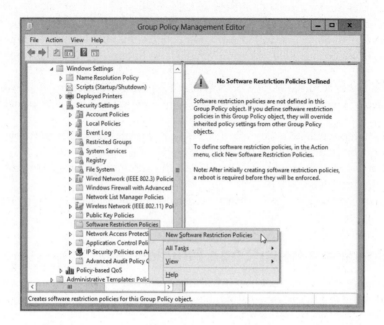

Software Restriction Policies' "Philosophies"

Using Software Restriction Policies with your Windows users involves three primary philosophies. You can choose your philosophy by selecting the Security Levels branch of Software Restriction Policies, as shown in Figure 8.20.

Philosophy 1 (aka "The Black List") *Allow everything to run except specifically named items.* Here, we've chosen the default that the Unrestricted option is selected. Windows will allow all programs to run, like normal. However, if the administrator names certain applications, such as a virus or a game, it will be prevented from running. It's as if you're putting the things you don't want on the "black list" but allowing everything else to run.

Philosophy 2 (aka "The Doggie Door") *Don't allow programs of a certain type to run.* Allow only specifically named items of that type to pass. I nickname this one "The Doggie Door." The Unrestricted option is selected. You can choose to squelch all files of a certain type, say, all .VBS files. However, you can instruct Windows to allow .VBS files that are digitally signed from your IT department to run.

Philosophy 3 (aka "The White List") *Nothing is allowed to run but the operating system and explicitly named items.* This is the "Full Lockdown" approach. The Disallowed option is selected. This is the most heavy-handed approach but the safest. Only operating system components will run, unless you specifically open up ways for programs to be run. Be careful when using this method; it can get you into a lot of trouble quickly.

FIGURE 8.20   The Security Levels branch of Software Restriction Policies sets your default level of protection.

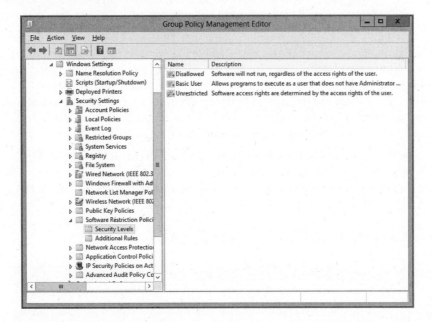

You can also specify that certain software can only be run with Basic User credentials. That is, if you decide that you want to run a specific application but are concerned that in doing so it might run with too many rights, you can specify it to run as a "Basic User."

You cannot select the Basic User security level for a certificate rule (described next).

Software Restriction Policies' Rules

Once you've chosen your philosophy, you can choose how wide the door is for other stuff. There are four rules to either allow or deny specific software:

- Hash
- Path
- Certificate
- Network zone

To create a new rule, select the Additional Rules folder, and right-click in the right pane to see your choices, as shown in Figure 8.21.

 By default, some path rules are set that enable access to critical portions of the Registry. These are enabled so that the operating system can write to the Registry even if the Disallowed option is set in the Security Levels branch.

Hash Rule In computer science terms, a hash value is a numeric representation, or fingerprint, that can uniquely identify a file should it be renamed. It's sort of like a "checksum" value. For instance, if I rename Doom.exe to Gloom.exe, the actual bits, the 1s and 0s, contained within the .EXE file are the same. Therefore, the hash value is the same. However, if any changes are made to the file (even if one bit is changed), the hash value is different. Hash rules are quite useful in containing any application that's an .EXE or a .DLL.

Sure, it's true that a user could use a hex editor (such as FRHED from http://frhed .sourceforge.net/) and change just one bit in an .EXE or .DLL file to get a new hash value, but it's bloody unlikely. And, the .EXE could be damaged and unusable in the process! And that's reasonably good protection for most of us.

FIGURE 8.21 The rules of Software Restriction Policies

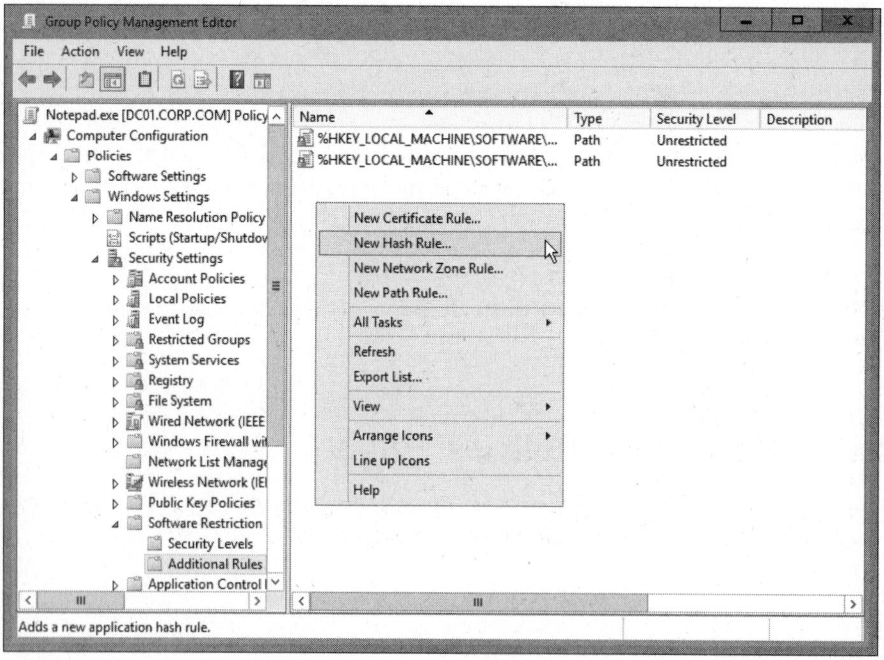

Path Rule   You can specify to open (or restrict) certain applications based on where they reside on the hard drive. You can set up a path rule to specify a specific folder or full path to a program. Most environment variables are valid, such as %HOMEDRIVE%, %HOMEPATH%, %USERPROFILE%, %WINDIR%, %APPDATA%, %PROGRAMFILES%, and %TEMP%. Additionally, path rules can stomp out the running of any file type you desire, say, VBScript files. For example, if you set up a path rule to disallow files named *.vb*, all VBScript file variants will be unable to execute.

Certificate Rule   Certificate rules use digitally signed certificates. You can use certificate rules to sign your own applications or scripts and then use a certificate rule to specify your IT department as a Trusted Publisher. Users, admins, or Enterprise Admins can be specified as Trusted Publishers. Be sure to read the sidebar "Software Restriction Policies and Digital Signatures" before rolling out certificate rules. Note that these rules are unable to specify the Basic User security level as previously described.

Network Zone Rule   Users will download crap off the Internet. This is a fact of life. However, with Network Zone Rule you can specify which Internet Explorer zones are allowed for download. You can specify Internet, Intranet, Restricted Sites, Trusted Sites, and My Computer. The bad news about zone rules, however, is that they simply aren't all that useful. They prevent downloads of applications with the MSI format but nothing else. So, in my opinion, they're not quite ready for primetime use. (Note that we talk more about MSI files in Chapter 11.)

Setting Up a Software Restriction Policy with a Rule

As stated, you can craft your Software Restriction Policies in myriad ways. Space doesn't permit explaining all of them, so I'll just give you one example. We'll test our Software Restriction Policies by locking down a not-so-nefarious application: Windows Notepad.

To restrict Notepad from your environment, follow these steps:

1. Create a new hash rule, as seen in Figure 8.21, earlier in this chapter.

2. Click Browse and locate notepad.exe.

> You might have to type **\\Win10\c$\windows\system32\notepad.exe** to point to a copy of Notepad on one of your Windows 10 machines if you yourself are not on a Windows 10 machine with the same version of Notepad.

So, the "File information" field (shown in Figure 8.22) shows notepad.exe and holds (but doesn't show) the actual file hash value.

In the updated GPMC, there isn't a file hash that's shown, but it's still doing the work.

Under the hood, the Software Restriction Policies editor actually created *two* file hashes. One hash is an MD5 hash (for older Windows XP and Windows Server 2003 clients), and another is an SHA-256 hash for newer XP, Windows Server 2003, and Windows Vista and later clients. Windows Vista and later still reads MD5 hashes created using older Windows XP management stations.

Now let's be super clear: the hash value for notepad.exe on Windows 8.1 won't equal the hash value for notepad.exe on Windows 10. With that in mind, if you want to restrict notepad.exe everywhere, you'll need to get a hold of each and every notepad.exe variant and add it as a hash value.

Testing Your Software Restriction Policies

In the previous example, you could create a Software Restriction Policies item that affects users or computers. If your policy is for users, for this very first test, log off. If your policy is for computers, run gpupdate or reboot the machine.

Then just launch Notepad and see what happens.

On Windows 10, a whole lot of nothing happens. It just prevents Notepad from launching. There's so much "nothing" that there's not even anything to show you in a screen shot.

FIGURE 8.22   Once you specify the file, the hash value is filled in.

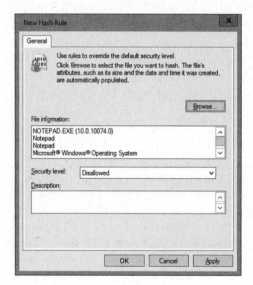

That being said, if you try to run notepad.exe from a command prompt, you'll get what's seen here.

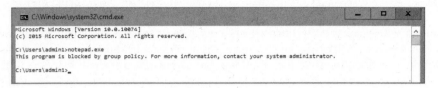

Software Restriction Policies and Digital Signatures

Note that there is a security policy setting named **System settings: Use Certificate Rules on Windows Executables for Software Restriction Policies** located in Computer Configuration ➤ Policies ➤ Windows Settings ➤ Security Settings ➤ Local Policies ➤ Security Options.

You'll need to enable this policy setting if you create a certificate rule on a *digitally signed* .EXE. You can tell if a file is digitally signed by checking out its properties and looking for a Digital Signatures tab, as seen here in the file's properties. WINWORD.EXE has a Digital Signatures tab, whereas, say the old Solitaire for Windows XP, sol.exe has none.

If you were to restrict a digitally signed .EXE, such as WINWORD.EXE, this policy setting would be necessary for the certificate rule to be embraced by your client systems.

As stated, this policy setting is only necessary for digitally signed .EXE files. However, if you only deal with digitally signed .VBS or .MSI files, you don't have to worry about this setting at all.

Understanding When Software Restriction Policies Apply

When you log onto a machine, you're running a shell program that launches other programs. This is sometimes called a "launching process." That shell program (or launching process) is familiar—Explorer.exe. Whenever Explorer.exe (or another launching process) launches restricted software, it checks a portion of the Registry for any restrictions. How does this help determine when Software Restriction Policies applies?

> **TIP** Software Restriction Policies are housed in HKEY_LOCAL_MACHINE\ SOFTWARE\Policies\Microsoft\Windows\Safer\CodeIdentifiers.

A Software Restriction Policy item affects a machine as soon as it's downloaded via the Group Policy engine. After that, no new instances of that application are possible. It doesn't matter if the launching program (i.e., Explorer) has already been started; it doesn't need a refresh. It just restricts the software as specified in the Software Restriction Policies as soon as the Group Policy containing the Software Restriction Policies is applied. Note, however, that programs *already* running don't magically stop running. This will only prevent future instances of the specified application from running. So, if notepad.exe is already running, then a Software Restriction Policy comes down to disable it—as long as notepad.exe is running, it stays running. When you close it, however, it cannot be reopened again because Explorer has checked in with the Registry and prevents it.

Troubleshooting Software Restriction Policies

You can troubleshoot Software Restriction Policies in two primary ways:

- Inspect the Registry to see if the Software Restriction Policies are embraced.
- Enable advanced logging.

Inspecting the Software Restriction Policies Location in the Registry

If Software Restriction Policies aren't being applied, and you logged off and back on, log on again as the administrator at the target machine and check KEY_LOCAL_MACHINE or:

HKEY_CURRENT_USER\SOFTWARE\Policies\Microsoft\Windows\Safer\CodeIdentifiers

Inside, you'll see numbered branches containing the rules. In Figure 8.23, you can see notepad.exe restricted by a hash rule.

Note that operating system files change with a Windows Update or a service pack— sometimes even innocuous things like notepad.exe! If after an update your client isn't restricting applications as you expect (because the hash value changes even after a tiny change), make sure the version number of the restricted application matches the version located on the client. More specifically, make sure the hash values match.

Software Restriction Policies Advanced Logging

You can troubleshoot Software Restriction Policies via a log file. To do so, follow these steps:

1. In the Registry, traverse to:

   KEY_LOCAL_MACHINE\SOFTWARE\Policies\Microsoft\Windows\Safer\CodeIdentifiers

2. Create a new string value named LogFileName.

3. In the Data field of the new Registry key, enter the full path and name of a log file—for example, **C:\temp\srplog.txt**.

FIGURE 8.23   The Registry lays out what will be restricted.

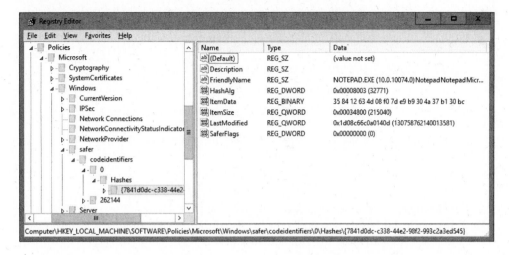

Now whenever an application runs, a line is written to the log file explaining why it can or cannot run. Here are two lines from that log file: the first when I run dogfood.exe (which is free to run) and the second when I run notepad.exe (which is restricted):

```
cmd.exe (PID = 1576) identified C:\WINDOWS\system32\dogfood.exe as Unrestricted
    using path rule, Guid = {191cd7fa-f240-4a17-8986-94d480a6c8ca}

cmd.exe (PID = 1576) identified C:\WINDOWS\system32\notepad.exe as
Disallowed using
    hash rule, Guid = {e669efa3-96d8-4c16-b506-2fec88fbee33}
```

You'll find a great article on Software Restriction Policies in TechNet at http://technet.microsoft.com/en-us/library/bb457006.aspx. If it's not there, then just search for an article named "Using Software Restriction Policies to Protect Against Unauthorized Software." Also check out this small article series on the subject by my pal Jakob H. Heidelberg called "Default Deny All Applications" (part 1 at http://tinyurl.com/ysb6wu and part 2 at http://tinyurl.com/2hdz7s).

Oops, I Locked Myself Out of My Machine with Software Restriction Policies

If you make a Software Restriction Policy too tight, you can lock yourself right out of the system! Don't panic. If the policy is a GPO in Active Directory, remove the policy setting or disable the GPO. After Group Policy processes on the client, log on again as the user and you should be cleared up.

However, if you make a Software Restriction Policy using the local policy editor (gpedit.msc) and you lock yourself out, you have a slightly longer road to recovery. Follow these steps:

1. Reboot the machine, and press F8 upon startup to open the Advanced Options menu at boot time.

2. Select SAFE MODE and allow the computer to to finish booting.

3. Log on as the machine's local administrator.

4. Dive in to:

    HKLM\Software\Policies\Microsoft\Windows\Safer\CodeIdentifiers

    Delete everything below the CodeIdentifiers key.

5. Reboot the machine.

You should be out of the woods now.

However, if the policies were set on a given user, the steps are a bit different. Just drill down to that user's HKCU hive file and nuke them there.

More Software Restriction Policies resources can be found at:

www.microsoft.com/technet/security/prodtech/windowsxp/secwinxp/xpsgch06
.mspx

(shortened to http://tinyurl.com/mx96v).

Restricting Software Using AppLocker

AppLocker is the next generation of Software Restriction Policies. It's available for Windows 7 (Enterprise or Ultimate, and not Professional), Windows 8 Enterprise, and Windows 10 Enterprise. It's also available on Windows Server 2008 R2 and later.

Not that I think that you'll use it very much, if ever, on a Windows Server. The only foreseeable time would be if you're using Windows as a Terminal Server where real users log on.

AppLocker enables you to control both standard apps (those apps we've run for years) and "Packaged" apps, what used to be known as Metro Apps. Now Microsoft is calling them "Modern" apps or sometimes "Universal" apps.

These applications are very different from your traditional desktop-style apps as they are all downloaded from an app store. Having access to these apps via an app store can be very useful; however, in a corporate environment, allowing staff to install and run any Metro, I mean Packaged (or Modern or Universal), application, no matter how benign, is just not something that is desirable.

AppLocker is an important evolution compared to Software Restriction Policies. AppLocker has three "laws" to determine whether files should execute on the system. *Laws* is my word, not Microsoft's, but I think it explains AppLocker's "brain" pretty well.

AppLocker vs. DeviceGuard

To be honest, my plan in this book was to have a section on Windows 10's DeviceGuard, but it's simply not ready yet to do a full demonstration in print.

But that being said, by the time you read this, there should be some stuff you can try with regard to DeviceGuard, so I wanted you to be aware of what it does and how it relates to AppLocker.

First, DeviceGuard is scheduled only to work with Windows 10 Enterprise clients. This might change, but I doubt it.

Second, DeviceGuard is tied to the TPM (Trusted Platform Module) chip found in many modern machines and tightly locks down a system to thwart malware threats. So if you don't have a TPM chip, stop right here—DeviceGuard isn't going to work for you.

Even then, DeviceGuard isn't really supposed to be utilized on all systems.

My general feeling is that AppLocker is for more "general purpose" machines, where you want to allow or deny applications from running. You know, regular end-user machines.

DeviceGuard, in contrast, appears to me to be a way to ensure the entire integrity of the system, like cash registers, ATM machines, shop-floor machines, and so on, where the configuration hardly changes at all and you want it to stay that way.

DeviceGuard will be manageable via Group Policy. The general flow is something like this:

- Use PowerShell to create policy from your master or "golden" systems.
- You get back an XML file.
- You convert it to a binary file with another PowerShell script.
- You then use a Group Policy setting to point to this binary file.

Then only signed code is going to run on that system. Microsoft is fleshing out Device-Guard to have a service where you can upload binaries that aren't digitally signed, and Microsoft will sign it for you.

Then, if any malware or anything else on the machine tries to run... splat! Because the code isn't signed, it doesn't run.

You can get a preview of DeviceGuard from a talk at Ignite 2015 at `http://channel9 .msdn.com/events/Ignite/2015/BRK2336`. The talk covers theory, use cases, and how to implement it, generally.

Here are the AppLocker laws:

- Law 1: Explicit deny—A specific rule that denies an action.
- Law 2: Explicit allow—A specific rule that allows an action.
- Law 3: Implicit deny—All files that are not specifically named by an Allow rule are automatically blocked.

So, Software Restriction Policies did a reasonable job at controlling applications (in the Windows XP timeframe). But, on the other hand, it was missing (in my opinion) two key ingredients to make it a blockbuster:

- One problem is that there was no easy way to state, "Allow software to run from Manufacturer X, Product ABC, if Product ABC is above a certain revision."
- The other problem was that while Software Restriction Policies had the concept of "Allow" and "Deny," there was no great way of quickly telling Software Restriction Policies about all the "good" software you had. It was tedious, if not impossible, to make the list so that it worked well. With AppLocker, we can quickly spawn a list of "good stuff" we want to allow to run based on a "template machine."

So, we'll try to put both of these Software Restriction Policies problems behind us and bury them using AppLocker in these examples.

To prepare for these examples, we'll need Google Chrome. For these examples, perform the following steps (if you want to follow along):

1. Download the MSI version of Google Chrome here: www.google.com/intl/en/chrome/business/browser/.
2. As Administrator, install it on WIN10.
3. As Administrator, install it on WIN10MANAGEMENT.

When you install as Administrator, Chrome correctly writes itself to "Program Files." Now that it's installed in both places, we'll be able to manage it around the bend.

AppLocker has three required pieces we need to configure in order to make it work:

- The AppLocker policy itself, which describes the applications and circumstances to be on the lookout for.
- An "overall" policy describing if you want to lock out or just perform an "audit" (more later).
- AppLocker's service that must be actively running on the target machine. (The trick is that the service is *not* named AppLocker.)

We'll break down each piece, and additionally walk through where AppLocker has a leg up on its predecessor, Software Restriction Policies.

AppLocker: Rules and Rule Conditions

Let's start out by creating and linking a GPO to our **Human Resources Computers** OU and call it AppLocker Tests. You'll find AppLocker abilities tucked under Computer Configuration ➢ Policies ➢ Windows Settings ➢ Security Settings ➢ Application Control

Policies ➤ AppLocker. (Why they chose to use a separate subnode called AppLocker underneath Application Control Policies, I will never know.) Inside, you'll see there are four types of *rules*: Executable Rules, Windows Installer Rules, Script Rules, and Packaged app Rules. Let's review each before we dive into them for testing:

Executable Rules   Allow or Prevent specific types of files to run, such as `.EXE`, `.COM`, `.DLL`, or `.OCX`.

Windows Installer Rules   Allow or Prevent specific `.MSI` (Windows Installer) and `.MSP` (Windows Patching) setup files to run.

Script Rules   Allow or Prevent scripts to run. Limited to `.PS1`, `.BAT`, `.CMD`, `.VBS`, and `.JS` files only.

Packaged app Rules   Allow or Prevent the running of Packaged (previously known as Metro) applications. Interestingly, in the user interface, they're still called Packaged apps, instead of Microsoft's preferred word *Universal*.

Now, in a second, we'll create a rule. For the first three rules, there are three types of *rule conditions*; however, the Packaged app Rules will only use the Publisher Rule Condition:

Path Rule Condition   Similar to what you've learned about in Software Restriction Policies, you can Allow or Deny based on where the file resides.

File Hash Rule Condition   Again, similar to what you've learned about in Software Restriction Policies, you can Allow or Deny based on the hash of a file.

Publisher Rule Condition   This is unique to AppLocker and allows you to specify a publisher you want to Allow or Deny. This assumes the files you want to run are digitally signed by the publisher.

Using the GPO we have open, let's right-click Executable Rules and immediately select "Create Default Rules," as seen in Figure 8.24.

The Default Rules won't come into play right now, but they're a good habit to get started with. The Default Rules ensure that (at least) Windows system files will always be able to run, when you start to put the smack down on your applications.

But, since we're looking at them now, anyway, let's examine the Default Rules and understand what they allow us to do:

- Allow anything to run that's already installed in Program Files
- Allow anything to run if it's in the Windows folder
- Allow local administrators to run any file

Remember AppLocker's Law 3: Everything is denied unless we've specifically set up a rule to allow it. So, setting up the Default Rules is a good idea, so that anything and everything running inside Program Files will just work.

Now let's right-click Packaged Apps and do the same thing and select "Create Default Rules," as shown in Figure 8.25. As you can see, there is exactly one rule created when you do this: "Allow all Packaged Apps to run, by Everyone."

FIGURE 8.24   Choose "Create Default Rules" to ensure safe passage using AppLocker.

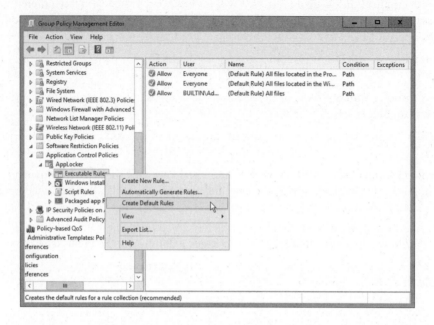

FIGURE 8.25   Choose "Create Default Rules" to ensure that Packaged apps will run using AppLocker.

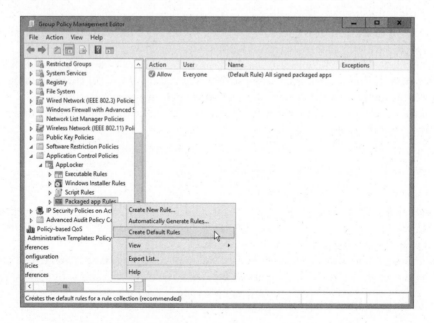

Why only one default rule and not three like before?

Packaged Apps are somewhat different from your normal desktop apps, as the built-in Administrator account is prohibited to run them. So having a default rule to allow the built-in administrator account to run these apps is not required (nor would it do anything).

Packaged Apps are also not stored in Program Files directories like traditional apps. Therefore, you also have no need for the Allow Path rule.

Leveraging Law 1: Blacklisting Specific Applications with an Explicit Deny

You've already installed Chrome on your WIN10 machine. It's already inside the Program Files directory, running along. And you've got a default rule in place that enables you to run it. (Remember, one of those rules allows anything inside Program Files to run.)

And, you've got a Packaged app, Weather, preinstalled on that same machine.

But these two apps are out there and installed already; how can we control them using AppLocker? In our two examples, we'll want to take these two steps:

1. Restrict the Google Chrome web browser using an executable rule based on who published it—Google.

2. Prohibit the running of the Weather Packaged app that comes preinstalled with Windows 10.

To do this, we'll create an Explicit deny to put the kibosh on Chrome and also Weather.

On your WIN10MANAGMENT machine, use the Group Policy editor within the AppLocker node. Right-click over Executable Rules and select "Create New Rule." When you do, you'll be prompted with a wizard and Before You Begin page (not shown). Click Next to get started. You'll then see a Permissions page where you can select to Allow or Deny applications. Let's select Deny (not shown), leave the "User or Group" selection set to Everyone (the default), and click Next.

When you do, you'll see the Conditions page shown in Figure 8.26.

Ensure that Publisher is selected and click Next. Then in the Create Executable Rules page (Figure 8.27), click Browse and locate and select chrome.exe within Program Files (or `Program Files x86`)\Google\Chrome\Application).

When you do, you'll see the Publisher, Product name, File name, and File version fields all automatically populate. This is because AppLocker is reading the digital signature within the Google Chrome file.

There are lots of ways to use this page, but here are some examples. If you leave the slider as is, making no changes, as seen in Figure 8.27, you're basically saying "Deny Google Chrome 42.0.0.0, with the file name Chrome.exe, published by Google." That's great, but maybe that's not what you want. You can move the slider up one notch, and the screen should look like this:

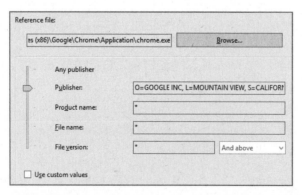

The "File version" selection goes to "*" which means "all versions." So, now you're saying "Deny All Versions of Google Chrome, with the file name Chrome.exe published by Google."

What happens if you move the slider up *another* notch, as seen here?:

Now you're saying "Deny all products by Google that are known as Google Chrome."

Move it up one more notch, as seen here, and you're saying "Deny all applications by the publisher Google":

FIGURE 8.26 Select Publisher to restrict based on digitally signed applications.

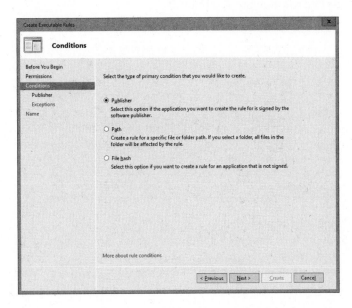

FIGURE 8.27 You can select a file that contains a digital signature and then dictate which values you want to restrict against.

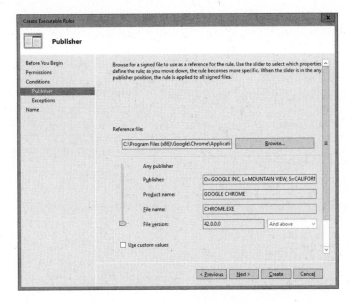

And, you can put it one *more* notch up, and deny all publishers, as seen here! (Don't really do this; I don't advise doing so right now.):

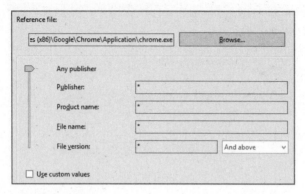

Wow! That's some serious power!

Turns out, though, none of these configurations is what I want us to work through for the real example. So, click the "Use custom values" check box. Then change the file version from whatever version you're running, say, 41.0.1180.60 to 42.0.0.0, and select "And below," as shown here:

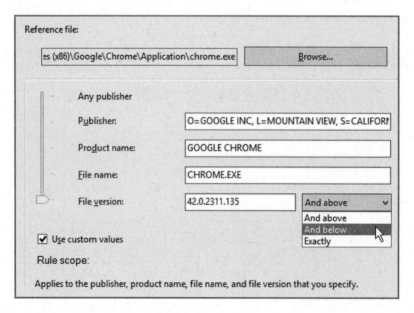

Now our rule says "Deny Google Chrome from Google when the file version is below 42.0.0.0."

Click Next to visit the Exceptions page (not shown). Here you can make an exception to your rule. We're not going to do this for now, but it's good to know there are ways we can permit specific applications from publishers if we really crank down, say, denying all applications based on Publisher. So on the Exceptions page, click Next.

The final page is called "Name and Description." The system guesses at a good name for your AppLocker rule. Feel free to change if you like and/or add a description. This page is not shown here. Click Create to finish up and present the rule. When you do, you'll see the rule created, as shown in Figure 8.28.

FIGURE 8.28   Your Deny rule is set to restrict Google Chrome 42.0 and below.

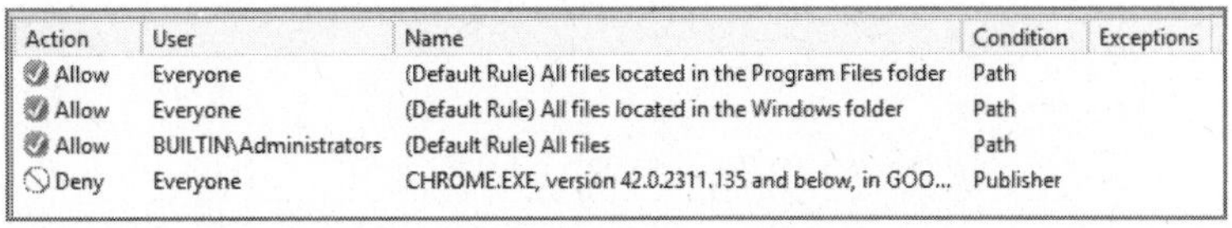

Action	User	Name	Condition	Exceptions
Allow	Everyone	(Default Rule) All files located in the Program Files folder	Path	
Allow	Everyone	(Default Rule) All files located in the Windows folder	Path	
Allow	BUILTIN\Administrators	(Default Rule) All files	Path	
Deny	Everyone	CHROME.EXE, version 42.0.2311.135 and below, in GOO...	Publisher	

Now, let's switch gears back to restricting Packaged applications. Simply right-click within Packaged app Rules and select "Create new rule"; then you will have an experience similar to standard applications.

You can see the differences in the Packaged App dialog box, as seen in Figure 8.29. Specifically, Packaged App Rules do not have "File name" as an option.

Simply click Select and specify the Packaged app, in this case Weather. The slider works the same as it did with regular applications. You can slide the slider up and put "*" characters next to each field to specify which items you want to make universal.

You might think that you're ready to go and get started testing AppLocker. Oh, no. There are two more big steps you must do before testing can commence.

AppLocker Actions: Enforcement or Auditing

AppLocker does nothing at all once you've created your rules.

It can be kind of a letdown if you're not prepared for it.

You have to determine what actions you want to take when your AppLocker rule comes to pass. So, to get the party started (or, more accurately, be the wet blanket *on* the party), you need to turn on Enforcement rules.

You find this by again locating Computer Configuration ➤ Policies ➤ Windows Settings ➤ Security Settings ➤ Application Control Policies ➤ AppLocker, right-clicking it, and selecting Properties. When you do, you'll see what's in Figure 8.30.

FIGURE 8.29 Packaged App Rule for the preinstalled Weather app

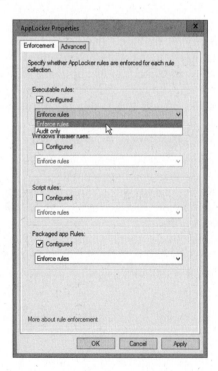

FIGURE 8.30 You can decide to start enforcement or simply audit for who is actually running your application.

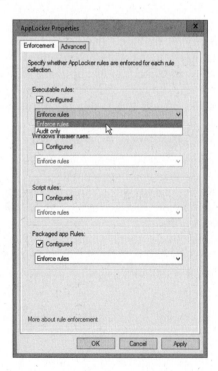

For our example, we've only configured an Executable rule and a Published app rule (both with a Publisher Rule Condition). So, we have to decide what action we want: Enforcement or Auditing.

Auditing will simply log results to the target machine's event log. Specifically, the results will go into the AppLocker log (which can be found in Event Viewer). If you want to see them, drill down into "Application and Services Logs" and select Microsoft ➤ Windows ➤ AppLocker. There, you'll find the logs for "EXE and DLL." There's another log as well for "MSI and Script."

If you'd like to try AppLocker in Auditing mode, you're on your own; I don't have enough space to cover it. You can also read this document from Microsoft about AppLocker and auditing to see the Event IDs generated: http://tinyurl.com/yjdm8j6.

For our example, we'll select "Enforce rules" for executable rules. Do that now and click OK.

Note that you can optionally enable DLL and OCX blocking if you choose to peek at the Advanced tab. There's a warning about some potential slowdowns when engaged, but I feel it's worth it in the name of security. Additionally, you'll have to be diligent. If you select to enable the stomping of DLLs, you'll need to ensure that every DLL that is used by your approved applications is in there. That could get difficult, fast. An application can just stop working if you forget to add a DLL.

Anyway, you would think that now you're done and ready for testing, right? Nope. One more big hurdle to overcome.

AppLocker: The AppID Service

It's almost as if Microsoft doesn't want you to use the AppLocker service. They've made it so you have to first create a rule, turn on the rule action (Auditing or Enforcement), and now, one last hurdle. And that hurdle must be performed on each and every Windows machine on which you wish AppLocker to work.

You need to turn on and change the startup mode for the AppLocker service. Really, it's called the Application Identity, or AppID service.

There are two ways I will suggest for you to accomplish this task: manually or using the Group Policy Preferences.

Turning On the AppID Service Manually

If you want to turn on the AppID service manually, on your target machine (WIN10) right-click Computer from the Start menu. Then select Manage.

Drill down to Computer Management ➤ Services and Applications ➤ Services and select Application Identity, as seen in Figure 8.31.

Change the service startup type to Automatic, click Start, and then click OK. When you do, you should see the service start right up and be set to Automatic startup going forward.

This technique is great if you want to test one or two machines. But it falls down if you have 10, 100, or 10,000 machines you want to use with AppLocker.

Turning On the AppID Service "En Masse" Using Group Policy Preferences

Instead of running around from machine to machine, you can optionally use the Group Policy Preferences' Services extension to mass-change and enable the AppID service (Application Identity Service).

As you can see in Figure 8.32, I'm using the Group Policy Preferences to select the AppID service. You'll change Startup to Automatic, and set "Service action" from "No Change" to "Start service."

FIGURE 8.31   The Application Identity service must be started (and configured to start at startup) in order to process AppLocker edicts. Be sure to change the startup type to Automatic and, if you want to start it immediately, click Start.

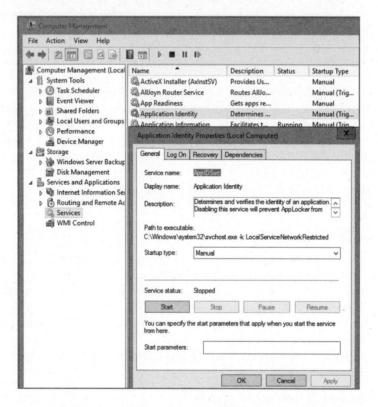

Use the same GPO you've already used for this AppLocker exercise, or create a new GPO. Just make sure your edict is linked to where your target machines are (Windows 7 and later) and you're golden. The next time Group Policy refreshes on those machines, the AppID service will start up and be ready to start on every reboot thereafter.

FIGURE 8.32   Use the Group Policy Preferences to mass-enable the AppID service (Application Identity) service on your supported Windows machines.

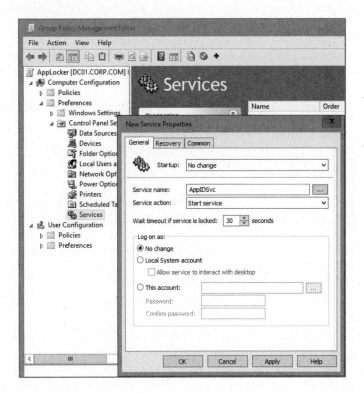

AppLocker: Testing It Out

Whew. Now that your rule is set up, your actions are set, and your service is started, you're finally ready to test AppLocker in action.

Log on as Frank Rizzo to WIN10. Now, remember that AppLocker policies are Computer side, not User side. And it could take up to 120 minutes before this policy becomes active on the computer.

Or, you could run gpupdate after you log on as Frank and get the latest policies for both Frank (who just logged on anyway) and the computer (which might have just been sitting around a while). Or you can reboot the computer. Your choice.

When you try to launch Chrome as Frank, it's entirely possible that a whole lot of "nothing special occurs" and Chrome simply continues to run. Even if you've done everything right and performed all the steps perfectly, it might not actually work.

It appears that the AppID service has a delay before it kicks in and performs the work. In my testing, the delay is about two minutes (usually) before AppLocker is fully engaged and actual smackdown occurs. This drove me totally nuts in my testing; but hopefully you're reading this and will go less nuts than I did.

After the little "game delay," users should encounter roadblocks, as seen in Figure 8.33, for Chrome. And if you try to launch the built-in Packaged Weather app, users should see what's shown in Figure 8.34.

FIGURE 8.33   The default message when AppLocker kicks in when a user tries to install Chrome

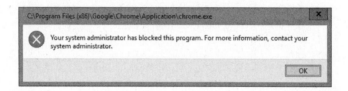

This is expected because the rule matched, and you have enforcement enabled. Success!

AppLocker: Modifying What the Client Sees

Users see the default message when an AppLocker rule kicks in, as you saw in Figure 8.33. However, there is an alternate message you can display for users if you like.

You can set the policy found at Computer ➢ Policies ➢ Administrative Templates ➢ Windows Components ➢ File Explorer ➢ **Set a Support Web Page Link**.

The goal is to point users to click on a custom URL, which, for instance, has your corporate rules listed in clear language, or a phone number for the help desk, or some other explanation as to why they were denied the ability to run the application.

Now, when users encounter a rule that blocks them, they'll get a different message, as shown in Figure 8.35.

The user now can be redirected to your URL by clicking the "More information" link as you've defined it.

AppLocker: Wrapping Up Our Tests

We've created a rule that blocks the execution of Google Chrome 42.00 and below. So our Google Chrome 41.0 is stopped dead in its tracks. To complete the test, on WIN10 upgrade Google Chrome to a version greater than 42.0, say, version 43.0 (or 172.0 by the time you read this).

You should see it run, because the rule was set to restrict only Google Chrome 42.0 and earlier.

FIGURE 8.34 The default message when AppLocker kicks in when a user tries to run the Weather app

FIGURE 8.35 Alternative AppLock message with "More information" link

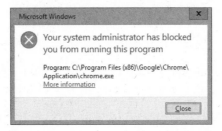

Leveraging Laws 2 and 3: Whitelisting Only Known Good Applications

In the previous example, we denied one publisher and its one application: Google. That Explicit deny rule would be helpful in two circumstances:

- If Google Chrome 42 was already installed in Program Files
- If Google Chrome 43 was already installed anywhere else

I know that seems like a weird way to describe what we did, but logically, that's the way we must express it. That's because we already had the default rule that would allow it to run inside Program Files. And our new Explicit deny rule stomps it out both in Program Files and anywhere else it's ever discovered (say, in some alternate directory).

Okay, great. We've now stamped out *one* little fire. Yippee.

What about the zillions of other applications we might want to protect ourselves against? And then, how can we specifically okay the apps we know are good?

Well then, you might want to consider AppLocker's "whitelist" approach. Let's recall our three AppLocker laws from earlier:

- Law 1: Explicit deny—A specific rule that denies an action.

- Law 2: Explicit allow—A specific rule that allows an action.

- Law 3: Implicit deny—All files that are not specifically named by an Allow rule are automatically blocked.

So, if we look at the laws carefully, we can see that if we turn AppLocker on, and, well, "do nothing," then all files that are not specifically named are going to be automatically blocked.

Wow, can that really be true? Let's try it out.

Testing AppLocker's Law #3: Default Deny

Let's start out by editing the one AppLocker GPO you created and removing the one Deny rule you had. At this point you should have nothing but the Default Rules again, as seen in Figure 8.24.

On WIN10, make sure you're logged in as Frank Rizzo. Run gpupdate to get the changed AppLocker rules from the GPO. Now, you should be able to run Chrome. Again, this runs because the Default Rules are saying, "Go ahead and let anything in Program Files run A-OK." And since Chrome is already installed there, it runs A-OK.

Now, as Frank, download the latest WinZip setup program. I found it here: www.winzip .com/downwz.htm. Next, as Frank, try to run the setup .EXE. You should get what's shown in Figure 8.36.

See? AppLocker specifically denies WinZip's setup program. It's not already installed and living in Program Files, so the default rule doesn't apply. It's immediately blocked.

Automatically Generating Rules for AppLocker Whitelisting

So, we can see that AppLocker will just auto-smackdown anything that isn't expressly listed by an Allow. You've likely come to the conclusion, however, that you'll have to generate some lengthy "Allow" list that contains all your applications.

And you're right. That's the hard part. You will have to figure out what the Sales team is using, and the Marketing team, and Human Resources, and so forth. It's not easy or fun. But there is good news: AppLocker can automatically generate rules and then add them to a whitelist, as shown in Figure 8.37.

FIGURE 8.36   AppLocker's Law 3 ensures that anything that isn't specifically listed is automatically denied.

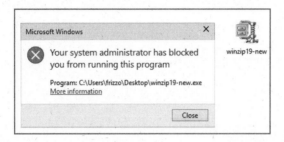

FIGURE 8.37   Automatically generate rules to add them to the whitelist.

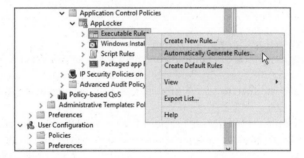

What you'll do is this:

- Find a representative machine from the department you want to control—say, Human Resources. We'll call this your AppLocker "template machine."

- On this machine, you'll need to have the GPMC running.

- You'll use the Automatically Generate Rules Wizard.

When the wizard is over, you'll have (at least) a start of the applications you know are good and should pass through and allow to run. Sure, you'll have to trim a bit, use your brains for a little while, as well as use a little elbow grease to make sure nothing bad slipped through.

But it's a quick way to get started. Right-click over Executable Rules and select Automatically Generate Rules to open the wizard to the "Folder and Permissions" screen shown in Figure 8.38.

FIGURE 8.38 Specify where you want to start your analysis.

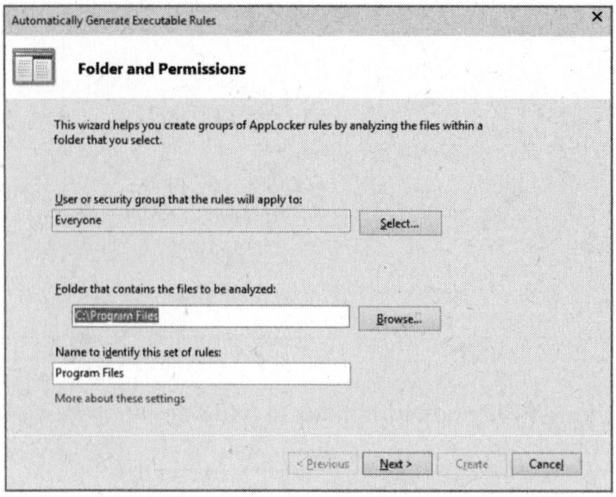

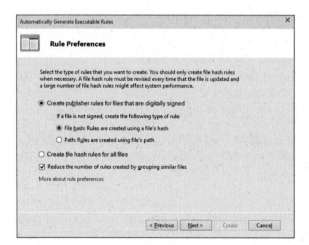

The default is C:\Program Files, but you're welcome to create rule sets for anyplace you wish. Indeed, for x64 machines, you should run the wizard again, and be sure to include, say, C:\Program Files (x86) because otherwise all 32-bit apps on the 64-bit system will be missed. Additionally, be sure to add in any custom applications in C:\DogFoodMaker or the like.

The next screen is Rule Preferences, as seen in Figure 8.39. I recommend accepting the defaults as they do a pretty decent job, but you're welcome to try other options.

FIGURE 8.39 Use the defaults to create rules based on signed files with file hashes as a backup.

You'll then come to the Review Rules screen, shown in Figure 8.40. At this point the rules aren't yet created. You can select "Review files that were analyzed" if you want to explicitly remove a file from consideration. You can also preview the rules before they get codified.

FIGURE 8.40   You can explicitly remove a file from consideration using the "Review files that were analyzed" selection.

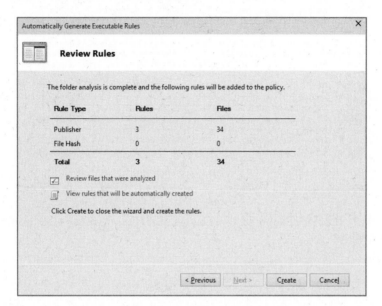

When ready, click Create. When you do, the rules for your particular machine will be populated into the GPO, as seen in Figure 8.41.

AppLocker: Importing and Exporting Rules

Since you're doing all of these wonderful tests in the test lab, you might be wondering how you're going to take your (potentially complex) rule set and export those rules—then, in the real world, how you're going to import them. It's easy. Look at Figure 8.42.

You can also utilize Export and Import to take one GPO's rules in the real world, export them, and import them into another one for transfer or cleanup.

AppLocker Final Thoughts and Resources

We used AppLocker in two ways: we explicitly denied an application (blacklisting), and we also implicitly denied everything and specified the good applications (whitelisting).

FIGURE 8.41   AppLocker allows you to auto-generate rules for whitelisting.

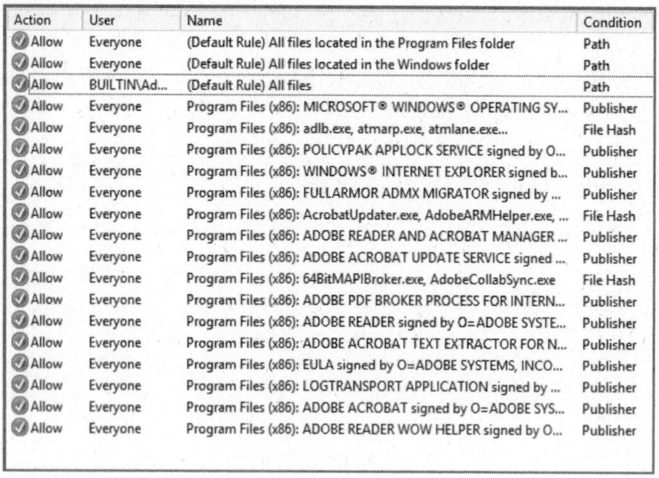

Action	User	Name	Condition
Allow	Everyone	(Default Rule) All files located in the Program Files folder	Path
Allow	Everyone	(Default Rule) All files located in the Windows folder	Path
Allow	BUILTIN\Ad...	(Default Rule) All files	Path
Allow	Everyone	Program Files (x86): MICROSOFT® WINDOWS® OPERATING SY...	Publisher
Allow	Everyone	Program Files (x86): adlb.exe, atmarp.exe, atmlane.exe...	File Hash
Allow	Everyone	Program Files (x86): POLICYPAK APPLOCK SERVICE signed by O...	Publisher
Allow	Everyone	Program Files (x86): WINDOWS® INTERNET EXPLORER signed b...	Publisher
Allow	Everyone	Program Files (x86): FULLARMOR ADMX MIGRATOR signed by ...	Publisher
Allow	Everyone	Program Files (x86): AcrobatUpdater.exe, AdobeARMHelper.exe, ...	File Hash
Allow	Everyone	Program Files (x86): ADOBE READER AND ACROBAT MANAGER ...	Publisher
Allow	Everyone	Program Files (x86): ADOBE ACROBAT UPDATE SERVICE signed ...	Publisher
Allow	Everyone	Program Files (x86): 64BitMAPIBroker.exe, AdobeCollabSync.exe	File Hash
Allow	Everyone	Program Files (x86): ADOBE PDF BROKER PROCESS FOR INTERN...	Publisher
Allow	Everyone	Program Files (x86): ADOBE READER signed by O=ADOBE SYSTE...	Publisher
Allow	Everyone	Program Files (x86): ADOBE ACROBAT TEXT EXTRACTOR FOR N...	Publisher
Allow	Everyone	Program Files (x86): EULA signed by O=ADOBE SYSTEMS, INCO...	Publisher
Allow	Everyone	Program Files (x86): LOGTRANSPORT APPLICATION signed by ...	Publisher
Allow	Everyone	Program Files (x86): ADOBE ACROBAT signed by O=ADOBE SYS...	Publisher
Allow	Everyone	Program Files (x86): ADOBE READER WOW HELPER signed by O...	Publisher

FIGURE 8.42   Use AppLocker's Export and Import Policy to move rules from your test lab to the real world.

I want you to think about that for a moment. Here's why: Let's assume you add a rule you didn't want to add, but then think "No problem, I'll just stop AppLocker by killing the service!" it doesn't work. The rules are already moved onward into the kernel for processing. That being said, turning off the AppID service then rebooting will flush the AppLocker rules in memory and get the affected computer without restrictions.

You would use the Group Policy editor to add or "back out" your rules. Then, turn back on the AppID service and reapply Group Policy on the client apply and see your updates take effect.

My parting thought here is to use AppLocker with as many "Allow" rules as you can. That's because denying specific things (Law 1) is going to be less secure than relying on Law 3 to auto-smackdown stuff that shouldn't be running.

If a really smart user wanted to subvert your AppLocker policies, here's how they could do it:

Path Rules   They could figure out where an application *isn't* allowed to run and move it to a place where it *is* allowed to run. This could take some trial and error, but it's certainly in the realm of possibility.

File Hash Rules   A user could use a hex editor (explained earlier) to modify the file hash. This does increase the risk of the application breaking, however.

Publisher Rules   A user could inject the executable with a signed (Allowed) certificate. They would need the private key of the certificate, which would not be possible under almost all circumstances. This is a pretty low-probability problem.

True, most places won't have to worry about these kinds of attacks. But if you use whitelisting (Law 3), you won't have to worry about them at all. I've provided a thorough workout of AppLocker here, but if you're still hungry for more, here are some pointers:

- Here's a big speech I gave on AppLocker at Microsoft TechEd in 2010. In it, I also go over some PowerShell with regard to AppLocker. Check it out:

  http://channel9.msdn.com/Events/TechEd/NorthAmerica/2010/WCL303

- TechNet article by Greg Shields:

  http://technet.microsoft.com/en-us/magazine/2009.10.geekofalltrades.aspx

  (shortened to http://tinyurl.com/ylkrs5z)

- A five-part series by Brien Posey:

  www.windowsnetworking.com/articles_tutorials/Introduction-AppLocker-Part1.html

- Microsoft Technical Documentation on AppLocker: http://tinyurl.com/yhcw83f
- PowerShell and AppLocker: http://tinyurl.com/otdo8a and http://tinyurl.com/yj2cfv8

Controlling User Account Control with Group Policy

UAC is the User Account Control feature for Windows Vista and later. You might see it as the "annoying extra pop-up box I need to click in order to do anything useful!" Well, sometimes it might seem that way. But that's not exactly accurate. What's really happening is that you're seeing a prompt for anything that requires administrator rights (that is, that affects the entire computer and all users on that computer).

Since UAC is available for Windows Vista and later, instead of saying "Windows Vista and later" each time it comes up, I'll just say "for Windows" in the general case, and if there's something specific about a particular version of Windows, I'll let you know.

For instance, on Windows Server you might not see the prompts as much because if you log on with the local Administrator account, UAC prompts are largely not presented. However, if you log on as just about anyone else, like a Server Operator, you will see the UAC prompts that we'll discuss here using Windows 10 examples.

In reality, it's not that bad; UAC is designed to put a (small) roadblock in front of administrative tasks and applications so that only administrators can do anything with these items.

An example of a UAC dialog box that can pop up based on the types of actions and programs you want to run is shown in Figure 8.43. For example, anytime mere mortals want to manipulate the firewall, they are prompted for local administrator credentials.

FIGURE 8.43 Anytime a user clicks on an action with a shield icon (as seen above), they are prompted for credentials (as seen below).

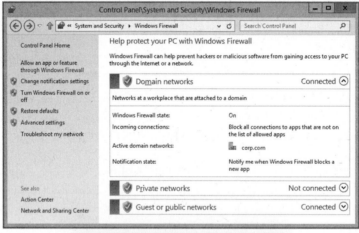

In UAC parlance, a mere mortal, or regular user, is officially called a *Standard User*. There are three types of prompts you might get when UAC is active:

Teal Bar Plus a Shield   This program is a part of Windows.

Gray Plus a Shield with an Exclamation Mark   This is signed and trusted by Windows. Trusted means that the certificate used to sign the application "chains" to a certificate in the computer's Trusted Root Certificate Store. The Trusted Root Certificate Store can also be managed via Group Policy.

Orange Plus a Shield with an Exclamation Mark   This program isn't part of Windows and is either unsigned or signed but not yet trusted.

And, at first blush, you might be right. It might be annoying to provide that one extra click or provide alternate credentials. But the underlying idea of UAC is a really good one: regular users need permissions to do the more privileged operations on a Windows machine.

In the short term, you might see the UAC prompts a lot. That's because when you're first configuring Windows, there will be a lot of system-wide changes you'll want to make. But over time, how often are you really making those kinds of changes? Once the computer is configured for your specific environment and the bulk of the software is installed, you will rarely ever see a UAC dialog box again.

Additionally, when you log on as an Administrator (local or Domain Administrator), you get "stripped" of your admin rights until you click to say you want to leverage them. UAC's goal is to implement the "Principle of Least Privilege": only use privileged user rights when needed.

The UAC prompts leverage of a technology called UIPI (UI Process Isolation) and another called MIC (Mandatory Integrity Control). The idea is that the operating system is protected from nonprivileged processes. Only certain types of Windows messages and input are permitted to interact with this dialog box. Therefore, previous attacks where the malware would simply click the security dialog box before the user ever saw the prompt are thwarted—only privileged processes can interact with the UAC dialog boxes. This helps prevent what is known as process injection and shatter attacks.

Learn more about process injection and shatter attacks at http:// en.wikipedia.org/wiki/Code_injection and http://en.wikipedia .org/wiki/Shatter_attack.

What's the upshot? Sure, it's one extra click (as an admin) or the fuss of providing admin credentials (for users who aren't admins). But what's the benefit? In short, even admins get the benefit of not doing something potentially harmful because there's one extra click in the way. (How many times have you wished you could have taken an extra "beat" before doing something potentially harmful?)

The other big goodness is that all applications run without admin privilege by default; therefore, scenarios like web browsing and e-mail become much more secure without any changes to the applications. You cannot have "Protected Mode IE" without UAC.

So I encourage you to find it in your heart to try to love this feature. Here's the idea (which is only partially related to UAC): You want all your users to run as Standard User (or, as they're sometimes called, mere mortals). That is, they are in the local Users group of the workstation or in the Domain Users group and not in the local Administrators group of the workstation or the Domain Admins group in the domain. In short, they're just users. Additionally, if you want to throw some numbers at the managers in your corporations, the Gartner Group states that running your desktops as Standard User can reduce total cost of ownership (TCO) by as much as 40 percent versus running those same desktops with administrative credentials. The idea is that if the user, I mean, administrator of that local machine could just stop making all those darned changes, you would be at their desk fixing their computer a whole lot less. Get it?

So, what does UAC do? It prompts the users for credentials under specific conditions. Take a quick gander at the general UAC document on Microsoft's website here:

`http://technet.microsoft.com/en-us/library/cc772207%28WS.10%29.aspx`

And, if you like, check out this older but very geeky "internals about UAC" article from Mark Russinovich, "Inside Windows Vista User Account Control," found here:

`http://technet.microsoft.com/en-us/magazine/2007.06.uac.aspx`

(shortened to `http://tinyurl.com/as3oy2`).

There is also an article called "Inside Windows 7 User Account Control," which is an interesting read, found here:

`https://technet.microsoft.com/en-us/magazine/2009.07.uac.aspx`

And, as far as I know there are no UAC changes between Windows 7 through 10.

The manual way to manage UAC is seen in Figure 8.44.

But that doesn't help you if you have 10,000 machines to configure manually. So in a bit, you'll learn about the 10 different Group Policy controls you have at your disposal to configure it the way you want it to work.

Finally, we'll wrap up our talk on UAC with some prescriptive guidance for certain scenarios to help you configure users based on what they're trying to accomplish.

Just Who Will See the UAC Prompts, Anyway?

The point of UAC is to have "administrative" type users run as mere mortals until they need to use their superpowers. To that end, you'll likely want to get a handle on just who is going to be affected by UAC prompts and will have to run as mere mortals on Windows (until they elevate their credentials and use that superpower).

There are two categories of folks: anyone who's a member of some special Active Directory or local Security Accounts Manager (SAM) groups and anyone who has one of nine special rights.

FIGURE 8.44 The updated UAC interface for Windows 7 and 8

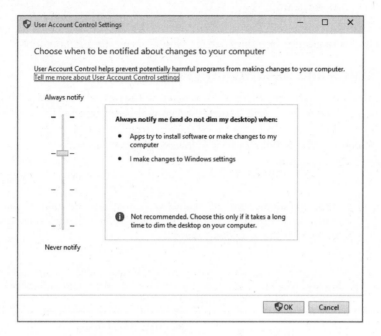

Groups That Are Affected by UAC

There are 16 accounts and related SIDs that are affected by UAC:

- Built-in Administrators
- Power Users
- Account Operators
- Server Operators
- Print Operators
- Backup Operators
- RAS Servers Group
- NT 4 Application Compatibility Group
- Network Configuration Operators
- Cryptographic Operators
- Domain Administrators
- Domain Controllers
- Certificate Publishers
- Schema Administrators

▪ Enterprise Administrators

▪ Group Policy Administrators

UAC sometimes call these users Split Token Users or Hybrid Users as they have two user tokens (nonadmin and admin). See the sidebar "How Token Filtering/Split Token Works."

Elevated Rights and Security (SE) Privileges

If the user does not belong to any of the groups listed in the preceding section but has any of the E privileges listed in Table 8.2, a filtered token will be created for the user with these privileges removed. These privileges are found in the Group Policy Management Editor in Computer Configuration ➤ Policies ➤ Windows Settings ➤ Security Settings ➤ Local Policies ➤ User Rights Assignment.

 You can get these rights from any level: local, site, domain, or OU. Additionally, many rights are predefined in the default Group Policy Objects (discussed in the previous chapter).

TABLE 8.2 Rights and SE names that generate a filtered token user experience

Right	Security (Se) Name
Create a token object	SeCreateTokenPrivilege
Act as part of the operating system	SeTcbPrivilege
Take ownership of files or other objects	SeTakeOwnershipPrivilege
Back up files and directories	SeBackupPrivilege
Restore files and directories	SeRestorePrivilege
Debug programs	SeDebugPrivilege
Impersonate a client after authentication	SeImpersonatePrivilege
Modify an object label	SeRelabelPrivilege
Load and unload device drivers	SeLoadDriverPrivilege

You can check to see if a currently logged-in user has one of these privileges by typing **whoami /priv** at a command prompt.

How Token Filtering/Split Token Works

If you log in with Domain Administrator rights to a Windows XP machine, you can "do" just about anything you want, including shooting your foot off, easily. This is because if you're assigned rights at some level of Active Directory or SAM, Windows XP just lets you use them. Sounds good, until you start making a mistake while web surfing or using e-mail.

Starting with Windows Vista, things get a little more cautious. Again, the idea in modern Windows is that if you've got one of the special rights listed in Table 8.2, you will get a "split token." That means that in your daily life, you're running around as a mere mortal. When you need to rip off your shirt and become Superman, you can do that, too—but you have to find a close phone booth, er, UAC prompt to help you with that.

So, for instance, if a user is a member of the Administrators group, the filtered token will have the Administrators group membership set to "deny only." Yep, you read that right. As they're running around as a mere mortal, anything they try to do on the system is expressly Denied.

Meanwhile, a second protection mechanism kicks in. All the machine-impacting privileges are removed from the token. Therefore, as the Domain Administrator is going about his daily life on a Windows Vista and later machine, when he starts up things like explorer.exe, it's using a nonelevated process token.

You can look at this token using whomai.exe, which is included in Windows. First run whoami /groups in a command window when logged in as Domain Administrator, as shown here:

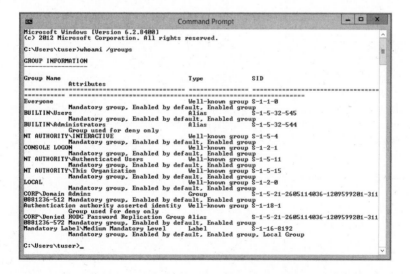

If you look closely you'll see that the BUILTIN\Administrators and the CORP\Domain Admins groups both have a special Deny token—just for them. Kooky! Again, this is reinstated once UAC prompts are satisfied.

Additionally, you can see what privileges are being used at any time with whoami /priv, as shown here:

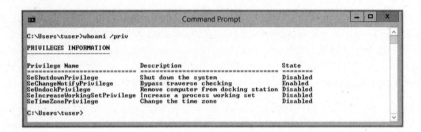

Compare this to the whoami /priv command when run on a Windows XP machine shown here:

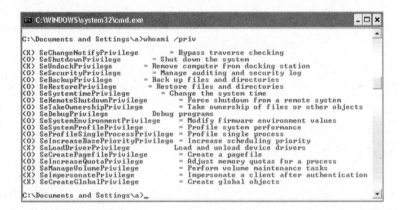

So, Windows XP doesn't "filter" anything. Windows goes the extra mile to strip out unused rights until you actually need them. Note that the whoami tool isn't built into Windows XP as it is in Windows Vista and later. You can load the whoami tool from the Windows XP support tools here: http://tinyurl.com/4uhnu.

Understanding the Group Policy Controls for UAC

There are 10 Group Policy controls for UAC. They are all found within Computer Configuration ➤ Policies ➤ Windows Settings ➤ Security Settings ➤ Local Policies ➤ Security Options, and all start with "User Account Control:" as seen in Figure 8.45.

FIGURE 8.45   The User Account Control entries are all found under Security Options.

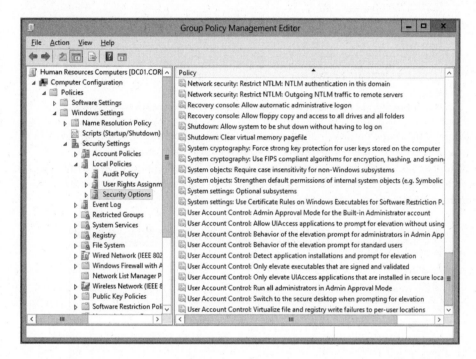

Let's examine each policy setting so you can decide if you want to change the default behavior.

What? No Usable Local Administrator Account on Modern Windows?

By default, the Windows Vista and later built-in Administrator account is disabled. Yep, you read that right—there is no usable built-in Administrator account on Windows. It's there; it's just disabled. Indeed, check out the following figure, where I'm simply typing **net user administrator** at a Windows command prompt. Note that the "Account active" flag is set to No.

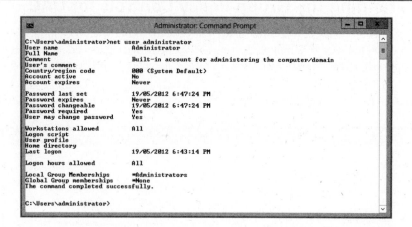

However, if you create a new Windows machine (that isn't joined to the domain), the first user you create by default has permissions equivalent to those of a local administrator and all subsequent users are Standard Users—see the following figure where my first user on this fresh Windows installation is named Alan but is still a local Administrator. Confusing, right?

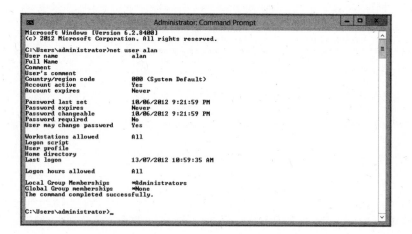

So, be careful when you give that first local user account's name and password. That first user account really has administrator rights! Yikes!

However, if, during setup, you join the domain directly, you won't have any local user accounts created, and hence, you won't have any accounts you can log onto as a local administrator. Of course, you could always log onto the Enterprise or Domain Administrator accounts (but we're talking about local accounts here).

So, what about that disabled local Administrator account? Well, again, ask yourself if you really need it. In a domain environment, you could always just log in as a Domain Administrator. And, if the machine wasn't joined to the domain during setup, you could log in with that first user. So all bases are covered.

But, if you felt like you wanted to bring back that local Administrator account, you could do so. Historically, this account has been used for pure maintenance. That's why, by default, it's not enabled and has special behavior once enabled. So before I tell you how to enable the local Administrator account, I want to pass on a big ol' cautionary note: the local Administrator account is exempt (by default) from all UAC prompts.

The behavior is the same on Server 2008 and later should you log on with the local Administrator account or Domain Administrator account.

You won't see any prompts. If you enable the Administrator account and romp around within Windows while using it, there are absolutely no safety checks. If you wanted to change this behavior, you would manipulate the User Account Control: Admin Approval Mode for the **Built-in Administrator account** policy setting.

Again, it's not recommended that you enable the local Administrator account, but if you wanted to, the command line you would type is this:

```
net user administrator complexp@ssw0rd /active:yes
```

And again, I'm not suggesting you should run out and enable all your local Administrator accounts. But if you do have some "corporate-wide" reason to do this, it would be wise to set a complex password during machine creation time (with an answer file).

But there's another way to enable the local Administrator account. Assuming the password is set on the local Administrator account (say, via the answer file at machine creation time), you can use Group Policy to just "turn it on." You'll find the setting to turn this on in Computer Configuration ➢ Policies ➢ Windows Settings ➢ Security Settings ➢ Local Policies ➢ Security Options ➢ **Accounts: Administrator account status**.

Before we finish talking about the local Administrator account, there is one more local Administrator–related change you need to be aware of. In pre–Windows Vista, you could, if you wanted to, boot into Safe Mode logon with the *disabled* built-in Administrator account. Don't know why you'd want to, but it is possible.

Because Windows is now trying to encourage Standard Users on desktops (in businesses) and engaging parental controls (in the home), Safe Mode had to undergo some security changes:

On Workgroup or Nondomain Joined Computers   If there is at least one active local Administrator account, Safe Mode will not allow logon via the disabled built-in Administrator account. But there's no issue logging in with any active Administrator account. If there are no other active local Administrator accounts, Safe Mode will allow the disabled built-in Administrator account to log on for disaster recovery. From that point, it is suggested that you create a new Administrator account before the computer is rebooted.

On Domain Joined Computers   The disabled built-in Administrator account cannot log on in Safe Mode under any circumstances. Here's where it gets tricky: If a user whose account is also in the Domain Administrators group has ever logged onto that machine before, they can log on again using Safe Mode, no problem. But what if no one from the Domain Administrators group has ever logged onto that machine? Then the computer must be started in "Safe Mode with Networking" since the credentials will not have been cached. Hopefully, Windows will not be "so broken" that networking support won't work in this case. If the machine is disjoined from the domain, it reverts back to the nondomain joined behavior.

User Account Control: Admin Approval Mode for the Built-in Administrator Account

As we've already discussed, both users and administrators have to "say yes" or provide administrator credentials.

> Only admins can "say yes." Standard Users must obtain administrator credentials. Standard Users cannot just "say yes."

This prevents them from doing things that could be potentially harmful to the machine. So, this setting dictates the "Admin Approval mode" for the built-in Administrator account. What built-in Administrator account? Check out the sidebar "What? No Usable Local Administrator Account on Modern Windows?"

If you choose to enable this built-in Administrator account, this policy setting affects this account.

Enabled   When this setting is Enabled, the built-in Administrator will be forced to honor UAC prompts.

Disabled (Default)   By default, if you choose to leave this feature disabled (the default) and log in with the local Administrator account, then that account is exempt from UAC prompts.

User Account Control: Allow UIAccess Applications to Prompt for Elevation without Using the Secure Desktop

UIAccess, or UIA, is a category of features designed to make using Windows easier for persons with disabilities. The problem is that applications that interface with the desktop might need to ask the user about security credentials, and any user needs to be able to enter the answer to UAC security prompts.

And, as it turns out, one application that many people often use is categorized as a UIA application. That's the Windows Remote Assistance application.

What happens if you try to provide remote assistance to a user by default? Everything goes fine until a UAC prompt occurs at the machine needing help. In this case, any UAC prompts will appear on the interactive user's desktop (the person needing help) instead of the secure desktop (the person providing the help).

Oh, the catch-22 of it all!

That's what this policy setting is meant to help with.

Enabled (Default)   If you enable this setting, the person needing help will see the UAC prompt, but the person providing help will see what the person needing help is doing. This means that the person needing help (Joe User) will need to know a local Administrator account's password to get through this prompt. Note that the Explain text of this setting incorrectly suggests that Disabled is the default, which it isn't.

Disabled   If you disable this policy setting, you don't have to worry about Joe User knowing a local administrator password in order for him to get remote help. Again, this setting is mislabeled as the default. It's not. Enabled is really the default.

User Account Control: Behavior of the Elevation Prompt for Administrators in Admin Approval Mode

As stated, even if you log on as a Domain Admin to a local Windows 10 box, you're still going to get UAC prompts.

Actually, if you log on with any of 16 different privileged SIDs, you'll get UAC prompts as an Admin. Or, if you log in with any of nine user rights, you're also going to see the prompts.

We saw these accounts in a list earlier in this chapter and the user rights in Table 8.2.

This policy setting controls how, when logging in as a member of one of those groups or with one of those rights, you'll see prompts.

If you're an admin, the system already knows you're an admin. It won't (by default) re-ask you to supply credentials. It will, however, ask you (essentially) to acknowledge you're about to do a potentially harmful or impactful thing, like installing an application or creating a new user.

Prompt for consent (Default)   Because you're already an admin, by default you don't need to resupply your username and password; you just have to click the Continue button or use Alt+C.

Prompt for credentials   This requires an admin to reenter their username and password or provide the username and password of any other Administrator account.

Elevate without prompting   Use with caution: this will silently "say yes" to any prompt if you're logged in as an admin. Microsoft suggests that this only be used in the most secure (they call it *constrained*) environments.

User Account Control: Behavior of the Elevation Prompt for Standard Users

As expected, mere mortals have to supply some additional credentials to perform administrative tasks. When will mere mortals be asked for administrative credentials?

Prompt for credentials (Default)   Users logging into non–domain joined machines will always be prompted for administrative credentials. If the user enters valid administrative credentials, the user will be permitted to continue.

Prompt for credentials on the secure desktop   Similar to the previous setting but prompts users on the secure (grayed-out) desktop, which proves that the request is coming from UAC and not a bad guy. What's weird about this setting is, the Explain text says this is the default, but in reality the previous setting (Prompt for credentials) is set up on the multiple workstations and servers I tested. And, moreover, the default action does, indeed, seem to be what this setting says—Prompt for credentials on the secure desktop. Not exactly sure why there's a discrepancy here, but I thought I would point it out.

Automatically deny elevation requests   If users shouldn't access certain stuff, why even prompt for credentials? If you set this policy setting to "Automatically deny elevation requests," users will simply get an "Access Denied" anytime they try to do something privileged. I discuss this a bit later in the section "UAC Policy Setting Suggestions."

This setting's Explain text says, "Default for enterprise," but it's really a "strong suggestion" for the enterprise. See the scenarios a little later for more information about why this is recommended.

User Account Control: Detect Application Installations and Prompt for Elevation

This security setting determines the behavior of application installation detection for the entire system.

Enabled (Default)   Applications that start with the words *setu* (yes, that's right, *setu*, as in setup.exe, setupnow.exe, and others), *instal* (yes, again, it's *instal*), or *update* will be automatically detected by UAC and prompted for credentials. Note that the policy setting Explain text says, "Default for home," but it's really default for everyone.

Disabled   If you're using GPSI or SCCM to deploy your software, this feature isn't needed. It's only required when Junior or Grandma tries to run setup.exe for EvilApp6. GPSI and SCCM automatically work around this, so you can safely set this to Disabled here if you want to.

This policy setting says, "Default for enterprise," but it's really a "strong suggestion" for the enterprise. See the scenarios a little later for more information about why this is recommended.

User Account Control: Only Elevate Executables That Are Signed and Validated

You can set up UAC such that applications only run if they are digitally signed via a PKI (Public Key Infrastructure) and Trusted. Enterprise administrators can control the allowed applications list by populating certificates in the local computer's Trusted Root Store.

 Population of this store is supported by Group Policy.

Enabled   Only applications signed by a trusted PKI certificate are permitted to run.

Disabled (Default)   It doesn't matter if the application is signed via PKI.

User Account Control: Only Elevate UIAccess Applications That Are Installed in Secure Locations

We talked about UIAccess (UIA) programs when we checked out the **User Account Control: Allow UIAccess applications to prompt for elevation without using the secure desktop** setting earlier.

Again, UIAccess is a category of features designed to allow persons with disabilities to more easily use Windows. The problem is that these same applications have the potential to be places where an attacker can gain a toehold in the system and do nefarious things. So, this policy setting manages UIAccess programs and ensures that they can be run only in secure locations. This policy setting takes advantage of IL (Integrity Level) and MIC (Mandatory Integrity Control).

 IL (Integrity Level) and MIC (Mandatory Integrity Control) are whole new concepts in modern Windows (and simply too deep to go into here). In short, these facilities let certain users and programs have certain rights to files based on their "trust level." An ever-so-brief overview of MIC can be found at http://tinyurl.com/y8753w, though decent online information on this subject is kind of hard to come by. One such decent, but not online, source is Mark Minasi's book *Administering Windows Vista Security: The Big Surprises* (Sybex, 2006). Yes, it's about Windows Vista, and we're up to Windows 10, and as far as I know, there is no better book on the subject, and all the information should be valid through Windows 10.

Enabled (Default)   Specifies that an application will only launch with "UIAccess integrity" if it resides in a secure location in the file system. The secure locations in Windows are limited to the following directories:

- `\Program Files\`, including subdirectories
- `\Windows\system32\`
- `\Program Files (x86)\`, including subdirectories for 64-bit versions of Windows

Windows enforces a PKI signature check on any interactive application that requests execution with UIAccess integrity level regardless of the state of this security setting.

Disabled   An application will start with UIAccess integrity *even if it does not* reside in one of the three secure locations in the file system.

User Account Control: Run All Administrators in Admin Approval Mode

This is the "master switch" for UAC.

Enabled (Default)   If this setting is Enabled, all UAC prompts are possible (although they might not all happen, based on other things you set). However, at least this switch needs to be Enabled. Changing this setting requires a system reboot.

Disabled   If you Disable this policy, UAC and all of its supporting functionality just goes away. Not suggested.

The Security Center feature in Windows will demonstrate that the overall security of the operating system has been reduced.

User Account Control: Switch to the Secure Desktop When Prompting for Elevation

When you try to perform any administrative task, including taking remote control of a PC, you are prompted for authorization. This security setting determines whether the elevation request will prompt for the user's Interactive Desktop or the Secure Desktop.

You might be wondering what the difference is between prompting for the *Secure Desktop* versus the *Interactive Desktop*. The Secure Desktop only allows trusted System processes to run on it, which means that an application must have already been approved by an Administrator to be installed and run with System-level privilege. The Interactive Desktop allows User processes to run (such high-level approval isn't required to install and run User processes). The interesting part of all this is that it only requires User-level privilege to spoof users into believing they are seeing and/or clicking on something that is being generated, legitimately, from Windows. Therefore, by placing the elevation dialog box on the Secure Desktop, only a highly privileged process can hope to run there, which means that the dialog box the user is seeing and interacting with is a genuine one that Windows has generated (not some bad guy hoping you'll click OK).

The Secure Desktop protects against input and output spoofing when a user interacts with the UAC elevation dialog box.

Enabled (Default)   All elevation requests by default will go to the Secure Desktop. The Secure Desktop is used here as an "antispoofing" technology, so it is recommended that you leave this on.

Disabled   All elevation requests will go to the user's Interactive Desktop. In some specific cases (e.g., an enterprise that leverages Remote Assistance and doesn't allow their Standard Users the ability to approve an elevation request), it may be all right to disable this policy.

User Account Control: Virtualize File and Registry Write Failures to Per-User Locations

Windows Vista and later machines have a feature called File and Registry Virtualization. The idea is that for years programmers have been told, "It's okay to dump your garbage anywhere in Windows." Now, in modern Windows, it's not. But what about those poor applications? They need to keep working, too. This feature will redirect potentially harmful file and Registry writes to "okay" locations.

The idea is that some applications might try to write to profile and Registry locations they don't have access to, so a modern Windows system will redirect (or, as Microsoft calls it, *virtualize*) these writes to writable places in the profile and Registry. So, if an application tries to write application data to %ProgramFiles%, %Windir%, %Windir%\system32, or HKLM\ Software\, this virtualization feature kicks in and gently places the data into the kosher places in the file system and Registry. Don't panic for now; I discuss file and Registry virtualization in detail in the next chapter.

This will happen automatically when anyone is logged in as a Standard User.

An administrator may choose to disable this feature—if she's sure she's running all modern Windows-compliant applications. But how would you really be sure?

Enabled (Default)   Facilitates the runtime redirection of application write failures to defined user locations for both the file system and Registry.

Disabled   Applications that write data to protected locations will simply fail as they did in previous versions of Windows.

There is a neat roundup of File and Registry virtualization issues found in one Knowledge Base article here: http://support.microsoft.com/ default.aspx/kb/927387.

UAC Policy Setting Suggestions

There are 10 UAC settings, which we just explored. That means you've got a lot of power to control UAC. As we stated, you really don't want to just "turn it off." You want to tune it based on your situation.

Let's examine some cases, the default behavior, and perform a suggested remediation.

Case 1: Enterprise Desktop: Standard User (Who Gets Help Remotely When Needed)

This is the type of user who will never need to perform an elevated or privileged administrative task. The majority of users fall into this category. If you need to help them, how will you? Likely, you'll simply use Remote Desktops and perform desktop management remotely.

Suggestion 1: Set "UAC: Behavior of the elevation prompt for Standard Users" to Disabled.   If the user should never perform an administrative task, then why present them with the opportunity? If you perform this simple change, they simply won't see the UAC prompts, and it will be denied. By performing this step, you're reducing the overall "attack surface."

Additionally, if users see the credential dialog box, it can motivate them to call the help desk and beg for a valid Administrator account. You don't want to get caught in this trap. You can eliminate this type of support call.

Suggestion 2: Set "UAC: Switch to the Secure Desktop when prompting for elevation" to Disabled.   The Secure Desktop can be disabled if the logged-on Standard User never elevates. The technology is designed to protect elevations; if the logged-on user never elevates, the Secure Desktop protection is not needed. Be sure you're positively using suggestion 1 along with suggestion 2 in this two-part tip. Otherwise, you're possibly opening up a security hole.

Case 2: Enterprise Desktop: Standard User (Who Gets "Over-the-Shoulder Help" When Needed)

In some environments, the user puts in a request, and the administrator walks over to the desk and, while the user is logged in, helps adjust or install applications. This is sometimes called "over-the-shoulder" (OTS) assistance. OTS assistance often takes place in doctor and lawyer offices and other smaller offices that occasionally need tuning.

Main suggestion: Set "UAC: Behavior of the elevation prompt for Standard Users" to "Prompt for credentials."   In smaller organizations it may be preferable to leave this policy enabled to facilitate administrative help without requiring the administrator to perform a Fast User Switch and log on as himself.

Case 3: Enterprise Desktop: Protected Administrator

This is the case where you've been forced into giving Sally local administrative privileges on her own machine. You don't want to do it, but you have to for some reason. This can happen if Sally is already an administrator of her Windows XP machine before you upgrade it to Windows Vista. Or, you install Windows 10 for her, and you're forced to give her administrator rights.

In UAC parlance, Sally would be called a *Protected Administrator* because she is a user who is either directly or indirectly a member of the local administrators group of the client workstation.

Main suggestion: Set all UAC policies at the default.   Windows UAC policy defaults are optimized for the Protected Administrator user account type. Do the dirty deed: give Sally the admin rights she needs (Boo! Hiss!). The good news, though, is that the default UAC policies will force the applications that previously ran on XP with administrative privileges to run with the equivalent privilege of a Standard User.

So now, your e-mail editor and web browser will no longer run with administrative privileges unnecessarily. Rejoice in attack surface reduction!

Case 4: Enterprise Desktop (Running Only Windows "Logo'd" Software)

In this case, we're not talking about Universal, Metro, or "Modern" apps. We're talking about desktop apps still, but Logo'd for Windows.

If all your applications are Windows Logo'd, you could set the following policy settings as follows:

1. Set "UAC: Behavior of the elevation prompt for Standard Users to Automatically deny elevation requests" to Disabled.

2. Set "UAC: Switch to the secure desktop when prompting for elevation" to Disabled.

3. Set "UAC: Virtualize file and registry write failures to per-user locations" to Disabled.

So, if you are running applications that are designed for the Standard User, you will not use or require the virtualization feature. This feature was designed as legacy application compatibility mitigation but comes with a price.

Applications that leverage virtualization perform a "double read" when accessing data that could potentially be in a virtualized location.

So, if the application was installed to %ProgramFiles%\ApplicationX\ and under that folder are FileX and FileY, if during runtime ApplicationX modifies and saves FileY, this forces FileY to be virtualized to %userprofile%\..\..\VirtualStore\Program Files\ApplicationX\FileY.

The next time ApplicationX tries to access FileX, it must first look in the user "VirtualStore" as FileX could have potentially been virtualized. If FileX is not found, it will then query the "real" %ProgramFiles%\ApplicationX\FileX.

That's going to be a performance hit. But with these settings, you would increase performance. Again, this is only a good idea if all the applications are modernized.

Case 5: Enterprise Desktop: Protected Administrator (All Applications Are Signed)

Again, this is a long-term goal for you to reach in your environment. The goal is that all applications are signed by the organization and only a restricted set of "Application signing certificates" are trusted by the client computer.

Main suggestion: Set "Only elevate executables that are signed and validated" to Enabled. This configuration will ensure that only those applications that either ship with Windows or are explicitly signed and trusted by the organization will be allowed to run with administrative rights.

If you invoke an elevated cmd.exe "command host," you can then launch most applications from within the command host environment, thus bypassing this policy check.

Case 6: Power User–Style User Who Shares Computers with Standard Users

In this case, you would want the power user to be prompted when they do an administrative action. Give the right credentials, then, poof! They're in. But you also want to silently deny the regular user. Don't let them even see what they shouldn't play with.

Main suggestion: Set "Behavior of the elevation prompt for administrators in Admin Approval Mode" to "Elevate without prompting." If the user wants to gain the benefits of the "Split Token" but never see a UAC elevation dialog box, this configuration is better than disabling UAC altogether.

Remember that when UAC is disabled, all its supporting technologies are also disabled. In most cases this is not desirable.

Case 7: Your Users Request Assistance with Windows Remote Assistance

In this case, you would want to ensure that users don't have to know a local administrator password to get help.

Main suggestion: Use the default and ensure "Allow UIAccess applications to prompt for elevation without using the secure desktop" is set. This way, it's a clear path for users to ask for help and for you to provide help.

UAC Final Thoughts and References

As I stated in the introduction, UAC hasn't changed, internally, too much since Windows Vista. But if you want to get a leg up and learn what's different, here are some additional articles I suggest you read. The information here shouldn't change and should be valid for Windows 7 and later.

"Inside Windows 7 User Account Control," by Mark Russinovich:

`http://technet.microsoft.com/en-us/magazine/2009.07.uac.aspx`

(shortened to `http://tinyurl.com/mokz59`).

"Engineering Windows 7 (UAC), Post 1":

`http://blogs.msdn.com/e7/archive/2008/10/08/user-account-control.aspx`

(shortened to `http://tinyurl.com/3jn5g3`).

"Engineering Windows 7 (UAC), Post 2":

`http://blogs.msdn.com/e7/archive/2009/01/15/user-account-control-uac-quick-update.aspx`

(shortened to `http://tinyurl.com/9a8vrj`.

"Engineering Windows 7 (UAC), Post 3":

`http://blogs.msdn.com/e7/archive/2009/02/05/update-on-uac.aspx`

(shortened to `http://tinyurl.com/dyp9s8`).

"Engineering Windows 7 (UAC), Post 4":

`http://blogs.msdn.com/e7/archive/2009/02/05/uac-feedback-and-follow-up.aspx`

(shortened to `http://tinyurl.com/ct8wt6`).

Wireless (802.3) and Wired Network (802.11) Policies

Built-in support for wireless networks was introduced for Windows XP and Windows 2003 and is now enhanced for Windows Vista and later. Additionally, Windows Vista and later has a Wired policy that is neat. And Windows 7 and 8 added a few more bells and whistles (which can be found in the same place as the Windows Vista settings).

You can see two new nodes in Computer Configuration ➤ Policies ➤ Windows Settings ➤ Security Settings ➤ **Wired Network (IEEE 802.3) Policies** and **Wireless Network (IEEE 802.11 Policies)**, as shown in Figure 8.46.

Here's the trick, though: to make the examples in this section work, you need to have an updated schema of at least Windows Server 2008 or later.

Note that if you try to create new Wireless Network (IEEE 802.11) policies for Windows XP *without* updating the schema, these policies will succeed, because Windows XP doesn't require the updated schema. Do note, however, that this still requires (at least) the Windows Server 2003 Active Directory schema.

However, if you don't have the schema update, and you attempted to create a new Wireless policy for Windows Vista or later or new Wired policy (which is Windows Vista and later–only anyway), you'll encounter what you see in Figure 8.47.

Assuming you've modified the schema as required, you're ready to move on.

802.11 Wireless Policy for Windows XP

When you right-click **Wireless Network (IEEE 802.11) Policies,** you can select "Create a New Windows Network Policy for Windows Vista and Later Releases" or "Create a New Windows XP Policy," as seen in Figure 8.46. For XP, you know which one to pick.

You can set all sorts of wireless parameters for your Windows XP or Windows 2003 computers (though it's unlikely you'll have many Windows 2003 computers with wireless cards). The policy settings themselves are beyond the scope of this book and include options such as WEP, EAP/Smartcard usage, and other scary-sounding wireless settings. However, you can learn about the controllable settings in "Securing Wireless LANs with Certificate Services." At last check it was found here: `http://tinyurl.com/yzm3tv`.

FIGURE 8.46   Wired and Wireless policies nodes

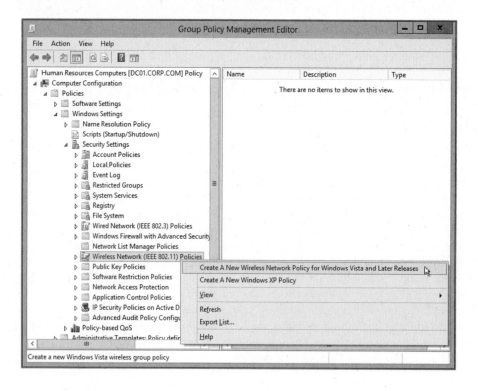

FIGURE 8.47   What happens if you try to create a new Wired or Wireless policy for Windows Vista and later without the schema update

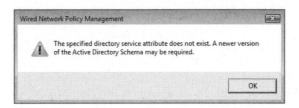

Note that your users need to be connected to the hard-wired network at least one time and download Group Policy from a Domain Controller to get the appropriate certificates for Wireless policy.

802.11 Wireless Policy and 802.3 Wired Policy for Modern Windows

For Windows Vista and later, the Wireless policy has some new bells and whistles, and the Wired policy is specific to Windows Vista and later. And, for Windows 7 and later, both the Wired and Wireless policies have even more bells and whistles than they do for Windows Vista. When you create a new policy for each, you'll clearly see a little subsection that houses the Windows 7–specific features that only Windows 7 and later clients can utilize.

However, in the new goodies for Wireless you get things like "Mixed Security Mode" (where you can configure several settings to single SSID) and "Allow and Deny Lists" (where you can dictate specifically which SSIDs they can connect and not connect to).

At last check, a good starting point for leveraging these policies (the Windows Vista and later versions, anyway) can be found here:

`http://technet.microsoft.com/en-us/magazine/2007.04.cableguy.aspx`

(shortened to `http://tinyurl.com/ykfmkax`).

Note that machines always need to first make contact with a Domain Controller to download Group Policy over the wired Ethernet at least one time before this Wireless policy can kick in.

Additionally, the Wired policies don't look all that exciting at first blush. But they're the backbone for Network Access Protection (NAP)—a feature for Windows Server 2008 and later (with Windows XP/SP3 and later clients) that will prevent rogue machines from getting on your network.

Again, while they're not shown here, there are several Wired and Wireless policy settings just for Windows 7 and later target computers. When you create a new Wired or Wireless policy, you won't miss 'em. They're cordoned off in a category labeled "Windows 7 and later policy settings."

Configuring Windows Firewall with Group Policy

Since XP/SP2, all operating systems that Microsoft shipped have the firewall enabled by default.

But really, what's the point? The point of a firewall on your machine (whatever kind it is) is to allow certain kinds of traffic to pass through and certain kinds of traffic to be prevented. That's it. Nothing mysterious here about a firewall.

Well, since Windows XP/SP2, all inbound communication was filtered (blocked) by a firewall. We saw this phenomenon in Chapter 2 when we tried to perform a "Group Policy Results" to our Windows XP or later client system and got an RPC error (which is the same error we'd get if the machine were off).

So, since Windows Vista, there's an updated firewall and a killer updated way via Group Policy to control it. This technology is dubbed WFAS: Windows Firewall with Advanced Security.

Let me declare right now that it's simply not possible for me to go into every single thing you can do with WFAS. That's (at least) a whole book in and of itself.

My goal is to acquaint you with the WFAS mechanism vis-à-vis Group Policy. That way, when you know the underlying geeky firewall technology, protocols, encryption, certificates, and so on, you'll be ready to implement it all because your Group Policy knowledge will be solid enough to allow you to do what you want.

The other big part is helping you understand precedence order. With a lot of things in Group Policy-land, understanding why a policy (Group Policy or IPsec policy or Connection Rule Policy, and so on) takes effect is paramount to being a master troubleshooter.

Again, the Windows Firewall is a big, big topic, and you should read everything you can here:

http://technet.microsoft.com/en-us/network/bb545423.aspx

(shortened to http://tinyurl.com/5rvb62).

Before you go headlong into manipulating and changing the default firewall settings, I recommend that you use caution. In other words, the firewall is, in fact, turned on by default in these operating systems for a reason.

It provides the most protection from the bad guys trying to infect and hack your Windows machines. And it makes sure you'll be mindful about opening up just the ports you want to use, even on a server.

So, if you're going to start opening ports on your machines (or kill the firewall altogether), please use these policy settings with caution.

Know what you're changing and why you're changing it.

Again, the defaults are there for a reason!

Everything Old Is New Again: The Windows XP vs. WFAS Firewall Controls

Before we get too far down the pike here, let me describe one potential pitfall about what's happened here since Windows Vista: because Windows XP (and Windows Server 2003 for that matter) already had a firewall (with one set of Group Policy controls), and now Windows Vista and later have an updated firewall (with an updated set of Group Policy controls), it can sometimes be a little confusing just what you're controlling and where you're supposed to go in the Group Policy Management Editor in order to control it.

Now there are two sets of firewall settings:

- The "older" Windows XP firewall settings (where both Windows XP and Windows Vista and later machines can embrace most of these settings)

- The "newer" WFAS settings for Windows Vista and later (which Windows XP does not know how to handle)

Indeed, in Chapter 2, we used the policy **Windows Firewall: Allow Inbound Remote Administration Exception** when we wanted to allow the required ports to open up so we could perform a Group Policy Results analysis.

Yep, that one worked! But I haven't tested all the Windows XP policy settings against a Windows Vista and later machine. And, indeed, there's a more specific, targeted way to achieve the same goals with the WFAS firewall.

So, my humble suggestion, before you start creating lots and lots of GPOs with Windows Firewall policies in them, is to name them based on which operating system they're supposed to target. Then, you have a very clearly named GPO that you can link to proper places in your hierarchy.

Therefore, I suggest you keep your GPOs separate. Have GPOs that affect only the Windows XP firewall, GPOs that affect only the Windows Vista and later firewall, and maybe others that affect only the Windows Server 2008 and later firewall. In this example, you can see two GPOs linked to two OUs. We have "Sales Firewall Policy for Windows XP" and "Sales Firewall Policy for Vista and later Computers" and they're only affecting the specific type of computers inside the OUs. I think, in the long run, this is the cleanest and least-confusing path.

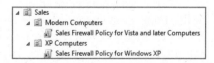

This might not always be possible, but it is by far the cleanest implementation.

The other way to specify which GPOs affect which machines is via WMI filtering (explored in detail in Chapter 4, "Advanced Group Policy Processing"). With WMI filters you can "target" a machine based on various characteristics. Here are the WMI queries you'll need to target a specific GPO to a specific machine type.

For Vista RTM:

```
Select * from Win32_OperatingSystem Where BuildNumber=6000
```

For Windows XP:

```
Select * from Win32_OperatingSystem Where BuildNumber =2600
```

Windows Server 2008 and Windows Vista/SP1 systems both share build number 6001. You can use the same query to address both Windows Server 2008 and Windows Vista/SP1 machines:

```
Select * from Win32_OperatingSystem Where BuildNumber = 6001
```

For Server 2008/SP2 and Windows Vista/SP2:

```
Select * from Win32_OperatingSystem Where BuildNumber = 6002
```

For Windows 7 and Windows Server 2008 R2:

```
Select * from Win32_OperatingSystem Where BuildNumber = 7600
```

For Windows 7/SP1 and Windows Server 2008 R2/SP1:

```
Select * from Win32_OperatingSystem Where BuildNumber = 7601
```

For Windows 8 and Windows Server 2012:

```
Select * from Win32_OperatingSystem Where BuildNumber = 9200
```

For Windows 8.1 and Windows Server 2012 R2:

```
Select * from Win32_OperatingSystem Where BuildNumber = 9600
```

For Windows 10 and Server 2016, the issue gets more complex. To save space, Alan Burchill, technical editor for this book, put together a little tutorial to help you understand the issue and syntax you'll need. It's a great resource, and that article is found at:
```
http://www.grouppolicy.biz/2015/05/how-to-apply-wmi-filter-to-windows-10-
or-windows-server-2016/
```

These are just some examples. If you have alternate operating systems not listed here, be sure to use the tools in Chapter 4 to glean the `BuildNumber` for the operating system you want to target.

Manipulating the Windows Firewall (the Old Way)

Most of the techniques we'll perform here should work just fine if the target machine is Windows Vista or later. But I haven't specifically tested each of these settings against a modern operating system.

Again, we already delved into some of these ideas in Chapter 2, where I used the old (non-WFAS) way to open up firewall ports.

Domain vs. Standard Profiles

If you dive down into the new firewall policy settings, contained within Computer Configuration ➢ Policies ➢ Administrative Templates ➢ Network ➢ Network Connections ➢ Windows Firewall, you'll notice two branches: Domain Profile and Standard Profile. You can see them in Figure 8.48.

FIGURE 8.48   The Domain Profile is used when the machine can make contact to a Domain Controller. The Standard Profile is used when the machine is in someplace like a hotel room or Starbucks.

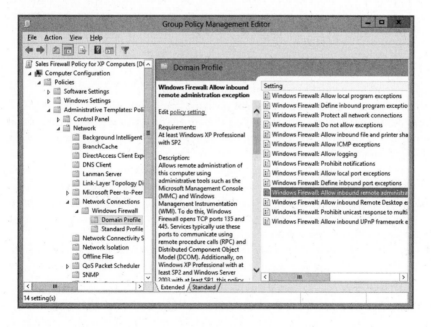

Inside each branch, you'll see a gaggle of settings that are exactly the same. So, what gives?

When policy settings within the Domain Profile are enabled, they affect the Domain Controller's firewall. This is usually when a computer is at the central office and a normal logon occurs.

When policy settings within the Standard Profile are enabled, they affect the firewall when Windows *cannot* authenticate to a Domain Controller. This might happen when the user is in a hotel room, an Internet cafe, or other areas with public connectivity.

You might set up your Domain Profile settings to have additional port exceptions to be used by the central office administrative team for scanning and remote administration. And you can leverage your Standard Profile settings to ensure that the firewall is at its maximum enforcement. In short, you get to choose how strong the firewall will act in each of these circumstances.

Microsoft has a great little article on how the computer fundamentally determines if it should use the Domain Profile or the Standard Profile. Check it out here: `http://tinyurl.com/cao73`.

Again, these settings here originated with the Windows XP/SP2 firewall, but they should also work with modern Windows. Here are some tips if you choose to affect Windows Vista and later machines with Windows XP/SP2 settings:

- Standard Profile settings apply to both the private and public profiles for Windows Vista and later.

- If you configure the more modern "Advanced Firewall Policy" (up next), then the Standard Profile settings will stop applying. The assumption is that if the computer is getting a new policy, you must have started using the new policy model.

Killing the Firewall (the Old Way)

There might be times when you just want to outright kill the Windows firewall. Additionally, you can prevent an inadvertent mishap should someone try to enable it.

I explained this in Chapter 2, but since we're here again, let's review. Again, note that the recommended course for manipulating the Windows Vista and later firewall will be discussed later, even though this technique will, in fact, work.

To kill the XP/SP2 (or later) firewall, drill down to Administrative Templates ➢ Network ➢ Network Connections ➢ Windows Firewall ➢ Domain Profile and select **Windows Firewall: Protect All Network Connections**. But here's the thing. You don't choose to *Enable* this policy. No, no. You *Disable* it. Yes, you read that right—you Disable it. Read the Explain text inside the policy for more information on specific usage examples.

Before you do this, though, remember that it's a better idea to leave it on and just filter based on the traffic you know you want. Only kill the firewall as a last resort.

Windows Firewall with Advanced Security WFAS

Now let's take a bite-sized tour of what we can do with the modern Windows Firewall with Advanced Security (WFAS). This firewall is included since Windows Vista, including of course Windows 10 and Windows Server 2016.

WFAS's two "prime directives" in life are as follows:

- To block all incoming traffic (unless it is requested or it matches a configured rule)

- To allow all outgoing traffic (unless it matches a configured rule to prevent it)

> As you go along in these examples, you'll see UI references to "Location" type, which can be "Domain Location," "Public Location," and "Private Location." To help you understand Network Location Types, read the article "Network Location Types in Windows Vista" here: http://tinyurl.com/669qxb. Because the Windows 10 machines we'll be manipulating are joined to the domain, they will be considered a part of the "Domain Location" where we can control the WFAS via Group Policy.

Additionally, the IP security (IPsec) function (discussed in more detail next) is also part of WFAS (where it was a separate node of the UI in the Group Policy Management Editor for pre-Vista management stations). You'll see how this all fits together as we go along.

Holy Cow! Three Ways to Set WFAS Settings!

There are three different *stores* for Windows Firewall for Advanced Security policies and four different ways to make that happen:

- The Active Directory–based Group Policy you know and love

- Local Group Policy accessible via gpedit.msc

- By running WF.MSC, which opens a GUI to the "local WFAS store"

Here's where it gets confusing, so stay with me: the store hosting rules from WF.MSC and from Local Group Policy are in fact *separate*.

If you crack open WF.MSC, you'll see that there are a number of Default Rules in WF.MSC (as shown here):

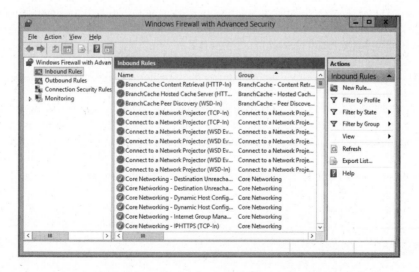

But open the Local Group Policy Editor, and you won't see those rules at all!

You can also see this behavior via the command line. The command is Netsh (then press Enter) advfirewall (then press Enter). Once inside, you can poke around. This is the command-line interface for all the goodies you're looking at in the Group Policy editor.

By default you're poking around the "local Windows Firewall store" (the same thing you'd see when you use WF.MSC), but you can use the set store command to change focus to, say, the local GPO or even an Active Directory–based GPO. The idea is that once you've "set store" to another place, say a particular GPO, you can do everything via the command line you could do via the GUI.

Nice touch!

Getting Started with WFAS "Properties"

The first place you might want to check out on your WFAS journey is the "Properties" of the WFAS node. Now, I say "Properties" with quotes because there isn't a precise name for them. But I'll call them "WFAS Properties" for our purposes. You find them by right-clicking over the "Windows Firewall with Advanced Security" node (with the little brick and the world icon) and selecting Properties, as seen in Figure 8.49.

Once there, you'll have lots of settings to play with. These settings specify certain behavior types based on how the machine is connected and some IPsec settings. You can see this in Figure 8.50. However, the trick about all of the WFAS Properties settings is that they act exactly like regular Administrative Templates policies. So, recall how in all Administrative Templates policy settings there is an "Enabled," "Not Configured," and "Disabled" ability? Well, all the settings contained here work exactly the same way across multiple GPOs, if configured. You can see an example of a subproperties page in Figure 8.50 where it demonstrates "Yes," "No," and "Not Configured." Each setting also displays the default setting if you do nothing (which is a nice touch).

Again, the point is that all the settings contained at this level are just like normal, everyday, garden-variety Group Policy. If stored at the local or domain-based levels, the regular Group Policy precedence rules will apply.

What we'll learn about *next* is a little different, because, while it uses the Group Policy interface, it's not exactly the same "Group Policy rule precedence" that you've come to know and love with the kinds of settings in here. Stay tuned—I'll explain it as we learn more and more, and then I'll wrap up our discussion about WFAS with an overall cheat sheet to help you grasp which rules come from where and what will win.

FIGURE 8.49   The Windows Firewall with Advanced Security has "Group Policy–like" properties inside.

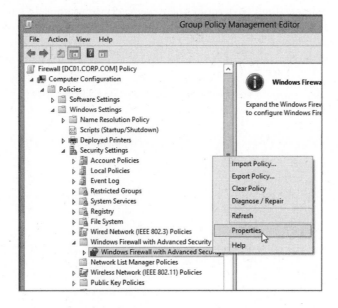

FIGURE 8.50   Imagine that all the settings in the WFAS Properties are just like Administrative Templates settings in other areas of Group Policy.

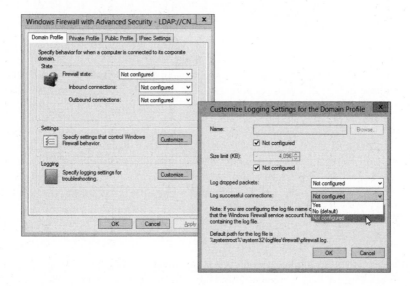

Creating New Inbound and Outbound Rules with the WFAS

WFAS is updated to support a neat-o new UI as well as some amazing under-the-hood features. Again, we simply don't have room to go over everything, so we'll have to make do with a brief tour. One important point to note is that WFAS has both inbound and outbound rules (where Windows XP's firewall had only inbound rules). You can see where to create rules in Figure 8.51 and simply right-click over the rule type to create a new rule.

FIGURE 8.51   Once you locate the Inbound and Outbound Rules nodes, you can right-click to select New Rule.

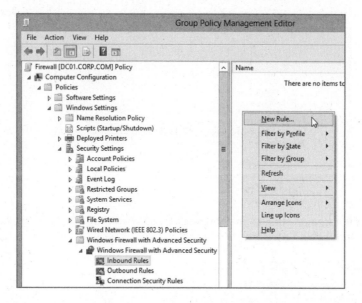

Inbound Rules   The goal of inbound rules is to prevent the bad stuff from reaching your machine and allow only traffic you request to reach you. This is the kind of thing most firewalls are used for.

Outbound Rules   At first blush, outbound rules seem counterintuitive. Why would you ever want to restrict outbound communication, right? Well, you might want to lock down a workstation from opening connections outbound to particular services. For example, you might have a specialty workstation that is only supposed to be used as a web-browser machine. Well, you can then lock out all outbound remote ports except port 80 (HTTP) and 443 (SSL/HTTPS). This would potentially allow you to squelch a virus or malware program that was trying to "phone home" or otherwise be a baddie. (Note that this works only if you lock out remote ports. If you locked out the local ports, this trick won't work.)

Connection Security Rules   These rules dictate if this machine is going to be able to talk to other machines at all. You can create all kinds of rules here, including only being able to talk with machines that are on the same domain, or just enable specific machine-to-machine contact. This is the new way to perform IPsec rules, though there's little mention of the word *IPsec*, actually. Additionally, there are settings here that work in conjunction with an advanced feature (which we cannot cover here) called Network Access Protection (NAP). The idea is that if your machine doesn't meet certain criteria, then it shouldn't be allowed to talk with its brothers and sisters. This is configured via the NAP MMC snap-in. Learn more about NAP at https://technet.microsoft.com/en-us/network/bb545879.aspx.

WARNING The rules you create should be ignored by pre-Vista machines (such as Windows XP). Be sure to read the sidebar "Everything Old Is New Again: The Windows XP vs. WFAS Firewall Controls."

Inbound and Outbound Rule Types

Once you've elected to create a rule, there are four rule types to choose from, as seen in Figure 8.52.

FIGURE 8.52 After creating an inbound or outbound rule, you must select the type. Most often, you'll select Predefined.

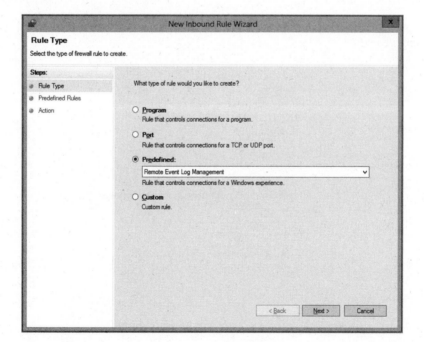

Program   You can dictate which programs (specified by path and executable name) you want to allow traffic to flow between. You need to also specify an action (Allow, Block, or "Allow the connection if it is secure"). Note that the "Allow the connection if it is secure" setting requires a valid connection security configuration as well as IPsec rules deployed to handle the IPsec portion of the enforcement.

Port   This is a specific rule based on TCP or UDP ports. You must also specify which ports (separated by commas). Specific ranges, say, 80–100, won't work unless the ports are individually listed with commas separating them.

Predefined   This will likely be where most people spend their time. This is a collection of "well-known" services and which ports to open up if you want traffic to flow. There are some new predefined collections for many client and server scenarios.

Custom   This is the kitchen sink. If you want to go whole hog and tweak until you're blue in the face, this is the place for you. If you couldn't configure the settings using one of the other three ways, this is where you do it.

If you want to try this out for a WFAS machine, select Predefined, then use the pull-down to see the various Predefined options, as seen in Figure 8.53. If we want to closely parallel the example in Chapter 2 (where we set the policy settings **Allow Inbound Remote Administration Exception**), we could simply select "Remote Event Log Management," as seen in Figure 8.53.

FIGURE 8.53   Use the Predefined rules to allow the kinds of "well-known" traffic your people might need.

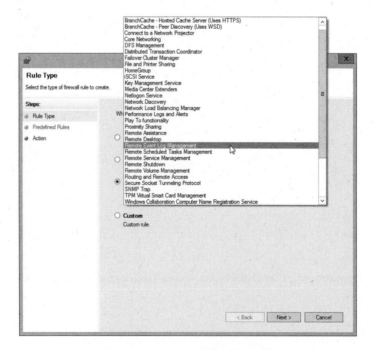

If you'd like to find the older "XP" way to do this (which still works for Windows 7 and later), see Chapter 2 in the sidebar "Understanding Windows Firewall Settings (and Dealing with Group Policy Results)."

By clicking Next in the wizard, you'll zip past all the predefined rules, saving you oodles of time. Once the wizard is complete, you'll see the new inbound rule and its name, as seen in Figure 8.54. To see what that rule is really doing, just check out the Properties for each line item.

FIGURE 8.54 When the rule is complete, you'll see the results in the right pane.

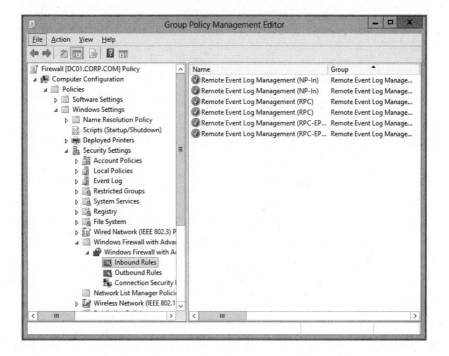

Connection Security Rules

In the previous example we leveraged an inbound rule to open up WFAS to allow a remote administration exception. And the procedure would be pretty similar if we wanted an outbound rule as well.

However, Connection Security rules are different. Connection Security rules define how and when computers authenticate using IPsec or Authenticated IP. Connection Security rules are used in establishing server and domain isolation as well as in enforcing NAP policy.

These allow you to specify which other computers you can talk with. Again, the idea here is to prevent your target machines from talking with the bad guys.

You can see the list of available Connection Security rule types in Figure 8.55.

FIGURE 8.55 WFAS Security rules offer lots of flexibility.

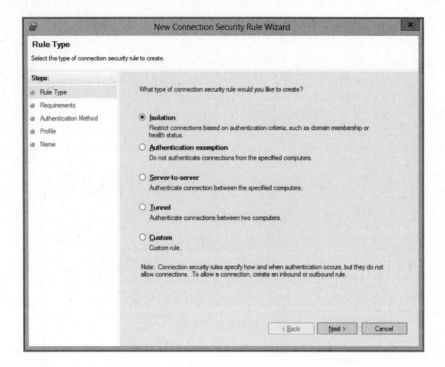

You can find more information on Authenticated IP at http://tinyurl .com/yelj7a and more on rule types at http://tinyurl.com/yx4rkk.

Rule Precedence

What if you have multiple WFAS rules applying? Which WFAS rule is going to win to restrict the traffic?

Additionally, what if you have multiple GPOs that affect this target machine with multiple rules? Turns out, it doesn't matter. All rules are simply "additive" among all GPOs—for the type of rule it is.

So, all inbound rules are all added up. All outbound rules are all added up, and so on. What you might care about is if a conflict exists between, say, an inbound rule and an outbound rule. Which will win there?

Again, the list of WFAS rules is merged from all sources and then processed in the order shown next from top to bottom. This rule process ordering is always enforced, regardless of the source of the rules:

Windows Service Hardening   This rule restricts services from establishing connections. These are generally automatically configured out of the box so that Windows Services can only communicate in specific ways (that is, restricting allowable traffic through a specific port). However, until you create a firewall rule, traffic is not allowed.

Connection Security Rules   This type of rule defines how and when computers authenticate using IPsec. Connection Security rules are used in establishing server and domain isolation as well as in enforcing NAP policy.

Authenticated Bypass Rules   This type of rule allows the connection of particular computers if the traffic is protected with IPsec, regardless of other inbound rules in place. Specified computers are allowed to bypass inbound rules that block traffic. For example, you could allow remote firewall administration from only *certain* computers by creating an "Authenticated bypass" rule for those computers. Or, you could enable support for Remote Assistance by the help desk *only* from the help desk computers.

Block Rules   This type of rule explicitly blocks a particular type of incoming or outgoing traffic.

Allow Rules   This type of rule explicitly allows a particular type of incoming or outgoing traffic.

IPsec (Now in Windows Firewall with Advanced Security)

The Internet Protocol security function, or IPsec for short, has a big job: securing the exchange of packets on your TCP/IP network. Its primary mission is host-to-host authentication. However, you can additionally choose to encrypt the traffic via tunneling or network encryption so others can't "spy" on the data flying by.

Maybe you have one super-important Human Resources server. And you want to ensure that no one except the Human Resources people can talk with that server. That's IPsec's job: ensuring that only the right people on the right computers can talk with the other computers you specify.

IPsec is based on IKE. The RFCs on IKE only support the concept of *computer authentication*. Microsoft, however, has gone the extra mile and introduced an extension to IKE called Authenticated IP (AuthIP). This new feature introduces the ability to support *user* authentication *as well as* computer authentication. Additionally, the administrator can choose to use *both* user and computer authentication if desired.

IPsec General Resources

IPsec is a big, big topic, and not one we can cover in enormous detail here. However, my goal for this section is to get you up to speed on the WFAS implementation of IPsec and explain how "legacy" IPsec interacts with the "new" IPsec. So, if you're not familiar with IPsec and want to follow along, you'll have to spend some quality time at the following websites:

- `www.microsoft.com/ipsec`

- `http://technet.microsoft.com/en-us/network/bb545651.aspx`

- A great document from Microsoft titled "Introduction to Windows Firewall with Advanced Security," found at `http://tinyurl.com/yx4rkk`

Server and Domain Isolation with IPsec

IPsec, at its core, restricts who is talking to whom. Okay, great. So, armed with that knowledge, you can take it to the next level and make sure that machines you know nothing about can't talk to machines you do know.

For instance, imagine a consultant comes into your business with a laptop and plugs in. Chances are, with enough poking around, he could figure out your IP address scheme. Now he's able to ping servers and see what's going on over there on machines without a firewall. And, what if he brought a virus in with him from the cold, dark, outside world? Oops, you've got a problem.

To combat this, let's assume instead you want to create "rings of protection" among machines you trust and machines you really trust. That's the idea of server and domain isolation with IPsec. You can see the general idea here in this graphic:

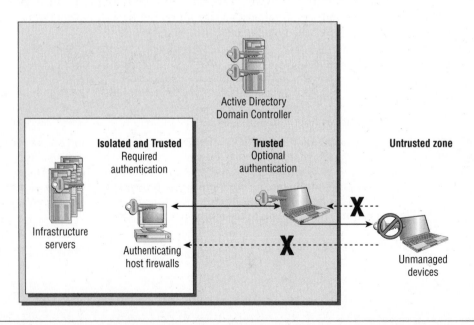

What sounds like a swell idea (and it is) can be a big project. Indeed, to protect your Windows machines from outside invaders (so they'll talk only with other machines you trust) takes about 300 pages of reading and implementing. You can find the big guide for this here:

    www.microsoft.com/technet/security/guidance/architectureanddesign/ipsec/
    default.mspx

(shortened to http://tinyurl.com/yywxas).

Again, it's something like 300 pages to do this for pre-Vista.

But if you check out:

    http://support.microsoft.com/default.aspx/kb/914841

you'll find information on the Simple Policy Update that adds more Windows Server 2003 and Windows XP IPsec support—specifically to reduce the amount of IPsec filters you need to pull this off.

In Windows Vista and later, it's simpler. There's a great Microsoft document called "Step-by-Step Guide: Deploying Windows Firewall and IPsec Policies," which is found at http://tinyurl.com/2rmd7u and covers this specific topic in depth.

Getting Started with IPsec with WFAS

Here's where it starts to get a little confusing. That's because there are two types of IPsec rules. I don't know if they have "proper" names, so we'll just call them "older" and "newer" rule types.

Older rule types are found in the node Computer Configuration ➤ Policies ➤ Windows Settings ➤ Security Settings ➤ **IP Security Policies on Active Directory**.

Newer rule types are found inside the new WFAS. Specifically, again, it's Computer Configuration ➤ Policies ➤ Windows Settings ➤ Security Settings ➤ **Windows Firewall with Advanced Security**. You can see both nodes highlighted in Figure 8.56.

To configure "old" IPsec policies, you right-click **IP Security Policies on Active Directory** and select "Create IP Security Policy."

To configure "new" IPsec policies, you right-click **Connection Security rules** and just get started with "New Rule." If IPsec is required it will just automatically be part of that rule.

Note that advanced IPsec configurations may require some additional "global" settings. To do this, right-click **Windows Firewall with Advanced Security** and select Properties, and then click the IPsec Settings tab, as seen in Figure 8.56. Then, when you click the Customize button in the IPsec Settings tab, you'll have the range of additional IPsec options to play with, as you can see in Figure 8.57.

FIGURE 8.56 You can see both the "old" and "new" places to configure IPsec policies.

 Note that the "old" IPsec policies' "Default Response Rule" is not valid for Windows Vista and later. The Group Policy editor will warn you of this if you try to create an IPsec policy using an updated GPMC management station. In short, don't mix old and new policies on the same computer.

Understanding How WFAS IPsec Rules Work

There are now two types of IPsec rules that can be applied to a machine with WFAS (Windows Vista and later).

Again, we're calling these the old IPsec rules and the new IPsec rules here. The old IPsec rules are configured in the IP Security Policy Management MMC snap-in.

Old IPsec Rules These are IKE rules that support only machine-based Kerberos, x.509 certificates, and preshared key authentication. Old IKE-based rules are applied in the same way to Windows Vista and later as they were in pre–Windows Vista operating systems: while multiple policies can be applied to a given machine, the last writer wins and there is no merging of IKE policy settings. So, if you had a policy set at the domain level and another set at the OU level, the OU level would win because there is no merging of any old IPsec rules.

FIGURE 8.57   Some "base" IPsec settings for a GPO can be found in the **Windows Firewall with Advanced Security** properties.

New IPsec Rules   Again, the new IPsec rules are created on machines with WFAS and applied to machines with WFAS (for Windows Vista and later). These rules are supported by an extension to IKE called Authenticated IP (AuthIP). As stated, a seriously good read on AuthIP can be found here: http://tinyurl.com/yelj7a. Here are some helpful tidbits as you explore the new WFAS IPsec. These (really geeky) tidbits are coming (nearly verba-tim) from the IPsec team at Microsoft, so, thank them (not me) if you get a nice tip here.

- With the new IPSec Rules, you can now leverage Interactive user, Kerberos/NTLMv2 credentials, User x.509 certificates, Machine X.509 certificates, NAP Health Certifi-cates, and Anonymous Authentication (optional Authentication) for authenticating an IPsec connection.

- When configuring GPOs for connection security and firewall policies, you could dis-able the use of local firewall and Connection Security rules. That way, only the Group Policy objects linked to the site, domain, or OU GPOs could control the Windows Fire-wall behaviors.

- Like other firewall and Group Policy rules, Connection Security rules are merged from all applicable GPOs (and processed according to the Rule Precedence list discussed earlier).

- Connection Security policies can be configured to create "old" (compatible) policies as well as Windows Vista and later (see the sidebar "Super-Geeky Note from the Microsoft IPsec Team #1: What's Going on Under the Hood").

- Only AuthIP policy is created for Windows Vista and later because IKE doesn't support User Authentication. Again, see the sidebar "Super-Geeky Note from the Microsoft IPsec Team #1: What's Going on Under the Hood."

- As noted earlier, Connection Security rules are merged from all applicable GPOs. However, there is a related group of settings for IPsec/Authenticated IP that manage the default IPsec behaviors that are not additive. The settings include the global authentication sets, Quick Mode and Key Exchange settings, and ICMP exemptions.

- On a WFAS client, Connection Security and IPsec rules can come from multiple GPOs. That is, all Connection Security rules on the client that make use of default auth/crypto sets will use the sets from the highest precedence GPO. If you need more flexibility, you have the three options. For authentication sets, configure the authentication through the Connection Security rule instead of using the default authentication. For Quick Mode crypto, use the command `netsh advfirewall` to configure Quick Mode crypto settings on a per–Connection Security rule basis as needed. For Main Mode, only one set is supported per policy. In the case where multiple Main Mode crypto sets are received, the one from the highest precedence GPO will be applied to all Connection Security rules in the policy. There is unfortunately no way to customize the rules to use different Main Mode crypto sets.

> Honestly, these tips are more for the IPsec "superstars" out there than us normal people (me included), so don't panic if it's not 100 percent evident or relevant to your situation.

How Windows Firewall Rules Are Ultimately Calculated

Hopefully by now you understand that there are two categories of "things" that can be set by WFAS policy: properties and rules.

Precedence Order for Properties

Properties are found in three ways:

- Running `WF.MSC` and right-clicking over the **Windows Firewall with Advanced Security** node (topmost node) and selecting Properties. This is the "local WFAS" store.

- Editing the local GPO of the machine and right-clicking over the Windows Firewall Advanced Security node and selecting Properties.

- Creating a new Active Directory–based GPO, then right-clicking over the **Windows Firewall with Advanced Security** node and selecting Properties.

Again, these properties all act like regular Group Policy Administrative Template settings.

Super-Geeky Note from the Microsoft IPsec Team #1: What's Going on Under the Hood

With WFAS, an admin can create IKE-based IPsec policies through the IP Security Policy Management snap-in. An admin can also create Connection Security rules that will be compatible with down-level IKE-based policies.

So, when the policy is created, here's what's happening under the hood:

- If no WFAS-specific features are required, the policy will be created with both a set of AuthIP (Vista and later) rules and a set of IKE rules for when the Vista (and later) system needs to connect to IKE-based 2000, XP, and 2003 systems.

- If there are WFAS-specific features (like requiring the use of a second User Authentication), then the system will *not* create pre–Windows Vista IKE rules.

What? Why not?

Simple: Since IKE on XP can't do User Authentication, there's no need to create extra policies where only Windows Vista and after features are used.

See! Told you this was geeky!

Super-Geeky Note from the Microsoft IPsec Team #2: Get the Right Certs to Do the Right Job

There is a particular nuance with regard to certificates that you'll need to know about before you plunge headlong into using IPsec and AuthIP. Again, the IPsec/AuthIP policies that are created by WFAS will use AuthIP by preference.

- If both machines are Windows Vista and later, then they'll use AuthIP to negotiate and authenticate.

- If one of the two talking machines is pre–Windows Vista, then the system will use IKE-based functionality.

- AuthIP uses SSL certs with client and/or server authentication settings configured.

- SSL certs can be client authentication or client and server authentication certs. And either should work.

What this means is that if you are constructing policies to use certificate authentication for Windows Vista and later, you'll need certificates that will work with AuthIP. That means the certificates you deploy to the clients need to be SSL certs with client and/or server authentication (depending on if you want one-way or mutual authentication).

Note that these certs differ from the standard digital certs used in Windows XP/2003.

Now, the one thing I waited to explain until now is this: you can "block" the local WFAS store from being added to the calculations. To do this, in any GPO that has Windows Firewall settings that apply to the computer, right-click the **Windows Firewall with Advanced Security** node and select Properties. Then, in, say, Domain Profile (or the other profiles), click Customize. Locate the Rule merging section and select No, as seen in Figure 8.58.

FIGURE 8.58 You can block the application of the local WFAS firewall rules or local Connection Security rules by setting the Rule merging settings.

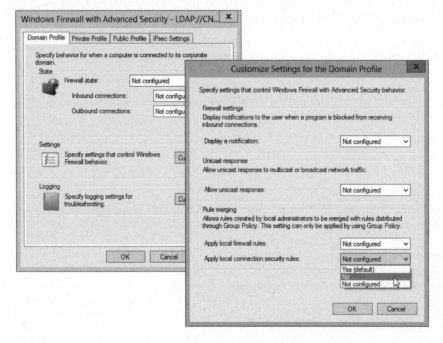

This will only block a rule merge. Or, additionally, you could choose No from the "Apply local connection security rules" drop-down to block those.

However, it should be noted that you could prevent a local admin from being able to control a property just by setting it in the GPO.

Again, the default is "Yes" that local WFAS store settings (and rules) would apply. Change this only if you do not want local rules to apply. However, note that WFAS has a zillion built-in firewall rules. And, if you set this to "No," then all those rules suddenly— poof!—turn off. And WFAS's default action would be to block all incoming traffic. To change this you would need to set specific rules (I suggest the Predefined rules) to specify which inbound traffic you would allow through.

 You could export the local WFAS store first and then import it into a domain-based one if you so choose.

Precedence Order for Rules

We've already discussed rule precedence (see the section "Rule Precedence" earlier). Even though the specific "what rule will win" aspect is pretty complicated, the overall Group Policy "rules" are simple.

Basically, all Group Policy Objects that contain any WFAS rules are added up. There isn't even a concept of a "conflict" with WFAS rules, because the rules are just "separated" into buckets:

- So, all the inbound rules are added up from the local store, then all GPOs.
- Then, all the outbound rules are added up from the local store, then all GPOs.
- And all the Connection Security rules are added up from the local store, then all GPOs.
- If there's a Deny/Block policy for *any* rule, that's always going to win for that rule type.

You can, if you want to, disable the local WFAS store and ignore those rules. That way, you just guarantee that Group Policy is doing all the dirty work to configure everything. In my opinion, this seems like a good way to go, so you don't have to remember if there even is a local WFAS store.

Again, you can see how to kill the WFAS local store's rule application in Figure 8.55.

What I Didn't Cover

Unfortunately, space limitations restrict me from delving into *all* security functions of Group Policy. Of note, two categories are missing from this Group Policy security roundup that can affect all computers:

- Certificate Services and Public Key Infrastructure (PKI)
- EFS and the EFS Recovery Policy

For More on Certificate Services and PKI

For getting a grip on Certificate Services and PKI, check out the free Microsoft Virtual Academy online training. It's at:

> http://www.microsoftvirtualacademy.com/training-courses/windows-server-2012-r2-implementing-a-basic-pki 549.aspx

For More on EFS and the EFS Recovery Policy

You'll find information on the Encrypting File System in Windows XP and Windows Server 2003 at http://tinyurl.com/576kx.

Additionally, see the Microsoft Knowledge Base article "Best Practices for the Encrypting File System" (KB 223316) at https://support.microsoft.com/en-us/kb/223316.

One final parting WFAS tip. If you check out the local WFAS editor by clicking Start and then typing **WF.MSC** in the Start Search dialog box, you'll also have the ability to see the WFAS "monitor," which can be useful for troubleshooting.

Final Thoughts

To know security, you need to know Group Policy. To that end, we've toured some of the major sights along the Group Policy security highway. From the "Default Domain Controllers Policy" and "Default Domain Policy" GPOs to Software Restriction Policies to AppLocker—a lot can be accomplished in there.

Walking up to a specific machine and applying local security sounds like a great, straightforward idea—until you have so many machines you couldn't possibly walk up to them all. This chapter covered some alternate methods for asserting your will across the network.

I covered this back in Chapter 3, but remember that most items in the security branch of a GPO will take effect, maximally, every 16 hours—even if the Group Policy doesn't change in Active Directory. This ensures that if a nefarious local administrator changed the policies on his workstation, they'll eventually be refreshed. However, recall that this "Security Background Refresh" will not affect other areas of Group Policy by default. If you want similar behavior, be sure to read Chapter 3 where I discuss the implications of the setting named **Process even if the Group Policy objects have not changed.** You can enable different sections of Group Policy to do this by drilling down in the Group Policy Management Editor within Computer Configuration ➢ Policies ➢ Administrative Templates ➢ System ➢ Group Policy.

Again, this was covered in Chapter 3. So, for fullest security and protection, reread that chapter to understand why and how to enable those settings.

When it comes to restricting software, Software Restriction Policies are fine for Windows XP and later, but AppLocker (Windows 7 and later) has a real leg up. Be careful not to lock yourself out "too much" lest you need to revert your policies or recover your machines. Other than that—they're great.

Finally, remember that Fine-Grained Password Policy (FGPP) isn't really related to Group Policy, but there is a tie-in: if no FGPP is assigned to a user or group, the domain-wide defaults take effect. You might want to consider choosing one or the other: either keep using the Default Domain GPO to store the passwords for everyone in the domain, or consider assigning FGPPs for positively everyone in the domain. That way, you only have to troubleshoot one area if you suspect a problem.

9

Profiles: Local, Roaming, and Mandatory

When a user logs onto a Windows machine, a profile is automatically generated. A *profile* is a collection of settings, specific to a user, that sticks with that user throughout the working experience. In this chapter, I'll talk about three types of profiles.

First is the *Local Profile*, which is created whenever a user logs on. Next is the *Roaming Profile*, which enables users to hop from machine to machine while maintaining the same configuration settings at each machine. Along our journey, I'll also discuss some configuration tweaks that you can set using certain policy settings—specifically for Roaming Profiles.

The third type of profile is the *Mandatory Profile*. Like Roaming Profiles, Mandatory Profiles allow the user to jump from machine to machine. But Mandatory Profiles force a user's Desktop and settings to remain exactly the same as they were when the administrator assigned the profile; the user cannot permanently change the settings.

That said, a way to eschew Roaming Profiles altogether and replace them with a tool that changes the game is gaining popularity. A Roaming Profile enables a user to hop from machine to machine, and when they do, the entirety of that profile comes down in one chunk. A variety of User Profile Management tools (one from Microsoft and several from third parties) can do the opposite: when the user logs on, almost nothing is downloaded. Then as users start to work, the tools download the pieces of the profile the user needs, as they need it. To learn more about User Profile Management tools, check out the section entitled "Are Roaming Profiles 'Evil'? And What Are the Alternatives?" in the section when we talk specifically about Roaming Profiles.

Setting the Stage for Multiple Clients

Here's a little "cheat sheet" before we go much further. You need a guide to understand which operating system's profiles are compatible and which are not.

- Version 0: Windows NT
- Version 1: Windows 2000, Windows 2003, and Windows XP
- Version 2: Windows Vista, Windows 7 and Server 2008 and Server 2008 R2

- Version 3: Windows 8 and Server 2012

- Version 4: Windows 8.1 and Server 2012 R2

- Version 5: Windows 10 and Windows Server 2016

We'll barely be talking at all about Version 0 profiles here. But we will be getting into Version 1 and Version 2 and later

Before we get too far down the line, let's just break the bad news: if you're interested in setting up Roaming Profiles between different groups of computers, you're really going to be setting up "parallel worlds."

That is, you'll set up multiple Roaming Profile infrastructures (one for Version 1, one for Version 2, one for Version 3, one for Version 4, and one for Version 5) and the five profile types shall never meet.

This really does mean that if you set this up properly, when a user roams from Windows 7 to a Windows 8.1 to a Windows 10 machine and back again, they will actually be creating three roaming profiles.

Wait a minute. This sounds awful.

If the profiles shall never meet, how will you share data for users if they roam from a Windows 7 machine to a Windows 8.1 machine to a Windows 10 machine and back again? That's the next chapter, where we take on redirected folders. So, stay tuned for that after you've successfully set up your Roaming Profiles universe for your machines.

In the previous edition, I didn't know something that I know now: there was a "secret" way to tell Windows 8 (and then later 8.1) *not* to share the same profile with Windows 7. The idea is that by avoiding co-mingling of profile data, profiles wouldn't become corrupt.

For me, in all my testing, I never had any problems roaming between Windows 7 and Windows 8. Even now, as I write these words, having just retested the heck out of it, I still couldn't break any roaming scenarios between Windows 7, Windows 8, and Windows 8.1 in any way at all. Yet, since I wrote the last edition, I've learned that Microsoft says roaming between Windows 7, Windows 8, and Windows 8.1 is not supported when using the exact same Roaming Profile. And, what's more, I never had anyone report to me that this didn't work for them.

Said another way: there's Microsoft documentation that goes out of its way to explain how to make Windows 8 and Windows 8.1 forcefully get their own profiles, so the profiles don't blow up when users roam from Windows 7 to later operating systems and back again.

For me: I cannot reproduce this possible problem. But I do understand how it can exist, and therefore, I'm going to assume Microsoft knows more than me, and I'm going to show you the "right" way to set up Roaming Profiles between the various types (Version 1 through Version 5).

I think it's best to set this up, right here, right now, before we continue further into the chapter. That way, if you're coming into this topic fresh, you'll get it right the first time. Or, if you're reviewing this section and, as with me, this is news to you too, you can experiment with "the right way" here in the test lab before you continue onward and fix your real network.

Here are the two articles that bring this to light:

- "Incompatibility between Windows 8 roaming user profiles and roaming profiles in other versions of Windows," http://support.microsoft.com/kb/2887239

- "Incompatibility between Windows 8.1 roaming user profiles and those in earlier versions of Windows," http://support.microsoft.com/kb/2890783

The only difference between these two articles is that the first one refers to "plain" Windows 8 and the second refers to Windows 8.1.

The Windows 8 one (KB 2887239) requires a hotfix first; then a Registry entry placed on all Windows 8 machines.

The Windows 8.1 one (KB 2890783) requires only the Registry entry.

So, what does this magical Registry entry do?

Nothing at all, until you start using Roaming Profiles (again, explained in detail a little later). Right now, we're just making sure that what we do later will work the way Microsoft wants it to work.

In order to have these totally separate, non-intersecting profiles, Windows 8 and 8.1 need to be told to look for special suffixes.

- Version 1 profiles have no suffix.

- Version 2 profiles automatically have a .v2 suffix.

- You would expect that Windows 8 (and Server 2012) would automatically create and look for the .v3 suffix. Bzzzzt. Wrong. (See? That's a problem. It requires a hotfix and a Registry entry to fix!)

- You would also expect that Windows 8.1 (and Server 2012 R2) would automatically create and look for the .v4 suffix. Bzzzzt! Wrong again! (Same problem! No hotfix this time, just a Registry entry.)

- You would also expect that Windows 10 and Windows Server 2016 would automatically create and look for the .v5 suffix. Ding ding ding! By the time Windows 10 went out the door, they got it right!

So, the problem is only for Windows 8 and Windows 8.1 so they know to look for their own profile types.

Said another way, you can skip this step if you only have Windows 7 (v2 profile) and Windows 10 (v5 profiles) because those two operating systems will automatically and correctly create, look for, and use their own profile type.

That being said, there's zero downside at all to applying this Registry item everywhere if you wanted. That would work because machines like Windows 7 and Windows 10 or Windows XP don't care about this Registry key. So the point is that you should take the time to implement this Registry key now and deliver it to all computers and therefore make all computers perform their correct (and respective) profiles. The key to deliver is HKEY_LOCAL_MACHINE\System\CurrentControlset\Services\ProfSvc\Parameters, and then you create a DWORD value UseProfilePathExtensionVersion with a value of 1.

Using Group Policy Preferences is the most logical way to mass-deliver this, and you can see it in Figure 9.1. Just link the Group Policy Object to the domain and enforce it (in case the Group Policy Object is being blocked from a lower level).

FIGURE 9.1   Use Group Policy Preferences to deliver a Registry value to Windows 8 and Windows 8.1 machines so they will honor their profile type.

At this point you've told all Windows clients to "flock together" and create and use their own correct profile types. Now you can be sure there won't be profile corruption when you roam from Windows 7 to Windows 8.1 to Windows 10 and back.

In general, your users will use desktop machines when roaming. However, users could, of course, roam to a server, like Windows Server 2008 R2, Windows Server 2012, or Windows Server 2016. Just remember that a Windows server will correspond to a specific profile type as seen earlier in this section.

Note that for some of the examples in this chapter, you'll need to create a new, mere-mortal user in the domain. In this example, we'll assume you created a user named Brett Wier. Take the quick second to do that now before continuing onward.

What Is a User Profile?

As I stated, as soon as a user logs onto a machine, a Local Profile is generated. This profile is two things: a personal slice of the Registry (contained in a file) and a set of folders stored on a hard drive. Together, these components form what we might call the *user experience*—that is, what the Desktop looks like, what style and shape the icons are, what the background wallpaper looks like, and so on.

The *NTUSER.DAT* File

The Registry stores user and computer settings into a file named NTUSER.DAT, which can be loaded and unloaded into the current computer's Registry—taking over the HKEY_CURRENT_USER portion of the Registry when the user logs on.

This is one of those times when I think taking a stroll down memory lane to XP will be helpful. This way, we can see and understand Microsoft's original profile guts and see what they did later in changing those guts.

In Figure 9.2, you can see a portion of a Windows XP machine's HKEY_CURRENT_USER; specifically, the Control Panel ➢ Desktop ➢ Wallpaper setting, which shows C:\WINDOWS\web\wallpaper\Bliss.bmp in the Data column.

FIGURE 9.2   A simple Registry setting shows the entry for the wallpaper.

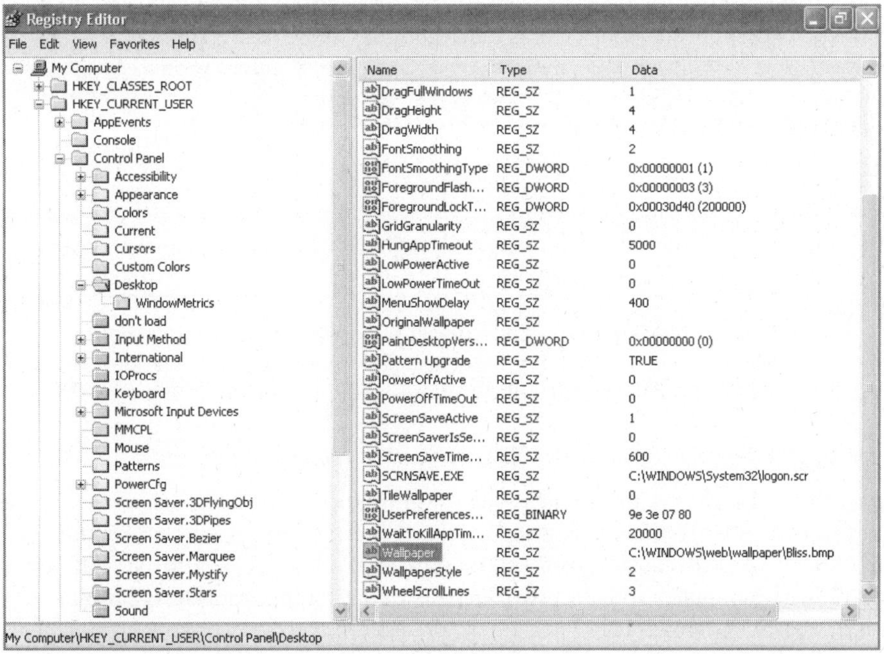

This portion of the Registry directly maps to a file in the user's profile—the NTUSER. DAT file. You'll find that many of a user's individual settings are stored in this file. Here are detailed descriptions for some of the settings inside NTUSER.DAT:

Accessories   Look-and-feel settings for applications such as Calculator, Clock, HyperTerminal, Notepad, and Paint.

Application   Settings for things like toolbars for Office applications and most newer applications.

Control Panel   The bulk of the settings in NTUSER.DAT. Settings found here include those for screen savers, display, sounds, and the mouse.

Explorer   Remembers how specific files and folders are to be displayed.

Printer   Network printer and local printer definitions are found here.

Drive Mappings   Stored, persistent drive mappings are stored here.

Taskbar   Designates the look and feel of the Taskbar.

Profile Folders for Type 1 Computers (Windows XP and Windows 2003 Server)

By default, Type 1 computers (Windows XP, Windows 2003 Server) have profiles that are stored in a folder under the C:\Documents and Settings folder.

Ultimately, what users "see" as their profile is an amalgam of two halves: their own personal profile and components from what is known as the "All Users" profile.

So, each user has a unique profile, and each user leverages a shared profile.

Understanding the Contents of a User's Profile (for Type 1 Computers)

Items in the profile folders can be stored in lots of nooks and crannies. As you can see in Figure 9.3, both visible and hidden folders store User Profile settings.

To show hidden files in an Explorer window, choose Tools ➢ Folder Options to open the Folder Options dialog box and click the View tab. Click the "Show Hidden Files and Folders" radio button, and then click OK.

Here are the folders and a general description of what each contains:

Application Data   Used by many applications to store specific settings, such as the Microsoft Office toolbar settings. Additionally, items such as Word's Custom Dictionary are stored here. MST (Microsoft Transform) files are stored here by default. MST files modify Windows Installer applications by providing customized application installation and runtime settings. (See Chapter 11, "The Managed Desktop, Part 2: Software Deployment via Group Policy," for more information on MST files.)

FIGURE 9.3   A look inside Frank Rizzo's profile reveals both visible and hidden folders.

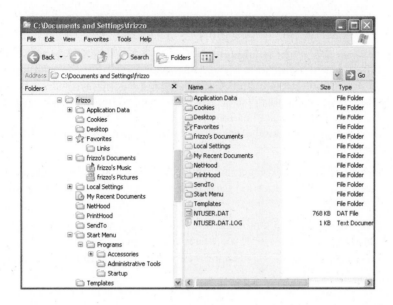

Cookies   Houses Internet Explorer cookies so that pages on the Internet can remember specific user settings.

Favorites   Houses Internet Explorer Favorites—the list of saved web page links.

Desktop   Contains only files that users store directly on the Desktop. Special icons such as My Network Places, My Computer, and the Recycle Bin are not part of the Desktop profile.

Local Settings   Contains application data specific to the user's machine, such as Internet Explorer History, temporary file storage, and other application data. This folder does not roam when Roaming Profiles are set up (see the section "Roaming Profiles" later in this chapter). Like the Application Data folder, this folder is to be used at an application vendor's discretion.

My Documents   Now, users of all sophistication levels can leverage this centralized repository for their data files. The My Documents folder has the advantage that it's easily understood by end users, instead of them having to wonder about which file goes in which drive letter path. In fact, the default Microsoft Office "Save as" path is to My Documents. This will come in handy, as you'll see in the next chapter. My Documents contains My Pictures, and Windows XP Profiles also contains My Music.

NetHood   Contains shortcuts to network drives. Even though the old-and-crusty NT 4.0 Network Neighborhood was renamed My Network Places, the NetHood folder is still around and performs the same functions.

PrintHood   Contains shortcuts to network printers; similar to NetHood.

Recent   Contains a list of the most recently used application files and user data files like .TXT and .DOC files.

SendTo   Contains icons that applications can use to tie into Explorer to allow file routing between applications (such as Outlook) and folders.

Start Menu   Contains the shortcuts and information that users see when they choose Start ➤ All Programs. Each user's Start Menu folder is different. For example, if Joe installs DogFoodMaker 4 and Sally installs CatFoodMaker 8.1, neither will see the other's icons. To allow them to see each other's icons, the icons need to live in the All Users ➤ Start Menu folder Note that if the application does a per-user installation, shortcuts will be present in the user's profile. If the application does a per-machine installation, the shortcuts are in the All Users profile.

Templates   Contains the templates that some applications, such as Excel and Word, use to perform conversions. Like the Application Data folder, this folder is to be used at an application vendor's discretion.

The All Users profile (for Type 1 Computers), which is found at the variable location %ALLUSERSPROFILE%, typically maps to C:\Documents and Settings\All Users.

Applications often add icons to %ALLUSERSPROFILE%\Start Menu to ensure that all users can run them.

Again, users end up seeing the combination of their own profile plus whatever is presented in the All Users profile.

Profile Folders for Type 2–5 Computers (Windows Vista and Later)

As I stated earlier in the chapter, the profiles for Windows XP and Windows Vista (and later) are basically incompatible.

But here's where it starts to get weird. Actually, it already got weird. In the section "Setting the Stage for Multiple Clients," I explained something important, but let's re-explain it just to be on the safe side.

The guts and contents of profiles got changed when Windows Vista rolled out the door, and its basic structure is maintained through Windows 10. But, just to make things super annoying, Microsoft won't support roaming from Windows 7 to Windows 8.1 to Windows 10 and back again. Yep, that's right: The guts are essentially the same, but if you try to attempt that feat, you're setting yourself up for profile corruption and cranky users. Again, that said, I was able to (personally) successfully roam from Windows 7 to Windows 8.1 to Windows 10 and back again without any fuss. But *that* being said, even though the profile guts are the same, you shouldn't be intermingling profile types.

And this is why we went through the motions at the top of the chapter:

- For Windows 8 and its patch plus a Group Policy Preferences Registry adjustment
- For Windows 8.1 (with only a Registry adjustment)

Both Windows 8 and Windows 8.1 need to be told, "Hey, you ... yes, you Mr. Operating System, you should create and honor different profile suffixes even though your profile guts are basically the same."

For our examples, we'll be poking around Windows 10, but any machine (Windows Vista and later) is a perfectly acceptable substitute if that's what's available to you to peer inside.

The items we'll be looking at here have moved from their original place in Windows XP to a new place in modern Windows—the Users folder, which is typically found hanging off of C:\. The \Users folder in Windows 7 and later is the equivalent of the Documents and Settings directory in Windows XP.

Additionally, again, all this information is valid for all versions of Windows Server 2008 and later. However, we'll be concentrating on Windows 10 because it's what your users will mostly be logging onto.

Understanding the Contents of a User's Profile (for Type 2–5 Computers)

Inside the Windows Vista and later profile are a lot of new folders and some that simply look familiar. Let's take a glance at what's inside the modern Windows profile.

Contacts   This is new for Windows Vista and later. This folder stores what are known as "Windows Contacts."

Desktop   Similar in function to Windows XP's Desktop (see earlier).

Documents   Was known as My Documents in Windows XP and serves the same basic function. Stores basic documents such as Word documents and such.

Downloads   This is new for Windows Vista and later. It becomes a storage spot for users' downloads.

Favorites   Similar in function to Windows XP's Favorites (see earlier).

Links   This is where Explorer's Favorite Links are stored. You'll see these down the left pane of Explorer.

Music   Was known as My Music in Windows XP.

Videos   Was known as My Videos in Windows XP (though not officially part of the Windows XP profile).

Pictures   Was known as My Pictures in Windows XP.

Saved Games   This is a folder where users can place their saved games. I'm sure network administrators everywhere are just *thrilled* about this.

Searches   This is new for Windows Vista and later, and it saves stored searches for Explorer.

UserTiles   This is new for Windows 8. If a user changes their logon picture (also known as a Tile), it will be saved here.

AppData   Was known as Application Data in Windows XP. Since Windows Vista, AppData is bifurcated into two parts: Local (to the computer only) and Roaming (for the specific user). We'll be talking more about Roaming Profiles in a bit, but this part is important to understand for when we do tackle them.

The `AppData\Roaming` folder performs the same function as the `Documents and Settings\<username>\Application Data` folder in Windows XP.

The `AppData\Local` folder is now meant to hold machine-specific application data that isn't supposed to roam with the user. This folder is to be the equivalent for `Local Settings\Application Data` in Windows XP.

The `AppData\LocalLow` folder is a special directory with "low integrity" rights. So files that get stored here will have a lower integrity level than files in other areas of the operating system. See the sidebar "The LocalLow Folder within `AppData`" for more information.

OneDrive   (Windows 10 only) Once you start using OneDrive, your OneDrive data gets synchronized here.

The LocalLow Folder within AppData

Within a user's AppData folder are two obvious entries: Local and Roaming. These make sense and are used when the corresponding condition is true. However, also note the presence of a LocalLow folder.

Windows Vista and later has various ways applications can run. One way is Protected Mode, which guarantees that a program will run with low rights. When running in this way, the application only has access to this portion of the User Profile. Internet Explorer in Windows Vista and later is one such application. Internet Explorer in Windows Vista and later runs in Protected Mode, which prevents malware and other various nasties from infecting your computer, or possibly compromising user-specific information.

Protected Mode uses the LocalLow profile folder.

Also note that there are low-integrity folders for Cookies, History, and Favorites.

I know this sounds weird, but the best book on the subject is an old Windows Vista book. But at least it's from my pal Mark Minasi. If you can get a copy of it, I strongly recommend *Administering Vista Security: The Big Surprises* from Sybex (2006).

In the next section, I talk about how several Windows XP holdovers are mapped to directories within AppData.

Adjusting for Windows XP Holdovers

Even though we're exploring the Windows Vista and later profile guts, something interesting should be noted: Windows Vista and later profiles are set up to automatically handle older applications that are still looking for Windows XP locations. For instance, if an application wanted to expressly save something in My Documents, it would have a problem. My Documents doesn't exist anymore, right? It's just Documents for Windows Vista and later. To that end, the Windows Vista and later profile has what are called Junction Points, so when an application visits My Documents, it's really going to Windows Vista's Documents.

To see these pointers, we need to see the hidden files inside a Windows Vista and later profile. You can perform this by going to the user's profile and typing **dir /ah /og** (to show hidden files and to sort by directories first). You can see this in Figure 9.4.

FIGURE 9.4   A view inside a Type 2–5 profile (dir /ah /og)

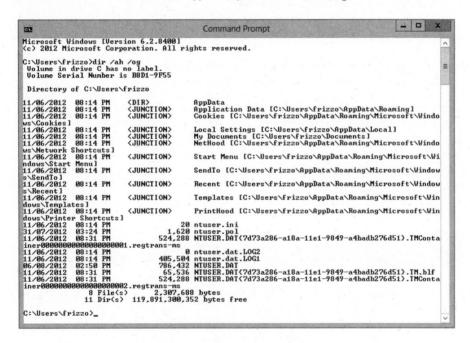

If you look closely at the folders in Figure 9.4, you'll see many that 4 *appear* at the top level of the profile, but really they are placed (junctioned) to either AppData\Roaming or AppData\Local.

Curious about what those regtran-ms, .TM.blf, and .LOG files are in Figure 9.4? I was! According to my sources at Microsoft, these are the files generated by Kernel Transaction Manager (KTM). The Vista and later Registry uses KTM to avoid corruptions, so you should never see Registry corruption (with regard to profiles) anymore. Let's hope, anyway.

Virtualized Files and Registry for Programs

Some applications try to do bad, bad things. And Windows XP will (usually) let them. For instance, an application could try to write program data to:

```
C:\program files\dogfoodmaker5\settings.ini
```

This DogFoodMaker application has no business writing settings there. In reality, settings should be in the user's profile, specifically in the Application Data (AppData) section (either user or machine based).

To that end, Windows Vista and later will redirect writes like this to a location where the application should be writing. Microsoft calls this redirection *virtualization—file virtualization* and *Registry virtualization*. Here's an example:

```
C:\users\<username>\AppData\Local\VirtualStore\Program Files\dogfoodmaker5
```

And, because multiple users could be using the same machine, a separate copy of the virtualized file is created for each user who runs the application.

Indeed, if you wanted to see these redirected files right away, Windows Explorer in Windows 7 (only) has its own button that lets you see them. If there is a virtualized version of a file related to the current directory, a Compatibility Files button appears that will take you to the virtual location to view that file. In this example, you can see that someone tried to put junk in the \Windows directory on this Windows 7 (specifically, Windows 7) machine.

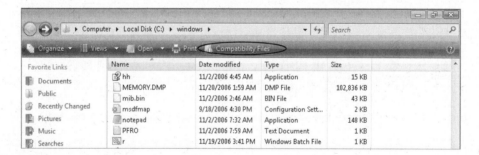

Note that this button is only available in Windows 7's Explorer and not in Explorer in Windows 8 or later.

Writes to incorrect places to the Registry work the same way. Bad writes get redirected to:

```
HKEY_CLASSES_ROOT\VirtualStore\MACHINE or USER\SOFTWARE
```

This automatically takes effect if the application isn't UAC compliant. So, file virtualization doesn't affect applications that are run with full administrative rights (when, say, someone elevates it to run as an Admin).

This technology is, of course, a stop-gap measure at best. It permits pre–Windows Vista applications to run in a predictable way. But it should be considered a short-term fix rather than a long-term solution. The goal is to ensure that your application developers modify their applications so that they meet the guidelines of the Windows Logo program instead of depending on file and Registry virtualization.

Note that file and Registry virtualization is disabled under some circumstances:

- File and Registry virtualization is simply not supported for Windows 64-bit applications. These applications are expected to be UAC compliant and to write data to the correct locations.

- Virtualization is disabled for applications that include an application manifest with a desired execution level attribute. If you're a developer, you can learn more about application manifests here:

  ```
  http://msdn.microsoft.com/en-us/library/windows/desktop/
  aa374191(v=vs.85).aspx
  ```

Additionally, note you can turn off virtual file and Registry abilities. That security policy is located in Computer Configuration ➢ Policies ➢ Windows Settings ➢ Security Settings ➢ Local Policies ➢ Security Options ➢ **User Account Control: Virtualize file and registry write failures to per-user locations**. You need to click "Define this policy setting" and then select Disabled to turn it off.

One side note: Windows 7 and later adds the C: drive as another area for file virtualization, whereas Windows Vista didn't do that. Nice update.

The Public Profile (for Type 2–5 Computers)

The Public profile in Windows Vista and later replaces the All Users concept in Windows XP and previous machines. However, it provides the same basic function: the end user's experience becomes their own profile *plus* the contents of the Public profile. Again, categories like the Desktop and Start Menu become good candidates here, because the icons you place here affect everyone.

The Default Local User Profile

The Default Local User Profile folder contains many of the same folders as any user's own Local Profile. Indeed, the Default User Profile is the template that generates all new local User Profiles when a new user logs on.

When a new user logs on, a copy of the Default Local User Profile is copied for that user to C:\users\%*username*%. As will often happen, the user changes and personalizes settings through the normal course of business. Then, once the user logs off, the settings are preserved in a personal local folder in the C:\users\%*username*% folder.

> **NOTE** This Default Local User Profile is different from the Default Network User Profile described later.

As an administrator, you can create your own ready-made standard shortcuts or stuff the folders with your own files. You can also introduce your own NTUSER.DAT Registry settings, such as a standard Desktop for all users who log onto a specific machine. In the following example, you can set up a background picture in the Default Local User Profile. Then, whenever a new user logs on locally to this machine, the background picture is displayed.

For Type 1 computers (Windows XP, Windows 2003), the Default User Profile is stored in C:\Documents and Settings\Default User.

For Type 2–5 computers (Windows 7, Windows 8.1, Windows 10, etc.), the Default User Profile is stored in C:\users\Default.

To set up your own Registry settings in NTUSER.DAT, follow these steps:

1. Choose Start ➢ Run to open the Run dialog box. In the Open box, type **regedit.exe** and press Enter to open the Registry Editor.

2. Select HKEY_USERS, as shown in Figure 9.5.

FIGURE 9.5 Load the NTUSER.DAT file into the Registry.

3. Choose File ➤ Load Hive.

4. For Type 1 computers, browse to the `C:\Documents and Settings\Default User` folder, shown in Figure 9.5. For Type 2–5 computers, browse to `C:\Users\Default`. You might have to specifically type in the path, as the file requester may hide it from you if you are not displaying hidden files and folders.

5. Select `NTUSER.DAT`.

6. When prompted to enter a key name, anything will work, but for our example let's use **This is a dummy key name,** and click OK. Figure 9.6 shows an example. The key name is only temporary, so it doesn't particularly matter.

FIGURE 9.6   It doesn't matter what the temporary dummy key is called.

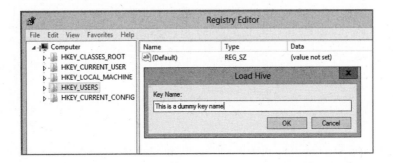

7. Traverse to any Registry key and value. In this case, we'll change all future wallpaper in Windows XP to `Coffee Bean.bmp` and `C:\windows\web\Wallpaper\Windows\img0.jpg` for Windows 8 and later. To do that, traverse to Dummy Key Name ➤ Control Panel ➤ Desktop and double-click `Wallpaper`. If you're using Windows XP, enter the value in this example, **`C:\windows\coffee bean.jpg`**. If you're using Windows 8 and later, enter **`C:\windows\web\Wallpaper\Windows\img0.jpg`**, as shown in Figure 9.7. Note that there might already be a default image set, but you're now changing it.

8. After you complete your changes, select your dummy key name, unload it by choosing File ➤ Unload Hive, and click OK to save the changes. Again, you must highlight your dummy key name to unload the hive.

You can load the hive of any User Profile that is not currently logged on using the previously described method. This can be very useful in some situations, such as if you want to make a Registry hack as an Admin on behalf of the user. Just remember to unload the hive or else you are blocking the profile.

Actually, you can also load hives from within a script (with `REG.EXE`). Jakob H. Heidelberg has a pretty cool article on this called "Efficient Registry Cleanup," which you can check out here: `http://tinyurl.com/24dm5v`.

Every time a new user generates a Local Profile, it pulls the settings from the Default Local Profile, which now has the coffee bean background picture. (Current users do not see the change because they already generated Local Profiles before the coffee bean picture was set in the default Local Profile.)

FIGURE 9.7 Enter the full path where the desired wallpaper is stored.

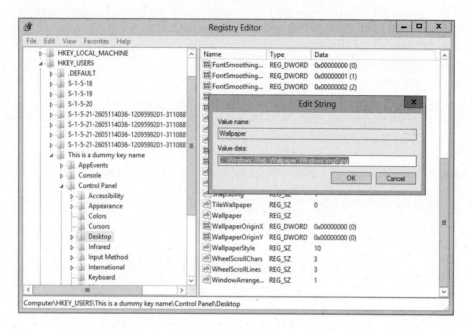

Test your changes by creating a new local user and logging on. Since this user has never logged on before, this should create a new User Profile from the default profile. See if the new user gets the coffee bean background for Windows XP, the neat landscape background for Windows 8, or in Windows 10 the shiny-new Windows 10 desktop background.

The Default Network User Profile

The Default Network User Profile is similar to the Default Local User Profile, except that it's centralized. Once a Default Network User Profile is set up, new users logging onto workstations in the domain will automatically download the centralized Default Network User Profile instead of using any individual Default Local User Profile. This can be a way to make default centralized settings, such as the background or Desktop shortcuts, available for anyone whenever they first log onto a machine.

I want to be super clear here. My suggestion is to use as much Group Policy, Group Policy Preferences, and PolicyPak stuff you can to make this whole experience *dynamic*.

So, although it's possible to "prebake" lots of settings into the user profile, I suggest instead that you have your profile as clean as possible and then deliver everything you can dynamically using Group Policy, Group Policy Preferences, and PolicyPak. Remember, with Group Policy you can deliver things like Desktop backgrounds and perform Start Menu lockdowns. With Group Policy Preferences, you can deliver Internet Explorer settings, shortcuts, printers, and more. And, if you change your mind or your requirements change, you don't have to re-crack open the original profile, make a change, and re-upload it to the server.

That being said, there are some items that simply cannot be delivered using Group Policy or Group Policy Preferences, and you might want to prebake those settings in. For example, you may want to set the regional setting inside the default profile instead of via Group Policy Preferences. Group Policy Preferences options sometimes "lose their mind" when applying non-USA settings.

So, by prebaking the regional and language settings into the default profile, you'll be sure users will always have the correct language when they first log on.

Default Network User Profiles for Type 1 Computers

Every once in a while, I have an "everything I know is wrong" moment. This is where I think I know exactly how something is supposed to work, and I've described it about a billion times to people, then later I find out I have to make a blog post or correction about some advice I've given. This is one of those moments.

So for years there was a procedure to take an existing user account's profile (on Windows XP) and copy it up to the server to use as the Default Network User Profile. Here were the basic (wrong) steps:

1. Create a new, mere-mortal user in the domain. From any Windows XP workstation in your domain, log on as this standard user.

2. Modify the Desktop and profile as you wish.

3. Log off as the user.

4. Log back onto the workstation as the Domain Administrator.

5. Click Start, and then right-click My Computer and choose Properties from the context menu to open the System Properties dialog box.

6. Click the Advanced tab, and then click the Settings button in the User Profiles section to open the User Profiles dialog box.

7. Select the user, as shown in Figure 9.8.

8. Click the Copy To button as seen in Figure 9.8 to open the Copy To dialog box, and in the "Copy profile to" field, enter the full path, plus the words **default user**, of the NETLOGON share of a Domain Controller, as shown in Figure 9.9. In this example, it's \\dc01\netlogon\Default User. The Default User folder is automatically created.

9. Click the Change button in the "Permitted to use" section, and change the default from the original user to Everyone, as shown in Figure 9.9. This lets all Type 1 computers use this as your baseline profile in the domain.

10. Click OK to copy the profile to the new folder and to close the Copy To dialog box.

11. Click OK to close the System Properties dialog box.

Okay. Why did I just show you all the wrong steps here?

FIGURE 9.8   This is the "incorrect" way to copy a Windows XP profile to be used as the Default Network Profile.

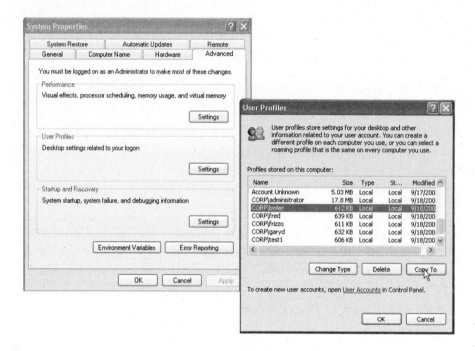

FIGURE 9.9   This is the old way to enable Everyone to use the profile.

Because, honestly, they usually just work. And it's worked for me every single time. But that being said, Microsoft has updated documentation on how to do these steps for Windows XP.

The KB article is 959753, "How to customize the default local user profile when you prepare an image of Windows XP or Windows Server 2003." In the article is the section "How to configure the default network profile."

It turns out that using "just any" user account and then clicking Copy To was the wrong way to do this all long. In KB article 959753, the rationale for the procedure update is as follows: "These procedures caused information to be left behind in the Default User Profile that caused the Windows shell to behave incorrectly. This led to problems with application compatibility and with the user experience. Therefore, do not advise customers to copy profiles over the Default User Profile. This method is no longer supported."

Ohhh kaay.

Well, if we want to do this the "supported way," we need to perform the steps in KB 959753. Without going too deep into the how-to, it kind of goes like this:

- Configure the Default Local User Profile. Run SYSPREP to neuter the machine.
- Only use the Default Local User Profile as the source profile, (to be copied to Default Network Profile)—not some random user account.

Sorry about the bad news. And, what's worse is that the procedure doesn't get any better for Windows 7 and later.

Default Network User Profiles for Type 2–5 Computers

We just learned that Windows XP has a Copy To button, but it shouldn't be used to copy a regular user's profile directory and make it the Type 1 Default Network Policy.

Turns out that Copy To button is still there for Windows Vista, Windows 7, Windows 8, and Windows 10. On Windows Vista, it worked just like Windows XP—but it turns out, again, using it on "regular users" and uploading their profiles was not a supported item.

So, that's why, starting in Windows 7, and continuing on through Windows 10, the Copy To button only works with the Default Profile. Indeed, if you try to click on any user listed in the User Profiles dialog, the Copy To button grays out—unless you select the Default Profile, and then it works!

So, how do we configure the Default Profile before we use that Copy To button? That's the discussion in this section. But before we talk about that, remember how profiles between Windows XP (Type 1) and Windows Vista, Windows 7, and Windows 8 and 8.1, and Windows 10 (Types 2–5) are incompatible?

Well, that's about to matter a whole lot, right here. And we need to cover this first. This is a little weird, so stay with me.

We need to know a certain piece of Windows magic. That is, Windows Vista and later will read profile directories from the network only if they end in a special moniker: .v2. That's right—the directory names must have a .v2 hanging off them for Windows Vista and later to read it.

Buuut … Remember what I said at the beginning of the chapter and reiterated later: There are really multiple types of "v2" profiles, which are .v3, .v4, and .v5.

So now, we'll provide our name with the special "v-something" designation.

Version 2   Windows Vista, Windows 7, and Server 2008 and Server 2008 R2 use designation .v2.

Version 3   Windows 8 and Server 2012 use designation `.v3`.

Version 4   Windows 8.1 and Server 2012 R2 use designation `.v4`.

Version 5   Windows 10 and Windows Server 2016 use designation `.v5`.

Then, when users log onto modern machines for the first time, Windows will recognize the special directory (Default User) with the extra-special `.v2`, `.v3`, `.v4`, or `.v5` moniker and download the profile just for that operating system.

There's a very lengthy, visceral thread if you want to read about it here: `http://tinyurl.com/mzwnos`.
(Though there is no mention of the monikers past `.v2`.)

But, ultimately, there is a specific set of rather lengthy and arduous instructions to create a local user profile on Windows 7 and later then upload it to the network as the Default Network Profile for Type 2, 3, 4, or 5 machines.

That KB article is 973289, and without going into the excruciating details, here's the gist. Again, these are the general steps—please consult the actual article for specific step-by-steps:

- Log on as the local administrator, and craft the profile the way you want to.

- Create an `Unattend.xml` file with a special parameter, called `Copy Profile = True`.

- Use an elevated command prompt and run SYSPREP to neuter the machine.

- When the computer starts up, it will magically copy the administrator's settings into the Default User's local profile.

But then there are still two more steps so that everyone can use the profile that was just copied up:

- Click the Copy To button to open the Copy To dialog box, and in the "Copy profile to" field, enter the full path plus the default user of the NETLOGON share of a Domain Controller, as shown previously in Figure 9.9. Now, to create your Type 2 profile (say, for a Windows 7 machine), you would type in `\\dc01\netlogon\Default User.v2`. Or if you were on Windows 10, it would be `\\dc01\netlogon\Default User.v5`. Note that no quotes are needed (as is often the case with items that have spaces in them). You can see an example in Figure 9.10. The `Default User.V5` folder will be automatically created.

- Click the Change button in the "Permitted to use" section, and change the default from the original user to Everyone. This lets everyone use the profile in the domain.

You can test your Default Network Profile by creating a new user in the domain and logging onto any corresponding machine type (`.v2`, `.v3`, `.v4`, or `.v5`). Remember, you'll only see the magic for users who have no Local Profiles already on their own PCs.

Now that you're familiar with the files and folders that make up Local Profiles, you're ready to implement Roaming Profiles.

FIGURE 9.10   Be sure to put the .v5 extension in, because this is a Windows 10 (Type 5) profile.

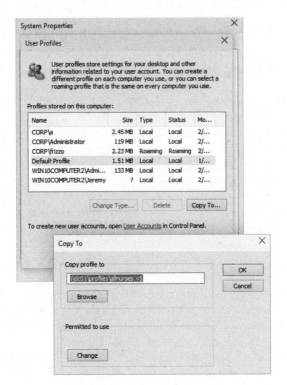

Roaming Profiles

Roaming Profiles are a logical extension to the Local Profiles concept. When users hop from machine to machine, the customized settings they created on one machine are automatically placed on and displayed at any machine they log onto.

For instance, you might have an organization in which 30 computers are at each site for general use by the sales team. If any member of the sales team comes into any office, they know they can log onto any machine and be confident that the settings from their last session are patiently waiting on the server.

Setting up Roaming Profiles for users in Active Directory is a straightforward process: share a folder to house the profiles, and then point each user's profile toward the single shared folder.

But again to be ludicrously clear (third time now): Microsoft doesn't think you should roam profiles between types. So, Windows Vista and Windows 7 are Type 2. Windows 8 is Type 3, Windows 8.1 is Type 4, and Windows 10 is Type 5.

I'm going to assume that you took my advice at the top of the chapter and applied the patch (if necessary) and dictated the Registry key to Windows 8 and Windows 8.1 so you will do Microsoft's best practice and keep each type in its own silo. (Again, to reiterate, Windows 7 and Windows 10 already self-silo by automatically using the .v2 and .v5 suffixes.)

Assuming you did that, let's proceed.

By default, a copy of the Roaming Profile is saved to the local hard drive. That way, if the network or server becomes unavailable, the user can use the last-used profile as a cached version. Additionally, if the user's Roaming Profile on the server is unavailable (and there is no locally cached copy of the Roaming Profile), the system downloads and uses a temporary Default User Profile as an emergency measure to get the user logged on with some profile.

As you'll see in the next chapter, another advantage associated with Roaming Profiles is that if a machine crashes, the most recent "set" of the user environment is on the server for quick restoration.

For those of you who threw up your hands and gave up using Roaming Profiles in Windows NT, I encourage you to try again with the newer operating systems.

For Windows 2000 and later, the Roaming Profile algorithm has been much improved since the NT 4 days. Specifically, there are three reasons the improved algorithm is better than the old NT 4 counterpart. I know it's kind of odd in 2015 to have a book that still refers to NT 4.0, but "perception" is a weird thing. People's memories of the "bad old days" can remain and linger on, for a lot longer than we might think. Anyway, here are the main differences between then and now:

Roaming Profiles now account for multiple logins.   Most people had problems when a single user logged onto multiple machines at the same time. In NT 4, the profile was preserved only from the last computer the user logged off from—potentially losing important files in the profile. Modern Windows systems don't work that way. They do a file-by-file comparison of files *before* they get sent back to the server—sending only the latest time-stamped file to help quell this problem. So, give it another go if you despaired in the past.

However, one warning should be noted. All the user's Registry settings are represented as a single file: NTUSER.DAT. Because the last writer wins, the NTUSER.DAT with the latest time stamp overwrites all others. If you make two independent changes to a setting on two different machines, you can lose one because only the NTUSER.DAT with the latest time stamp "wins."

Roaming Profiles now only pull down and push up changed files.   NT 4 Roaming Profiles were on the slow side—especially over slow links. The good news about profiles from modern systems is that only new and changed files are specifically moved around the network. So, if someone logs onto the same machine over and over again, the user is not waiting for the whole gamut of profile files to be downloaded. Logging in is now faster than ever.

Better Remote Desktop Services/support is available for Roaming Profiles. In Windows 2000, when the user logs off a session, the system tries 60 times—about once a second by default—to tidy up the `NTUSER.DAT` file and send it back to the server to be housed in the Roaming Profile. Usually, it only needs one try (and about one second) to do this task.

Are Roaming Profiles "Evil"? And What Are the Alternatives?

Roaming Profiles get a bad rap. People think they're:

* Slow

* Easily corrupted

* Hard to manage because of the siloing situation (where each machine type must not use another machine's profile type)

Well, maybe I'm in the minority, but I just don't think Roaming Profiles are all that bad. Let me break down each issue as I see them.

Problem 1: Roaming Profiles Are Perceived as Slow

Roaming Profiles can be slow, but it's usually at the first logon, and not the consecutive ones. Think about it: If you get a brand-new machine (of the same type), that machine must download the whole contents of the Roaming Profile at login time. Not a great way for the user to experience their first logon. But, after that, consecutive logons only have to download file changes, and that's not usually too bad.

Problem 2: Roaming Profiles Are Perceived as Being Easily Corrupted

I hear about this from time to time but can never pin someone down to explain to me, in super technical terms, what they think has caused "profile corruption." We did already establish that Microsoft wants you to keep profile types (v2, v3, v4, and v5) separate and siloed, specifically to prevent cross pollination and problems. But even then, I was never able to make a problem occur when intermingling between v2–v4 (Windows Vista to Windows 8.1). If we do Roaming Profiles in the prescribed, Microsoft way, we can safely take that out of the "corruption equation." But even then, I think some folks have misintrepreted what is happening and simply throw their hands up and say, "It's profile corruption" without getting to the bottom of what really might have occurred. This blog entry from my pal Mike Stephens at Microsoft really says it all, and it is worth a read. It's entitled "Mythical Creatures – Corrupt User Profiles" and is found at:

```
http://blogs.technet.com/b/askds/archive/2010/10/20/mythical-creatures-
corrupt-user-profiles.aspx
```

If you want a second opinion from a profile expert, read "Corrupt User Profiles - Do They Even Exist?" at:

```
https://www.sepago.com/blog/2008/07/02/corrupt-user-profiles-do-they-even-
exist
```

Problem 3: Roaming Profiles Require Siloing

Okay. You got me on this one. I really hate the fact that I have to have a whole different universe for my Windows 7, Windows 8.1, and Windows 10 machines. So when I roam from Windows 7 to Windows 10, I have to start all over again. That's just rotten, and I hate it. But if I'm able to keep on top of my rollouts and ensure that people roam only within one type of machine, this isn't really a problem at all.

Solutions to Problems 1–3

So to solve these problems (real and perceived), there are a variety of tools that can come to your aid.

Let's start back with Problem 1, where the first logon to a new machine with an existing roaming profile means an almost guaranteed longer login time than the second login. Where is this problem the most severe? Not at the desktop or the laptop, but with a VDI session. Many VDI systems are architected to give you a nice clean system every time. (Hurray!) Until you need your documents and data settings. (Boo.) So that login to a VDI feels like the first time every time. And if that's the case, we need to make things go quicker. How do we do that? Easy: Don't download the Roaming Profile now, but do it as needed, on demand, as the user "does stuff."

So the user needs to open up HugeFile.PDF? No problem. Grab that file as needed, instead of roaming it inside the profile.

So the user runs Acrobat Reader or Internet Explorer or Microsoft Word? Great! Simply pull down the configuration settings that the user himself made from his portion of the roaming profile that contains these settings.

These Profile Management tools definitely help here, because they spread the download over the whole user's working session instead of pre-downloading them all at once. When a user makes a change, only those small changes are uploaded back to the tool's storage point.

Pretending for a second that profile corruption was a real thing, these tools help here, too. Because you're essentially throwing Roaming Profiles out the window, and hence, you're also throwing profile corruption out the window (if it existed at all).

As for Problem 3, here is where these tools shine. They can ensure that when you roam from Windows 7 to Windows 8.1 to Windows 10, your look and feel settings get mapped. And if you've got applications' settings, those user's own changed settings will just "be there" when the user runs the application.

I call these tools "Un-Roaming Profile" tools. The following tools would be in this family:

- Microsoft User Experience Virtualization (UE-V), which is available as part of Microsoft's MDOP. A good demo video can be seen here: https://technet.microsoft.com/en-us/windows/hh925634.

- Citrix Profile Management, which comes with some Citrix purchases.

- VMware Persona Management, which comes with some VMware purchases (though VMware will likely be changing gears to leverage their new acquisition from a company called Immedio).

There are others. But these are the ones I've used. Note that I didn't mention PolicyPak in this list. That's because PolicyPak (and Group Policy at large) does the *counterpart* of what these "Un-Roaming Profile" tools are doing.

Remember, Roaming Profiles (and Un-Roaming Profile tools) give the user's *own* changed settings back to them as they roam from machine to machine. (A user changes the Firefox home page to www.GPanswers.com? They're going to want to see that again on the next computer they log on to.)

But Group Policy and/or PolicyPak, on the other hand, don't care what the *user* wants. Group Policy and PolicyPak care about what *you* want them to get.

So the job of Group Policy at large (and also PolicyPak) is that you get to dictate (and lock down) settings for operating system and applications that you want to ensure and stay set that way. (You want to prevent people from using the Control Panel? Great! Use in-the-box Group Policy. Want to maintain a corporate standard that the Firefox home page is set to www.Corp.com? Great. Use PolicyPak to dictate that setting and enforce it so users cannot work around it.)

So that being said, Roaming Profiles and "Un-Roaming Profile" tools do have an important job. You want users to feel that when they roam from machine to machine, their own changes (sometimes called a *persona*) follows them. That's cool by me.

But I also want to ensure that IT settings for applications and the operating system get set and stay set and that's what Group Policy and PolicyPak are for.

In a competition, remember that Group Policy (and PolicyPak) will "win" when both you and the end user want something—Because a user's settings are really preferences, and only policy is policy.

To see PolicyPak and Microsoft UE-V or VMware Persona Management working together, check out the videos we have here:

www.policypak.com/integration/policypak-user-environment-uem-utilities.html

On another note, back in October 2014, two other MVPs (Helge Klein and Aaron Parker) took some time to delve into Roaming Profiles, and they wrote a five-part article series on them plus a 90-minute webinar talking about their discoveries. They stress-tested Folder Redirection under extreme server loads and conditions. I'll give you the URLs to the articles and webinar in a moment, but here are my takeaways summarizing all five articles:

- Point 1 (found in Article 4): Folder Redirection logon times are not affected by the size of the redirected folders. So if you have 10MB, 20MB, 500MB of data, your second (and onward) logon will be about the same speed, regardless of profile size.

- Point 2 (found in Article 2): If you redirect your folders, be sure your servers aren't overloaded. At high loads, redirected experience is super painful for end users because the server is having to serve redirected items, and it does it poorly.

- Point 3 (found in Article 4): If you use an "Un-Roaming Profile" tool then a typical logon, could be *slower* than even straight Folder Redirection. (This depends on the

Un-Roaming Profile product, so your results could vary.) But then *after* you make a request that needed to talk with the server, since that stuff has come down from the server and is now cached locally, things start to speed up.

- Point 4 (found in Articles 2 and 3): Redirecting AppData seems to be the sore spot when it comes to Folder Redirection and the user experience slowdown. The sore spot specifically comes as applications take a while to launch, because they're trying to read and write from redirected AppData.

- Point 5 (found in Article 5): If you're redirecting to an older server that doesn't support SMB 2 (or SMB 2 isn't working or is specifically disabled for some reason), then Folder Redirection and the user experience is going to be very slow.

So before I give you the name and URLs of these articles and resources, I want to just say up front that while I generally agree with their findings, I don't agree with what they *named* the series and the corresponding webinar.

Article 1 and the webinar is entitled "How Folder Redirection Impacts UX & Breaks Applications." I don't see any evidence in these findings of the later part of the statement, that Folder Redirection *breaks* applications. I would suggest interpreting the word *breaks* to mean *hurts* or *slows down*. But in my opinion, *break* might not be the word I would have selected, as I didn't see any true application failures caused by Folder Redirection in their findings and demonstrations.

So that being said, start reading the articles here:

https://helgeklein.com/blog/2014/10/folder-redirection-impacts-ux-breaks-applications/

And watch the webinar replay here:

http://stealthpuppy.com/webinar-replay-folder-redirection-impacts-user-experience-breaks-stuff/

Setting Up Roaming Profiles

The first thing we need to do on our server, DC01, is to create and share a folder in which to store our profiles. In this example, we'll choose a novel name: Profiles. Normally, you'd do this procedure on a file server somewhere, not on a Domain Controller. But we'll continue on, because there's no harm here in our test lab. Again, I'll assume our server has two drives, C: and D:, and we'll perform these functions on our D: drive.

To create and share a folder in which to store Roaming Profiles, follow these steps:

1. Log on to DC01 as Administrator.

2. From the Desktop, click My Computer to open the My Computer folder.

3. Find a place to create users' folders. In this example, we'll use D:\PROFILES. After entering the D: drive, right-click and select New ➤ Folder. Name your new folder **Profiles**.

 You can substitute any name for Profiles. Additionally, you can hide the share name by placing a **$** after the name, such as **Profiles$**.

4. Right-click the newly created Profiles folder, and choose "Share with"; then select "Specific people" to open the File Sharing dialog box. Pull down the drop-down box and select Everyone, and then click Add. Change the permissions for Everyone from Read to Read/Write, as shown in Figure 9.11.

FIGURE 9.11   Share the Profiles folder so that Everyone has Read/Write permissions.

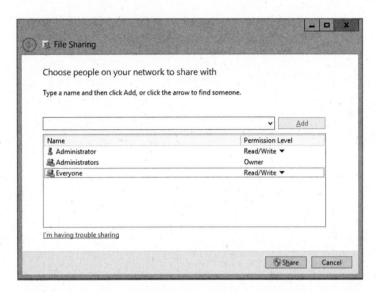

Now you need to specify which network user accounts can use Roaming Profiles. In this example, you'll specify the user Brett Wier, who you created at the beginning of the chapter. Brett will now be able to hop from workstation to workstation. When he logs off one workstation, the changes in the profile will be preserved on the server. He can then log on to any other workstation in the domain and maintain the same user experience.

To modify accounts to use Roaming Profiles, you'll leverage Active Directory Users and Computers as follows:

1. Choose Start ➢ All Programs ➢ Administrative Tools ➢ Active Directory Users and Computers.

2. Expand Corp.com in the tree pane, and double-click Brett Wier's account to open the Brett Wier Properties dialog box; click his Profile tab.

3. In the Profile Path field, specify the server, the share name, and folder you want to use, such as **\\dc01\profiles\%username%**. After you enter that, click OK. Then, just as a quick test, go back into the user account and look again at the Profile tab. When you do, you should see the *username* automatically filled in, as shown in Figure 9.12. For our purposes, you can leave all other fields blank.

4. Click OK.

FIGURE 9.12   Point the user's profile path settings at the server and share name.

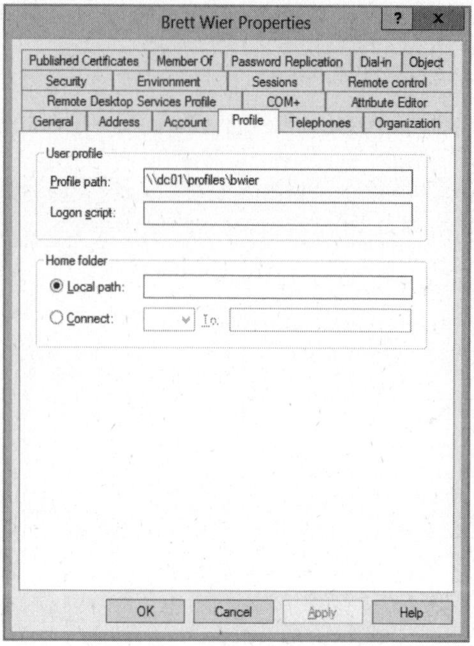

The syntax of *%username%* is the secret sauce that allows the system to automatically create a Roaming Profiles folder underneath the share. The *%username%* variable is evaluated at first use, and Windows springs into action and creates the profile. Windows is smart, too—it sets up the permissions on the folder with only the required NTFS permissions so that only the user has access to read and modify the contents of the profile. If you want administrators to have access along with the user, see the information in the section "Add the Administrators Security Group to Roaming User Profiles" later in this chapter.

Modifying Multiple Users' Profile Paths

After you set up Roaming Profiles and get comfortable with their use, you'll likely want the rest of your users to start using Roaming Profiles as well. The Active Directory Users and Computers tool allows you to modify the profile paths of multiple users simultaneously. To do so, follow these steps:

1. Select the users (hold down Ctrl to select discontiguous users).

2. Right-click the selection, and choose Properties from the context menu to open the "Properties for Multiple Items" (previously called Properties On Multiple Objects) dialog box.

3. Click the Profile tab, if necessary.

4. Click the "Profile path" check box, and enter the path.

5. Click OK to give all the selected users the same path, making sure you use the *%username%* convention in the path you specify.

If you'd like to put on your coding hat, you can use the following sample PowerShell code to run through all the users in the domain Corp.com in the **Employees** OU and change their profile path so that they have access only to their own profile folder. Upon first use by the user, the folder is automatically created, and the user is granted exclusive access to that folder.

```
$ou="ou=Employees,DC=corp,DC=com"
$profileserver="dc01.corp.local"
Import-Module ActiveDirectory
$users=Get-ADUser -filter * -searchbase $ou -properties profilepath
foreach ($user in $users) {
  If ($user.profilepath) {
    Write-Host "Profile for $($user.name) already has a profile: $($user.
profilepath)"
    }
```

```
else {
    $UserProfilePath=Join-Path -path "\\$profileserver\profiles" -childpath
$user.samaccountname
    Write-Host "Profile for $($user.name) has been set to: $userProfilePath"
    $user | Set-ADUser -profilepath $userProfilepath
  }
}
```

Testing Roaming Profiles

You can easily test Roaming Profiles if you have multiple workstation machines.

Provided you did the homework at the top of the chapter, all machine types will be automatically siloed, and you can roam from machine type to machine type.

I suggest you log on as Brett on all the machine types you want to test, say Windows XP machine (Type 1) and a Windows 8.1 machine (Type 4) and Windows 10 (Type 5). Make sure these workstations are members in your domain.

A quick test might be to do the following:

- Log on to a Windows 7 machine as Brett Wier. In the My Documents folder, create **WIN7.TXT** and save some dummy data inside. Change the color scheme to something different. Log off as Brett Wier.

- Log on to a Windows 8.1 machine. In the My Documents folder, create **WIN81.TXT** and save some dummy data inside. Change the color scheme to something different. Log off as Brett Wier.

- Log on to a Windows 10 machine. In the My Documents folder, create **WIN10.TXT** and save some dummy data inside. Change the color scheme to something different. Log off as Brett Wier.

Now log back on to each machine as Brett. Right-click the dummy text file you created on each and choose Properties from the context menu to see the file's properties.

Take note of the path where the file is actually residing. You can compare that file's location now (the local hard drive) with the file's location after the next chapter is completed when we combine this with Offline Files.

Additionally, notice how a file created on one type of computer is not present on the other type. Again, this is because the various profile types are not supposed to intermingle.

Back on the Server

If you check out what's transpired on the server, three unique directories are created for Brett, one for each type of computer he logs on to (Type 2, Type 4, and Type 5), as seen in Figure 9.13.

FIGURE 9.13   On the server, a folder for each computer type has been generated.

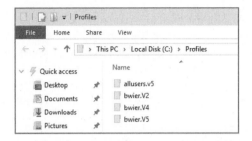

Additionally, note that even if you're an administrator, you cannot dive into Brett's profile folders. An example of this failure can be seen in Figure 9.14. This is a safety mechanism that gives Brett exclusive permissions over his personal sensitive stuff. If you want administrators to have access along with the user, see the information in the section "Add the Administrators Security Group to Roaming User Profiles" later in this chapter.

FIGURE 9.14   Administrators cannot poke around User Profiles (by default).

Upshot of Roaming Profiles in a Mixed Windows World

It's kind of bad news for mixed environments. As you saw, logging onto one type of machine, then another type of machine means you don't get to "share" information in any way.

For instance, as we saw, `WIN7.TXT` was created (and available) only in the Windows 7 profile. And `WIN10.TXT` was created (and available) only in the Windows 10 profile. So, by default, between machine types, profile data doesn't get to be shared.

What a bummer (on the surface at least). But don't worry; we'll overcome it.

To that end, if we want a "one-stop shop" place for our documents, Start Menu icons, and more, we'll have to leverage the Folder Redirection mechanism in the next chapter. Not to get too far ahead of ourselves, but Folder Redirection's goal is to make various items (like Documents) point to the *same place* on a network share. That way, regardless of the kind of machine you log in with (Windows 7, Windows 8.1, or Windows 10), your data will *always* be available.

So, stay tuned for that in the next chapter.

Migrating Local Profiles to Roaming Profiles

In some situations, you might already have lots of machines with Local Profiles. That is, you didn't start off your network using Roaming Profiles, and now you have either many machines with Local Profiles or just pockets of machines with a combination of Roaming Profiles and Local Profiles. You can, if you want, maintain the user's Local Profile settings and transfer them to the spot on the server you set up earlier. You first need to set up a share for the Profiles on a server, and we already did this back in Figure 9.11.

In general, this step couldn't be easier. As we did earlier, on each user's Profile tab, point the profile path to *servername*\share\%*username*%, as seen earlier in Figure 9.12. The next time the user logs onto a machine with a Local Profile (and then logs off), the Local Profile is automatically uploaded to the server to become their future Roaming Profile. For most users, this is the way to go.

And, remember, profiles are zapped up to their source on the server independently. If a user has used multiple machines, then travels back to these Desktops, each computer's profile is zapped up into their own siloed directory.

You saw those directories in Figure 9.13, shown earlier.

But what if the same filename exists, say, on the Desktop on three machines the user has logged onto in the past? The system will automatically figure out which is the last-written file based on the file date. And that file will end up being the only copy placed in the directory. In other words, you won't see three files with the same name in the profile directory—even if it exists on three local machines.

Roaming and Nonroaming Folders

Oftentimes, you'll want to get a handle on specifically what, inside the Roaming Profile, is roaming and what isn't roaming. Things are different for Type 2–5 computers (like Windows 8, 8.1, and Windows 10) versus Type 1 computers (Windows XP). Let's check out those differences here.

Roaming and Nonroaming Folders for Type 1 Computers

Now that you have a grip on which folders constitute the profile and how to set up a Roaming Profile, it might be helpful to know a bit about what's going on behind the scenes. Remember that several folders make up our profile.

Type 1 Profile Directories That Do Not Roam

Local settings, including local machine-specific application folders and information, do not roam when Roaming Profiles are enabled. This is true for the local computer's Application Data. Some applications write information specific to the local computer here. The Application Data folder is located in `\Documents and Settings\<username>\ Local Settings`. Any subfolder below this folder also does not roam, including these:

- History
- Temp
- Temporary Internet Files

Type 1 Profile Directories That Do Roam

All other folders do roam with the user.

There's an Application Data directory that does roam with the user. This Application Data folder is located in `Documents and Settings\<username>`. This is typically a per-user store for application data, such as Microsoft Office custom dictionary. These are the kinds of things you would want to roam with the user:

- Cookies
- Desktop
- Favorites
- My Documents
- My Pictures
- NetHood
- PrintHood
- Recent
- Send To
- Start Menu
- Templates

Indeed, My Documents, My Pictures, Desktop, Start Menu, and Application Data have an additional property; they can each be redirected to a specific point on the server, as you'll see in the next chapter.

Roaming and Nonroaming Folders for Type 2–5 Computers

If we crack open a Windows 10 Roaming Profile, we can see that some things are similar and some things are different compared to a Type 1 profile.

Figure 9.15 shows what the profiles look like when viewed from a pre-Vista machine. Note how the "My" prefix magically appears when viewed here, even though under the hood there is no "My" prefix. You can see this in Figure 9.16 when viewed directly from a Windows 10 machine.

FIGURE 9.15 Some of the contents of a Type 2–5 computer are similar to a Type 1 computer. Note that when viewed on a pre-Vista machine, Type 2 profiles have the "My" prefix because they're viewed within a pre-Vista machine's Explorer.

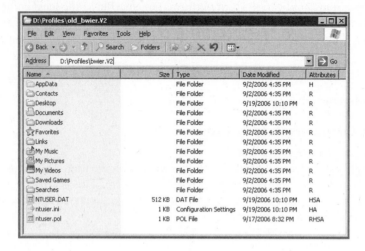

FIGURE 9.16 The same folder, when viewed directly from the command line. Note the absence of the "My" prefix for Music, Pictures, and Videos.

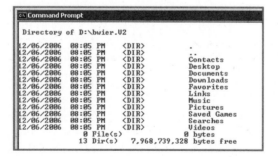

    To see the contents in Figure 9.15, you need to be logged in as Brett Wier or take ownership of the directory as the Administrator.

Let's get a grip on which directories roam and which don't roam.

Type 2–5 Profile Directories That Do Not Roam

Local settings, including local machine-specific application folders and information, do not roam, even when Roaming Profiles are enabled. The nonroaming directories will stay on each local computer in the \Users\<*username*>\AppData\ directory. Inside \AppData are two directories that contain this nonroaming data: Local and LocalLow. Any subfolders within Local or LocalLow do not roam, including these:

- History
- Temp
- Temporary Internet Files

 See the sidebar "The LocalLow Folder within AppData" for more information about LocalLow.

Type 2–5 Profile Directories that Roam

All other folders do roam with the user. When a Roaming Profile is enabled, these directories are shot up to the server and stored within a user's own private directory.

Again, depending on the version of the operating system where the user logs in, the folder might be called <*username*>.v2 - .v5 and contain the following items:

- Contacts (New for Windows Vista and later.)
- Desktop
- Favorites
- Documents (Was My Documents in Windows XP.)
- Pictures (In Windows XP, this was under My Documents, and since Windows Vista, it's at the root of the profile.)
- Music (In Windows XP, this was under My Documents, and since Windows Vista, it's now found at the root of the profile.)
- Videos (New for Windows Vista and later machines.)
- Under \AppData\Roaming\Microsoft you will find these:
  - **Credentials**
  - **Crypto**
  - **Internet Explorer**
  - **Protect**
  - **SystemCertificates**

Of course, your users will need their day-to-day goodies as they roam from machine to machine. This is known as Per-User Application Data. This stuff is stored within the Roaming Profile's \AppData\Roaming\Microsoft\Windows directory. Here, you'll see lots of stuff you know and love, such as the following Desktop attributes, as shown in Figure 9.17:

- Network Shortcuts
- Printer Shortcuts

- Recent
- SendTo
- Start Menu
- Templates
- Themes
- Cookies (hidden for some reason)
- PrivacIE (for InPrivate browsing)

FIGURE 9.17   The AppData\Roaming directory in the Type 2–5 computer contains the only directories that will roam with the user.

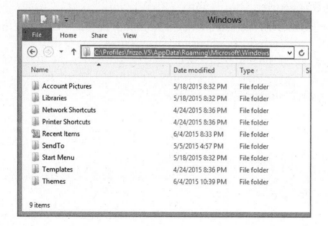

Managing Roaming Profiles

We've just been through how to set up and use Roaming Profiles. But don't leave home without these parting words about managing them day to day.

Merging Local Profile and Roaming Profile

Once a Roaming Profile is established, users can hop from machine to machine, confident that they'll get the same settings. However, if a user with a Roaming Profile hops to a machine of the same type (Type 1 to Type 1, or Type 2 to Type 2), something special happens: the previous Local Profile and the existing Roaming Profile are merged (except for the NTUSER.DAT settings). This data is then saved to the Roaming Profiles folder on the server at logoff time.

This is helpful should a user have just the one copy of a critical document stored in the Documents folder of one computer, say, WIN10A, and has other critical files on his second computer, say, WIN10B.

The next time the user logs onto WIN10B, missing documents will appear in My Documents in his Roaming Profile. Oh, and you don't have to worry about overwriting existing, exactly named files in the profile, either; the latest time-stamped file is preserved.

You can prevent this behavior if you want. Check out the section "Prevent Roaming Profile Changes from Propagating to the Server" later in this chapter.

Guest Account Profile

Who uses the Guest account anymore? If it's you, there's some interesting behavior you should know. The profile of a guest user is deleted at logoff—but only when the computer is joined to a domain. If the machine is in a workgroup, no guest profiles (of users in the Guests group) are deleted at logoff.

If the Windows computer is in a domain, and a user is a member of both the Guests and the Local Administrators groups, the profile is not deleted—quite an unlikely scenario.

Additional System Profiles

There are two profiles that are meant to be used by newly installed services: Local Service and Network Service.

Local Service   Meant to be used by services that are local to the computer but do not need intricate local privileges or network access. This is in contrast to the System account, which pretty much has total authority over the system. If a service runs as Local Service, it appears to be a member in the local users group. When a service runs as Local Service across the network, the service appears as an anonymous user.

Network Service   Similar to Local Service but has elevated network access rights—similar to the System account. When a process runs under Network Service rights, it does so as the SID (Security ID) assigned to the computer (which in an Active Directory environment is a member of Domain Computers, and therefore also a member of Authenticated Users).

Windows automatically creates these profiles, which are basically normal but still a little special. For instance, you will not see the Local Service or Network Service in the listing of Profiles in the System Properties dialog box. You can see them in the Documents and

Settings folder; however, they're "super-hidden" so that mere mortals cannot see them by default. You can see them in the top window here:

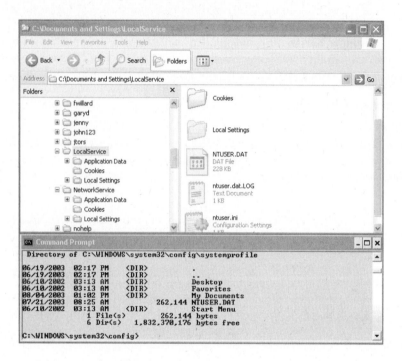

On Windows Vista and later, the Local Service and Network Service profiles have moved to the %windir%\ServiceProfiles directory. Windows can also load software, services, and its own profile when the computer starts up. Indeed, you see this profile in the "Log on to Windows" dialog box, in which you are prompted to press Ctrl+Alt+Del. Basically, this is the profile for when no one is logged on.

When this happens, Windows loads what is called the .DEFAULT (pronounced "dot default") profile. Windows has the .DEFAULT profile in:

```
C:\windows\system32\config\SystemProfile
```

You can see the System Profile in the command prompt window in the lower half of the previous screen shot.

Cross-Forest Trusts

Roaming Profiles, like GPOs, are affected by cross-forest trusts. Whether a user gets a Roaming Profile depends on the client operating system they're logged on to. (This operating system–specific variance is documented in Chapter 4, "Advanced Group Policy Processing.") When clients log on to computers that enforce the rule, you'll get the message shown in Figure 9.18.

FIGURE 9.18   Users roaming within cross-forest scenarios receive this message.

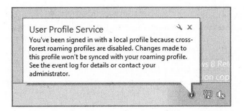

You can use a policy setting to prevent this from affecting your client computers. To do this, locate the **Allow Cross-Forest User Policy and Roaming User Profiles** policy setting by drilling down in Computer Configuration ➢ Policies ➢ Administrative Templates ➢ System ➢ Group Policy.

Manipulating Roaming Profiles with Computer Group Policy Settings

Roaming Profiles are simple to set up and maintain, but sometimes you'll want to use certain policy settings to affect their behavior. The policies you'll be setting appear in the Computer Configuration section of Group Policy. Drill down into Policies ➢ Administrative Templates ➢ System ➢ User Profiles, as shown in Figure 9.19.

Some policy settings here only affect older Type 1 profiles and others affect only Type 2 and later profiles; still others will work with all profile types (Type 1 and Type 2 and later profiles). To save space, I won't be covering any of the items that *only* affect Type 1 profiles. If you need coverage on that, feel free to read the help text within the policy settings in this category or pick up an older copy of this book.

Recall that computers must be in the OU that the GPO affects (or in a child OU that inherits the setting). Or the GPO could be linked to the root of the domain and scoped to a security group that the computer is a member of.

If a user is moved to a new OU, the user needs to log off and back on. If a machine is moved to a new OU, the machine needs to reboot.

FIGURE 9.19   There are many policy settings that affect profiles.

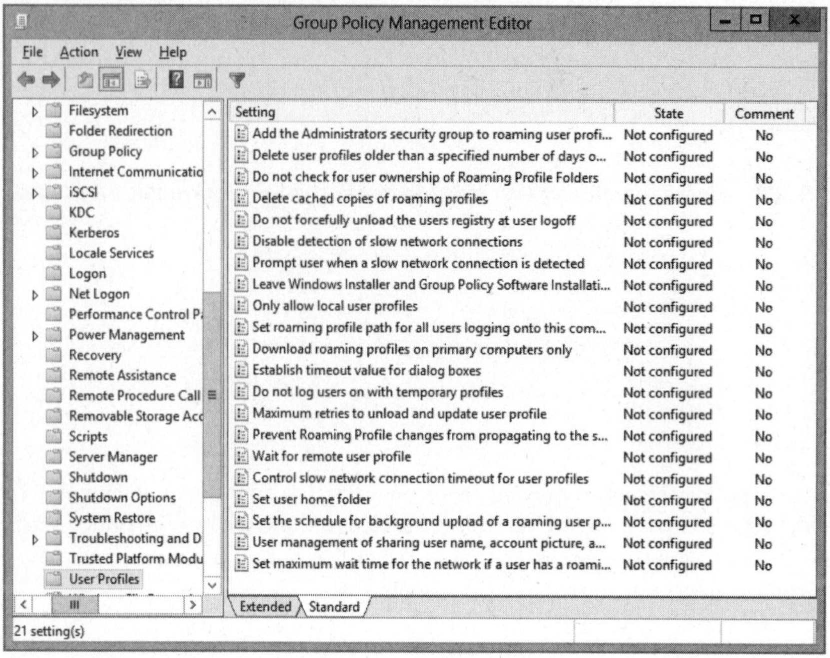

Before implementing any policy setting that affects Roaming Profiles, read through the following sections to determine if it adds value to your environment. Then, create a test OU and ensure that the behavior is as expected.

Delete Cached Copies of Roaming Profiles

This is a space-saving and security mechanism that automatically deletes the user's locally cached profile when the user logs off. The default behavior is to allow files to be downloaded and pile up on each and every hard drive to which the user roams. You can enable this policy setting to (as the forest rangers say) "Leave only footprints and take only memories." Heck, you won't even be leaving any footprints.

This policy setting has two downsides, however; let's walk through two scenarios to examine these potential problems.

Problem Scenario 1: Server Down at Login Time   This policy setting is set to delete cached copies of Roaming Profiles. The user logs on, makes some changes, and logs off. The profile is automatically sent back to the server, and the footprints are washed away on the local machine.

Now, let's say that the server that houses the Roaming Profiles goes down. By default, if the user tries to log on and the server is unavailable to deliver the Roaming Profile, the locally cached copy of the profile is summoned to take its place. Once you enable this policy setting, you're severing a potential lifeline to the user if the server that houses the Roaming Profile becomes unavailable. Enabling this policy setting sweeps up after the user on the local machine at logoff. If the server goes down, the user will not get their locally cached version of the Roaming Profile because there is no locally cached version of the profile. Rather, the only profile the user will get is a temporary Local Profile that is not saved anywhere when the user logs off.

Problem Scenario 2: Up and Back and Up and Back   Again, by setting this policy setting, you're deleting all cached files. So, when the user logs back onto the same machine, all the Roaming Profile files need to get redownloaded from the Roaming Profile on the server, which means you're killing the caching inherent in the Roaming Profile system. In essence, you're making your machine act like NT 4, where the whole profile gets redownloaded at login. Note, however, that at logoff time things should still be faster than NT 4 because you're pushing up only changes (where NT 4 would have pushed up *all* the files).

So those are the major problem scenarios. Let's take a look at a scenario where this setting is extremely useful.

This policy setting is useful in high-security environments where you need to make sure that no trace of potentially sensitive data in the profile is left behind. Be careful when using it with laptops, however, because users frequently need to use their copy of the locally cached version of the profile to get their work done. Additionally, enabling this policy setting does not prevent third-party tools from "resurrecting" deleted files inside the profile. It deletes the files but doesn't obliterate them to prevent industrious hackers from any possible recovery.

Once this policy setting is Enabled, the profile is erased only on logoff. And then it erases only profiles from machines on which users don't already have an existing cached copy! If you need to maintain a high-security environment, be sure to enable this policy setting early so that users don't have time to roam from machine to machine sprinkling copies of their profiles around (which won't get erased later by use of this policy setting).

 WARNING   To use this policy setting, you'll need to disable (or not configure) the **Do not detect slow network connection** policy setting, as described shortly. If a network connection is determined to be slow, it automatically tries to grab the locally cached copy of the profile, which doesn't exist if you've enabled this **Delete cached copies of roaming profiles** policy setting.

Delete User Profiles Older Than a Specified Number of Days on System Restart

This policy setting is handy and applies only to Windows Vista and later computers.

What happens when Sally User logs onto a Windows 10 machine on the 4th floor—one time? All her profile junk gets downloaded on that machine and sits there—forever. Just eating up disk space, never to be reclaimed again. Until now.

If you enable this policy setting and specify a certain number of days, the Roaming (and Local) Profiles on that Windows 10 machine will be wiped clean—automatically. The user doesn't have to do anything. The system will automatically flush them down the, er, wherever it flushes them. But it only does this when the system is rebooted.

Here's a huge warning: Be careful with this setting. Any data that is, say, only in a Local Profile (like the Documents folder) will be gone once the profile is wiped clean. Note that the data stored in the server-side copy of a Roaming Profile, and also any data redirected using Redirected Folders, is not touched. Figure 9.20 shows a before-and-after picture of how drastic profile cleanup is.

FIGURE 9.20   A typical Windows Type 2 (and later) computer after multiple users have logged onto it over time (left). The same computer (right) after this policy kicks in within 24 hours. Note even local User Profiles are gone.

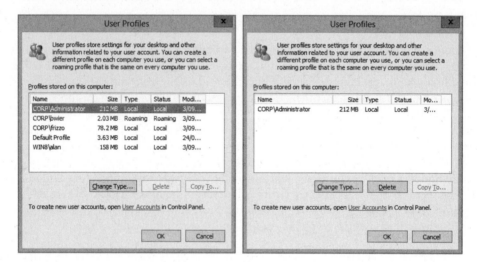

Control Slow Network Connection Timeout for User Profiles

Enabling this entry performs a quick ping test to the profiles server. If the speed is greater than the minimum value, the Roaming Profile is downloaded. If, however, the speed is not fast enough, the locally cached profile is used unless you've enabled the previous entry (**Delete cached copy of local profiles**). In that case, the user ends up with a temporary profile, as described earlier.

WARNING   Enabling the **Disable Detection of Slow Network Connections** policy setting, as described in the next section, forces anything specified in this policy setting to be ignored.

This policy setting is a bit strange: even if it's not configured, it has a default. That default "fast enough" speed threshold is 500Kbps, and the default "fast enough" ping time is 120ms. So if the test is slower than either of these values, the Roaming Profile is skipped and the locally cached profile is used.

You might want to enable this policy setting and decrease the value thresholds if you want to increase the chances of a dial-up connection receiving the Roaming Profile instead of the locally cached profile. If you enable this policy setting, you'll need to manually specify both an IP ping time test and a non-IP ping millisecond test. As you can see, this setting can also affect machines that aren't using TCP/IP, but that's a pretty rare event nowadays. See the Explain text for more information if you have a non-IP situation.

 Unrelated speed tests can verify the ability to apply GPOs for both the user and computer. They are in the Group Policy Editor under Computer or User Configuration ➤ Administrative Templates ➤ Policies ➤ System ➤ Group Policy ➤ **Group Policy Slow Link Detection**.

Disable Detection of Slow Network Connections

Like the previous policy setting, this one is a little strange. If it's not configured, it still has a default; the users affected by this policy setting check the **Slow network connection timeout for user profiles** setting to see what a "slow network" actually means. If you enable this policy setting, you're disabling slow network detection, and the values you place in the **Slow network connection timeout for user profiles** policy setting don't mean a thing.

Wait for Remote User Profile

Again, even if this policy setting is not defined or disabled, there is still a default; if the speed is too slow, it will load the locally cached profile. If you enable this policy setting, the system waits until the Roaming Profile is downloaded—no matter how long it takes. You might turn this on if your users hop around a lot and the connection to the computer housing the Roaming Profiles is slow but not intolerable. That way, you'll still use the Roaming Profile stored on the server as opposed to the locally cached profile.

Prompt User When a Slow Network Connection Is Detected

When the ping test determines that the link speed is too slow, the user can be asked if they want to use the locally cached profile or grab the one from the server. If this policy setting is not configured or it's disabled, the user isn't even asked the question. If the **Wait for remote user profile** policy setting is enabled, the profile is downloaded from the server—however slowly.

For pre-Vista machines, if this policy setting is enabled, the user can determine whether they want to accept the profile from the server or utilize the locally cached profile.

For modern Windows machines, if this policy setting is enabled, the user must determine before logon time (by using a check box at logon time) to use the local or remote profile, as seen in Figure 9.21.

FIGURE 9.21 You can specify to allow users to download their profile over a slow network connection before they actually log on using Windows Vista or Windows 7. This check box doesn't appear on Windows 8 or later.

 This setting worked great in my tests for Windows Vista and Windows 7, but the check box never showed up on my Windows 8 or later machine.

If this setting is not configured (or it's set to disabled), the system always uses the Local Profile instead of the Remote Profile when the link is slow.

If you've enabled the **Delete cached copies of roaming profiles** policy setting, there won't be a local copy of the Roaming Profile, so the user will be forced to accept the Default User Profile. If the **Disable Detection of Slow Network Connections** policy setting is enabled, this GPO is ignored.

Do Not Log Users on with Temporary Profiles

This is the harshest sentence you can offer the user if things go wrong. By default, if the server is down (or the profile is corrupted), the user first tries to load a locally cached profile. If there is no locally cached profile, the system creates a TEMP profile from the Default User Profile.

However, if you choose to enable the setting, the behavior changes. If no Roaming Profile or locally cached profile is available (presumably because you've enabled the **Delete cached copies of roaming profile** policy setting), the user is not permitted to log on.

Add the Administrators Security Group to Roaming User Profiles

As you saw in Figure 9.14 earlier in this chapter, only the user can dive in and poke around their personal User Profile. However, you can specify that the administrator and the user have joint access to the folder.

Oddly, this policy setting is found under the Computer side of the house—not the User side. Therefore, it's somewhat difficult to implement this policy setting on a small scale, because it's sometimes a mystery as to which client machine users will log on to. If you want to use this policy setting, I recommend creating a GPO with this policy setting at the domain level to guarantee that any client computers that users log on to will be affected. Modifying this policy setting so that it affects the file server housing the profiles doesn't do anything for you. It's the target client computers that need to get this policy setting.

This policy setting *only* takes effect when new users first log on to affected client computers. Once they're on, they'll make some changes that affect the profile and then log off. When they log off, a signal is sent back to the directory housing the profile, which then finalizes the security on the directory so that both the user and the administrator can play around in there.

To be especially clear, as I implied, this policy setting works only for new users—those users who don't already have a Roaming Profile. Users who *already* have established Roaming Profiles are essentially left in the dark with regard to using this—but there is a ray of light. If you want the same effect, you can take ownership of a profile and manually establish administrative access for the administrator and the user, as described in the upcoming section "Mandatory Profiles."

Prevent Roaming Profile Changes from Propagating to the Server

As previously discussed, when a user jumps from machine to machine and lands on one with an existing Local Profile, the system merges the Local Profile as a favor to the user. The idea is that if this Local Profile has a data file, say, RESUME.DOC, that's missing in the user's Roaming Profile, this is a perfect time to scoop it up and keep it in the Roaming Profile. You can dictate specific machines for which you don't want this to happen.

In general, you set this policy setting only on computers that you are sure you don't want the merge between Local Profiles and Roaming Profiles—perhaps because the Local Profiles contain many unneeded files. With the policy enabled, changes made to the profile are lost because the Roaming Profile is downloaded from the server logoff and not merged with the Local Profile.

 In case you missed it, this policy setting makes the profile work like a Mandatory Profile, so don't save anything valuable in the profile, because it is going to be lost!

Only Allow Local User Profiles

This policy setting is useful when you have set up specialty machines, such as lab machines, library machines, kiosk machines, and so on. By enabling this policy setting on your machines, you can ensure that a user's Roaming Profile doesn't get downloaded onto a particular machine.

Leave Windows Installer and Group Policy Software Installation Data

Earlier, we explored the **Delete cached copies of roaming profiles** policy setting. The idea was to "clean up" behind a user when he or she logged off. This was a great idea in theory but had an unintended consequence.

If you opt to delete Roaming Profiles at logoff time, the information regarding applications deployed via Group Policy Software Installation (explored in Chapter 11) is also lost (by default).

This policy, once enabled, will ensure that at least the Group Policy Software Installation data remains on the hard drive, so subsequent logins for users are much faster.

Do Not Forcefully Unload the Users Registry at User Logoff

In versions of Windows previous to Vista, the logging-off process sometimes just "hung" there. In Windows's defense, it was usually a service or something similar that kept the user's profile open. Windows Vista and later goes the extra mile and should automatically do this.

So, the only time to enable this policy is if you think something is getting broken by this automatic process. For instance, you log on a second or third time and notice your application didn't save settings that would normally be stored in the user's Registry hives.

In other words, only enable this policy setting if you suspect some issue with the behavior of forcefully unloading the user's Registry at logoff.

This policy setting works with Windows Vista and later.

Set Roaming Profile Path for All Users Logging Onto This Computer

The policy setting enables you to establish a shared User Profile path for a specific computer. Think of it as "Everyone who logs onto this computer gets the same profile."

But just because you enable this policy setting doesn't mean it's 100 percent guaranteed to be embraced. That's because other values might have precedence before this one takes effect.

Windows reads profile configurations in the following order and uses the first configured setting:

1. The Roaming Profile path specified in the Terminal Services policy setting found at Computer Configuration ➢ Policies ➢ Administrative Templates ➢ Windows Components ➢ Remote Desktop Services ➢ Remote Desktop Session Host ➢ Profiles ➢ **Set path for Remote Desktop Services Roaming User Profiles**

2. The Roaming Profile path specific to the Terminal Server user object in Active Directory Users and Computers

3. The per-computer Roaming Profile path specified (using this policy setting)

4. The per-user Roaming Profile path specified in the user object in Active Directory Users and Computers

This policy setting works with Windows Vista and later.

Set Maximum Wait Time for the Network if a User Has a Roaming User Profile or Remote Home Directory

This is a wordy policy setting, for sure, but what it does is simple: you can increase the network timeout if you know the computer may not find the network right away after a user chooses to log on. This can happen a lot in the cases where a wireless card is searching, searching, searching for the wireless access point but, meanwhile, the user has already pressed Ctrl+Alt+Del to log on!

Ouch!

When you set this policy, the computer waits a bit first to see if the network suddenly becomes present.

If the network still isn't available (based on this value, or 30 seconds by default), the cached profile is used and the user won't have access to the network home drive.

This policy setting works with Windows Vista and later.

Set the Schedule for Background Upload of a Roaming User Profile's Registry File While User Is Logged On

Another wordy policy setting, but this one only applies to Windows 7 and later.

This policy is neat: it solves an interesting problem.

Remember that a user's profile is made up of a bunch of items: user data, documents, and a lot of other stuff. Arguably, the most important part of the profile is the NTUSER.DAT file—the user's portion of the Registry that is loaded in and out every time she logs on and off.

But if the user is over a slow link, maybe you don't want to move all the junk up and back and up each time. Just one trip could take a long time—even just the new files, since Windows Vista and later only send up and back changes.

So, is there a middle ground? This policy setting's goal, when active, is to say: "Don't send up the user's data over a slow link. Send up only the NTUSER.DAT file."

Why is this a neat idea? Because you'll be able to roam to a different machine and get the same look and feel. True, the files might not be up-to-date, but maybe you're okay with that, or with using some other technique to save data files (like mapped network drives or thumb drives or something).

This policy setting might not be needed for your environment, but it's a neat idea for at least some people.

You can see how to configure it in Figure 9.22.

FIGURE 9.22   Use this Windows 7 and later policy setting to upload only the NTUSER.DAT file over a roaming profile.

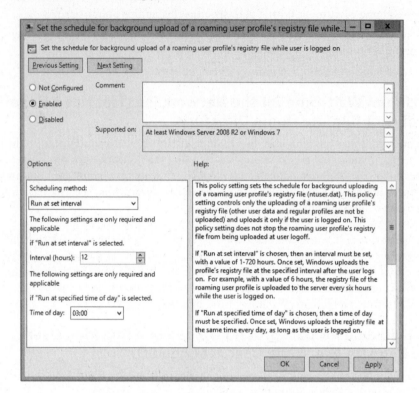

Download Roaming Profiles on Primary Computers Only

This setting only works with Windows 8 and later (or Windows Server 2012 and later machines).

This setting basically says, "If the user isn't on their 'usual' machine, then don't deliver a roaming profile."

To use this setting, you need to first describe to Active Directory which computers are "usual" for which users. If you want to do this, see the sidebar "Specifying a User's Primary Computer(s)." The skills you learn in that sidebar you'll also utilize in the next chapter, because there's a similarly named policy setting called **Redirect folders on primary computers only.** Again, that's the next chapter.

So, again, when this setting is set, and the computer gets the policy setting, it's looking next to see which user is its primary user. Again, see the sidebar "Specifying a User's Primary Computer(s)" for the how-to.

Set User Home Folder

This one also only works with Windows 8 and later (and Windows Server 2012 and later) machines.

When the computer picks up this setting, it will create a user's home directory and map a drive letter for them. Of course, you've been able to do this for years using the user's Profile attribute in Active Directory Users and Computer, but now there's a sexy Group Policy way.

If the user logs onto a computer that also gets this setting, and they also have the Active Directory Users and Computers attribute set, then this Group Policy setting wins.

To use this policy setting, simply specify that all the users on the affected computer will get the location set to "On the network" or "On the local computer."

Then set the path and drive letter. Note that setting the drive letter only works when the location is set to "On the network."

User Management of Sharing User Name, Account Picture, and Domain Information with Apps (Not Desktop Apps)

This one also only works with Windows 8 and later (including Windows Server 2012 and later).

This setting enables admins to decide how much information about the user a Universal app can read. For more information on this, read the help text inside the policy setting.

Turn Off the Advertising ID

This one only works with Windows 8 and later (including Windows Server 2012 and later).

This setting mirrors one that is also on Windows Phone 8 and later.

The idea here is that each phone (or computer in this case) has an advertising ID that can be used to share information about you or your users to applications.

Leave it on, or turn it off using this policy setting.

One More Policy Setting That You Might Like

This policy setting isn't specifically profile related, but it does relate to the logon experience.

Check out **Report when logon server was not available during user logon** found in Computer Configuration (and User Configuration) ➤ Policies ➤ Windows Components ➤ Windows Logon Options. They both work the same way.

Once enabled, this policy setting displays an informative dialog box telling the user if, more or less, she's working online or offline. This can be a great first step in knowing what's going on and whether or not a problem exists. Here is what it looks like for users logging in to Windows 10.

Specifying a User's Primary Computer(s)

One of the settings that Windows 8 and later can use is called **Download roaming profiles on primary computers only**. I talked about it earlier.

In the next chapter, you'll encounter another similarly named policy setting: **Redirect folders on primary computers only**.

Again, both of these policy settings only function when the target computer is Windows 8 and later (including Windows Server 2012 and later machines as well). So, what the heck is a "primary computer"?

In short, you can "teach" a user account which computers are "normal" for that user. A user might use one, two, or more machines normally. And when he's on those normal machines, maybe you want normal stuff to happen, like he gets his Roaming Profile and, in the next chapter, he gets Folder Redirection.

But if he's not on his normal computer, what then? Well, if he's roamed to some other "unusual" computer, then maybe you don't want to download the Roaming Profile and/or folder redirected files.

Microsoft has a lengthy document on how to describe to user accounts what their primary computer(s) are. That doc is here: http://tinyurl.com/win8primary.

But I'm going to give you the quick rundown of what you need and a super-fast example of how to marry up a user to one or more primary computers.

To start out, you don't need any Windows Server 2012 machines, but you do need at least the Windows Server 2012 schema. That's because the Windows Server 2012 (and later) schema has two attributes that do the "marrying" we talked about.

Next, fire up Active Directory Users and Computers and select View ➤ Advanced Features. Then select a computer, such as WIN10. In the properties page, select the Attribute Editor tab, as seen here, and find the value `distinguishedName`. Then right-click over the value and select Copy.

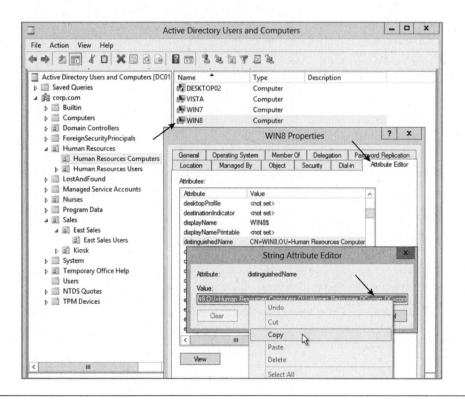

Paste what you copied into Notepad if you wish.

Next, find the user account, such as Frank Rizzo, and in his Attribute Editor tab, find msDS-PrimaryComputer, click Add, and select Paste, as seen here.

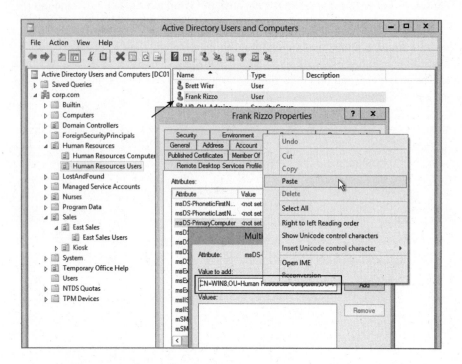

If you want Frank to have more than one primary computer, you simply paste the other computer's Distinguished Names (DNs).

Now you're all set. The policy settings **Download roaming profiles on primary computers only** (which I talked about in this chapter) and **Redirect folders on primary computers only** (which I'll talk about in the next chapter) will actually honor your request!

Manipulating Roaming Profiles with User Group Policy Settings

As you have just seen, most policy settings regarding Roaming Profiles are associated with the computer itself. Two policy settings, however, affect Roaming Profiles but are located on the User side of the fence: **Limit profile size** and **Exclude directories in roaming**

profile. These policy settings are found under User Settings ➢ Policies ➢ Administrative Templates ➢ System ➢ User Profiles, as shown in Figure 9.23.

FIGURE 9.23 Some entries for profiles are found under the User Profiles node in Group Policy.

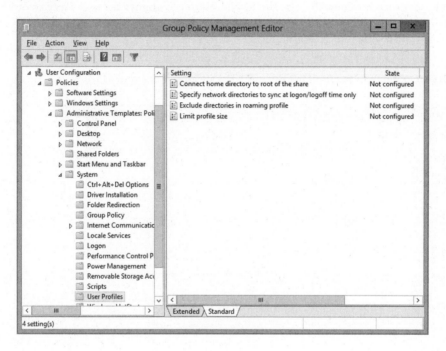

Limit Profile Size

This setting limits how big the profile can grow. Remember, now the My Documents folder is part of the profile. If you limit the profile size, the profile can hit that limit awfully quickly.

 I recommend that you avoid using this setting unless you use the techniques described in the next chapter for redirecting folders for the My Documents folder. When that technique is applied, the redirected My Documents folder is no longer part of the profile, and the size can come back down to earth.

Once enabled, the setting provides three other options:

"Show registry files in the file list" If selected, the user will see the NTUSER.DAT as part of the total calculations on space. I suggest you leave this unchecked because most users won't know what the NTUSER.DAT file is. And, when it's left unchecked, the NTUSER.DAT file doesn't count toward the space used.

"Notify user when profile storage space is exceeded"   This option notifies the user about size infractions.

"Remind user every *X* minutes"   Use this setting so that it annoys the user every so often. This setting is only valid if the "Notify user when profile storage space is exceeded" box is checked, as shown in Figure 9.24.

FIGURE 9.24   You can limit the Roaming Profile size, if desired.

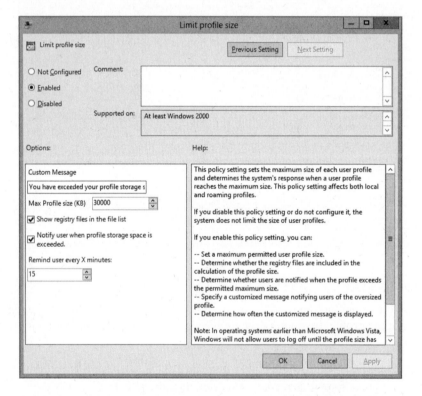

Once this policy setting is configured, the affected users on Windows XP cannot log off until the files that compose their profile take up less than the limit. They are presented with a list of files in their profile, as shown in Figure 9.25, and from this list they must choose some to delete.

Windows 7 and later machines get a pop-up. You can see it in Figure 9.26. To see the list of files, they have to double-click the X. (You might want to mention this in your custom message.)

FIGURE 9.25 Once the Roaming Profile size is set, Windows XP users can't log off until they delete some files.

FIGURE 9.26 Windows 7 and later pop up a message for the user when you restrict profile size.

Additionally, for Windows Vista and later, users can log off, but their changes aren't synchronized back to the server. At logoff, they are greeted with the message you see in Figure 9.27. It stays on the screen for a few seconds and then goes away, allowing the next user to log on.

FIGURE 9.27 Users are notified that their profile isn't completely synchronized.

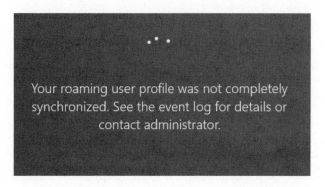

In general, this is a blunt instrument. The original use of this entry was for situations in which users stuffed lots of documents into their Windows NT Roaming Profile—onto the Desktop, for instance. Recall that Windows NT pushes the entire profile up and back, causing major bandwidth headaches. Indeed, because users rely heavily on the My Documents folder (which is part of the profile), there's even more reason to be concerned.

 WARNING   Don't try to place disk quota restrictions on Roaming Profiles. Because applications sometimes put their own data inside the profile, users have a hard time tracking down files to delete if the quota prevented them from writing. Instead, use disk quotas on redirected folders, such as the My Documents folder.

But instead of being forced to use this policy setting as your only weapon to fight disk space usage, you have an ace in the hole; in the next chapter, you'll learn how to use Folder Redirection to redirect My Documents. You can then place a disk quota on the redirected My Documents folder.

In Windows Vista and later, this policy setting will automatically exclude \AppData\ Local and AppData\LocalLow directories (and all their subdirectories).

Exclude Directories in Roaming Profile

As previously stated, several folders in the profile will not roam. For pre–Windows Vista machines, these folders are:

Documents and Settings\<*username*>\Local Settings\Application Data

(and everything below it, including Local Settings, History, Temp, and Temporary Internet Files).

For Windows Vista and later machines, these folders are \AppData\Local, AppData\ LocalLow, and all their subfolders (like \Temporary Internet Files).

You can add additional folders to the list of those that do not roam, if you want. You might do this if you want to fix a specific file to a Desktop (if you maintain locally cached profiles). For instance, you can exclude Desktop\LargeZipDownloads if you want to make sure those types of files do not roam with the profile.

 NOTE   Enter additional entries relative to the root of the profiles. For instance, if you want to add the Desktop, simply add **Desktop** (not **C:\Documents and Settings\Desktop** or anything similar), because the Desktop folder is found directly off the root of each profile.

Connect Home Directory to Root of the Share

I'm pretty sure that by the time you get to the end of this book, you won't want to use old-style "Home Drives" anymore. That's because the changes in Roaming Profile behavior and redirected folders (see the next chapter) present a better way for users to store their files. However, if you do end up using Home Drives for each user (located in the Account tab of each user account's Properties dialog box), you can specify a location for users to store their stuff.

Those two environment variables, *%HOMEDRIVE%* and *%HOMEPATH%*, are automatically set when you set up, share, and assign a home directory for a user. NT 4 client computers aren't as smart as Windows 2000 computers, and they understand the meaning of the *%HOMEDRIVE%* and *%HOMEPATH%* shares a bit differently. To make a long story short, the fully qualified name path to the share isn't represented when those variables are evaluated on NT 4 clients, but it is for Windows 2000 and later clients. You can "dumb down" clients by applying this policy setting and making new clients act like old NT 4 clients.

This policy is not supported on Windows Vista or later. Those operating systems *always* set *%HOMEDRIVE%* and *%HOMEPATH%* in the new way.

Mandatory Profiles

Mandatory Profiles enable the administrator to assign a single user or multiple users the same, unchanging user experience regardless of where they log on and no matter what they do. In non–mumbo-jumbo terms, Mandatory Profiles ensure that users can't screw things up. When you use Mandatory Profiles to lock down your users, you guarantee that the Desktop, the files in the profile, and the Registry continue to look exactly as they did when they were set up.

Mandatory Profiles are great when you have general populations of users—such as call centers, nursing stations, or library kiosks—on whom you want to maintain settings.

Once the Mandatory Profile is set for these people, you know you won't be running out there every 11 minutes trying to fix someone's machine when they've put the black text on the black background and clicked Apply. Actually, they can still put the black text on the black background and click Apply, and it *does* take effect. But when they log off or reboot (if they can figure out how to do that in the dark), the values aren't preserved. So, voilà! Back to work!

If you previously set up the **Add the Administrators security group to roaming user profiles** policy setting, you won't need to worry about not being able to dive into the profile. However, the policy setting must be placed before the Roaming Profile is placed.

Establishing Mandatory Profiles for Windows XP

Remember earlier when I confessed that I had an "everything I knew was wrong" moment? This is Part II of that. Sort of.

You'll recall that earlier we talked about Windows XP's Copy To button, which appears to work fine (for me) when establishing a Default Network Profile. But, as I described, there was a "superseding" KB article 959753 that described updated, supported steps for how to establish the Default Network Profile.

In other words, the Copy To button appears to be the "wrong" way to do it, and the KB article gives new directions for establishing the Default Network Profile.

So, I would also think that the Copy To button would be frowned upon to establish a Mandatory Profile in Windows XP. However, I can find no evidence for this in my research. That is, there is a pretty old (2006) KB article titled "How to assign a mandatory user profile in Windows XP" that describes how to use the Copy To button to establish a Mandatory Profile in Windows XP.

But we already know there is updated thinking about the Copy To button with regard to Default Network Profiles and regular user accounts. So, we can also assume that the same updated thinking should also hold true for Windows XP Mandatory Profiles—even if there isn't a KB article on it at all.

With that in mind, here's my advice: Start out by using the information in KB 959753 (the one that describes the steps for creating a Default Network Profile). However, rather than creating a Default Network Profile, use the Copy To button in conjunction with the configured Default Local User Profile as the basis for establishing your Mandatory Profile for Windows XP.

Once you're ready to click Copy To, enter the full path plus a folder for the common users who will use the Mandatory Profile, as shown in Figure 9.28. This example has \\Dc01\profiles\allnurses. The allnurses folder is automatically created under the Profiles share.

FIGURE 9.28   For Windows XP, use the Copy To dialog box to copy the prepared Default User Profile as a Mandatory Profile.

Click the Change button in the "Permitted to use" section to open the "Select User or Group" dialog box, and change the default from the original user to Authenticated Users. This lets everyone use the profile in the domain.

Next, use Explorer to locate the share we created earlier, named Profiles. Inside the Profiles directory, you should now see allnurses. Locate NTUSER.DAT and rename it to **NTUSER.MAN**, as shown in Figure 9.29.

FIGURE 9.29 Change a Roaming Profile to a Mandatory Profile by renaming NTUSER.DAT to NTUSER.MAN.

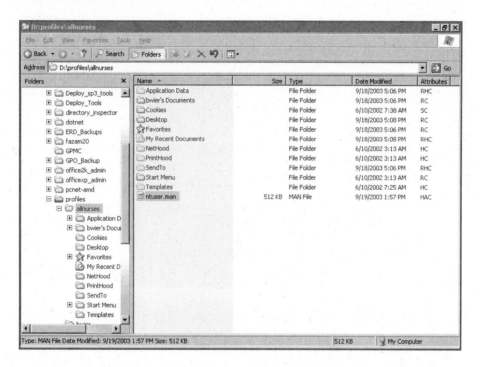

At this point, if you're not planning on establishing Mandatory Profiles for your modern Windows, then skip over the next section and meet me at "Mandatory Profiles—Finishing Touches."

Because NTUSER.DAT is hidden by default, you might have to change the default view options. In Explorer, choose Tools ➢ Folder Options to open the Folder Options dialog box. Click the View tab, click the "Show Hidden Files and Folders" button, clear the "Hide File Extensions for Known File Types" check box, and click OK.

Establishing Mandatory Profiles for Modern Windows

The advice for establishing a Mandatory Profile for modern Windows is, again, found in KB 973289.

Again, the basic steps start out the same as what we talked about with regard to creating a Default Network Profile for a modern Windows machine:

- Log on as the local administrator, and craft the profile the way you want to.

- Create an Unattend.xml file with a special parameter, called Copy Profile = True.

- Using an elevated command prompt, run SYSPREP and neuter the machine.

- When the computer starts up, it will magically copy the administrator's settings into the Default User's local profile

At this point, you're ready to use the Copy To button to copy the Default User's local profile to be the Mandatory Profile. In Figure 9.30, you can see that we're copying the profile to \\dc01\profiles\allnurses.v5. The .v5 extension is required, because we're using Windows 10 and this is a Type 5 machine and a Type 5 profile.

FIGURE 9.30   Be sure to put the .v5 extension in, because this is a Windows 10 (Type 5) profile.

Next, use Explorer to locate the share we created earlier, named Profiles. Inside the Profiles directory, you should now see allnurses.v5. Locate NTUSER.DAT and rename it to **NTUSER.MAN**, similar to what was shown earlier in Figure 9.29.

Mandatory Profiles—Finishing Touches

At this point you've established a Mandatory Profile. Now you need to point some user or users toward the Mandatory Profiles you created. This is done quickly in Active Directory Users and Computers.

Simply open up the user (or multiselect user accounts) and in the Profile tab, specify exactly what you see in Figure 9.31.

FIGURE 9.31   Point all similar users to the new Mandatory Profile.

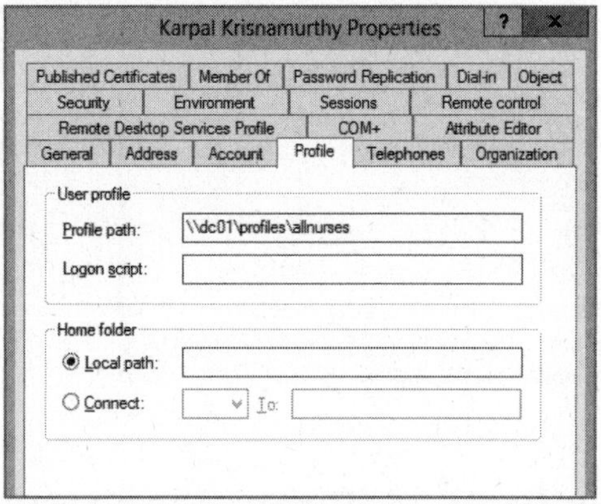

This is kind of weird, of course, because you know you have (up to) five folders: allnurses for Type 1 computers and allnurses.v2 for Type 2, allnurses.v3 for Type 3 computers, and so on.

But it doesn't matter. In Active Directory Users and Computers, as seen in Figure 9.31, you simply type in the name of the older Type 1 computer folder— even if you have no Windows XP at all and have nothing but, say, Windows 7 and Windows 10.

It doesn't matter.

You leave off the .v2 or .v5 at the end when pointing users toward the Mandatory Profile folder. Each machine type will automatically find the right directory regardless of the computer type.

Last, since you copied the profile to the server with permissions for Authenticated User to use, you'll also want to modify the NTFS permissions of the allnurses folder under the Profiles share to make sure it's protected. You might choose to protect the allnurses and allnurses.v5 folders by setting the permissions, as shown in Figure 9.32 (one time for each directory).

FIGURE 9.32   You can prevent people from inadvertently modifying the newly established profile.

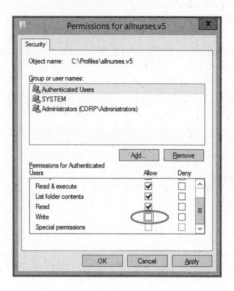

Forced Mandatory Profiles (Super-Mandatory)

Mandatory Profiles might not always be so—if the server is down or a user unplugs their network cable, the Mandatory Profile does not load. Indeed, the user will get the Default Local User Profile. This could be a potential security problem and possibly a violation of your corporate policy.

In instances like this, you need to determine if it's more important that a user logs on (and gets the Default Local User Profile) or that, if they don't get the Mandatory Profile, they don't get to log on at all. Microsoft calls this type of profile "Super-Mandatory." In Figure 9.29 earlier, we used a folder named allnurses as our Mandatory Profile folder. We can take this to the next step and ensure that users who would use the allnurses folder can only log in if they can connect to the share on the server.

Don't forget: profiles are different for Type 1 (pre–Windows Vista) and Type 2 and later (Windows Vista and later). To that end, you'll need to set up Mandatory Profiles that fit for each type.

To force users who log on to Windows Vista and later to use a Mandatory Profile or lose logon capability, you need to first rename the allnurses.v2 folder so that it has .man.v2 instead. So, the final folder name for Windows 7 would be allnurses.man.v2.

For Windows 8.1, it would be allnurses.man.v4.

For Windows 10, it would be allnurses.man.v5.

To force users to use the Mandatory Profile or lose logon capability, simply follow these steps:

1. Create a Mandatory Profile as described earlier, including renaming the NTUSER.DAT to **NTUSER.MAN**.

2. For Type 1 machines, rename the entire folder from allnurses to **allnurses.man**. For Type 2 machines, rename the entire folder from allnurses.v2 to **allnurses.man.v2** (or use the correct corresponding suffix based upon machine and profile type).

3. Change the affected users' Profile tabs to point to the new location, such as \\Dc01\ profiles\allnurses.man, as shown in Figure 9.33.

Once the forced Mandatory Profile is introduced onto a system, the system always checks to see if the profile is available. If the forced Mandatory Profile is unavailable, the user is not permitted to log on.

FIGURE 9.33   You can force a Mandatory Profile if absolutely necessary.

Technically, you can couple a Mandatory Profile with the **Log users off when roaming profile fails** policy setting to create the same effect. However, the method detailed here is preferred.

Final Thoughts

In this chapter, you learned about the three profile types: Local, Roaming, and Mandatory.

Local Profiles alone are great—for only the smallest of environments. However, remember that there's a lot you can do to get a similar look and feel for when new users show up on the job. You can craft a Default Local User Profile or, even better, a Default Network User Profile.

Step up to Roaming Profiles when you have even a handful of users and you want to allow them to bounce from machine to machine and keep their look and feel. Roaming Profiles have grown up since the days of Windows NT. The algorithm to move the profiles up and back is much improved, and you should give it another try if you once gave up in frustration.

Roaming Profiles are especially useful if you want to bring users' Desktops and laptops back from the dead, as we'll explore in the next two chapters. Indeed, you can use Roaming Profiles as a handy way to upgrade users' machines while preserving their Desktops.

Remember that the Active Directory Users and Computers tool allows you to select multiple users at once and set their Roaming Profile path to a server. And as stated earlier, there's no need to create the folder underneath the shared directory first—the system will automatically do that once the *%username%* variable is encountered.

Even though we set up Roaming Profiles for various computer types (From Type 1 for Windows XP to Type 5 for Windows 10), we have no way to exchange data between the two. If someone logs onto Windows 8.1 and drops some music files in their profile, then log onto a Windows 10 machine, they simply won't see those music files.

You also learned about Un-Roaming Profile tools, like Microsoft UE-V, which can spread out the download of the parts of the profile across the time of the user's session instead of all at once at login time.

In the next chapter, we'll discuss Redirected Folders. The idea is that instead of saving critical data in our profile, we save it on a point on our server. That way, as we roam from type to type, we'll be able to just reach out and touch the data that lives on the server. We'll get there right around the corner.

As stated earlier, there are a lot of policy settings you can utilize to hone how profiles work. You can set up your environment to be moderately secure when using the **Delete cached copies of roaming profiles** policy setting. And you can allow joint ownership of the user's Roaming Profile directory on the server by utilizing the **Add the Administrators security group to roaming user profiles** policy setting.

Use Mandatory Profiles sparingly. With Group Policy settings available to tie down all sorts of settings, Mandatory Profiles are really only a last resort. And Forced Mandatory Profiles are a really, really last resort (if there's such a thing).

10

The Managed Desktop, Part 1: Redirected Folders, Offline Files, and the Synchronization Manager

You get Active Directory, you get Group Policy. That's the good news. The better news is how you can put your knowledge of Group Policy to use to keep your users happy. Here's the idea: easily create a consistent environment for your users no matter where they roam.

In the previous chapter, you used Roaming Profiles to kick off your journey to a consistent environment. But that only got you so far—especially if you had both Windows XP and, say, Windows 7, 8.1, and/or 10 machines. That's because when you roamed from Windows XP to later machines (or vice versa), you didn't maintain the goodies, like the stuff you put in My Documents (for XP) and Documents (for Windows Vista and later). Each computer type became its own island.

In fact, as a reminder, to put a fine point on it, Microsoft encourages you to "silo" your machines so the profiles never meet. The profiles should be set up such that they are only used within the same version. Again, this was covered in great detail in the last chapter, and simply as a reminder, here are the Windows profile types:

- Version 1: Windows 2000, Windows 2003, and Windows XP
- Version 2: Windows Vista, Windows 7 and Server 2008 and Server 2008 R2
- Version 3: Windows 8 and Server 2012
- Version 4: Windows 8.1 and Server 2012 R2
- Version 5: Windows 10 and Windows Server 2016

So if these profiles can never meet, how will you get a unified experience?

That's one of the points of a *managed desktop*.

A managed desktop is one where you can create a predictable environment for your users to log into and enjoy. It's not put together with wacky applications and icons all over the place. You know what to expect when your users log on, and so do they.

I like to call this "my documents follow me" and "my settings follow me."

Again, you built a bit of a foundation for your journey toward a managed desktop in the last chapter when you implemented Roaming Profiles. This enabled the basics of the "my documents follow me" and the "my settings follow me" philosophies. In this chapter, we'll explore the implementation of some of the other features needed to create a managed desktop: Redirected Folders, Offline Files, and the synchronization capabilities.

 In normal use, people may call Offline Files something else—Offline Folders and also CSC (for Client-Side Caching). In regular use, they're all the same thing, but strictly, Microsoft documentation refers only to Offline Files and not Offline Folders. So, to be consistent, we'll also call the feature Offline Files.

Previously, the concept of a managed desktop was called IntelliMirror. It seems like the marketing folks in Redmond have put that term to pasture, though. I bring it up here in case you have my original book, which had the word *IntelliMirror* in the title. So, we'll just refer to IntelliMirror as a "managed desktop."

In the next chapter, I'll continue creating a managed desktop with a discussion of software deployment via Group Policy. Finally, in Chapter 12, "Finishing Touches with Group Policy: Scripts, Internet Explorer, Hardware Control, Printer Deployment, Local Admin Password Control," you'll see how the "circle of life" for a computer comes together with more Group Policy preference extensions, tricks, and more.

Redirected Folders

Redirected Folders allow the administrator to provide a centralized repository for certain noteworthy folders from client systems and to have the data contained in them reside on shared folders on servers. It's a beautiful thing. The administrator gets centralized control; users get the same experience they always did. It's the best of both worlds.

Available Folders to Redirect

Windows XP and its newer cousins (Windows Vista and later) have different folders that are available for redirection. In Windows XP, you can set Redirected Folders for the following:

- My Documents
- My Pictures
- Start Menu
- Desktop
- Application Data

In Windows Vista and later, you can redirect the following folders:

- Contacts (not previously available in Windows XP)
- Start Menu (like Windows XP, but see the note following this list)
- Desktop (like Windows XP)
- Documents (was called My Documents in Windows XP)
- Downloads (not previously available in Windows XP)
- Favorites (not previously "redirectable" in Windows XP, but available in the Roaming Profile)
- Music (was called My Music in Windows XP)
- Videos (was called My Videos in Windows XP)
- Pictures (was called My Pictures in Windows XP)
- Searches (not previously available in Windows XP)
- Links (not previously available in Windows XP)
- AppData (was called simply Application Data in XP); note you can only redirect the Roaming folder of AppData and not the Local or LocalLow folders
- And (Lord help us) Saved Games (not previously available in Windows XP)

> **NOTE**   The Start Menu redirection support in Windows Vista and later is better than XP, because in XP you didn't have the ability to redirect each user's Start Menu folder to a different location. You could only do it to a shared location. It wasn't as flexible as My Documents.

For each of these settings, there is a Basic and an Advanced configuration.

The idea is to set up a GPO that contains a policy setting to redirect one or more of these folders for clients and "stick them" on a server. Usually the GPO is set at the OU level, and all users inside the OU are affected; however, there might occasionally be a reason to link the GPO with the policy setting to the domain or site level.

In the *Basic* configuration, every user who is affected by the policy setting is redirected to the same shared folder. Then, inside the shared folder, the system can automatically create individual, secure folders for users to store their stuff.

In the *Advanced* configuration, Active Directory security group membership determines which users' folders get redirected to which shared folder. For instance, you could say, "All members of the **Graphic_Artists** Global security group will get their Desktops redirected to the ga_Desktops shared folder on Server 6," or "All members of the Sales Universal security group will get their Application Data redirected to the AppData share on Server Pineapple."

Redirected Documents/My Documents

For our journey through Redirected Folders, we'll work primarily inside the Documents folder. All the principles that work on the special Documents folder work equally well for the other special "redirectable" folders, unless otherwise noted. At the end of this section, I'll briefly discuss why you might want to redirect some other folders as well.

In the last chapter, we explored how to leverage Roaming Profiles to maintain a consistent state for users if they hop from machine to machine. Roaming Profiles are terrific, but one significant drawback is associated with using Roaming Profiles. Recall that My Documents (for Windows XP) and Documents (for Windows Vista and later) are now part of the profile. On the one hand, this frees you from the bondage of drive letters and home drives. No more, "Ursula, put it in your U: drive," or, "Harry, save it to the H: drive."

On the other hand, once the user data is in Documents/My Documents, your network will be swamped with all the up-and-back movement of data within Documents/My Documents when users hop from machine to machine—20MB of Word docs here, 30MB of Excel docs there. Multiply this by the number of users and it'll add up fast! Not to mention that (for XP, at least) that data is synchronized at logon and logoff, and hence, the user may have to wait until it's all completed. As you learned in the previous chapter, the Roaming Profiles algorithm does its best to mitigate that, but it's still got to move the changed files.

But with Redirected Folders, you can have the best of both worlds. Users can save their files to the place they know and love, My Documents (for Windows XP) and Documents (for Windows Vista and later) and anchor the data to a fixed location so it *appears* as if the data is roaming with the users. But it really isn't; it's safe and secure on a file share of your choice. And, since the data is already on the server, there's no long wait time when logging on or logging off.

There are two added bonuses to this scheme. Since all the Documents/ My Documents files are being redirected to specific fixed-shared folders, you can easily back up all the user data in one fell swoop. Perhaps you can even make a separate backup job specifically for the user data that needs to be more closely monitored.

Basic Redirected Folders

Basic Redirected Folders works best in two situations:

- Smaller environments—such as a doctor's office or storefront—where all employees sit under one roof

- In an organization's OU structure that was designed such that similar people are not only in the same OU but also in the same physical location

The reason these simple scenarios make a good fit with the basic option is that such situations let you redirect the users affected by the policy setting to a server that's close to them. That way, if they do roam within their location, the wait time is minimal to download and upload the data back and forth to the server and their workstation.

In the following example, I've created an OU called **LikeUsers** whose users are all using the same local server, DC01. Setting up Redirected Folders for Documents/My Documents is a snap. It's a three-step process:

1. Create a shared folder to store the data.

2. Set the security on the shared folder.

3. Create a new GPO and edit it to contain a policy setting to redirect the Documents/My Documents folder.

To create and share a folder to store redirected Documents/My Documents data, follow these steps:

1. Log onto DC01 as Administrator.

2. From the Desktop, double-click My Computer to open the My Computer folder.

3. Find a place to create a users folder. In this example, we'll use C:\DATA. Once you're inside the C: drive, right-click C:\ and select the Folder command from the New menu, and then type **Data** for the name.

> You can substitute any name for Data. Some use DOCS, MYDOCS, or REDIRDOCS. Some administrators like to use hidden shares, such as Data$, MYDOCS$, or MYDOCUMENTS$. This works well, too.

4. Right-click the newly created Data folder, and choose Share with ➢ Specific People, which opens the Properties of the folder, focused on the Sharing tab. Pull down the drop-down menu and select Everyone, and then click Add. Note that the default is such that the share is Everyone:Read. Change this so that Everyone has Read/Write permissions, as seen in Figure 10.1.

FIGURE 10.1   Share the Data folder such that Everyone has Read/Write permissions.

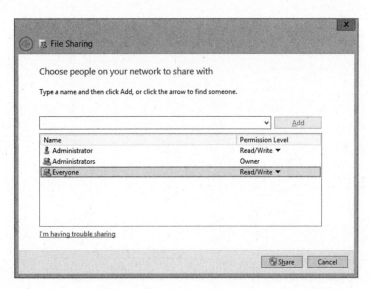

Be sure that the NTFS permissions allow write access for the users you want as well. In other words, both the share level and NTFS permissions must allow the user to write.

Now that the share is created, you're ready to create a new GPO to do the magic. Again, you'll want to do this on your Windows 10 management station, WIN10MANAGEMENT. This machine should have Windows 10 along with the RSAT tools, which contain the updated GPMC.

To set up Redirected Folders for Documents/My Documents, follow these steps:

1. In the GPMC, right-click the OU on which you want to apply Folder Redirection (in my case, the **LikeUsers** OU), and choose "Create a GPO in this domain, and Link it here."

2. Name the GPO, say, "Documents Folder Redirection."

3. Right-click the new GPO, and choose Edit from the context menu to open the Group Policy Management Editor.

4. Drill down to Folder Redirection by choosing User Configuration ➢ Policies ➢ Windows Settings ➢ Folder Redirection. Right-click the Documents entry in the Group Policy Management Editor, and choose Properties to open the Documents Properties dialog box, as shown in Figure 10.2.

FIGURE 10.2   Use the Group Policy Editor to find Folder Redirection and right-click the folder and choose Properties.

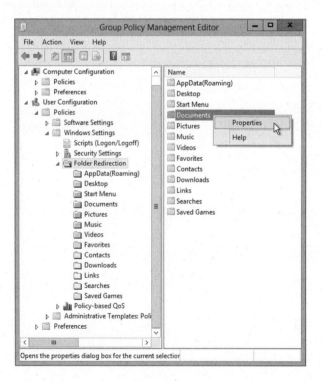

5. In the Setting drop-down list box, select "Basic—Redirect everyone's folder to the same location" as seen in Figure 10.3.

FIGURE 10.3　The Basic settings redirect all users in the OU to the same location.

Don't click OK (or Apply) yet. There's more to do. If you do click OK or Apply, you're going to get a warning (which we'll talk about in the sidebar "What Happens When You Edit a GPO from an Older GPMC?" later in this chapter).

The Target Tab

The "Target folder location" drop-down list box has the following four options:

Redirect to the user's home directory　Many companies use home drives for each user and have the users store all their stuff there. To set a home drive for each user, in Active Directory Users and Computers, click the Profile tab for the user and enter a path in the "Home folder" section. The idea behind this setting is that it's an easy way to help users continue to use a drive letter they already know and love, say, H: (for Home directory) in addition to the Documents/My Documents redirection. If you choose this setting, both H: and Documents/My Documents point to exactly the same place—the path you set in the "Home folder" section in Active Directory Users and Computers. In this book, we didn't set up home drives because Documents/My Documents redirection frees us from the need to do so. This setting is provided here only as a convenience for organizations that want to continue to use home folders. If you plan to eventually get rid of home drives in your company in lieu of just a redirected Documents/My Documents folder, my advice is not to use this setting; instead, use the "Redirect to the following location" setting (explored shortly). Note that this setting is only available when you're using Documents redirection and is not available for the other folders.

If the user has no home folder, this option is ignored, and the folder stays in its current location.

Share Permissions: Full Control vs. Read/Write

In the previous chapter, we set up a shared folder for our Roaming Profiles and set it to Read/Write permissions.

Interestingly, here, on the share that will house our Redirected Folders, we need Full Control permissions or the Folder Redirection will fail. So, is there a problem using Full Control or Windows Server 2012's "Read/Write" rights? Is there a way to exploit an attack on a share like these?

Not really, unless the underlying NTFS permissions are open for an attack. Basically, as long as the root folder of the share is an NTFS folder with appropriate permissions, there is no concern for having the share "wide open."

Some people used to insist on using specific share permissions for specific people or groups, but it was often because they instituted the practice in the dark days of OS/2 and Microsoft's LAN Manager and got used to it (and maybe they had the "insecure" FAT file system running). The share permission is simply a security descriptor stored in the Registry entry for the share in the LanManServer entries on the server. It doesn't matter if everyone has Full Control rights. It doesn't change the permissions on the Registry entry itself, so it cannot be used as an exploit for getting a toehold on the server.

The moral of the story: Have the correct NTFS permissions under the folder that contains the share. Indeed, share permissions aren't sufficient if someone gets physical access, or near-physical access, to the box—for example, via Remote Desktop Services (what was known as Terminal Services) access.

Create a folder for each user under the root path   If you plan to redirect more than just the Documents/My Documents folder (say, the Application Data or Desktop), you might want to select this option. This creates secure subfolders underneath the point you specify. As you can see in Figure 10.3 earlier in this chapter, entering \\DC01\data in the Root Path box is an example of how all users affected by this policy setting are redirected.

In the example, you can see that Documents for a user Clair will be redirected to her own folder in the Data share. Go ahead and perform this now.

This choice might be good if you don't want to have to remember what the specific environment variables point to.

In our example, we're using DC01, a Domain Controller. You usually wouldn't do this; rather, you'd use a regular run-of-the-mill file server (as a member server, not a Domain Controller). We're doing that here simply for the sake of example.

Redirect to the following location   This option makes sense if you plan to redirect only Documents/My Documents or just one other redirectable folder.

It also makes sense if you want to leverage the maximum flexibility. This selection allows you to specifically dictate where you want the folder placed. That's because you can use environment variables here.

For instance, to use this setting, type **\\DC01\data\%username%** in the Root Path text box. Then, a subfolder for the user is created directly under the Data shared folder. This is the selection to choose when none of the others are to your liking; you have the most flexibility with this option.

 In advanced configurations, you can use this setting to (get this) co-share a Documents/My Documents folder between multiple users. Crazy! But you need to ensure that you set the right ACLs on the folder as well as enable the policy named **Do not check for user ownership of Roaming Profiles**, which is located in Computer Configuration ➢ Policies ➢ Administrative Templates ➢ User Profiles.

Redirect to the local *userprofile* location   With this option, you redirect the folder for the user back to their Local Profile. It's useful when you want to remove redirection for a particular folder without affecting the rest of the other Redirected Folders.

Don't click OK (or Apply) yet. There's more to do. If you do click OK or Apply, you're going to get a warning (which we'll talk about in the sidebar "What Happens When You Edit a GPO from an Older GPMC?").

The Settings Tab

When you click the Settings tab, you have access to additional options for Folder Redirection. The Settings tab is the hidden gem of Folder Redirection; it activates a bit of magic. Figure 10.4 shows the Settings tab for Documents.

By default, users have exclusive NTFS permissions to their directories, and the contents of their Documents/My Documents folders are automatically moved to the new directory. You can change this behavior, if desired, by making the appropriate choices on the Settings tab.

Because we're discussing My Documents (for Windows XP) and Documents (for Windows Vista and later) at this point, we'll dive into the Settings tab specifically for Documents for Windows Vista and later. However, each setting discussed here affects the other potentially Redirected Folders in exactly the same way. Let's take a look at some of the options available on this tab.

Grant the user exclusive rights to Documents   By default, this check box is checked. You're instructing the system to create a secure directory under the redirection. This check box sets NTFS permissions on that directory so that only the owner (the user) can enter the directory. This keeps prying eyes, even those of nosy administrators, out of people's personal business. If you want to change this setting, uncheck the box.

Deselecting the "Grant the user exclusive rights to Documents" check box sets no additional permissions, nor does it modify the target directory permissions in any way. When the folder gets created, it inherits its parent folder permissions instead of creating its own, exclusive, noninherited permissions. The NTFS permissions are not modified. Because Windows Server uses NTFS inheritance, newly created folders receive the same permissions as the parent folder.

If the "Grant the user exclusive rights to Documents" is checked and you do need to dig into someone's personal directory, you'll have to take ownership of the directory, as described in the previous chapter. Or, if you set it up in advance—using the information in the sidebar "How to Grant Administrators Access to Documents/My Documents (or Other Redirected Folders)"—you'll be able to get in whenever you want! (Again, though, you need to set it up in advance.)

FIGURE 10.4   The Settings tab in Folder Redirection holds all sorts of magical powers!

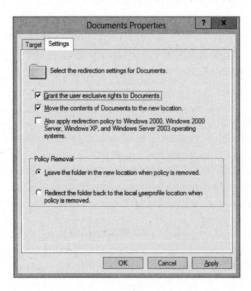

Move the contents of Documents to the new location By default, this check box is selected. When you start out creating a managed desktop, Microsoft is betting that the first thing you do is set up Roaming Profiles and then move on to setting up Redirected Folders. In between those two time periods, however, users have surely created their own documents and started putting them in their Documents folder in their Local or Roaming Profile. Enabling this option magically moves (not copies) their documents from their profile (Roaming or Local) to the appointed place on the server the next time they log on.

If users have bounced from machine to machine and sprinkled data in the local Documents folder, the files in Documents will move users' documents to the redirected location the next time the user logs onto that machine. The only time to worry is when two files have the same name— the latest time-stamped file wins and stays on the server.

Also apply redirection policy to Windows 2000, Windows 2000 Server, Windows XP, and Windows Server 2003 operating systems This setting gets the prize for greatest number of characters in a dialog box with just one check box. You'll only see this option when you create a GPO using a modern GPMC.

This check box turns on or off what is called (unofficially) "downlevel compatible" Folder Redirection mode. This addition helps bridge the differences between the pre-Vista and Vista and later system profile hierarchies.

Here's what happens if you enable this box (which implies if you have Windows XP machines):

- The target folder name for the Documents folder will automatically be set to My Documents; of course, you can change it to whatever you like.

- The Music and Videos folders will also automatically be redirected to the Follow the Documents folder, which means its target location will be <MyDocPath>\My Music and <MyDocPath>\My Videos. This is because pre-Vista Folder Redirection does not support individual redirection for these two folders.

- The Pictures folder, by default, will be set to follow the Documents folder. But there are some differences: since you can specify different locations in the pre-Vista system, you can do it on Vista and later as well. This means you can still change the Pictures folder to other places (including back to the Local Profile) as well.

Here's what happens if you disable this box (which implies you have only Windows Vista and later machines):

- The target folder name will be Documents by default—you can still change it to other names.

- Pictures/Music/Videos will not automatically be placed within Documents as a parent. They remain where they are. You can configure them to redirect to any location you want, and the target folder name is also the new name without the "My" prefix.

The pure Vista and later mode gives the customer more flexibility; if you don't have pre-Vista systems in your environment, then it is better to use this mode.

Policy Removal   You must select one of the two settings under the Policy Removal heading. The point of having OUs is that you can move users easily in and out of them. If the user is moved out of an OU to which this policy applies, the following options help you determine what happens to their Redirected Folder contents:

> **Leave the folder in the new location when policy is removed**   If this option is selected and the user is moved out of the OU to which this policy applies, the data stays in the shared folder and directory you specified. This is the default. The user will continue to access the contents of the Redirected Folder. However, there is one potential pitfall when using this option. To get a grip on it, read the sidebar "Folder Redirection Pitfalls" later in this chapter.

> **Redirect the folder back to the local userprofile location when policy is removed**   If this check box is selected and the user moves (or the policy no longer applies), a copy of the data is sent to the profile.

If Roaming Profiles is not set up, a copy of the data is sent to every workstation the user logs on to. If you've set up Roaming Profiles, the data gets pushed back up to the server and shared folder that houses the user's Roaming Profile when the user logs off.

This setting is useful if a user under your jurisdiction moves to another territory. Once this happens, you can eliminate their junk cluttering your servers (as long as you're not the administrator of the target OU). Use this option with care, though; since the user's data isn't anchored to a shared folder, the network traffic will increase when this data roams around the network.

I recommend that you check with the target OU administrator to ensure that some Folder Redirection policy will apply to the user. This eliminates all the "up and back" problems associated with maintaining user data inside regular Roaming Profiles.

Don't click OK (or Apply) yet. There's more to do. If you do click OK or Apply, you're going to get a warning (which we'll talk about in the sidebar "What Happens When You Edit a GPO from an Older GPMC?").

Folder Redirection Pitfalls

Earlier, you learned about the "Leave the folder in the new location when policy is removed" check box that is used when redirecting folders. However, let's work through a quick example—we'll assume that the check box is checked, and a user is being asked to use two machines.

Let's imagine the following scenario:

- There is a user Fred in the **Sales** OU.

- Fred uses ComputerA.

- There is a GPO linked to the **Sales** OU that contains a Folder Redirection policy. This policy redirects his Documents folder and has the "Leave the folder in the new location when policy is removed" setting enabled.

Fred logs onto ComputerA, and the Documents folder is redirected to \\server1\share1\Fred\documents. As expected, Folder Redirection is working fine and dandy.

Now, let's assume Fred gets transferred to another job in Marketing, say, and his account is moved from the **Sales** OU to the **Marketing** OU. Let's assume Marketing does not have a Folder Redirection policy for Documents in place.

What happens the next time Fred logs onto ComputerA?

Well, because the GPO doesn't apply to him, the policy for Folder Redirection will be removed. However, the Documents folder is still pointing to the server, and he can see all of his data on the server. Fred clicks his Documents folder and all is well. He sees the files on the server just fine. As far as the user is concerned, nothing "changes" because "Leave the folder in the new location when policy is removed" was selected.

A week later, ComputerA catches fire. Fred gets a brand-new machine, ComputerB, which he has never logged onto before.

When Fred logs onto ComputerB, his Documents folder will be pointing to C:\users\%username%\Documents—not the server location as it was on ComputerA.

This makes sense: there isn't a Folder Redirection policy that affects Fred anymore. Remember—he's moved to Marketing, and they don't have a Folder Redirection policy. So, he never got the "signal" to use the server location he once did.

So, when Fred clicks Documents on ComputerB, he sees...nothing. However, Fred still has *rights* to get his files. So, if he wanted access to his files on ComputerB, he would have to navigate to \\server1\share1\%username%\documents via an Explorer window to be able to see his data.

How to Grant Administrators Access to Documents/My Documents (or Other Redirected Folders)

As you learned in the last chapter, it's possible to grant administrators access to the folders where users store their Roaming Profiles. In that chapter, you set up a policy setting that affects the client computers; the first time the user jumps on the computer, the file permissions are set so that both the user and the administrator have joint access. However, that's not the case with Redirected Folders.

If you want both the user and the administrator to have joint access to a Redirected Folder such as Documents, you need to perform two major steps:

1. Clear the "Grant the user exclusive rights to Documents" setting (seen in Figure 10.4).

2. Set security on the subfolder you are sharing that will contain the Redirected Folders.

In the Security Properties dialog box of the folder you shared, select Advanced. Uncheck the "Allow inheritable permissions from parent to propagate to this object" check box. Now, remove the permissions, and then add four groups, assign them permissions, and dictate where those permissions will flow. Here's the breakdown:

Administrators   Full Control, which applies to "This folder, subfolders, and files"

System   Full Control, which applies to "This folder, subfolders, and files"

Creator Owner   Full Control, which applies to "This folder, subfolders, and files"

Authenticated Users   Create Folders/Append Data, Read Permissions, Read Extended Attributes, which apply to "This folder only" (as seen here):

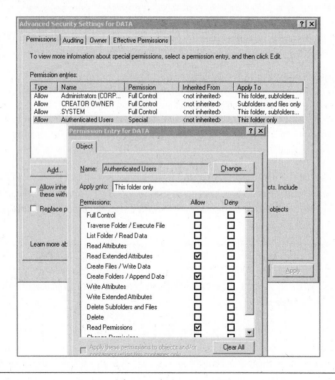

This information is valid for Windows 2003 and later. You can find more details in the Knowledge Base article Q288991. Adding these groups and assigning these permissions appears to remove the automatic synchronization of Redirected Folders, as you'll see a bit later. However, you can restore this functionality with the **Administratively Assigned Offline Files** policy setting—again, we'll explore that later.

But we have a problem. What if you've already set up Redirected Folders and users already have their own protected subfolders? How do you go back in time and fix the ones that already were created?

It could require a bit of work, but you could take ownership of the files and then add in the rights for both you and the user to have access to the files. Finally, for good measure, you should use the `subinacl` command (with the `/setowner` flag) to grant ownership access of the files back to the user (because the ownership rights are stripped when you take ownership).

Advanced Redirected Folders

Anything beyond the basics, as previously described, isn't required. However, you can set up some advanced options using the Setting drop-down list box, as shown in Figure 10.3 earlier in this chapter. Advanced Redirected Folders works best in two situations, both larger environments:

- A campus with many buildings. You'll want to specify different Redirected Folders locations that are closest to the biggest groups of users.

- More likely, a specific department that is charged with purchasing its own server and storage. In this scenario, there's usually a battle over who can store what data on whose server. With this mechanism, everyone can have his or her own sandbox.

In either case, you can still have an OU that affects many similar users but breaks up where folders are redirected, depending on the users' respective security groups. For example, we have an OU called **Sales** that contains two global security sales groups: **East_Sales** and **West_Sales**. Each Sales group needs its folders redirected to the server closest to it, either East_Server or West_Server. First, you'll want to create the shares on both the East_Server and West_Server as directed earlier. For this example, they're each shared out as Data. To perform an Advanced Folder Redirection, follow these steps:

1. Log onto WIN10MANAGEMENT as Administrator (if you haven't already).

2. Start the GPMC.

3. Right-click the OU on which we want to apply Folder Redirection, in this case the **Sales** OU, and select "Create a GPO in the domain, and Link it here."

4. Enter a descriptive name, such as "Advanced Folder Redirection for the Sales OU," for the GPO. Select it, and click Edit to open the Group Policy Management Editor.

5. The GPO for the OU appears. Drill down to Folder Redirection by choosing User Configuration ➤ Policies ➤ Windows Settings ➤ Folder Redirection.

6. Right-click the Documents folder in the Group Policy Management Editor, and choose Properties from the context menu to open the Documents Properties dialog box. In the Setting drop-down list box, select "Advanced—Specify locations for various user groups." The dialog box changes so that you can now use the Add button to add security settings, as shown in Figure 10.5. Click OK.

FIGURE 10.5   Use the Advanced redirection function to choose different locations to move users' data.

7. Click the Add button in the My Documents Properties dialog box to open up the "Specify Group and Location" dialog box. Click Browse under Security Group Membership, and locate the **East_Sales** Global security group.

8. From the "Target folder location" dropdown, choose "Redirect to the following location" and enter the UNC path of the Redirected Folder. In this case, it's **\\east_server\data\%username%**. Click OK to close the "Specify Group and Location" dialog box.

9. Repeat steps 7 and 8 for the **West_Sales** Global security group.

Don't click OK (or Apply) yet. There's more to do. If you do click OK or Apply, you're going to get a warning (which we'll talk about in the sidebar "What Happens When You Edit a GPO from an Older GPMC?").

When you're finished, you should have both **East_Sales** and **West_Sales** listed.

The next time the user logs on, the settings specified in the Settings tab take effect; by default, a new folder is generated specifically for each user, and the current documents in the user's Documents folder are transported to the new Redirected Folder location. Note that if the user is an inadvertent member of both groups, then the membership of the upper group wins.

What Happens When You Edit a GPO from an Older GPMC?

As I've suggested, you should be using a Windows 10 (or at least a Windows 7) management machine to do your GPO creation. Why? Because you'll always have the full ability to edit whatever new goodies are in the Group Policy Object Editor.

And for Folder Redirection, this isn't any different. As you saw in Figure 10.2, Windows Vista and later has a lot more folders it can possibly redirect (like Links, Searches, and others listed previously) and some that are more familiar (like Start Menu and Documents).

So, whenever you click OK after editing any Folder Redirection policies on an updated GPMC, you'll always get a warning like this one:

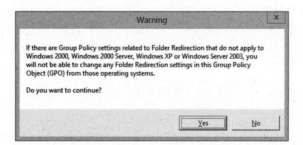

This warning is saying "You're editing this GPO on an updated GPMC. If you edit it on an older (Windows XP / Server 2003) GPMC, you're going to be in for a world of hurt."

Indeed, this is true. Take a look at the same GPO when viewed on a Windows Server 2003 GPMC if you had a policy for, say, the Links folder. The GPMC on that older machine doesn't know how to interpret the settings. This makes sense: the updated GPMC has newer settings for Vista and later; older management stations don't know what to do with this information. Sometimes, the GPMC displays only the information it can. For instance, older GPMCs can still sometimes figure out what's going on in the Documents folder when it's redirected—but not always, as you can see here:

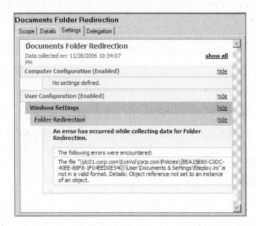

Then, if you decide to try to use an older GPMC to edit Folder Redirection policies, again, it's a world of hurt. Take a look at what happens when you try to make a change in, say, My Documents (if this was originally created on an updated GPMC). The system throws an "Access is denied" message—which is pretty elegant, considering the circumstances.

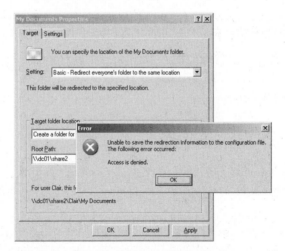

So, the message is clear: Create and edit your GPOs using a modern GPMC. Don't create the GPOs using a modern GPMC and then return to the older GPMC.

In case you're interested, here's what's happening under the hood: The updated GPMC's Folder Redirection routine writes a new file into the GPT called `fdeploy1.ini` that doesn't overlap with the old one (called `fdeploy.ini`). However, it does populate `fdeploy.ini` when you select downward-compatible mode. But you see this message on an older GPMC because the newer GPMC sets the "old" fdeploy.ini file that it creates for downward compatibility as Read-only in the GPT, effectively preventing the older (downlevel) GPEditor from writing to it.

It's a pretty low-tech solution, but it works.

Testing Folder Redirection of *Documents/My Documents*

In the previous chapter, you used Brett Wier's account to verify that Roaming Profiles were working properly.

If it all went right, each operating system was put into a silo where it couldn't see the other operating systems' roaming profile files.

Now, we're going to fix that problem and after we're done as you roam from machine to machine you should be able to see all files.

 You will need to log off and back on as Brett to see the changes take effect. Group Policy background refresh (as detailed in Chapter 3, "Group Policy Processing Behavior Essentials") does not apply to Redirected Folders.

In this example, I'm going to do something here I haven't done yet. I'll show you the results of Folder Redirection on all five machine types with just one file called FILE1.txt using the following machine types: Windows 2000, Windows XP, Windows 7, Windows 8, and Windows 10. Why? Because they're each a little different. And, yes, Windows 2000 is old, but it's good to understand *original* behavior before trying to understand *current* behavior.

Let's first see what happens when we log onto a Windows 2000 machine as Brett Wier and open My Documents. If he was to right-click upon FILE1.TXT and note its location, he would see this, as shown here:

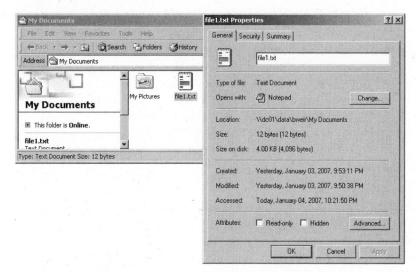

The file was automatically transported from the Roaming Profile and anchored to the fixed point on the server, in this case \\DC01\data\bwier\Documents.

If you perform the same experiment on a Windows XP machine, you'll see this:

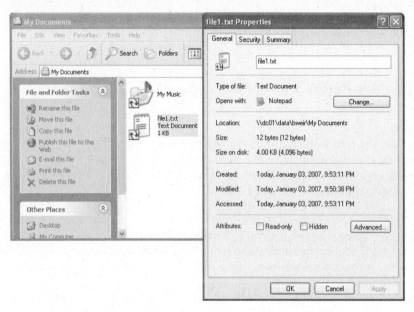

On a Windows 7 machine, you'll see this:

On a Windows 8 machine, you'll see this:

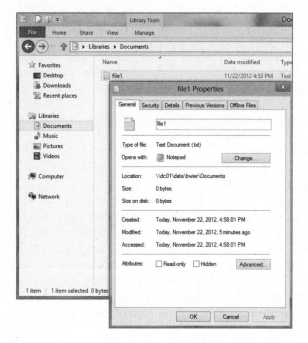

On a Windows 10 machine, you'll see this (though I added a little arrow to point something out to you):

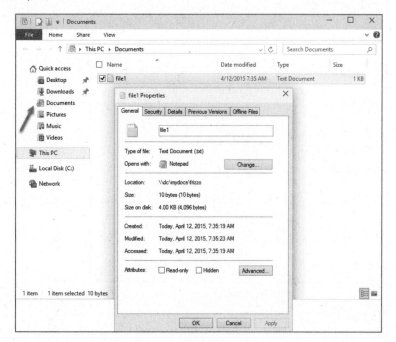

Each figure (more or less) demonstrates the same thing, another managed desktop feature of a feature that's already working for you—Offline Files, which I'll talk about in the next major section.

However, one point should be gleaned from these five figures. The behavior of Windows XP and later is different from that of Windows 2000. When a Windows XP or later machine uses a Redirected Folder, the entire contents are automatically cached offline. Thus, when the network is offline, your users still have total access to the files they need.

However, in Windows XP it's very, very clear that Offline Files is engaged. Oddly, in my opinion, it's less clear that it's on in Windows 7 and pretty unclear that it's engaged on Windows 8. If you look at the Windows 8 screen shot, you will see no immediate indication that the file is available offline.

In Windows 10 the notification that Offline Files is engaged got a little better (which is why I used an arrow to show it to you).

In all cases and operating systems, you need to right-click over the file and look at its properties to see that the location is truly on the server. Alternatively, savvy users could also right-click over the file and see that the "Always available offline" setting is already pre-checked and hard-coded on, as seen in Figure 10.6. Another strategy savvy users might utilize is to add the Folder Path column to the file list, as also seen in Figure 10.6.

FIGURE 10.6   The Folder Path column can show when a file is redirected. Additionally, you can force files to stay with the user offline by selecting "Always available offline."

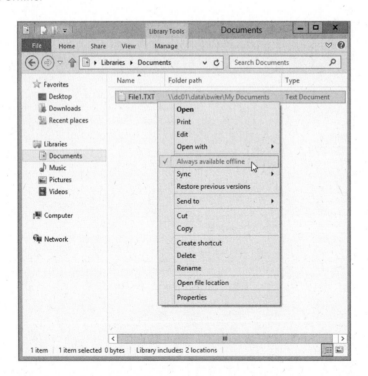

In this one guy's opinion, the icon indications in Windows XP were very clear, but in Windows 8 and later, I feel it's harder for a user to know if specific files are set to be used offline or not. More on this later, when I discuss this further in the section titled "Offline Files and Synchronization."

You will not see the arrows if you performed the procedure in the sidebar "How to Grant Administrators Access to Documents/My Documents (or Other Redirected Folders)" earlier in this chapter. However, you will see these arrows if you follow these instructions in the section "Administratively Assigned Offline Files" later in this chapter.

Redirecting the Start Menu and the Desktop

The Start Menu and Desktop might seem like weird items to redirect. However, in some cases, you might want to.

One case is in a common computing environment—such as a nursing station, library computer, or kiosk—where you want to make sure the same Start Menu and/or Desktop is always presented. Then, you can lock down the target location of the redirected items to ensure that they cannot be changed.

In cases like these, you specify a shared folder with Read-only access for the security group who will use it and Full Control for just one person who can change the Start Menu or Desktop (such as a fake account that no one uses within that security group). That way, no one in the affected group can normally change the common Start Menu or Desktop except for the administrative user of the bogus account you created, who has Full Control permissions over the share.

Instead of using the *%username%* variable, you fix the redirection to a specific shared folder and directory, as shown in Figure 10.7. Since all users are to use the same settings, there's no need to use *%username%*. Indeed, because you're locking the shared folder down as Read-only for the security group, the username is moot.

You could also argue that redirecting the Desktop is good for those who have users who think the Desktop is a perfect dumping ground for big documents. If you redirect the Desktop, you're reducing the size of the Roaming User Profile. It's up to you if you want to explore this option.

You'll find additional Group Policy settings regarding the configuration of the Start Menu in User Configuration ➢ Policies ➢ Administrative Templates ➢ Start Menu & Taskbar.

FIGURE 10.7   Use one static path to ensure that all Desktops receive the same setting.

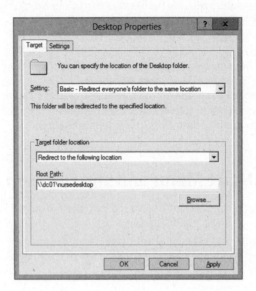

Redirecting the Application Data Folder

Because application designers can decide what to put in the Application Data folder in the profile, an administrator never knows what size this folder could grow to. When you redirect the Application Data folder, files—such as custom dictionaries or databases—can be firmly planted on the server instead of having to go up and back with each logon with the Roaming Profile.

I mentioned this in Chapter 9, but two other MVPs (Helge Klein and Aaron Parker) wrote a five-part article series about Roaming Profiles and also some items around folder redirection.

One of the key takeaways, which I firmly agree with, is that redirection of Application Data will cause end-user experience slowdown. This is because, again, Application Data could be really big. For instance, a (pretend) application called DogFoodMaker Reader might have an Application Data XML file that's 36MB to configure its "look and feel settings." If you had to read that file every time you launched DogFoodMaker Reader, and that file was redirected across the network, that could be a slowdown for the user at every launch.

That being said, Windows XP and later should automatically cache this folder when redirected and there shouldn't be any slowdowns.

But I have seen it, and the other MVPs proved it during their tests. Again, Parts 2 and 3 in this five-part article help illuminate the issue:

```
https://helgeklein.com/blog/2014/10/folder-redirection-impacts-ux-breaks-
applications/
```

And watch the webinar replay here:

```
http://stealthpuppy.com/webinar-replay-folder-redirection-impacts-user-
experience-breaks-stuff/
```

Group Policy Setting for Folder Redirection

There are only a handful of settings that control Folder Redirection. They're located in Computer *and* User Configuration ➢ Policies ➢ Administrative Templates ➢ System ➢ Folder Redirection. If there's a conflict between the User and Computer side, the Computer side will win.

Do Not Automatically Make Redirected Folders Available Offline (User Side Only)

As you're about to discover, Windows XP and later go the extra mile and automatically cache every scrap of data you have in, say, Documents/My Documents (or any other Redirected Folder). The idea is that if you're offline, you might need the data on the road. (Don't worry; we'll get to this topic in excruciating detail soon.)

This setting lets you disable that behavior. You might want to do this if you have laptops that travel to places with slow links because all of the user's data will be downloaded over that slow link. See the section "Using Folder Redirection and Offline Files over Slow Links" later in this chapter.

Because this policy is a User-side policy, it becomes difficult to implement on a system-wide level.

> If you really wanted to though, you could use either Group Policy Loopback policy processing or PolicyPak Admin Templates Manager, which enables you to take User-side policy settings and apply them to any computer you like. (Note that Loopback would deliver all User-side settings to the computer, where PolicyPak Admin Templates Manager would deliver exactly this setting, if that's what you wanted.)

Use Localized Subfolder Names When Redirecting Start Menu and My Documents (Both User and Computer)

This setting is one that you might consider using in a multilingual corporate environment. However, it's quirky.

The policy affects only legacy subfolders of My Documents (My Music, My Pictures, and My Videos) and the Start Menu subfolders. This policy *does not* affect the root Documents or Start Menu folders.

It supports the legacy scenario where users may be sharing data between a multilingual Windows Vista and later machine and a localized Windows XP machine. In that scenario, the legacy folder structure is preserved. The subfolders like My Music also map correctly to the localized name on the localized downlevel OS. The supported scenario is only when the user goes across the same languages—that is, Vista (and later) French to XP Localized French (but *not* across languages). This policy setting affects only Windows Vista and later. As you're about to discover, Windows XP and later go the extra mile.

Enable Optimized Move of Contents in Offline Files Cache on Folder Redirection Server Path Change (Computer Side)

This policy setting takes a bit of explanation to understand. First, it will only work on Windows 8 and later. Here's the idea: remember earlier, in Figure 10.3, we specified a location for our redirected folder, and in Figure 10.4, we saw the settings for that redirected folder.

Here's the scenario: you change your mind, and instead of using \\dc01\data you decide to use \\server12\mydata—a totally different server and/or share name.

Now what?

Well, if you were to change the server and share seen in Figure 10.3 from \\dc01\data to \\server12\mydata, the client suddenly has a lot of work to do. That's because when the change occurs, it's not like server DC01 magically makes contact with SERVER12 and transfers the files on behalf of the user. No, no, that's way too easy.

Instead, what happens is that the files are "re-stamped" locally on the Windows machine with the new server and share name. And eventually, in the background, all those files are copied up—from the Windows client up to the server. That's right—the Windows client is really in charge here.

So, if you change your mind and want users' redirected folders to live on \\server12\mydata instead of \\dc01\data, you don't have to do anything except change the UNC path within the Folder Redirection policy.

Except now you have a problem. And that problem is that all those Windows client computers that were using \\dc01\data to store their redirected folders are now madly copying gigabytes of files from your Windows client to \\server12\mydata.

If this copying takes place over a WAN link or slow network connection, and you have lots of client machines, you could have a major problem.

So, now we get to talk about this policy setting: **Enable optimized move of contents in Offline Files cache on Folder Redirection server path change**. If this setting is enabled, and your Windows 8 and later client machine gets this setting, and then you change your mind and want to use another server, something special happens. That is, your client machine won't do all that copying of gigabytes of files from your Windows client up to the new server. Instead, what happens is that all the redirected files are simply "repointed" to the new location—and no copying occurs.

In order for this magic to work, however, the files need to somehow already be copied (presumably by you, the Administrator) from the original server and share to the new server and share. And since you did this manually (server to server), when the client gets the signal to start using the new server and share, then—bingo. The data is already there, and the client just sees the files. No copying from your Windows 8 (or later) client to the new server required.

So, this means you will definitely need to have the files in place on the new server, with the right permissions and even the right time stamps on the files preserved. Again, the Windows client will be looking for differences, and if the files are newer on the updated server, then those files will be downloaded from the server back down to the client—causing the bandwidth issues you wanted to avoid in the first place.

> If you use Robocopy, you can copy ACLs and time stamps from the original server to the target server. Check out the switches /DCOPY:T and /COPYALL. Be sure to verify that both permissions and time stamps came across the way you expected.

Troubleshooting Redirected Folders

Occasionally, Folder Redirection doesn't work as it should. Or maybe it does. We'll check out some cases in which it appears not to be working but really is.

Windows XP (and Later) Fast Boot and Folder Redirection

If you see the message in Figure 10.8, you might initially think that Folder Redirection isn't working as it should. This event tells us that, by default, Fast Boot is enabled in Windows and Folder Redirection will not take effect until the next logon.

FIGURE 10.8   Fast Boot in Windows XP (and later) can delay Folder Redirection until multiple reboots.

With the default (that Fast Boot is enabled), Basic Folder Redirection needs two logons to take effect and Advanced Folder Redirection can take three logons to take effect (see Chapter 3 for more information).

Permissions Problems

Be sure that the user has access to the folder; specifically, make sure that the share you use for Folder Redirection is set so Authenticated Users has Full Control. Without it, you might encounter Event ID 502, as shown in Figure 10.9 Again, the idea is that there are some permissions problems—usually share-level permissions where the Authenticated Users group wasn't set up properly for Full Control (or Co-owner).

FIGURE 10.9   Windows 7 and later's Application log (event ID 502) shows that the user requires permissions to write to the share you set up.

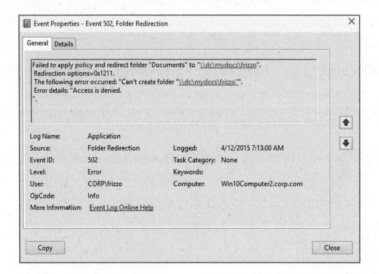

Use *GPResult* for Verification

First, make sure the user is being affected by the GPO you set up that contains your Folder Redirection policy. Use the GPResult tool we explored in Chapter 7, "Troubleshooting Group Policy." Figure 10.10 shows a snippet from the output of GPResult /R /v when Folder Redirection is working.

If no Folder Redirection policy displays in the output when you run GPResult /R /v, chances are the user is not being affected by the policy. Check to see if the user has permissions on the GPO for both Read and Apply Group Policy. If the user is getting the GPO as indicated via GPResult /R /v, also make sure that the target server is still available, that the share is still shared, and that the user has rights to write to that share and folder. Last, make sure the user isn't hitting a disk quota on the volume on which the shared folder resides, as this can generate mixed results.

FIGURE 10.10 GPResult can help you determine whether Folder Redirection is working.

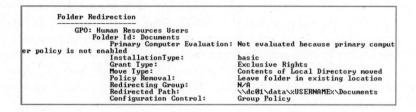

```
            Folder Redirection
            ------------------
                GPO: Human Resources Users
              Folder Id: Documents
                      Primary Computer Evaluation: Not evaluated because primary comput
er policy is not enabled
                      InstallationType:              basic
                      Grant Type:                    Exclusive Rights
                      Move Type:                     Contents of Local Directory moved
                      Policy Removal:                Leave folder in existing location
                      Redirecting Group:             N/A
                      Redirected Path:               \\dc01\data\%USERNAME%\Documents
                      Configuration Control:         Group Policy
```

Enabling Advanced Folder Redirection Logging

Folder Redirection has built-in detailed logging.

For Windows 7 and later, there are two places you'll want to check out for any interesting events:

- Windows Logs ➢ Application Log
- Application and Services Logs ➢ Microsoft ➢ Windows ➢ Folder Redirection ➢ Operational log

In Figure 10.11, you can see the Folder Redirection Operational log, where you can see what Folder Redirection is "thinking" as it goes about its business. If it stumbles, you can try to determine where that occurred. This log is always on and working all the time.

FIGURE 10.11 The Folder Redirection Operational log

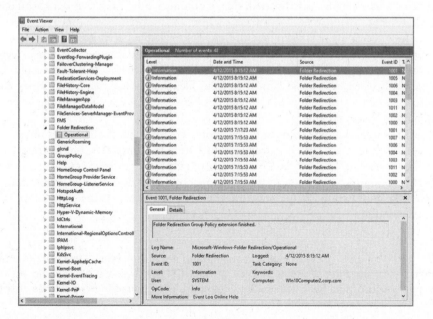

Offline Files and Synchronization

We've mitigated the amount of traffic our network will have to bear from Roaming Profiles by implementing Redirected Folders—especially for My Documents (for Windows XP) and Documents (for Windows Vista and later). But we still have another hurdle. Now that we're anchoring our users' data to the server, what's to happen if the server goes down? What happens if our network cable is unplugged? What if our top executive is flying at 30,000 feet? How will any of our users get to their data? The answer, in fact, comes from another feature—Offline Files.

The Offline Files feature seeks to make files within shares that are normally accessed online available offline. You can be sitting under a tree, on an airplane, in a submarine—anywhere—and still have your files with you.

Here's a brief overview of the magic: Once you enable a particular share to support the function, the client's Offline Files cache maintains files as they're used on the network. If the share is redirected, as we did in the previous section, Windows XP and later will automatically cache all the files within that share. No action or setup needed.

What's the payoff? When users are online and connected to the network, nothing really magical happens. Users continue to write files on the server as normal. However, in addition to the file writes at the server, the file writes get reflected in the local cache, too, as a protection to maintain the files in cache. Moreover, reads are satisfied from the client, thus saving bandwidth.

You can use Offline Files for any share you like and practically guarantee that the data users need is with them. Again, as we've noticed, Windows XP and later already seem to do something special when you're using Redirected Folders. That is, when these operating systems notice that a user's folder is redirected, they'll automatically make that data available offline for that folder.

Additionally, it's certainly possible to use Offline Files for public "common" shares. For example, an Administrator can set up shares for customer data, and a server can have a "general repository" from which multiple users can access files. We'll see how this works around the bend (especially when two people change the same file). Sounds bad, but it's not crazy-bad.

We'll also explore the differences in Offline Files between Windows XP and the newer cousins, Windows Vista and later.

So, for these examples, if you want to follow along, create a share called Sales on \\ DC01. You wouldn't normally stick shares on your Domain Controller, but for our working example here, it'll be just fine. Also, stick 10 text files—salesfile01.txt through salesfile10.txt—in there, so you can watch the reaction as various flavors of Windows try to touch these files. Finally, map a network drive over to \\DC01\sales from a test machine (say, Windows 10).

 There are three shares that you should not place Offline Files on. Don't use Offline Files with the SYSVOL or the NETLOGON share. Nor should you use Offline Files with the Profiles share you created in the previous chapter (more on this later).

Making Offline Files Available

When you set up any shared folder on your server, you'll be able to set up the Caching parameters. In Figure 10.12, which is on Windows Server 2016, you click over the share, click Advanced Sharing, and then click the Caching button (not shown) to get to the Offline Settings.

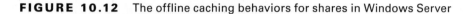

FIGURE 10.12   The offline caching behaviors for shares in Windows Server

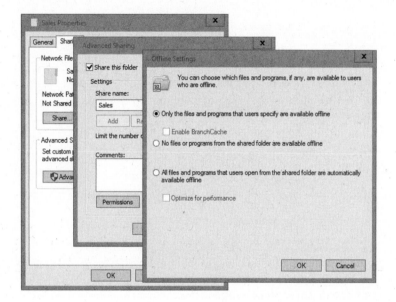

The default setting, "Only the files and programs that users specify are available online," may not be the most efficient setting for this feature. The three settings are described in the following sections.

Only the Files and Programs that Users Specify Are Available Offline

With this setting, users must specify which files they want to keep with them offline. They can do this in the Documents/My Documents folder by right-clicking a file (or, more commonly, a folder) and choosing "Always available offline" in Windows Vista and later (see Figure 10.13) from the context menu. The unofficial term for this is *pinning* a file, but you won't see that term in any official Microsoft documentation. Users can pin as many files as they like, though there is a "max space" limit that can be imposed by Group Policy (explored a little later). In Windows 8 and later, a "roundtrip/offline files" icon appears for files that are specifically told to be "Always available offline" by the user. In Figure 10.14, I've added a little arrow for emphasis.

FIGURE 10.13 Windows 8 and later shows files that are forced offline via "Always available offline."

FIGURE 10.14 Users can pin files by right-clicking them and making them available offline.

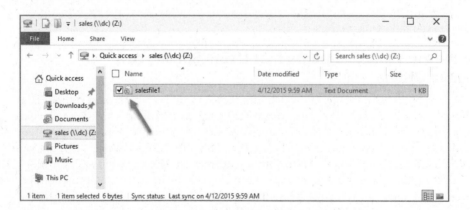

All Files and Programs that Users Open from the Shared Folder Are Automatically Available Offline

If you plan to use Offline Files for "regular shares" (as opposed to, say, Redirected Documents), you might want to select this option. When users access any files in a share with this setting, the files are copied and stored in a local cache on the workstation.

In Windows XP, by default, 10 percent of the C: hard drive space is used to maintain files in a first-in, first-out fashion.

For Windows Vista and later, that default is changed to 25 percent of free disk space when the drive cache is first created. This could mean that if you have only a little space left when the drive cache is created, it won't be 25 percent of the drive.

Before turning this on for any share or shares, be sure to read the sidebar "Autocache vs. Administratively Assigned Offline Files" a bit later.

Later in this chapter, in the section "Manually Tweaking the Offline Files Interface for Windows Vista and Later Machines," you can see this "25 percent of available disk space" formula in action. In Figure 10.24, later on, you'll see that my offline cache size is only 22.4 percent. This number was calculated because it was 25 percent of free disk space at that time.

For example, let's say you created a 1GB partition. Let's also say that you have 11 files, each 10MB in size, named FILE1.DOC through FILE11.DOC. You consecutively click each of them to open them and bring each into the cache. FILE1.DOC through FILE10.DOC are maintained in the cache until such time as FILE11.DOC is read. At that time, since FILE1.DOC was first in the cache, it is also the first to be flushed from the cache to make way for FILE11.DOC.

The files are ejected in a background thread called the CSC Agent. The agent periodically makes a pass over the cache, removing autocached files as necessary. If a Write operation grows the cache size beyond the established limit, it doesn't immediately evict the least recently used auto-cached file. The CSC Agent is only periodically brought into memory for execution.

Additionally, files can be pinned, as they were in the "Only the files and programs that users specify are available online" option. Pinned files don't count toward the cache percentage in Windows XP, but they *do* count toward pinned cache size in Windows Vista and later.

In all cases, though, pinned files are exempt from being flushed from the cache and are protected, and thus "always available" to your users when working offline.

You'll also note a suspicious-looking entry called "Optimize for performance."

For Windows XP machines, what this would do is look first in the local cache to save bandwidth when it can use either the locally cached version or the network version.

In Windows Vista and later, this setting literally does nothing, so there's never a reason to check it if you only have Windows Vista and later machines.

No Files or Programs from the Shared Folder Are Available Offline

If you choose this option, no files are cached for offline use, nor can they be pinned. This doesn't prevent users from copying the files to any other place they might have access to locally or to another network share they have access to that does have caching enabled.

Inside Windows 10 File Synchronization

Starting in Windows Vista, the Offline Files synchronization engine was rewritten in several ways to address some of the shortcomings of the Windows XP version. To save space, I've removed the nuts and bolts on how the Windows XP File Synchronization engine worked. You're welcome to find a previous edition of the book if you need those details. I have, however, left comparisons to Windows XP to help you understand why things have progressed since Windows XP.

Better Handling of Downed Shares

If a user was using a Windows XP machine and was leveraging several offline-enabled shares, and one network share went down, XP always thought the whole server went down. So, the upshot was that other shares (that you likely didn't set to be available offline) were then suddenly also not available. Again, that server itself really never went down—just one share on that server. Though bad, it doesn't sound *that* bad on first blush. But if you were using a domain-based DFS (Distributed File System), this could be a major problem—especially if you put your redirected My Documents folder in a domain-based DFS. If even one share in the DFS went offline, XP would assume the whole caboodle wasn't available.

In Windows Vista and later, things get smarter. If one share goes down, it doesn't assume (thankfully) that the whole server up and died. It just transitions that one share to offline and keeps trying the other shares. The same goes for domain-based DFS shares. If you can't access one, it doesn't assume the whole DFS up and died—it will make just the parts that appear to be offline now available offline.

 For more information on DFS, check out Microsoft's Distributed File System Technology Center at https://technet.microsoft.com/en-us/library/jj127250.aspx.

Better Handling of Synchronization

Synchronizing files got much smarter in Windows Vista and later. In Windows XP, you had to close *all* your open files (handles, really) in order for synchronization to start. In Vista and later, it's supposed to be "absolutely seamless," to quote a Microsoft employee. Since

Vista, changes are just synchronized in the background, and the user doesn't notice anything has happened. Of course, a file cannot be synchronized while it is held open for write. All files need to be closed, and then they're automatically synchronized.

Also, modified files, or files currently in conflict, continue to stay offline while all other files and folders are transitioned online. The conflicting files are transitioned online after the conflict is resolved.

No More Logon/Logoff Syncing Files Dialog Boxes

On Windows XP, when you logged off your machine, you would see your files synchronizing (provided "sync at logoff" was turned on). This was often confusing for a new user who had no training about what was going on. In Windows Vista and later, there are no more synchronization dialog boxes during logoff (or logon, for that matter).

In fact, with Windows Vista and later, there's no more synchronization of files at logoff. This is a big, big change from the Windows XP behavior.

I make note of this in case you have some reliance that absolutely guarantees that your files need to be synchronized at logoff in Windows Vista and later as they were in Windows XP.

You can read more about the engine internals using this article:

```
http://blogs.technet.com/b/netro/archive/2010/04/09/how-the-synchronization-
in-windows-7-offline-files-works.aspx
```

Better Transfer Technology

In Windows XP, the following file types cannot be cached:

* .PST (Outlook personal folder)
* .SLM (Source Library Management file)
* .MDB (Access database)
* .LDB (Access security)
* .MDW (Access workgroup)
* .MDE (Access compiled module)
* .DB? (Everything that has the extension .DB plus anything else in the third character, such as .DBF, is never included in the cache.)

In Windows Vista and later, those limitations are out the window. Not only is there a brand-new algorithm to help determine which files and directories are different, but also this same technology sends over *just the changed data* in a file. So, previous limitations on the types of files are gone. The new technology is called *Bitmap Differential Transfer (BDT)*. BDT is so amazing, it keeps track of what *disk pages* of the files have changed. So, if you change 8 bytes in a 2GB file, only that block of data is sent to the server, instead of the whole 2GB.

And, did you catch that Outlook .PST files are no longer unsupported? That is, you can use Offline Files with 2GB .PST files and Microsoft will support you.

The BDT technology only works when you change a file on the *client* and want to sync it back to the *server*. This is fine, as this is the usual case. However, should someone work directly on a file on the server (and hence, your file on Windows Vista and later is out of date), sadly, the entire file is pulled down to the client. BDT can't send just the changed bytes.

The other BDT limitation is that it isn't effective on *new* files. All of the new files are synchronized back to the server. And this can be a pitfall, because some applications (like Microsoft Word) insist on creating new files sometimes—even though you're editing what *feels* like the same .DOC file. There is a good blog entry here:

https://blogs.technet.com/filecab/archive/2006/07/11/441131.aspx

---

What's Really Happening in the Background?

The Offline Files service on Windows Vista and later automatically synchronizes files in several scenarios:

- If the user is working online, every five minutes the service "fills" in any sparsely cached files. This helps reduce the chance of transitioning offline and sparse files becoming unavailable to the user.

- Approximately one minute after user logon, the Offline Files service performs a full two-way synchronization of all content cached by that user. This is essentially the "logon sync" that was prominent in XP.

- Whenever a share transitions from offline to online, the Offline Files service performs a full two-way synchronization of that scope for each logged-on user.

Because of these background activities, the need to sync at logoff is reduced. Since sync-at-logoff is not officially exposed in either the Offline Files or Sync Center UI, users must manually sync using Sync Center before logging off if they wish to ensure that they have (in their local cache) all of the latest content from the server(s).

Better User Interface Design and Experience

Windows Vista and later doesn't show a pop-up and tell clients they are now offline. This is good. We don't need to scare the users any more than usual. Because the experience is now "seamless," there's nothing that needs to be said to the user.

There's no pop-up window at logoff telling users anything about the offline synchronization—because there is no synchronization at logoff. Synchronization is just quietly happening in the background. The downside, as stated earlier, is that Windows Vista and later might not have all the files synchronized when a user logs off if synchronization hasn't recently occurred.

Windows 8 and later does introduce a new UI feature, where you can manually select files and right-click to "Sync selected offline files," as seen in Figure 10.15.

FIGURE 10.15   Windows 8 users can manually "Sync selected offline files."

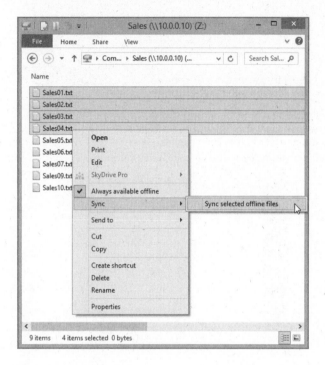

Windows Vista and later also has a new Sync Center. It's a complete redesign/rewrite, but it serves a similar function.

This Sync Center can be found in several ways. In Windows 8 and later, it's actually hiding in the system tray, as seen here:

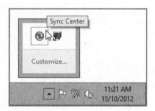

Double-clicking it will launch the Sync Center on Windows 8 and Windows 10.

You might want to consider always showing all icons so this important item isn't hidden by default.

In Windows 8, you can also launch it from the Start screen by typing **Sync** in the Search Apps bar under Settings and selecting Sync Center, as seen here:

In Windows 10, you can also launch it from the Start Menu by typing **Sync Center** in the "Search the web and Windows" box in the task bar, as seen here:

The idea of the Sync Center is that it's a common user interface where all files and devices can get synchronized. You can see the Sync Center in Figure 10.16.

FIGURE 10.16   The Windows Sync Center

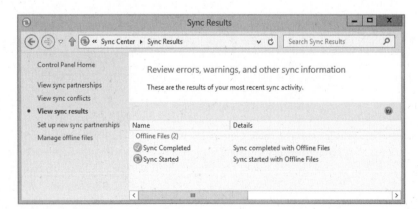

We'll explore more of the options here in the upcoming section "More to Tweak: Offline Files Sync Schedule."

Better Offline Experience (Unified "Namespace" View)

Here's a common problem scenario with Windows XP. Let's assume Xavier chose to make three files out of 10 available offline. When Xavier's computer went offline, the three files Xavier chose to keep offline were, of course, still there for Xavier to play with. However, the remaining seven files (which he didn't choose to make available offline) simply—poof!— disappeared. This behavior could be confusing for users who weren't sure what the heck was going on. Windows Vista and later use "ghosting" (which has nothing whatsoever to do with a product by Symantec).

Let's take the same scenario for Ben on his Windows 10 machine. If he chooses to make those files "Always available offline," then he gets a different experience. Windows Vista and later Offline Files Ghosting will show the files that are not available online as "ghosted," as shown in Figure 10.17. Ghosts are namespace holders; they are visually different and are grayed out, plus they have an X icon overlay showing that they're not accessible. The files are on the server, but because they're only on the server, Ben can't access the files until he reconnects and makes them available offline.

FIGURE 10.17   Files that are not available while offline show a "ghosted" icon with a little *X*.

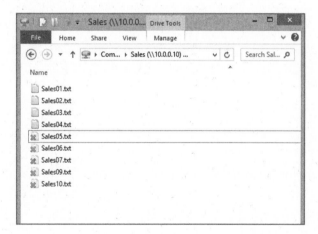

Here's a tip: You can learn the Online/ Offline status of specific files in two additional ways. One way is to use the Explorer Details pane, as seen in Figure 10.18.

In Windows 10, this behavior has changed to be more in line with the behavior of the OneDrive client (as shown in Figure 10.19). The idea is to reduce confusion for users so they don't accidently think that the files are available on the computer when they're really not present at all.

FIGURE 10.18   When you are offline, Windows 8 shows the files that are not currently cached.

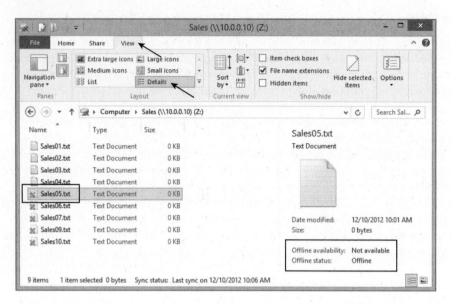

FIGURE 10.19   When you are offline, Windows 10 shows only the files that are currently cached.

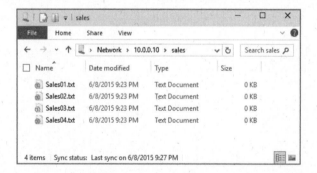

Additionally, you can add two columns to Explorer's list view. Try adding in the columns of "Offline availability" and "Offline status" to get a quick at-a-glance view.

Better Cache Encryption

In Windows XP, offline files had the ability to be encrypted. This way, if the laptop was stolen and the bad guy rooted around the file system, those offline files couldn't be seen in the clear. However, it wasn't long before it was realized that the encryption was based on the system account. Once you hijacked the system account, it was a trivial matter to see inside this encrypted cache. Just run a command prompt as the system account and—poof!—you're in!

First things first: you should be using some kind of full drive encryption on your machine (like BitLocker for Windows 7 and later) should it get stolen. But there's also an interesting part of offline files—the cache of offline files can be encrypted, too. In Windows Vista and later, offline files are now encrypted with the credentials of the first user who wants to encrypt a file. Using the user certificate is more secure (as hacking the system account is trivial), and this has a side benefit where multiple users of the same machine cannot see one another's encrypted cached files. However, this has a negative side detractor. What if Xavier and Ben both have access to an encrypted file on a file server? Actually, this isn't a big deal if both Xavier and Ben are online using different systems. XP and later all have provisions for multiple certificates to be inside a file, allowing both users access to the file.

The problem comes in if Xavier or Ben wants to use that file while offline, and they both use the same Windows 10 laptop. Here's where it gets sticky. If you choose to enable encrypted offline cache in Windows Vista and later, you cannot share the same encrypted file with another user *on the same machine* (when that file transitions to offline). Only the user who initially encrypted the file can access that file when offline. The file is encrypted using only one certificate, and that is the reason multiple users cannot access them offline.

Again, this isn't a problem when Xavier and Ben are *online* (and use the same Windows 10)—both users can continue to access the server version from the same client and get in using their certificate.

So, you could argue that with full disk encryption (like BitLocker), you wouldn't need to encrypt the offline files cache—and you'd be right. But it's interesting to know about the encrypted cache if you come across it in the user interface.

Other Random Offline Files Goodies

Here's a smattering of additional goodies you get with Offline Files in Windows Vista and later:

- One of the key problems with Windows XP's Offline Files feature was that it was never quite sure whether you were using a slow link. That is, if you had connectivity but the connection was slow, Windows XP would still use the file over the network rather than just use the copy it had cached locally. This would get really, really bad if you had lots of files over the network and even just looked at a thumbnail view (in Windows XP). The whole file would be downloaded. In Windows Vista and later, this can change. It's not changed by default, but see the section "Using Folder Redirection and Offline Files over Slow Links" a little later.

- Offline Files in Windows Vista and later is much smarter about detecting a slow-link condition—but only if you "explain" to Windows Vista and later what a slow link is; more on this later. And, during a slow link, it will simply transition to working offline. However, a user can, if desired, manually initiate a sync in the Sync Center. Finally, the user may force a transition to online mode if desired.

- You can, if you want, write your own scripts to manage the offline cache. Basically, all Offline Files functionality is scriptable and/or available via APIs. For instance, you could write a script to delete all files in cache, or initiate a sync, and other goodies as you wish. See the note after these bullet points for some additional geeky info about scripting.

- Windows XP had a 2GB maximum Offline Files limit. That limit is gone with Windows Vista and later.

- In case you missed it before, Windows Vista and later machines send only the changed bits back to the server—not the whole file. This is via the Bitmap Differential Transfer (BDT) protocol. And, this new BDT magic works with (get this) any SMB server share back as far as Windows 2000 Server! That's right. You don't need a Windows Server 2008 or Windows Server 2012 machine to take advantage of this. Your Windows Vista and later clients do all the magic on their own.

 Not to get too geeky, but the script support is implemented as a Windows Management Instrumentation (WMI) provider. You can learn more about the `Win32_OfflineFiles` class by looking here: http://tinyurl.com/yezar8j.

Roaming Profile Shares and Offline Cache Settings

You should not use any caching with shares for Roaming Profiles. If any caching is enabled for profiles, Roaming Profiles can fail to act normally. Roaming Profiles has its own "internal" caching that is incompatible with Offline Files caching.

The correct choice for Roaming Profile shares is to select "Files or programs from the share will not be available offline."

If you did set up a profile share in the previous chapter, go back to that share and ensure that it is set to disallow all caching.

Handling Conflicts

But a potential problem lies in these public "common" shares: what if someone on the road and someone in the office change the same document? In that event, the Windows XP Synchronization Manager or Windows Vista and later Sync Center will handle conflict resolution on behalf of the Offline Files component.

When conflicts occur between a file on the Windows 8 and later client and what's on the server, users see incredibly little information. Here's what they see:

Can you see it? Can you spot the icon change? I would argue that, unless you knew what you were looking for, it would be quite easily overlooked.

Windows XP and Windows 7 displayed a huge dialog box explaining that there were synchronization conflicts. But Windows 8 and later does away with this dialog and shows only a small triangle inside the Sync Center icon to alert the user of sync conflicts.

Once the user clicks the icon, the Sync Center opens and there is more info to be found, as seen in Figure 10.20. Clicking on the link, as seen in Figure 10.20, or clicking "View sync conflicts" (also in Figure 10.20) will show the conflicts that occurred. The user is then presented with a list of items that need resolution. A user can then view the options to resolve the conflict, as seen in Figure 10.21.

In Figure 10.22, the user is presented with what has occurred on this computer and also on the server.

FIGURE 10.20   The Windows Sync Center shows users' file conflicts.

FIGURE 10.21   Users can manually resolve file conflicts.

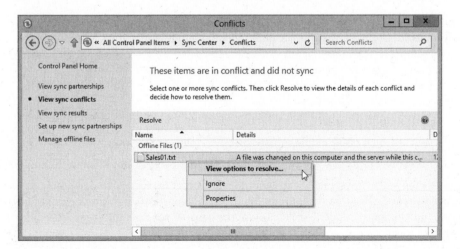

FIGURE 10.22   Conflicts are presented to the user at sync time.

As you can see, the user can inspect the contents of each version of the file, although that's usually not much help because there's no "compare changes" component to this resolution engine, and there's no way to "merge" the documents. But you can paw through the file yourself if you can remember where the last change was. It's not much, but it's a start.

In general, the Offline Files handler is fairly smart. If a file is renamed on either side (network or local cache), the engine wipes out the other instance of the file (because it thinks it's been deleted) and creates a copy of the new one. Hence, it appears a rename has occurred.

Client Configuration of Offline Files

You might want to default your shares to "All files and programs that users open from the share will be automatically available offline"—also known as Autocache. We're about to explore what happens if you leverage Autocache, but before we dive into it, be sure to read the sidebar "Autocache vs. Administratively Assigned Offline Files."

If you decide to use Autocache, you can configure clients to use Offline Files with the aforementioned setting in three ways:

- Take the "do nothing" approach.

- Run around to each client and manually specify settings.

- Use Group Policy to do the work (insert fanfare music here).

The following sections explore the options clients can set on their own computers (or with your assistance). Then, in the later section "Using Group Policy to Configure Offline Files (User and Computer Node)," we'll explore the broader scope of GPOs to see what sort of configuration we can do.

Another option is that you can script your changes via the Offline Files WMI provider described earlier. Of course, that only works for Windows Vista and later clients.

The "Do Nothing" Approach

If you do absolutely nothing at all, your clients will start to cache the files for offline use the first time they touch files in a share. This is called autocaching. The underlying Offline Files behavior is the same for all versions of Windows. However, as expected, some subtle differences can be found in each.

Autocache vs. Administratively Assigned Offline Files

In previous editions of the book, and in some articles I wrote, I suggested that you simply enable "All files and programs that users open from the share will be automatically available offline" for every share. In retrospect, I think I could have given you better advice.

Here's why.

Once that setting is enabled on a share, *everyone* who connects to this share will autocache the files. So, for instance, if you set Autocache on the Sales share, an errant Human Resources person just poking around and opening up that share will start to stream those Sales files into the cache—even if that person doesn't plan on using them. Sure, eventually those files will be ejected after nonuse, but why get the user into a situation where he's merely looking at a share and then downloading all the junk in it? (Of course, it isn't junk to the Sales folks—but the HR person certainly doesn't care about it much.)

A better approach is to specify that Sales folks need to autocache the Sales share. And you can't do that directly in the share. To do that, you'll need a policy setting named **Administratively Assigned Offline Files**. Now, before I get too far ahead of myself, I will say that enabling this policy setting takes work. That is, every time you create a new share for the Sales folks, you'll have to edit the GPO and specify the additional share. That way, only the Sales folks will autocache the Sales shares. Ditto for HR and other folks around your Active Directory.

So, setting Autocache on all your shares (except the Profiles share) sounds like a good thing—but it's a better thing (if you can keep on top of it) if you hone in on the focus of *who* autocaches *which* shares with **Administratively Assigned Offline Files,** explored a bit later in the chapter.

Windows Servers acting as client computers are not enabled to cache files; this feature is specifically disabled in the operating system but can be turned on if desired. See the sidebar "Offline Files for Windows Server."

Keep this difference in mind if you plan to enable caching for your shares to use Offline Files. In the examples in this section, we have a share called Sales, which contains some important files for our Sales users. For this example, again, ensure that the "All files and programs that users open from the share will be automatically available offline" caching option is set on the share on our server.

Note that Windows XP and Windows Vista behavior here is definitely different. To save space, I've cut it from this edition of the book. If you need to know precisely how Windows XP and Windows Vista will behave, you'll need to refer to previous editions of the book.

After connecting to the share and opening a specific file (Windows 7 and later), you can see which files it cached. It's more than a little cumbersome to see the list of offline files.

Remember, you have several options to see what's happened:

- In the Details view, add in the column "Offline availability."

- On the Start menu, type **Offline**, and in the Settings category, select "Manage offline files."

- If you're already in the Sync Center (see our discussion earlier), you can click "Manage offline files," as seen earlier in Figure 10.16.

Control Panel also has a search bar. You can type **offline** there and it will take you to the Offline Files Control Panel applet.

Then, you can click through and hit the button "View your offline files." You'll see a screen shot of this a bit later in Figure 10.24.

Then, click through the mapped network drives and find Sales. Tucked away in the far right is a column labeled Offline Availability (though you might have to move around the columns a bit). In Figure 10.23, you can see the Availability column.

FIGURE 10.23   The Windows Vista and later Offline Availability column shows you the status of your files.

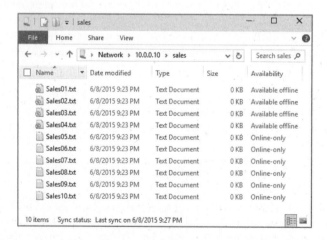

Running Around to Each Client to Tweak Offline Files and the Synchronization Manager

If you wanted to, you could teach your users how to manage Offline Files themselves. (I'll wait a minute or two until the laughter stops.) Okay, maybe not, but if you ever needed to manage a computer that was using Offline Files but not using Group Policy, here's how you'd do it.

Offline Files for Windows Server

By default, Offline Files is enabled only on the workstation versions of the operating system.

It can, however, be enabled via the Offline Files Control Panel applet. But you'll also need the Desktop Experience Feature installed using Server Manager. Without the Desktop Experience feature, there is no access to the Sync Center UI.

Manually Tweaking the Offline Files Interface for Windows Vista and Later Machines

Once you're in the Sync Center, you can select "Manage offline files" and see what's in Figure 10.24.

FIGURE 10.24 You can manually turn off Offline Files with Local Administrator credentials.

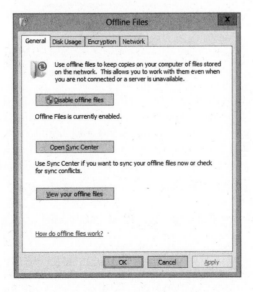

General   On the General tab, you can select "Disable offline files," which, when presented with Local Administrator credentials, will do just that.

You can also open the Sync Center (previously discussed) or view all the files from all shares that are available offline.

Disk Usage   The Disk Usage tab has two main items: changing the disk usage limits and flushing the cache with "Delete temporary files." This only deletes any unpinned files from the cache. You can see this in Figure 10.25.

FIGURE 10.25   You can use the sliders to manage your hard disk usage.

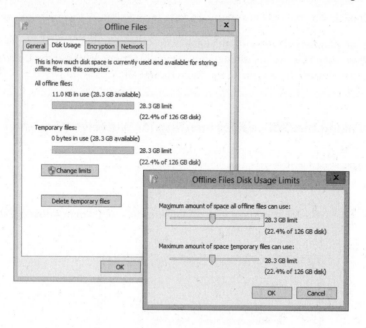

In Windows Vista and later, both pinned files and automatically cached files must fit neatly into a container size you specify. The first slider (shown in Figure 10.25) is the total space that all offline files will use on this machine (including pinned files). The lower slider is just for automatically cached files. You can use Group Policy to guarantee these numbers via the policy setting **Limit disk space used by offline files** (for Windows Vista and later only).

Encryption   This tab literally has only two buttons on it: Encrypt and Unencrypt. Here, in the user interface, a user can do this manually. You'll also see later that Offline Files supports a Group Policy setting (**Encrypt the Offline Files cache**) that causes the cache to become encrypted.

I described this already, but here's the breakdown: when that policy setting is enabled, or the Encrypt button is clicked, the Offline Files service performs the encryption automatically on behalf of the first user who logs on, shortly after he logs on. But what if multiple users use the same Windows Vista and later machine, say, as a traveling laptop?

If User 1 encrypts the redirected Documents folder, everything is hunky-dory for any user on a particular Windows Vista and later machine. So, User 2, User 3, and so on who are on the same machine will have no problems accessing that file—that is, provided the file is network accessible. But, when the machine is offline, User 1 (the one who encrypted the file cache) will be the only user who can access those Offline Files while offline.

That's a subtle behavior, but it may be important if you share a specific laptop, encrypt the offline files that reside on a public share, and expect everyone to be able to read it when those users are offline.

Network   The Network tab allows you to choose how often you want to verify you're working on a fast or slow connection.

In Figure 10.26 you can see Windows 8's Network tab.

FIGURE 10.26   The Offline Files Network tab

You'll see that "On slow connections, automatically work offline" is both checked on and grayed out. What's especially weird is that not even an administrator can modify the setting.

One more note here: This setting is a bit irregular. *Any* user of the client machine is allowed to change that time value setting. And that time value affects *all* users of the client computer. The rationale is that the setting must be per-machine to correspond with the per-machine cache, but any user of the client should be able to set it.

And because on Windows 7 and later, the check box is automatically checked, all users on the same machine can optionally manually change how often the machine looks for a slow connection.

But here's the trick about slow connections: you have to be ridiculously specific and explain to it (like to a two-year-old) exactly what servers and what shares and what speeds constitute a slow network connection. To determine if a link is slow, Windows 7 and later uses link latency (basically, the "round-trip time") it takes for a packet to go back and forth. It's a pretty coarse measurement, which we'll talk about a little later.

The Group Policy setting you'll use to teach Windows 7 and later what is defined as a slow link is called **Configure slow-link mode**. I'm telling you this so you don't get confused with the unfortunately named **Configure Slow link speed** (which is a Windows XP–only setting).

More to Tweak: Offline Files Sync Schedule

Again, the Sync Center is where users can go to see what has synchronized or to manually kick off a synchronization. There are, however, some tweakable features.

I've already expressed how Windows Vista and later positively do not synchronize files at logoff (whereas Windows XP did). However, you can specify some options for the user in order to dictate when Offline Files performs its syncing.

In the Sync Center, click the Schedule button, as seen in Figure 10.27. When you do, you'll be presented with the "Which items do you want to sync on this schedule?" dialog box, also shown in Figure 10.27. The check box called "Sync item name" is intended for selecting All or Nothing.

FIGURE 10.27 The Windows Vista and later Sync Center has options you can set for each item under Schedule.

Next, you'll be asked, "When do you want this sync to begin?" and you can choose "At a scheduled time" or "On an event or action." (This screen isn't shown here in the book.) You can see the options for "At a scheduled time" in Figure 10.28 (with its "More scheduling options" dialog box, also shown). You can see the options for "On an event or action" in Figure 10.29 (with its "More scheduling options" dialog box shown).

FIGURE 10.28   The time-based schedule synchronization options

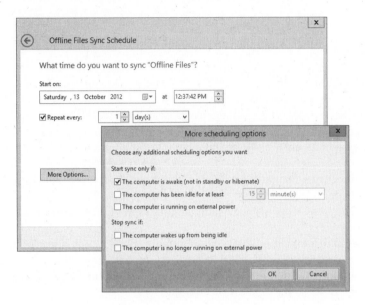

FIGURE 10.29   The action-based schedule synchronization options

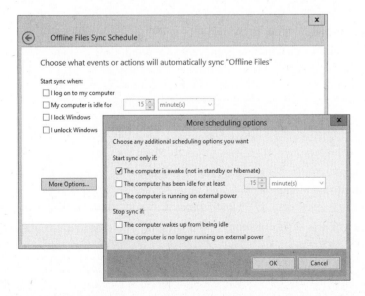

Again, these are optional settings for each Windows Vista and later machine. The bad news is that there is currently no direct way to dictate these settings using Group Policy.

Using Folder Redirection and Offline Files over Slow Links

Windows wants to make you happy.

Well, not you. But your users when they're over slow links.

Let's think about what happens when a user utilizes a private folder like a redirected Documents/My Documents when using Offline Files over a slow link, and also the consequences of using a regular share, like our Sales share.

The "normal case" is easy. That is, a user has already been to the main office and received a GPO that says "Use Folder Redirection for your Documents/My Documents folder," and the system automatically creates a copy of the files in the Offline Files cache. Then, when the user is traveling with his Windows machine, the computer simply uses the local copy before using the network. Again—that's the super-easy, most-used case for Redirected Folders plus Offline Files.

The hard stuff happens when we are using "regular shares" with Offline Files.

What happens then?

Or, what happens to a user if he shows up in another country with a totally new laptop handed to him—and he never, ever downloaded anything into his Offline Files cache?

In the following sections, we cover those hard cases. The bad news is that you will see different behaviors for different versions of Windows:

- Windows 2000
- Windows XP
- Windows Vista
- Windows 7, Windows 8, and Windows 10.

And the worse news is that I'm only going to cover Windows 7 and later here. For previous operating systems, refer to previous editions of the book.

Before we continue, let's quickly define what a "slow link" is in the first place. Windows 7 and later define a slow link when one of two things is true:

- It takes a long time for a response when communicating from the client to the server and back again. That's called *latency*. Windows 7 has a slightly different definition of how slow it will tolerate vs. Windows 8 and 10. We'll get to that in a bit.

- The actual bandwidth is slower than a defined value. This is about "how much" data you can push through the pipe. As you'll learn, Windows 7 and later don't use bandwidth (by default), but they can "learn" to use it. Again, more on this later.

But the point right now is pretty simple: there are only two things we care about when it comes to our network's speed—latency and bandwidth. Stay tuned for the rest of the story.

Now, here's a big ol' warning for this whole "Using Folder Redirection and Offline Files over Slow Links" section. I was able to test some, but not all, configurations between Windows clients and fast- and slow-link scenarios. I'm going to describe what should happen, but your experiences may vary. Offline Files does have a (well-earned) reputation for having odd and sometimes unexpected behaviors. My goal here is to document what I know *should* happen, even if it doesn't always happen that way for you.

Synchronizing over Slow Links with Redirected My Documents

The first place you can run into trouble is if the user has never synchronized on a particular machine. For example, Charles is a member of the Marketing group. He's given a generic "workgroup" laptop to take to an emergency meeting in China. But Charles doesn't synchronize with the fast LAN before he runs out the door to catch his plane. Of course, he won't have any files while he's on the long flight to China.

But worse, when he gets to China and uses the VPN over a slow link, what is going to happen? Will it be a long login time for Charles? What will he see and what won't he see?

Remember: the Group Policy engine won't process new and changed Folder Redirection directives when the Group Policy engine learns that the link speed is less than 500Kb. You learned in Chapter 3 about the Group Policy engine and how it won't process many items over a slow link, including Group Policy Software Installation directives, Folder Redirection directives, and others.

So if Charles is using a slow link, then Folder Redirection will not engage Folder Redirection (see Chapter 3). Therefore, Charles won't see anything in his Documents/My Documents folder when in China (over a slow link).

Now, Charles could just map a network drive over to his Documents/My Documents and grab the files he needed that way. That would totally work, and, hence, Charles is no longer in the cold.

Again, to be super clear, we're talking about a unique case: Charles has a totally new laptop, and he's using it over a slow link for redirected My Documents. Arguably, this doesn't happen that often.

So, what if you wanted Charles to automatically "work" with this weird case and ensure that he is able to get to his redirected Documents/My Documents the very first time?

If you'd like to make redirected Documents a reality over slow links (for users who have never synchronized with the LAN), you'll need to set up a GPO that affects target computers.

You'll set up a GPO that enables the policy under the Computer Configuration ➢ Policies ➢ Administrative Templates ➢ System ➢ Group Policy ➢ **Folder Redirection policy processing** policy setting and, inside, set it to "Allow processing across a slow network connection."

A-ha! So this setting will now tell our Windows XP and later machines, "Go ahead and do that Folder Redirection thing, even over a slow link, even if I have never synchronized before."

So, again, if you don't enable this policy setting, users won't see their files in Documents/My Documents if they use a slow connection.

The only time they would see stuff in Documents/My Documents is if they have already performed a synchronization with the Synchronization Manager before they left for the trip.

Whew. Complicated!

Now, let's assume you had the forethought to enable the Folder Redirection policy processing policy setting and, inside, set it to "Allow processing across a slow network connection."

What happens now when Charles starts up for the first time in China? And what happens if Charles has 12GB of stuff in his Documents/My Documents folder?

We have two cases to consider. Did Charles grab a Windows 7 laptop or a Windows 8 or later laptop before he ran off to China?

Windows 7 Latency Behavior   If Charles grabbed a Windows 7 laptop, then Windows 7 will look at the network connections and inspect the wire. Windows 7 will then try to evaluate the latency—that is, how long communication between the client and server and back again takes.

If the latency is less than 80ms "round trip," then Windows 7 says "Awesome! That's fast enough for me!" and all 12GB of Charles's files will come down over the network—even if the overall bandwidth (pipe size) is very little and slow.

If the latency is greater than 80ms "round trip," then Windows 7 says "Whoooa Nelly! That's too slow for me!" and all of Charles's files will stay over the network. The share transitions to Offline status.

Windows 8 and Windows 10 Latency Behavior   If Charles grabbed a Windows 10 laptop, then Windows 10 will look at the network connections and inspect the wire. Windows 10 will also try to evaluate the latency.

If the latency is less than 35ms "round trip," then Windows 10 says "Awesome! That's fast enough for me!" and all 12GB of Charles's files will come down over the network—even if the overall bandwidth (pipe size) is very little and slow.

If the latency is greater than 35ms "round trip," then Windows 10 says "Sorry, Charley! That's too slow for me!" and all of Charles's files will stay over the network. The share transitions to Offline status.

So both Windows 7 and Windows 8 (or Windows 10) check just that one item: latency. Neither Windows 7 nor Windows 8 (or Windows 10) cares if the bandwidth pipe is teeny-weeny or jumbo huge. It only cares about latency—by default.

Now, note that you could have set the policy setting **Do not automatically make redirected folders available offline**, which will return clients to the older "Windows 2000–style" behavior. That is, redirected folders like Documents/My Documents will simply not be downloaded and utilized with Offline Files.

Remember, though, that unless users copy the files they need locally or manually pin them, the files in Documents/My Documents will not be available offline.

Now that we've got a grip on how to deal with Folder Redirection and Offline Files for the special folders like Documents/My Documents, let's move on to Folder Redirection and Offline Files for "regular shares."

Synchronizing over Slow Links with Regular Shares

Let's look at another example.

Sven and Ben are sometimes in the office and sometimes on the road. Sven uses a Windows 7 laptop. Ben uses a Windows 10 laptop. Clever, right?

When in the home office, all employees plunk files into the share \\east_server\sales-figures, which is configured to use "All files and programs that users open from the share will be available offline."

They all use a file called Frankfurt.doc. Because Sven uses Windows 7 and Ben uses Windows 10, their files are automatically synchronized in the background.

Sven and Ben leave for Frankfurt, Germany, to woo a prospective account. During the time that Sven and Ben are on the plane, Harold (who's back in the office) modifies the Frankfurt.doc file with up-to-the-minute information on their prospective customer.

Sven and Ben get drunk on the plane ride over and sleep the entire way. They don't even crack open their laptops to look at the Frankfurt.doc file. In short, they don't modify their copies on the laptops; only Harold modifies a copy at the home office.

Sven and Ben check into different hotels and use the VPN to connect to the home office. They all want to ensure that the latest copy of Frankfurt.doc on the server is downloaded to their laptops to present to their client in the morning.

The Windows 7 and Later Synchronization Engine over Slow Links

Sven uses the VPN and connects back to the office. Will Frankfurt.doc (and the other potentially large files in the share) automatically come down over the slow link?

The answer is maybe. But under most normal circumstances, the answer is no.

If Sven looks at the share in Large or Extra Large icon view, then, yes, he's officially "touched the files" and it comes down. If Sven looks at the share in List or Small Icon view, then Windows 7's Explorer doesn't seem to officially "touch" the file to bring it down.

Now, it is possible that Windows 7 could make a "snap judgment" call and say, "Actually, Sven, the link *is* fast. Even though *you* think it's slow, *I* can tell the link is really fast."

So, what does Windows 7 "know"? Again, Windows 7 checks out the "latency speed" of the line. Latency is, more or less, the round-trip time that a Ping packet takes. If that round-trip speed is 80ms or less, the link is considered "fast." If it's 80ms or more, then it's considered "slow."

Latency is kind of a weird measurement to bank on, though. Technically, your link could be 30Kbps (half the speed of a dial-up modem from 1996), but the latency could be super-zippy. Windows 7 will then cheerfully interpret that type of connection as a "fast connection" and download all the files. Not so smart after all. But you can teach them (Windows 7, Windows 8, and Windows 10) how to be smart-er.

Ben on his Windows 10 machine has a different value. The Latency value on Windows 8 and Windows 10 is hard-coded to check at a 35ms round-trip.

So, it's conceivable that Ben automatically gets the Frankfurt.doc but Sven doesn't!

Or, vice versa!

Oh if only there was a way to make this more predictable! (Hint, hint: Read onward.)

Teaching Windows 10 How to React to Slow Links

Let's recap what we've learned so far:

* Windows 7 thinks that all links are fast unless the link's latency is less than 80ms.

* Windows 8 and Windows 10 think that all links are fast unless the link's latency is less than 35ms.

These facts of life are not ideal. Using latency round-trip speed as the only data point might not be the best idea.

You might want some shares on certain servers to act as "fast"—always—and yet other shares on specific servers, as "slow"—always. Or some shares to act as fast under certain conditions and slow under other conditions.

The other piece of the puzzle we need to explore is some special magic that Windows 7 and later clients will do when they have detected a slow link and (theoretically) wouldn't be able to talk back to the servers.

Let's dig in.

Using the Configure Slow-Link Mode Policy Setting

Again, using only latency to decide if a link is slow or not appears a little silly and short-sighted. But Microsoft did this because it's determined very, very quickly. If the latency is too big, then, bingo...the link is evaluated to be slow, and it's transitioned offline. But it doesn't need to only use latency. As Yoda said to Obi-Wan, "There is another."

You can reteach your Windows 7 and later four things in order to understand how you've defined "slow":

* The name of the server with the share(s)

* The name of the share(s)

* What constitutes slow latency (round-trip time for Ping)

* What constitutes a slow link (speed)

Once your Windows client "gets" this, it starts being *much* smarter about not down-loading humongous files over slow links.

You do this with the **Configure slow-link mode** policy setting located in Computer Configuration ➢ Policies ➢ Administrative Templates ➢ Network ➢ Offline Files, as seen in Figure 10.30. Figure 10.31 shows an example of how to precisely set up one server's characteristics; you can see \\server1 and share1 being set to a slow link speed of 600Kbps and Latency of 50ms.

So, when should you use throughput or latency thresholds?

Well, this policy can be set to use *either* throughput *and/or* latency thresholds. So, you can decide to use throughput, latency, or both.

What should you use? Throughput, latency, or both? The short answer: both.

FIGURE 10.30 The description of the **Configure slow-link mode** policy setting expresses this, but you can specify a single lone * (asterisk) to turn on slow-link mode for all shares on all servers.

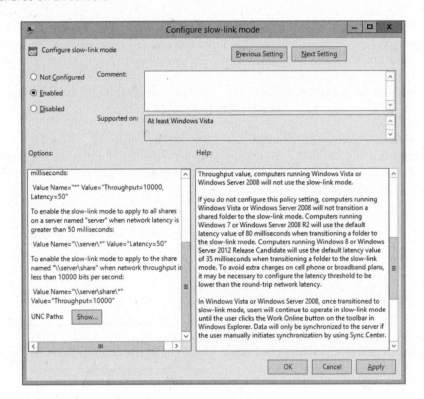

FIGURE 10.31 Specify Throughput = for 600Kbps and Latency = 50 for 50ms, for instance, to define your slow link threshold. Note that all paths should have an ending slash (\) and asterisk (*) even if you're just specifying one server and one share.

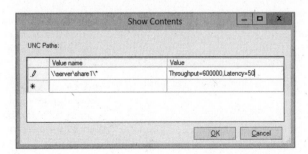

Sven on Windows 7 could have a dog-slow link but peppy latency. So, by default, Windows 7 (unfortunately) sees that as "A-OK" and, *oops!*, tons of files downloaded by accident (if, say, he used Large Icons to view the files).

And what about Ben on Windows 10? He could have a pretty fast network (bandwidth wise), and *oops!*, not get the Frankfurt.doc file at all.

So using this policy setting, **Configure slow-link mode**, we can guarantee that Windows 7 and later will uniformly accept our meaning of what slow means.

To use this policy setting, you add additional items for each server and share combination you needed to define individually. Or, you can also perform this operation en masse based on specific servers or, heck, have all Windows Vista and later clients react to all servers the same way.

Table 10.1 gives you some examples of values you might want to specify using the **Configure slow-link mode** policy setting when entering in the "Enter the name of the item to be added" block and the "Enter the value of the item to be added" block and what the result would be if you used these suggestions.

 A good blog entry on the **Configure slow-link mode** policy setting can be found at http://tinyurl.com/ydoekex.

TABLE 10.1 Configure Slow-Link Mode policy setting examples

The "Enter the name of the item to be added" block	The "Enter the value of the item to be added" block	Result of these settings
\\server1\share1*	Throughput = 600000, Latency = 50	Only \\server1\share1 would react for Windows Vista+ clients affected by this policy setting. The share will automatically transition to offline if the speed is less than 600Kbps or the latency is less than 50ms.
\\server1*	Throughput = 128000	All shares on \\server1 would react for Windows Vista+ clients affected by this policy setting. The share will automatically transition to offline if the speed is less than 128Kbps. Note that Windows Vista+ clients affected by this policy would not test for latency.

The "Enter the name of the item to be added" block	The "Enter the value of the item to be added" block	Result of these settings
**	Throughput = 400000, Latency = 20	All shares on all servers would react for Windows Vista+ clients affected by this policy setting. All shares would automatically transition to offline if the speed was less than 400Kbps or the latency was less than 20ms. Note the trailing star (*) at the end of the expression to signify all shares.
**	Latency = 30	All shares on all servers would react for Windows Vista+ clients affected by this policy setting. All shares would automatically transition to offline if the latency were 30ms. Note the trailing star (*) at the end of the expression to signify all shares.

> None of the **Configure slow-link mode** values require quotes, which can be confusing if you read the Explain text in the policy setting.

Windows 7 and later Offline Files Background Sync

Windows 7 and later clients have a little something special going on when they've detected that a share is "too slow" to use.

As I've mentioned, the official term for when the share automatically pops offline is *Transitioned to Offline.*

This means that normal requests to the share, which has transitioned to offline, simply won't work.

But there is some extra magic here: Windows 7 and later will still try to synchronize any changed data in offline files back up to the server in the background—every 360 minutes (with a 0–60-minute random offset).

Here's why this is a cool idea: the share transitions to "offline" because Windows is saying, "Look, User, if you try to grab huge files from my dog-slow network, it's going to hurt everyone using that dog-slow connection. So, I'll just turn that share 'off' to you, until you're on a fast connection again."

But what happens if a user then makes changes to the local version of the file (say, she gets 10 new emails in a big PST file) or changes one line in a giant AutoCAD file or just adds a sentence to a Word doc? Well then, you'll want to make sure that those changes (and only those changes) are delivered to the server for safekeeping (and merged with the original file).

So, Windows 7 and later have this superpower. It will automatically sync up all the new stuff in the background every 360 minutes or so—even over a slow link. That way, users won't auto-download big new files from the "offline" share, but they will auto-upload any small changes from the documents they already have in their cache.

This Windows 7 and later behavior is configurable via Group Policy using the **Configure Background Sync** policy setting, as you'll see in a bit.

You may be asking yourself, "What if a user needs to get to a new (big) file on a share? Can he do that, even though the share now appears to be offline?" Yes. I'll show you how to do that in a second with the Work Offline/Work Online button.

Using Group Policy to Configure Offline Files (User and Computer Node)

Asking users to configure their own Offline Files settings can be—to say the least—confusing. This isn't the fault of Microsoft—there are just a lot of options to play with. The good news is that most Offline Files settings can be delivered from up on high.

The policy settings for the Offline Files are found in two places in the Group Policy Management Editor. Some settings affect users specifically. To get to those settings, fire up the Group Policy Management Editor and traverse to Computer Configuration ➢ Policies ➢ Administrative Templates ➢ Network ➢ Offline Files, as shown in Figure 10.32.

Nearly all the same settings are also found in the User side of the house, at User Configuration ➢ Policies ➢ Administrative Templates ➢ Network ➢ Offline Files, as shown in Figure 10.33.

These settings give you flexibility in how you configure Offline Files. You can mix and match—within the same GPO or from multiple GPOs. The general rule is that if both computer and user settings are specified on the target, the computer settings win.

In the following sections, I'll briefly detail what each Offline Files policy setting does. Since most of the policies overlap in both User and Computer nodes, I'll discuss all the User and Computer configuration settings and then focus on those that apply only to the Computer configuration settings.

I will be discussing all the settings that will apply only to Windows 10, 8, and 7 first.

I will also talk about settings specific to Windows Vista and later. Then I will describe policy settings that are older and continue to work on Windows 7 and later.

But what I won't be talking about is a wider variety of settings that *only* work on Windows XP. For that information, you'll need to pick up a previous edition of the book.

So, in other words, I won't be describing every policy setting in Figure 10.32 and Figure 10.33.

FIGURE 10.32   You'll find a slew of Offline Files options under the Computer node.

FIGURE 10.33   Many Offline Files options can also be found under the User node.

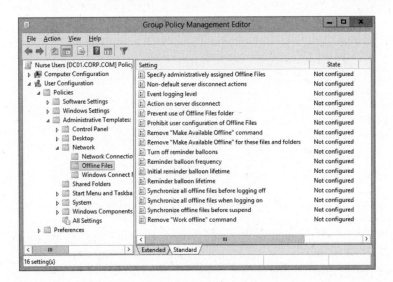

Configure Background Sync

We just talked about **Configure Background Sync,** which is a policy for Windows 7 and later.

Again, the brief recap is that when Windows 7 and later shares have transitioned to offline, then Windows will still keep local files updated with the server, even on a slow link, "every so often."

Although it's true that most of the time the changes will originate from the laptop and need to be saved to the server, there are also going to be times when the data on the server has changed and it needs to update the laptop. Background Synchronization is indeed a two-way sync.

Remember: when changes go up to the server, they're quick, because only the changed blocks are uploaded. However, changes from the server *down* to the laptop could be slower, because in those cases, the whole file needs to come down.

On Windows 7, this process happens every 360 minutes, by default, with a random offset of 0–60 minutes.

On Windows 8 and Windows 10, this process happens every 120 minutes, by default, with a random offset of 0–60 minutes.

There's also an (almost secret) check box in this policy setting: "Enable Background Sync for shares in user selected 'Work Offline' mode," as seen in Figure 10.34. This setting also ensures that when users use a Windows 7 machine to manually flip a share to "Offline," those shares are *also* synchronizing changed data as well.

FIGURE 10.34　Use this policy setting to configure Windows 7's (and later) slow-link background sync.

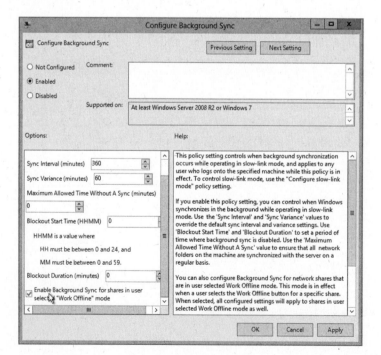

Note that every user on Windows 7 and later is affected by this policy setting, because it affects the Computer side.

Enable Transparent Caching

Another policy, which only works for Windows 7 and later clients, is **Enable Transparent Caching**.

This policy is another Windows 7 and later optimization, but it must be enabled for it to work. In short, if you enable the **Enable Transparent Caching** policy setting, Windows 7 and later will create a local cache of files that users use often. If the link is slow, it will not use the slow network to read the file the user wants but instead use the local, secret copy it created.

In a way, this is kind of like Offline Files for files that you haven't specified be available temporarily (via share settings) or permanently available online (by pinning a file).

This policy is a nice catchall for all sorts of file types, and I can't see a good reason not to have it enabled at all times.

Once again, this policy setting uses network latency as the speed verification—which could be a pitfall. Again, you can have very low speeds but perfectly decent network latency, so you may want to test this out.

Note that the value appears to be requested in milliseconds, like "60" for 60 milliseconds. But when you go to enable this policy setting, it defaults to 32,000 milliseconds (32 seconds), which is the maximum possible time to wait before giving up. This behavior is just a bug in the UI of the policy setting. Just put in the number of milliseconds that's appropriate.

A little side note: My friends on the Offline Files team at Microsoft once told me that their ideal value for this setting has tested out to be 35ms for most networks. I never tested that out end to end, but it seems reasonable to me.

Remove "Work Offline" Command

This is a Windows 8 and later policy setting.

When shares transition to offline, Windows 7 and Windows 8 have a button that permits users to forcefully put their shares back online. When this setting is enabled, the button is grayed out (and not really removed) on Windows 8 and later. Note that this policy setting only works for Windows 8 and later and not Windows 7.

You can see where the "Work offline" button is (and would be grayed out) in Window 10. It's in Explorer, tucked away in Home ➤ Easy Access, as seen here.

Note that when you are working Offline, the button name doesn't change to "Work online". It just always says "Work offline," regardless of the state.

Remove "Make Available Offline" Command

Enabling the **Remove "Make Available Offline" command** policy setting prevents users from pinning files by right-clicking them and selecting Make Available Offline. Files are still cached normally as dictated through other policies or by the defaults. Additionally, enabling this policy setting will not unpin already pinned files. Therefore, if you think you might not want users pinning files, you'll need to turn this setting on early in the game or you'll be forced to run around from machine to machine to unpin users' pinned files.

Enabling this setting does not interfere with the "Offline Settings" entries seen in Figure 10.12

Specify Administratively Assigned Offline Files

Specify Administratively assigned offline files is arguably the most useful setting in the bunch. Recall that Windows XP and later will automatically pin all files in Redirected Folders.

But what about other shares? If you want to ensure that non–Redirected Folders are *also* always available offline, this policy setting is your new best friend.

Remember, though, that in Windows XP, since these files are pinned, they are exempt from the percentage cache used (10 percent by default). That is, all files that are pinned are guaranteed to be available on the hard drive if the user transitions to offline. You can use the **Specify administratively assigned Offline Files** policy setting to force specific files or folders to be pinned, as seen in Figure 10.35.

FIGURE 10.35   Use the Specify administratively assigned Offline Files policy setting to force specific files or folders to be pinned.

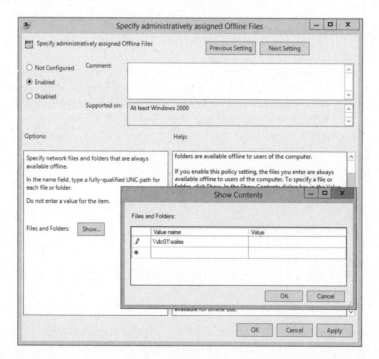

The next time your users get this policy setting assigned, all the files affected will be pinned. Every newly created file will be pinned as well, as shown in Figure 10.36.

FIGURE 10.36 All files and folders specified by the **Specify Administratively assigned offline files** policy setting are now pinned. You can see this by looking at the "Availability" column of any file.

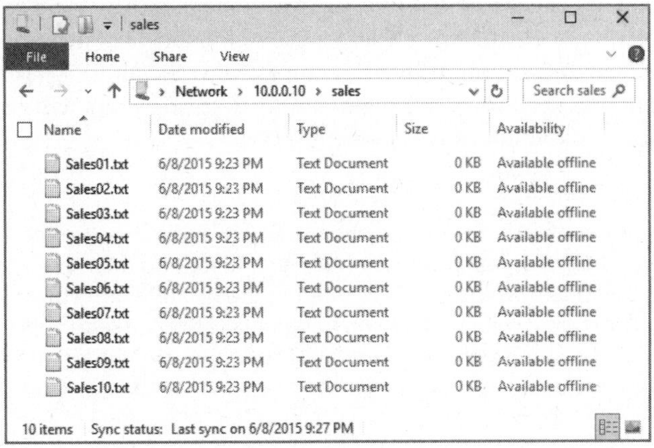

So, again, the reason I find this policy setting so useful is that you can ensure that the vice president of sales always has her sales figures available. This is useful when network connectivity is spotty or absent (like on airplanes). In short, you can look like a superhero because you thoughtfully pinned these important files—and your users didn't have to do any thinking at all. The files were just "there." Magic.

Do Not Automatically Make All Redirected Folders Available Offline

I get several emails a month asking me how to prevent Windows from pinning all files in Redirected Folders, such as Documents. Here it is: ensure that it affects all the users you want. Of course, this trick should work for Windows Vista and later as well.

Actually, the **Do not automatically make all redirected folders available offline** policy isn't found (anymore) in Computer Configuration ➤ Policies ➤ Administrative Templates ➤ Network ➤ Offline Files. In Windows Vista and later, it's been moved to User Configuration ➤ Policies ➤ Administrative Templates ➤ System ➤ Folder Redirection (and we discussed it earlier). But I'm bringing it up again here because this policy does directly relate to Offline Files—even though it's been moved to the Folder Redirection section.

Because this policy is a User-side policy, it becomes difficult to implement on a system-wide level. See the upcoming section, "Turning Off Folder Redirection's Automatic Offline Caching for Desktops," which describes how to use the **Do not Automatically Make Redirected Folders Available Offline** policy setting by strapping on a set of fangs.

Allow or Disallow Use of the Offline Files Feature

This policy setting is only found on the Computer side.

The **Allow or Disallow use of the Offline Files feature** policy is the "master switch" for Offline Files. This policy can affect Windows XP and later. Once a machine embraces this policy setting, a reboot is required. Disable (yes, disable) this policy setting and you effectively turn off Offline Files. Note that a restart is required.

Recall that Offline Files is enabled only for workstation machines. It's disabled for servers by default. You can use the **Allow or Disallow use of the Offline Files feature** policy setting to your advantage to turn on Offline Files on all your Windows Server computers easily—not that you would need to, as it's highly unlikely your servers will often be offline. See the earlier sidebar "Offline Files for Windows Server."

> If you enable this feature, it should kick in right away (when the background refresh interval hits). However, disabling this feature is another story. If one or more files are open in the cache when you try to disable the feature, that disable operation will fail; a reboot is required. You can experience the same behavior when trying to disable the feature through the user interface.

Exclude Files from Being Cached

This policy setting is only found on the Computer side.

So, if you have Windows 7 and later machines and you want them to exclude a specific file type or types, like all *.FOO and *.BAR files, just add them to this policy setting as a list with semicolons separating them.

Note that this policy setting is very similar to an older policy on Windows XP entitled **Files not cached**, which is only valid for Windows XP, 2003, and the like.

Configure Slow-Link Mode

This policy setting is only found on the Computer side.

We explored **Configure slow-link mode** earlier in the section "Using the Configure Slow-Link Mode Policy Setting." Check out that section for detailed usage examples.

Turn On Economical Application of Administrative Assigned Offline Files

This policy setting is only found on the Computer side.

Read the name of the policy setting again. Then forget it.

It should have been called **Turn *off* economical application of administrative assigned Offline Files**. Yes, off.

Here's the history of this setting. Recall that you can use the Specify **Administratively assigned offline files** policy setting to guarantee a share be offline for a user. This is great, except that with Windows XP, people found that their servers were experiencing very high file loads when users would log onto their clients (that is, at 9 a.m.). What was happening was that each client was trying to process his or her **Administratively assigned offline files** policy. Windows XP/SP2 had a Registry punch (found in KB 830407) to ease this problem. It was called "economical administrative pinning." Once it was enabled, any client with this behavior would perform the full pinning operation *only* if the top-level folder was not yet pinned in the Offline Files cache.

The result is that when the policy is processed once, subsequent logons to the server do not jam up the server.

This behavior was added and turned on, by default, in Windows Vista and later. However, the policy title really should be **Turn *off* economical application of administratively assigned Offline Files**. Once this policy setting is Disabled (yes, Disabled), the policy setting reverts back to pre–Windows XP/SP2 behavior.

This policy setting applies only to Windows Vista and later.

Limit Disk Space Used by Offline Files

This policy setting is only found on the Computer side.

In Windows XP, files expressly pinned weren't counted toward Offline Files usage. In Windows Vista and later, with the **Limit disk space used by Offline Files** policy setting, you can dictate how many megabytes you want to set aside for *all* Offline Files—those automatically cached and those pinned.

There are two settings here:

- One for total size of Offline Files (including those that are pinned)
- One for the size of autocached files

The Group Policy interface allows you to set the second number higher than the first— but that setting isn't possible in real life. Indeed, if you go back to Figure 10.25, you'll see the sliders for this setting in the interface. If you try it out, you'll notice you can't slide the second slider past the first. That's because you can't have a size bigger than the "Maximum amount of space all offline files can use." If you do that, the second number will automatically be set to the first number.

This policy setting applies only to Windows Vista and later machines.

Enable File Synchronization on Costed Networks

This policy only works for Windows 8 and later.

Windows 8 and later has some magic in it to prevent offline file synchronization when users are using a data plan, like 3G, 4G, or LTE. That is, Offline Files will not sync when a Windows 8 or later device is using a paid data plan. You would need to specifically enable it using this policy setting.

You can express to Windows 8 and later which networks are costed by clicking the network icon in your system tray and then right-clicking on the network connection and clicking the "Set as metered connection" option.

You can see some nice, detailed information on metered/costed networks, some shots, and Windows 8 and later Group Policy information in two places:

- The Engineering Windows 8 blog has information here:

  http://blogs.msdn.com/b/b8/archive/2012/01/20/engineering-windows-8-for-mobility.aspx

- My friend Alex Verboon has gone into some extra details with Group Policy how-tos here:

  www.verboon.info/index.php/2012/10/windows-8metered-connections/

Troubleshooting Sync Center

The event log in Windows Vista and later is a deep and rich place. To that end, there are two places in particular to go when troubleshooting Sync Center problems.

Enabling the Offline Files Log

The Offline Files log file is located in Event Viewer ➢ Applications and Servers Logs ➢ Microsoft ➢ Windows ➢ Offline Files. Once there, dive one level deeper into the Operational log. In Figure 10.37, you can see a Windows 8 event from the OfflineFiles Operational log.

FIGURE 10.37   Information found in the OfflineFiles Operational log. To see data here, you must enable the log first.

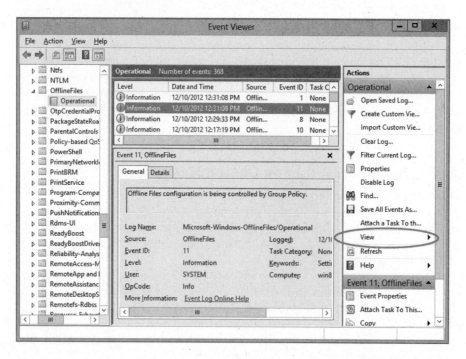

The events you'll find here are mostly the successful or unsuccessful startup/shutdown of the Offline Files feature as well as online/offline transitions. In the events (like what's seen in Figure 10.37), you can see the speed at which the machine believes the link is in terms of latency and bandwidth.

Enabling the Sync Log

There is also a Sync Log, but you need the super-secret entry key to know it's there. The thing to know how to do is called Show Analytic Channels, and here's how to do it. This trick works on Windows Vista and later, including Windows 10.

As shown previously in Figure 10.37, the rightmost pane of the Computer Management Console's log view contains a View action. Click that View option and select "Show Analytic and Debug Logs." (You can see "View" highlighted in Figure 10.37 for quick reference.) Once you do, you'll then be able to find the Sync Log hiding under Microsoft ➤ Windows ➤ Offline Files. Right-click Sync Log and you can click the Enable Log item.

This is an analytic channel that reports sync activity *as it is happening* in the Offline Files service.

It is not intended for use by end users, but it should prove valuable to administrators to gather specific information about what's going on. (Microsoft Product Support Services could ask you for this information, too.)

When that log is enabled, log entries appear for items that are being synchronized within the service. This means that any item synchronized by the service will be reported, not only items synchronized through Sync Center. You can see one of these events in Figure 10.38.

FIGURE 10.38 You can get blow-by-blow details of what is being synced via Offline Files.

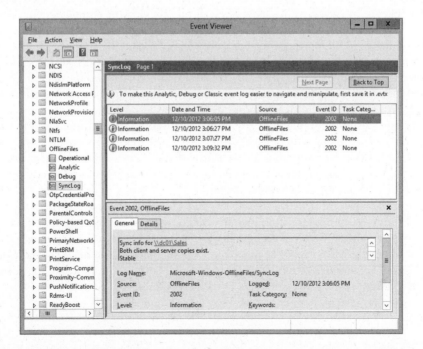

If you open one of these sync events to the Details tab in the Event Viewer, you can see the XML format containing the details; then, you can buy your favorite scripting pal some lunch to make some killer reports for you based on the XML data!

Turning Off Folder Redirection's Automatic Offline Caching for Desktops

I've never met a policy setting I didn't like. But I have met a few that missed their calling. The policy setting at User Configuration ➤ Policies ➤ System ➤ Folder Redirection ➤ **Do not Automatically Make Redirected Folders Available Offline** has missed its calling.

What on earth am I talking about?

Well, let's take a minute and analyze the normal function of Offline Files: its primary mission is to maintain files when you're not on the network so you can keep working. Super. So, what kinds of computers are off the network a lot? Laptops and tablets, of course. And desktops generally *stay* on the network.

Assuming your laptops represent 30–50 percent of your workforce, do you need those files automatically cached on *every* machine in your enterprise like the remaining 50 percent of your desktops?

Why should you care about turning it off?

Because, depending on whom you ask, it could be a security risk. Do you want cached copies of your precious documents on every machine to which your users roam? Likely not. Isn't putting your user's documents on every desktop they roam to a security risk? In a way, yes!

Sure, you could encrypt the Offline Files using EFS or BitLocker, but let's face it, most people simply don't use EFS today. BitLocker deployment is growing all the time. And, even then, if BitLocker is implemented, it's most likely not on the desktop computers but rather laptops (because it's usually only laptops and pricier desktops that have the special Trusted Platform Module [TPM] chip needed for BitLocker—but I digress).

Finally, let's not forget that every time a user roams to a desktop, he's just wasting space on the local hard drive. Remember, desktops are *normally* connected to the network just fine. Do they need *another* copy of their documents clogging up the local disk when they roam and Redirected Folders autocaches your documents?

So, in my analysis (and I'm just one guy with an opinion here), Offline Files doesn't make sense on a well-running network where your desktops and servers are on a fast LAN. Let me be clear: it won't hurt anything, either. But with files flying around everywhere, being sprinkled from desktop to desktop, it can be a security risk, waste space, and promote unnecessary synchronization and bandwidth.

Let me be a zillion percent clear: I positively love this feature for my *laptops*. I'm just not that wild about it for my *desktops*. However, I likely would keep it on my desktops if I were connected to servers on a slow WAN, like a branch office (especially if that WAN link was flaky).

So, my first thought when I read the name of this policy setting (**Do not Automatically Make Redirected Folders Available Offline**) was "A-ha! They're thinking what I'm thinking! There's a policy setting that enables me to turn it off for desktops!"

Except that's not how this policy setting works. This policy setting is not on the Computer side; it's on the User side. So, inherently, it cannot simply be put in a GPO and linked to, say, the **Desktops** OU to turn it off.

With this policy setting, you can only say, "The users in Sales don't automatically make their Redirected Folders available offline." But that's not the point, is it? You want the Sales folks to cache their documents on their laptops and tablets but *not* cache them on the various desktops they roam to (especially if they're public computers).

So, **Do not Automatically Make Redirected Folders Available Offline** doesn't work to turn it off for particular computers. But there is a work-around for Windows XP and Windows 7.

And, now for Windows 8 and 10, there's a policy setting called **Redirect folders on primary computers only**, which is a welcome addition—with no work-around required.

Turning Off Folder Redirection's Automatic Caching for Windows XP and Windows 7

Now, cracking open the underlying ADMX file that describes the **Do not Automatically Make Redirected Folders Available Offline** policy setting, I learned that the Registry key for this policy setting is a value called:

```
HKEY_Current_User\Software\Policies\Microsoft\Windows\NetCache
```

and it sets a REG_DWORD of DisableFRAdminPin to 1.

And then, it came to me in a dream: if I could somehow apply this policy setting (or the underlying Registry setting) to only my desktops, then, bam! I could turn off Offline Files for desktops (which would leave it on for laptops) and I would get the effect I wanted! I needed to find a way to drop a *user-based* Registry item onto specific *computers*.

Let me jump to the end of the story and tell you what I found when I applied this policy setting (or the underlying Registry entry) on Windows XP and Windows Vista and later machines.

Turns out, when I did this, Windows XP and Windows Vista and Windows 7 didn't react the same way. For Windows 8 and later, there's an alternate procedure, which we'll talk about next.

Here's what I found, with Jakob Heidelberg, to back me up (your mileage may vary):

When we applied the Registry value to Windows XP...   Windows XP just eats the policy setting (or Registry value) and, bang! Offline Files goes out like a light. It's awesome. If you've never told Windows XP to try to use Offline Files, you'll be 100 percent successful immediately: Windows XP just won't try to use Offline Files with Redirected Folders.

However, there's a catch. If you have the Registry tweak set, and the desktop goes offline for some reason for a period of time (you experience a network failure or the server goes offline, for instance), *and* the user creates or edits a document while offline, that document will be synchronized the next time the client is online (which is good). However, it will also stay in the local cache from that point.

That's not what we wanted. However, since we're talking about desktops (and they're usually online all the time), this shouldn't happen too much.

Now, with a little extra elbow grease and magic, you might be able to flush the cache using the downloadable XP tool, CSCCMD.EXE, which you can still download at http://support.microsoft.com/kb/884739. But you're on your own for that.

When we applied the Registry value to Windows Vista and Windows 7...   Windows Vista and Windows 7 react kind of like Windows XP to the policy (or Registry addition), but it gets a little better.

The next time you log on, those redirected files are flushed from the local cache forever. So, with Vista and Windows 7, you will be sure no Offline Files are stored locally once the policy setting (or Registry item) is set.

You may have to perform one more sync via Sync Center to get the flush to occur. Whew. Figuring all that out made both Jakob's and my head spin! Be sure to test our findings out thoroughly in your environment before you roll out one of our proposed plans in a widespread way. Now, once we know the predicted behavior, how do we get the user-based policy setting (or the underlying Registry entry) applied to *just* our desktops?

There are three ways to get this setting applied just on desktops (that is, turn it off just for desktops) but leave it on for laptops. Here are the three tricks I have up my sleeve:

- Create a custom WMI filter to apply to a GPO (with the policy setting contained within it).

- Use Group Policy Preference Extensions to jam in the same Registry value that the policy setting would, but ensure that only users on desktops get the setting.

- Use PolicyPak Admin Templates Manager to deploy the setting and specifically get to particular computers you want.

Figure 10.39 shows an example of what happens after a user logs onto a Windows 7 machine after we make our setting. You can see that synchronization has been turned off, but folder redirected files are still stored on the server but not cached to the desktop (no little yin-yang symbols on the file icons).

Any of these will work, so, let's get started!

If you've figured out a more creative or alternate way to do this, let me know, and I'll include it in a GPanswers.com newsletter.

Using WMI Filters to Forcibly Apply This Setting Specifically to Desktops

This technique assumes you understand how to create WMI filters. If you need a refresher, please check out Chapter 4, "Advanced Group Policy Processing," where I cover it in depth.

Here are the short steps you'll need to forcibly disable Redirected Folders from automatically making the contents available offline on desktops:

1. Create a new GPO that enables the **Do not Automatically Make Redirected Folders Available Offline** policy. You don't need to configure any other settings in the GPO.

2. Link the GPO to OUs containing user accounts. Again, please, please read my warnings about how WMI filters can slow you down in Chapter 4.

FIGURE 10.39   Documents are still redirected to the server, but for users on desktops, you can avoid the synchronization (copy) to the local computer.

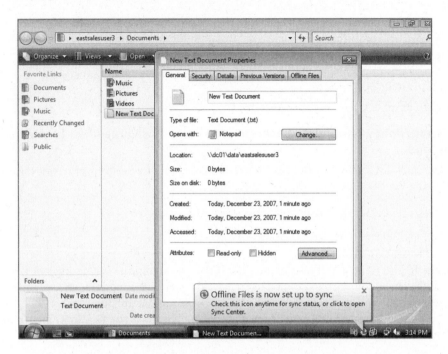

3. Create a WMI filter that determines if a machine meets certain criteria. My suggestion is to check to see if it's a desktop (and not a laptop).

   ▪ If it's a desktop, then the users on those desktops will successfully embrace this GPO (and the adjusted synchronization behavior as described earlier will be performed).

   ▪ If it's not a desktop, then the standard behavior to sync Redirected Folders will continue (this is what we want).

All you need is a sample WMI query (once you've learned the basics). This query will work a lot of the time (although perhaps not all of the time):

```
Select * From Win32_PhysicalMemory Where FormFactor != 12
```

This query returns `True` on computers that do not have SODIMM form factor memory and `False` on computers with SODIMM form factor memory. The assumption is that pretty much all laptops will have this style memory and that your desktops will not. Though it's true some desktops do use SODIMM memory, most don't—so it's a pretty good bet, and will work a high percentage of the time. We've tested this out and it seems to work for most cases.

To learn more about the `Win32_PhysicalMemory` class, visit `http://tinyurl.com/2hq6e6`.

How did we figure out this query? Hats off to Jakob for launching a worldwide search for the answer. Check out the thread at:

`http://heidelbergit.blogspot.com/2008/02/wmi-filter-contest-are-you-knight-in.html`

(shortened to `http://tinyurl.com/yvpshy`).

Using Group Policy Preference Extensions to Force the Value (Just for Users on Desktops)

Because we can't just apply the policy setting to the User side, we need to get tricky. Again, the underlying Registry entry for the policy setting is:

`HKCU\Software\Policies\Microsoft\Windows\NetCache`

and it sets a REG_DWORD of `DisableFRAdminPin` to 1.

We need to get this to our desktops.

Now, the Registry entry itself can't figure out if the user's machine is a desktop or laptop. But with some of our Group Policy preference extensions superpowers, we can set the same Registry value and ensure that it *only* affects machines that are desktops!

So, create a GPO and link it to your user population. Then, use the Registry extension on the User side to specify the Registry value, as seen in Figure 10.40.

FIGURE 10.40 This is the same Registry entry that **Do not automatically make all redirected folders available offline** would put in place.

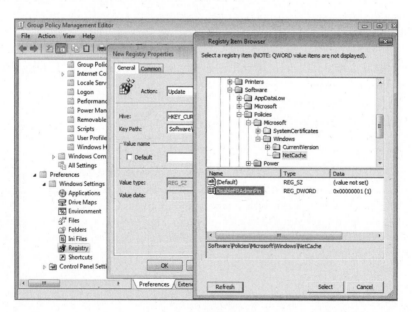

However, at this point, you need to target the value so only users logged onto desktops get the preference setting containing the Registry entry. In Figure 10.41, you can see my suggested target. In short, I'm saying three things must be true for it to be a desktop:

* It is not a laptop (because the hardware profile says so).

* It has no battery.

* It has no PCMCIA slots.

FIGURE 10.41   If you use this query, it will usually determine that your machine is a desktop and not a laptop.

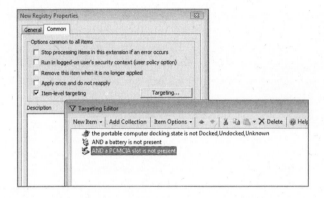

Again, this might not be perfect in all situations, but it should suffice for most.

Alternatively, if all of your desktops had the word *Desktop* or some other distinguishing factor in the name, you could use a query like the one shown in Figure 10.42.

FIGURE 10.42   If you have a uniform naming convention for your desktops, this job is even easier.

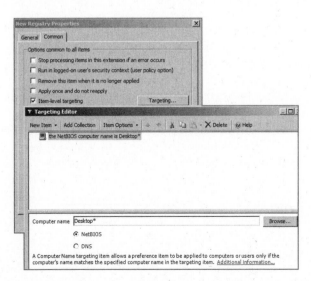

Using PolicyPak Admin Templates Manager to Apply This Setting to Specific Computers

PolicyPak Suite contains PolicyPak Admin Templates Manager, which we visited in Chapter 4.

There, we learned that PolicyPak Admin Templates Manager can deliver any User-side setting and dictate it to the computers you want.

As such, it takes about five clicks to get what you see in Figure 10.43.

FIGURE 10.43 You can use PolicyPak Admin Templates Manager to deliver **Do not Automatically Make All Redirected Folders Available Offline** (user setting) apply to computers.

One of PolicyPak's superpowers is to enable you to target User-side policy settings to all users on a specific machine. PolicyPak can simply process user settings for every user on a specific computer, if that's what's needed. And that's precisely what's needed in this case.

Turning Off Folder Redirection's Automatic Caching

As stated earlier, Windows 8 and later has a new policy setting named **Redirect folders on primary computers only.** This setting is located in the Group Policy editor under Computer Configuration ➢ Policies ➢ Administrative Templates ➢ System ➢ Folder Redirection and also User Configuration ➢ Policies ➢ Administrative Templates ➢ System ➢ Folder Redirection.

Here's the idea: once a computer (or user) gets this policy, the user (or all users on a computer) perks up and then is looking for *another* directive.

The user then looks to see what his "primary computer" is. And if he's on his designated primary computer, then…bingo! Folder Redirection kicks on—just for this computer (and Offline Files automatic caching also occurs). If users are not on their primary computer, then a whole lot of nothing occurs.

This solves the big problem I had all along: ensuring that Offline Files can be on for laptops and off for desktops.

So, how do you associate users with their primary computer? It's an attribute stored in Active Directory, and the Active Directory schema must be Windows Server 2012 or later or this won't work. Again, just the schema needs to be Windows Server 2012 or later; you don't need any actual Windows Server 2012 (or later) Domain Controllers or servers.

Next, you'll use Active Directory Users and Computers (in Advanced mode) and right-click over the computer, and inside its properties, you'll find the Attribute Editor, as seen in Figure 10.44. Then find the distinguishedName attribute and copy it, as also shown in Figure 10.44.

FIGURE 10.44   Find the DN of the computer before you associate it with a particular user.

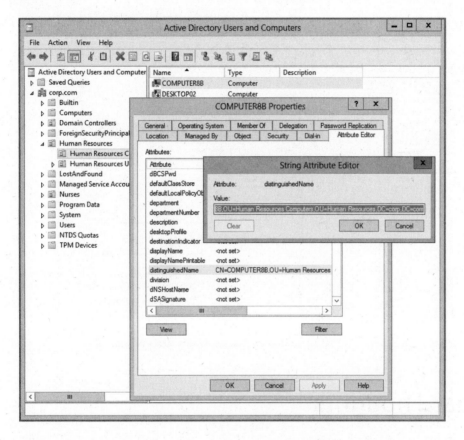

Then, using Active Directory Users and Computers, find the user account, as seen in Figure 10.45, and again, within the account properties, find the Attribute Editor and select msDs-PrimaryComputer. Then paste in the DN from the computer the user uses.

Now, users get Folder Redirection only when they are at their primary computer and not anywhere else.

Magical!

FIGURE 10.45   Paste in the DNs of the user or users who should be able to utilize Folder Redirection on this computer.

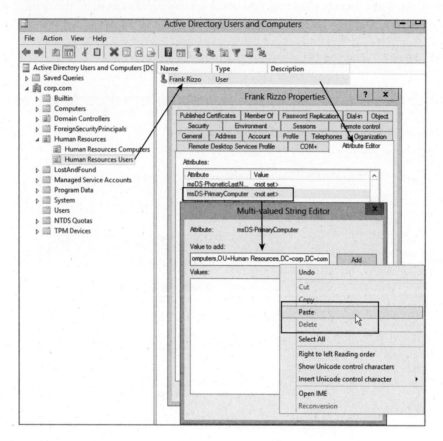

Final Thoughts

In the previous chapter, you set up Roaming Profiles. But there was a problem. If you had any mix of Windows XP, Windows 7, Windows 8, and Windows 10 (and Roaming Profiles was set up correctly), you wouldn't "see" files, say, in the Documents folder on the Windows 7 machine and see them also on the Windows 10 machine.

Here, you set up Redirected Folders, which anchored My Documents (for Windows XP) and Documents (for Windows Vista and later) to the same place.

This strategy gave you several key features: a centralized backup place for critical files, the ability for users' Documents contents to be available on any workstation, and the ability to mitigate the generated traffic caused by Documents being located within the profile. By default, the Documents folder is located within the profile.

You also set up Offline Files so that files work offline as though they were online. You used Group Policy to specify how your users and computers would use this function. Recall that Documents/My Documents is already automatically pinned if you use Windows XP and later.

Windows 7 and later automatically use latency to determine if a link is slow or not, but it's not a great measurement. Be sure to use the Group Policy settings we explored in this chapter to teach Windows 7 and later how to correctly determine if a link is fast or not.

If you just can't get enough information on Offline Files, be sure to check out the following resources, which are still useful for Windows 8 and later:

- "What's New in Offline Files for Windows Vista," at http://tinyurl.com/mweeq8q.

- "Changes to Offline Files in Windows Vista," (written by me), in *TechNet Magazine*: http://tinyurl.com/2zkk8p.

- "What's New in Offline Files" just Goog..., I mean, Bing for it. It seems to move around a lot.

Creating a managed desktop isn't easy; there's a lot to configure. And you're well on your way to making your Windows life more livable. In the next chapter, we'll continue our desktop management story. You'll learn how to distribute software to your users and computers. So, turn the page and get started!

11

The Managed Desktop, Part 2: Software Deployment via Group Policy

Two chapters ago, I discussed and implemented the first big feature of getting your managed desktop story in gear: Roaming Profiles. Once Roaming Profiles are enabled, users can roam from machine to machine, comfortable that their working environment will follow wherever they go.

In the previous chapter, I discussed and implemented more features to get your managed desktop handled. First, we tackled Redirected Folders, which took Roaming Profiles one step further and anchored the user's Documents or My Documents folder to a share on a server. We then used the Group Policy settings on Offline Folders and the Synchronization Manager to ensure that certain files are always available in the cache if our connection to the server goes offline or if the server itself goes offline.

We're well on our way to implementing a fully managed desktop. We want our users to roam freely across our entire environment and take all their stuff with them. But we're missing a fundamental piece of the equation: how can we guarantee that a specific application is ready and waiting for them on any given machine? What good is having your user data follow you if an application needed to access the data isn't available? That's what we're going to handle in this chapter.

That being said, we're going to be talking about MSI-based applications. We're not going to be tackling the installation of the family of apps known as modern, Metro, or Universal (all the same thing). A good first article to read on those kinds of applications would be found at:

    http://blogs.msdn.com/b/mvpawardprogram/archive/2014/03/24/side-loading-
    deployment-of-windows-store-apps-in-enterprises-step-by-step.aspx

We are, however, going to tackle something unique called Office Click-to-Run, which is a different way to install modern versions of Microsoft Office. So, stay tuned for that.

Group Policy Software Installation (GPSI) Overview

Without any Microsoft software distribution mechanisms, such as Intune or System Center Configuration Manager (what was known as SMS), or third-party software such as Altiris (or something similar), most environments require that you spend a lot of your time running from desktop to desktop. In a typical scenario, a user is hired and fills out the human resources paperwork, and a computer with the standard suite of software is dropped on his or her desk.

Usually, this machine comes from some sort of "deployment farm" in the back office, where scads of machines are imaged (à la Symantec's Ghost) by the scores. Or maybe the team is using Microsoft deployment techniques like the Microsoft Deployment Toolkit (MDT) to blast images out there.

The user then starts to surf the Internet—er, I mean—get to work. Soon enough, it's discovered that the user needs a specific application, and a desktop technician is dispatched to fulfill the user's request for new software. When the desktop technician arrives, he either loads the user's special software via the DVD drive or USB port or connects to a network share to pull down the software.

That's a lot of manual labor; let's make the pain stop.

Group Policy Software Installation (GPSI) is the next big feature we'll set up. This feature allows users to automatically pull applications through the network. GPSI further chips away at the workstation maintenance total cost of ownership (TCO).

There are essentially four steps to going from 0 to 60 in four seconds when it comes to deploying software with GPSI features:

1. Acquire a software setup package with an .MSI extension.

2. Share and secure a software distribution shared folder.

3. Set up a GPO to deliver the software.

4. Assign or Publish the software.

We will approach each of these steps in our software configuration journey in the next few pages.

Software installed this way—via Group Policy—is referred to in many Microsoft documents as *managed* software. Group Policy can perform what is generically known as an *advertisement* of software, and the Windows Installer Service picks it up and runs with it to perform the installation. Let's get started by understanding the Windows Installer Service.

Now, I'm guessing that some large percentage of people are flipping to this chapter to find out how to deploy "the big one"—Office—to their client machines using Group Policy. That's great. I'm going to show you how to do that. But I have to begin by explaining exactly how we're going to address the problem that is Microsoft Office:

Office 2003 was "normal."   We'll be using Office 2003 as our "working example" throughout the chapter. This will get you familiar with the normal constructs of GPSI. We'll cover .MSI files, how to create what's known as "transform files" (.MST files), how to patch .MSI files, and a whole lot more.

The material you learn here will be valid for 99 percent of the software packages out there, except (mostly) for its newer siblings: Office 2007 and later.

Note that for our working examples in the chapter, you could also substitute Office 2000 and Office XP for Office 2003, as all three of those packages are "normal."

And again, almost all other packages you'll encounter out there are "normal."

Office 2010 and later are "abnormal."   For Office 2010 and Office 2013, I'll have a section specifically after we learn a "normal" application like Office 2003.

Note that in previous editions I showed how to deploy Office 2007 using Group Policy. Although it's possible (barely) to deploy Office 2007 using GPSI, with Office 2010 it's not possible at all. So in this edition, I've taken out all the Office 2007 stuff.

You might think—"Okay, Moskowitz. It's not 2003 anymore. So get a grip on reality and teach us something more 'useful' than Office 2003 as the main example." I would. It's just that Office 2003 is so "perfect" as the prime example of how most applications deploy correctly. And because Office 2010 and later do things so totally differently, it makes sense to learn a normal application first (like Office 2003) before we go downtown to Crazytown with Office 2010 or later.

Trust me. Remember, the goal isn't about how to deploy Office 2003. I know you're not actively trying to perform a deployment of Office 2003. I get that. The goal is to have you understand how a "normal" application does its thing—and you can take the information you learn with you to a huge variety of common applications you're likely to encounter. And, don't worry—you'll learn how to deploy Office 2010, Office 2013, or Office 2016 in this chapter, too, if that's specifically what you're after.

In the chapter, I'll show you how to deploy Office 2013, but as I write this, some early betas of Office 2016 are coming out. If that's the case, why am I showing you how to deploy Office 2013 and not Office 2016? At the time of this writing, the Office 2016 beta is only available as what's known as the *Click-to-Run* version and not yet available as an MSI (the file format most applications are packaged in and the substance of what this chapter is all about). So, I reached out to my friends at Microsoft who told me that MSI versions of Office 2016 will only be available for Volume License customers and that all other instances of Office 2016 will be Click-to-Run.

If you want to learn more about the Click-to-Run version of Office 2013 and 2016, start out here:

`https://technet.microsoft.com/en-us/library/jj219427.aspx`

Then read this:

`https://www.microsoft.com/en-us/download/details.aspx?id=36778`

So in summary, if you want to deploy the MSI version of Office 2016, I can't show that to you here in this chapter, because it doesn't exist yet for me to show. That being said, my friends at Microsoft have explained to me that all the steps I've shown you for Office 2013 and its MSI will be precisely the same steps for Office 2016 and its MSI when it's released.

With that in mind, let's get started.

The Windows Installer Service

A background service called the *Windows Installer Service* must be running on the client for the software deployment magic to happen. The Windows Installer Service can understand when Group Policy is being used to install or revoke an application and react accordingly. The Windows Installer Service has a secret superpower: it can run under "elevated" privileges. In other words, the user does not need to be a local administrator of the workstation to get software deployed via Group Policy.

So, the Windows Installer Service installs the software with administrative privileges. Once installed, however, the program is run under the user's context.

Windows Installer can install applications via *document invocation*, or *auto-install*. Windows Installer is automatically started when you choose a specific extension or extensions. For instance, if you are e-mailed a file with a .PDF extension and then double-click to open it (but don't yet have Acrobat Reader installed), the Windows Installer Service can be automatically invoked to bring down Adobe Acrobat Reader from one of your servers. This is described in more detail in the section "Advanced Published or Assigned" later in this chapter. Additionally, Windows Installer can determine when an application is damaged and repair it automatically by downloading the required files from the source to fix the problem.

> You might have heard the phrase *advertising a package* or, in short, *an advertisement*. *An advertisement* is a generic term that means software is "offered" by Active Directory to the client machine. But the client has three ways to accept that advertisement. You'll see later that the shortcut can be selected, which will download the application (that's one way). Another way is to click a file extension that is registered for GPSI (we already mentioned this one), and, finally, you can invoke an advertised COM object (which we won't be discussing here).

Understanding .*MSI* Packages

About 99 percent of the magic in software deployment with Group Policy is wrapped in a file format called .MSI. The .MSI file has two goals: to increase the flexibility of software distribution and to reduce the effort required to make new packages. When a software application is rolled out the door, files in the .MSI format are often "standard issue" (though sometimes they are not). For instance, every edition of Office since Office 2000 has shipped as an .MSI distribution.

On the surface, .MSI files appear to act as self-expanding distribution files, like familiar, self-executing .ZIP files. But under the surface, .MSI files contain a database of "what goes where" and can contain either pointers to additional source files or all the files rolled up inside the .MSI itself. Additionally, .MSI files can "tier" the installation; for instance, you can specify, "Don't bother loading the spell checker in Word, if I only want Excel." Sounds simple, but it's revolutionary.

Moreover, because .MSI files are themselves a database, an added feature is realized. The creator of the .MSI package (or sometimes the user) can designate which features are loaded to the hard drive upon initial installation, which features are loaded to the hard drive the first time they are used, which features are run from the CD or distribution point, and which features are never loaded. This lets administrators pare down installations to make efficient use of both disk space and network bandwidth.

With .MSI files, the bar is also raised when it comes to the overall management of applications. Indeed, two discrete .MSI operations come in handy: Rollback and Uninstall. When .MSI files are being installed, the entire installation can be canceled and simply rolled back. Or, after an .MSI application is fully installed, it can be fully uninstalled. You are not guaranteed exactly the same machine state from Uninstall as you are with Rollback, however. The GPSI features in Active Directory are designed mainly to integrate with the new .MSI file format. There is other legacy support, as you'll see later.

Utilizing an Existing *.MSI* Package

As stated, lots of applications come as .MSI files. Some are full-blown applications, such as Office 2000 and later. Others are smaller programs downloaded from the Internet or utility packages and the like.

Be forewarned: just because an application comes as an .MSI doesn't necessarily mean it can always be deployed via GPSI; however, that's a pretty good indication. Yet, even though versions of the Norton AntiVirus client shipped as an .MSI, it wasn't installable via GPSI until version 9. Ditto for Adobe Acrobat. Until Acrobat version 7, the Reader Program didn't ship as an .MSI, but the full version did. But even though earlier versions of Adobe Acrobat shipped as .MSI files, they simply weren't deployable via GPSI.

Additionally, some .MSI applications (Office 2003) can be deployed to *either* users or computers. However, some applications are coded to *only* be deployed successfully to computers.

You'll want to check with the manufacturer of the .MSI file to understand how it needs to be installed. The .MSI files that can be deployed via GPSI usually come in three flavors:

- Some .MSI packages are just one solitary file, and they come ready to be deployed.

- Some .MSI packages have one file to "kick off" the installation. Then, there are a gaggle of other files behind it. The .NET Framework (netfx.msi) is an example in this category.

- Other .MSI files need to be "prepared" for installation. Usually, these applications are more complex. Office 2003 is an example in this category.

Many people want to deploy big applications, such as the Office suite. Again, for the majority of this chapter, I'm going to be using the older Office 2003, because it's very "normal" in the way it's deployed. And, by learning Office 2003, you'll be able to take the knowledge and deploy many other applications (just not Office 2010 and later sadly).

So, for these examples, I'll assume you have a copy of Office 2003. Note that only the Enterprise versions of these applications are guaranteed to work using GPSI. Other editions, like Home and School, may not work properly deployed via GPSI.

Setting Up the Software Distribution Share

The first step is to set up the software distribution shared folder on a server. In this example, we'll use DC01 and create a shared folder with the name of Apps. We want all our users to be able to read the files inside this software distribution share because later, we might choose to create multiple folders to house additional applications' sources. Later, we'll also create our first application subfolder and feed Office 2003 into its own subfolder.

To set up the software distribution shared folder, follow these steps:

1. Log onto DC01 as Administrator.

2. From the Desktop, click My Computer to open the My Computer folder.

3. Find a place to create a users folder. In this example, we'll use C:\Apps. Once you've opened the C: drive, right-click C: and select the Folder command from the New menu; then, type **Apps** as the name. (You can substitute any name for Apps.)

4. Share the Apps folder so that Everyone has Read access. Note that the Domain Users group isn't sufficient here because computers also must have access. While you're in the Permissions dialog for the Apps folder, also ensure that the Administrators group has Full Control permissions on the share.

You can use Share permissions, NTFS permissions, or both, to restrict who can see which applications. The most restrictive permissions between Share-level and NTFS-level permissions are used. Here, at the Apps share, you want everyone to have access to the share. You'll then create subfolders to house each application and use NTFS permissions to specify, at each subfolder level, which groups or users can see which applications' subfolders.

Again, in this example, we're using a simple share on a simple server. Here, we'll be installing from a Domain Controller in our examples, which you wouldn't normally do in real life, but it's okay for our examples. Indeed, the best thing to do is to use Distributed File Systems (DFS) Namespaces to ensure that users can get to this share from another server, even if this server is down. DFS Namespaces is beyond the scope of this book, but read the sidebar "Normal Shares vs. DFS Namespaces."

 It's a good idea to exclusively use DFS Namespaces for package installation points. This is because if you move a package, you will likely cause a product reinstallation on your target machines. This happens whenever the original source location changes. By using DFS Namespaces, you can avoid this problem.

Setting Up an Administrative Installation (for *.MSI* Files That Need Them)

As stated, not all .MSI files are "ready to go"; some need to be prepared. To prepare Office 2003, you must perform an *Administrative Installation* of its .MSI file. In this procedure, the system will rebuild and copy the .MSI package from your CD-ROM source to a destination folder for use by your clients. While the package is being rebuilt, it injects the serial number for your users and other customized data. Again, to be clear, not all `.MSI` packages must be prepared in this manner. Be sure to check your documentation.

To perform an Administrative Installation of Office 2003, you'll use the `msiexec` command built into Windows 2000 and Windows 2003. The generic command is `msiexec /a whatever.msi`. For Office 2003, the command is `msiexec /a Pro11.MSI`.

When you run this command, Office is *not* installed on your server (or wherever you're performing these commands). This can be confusing because the Office Installation Wizard is kicked off and it will write a bunch of data to your disk. Again, to be clear, an Administrative Installation simply *prepares* a source installation folder for future software deployment.

The Office Installation Wizard will show that it's getting ready for an Administrative Installation, as you can see in Figure 11.1.

FIGURE 11.1   You need to perform an Administrative Installation to prepare a source installation folder for Office.

Your next steps in the Installation Wizard are to specify the organization and the installation location and to enter the product key. For the installation location, choose a folder in the share you already created, say, `C:\Apps\office2003distro`. Be sure to enter a valid product key or you cannot continue. The next screen asks you to confirm the End-User License Agreement. Finally, the Administrative Installation is kicked off, and files are copied to the share and the folder, as shown in Figure 11.2.

FIGURE 11.2 The files are simply copied to the share; Office isn't being installed (despite the notification that it is).

Remember that not every application requires any "preparation" for an Administrative Installation as Office 2003 does.

Many applications are "ready to rock" with no preparation necessary. In those cases, I suggest you just create a subdirectory under Apps, based on the package name, and dump the installation files to that directory. Even more ideal is to have a version number within each application's directory to further segregate.

You'll have to check with each package manufacturer to see whether or not an Administrative Installation is required.

About Underlying Share Permissions

When you set up shared folders, also lock them down with NTFS permissions to prevent unauthorized users from accessing the installations. Even though GPSI can *target* specific users, it makes no provisions for security. Rather, if your users discover the distribution shared folder, they'll have the keys to the candy store unless you put security on the shared folder or, even better, utilize NTFS permissions as a dead bolt on the lock.

You can expose or hide your shared folders; to hide them, add a $ (dollar sign) to the end of the share name. You can have one shared folder for each package or one shared folder for all your software with subfolders underneath, each with the appropriate NTFS permissions.

I do not recommend (nor is it possible) that you dump all the installations in one shared folder without using subfolders. Using subfolders lets you differentiate between two applications that have the same name (for example, Setup.msi) or two versions of the same application.

Creating Your Own *.MSI* Package

It's great when applications such as Office 2003 come with their own .MSI packages, but not every vendor supplies .MSI packages. You can, however, create your own .MSI packages to wrap up and deploy the software you've already bought that doesn't come with an .MSI package.

Here are some of the popular repacking tools:

AdvancedInstaller http://www.advancedinstaller.com/

SmartPackager from Scalable Software: http://scalablesmartpackager.com/smart-packager-ce-free-msi-packager/

Flexera AdminStudio: http://tinyurl.com/yc27wbt

The general steps for using a repackaging tool are as follows:

1. Take a snapshot of a clean source machine.

2. Run the current setup program of whatever you want to wrap up.

3. Fully install and configure the application as desired.

4. Reboot the machine to ensure that changes are settled in.

5. Take a snapshot again, and scour the hard drive for changes.

Once the changes are discovered, they're wrapped up into an .MSI file of your choice, which you can then Assign or Publish.

The third-party tools have some fairly robust features to assist you in your .MSI package creation. As I stated, the .MSI format lets you detect a damaged component within a running application. This feature is called *keying* files for proper operation. For example, if your Ruff.DLL gets deleted when you run DogFoodMaker 7, the Windows Installer springs into action and pulls the broken, but keyed, component back from the distribution point—all without user interaction.

Additionally, if you're looking for some heavy-duty .MSI training, consider my pal Darwin Sanoy, who can be found at:

  http://desktopengineer.com/windowsinstallertraining

(Let him know I sent you.)

Assigning and Publishing Applications

Once you have an .MSI package on a share, you can offer it to your client systems via Group Policy. GPSI is located under both Computer and User Configuration directories and then Policies ➢ Software Settings ➢ Software Installation. Before we set up our first package, it's important to understand the options and the rules for deployment. You, the administrator, can offer applications to clients in two ways: *Assigning* or *Publishing*.

Assigning Applications

The icons of Assigned applications appear in the user's Start Menu. More specifically, they appear when the user selects Start ➢ All Programs. However, colloquially, we just say that they appear on the Start Menu. You can Assign applications to users or computers.

What Happens When You Assign Applications to Users

If you Assign an application to users, the application itself isn't downloaded and installed from the source until its initial use. When the user first clicks the application's icon, the Windows Installer (which runs as a background process on the client machine) kicks into high gear, looks at the database of the .MSI package, locates the installation point, and determines which components are required.

Assigning an application saves on initial disk space requirements since only an application's entry points are actually installed on the client. Those entry points are shortcuts, CLSIDs (Class Identifiers), file extensions, and, sometimes, other application attributes that are considered .MSI entry points.

Once the icons are displayed, the rest of the application is pulled down only when necessary. Indeed, many applications are coded so that only portions of the application are brought down in chunks when needed, such as a help file that is only grabbed from the source when it's required the first time.

When portions of an application are installed, the necessary disk space is claimed. The point is that if users roam from machine to machine, they might *not* choose to install the Assigned application, and hence, it would not use any disk space. If users are Assigned an application but never get around to using it, they won't use any extra disk space. Once the files are grabbed from the source, the application is installed onto the machine, and the application starts. If additional subcomponents within the application are required later (such as the help files in Office 2003 Word, for example), those components are loaded on demand in a *just-in-time* fashion as the user attempts to use them.

What Happens When You Assign Applications to Computers

If the application is Assigned to computers, the application is *entirely* installed and available for all users who use the machine the next time the computer is rebooted. This won't save disk space, but it will save time because the users won't have to go back to the source for installation.

Publishing Applications

The icons of Published applications are placed in the Add or Remove Programs folder in Control Panel in Windows XP or in the "Install a program from the network" window in Windows 8 and later, as seen in Figure 11.3.

FIGURE 11.3 Windows applications can be Published in the (very) hard to find "Install a program from the network," as seen here (Windows 8 and later).

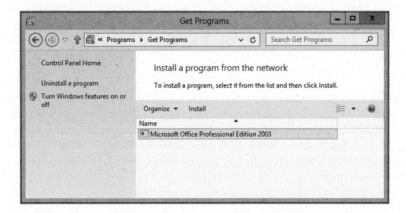

You can Publish to users (but not computers). When you Publish applications to users, the application list is dynamically generated, depending on which applications are currently being Published. Users get no signals whatsoever that any applications are waiting for them in Control Panel.

Once the application is selected, all the components required to run that application are pulled from the distribution source and installed on the machine. The user can then close Control Panel and use the Start Menu to launch the newly installed application.

By default, the icons of Assigned applications are also placed in the Add or Remove Programs folder (or "Install a program from the network") for download. In other words, by default, all Assigned applications are also Published. The "Do Not Display this Package in the Add/Remove Programs Control Panel" option is unchecked by default; therefore, the application appears in both places by default upon Assignment. (I'll discuss this option in the section "Advanced Published or Assigned.")

 Published apps are also advertised to be run automatically via document invocation (again, also known as auto-install).

Rules of Deployment

Some rules constrain our use of GPSI, regardless of whether applications are Assigned through the Computer or User node of Group Policy. As just stated, the icons of Assigned applications appear on the Start Menu, whereas the icons of Published applications appear in the Add or Remove Programs folder (or "Install a program from the network"). With that in mind, here are the deployment rules:

Rule 1   Assigning to computers means that anyone who can log onto machines affected by the GPO sees the Assigned application on the Start Menu. This is useful for situations such as nursing stations. You can also Assign applications to users in the GPO, which means that whenever users roam, their applications follow them—no matter which machine they reside at physically.

Rule 2   You can't Publish to computers; you can only Assign to computers within a GPO.

Why the funky rules? Although I have no specific confirmation from Microsoft, I'll make an observation that might help you remember these rules: Most users can use the Start Menu to launch applications. Therefore, Assigning applications to users makes sense.

Additionally, since applications Assigned to computers apply to *every* user who logs onto a targeted machine, the users in question can also surely use the Start Menu to launch the Assigned applications. But using Published applications takes a little more computer savvy. Users first need to know that applications are Published at all and then check the Add or Remove Programs folder (or "Install a program from the network") to see if any applications are targeted for them. A specific user might know that applications are waiting for her, but it's unlikely that all users using a computer would know that. In any event, just remember the following rules:

- You can Assign to users.
- You can Assign to computers.
- You can Publish to users.
- You cannot Publish to computers.

Since this level of sophistication isn't really the norm, I bet Microsoft avoided providing Publishing capabilities for computers because there is no guaranteed level of sophistication for a specific user of a specific computer.

Package-Targeting Strategy

So far, we've set up our software distribution shared folder, prepared the package to the point of distribution, and (optionally) tied it down with NTFS permissions. Now, we need to target a group of users or computers for the software package. Here are some possible options:

- Leverage an OU for the users you want to get the package, move the accounts into this OU, and then Assign or Publish the application to that OU. Whenever members of the OU log on, the application is available for download. Each user can connect to the distribution source and acquire a copy of the installation. This is best for when your users are mostly using desktops. Because desktops are connected to the network, the just-in-time fashion of the download really makes sense here.

- Leverage an OU for the computers that you want to get the package, and then Assign the application to the computers in that OU. When the computer is rebooted, then, whenever any user logs onto the targeted machines, the application is fully downloaded and ready to go. This isn't true for every application; it's not true for Office 2010 and later (shown later), but it is true for just about everything else. This is best if you have a gaggle of laptop users. You'll want to ensure that the entire application is loaded before users go on the road with their machines. This strategy is ideal for this scenario.

- Assign or Publish the application at the domain or OU level, and then use GPO Filtering with security groups (see Chapter 2). This is a more advanced technique, but it can be very useful when you want to give someone only the ability to modify group memberships and (by modifying the group membership) also deploy software to a group of users (or even computers).

- Assign or Publish the application at the domain or OU level, and then use WMI (Windows Management Instrumentation) Filtering based on specific information within machines. (See Chapter 4 in the section "Fine-Tuning When and Where Group Policy Applies.") This is most useful if you want to strategically target machines based on specific criteria—for instance, "Only deploy this software to users with 6GB of RAM and hotfix Q24601."

> There's also the ability to set permissions upon individual packages within a GPO for more fine-grained targeting. Check out the Security tab for each package.

We could use any of these methods to target our users. The first two options are the most straightforward and most common practice. In our first example, we'll leverage an OU and Assign the application to our computers. We'll use the **Human Resources Computers** OU and Assign them Office 2003.

Normal Shares vs. DFS Namespaces

The GPSI features are like the postal service; they're a delivery mechanism. Their duty is to deliver the package and walk away. But it's something of a production before that package is delivered to your users (or computers.)

Before we get there, however, you need to prepare for software distribution by setting up a *distribution point* to store the software. You can choose to create a shared folder on any server—hopefully, one that's close to the users who will be pulling the software.

The closer to the user you can get the server, the faster the download of the software and the less saturated your network in the long run.

In a nutshell, GPSI delivers a message to the client about the shared folder from which the software is available. However, if you are concerned that your users will often roam your distributed enterprise, you can additionally set up *DFS Namespaces*.

DFS Namespaces is the *Distributed File System* technology that, when used in addition to Active Directory Site Topology definitions, can automatically direct users toward the share containing the software closest to them. The essence of DFS Namespaces is that it sets up a front end for shared folders and then acts as the traffic cop, directing users to the closest replica. To explore DFS technology, visit https://msdn.microsoft.com/en-us/library/bb727150.aspx.

DFS Namespaces has an extra huge benefit over using normal shares. If a normal share on a normal server goes down (and the client application needs a repair), the client can just find another node (the next closest node) on the network that contains the software. Or, if you want to repurpose that server for something else, you don't have to worry about the gruesome problem of removing the software from everywhere, putting the share on the new server, and redeploying the application. With DFS, you just add a server with the share contents and change a few pointers around on the back end.

Creating and Editing the GPO to Deploy Office

We are now ready to create our GPO and Assign our application to our users. In this example, we'll Assign Office 2003 to computers, but this procedure works for just about every application that's "Group Policy deployable." Again, Office 2010 and 2013 break the rules, so learn now with Office 2003, and you'll be good to go for almost all "normal" applications.

Open the GPMC, and then follow these steps:

1. To create a GPO that deploys Office 2003 to the **Human Resources Computers** OU, right-click the OU and choose "Create a GPO in this domain, and Link it here" from the context menu to open the New GPO dialog box. Enter a descriptive name in the New GPO dialog box, such as **Deploy Office 2003 (to computers)**. The GPO should now be linked to the **Human Resources Computers** OU.

2. Right-click the link to the GPO (or the GPO itself), and choose Edit from the context menu to open the Group Policy Management Editor.

The software distribution settings are found in both Computer Configuration and User Configuration; Figure 11.4 shows them under User Configuration.

FIGURE 11.4 Right-click the GPSI settings to deploy a new package.

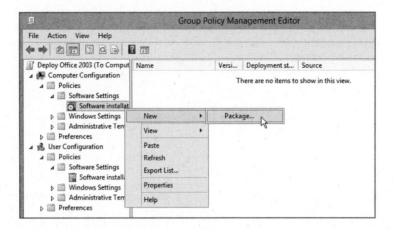

For this first package, we will Assign the application to the computers in the **Human Resources Computers** OU.

1. Choose Computer Configuration ➢ Policies ➢ Software Settings.

2. Right-click "Software installation" and choose New ➢ Package, as shown in Figure 11.4, to open the Open dialog box, which lets you specify the .MSI file.

Do not—I repeat—do not use the Open dialog box's interface to click and browse for the file locally. Equally evil is specifying a local file path, such as D:\apps\office2003distro\Pro11.msi. Why is this? Because the location needs to be from a consistently available point, such as a UNC path. Entering a local file path prevents the Windows Installer at the client from finding the package on the server. Merely clicking the file doesn't guarantee that the package will be delivered to the client. Again, entering the full UNC path, as shown in Figure 11.5, is the *only* guaranteed method to deliver the application to the client.

You will need to specify the full UNC path on the shared folder for the application. Let me say that again: you will need to specify the network path, not the "local" path, or the installation will fail.

Earlier, we put our Office 2003 Administrative Installation inside the Apps share on the DC01 server inside the Office2003Distro directory. If you take a look at the Office 2003 media, you'll note there are lots of .MSI files that might work. However, there is only one that is meant for GPSI distribution. The precise name will vary depending on the version of Office 2003 you have. In my case, I have Office 2003 Professional Edition. The file that I'll need to deliver using GPSI is named Pro11.msi. Therefore, the full UNC path to the application is \\DC01\Apps\Office2003Distro\Pro11.MSI, as shown in Figure 11.5.

FIGURE 11.5 Always use the full UNC and never the local path when this dialog box requests the file.

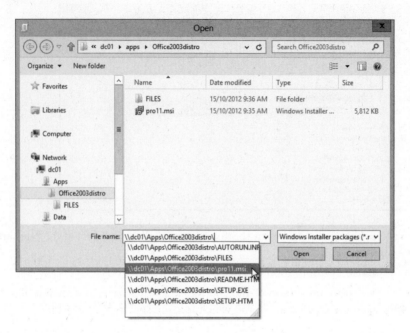

Before You Ramp Up, Let's Talk about Licensing

A question I often get when I teach my live Group Policy Intensive course is this: "If I use GPSI to deploy applications to my users, how does this affect my licensing agreements with Microsoft or other software vendors?" The next most frequently asked question about GPSI is this: "If I use GPSI to do mass rollouts, how can I keep track of licensing for reporting during audits?" Bad news on both fronts, friends.

Occasionally, the Microsoft technology doesn't work in lockstep with usable licensing agreements. Specifically, if you use GPSI as your mechanism to get software to the masses, you need to be especially careful with your Microsoft licensing agreements or any other licensing agreements. When you deploy any software via GPSI, you have the potential to load the software on a machine and make it available to any number of users who can log onto that machine. As I discussed, using GPSI to deploy to computers gives everyone who logs onto the machine (via the domain) access to the icons on the Start Menu. And, if you target users, whether the application is available only for a specific user depends on the application. For instance, a well-written .MSI prevents users who aren't Assigned the application from using it—but other .MSI applications (especially those you create with third-party tools) may not. And when you use GPSI to deploy an application to, say, users in an OU, you won't know how many users accept the offer and how many users don't end up using the application.

With that in mind, GPSI is a wonderful mechanism for deploying software. But in terms of licensing and auditing, you're on your own. My advice is that if you're planning to use GPSI for your installations, check with each vendor to find out the vendor's licensing requirements when you Assign to users and Assign to computers.

Remember, you have a large potential for exposure by doing a GPSI to users and/or computers; protect yourself by checking with your vendor before you do a mass deployment of any application in this fashion. Additionally, it's important to remember that there is no facility for counting or metering the number of accepted offers of software for auditing purposes.

That's where Microsoft's System Center Configuration Manager is supposed to come into play, to help you determine "who's using what."

Finally, if you're looking for an all–Group Policy solution to help mitigate these (and other) problems, check out Specops Software's Specops Deploy (www.specopssoft.com). But stay tuned—more on that later.

Once the full UNC path is entered, a dialog box will appear, asking which type of distribution method we'll be using: Assigned or Advanced. Published will be grayed out because you cannot Publish to computers.

For now, choose Assigned and click OK. When you do (and you wait a minute or two), you'll see the application listed, as shown in Figure 11.6. Hang tight—it'll show up.

FIGURE 11.6   The applications you assign are listed under the node you chose to use (Computer Configuration ➤ Software installation or User Configuration ➤ Software installation).

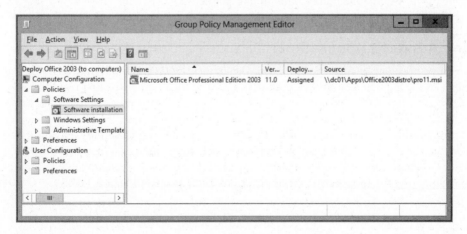

Understanding When Applications Will Be Installed

Once you've Assigned or Published an application, you'll need to test it to see if it's working properly. Here's how users and computers should react:

- Applications Published to users on any operating system should show up right away in Control Panel. No rebooting or logging (and logging back in) should be required, but you might have to refresh the Add or Remove Programs folder (or "Install a program from the network"). An application isn't installed until a user specifically selects it or the application is launched via *document invocation* (also called *install-on-first-use* or *advertisement*). Recall that document invocation allows the application to be installed as soon as a file associated with the application is opened.

- Applications Assigned to users on servers should show up on next logon on the Start Menu. Applications Assigned to server computers should install upon next reboot. All users logging onto those computers will see the icons on the Start Menu.

- If you're deploying to users on Windows XP or later, you need to know whether Fast Boot is turned on. Recall from Chapter 3 that Fast Boot is enabled by default for Windows XP and later, and you will need to explicitly turn it off. To review:

  - If Windows XP or later Fast Boot is enabled and you Assign applications to users, it will take two logoffs and logons for the icons to appear on the Start Menu.

  - If Windows XP or later Fast Boot is enabled and you Assign applications to computers, it will take two reboots before the assignment is installed. Afterward, icons appear for all users on the Start Menu. If you want to turn off this behavior for Windows XP and later, you can do so. Just check out Chapter 3 to learn how.

  - Note, however, that Windows XP and later Fast Boot is always off if a Roaming Profile is used.

 WARNING   You'll need to adjust the deployment properties before certain applications will deploy properly to users. (More on this in the section "Advanced Published or Assigned" later in this chapter.)

Testing Assigned Applications

Before you go headlong and try to verify your deployment of Office 2003, first verify that a machine is in the **Human Resources Computers** OU, and then reboot the first test machine in the OU.

If you're Assigning an application to a Windows 7 or later machine, by default you won't see anything during startup except a "Please wait..." and a lot of disk activity. However, if you enable the policy setting **Display highly detailed status messages** located within Computer Configuration ➢ Policies ➢ Administrative Templates ➢ System, you'll see more information during startup, such as the application's title, as seen in Figure 11.7.

FIGURE 11.7 If you enable the Display highly detailed status messages policy setting to affect your Windows 7 or later machines, you'll see the name of the software installing instead of a lousy "Please wait..." message at reboot time.

Go ahead and get a cup of coffee while this is installing. It takes a while. Really. Go ahead. I'll wait.

Once the application is fully installed, you can log on as any user in the domain (or the local computer) and see the application's icons on the Start Menu.

On Windows 7, icons will show up on the Start Menu, as seen in in Figure 11.8.

FIGURE 11.8 The Office icons and program names will appear on the Start Menu (more specifically on the Start ➢ All Programs menu) on Windows 7.

On Windows 8, new applications appear on the Start screen, as seen in Figure 11.9. On Windows 10, the application icons appear in a folder called Microsoft Office on the Start menu, as seen in Figure 11.10.

FIGURE 11.9   On Windows 8, the application icons appear on the Start screen.

FIGURE 11.10   On Windows 10, the application icons appear in a folder called Microsoft Office on the Start menu. (I added a little arrow to help you find it.)

At this point, any user can select any Office application, and the application is briefly prepared and then displayed for the user. In Windows 10, clicking on the folder reveals the applications inside, as seen here:

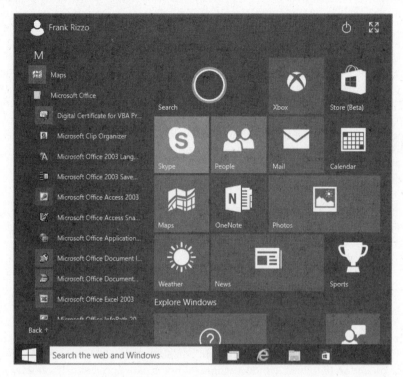

Stay tuned for more information on Assigning and Publishing .MSI applications (particularly to users).

Testing Publishing Applications (to Users)

You can also test the process of Publishing applications before continuing. Recall that the icons of Published applications appear in the "Install a program from the network") in Control Panel. However, the usefulness of Published applications is minimal, which is why it's relegated to such a small section for discussion. Users must be specifically told there's something waiting for them, hunt it down themselves, and install it. And applications can only be Published to users, not computers, so a user who is getting a Published application must be logged in.

To test this for yourself, simply select Publish when adding a new application, or right-click an existing package Assigned to users and choose Publish from the context menu.

To see a Published application in action on a Windows 7 or later machine, follow these steps:

1. Choose Start ➤ Control Panel ➤ Programs ➤ Get Programs ➤ "Install a program from the network."

2. Select the application and select Install, as shown in Figure 11.3.

A Published application needn't be fully relegated to lying dormant until a user selects it. Indeed, the default is to specify that the application automatically launch via document invocation (also known as auto-install) as soon as an associated file type is opened. In this way, you can have the application available for use but just not have the application's icons appear on the Start Menu as you do when you Assign it. However, you can turn off document invocation by clearing the "Auto install this application by file extension activation" check box as specified in the section "The Deployment Options Section" a bit later.

You'll need to adjust the deployment properties before certain applications will deploy properly to users. (More on this in the section "Advanced Published or Assigned" later in this chapter.)

Application Isolation

In many circumstances, applications are *isolated* for their intended use. This means that if an application is deployed, another user shouldn't be able to use it. Here are some examples to help you understand how Windows Installer helps with application isolation:

- Users do not share Assigned or Published applications that an administrator has set up. For instance, User A is Assigned an application and installs it. User B can use User A's machine but is not Assigned the application via Group Policy. Therefore, when User B logs onto that machine, User B does not see the Assigned icons for User A.

- Users require their own "instance" of the application. If User A and User B are Assigned the same application, each user must contact the source and perform a one-time/per-user customization that some applications require. In most circumstances, this will not double the used disk space, and the time for installation for the second user is not very long because portions of the application are already installed for User A.

- If two users are Assigned different applications that register the same file types, the correct application is always used. For instance, Joe and Dave share the same machine. Joe is Assigned WinZip and Dave is Assigned UltraZip. When Joe opens a .ZIP file, WinZip launches. When Dave opens a .ZIP file, UltraZip launches.

- Depending on the .MSI application, users might not be able to go "under the hood" and select the EXEs of installed programs. For instance, if User A is Assigned an application, User B (who is not Assigned the application) cannot just use Explorer, locate the application on the hard drive, and double-click the application to install it. This is not a hard-and-fast rule and is based on how the .MSI application itself is coded.

- Users can uninstall applications that they have access to in the Add or Remove Programs folder (or "Uninstall or change a program" in Windows Vista and later parlance). This has a two-part implication. First, by default, all Assigned applications are also Published, and thus, users can remove them using the Add or Remove Programs folder. The icons for the applications will still be on the Start ➢ All Programs menu the next time the user logs on. The first time the user attempts to run one of these applications by choosing Start ➢ All Programs ➢ *application*, the application reinstalls itself from the distribution point. The second implication deals with who, precisely, can remove Assigned (or Published) applications. First, users cannot delete applications that are directly Assigned to computers. Next, users cannot delete applications that aren't directly Assigned to their user account.

Advanced Published or Assigned

When you attempt to Publish or Assign an application to your users or computers, you are given an additional selection of Advanced. If you didn't choose Advanced when you initially deployed the application, that's not a problem. You can simply right-click the package and choose Properties from the context menu to open the Properties dialog box. The only option that is not available in this "after the fact" method is the ability to add Microsoft Transform Files, which I'll describe in the section "The Modifications Tab" later in this chapter.

The Properties dialog box has six tabs: General, Deployment, Upgrades, Categories, Modifications, and Security. In Figure 11.11, the Properties dialog box is focused on the Deployment tab, which is discussed in detail in a bit.

FIGURE 11.11   These are the options on the Deployment tab when you're Assigning to computers. Note how just about everything is grayed out.

The General Tab

This tab contains the basic information about the package: the name that is to be displayed in the Add or Remove Programs folder (or "Install a program from the network"), the publisher, and some language and support information. All this is extracted from the .MSI package.

Under the General tab, you'll find another little goodie: you can specify the URL of a web page that contains support information for the application. For instance, if you have specific setup instructions for the user, you can place the instructions on a page on one of your intranet servers and include the URL with the package. The client's Add or Remove Programs folder displays a hyperlink to the URL next to the package.

The Deployment Tab

This tab, as shown in Figure 11.11, has three sections: "Deployment type," "Deployment options," and "Installation user interface options." There is also an Advanced button at the bottom of the tab. Which options on the Deployment tab you choose depends on how you want to deploy the application and whether you are Assigning to computer or Assigning or Publishing to users. Figure 11.11 earlier shows the options when you're Assigning to computers.

Figure 11.12 shows the options on the Deployment tab when you're Assigning an application to users. You'll notice that many more options are available than when you're Assigning to computers. The options in the "Installation user interface options" section are critical, and you will likely need to change them before applications are correctly Assigned or Published to users.

FIGURE 11.12   These are the options on the Deployment tab when you're Assigning or Publishing to users.

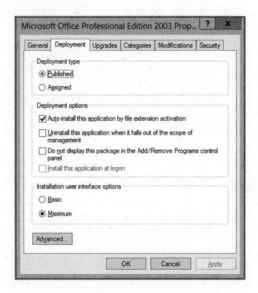

The Deployment Type Section

The options in this section let you instantly change the deployment type from Published to Assigned, and vice versa, and are available only when you are deploying applications to users. When you are deploying applications to computers, Assigned is the only option. If you're deploying to user accounts, you can also change the deployment type by right-clicking the package definition. You can see a package definition of an application in the Group Policy Management Editor dialog box in Figure 11.6, earlier. Then, you can select the deployment type, Assign or Publish, from the context menu.

The Deployment Options Section

This section has four check boxes:

Auto-install this application by file extension activation   When .MSI applications are Published or Assigned (or .ZAP packages are Published), each of their definitions contains a list of supported file types. Those file types are actually loaded inside Active Directory.

When a GPO applies to a user or a computer and this check box is selected, the application is automatically installed based on the extension. This is, essentially, application execution via document invocation. Note that this option is always automatically selected (and cannot be unselected) if you Assign the application. That is, document invocation is only optional when Publishing.

Document invocation is most handy when new readers and file types are released, such as Adobe Acrobat Reader and its corresponding .PDF file type. Simply Assign or Publish an application with this check box enabled and Acrobat Reader will be automatically shot down to anyone who opens a .PDF file for the first time. This check box is selected by default when you are Assigning applications to users or computers.

Uninstall this application when it falls out of the scope of management   GPOs can be applied to Sites, Domains, or OUs. If a user is moved out of the scope to which this GPO applies, what happens to the currently deployed software? For instance, if a user or computer is moved from one OU to another, what do you want to happen with this specific software package? If you don't want the software to remain on the workstation, click this check box. Remember—the applications aren't removed immediately if a user or computer leaves the scope of the GPO. As you'll see shortly, computers receive a *signal* to remove the software. (This is described in the section "Removing Applications" later in this chapter.)

Do not display this package in the Add/Remove Programs control panel   As mentioned, icons and program names for Assigned applications appear in the Start ➢ All Programs menu, but, by default, they also appear as Published icons in the Add or Remove Programs applet in Control Panel. Thus, users may choose to install the application all at once or perform an en masse repair. However, the dark side of this check box is that users can remove any application they want. To prevent the application from appearing in the Add or Remove Programs folder or "Install a program from the network," select this check box. When the application is then earmarked for being Published, the application is available only for loading through document invocation.

Install this application at logon   See the section "Using Group Policy Software Installation over Slow Links" later in this chapter for a detailed explanation.

The Installation User Interface Options Section

Two little innocuous buttons in this section make a world of difference for many applications when you're Assigning or Publishing applications to users. Some .MSI packages can recognize when Basic or Maximum is set and change their installation behavior accordingly. Others can't. Consult your .MSI package documentation to see if the package uses this option and what it does.

Assigning most normal MSIs to users can be disastrous if you retain the default of Maximum. If we keep on the same idea using Office 2003, instead of the application automatically and nearly silently loading from the source upon first use, the user is prompted to step through the application's own Installation Wizard.

Simply choosing Basic remedies this problem: most normal apps are magically down-loaded and installed for every user targeted in the OU. Why is Maximum the default? I wish I knew. For now, if you're Assigning applications to users, be sure the Basic check box is checked. For information about how to change the defaults, see "Default Group Policy Software Installation Properties" later in this chapter.

The Advanced Button

Clicking the Advanced button opens the Advanced Deployment Options dialog box, shown in Figure 11.13. This dialog box has two sections: "Advanced deployment options" and "Advanced diagnostic information."

FIGURE 11.13   The options in the Advanced Deployment Options dialog box

The Advanced Deployment Options Section

In the modern GPMC, this section has three options, and in the old GPMC, it has four options:

Ignore language when deploying this package   If the .MSI package definition is coded to branch depending on the language, selecting this option can force one version of the language. Normally, if the language of the .MSI package doesn't match the language of the operating system, Windows will not install it. The exceptions are if the application is in English, if the application is language-neutral, or if this check box is checked. If there are multiple versions of the application in different languages, the .MSI engine chooses the application with the best language match.

Make this 32-bit X86 application available to Win64 machines   Modern 64-bit clients ignore this setting. It was used for older computers, like Windows Server 2003 targets.

Include OLE class and product information   I've never needed this switch, but here's the idea: if the application you're deploying uses COM classes, and that COM class is triggered, then the application is pulled down automatically. Again, I never needed it. Check with your application vendor to see if you need this switch.

The Advanced Diagnostic Information Section

You can't modify anything in this section, but it does have some handy information.

Product code   As mentioned, if the unique product code of the application you are deploying matches an existing installed product, the application will be removed from the client.

Deployment count   A bit later in this chapter, you'll learn why you might need to redeploy an application to a population of users or computers. When you do, this count is increased. See the section "Patching a Distribution Point" a bit later for more information.

Script name   Whenever an application is Published or Assigned, a pointer to the application, also known as an .AAS file, is placed in the SYSVOL in the Policies container within the GPT (Group Policy Template). The .AAS files are application advertisement script files and are critical to an application's ability to install on first use. This entry shows the name of the .AAS file, which can be useful information if you're chasing down a GPO replication problem between Domain Controllers.

The Upgrades Tab

You can deploy a package that upgrades an existing package. For instance, if you have "Super App 1.0" and want to upgrade it to "Super App 1.5," this is the place. Upgrades can be either mandatory or optional.

Moreover, you can "upgrade" to totally different programs. For instance, if your corporate application for .ZIP files is WinZip but changes to UltraZip, follow these steps to upgrade:

1. Create the UltraZip .MSI package, Assign or Publish the application, open the Properties dialog box, and click the Upgrades tab.

2. Click the Add button to open the Add Upgrade Package dialog box, as shown in Figure 11.14.

3. In the "Package to upgrade" section, select the package definition. Note that WinZip doesn't specifically appear in our example in Figure 11.14; it's just the dialog box you would use.

FIGURE 11.14   Use the Upgrades tab to migrate from one application to another.

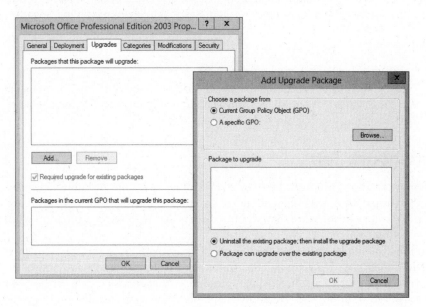

Although you can click the Browse button to open the Browse dialog box and select another GPO for this to apply to, it's easier to keep the original package and upgrade in the same GPO scope.

4. Use the options at the bottom of the Add Upgrade Package window to choose either to uninstall the application first or to plow on top of the current installation, and then click OK.

5. Back in the Upgrades tab, check the "Required upgrade for existing packages" check box and click OK to force the upgrade.

If the "Required upgrade for existing packages" check box is cleared, users can optionally add the program using the Add or Remove Programs applet in Control Panel. This can cause grief for applications that shouldn't really ever be installed on the same machine at the same time. An old example might be Office 2003 and Office XP; if they're together on the same machine, bad things happen. Moreover, if the check box is not checked, the old application is started whenever an associated file extension (such as `.DOC`) is invoked.

It is best if your package is specifically written to upgrade earlier (or different) products; sometimes, it may not actually remove the previous application.

When you're Assigning to computers, the "Required upgrade for existing packages" check box is always checked and not available for selection.

The Categories Tab

The Categories tab allows administrators to give headings to groups of Published software, which are then displayed in the Add or Remove Programs applet in Control Panel. Users can select the category of software they want to display and then select a program within the category to install.

For example, you might want to create the category Archive Programs for WinZip and UltraZip and the category Doc Readers for Adobe Acrobat Reader and GhostScript. If you want, you can list a package in multiple categories. You can also create categories. For information on how to do so, see "Default Group Policy Software Installation Properties" later in this chapter.

The Modifications Tab

The Modifications tab is used to deploy Microsoft Transform Files (.MST) files, or just Transform Files for short. For "normal" applications, Microsoft Transform Files are applied on current .MSI packages either to filter the number of options available to the end user or to specify certain answers to questions usually brought up during the .MSI package installation.

Some applications ship with preconfigured MST files. Others ship with their own "transform generator" utilities. Others ship with none of these.

Ask your application vendor if a transform-generation utility for your package is available. If not, you might have to step up to a third-party .MSI/.MST tool, such as InstallShield by Flexera. Some applications, such as Office 2003, come with their own .MST generation tool.

Handy! But, again, that situation is unique. Often, vendors just assume you will be able to use an .MST transform-creation program to create MSTs.

Office 2010 and 2013 do not ship with an MST-generation tool. See the section "Deploying Office 2010 and Later Using Group Policy (MSI Version)" later for more information.

In Figure 11.15, you can see I've loaded an .MST file named NOMSACCESS.MST (but I haven't yet pressed OK.) This .MST will prohibit the use of Microsoft Access 2003 from Office 2003 but allow all other functions of Office 2003 to run.

FIGURE 11.15   You can only add .MST files during the package definition.

The Modifications tab is available for use only when Advanced is selected when an application is to be initially Published or Assigned. Once you press OK after adding the MST files, then all of the buttons in the Modifications tab in Figure 11.15 will be grayed out. Again, this is because the .MST file must be loaded at package deployment time, and after deployment time, there is no way to add or remove (revoke, really) .MST files after the fact.

Note that if you wanted to, you could add multiple .MST files before clicking the OK button to lock in your selection. You can see this ability and the Move Up and Move Down buttons in Figure 11.15. But why would you do this?

Multiple autonomous administrators can individually create .MST files and layer them so that each Transform File contains some of the configuration options. These files are then ordered so that the options are applied from the top down. If configured options overlap, the last-configured option wins.

However, in my travels, I haven't seen administrators choose to add multiple .MST files for the same .MSI. Typically, only one .MST file is used for the package, and that's that.

You might be wondering how you can create your own .MST files for Office. Again, the last "normal" version of Office that used MST files was Office 2003. The short answer is to use the Microsoft Custom Installation Wizard, which is part of the Office 2003 Resource Kit.

If you want to see precisely how it's done, you can refer to the first edition of the book, or use an article I found at http://tinyurl.com/k7fx7r2.

The Security Tab

Individual applications can be filtered based on computer, user, or Security group membership. For instance, if you Assign WinZip to all members of the **Human Resources Users** OU, you set it up normally, as described earlier.

> If a user who happens to administer the application in the GPO is not given Read access, that user will no longer be able to administer the application. Therefore, don't use filtering based on user or security group membership on the administrators of the application.

If, however, you want to exclude a specific member, say, Frank Rizzo, you can deny Frank Rizzo's account permissions to Read the package. A better strategy is to create a security group—say, DenyWinZip—and put the people not allowed to receive the application inside that group. You can then set the permissions to Deny the entire security group the ability to read the package, as shown in Figure 11.16.

FIGURE 11.16   Use the Security tab to specify who can and cannot run applications.

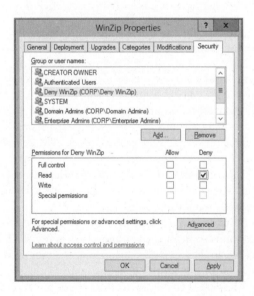

Default Group Policy Software Installation Properties

Each GPSI node (one for users and one for computers) has some default installation properties that you can modify. In the Group Policy Management Editor, simply right-click the GPSI node and choose Properties from the context menu, as shown in Figure 11.17, to open the "Software installation Properties" dialog box (also shown in Figure 11.17), which has four tabs: General, Advanced, File Extensions, and Categories.

FIGURE 11.17   Use the GPSI Properties dialog box to set up general deployment settings.

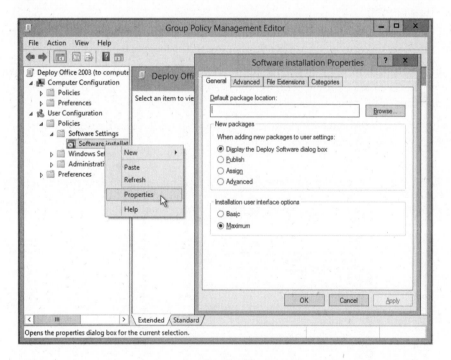

The General Tab

Most settings on the General tab are self-explanatory. Note that you can specify a default package location, such as \\DC01\Apps, so that you can then use the GUI when adding packages. Avoid using direct paths such as C:\Apps since C:\Apps probably won't exist on the client at runtime.

You can also specify the behavior of what happens when you add in new packages (and the Assign action is chosen). That is, a collection of defaults you specify is automatically selected.

Last, you can establish the critical setting of either Basic or Maximum here (when Assigning applications to users). The bummer is that these default setting changes are local only for this specific GPO; the next GPO you create that uses GPSI will not adhere to the defaults you set in this GPO.

The Advanced Tab

The Advanced tab, as shown in Figure 11.18, allows you to set default settings for all the packages you want to deploy in this GPO. You saw settings with similar names earlier in the Advanced Deployment Options dialog box (Figure 11.13). The Advanced tab contains the following options:

Uninstall the applications when they fall out of the scope of management   I'll discuss this setting in the section "Removing Applications" later in this chapter.

Include OLE information when deploying applications   Again, an application might have COM components called by some other action. Selecting this check box will auto-download the deployed application if the trigger occurs.

The "32-bit applications on 64-bit platforms" section   Again, the options in this section seem to do nothing on modern 64-bit systems.

FIGURE 11.18   You can set up some default settings for new packages in this GPO.

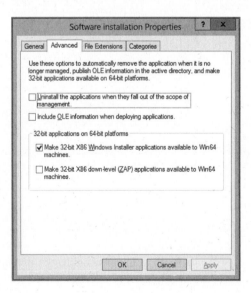

The File Extensions Tab

As stated earlier, you can install and start applications by double-clicking or by invoking their document type. For instance, double-clicking a .ZIP file can automatically deploy a Published or Assigned WinZip application. The correspondence of a file type to a package is found in either the .ZAP file definition or the .MSI file database. Once the application is set to be deployed, the file types are automatically entered into Active Directory.

Occasionally, two Published or Assigned applications are called by the same file extension. This can occur if you're upgrading a package from, say, WinZip to UltraZip and both are using the .ZIP extension, or if you're upgrading from Acrobat Reader to FoxIT Reader and both applications use the .PDF extension.

In those cases, you need to specify which extension fires off which application. To do so, follow these steps:

1. In the "Software installation Properties" dialog box, click the File Extensions tab.

2. Click the "Select file extension" drop-down list box, and select the extension to display all the applicable Assigned or Published applications in the Application Precedence list.

3. Select an application, and then click the Up or Down button to change the order.

The Categories Tab

Categories is a domain-wide property that puts Published or Assigned software into bite-sized chunks, instead of one giant-sized alphabetized list, in the Add or Remove Programs folder or "Install a program from the network" window. As noted earlier, you might want to group WinZip and UltraZip in the Archive Programs category or put Adobe Acrobat Reader and GhostScript in the Doc Readers category. On this tab, simply click the Add button to enter the names of the categories in the "Enter new category" dialog box.

Therefore, if possible, select one administrator to control this property, set it up to be centrally managed, and then use the Properties dialog box to associate a package with a category or categories.

Removing Applications

You can remove applications from users or computers in several ways. First, under some circumstances, users can manually remove applications, but as an administrator, you hold the reins. Therefore, you can set applications to automatically or forcibly be removed.

Users Can Manually Change or Remove Applications

If an application is Assigned (and also Published) to users, they can use Control Panel to change the installed options or remove the application to save space. However, Microsoft's position is that this ability provides the best of both worlds: the user can remove the application's installation (and save space), but since the application is Assigned, the icons and program names are always forced to appear on the Start ➤ All Programs menu.

But, in practice, I've found that this is a bad thing. Users can remove their applications and then go on the road with their laptops. What happens when users actually need those applications? Uh-oh. You get the picture. Again, you may wish to prevent users from being able to change this setting if you have users who like to poke around a lot.

Note, however, that applications Assigned to the computer cannot be changed or uninstalled by anyone but local computer administrators. This is a good thing.

Automatically Removing Assigned or Published
.*MSI* Applications

Applications can be automatically uninstalled when they no longer apply to the user. Earlier, in the "Advanced Published or Assigned" section, while deploying an application, you saw the Deployment tab has a check box entitled "Uninstall this application when it falls out of the scope of management" (Figure 11.12). You can specify that the application is to be uninstalled if any of the following occurs:

- The user or computer is moved out of the OU to which this software applies.
- The GPO containing the package definition is deleted.
- The user or computer no longer has rights to read the GPO.

The software is never forcibly removed while the user is logged onto the current session but is removed a bit later in the following manner:

- Applications Published to users are removed upon next logon.
- Applications Assigned to users are removed upon next logon.
- Applications Assigned to computers are removed upon next reboot.
- Applications Assigned to computers that are currently not attached to the network are removed the next time the computer is plugged into the network and rebooted and the computer account "logs on" to Active Directory.
- Applications Assigned or Published to users on computers that are currently not attached to the network are removed the next time they log on and are validated to Active Directory.

In these cases, the software is automatically removed upon next logon (for users) or upon next reboot (for computers). For example, Figure 11.19 shows what happens when a computer is moved out of an OU and then rebooted. Moving users and computers in and out of OUs might not be such a hot idea if lots of applications are being Assigned.

FIGURE 11.19 Applications can be set to uninstall when they fall out of scope of management.

Removing managed software Microsoft Office Professional Edition 2003...

These rules assume Fast Boot is not enabled—that you've specifically *disabled* Fast Boot. If Fast Boot is enabled (the default), these rules don't apply; expect two logons or two reboots for the change to take effect.

Here's one final warning about the automatic removal of applications: GPSI cannot remove the icons and program names for the application if the GPO has been deleted and the user has a Roaming Profile and has roamed to a machine after the application was uninstalled. In this case, there is not enough uninstall information on the machine, and therefore, the icons and program names will continue to exist, though they will be nonfunctional.

Forcibly Removing Assigned or Published .*MSI* Applications

You have seen how applications can be automatically removed from users or computers when the user or computer object moves out the scope of management. But what if you want to keep the user or computer in the scope of management and still remove an application? You can manually remove Published or Assigned applications. To do so, simply right-click the package definition, and choose All Tasks ➢ Remove, as seen in Figure 11.20. This will open the Remove Software dialog box. The options presented in this dialog box depend on whether you deployed .MSI or .ZAP applications.

FIGURE 11.20 You can revoke deployed applications by selecting Remove.

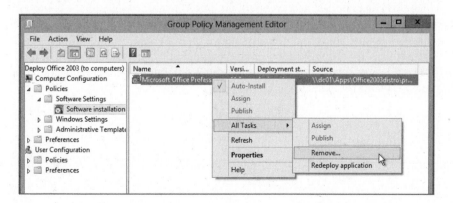

If you are removing an .MSI file, you have two options, as discussed in the next sections.

Immediately Uninstall the Software from Users and Computers

If you choose the option "Immediately uninstall the Software from Users and Computers," then all connected computers receive a signal to uninstall the software, and they follow the rules for uninstalling you learned in the previous section.

The signal to remove an application lives in the actual GPO definition. Therefore, if you're looking for success in the forcible removal of applications, don't delete the GPO right after selecting this option. If you do, the signal to remove the application won't be available to the workstations. Rather, remove the application, and leave the GPO definition around for a while to ensure that the computers get the signal to remove the software. If you remove the GPO before the target user receives the signal (upon next logon) or the computer receives the signal (upon next reboot), the application is orphaned on the Desktop and must be manually unloaded via Control Panel or by some other means (for instance, MSIEXEC, as described later in this chapter).

WARNING   This is a second warning in case you overlooked the ominous message in the previous paragraph: If you remove the GPO definition before a target user or computer receives the signal, the application is orphaned on the Desktop. You can, however, likely get out of this trap if the application was specified with the "Uninstall this application when it falls out of the scope of management" check box. You can move the user or computer out of the scope of management to remove the application and then bring it back in when the application removal is completed. It's a bit rough, but it should work.

Allow Users to Continue to Use the Software, but Prevent New Installations

When you remove applications using the option "Allow users to continue to use the software, but prevent new installations," current installations of the software remain intact. Users to which this edict applies, however, will no longer be able to install new copies of the software. Those who do not have the software will not be able to install it. Those who do have it installed will be able to continue to use it.

The self-repair features of the Windows Installer will still function (for example, if Winword.exe gets deleted, it will come back from the dead), but the application cannot be fully reinstalled via Control Panel.

Once you use this option, you will no longer be able to manage the application and force it to uninstall from the machines on which it is installed.

Using Group Policy Software Installation over Slow Links

First things first: applications Assigned to computers cannot ever be installed over slow (old and crusty) dial-up links, slow 3G connections, or slow VPN (virtual private network) connections.

Why?

Because the computer must see the network, log onto it, and then start to download the program. If you're using any kind of slow connection, manual intervention to connect to the network must be involved. Therefore, in general, no applications Assigned to computers will ever install unless the computer is connected to the LAN.

 I say "in general" in the previous sentence because it does depend a bit on your VPN technology. For instance, you could have a hardware VPN, separate from the client, and a computer assignment could work over that should a slow link not be detected. Indeed, Microsoft's newest "VPN-less" technology DirectAccess might be able to overcome this limitation. I have not set up DirectAccess myself to test this theory.

However, when applications are Assigned or Published to users (not computers), it's a different story. When users connect via a slow link, they will not see new Assignment offers. By default, only users connected at 500Kbps or greater will see new Assignments on the Start ➢ All Programs menu. This is a good thing, too, as you wouldn't want someone to VPN in over a slow link and try to accept the offer for a large application.

You can change this behavior by modifying the GPO at Computer Configuration ➢ Policies ➢ Administrative Templates ➢ System ➢ Group Policy ➢ "**Configured software Installation policy processing,**" as shown in Figure 11.21.

FIGURE 11.21 Use Group Policy to change the default slow-link behavior.

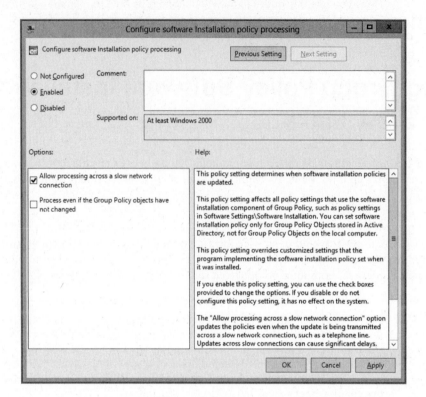

Checking the "Allow processing across a slow network connection" check box forces all clients, regardless of their connection speed, to adhere to the policy setting. If you want to be a bit less harsh, you can change the definition of a "slow link" and modify the **Group Policy Slow Link Detection** policy setting. After you enable the policy setting, set a value in the "Connection speed (Kbps)" spin box.

One word of warning with regard to slow links: Users who are Assigned or Published applications can find other ways to install applications over slow links. First, they can trot out to the Add or Remove Programs applet and select the application. Sure, the offer isn't displayed on the Start ➢ All Programs menu, but it's still going to be available in the Add or Remove Programs applet in Control Panel. To prevent this, select the "Do not display this package in the Add/Remove Programs control panel" check box, which is found in the Deployment tab of the application's Properties (see Figure 11.12).

Last, check out this scenario. Imagine that while on a fast link, a user named Wally accepts the offer for Excel. Super-duper—Excel is now installed. Now, Wally is VPNed in (on a slow link) and receives a Word document in e-mail. And Wally hasn't yet installed Word. Look out! Because .DOC is a registered file type for Microsoft Office, Word will attempt to install over a slow link (if Assigned to a user).

This happens because Wally has accepted the "offer" for Office (he got Excel over a fast link) and now selects to get Word via document invocation. To prevent this, simply clear the "Auto-install this application by file extension activation" option in the Deployment tab in the Properties dialog box of the application (again, see Figure 11.12).

As I stated earlier, users who have dialed up or VPNed over a slow link will not see *new* Assignment offers. The key word here is *new*.

However, this wasn't Wally's problem. He wasn't accepting a new offer over a slow link; rather, Wally had already accepted an offer before he left and VPNed in. If something like that should occur, you'll see something like this:

What you're seeing here is the user being asked where the installation source is—even if he's not connected to the network. Not great, because users (a) don't have a connection to the network and (b) wouldn't know the location or (c) wouldn't know what to type in even if they knew the location (usually).

The best way to handle this is to simply avoid the problem entirely.

So, we could have prevented Wally's problem if the application were already fully installed. But I already said that when you Assign applications to users, the .MSI file is downloaded in chunks—not all at once—which is precisely why Wally had problems when he tried to download Word. He had the "chunk" for Excel but not for Word. Therefore, he needed to reach the original source for a download.

There are two ways to solve this problem:

Assign applications to computers (laptop OUs).   Again, if you Assigned the application to the OU where Wally's laptop lived, the next time he rebooted, he would have the full installation of the application, thus preventing the issue.

Leverage the "Install this application at logon" option.   If you take a peek back in Figure 11.12, you'll see the option "Install this application at logon." What it should say is "Install this application, in full, every time the user logs on to a new machine." The idea is that whenever Wally logs onto a new machine, he will be force-fed the entirety of the application. Then, he'll be sure to have it on his laptop. Again, this setting is only available when you're assigning applications to users.

WARNING   If the user opens the Add or Remove Programs folder (or the "Install a program from the network" window) and manually uninstalls the application, neither the logon script nor the "Install this application at logon" setting will kick back into high gear and install the application. This might be a big deal if your users fool around trying to add or remove stuff. You might also want to select the "Do not display this package in the Add/Remove Programs control panel" check box, also on the Deployment tab in the Properties dialog box.

MSI, the Windows Installer, and Group Policy

Understanding all the nuances of the Windows Installer could be its own book. So instead of giving you pages and pages of stuff that might not be all that useful to you right now, I'm going to cherry-pick some random facts that will likely help you out.

So, in this section, here's what we'll tackle:

- Manually installing or repairing an application on a machine (or multiple machines).

- Patching your installation source.

- Some of the Group Policy settings that affect Windows Installer. Not all of them—just some.

Inside the *MSIEXEC* Tool

MSIEXEC is a command-line tool, which helps you get applications installed.

You can use MSIEXEC in several ways, but here, we're going to look at how to use it to manage existing .MSI packages. Indeed, you can use MSIEXEC to script an installation of an .MSI package at a workstation, but why bother? You're already using the power of Group Policy. However, you might need to check out how an installation works by hand or enable additional logging for deeper troubleshooting. Or you could trigger a preemptive repair of an application at specific times. You can even use MSIEXEC to remove a specific application.

You can also use MSIEXEC as a maintenance tool for existing packages on distribution points. We'll explore a bit of both uses.

Instead of diving into every MSIEXEC command, I'll highlight some of the most frequently used. Indeed, you may never find yourself using MSIEXEC unless specifically directed to do so by an application vendor's Install program.

Using *MSIEXEC* to Install an Application

The first function of MSIEXEC is to initiate an installation from a source point. This is essentially the same as double-clicking the .MSI file, using the /I switch (for Install). The syntax for your application might be as follows:

```
Msiexec /I \\DC01\Apps\yourapp.msi
```

Using *MSIEXEC* to Repair an Application

You can script the repair of applications by using MSIEXEC with the /f switch and an additional helper switch, as indicated in the Windows help file. For instance, you might want to ensure that Pro11.msi (Office 2003) is not corrupted on the client. You can do so by forcing all files from inside the Office 2003 .MSI to be reinstalled on the client. Use the following command from the client (which overwrites older or equally versioned files):

```
Msiexec /fe \\DC01\Apps\officc20e003distro\Pro11.msi
```

If you want to ensure that no older version is installed, you can execute the following command:

```
Msiexec /fo \\DC01\Apps\officc20e003distro\Pro11.msi
```

Again, be sure to consult the Windows help file for the complete syntax of MSIEXEC in conjunction with adhering to your specific application vendor's directions.

Patching a Distribution Point

You can also use MSIEXEC to *patch*—that is, to incorporate vendor-supplied bug fixes and the like to the code base of an existing package. The vendor supplies the patches by using an .MSP file, or *Microsoft Patch* file. Office XP's service packs, for instance, come with several .MSP files that update the original .MSI files.

Office 2003 has multiple service packs. You can download the latest one (SP3) from http://support.microsoft.com/kb/923618. It contains mainsp3.msp, owc11sp3.msp, and owc102003sp3.msp.

Be sure to check with your vendors to see how they want patches applied. In some cases, you would apply all successive service packs. In other cases, you simply apply the last one.

Throughout this chapter, we've leveraged our Office 2003 administration point. We'll continue with that trend. In the following example, the Office 2003 distribution, located at \\DC01\Apps\officc20e003distro, is to be patched with the MAINSP3.msp patch that comes with Office 2003 Service Pack 3. The resulting log file will be called logfile.txt.

Because each vendor may have a different way of patching, be sure to check out the Readme file that comes with the patch files.

The following command line is written as directed from the Office 2003 SP3 whitepaper:

```
Msiexec.exe /a \\<path>\Pro11.MSI /p
    \\<path>\MAINSP3.msp SHORTFILENAMES=True
    /qb- /Lv* C:\Logfile.txt
```

 Again, you'll have to run the command for each and every included patch file to update an Office 2003 distribution point to SP3. However, the good news is that included in the download are all updates that were contained in the previous service packs. So, at least you don't have to download and install Office 2003 to SP1, or SP2 for that matter. Just install all the patch files in SP3 and you're good to go.

Note the following important point: Once the .MSI is patched, all your users (or computers) need to reinstall the application. The underlying application has changed, and the client system doesn't know about the change until you tell it. You can see how to redeploy an application in Figure 11.22. Again, this is only required after an .MSI source is patched.

FIGURE 11.22 Once you patch an .MSI source, be sure to select "Redeploy application."

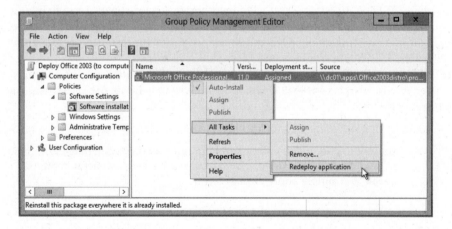

Users also need to do this because of what is termed the "client-source-out-of-sync" problem. Until the client reaches and reinstalls from the updated administrative image, it won't be able to use the administrative image for repairs or on-demand installations. This is because a source location is validated by the Windows Installer before use. The criteria for validation are the name of the package file and the package code (seen as a GUID) of the package. When you patch the administrative image, you change the underlying package code GUID. Thus, the client needs the recache and reinstall in order to pick up the updated package code information.

So, specifically, after you patch a distribution point (or otherwise change the underlying .MSI package in a distribution point), you need to right-click the offer and choose All Tasks ➤ "Redeploy application," as shown in Figure 11.22.

Affecting Windows Installer with Group Policy

You can use several policy settings to tweak the behavior of the Windows Installer. Most tweaks do not involve how software is managed or deployed via GPSI because there's not much to it. You deploy the application, and users (or computers) do your bidding. Rather, these settings tweak the access the user has when software is not being Assigned or Published.

There are two collections of policy settings for the Windows Installer; one is under Computer Configuration, and the other is under User Configuration. As usual, to utilize these policy settings, just create a new GPO, enable the policy settings you like, and then ensure that the corresponding user or computer account is in the scope of management of the GPO.

There are a lot of policy settings that affect Windows Installer. But we're not going to cover all of them. I just want to explain some of them—the ones that really matter. Here they are in no particular order.

Computer-Side Policy Settings for Windows Installer

To display the settings in Computer Configuration, as shown in Figure 11.23, choose Computer Configuration ➤ Policies ➤ Administrative Templates ➤ Windows Components ➤ Windows Installer.

FIGURE 11.23   Use Group Policy to affect the Windows Installer settings.

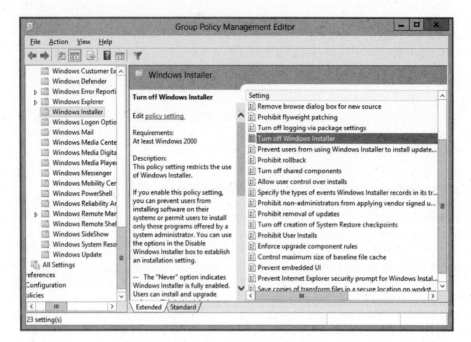

Specify the Types of Events Windows Installer Records in Its Transaction Log

This setting used to be called "Logging." Yep, just "Logging." Now it's got a huge (but very descriptive) name.

Applications Assigned or Published using Windows Installer do not provide much information to the administrator about the success of their installation. By default, several key tidbits of information are logged about managed applications that fail. The log files are named `.MSI*.LOG`; the `*` represents additional characters that make the log file unique for each application downloaded.

Per-computer logs are in `C:\windows\temp` and per-user logs are in `%temp%`.

Thus, centralized logging and reporting is an arduous, if not impossible, task for anything more than a handful of users who are using Windows Installer. For additional logging and reporting, Microsoft recommends its Systems Management Server, as described in the section "Systems Center Configuration Manager vs. Group Policy (and Alternatives)" later in the chapter.

To add logging entries, modify this policy setting. Some settings that might come in handy are Out of Memory and Out of Disk—two common reasons for Windows Installer applications failing to load.

You can also turn on Application Management debugging logs by manually editing the Registry of the client machine. Simply run `regedit` or `regedt32` and edit the following key: `HKEY_LOCAL_MACHINE\Software\Microsoft\Windows NT\CurrentVersion`. Create a key called `Diagnostics`, and then add a `Reg_DWORD` value called `AppMgmtDebugLevel` and set it to `4b` in hexadecimal. You'll then find a log in the local `%windir%\debug\usermode` folder named `appmgmt.log`, which can also aid in finding out why applications fail to load.

Turn Off Logging via Package Settings

If this property is turned on within the package, `.MSI` packages can choose to log their own actions if the property is turned on within the package. With this policy setting you can let that behavior stand or turn it off.

This setting is valid only on machines that have Windows Installer 4 or later, which is on Windows Vista and later.

User-Side Policy Settings for Windows Installer

To display the Group Policy settings that affect the Windows Installer, as shown in Figure 11.24, choose User Configuration ➢ Policies ➢ Administrative Templates ➢ Windows Components ➢ Windows Installer. These settings affect the behavior of the users in the scope.

FIGURE 11.24   The Windows Installer user settings

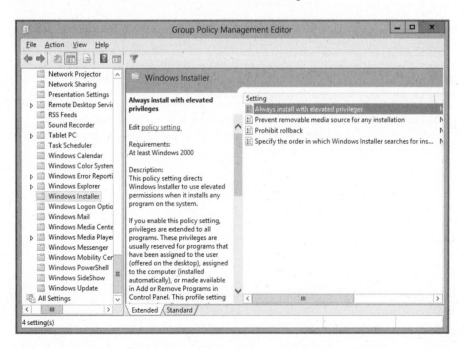

There aren't any settings I wish to call out for your use. Again, for normal Group Policy operations, you should be just fine with the defaults. Many of the settings on both the User and Computer side deal with strange use cases of users installing software under the most bizarre of conditions.

If you use Group Policy Software Installation to deploy your software, it isn't bizarre at all, and therefore you simply won't need to employ many (or any!) of these policy settings.

One for the Road—Leave Windows Installer and Group Policy Software Installation Data

Back in Chapter 9, "Profiles: Local, Roaming, and Mandatory," we discussed a specific problem with regard to GPSI and roaming user profiles. That is, if you choose to enable the **Delete Cached Copies of Roaming Profiles** policy setting, the machine "cleans up" as a user logs off.

This has an unintended consequence with regard to GPSI.

Specifically, if the Roaming Profiles data is deleted at logoff time, the information regarding applications deployed via Group Policy Software Installation is also lost (by default). To that end, you should enable a policy that affects users on Windows XP/SP2 or later called **Leave Windows Installer and Group Policy Software Installation Data**. Once that policy is enabled, the Group Policy Software Installation data remains on the hard drive, so subsequent logins for users are much faster.

Again, enable this setting if you're also choosing to wipe the Roaming Profile away when the user logs out. Note that it is not a Windows Installer setting per se, so it's located in a different area. Specifically, you'll find the policy you need at Computer Configuration ➢ Policies ➢ Administrative Templates ➢ System ➢ User Profiles ➢ **Leave Windows Installer and Group Policy Software Installation Data.**

If you're interested, this problem is specifically discussed in Knowledge Base article 828452, "An Assigned Package Is Reinstalled Every Time Clients Log on to the Domain" (http://support.microsoft.com/kb/828452).

Deploying Office 2010 and Later Using Group Policy (MSI Version)

In the previous examples, we used Office 2003 as the "main example" of how to deploy software, in the normal case. By normal, I'm talking about, well, normal stuff:

- `.MSI` files for deployment. Using `msiexec /a <`*`filename`*`.msi>` to prepare installations in some cases, like we saw in Office 2003.

- `.MST` files for transforming applications. In the case of Office 2003, we created a `NOMSACCESS.MST` to prevent our users from receiving Microsoft Access.

- `.MSP` files for patching applications.

It all makes "sense." Rather, *made* sense. Until Office 2007 came along. Again, to be clear, the stuff you learned earlier in this chapter is indeed valid for almost all applications under the sun.

For some reason, the Office 2007, Office 2010, Office 2013, and the upcoming Office 2016 teams decided not to follow the rules. Let's see how we can work around this limitation and use Group Policy in some form to deploy Office 2010, Office 2013, or Office 2016.

> If you happen to be interested in deploying Office 2007 and not Office 2010 or later, then please refer to earlier editions of this book, which detail the process.

What we're about to talk about will work for Office 2010 and later (including Office 2016, Volume License Edition), but I'll be showing you Office 2013. That's because as of this writing, Office 2016's MSI was not yet released, so I couldn't show you the latest and greatest. That being said, my friends at Microsoft have explained to me that all the steps I've shown you for Office 2013 and its MSI will be precisely the same steps for Office 2016 and its MSI when it's released.

Let me jump to the end of the story. To perform an Office 2013 and later installation correctly using Group Policy, we'll be using Group Policy with computer startup scripts. So, no GPSI involved. We'll be using computer startup scripts to do the heavy lifting.

That's the deal, so let's check it all out.

> Office 2013 comes in a variety of formats. One of them is called Click-to-Run, which actually streams the Office download from Microsoft instead of actually installing it. We'll cover that in the section "Installing Office using Click-to-Run."

Steps to Office 2013 and 2016 Deployment Using Group Policy

Before we get going, let me just state that there might be other ways to perform the task of Office 2013 or 2016 deployment using scripts. In short, this is simply my recipe, and it may or may not be perfect in your world. It should be sufficient for most people and most circumstances, though.

So, here are the general steps we're about to undertake using my recipe. In this document, I'm not going to say the words "Office 2013 and Office 2016" over and over again. I'm just going to say "Office" and you should think "Office 2013 or 2016" unless otherwise noted.

Step 1: Download or acquire the MSI version of Office.   There are a lot of versions of Office. Knowing which version you're using is going to be important in upcoming steps. Note that Office comes in MSI and Click-to-Run versions. In this section, we'll tackle the MSI version.

Step 2: Once it's downloaded, expand Office.   Should you download Office, it may come in a compressed (packed) format, which needs to be expanded to be used.

Step 3: Acquire the Office Customization Tool components.   The Office Customization Tool (OCT) is similar to what we saw earlier in Office 2003's Custom Installation Wizard. Sometimes the version of Office you downloaded in step 1 doesn't have the OCT components. I'll show you where to track these down.

Step 4: Create an .MSP file for Office customization.   Here's where it starts to get weird. To modify Office, we'll be creating an .MSP file (and not an .MST file) using the OCT.

Step 5: (optional) Configure the existing config.xml.   There's a secondary file called config.xml that can have additional configuration options during the deployment process. We'll learn how to configure it.

Step 6: Create a share to deploy Office.   The Office files will be stored and shared for deployment. This is a quick step.

Step 7: Create a share to house the log files.   During deployment, we'll learn which machines succeeded and which failed. We'll create an incoming share for those log files.

Step 8: Utilize and modify Microsoft's suggested deployment script.   Microsoft has a script that we'll use and modify for deploying Office using startup scripts. We'll see where to get it and how to do it.

Step 9: Tweak some Group Policy settings to aid in Office deployments.   There are a handful of settings I will recommend we use to ensure smooth sailing for deployment.

Step 10: Watch the magic.   If all goes well, Office will install.

Step 11: Troubleshoot the mayhem.   If it doesn't go well, we can analyze what went wrong using various logs and reports.

Step 1: Download or Acquire the MSI Version of Office

This part is fairly obvious. If you already have Office and want to skip this step, great. If you're flirting with Office or just want to practice along, you could visit http://office .microsoft.com/en-us/try and download a copy. Or if you have an MSDN subscription you could download it there. I recommend Office Professional 2010 or 2013 for these examples.

 When I last tested downloading Office Professional 2010, the file was named (literally) X17-75058.exe. Nice name. Reminds me of the title of George Lucas's first student film.

Don't forget the Office keycode. We'll need it soon, too.

Step 2: If Downloaded, Expand Office

If your download is compressed (that is, it's downloaded as a single .EXE file as I described in step 1), then you'll need to extract it. I suggest you extract it directly onto your server, since you'll be sharing it from a share on a server in a future step.

The command to extract it could be something like this (by using the /extract switch, adding a colon, and specifying a target directory): X17-75058.exe /extract:\ OfficeDistro.

Step 3: Acquire the Office Customization Tool Components

Now that Office is extracted, try running the Office Customization wizard. Run setup / admin from within the Office folder you expanded.

If the OCT runs, great. Skip the rest of this step. That means your version of Office came ready to go with the OCT pieces.

If you got an error stating that the OCT won't run, that's expected. Here's what to do next. Download a collection of files with a huge title. It's called "Office 2013 Administrative Template files (ADMX/ADML) and Office Customization Tool." You'll find it here: www.microsoft.com/en-us/download/details.aspx?id=35554.

Since Office 2016 doesn't exist in MSI form at the time of this writing, there's also no Office 2016 Office Customization Tool (yet).

Inside the download, you'll find a folder named Admin. Don't confuse it with the other folders; you're simply looking for the one called Admin. Take the folder—in its entirety—and copy it to the Office folder you expanded.

In Figure 11.25 (left side), you'll see the expanded folder structure without the Admin folder. In Figure 11.25 (right side), you'll see what you have to do: copy the Admin folder from the download into the expanded Office directory.

FIGURE 11.25   The OCT won't work out of the box with some versions of Office. The Admin folder is missing (left) and must be downloaded. Copy the Admin folder from the download so it looks like the screenshot on the right.

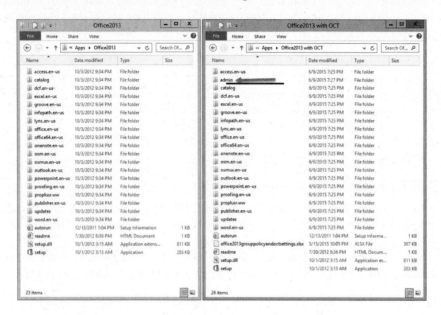

Now, rerunning `setup /admin` should succeed, as seen in Figure 11.26, because the required components for the OCT are now present.

FIGURE 11.26   The Microsoft Office Customization tool will work after the right files are introduced to Office.

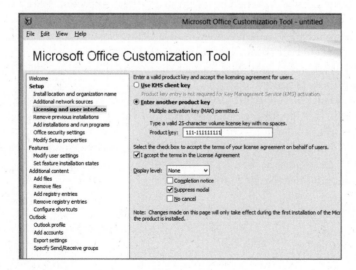

Step 4: Create an *.MSP* File for Office Customization

The OCT is now up and running. Here is where you'll be able to make your tweaks and create a customized Office installation. I don't have space to go into every bell and whistle here, so let me just give you some general guidance:

- In the "Licensing a user interface" section, be sure to enter the key you have, use the Key Management Service (KMS), or use a Multiple Activation Key (MAK). Learn more about KMS and MAKs here:

  http://technet.microsoft.com/en-us/library/ee624358.aspx

- In the same section, I recommend you do three things: select "I accept the terms of the License Agreement" on behalf of the user, set Display Level to None, and uncheck "Completion notice." Doing so will make the installation go smoother because the user will not be able to see anything during the install process.

- You are welcome to do what we did earlier with Office 2003. That is, you can prevent, say, Microsoft Access from being installed by clicking "Set feature installation states" and specifying that Microsoft Access will be set to "Not Available."

For more information on the OCT and configurable options, check out http://technet.microsoft.com/en-us/library/cc179097.aspx.

When you're done creating your customizations, use File ➢ Save As and save it using any filename you want in the folder named Updates, which already exists in your expanded Office folder.

          The file is saved as an .MSP (Microsoft Patch File) and not an .MST file.

Step 5: (Optional) Configure Existing *Config.xml*

You just created and saved an .MSP file in the Updates folder in step 4.

There's a secondary file called config.xml that can have additional configuration options during the deployment process.

This file is optional, and most items can be safely taken care of using the MSP file that was created using the OCT. However, if you want to dive into its capabilities, you're welcome to check out this article:

http://technet.microsoft.com/en-us/library/cc179195.aspx

There are four important notes about the config.xml file (even if you're not planning on using it):

- If there's a conflict between the config.xml file and the .MSP file, then the settings in the config.xml file win.

- All the settings in config.xml are commented out. Commented lines start with <!-- and end with -->.

- The first line in the file is not commented and must match the internal name of the office product. You'll see names like ProPlus or SingleImage here.

- The file is actually required, and the first and last lines must exist or the startup script we'll be using in a bit will fail. The first and last lines are the only two un-commented. So, in short, even if you don't plan on modifying this file, just leave it where it is—as it is—and you should be A-OK.

Step 6: Create a Share to Deploy Office

You've unpacked the Office files. You've created your MSP file. You've (optionally) modified the config.xml file.

Now, share the folder you've been working in. My example is seen in Figure 11.27. Enable the share for Everyone:Read.

FIGURE 11.27   Share your Office deployment folder.

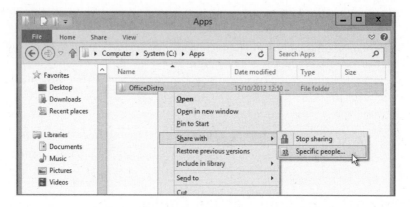

In my example, I'll be using a folder and share called OfficeDistro that lives on the DC. Set the share to Read-only for Everyone.

Step 7: Create a Share to House the Log Files

When we set up the script for deployment (next), we'll be able to know what machines succeeded and which failed during the deployment.

So, create a new folder, and share it so we can receive log files. In my example, I'll be using a folder and share called OfficeLogs that lives on the DC. Set the share to Read/Write for Everyone.

Step 8: Utilize and Modify Microsoft's Suggested Deployment Script

The next step has a lot of little steps. First, Microsoft has created a recommended script to help with deploying Office.

First, get the script (originally written for Office 2007) here:

`https://technet.microsoft.com/en-us/library/cc179134%28v=office.12%29.aspx`

Ignore all the text in the article, and just grab the script and call it something like `officedeploy.bat` and keep it handy.

Next, we need to modify four lines at the beginning of the script. In Figure 11.28, you'll see the script as provided by Microsoft. We need to change the highlighted areas to reflect "our world," not Microsoft's world.

FIGURE 11.28   The login script as provided by Microsoft

```
setlocal

REM ***************************************************************
REM Environment customization begins here. Modify variables below.
REM ***************************************************************

REM Get ProductName from the Office product's core Setup.xml file.
set ProductName=Enterprise

REM Set DeployServer to a network-accessible location containing the Office source files.
set DeployServer=\\server\share\Office12

REM Set ConfigFile to the configuration file to be used for deployment REM (required)
set ConfigFile=\\server\share\Office12\Enterprise.WW\config.xml

REM Set LogLocation to a central directory to collect log files.
set LogLocation=\\server\share\Office12Logs

REM ***************************************************************
REM Deployment code begins here. Do not modify anything below this line.
REM ***************************************************************

IF NOT "%ProgramFiles(x86)%"=="" SET WOW6432NODE=WOW6432NODE\
```

Here are the changes I would make for my test lab. The four things I need to reconfigure the file are as follows:

ProductName   My ProductName is called SingleImage. There are others, like ProPlus, but mine is called SingleImage. When deploying Office 2013, be sure to put in the right ProductName, which will start with Office15 and not Office14 because the script was originally developed for Office 2007. Again, for Office 2013, the right ProductName will be something like Office15.ProPlus.

DeployServer   The server and share in which the Office files are stored. This is `\\DC01\OfficeDistro`.

ConfigFile   This is a pointer to the `config.xml` file, which is required even if not used. My pointer would be `\\DC01\OfficeDistro\SingleImage.WW\config.xml`.

LogLocation   This is the server and share for the logs when Office is installed. Mine would be set to `\\DC01\OfficeLogs`.

In Figure 11.29, you can see the script with my changes. This should work great if you've downloaded Office and are also using the recommended test lab setup from the book. Your changes might be different in your real world.

FIGURE 11.29   The script modified as necessary (with underlines showing where the modifications were made)

```
setlocal

REM *********************************************************************
REM Environment customization begins here. Modify variables below.
REM *********************************************************************

REM Get ProductName from the Office product's core Setup.xml file.
set ProductName=SingleImage

REM Set DeployServer to a network-accessible location containing the Office source files.
set DeployServer=\\DC01\OfficeDistro

REM Set ConfigFile to the configuration file to be used for deployment REM (required)
set ConfigFile=\\DC01\OfficeDistro\SingleImage.WW\config.xml

REM Set LogLocation to a central directory to collect log files.
set LogLocation=\\DC01\OfficeLogs

REM *********************************************************************
REM Deployment code begins here. Do not modify anything below this line.
REM *********************************************************************

IF NOT "%ProgramFiles(x86)%"=="" SET WOW6432NODE=WOW6432NODE\
```

Next, you'll create a Group Policy Object and link it over where your computer accounts reside. For these tests, create and link a Group Policy Object on the **Human Resources Computers** OU, which we'll use to deploy Office and tweak some settings. In Figure 11.30, I've created a GPO named "Deploy Office (to computers)" and linked it over to the **Human Resources Computers** OU.

FIGURE 11.30   Create a link to a Group Policy Object to deploy Office to computers and make configuration tweaks.

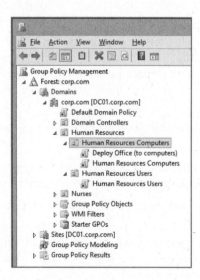

Edit the Group Policy Object and add the startup script. Do this by drilling down to Computer Configuration ➢ Policies ➢ Windows Settings ➢ Scripts (Startup/Shutdown). Then in the Startup section, select Show Files. Here, you'll now be looking at the "guts" of the Group Policy Object. This is where the script has to go. You could copy and paste the script into a new file that you create here. You could drag and drop the script here (if it's already saved).

 It can be a little maddening, because Notepad insists that things be saved with a .TXT extension. In other words, be careful *not* to save or rename your file with a .TXT extension—or the file won't run as a script!

In short, however, ensure that the script is actually here (saved as a .BAT file)—inside the Group Policy Object before continuing.

When done, your script should show up as it does in Figure 11.31.

FIGURE 11.31   Be sure your Office deployment script is in the Group Policy Object, with a (correctly named) .BAT extension.

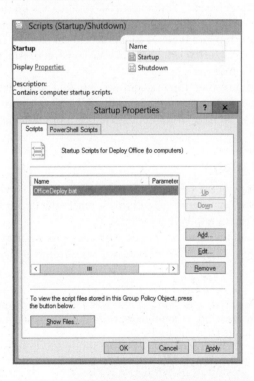

Step 9: Tweak Some Group Policy Settings to Aid in Office Deployments

In order for Office to successfully deploy during startup, there are some tweaks that you must have. Group Policy has a natural "time out" of 5 minutes for scripts. So because it can often take longer (a lot longer) for Office to deploy when the computer is starting up (sometimes 5–30 minutes), you need to configure Group Policy so the engine doesn't kill the process midstream.

The policy setting you need to use is Computer Configuration ≻ Administrative Templates ≻ Policies ≻ System ≻ Scripts ≻ **Specify maximum wait time for Group Policy scripts**. I suggest you start out by Enabling this policy and set it to 0, which will turn it off and therefore ensure that no matter what happens, the installation always finishes. There is a downside here, which is that if the script does hang, some users won't be able to log on. The middle ground would be to try to get a baseline of how long Office takes to install on your machines and then configure this setting with a little wiggle room.

The other policy setting you need to use is Computer Configuration ≻ Policies ≻ Administrative Templates ≻ System ≻ Scripts ≻ **Run startup scripts asynchronously** and set it to Disabled (yes, Disabled). When you do this, you ensure that if you do have other scripts, they aren't running concurrently alongside this script and gunking up the works.

These next two are "nice to haves." You might also want to ensure that Computer Configuration ≻ Policies ≻ Administrative Templates ≻ System ≻ Logon ≻ **Always Wait for network at computer startup and logon** is Enabled. This makes the computer process GPOs synchronously and ensures that the next time the computer restarts, it's definitely going to run your script, the first time.

The last one I recommend is something (again) we've talked about. It's called **Display highly detailed status messages** located within Computer Configuration ≻ Policies ≻ Administrative Templates ≻ System, which could give you more information during the installation process.

Step 10: Watch the Magic

Make sure your target computer is in the right OU. In my examples, my computer (WIN10) is in the **Human Resources Computers** OU, and this is where the Group Policy Object is linked with the script and the Group Policy settings.

If all goes well, Office will install—except you won't see a thing on your target machine, except what you see in Figure 11.32. That's because it's the Scripts policy that is processing the Office install.

FIGURE 11.32   Because Office is being deployed by a Startup script, Windows shows the Scripts policy processing, as seen here. Note that you could see "Please wait" or something unrelated, too, as Office installs.

However, you should notice your hard drive being pounded away during the install. If all goes perfectly, between 5 and 30 minutes later you should have Office fully installed. Anyone logging onto that machine should see Office in the Windows 10 Start screen seen in Figure 11.33.

FIGURE 11.33   Windows 10 shows the Office icons using the Group Policy installation techniques in this chapter.

Additionally, remember that the script we used will put something in the logs folder we designated in the script. In our example we used \\DC01\OfficeLogs. Look there to see if there's anything useful from the target computer. If you see a computer name for a file, excellent! You've got something! Open it up, and see what the code is. If it's 0, then, well, 0 means "Success!"

If you see any other code in that file, then oops! Possible problem (and a clue!).

Step 11: Troubleshoot the Mayhem

If you feel you've waited a long, long, long…too long of a time, and it doesn't appear it went well, you can analyze what went wrong using various logs, reports, and a trouble-shooting tip.

Let's again first look in the OfficeLogs folder on the server. If the script ran and didn't finish, it might have left you a clue. You should find a log file with the name of the computer on which the script ran. Inside that name is a code. You can look up this code here: http://support.microsoft.com/kb/290158 (even though the article refers to Office 2003 and XP). That might help you learn that the computer was out of space (common) or memory (less common), or had some other issue.

Next, let's see what's actually going on. In the Group Policy Object you used for deployment, Enable the policy setting at Computer Configuration ➢ Policies ➢ Administrative Templates ➢ System ➢ Scripts ➢ **Display instructions in startup scripts as they run**.

Now, again, this is not something you would want to leave on—it's only for testing. The idea is that you will be able to see what's going on with the script. Is it hanging? Where? Did it show an error? What was it? Know that during the time the script is able to be displayed, users can be naughty, cancel the script, or possibly use it to be extra-naughty and run commands as System. In Figure 11.34, you can see an error being displayed. Oops, I forgot to share the OfficeDistro folder as a share, silly me.

FIGURE 11.34 By showing the commands in the startup script, you can see any visible, obvious errors during deployment.

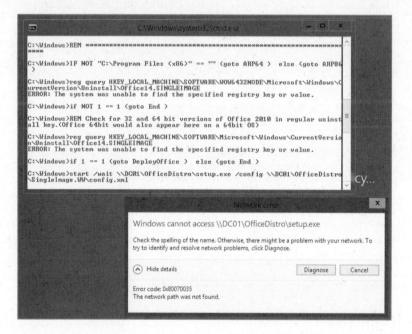

Result of Your Office Deployment Using Group Policy

If you have the success I hope you have, when users are able to next log on, all users should see what's in Figure 11.33.

Installing Office Using Click-to-Run

As I mentioned at the top of the chapter, Office comes in two versions: the MSI version (unusual as it is) and also in a version called Click-to-Run.

The Click-to-Run version of Office is available based upon what version of office you purchase. Why is one method better or worse than another?

Well, when the MSI version is used, it's installed all at once. The install files are pretty huge and it takes a long time to install. Admins also need to stay on top of updates manually.

When the Click-to-Run version is used, its pieces are installed "as needed." The install file is unbelievably small, and updates are automatic and slipstreamed without clients even knowing about updates or admins having to think about anything. Click-to-Run also enables "side-by-side" scenarios of old-and-crusty versions of Office alongside the latest versions of office.

Click-to-Run is based upon Microsoft App-V technology, which takes applications and puts them in a "bubble" or "sandbox," and, well, the application is never really *installed* in the traditional sense. The files are there, semi-hidden, and the whole thing just works without really being installed at all. This is why you can have an old-and-crusty version of Office installed and then have a new version of Office alongside it; the Click-to-Run version isn't really installed, so the old-and-crusty version of Office simply doesn't know it's there.

Again, there are various versions of Office that ship as Click-to-Run, including Office 2000, 2010, 2013, and (coming soon) Office 2016.

If you want to walk along exactly with me, I signed up for a trial of Office 365 Business Premium, which would normally cost $12.50 user/month and includes the Click-to-Run version of Office 2013, which can be installed on endpoints. You don't need a credit card to get started if you want to simply buzz through my walk-through.

Here's the road map for this section:

- Get the Click-to-Run Office.
- Test-install Office Click-to-Run "by hand."
- Tweak the setup of Office's features and settings using the Office Deployment tool.
- Use Group Policy to "mass-install it."

Note that by the time you read this, Office 365's version of Office could be Click-to-Run Office 2016 instead of Click-to-Run Office 2013.

Note that before continuing, you might want to manually uninstall Office from your test client machine. You should also unlink any GPOs that are performing deployment of Office from previous examples in this chapter. That way you can perform this example cleanly without having Office install next to an existing copy of Office.

Getting Office Click-to-Run

After signing up for an Office 365 trial, you can immediately go to the little gear icon seen in Figure 11.35 and then click on Office 365 (not shown).

FIGURE 11.35   Use the "Office 365 settings" location to start to download Click-to-Run Office

Then click Software (not shown). The next screen is where you would be able to install Office because of your Office 365 subscription. Office, as seen in Figure 11.35, is already selected and you simply click Install.

At this point you'll want to save and not actually run Office Click-to-Run. The name I got during download was Setup.X86.en-us_0365BusinessRetail_fd99458f-200e-4f59-98da-2ed4459a9c13_TX_PR_.exe.

Yours might be different. At this point you can get it to any client machine you want.

Installing Office Click-to-Run by Hand

As an initial test, on one machine you might want to see how Office Click-to-Run works when you run it manually. In Figure 11.36 you'll see three things:

- The Office Click-to-Run icon (left).

- The amazingly small file size of the Office Click-to-Run install (middle). It's only 1.02 MB!

- What happens when you click the icon and select to start the installation (right).

FIGURE 11.36   Note the amazingly small Office Click-to-Run installation file size

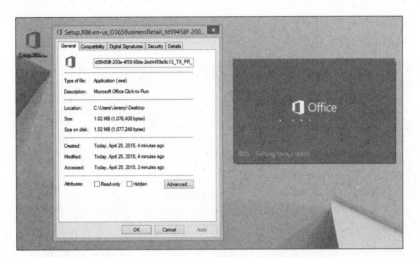

Of course, Office isn't a mere megabyte. This is a "bootstrapper program," something that gets you kickstarted to the bigger thing. The idea here is that Office is then installed over the Internet, its pieces downloaded as needed.

What's neat is that Office Click-to-Run doesn't have to be fully installed for it to be ready to rock. In Figure 11.37, you can see Office is still installing and downloading, but applications were ready to work for me reasonably quickly.

FIGURE 11.37   Office Click-to-Run enables you to run Office even before it's fully installed.

In Windows 10, you can see Office Click-to-Run in the Start Menu, as seen in Figure 11.38.

FIGURE 11.38   You can see Office Click-to-Run in the Windows 10 Start Menu.

Deploying Office Click-to-Run via Group Policy

Running around from machine to machine to install Office Click-to-Run isn't the ideal way. If you did this, first your arms and legs would get tired. Second, it would take a long time. And third, each and every machine would have to download all of Office over the Internet—each and every time.

Instead, let's fix all three problems.

If you want to use Group Policy to deploy Office Click-to-Run, the steps are reasonably similar to what we talked about with the Office MSI version:

- We need a share that contains the Office Click-to-Run install/bootstrapper program.

- We need a share to receive log files about how the deployment went.

- We need to download the Office Click-to-Run "guts" and store them locally on a server (instead of relying on the Internet).
- We need to customize the Office Click-to-Run experience (more on this in a bit).
- We need a script to launch the Office Click-to-Run installation as a startup script.
- We need to throw the script in a Group Policy Object and link it to computers so when they start up, they run the script.

That's it. So, let's do it.

Step 1: Creating the Share for Office Click-to-Run

On your server (in my case, DC01), create a folder with a name that makes sense. I'm using OfficeClickToRun (pointed to by an arrow) and then sharing it so Everyone has Read permissions, as seen in Figure 11.39.

FIGURE 11.39   Create a share to house Office Click-to-Run setup (bootstrapper) and customization files.

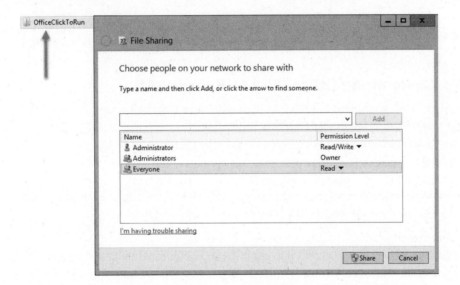

Step 2: Creating the Share for Receiving Log Files

Next, create another folder with a name that makes sense to receive log files from the installation. I'll use OfficeClickToRunLogs, as seen in Figure 11.40 (pointed to by an arrow). This share needs to be Read/Write so the computer can write there when the installation is done.

FIGURE 11.40 Create a folder and share it as Read/Write to accept the Office Click-to-Run results logs.

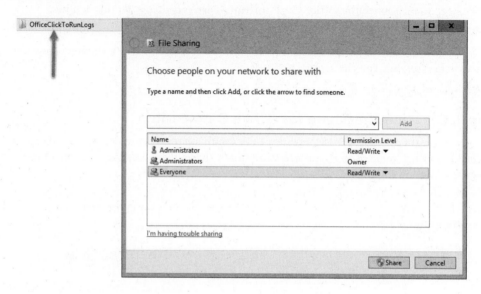

Step 3: Customizing Office Click-to-Run via XML

You need an XML to explain to Office Click-to-Run how to install.

The various configuration possibilities are found here:

`https://technet.microsoft.com/en-us/library/jj219426.aspx`

But if you go to the very bottom of this page, you can copy and paste a Click-to-run Configuration XML example and then customize it for your world.

The example has references to a bogus server and refers to installing both Office and Visio. So, change the right lines so the file ends up looking like this:

```
<Configuration>
  <Add SourcePath="\\DC\OfficeClickToRun" OfficeClientEdition="32" >
    <Product ID="O365ProPlusRetail">
      <Language ID="en-us" />
    </Product>
  </Add>
  <Display Level="None" AcceptEULA="TRUE" />
  <Logging Level="Standard" Path="%temp%" />
</Configuration>
```

Note that the items are case sensitive, so be sure to copy, paste, and then modify carefully.

You could specify preventing updates, but I'm going to advise against it.

In my example, I've saved the file as `config.xml` and put it in the same folder and share as the Office Click-to-Run bootstrapper and Office Click-to-Run downloaded files.

Note that three values that are detailed here:

`https://technet.microsoft.com/en-us/library/jj219420.aspx`

are likely the most commonly changed ones.

`Enabled`   When this is TRUE, Office Click-to-Run will automatically install updates as needed. (Note: This is the default.) If Enabled is set to FALSE, Office won't check for updates and will remain at the installed version.

`UpdatePath`   This was in Microsoft's example XML, but I stripped it out in the example I think you should use for testing. If present, it can specify a network, local, or HTTP path for updates. If UpdatePath isn't set (or set to the special word *default*), then the Office Click-to-Run source on the Internet is used.

`TargetVersion`   Click-to-Run for Office can be "dialed in" to a specific product build number; such as 15.0.0.0. When the version is set, install the specified version. If TargetVersion isn't set (or is set to the special word *default*), then Office Click-to-Run updates to the latest version advertised at the source path.

Step 4: Using the Office Deployment Tool to Download Office Click-To-Run

I'm going to suggest you do this step on the server.

In this step, you first need to download the Office Deployment tool for Click-to-Run. It's found here:

`http://www.microsoft.com/en-gb/download/details.aspx?id=36778`

Once it's downloaded, you need run the program to unpack it. Put the files in the folder with the Office Click-to-Run bootstrapper.

Once that's all set, this next step is optional. In the previous example, we hand-downloaded Office Click-to-Run and it downloaded over the Internet. But if you have 500 or 10,000 machines all trying to do this at the same time, that might be a problem.

So, instead, you can download the Office Click-to-Run "guts" by running `setup /download <config.xml>`, where `<config.xml>` is the name of the file you created earlier.

And inside that config file, you specified where you want to download the guts. If you took my advice and stored the Office Deployment tool files in the same place as the Office Click-to-Run bootstrapper, you simply need to run:

`setup /download \\dc\officeclicktorun\config.xml`

You can see this in Figure 11.41.

FIGURE 11.41 When you run the Office Deployment tool setup, it will create a folder called Office, as seen here.

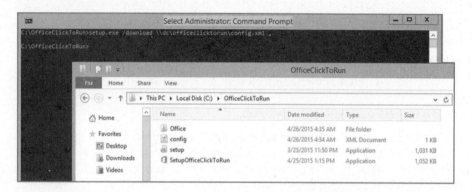

Note that I've seen the setup download hang in two places: First, if you fail to give it a place inside the config.xml file that is writeable, that becomes a problem. Second, I've seen the setup download fail to download the full required 1GB of files or so. In my tests, I got 2MB and 200MB before trying another machine that (correctly) downloaded a little over the required 1GB of Office setup files.

Again, this step is totally optional. If you didn't do this, Office Click-to-Run will cheerfully, each and every time, on every Windows PC, use the Internet version and download itself.

Step 5: Using a Script to Launch the Office Click-to-Run Bootstrapper File with XML Configuration

I like it when other people do my homework for me.

Fellow MVP in Exchange, Brian Reid from C7 Solutions, has a great batch file (and overall basic tutorial) for launching Office Click-to-Run via Group Policy (specifically using a computer startup script):

```
http://www.c7solutions.com/2014/09/installing-office-365-proplus-click-to-
run-via-gpo-deployment
```

I asked Brian if I could copy his script and put it on GPanswers.com as a backup. It's in this book's resources with permission if you need a backup: www.gpanswers.com/books/book-resources/.

This script looks like it was based on the Office 2007, 2010, and 2013 MSI computer startup script from Microsoft. Or if not, it basically does the same thing:

- At computer startup time, see if Office Click-to-Run is already installed.
- If not, install it.
- If yes, don't bother.

You simply need to change it a little to point to your deployment server and share, configuration XML file, and log location.

So the three lines to change (and what they should be changed to) will be:

```
set DeployServer=\\DC\OfficeClickToRun
set ConfigFile=\\DC\OfficeClickToRun\config.xml
set LogLocation=\\DC\OfficeClickToRunLogs
```

You can see the changes in Figure 11.42.

FIGURE 11.42   Modify the Office Click-to-Run installer batch file to point toward your server and config file.

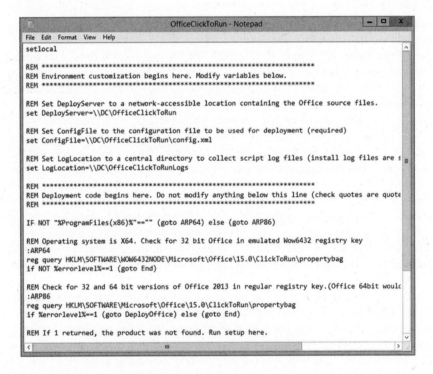

Step 6: Deploy the Script via Group Policy

These next steps should be familiar. (It's similar to what we did in the MSI version of Office; the same idea.)

You'll create a Group Policy Object and link it over where your computer accounts reside. For these tests, create and link a Group Policy Object on the **Human Resources Computers** OU, which we'll use to deploy Office and tweak some settings.

Edit the Group Policy Object and add the startup script. Do this by drilling down to Computer Configuration ➢ Policies ➢ Windows Settings ➢ Scripts (Startup/Shutdown). Then, in the Startup section, select Show Files. Here, you'll now be looking at the "guts" of the Group Policy Object. This is where the script has to go. You could copy and paste the script into a new file that you create here. You could drag and drop the script here (if it's already saved).

In short, however, ensure that the script is actually here (saved as a .BAT file)—inside the Group Policy Object—before continuing.

When you're done, your script should show up as it did back in Figure 11.31 when we deployed a startup script for the MSI version of Office.

Step 7: Tweak Some Group Policy Settings to Aid in Office Deployments

When we deployed Office via MSI, we established some tweaks to help ensure Office's smooth deployment via script.

To recap: Group Policy has a natural "time-out" of 5 minutes for scripts. And since it can often take longer (a lot longer) for Office to deploy when the computer is starting up (sometimes 5–30 minutes), you need to configure Group Policy so the engine doesn't kill the process midstream.

The policy setting you need to use is Computer Configuration ➤ Administrative Templates ➤ Policies ➤ System ➤ Scripts ➤ **Specify maximum wait time for Group Policy scripts**. I suggest you start out by Enabling this policy and setting it to 0, which will turn it off and therefore ensure that no matter what happens, the installation always finishes. There is a downside here: if the script does hang, some users won't be able to log on. The middle ground would be to try to get a baseline of how long Office takes to install on your machines and then configure this setting with a little wiggle room. Maybe 15–20 minutes.

The other policy setting you need to use is Computer Configuration ➤ Policies ➤ Administrative Templates ➤ System ➤ Scripts ➤ **Run startup scripts asynchronously** and set it to Disabled (yes, Disabled). When you do this, you ensure that if you do have other scripts, they aren't running concurrently alongside this script and gunking up the works.

These next two are "nice to haves" that we already talked about, but it's good to repeat them here. You might also want to ensure that Computer Configuration ➤ Policies ➤ Administrative Templates ➤ System ➤ Logon ➤ **Always Wait for network at computer startup and logon** is Enabled. This makes the computer process GPOs synchronously and ensures that the next time the computer restarts, it's definitely going to run your script the first time.

The last policy setting I recommend is the second "nice to have." It's called **Display highly detailed status messages** and it's located within Computer Configuration ➤ Policies ➤ Administrative Templates ➤ System. It could give you more information during the installation process.

Step 8: Troubleshoot the Mayhem

As with the MSI version of Office, if you feel you've waited a long, long, long…too long of a time, and it doesn't appear it went well, you can analyze what went wrong.

Check out the earlier "Troubleshoot the Mayhem" section when I talked about deploying the MSI version of Office.

System Center Configuration Manager vs. Group Policy (and Alternatives)

Microsoft's System Center Configuration Manager (formerly known as Microsoft Systems Management Server [SMS]) is a big deal in corporations around the world. Configuration Manager (for short) is part of the overall package you purchase when you purchase Microsoft System Center. Configuration Manager requires a client component on every Windows PC and server on your network and a distributed big-ish server architecture to cover all your sites, plus at least one SQL server. But if you can get over these drawbacks, it houses a pretty amazing collection of core features. The entire list of capabilities and features is listed on Microsoft's website here:

```
www.microsoft.com/en-us/server-cloud/system-center/configuration-manager-
2012-capabilities.aspx
```

Here are the major ones:

- Software deployment
- Software and hardware inventory
- Client health and monitoring
- Operating system deployment
- Software/patch management
- Power management
- Windows phone and non-Windows phone management

Most of these features would be a welcome addition to any managed environment.

There are, of course, other management systems that don't ship from Microsoft. The people at companies like Symantec and LANDesk make their living selling similar tools. These all have one thing in common: more moving parts on your client and, usually, additional servers and components to move things around. They get the moniker of enterprise management systems because they scale pretty well.

But what's also true about these tools is that they don't, fundamentally, use the Group Policy infrastructure that's already there. In other words, the "moving parts" of Group Policy are already installed on every client computer.

So, the question often comes up: Do you need a "big" management tool if you're already using Group Policy?

If you look at the list I just showed you and compare it against the built-in Group Policy and Group Policy Preferences items, you'll see that there is very little overlap. For instance, Configuration Manager doesn't try to address items like these:

- Printers
- Shortcuts
- Drive maps

- "Look and feel" settings (à la the Administrative Templates and many Group Policy Preferences items)

- Operating system security settings

Or just about any other of the 39 Group Policy and Group Policy Preferences categories. There is some overlap, however, say, in operating system power management and application deployment (the subject of this chapter), and Center 2012 Configuration Manager SP1 is scheduled to have some overlap with Folder Redirection and Offline Files. As we explored in this chapter, Group Policy has a decent set of features when it comes to deploying software to clients.

Several facets of Configuration Manager software deployment are simply better than the GPSI. Specifically, Configuration Manager can do the following that GPSI cannot:

- Deploy software to users or computers any time of the day or night—not just on logon or reboot.

- Compress the application and send it to a distribution point close to the user. Even if we set up GPSI with DFS Namespaces, Group Policy cannot do this. However, the replication that DFS Namespaces uses, called *DFSR*, does have the superpower of only sending over the changed bytes if possible (and that's really sweet).

- Once a machine is targeted for a delivery and the package is received, the machine can send back detailed status messages describing success or failure of the transaction.

- Dribble the applications to clients over slow links without slowing down the connection. Only when the software is fully downloaded is the install initiated.

- Get detailed, central logs about which users or computers did or did not get the package.

So, Configuration Manager has the upper hand here. However, with a little elbow grease, you can get an amazing amount of mileage out of GPSI—even in large environments. The big hit Group Policy takes in GPSI seems to be that the Office team basically abandoned GPSI as a viable deployment method for Office 2007 and later. However, in the section "Deploying Office 2010 and Later Using Group Policy (MSI Version)," we saw some neat workarounds that get the job done.

Even though Configuration Manager has a lot of killer features, what I often see is that people implement Configuration Manager for *one* killer feature—application deployment. If you're contemplating making the plunge to Configuration Manager and using all (or most) of it, great. However, if you're looking at Configuration Manager for only its application deployment features, I suggest another avenue for inspection.

I'd like to formally recommend two products that might be a better fit if you only want a tool that performs software installation.

First, check out PDQ Deploy (www.adminarsenal.com/pdq-deploy). The software has free and pay versions (even the pay version is super inexpensive).

The software is licensed "per admin who wants to use the software" and not per endpoint, which makes it very affordable. That being said, PDQ Deploy doesn't use Group Policy as its transport and just "talks directly" to clients from your admin station.

Another fine choice, and one that does use Group Policy as its transport, is from my friends at Specops Software. It's called Specops Deploy (www.specopssoft.com). And it overcomes some of the thorniest problems that Group Policy out of the box cannot solve. Specops Deploy can do the following:

- Deploy MSIs and EXEs to client computers or users (where normal GPSI only targets MSIs)
- Target based on time of day
- Deploy applications without requiring a reboot
- Use the Background Intelligent Transfer Service (BITS) protocol to dribble applications to clients over slow links
- Give you detailed reports about which machines and users received the software and which ones didn't

Sometimes, I get the question "What's better? Group Policy or SCCM?"

That's an age-old question—but it's the wrong question to ask.

So, for me, I don't even see a competition between Configuration Manager versus Group Policy.

Group Policy is meant to manage the settings of Windows: look and feel, desktop, and security settings.

Configuration Manager is about deploying operating systems, software, patching, and other tasks.

In other words, lead your desktop, laptop, and VDI management with Group Policy first. Use it to configure the desktop experience and operating system configuration settings. Then after that, layer Configuration Manager upon it next with its excellent reporting features to help you gain insight into what needs additional management.

The only real "Configuration Manager vs. Group Policy" question at all is "Which should I use—GPSI vs. Configuration Manager's application management?" (Again, this is assuming you own Configuration Manager.)

Some organizations use either GPSI or Configuration Manager for software deployment. And some use both. You might want to use, say, both GPSI and Configuration Manager depending on the use case. GPSI can handle smaller applications that need to be rapidly fired off due to document invocation. For example, if a user is sent an Adobe Acrobat .PDF file via e-mail but doesn't have Adobe Acrobat Reader, double-clicking the document automatically installs the application on the machine.

Configuration Manager could then be used to deploy larger applications, such as the Office suite, when you need definitive feedback about what went wrong (if anything). This philosophy provides a good balance between the "on-demand" feel of GPSI and the "strategic targeted deployment" feel of Configuration Manager.

Again, it's just one possible strategy.

As you've seen, most of the features do not overlap, making a bigger management tool, like Configuration Manager, an addition to any medium-sized or large environment. My opinion is that if you're only going to use Configuration Manager for one thing, specifically software deployment, it's a bit overkill. And in that case, purchasing a moderately priced third-party tool that does one thing really, really well—software deployment—can help you avoid having to spin up a whole infrastructure for a tool you might use to do only one thing.

Final Thoughts

In this chapter, we inspected Software Installation using Group Policy (GPSI) and also deploying Microsoft Office—both MSI and Click-to-Run versions.

To make the most of GPSI, you need to leverage .MSI applications. You can either get .MSI applications from your software vendor or wrap up your own with third-party tools (listed in this chapter).

Share a folder on a server you want to send the package from. Plop the application in its own subfolder, and use both share and NTFS permissions to crank down who can read the executables and install files. Remember, though, that not all .MSI applications are ready to be deployed. Some are indeed ready to go (like the .NET Framework), others require an Administrative Installation (like Office 2003), and still others ship as .MSI files but cannot be deployed via GPSI (such as older versions of Adobe Acrobat Writer).

Once you have your package, you can Assign or Publish your applications. Assign applications when you want application icons to appear on the Start ➢ All Programs menu; Publish applications when you want users to dive into the Add or Remove Programs folder or the "Install a program from the network" window to get the application. You can leverage Microsoft Transform Files (.MST files) to hone an .MSI and customize it. (Note that Office 2007 and later don't use .MST files.) You can patch existing .MSI applications with Microsoft Patch Files (.MSP files), but afterward, you need to redeploy the application.

Try not to orphan applications by removing the GPO before the target computer gets the "signal" upon the next reboot (for computer) or logon (for user). If you think you might end up doing this, it's best to ensure that the "Uninstall this application when it falls out of the scope of management" check box is checked, as seen in Figure 11.12.

Darren Mar-Elia, on his SDMSoftware.com website, has a free tool called GPSIViewer that provides a nifty list view of all deployed applications in a domain and has some printout and .CSV reporting capability, as well. Check it out at:

```
https://sdmsoftware.com/gpoguy/free-tools/library/group-policy-software-
installation-viewer-utility/
```

Use the material in Chapter 4 (on creating WMI filters) to change the scope of management for when a GPO will apply. You can use WMI filters for any GPO you create—not just ones that leverage GPSI. However, the most common use for WMI filters is usually for GPOs that leverage GPSI. Additionally, Windows XP and later clients set to evaluate a WMI filter will take some extra processing time for each filter they need to work through. Be sure to test all your WMI filters in the test lab first.

On the downside, Office used to be "normal." It used MSIs, MSTs, and MSPs, all in the normal way. Then, one day, with Office 2007, it all changed. In order to deploy Office, you'll need to pick a version: MSI or Click-To-Run. Then, you'll use computer startup scripts to get it out there.

Finishing Touches with Group Policy: Scripts, Internet Explorer, Hardware Control, Printer Deployment, Local Admin Password Control

We've come a long way so far in this book.

We've got Group Policy handled. We've set up Roaming Profiles, Redirected Folders, and Offline Files. We've deployed software using Group Policy Software Installation.

We've made a pretty big cake—but no frosting. Now it's time for the finishing touches.

In this chapter, we'll cover five big topics to round out your desktop experience:

Using Scripts   You can deploy startup, shutdown, logon, and logoff scripts. And there are three ways to do it.

Configuring Internet Explorer   You can deploy settings to your favorite (er, maybe not-so-favorite) application. We'll review the in-the-box ways to manage Internet Explorer. And one "out-of-the box" way, too.

Restricting Access to Hardware   Want a way to ensure that only the hardware you sanction gets onto your network? Well, giddyup!

Setting Up Printers   The Group Policy Preferences have some special ability to help with printer management. I'll show you the ropes.

Managing Local Administrator Passwords   Well, you cannot manage local administrator passwords anymore using Group Policy Preferences because it's a security risk. So, what's the right way to do it? Find out in this section.

So, let's get started with the finishing...touches, that is!

Scripts: Logon, Logoff, Startup, and Shutdown

Users have always been able to process logon scripts. Active Directory Users has a "holdover" way to deploy login scripts from the old Windows NT days.

However, you can step up to the next level using Group Policy and get more than just logon scripts:

- Users can process logon and logoff scripts.

- Computers can process startup and/or shutdown scripts.

And, the best part is, you're not limited to old DOS-style batch files. Scripts deployed via Group Policy can use DOS-style .BAT or .CMD scripts, VBScript (.VBS files), JavaScript (.JS files), or even executables.

Also, you can also use PowerShell (.PS1) scripts when your target machine is Windows 7 or later. As you'll see, however, there are some caveats to delivering PowerShell scripts via Group Policy.

Non-PowerShell-Based Scripts

In the following sections, we're going to explore all the non-PowerShell ways to deploy scripts. Look at the list in the previous section; most people use .VBS or DOS-style batch files.

In these examples, I'll use basic DOS-style .BAT commands to explain the concept. First is an example of a script that displays "Hello World" and then pauses for a key press before removing the files from the %temp% folder.

In Notepad, create the following file:

```
Echo "Hello World."
Pause
Del /Q /S %temp%
Pause
```

Okay, my example is kind of lame. In the real world, you can do all sorts of things, like automatically fire up Excel at logon or kick off a full-drive sweep of your virus scanner at shutdown. We're going to keep it simple for these examples.

To use scripts with Group Policy, users must be in the Site, Domain, or OU linked to a GPO that contains a logon or logoff script. As the name of the script implies, users execute the script only at logon or logoff. Computers must also be in the Site, Domain, or OU linked to a GPO that contains a startup or shutdown script, which they run only at startup or shutdown.

User and computer scripts delivered via Group Policy do not run "visibly" to the user, which prevents users from canceling them. Scripts run silently in the background unless there is a problem. At that point, you have to wait until the script times out (10 minutes by default). I'll show you a bit later how to expose the scripts to run visibly.

Startup and Shutdown Scripts (Non-PowerShell)

The startup and shutdown script settings are found under the Computer Configuration ➢ Policies node in the Windows Settings ➢ Scripts (Startup/Shutdown) branch. You can get your proposed script into the proper GPO in many ways; however, I think I have found the ideal way, as follows:

1. Once you're in the Group Policy Management Editor, drill down to the Scripts (Startup/Shutdown) node and double-click Startup. The Startup Properties dialog box will appear.

2. Click the Add button to open the "Add a Script" dialog box.

3. In the Script Name field, you can enter a filename or click Browse to open the Browse dialog box, shown in Figure 12.1.

FIGURE 12.1　You can create .BAT or .VBS files on the fly with this little trick.

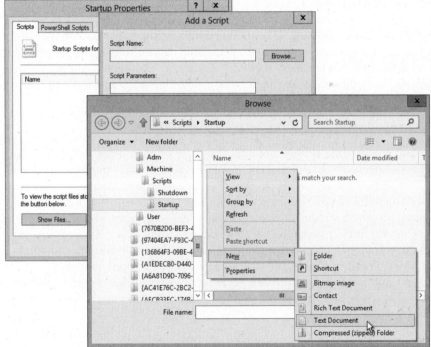

4. To create a new file, right-click in the Browse dialog box, and choose New ➢ Text Document, for example.

5. Enter a name for the file, such as **myscript.bat**.

6. When asked if you want to change the file extension, click Yes, right-click the file, and choose Edit from the context menu to open Notepad.

7. Type your script, and save the file.

8. Select the new file as the proposed script.

Again, the computer account must be in an OU with a linked GPO that contains a script. However, don't reboot yet. By default, you won't see the script run. And, since our script contains a Pause statement, your users will wait a really long time before the script times out. To allow the script to be visible (and enable you to press any key at the pause), enable a policy setting that also affects the machine. Traverse to Computer Configuration ➤ Policies ➤ Administrative Templates ➤ System ➤ Scripts, and select either **Run startup scripts visible** or **Run shutdown scripts visible,** or enable both options. Note that, oddly, in Windows Vista and later, neither of these policy settings will do anything unless you also force the scripts to run synchronously.

Next, it's important to understand the context in which startup and shutdown scripts run. Specifically, they run in the LocalSystem context. If you want to connect to resources across the network, you'll need to ensure that those resources allow for computer access across the network (not just user access), because the script will run in the context of the computer account when it accesses network resources (such as the Domain Computers group).

Last, be careful in granting users the ability to see logon or startup scripts. This is because, when the script is running, it is running with administrative credentials. So, if there is anything the user might be able to do that would halt the script from processing and then *remain* in the command prompt, they will continue to have access. And that access is local system access, god-like access, which is not a good thing. So, only show the startup or login scripts during testing, and rescind during your real rollout.

Logon and Logoff Scripts (Non-PowerShell)

The Logon and Logoff script settings are under the User Configuration ➤ Policies node in the Windows Settings ➤ Scripts (Logon/Logoff) branch. If you're implementing new logon scripts, I suggest you follow the steps in the previous section. Again, the user must be in an OU with a linked GPO with a script. However, don't log off and log back on yet. By default, you won't see the script run. To allow the script to be visible (and enable you to press any key at the pause), you need to enable a Group Policy. Traverse to User Configuration ➤ Policies ➤ Administrative Templates ➤ System ➤ Scripts, and select either **Run logon scripts visible** or **Run logoff scripts visible,** or enable both options.

Logon and logoff scripts run in the user's context. Remember that a user is just a mere mortal and might not be able to manipulate Registry keys that you might want to run in a logon or logoff script.

Script Processing Defaults (and Changing Them)

One final note about scripts before we move on: different scripting types run either synchronously or asynchronously. Here's the deal:

Logon scripts run asynchronously by default.   By default, logon scripts run asynchronously. That is, all scripts at a certain level will fire off at the same time. There is no precedence order for scripts at the same level, and there is no knowing which script will finish before another. If you want to change this behavior to help "link" one script after another, you have to tell the client computer to run the scripts *synchronously*. If you want to change this (and many times you'll want to), then find Computer Configuration ➢ Policies ➢ Administrative Templates ➢ System ➢ Scripts, and enable **Run logon scripts synchronously**.

Bizarrely enough, there is also a setting that does exactly the same thing located on User Settings ➢ Policies ➢ Administrative Templates ➢ System ➢ Scripts ➢ **Run logon scripts synchronously**. Again, recall that if there's a conflict between these settings, the ones that affect the computer will "win."

Startup scripts run synchronously by default.   By default, startup scripts run synchronously: all scripts are processed from lowest to highest priority order. Then, each script is run—consecutively—until they're finished. This usually makes the most sense, so I tend to leave it as is. However, if you want to change it, locate Computer Configuration ➢ Policies ➢ Administrative Templates ➢ System ➢ Scripts, and enable **Run startup scripts asynchronously**.

Group Policy scripts time out in 10 minutes.   As stated, if a script just hangs there, you'll have to wait a whopping 10 minutes for it to time out. You can change this with the policy setting found at Computer Configuration ➢ Policies ➢ Administrative Templates ➢ System ➢ Scripts called **Specify maximum wait time for Group Policy scripts**.

Also, before we move on, let's take a second to talk about "perceived slow" performance when scripts are used with Group Policy. In previous chapters, I suggested you might want to make your Windows machines act like Windows 2000. That is, use the **Always wait for the network at Startup and Logon** policy setting, which throws Windows into "synchronous" processing mode. There can be a problem with this approach: It can affect you if you have laptops that are not always on the network at bootup. This *can* cause slower performance. Imagine you have traveling users on laptops with startup and login scripts. By default, the scripts are stored on the Domain Controller. So, during bootup or login time, the laptop tries to connect to the Domain Controller for the script. You may want to dictate to the client to use a local path (like C:\scripts\blah.vbs) instead of the default, which will go to the server. Ensure that the script is contained within a path that clients cannot write to or they could do nefarious things to the system by replacing the script (which runs as System).

Deploying PowerShell Scripts to Windows 7 and Later Clients

Windows 7 and later machines can accept PowerShell as scripts via Group Policy.

In Figure 12.2, we can see the properties of the Logon script dialog box found under User Configuration ➢ Policies ➢ Windows Settings ➢ Scripts (Logon/Logoff). Similar settings for the computer are found in Computer Configuration ➢ Policies ➢ Windows Settings ➢ Scripts (Startup/Shutdown).

You can add in the script here. PowerShell scripts must have the extension .PS1 or they will fail to execute on the client.

FIGURE 12.2   Group Policy can deploy PowerShell scripts.

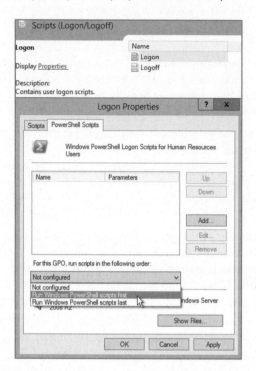

You can decide if you want this PowerShell script to run before or after regular (non-PowerShell) scripts. This setting can be performed on a per-GPO basis (seen here). Or, you can have an overarching policy setting for logon, logoff, startup, and/or shutdown scripts with policy settings located at User Configuration ➢ Policies ➢ Windows Settings ➢ Administrative Templates ➢ System ➢ Scripts ➢ **Run Windows PowerShell scripts first at user logon, logoff.** And, on the Computer side, there's **Run Windows PowerShell scripts first at user startup, shutdown.** Again, the idea is that you might set one of these overarching policies first as a general case but then make an exception right in the script, as seen in Figure 12.2.

Managing Internet Explorer with Group Policy

In the previous edition of the book, I explored four ideas:

1. The death of Internet Explorer Maintenance policy settings
2. Managing IE using Group Policy Preferences

3. Managing IE using Group Policy settings

4. Managing IE using the Internet Explorer Admin Toolkit.

I'm going to drop items #1 and #4 on the list and add in something new for you. In the following sections, we'll talk about managing Internet Explorer 11's Enterprise Mode and also managing Internet Explorer using PolicyPak Application Manager.

Let's get started!

Managing Internet Explorer with Group Policy Preferences

You can set some Internet Explorer preferences settings for users by traversing down to User Configuration ➢ Preferences ➢ Control Panel Settings ➢ Internet Settings and selecting a new Group Policy Preferences item for Internet Explorer 5 and 6, 7, 8 and 9, or 10. It's a little weird how they're grouped together that way, but that's how they are.

But isn't there Internet Explorer 11? If yes, why don't we see it in the Group Policy Preferences possibilities in Figure 12.3?

It turns out that when you see Internet Explorer 10, you should really think "Internet Explorer 10 and later," which of course includes Internet Explorer 11.

FIGURE 12.3 Note how Internet Explorer 11 is conspicuously missing.

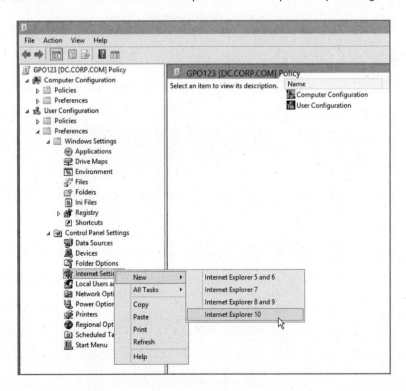

Underneath the hood, some Group Policy Preferences have what's called "hidden filters." By revealing the under-the-hood XML of a Group Policy Preferences item, you can see the hidden filter, as seen in Figure 12.4.

You can see in Figure 12.5 where I'm using Group Policy Preferences to set the home page to www.GPanswers.com.

FIGURE 12.4   Internet Explorer 10 items will work for versions 10 to 99.

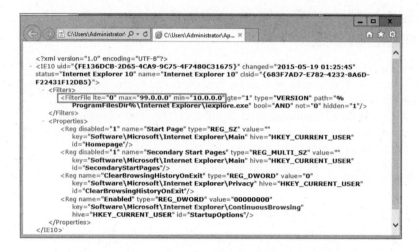

FIGURE 12.5   Group Policy Preferences Internet Explorer settings

We've already covered Group Policy Preferences Internet Explorer settings in Chapter 5, but since we're here anyway, I want to remind you of something.

As you learned in Chapter 5, all Group Policy Preferences items automatically reapply if users try to change them—provided the computer is online and can reconnect to a domain controller to request a refresh of the Group Policy Preferences items.

To change the behavior, and to make it a "one time delivery only" inside the Group Policy Preferences item, select the Common tab and then select "Apply once and do not reapply," as seen in Figure 12.6.

Again, for more information on this procedure, and also the Group Policy Preferences Internet Settings node, check out Chapter 5.

FIGURE 12.6   Select "Apply once and do not reapply" to have your IE preferences settings delivered only one time.

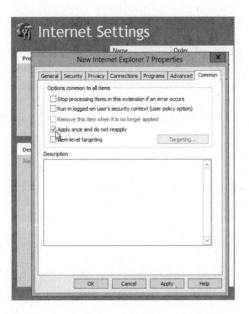

Internet Explorer's Group Policy Settings

The Group Policy settings for Internet Explorer are found in (User and Computer Configuration) ➢ Policies ➢ Administrative Templates ➢ Windows Components ➢ Internet Explorer. Remember, only Group Policy settings are something that users cannot work around.

In contrast, preferences (what we just breezed by again) simply "suggest" a setting and users can work around it. Be sure to read both the Explain text for each Group Policy setting and the requirements. Not every setting is valid for every version of Internet Explorer. So be sure to read and test.

Understanding Internet Explorer 11's Enterprise Mode

To help organizations walk away from Internet Explorer 8, Internet Explorer 11 has a special compatibility mode called Enterprise Mode.

Enterprise Mode's job is to accept a list of websites that should be handled differently and then try to format them to be more like what they would look like in IE 8 as opposed to IE 11.

The way this works is a little roundabout, so stick with me. Here's the basic steps:

- You download the Enterprise Mode Site List Manager tool.
- Using the tool, you specify the sites you want to render differently.
- You specify any special modes.
- This list becomes an XML file.
- This XML file lives on a web server or can be copied locally to the client machine.
- You then use a Group Policy setting to point to where this file lives.

Why the roundabout method? Why not just have a policy setting that could accept a simple list of URLs? Well, Group Policy (in the box) has no way to handle the manipulation of XML files. So there was no way to do this except to first pre-create the file, then use Group Policy to point to that file.

The Enterprise Mode Site List Manager can be found at:

`https://www.microsoft.com/en-us/download/details.aspx?id=42501`

When it runs, it looks like what's seen in Figure 12.7.

FIGURE 12.7   Use Enterprise Mode Site List Manager to dictate which websites should be rendered differently.

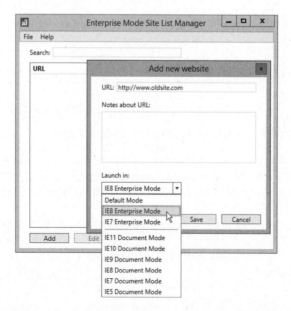

Once your rules are established, save the file. The usual next step would be to store this on a website somewhere, say `http://corp.com/your-old-sites.xml`.

You could also copy it to a file share, like `\\DC\share\your-old-sites.xml`, or copy it locally to each machine, say, using Group Policy Preferences, and deliver it to, say, `C:\sites\your-old-sites.xml`.

Then use Group Policy on either the User or Computer side: navigate to Administrative Templates ➢ Windows Components ➢ Internet Explorer and use the Enterprise Mode IE website list policy setting and point to the file, as seen in Figure 12.8.

FIGURE 12.8   Use Computer- or User-side Group Policy for Enterprise Mode to point to the XML file made with Enterprise Mode Site List Manager.

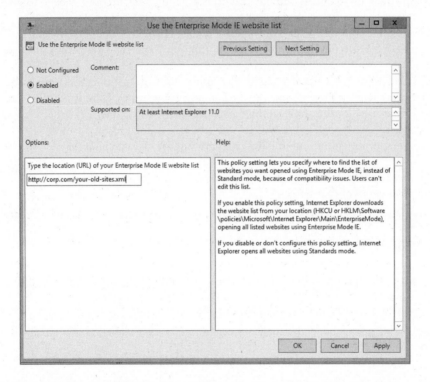

You can read more about this from Microsoft at `https://msdn.microsoft.com/en-us/library/dn640699.aspx`.

Three little sidenotes: First, when the target machine picks up the Group Policy Object that points to the list and then processes the list, an unusual thing happens. Internet Explorer takes upward of 65 seconds after Internet Explorer launches. Sixty-Five seconds? Yep, 65 seconds. I read it at the Microsoft link I just mentioned, and then I also confirmed with someone who wrote parts of the code for this within IE 11. So don't freak out when you don't see Enterprise Mode for IE 11 work right away as expected.

Second, it should be noted that the Enterprise Mode Site List Manager (and IE 11 itself) gets updated from time to time to handle new modes. Therefore, I would recommend checking out the IE blog and signing up for an RSS feed subscription to any changes. The blog with archived posts is at http://blogs.msdn.com/b/ie/, and the newer one is at http://blogs.windows.com/msedgedev/feed/.

Third, the Windows 10 "modern browser" Microsoft Edge is also supposed to utilize the Enterprise Mode site list and try also to render sites in compatible mode.

Managing Internet Explorer 11 Using PolicyPak Application Manager

When I took a hard look at how fragmented the management experience is between Group Policy, Group Policy Preferences, and now Enterprise Mode, I decided we needed to do something.

So, without going into insane detail, we made a huge effort to "Conquer Mount IE." We tried to figure out how to manage every aspect of Internet Explorer—versions 8 and later, including IE 11.

Instead of having some preferences items that users can work around and some policy settings that don't work with different versions of each browser, we have a "Unified Pak for IE" available that handles the ability to manage darn near everything in Internet Explorer and lock it down.

I wanted to especially point out the ability to manage IE 11 Enterprise Mode. We eliminate the need to pre-create the XML site list and give you the ability to dictate the list, on the fly, to either users or computers, directly inside a Group Policy Object.

You can see a demo of that here:

http://www.policypak.com/video/policypak-internet-explorer-11-enterprise-mode.html

A lot of people have told me it was "a real game changer" for them.

The PolicyPak Pak for IE can do a lot, including dictating favorites, certificates, and LAN settings; delivering and removing add-ons; managing pop-ups; and a whole lot more. Again, it will do darn near everything you would want to do with IE.

You can see all the stuff that's possible in one place here:

www.policypak.com/products/manage-internet-explorer-using-group-policy-policypak.html

Restricting Access to Hardware via Group Policy

You know it's true: those USB thumb-disk keys and removable media doodads make your personal life easier but your professional life harder. You want a way to control which hardware devices can be installed by users and which can't.

Thank you, Group Policy, for coming to the rescue.

Imagine this scenario: You allow users to have USB mice but disallow USB thumb drives. You could allow CD-ROM readers but not DVD writers. You could allow Bluetooth but disallow PC Card devices.

You're in control, letting Group Policy do the work for you.

There are two ways to make this magic happen: one way disables the device, which is nice, but the other way restricts the driver itself from even loading.

The first way uses the Group Policy Preferences Devices extension. The second way is via Group Policy's Administrative Templates.

Table 12.1 will be the basis of our discussions. Here, we'll be able to see how the two Group Policy technologies compare and contrast. And when you're done reading this big section, come back to this table to make your final decision about which one to use. (Or, heck, maybe you'll decide to use 'em both!)

TABLE 12.1   GPPrefs Devices vs. Group Policy device installation restriction

Feature evaluation	GPPrefs Devices extension	Device installation restriction
Valid for	XP+	Vista+
Mechanism	Disables the device	Prevents the driver from loading
Requirements	Machine must have Group Policy Preferences CSE installed.	Vista+
User can avoid?	Possible: With admin rights, can re-enable	Possible: With admin rights, can avoid the Group Policy altogether, but more difficult
Notification of restriction	None	Pop-up balloon
Granularity	Works only to restrict device class and device type	Works to restrict from very specific hardware ID or generic device IDs up to restricting the entire hardware class

Group Policy Preferences Devices Extension

In Chapter 5, you learned about the Group Policy preference extensions (and how to install them). One of those extensions is the Devices extension. The Devices extension works for Windows XP and higher, provided the GPPref CSE is already loaded.

The Devices GPPref disables the device or port but *doesn't* prevent the driver from loading. The new Devices extension node is found by navigating to Computer Configuration ➢ Preferences ➢ Control Panel Settings ➢ Devices or User Configuration ➢ Preferences ➢ Control Panel Settings ➢ Devices. You can see the Devices extension in Figure 12.9.

FIGURE 12.9   The Group Policy preference extensions have the ability to restrict devices and device classes. Here, I'm selecting a whole class to disable.

Why is it on both sides?

You'll use the Computer side when you want all users on the same machine to be affected by your edict. Use the User side when you want a specific person to be affected by your edict.

Most organizations will choose the Computer side. That way, everyone on the machine can be restricted from using, say, USB flash disks or CD-ROMs.

Deciding to Disable the Device Class or Device Type

In Figure 12.9, we can see the "Select a Device Class or a Device" dialog. Here you can select a root class, like Ports (COM & LPT), or a specific device, like Communications Port (COM1).

If you choose just the device class, only the "Device class" block gets filled in. If you choose the actual device, then both "Device class" *and* "Device type" are populated, as seen in Figure 12.10.

FIGURE 12.10   Restricting a specific device

What Happens When a Device Is Restricted?

When a specific device is restricted, it is simply disabled, indicated by the little down-arrow icon in Figure 12.11.

However, if you went the extra mile and disabled the class, then, usually, *all* devices within that class are restricted, as seen in Figure 12.12.

The issue is that, with proper rights, any user could right-click and re-enable the device (also seen in Figure 12.11). Now, by default, regular users (on Windows XP and later) cannot re-enable devices that are disabled like this. But because many organizations run their users as local admins, this could be easy for any admin-user to do. However, because Group Policy preference extensions leverage the Group Policy infrastructure, they take effect during the background refresh (about every 90 minutes or so). At that time, the device will once again be restricted (provided the DC can be reached and the Group Policy Preferences settings redownloaded).

You cannot disable some devices. For example, on my Windows machines, I was unable to disable processors. I'm pretty sure this is a "Good Thing."

FIGURE 12.11 The Devices extension simply disables devices.

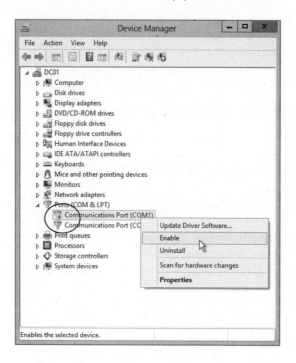

FIGURE 12.12 Disabling the whole class will disable all devices within that class.

Dealing with Devices That Aren't Listed

This is kind of a problem with the Devices extension: you cannot specify a piece of hardware that you don't already have on your management station.

So, while it's a snap to disable USB ports altogether, it's a lot harder to eliminate just thumb drives, or something specific like a 30GB color video iPod. In short, the easiest way to disable a device is to track one down and get it hooked into your management station. Then, you'll be able to just point to it and you're done.

Now, if you can't get a hold of the device but you know someone who has one, you might still be in luck. That's right! Just the very act of knowing someone with the device might be able to help you get out of a jam. Instead of having to schlep that device over to your management station (or make the machine with the device a temporary management station), you can simply ask your pal to tell you what the device properties are and jam them into the XML code of the preference you created. (We covered how to edit the underlying XML code of a preference in Chapter 5.)

Table 12.2 shows what you need from the device property details and how to set them within the XML attribute.

TABLE 12.2 Device property details and their appropriate XML attributes

XML attribute	Device property from Details tab of device properties
deviceClass	Class long name
deviceType	Device description
deviceClassGUID	Device class GUID
deviceTypeID	Device instance path

The CSE has to have the deviceClassGUID and the deviceTypeID exactly as they are displayed in the device properties to correctly enable or disable the device.

Why Is There an Option to Disable and Enable?

A keen eye will spot that the Devices extension has both Disable *and* Enable.

The idea is simple: you can use GPO filtering or Group Policy preference extensions item-level targeting to decide, perhaps, who should get which hardware enabled or disabled. For instance, everyone who gets the GPO will have their USB ports disabled, except for lab technicians, who need USB ports enabled.

To do something like this, you might set the GPO at a high level (maybe a high-level OU or at the domain level) and then set it to Disabled. Then, lower down, say, at the **Lab Technicians** OU, set the USB ports as Enabled.

In my testing, the Devices GPPrefs item worked perfectly when I used Computer Configuration ➤ Preferences ➤ Control Panel Settings ➤ Devices. I restricted the hardware and ran the gpupdate.exe command, and my hardware was disabled. However, when I did the same thing using User Configuration ➤ Preferences ➤ Control Panel Settings ➤ Devices and restricted the same hardware, it didn't always take effect right away.

Restricting Driver Access with Policy Settings

In the previous section, we talked about the Group Policy preference extensions and how, in using that technology, you can disable devices. That's great. But you can take it to the next level with two areas of Group Policy. There are two sections of Group Policy that we're going to talk about now to help you secure your hardware even further:

- Computer Configuration ➤ Policies ➤ Administrative Templates ➤ System ➤ Removable Storage Access (seen in Figure 12.13)

- Computer Configuration ➤ Policies ➤ Administrative Templates ➤ System ➤ Device Installation ➤ Device Installation Restrictions (seen in Figure 12.14)

FIGURE 12.13 There are some predefined hardware restrictions you can leverage in Group Policy.

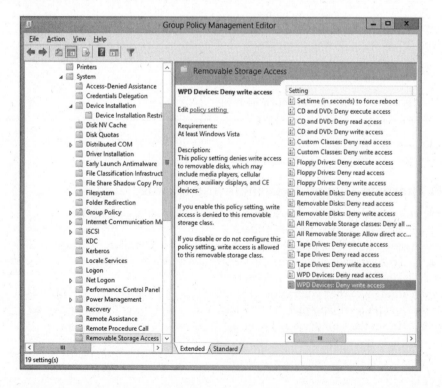

FIGURE 12.14   You can customize the kinds of hardware you want to restrict.

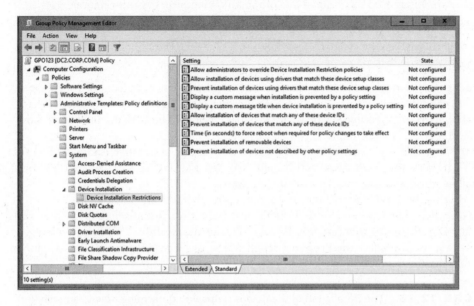

The first set (Removable Storage Access) is fairly self-explanatory. If you enable a policy setting for that kind of removable storage (CD/DVD, floppy, and so on), you can make it so that the whole device type cannot be read or written to. But it doesn't have the "super-power" the second set (Device Installation Restrictions) has.

In the first set, there is a policy setting named **Custom Classes: Deny read access** and another one named **Custom Classes: Deny write access**.

There is a difference between the sets.

The Removable Storage Access policy set doesn't prevent the drivers from being installed. So, the driver for the class will be installed when the hardware is detected, but this policy prevents it from being read or written to.

So we're about to explore the Device Installation Restrictions policy settings, where we'll put the real smackdown on the driver itself.

Getting a Handle on Classes and IDs

First, you need to know what you want to restrict. You can think big or you can think small. As with the Devices extension, you can restrict a specific "class" of devices or get super-specific and restrict a single hardware type. Or you can allow only specific device classes, like USB mice.

Here's the trick: to really be effective, you're, once again, going to need to track down the hardware you'll want to restrict.

So, if you want to say, "No joystick drivers can be installed on my Windows 7 machines," and "Only USB mice can be installed on my Windows 10 machines," you'll likely need to get hold of a joystick and a USB mouse. Now, this isn't always true. You can try to use the Internet to track down one of the following pieces of information:

- Hardware ID
- Compatible ID
- Device class

But, again, it's much easier if you just have one of these devices in front of you. That way, you can introduce it to a Windows Vista or later machine and see for yourself what the hardware ID, compatible ID, or device class is. Once you know that, you'll know how to squash it (or leave it available).

In this example, we'll squash a specific sound card family: a Creative AudioPCI ES1371/ES1373. If you want to squash something else (like specific USB devices or even USB ports), just follow along and substitute the device you want.

To do this, fire up Device Manager on a machine that already has the hardware items installed. Then, when you find the device, right-click it and select Properties and click the Details tab. By default, you'll see a "Device description." While interesting, it's not that useful. Select the Property dropdown and select "Hardware Ids," as shown in Figure 12.15.

FIGURE 12.15   The Details tab of the device helps you determine how to squash it.

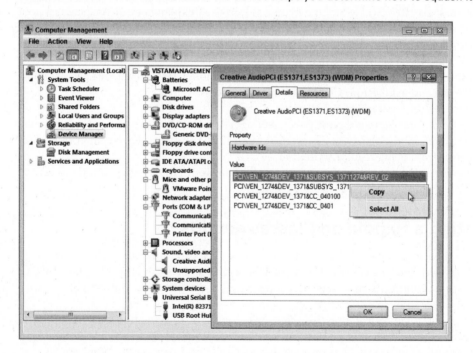

The "Hardware Ids" page shows you, from top to bottom, the most specific to least specific device ID. If you look closely at the topmost item in the "Hardware Ids" value list, you'll see that this sound card is specifically a Rev 2 of the ES1371 soundboard. That's pretty darned specific. As you go down the list, the description becomes less specific to encompass the whole family.

Additionally, you can change the Property setting to "Compatible Ids." These IDs also describe the hardware and are considered less specific than what you'll find in "Hardware Ids." You might choose to use the information found in "Compatible Ids" to try to corral more hardware that's similar into the "don't use" list—because it's less specific and might net you more results. The trade-off is that you might restrict something you didn't want to as you get less specific.

And, finally, the least specific category can be found by selecting Device Class from the Property dropdown. In my case, the sound card shows up as simply Media. But lots of things could be considered Media, so, again, caution should be used the less specific you go.

Once you've decided which value you want to leverage, right-click it, select Copy, and paste it into Notepad for safekeeping. Copying it directly as it's presented is important because, in the next steps, the value must be entered exactly. If there are upper- and lower-case characters in the value, they must be transferred precisely.

If you wanted to be a command-line commando instead of using the Device Manager to capture the hardware IDs or device classes, check out the DevCon command-line utility at http://support.microsoft.com/kb/311272.

Microsoft has a bunch of identifiers for common classes here that may be helpful if you don't have any physical access to the device: http://msdn.microsoft.com/en-us/library/ff541224.aspx.

Restricting or Allowing Your Hardware via Group Policy

Although we'll explore all the policy settings located in Computer Configuration ➢ Administrative Templates ➢ System ➢ Device Installation ➢ Device Installation Restrictions (seen in Figure 12.14), there is really only one policy setting we'll need to complete this initial example.

Create a GPO and link it to an OU (or domain, and so on) that contains the Windows Vista and later machines you want to control. Then, edit the GPO and drive down into Computer Configuration ➢ Administrative Templates ➢ System ➢ Device Installation ➢ Device Installation Restrictions ➢ **Prevent installation of devices that match any of these device IDs**. Select Enabled in the policy setting, click Show (also in the policy setting), which opens up the Show Contents dialog, then paste in the information from the device you got before. All this can be seen in Figure 12.16.

FIGURE 12.16 Paste the device ID to ensure that you've captured the device description exactly.

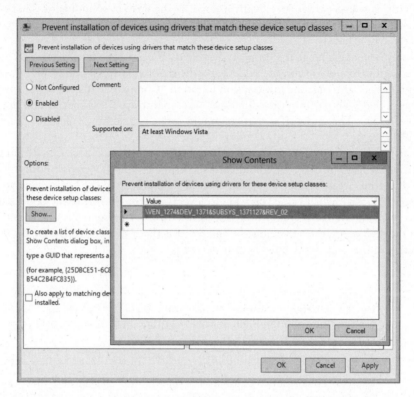

There's also a switch inside this policy setting, "Also apply to matching devices that are already installed." Enabling this switch is a good idea if you want uniform restrictions. As soon as the next Group Policy update occurs, blammo! The hardware is locked out.

When you turn on a machine that has never seen the hardware device, you'll see the machine try to install the hardware device and provide pop-up balloon status information as to its progress. When it's completed, the goal is that the hardware is restricted, as you can see in Figure 12.17.

FIGURE 12.17 When implemented properly, the device driver will be prevented from installing.

Understanding the Remaining Policy Settings for Hardware Restrictions

In the example we just went through, we squashed the use of just one device. You could, if you wanted, go the opposite route, which is to restrict *all* hardware by default and allow only *some*. This can be done using the policy settings described next. Again, you can see a list of these policy settings in Figure 12.14, which shows the Computer Configuration ➢ Administrative Templates ➢ Device Installation ➢ Device Installation Restrictions branch of Group Policy.

Allow Administrators to Override Device Installation Restrictions

By default, local administrators on Windows Vista and later machines must honor the restrictions that are put in place. If you enable the **Allow administrators to override device installation restrictions** setting, local administrators can install whatever hardware they want.

Allow Installation of Devices Using Drivers That Match These Setup Classes

By entering device descriptions in this policy setting, you're expressly allowing these hardware devices as "allowed" into the system. Note that the **Allow installation of devices using drivers that match these setup classes** policy setting honors only setup classes and not device IDs (like those we used in the working example). You can learn more about setup classes at:

```
http://msdn.microsoft.com/en-us/library/windows/hardware/ff553426(v=vs.85).
aspx
```

Prevent Installation of Devices Using Drivers That Match These Device Setup Classes

In our earlier example, we used the device ID to describe our hardware and enabled another policy setting, **Prevent Installation of devices that match any of these device IDs**. Note that the setting we used does not honor class ID descriptions. To use class ID descriptions, you need to use the **Prevent installation of devices using drivers that match these device setup classes** policy setting.

There's also a switch inside this policy setting, "Also apply to matching devices that are already installed." This is a good idea if you want uniform restrictions.

Display a Custom Message When Installation Is Prevented by Policy (Balloon Text) and Display a Custom Message When Installation Is Prevented by Policy (Balloon Title)

These are two policy settings that help you customize the message, as shown in Figure 12.17. It's super fun to scare the pants off people with these messages. On second thought, don't do that.

Allow Installation of Devices That Match Any of These Device IDs

In our earlier example, we used the device ID to describe our hardware. However, I also stated that the least specific way to describe our hardware is based on hardware class. It should be noted that the **Allow installation of devices that match any of these device IDs** policy setting does not honor class ID descriptions. To use class ID descriptions, use the policy settings **Allow installation of devices using drivers that match these device setup classes** or **Prevent installation of devices using drivers that match these device setup classes**.

This setting is best used with another setting, **Prevent installation of devices not described by other policy settings**. By preventing everything (by default), then using this setting, you can specify precisely which devices you want to allow to be installed.

Prevent Installation of Devices that Match Any of These Device IDs

In our example, **Prevent installation of devices that match any of these device IDs** is the policy setting we used to restrict a specific type of hardware based on device IDs. If we wanted to restrict using device classes, we would have to leverage other specific policy settings, such as **Allow installation of devices using drivers that match these device setup classes** or **Prevent installation of devices using drivers that match these device setup classes**.

Prevent Installation of Removable Devices

The **Prevent installation of removable devices** setting is a generic and quick way to restrict any hardware device that describes itself as "removable," including USB devices. I wouldn't count on this particular policy setting that often. Use the techniques described earlier to get moderately restrictive device IDs and lock them down specifically. This setting is vague enough and there's no telling what the hardware is telling Windows about itself to be sure it's locking down what you think it is.

Prevent Installation of Devices Not Described by Other Policy Settings

The setting **Prevent installation of devices not described by other policy settings** is the catchall policy setting that basically restricts all hardware, unless you've specifically dictated that something can install. This policy, in conjunction with the various "Allow" policies (such as **Allow installation of devices that match any of these device IDs**), can make a powerful combination you can use to allow only the hardware you want in your environment.

Time (in Seconds) to Force Reboot When Required for Policy Changes to Take Effect

The **Time (in seconds) to force reboot when required for policy changes to take effect** setting appears to be used when removing a driver would require a reboot to take effect. I didn't have a specific way of testing this, but it seems like a good idea to turn on this setting if you're about to restrict a lot of various hardware. Note that this policy affects Windows 7 and later machines.

Assigning Printers via Group Policy

Let me guess what another of your biggest headaches is printers, right? Wouldn't it be great if we could just zap printers down to our Windows machines? Or, whenever Sally roams from Desktop to Desktop, she had access to the same printers?

Those are two different goals, and we're about to approach both of them here.

Ideally, you'll use the Group Policy preference extensions to zap printers to your users and computers. With that in mind, let's explore how to zap printers down to your users.

Zapping Down Printers to Users and Computers (a Refresher)

We explored this subject briefly in Chapter 5, but here's a quick review.

The Printers Group Policy preference extension exists on both the Computer and User sides. On the Computer side, however, you can't map shared printers, but only TCP/IP and local printers, as you can see in Figure 12.18. On the User side, you can map all three kinds of printers, as Figure 12.19 shows.

Setting up a shared printer on the User side is easy, as seen in Figure 12.20. Just set the share path to the printer share, and voilà—instant printer for the user. The bonus is that the user doesn't need to be an administrator to install the drivers that will come down from the server when this connection happens. The Group Policy engine does it on the user's behalf, so it's just done, lickety-split.

FIGURE 12.18   The Printers extension on the Computer side allows only for mapping TCP/IP and local printers.

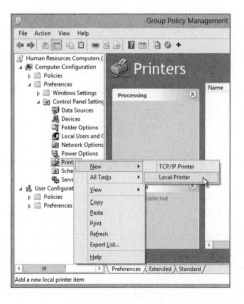

FIGURE 12.19 The Printers extension on the User side can deploy all three types of printers.

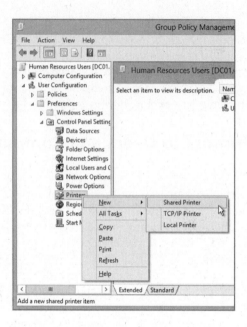

FIGURE 12.20 Shared printers are usually what most people set up.

Trickier: Zapping Down Specific Printers to Users on Specific Machines

Oh, sure, you can use the Printers extension to map a specific printer to a specific user. But that means that no matter which computer a user travels to, he gets exactly the same printers.

But maybe that's not what you want. I talk with lots of people who have the same problem: how to map printers based on the computer the user is on at that moment.

Take Figure 12.21, for example. Here, you can see four zones:

- Zone 1 with Printer 1: IT computers
- Zone 2 with Printer 2: Human Resources
- Zone 3 with Printer 3: Sales
- Zone 4 with Printer 4: Marketing

FIGURE 12.21   In our sample company, we have four zones and one special shared printer requirement.

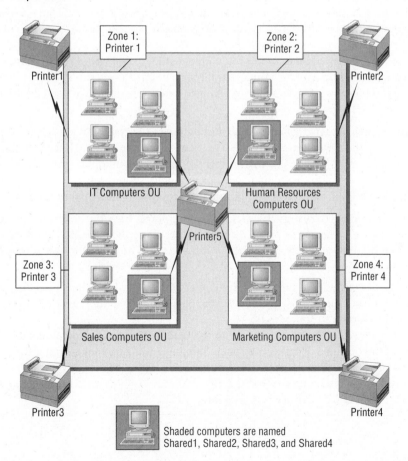

And, just for fun, I'm adding an additional challenge: a special circumstance where I have a shared computer in each zone that should not only print to the normal printer in that zone but also map to an additional shared printer specific to the shared computers.

In Figure 12.21, our shared computers are shaded and have the word "shared" in their names. This will be helpful later, as we craft our printing experience.

So the goal is that whenever anyone logs onto any computer in the zone, they get mapped to the printer for that zone.

To achieve the goal, we'll break this out into two steps:

1. Deploy the specific zone printer to all computers in the same zone.

2. Deploy the shared printer to only the shared computers in all zones.

Deploying the Same Printer to All Computers in the Zone

To accomplish our first goal, we want to make sure all computers in Human Resources get the same printer, Printer 2. You'll repeat the same procedure for other areas of your universe, but we'll just show Human Resources as an example.

We've already seen how you can't deploy Shared Printers to computers. That's a bummer, because our goal is that whenever anyone logs onto a Human Resources computer, he or she gets Printer 2.

And, natively, you can't do that. (You could do it with Group Policy Loopback in Merge mode, but you may end up getting unintended Group Policy Objects this way.)

But with a little one-two Group Policy preference extensions punch, we can do it without any Loopback hassle.

Punch 1: Put an environment variable on all computers in the zone.   What we need is a way to tag the specific computers with a little marker, so that once we can see this marker, we can take action on it. We can use environment variables to make this little tag on specific computers, which will indicate that specific computers should use specific printers. We'll use the Group Policy Preferences Environment extension to do this for us.

Punch 2: Map shared printers only to users whose computers have the environment variable.   Once we have the little tag on each computer, we'll use the GPPref Printers extension. We'll map shared printers to users, but only if the tag is present on the machine that specifies a printer.

Before we get started, make sure your **Human Resources** OU looks like mine does in Figure 12.22. You can see I've got **Human Resources Computers** and **Human Resources Users** within the **Human Resources** OU.

Next, we'll create a GPO and link it over to the **Human Resources Computers** OU. We'll use the GPPref Environment extension to put a System variable on the computer called PRINTER2, and give it a value of 1 (which means true).

The idea is that if a computer in Zone 2 sees a variable with Printer2, that computer should get that printer. You can see this in Figure 12.23.

FIGURE 12.22   Make sure your Human Resources structure looks like mine.

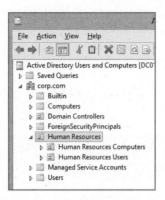

FIGURE 12.23   Use a System variable to tag computers to use specific printers.

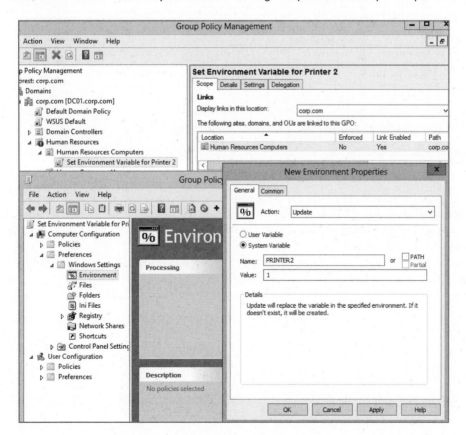

Then, create a GPO and link it to the domain level (or any higher level such that all the zones you want are covered). I'm calling my GPO "Universal Printer Map for Users." This GPO will affect all user accounts. It will use the GPPref Printers extension on the User side to map a shared printer, as seen in Figure 12.24.

FIGURE 12.24   Use the GPPref Printers extension to map a printer to everyone.

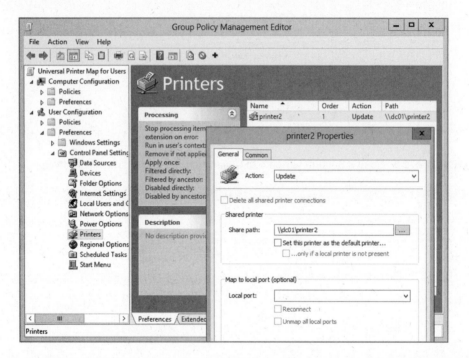

Now, if we stopped here, we'd have a problem. That's because, right now, we're saying, "Everyone should get \\dc01\printer2," and that's not right. What we want to say is, "Everyone should get \\dc01\printer2—if they're using a computer that's tagged with the environment variable PRINTER2=1."

So, now, click the Common tab in the Printer extension properties. Then, click "Item-level targeting," as seen in Figure 12.25, and select the Targeting button to open the Targeting Editor.

FIGURE 12.25   Use item-level targeting (ILT) to specify that the PRINTER2 environment variable must be set to 1.

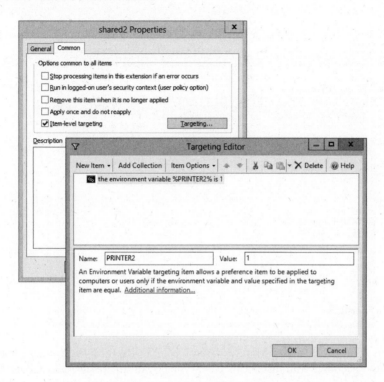

Add a new item, select the environment variable, and specify that the PRINTER2 environment variable must be set to 1, as seen in Figure 12.25.

If all goes well, two things happen on the client system: the system gets the message that produces the environment variable (and sets its value), and, because of that environment variable's value, anyone who logs onto that computer with the variable set with the value gets the printer.

Magic!

You can see this magic in Figure 12.26. The command prompt shows the environment variable PRINTER2=1, and the Devices and Printers dialog box shows the newly mapped printer based on the environment variable.

FIGURE 12.26 Based on the environment variable, anyone who uses this computer gets the printer.

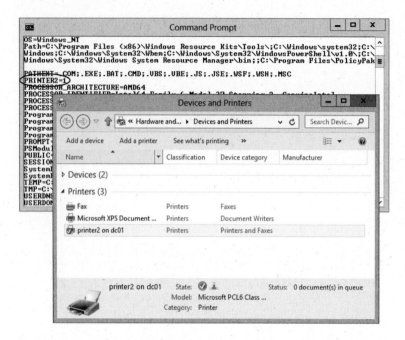

Because this "Universal Printer Map for Users" GPO is linked to the domain, it already affects every user account. And inside this GPO, you'll want to create a new Group Policy Preferences item *for every printer*. The goal, again, is to make it such that the mapping of the printer only happens when computers have the environment variable present.

Deploying a Shared Printer to Only the Shared Computers in All Zones

In the previous example, we got everyone to use the specific printer for the computers in their zone.

However, remember that we have one special requirement: we want all the shared computers (in our examples, they're named Shared1, Shared2, Shared3, and Shared4) to use the same printer: Printer 5. So, this time, we'll use a trick in the ILT feature to specify that all computers with "shared" in the name will map to the same printer.

To do this, we'll create a GPO at the domain level called "Special Map for Public Computers" and use the Printers extension on the Users side to map \\dc01\printer5, but only when the computer name is SHARED-something.

We accomplish this by using the * indicator, as in SHARED*. You can see this in Figure 12.27.

FIGURE 12.27   You can map printers to users based on the computer name.

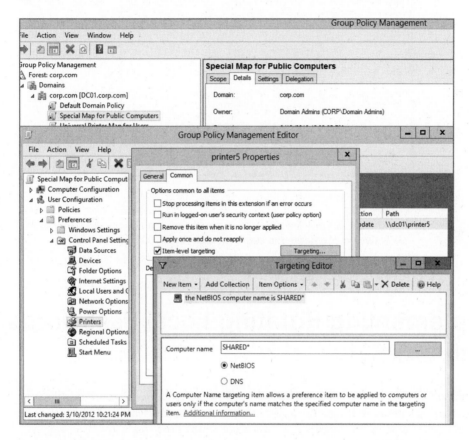

The star will evaluate to true for any computer named SHARED1, SHARED2, and so on.

Now, you've done it! You've got a universal way to ensure that people get a specific printer based on the specific computer they're logging onto. Indeed, if you were to log onto SHARED2, which is in the **Human Resources Computers** OU, you would now get two printers: you'd get Printer2 because you were in Zone 2 (from the first example), and Printer5 because you were on a shared computer, as seen in Figure 12.28.

FIGURE 12.28 Because you logged onto SHARED2, you got two printers.

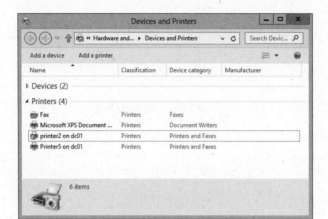

For PolicyPak On-Premise suite users, there's an equally, arguably more effective way to get these same results. Check out the video at:

`www.policypak.com/video/policypak-deliver-gpprefs-items-without-using-loopback-mode.html`

Implementing Rotating Local Passwords with LAPS

It's not a great idea to have the same local administrator account's password on all your machines. Think about it: If I get the password to one of these machines, I own all of your machines with the same local password. This is one of the problems with the so-called Pass-the-Hash security attack.

You can learn more about Pass-the-Hash attacks and how to mitigate them from Microsoft's docs at `www.microsoft.com/en-us/download/details.aspx?id=36036`.

Remember back in Chapter 5 when we talked about Group Policy Preferences having the ability to manage passwords in local accounts? Well, also remember that functionality is gone, because there was an easy way to reverse and reveal any passwords created with Group Policy Preferences and stored within a Group Policy Object.

So now what do we do?

We don't want to bake the same local admin password into our build.

We don't want to (really, can't set) the local admin password via Group Policy Preferences.

Well there's a third option and it's called LAPS: Local Administrator Password Solution.

LAPS is a free add-on from Microsoft that installs (wait for it!) as a Group Policy extension! So it's very easy to set up and easy to manage.

The general idea of LAPS is that it takes a series of rules (stored in a Group Policy Object) and then based upon those rules, rotates the password and stores them in Active Directory in a special, protected place. And then only the people with security clearance can read those passwords! So even though the passwords are stored in cleartext, only authorized people can view them.

To get started with this walk-through, download LAPS at www.microsoft.com/en-us/download/details.aspx?id=46899.

What to Install from LAPS

There are different pieces you must install to make LAPS operate.

You need to install LAPS (same installer) twice: Once on your machine to manage LAPS and once on the target machines you want to manage. Let's do these both now.

You'll want to use the Windows Installer packages that LAPS contains. There's one for 32-bit machines and one for 64-bit machines.

Installing LAPS on Your Machine to Manage LAPS

Once you click to run the LAPS installer on your management station, you will need to change the defaults so you are only installing the management pieces and not the CSE.

See Figure 12.29 for the ideal configuration.

FIGURE 12.29 Change the default installation to match this for your management station.

Installing LAPS on Target Machines to Install the CSE

Then on one endpoint, say Win10, install the LAPS MSI installer, which will install the CSE. In Figure 12.30, see the configuration for installing only the CSE on the target machine.

FIGURE 12.30   This is what is needed on the client computer to install the LAPS CSE.

Extending the Schema and Setting LAPS Permissions

Remember that LAPS has no database. Passwords are delivered from the client computers to a special place in Active Directory. That special place, however, requires a schema extension to Active Directory.

To perform the work, you'll need to be logged in as the Enterprise Administrator of your organization and then use PowerShell. Start out by importing the LAPS cmdlets as seen in Figure 12.31.

FIGURE 12.31   Import the LAPS cmdlets

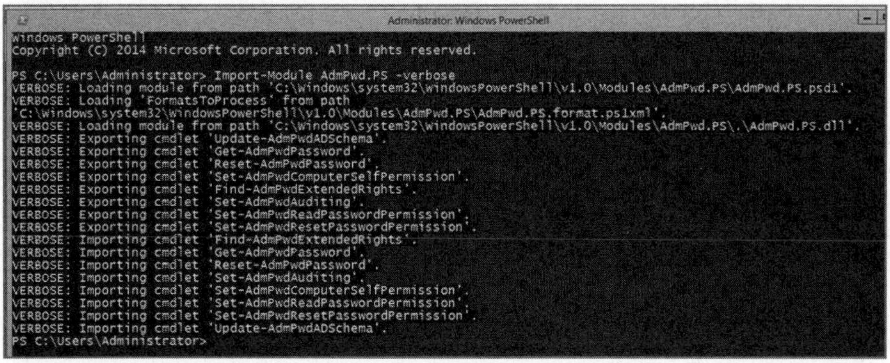

Use the PowerShell command:

`Import-Module AdmPws.PS -verbose`

and you'll see all the cmdlets that are imported.

Then run the cmdlet `Update-AdmPwdADSchema`, as seen in Figure 12.32. When you do, the Active Directory schema is updated to hold the fields. After you do this, the Computer attributes in Active Directory will have these new fields in which to store passwords. The permission on the password field is set as "Confidential."

FIGURE 12.32   LAPS updates your Active Directory schema to hold the local admin passwords.

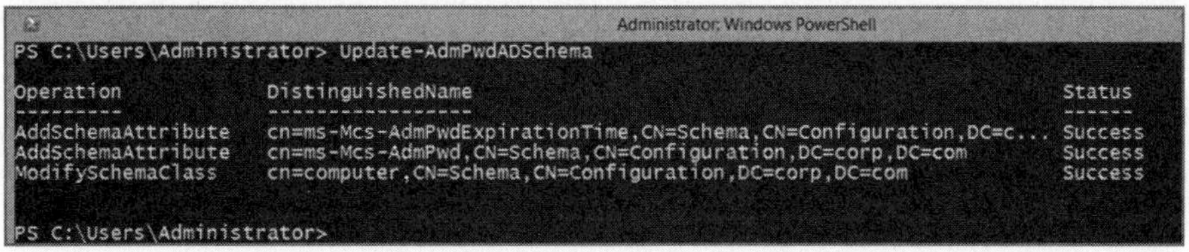

Computers need the rights to update this password when it changes. To configure the rights, run the cmdlet `Set-AdmPwdComputerSelfPermission` against each container and OU, which contains computer accounts. In Figure 12.33, I delegated the rights against the Computers folder (not an OU) and also the **Human Resources Computers** OU within Human Resources OU.

FIGURE 12.33 Delegate which computers have the rights to deliver updated passwords into Active Directory.

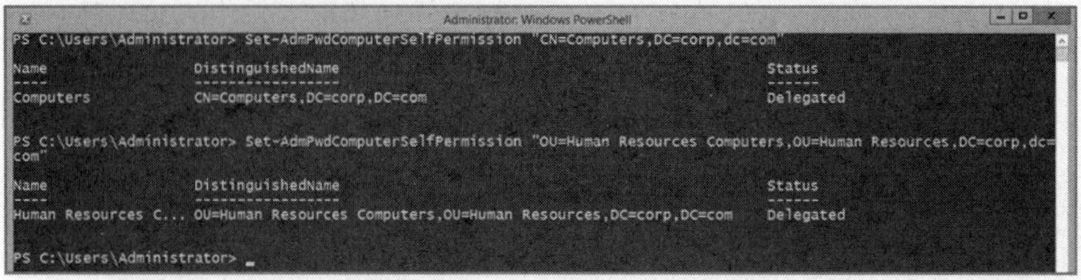

The last step is delegating Read access. You need to delegate twice here: once for the computers that need access to this field and once for admins who should be allowed to read this field.

So in Figure 12.34 we delegated Write access for the Computers folder (not OU) and also the **Human Resources Computers** OU. We should now delegate Read access for these same locations. Additionally, delegate Read access for the Active Directory security group you want to have access to read these passwords. In my examples, I've pre-created a group called PasswordReaders, but you can call it anything you like.

FIGURE 12.34 Set read permissions upon the locations and grant who can read the passwords.

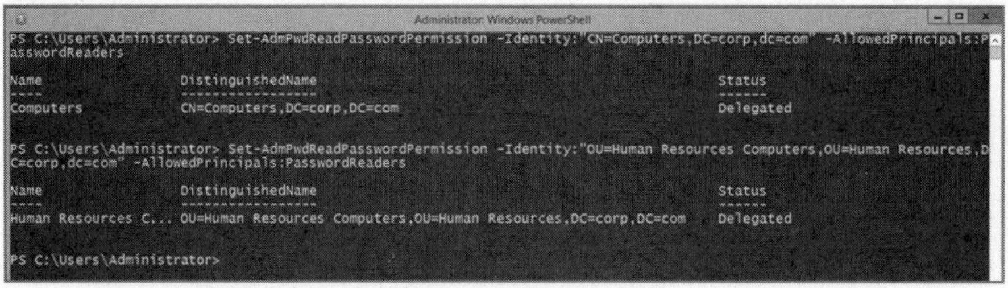

The syntax would be something like:

```
Set-AdmPwdReadPasswordPermission -Identity:<DN> -AllowedPrincipals:<GroupName>
```

So, in Figure 12.34, you can see the two commands:

```
Set-AdmPwdReadPasswordPermission -Identity:"CN=Computers,DC=corp,dc=com"
-AllowedPrincipals:PasswordReaders
```

and:

```
Set-AdmPwdReadPasswordPermission -Identity:"OU=Human Resources Computers,
OU=Human Resources, DC=corp,  DC=com" -AllowedPrincipals:PasswordReaders
```

Using a Group Policy Object to Manage LAPS

If you have no ADMX Central Store set up and are using only local storage, then when you install the LAPS management station pieces, the ADMX files are already in the right place.

If you are using an ADMX Central Store, you'll need to copy the files named AdmPwd.Admx and AdmPwd.Adml to their proper location. For more information on how to utilize a Central Store, see Chapter 6.

The Group Policy settings appear in Figure 12.35.

FIGURE 12.35   The LAPS Group Policy settings

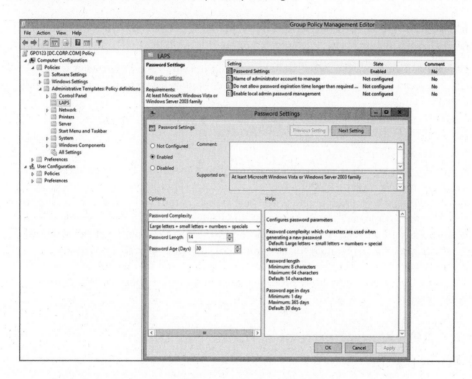

Here is a rundown of each Group Policy setting for LAPS.

Password Settings

Inside this policy setting you can set Password Complexity (there are four options), described here from weakest to strongest:

- Large letters
- Large letters + small letters
- Large letters + small letters + numbers
- Large letters + small letters + numbers + specials

Also present are Password Length, and Password Age (Days).

If this is not configured, the default is the strongest type with 14-character passwords and a password age maximum of 30 days.

Name of Administrator Account to Manage

LAPS can only set and manage one local account password. By default, when this value is un-set, it will hit the default local administrator account, even if it's been renamed. This is because the local administrator account's SID never changes, even if the account is renamed.

That being said, if you want to dictate another account name to rotate, you can do that in this policy setting.

Do Not Allow Password Expiration Time Longer than Required by Policy

If your actual domain-wide password policy is configured differently than what is set in the LAPS **Password Settings** policy setting, you can configure LAPS to honor that setting should the two conflict.

Enable Local Admin Password Management

This is the "Master Switch."

This must be set to Enabled for LAPS to actually do something. This is basically "Turn LAPS on," and it must be set to Enabled.

The Group Policy Object you create with these settings needs to be linked to a place that contains computer accounts. There's nearly no downside in linking it to the whole domain, since this process will only work (again) when the CSE is installed on the client machine and proper permissions are granted to the computers you want to perform writes.

Once the Group Policy Object's settings are set and the Group Policy Object is linked, simply wait for Group Policy to apply on target machines, or run gpupdate manually on your test client.

Using LAPS Management's Tools: Fat Client and PowerShell

So how do you know if it's working or not?

LAPS ships with two ways to query the password, which is stored in Active Directory. One is called the *Fat LAPS UI* (nice name) and the other is a PowerShell cmdlet, Get-AdmPwdPassword.

The Fat LAPS UI is (wait for it...) named "LAPS UI" and can be found right on the Start Menu of your management station. When you run it, it's a simple dialog box where you enter in the computer name and click Search.

If the computer account is found in Active Directory, and the password value has been set by the computer, you'll see something like what's seen in Figure 12.36. You can also use the Fat LAPS client to immediately force a password change request, by leaving the "New expiration time" field blank and clicking Set. Alternatively, you can set a new date/time here for the password to expire if you so desire.

FIGURE 12.36 LAPS has a GUI and a PowerShell method for retrieving passwords stored in Active Directory.

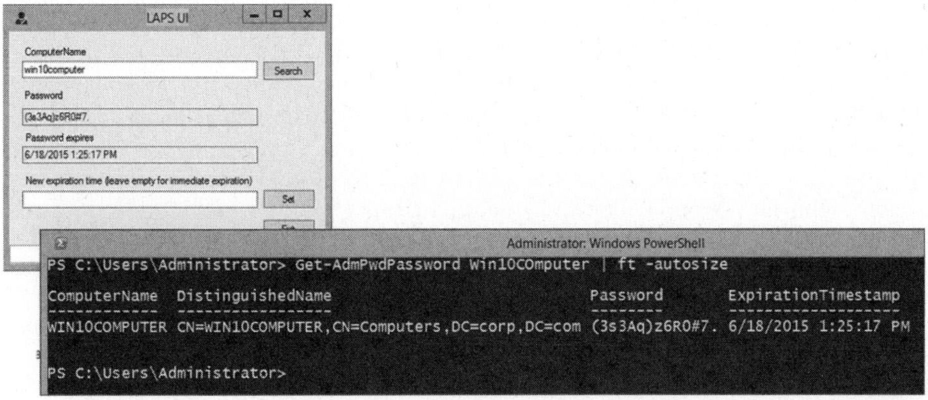

You can also see in Figure 12.36 the PowerShell cmdlet that does the same thing. Use `Get-AdmPwdPassword` *<computername>* and, if desired, some optional parameters for formatting the output.

LAPS is a great idea and easy to set up and use. Everyone should be using it to dictate strong local admin passwords. The only hitch I can see is that it does require an Active Directory schema update, but that shouldn't be a big barrier as it's nothing to be afraid of.

For more information on LAPS, here are some links:

Security advisory

`https://technet.microsoft.com/en-us/library/security/3062591`

LAPS blog

`http://blogs.msdn.com/b/laps/`

For a great walk-through of Pass the Hash and how using LAPS can prevent you from being hacked, check out "Barbarians Inside the Gates: Protecting against Credential Theft and Pass the Hash Today" by Aaron Margosis and Mark Simos from the Ignite 2015 conference. It's found at:

`https://channel9.msdn.com/Events/Ignite/2015/BRK2334`

And, again, the actual download of LAPS is at:

`www.microsoft.com/en-us/download/details.aspx?id=46899`

Final Thoughts for This Chapter and for the Book

The cake might be yummy, but we appreciate the frosting first.

In this chapter, we added some frosting to our already hearty, secure, and managed desktop cake. We leveraged login and startup scripts to automate user tasks. We managed Internet Explorer settings using some new techniques. We used hardware control to keep the bad devices off our network and ensured that users had printers exactly when they needed them. And we used LAPS to manage the local admin passwords and store their values in Active Directory in a secure manner.

I hope you enjoyed this book. It was fun to share with you some of my favorite tips, tricks, and insights into Group Policy and Desktop nirvana.

If you're looking for more stuff from me, here's the breakdown at both www.GPanswers .com and www.PolicyPak.com.

At www.GPanswers.com, explore the resources like:

- A killer newsletter with Group Policy updates.
- Constantly updated FAQ and "Tips and Tricks."
- A video series.
- A community room to help get your most pressing questions answered.
- And, of course, my hands-on training to take your game to the next level. You can do this with me or online using my Group Policy Online University (where I'm *still* available one-on-one to help you through your toughest challenges!). Both classes are hands-on to take your skills even further.

As for PolicyPak, explore the software I've helped to create to make you "more awesome" as an administrator:

- PolicyPak On-Premise Suite enhances your ability to manage your applications and maintain your important IT settings on premise.
- PolicyPak Cloud helps manage applications plus extend Group Policy to the cloud.
- PolicyPak Group Policy Compliance Reporter (which we didn't get a chance to talk about in the book) can help finally answer the question "Did my GPOs and my settings actually make it to my endpoints?"

All PolicyPak Policy enhancements have videos at www.PolicyPak.com and free trials.

Thanks for making it to the end of the book. I hope to meet you in person at a conference or when you take one of my live training classes.

For sure, I'll see you at GPanswers.com—where *smart* Group Policy admins come to get *smarter*!

Jeremy

Moskowitz

Scripting Group Policy Operations with Windows PowerShell

In Chapter 2 ("Managing Group Policy with the GPMC and via PowerShell"), we discussed how to perform many of our day-to-day operations using the Group Policy Management Console (GPMC). Also in Chapter 2, we discussed how to use PowerShell to perform many (but not all) functions that the GPMC can perform.

In this appendix, we'll spend some time discussing how to use Windows PowerShell to go the extra mile. Some of the scripts here are a little longer but, as such, do more and are more powerful.

In this appendix, the goal is to use PowerShell to enable us to document, manage, and interact with Group Policy. By the time you're done, you might even say that this was fun (well, almost fun.)

There are two ways administrators can use PowerShell with regard to Group Policy. One way is to use PowerShell to deploy PowerShell scripts to client machines. We described how to do that in detail in Chapter 12, "Finishing Touches with Group Policy: Scripts, Internet Explorer, Hardware Control, Printer Deployment, Local Admin Password Control."

Again though, the journey we are after here is to leverage PowerShell to do more "Group Policy stuff."

A cmdlet (pronounced "command-let") is like PowerShell commands in a prepackaged snack pack.

This appendix was written by Jeffery Hicks, PowerShell MVP, with Jeremy Moskowitz, Group Policy MVP.

Using PowerShell to Do More with Group Policy

Before we get into heavy lifting with PowerShell, we'll cover some basics to get you up and running. First, we'll briefly discuss installing PowerShell. Then, we'll dive into doing some cool stuff with Group Policy, including automating our documentation and manipulating our GPOs. Finally, we'll deal with the sticky business of importing GPOs so that we can utilize them in a test lab before we import them into production.

Everything we are going to be discussing in this chapter is based on PowerShell v4.0, which you get automatically with Windows 8.1 and later and/or Windows Server 2012 R2 and later. Windows 10 ships with PowerShell v5.0, but for our purposes working with Group Policy, there is nothing relevant in the latest PowerShell version. That said, we will be using a Windows 10 desktop, which at the time of writing this chapter is still in late-stage technical preview.

We should point out that the stuff we talk about in this chapter should also work on Windows 7, Windows Server 2008, and Windows Server 2008 R2, although you'll have to download PowerShell v3 for Windows 7 and Windows Server 2008 platforms. Hopefully you aren't stuck with these legacy systems. We're also going to assume you want to manage Group Policy from the comfort of your cubicle without resorting to remote desktop sessions and the like.

For the most part, everything you need to accomplish can be done with any Active Directory domain flavor. We've tested Windows 2008 R2 and later. In the book, you mainly use Windows 7, 8.1, or 10 as your management machine, and now you'll continue to use the same as your PowerShell management machine. We'll explain how to set up your machine for this job in a page or so.

There are a few instances where we want to take advantage of a little something extra: add-ons are available that enable Active Directory management using PowerShell. Those goodies are wrapped inside the Active Directory cmdlets from Microsoft.

To use these new Active Directory cmdlets, you will need one of two things:

- A Windows Server 2008 R2 or later domain controller.
- If you only have Windows Server 2008, you can download and install the free Active Directory Management Gateway Service (ADMGS) from Microsoft at `http://tinyurl.com/ps423h`.

You can find a helpful blog entry on getting this all set up at

`http://technet.microsoft.com/en-us/library/dd391908(v=ws.10).aspx`

With the ADMGS, you'll still need a Windows 7 or later client to "ask" the ADGMS machines about Active Directory, when needed.

Again, the only reason you need a Windows Server 2008 or later domain controller (or the ADMGS) is if you plan on using the Microsoft Active Directory cmdlets to work with objects like users, groups, and organizational units.

Otherwise, the "built-in stuff" in the box with Windows 8 and later will handle all the Group Policy stuff perfectly well—no additional installs required.

Preparing for Your PowerShell Experience

We recommend you continue to use your Windows 10 machine as your PowerShell management machine. That's because it has everything you'll need to be successful—immediately. You could also use a Windows 7 or Windows Server 2008 R2 machine—because the "guts" of Windows 10, Windows 8, Windows 7, and Windows Server 2008 R2 are all equivalent, and they can run the same PowerShell version and have the built-in stuff we need to manage GPOs.

For this chapter, we'll assume you'll use Windows 10 as your GPMC and your PowerShell management machine.

Running PowerShell for the First Time

Before we proceed, let's make sure you can launch PowerShell. On Windows 10, to run PowerShell you have two options. When PowerShell is installed, the system path is added, so you can simply right-click on Start and in the "Search the web and Windows" dialog type **PowerShell**. Specifics may vary by operating system. If you are running a 64-bit operating system, you will most likely see options for 32- and 64-bit. For now, select the version that corresponds to your architecture.

Once PowerShell is launched, you should see a PowerShell window like the one shown in Figure A.1.

FIGURE A.1   PowerShell is up and running (with a late beta of Windows 10).

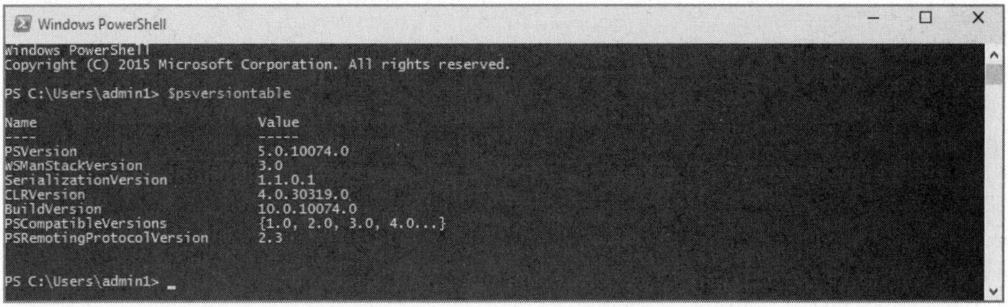

Preparing to Run Our Scripts

Finally, there is one last thing to do. By default, as a security feature, PowerShell will not run *any* scripts. You can use PowerShell as a command-line interface (CLI) to run interactive commands, but it stops short of running scripts.

That's right. It's like having a Ferrari you can't drive unless you have a special set of keys cut. And that's what you're going to do with this next command. You'll be able to drive the Ferrari after you "cut the keys" by running a cmdlet called `Set-ExecutionPolicy`. PowerShell supports six modes:

Unrestricted   All scripts will run.

RemoteSigned   If a script is downloaded from the Internet or from any site that is considered an Internet Zone, it must be digitally signed with a trusted code signing certificate.

AllSigned   All scripts must be digitally signed with a trusted code signing certificate.

Restricted   No scripts are allowed (this is the default).

Bypass   Nothing is blocked and there are no warnings or prompts.

Undefined   This mode removes the execution policy from the current scope as long as it wasn't defined by a Group Policy.

You can learn more about these settings by using Help.

```
PS C:\> help about_execution_policies -showwindow
```

To change the mode, you need to run a simple command. We recommend setting the mode to at least RemoteSigned. You do that with this command in an elevated PowerShell session:

```
PS C:\> Set-ExecutionPolicy RemoteSigned
```

We're choosing RemoteSigned because it ensures that we can't inadvertently run scripts downloaded from the Internet. (We all know where that could lead.) We'll be writing and running our own scripts, so this is the perfect level of protection.

You can download the chapter's scripts from us at www.GPanswers.com in the "Book's Resources" section.

Getting Started with PowerShell

Of course, you don't want to, and shouldn't need to, log onto a Domain Controller to manage your network. Instead, you will want to use your Windows management station. All the examples in this chapter will be done from a Windows 10 desktop. There are a few steps you need to take to get ready.

Windows 10 Remote Server Administration Tools

The first step is to download and install the Remote Server Administration Tools (RSAT) for Windows 10. You did that way back in Chapter 1.

However, let's review in case you've jumped right ahead here.

If you're using Windows 10, install the RSAT for Windows 10, which (at last check) was here (it could move by the time you read this though):

www.microsoft.com/en-us/download/details.aspx?id=44280

If you're using Windows 8, install the RSAT for Windows 8, which (at last check) was here: http://tinyurl.com/9dz427g.

If you're using Windows 7, then install Windows 7's RSAT from (at last check) here: http://tinyurl.com/klycep.

Open Control Panel and then the Programs applet. Click "Turn Windows features on or off." Scroll down to the Remote Server Administration Tools and expand the list.

When you install RSAT on Windows 8 or later, everything should be ready to go for what we need for this chapter. But let's verify that everything is there. Expand Feature Administration Tools and check Group Policy Management Tools. While you're at it, expand Role Administration Tools and then AD and LDS Tools, in case you may also want to enable the Active Directory Module for PowerShell. Although we don't need it for our work in this chapter, you probably will be using it for other tasks. Of course, enable support for anything else you need to manage. You can see my result in Figure A.2.

FIGURE A.2   Turn Windows features on or off.

Adding the Group Policy Module

Now that you have the Group Policy RSAT tools, you need to load them into PowerShell. Open a PowerShell session. When you do a directory listing of your modules directory, you should see Group Policy:

```
PS C:\> dir $pshome\modules\g*


    Directory: C:\Windows\System32\WindowsPowerShell\v1.0\modules
```

```
Mode               LastWriteTime      Length Name
----               -------------      ------ ----
d----          4/10/2015   3:14 PM           GroupPolicy
```

PowerShell v3 and later will auto-load modules as soon as you use any of the commands within the module. But you can always manually import the module:

```
PS C:\> import-module grouppolicy
```

What goodies do we get with this module? Let's ask PowerShell:

```
PS C:\> get-command -module grouppolicy | select name | sort name

Name
----
Backup-GPO
Copy-GPO
Get-GPInheritance
Get-GPO
Get-GPOReport
Get-GPPermission
Get-GPPermissions
Get-GPPrefRegistryValue
Get-GPRegistryValue
Get-GPResultantSetOfPolicy
Get-GPStarterGPO
Import-GPO
Invoke-GPUpdate
New-GPLink
New-GPO
New-GPStarterGPO
Remove-GPLink
Remove-GPO
Remove-GPPrefRegistryValue
Remove-GPRegistryValue
Rename-GPO
Restore-GPO
Set-GPInheritance
Set-GPLink
Set-GPPermission
Set-GPPermissions
Set-GPPrefRegistryValue
```

To be clear, in Chapter 2, we already reviewed and gave examples for the following cmdlets.

Group Policy PowerShell cmdlet	What it does
New-GPO	Creates a new Group Policy Object.
New-GPlink	Creates a new link to a Group Policy Object.
Get-GPO	Gets information (name, etc.) about GPOs.
Get-GPOReport	Produces HTML reports of a Group Policy Object's "guts."
Set-GPlink	Sets a GPO's link status to Enable or Disable.
Remove-GPlink	Deletes a GPO's link.
Set-GPinheritance	Performs Block Inheritance upon a Group Policy level (usually OU).
Set-GPPermissions	Sets the permissions upon a Group Policy Object.
Get-GPPermission	Reads the permissions upon a Group Policy Object.
Add-SDMSOMSecurity	From SDM Software's free PowerShell cmdlets, not a Microsoft built-in cmdlet. Enables you to specify "who can do what" within the Group Policy infrastructure.
New-GPStarterGPO	Creates new Starter GPOs.
Backup-GPO	Backs up your GPOs.
Restore-GPO	Restores your GPOs.
Import-GPO	Transfers GPOs from another domain to your domain.

As you can see, cmdlet names follow a verb-dash-singular noun naming convention, which makes it pretty easy to figure out what to use. If you want more information, simply ask PowerShell for help, as seen in Figure A.3.

In the preceding table, you'll see a quick summary of the cmdlets we already covered and what they do (in a nutshell). If you want even more help information about cmdlets we already explored or cmdlets we haven't explored yet, simply ask PowerShell for full help about the cmdlet like this:

```
PS C:\> help get-gpo -full
```

FIGURE A.3   Getting cmdlet help in PowerShell

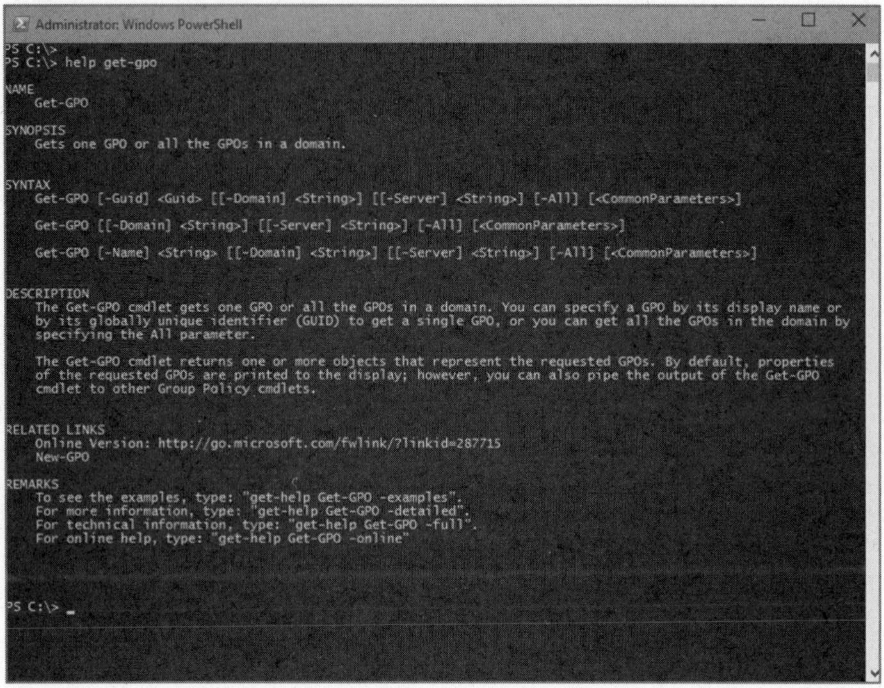

At the end of the help output, there will be a number of examples on how to use the cmdlet.

We won't go through every single cmdlet you see listed in the GroupPolicy module; instead, we'll focus on some common Group Policy management tasks.

Documenting Your Group Policy World with PowerShell

One of the most complicated and annoying parts of managing GPOs is the need to document them. Without clear documentation, troubleshooting can be quite complicated. In the following sections, we'll show you how easy it is to create useful documentation with the Group Policy cmdlets and PowerShell. You'll be amazed at how much you can accomplish with having to write a single script.

Listing GPOs

Let's start by listing all the GPOs within the domain. And in that list, we will, of course, retrieve some specific information about the GPO. We'll get things like the name, where it's linked in Active Directory, creation time, modification time, and much, much more:

```
PS C:\> get-gpo -all -domain corp.com
```

```
DisplayName      : Kill Control Panel
DomainName       : corp.com
Owner            :
Id               : 01f223e8-ba95-488f-ad7d-7b33a1f3c9aa
GpoStatus        : UserSettingsDisabled
Description      :
CreationTime     : 6/13/2012 8:56:25 AM
ModificationTime : 4/14/2015 2:21:32 PM
UserVersion      : AD Version: 0, SysVol Version: 0
ComputerVersion  : AD Version: 0, SysVol Version: 0
WmiFilter        :

DisplayName      : Custom Registry
DomainName       : corp.com
Owner            :
Id               : 1b974e46-2f06-4e97-9c12-a0fcfc5e7268
GpoStatus        : AllSettingsDisabled
Description      : Demo custom registry settings in a GPO
CreationTime     : 11/22/2011 2:08:27 PM
ModificationTime : 4/14/2015 2:22:40 PM
UserVersion      : AD Version: 13, SysVol Version: 13
ComputerVersion  : AD Version: 1, SysVol Version: 1
WmiFilter        :

DisplayName      : Script Test
DomainName       : corp.com
Owner            :
Id               : 21c79adb-9f4d-48e1-8329-4e8a81cd017a
GpoStatus        : ComputerSettingsDisabled
Description      : sample policy for script processing
CreationTime     : 9/28/2011 9:32:40 PM
ModificationTime : 2/13/2013 10:25:38 AM
UserVersion      : AD Version: 2, SysVol Version: 2
ComputerVersion  : AD Version: 0, SysVol Version: 0
WmiFilter        :
...
```

The output has been truncated to save space, but you get the idea. We're using the Get-GPO cmdlet and the -all parameter to list Group Policy Objects for every GPO in the corp.com domain. The cmdlet would have used the current, default domain, but we wanted to demonstrate how you query a specific domain. The output looks like text, but these are objects with properties, like DisplayName and GPOStatus.

Leveraging Objects for Fun and Profit

We'll talk a lot about objects in this chapter. Let's take a second to discuss the power of outputting an object instead of just text.

What is an object?

An object is a logical representation of a "thing." This thing could have properties and, possibly, methods. This thing could be anything from a car to a file located on a hard drive. In PowerShell, these things are .NET classes or COM objects.

Why does this matter?

Dealing with objects instead of text gives us a huge advantage. Let's take a car, for example. A car has a type, model, tires, color, and a slew of other properties. It also has functions (or methods), like start, stop, drive, and shift. When dealing with text, we could just have the following:

Make	Type	Color
Mazda	MPV	White
BMW	328i	Gray
Mazda	Mazda3	Gray

This is fine if we don't need to do anything with this data, but what if we do? What if we just wanted to see the cars that are gray or cars that are made by Mazda? We would have to search the text and find the lines that have the information we need and manipulate the results to output what we are after.

In PowerShell, this is very simple—because each car is an *object* with properties that we can easily filter according to any one individual property. Let's consider the following example.

This line will get all the cars made by Mazda and output only the type:

```
PS> Get-Cars | where{$_.Make -eq 'Mazda'} | select-object Type
```

What if we want all the gray cars? We'd simply type this line:

```
PS> Get-Cars | where-object {$_.Color -eq 'Gray'}
```

As you can see, this is much easier to manage and much more powerful than messing with raw text.

Here's an interesting example for us to hang our hats on. Let's say your boss comes in and asks you for a list of every GPO you have in the domain. He doesn't want to see all the fluff, just the names. You'll have it for him before he leaves the room by running this:

```
PS C:\> get-gpo -all -Domain corp.com | select Displayname

DisplayName
-----------
Kill Control Panel
Custom Registry
Script Test
Configure PowerShell Remoting
Profile Policy
Default Domain Policy
PowerShell Scripts
WMI Remote Management
...
```

All we're doing is piping the output from Get-GPO to the select-object cmdlet (using the alias select) and stripping off everything but the DisplayName property. The boss is clearly impressed, but he says, "You know … I wonder when they were created."

You turn around to your computer and you run this command, based on (you guessed it) the same Get-GPO cmdlet:

```
PS C:\> get-gpo -all -Domain corp.com | select Displayname,CreationTime

DisplayName                         CreationTime
-----------                         ------------
Kill Control Panel                  6/13/2012 8:56:25 AM
Custom Registry                     11/22/2011 2:08:27 PM
Script Test                         9/28/2011 9:32:40 PM
Configure PowerShell Remoting       7/20/2011 5:54:31 PM
Profile Policy                      8/19/2011 5:00:09 PM
Default Domain Policy               4/26/2011 12:06:59 PM
PowerShell Scripts                  5/21/2014 5:03:00 PM
WMI Remote Management               10/31/2011 3:37:39 PM
...
```

This time, you tell Select-Object to only select the DisplayName and CreationTime properties. Again, before the boss leaves, you get him what he asked for. As he picks his jaw off the floor, he says, "I don't suppose you could get me all the GPOs that have been changed in the last week?" You say, "Sure, one sec." Back to the Get-GPO cmdlet again with this command:

```
PS C:\> get-gpo -all -domain corp.com | where {$_.ModificationTime -ge (Get-Date).AddDays(-7).Date} | Select Displayname,ModificationTime


DisplayName       ModificationTime
-----------       ----------------
Kill Control Panel 4/14/2015 2:21:32 PM
Custom Registry    4/14/2015 2:22:40 PM
```

The Where filter says, "Look at the modification time of each GPO and if it is greater or equal to the date 7 days ago, keep it in the pipeline." The $_ is a placeholder for each object as it comes through the pipeline. You might also see the filter written like this:

```
where {$psitem.ModificationTime -ge (Get-Date).AddDays(-7).Date}
```

Which would still give you the same results. Whether you use $_ or $psitem is up to you. Just pick one and stick with it.

Regardless of how you did it, your boss is clearly impressed at your speed and agility, and he doubles your salary! Okay, maybe not, but he will definitely know who has the information he needs, and he will remember that come review time.

 NOTE You can type the command as one line, letting PowerShell wrap as necessary, or you can manually break the line to make it easier to read or to fit on a printed page, as we've done here. The best approach is to press return after a pipe character, an open curly brace, or an open parentheses.

Getting Information about Objects

In the Get-GPO examples, we used Select-Object to filter out some properties. You may be curious about how we even knew what properties were available.

The easiest way to get a list of what properties and methods an object has is to pipe the object to a cmdlet called Get-Member.

Get-Member is used to "reflect" the object and list the properties and methods it finds.

Here is an example:

```
PS C:\> get-gpo "Default Domain Policy" | Get-Member
```

```
   TypeName: Microsoft.GroupPolicy.Gpo


Name                    MemberType   Definition
----                    ----------   ----------
Backup                  Method       Microsoft.GroupPolicy.GpoBackup Backup(string...
CopyTo                  Method       Microsoft.GroupPolicy.Gpo CopyTo(Microsoft.Gr...
Delete                  Method       void Delete()
Equals                  Method       bool Equals(Microsoft.GroupPolicy.Gpo other),...
GenerateReport          Method       string GenerateReport(Microsoft.GroupPolicy.R...
GenerateReportToFile    Method       void GenerateReportToFile(Microsoft.GroupPoli...
GetHashCode             Method       int GetHashCode()
GetSecurityInfo         Method       Microsoft.GroupPolicy.GPPermissionCollection ...
GetType                 Method       type GetType()
Import                  Method       Microsoft.GroupPolicy.Gpo Import(Microsoft.Gr...
IsAclConsistent         Method       bool IsAclConsistent()
MakeAclConsistent       Method       void MakeAclConsistent()
SetSecurityInfo         Method       void SetSecurityInfo(Microsoft.GroupPolicy.GP...
ToString                Method       string ToString()
Computer                Property     Microsoft.GroupPolicy.ComputerConfiguration C...
CreationTime            Property     datetime CreationTime {get;}
Description             Property     string Description {get;set;}
DisplayName             Property     string DisplayName {get;set;}
DomainName              Property     string DomainName {get;}
GpoStatus               Property     Microsoft.GroupPolicy.GpoStatus GpoStatus {ge...
Id                      Property     guid Id {get;}
ModificationTime        Property     datetime ModificationTime {get;}
Owner                   Property     string Owner {get;}
Path                    Property     string Path {get;}
User                    Property     Microsoft.GroupPolicy.UserConfiguration User ...
WmiFilter               Property     Microsoft.GroupPolicy.WmiFilter WmiFilter {ge...
```

Even if you don't see the property name by default when you run a cmdlet, if you see it in this list, you can use it.

We can also use Get-GPO to examine details about a specific GPO:

```
PS C:\> get-gpo 'default domain policy'



DisplayName       : Default Domain Policy
```

```
DomainName        : CORP.com
Owner             : CORP\Domain Admins
Id                : 31b2f340-016d-11d2-945f-00c04fb984f9
GpoStatus         : AllSettingsEnabled
Description       :
CreationTime      : 4/26/2011 12:06:59 PM
ModificationTime  : 2/4/2015 11:08:16 AM
UserVersion       : AD Version: 0, SysVol Version: 0
ComputerVersion   : AD Version: 14, SysVol Version: 14
```

There's a lot of useful information here!

You'll notice that, instead of Name, this cmdlet uses DisplayName.

How did we know? Simple; we used Get-Member to discover the property names for the objects that Get-GPO writes to the pipeline as we demonstrated earlier.

We hope you realize we haven't run a single PowerShell script. Who says using PowerShell is difficult?

Operators in PowerShell

In PowerShell, there are comparison operators, which are used to compare one object to another object. Understanding the operators' functionality is key. There are about 26 operators that you can use, but we want to cover only a few of them:

-eq: Equal

-ne: Not equal

-ge: Greater than or equal

-gt: Greater than

-lt: Less than

-le: Less than or equal

-like: Wildcard comparison

-notlike: Wildcard comparison

-match: Regular expression comparison

-notmatch: Regular expression comparison

-contains: Containment operator

-notcontains: Containment operator

These are case insensitive by default, so most of these operators have case-sensitive equivalents. You can access them by adding a c in front of the operator—for instance, -ceq. You can find more information in the help file by running this command:

```
PS C:\> get-help about_operators
```

Creating GPO Reports

Creating printed documentation for all your GPOs couldn't be easier in PowerShell using the Microsoft `Get-GPOReport` cmdlet. You can dump the data to an XML file (or create a pretty HTML report). We explored this in Chapter 2, but to recap, try this:

```
PS C:\>Get-GPOReport 'Default Domain Policy' -ReportType HTML  -Path \\File01\
GPReports\DefaultDomain.html
```

This command will create an HTML report for the Default Domain Policy GPO, saved to the specified file. The cmdlet assumes the GPO is in the current domain, although you can specify a specific domain and/or Domain Controller:

```
PS C:\> Get-GPOReport 'Firewall Settings' -domain corp.com -server DC01
-ReportType XML -Path C:\Work\GPReports\Firewall.xml
```

The `Get-GPOReport` cmdlet includes an –All parameter. When used, it will create a single XML or HTML report for every GPO in your domain. If you prefer to generate reports for all GPOs, but with each GPO as a separate file, combine a few cmdlets in a single PowerShell expression:

```
PS C:\> Get-GPO -all | Foreach-Object {
>> $report='C:\Work\GPReports\{0}.htm' -f $_.displayName.Replace(" ","")
>> Get-GPOReport $_.DisplayName  -ReportType HTML -Path $report
>>}
```

Each GPO from `Get-GPO` is piped to the `ForEach-Object` cmdlet. We're creating a variable called `$report` to indicate the filename. Using a little PowerShell sleight of hand, we're incorporating the display name of each GPO that is piped in, stripping out any spaces. The second step in the loop calls `Get-GPOReport` and creates the report for the pipelined GPO using the variable we just created. You can view a sample HTML report in Figure A.4. Note that you might be prompted to allow protected content. It's OK.

Documenting GPO Links

In the following sections, you'll learn how to document GPO links. We're going to find all the GPOs and their links. Again, because we're using PowerShell, we have the ability to output objects, not just straight text. While the power of this may not immediately be evident, you'll soon see why this is such a huge benefit.

When you look through the list of new GPO cmdlets, you'll see some to create and set links, like `New-GPLink`. But there is no cmdlet called `Get-GPLink`. On one hand, this makes perfect sense. Even though we can retrieve a GPO, the link is part of the Active Directory object. Fortunately, the Active Directory cmdlets return linked GPO information. Here's a PowerShell script (Listing A.1) you can run to get Group Policy link information for Sites, Domains, and OUs. This script will require that you have configured RSAT to manage Active Directory, *and* you will need either a Windows Server 2008 R2 Domain Controller or an older DC running the ADMGS that we talked about earlier.

FIGURE A.4   HTML GPO report

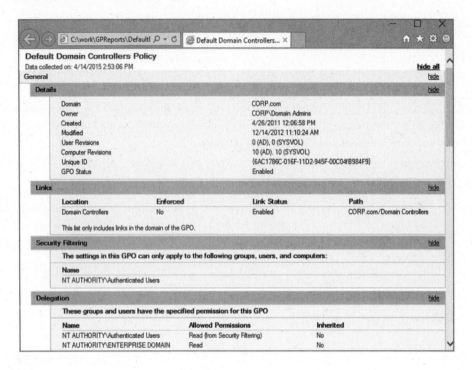

 NOTE   Don't try to type this script. It's in this chapter's "Book Resources" section on GPanswers.com.

Listing A.1: Group Policy documentation script using PowerShell

```
#requires -version 3.0
#requires -module ActiveDirectory,GroupPolicy

Function Get-MyGPLink {

#download version includes help and examples
[cmdletbinding()]

Param(
    [Parameter(Position=0)]
    [ValidateSet("All","Site","Domain","OU")]
```

```
    [string]$Filter="All"
    )

#a nested function to get link data
Function Get-GPOLinkData {

[cmdletbinding()]

Param([string]$link,[string]$dn)

    Write-Verbose "$(Get-Date) Starting $($myinvocation.mycommand)"
    #split link at ;
    $data=$link.split(";")

     #get link state from $link
     #a value of 0 means link enabled, 1 means link disabled.

    $linkstate=$data[1]
     Write-Verbose "Linkstate = $linkstate"
    if ($linkstate -eq 0) {
        $linked=$True
    }
    else {
        $linked=$false
    }


    #define a REGEX pattern for a GUID
    [Regex]$RegEx = "(([0-9a-fA-F]){8}-([0-9a-fA-F]){4}-([0-9a-fA-F])
{4}-([0-9a-fA-F]){4}-([0-9a-fA-F]){12})"
    [System.GUID]$gpoGuid=$regex.match($link).value


    if ($gpoGUID) {
        #get the GPO and add a custom property to show the linked OU
        $gpoid= Get-GPO -id $gpoGuid
        $gpoid | Add-Member -memberType NoteProperty -Name "LinkEnabled" -value
$linked
        $gpoid | Add-Member -memberType NoteProperty -Name "CanonicalLink"
-value (Get-ADObject $dn -property CanonicalName).CanonicalName
        $gpoid | Add-Member -memberType NoteProperty -Name "GPLink" -value $dn
-passthru | Select *
    }
```

```
    Write-Verbose "$(Get-Date) Ending $($myinvocation.mycommand)"

} #end Get-GPOLinkData

#a nested function to get SOMs linked to a GPO
Function Get-GPOLink {
[cmdletbinding()]
Param([string]$identity)
    Write-Verbose "$(get-date) Starting $($myinvocation.mycommand)"
    $results=Get-ADObject -identity $identity -Properties gplink
    if ($results.gplink) {
     #split gplink since all links are passed as one string
     $results.gplink.split("][") | Where {$_}
    }
    else {
        Write-Verbose "$(Get-Date) No GPO Links found"
    }
    Write-Verbose "$(Get-Date) Ending $($myinvocation.mycommand)"
} #end Get-GPLink

#main function code
Write-Verbose "$(Get-Date) Starting $($myinvocation.mycommand)"
Write-Verbose "$(Get-Date) Filter is $($filter.toUpper())"

#Process SITES
if ($filter -eq "All" -or $filter -eq "Site") {
    #Get Site linked GPOs
    #get configuration naming context

    $config=(Get-ADRootDSE).ConfigurationNamingContext

    #get sites
    Write-Verbose "$(Get-Date) Getting site links"
    $sites=get-adobject -LDAPFilter "(Objectclass=site)" -searchbase $config
-properties gpLink

    Write-Verbose "$(Get-Date) Processing site links"

    foreach ($site in $sites) {
        Write-Verbose "$(Get-Date) $($site)"
```

```
        $links=Get-GPOLink $site.distinguishedname
        if ($links) {
            Foreach ($link in $links) {
                Get-GPOLinkData $link $site.distinguishedname
            } #end foreach $link
        }
    } #end foreach $site
}


#Process DOMAIN
if ($filter -eq "All" -or $filter -eq "Domain") {
    Write-Verbose "$(Get-Date) getting domain object"
    $domain=Get-ADDomain

    #Get Domain linked GPOs
    Write-Verbose "$(Get-Date) processing domain links"

    $links=Get-GPOLink $domain.distinguishedname
    if ($links) {
        Foreach ($link in $links) {
            Get-GPOLinkData $link $domain.distinguishedname
        } #end foreach $link
    }
}


if ($filter -eq "All" -or $filter -eq "OU") {
    Write-Verbose "$(Get-Date) getting OUs"

    if (-not $domain) {
        Write-Verbose "$(Get-Date) getting domain object"
        $domain=Get-ADDomain
    }

    #Get OU Linked GPOs
    Get-ADOrganizationalUnit -filter * -searchBase $domain | foreach {

      #assign the current OU object to a variable to make it easier to follow
      $OU=$_

      #get GPO Links for the OU
```

```
    Write-Verbose "$(Get-Date) $($OU)"

    Write-Verbose "$(Get-Date) processing linked GPOs"

   $links=Get-GPOLink $ou.distinguishedname
   if ($links) {
      Foreach ($link in $links) {
         Get-GPOLinkData $link $ou.distinguishedname
      } #end foreach $link
   }
  } #end foreach OU
}
 Write-Verbose "$(Get-Date) Ending $($myinvocation.mycommand)"

} # End Function
```

If you run the script, nothing will happen. The script loads the necessary modules and then defines a function called Get-GPOLink. To use the script, you need to *dot-source* it in your PowerShell session or your PowerShell profile. The function includes help information just like a cmdlet. Run help get-mygplink to see for yourself. By the way, you probably noticed that we didn't call the function Get-GPLink. That was on purpose. It is possible that Microsoft will add a Get-GPLink cmdlet to a future version of the GroupPolicy module. By adding the "my" prefix, we avoid future naming collisions.

Dot-sourcing

Normally, when you run a script or function, anything you define, from the function itself to variables or PSDrives, disappears when the script or function finishes. One way to keep items such as functions and variables is to dot-source the file. To accomplish this, insert a period before you run the script. Using the script in Listing A.1, to load the Get-GPOLink into your PowerShell session, you would type this command, assuming you were in the same directory as the script file:

```
PS C:\>. .\Get-MyGPLink.ps1
```

It might look a little funny, and don't forget a space after the first period. What that dot says is, "Run this script, but keep everything it creates and defines right here."

The function uses several Active Directory functions to discover Sites, the Domain, and OUs. These Active Directory objects include a property that reflects the Group Policy link. The script does some fancy parsing of this string to pull out the GPO GUID and its domain, because it's conceivable you have a cross-domain linked GPO! With this information, we can use Get-GPO to retrieve the object. The function returns that object with an extra property to show the connected target. By the way, this script requires PowerShell v3 or later.

Because the function acts like a cmdlet, you can use it in a pipelined expression like this:

```
PS C:\> Get-MyGPlink | Sort Target | Select Target,DisplayName,DomainName,
GPOStatus,*Time


Target            :
DisplayName       : Default Domain Controllers Policy
DomainName        : CORP.com
GpoStatus         : AllSettingsEnabled
CreationTime      : 4/26/2011 12:06:59 PM
ModificationTime  : 12/14/2012 11:10:25 AM

Target            :
DisplayName       : PowerShell Scripts
DomainName        : CORP.com
GpoStatus         : AllSettingsEnabled
CreationTime      : 5/21/2014 5:03:00 PM
ModificationTime  : 5/27/2014 12:27:20 PM

Target            :
DisplayName       : Configure PowerShell Remoting
DomainName        : CORP.com
GpoStatus         : AllSettingsEnabled
CreationTime      : 7/20/2011 5:54:31 PM
...
```

You can take these objects and do anything else you need, such as filtering further, exporting, printing, or saving to a file.

Of course PowerShell never ceases to amaze us. The function we just showed is designed to give you full GPO information. But you can also get linked information via the Get-GPInheritance cmdlet:

```
PS C:\> Get-GPInheritance -Target (get-addomain).distinguishedname

Name                 : corp.com
ContainerType        : Domain
Path                 : dc=corp,dc=com
GpoInheritanceBlocked : No
```

```
GpoLinks              : {Default Domain Policy, CredSSP, Profile Policy, Script
                        Test...}
InheritedGpoLinks     : {Default Domain Policy, WMI Remote Management, WSUS
Config,
                        Domain PKI}
```

We used a nested command with `Get-ADDomain` to avoid having to hard-code the domain distinguished name, or path. We could also specify the distinguished name of an OU. See that `GpoLinks` property? That's what we want. Let's "unroll" it:

```
PS C:\> (Get-GPInheritance -Target (get-addomain).distinguishedname).gpolinks
```

```
GpoId       : 31b2f340-016d-11d2-945f-00c04fb984f9
DisplayName : Default Domain Policy
Enabled     : True
Enforced    : False
Target      : dc=corp,dc=com
Order       : 1

GpoId       : 77480092-642d-4843-8b77-50029a56399f
DisplayName : CredSSP
Enabled     : False
Enforced    : False
Target      : dc=corp,dc=com
Order       : 2

GpoId       : 31685888-184a-4a6d-a52c-a091d4b75e69
DisplayName : Profile Policy
Enabled     : False
Enforced    : False
Target      : dc=corp,dc=com
Order       : 3
...
```

Clearly not as much detail as `Get-MyGPLink`, but we can build on this. Here's another function you can download and try out:

```
#requires -version 4.0
#requires -module GroupPolicy,ActiveDirectory

#get basic GPO link information
Function Get-MyGPLinkBasic {
[cmdletbinding(DefaultParameterSetName="All")]
```

```
Param(
[parameter(Position=0,HelpMessage="Enter a GPO name. Wildcards are allowed")]
[string]$Name,
[string]$Server,
[string]$Domain,
[Parameter(ParameterSetName="enabled")]
[switch]$Enabled,
[Parameter(ParameterSetName="disabled")]
[switch]$Disabled

)

#hashtable of parameters
$paramhash = @{
ErrorAction = "Stop"
}

if ($Server) {
    $paramhash.add("Server",$Server)
}


if ($domain) {
    $paramhash.add("Identity",$domain)
}

Try {
    $mydomain = Get-ADDomain @paramhash
    #add the DN to the list
    $targets = @($mydomain.distinguishedname)
}
Catch {
    Write-Warning $_.exception.message
    #bail out
    Return
}

if ($targets) {
    #revise parameter hashtable
    if ($domain) {
```

```
        $paramhash.remove("identity")
        $paramhash.add("Domain",$domain)
    }


    #get OUs
    $targets+= Get-ADOrganizationalUnit @paramhash -filter * | Select
-ExpandProperty Distinguishedname

    #get all the links
    $links = ($Targets | Get-GPInheritance @paramhash).gpolinks

    #filter for Enabled or Disabled
    if ($enabled) {
        $links = $links.where({$_.enabled})
    }
    elseif ($Disabled) {
        $links = $links.where({-Not $_.enabled})
    }
    if ($Name) {
        #filter by GPO name using v4 filtering feature for performance
        $links.where({$_.displayname -like "$name"})
    }
    else {
        #write all the links
        $links
    }
}

} #end function
```

This function gets all links from your domain and organizational units. But you can also use it to filter by GPO name and/or whether it is enabled or not:

```
PS C:\> get-mygplinkbasic *Powershell* -Disabled | select
Displayname,Target,enabled

DisplayName              Target                    Enabled
-----------              ------                    -------
PowerShell Configuration dc=corp,dc=com             False
PowerShell Scripts       ou=employees,dc=corp,dc=com False
```

Documenting WMI Filters and Links

The `Get-GPO` cmdlet will return WMI filter information:

```
PS C:\> get-gpo "engineering desktop"

DisplayName        : Engineering Desktop
DomainName         : CORP.com
Owner              : CORP\Domain Admins
Id                 : 0205d134-9a2b-4f28-b2c2-cc77fc620248
GpoStatus          : AllSettingsEnabled
Description        :
CreationTime       : 4/14/2015 3:56:06 PM
ModificationTime   : 4/14/2015 3:56:46 PM
UserVersion        : AD Version: 0, SysVol Version: 0
ComputerVersion    : AD Version: 0, SysVol Version: 0
WmiFilter          : Windows 10
```

But if you try to select just the `WMIFilter` property, you'll get a little surprise:

```
PS C:\> get-gpo "engineering desktop" | Select WmiFilter

WmiFilter
---------

Microsoft.GroupPolicy.WmiFilter
```

The cmdlet output is pulling the WMI filter name from the underlying object, but the property itself is another object. If you only need a single nested property like this, you can expand it:

```
PS C:\> get-gpo "engineering desktop" | Select -expandproperty WmiFilter

Description Name        Path
----------- ----        ----
           Windows 10 MSFT_SomFilter.ID="{9BBB0E48-0066-4E76-A776-
08B57529F031}",...
```

Or you can use a hash table with `Select-Object` to pull out the filter information nestled away:

```
PS C:\> get-gpo -all | Where {$_.WMIFilter} |
>> Select Displayname,@{name="WMIFilter";Expression={$_.WMIFilter.name}},
>> @{Name="WMIDescription";Expression={$_.WMIFilter.Description}}
>>
```

```
DisplayName         WMIFilter            WMIDescription
-----------         ---------            --------------
Engineering Desktop Windows 10
MyTestGPO           PowerShell v4        Running PowerShell 4.0
Win2012Config       Windows Server 2012 running 2012 or later
```

The expression gets all GPOs and filters them using `Where-Object` to keep only GPOs with a `WMIFilter` defined. The hash tables create custom properties with values pulled from the `WMIFilter` object.

There's one minor "gotcha" here. This expression will return all WMI filters currently linked; it won't show you other filters you may have defined. However, you can easily get that information by querying Active Directory (assuming you have the Active Directory module ready and the requisite domain controllers or ADMGS on the back end).

```
PS C:\> get-adobject -LDAPFilter "(ObjectClass=msWMI-som)" -properties * |
>> Select @{Name="GUID";Expression={$_.Name}},
>> @{Name="Name";Expression= {$_.'msWMI-Name'}},
>> @{Name="Description";Expression={$_.'msWMI-Parm1'}},
>> @{Name="WMIQuery";Expression={$_.'msWMI-Parm2'.Split(";")[-2] }},
>> Created,Modified
>>


GUID        : {17B0BE91-3446-4D07-B4DB-A11B33378C9D}
Name        : PowerShell v4
Description : Running PowerShell 4.0
WMIQuery    : Select * from CIM_Datafile where drive='c:' AND path=
              '\\windows\\system32\\windowspowershell\\v1.0\\' AND
              extension='exe' AND filename='Powershell' AND version LIKE
              '6.3%'
Created     : 11/12/2013 3:35:52 PM
Modified    : 11/12/2013 3:50:36 PM


GUID        : {9BBB0E48-0066-4E76-A776-08B57529F031}
Name        : Windows 8
Description :
WMIQuery    : Select * from win32_operatingsystem where version Like "6.2%"
Created     : 11/12/2013 3:40:29 PM
Modified    : 11/12/2013 3:50:36 PM


GUID        : {B2AD75F7-0D03-4599-A6A9-D926B34309F4}
Name        : Windows Server 2012
Description : running 2012 or later
```

```
WMIQuery     : select * from win32_operatingsystem where caption like
               "Microsoft Windows Server 2012%"
Created      : 4/14/2015 4:07:55 PM
Modified     : 4/14/2015 4:11:09 PM
```

Using the `Get-ADObject` cmdlet, you search for objects that are of the `msWMI-som` class. You need to tell the cmdlet to return all properties. You might want to do something else with the default results, but in our example we piped the results to `Select-Object` and displayed a number of properties, some of which were calculated from the raw property values. Now we can see all of our WMI filters, regardless of their link state.

Listing GPO Permissions

A big part of troubleshooting Group Policy is dealing with permissions on the actual Group Policy Object. Let's see what we can do with the `Get-GPPermissions` cmdlets:

```
PS C:\> Get-GPPermissions -name "default domain policy" -all

Trustee     : Authenticated Users
TrusteeType : WellKnownGroup
Permission  : GpoApply
Inherited   : False

Trustee     : Domain Admins
TrusteeType : Group
Permission  : GpoCustom
Inherited   : False

Trustee     : Enterprise Admins
TrusteeType : Group
Permission  : GpoCustom
Inherited   : False

Trustee     : Help Desk
TrusteeType : Group
Permission  : GpoRead
Inherited   : False

Trustee     : ENTERPRISE DOMAIN CONTROLLERS
TrusteeType : WellKnownGroup
Permission  : GpoRead
Inherited   : False
```

```
Trustee      : SYSTEM
TrusteeType  : WellKnownGroup
Permission   : GpoEditDeleteModifySecurity
Inherited    : False
```

Here, we can see all permissions for the Default Domain Policy GPO. If you prefer to limit your results to a specific user or group, use the -TargetGroup and -TargetName parameters:

```
PS C:\> Get-GPPermission "Engineering Desktop" -TargetType Group -TargetName
"Help Desk"
```

```
Trustee      : Help Desk
TrusteeType  : Group
Permission   : GpoEdit
Inherited    : False
```

Here's a (relatively) simple one-liner to get permissions for all GPOs and export the results to a plain CSV, which you could later open in Microsoft Excel:

```
Get-GPO -All -PipelineVariable p | Get-GPPermission -all |
Select @{Name="Name";Expression={$p.Displayname}},
@{Name="Trustee";Expression={$_.Trustee.name}},
@{Name="TrusteeType";Expression={$_.Trustee.SIDType}},
Permission,Inherited | Export-csv c:\work\AllGPOPermissions.csv
-NoTypeInformation
```

This expression takes advantage of the new common PipelineVariable, which obviates the need for a more complicated ForEach statement.

If you want to find a specific security principal, say Help Desk, you can modify this expression filter with Where-Object:

```
get-gpo -all | Where { $_ | Get-GPPermission -TargetName "Help Desk" -TargetType
Group -erroraction SilentlyContinue} | Select Displayname
```

This expression gets all GPOs and pipes them to Where-Object. Each pipelined GPO is passed to Get-GPPermissions, looking for the Help Desk group. If we were looking for a domain group, we would use the domain\groupname format. Because the Get-GPPermissions cmdlet will raise an exception if the group is not found, we temporarily turn off the error pipeline with the -ErrorAction parameter. If the group is found, then the GPO object is passed on in the pipeline and, finally PowerShell will return the GPO's display name.

You may also want to find GPOs where a particular user or group does *not* have permissions. This is a little trickier, but we won't make you figure it out:

```
get-gpo -all | where { ($_ | Get-GPPermissions -all).Trustee.name -notcontains
"Authenticated Users"} | Select Displayname
```

This code listing takes advantage of a feature introduced in PowerShell v3 that automatically expands properties of nested objects, like the trustee object that is part of each permission. In this snippet, if Authenticated Users isn't found, PowerShell will display the name of the GPO.

Setting GPO Permissions

The Group Policy module includes a cmdlet called Set-GPPermission, which you can use to modify permissions for one or more GPOs in your domain. We hope it goes without saying that whenever you start messing with permissions, you should test thoroughly in a nonproduction environment. Also, read through all the help and examples for this cmdlet.

The cmdlet has a PermissionLevel parameter that sets the appropriate access control on the GPO. Valid values for this parameter are GpoRead, GpoApply, GpoEdit, GpoEditDeleteModifySecurity, and None.

Let's say we have a GPO called "Desktop Additions" we're developing. Here are the current permissions:

```
PS C:\> Get-GPPermission "Desktop Additions" -all


Trustee      : Authenticated Users
TrusteeType  : WellKnownGroup
Permission   : GpoApply
Inherited    : False

Trustee      : Domain Admins
TrusteeType  : Group
Permission   : GpoEditDeleteModifySecurity
Inherited    : False

Trustee      : Enterprise Admins
TrusteeType  : Group
Permission   : GpoEditDeleteModifySecurity
Inherited    : False

Trustee      : ENTERPRISE DOMAIN CONTROLLERS
TrusteeType  : WellKnownGroup
```

```
Permission  : GpoRead
Inherited   : False


Trustee     : SYSTEM
TrusteeType : WellKnownGroup
Permission  : GpoEditDeleteModifySecurity
Inherited   : False
```

Using `Set-GPPermissions`, we want to remove Authenticated Users and give the Help Desk group permissions to apply the GPO.

```
PS C:\> Set-GPPermission "Desktop Additions" -TargetName "Help Desk" -TargetType
Group -PermissionLevel GPOApply -whatif
What if: Set the permission level to GpoApply for the security group "Help Desk"
on the "Desktop Additions" GPO in the CORP.com domain. (Set-GPPermissions)
```

Well, we didn't quite do it. We wanted to demonstrate another useful PowerShell feature, the `-WhatIf` parameter. Cmdlets that make changes, such as the Set and Remove cmdlets, support this parameter. Think of it as a sanity check; the cmdlet is telling you, "This is what I would have done, if you'd let me."

Now, let's do it for real by rerunning the previous command without `-Whatif`:

```
PS C:\> Set-GPPermission "Desktop Additions" -TargetName "Help Desk" -TargetType
Group -PermissionLevel GPOApply
```

```
DisplayName      : Desktop Additions
DomainName       : CORP.com
Owner            : CORP\Domain Admins
Id               : fc88b833-5ba4-415e-9d52-c13124afe434
GpoStatus        : AllSettingsEnabled
Description      :
CreationTime     : 4/14/2015 5:06:28 PM
ModificationTime : 4/14/2015 5:06:28 PM
UserVersion      : AD Version: 0, SysVol Version: 0
ComputerVersion  : AD Version: 0, SysVol Version: 0
WmiFilter        :
```

Next, let's remove Authenticated Users by setting their permission level to None:

```
PS C:\> Set-GPPermission "Desktop Additions" -TargetName "Authenticated Users"
-TargetType Group -PermissionLevel None
```

```
DisplayName       : Desktop Additions
DomainName        : CORP.com
Owner             : CORP\Domain Admins
Id                : fc88b833-5ba4-415e-9d52-c13124afe434
GpoStatus         : AllSettingsEnabled
Description       :
CreationTime      : 4/14/2015 5:06:28 PM
ModificationTime  : 4/14/2015 5:09:32 PM
UserVersion       : AD Version: 0, SysVol Version: 0
ComputerVersion   : AD Version: 0, SysVol Version: 0
WmiFilter         :
```

Now when we check permissions, they are exactly what we want:

```
Trustee     : Help Desk
TrusteeType : Group
Permission  : GpoApply
Inherited   : False


Trustee     : Domain Admins
TrusteeType : Group
Permission  : GpoEditDeleteModifySecurity
Inherited   : False


Trustee     : Enterprise Admins
TrusteeType : Group
Permission  : GpoEditDeleteModifySecurity
Inherited   : False


Trustee     : ENTERPRISE DOMAIN CONTROLLERS
TrusteeType : WellKnownGroup
Permission  : GpoRead
Inherited   : False


Trustee     : SYSTEM
TrusteeType : WellKnownGroup
Permission  : GpoEditDeleteModifySecurity
Inherited   : False
```

Manipulating GPOs with PowerShell

Another task that administrators spend a large amount of time on is the actual manipulation of GPOs themselves. But creating, linking, and backing up GPOs are all things we should be able to script. Now that we have shown you some scripts that enable you to document GPOs, you're ready to take on some of these new challenges.

Creating New GPOs

One of the most common tasks for GPO administrators is creating new GPOs. We can easily create a new GPO with the New-GPO cmdlet from the Group Policy module:

```
PS C:\> New-GPO "Executive Desktops" -Comment "C-level desktop configurations"
```

```
DisplayName       : Executive Desktops
DomainName        : CORP.com
Owner             : CORP\Domain Admins
Id                : 4c8ad76c-72d4-41ac-a840-81aa2e314f2b
GpoStatus         : AllSettingsEnabled
Description       : C-level desktop configurations
CreationTime      : 4/14/2015 5:14:08 PM
ModificationTime  : 4/14/2015 5:14:08 PM
UserVersion       : AD Version: 0, SysVol Version: 0
ComputerVersion   : AD Version: 0, SysVol Version: 0
```

The only part that is required is a GPO name, but we went ahead and added a comment as well. We can take this a step further and combine some of the cmdlets we've already looked at. Assuming the "Executive Desktops" GPO doesn't exist, look at this:

```
PS C:\> New-GPO "Executive Desktops" | New-GPLink -target "ou=executive,ou=depar
tments,ou=employees,dc=corp,dc=com" |
Set-GPPermission -permissionlevel gpoedit -targetname "corp\help desk"
-targettype group
```

```
DisplayName       : Executive Desktops
DomainName        : CORP.com
Owner             : CORP\Domain Admins
Id                : f2868820-8e44-4443-b0b3-7e4898fdac22
GpoStatus         : AllSettingsEnabled
Description       :
CreationTime      : 4/14/2015 5:18:04 PM
ModificationTime  : 4/14/2015 5:18:04 PM
```

```
UserVersion      : AD Version: 0, SysVol Version: 0
ComputerVersion  : AD Version: 0, SysVol Version: 0
WmiFilter
```

With one command, we created a new GPO, linked it to an OU, and added the Help Desk group as GPO editors. That's the power of the PowerShell pipeline!

Modifying GPO Settings

Microsoft doesn't offer much in the way of cmdlets to define settings *within* a GPO. Even with all this PowerShell scripting power, you still (mostly) need the GPMC for that.

However, there are two cmdlets you can use in the GroupPolicy module to set and get Registry settings. In the GPMC, you can define Registry values for a GPO's computer and user nodes. You can make the Registry value a policy setting or a preference. Which you use depends on your needs, but you can manage either with PowerShell.

Get-GPPrefRegistryValue

The Get-GPPrefRegistryValue cmdlet will return Registry information in a GPO, configured as a preference. You need to specify the GPO name, the GPO context, and the Registry key path:

```
PS C:\> Get-GPPrefRegistryValue -Name "Sales Desktops" -Context User -Key
HKCU\Corp
```

```
KeyPath            : Corp
FullKeyPath        : HKEY_CURRENT_USER\Corp
Hive               : CurrentUser
Action             : Create
Order              : 1
DisabledDirectly   : False
DisabledByAncestor : False
Value              : Philadelphia
Type               : String
ValueName          : Office
HasValue           : True

KeyPath            : Corp
FullKeyPath        : HKEY_CURRENT_USER\Corp
Hive               : CurrentUser
Action             : Create
Order              : 2
DisabledDirectly   : False
```

```
DisabledByAncestor : False
Value              : Sales
Type               : String
ValueName          : Dept
HasValue           : True
```

There is no way to guess at the Registry key, say, by using a wildcard. You have to know that a setting exists beforehand.

Figure A.5 shows the same settings in the GPMC.

FIGURE A.5   Group Policy Registry preferences

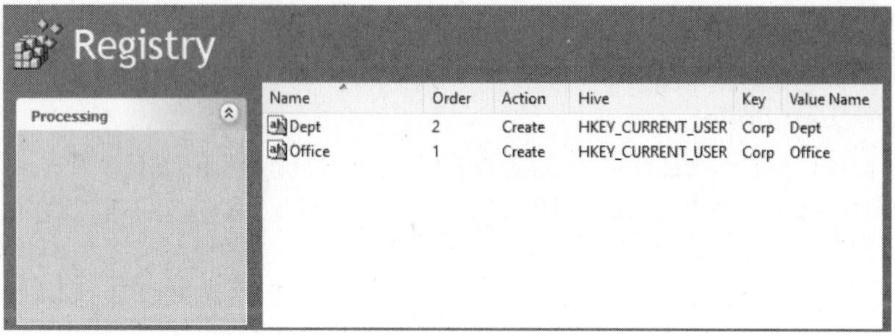

If you know the exact value name, you can ask for it alone:

```
PS C:\> (Get-GPPrefRegistryValue -Name "Sales Desktops" -Context User -Key
HKCU\Corp -ValueName Office).Value
Philadelphia
```

Set-GPPrefRegistryValue

More than likely, you might want to modify or create a Registry preference. You can accomplish this task with Set-GPPrefRegistryValue. As with its counterpart, Get-GPPrefRegistryValue, you will need to supply a GPO name, a context, and the Registry path. You will also need to define a ValueName, the assigned value, its type, and an action (Create, Replace, Update, or Delete):

```
PS C:\> Set-GPPrefRegistryValue "Executive Desktops" -Context User -Key  "HKCU\
Corp" -ValueName EVP -Value "Jeremy Moskowitz" -Type String -Action Create
```

```
DisplayName        : Executive Desktops
DomainName         : CORP.com
Owner              : CORP\Domain Admins
Id                 : f2868820-8e44-4443-b0b3-7e4898fdac22
GpoStatus          : AllSettingsEnabled
```

```
Description        :
CreationTime       : 4/14/2015 5:18:04 PM
ModificationTime   : 4/14/2015 5:40:18 PM
UserVersion        : AD Version: 1, SysVol Version: 1
ComputerVersion    : AD Version: 0, SysVol Version: 0
WmiFilter          :
```

Normally, you will want to use String or Dword, but other possible choices are ExpandString, Binary, MultiString, and Qword. In this example, we've added another Registry preference under HKCU\Corp called EVP. Let's verify:

```
PS C:\> Get-GPPrefRegistryValue "Executive Desktops" -Context "User" -ValueName
"EVP" -Key "HKCU\Corp"
```

```
KeyPath            : Corp
FullKeyPath        : HKEY_CURRENT_USER\Corp
Hive               : CurrentUser
Action             : Create
Order              : 1
DisabledDirectly   : False
DisabledByAncestor : False
Value              : Jeremy Moskowitz
Type               : String
ValueName          : EVP
HasValue           : True
```

You can manage any GPO Registry preference with these PowerShell cmdlets from the GroupPolicy module or the GPMC.

Using PowerShell is exactly like using the "click-click-click" method of the Group Policy Preferences Registry extension. Anything you can do with "click-click-click" you can do with Set-GPPrefRegistryValue.

Neat!

Get-GPRegistryValue

You can also define Registry values as part of a GPO policy. To retrieve existing settings, you need to know at least the start of the Registry path. Let's find the screen saver settings in the "Sales Desktops" GPO:

```
PS C:\> Get-GPRegistryValue -Name "Sales Desktops" -key HKCU\Software\policies\
Microsoft\Windows\
```

```
KeyPath      : Software\policies\Microsoft\Windows\\Control Panel
FullKeyPath  : HKEY_CURRENT_USER\Software\policies\Microsoft\Windows\\Control Panel
Hive         : CurrentUser
```

We knew at least part of the Registry name. Since we see a value for KeyPath, there's probably something there, so we keep drilling:

```
PS C:\> Get-GPRegistryValue -Name "Sales Desktops" -key 'HKCU\Software\policies\
Microsoft\Windows\Control panel'
```

```
KeyPath     : Software\policies\Microsoft\Windows\Control panel\Desktop
FullKeyPath : HKEY_CURRENT_USER\Software\policies\Microsoft\Windows\Control
panel\Desktop
Hive        : CurrentUser
```

Eventually we'll end up with this:

```
PS C:\> Get-GPRegistryValue -Name "Sales Desktops" -key 'HKCU\Software\policies\
Microsoft\Windows\Control panel\Desktop'
```

```
KeyPath     : Software\policies\Microsoft\Windows\Control panel\Desktop
FullKeyPath : HKEY_CURRENT_USER\Software\policies\Microsoft\Windows\Control
panel\Desktop
Hive        : CurrentUser
PolicyState : Set
Value       : 1
Type        : String
ValueName   : ScreenSaveActive
HasValue    : True

KeyPath     : Software\policies\Microsoft\Windows\Control panel\Desktop
FullKeyPath : HKEY_CURRENT_USER\Software\policies\Microsoft\Windows\Control
panel\Desktop
Hive        : CurrentUser
PolicyState : Set
Value       : 900
Type        : String
ValueName   : ScreenSaveTimeOut
HasValue    : True

KeyPath     : Software\policies\Microsoft\Windows\Control panel\Desktop
FullKeyPath : HKEY_CURRENT_USER\Software\policies\Microsoft\Windows\Control
panel\Desktop
Hive        : CurrentUser
PolicyState : Set
```

```
Value      : CorpScreen.exe
Type       : String
ValueName  : SCRNSAVE.EXE
HasValue   : True
```

Or we can select a single value:

```
PS C:\> Get-GPRegistryValue -Name "Sales Desktops" -key 'HKCU\Software\policies\
Microsoft\Windows\Control panel\Desktop' -ValueName ScreenSaveTimeout
```

```
KeyPath     : Software\policies\Microsoft\Windows\Control panel\Desktop
FullKeyPath : HKEY_CURRENT_USER\Software\policies\Microsoft\Windows\Control
panel\Desktop
Hive        : CurrentUser
PolicyState : Set
Value       : 900
Type        : String
ValueName   : ScreenSaveTimeout
HasValue    : True
```

You can see this is the same value when looking at the GPO in the GPMC, as shown in Figure A.6.

FIGURE A.6   GPO Registry policy

Set-GPRegistryValue

Setting Registry values as a policy can also be done with PowerShell, but you need to think ahead. If you know the Registry key that is being modified when you configure something in a GPO, you can use `Set-GPRegistryValue` and configure that setting. For example, since we know the Registry key and values for the screen saver time-out, we can modify them with PowerShell. The syntax is similar to `Set-GPPrefRegistryValue`:

```
Set-GPRegistryValue "Sales Desktops" -key "HKCU\Software\Policies\Microsoft\
windows\control panel\desktop" -ValueName ScreenSaveTimeOut -Value 600
-type string
```

You can see the changed result in the GPO report in Figure A.7.

FIGURE A.7   GPO Registry policy change

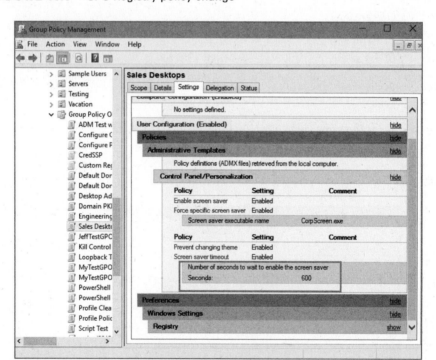

But wait, there's more. You can also set a Registry policy that doesn't exist in the Group Policy editor. Here's how that might happen.

Suppose you have a homegrown custom application and you want to set some Registry values for that application using Group Policy.

It's easy … here's one way:

```
Set-GPRegistryValue "Sales Desktops" -key "HKLM\Software\MyCompany\CustomApp"
-ValueName InstallPath -Value "\\file02\installs\customapp.msi" -Type String
```

We can verify this with Get-GPRegistryValue:

```
PS C:\> Get-GPRegistryValue "Sales Desktops" -key "HKLM\Software\MyCompany\
CustomApp"
```

```
KeyPath      : Software\MyCompany\CustomApp
FullKeyPath  : HKEY_LOCAL_MACHINE\Software\MyCompany\CustomApp
Hive         : LocalMachine
PolicyState  : Set
Value        : \\file02\installs\customapp.msi
Type         : String
ValueName    : InstallPath
HasValue     : True
```

Great. We can see that the data is set and ready to be deployed via Group Policy. But what's happening under the hood? How does the GPMC report this? Look at Figure A.8.

FIGURE A.8   GPO custom Registry policy setting

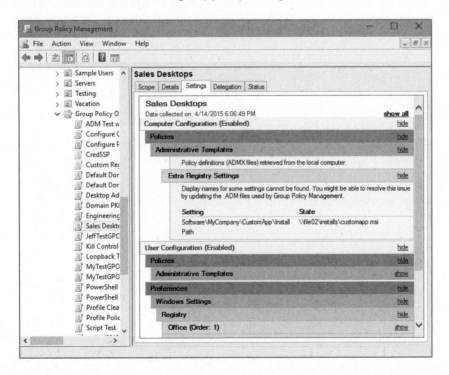

The setting shows up in the report as "Extra Registry Settings" because the GPMC doesn't have any ADM or ADMX file to "match" the setting with.

To be clear: The setting will be deployed just fine. But the only way you can actually *edit* the setting again is via PowerShell. Alternatively, you could create a custom ADM or ADMX template for your application settings and match up the missing setting. But then, what would be the point?

This can get a little confusing, and Microsoft's terminology doesn't make it any easier.

Policy vs. Preferences Using PowerShell Cheat Sheet

If your head is spinning about which to use—Set-GPRegistryValue or Set-GPPrefRegistryValue—here's your cheat sheet.

- In both cases: Registry data can be created and modified using PowerShell.

- Using GPPrefs and Set-GPPRefRegistryValue, you can modify data directly using the Group Policy editor and view it correctly in the GPMC GPO reports.

- Using Group Policy "Registry" settings, you cannot data modify data directly using the Group Policy editor (unless there's a matching ADM or ADMX template). Likewise, reporting shows only "Extra Registry Settings" unless there's a matching ADM or ADMX template.

Linking a GPO

We created a GPO, we edited a GPO, but what good is a GPO if you can't link it? We briefly showed you this earlier in this appendix and explored linking a Group Policy Object with PowerShell in Chapter 2, but let's make sure we really cover both New-GPLink and Set-GPLink. The former will link a GPO with a target:

```
PS C:\> new-gplink "MyTestGPO" -Target "OU=testing,DC=corp,DC=com"
```

```
GpoId        : 9061e2e6-0385-436d-a17e-d1b2f41c6b08
DisplayName  : MyTestGPO
Enabled      : True
Enforced     : False
Target       : OU=Testing,DC=CORP,DC=com
Order        : 2
```

This cmdlet also has parameters that take Yes/No values: -Enforced and -LinkEnabled. They should be self-explanatory.

If you already have a link and want to modify it, you can use `Set-GPLink`. Let's enforce the link we just created:

```
PS C:\> set-gplink "MyTestGPO" -Target "OU=Testing,DC=corp,DC=com" -enforced yes
```

The syntax is very similar. Remember, if you forget how to use a cmdlet, ask PowerShell for help:

```
PS C:\> help set-gplink -full
```

Removing a GPO Link

We bet by now you can make a pretty good guess about what cmdlet to use to remove a GPO link:

```
PS C:\> remove-gplink "MyTestGPO" -Target "OU=testing,DC=corp,DC=com"
```

This cmdlet also supports `-Whatif` so you can avoid shooting yourself in the foot. But you will need to know where the GPO is linked. That's where the functions we shared earlier come in handy.

Suppose you have GPO like this, linked to multiple locations:

```
PS C:\> Get-MyGPLinkBasic -Name Restricted


GpoId       : 915b940f-683d-461b-beae-edb50fc996bf
DisplayName : Restricted
Enabled     : True
Enforced    : False
Target      : ou=mytest,dc=corp,dc=com
Order       : 2

GpoId       : 915b940f-683d-461b-beae-edb50fc996bf
DisplayName : Restricted
Enabled     : True
Enforced    : False
Target      : ou=temporaryhires,ou=employees,dc=corp,dc=com
Order       : 1
```

You want to remove all the links but you don't want to have to know where they all are. Our function makes your life easier and can work with `Remove-GPLink`:

```
PS C:\> Get-MyGPLinkBasic -Name Restricted | remove-gplink -WhatIf
What if: Remove the link between the GPO with ID {915b940f-683d-461b-beae-
edb50fc996bf} in the CORP.com domain and the Active Directory container with
 the LDAP path "ou=mytest,dc=corp,dc=com".  (Remove-GPLink)
```

```
What if: Remove the link between the GPO with ID {915b940f-683d-461b-beae-
edb50fc996bf} in the CORP.com domain and the Active Directory container with
  the LDAP path "ou=temporaryhires,ou=employees,dc=corp,dc=com".  (Remove-GPLink)
```

Or perhaps you want to remove links for all GPOs that aren't even enabled:

```
PS C:\> Get-MyGPLinkBasic -Disabled | Remove-GPLink -whatif
What if: Remove the link between the GPO with ID {77480092-642d-4843-8b77-
50029a56399f} in the CORP.com domain and the Active Directory container with
  the LDAP path "dc=corp,dc=com".  (Remove-GPLink)
What if: Remove the link between the GPO with ID {31685888-184a-4a6d-a52c-
a091d4b75e69} in the CORP.com domain and the Active Directory container with
  the LDAP path "dc=corp,dc=com".  (Remove-GPLink)
What if: Remove the link between the GPO with ID {21c79adb-9f4d-48e1-8329-
4e8a81cd017a} in the CORP.com domain and the Active Directory container with
  the LDAP path "dc=corp,dc=com".  (Remove-GPLink)
What if: Remove the link between the GPO with ID {5ea7e3ea-14e5-47c9-9180-
afa97845b0b8} in the CORP.com domain and the Active Directory container with
  the LDAP path "dc=corp,dc=com".  (Remove-GPLink)
What if: Remove the link between the GPO with ID {cd73c562-5bfe-40e2-b81e-
28da10da425c} in the CORP.com domain and the Active Directory container with
  the LDAP path "ou=servers,dc=corp,dc=com".  (Remove-GPLink)
What if: Remove the link between the GPO with ID {4ac440d7-bed7-447f-882a-
9cc930bf28df} in the CORP.com domain and the Active Directory container with
  the LDAP path "ou=employees,dc=corp,dc=com".  (Remove-GPLink)
```

We didn't really want to remove any of the links, but you can by omitting the -WhatIf parameter.

Performing a Remote *GPupdate* (Invoking *GPupdate*)

Up until this point all the Group Policy cmdlets were available since Windows 7.

If you'll recall in Chapter 3 in the section "Manually Forcing Background Policy Processing (Remote GPupdate)," we learned that the Windows 8 and later GPMC has a function where you can right-click upon an OU and specify which computers will receive GPupdate.

Well, there's a PowerShell cmdlet for that too: Invoke-GPupdate. In order for it to be used, the same rules as running the command from the GPMC apply. So, let's review:

- Target machine must be Windows 7 or later.
- Target machine must be on.
- The firewall has to have ports 135 and 445 poked through.

For more information on that last one, see the sidebar in Chapter 3 entitled "Under the Hood with Remote Group Policy Processing."

Now, let's take a look at the `Invoke-GPupdate` cmdlet to see how it works.

First, you can use this cmdlet in place of the traditional gpupdate.exe and force an update of the local machine:

```
PS C:\> invoke-gpupdate
```

If you prefer to limit the refresh to either user or computer settings, then specify it:

```
PS C:\> invoke-gpupdate -Computer client8 -Target User
```

This will remotely update GPO user settings on Client8. You can also apply an update to multiple computers using any of these techniques:

```
PS C:\> "client1","client2","client3" | invoke-gpupdate -Target Computer
PS C:\> get-content c:\work\computers.txt | invoke-gpupdate -Computer  -Target
computer
PS C:\> get-adcomputer -filter * -SearchBase "OU=desktops,DC=corp,DC=com" |
>> Where {Test-Connection $_.name -Quiet -Count 1} |
>> Select -ExpandProperty Name |
>>Invoke-GPUpdate -randomdelayinminutes 5 -Target computer
```

The last example will get all computers in the **Desktops** OU and send a test ping to each one. If the computer responds to the ping, the name property is passed on in the pipeline and sent to `Invoke-GPUpdate`, which will update Group Policy settings for the Computer side using a delay of 5 minutes plus a random offset.

This cmdlet also has parameters to force a computer to reboot (`-Boot`) or log off the user (`-Logoff`), but use these with caution. Be sure to take the time to read full help and examples for this cmdlet and test in a nonproduction setting as `Invoke-GPUpdate` doesn't write anything to the pipeline.

Replacing Microsoft's GPMC Scripts with PowerShell Equivalents

Microsoft has an army of interesting Visual Basic scripts that perform many of the functions of the GPMC. You can download the original Microsoft GPMC scripts at http://tinyurl.com/23xfz3.

However, you'll be better served by using the new PowerShell equivalents. Table A.1 shows the original Microsoft script, what it does, and the equivalent PowerShell cmdlets. Some of the cmdlets may need to be part of an expression using standard PowerShell cmdlets, such as `Where-Object` and `Select-Object`.

TABLE A.1   PowerShell equivalents for Microsoft scripts

Microsoft Script	What It Does	PowerShell Cmdlet
BackupAllGPOs.wsf	Backs up all GPOs	Backup-GPO
BackupGPO.wsf	Backs up a GPO	Backup-GPO
CopyGPO.wsf	Copies GPO	Copy-GPO
CreateGPO.wsf	Creates GPO	New-GPO
DeleteGPO.wsf	Deletes GPO	Remove-GPO
DumpGPOInfo.wsf	Dumps GPO information	Get-GPO
FindDisabledGPOs.wsf	Finds all disabled GPOs	Get-GPO
FindDuplicateNamedGPOs.wsf	Finds duplicate named GPOs	Get-GPO
FindGPOsByPolicyExtension.wsf	Finds GPOs by policy extension	None
FindGPOsBySecurityGroup.wsf	Finds GPOs by security group	Get-GPPermissions
FindGPOsWithNoSecurityFiltering.wsf	Finds GPOs with no security filtering	Get-GPPermissions
findorphanedGPOsInSYSVOL.wsf	Finds orphaned GPOs in SYSVOL	None
FindUnlinkedGPOs.wsf	Finds GPOs with no links	None
GetReportsForAllGPOs.wsf	Gets reports for all GPOs	Get-GPOReport
GetReportsForGPO.wsf	Gets reports for a GPO	Get-GPOReport
GrantPermissionOnAllGPOs.wsf	Grants the permissions for all GPOs	Set-GPPermissions
ImportAllGPOs.wsf	Imports all GPOs in a path	Import-GPO
ImportGPO.wsf	Imports a GPO in a path	Import-GPO

Microsoft Script	What It Does	PowerShell Cmdlet
ListAllGPOs.wsf	Lists all GPOs	Get-GPO
QueryBackupLocation.wsf	Lists all GPOs in a backup	
RestoreAllGPOs.wsf	Restores all GPOs in a path	Restore-GPO
RestoreGPO.wsf	Restores a GPO in a path	Restore-GPO

Any scripts you need can be found in the Book Resources section of www.GPanswers.com, as well as any updates and notes if they're available.

Final Thoughts

Here's a great idea! Let's manually configure the permissions on 500 GPOs and adjust them to our needs. Or document them. Or back them up. If that sounds like a good time to you, then knock yourself out.

But we think you're smarter than that and realize how much time and energy you can save with PowerShell. In fact, if you look around we're sure you'll find some cool stuff from vendors like Specops Software and SDM Software that offer PowerShell-centered solutions. Granted, their offerings may require a financial investment, but when you think about the investment you've already made in learning PowerShell, it is a pretty good deal.

PS: You can see a talk Jeff and I did at TechEd 2012 on Group Policy + PowerShell. The link is

    http://channel9.msdn.com/Events/TechEd/NorthAmerica/2012/WSV415

If you are curious about learning more about Windows PowerShell, pick up a copy of *PowerShell in Depth, Second Edition,* by Don Jones, Richard Siddaway, and Jeffery Hicks (Manning Publications, 2014). Or grab a copy of *Learn PowerShell in a Month of Lunches, Second Edition,* by Don Jones and Jeff Hicks (Manning Publications, 2012). Jeff has also published a number of PowerShell training videos for Pluralsight.

B

Group Policy and VDI

Not everyone is flocking to virtual desktop infrastructure (VDI). Most still have a standard desktop and laptop running the operating system on the actual machine itself.

Your non-Microsoft tablet (dare I say it?), an iPad or Android, for instance, won't run Windows. So if you want to give someone a remote desktop experience, you can use traditional Remote Desktop Services (RDS)/Terminal Services or create a VDI infrastructure.

A VDI infrastructure is loosely defined as a desktop PC running in a virtual machine on a server using a hypervisor (like Microsoft Hyper-V, Citrix XenApp, or VMware vSphere). These "desktops" can be either *persistent* or *nonpersistent*. Persistent means that the user experience feels like a regular desktop. Users' data and settings are preserved from session to session. Nonpersistent means that users' changes are wiped out when the session is over.

Creating a VDI infrastructure is way beyond the scope of this book. You can create a VDI infrastructure from only Microsoft components or by using Microsoft and Citrix, VMware, Quest, and many others. You're on your own for that part. If you're interested in Microsoft-specific virtualization, check out *Mastering Microsoft Virtualization* by Tim Cerling and Jeffrey L. Buller (Sybex, 2009).

Also, for the record, I got a lot out of Brian Madden's "The New VDI Reality" which you can pay for, or get for free here:

http://www.bitpipe.com/detail/RES/1368201274_443.html

However, what I want to do in this appendix is highlight some Group Policy specifics with regard to VDI. We'll tackle the following topics:

- What is VDI and why is it different?
- Tuning your images for VDI
- Group Policy settings to set and avoid for maximum VDI performance
- Group Policy tweaks for fast VDI video
- And some final thoughts to help you along with your VDI journey

I want to say up front that this appendix was primarily based on two sources from two Group Policy friends.

Source #1 is a great speech that Darren Mar-Elia, fellow Group Policy MVP, did at TechEd 2011. You can find that speech here:

`http://channel9.msdn.com/Events/TechEd/NorthAmerica/2011/WCL309`

Source #2 is a great article that Alan Burchill, fellow Group Policy MVP, wrote; you can find it here:

`www.grouppolicy.biz/2011/11/best-practice-group-policy-for-virtual-desktops-vdi/`

I'll be sprinkling in as much additional wisdom as I can, but hats off to these guys for doing the hard work for me.

Why Is VDI Different?

VDI is a somewhat different animal than individual desktops and laptops by themselves. That's because any given desktop or laptop user could be doing something that makes their own machine slower, and no one else really cares.

With VDI, everyone is sharing the same hypervisor and storage. One bad apple makes the whole cart rotten.

Additionally, if you don't have enough memory allocated per VDI session, those sessions will simply page to disk, causing more disk operations and slowing down *everyone* on the VDI system.

Before we get going, let's visualize what happens in a VDI session.

When a VDI session starts up for the very first time from an image, it wakes up, boots, downloads the Computer-side GPOs perfectly normally, and gets fully warmed up. Then a user logs on to the VDI session and processes all User-side GPOs perfectly normally and gets the Start Menu going.

See? The VDI world is not that different than what you already know.

What is a little different between VDI machines and normal machines is that the sessions can either be persistent or nonpersistent. If the session is persistent, then the user gets only the changed GPOs the next time the computer starts and the user logs on. If the session is nonpersistent, the computer throws everything out the window and redownloads all the GPOs (since it's never seen any GPOs before—as far as it remembers).

So, I want to say that mostly everything you've learned so far in this book is perfectly valid. That is, I don't want you to think too hard about re-crafting your Group Policy world for a VDI rollout. Group Policy will apply normally to VDI sessions as it will for desktops and laptops. What you're already doing for them (desktops and laptops) is (almost) equally valid for VDI. The dynamic-ness (if that's even a word) is what you love about Group Policy, and it applies equally to real and virtual machines.

The only big difference is that if you're using a nonpersistent VDI session, you might want to prebake in some additional settings instead of relying on Group Policy to dynamically deploy them. That way, you're not downloading the same GPOs again and again—as if it were the first time the computer has ever seen them.

I want to be clear: I'm not saying don't use GPOs to make dynamic adjustments to your nonpersistent VDI sessions. There are oodles of opportunities to have groups of users get different look-and-feel settings on the fly using Administrative Templates, shortcuts and printers (via Group Policy Preferences), or Firefox settings and UI lockout using PolicyPak. Given all those choices, it still makes sense to use Group Policy with nonpersistent desktops. In this appendix, however, I'll suggest areas where, especially for nonpersistent desktops, you might want to prebake the settings directly into the image instead of necessarily relying on Group Policy for its dynamic abilities.

And, for persistent VDI sessions, almost certainly do use Group Policy for nearly everything you do now. Because the real Group Policy "speed penalty" occurs only when a machine and user have never seen the GPOs before, there's little downside to doing precisely what you're doing now with GPOs. Craft your perfect VDI GPO universe (specifically for VDI machines) and you're golden.

Tuning Your Images for VDI

All VDI sessions start out life as images. These images then get moved to the hypervisor, and end users "run" them and see a desktop.

So, in the theme of keeping unnecessary disk activity to a minimum, you'll want to turn off items inside the VDI image that would scan, scrub, or write to the whole disk.

Remember that all VDI sessions start out as some image, which was frozen in time.

The best approach is to plan ahead and turn off the unused services you might or might not want to use. But, ultimately, always, you'll forget something. Or, you turned something off, and now—oops, some percentage of your VDI population wants it back on.

Good news: I already showed you exactly how to deal with this in Chapter 5, "Group Policy Preferences," when we leveraged the Group Policy Preferences. You'll use Group Policy Preferences' Services extension and specify which users or computers get what directives.

As shown in Figure B.1, use Group Policy Preferences to turn off (disable) any services after the image is finalized.

Remember, anything you bake into your image is static, which means it'll be faster inasmuch as the service is already off in the finalized image. However, also remember that using Group Policy is the most *flexible* way to handle turning on or off services.

FIGURE B.1 Using Group Policy Preferences to turn off (disable) unused services works for real and VDI machines.

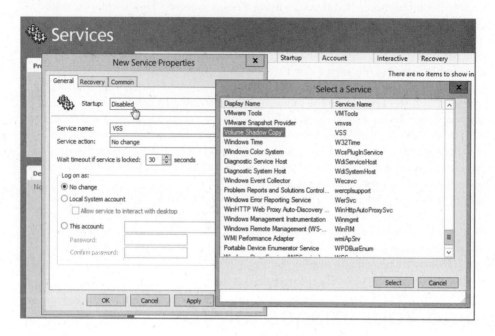

Specific Functions to Turn Off for VDI Machines

There are a bunch of unnecessary tasks that your system does—tasks that would make total sense if it was a real desktop or laptop but that have little utility in a VDI machine. To that end, to save memory and disk operations, turn off (or don't install) items like the following:

- Antivirus scans
- Windows Search Indexing
- Defragmentation tasks
- Windows Defender
- Windows Update

In Figure B.2, I'm deleting the unnecessary built-in defragmentation task that comes with Windows.

You might be surprised to see Windows Update and Windows Defender on the list, but here's the idea. If you're using nonpersistent desktops (those that ditch whatever users do within the session), then what's the point of keeping them "updated" and/or "defended"? You could argue that if your machines are unpatched for long periods, the bad guys could infect some other system, which affects your whole VDI population and they in turn become bad guys too. (I've seen this with desktops in real life, and it's not pretty.)

FIGURE B.2   Prepare to minimize your disk operations by killing unnecessary items, like disk defragmentation.

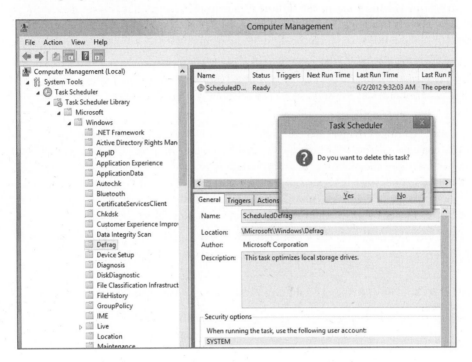

So, I'm not saying don't ever update your machines. You'll need some kind of process for updating that's specific to your VDI world. But you might be able to stop downloading and installing Microsoft patches and such—only to throw them away at the end of a session.

Group Policy Settings to Set and Avoid for Maximum VDI Performance

Again, some items make a lot of sense on the desktop but not on VDI sessions. Here are some favorites you'll want to make sure are prebaked into your VDI image or always delivered to VDI machines:

System Restore   VDI by its very nature enables you to snap back a machine to a known state. So, System Restore can be safely turned off. The policy setting is found at Computer Configuration ➢ Policies ➢ Administrative Templates ➢ System ➢ System Restore ➢ **Turn off System Restore.**

Offline Files   Users aren't taking data away with them. So there's no reason to have Offline Files enabled. This is especially important when it comes to nonpersistent desktops (where the whole system is reset the next time users utilize it). Because of this, there is literally zero utility in having this feature on in those cases. The policy setting is found at Computer Configuration ➢ Policies ➢ Administrative Templates ➢ Network ➢ Offline Files ➢ **Allow or Disallow use of the Offline files feature**. Ensure that you set this setting to Disabled to prevent Offline Files from operating. This policy setting is further discussed in Chapter 10, "Profiles: Local, Roaming, and Mandatory."

BitLocker Disk Encryption   Since the disk that users are writing to is in the data center, there's no reason at all for BitLocker to be enabled. Standard users on a system cannot perform BitLocker operations anyway, so there's nothing you need to do in Group Policy to turn it off.

Outlook and Exchange Offline Cached Mode   In a similar vein, if you're using Outlook and Exchange, consider turning off Exchange Cached Mode for Outlook. All it does is pull down the whole mailbox to the machine, which you definitely don't need. If you add the Office 2010 templates, the setting is located in User Configuration ➢ Policies ➢ Administrative Templates ➢ Outlook 2010 ➢ Account Settings ➢ Exchange ➢ Cached Exchange Mode ➢ **Use Cached Exchange Mode for new and existing Outlook profiles**. Set to Disabled.

Using File System or Registry ACLs   In Figure B.3, you can see two areas that are part of Group Policy Objects but are, in general, a terrible idea on VDI machines.

FIGURE B.3   File and Registry security within Group Policy should not be used on VDI machines.

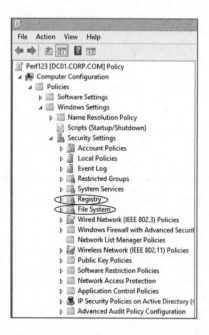

Those two areas are file system and Registry security settings.

While these two areas let you re-permission the file system or Registry, this is not something you would want to do inside Group Policy since it's soooo slooooow. And, moreover, as you learned in Chapter 3, "Group Policy Processing Behavior Essentials," all security settings reprocess every 16 hours, even if nothing has changed. There's no reason to saddle your VDI machines with that kind of burden.

Using the "Right" Screen Saver   Everyone loves those "bells and whistles" screen savers. Problem is, they're CPU and sometimes disk intensive. Really, anything that uses any visualizations and such eats CPU and ultimately bandwidth because VDI sessions' displays are remote to whatever device the user is using. To that end, consider setting the blank screen saver. Do this using User Configuration ➢ Policies ➢ Administrative Templates ➢ Control Panel ➢ Personalization ➢ **Force specific screen saver**. Set the value to scrnsave.scr, which will establish the blank screen saver for the user.

Group Policy Tweaks for Fast VDI Video

If you use a Microsoft VDI environment, your "work" is happening on the server, and your display is happening on the device your users are using.

Tweaking RDP Using Group Policy for VDI

That protocol performing the displaying is RDP. To that end, you should investigate the RDS settings available to you within Computer Configuration ➢ Policies ➢ Administrative Templates ➢ Windows Components ➢ Remote Desktop Services ➢ Remote Desktop Session Host ➢ Remote Session Environment, as seen in Figure B.4.

FIGURE B.4   Remote Desktop Session Host policy setting suggestions

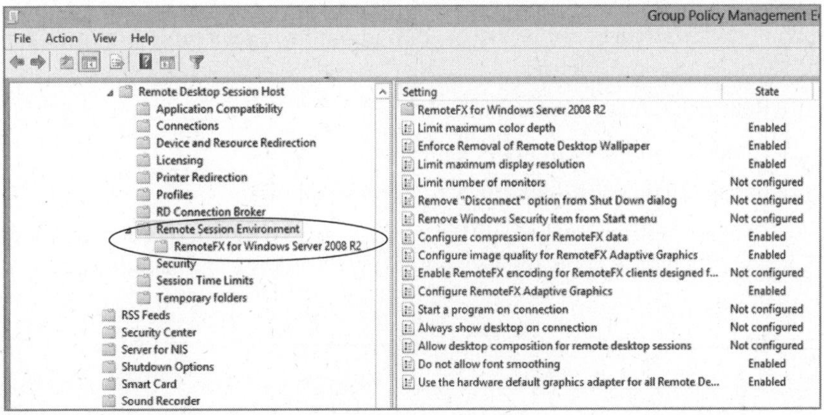

To maximize display performance, consider tweaking the following policy settings:

Limit maximum color depth   Every "bit" counts. You can reduce color depth and save bandwidth across every connection using this policy setting. However the benefit of this is somewhat limited as Microsoft already optimizes the compression for 32-bit color. Best to test this at 16-bit color and compare the difference, then make a call if the reduced quality of the screen is worth the marginal improvements. A good read on this idea can be found at

```
http://blogs.msdn.com/b/rds/archive/2009/03/03/top-10-rdp-protocol-
misconceptions-part-1.aspx
```

Enforce Removal of Remote Desktop Wallpaper   Those pretty desktop backgrounds look great. But when RDP has to paint them and all the pixels next to a background over and over again, it's costly. Enabling this setting makes the backgrounds go away.

Limit maximum display resolution   The tighter the resolution, the less is transmitted between the server and the client. Enable this setting and specify the resolution to guarantee that users cannot utilize a really big screen and pass around all that drawing data.

Use the hardware default graphics adapter for all Remote Desktop Services sessions   This setting can enable GPU (graphics processing unit) hardware acceleration if you have supporting hardware on your server, making drawing multiple sessions even faster.

Do not allow font smoothing   Enabling this policy setting could speed things up under some circumstances. Of all the tuning you could do, this would likely have the least impact if you wanted to try it.

Tweaking RemoteFX using Group Policy for VDI

In Computer Configuration ➢ Policies ➢ Administrative Templates ➢ Windows Components ➢ Remote Desktop Services ➢ Remote Desktop Session Host ➢ Remote Session Environment, you'll also see mention of Microsoft's RemoteFX protocol. This protocol can perform some fancy footwork and give high-resolution experiences to VDI and remote desktops.

The following policy settings can be tweaked to maximize speed (and minimize bandwidth) at the sacrifice of some fidelity:

- Configure RemoteFX Adaptive Graphics
- Configure compression for RemoteFX data
- Configure Image Quality for RemoteFX Adaptive Graphics

There are also three settings tucked within a node called "RemoteFX for Windows Server 2008 R2," (which only apply to Windows Server 2008 R2 and Windows 7, as seen in Figure B.5).

FIGURE B.5　Several of the RemoteFX policy settings are tunable so they can use less bandwidth.

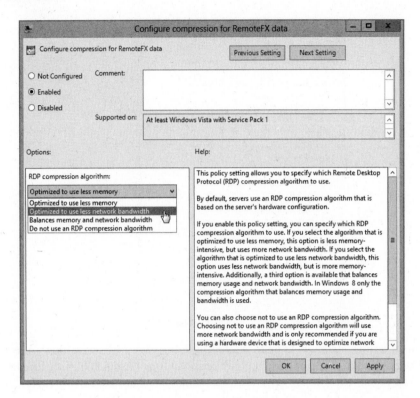

These settings specifically work with RemoteFX on Windows Server 2008 R2:

- Configure RemoteFX
- Optimize visual experience when using RemoteFX
- Optimize visual experience for Remote Desktop Service Sessions

Managing and Locking Down Desktop UI Tweaks

Windows provides a lot of desktop-driven UI settings that you can't manipulate using Group Policy. Figure B.6 shows the Performance Options Control Panel applet, available in Windows 7 and later. The figure shows the Visual Effects tab, featuring a menagerie of look-and-feel settings that make the desktop more pleasant but put a strain on the CPU and the bandwidth.

FIGURE B.6 Microsoft's Visual Effects tab within the Performance Control Panel applet

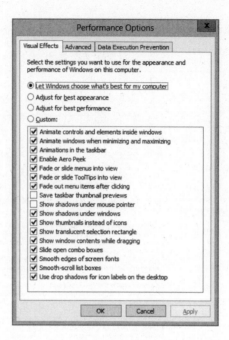

The optimal settings here would be to disable all things that produce shadows or transparency. The problem is, doing so is simply not possible using Group Policy settings in the box. Those settings are stored within the operating system as REG_BINARY values, and Group Policy doesn't have a way to deliver and tweak those specific bits.

It should be noted that PolicyPak can manage these; it has a preconfigured Pak for this that can flip every important bit and also lock down the user interface so users cannot work around it.

Final Thoughts for VDI and Group Policy

In this book, you've created OUs that mirrored who would be managing them. We had Frank Rizzo managing the **Human Resources** OU. And that OU contained sub-OUs—one for users and one for computers.

However, you might want to manage your VDI machines differently than a desktop or laptop. To that end, consider having a separate OU structure for your VDI machines that makes sense for you. I can't give you specific guidance here, but the point is to separate the computer accounts that represent the VDI computers from the ones that you already have for your real machines.

This arrangement gives you three big benefits:

- You can specifically link GPOs to this structure (and thus avoid affecting your real machines).

- These machines are different (by definition) and hence will be managed differently. And you won't be able to forget that these machines are different if they're in a different OU.

- If you use Loopback policy processing for VDI machines, it's way easier to do.

That final bullet is the next thing I want to talk about here. That is, like RDS machines (aka Terminal Services), VDI sessions are often a good choice to utilize Loopback mode (specifically Loopback—Replace). This enables you to have an environment in which people using the VDI machines get an experience specific to their VDI world. And, when they're in their normal desktop and laptop world, they get the normal desktop and laptop experience.

I've already talked about Loopback policy processing in detail in Chapter 4, "Advanced Group Policy Processing," and provided examples on when to use it and how it works. Be sure to reread Chapter 4 for more information on Loopback if you need to.

The final thought about VDI machines is that, as with regular machines, the information you learned about profiles in Chapter 9, "Profiles: Local, Roaming, and Mandatory," and the information you learned about Folder Redirection in Chapter 10, "The Managed Desktop, Part 1: Redirected Folders, Offline Files, and the Synchronization Manager," is 100 percent valid. That means, when you follow the instructions in this appendix properly, you can have a smooth roaming experience between real and VDI machines, and users will share their profile correctly and see all their redirected files.

And they'll still like you.

C

Advanced Group
Policy Management

Let's start with the bad news...because there's a lot of good news in this appendix, and I don't want anyone to say, "Hey! I'm 30 pages into this and he didn't tell me [this very important fact I'm about to tell you]."

That is, to use the stuff we're going to talk about in this appendix, you have to pay Microsoft a little extra. That's right. Everything we've talked about in this book so far is "free," inasmuch as it's in the box when you buy Windows and spin up an Active Directory, install your Windows clients, perform some downloads, and so on.

But this appendix is different. We're going to talk about a Microsoft tool called Advanced Group Policy Management (AGPM). Its goal is to help bigger companies with the challenge of GPO management. There's no "Are you sure you really want to do this?" inside the GPMC and Group Policy Object Editor. Everything happens in real time. If you make a mistake, there's no "Group Policy Undo" short of disabling or deleting the GPO and hoping you only have a few desktops to clean up.

AGPM puts a "Change Management" system around Group Policy within the GPMC. Change Management is the art of "not screwing things up." The idea is that some people request changes, others make editing choices, and others approve their changes. AGPM is involved with ensuring that your overall philosophy of Group Policy management is embraced. Here are the main things it's meant to do:

- Ensure that GPOs are configured correctly—before they're placed into production
- Reduce risk of Group Policy deployment errors
- Ensure that Group Policy management is done securely
- Track usage (that is, know what's going on, who made the change, and what was changed)

And it's a really cool tool. Which is why Microsoft is making you pay extra for it.

How do you get this tool? You must be a Microsoft Software Assurance (SA) customer. Being an SA customer means you pay a little extra insurance money up front hoping that Microsoft produces updates that you want to install. A misconception is that SA customers must be big companies. They don't have to be. You can be an SA customer with as few as 50 seats. You can learn more about becoming an SA customer here: www.microsoft.com/licensing/sa/.

Then inside of SA is also a bundle offering of programs called the Microsoft Desktop Optimization Pack (MDOP). You can see all the stuff in MDOP at www.microsoft.com/mdop.

This appendix isn't for everyone, because it assumes you're an SA customer and that you got a hold of MDOP. But AGPM is a great addition to the possibilities in Group Policy-land, so we'll explore what it has to offer.

The Challenge of Group Policy Change Management

Group Policy offers a huge amount of power. (That's why our logo at www.GPanswers.com looks like a deity hurling a lightning bolt.) Actually, some could argue that Group Policy has too much power. Not too much power in the hands of someone skilled in the ways of Group Policy kung fu. But rather, it can be too much power for someone who's a mere white belt.

With that in mind, Microsoft's AGPM product seeks to fill in several gaps within the GPMC when it comes to who can do what to Group Policy. In Chapter 2, "Managing Group Policy with the GPMC and via PowerShell," you learned about the Group Policy delegation model. Sure, it's possible to say, "Carl can create GPOs," "Ed can edit these GPOs," and, "Larry can link GPOs to the Sales OU." But that's not good enough for environments that have multiple administrators who need more granular levels of control.

The other challenge is that, sure, Ed can edit the GPOs. But does he know what he's doing? Wouldn't it be better if Alice approved the GPO that Ed edited? And what if Edward (a different dude than Ed) wanted to edit the same GPO that Ed just edited?

Additionally, with all this creating, editing, and linking, it can be hard to figure out what's happened over time if a problem occurs. If you really wanted to know, could you tell which Ed (Ed or Edward) had edited it, what the edit was, and which Ed edited it last?

So, with that in mind, AGPM brings several change control functionalities to the table to help solve these issues:

- Check In/Check Out workflow management
- Version control
- Difference reporting
- Role-based delegation
- Offline editing of GPOs
- GPO templates (super-stud cousin to Starter GPOs, which we learned in Chapter 2)

The best part is that once it's loaded, AGPM fits right into the GPMC. This means it's not another whole tool to learn (although it does have its ins and outs). In this appendix, we'll explore these major features of AGPM so you can get a feel for how you might use it in your environment.

It doesn't matter if you're using the Central Store with ADMX files or still using ADM files. AGPM works with GPOs created from any platform, but the best management station platform is a Windows 10 management station with the AGPM client installed. We'll talk about installation in the next section.

Architecture and Installation of AGPM

Actually, the first part of installing AGPM is downloading it. As an SA customer, ask your salesdude or salesdudette, or your Microsoft Technical Accounts Manager (TAM) if you have one, for a copy if you're entitled to it.

When you decide to make the leap to AGPM, be sure to read the Readme file and guidance about which is the latest version and what operating systems it can be installed on. AGPM is a little weird in that it works best when the operating system it is installed upon is the latest, and therefore AGPM itself must also be updated to suit.

Make sure you're getting the right (latest) version (whatever it is). Note that sometimes the latest AGPM will also ship with the older versions of AGPM, just to be confusing. Be sure to get off on the right foot and install the right version!

AGPM Architecture

The AGPM architecture is, in a word, elegant. It doesn't require any wacky schema extensions. You don't have to touch every DC. You just install two pieces: a server piece and a client piece.

The AGPM server piece should be installed on the latest version of Windows Server possible. This is because the server piece (and archive that lives within it) leverages the Group Policy client-side extensions registered within the machine it's run on. So, though you can install the AGPM server on an old server, or even a client system in a pinch, that's not really a hot idea. It's best to install the latest AGPM on the latest version of Windows Server, because the latest version of Windows Server has the most Group Policy extensions available, so it's the best place to house the archive.

The client part is a misnomer. It's not a client that needs to be installed on every desktop, just a little management piece that needs to be installed on your management stations where you run the GPMC. Since you're likely to use Windows 10 as your management station, this is where you would load your AGPM client.

Indeed, if you want to use Windows 7 as your AGPM client (that is, the client from which you manage AGPM), then you positively need to have Windows Server 2008 R2 to run the AGPM server piece. That's because their GPMCs "match" and will cause no errors in their interaction (as could happen with mismatched pieces, it's assumed). Additionally, it should be noted that AGPM 3.0 clients are prevented from connecting to AGPM server archives, for a similar reason.

> If for some reason you require mixed environments (such as an AGPM server on Windows Server 2016) but need, say, AGPM clients on Windows 7, you should read Microsoft's document on the subject. It should ship alongside AGPM in a PDF. You can also check out `https://technet .microsoft.com/en-us/library/dd553090.aspx`, which also appears to be up to date.

A little later, we'll discuss how to use the AGPM world as the exclusive place to create new GPOs and then manage them. But that means that soon after deployment of the AGPM server, you'll want to get the AGPM client piece out to all your administrators so they can continue managing GPOs (albeit in a new way).

Installing AGPM

Again, you'll get AGPM from your Microsoft contact if you're an SA customer. As of this writing, the installation of AGPM is contained within MDOP, but that should change soon. Again, the one we're concerned with is Advanced Group Policy Management, within the MDOP launcher seen in Figure C.1.

FIGURE C.1 The MDOP splash and installation screen

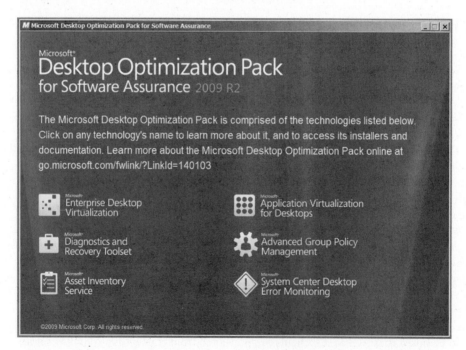

Installing the AGPM Server Service

AGPM performs much of its Check In/Check Out workflow management because it installs a simple service on the server of your choice. There are no schema changes, no Active Directory back-end changes, and no touching all of your Domain Controllers.

It's recommended that you install the AGPM server on a regular server (not a Domain Controller), but it appears to install and run just fine on a DC.

However, here's the trick (as previously stated): In order to make use of AGPM, you'll need to install the AGPM server piece on a Windows Server. That's because AGPM will track 100 percent of the Group Policy settings only when the server service is installed on the latest server operating system.

Again, AGPM is a little strange: it relies on the machine it's loaded on as the "backbone" for the CSEs it supports in the archive. So, then, you need to ask yourself, "Which Windows machines have the *most* (and latest) CSEs?" And the answer to that is easy: Windows Server 2016 and Windows 10. And, well, Windows Server 2016 is a *server*. So, it is the ideal candidate (though my understating is that it is possible to load the AGPM service on a Windows client if you need to, in a pinch, but I haven't tried it).

The first piece you'll install is the server, and you can do this by clicking Install Server (64-Bit), as seen in Figure C.2.

FIGURE C.2   Start out by installing the AGPM server.

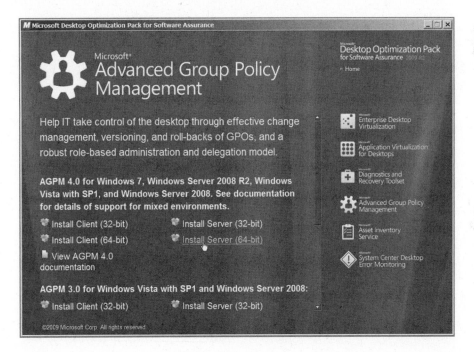

At this point, you'll see a wizard-driven Server Setup screen. You'll need to accept the license terms and give it a directory in which to install the AGPM server (the default is usually A-OK). The tricky question is when you're asked about the Archive Path, as seen in Figure C.3. The default for this is a little baffling to me, as it puts the Group Policy archive underneath the `ProgramData\Microsoft\AGPM` directory (also seen in Figure C.3), and on Windows Server, it puts the path as `C:\ProgramData\Microsoft\AGPM` (which is a little better). The files that AGPM puts here are just regular files. And, although you shouldn't need to poke directly around the archive (like, ever), if you did need to, it might be nice to have the archive set in a place that's obvious. So, I like to change the default to `C:\AGPM-ARCHIVE` (as seen in Figure C.4) or something similar, where I know I can easily get to it.

FIGURE C.3   The original path for storing AGPM data is a little obtuse.

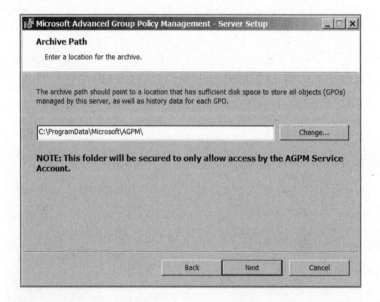

Next, you'll be asked about the AGPM service account, as seen in Figure C.5. If you have one domain and you install AGPM on a Domain Controller as a last resort, because you have no other servers in your environment that you can install it on, I suggest you choose Local System. If you have multiple domains or install on a member server, then select User Account and provide an account that you trust. This account will have rights over the AGPM system.

FIGURE C.4   This is my suggested path for storing AGPM data.

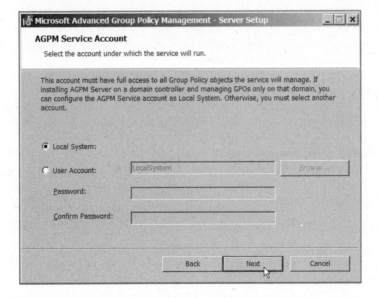

FIGURE C.5   If you're installing on a Domain Controller, choose Local System.

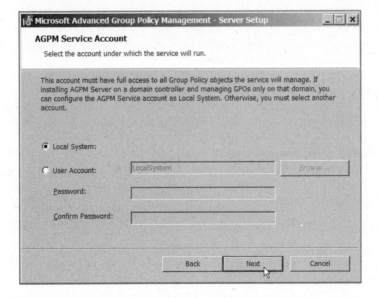

The next screen is the initial Archive Owner account, as seen in Figure C.6. You can choose a regular user account here or a security group (such as AGPM-OWNERS). This account doesn't need to have Domain Administrator rights. But note that this person will initially own all the material inside the archive. Later, this person will be able to delegate the stuff contained within the archive to other users of the AGPM system. More users or groups can be delegated these rights later.

FIGURE C.6   If installing AGPM on a member server, choose an Active Directory user account with a name reflective of what you're using. I suggest AGPM-OWNER or AGPM-SERVICE or something similar. In my examples, I'll use AGPM-OWNER.

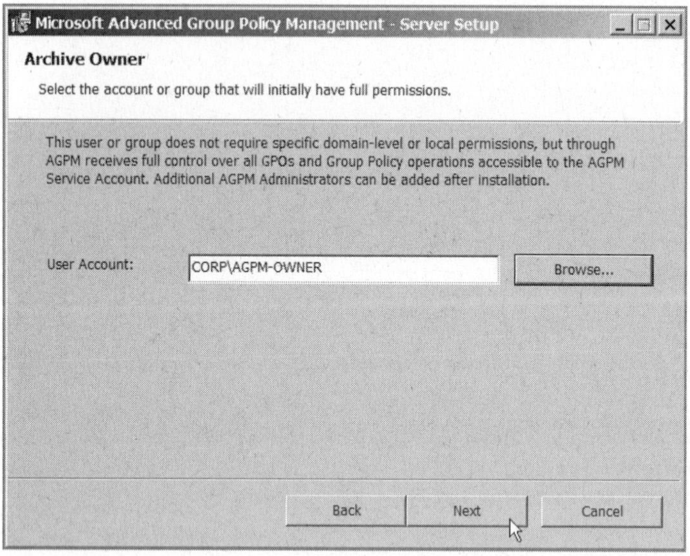

I suggest using a new, neutral, non-Administrator account. I'm calling mine AGPM-OWNER. I created this account in Active Directory Users and Computers, then selected it, as seen in Figure C.6.

You'll then be asked which port to communicate on. The default port is 4600. Because Windows Server has the firewall enabled by default, you will need to also open the Windows Server firewall to enable client-to-server communication. This wizard page allows you to do that. Note that this screen is not shown.

You'll also be able to specify which languages the server is available in. All languages are selected by default. I usually uncheck all and specify only my language. Note that this screen is not shown.

Finally, you'll be at the final screen and can click Install to install AGPM.

Sometimes, using a domain account like AGPM-OWNER can add some headaches because the AGPM-OWNER may not be able to access the original GPOs. If you start to have permissions issues that look unsolvable, read the section "Advanced Configuration and Troubleshooting of AGPM" toward the end of this appendix for some remediation.

Right now, the AGPM service could be considered a "single point of failure." That is, if the computer that the service is running on dies (or the service dies), the AGPM system will obviously fail to work. However, AGPM is not an officially "clusterable" service, meaning you cannot (right now) officially spin up Microsoft Cluster Services and get failover if the primary server dies. However, the "regular" method of manipulating GPOs (that is, directly and not through the AGPM system) will still work and can be used as an alternative until the AGPM system or service is back up and running.

We at www.GPanswers.com tested AGPM in a clustered environment and it seemed to work A-OK. Because it's not officially clusterable, your mileage and official support may vary.

When finished, you can install the next piece: the "client" piece that installs within the GPMC.

Installing the AGPM Client

Since we learned that the best management station is a Windows Server 2016 machine or, more likely, a Windows 10 client machine, that's precisely where we'll load our AGPM client.

You load the AGPM client on the machine from which you typically manage your Group Policy.

You saw the AGPM client installation option back at Figure C.2, so we'll select it now. Again, I recommend you do this both on the server on which you installed AGPM as well as on WIN10MANAGEMENT, the machine from which you do all your Group Policy manipulations. I'll only show (and talk about) installing it once, but again, I'm suggesting you install it in both places.

After you accept the license terms, you'll be prompted for the installation directory. The defaults are fine for this. You'll then have to tell the AGPM client which server the AGPM server is running on, as well as the communication port, as seen in Figure C.7.

You'll then need to select which languages you want to install.

At this point, the client will install and you'll be done. You'll need to install the AGPM client on each Group Policy administrator's computer or that individual won't be able to participate in the Check In/Check Out system.

FIGURE C.7   Specify the server and the server port for AGPM clients.

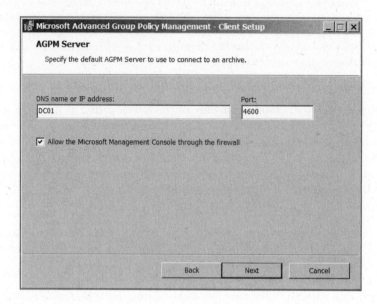

 You can also Deploy the AGPM client using Group Policy Software Installation. See Chapter 11, "The Managed Desktop, Part 2: Software Deployment via Group Policy," for more information.

What Happens after AGPM Is Installed?

Once AGPM is installed, you might want to start it up. But you'll notice there isn't any AGPM icon anywhere on the server. The server is just silently running the AGPM service, waiting as a "storage vault" for GPOs we're about to feed it.

GPMC Differences with AGPM Client

Now, if you start to plunk about in the GPMC, you'll see some subtle, but powerful, changes. First, note that if you click on a GPO or a link to a GPO, there's now a new tab, called History, as seen in Figure C.8. Indeed, you might also get an error similar to what's also seen in Figure C.8.

We'll get to that error in a second. But for now, let's finish the quick tour. You'll also notice a whole new node underneath Group Policy Objects called Change Control.

 Sometimes, the Change Control node mysteriously "floats" up to the domain level. So, be sure to check the domain level if you suddenly think, "Where's the Change Control node?"

FIGURE C.8 By default, anyone without rights will be denied access to the archive.

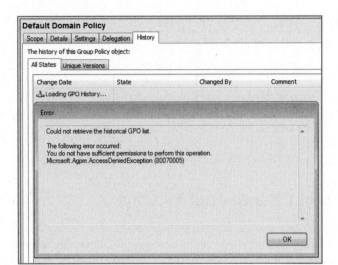

And within Change Control, there are four tabs: Contents, Domain Delegation, AGPM Server, and Production Delegation, as seen in Figure C.9. Indeed, if you click the Contents tab, you might get a similar error to what we just saw (basically, another type of Access Denied, as seen in Figure C.9).

FIGURE C.9 Access is denied for those without rights to the AGPM system.

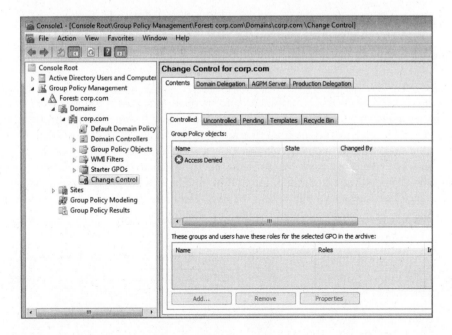

What's With All the Access Denied Errors?

So, why are you being denied? Because, even though you might be logged in as Administrator of Active Directory, you're not logged in as the person you designated to have the initial ability to own the stuff contained within the archive.

It's easy to clear this up. On your management station, log on as that user (in my case, I chose AGPM-OWNER).

Once you're logged in with that account (in my case, as AGPM-OWNER) on your management station (which already has the AGPM client installed), fire up the GPMC by selecting Start and typing `GPMC.MSC` in the Search box. Then, see if you still get those Access Denied errors.

You won't, because you're logged in as the person who owns the AGPM archive.

Does the World Change Right Away?

The goal of AGPM is to help you get a better handle on the way you create, approve, and manage GPOs. But installing the AGPM server component doesn't prevent you (immediately) from administrating Group Policy the way you always did. That is, by default, if you've got the ability to create GPOs, you can still create them. And if you've got the ability to link GPOs, you can still link them. Those powers don't go away until they're expressly taken away by the AGPM archive owner (in my example, AGPM-OWNER). By default, every GPO is considered *Uncontrolled*.

What we'll learn about next is the delegation model and how to make existing GPOs *Controlled*.

Understanding the AGPM Delegation Model

Again, each GPO can be either Controlled or Uncontrolled. The goal is to move from your current chaotic environment (Uncontrolled) to one that is orderly and neat (Controlled). To that end, we need to understand the roles that are available to us—who can do what. Once we understand that, we'll have a better chance of maintaining order going forward.

The point is to bring order from chaos. To do that, we need an ongoing process to manage our GPOs. You can start to think of the AGPM archive as a big library system. It's been *years* since I stepped into a public library (sorry, but I like the cappuccinos and lemon squares at book stores). But I remember the basic procedure:

- Find a book I want to read.
- Show my library card (which is my credential to "do something" with this book).
- Borrow the book by "checking it out" of the library. At this point, I have sole possession of this book. No one else can use it.

- Utilize the book.

- When I'm done, return it to the library in the drop slot. This doesn't mean the book immediately goes back on the shelf; it's just *pending* in the holding pen. The librarian will examine the book to make sure I didn't bend the pages or scribble in the book's margins. The book goes into the "book depository" or "book vault" or "book archive," or whatever that particular library calls it.

- If someone had requested this book while I had it checked out, it wouldn't go back on the shelf. The librarian would call the next book user and let her know the book was waiting for her behind the counter.

- If no one wanted the book, the book is put back on the shelf, sometimes called being "checked in." That way, it's ready to be leveraged by the next person.

So, neat, orderly, and systematic. That's your good ol' public library system. And that's the same idea you'll use when dealing with GPOs in AGPM. Here's the basic framework when dealing with GPOs once you get the hang of AGPM:

- Create a new GPO and put it under control (or Control a GPO that was previously uncontrolled).

- Check out the GPO so it cannot be modified by anyone else.

- Edit the GPO (again, only you have access right now).

- Return the GPO to the library by "checking it in." This doesn't mean the GPO is "live" and actively modifying clients. It's *pending* in the "holding pen" until it's approved.

- At this point, others might choose to "check out" the GPO to make more changes.

- Once all changes are made, someone Reviews the changes and makes comments.

- Finally, once all Reviews are made, someone Approves the changes and the GPO goes "live."

AGPM Delegation Roles

Because you can be one administrator in a larger company with dozens of administrators, you can have different roles for different people. You can assign different Active Directory groups to various AGPM roles, or you can assign specific people (without groups) to specific roles. Here are the AGPM roles:

Reviewer   You can see the GPO and what's been done to it. Think of this as Read-Only access to the history and settings of the GPO.

Approver   This role should have been called Approver/Reviewer, because you automatically get Reviewer rights when you get Approver rights. Approver rights allow you to "check in" GPOs from the archive into the real world. Ultimately, it's the Approver who can take offline GPO copies and make them "live" to affect the user population.

Editor   This role should be called Editor/Reviewer, because you automatically get Reviewer rights when you get Editor rights. This allows you to make changes to GPOs. But these changes aren't happening in the real world—they're being changed in an offline archive copy of the GPO, until an Approver performs a "check in," which takes the copy of the GPO and plunks it back down into the live-production GPO.

Full Control   You have full ability over all GPOs (and, of course, rights to Review all GPOs). You can dictate which GPOs are Controlled and Uncontrolled and can perform all roles with any GPOs. By default, only the named account during setup (in my world, AGPM-OWNER) is set up as Full Control.

The AGPM permissions can be a wee bit mysterious underneath the hood. There are various new levels of security within the AGPM system. On the surface, AGPM adds the following roles: Reviewer, Editor, Approver, and Full Control. In the following table, you can see the default permissions for these roles:

	Reviewer	Editor	Approver	Full Control
List Contents	X	X	X	X
Read Settings	X	X	X	X
Edit Settings		X		X
Create GPOs			X	X
Deploy GPOs			X	X
Delete GPOs			X	X
Modify Options				X
Modify Security				X
Create Templates		X		X

However, occasionally, you need to know exactly which actions a specific role is able to do. In other words, if someone is a Reviewer, Editor, Approver, or AGPM Administrator, which tasks are they able to perform (because of the permissions they have)? In the following tables, you can see the cross reference of the AGPM roles, the tasks they can perform, and the required permissions needed to perform that task.

This table shows the required permissions needed to perform domain-level tasks:

	Roles			
Domain-Level Tasks	Reviewer	Editor	Approver	Admin (Full control)
Delegate domain-level permissions				X
Configure e-mail notification				X
View mail notification settings	X	X	X	X
Create a GPO or approve creation			X	X
Request creation of a GPO	X	X		
Control an uncontrolled GPO			X	X
Request control of an uncontrolled GPO	X	X		
Create a template		X		X
Set default template for creating new GPOs		X		X
List GPOs	X	X	X	X

X—This task requires this permission.
1—Delegating GPO-level permissions requires List Contents permission at the domain level.
2—This task requires at least one of these permissions.

This table shows the required permissions needed to perform Group Policy–level tasks:

	Roles			
GPO-Level Tasks	Reviewer	Editor	Approver	Admin (Full Control)
Delegate GPO-level permissions			X	X
Deploy a GPO or Approve deployment			X	X
Change GPO links during deployment			X	X
Request deployment of a GPO		X		

	Roles			
GPO-Level Tasks	Reviewer	Editor	Approver	Admin (Full Control)
Delete a GPO archive (move to Recycle Bin/ uncontrol) or Approve deletion		X	X	X
Delete a deployed GPO or Approve deletion			X	X
Request deletion of a deployed GPO		X		
Delete a template			X	X
Destroy a GPO			X	X
Restore a GPO		X	X	X
Archive a GPO		X	X	X
Check Out a GPO		X	X	X
Edit a GPO		X	X	X
Rename a GPO		X	X	X
Label a GPO		X	X	X
Check In a GPO/undo Check Out		X	X	X
View GPO history	X	X	X	X
View reports or GPO links	X	X	X	X

3—This task requires at least one of these permissions. To perform this task, an individual who has only this permission must be the Editor who checked out the GPO.

4—Only the individual who checked out the GPO or an AGPM Admin can perform this task.

AGPM Common Tasks

In the following sections, we're going to conquer the big tasks that AGPM can do.

And we're going to do it as if we were the only administrator in the world. This isn't how AGPM is meant to be used. Indeed, it's meant to be used in a multi-domain-administrator environment—that's the point. But to get a grip on what's possible in the AGPM world, for now, anyway, we're going to leverage the AGPM-OWNER account and not one of our already-created OU admins from previous chapters.

We'll get to multiple-administrator environments just a little later in the section "AGPM Tasks with Multiple Admins." That way, you'll be able to see 100 percent of what's possible with the power of AGPM now. Then, in that section, we'll add others to the AGPM system so you can see how multiple administrators might interact with the system as a whole.

But since we know we want to use multiple administrators later, let's get set up for that and become forward-thinking. In those examples, we'll use the **Human Resources** OU with our trusty admin Frank Rizzo. In previous chapters, Frank was delegated the ability to create GPOs and also link them to the **Human Resources** OU. Figure C.10 shows what it might look like if Frank created and linked three GPOs to the **Human Resources** OU.

FIGURE C.10   Three example GPOs created outside of the AGPM system

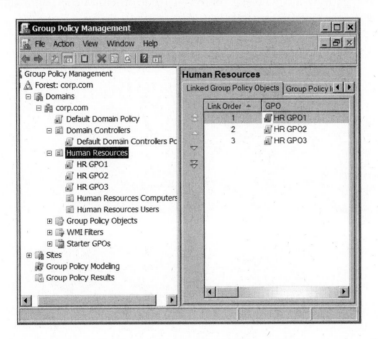

Before we go further, one key point bears repeating: only GPOs that are managed with AGPM can be checked out and checked in. GPOs that were created before AGPM was installed will continue to act as if AGPM *wasn't* installed. We'll see in a minute how to get these GPOs under *Control*.

Now, here's the kicker: Even with AGPM installed, it's still possible to shoot yourself in the foot. Using AGPM does not mean you've suddenly invested in a fail-safe method to prevent screw-ups. That's because, as we're about to learn, the only time GPOs cannot be edited (the original way) is when they're Checked Out via AGPM. We're about to work through these examples, so don't worry if you're a little confused.

Understanding and Working with AGPM's Flow

The point of AGPM is that it provides a way to wrap "history" around the birth, life, and death of a GPO. The AGPM system doesn't care as much about live GPOs as it does about GPOs that it has in its archive. Once AGPM has Control of a GPO (which really means a GPO has the ability to be manipulated by AGPM), *that's* when the magic happens. With Control, you're basically saying, "I give in, O great and powerful AGPM system!"

Once you Control a GPO with AGPM, you're ripping ownership away from the original creator. In this way, the original owner can no longer modify the live GPO, thereby affecting the GPO and making inadvertent changes everywhere it's linked. This, to me, is the biggest change between older generations of AGPM and current generations of AGPM. Again, as soon as you Control a GPO, it is no longer accessible outside of AGPM (by default).

Figure C.11 and Figure C.12 help express the flow of the birth and life of a GPO. Note that there are two paths to a GPO being "born"—outside of AGPM control (topmost circle) and inside AGPM control (leftmost circle).

FIGURE C.11   The first part of the AGPM "flow"

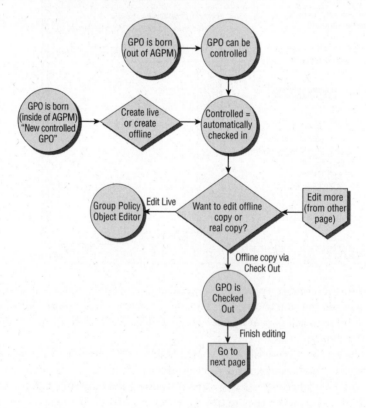

FIGURE C.12   The second part of the AGPM "flow"

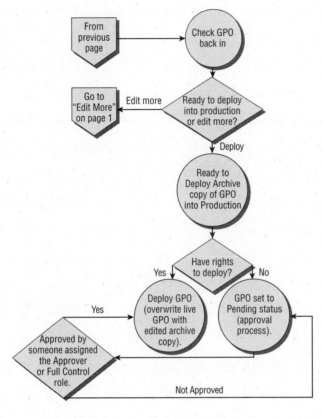

We're going to go over all the points of this flowchart now, but if you have 120 seconds, really read the flowchart to get a feel for where we're going before you continue.

At this point, if you'd like to run through these procedures with me, my suggestion is to be logged into the AGPM-OWNER account. That way, you have Full Control rights to everything we're about to try. Then, a little later, we'll see how to deal with multiple admins with various rights to the system.

Controlling Your Currently Uncontrolled GPOs

After AGPM is loaded, all GPOs are considered *Uncontrolled*. That just means that copies of the GPOs haven't been made into the archive for offline editing. And that's an important point to drive home here: the point of AGPM is to allow you to create a copy of your GPOs offline and edit the offline copies. Controlling those original uncontrolled GPOs is the first step in that process.

So, to that end, I can't see any reason not to control all GPOs. That way, you've got the ability to use the AGPM system to then Check Out GPOs (which will then prevent people from editing them) and do all sorts of awesome things.

However, for our examples, let's Control the three GPOs within Human Resources that we saw earlier in Figure C.10. To do that, we'll click the Change Control node, make sure we're on the Contents tab (at the top), and then click the Uncontrolled tab in the middle. All the GPOs in the domain should appear here. Find HR GPO1, HR GPO2, and HR GPO3. Then multi-select (by using the Ctrl key and left-clicking with the mouse) the three GPOs. Finally, right-click over them and select Control, as seen in Figure C.13.

FIGURE C.13   To get started with GPOs within AGPM, you need to take Control.

Group Policy Management	

File   Action   View   Window   Help

Change Control for corp.com

Contents | Domain Delegation | AGPM Server | Production Delegation

Search Group Policy objects

Controlled | Uncontrolled | Pending | Templates | Recycle Bin

Group Policy objects:

Name ▲	State	Changed By
AA Test	Uncontrolled	Domain Admins (CORP\Domain Admi..
Default Domain Controllers Policy	Uncontrolled	Domain Admins (CORP\Domain Admi..
Default Domain Policy	Uncontrolled	Domain Admins (CORP\Domain Admi..
HR GPO1	Uncontrolled	Domain Admins (CORP\Domain Admi..
HR GPO2	Uncontrolled	Domain Admins (CORP\Domain Admi..
HR GPO3		Domain Admins (CORP\Domain Admi..
Test123		Domain Admins (CORP\Domain Admi..

Context menu:
- History
- Control...
- Save as Template...
- Settings ▶
- Differences ▶
- Refresh
- Help

Tree (left pane):
- Group Policy Management
  - Forest: corp.com
    - Domains
      - corp.com
        - Default Domain Policy
        - Domain Controllers
        - Group Policy Objects
        - WMI Filters
        - Starter GPOs
        - Change Control
    - Sites
    - Group Policy Modeling
    - Group Policy Results

These groups ar... ...ed GPO in the archive:

Name		Roles	Inhe

Add... | Remove | Properties | Adva

Change Control

When you do, you'll be asked for a comment. You can put in anything you like here; it's just a comment for this point in time. Perhaps, "Taking control on [insert date here] by [your name]." When you do, you'll be presented (hopefully) with a Succeeded message, similar to what's seen in Figure C.14.

If you don't get a Succeeded message, read the section "Advanced Configuration and Troubleshooting of AGPM" later in this chapter for some tips that could help you out.

Now, click on the Controlled tab within the Change Control node. You'll see that these three GPOs are now Controlled. And because they're Controlled, they're automatically Checked In. You can see this status in Figure C.15.

FIGURE C.14   You can see the GPOs you just controlled.

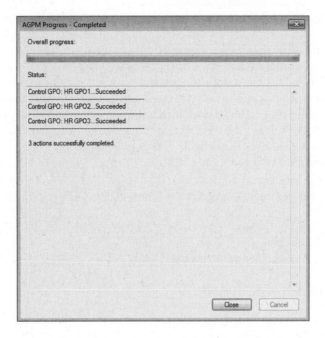

FIGURE C.15   Checked-In GPOs are now active within AGPM.

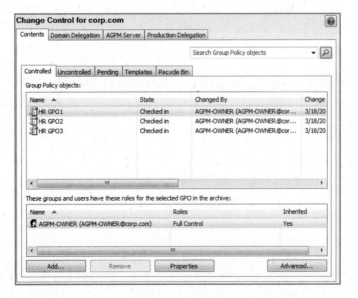

Now that they're Controlled and Checked In, you have the ability to make offline copies; it's the offline copies you can edit using AGPM.

Again, here's a big difference between older versions of AGPM and the current AGPM. That is, Frank Rizzo, who originally created these GPOs outside of the AGPM system, now cannot edit them. That's because they're Controlled by AGPM now. This is a major "hole" with previous versions of AGPM, and one I'm glad is now closed.

You can prove this in one of two ways (or you can try both). First, you can log onto another management station with the GPMC loaded and see if Frank can edit HR GPO1. Believe me, he can't. And the reason he can't is that the owner of the live GPO is changed to SYSTEM from Frank. You can see the owner by clicking the GPO, then clicking the Details tab and checking out the Owner field, as seen in Figure C.16. There, you can see that, indeed, the owner has changed to SYSTEM.

FIGURE C.16 Now that the existing GPO is Controlled, the original owner cannot modify it.

Creating a GPO and Immediately Controlling It

We just learned how we can take *existing* live GPOs and Control them. It's also possible to create brand-new GPOs directly within the AGPM system and immediately Control them. To do so, right-click over Change Control and select New Controlled GPO. When you do, you'll be prompted with what you see in Figure C.17.

Next, you can add a comment, and select "Create in archive and production" or "Create in archive only."

"Create in archive and production" will create the GPO in the archive and also put it in the Group Policy Objects node (the swimming pool). It's not linked anywhere, which means it's not affecting any levels of Active Directory yet. Note that GPOs created in this way are automatically protected from harm in the same way that other Controlled GPOs are. That is, GPOs created directly via AGPM are created with the owner as SYSTEM (or, depending on install options, the AGPM service account), as seen in Figure C.18. Again, this means only administrators who are part of the AGPM system can eventually edit them. That's because AGPM is now "in charge" of this GPO and it cannot be edited in the old (regular) way.

FIGURE C.17   Creating a new, Controlled GPO

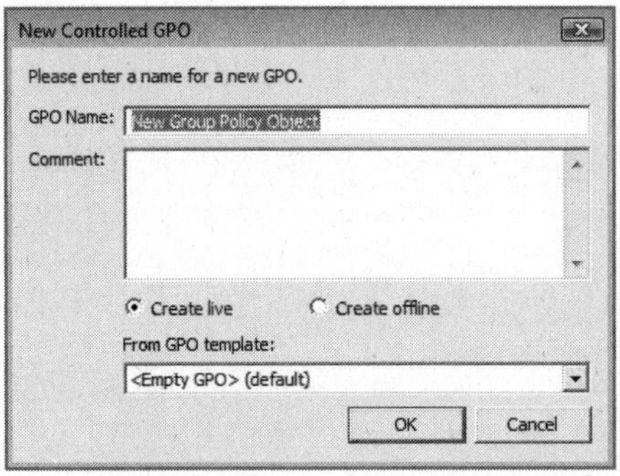

FIGURE C.18   The owner of new, Controlled GPOs will automatically be either SYSTEM or the AGPM service account.

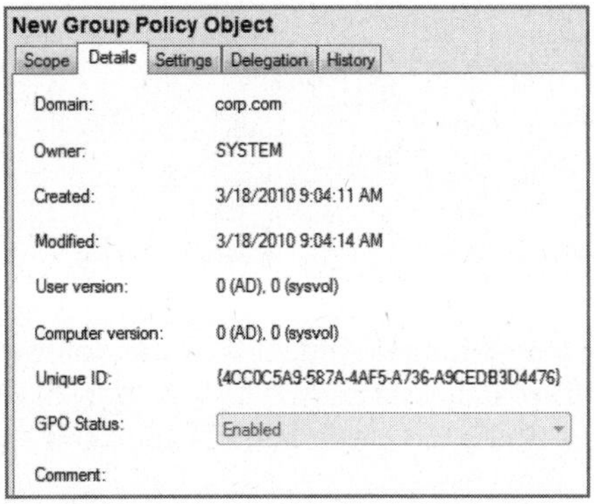

And this is what you want to strive for: ensuring that all administrators in your domain are consciously using the AGPM system for all Group Policy creation and editing functions (instead of the "live" native way directly). We'll see how to forcefully require compliance of your administrators a little later to ensure that they're using AGPM and not the native tools to manage your Group Policy universe.

Check Out a GPO

At this point, let's take AGPM for a real test-drive. Our goal is to take an original live GPO and then make a copy of it to work with offline, via Check Out. Then, we'll work with it offline.

Again, as soon as it's Controlled, only administrators within the AGPM system can manipulate it. Once it's Checked Out, then it's editable.

Let's get started. In the Change Control node, select the Contents tab (top), select the Controlled tab (middle), right-click over a GPO (like HR GPO1), and select Check Out, as seen in Figure C.19.

FIGURE C.19   You can work on a copy of a GPO if you perform a Check Out.

When you do, you'll be prompted for a comment. Perhaps you want to specify why you checked it out, say, to add Control Panel settings. The state now changes to Checked Out, a red outline surrounds the GPO, and a red check mark is added, as seen in Figure C.20.

FIGURE C.20   Checked-Out GPOs can be seen by the outline in the GPO icon (and a little check mark). This is a lot easier to see in color. The GPO is surrounded by a red border, noting that it's checked out.

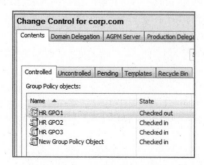

At this point, you'll be ready to edit the offline copy of the GPO that was just created.

Viewing Reports about a Controlled GPO

Now that you've got the GPO in Control, you can examine it a bit. One of the key things you'll likely want to do is to make sure it has the settings you think it has. By right-clicking over the GPO within Change Control ➢ Controlled (or other nodes within Change Control), as shown in Figure C.21, you'll be able to get a quick report of what's going on.

FIGURE C.21   You can report on GPOs in the archive in multiple ways.

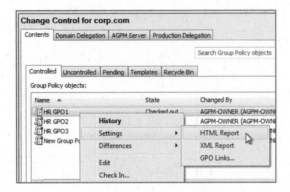

The HTML report is the most useful report here, though there might be some call for an XML report as well. Knowing where the GPO is linked is useful too, of course, and the report is a graphical demonstration of where the GPO is currently linked.

Editing a Checked-Out Offline Copy of a GPO

Again, the person who did the checking out (in our case, the AGPM-OWNER) will be able to Edit the offline copy of the GPO. But before we do that, let's understand why that's possible, and also what's happening to the "real Group Policy world" when we Check Out a GPO and make a copy of it in the archive.

What's Happening under the Hood during a Check Out

We know that when we Check Out a live GPO, we're really only creating an offline copy to work with. But where does that copy "live"? Turns out, it lives in exactly the same place all other GPOs live—the Group Policy Objects node (the swimming pool).

Here in Figure C.22, you can see that a copy of the original GPO (HR GPO1) was created and put in the archive for our editing. This is what we're about to manipulate: the Checked Out copy of HR GPO1 (the one labeled [AGPM] HR GPO1), not the live HR GPO1 itself.

FIGURE C.22   A copy of a GPO is created when it's Checked Out.

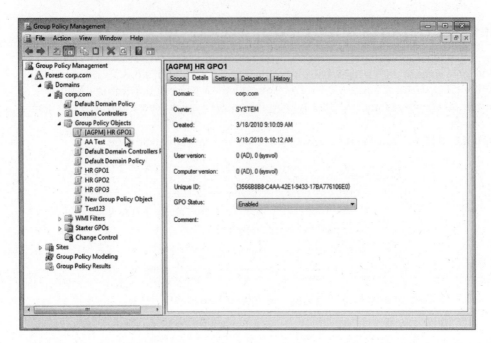

And now that the GPO is Checked Out, only the person who Checked Out the copy of the GPO can edit that offline copy.

 You may have to refresh the Group Policy Objects node to see this new Checked Out copy of the GPO.

And, looking at the Details tab of "[AGPM] HR GPO1," you can see who owns the GPO: SYSTEM or the AGPM service account. This really means that AGPM is in control of the GPO. And only those people with access rights, like AGPM-OWNER or Editors of the GPO, would have the ability to use AGPM to get to this offline copy.

And again, just to make sure we have it in our heads, let's click on the live version of the HR GPO1 and see who owns that. Back in Figure C.16, we can see that the SYSTEM also owns the *live* HR GPO1. This happened as soon as we Controlled it.

What's Not Controlled During a Check Out

When Check Out of a GPO is performed, an offline [AGPM] copy is made. But the following is still true:

- No one except AGPM participants can edit the real live GPO or the Checked-Out copy.
- Anyone, anywhere with link rights can still link or unlink to the real GPO where and when they want.

- Anyone, anywhere with link rights can Enforce or Un-Enforce the link to the GPO (in the place where they have link rights).

Therefore, don't be lulled into thinking, "Oh, if it's Checked Out, it can't do any harm to anyone." That's just not true. The Checked-Out copy is simply an offline *copy* used for editing and is not related to the live GPO until it's checked back in. Even though we're prevented from making changes to the GPO, others can still link that existing GPO and utilize it just the same.

Performing Your Offline Edit

Now that you know what's going on under the hood, let's perform an Offline Edit of the copy we made of HR GPO1. To do this, find the Checked-Out GPO in Change Control ➢ Contents ➢ Controlled, right-click over it, and select Edit, as seen in Figure C.23.

FIGURE C.23   Editing a GPO in the archive

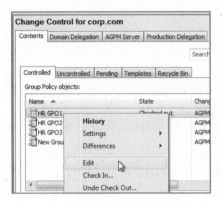

When you do, you'll see the usual Group Policy Editor (or Group Policy Management Editor). Here, let's add some settings for later use. Let's Enable the User Configuration ➢ Policies ➢ Administrative Templates ➢ Control Panel ➢ Display ➢ **Screen Saver timeout** and set it to 100 seconds.

When you're finished, exit the Group Policy Object Editor.

Again, at this point, you've edited only the offline copy of the GPO, not the live GPO. This is the point of AGPM—it allows you to perform your proposed changes offline before doing potential harm to the live GPOs.

Performing a Check In of a Changed GPO

Remember that the point of performing a Check Out of a copy of a GPO was to make sure no one else could modify that copy while I had it out. But to do anything else with this GPO (except additional editing), I have to perform a Check In.

Do this by finding the GPO within Change Control ➤ Contents ➤ Controlled, right-clicking over the GPO, and selecting Check In. When you do, you'll be able to make a comment about what you did to the GPO, like "Enabled Hide Settings Tab."

When you Check In a GPO, the little red band around the GPO icon in the Controlled tab will disappear, because it's no longer Checked Out.

Deploying a GPO into Production

Once the GPO you just edited is Checked In, you can potentially Deploy this (modified) copy into production.

The question is, are you ready? This is where you need to take a deep breath and say, "Okay, I'm ready to overwrite what's currently live in production with the changes I made offline." If you're ready to rock, just right-click over the Controlled GPO and select Deploy, as seen in Figure C.24.

FIGURE C.24   When you're ready, you can Deploy your GPO's changes into the live network.

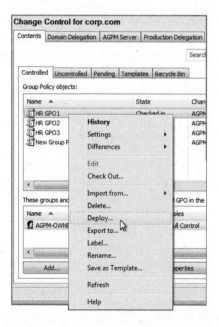

At this point, you'll be asked if you want to Deploy the GPO, as seen in Figure C.25. Clicking Yes will Deploy it immediately, maintaining the link state the links were in at the time that the *archive was created.*

FIGURE C.25   You can choose to restore original links if you so desire.

   Again, if you click Yes, it will Deploy the GPO immediately and re-link the GPOs back to the time that the *archive was created*. This is a key point. If the links for the live GPO were changed between the time the GPO was Checked Out (that is, when the offline copy was made) and *now*, you'll be rearranging links back to their original configuration.

You can click Advanced to get granular control over link restoration if you'd like. When the deployment is completed, you should get a message similar to Figure C.26.

FIGURE C.26   The output from a GPO Deploy command

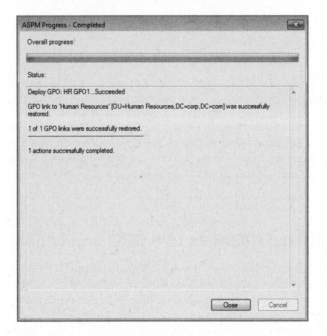

At this point, your GPO and its changes are in production, live, working hard for you!

> If you receive errors while Deploying the GPO, check out the section "Advanced Configuration and Troubleshooting of AGPM" for a tip that could help you.

Scripting AGPM Operations with PowerShell

As of this writing, AGPM isn't scriptable using PowerShell.

But it's coming. At Ignite 2015, I was given the ability to announce several updates to AGPM, specifically around the idea of scripting some of its operations.

The following pieces of AGPM will be scriptable in a (near) future version of AGPM (perhaps by the time you read this):

- View controlled GPOs

- Control a GPO

- Check-Out a GPO

- Check-In a GPO

- Deploy a GPO

- Undo Check-Out of a GPO

- Delete a GPO from AGPM

The "killer" scenario that's enabled with AGPM and PowerShell is to use some scheduled task or other trigger to use PowerShell to Deploy the GPO into Production. The trick is that the GPO will have to be all ready to go first; staged and prepped for deployment. Then after that, PowerShell can be used to Deploy that GPO live.

Making Additional Changes to a GPO and Labeling a GPO

At this point, you've got the ability to keep going back and forth. That is, you can Check Out a GPO to make an offline copy. Then, you can edit the offline copy. You can make some changes to that copy, then check it back in. You can then Deploy it on top of the live GPO.

Indeed, to continue with the next exercises, we'll need to have done that so we can inspect some additional features that AGPM provides. We'll be checking out some features like performing a rollback based on older GPOs and doing a comparison of GPOs over time.

With that in mind, let's edit the HR GPO1 by first using Check Out to create an offline copy. Then, we'll use AGPM to edit a change to the GPO copy. For instance, Enable User Configuration ➤ Policies ➤ Administrative Templates ➤ Control Panel ➤ Display ➤ **Prohibit access to Control Panel and PC settings**.

When you're ready, check in the GPO and then Deploy it into production, overwriting the live HR GPO1. Be sure to make comments so you'll know what you did during each step! You can make a comment at any time, without even making any changes to a GPO, by right-clicking the GPO and selecting Label (Figure C.27).

FIGURE C.27   You can always add a label to make your actions more clear.

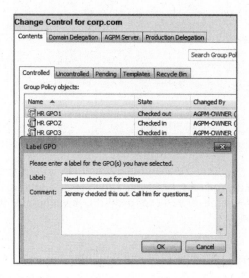

By creating a label, you get the added benefit of being able to roll back a GPO from when the label is created, a concept similar to other source control systems. We'll talk about Roll Back, well, right now.

Using History and Differences to Roll Back a GPO

So, at this point, you've modified your HR GPO1 twice. Once to Enable the **Screen Saver Timeout** policy setting and another time to Enable the **Prohibit access to Control Panel and PC settings** policy setting. You did this in three steps: Checking Out (creating a copy), Checking In the copy, and re-Deploying the copy of the GPO on top of the live GPO. So, now, the GPO is changed and live in the real world.

Now, the boss walks into your office and says he wants the Control Panel settings returned.

What are you going to do?

You're going to Roll Back the HR GPO1 GPO back to *before* you enabled the **Prohibit access to Control Panel and PC settings** policy setting. But lots of changes *could* have transpired since then. Your job now is to compare GPOs that have passed through the archive and determine which one is the right one. To get started, right-click over the GPO, select Change Control ➢ Controlled, and select History, as seen in Figure C.28.

FIGURE C.28   You can look back in time and see a GPO's history.

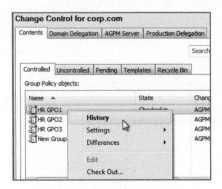

 Note that the full History view is added as an additional tab within the GPMC whenever you click on a GPO, even outside the Change Control node.

Inside the History View

The History view shows when the GPO was created and each time it was Checked In or Deployed plus the comments you added during those steps. Additionally, if you decided to label your check-ins and check-outs while working with the GPOs and their copies within AGPM, you would see an unchanged GPO with a new comment. You can see examples of the History view in Figure C.29.

 The Computer and User column display version number information. For more information about version numbers, see Chapter 7, "Troubleshooting Group Policy."

Performing a Difference Report

Assuming the comments weren't clear, this would be the perfect opportunity for you to leverage the History tab to see Difference information. To do that, hold down the Ctrl key, then click two "points in time" to compare. Right-click over one of them, and select Differences ➢ HTML Report, as seen in Figure C.30.

FIGURE C.29   A GPO's history contains time stamps, an indication of who owned the GPO, and comments. If you click on a history item, you can see its settings.

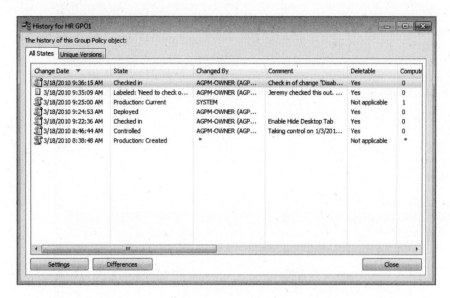

FIGURE C.30   You can create a History Differences report.

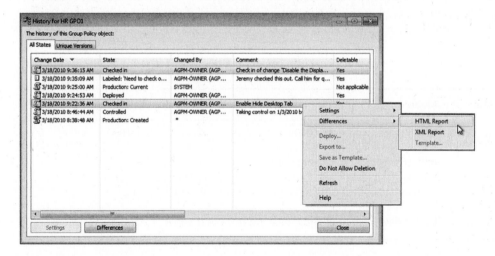

The report is displayed in a browser window as an HTML document, as seen in Figure C.31.

FIGURE C.31   History reports are color-coded to make differences easy to spot.

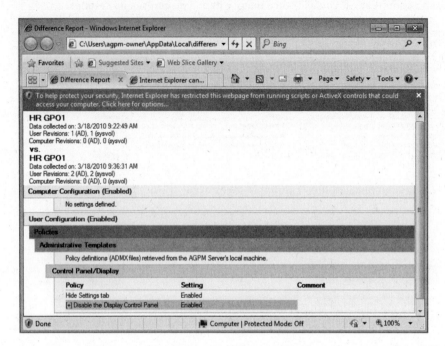

When you're comparing two GPOs, you'll see different symbols and corresponding colors to help you decipher the differences between them. Table C.1 has the breakdown of the meaning of each symbol along with its corresponding color.

TABLE C.1   AGPM reporting symbols, colors, and their meanings

Symbol	Meaning	Color
None	Same settings in both GPOs	Varies
[#]	Item in both GPOs, settings different between them	Blue
[-]	Item exists in first GPO (missing from second GPO)	Red
[+]	Item exists in second GPO (missing from first GPO)	Green

Performing a Rollback Based on a Difference

Now you've got a handle on which GPO in the history you want to Roll Back to (the one that was Checked In after the **Screen saver timeout** policy setting was Enabled but before the **Prohibit access to Control Panel and PC settings** was Enabled). Just right-click over the GP you want to Roll Back to in the History view and select Deploy, as seen in Figure C.32.

FIGURE C.32   You can use the Deploy command, which will perform a GPO Roll Back based on a History item.

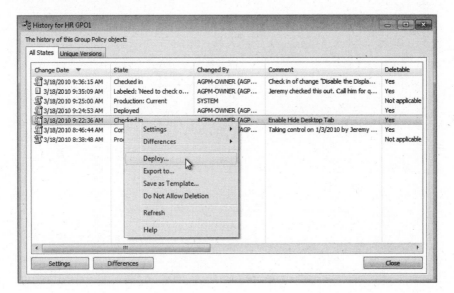

The newest History view should show that archived copy of the GPO as deployed. Just to be safe, inspect the settings of the (now live) GPO to make sure what's deployed is what you expected!

Using "Import from Production" to Catch Up a GPO

What happens if the AGPM server or service itself fails? In that instance, you would have to make live changes using the Domain Administrator account (which can *always* get into all live GPOs).

Now, when AGPM is restored (or the server comes back up, or whatever else fixes the problem), you've still got a little issue. The information in the *archive* is different (older) than what is live in *production* (newer).

If this should happen, you might want to suck the live version into the archive and compare it to one of the archived GPOs. Then, you can use the History tab to do your comparisons as you did earlier and figure out which GPO should live or die: the last known archive copy or the currently live GPO.

To bring a live GPO into the archive, you would select the controlled GPO and select "Import from Production," as seen in Figure C.33.

FIGURE C.33 Use the "Import from Production" command if the archive goes offline for a time.

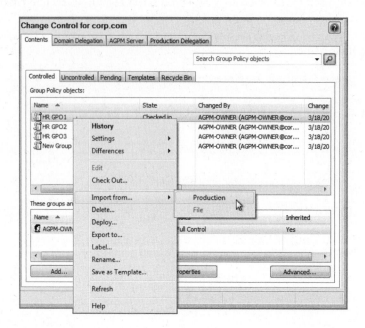

Note that we'll talk about "Import from File" a little later, and it is not related to this situation.

 You can only Import from production GPOs that are Controlled.

Uncontrolling, Restoring, and Destroying a GPO

If, for some reason, you want to take a GPO out of AGPM's universe, you need to delete it, although that's kind of a misnomer. I like to call it "Uncontrol" instead. Let's explore how to delete, I mean, Uncontrol it (and also bring it *back* into the archive, if we want to).

Uncontrolling a GPO (Deleting It from the Archive)

To do this, locate the controlled GPO in the Controlled tab and select Delete, as seen in Figure C.34.

FIGURE C.34 Deleting a controlled GPO doesn't really delete it.

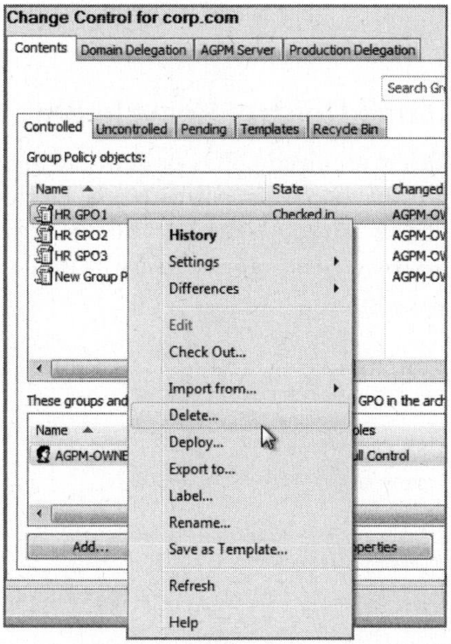

When you do, you'll be prompted with the choice you see in Figure C.35. That is, you can "Delete GPO from archive only" (uncontrol) or "Delete GPO from archive and production."

FIGURE C.35 You can choose what kind of deletion to perform.

If you select the "Delete GPO from archive only" option, the GPO moves from Controlled to Uncontrolled. All previous history is maintained; it's just not managed (right now) through the AGPM system. Interestingly, the History tab will not show all the history until the GPO is re-Controlled.

If you later want to Control it, just find the GPO (now within the Uncontrolled tab) and re-Control it.

If you select "Delete GPO from archive and production" (the second option in Figure C.35), the GPO doesn't move to Uncontrolled. This option unlinks it from anywhere it's currently deployed in the live, real world, then moves the archived GPO and its history to the Recycle Bin.

Restoring from the Change Control Recycle Bin

If you use AGPM's facility to Delete archived GPOs or to delete the GPOs from production, you're never far away from a backup. That's because the deleted archives of GPOs (or deleted GPOs themselves) end up in the AGPM Recycle Bin. If you want to recover a deleted GPO from the AGPM universe, just right-click it within the Recycle Bin tab, and select Restore, as seen in Figure C.36.

FIGURE C.36   You can use the AGPM Recycle Bin to recover old GPOs.

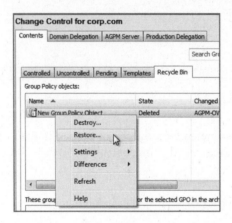

Restored GPOs from AGPM are always automatically set to Controlled.

Permanently Deleting a GPO and Its History

In the Recycle Bin, you can also right-click a deleted GPO and select Destroy. This really does delete the GPO and any surrounding history. There is no undo from this operation.

After you perform this, it's dead.

Searching for GPOs Using the Search Box

One AGPM feature is the "Search Group Policy objects" box seen anytime you're visiting the Contents tab (a good example appears in Figure C.15).

This box enables you to do a full text search across all columns for any data. For instance, if you wanted to search for "All Uncontrolled GPOs that have the word OUCH in them," then just click on the Uncontrolled tab, and in the "Search Group Policy objects," type **OUCH**.

Or, if you wanted to see which GPOs were in the Recycle Bin because of a certain person, then just click on the Recycle Bin tab and type in the person's name.

Again, the default behavior is to search across all text fields in all columns at once. If you want to get fancy and specify just one column for search, you can do things like entering **name:GPO**, which will show only the GPOs with "GPO" in the actual name.

For more help on this feature and more advanced search queries, click in the "Search Group Policy objects" box and hit F1 for detailed help.

AGPM Tasks with Multiple Admins

At this point, you've got a grip on all the major AGPM features. Between Check In/Check Out, offline editing, comparison reports, and so on, you're ready to use AGPM.

Well, that would be true if you worked on an island. But you don't. You work with other administrators.

In our previous example in this chapter, we assumed Frank Rizzo, who's in charge of the **Human Resources** OU, originally created three GPOs: HR GPO1, HR GPO2, and HR GPO3. Let's look at the whole (theoretical) gang within Human Resources):

- Eddy Cox: Eddy works for Frank. Eddy is the desktop engineer who knows the Human Resources users best. He is a good candidate for the Editor role, so he could request a new GPO (which Frank can create) and then edit the offline copy. He can then request it to go live. But, again, only Frank can Approve the GPO and put it in play. (These users weren't created in other exercises; they're new for these examples.)

- Reva Ewer: Reva is the IT department manager and is also in charge of quality assurance. She knows her way around GPOs enough to know what she's doing. Reva's a good candidate to be a Reviewer. So, Reva can see the copy of the GPO that's created and what's been done to it that makes it different from the live GPO. So, basically, we want to give her Read-Only access to the history and settings of the archived GPO. And, of course, because Reva can see what's changed, she can make recommendations to Frank if she thinks the GPO choices made within the **Human Resources** OU are unacceptable.

- Frank Rizzo is the Approver. Since it's the Approver who finally makes GPOs live, Frank will be the guy in trouble if something is put into production that wasn't sanctioned.

E-mail Preparations and Configurations for AGPM Requests

Requests for Reviewing and Editing are sent to Approvers to say yea or nay. This happens via e-mail. Exchange Server isn't *directly* supported as a transport medium. That is, you can't just say, "Here's my Exchange server," and have AGPM do all the under-the-hood connection stuff for you. But standard SMTP is, and Exchange Server can be (and is usually) set up to be an SMTP server. So, if you have an SMTP server set up already, you're almost there. Consult your Exchange admin to see if your Exchange server is honoring SMTP requests.

 If you really can't get Exchange to be an SMTP server, you might be able to set up your own SMTP server, which we explore how to do in the sidebar "Setting Up an SMTP Server for AGPM Testing." In that same sidebar, we'll set up a test SMTP server to handle our requests in the examples in this chapter.

For our purposes, just fill in the blanks in the Change Control ➤ Domain Delegation node. You can see some example values in Figure C.37. Just be sure to replace your SMTP server and username with valid names and passwords or no mail will make it to the server.

FIGURE C.37   You can specify where AGPM e-mails are sent. Note that in my testing, semicolons (not commas) were required for multiple recipients on the To e-mail address: line.

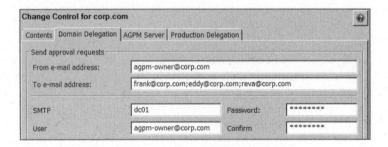

The most important line is the To: line. Only the people on the To: line will get the e-mails that the system generates (though the Requester can add people via an optional Cc:). But you'll want to be sure all Approvers are listed (or create an e-mail alias that contains the entire list of Approvers) as well as Editors and perhaps Reviewers. In my example in Figure C.37, I'm specifically listing the e-mail addresses of the AGPM participants. However, in the real world, you might want to simply have an e-mail alias for anyone participating in the AGPM system named something like "agpm-participants@corp.com," which would contain Eddy, Reva, and Frank.

Setting Up an SMTP Server for AGPM Testing

If you don't want to set up an Exchange Server with SMTP support to test AGPM requests, you can download one of about a dozen free SMTP/POP servers that will run on Windows.

I like hMailServer by a company of the same name, found at www.hmailserver.com. I like this one for several reasons:

- It's free.
- It runs on Windows Server 2003 and later.
- It works.
- It's small.
- It's super-easy to set up.
- Did I mention it was free?

There is one trick about setting it up when you want to run it on Windows Server. The Windows Firewall is turned on by default. This means if you choose to run your SMTP server (Office Mail or something else) on Windows Server, you need to also tell Windows Server to open the two mail ports we need: port 110 for POP and port 25 for SMTP.

There are multiple ways in Windows Server to achieve this goal. Perhaps the simplest is by clicking Start and, in the search box, typing **Firewall** to bring up the Windows Firewall with Advanced Security snap-in. Then right-click over Inbound Rules and select New Rule.

At the Rule Type screen, select Port, then click Next. At the Protocol and Ports screen, ensure that TCP is selected, and then, in the "Specific local ports" box, type **110,25**, as seen here.

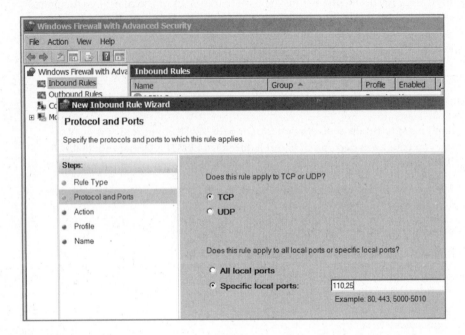

You can accept the rest of the defaults in the wizard, but at the end you must give it a name, like **MAIL PORTS**.

Once you're finished, mail can be sent to this SMTP server and then picked up with any SMTP email client (Outlook, Thunderbird . . .).

To make sure you're all set up correctly for my examples, I would set up three Active Directory users: Frank (already done), Reva, and Eddy. Then create mail accounts using Office Mail or your SMTP server. Finally, I would send test e-mails back and forth between all three to ensure that e-mail communication is flowing. After that, you can proceed to the section "Adding Someone to the AGPM System" confident that the e-mail part is working.

Adding Someone to the AGPM System

Anyone dealing with the AGPM system needs to be expressly granted access to it. And they also need to have the AGPM client installed. Let's review those pieces now.

Setting Permissions within the AGPM System

The best way to get started is to do what we did earlier. That is, map out who will use the system and which roles they will have. We've decided on the following roles for the following people:

- Frank: Approver
- Eddy: Editor
- Reva: Reviewer

Now, in this chapter, we're going to be dealing with these three people. But you could just as easily create three Active Directory groups, like these:

- AGPM_APPROVERS
- AGPM_REVIEWERS
- AGPM_EDITORS

Then use those groups and just add users to them. We're not going to do that here, but in real life, you might want to.

To add people to the AGPM system, you need to go to the Change Control node, and in the Domain Delegation tab, click Add. Once you do, you can add the three user accounts: Frank, Eddy, and Reva. Give them the permissions specified in the previous paragraph: Frank—Approver, Eddy—Editor, Reva—Reviewer.

You might also want to add the actual domain administrator as Full Control to the system, which would make it equivalent to the AGPM-OWNER. It's just a good idea in case the AGPM-OWNER is unavailable.

Right now, be sure you're using the Add button and not the Advanced button.

In Figure C.38, I've added all three users to the system, and their initial permissions are displayed under Roles.

As stated, each user is to get different permissions. And, what's more, the AGPM system doesn't automatically propagate the permissions you set (in the Domain Delegation tab) down to every GPO in the archive.

This is something we need to do manually (and it's a little tedious, so stay with me).

Click on each user, say, Frank Rizzo first, and then click the Advanced button.

You can granularly dictate the settings for Frank. Even though we're saying that Frank Rizzo is an Approver, it's likely best, in this case, to ensure that Frank has Editor rights (and also Reviewer rights) as well. You can see my suggested rights for Frank in Figure C.39. That way, if Eddy edits a copy of a GPO (offline, of course) that Frank later wants to modify, he can do so.

FIGURE C.38 These aren't the final permissions required. You'll need to click each user and select Advanced to fine-tune their security.

FIGURE C.39 Here, you can see Frank Rizzo and his permissions.

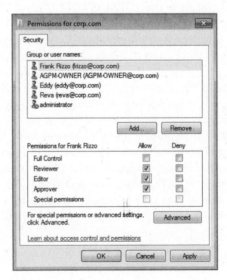

Eddy's account is fine as is, but double-check that he has only Editor rights (and Reviewer rights). You can see Eddy's rights in Figure C.40.

FIGURE C.40   Here, you can see Eddy and his permissions.

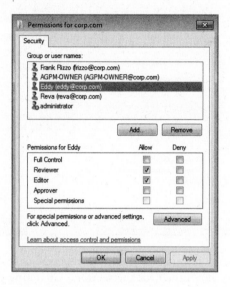

Reva's account should also be okay, but ensure that she has only Reviewer rights. You can see Reva's rights in Figure C.41.

FIGURE C.41   Here, you can see Reva and her permissions.

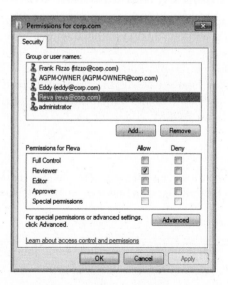

When you're finished, click OK. The total rights will be seen in Figure C.42.

FIGURE C.42   The finished permissions should look like this.

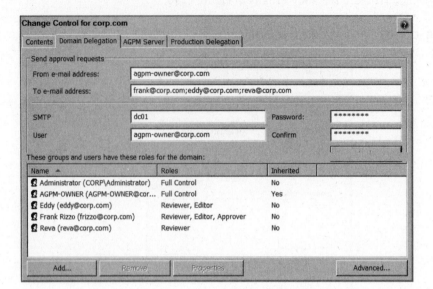

Maybe, in real life, granting Frank, Eddy, and Reva access across *all* GPOs isn't what you want. In that case, stay tuned for the section "Changing Permissions on GPO Archives," where we show you how to get even *more* granular if you have a situation where some AGPM users should have permissions to only some GPOs within the archive.

Installing the AGPM Client on Management Stations

It's likely that the AGPM system was installed by some domain administrator. And the intention, of course, is to start using AGPM as the focus point for all Group Policy management.

Therefore, all parties involved, Frank, Eddy, and Reva, have to install the AGPM client piece as we did earlier in Figure C.7. Again, the AGPM client needs to be the right one to match the operating system and match the version of the AGPM server. Usually, if you're using the latest AGPM, you want the latest client operating system, like Windows 10.

Alternatively, you can install the AGPM client on a machine with Windows Server plus Remote Desktop Services and then have everyone log on remotely.

Once the AGPM client is installed on all necessary management stations, Frank's, Eddy's, and Reva's GPMC will change so they all have the Change Control node (showing they have the potential ability to use AGPM).

Now that Frank, Eddy, and Reva all have access to the AGPM system, they should no longer get AGPM Access Denied messages as we saw in Figures C.8 and C.9.

> If, during your testing, you don't want to set up three Windows 10 management stations (one each for Frank, Eddy, and Reva), you can simply create one management station and install the AGPM client. Then use Windows's Switch User mode to allow each person to log on.

Setting Up Mail Accounts for Each AGPM User

This step has likely already been done in the real world. But if you're following along with the examples, don't forget to also set up e-mail accounts on your SMTP server for Frank, Eddy, and Reva.

Again, be sure e-mail is working between Frank, Eddy, and Reva before continuing. If mail isn't flowing correctly, your AGPM administrators won't get the signals that anything is waiting for them.

Requesting the Creation of New Controlled GPO

Eddy knows he wants to enable the **Remove Search link from Start Menu** policy setting to affect all the computers in Human Resources.

It's time for Eddy to request a new GPO.

After Eddy logs into his account, he can right-click the Change Control node and select New Controlled GPO. You can see what happens in Figure C.43.

But now that the request is coming from Eddy, who's a requestor, really an Editor, he gets prompted (again, check out Figure C.43).

At this point, Eddy can put in some comments that will go to all the people on the To: line; the most important person being the Approver (Frank Rizzo). You can see this in Figure C.43.

When Eddy clicks Submit, he'll see something similar to Figure C.44. That is, the request for a GPO gets sent into the system and an e-mail is sent of pending requests.

Even though Eddy requested a live (but Controlled) GPO, he didn't get that. He got the request submitted for that GPO. Now, it's time for the Approver to verify and Approve or Reject the request.

All he needs to do is to first check his e-mail's inboxes.

FIGURE C.43 Eddy is requesting a new GPO.

Submit New Controlled GPO Request
You do not have permissions to perform this action directly. Please complete this form and click Submit to notify the person designated to approve your request.
From:
agpm-owner@corp.com
To:
frank@corp.com;eddy@corp.com;reva@corp.com
Cc:
Subject:
AGPM : Request Creation "Remove Search Link from Start M
GPO Name:
Remove Search Link from Start Menu GPO
Comment:
The head of HR keeps asking for this for his department.
Create in archive and production
Create in archive only
From GPO template:
<Empty GPO> (default)
Submit
Cancel

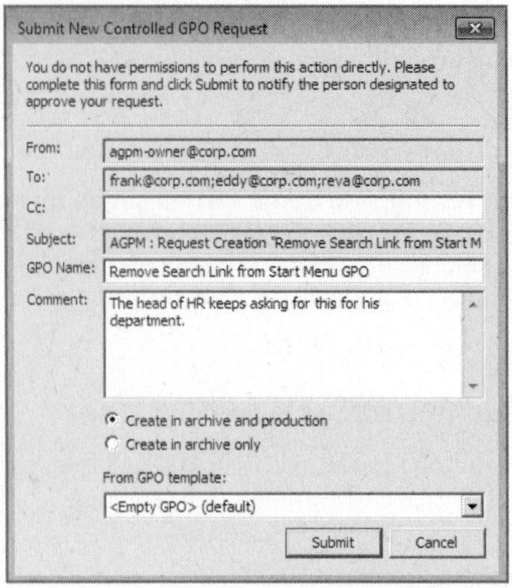

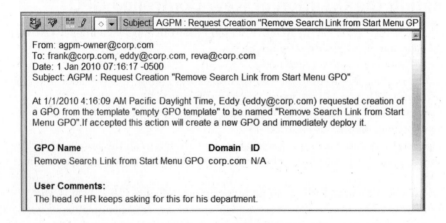

FIGURE C.44 Here's what Eddy's e-mail looks like when sent to the gang.

Subject: AGPM : Request Creation "Remove Search Link from Start Menu GP
From: agpm-owner@corp.com
To: frank@corp.com, eddy@corp.com, reva@corp.com
Date: 1 Jan 2010 07:16:17 -0500
Subject: AGPM : Request Creation "Remove Search Link from Start Menu GPO"
At 1/1/2010 4:16:09 AM Pacific Daylight Time, Eddy (eddy@corp.com) requested creation of a GPO from the template "empty GPO template" to be named "Remove Search Link from Start Menu GPO".If accepted this action will create a new GPO and immediately deploy it.
GPO Name
Domain
ID
Remove Search Link from Start Menu GPO
corp.com
N/A
User Comments:
The head of HR keeps asking for this for his department.

Approving or Rejecting a Pending Request

A pending request is Approved or Rejected in (generally) two steps. First, the Approver (Frank) receives the e-mail notifying him about a request. Then, the Approver can use the AGPM console to tend to the actual request.

E-mail Notifications from AGPM

AGPM sends notifications to everyone in the To: line. The e-mail looks like Figure C.44. It contains the following information:

- Who is doing the requesting (Eddy)
- What he wants (requested creation of a GPO)
- That he doesn't want to use a template (more on this later)
- What he wants to name the GPO
- Any comments left in the request

Tending to the Pending Request

At this point, Frank can log onto the GPMC, go to the Change Control node, and click Contents ➤ Pending to see any pending requests. Because Frank is an Approver, he can Approve or Reject the request (as seen in Figure C.45) and leave comments for Eddy in return (which will be logged in the GPO history). Some common comments can be seen in Figure C.46.

FIGURE C.45   Use the Pending tab to handle pending requests.

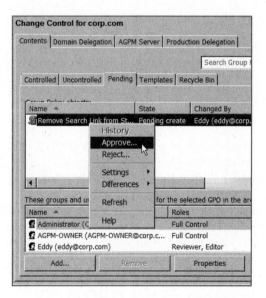

FIGURE C.46   Include a note during your approval (or rejection) of a pending request.

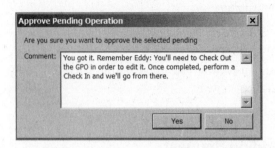

What's odd is that the original requester, Eddy, doesn't get an automatic e-mail response that this request has been tended to. This is just not something AGPM is capable of right now. So, unfortunately, Frank has to manually e-mail Eddy and tell him his request is done. This isn't the ideal workflow, and it's something you have to teach your AGPM admins to do right now.

Note that Frank could also Reject Eddy's request. The GPO is never created, and there is nothing added to the GPO's history.

Editing the GPO Offline via Check Out/Check In

As you'll recall, with AGPM, editing the actual GPO never happens live, online. To make proposed changes to the GPO, it must be Checked Out of AGPM first, where a copy is made. Then, during that time, no one else can edit the Checked-Out GPO.

This procedure is similar to what we just did. Except, this time, Eddy is performing the Check Out, since he was the one who requested the new GPO and who wants to edit the offline copy.

You can see a screen shot showing how to Check Out a GPO earlier in the chapter, Figure C.19. Once the GPO is Checked Out, Eddy can right-click it and select Edit. Eddy can now Enable the policy setting called **Remove Search link from Start Menu** as he wanted to in his request.

Once the policy setting is enabled, Eddy can then close the Group Policy Object Editor, return to the GPMC ➢ Change Control node, right-click over the GPO, and select Check In. He can leave comments about what he did for others to read, as seen in Figure C.47.

Requesting Deployment of the GPO

Now that Eddy has made his proposed changes to the GPO, he can request deployment. He simply right-clicks over the GPO and selects Deploy. You can see how to Deploy a GPO earlier in the chapter, in Figure C.24.

FIGURE C.47 You can add comments when Checking In a GPO.

When he does this, he can put comments in for the Reviewers, as seen in Figure C.48—though, again, the e-mails always go to everyone on the To: line. The system just isn't granular enough to send the e-mail *only* to Reviewers.

FIGURE C.48 AGPM users can submit deployment requests.

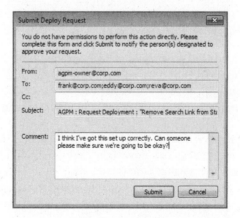

When Eddy clicks Submit, the e-mails go out. The example e-mail can be seen in Figure C.49. Reva, the quality-assurance (QA) person, reads the e-mail, so she knows she has something to do.

FIGURE C.49   Deployment requests get sent to all AGPM users via e-mail.

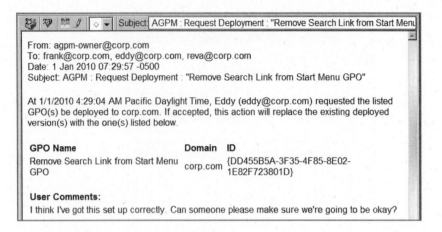

At this point, it's up to someone with Reviewer, Editor, or Approver rights to ensure that Eddy did what he was supposed to in the GPO.

> It's also possible for Eddy to realize he made an error while manipulating the GPO. If he wants to, he can right-click over the GPO again and Withdraw his request. The GPO will return to the Controlled tab.

Analyzing a GPO (as a Reviewer)

Eddy's e-mail made it to all Editors, Reviewers, and Approvers. Who's going to deal with Eddy's request? Well, that depends on who has the ability as a Reviewer over the GPO copy that Eddy has in the archive.

Reva, the QA person, is going to ensure that the Group Policy settings are valid before they go into production.

Earlier, we made Reva a Reviewer of all GPOs in the archive, and therefore, Reva should be able to review Eddy's changes. Reva can now right-click over a GPO that Eddy created and view the HTML report of the settings contained inside, as seen in Figure C.50.

Reva cannot Approve or Reject Eddy's work. But she could shoot an e-mail to the team expressing concern if need be. Only Approvers (like Frank) can ultimately Approve (Deploy) a GPO into production.

Deploying a GPO into Production

At this point, Frank can log on, find the GPO that Eddy created on the Pending tab, and choose to Approve or Reject it, as seen in Figure C.51. Approving will redeploy the GPO into production. Rejecting it will leave it Controlled but not put it into production.

FIGURE C.50   Reva can review the changes via an HTML report.

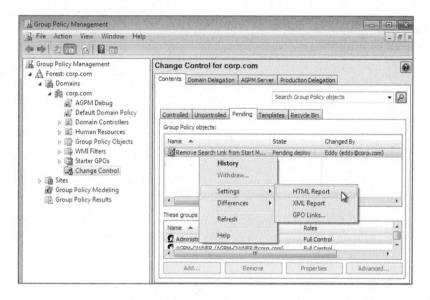

FIGURE C.51   Frank can Approve the GPO that was created.

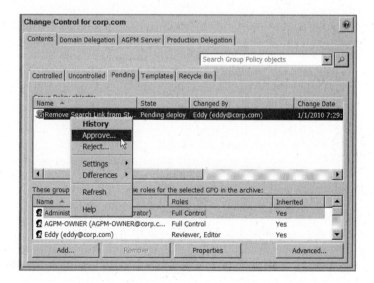

Advanced Configuration and Troubleshooting of AGPM

AGPM is a big place with some big power. In the following sections, we'll examine some less-often-used features, like templates and forest-to-forest migration, and also learn how to set up specific permissions within AGPM, perform some AGPM troubleshooting, and other odds and ends.

Production Delegation

This section, seen in Figure C.52, has a weird name. It's called "Production Delegation" but, in my opinion, should have been called "Permissions after Deployment."

FIGURE C.52　You can specify that you want to stamp these additional permissions upon a GPO when it's deployed.

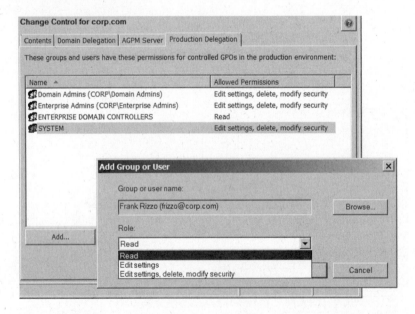

Because that's what this section does.

Remember, when the GPO is Controlled, the service account (seen as SYSTEM in the GPO's Owner field) owns the account and strips permissions away so that people in the live world cannot manipulate the GPO. Makes sense.

But when a GPO is Deployed from the archive into the real world, you may want to have certain rights upon that GPO stamped down. For instance, you might want certain people to be able to Edit the GPO, live, in production, even outside of AGPM. Usually not—but you can do it, here, using the Production Delegation tab. The folks listed in this section, with the rights alongside them, are stamped down upon the GPO when it finally goes live.

Auto-Deleting Old GPO Versions

If you have a lot of changes, you're storing a lot of old data in the archive. Maybe you don't care that two years ago, three changes were made. You're concerned about the last five changes, and that's it.

If you'd like, you can turn on auto-deletion of older archived GPOs, as seen in Figure C.53. This is a new feature of AGPM.

FIGURE C.53   You can specify how many old copies to keep in the archive before auto-deleting.

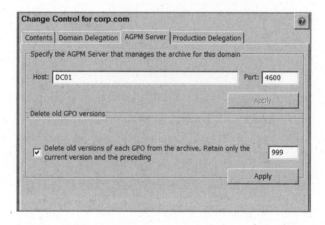

Export and Import of Controlled GPOs between Forests and/or Domains

In many bigger companies, having AGPM to be the "gatekeeper" isn't enough. Some companies want to test their GPOs in a test lab first (good idea) and then bring those GPOs from the test lab into the real world.

Great. But if in the real world you're using AGPM, how are you going to move those GPOs from the test lab AGPM system to the real-world AGPM system?

Export and Import, of course! (Again, a new feature of AGPM.)

You can Export any Controlled GPO in the archive. Just right-click and select "Export to," as seen in Figure C.54.

FIGURE C.54   You can Export to a plain old .CAB cabinet file.

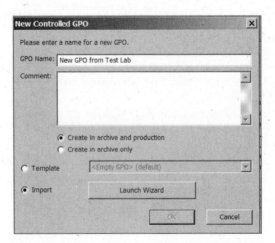

When you have the GPO (now a file) exported, you can then move it via USB stick, network cable, or carrier pigeon from your test lab AGPM setup to your real-world AGPM (or vice versa).

Then, in the target AGPM system, create a new GPO. Specify to Import and select Launch Wizard, as seen in Figure C.55.

FIGURE C.55   Use the Import Wizard to import an existing .CAB file.

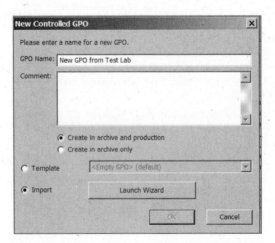

The Import Wizard can use exactly the same migration tables we already created in Chapter 2.

When finished, you'll have a fully copied (migrated) GPO from the source AGPM system, now in the target AGPM system. Note that you can also use the Import from ➢ File menu on any Checked-Out (existing) GPO and perform an Import. That way, you don't have to create a new GPO; you can leverage an existing GPO and wipe out its contents.

Here's the only "extra bonus" you get from using the AGPM Export and Import processes (as opposed to the "free" built-in migration tables stuff we learned in Chapter 2, specifically in the section "Migrating Group Policy Objects Between Domains." Group Policy Preferences' references will be processed by the AGPM migration tables' Import process. The built-in (free) migration tables process will not do this.

Troubleshooting AGPM Permissions

When setting up AGPM, you can either choose to use the SYSTEM account, if you're installing it on a Domain Controller, or choose a domain account, like AGPM-OWNER. Picking the latter option can sometimes mean additional headaches, which we'll solve here.

Trouble Deploying Controlled GPOs

Sometimes, it seems that you can't deploy controlled GPOs. You'll get an error stating, "Could not take ownership of the deployed GPO," like what you see in Figure C.56.

FIGURE C.56   A GPO permissions problem prevents Controlling GPOs.

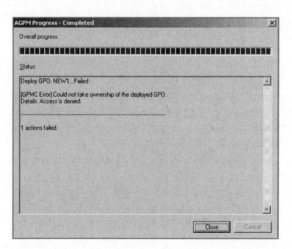

To fix this, you can change the permissions on the GPO itself so that the AGPM service account (such as AGPM-OWNER) has "Edit settings, delete, and modify security" on the particular Group Policy Object. You can do this by clicking on the GPO itself and selecting the Delegation tab to edit who has access to the GPO directly. We cover the how tos in detail in Chapter 2.

However, you can also use a script we developed in Appendix A, "Scripting Group Policy Operations with Windows PowerShell," with a quick trip backward to utilize a cmdlet we learned there.

The cmdlet is named Set-GPPermissions and can be executed with the -all, -user, and -permission switches together. This will append a selected user (the AGPM-OWNER account) to the ACL of all GPOs in the domain, with a chosen permission level: Full Control (also known as the fun-to-type GpoEditDeleteModifySecurity).

Here is how to use the GPO cmdlet (and you can see the run of the cmdlet in Figure C.57):

```
Set-GPPermissions -all -TargetName "Corp\AGPM-OWNER" -TargetType
User -PermissionLevel GpoEditDeleteModifySecurity
```

FIGURE C.57   Use a cmdlet from our scripting chapter to affect all exiting GPOs so the AGPM-OWNER account has rights to the "live" GPOs.

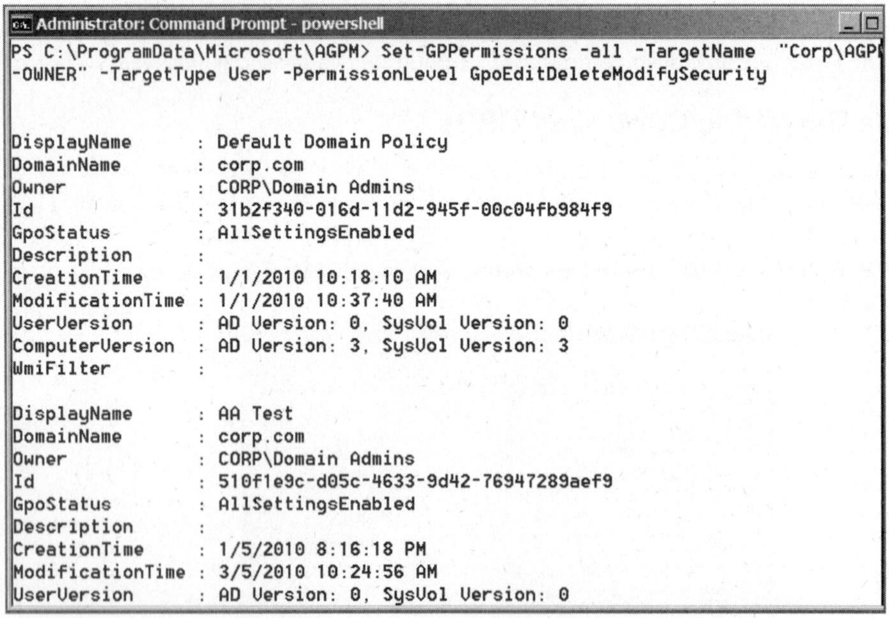

And voilà, the PowerShell script modifies the permissions of all GPOs in the domain, appending the selected user account.

After this, you will be able to Deploy your controlled GPOs using AGPM because the AGPM-OWNER account now has permissions to the real GPO.

Trouble Creating New Controlled GPOs

Similarly, you might encounter a situation where you cannot create new Controlled GPOs within AGPM. You might get an error similar to the one you see in Figure C.58, which is "Access is denied."

FIGURE C.58   An error you might see when creating new Controlled GPOs within AGPM.

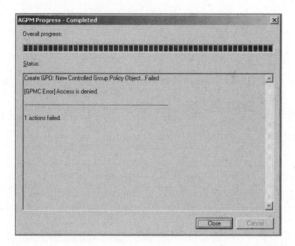

If you encounter this, you likely need to delegate the AGPM service account (such as AGPM-OWNER or AGPM-SERVICE) permissions to Create GPOs in the domain.

Again, this is in the Delegation node within the Group Policy Objects container, within GPMC. I describe how to set these permissions in Chapter 2.

Leveraging AGPM Templates

In Chapter 2, you learned about the concept of Starter GPOs. Starter GPOs are available when your management station has the updated GPMC loaded.

However, Starter GPOs are very limited. They only allow you to preserve the settings within Administrative Templates as the starting point when you're creating GPOs.

AGPM's Templates feature goes a lot further. It allows you to preserve just about every possible setting within a GPO. Then, when a new Controlled GPO is requested, a new GPO is stamped out with all those original settings.

Making a GPO into a Template

The first step in making a template is to make a new Controlled GPO. You might want to give it a name that's indicative of what you want to do with it. In this example, Frank Rizzo, who has Approver rights and therefore can immediately create new Controlled GPOs, can do just that—create a new Controlled GPO as a starting point.

Next, you'll need to Check Out the new GPO. You can't Edit a GPO unless it's Checked Out. Edit the GPO to preserve the template settings. You might want to create templates for all sorts of situations because you can plunk any Group Policy items within the template. Just think about it. You can have templates that consist of the following:

- Administrative Templates
- Security settings

- Deployed printers
- Group Policy Preference Extensions
- Or anything else your heart desires

Before you Check In the GPO, right-click over it and select "Save as Template," as seen in Figure C.59.

FIGURE C.59 You can create a template from an existing Controlled GPO.

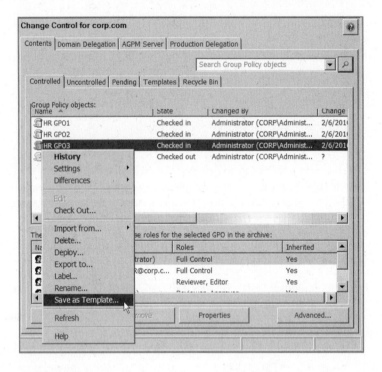

Then, you'll be able to give the template a name and add some salient comments, as seen in Figure C.60.

FIGURE C.60 Adding a comment to a new template

Spawning a New Controlled GPO Based on a Template

At this point, new Controlled GPOs can either be based on no template (or, really, the default template named "<Empty GPO>") or be based on the template you just created.

People making new requests for creating GPOs can choose the template. They can do this while in the Submit New Controlled GPO Request dialog box, as shown in Figure C.61, or by clicking the Templates tab, locating the template, right-clicking over it, and selecting New Controlled GPO.

FIGURE C.61   Creating a GPO from an existing template

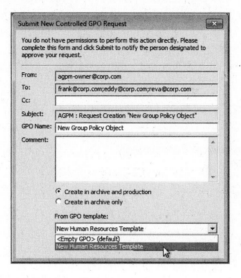

Setting the Default Template

If you'd like, you can set the default template, which is used whenever anyone creates a GPO, by right-clicking over the template and selecting "Set as Default." Note that anyone with Editor rights can set the default template.

Editing a Template

Briefly, once you save a template, you cannot edit it. It's essentially frozen in time forever. However, if you want to, you can do the following procedure, which is almost like editing a template:

1. Create a new Controlled GPO from the template.

2. Edit the GPO.

3. Save it as a template with a darn-similar name (because you can't have two templates with the same name).

4. Put the original template in the Recycle Bin.

5. Destroy the original template in the Recycle Bin.

6. Rename the new template with the original name.

Finding Differences between a Deployed GPO and a Template

One of the great things about templates is that you can do "spot auditing" for differences between a controlled GPO and a template. Indeed, you could consider some templates to be baseline security, depending on how you use them.

With that in mind, to see how far changed HR GPO1 is from a specific template (for instance, the one that created it), just right-click over the GPO and select Differences ➢ Template, as seen in Figure C.62; then pick the template you want to compare.

FIGURE C.62 You can create a Difference report between a GPO and a template to see variations from the original.

The output will be similar to other reports. Blue lines with pound signs (#) designate that the same GPO is in both. Plus signs (+) with green lines designate that some setting was added since the template was made. The minus sign (–) with red lines means that some setting was subtracted since the template was made.

See Figure C.31 for an example report that will be similar to Difference reports.

Changing Permissions on GPO Archives

In Figure C.42, we saw how Frank, Reva, and Eddy all had access to the AGPM system. We did this via the Domain Delegation tab. And adding them using the Add button made sure they received rights that allowed them to travel through the AGPM system Reviewing, Editing, and Approving requests.

However, you can, if you want, add someone else to a single GPO within the archive. This can be performed only on a Controlled GPO. So, for instance, if someone else (not normally part of the AGPM system) needed rights to manage one GPO in the archive, you could grant it to them.

To do this, click on the Controlled GPO, then click the Advanced button in the lower right. This will bring up the permissions for the GPO in the archive. Then, as seen in Figure C.63, I've added Nurse1 to the Controlled HR GPO2.

FIGURE C.63   You can grant permissions to an AGPM user for a single GPO.

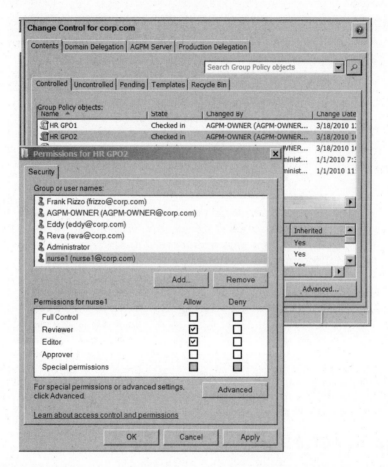

By default, when you click Add and select a user, the user gets Reviewer and Editor rights. After that, you can tailor the permissions to specifically what you need (again, seen in Figure C.63).

Backing Up, Restoring, and Moving the AGPM Server

Because AGPM is a single point of failure, you need a backup. And this backup can be moved/restored to any server. But it's certainly easier to bring up a server with the same name as the original AGPM server and restore it to the same location.

In my original example, I installed the AGPM server on DC01 and put the archive within C:\AGPM-ARCHIVE (a change from the defaults, which we talked about earlier). You can see the archive in Figure C.64.

FIGURE C.64   The GPOs in the archive are just files in directories.

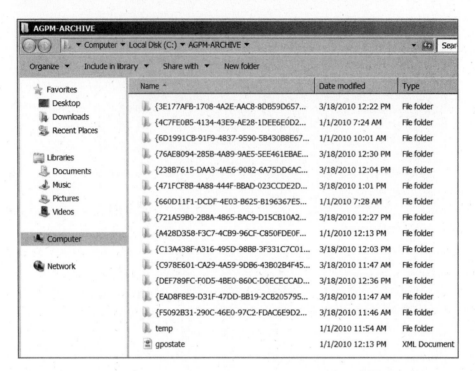

The AGPM archive consists of directories and a handful of files—just plain old regular directories and files, with backups of Group Policy Objects within them and some pointer files (gpostate.xml and manifest.xml) to help keep some order to the place.

Backing Up the AGPM Server

To back up the AGPM server, just copy the whole AGPM-ARCHIVE directory to another safe location for easy access. You can schedule this action.

It's likely a good idea to stop the AGPM service running on the server, though, to ensure that no users are currently in the middle of making Group Policy Check-Outs/Check-Ins.

Of course, the whole process can be scripted and scheduled to happen, say, nightly, if desired.

Restoring the AGPM Server

Restoring the AGPM server is simple: get a new machine to house the AGPM server. Then, install the server as you did earlier. Again, I suggest you specify a directory like C:\AGPM-ARCHIVE for the archive. You can specify the same service account you used earlier and the account that will own the AGPM archive (AGPM-OWNER).

Then, once it's fully installed, stop the AGPM service.

Traverse to the directory, and copy in the backed-up files. Make sure the gpostate.xml and manifest.xml files are in the root of the archive.

Finally, once they're all copied, start the AGPM service on the server.

> You might have one file in the newly created server called gpostate.xml. During a restore, just rename that file gpostateold.xml.

Changing the Location of the Clients to the New Server

During this period of restoring (or moving) the AGPM server, your AGPM administrators won't be able to access it. When they click on the Change Control node, they'll get a message similar to what's seen in Figure C.65. Actually, they'll see this message whenever the AGPM service is stopped for any reason.

FIGURE C.65   You'll get an AGPM error if you choose to restore to a different server.

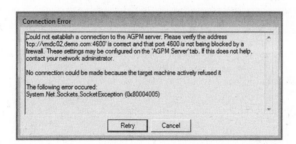

At this point, if you've restored back to the same server, your clients should be A-OK and seeing the same data in the archive they saw before the incident.

However, if you changed the name of the server, you'll need to change the AGPM client to point to the new AGPM server. If you don't get the updated server name correct, you'll see what's in Figure C.66.

FIGURE C.66 You'll get an AGPM client error if it cannot find the AGPM server.

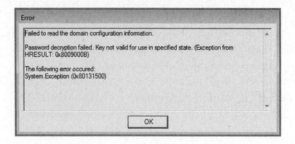

 WARNING Remember, you'll also need to explicitly open the AGPM port for inbound communications. The default is port 4600.

Finally, your restore isn't complete until you set the SMTP and e-mail settings, including spelling out who should be on the From: and To: lines as well as setting the SMTP server name and putting back in the password. Also remember to use semicolons, not commas, between names on the To: line. If you don't finish these steps, you might see what's in Figure C.67.

FIGURE C.67 Another AGPM error regarding SMTP configuration during restore

Once those steps are completed, you've successfully restored your AGPM server.

Changing the Port That AGPM Uses

If for some reason after AGPM server installation you need to modify the port that AGPM uses, the procedure is very simple. Just stop the AGPM service, locate the gpostate.xml file (in the root of the AGPM archive), locate the line that says Agpm:port="4600", change the port number, restart the AGPM service, and finally, change the port on the AGPM client to match.

Events from AGPM

I wish I could tell you that AGPM had rich event reporting in the Event Viewer. It doesn't. Take a look at Figure C.68.

FIGURE C.68   All AGPM events seem to be the same Event 2005, and they all seem to be about successful restores of GPOs.

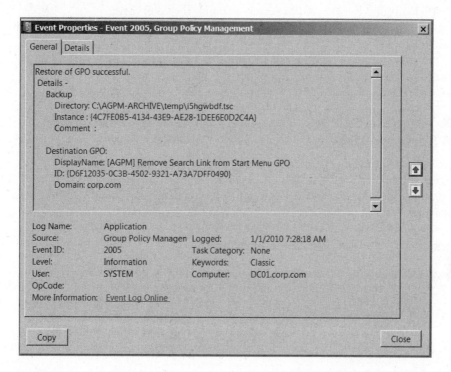

With AGPM, you'll see events from the source named "Group Policy Management." These events are not actually being generated by AGPM but instead are the results of actions taken by AGPM. You might also see events if you manually back up and restore Group Policy Objects via the Group Policy Management Console.

If you want detailed reports of what's transpiring between the AGPM client and AGPM server, you need to turn on AGPM tracing. See the section "AGPM Tracing Clients and Servers" a little later.

Leveraging the Built-in AGPM ADMX Template

In Chapter 6, "Managing Applications and Settings Using Group Policy," you learned about ADM and ADMX files and how ADMX files are the newer technology to control an application's settings. When you load the AGPM client, it also puts an ADMX file on your system in the \Windows\PolicyDefinitions directory. This file can help you manage both your AGPM servers and your AGPM clients. (Again, an AGPM client means a management station that has the AGPM management piece installed.)

To use the AGPM ADMX template, simply create a new GPO and link it to the location you want to manage. To leverage the policy settings on the User side, you might want to create an OU called **People who can manage GPOs via AGPM** and link the GPO there.

Or, to leverage the policy on the Computer side, you might want to create an OU called **Our AGPM clients** and/or **Our AGPM servers** and link the GPO there.

You can see the AGPM settings in Computer Configuration ➤ Policies ➤ Administrative Templates ➤ Windows Components ➤ AGPM and in User Configuration ➤ Policies ➤ Administrative Templates ➤ AGPM and also another node parallel to AGPM called Microsoft Management Console.

Let's run down the things the ADMX template is capable of performing.

ADMX Template Settings That Tell Your AGPM Client Which AGPM Server to Use

There are two curiously named settings within User Configuration ➤ Policies ➤ Administrative Templates ➤ Windows Components ➤ AGPM, as seen in Figure C.69. They're named **AGPM: Specify AGPM Servers** and **AGPM: Specify default AGPM Server (all domains)**.

FIGURE C.69   The two AGPM settings on the User side

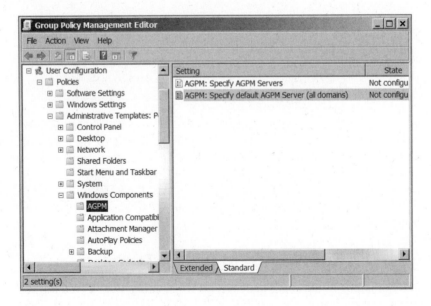

You can choose to use one, both, or neither of these settings.

Let's say you had OU administrators who all needed to use the same AGPM server. No problem—you might link a GPO to the domain level (therefore ensuring that every OU administrator got the GPO) and use agpm.corp.com as your AGPM server.

That's great. Except for a small handful of OU admins contained within an OU named **AGPM Testers**. In this OU, they need to use another AGPM server (testagpmserver.corp .com), which is online just for testing purposes.

So, you've got two policy settings. One policy setting, **AGPM: Specify default AGPM Server (all domains)**, would be used to tell the AGPM client which server to use normally (agpm.corp.com). Buuut you might consider linking a GPO containing settings within the policy setting named **AGPM: Specify AGPM Servers**, which overwrites any defaults that might be set via the **AGPM: Specify default AGPM Server (all domains)** setting.

You can see how to use the **AGPM: Specify AGPM Servers** policy setting in Figure C.70.

FIGURE C.70   Setting the AGPM: Specify AGPM Servers policy setting

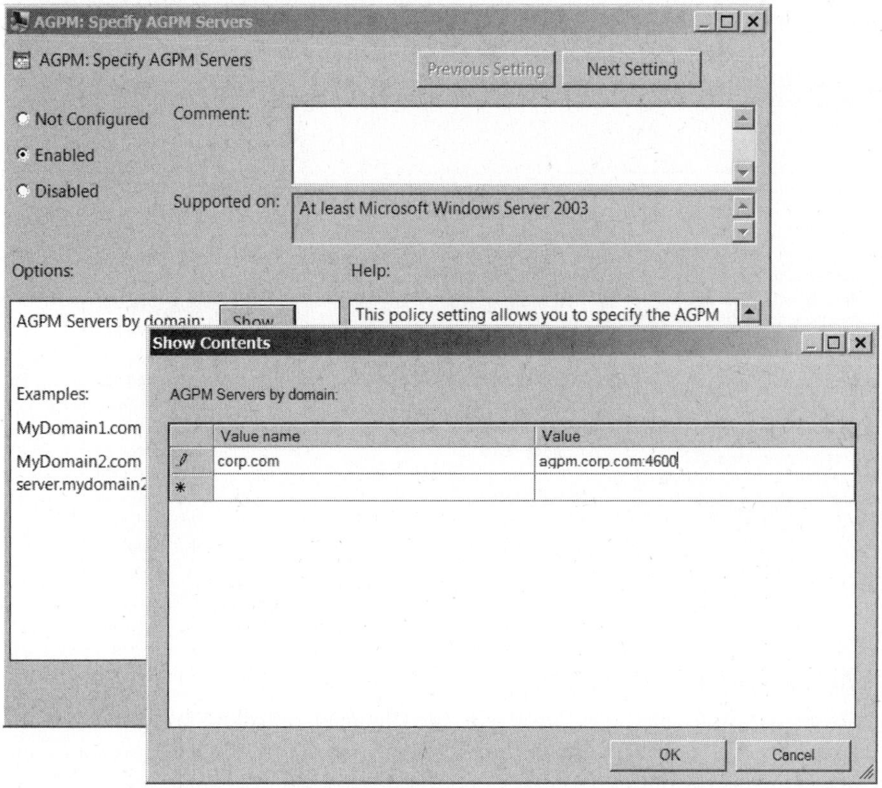

It's a little counterintuitive, I know. So, here it is in a nutshell: if you have a conflict between **AGPM: Specify AGPM Servers** and **AGPM: Specify default AGPM Server (all domains)**, then **AGPM: Specify AGPM Servers** is meant to be the more specific setting, so it will win.

And, a quick warning: In my tests, if the setting was already set locally, this policy setting didn't always apply. So be sure not to set up the AGPM client manually if you're planning on using these Group Policy ADMX templates and their settings.

Honing the AGPM Client View

Dive down into User Configuration ➤ Policies ➤ Administrative Templates ➤ Windows Components ➤ Microsoft Management Console ➤ Restricted/Permitted snap-ins ➤ Extension Snap-ins and there are three policy settings that let you further restrict who can do what within the AGPM client. You can see them in Figure C.71.

So, without further ado, here's the breakdown.

FIGURE C.71   You can further refine which snap-ins and tabs are shown within the GPMC and AGPM.

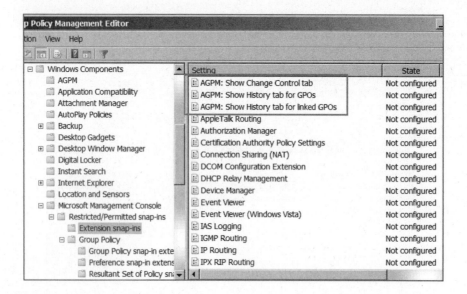

AGPM: Show Change Control Tab

If this policy setting is Disabled (yes, Disabled), the Change Control node will not be shown. Might be useful if anyone *except* the people part of the AGPM cabal in your company inadvertently installs the AGPM client. That way, they won't be tempted to click on the Change Control node and get an Access Denied error message.

AGPM: Show History Tab for Linked GPOs

If this policy setting is Disabled (yes, Disabled), the History tab goes away within the GPMC. This occurs for the History tab over linked GPOs and makes History unavailable within the Change Control node.

Might be useful when someone's job is just to request GPOs and they shouldn't see any history of past GPO implementations.

AGPM: Show History Tab for GPOs

If this policy setting is Disabled (yes, Disabled), the History tab is removed from GPOs that are not linked (just in the swimming pool). That is, you'll see the History tab only on GPOs that are linked.

AGPM Tracing Clients and Servers

In Figure C.72, you can see the setting for AGPM logging.

FIGURE C.72   You can set AGPM logging (for both server and client) using Group Policy.

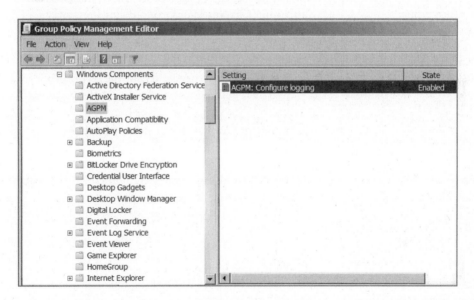

What's interesting about this policy is that the same policy (when Enabled) can affect either AGPM clients or AGPM servers. So, just create the GPO and link it over to the OU containing either AGPM clients or AGPM servers.

Enabling the policy setting and affecting an AGPM client turns on tracing and puts a log in %LocalAppData%\Microsoft\AGPM\agpm.log.

Enabling the policy setting and affecting an AGPM server turns on tracing and puts a log in `%ProgramData%\Microsoft\AGPM\agpmserv.log`.

You can experiment with this to see the logging levels. Indeed, I recommend you do this before there's an AGPM problem, so you can get a feel for what's possible when logging is enabled.

Final Thoughts

AGPM is neat. But it's an investment. Not only is it an investment in terms of money, it's also an investment in terms of time.

Remember that, by default, just because AGPM is deployed doesn't mean that the original owners can't modify the original live GPOs. To prevent that, you'll need to take Control of the GPO. When you do that, the original owner is changed to SYSTEM or the AGPM-OWNER account (or whatever you called it during setup). So in this way, the previous owner is prevented from manipulating that GPO, and that's a good thing.

AGPM doesn't care if you use technologies like the Central Store, ADM files, custom ADM files, or custom ADMX files (all within Chapter 6) or Group Policy Preference Extensions (Chapter 5).

When it comes to third-party Group Policy extensions and AGPM, not every Group Policy add-on is compatible. That's because the way those tools store their data could be outside of the way AGPM knows how to back it up and restore it. For the record, PolicyPak (Chapter 6) and AGPM work perfectly together, and there's a video on the PolicyPak website at

```
http://www.policypak.com/integration/policypak-group-policy-change-
management-utilities.html
```

to help demonstrate them working together.

Remember the key point: you want install AGPM on the latest Windows Server machine because that archive power relies on the underlying server host.

Also, before I forget, I also wrote an AGPM "Myths and Facts" article, which Microsoft picked up on their website. You can find it here:

```
http://tinyurl.com/agpm-myths
```

One final note: If AGPM isn't affordable or available to you, there are other non-Microsoft ways to accomplish similar tasks. Tasks such as working together as a team, checking out a GPO, deploying, roll-back, and so on.

If you look at the video link I gave you regarding AGPM and PolicyPak, I demonstrate several other AGPM-like systems which are available in the marketplace for you to check out.

Security Compliance Manager

Microsoft has a free tool called Security Compliance Manager (SCM) to help you get your desktops and servers more secure.

Its job is to give you prescriptive guidance from Microsoft, and that advice is automatically download it into the SCM tool. Once it's there, you can look up Microsoft's suggestions for how to secure, say, Exchange, Internet Explorer, Microsoft Office, Windows client and server, or anything else for which Microsoft produces a *baseline*.

A baseline is a collection of suggestions complete with documentation to help you make a system more secure.

As of this writing, the SCM doesn't yet have Windows 10 baselines, so I'll be using Windows 8 baselines in my examples.

If you love Microsoft's suggestions within the baseline, wonderful. You can export those suggestions as GPOs or other formats (we'll talk about those later).

If you think the suggestions are "too much" or "too little," you can copy a particular baseline and then modify the copy. For instance, maybe the Windows 8 Computer Security Compliance baseline has something locked down but you know you need it open. That's okay. You just copy the Microsoft version of the baseline and make the change in your copy.

Then, once that's complete, you export your changed version to a GPO (or other format).

The SCM tool, once up and running, looks like Figure D.1.

It's pretty easy to get SCM installed. Let's talk about that first before we do anything else.

FIGURE D.1   SCM once up and running. Note the three highlighted sections.

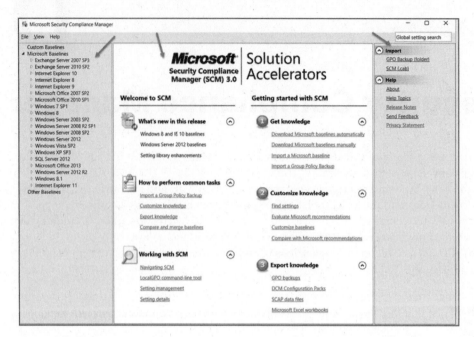

SCM: Installation

SCM itself can be installed on Windows 7 and later. These examples show how to install it on a Windows Server 2012 machine.

Download SCM here:

`www.microsoft.com/scm`

The installation requires the .NET Framework. On Windows Server 2012 and later, open the Server Manager, click "Add Roles and Features," select .NET Framework 3.5 Features, and then choose ".NET Framework 3.5 (includes .NET 2.0 and 3.0)," as seen in Figure D.2.

Once the preceding steps are performed, the SCM installation routine will continue. The routine will also usually install the Visual C++ 2010 runtimes as well as ask you about any SQL servers you have. And, if you have no SQL server or just want to make this a fully stand-alone version, the SCM installation routine will cheerfully go to the Internet and download SQL Express for you.

FIGURE D.2   SCM requires that you have the .NET Framework installed.

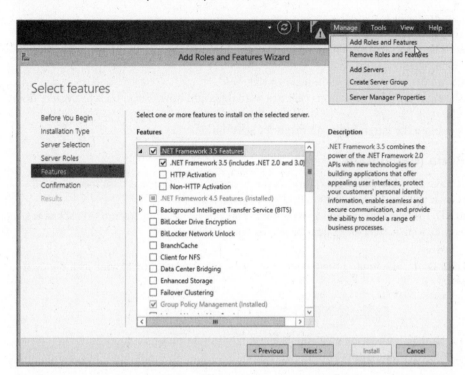

The installation is straightforward. To save space I've not included any screen shots. When you run SCM the first time, that's when it gets interesting. SCM will unpack the baselines it had within its installation, as seen in Figure D.3.

FIGURE D.3   SCM downloads all initial baselines from Microsoft at first run.

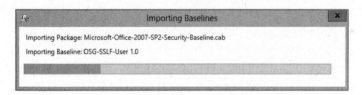

When that's complete, the SCM utility should look similar to what's shown in Figure D.1.

SCM: Getting Around

As seen in Figure D.1, there are three panes.

On the left pane, you see the baselines. There are categories for Microsoft Baselines, which will be autopopulated at first run. You can also see Custom Baselines, which we'll get to in a moment.

In the middle, you see the main meat of the tool.

On the right are various actions that are available right now, based on what you're doing within the tool.

Let's explore the left, middle, and right panes a bit.

Left Pane (Baselines)

The left pane is where you can explore all the *baseline sets*. Within a baseline set you'll usually find two things: documentation and specific baselines.

Figure D.4 shows two examples expanded. You can see documentation (Attachments \ Guides) as well as the constituent baselines within the set.

FIGURE D.4   Expanding the baseline set shows documentation as well as individual baselines.

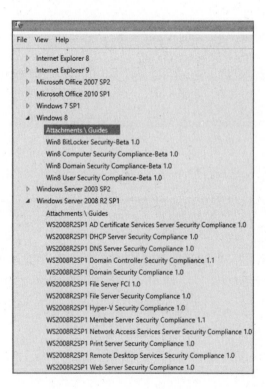

For instance, in the Windows 8 baseline, you'll see a guide, as shown in Figure D.5.

FIGURE D.5   Guidance is an important part of SCM.

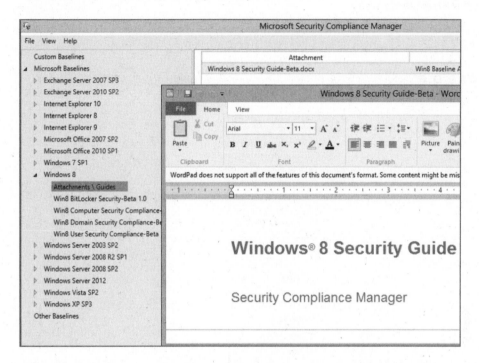

The guide explains why you might or might not want to configure something in the target product. For instance, the Windows 8 Security Guide goes into detail about which items you might want to set to make Windows 8 more secure. Out of those documents, Microsoft has also produced the various baselines for Windows 8 (seen in Figure D.4, directly under `Attachments \ Guides`).

We'll talk about the baselines themselves coming up.

Middle Pane

If you get lost and don't see the right pane with all the links in it, as seen in Figure D.1, simply click the words Microsoft Baselines in the left pane, and the middle pane will come back.

The middle pane is broken into two parts. The left part features help with using the tool itself. The left side has items like "What's new in this release," "How to perform common tasks," and "Working with SCM."

The right side lets you perform tasks within the tool. The right pane has three sections: "Get Knowledge," "Customize Knowledge," and "Export Knowledge."

We won't be able to go into all the functions this tool can do, but I'll give you the meat and potatoes.

Right Pane (Actions)

The right pane is always changing. Based on what you're doing in the tool, you could see the right pane look like what you saw in Figure D.1 or, for instance, what's seen in Figure D.6.

FIGURE D.6   The right pane reflects what you're currently doing in the other parts of the tool.

Again, it's context sensitive.

SCM: Usual Use Case

Let's walk through a use case of SCM. We'll locate the Windows 8 baseline and documentation, as already seen in Figure D.4.

If you look at Figure D.4, you'll see there are four baselines included for Windows 8. The first course of action would be to read the documentation in the Attachments \ Guides section. Sometimes the guidance describes specifically why certain recommendations are made. Other times, it's more general.

After reading the documentation, you decide that you're ready to inspect and possibly modify an existing baseline. After that, you'll be ready to deploy that baseline.

Let's use the Win8 BitLocker Security baseline.

Again, in these examples I'm using Win8 BitLocker Security but you could substitute the ideas you learn here for any of the baseline areas, like Office, Internet Explorer, Windows Server 2008 R2, Windows Server 2012, and so on.

Inspecting a Baseline

After clicking the Win8 BitLocker Security baseline, you'll see the list of settings Microsoft thinks is a good idea for you to implement, as shown in Figure D.7.

FIGURE D.7   This baseline has 38 suggested settings. One (or more) of these settings might not be something you want to implement.

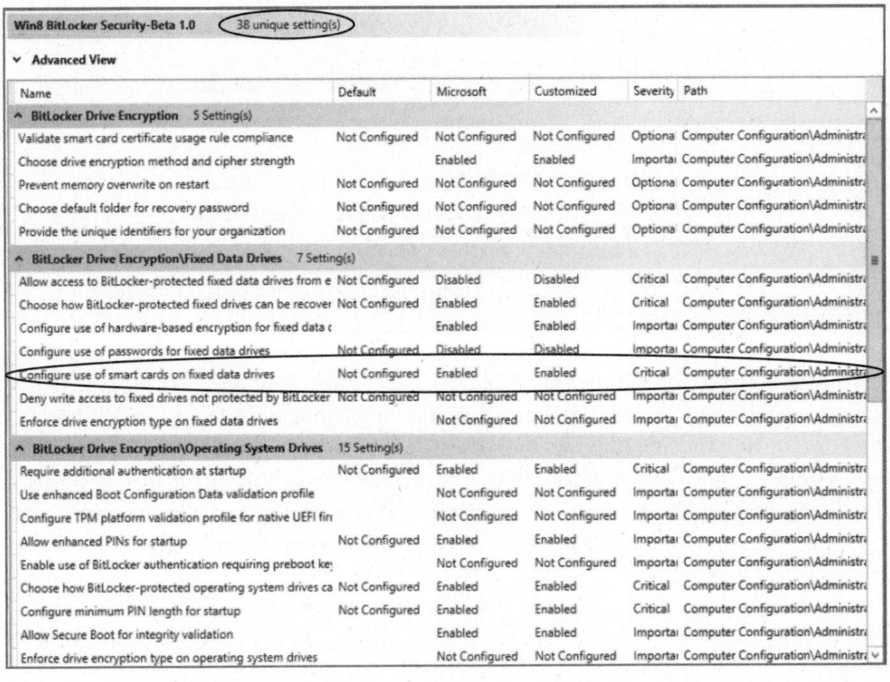

If you look at the list of all the settings within the baseline, some might jump out at you as good ideas and for others you might think, "I don't want to do that."

Let's zoom in and inspect one setting, "Configure use of smart cards on fixed data drives," highlighted in Figure D.7. Click on the setting, and it highlights. However, you'll also need to click on Setting Details (which isn't shown) to get what you'll see in Figure D.8. In Figure D.8, you'll see the expanded details of this setting.

FIGURE D.8 The expanded details of one particular baseline setting

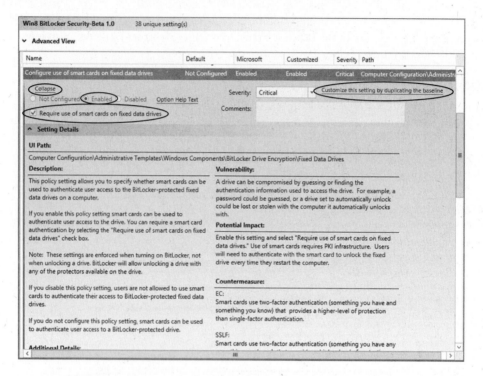

When you look at this baseline, you should see some interesting stuff. I want to draw your attention to the various categories within Setting Details. Inside, you'll find Microsoft's description of the policy setting (the same thing you would find within the Group Policy editor). But beyond that, you'll find Microsoft's rationale for why it wants this enabled: specifically, the sections Vulnerability, Potential Impact, Countermeasure, and Additional Details. These items are not found in the Group Policy editor and are only here in the prescriptive guidance of SCM.

The idea is that you can read for yourself why some setting might not be configured by default but the guidance suggests you enable it or disable it or prescribes some other remediation.

In this case, I saw that "Configure use of smart cards on fixed data drives" was set to Enabled. Then I looked a little deeper and also saw that there was an additional subsetting that required me to use smart cards when performing the encryption.

So, I like that this setting is set to Enabled. This means I can use smart cards. But having the additional setting "Require use of smart cards on fixed data drives" seemed very hard core to me. If I was going to implement this baseline in the real world, I might want to remove the required use of smart cards.

It might not be super clear in the screenshot in Figure D.8, but the Not Configured, Enabled, and Disabled items are all grayed out. So is the "Require use of smart cards on fixed data drives" item. That is, inside this Microsoft-provided baseline, you are not allowed to make changes.

However, in the upper-right corner of Figure D.8, you can see "Customize this setting by duplicating the baseline."

When I do this, I'm prompted to make a copy and give it a name and description.

Modifying a Baseline

Once the baseline is copied and named, you'll see it within Custom Baselines. You can see that mine is named "Corp copy of Win8 BitLocker Security" in Figure D.9.

FIGURE D.9   Microsoft baselines are read only. Your baselines are read/write.

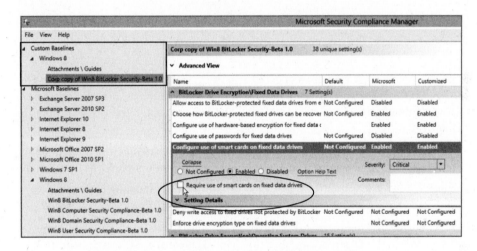

Again, the trick is that you cannot modify a Microsoft baseline.

You can however, modify a *copy* of a Microsoft baseline.

So, in this example, I'm locating "Configure use of smart cards on fixed data drives" within my baseline copy and then unchecking "Require use of smart card on fixed data drives."

When you make your change, there is no Save button or command. Just move on to examine other settings, or click Collapse and you'll be back at the list.

In practice you would continue going through a particular baseline looking for settings that didn't fit your world and change them as appropriate. When done, you would continue on to the next step, exporting a baseline.

Exporting a Baseline

Once you've got your baseline all set, you can use the right pane and select Export ≻ GPO Backup (folder). Then save the baseline export into a folder of your choice. The folder will contain a garden-variety GPO with your baseline in it.

In Figure D.10, I'm saving my baseline in a folder named Corp-Win8-BitLocker-Baseline to the Desktop.

FIGURE D.10   You can export your baseline to a GPO.

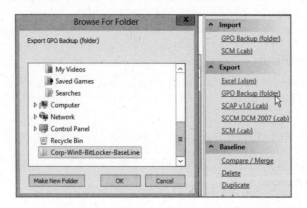

Note that there are other formats you could export to, including Desired Configuration Manager (DCM) for Microsoft System Center Configuration Manager, Excel, Security Content Automation Protocol (SCAP), and SCM "native" formats. Here are some notes on these formats:

SCM CAB Files   This format is handy if you want to exchange a baseline with a fellow administrator. This is the preferred way to transfer knowledge between multiple SCM installations.

Excel Format   This format requires Excel 2007 or later on the same box to produce an XLS sheet. Somewhat useful in case you want hard-copy documentation of a baseline.

SCCM DCM Format   This format is to be used in conjunction with System Center Configuration Manager's Desired Configuration Management (DCM) component. If you're interested, I wrote a whitepaper on the DCM component, and you can grab a free copy at www.policypak.com/itwhitepapers. The title of the free paper is "What most SCCM admins don't know about application management."

SCAP Format   I don't know of too many tools that can use the Security Content Automation Protocol (SCAP) format. IBM Tivoli BigFix can use this format and it's also a government standard. You can learn more about SCAP at http://scap.nist.gov/.

Importing a Baseline from an Exported GPO

Okay. Let's recap where we've been so far:

1. You found a baseline that was close to what you wanted, but not quite.

2. You copied and then modified your baseline to suit your needs.

3. You then exported your modified baseline. And you exported it as a GPO.

Now you're ready to take this export and get it into the GPMC.

You would think that you could simply "restore" the Group Policy you exported from SCM. But that approach usually doesn't work. Instead, you need to remember something we talked about in Chapter 2, "Managing Group Policy with the GPMC and via PowerShell": the idea of importing a GPO.

Backup and Restore is what's used when recovering GPOs backed up from the same domain.

Backup and Import is what's used when recovering GPOs from another domain or other source. To use the Import command, use the GPMC, and then create a blank GPO in the Group Policy Objects node. Finally, right-click and then select Import Settings, as seen in Figure D.11.

FIGURE D.11 You must take an exported SCM GPO and import it using the GPMC.

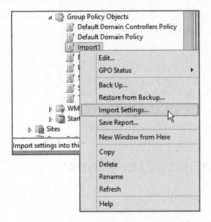

Run through the Import Wizard to import the files you exported earlier.

For a refresher on how to use the GPMC Import Wizard, go to Chapter 2 and read the section "Migrating Group Policy Objects between Domains."

When complete, you'll have a real, live GPO you can inspect, change, back up, and so forth. You can link this GPO over to your target OU and those settings that were in the baseline, which are now in the GPO, will affect your target users or computers.

Importing Existing GPOs

There might be times you want to reverse the process and take an existing, live GPO and bring its contents into SCM as a baseline.

The process is easy to understand. Start in the GPMC and create a normal, garden-variety backup of your GPO. Then, switch back to SCM. In the right pane, click Import ≻ GPO Backup (folder), seen in Figure D.1. Point SCM toward your GPO backup and perform the import. Your GPO will be converted (imported) into a baseline, as seen in Figure D.12.

FIGURE D.12   Your GPO can be imported to be an SCM baseline.

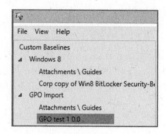

You might want to import an existing GPO for a variety of reasons. You might want to compare it to an existing baseline (coming up next). Or you might want to convert it to some other format (specifically, Excel, DCM, or SCAP).

Or, as you'll see later, you might want to take an existing machine's configuration, produce an export of that configuration as a GPO, and then import it for the same reasons. You'll learn more about this in the upcoming section "LocalGPO Tool."

Note that not every category in Group Policy will be properly mapped and imported into an SCM baseline. See the sidebar "Understanding SCM and LocalGPO's Export/Import Ability" for more information on what's supported.

Comparing and Merging Baselines

SCM doesn't really know anything about your real world. It only knows what you import into SCM.

So, a tool like Microsoft's AGPM (which we talk about in Appendix C, "Advanced Group Policy Management") can give you a comparison against two real, live GPOs.

However, SCM can do something quite similar: it can compare two *baselines*. The baselines might be a downloaded baseline from Microsoft or a GPO you previously imported and made into a baseline.

Said another way, you cannot compare GPO to GPO, or GPO to baseline. Only baseline to baseline.

So you might want to compare two Microsoft baselines to see the differences. To compare baselines, start by clicking on the baseline in the left pane. Then in the right pane find

Compare/Merge, as seen earlier in Figure D.6. Then, as shown in Figure D.13, select the second baseline to perform the comparison.

FIGURE D.13   You can compare settings between any two baselines.

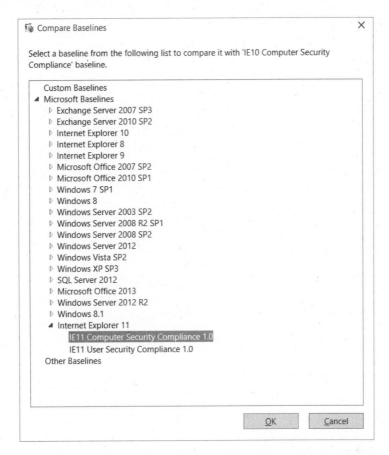

An example of the results of a comparison is shown in Figure D.14.

In Figure D.14, you can see the various categories, which you can expand and contract: "Summary," "Settings that differ," "Settings that match," "Settings only in Baseline A," and "Settings only in Baseline B."

You might have noticed that this section is named "Comparing and Merging Baselines." Why is there only "Export to Excel" and no "Merge Baselines" button?

The Merge Baselines button does make an appearance next to "Export to Excel" when SCM is able to perform the function. SCM won't perform a merge between two different product baselines (IE11 into a Windows 8 baseline).

FIGURE D.14   A baseline comparison can show you which settings are the same and differences between baselines.

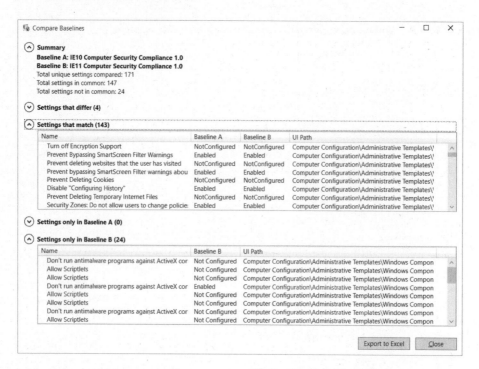

But you can see the Merge Baselines button appear when you're comparing two imported GPOs and Microsoft's baselines are not involved. Here is what it looks like:

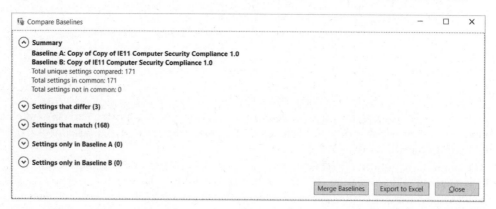

When the merge is complete (it takes only a moment), your baseline is combined and should look similar to Figure D.15.

FIGURE D.15   Your merged baseline is available inside SCM.

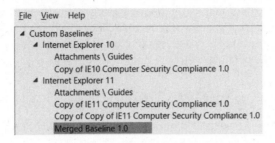

LocalGPO Tool

I get asked the following question fairly often over the course of a year: "Hey, Moskowitz, if I have machines that aren't domain-joined, can I use Group Policy with them?"

Well, "Yes" is the answer of course, because there's always Local Group Policy.

However, Local Group Policy (covered in detail in Chapter 1, "Group Policy Essentials," in the section "Understanding Local Group Policy") means you need to manually run around from machine to machine if you have an idea that you want to apply a policy to a non-domain-joined machine and use Local Group Policy to implement that idea.

So, SCM also ships with a tool called LocalGPO.

 There were some "unofficial" tools from Microsoft from my pal Aaron Margosis that performed a similar function. My understanding is that, again, those tools were not officially supported, and their functionality is subsumed by the SCM LocalGPO tool. But, in case you want to look at them for comparison, at last check they were at:

http://blogs.msdn.com/b/aaron_margosis/archive/2009/10/02/
utilities-for-local-group-policy-and-ie-security-zones.aspx

(shortened to http://tinyurl.com/8mqxq6t).

So, the LocalGPO tool that ships with SCM is meant to solve three problems:

- Testing or implementing baselines on computers that are not joined to a domain.

- Taking an existing LocalGPO and making a copy to be used on another machine.

- Reading in a local machine's existing policy and making a GPO from that. Optionally, importing that GPO back into SCM as a baseline or using it straight away in the GPMC.

And any other scenario where Local GPOs must be used ... This tool is the Swiss Army knife of Local Group Policy operations.

Note that LocalGPO cannot magically deliver settings over the Internet to non-domain-joined machines. If that's interesting to you, check out PolicyPak Cloud (http://www.policypak.com/products/policypak-suite-cloud-edition.html) if you need to do that. I also explore it in the next appendix.

Installing SCM's LocalGPO Tool

When you install SCM, the LocalGPO is not automatically installed. Look for the LocalGPO MSI installation program at C:\Program Files (x86)\Microsoft Security Compliance Manager\LGPO. I suggest you copy it over to a Windows XP or later machine and then install it there.

Once you've installed LocalGPO, you're ready to use it.

If you've installed on Windows 8 or Windows Server 2012, you won't immediately see the tool on the Start Menu. To run the program, right-click on the Start Menu and then click on "All apps." Then click on "LocalGPO Command-Line," which is how you'll be running LocalGPO anyway. When you do, you'll see something similar to Figure D.16.

FIGURE D.16 The LocalGPO command-line options

Using SCM's LocalGPO

So, the secret is, the SCM team did a pretty good job of documenting this tool, and I'm not going to repeat all the use cases they describe in the manual. To find the manual and their use cases, see Figure D.17 for an example of where to find precise step-by-steps for using the LocalGPO tool.

FIGURE D.17   The LocalGPO tool is documented in this guide and many other baseline guides.

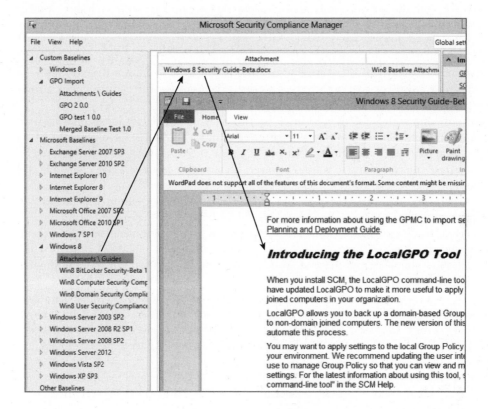

Here are the scenarios explicitly detailed in the guide:

- Exporting a GPO backup to the Local Group Policy of a computer
- Comparing a Local GPO of a machine to a previous Local Group Policy backup (without changing anything)
- Restoring a Local Group Policy to the default settings
- Exporting a Local Group Policy to a GPO backup
- Exporting MLGPO layers expressly as a GPO backup

- Creating a GPOPack (basically a GPO that can be "run" on a target machine without Local GPO itself being installed)
- Restoring a GPO backup specifically to a multiple Local Group Policy section
- Updating the Group Policy Editor UI with additional security settings

Honestly, all of these use cases are straightforward and clearly documented in the guide. This can jump-start your deployment of GP (at least using Local GPOs). If the machine is non-domain-joined, you might be able to avoid having to touch the computer again after Windows is installed.

However, with the last one, updating the Group Policy editor UI with additional security settings, it took me a while to figure out what to do and what to look for. Let me show you specifically how to do this one.

In a nutshell, there are a handful of "extra" Group Policy security settings that don't ship in the box from Microsoft. Actually, said another way, these are just Registry settings that have always existed in the target products themselves—there just isn't any Group Policy support for them within the Group Policy editor.

They only ship with SCM. Why? I think because they're only meant for specific use cases for US government requirements and aren't meant for the rest of us in general.

My pals at Microsoft recommend that you don't use these unless specifically required by some objective you're looking to solve. However, because this process can be confusing, I want to show you how it works.

These extra security settings can be exposed in the Group Policy editor. You can add these settings to your existing GPMC machine, which could then make GPOs for domain-joined machines. Or you can expose these settings for a stand-alone machine and see them only locally.

Let me show you what they are first. You can see the result of what I'm about to show you in Figure D.18.

And this is exactly how to do it. First, you need to have the LocalGPO handy, installed on a target machine. I'll be installing it on a machine with the GPMC installed. Just run the command Cscript LocalGPO.wsf /configsce. And, as seen in Figure D.19, the tool goes to work and modifies the Security Configuration Editor, which is part of the Group Policy editor.

Now, whenever you create new GPOs, you'll see the "MSS" settings located within Computer Configuration ➤ Policies ➤ Security Settings ➤ Local Policies ➤ Security Settings (shown in Figure D.18).

There is one caveat about these settings: the reports won't show correctly unless you're on a GPMC that has been specifically enhanced using the LocalGPO /configcse command.

In Figure D.20 on the top, you can see what happens when the GPMC has been enhanced. The reports are nice and pretty.

FIGURE D.18   The LocalGPO command can introduce a handful of additional security policy settings, all starting with MSS and a colon.

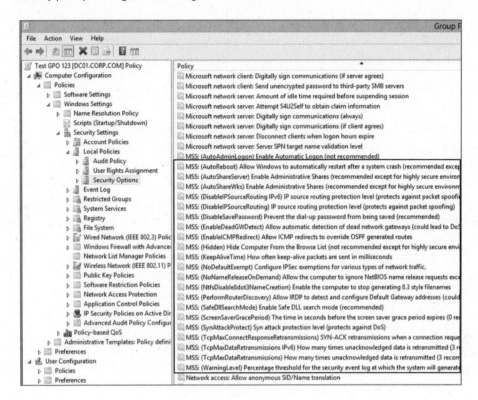

FIGURE D.19   Use the LocalGPO command with the /configsce switch to add more security policies to your Group Policy editor.

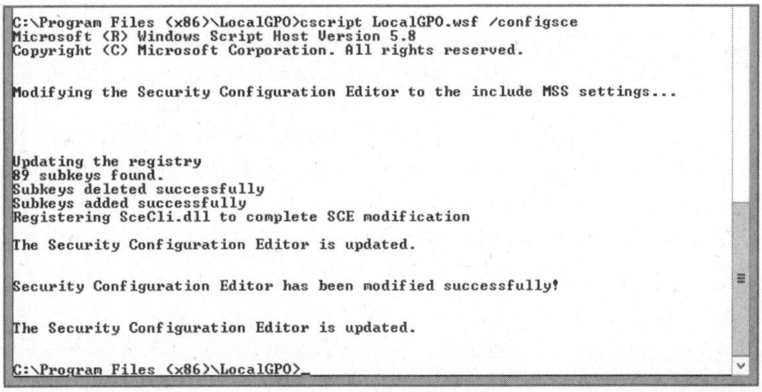

```
C:\Program Files (x86)\LocalGPO>cscript LocalGPO.wsf /configsce
Microsoft (R) Windows Script Host Version 5.8
Copyright (C) Microsoft Corporation. All rights reserved.

Modifying the Security Configuration Editor to the include MSS settings...



Updating the registry
89 subkeys found.
Subkeys deleted successfully
Subkeys added successfully
Registering SceCli.dll to complete SCE modification
The Security Configuration Editor is updated.

Security Configuration Editor has been modified successfully!

The Security Configuration Editor is updated.

C:\Program Files (x86)\LocalGPO>_
```

FIGURE D.20   On the top, the GPMC reports show the pretty name when the Group Policy editor is extended. On the bottom, the GPMC reports show what happens when the same GPO is seen using a GPMC that is not extended.

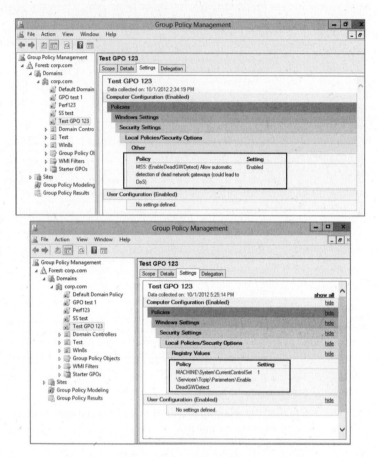

In Figure D.20 on the bottom is an example of the same GPO with the same setting. But since the GPMC on that computer wasn't extended, it can only show the changed Registry value.

There's no downside in having these extra settings showing up in the GPMC. But if you decide the extra settings are doing nothing for you, you can run `cscript LocalGPO.wsf /ResetSCE`.

Note that GPOs that have the settings already established inside them won't magically have those settings removed, though.

> **Understanding SCM and LocalGPO's Export/Import Ability**
>
> SCM and LocalGPO have something in common: they export and they import.
>
> SCM is able to import existing GPOs (and its own SCM-specific CAB files). SCM is able to export as CSVs, GPOs, DCMs, SCAPs, and its own SCM-specific CAB files. SCM never "touches" the real world. You feed SCM what it knows.
>
> LocalGPO, however, can touch the real world. It's able to take an existing machine's configuration and export those settings as a GPO. That GPO can then be applied later to other machines directly.
>
> So you can see the relationship:
>
> - SCM exports. LocalGPO imports.
> - LocalGPO exports and LocalGPO imports.
> - LocalGPO exports and SCM imports.
>
> Get it?
>
> But it's not a perfect export and import. There are some categories that cannot be exported from a Local GPO using the LocalGPO tool, specifically these:
>
> - IPsec
> - Scripts
> - Internet Explorer Maintenance (which is retired anyway)
>
> Everything else should export properly using LocalGPO and be imported back into SCM.
>
> It should also be noted that PolicyPak settings do play nicely with SCM and LocalGPO's export and import process. So if you wanted to mass-deliver PolicyPak application and security settings using PolicyPak, that will work fine.

Final Thoughts on LocalGPO and SCM

In a perfect world, you wouldn't have any non-domain-joined machines and wouldn't need LocalGPO.

But I see the need.

There are times when you have non-domain-joined machines and want to get some kind of Group Policy to them. Remember, though, it's not everything. It's most things, but not everything.

Again, one of LocalGPO's key functions is to take a machine's settings and export them for later use into SCM as a baseline or export them for later use on another machine.

We've talked about SCM in great detail in this appendix. Let's review some truths about SCM:

- The SCM downloads "advice baselines" from Microsoft.

- The SCM takes the baselines and outputs them as CSVs, GPOs, DCMs, SCAPs, and SCM-specific CAB files. Note that it's possible to have a baseline that doesn't support all the areas for export for all the settings. That is, you might not be able to export some baselines to DCM, and/or some settings could get dropped when exporting to SCAP.

- SCM enables admins to create copies of baselines and make their own baselines and to then output them as CSVs, GPOs, DCMs, SCAPs, and SCM-specific CAB files. The same caveat applies: not every baseline can be exported to every format.

- SCM is able to import GPOs and existing SCM CAB files.

- The SCM is able to compare any two baselines (A versus B) within the SCM system.

- The SCM itself has no management, compliance, remediation, live reporting, or knowledge of the actual world.

- SCM cannot perform live reporting or live differences between any baseline and anything that isn't previously imported. Said another way, SCM doesn't directly touch (or have direct knowledge of) the real world as the real world sits "right now."

- The SCM tool itself cannot perform changes within the real world or perform active compliance without a helper tool. Those tools are Group Policy, System Center Configuration Manager (SCCM), and third-party tools that can leverage a format SCM can export.

- Don't forget, also, to be sure to use the File menu and select "Check for Updates." When you do, you'll see if any new baselines are available for new products as they come out.

Additionally, here are some resources to help you gain more understanding of SCM:

- The main SCM web page is:

  http://microsoft.com/scm

- Here's a site with some SCM how-to videos:

  http://technet.microsoft.com/en-us/video/security-compliance-manager-with-chase-carpenter.aspx

- The SCM TechNet wiki can be found at:

  http://social.technet.microsoft.com/wiki/contents/articles/774.microsoft-security-compliance-manager-scm-en-us.aspx

- The SCM TechNet Forum can be found at:

  http://social.technet.microsoft.com/Forums/en-us/compliancemanagement/threads

Microsoft Intune and PolicyPak Cloud

Here are some scenarios you might have in your world:

- Roaming users with laptops. Yeah, you've got those.
- Non-domain-joined machines.
- BYOD (bring your own device) machines.
- Branch offices with or without their own domains.
- Multiple, unrelated customers, but with some shared common requirements.

And, oh yeah, it's up to you to manage these situations.

So in these cases, using "out-of-the-box" Group Policy might not be the best for you. This is because Group Policy (out of the box, anyway) means you'll need to have an on-premises domain controller and GPOs with directives for what you want to do.

Instead, if you have one of these situations you might want to check out a cloud-based way of getting Group Policy settings (or at least some Group Policy settings) out to your machines.

So in this appendix, we'll talk about two cloud options: Microsoft Intune and PolicyPak Cloud.

These two systems have pretty different goals and don't overlap that much.

Microsoft Intune

Microsoft Intune is Microsoft's pay-as-you-go endpoint and user management service (delivered as a cloud service). Here's the general idea:

- As of this writing, you pay between $6 and $11 a month per user. (That's in US dollars; your price may vary.) Any user can have five managed devices.
- You get a handful of common management features to manage desktops, laptops, and phone devices. Windows machines can be domain-joined or non-domain-joined.
- Some functions overlap with existing domain-based Group Policy. (We'll talk about that in a minute.)

Microsoft Intune consists of the following management features:

- Software updates (like WSUS)
- Hardware and software inventory
- Endpoint protection (like Forefront)
- Software deployment (like Group Policy or System Center Configuration Manager)
- License agreement maintenance
- Monitoring of endpoints
- Remote assistance
- Security policies: Intune agent settings, firewall, settings, and mobile security policy settings
- MDM settings for devices from phones to PCs (set lock screen, remote-wipe a device, etc.)

Along with your purchase, you get "upgrade rights" to Windows Enterprise editions if you've already paid for a lower version of Windows.

My goal is to give you a super-brief overview of Microsoft Intune, and as such, we won't be performing any advanced tasks.

Besides, Microsoft Intune is software as a service (SaaS) and there's a shorter time between what's out there now and what's coming next. In other words, learn Microsoft Intune in a general sense here, but know that the actual nitty-gritty details could change quickly because of Microsoft's faster than usual rollout schedule.

Getting Started with Microsoft Intune

To get started with Microsoft Intune, you'll find a free trial here:

www.microsoft.com/en-us/windows/windowsintune/try-and-buy.aspx

When you complete the signup, you'll get an e-mail that you'll need to confirm, and then you can log on. Once logged on, though, you're not really in Microsoft Intune yet, as shown in Figure E.1.

You're in the Online Services section, where you can make purchases (like Microsoft Intune or Office 365), add users and groups, or even synchronize your existing Active Directory with Microsoft's Online Services.

You might want to synchronize with Microsoft's Online Services because areas of Microsoft Intune are based on groups as well as users. Managing traditional Windows devices is based on groups. Managing mobile devices is based on users. So by synchronizing your Active Directory user groups with Microsoft Online Services, you can take advantage of those existing Active Directory groups and users inside Microsoft Intune without having to re-create them.

You get started with Microsoft Intune by clicking Admin Console, as seen in Figure E.1. Once you're inside Microsoft Intune, it looks like Figure E.2.

FIGURE E.1   Your Microsoft Online Services portal provides the gateway to Microsoft Intune but isn't Microsoft Intune itself.

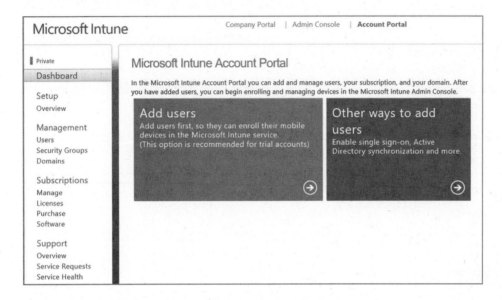

FIGURE E.2   This is the Microsoft Intune Admin Console. Menu items are on the left and quick-start items are on the right.

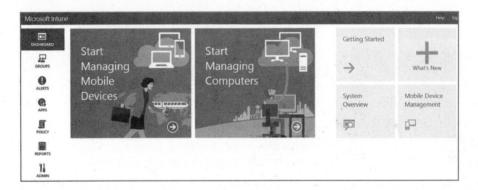

There are two main device types that you can manage: traditional Windows devices, like desktops and laptops, as well as mobile devices, like Windows phones, Android phones, or Apple iOS phones.

To manage traditional Windows devices, you need to install an agent on each machine. The agent is a setup file that is coded specifically to your Microsoft Intune account. Every time you install it on a client machine, it makes contact with Microsoft and *consumes* a license that you've purchased.

You download the agent, as seen in Figure E.3.

FIGURE E.3   Download and install the Microsoft Intune agent (client software) to consume a license.

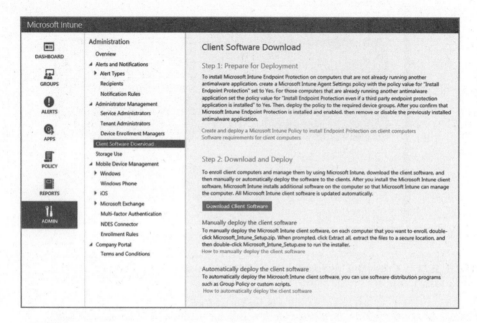

Once you download the setup file, you can deploy it in many ways, including manually installing it, using scripts, using Group Policy Software Installation, using System Center Configuration Manager, or whatever else you like. The MSI file can be installed on 32-bit or 64-bit machines. Of course, you cannot use Microsoft Intune itself to deploy its own agent.

You can get the MSI file from the download provided by using the `/Extract` command from the Microsoft Intune setup installer.

Once the Microsoft Intune setup is finished, the routine will put the Microsoft Intune agent and the Microsoft Intune Center on the machine. The agent enables updates, software deployments, and so on. The Microsoft Intune Center is a program users can run manually on their own machines to acquire applications, check for updates, start a malware scan, or request remote assistance.

You can do a lot with Microsoft Intune: way, way more than when I wrote this chapter back when Microsoft Intune was born; heck, it was called Windows Intune then.

As such I'm not going to cover, really, even a fraction of what's possible in Microsoft Intune and instead focus my attention strictly on Intune's policies capabilities for Windows PCs and how regular Group Policy is also dealt with at the same time.

I suggest you check out the following resource for in-depth Intune training:

`www.microsoftvirtualacademy.com/training-courses/microsoft-intune-core-skills-jump-start`

Additional tips and video are found at Channel 9, `https://channel9.msdn.com/`. Look for anything Intune related. Of course, newer information is always better than older information.

Using Microsoft Intune

Using Microsoft Intune is about two things: setting up groups and everything else.

That is, once you have defined your groups, the rest of what you can do with Microsoft Intune (with regard to managing PCs) falls into place. Because Microsoft Intune is a big place, and we're short on space, I'm only going to cover two items pertaining to using Microsoft Intune: setting up groups and setting policies.

Of course there is more to Microsoft Intune than that—features like malware protection, hardware and software inventory, and so on. But since this is a book on Group Policy, I want to focus specifically on where Microsoft Intune and Group Policy "touch." And that's in Microsoft Intune policies.

Setting Up Microsoft Intune Groups

Microsoft Intune uses device groups to "round up" both users and machines into neat categories. Once they're in groups, you are then able to dictate items like software deployment, malware settings, and firewall and policy settings and even configure the Microsoft Intune client itself.

Setting up groups is not hard at all. Simply click the Group icon on the left, shown in Figure E.4, and then click Create Group on the right.

FIGURE E.4   Creating groups is an important first step in using Microsoft Intune.

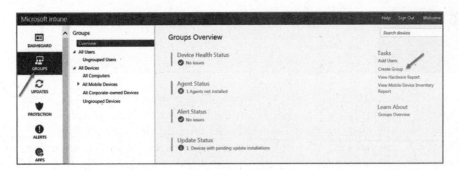

If you haven't synchronized to Active Directory, you can manually specify the names or set criteria to scan through computers, make a match, and add them to the group. This will autoplace computers based on names into a specific group.

If you have synchronized to Active Directory, you can do some magic tricks by specifying computers from a domain or a specific OU. In that way, you can ensure that when you get new computers in Active Directory, they're automatically synchronized to Microsoft Intune.

Note that groups can be nested. So you could have a group called "Sales Computers" and have other groups called "East Sales Computers" and "West Sales Computers" within it.

Doing so enables you to ensure that the policies and software (which we're just about to get to) can be generic or specific. For instance, you could deploy a common firewall setting to all the "Sales Computers" (including "East Sales Computers" and "West Sales Computers") but also have something specific as an exception for one or the other group.

Setting Up Policies Using Microsoft Intune

Microsoft Intune has policies for desktops and laptops, and it also has policies for mobile. I'll only be talking about policies for desktops and laptops. You can see the Policy Overview page in Figure E.5.

FIGURE E.5   Microsoft Intune policy overview

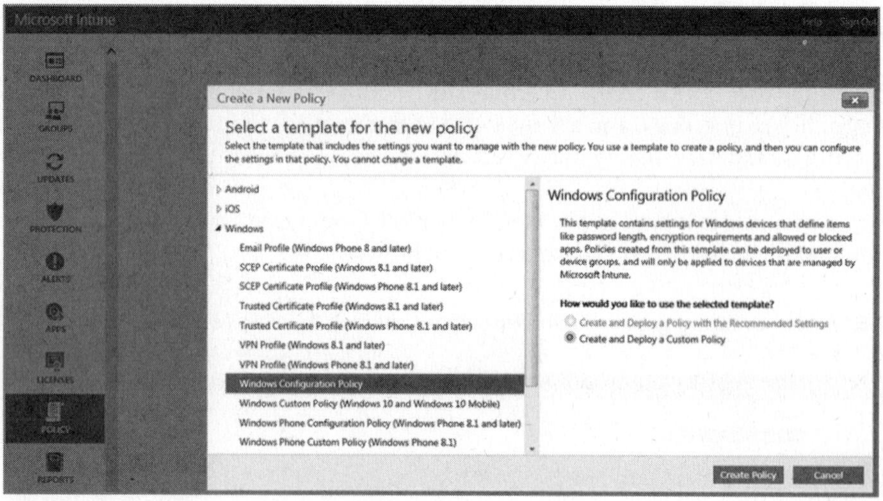

Microsoft Intune policies are a very, very small subset of what we know of as Group Policy settings. Specifically, there are policy settings for firewalls, some security settings, settings for email and malware agents, some browser settings, and some others.

In Figure E.6, you can see a Microsoft Intune policy requires the network firewall to be turned on.

FIGURE E.6   Creating a Microsoft Intune policy

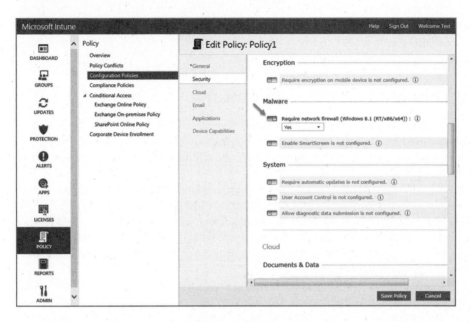

Once the policy is created, select the group that should accept this policy. It's a lot like creating a GPO and linking it—except with Microsoft Intune, you create the Microsoft Intune policy and then associate it with a Microsoft Intune group.

Microsoft Intune and Group Policy Conflicts

It's been a few years since Microsoft Intune has come out. And still, Microsoft Intune policies don't have Group Policy or Group Policy Preferences' power. There's a lot of other power; I'm not knocking on Microsoft Intune. I just kind of expected them to have more Group Policy–like things baked in by now.

That being said, there is some overlap, and Microsoft Intune policies are similar to what Group Policy delivers today—there's just not as many settings. But the policies they both deliver manipulate settings and tweak the same bells and whistles.

But what happens if you're using Group Policy and also Microsoft Intune and you happen to manage the same setting? The Microsoft Intune team has a little introduction on this topic, and you should definitely read it here:

http://blogs.technet.com/b/windowsintune/archive/2010/11/10/using-group-policy-and-windows-intune-to-manage-policy.aspx

However, here's the short answer: If there is a conflict between Microsoft Intune and Group Policy, then Group Policy wins. This makes sense to me, and I think Microsoft made the right decision in determining who wins.

Microsoft also has a great video here:

```
http://blogs.technet.com/b/windowsintune/archive/2011/08/02/handling-group-
policy-conflicts-in-windows-intune.aspx
```

It shows you exactly what happens within Microsoft Intune in these conflicting situations and shows you how to go about fixing them.

Final Thoughts on Microsoft Intune

Using the basics of Microsoft Intune to manage elements of a Windows PC isn't particularly difficult—which is nice. One of the key problems Group Policy or System Center Configuration Manager has is that it does take some dedicated time to learn how to "do it" before feeling confident.

That said, Microsoft Intune is growing by leaps and bounds, and trying to be a lot of things to a lot of different people. Still, the layout is relatively intuitive, and working with it is straightforward—at least for basic PC management. For some more advanced features, like application portals and mobile device management for Windows and non-Windows phones, plus connecting it all together (if you wanted) with SCCM on-premises, it is becoming a bigger animal every day.

But I want to emphasize that Microsoft Intune isn't *yet* a replacement for *either* Group Policy *or* System Center Configuration Manager.

To me, it just doesn't look like they're trying to bring all of Group Policy's functionality into Microsoft Intune. They're trying to compete with Airwatch and MobileIron—and ensure they have a great Windows phone and non-Windows phone (like iOS and Android) management experience.

But, that being said, who knows. Could Microsoft Intune be the future king and replace either Group Policy or System Center Configuration Manager? I think it's possible, but not likely for a long time.

Remember, Microsoft Intune doesn't do most Group Policy settings and it doesn't do Group Policy Preferences.

PolicyPak Cloud

So if Microsoft Intune doesn't give you the ability to get Group Policy settings to your machines over the Internet, what are you going to do?

That, my friend, is why we have PolicyPak Cloud.

PolicyPak Cloud's precise goal in life is to deliver Group Policy (and PolicyPak Application Manager) settings over the Internet to both domain-joined and non-domain-joined machines. So let's revisit the list of scenarios in which you might want to get Group Policy to machines over the Internet:

- Roaming users with laptops
- Non-domain-joined machines
- BYOD (bring your own device) machines

- Branch offices with or without their own domains
- Multiple, unrelated customers, but with some shared common requirements.

And if my goal is to get them Group Policy no matter what, then PolicyPak Cloud is the only way to go. If you like what you see here and want to try PolicyPak Cloud, we simply ask that you join us for a webinar (www.PolicyPak.com/webinar) and we'll get you started right after that.

PolicyPak Cloud 101

Getting started with PolicyPak Cloud is pretty simple. A lot of concepts are similar to Microsoft Intune.

- Like Microsoft Intune, PolicyPak Cloud has an agent you download as an MSI and install, and the computer "joins" PolicyPak Cloud.
- Like Microsoft Intune, PolicyPak Cloud has policies. These policies are XML files.
- Like Microsoft Intune, PolicyPak Cloud has groups.
- As with Microsoft Intune, you link policies to groups.
- Unlike Microsoft Intune policies, PolicyPak policies can be contents of a GPO.

So in this way you get the full power of Group Policy over the Internet to both domain-joined and non-domain-joined machines. To get a quick feel for PolicyPak Cloud, we'll go through the following quick tour:

- Understanding PolicyPak Cloud policies
- Creating and using groups
- Joining PolicyPak Cloud
- Group Policy and PolicyPak Cloud conflicts
  For a video overview of PolicyPak Cloud, check out the Quickstart video:

  www.policypak.com/video/policypak-cloud-quickstart.html

Understanding PolicyPak Cloud Policies

PolicyPak Cloud policies are really just pieces of existing GPOs. So, they're not entire GPOs; they are pieces of GPOs. The following pieces of a GPO can be uploaded to PolicyPak Cloud:

- Group Policy Admin Templates
- Group Policy Preferences
- Group Policy Security settings PolicyPak Application Manager settings (Flash, Firefox, Java, Office, etc.)

The ever-so-brief idea here is that you can take an existing GPO, with existing data, and export the pieces you need. So if you have Group Policy Security settings you want to export and then apply, great! Just export those as an XML file. If you have Administrative Template favorites you want to export and apply, great! If you have Group Policy Preferences ideas you want to export and apply, super-duper!

To do this, you'll use the PolicyPak MMC snap-in and export each type of Group Policy settings (see Figure E.7).

FIGURE E.7   Use the PolicyPak MMC snap-in to export the policy settings you want (Applications, Admin Templates, Group Policy Preferences, Security).

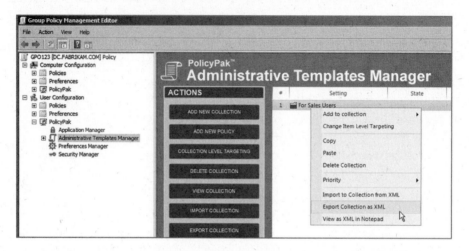

Once they're exported as a file, you simply upload it to the PolicyPak Cloud service with the results seen in Figure E.8.

FIGURE E.8   Upload XML files into the PolicyPak Cloud service.

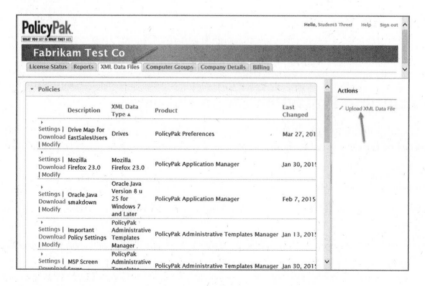

The directives then need to be linked to groups, which we'll discuss next.

Creating and Using PolicyPak Cloud Groups

Like Microsoft Intune, PolicyPak Cloud uses groups. The idea is super simple: Create a group, then link an XML directive (or multiple directives) to the group.

In Figure E.9, you can see Built-in Groups and Company Groups.

FIGURE E.9   In PolicyPak Cloud, create Company Groups and then link XML data files to them.

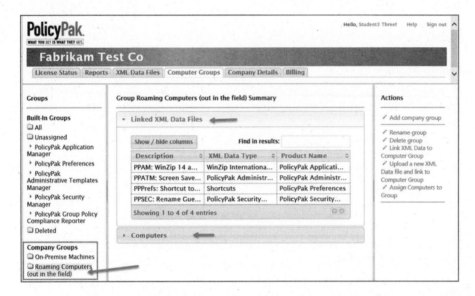

You are able to create Company Groups, and in Figure E.9, I've created two Company Groups and linked four XML data files to the "Roaming Computers (out in the field)" group.

Now when a computer is moved into the group, it picks up the directives.

Note the Built-in Groups of "All" and "Unassigned," which are special; so you can ensure that computers instantly get some kind of policy when they join PolicyPak Cloud.

Joining PolicyPak Cloud

Like Microsoft Intune, PolicyPak Cloud has an MSI installer that enables you to join the service. In Figure E.10, you can see the download ZIP (or singular MSIs) available in the Company Details tab.

Then on each machine you want to join PolicyPak Cloud, install the PolicyPak Cloud MSI. When you successfully join a computer to PolicyPak Cloud, you'll get what's seen in Figure E.11.

FIGURE E.10 Download your own PolicyPak Cloud MSI to join PolicyPak Cloud.

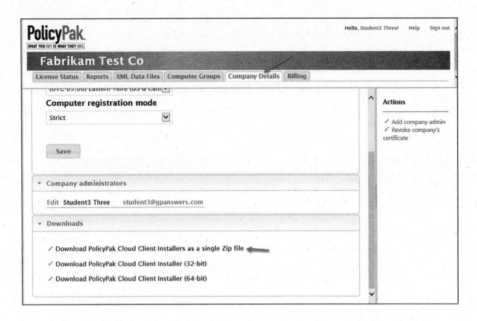

FIGURE E.11 When the computer joins PolicyPak Cloud, the computer goes into the All and Unassigned groups.

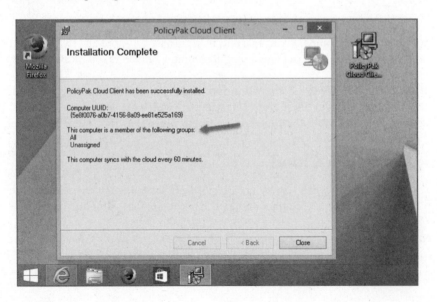

After the computer is joined, back in PolicyPak Cloud, select the group you want to move the computer to, then select "Assign Computers to Group" which appears back in Figure E.9.

If you don't want to wait for the client to synchronize with PolicyPak Cloud, at a command prompt on the computer, simply run the command line ppcloud /sync (not shown).

When you do, your directives from the group will be downloaded and processed by the computer (after about 10 seconds).

Final Thoughts on PolicyPak Cloud

As with many areas of Group Policy, PolicyPak Cloud will nicely revert policies back to the way they were should an XML data file no longer apply or the computer is moved out of a group.

Also, as with Windows Intune, there can be policy conflicts with PolicyPak Cloud directives and on-premises Group Policy directives. And as with Windows Intune, in a conflict, on-premises Group Policy directives win.

A good place to see more of PolicyPak Cloud in action would be:

www.policypak.com/support-sharing/policypak-cloud-getting-started.html

If you'd like to try out PolicyPak Cloud, then join me for a webinar:

www.PolicyPak.com/webinar

and you can try it out immediately after.

Final Thoughts on Microsoft Intune and PolicyPak Cloud

So, let's review this appendix.

Microsoft Intune does a lot of stuff: great stuff like trying to manage all devices, from Windows Phone and Windows PCs to non-Windows phones. It can deploy software, provide a company portal, help with patch management, and a whole lot more. Of course, Microsoft Intune has policies that can affect desktop machines, but it definitely doesn't offer what's possible using Group Policy.

On the other hand, PolicyPak Cloud isn't trying to compete with Microsoft Intune. PolicyPak Cloud doesn't try to manage phones or provide a company portal or deal with patch management.

PolicyPak Cloud's job is to get the Group Policy Admin, Group Policy Preferences, and Group Policy Security settings to your Windows machines (real Windows machines). PolicyPak Cloud simply enables you to take your on-premises Group Policy directives and get them to your machines, no matter where they are and regardless of whether they're domain-joined or non-domain-joined.

So, using each service on its own makes sense.

But can you use PolicyPak Cloud and Windows Intune together?

You bet.

A good one-two combo would be as follows:

- Use Windows Intune to manage your phones

- Use Windows Intune to deploy software to your PCs

- Use PolicyPak Cloud to deliver application settings (after those applications are deployed by Windows Intune)

- Use PolicyPak Cloud to deliver other Group Policy settings and to perform desktop lockdown and deliver security settings.

How's that for a better-together story?

Index

Note to the reader: Throughout this index **boldfaced** page numbers indicate primary discussions of a topic. *Italicized* page numbers indicate illustrations.

X